CW01370006

THE OXFORD HANDBOOK OF

GRAND STRATEGY

THE OXFORD HANDBOOK OF

GRAND STRATEGY

Edited by
THIERRY BALZACQ
and
RONALD R. KREBS

OXFORD
UNIVERSITY PRESS

OXFORD
UNIVERSITY PRESS

Great Clarendon Street, Oxford, OX2 6DP,
United Kingdom

Oxford University Press is a department of the University of Oxford.
It furthers the University's objective of excellence in research, scholarship,
and education by publishing worldwide. Oxford is a registered trade mark of
Oxford University Press in the UK and in certain other countries

© Oxford University Press 2021

The moral rights of the authors have been asserted

First Edition published in 2021

Impression: 1

All rights reserved. No part of this publication may be reproduced, stored in
a retrieval system, or transmitted, in any form or by any means, without the
prior permission in writing of Oxford University Press, or as expressly permitted
by law, by licence or under terms agreed with the appropriate reprographics
rights organization. Enquiries concerning reproduction outside the scope of the
above should be sent to the Rights Department, Oxford University Press, at the
address above

You must not circulate this work in any other form
and you must impose this same condition on any acquirer

Published in the United States of America by Oxford University Press
198 Madison Avenue, New York, NY 10016, United States of America

British Library Cataloguing in Publication Data

Data available

Library of Congress Control Number: 2020952298

ISBN 978–0–19–884029–9

DOI: 10.1093/oxfordhb/9780198840299.001.0001

Printed and bound in the UK by
TJ Books Limited

Links to third party websites are provided by Oxford in good faith and
for information only. Oxford disclaims any responsibility for the materials
contained in any third party website referenced in this work.

To the Memories of Colin Gray and Michael Howard—whose rigorous and provocative scholarship on strategy inspires us still.

ACKNOWLEDGMENTS

This Handbook on grand strategy is grand in scale: 44 essays, over 50 authors, over 300,000 words. As a result, we have only the foggiest idea whom we need to thank for engaging with, commenting on, conducting research for, and supporting—in financial and other ways—this Handbook and its essays. It is an immense chain of debt that we cannot ever hope to repay or even reconstruct. The countless people who constitute the chain's countless links know who they are and will have to be content with our rather impersonal thank you.

We, as editors, however, know the links in our own more personal chains, and we are grateful for the support we have received in a wide variety of congenial environments. Thierry Balzacq thanks the Asia-Pacific College (APCD) of Diplomacy at the Australian National University for hosting him during his sabbatical in 2017–2018, when the foundation stone of this Handbook was laid. He especially wants to thank Pauline Kerr, Greg Fry, Craig Hanks, Jochen Prantl, and Geoffrey Wiseman. He also acknowledges the generous financial support of the Francqui Foundation and the University of Namur in Belgium. He thanks Paul Wynants, former Dean at the University of Namur, who unfortunately passed away before this Handbook was completed, for his relentless trust in the ability of research in the social sciences to ameliorate the world. Thierry appreciates his many discussions with Peter Dombrowski and Simon Reich, whose unflagging enthusiasm has encouraged him to be attentive to the politics underlying grand strategy studies, though he wonders whether matters of ethics should not be brought into grand strategy studies, too. Sciences Po has offered Thierry an intellectual milieu that constantly pushes him forward, for which he is grateful. Finally, the first pitch for this Handbook looked completely different before Ron's splendid interventions. Thierry thanks Ron for the many invigorating conversations about grand strategy. Many colleagues report that, after a project of such a magnitude, they hate the person with whom they had to collaborate. Thierry, in contrast, feels lucky to have developed such a camaraderie with Ron while working on this Handbook.

Ron Krebs thanks Thierry Balzacq for his unsolicited email way back in February 2018, inviting him to collaborate on this Handbook. It is Thierry who properly gets the credit for this Handbook: it began with his vision and his initiative and would never have come to pass without his passionate commitment to grand strategy. Of course, given the work involved, perhaps blame, rather than gratitude, is more on point with respect to Ron's sentiments. Ron is, however, truly grateful to the University of Minnesota and its Department of Political Science, whose support of graduate research assistants helped make this project possible. In addition, the Beverly and Richard Fink Professorship in the Liberal Arts supported an in-person collaboration between the editors in the summer of 2019, at a crucial stage in the Handbook's development. Ron would also like to thank Robert Ralston and Pedro Accorsi for their fine and timely research assistance related both to his own contribution and to the Handbook as a whole.

The editors particularly would like to thank two programs and centers at the US Military Academy at West Point for providing opportunities for intensive exchanges among the Handbook's authors. In 2018–2019, Ron was an Adjunct Scholar of the Modern War Institute of the US Military Academy at West Point. The Institute's Director at the time, Col. Liam Collins, and its then Director of Research Lionel Beehner were intrigued by this Handbook and generously supported a workshop involving several authors in May 2019. The Rupert H. Johnson Grand Strategy Program at West Point, thanks to the initiative of its Director Max Margulies, provided further support for a second workshop, on The Future of Grand Strategy, held in September 2019. We are also immensely grateful to Lionel Beehner and Max Margulies for organizing these workshops. Numerous West Point faculty, staff, and students—too many for us to thank by name—thoughtfully engaged this Handbook's essays. If our experiences on the West Point campus are indicative, the future of the US Army is secure.

As always, Dominic Byatt of Oxford University Press has been a wonderful editor. He responded with great enthusiasm to our initial proposal and, over the years since, has ably and professionally shepherded the project, showing flexibility when necessary and delivering words of encouragement when circumstances have proved a bit more trying.

Working on this manuscript has been a pleasure, however, largely because we have been fortunate to have assembled so congenial and responsive a team of contributors. Herding these academic cats has not proved as difficult as we feared at the start. This Handbook bears the mark of their commitment to advancing the quality of research and teaching in the field of grand strategy.

This Handbook owes a great deal to our scholarly predecessors in the field. Two of these giants—the historian Michael Howard and the political scientist Colin Gray—passed away recently. We knew neither of these distinguished colleagues personally, but they had an outsized impact on the field and on our own thinking, even when we disagreed. We imagine they would have been pleased to see this *Oxford Handbook of Grand Strategy* in print, and we dedicate this Handbook to them.

CONTENTS

List of Figures   xiii
List of Tables   xv
List of Contributors   xvii

1. The Enduring Appeal of Grand Strategy   1
   THIERRY BALZACQ AND RONALD R. KREBS

PART I. HISTORY

2. Grand Strategy: The History of a Concept   25
   LAWRENCE FREEDMAN

3. Thucydides' Legacy in Grand Strategy   41
   NEVILLE MORLEY

4. Clausewitz, *DIE POLITIK*, and the Political Purpose of Strategy   57
   BEATRICE HEUSER

5. Liddell Hart's Impact on the Study of Grand Strategy   73
   LUKAS MILEVSKI

6. Grand Strategy beyond the West   89
   K.M. FIERKE

PART II. THEORETICAL APPROACHES

7. Rational Analysis of Grand Strategy   107
   CHARLES GLASER

8. Network Theory and Grand Strategy   123
   DANIEL H. NEXON

9. Making Grand Strategy in Practice   142
   CHRISTIAN BUEGER AND FRANK GADINGER

10. Ideas and Ideology in Grand Strategy 159
    THIERRY BALZACQ AND PABLO BARNIER-KHAWAM

11. Discourse, Language, and Grand Strategy 173
    MARKUS KORNPROBST AND CORINA-IOANA TRAISTARU

12. Governmentality and Grand Strategy 190
    ANDREW W. NEAL

PART III. SOURCES

13. Material Sources of Grand Strategy 205
    NORRIN RIPSMAN AND IGOR KOVAC

14. Technological Change and Grand Strategy 221
    SOPHIE-CHARLOTTE FISCHER, ANDREA GILLI, AND MAURO GILLI

15. The Domestic Sources of Grand Strategy 239
    JONATHAN D. CAVERLEY

16. Economic Interests and Grand Strategy 256
    KEVIN NARIZNY

17. Civil–Military Relations and Grand Strategy 271
    RISA BROOKS

18. Individual Psychology and Grand Strategy: Romancing the State 287
    BRIAN C. RATHBUN

19. Culture, Identity, and Grand Strategy 303
    DAVID M. McCOURT

20. Rhetoric, Legitimation, and Grand Strategy 322
    STACIE E. GODDARD

PART IV. INSTRUMENTS

21. Grand Strategy and Military Power 339
    PASCAL VENNESSON

22. Diplomacy and Grand Strategy 356
    OLE JACOB SENDING

23. Grand Strategy and the Tools of Economic Statecraft 370
    BRYAN R. EARLY AND KEITH PREBLE

24. Covert Action and Grand Strategy 389
    GREGORY MITROVICH

25. Intelligence and Grand Strategy 406
    JOSHUA ROVNER

26. Financing the Grand Strategy of Great and Rising Powers 422
    ROSELLA CAPPELLA ZIELINSKI

PART V. STRATEGIC MENUS AND CHOICES

27. American Grand Strategies: Untangling the Debates 441
    ROBERT JERVIS

28. Strategy on the Upward Slope: The Grand Strategies of Rising States 457
    JOSHUA R. ITZKOWITZ SHIFRINSON

29. Grand Strategies of Declining Powers 474
    PAUL K. MACDONALD AND JOSEPH M. PARENT

30. The Grand Strategies of Small States 490
    ANDERS WIVEL

31. The Grand Strategies of Violent Rebel Groups 506
    DANIEL BYMAN

32. Grand Strategy and the Challenge of Change 523
    WILLIAM D. JAMES

33. Rethinking Grand-Strategic Change:
    Overhauls versus Adjustments in Grand Strategy 539
    REBECCA LISSNER

PART VI. ASSESSING GRAND STRATEGY

34. Getting Grand Strategy Right 559
    HAL BRANDS AND PETER FEAVER

35. The Challenge of Evaluating Grand Strategy 575
    WILLIAM C. WOHLFORTH

36. Is Grand Strategy an Illusion? Or, the Grandiosity of Grand Strategy 590
    RICHARD K. BETTS

37. The Limits of Grand Strategy 604
    DAVID M. EDELSTEIN

38. Alternatives to Grand Strategy 620
    PETER DOMBROWSKI

39. Grand Strategic Thinking in History 637
    JOHN BEW, MAEVE RYAN, AND ANDREW EHRHARDT

PART VII. THE FUTURE OF GRAND STRATEGY

40. Grand Strategy in a Fractured Marketplace of Ideas 657
    DANIEL W. DREZNER

41. Pluralism, Populism, and the Impossibility of Grand Strategy 673
    RONALD R. KREBS

42. Grand Strategy Under Nonpolarity 690
    RANDALL L. SCHWELLER

43. Grand Strategy and Technological Futures 706
    ROBERT G. CANTELMO AND SARAH E. KREPS

44. Population Aging and Grand Strategy 721
    MARK L. HAAS

Index 737

FIGURES

8.1	Markets, hierarchies, and networks	124
8.2	Network density	130
8.3	Core–periphery structure	132
8.4	Different organizational logics of hegemonic orders	132
26.1	Outlays by the US Department of Defense and Department of State	424
28.1	Conceptualizing risers' grand strategies	464

TABLES

23.1	Grand strategy and the tools of economic statecraft	383
25.1	Intelligence postures and grand strategy	417
28.1	Shifting power among the European great powers, 1860–1910	460
33.1	Operationalizing grand strategy's first- and second-order elements	543
38.1	Grand strategy school (GSS) versus alternatives	624

LIST OF CONTRIBUTORS

Thierry Balzacq is Professor of International Relations at Sciences Po and Professorial Fellow at CERI-Sciences Po, Paris.

Pablo Barnier-Khawam is a PhD Candidate in Political Science at Sciences Po, Paris.

Richard K. Betts is the Leo A. Shifrin Professor of War and Peace Studies at Columbia University.

John Bew is Professor of History and Foreign Policy in the Department of War Studies at King's College London, where he also serves as Co-Director of the Centre for Grand Strategy.

Hal Brands is the Henry A. Kissinger Distinguished Professor of Global Affairs at Johns Hopkins University.

Risa Brooks is the Allis Chalmers Associate Professor of Political Science at Marquette University.

Christian Bueger is Professor of International Relations at the University of Copenhagen.

Daniel Byman is a Professor in the School of Foreign Service at Georgetown University and a Senior Fellow at the Center for Middle East Policy at the Brookings Institution.

Robert G. Cantelmo is a PhD Candidate in the Department of Government at Cornell University.

Jonathan D. Caverley is Associate Professor in the Department of Strategic and Operational Research at the Naval War College, and a Research Scientist in Political Science at the Massachusetts Institute of Technology.

Peter Dombrowski is Professor of Strategy at the US Naval War College.

Daniel W. Drezner is Professor of International Politics at the Fletcher School of Law and Diplomacy, Tufts University.

Bryan R. Early is the Associate Dean for Research and an Associate Professor of Political Science at the University at Albany, SUNY's Rockefeller College of Public Affairs & Policy.

David M. Edelstein is Associate Professor of International Affairs at Georgetown University.

Andrew Ehrhardt is a Postdoctoral Fellow with the Centre for Grand Strategy at King's College London.

Peter Feaver is Professor of Political Science and Public Policy and Director of the Program in American Grand Strategy at Duke University.

K. M. Fierke is Professor of International Relations at St Andrews University.

Sophie-Charlotte Fischer is a PhD Candidate at the Center for Security Studies, (ETH-Zurich) the Swiss Federal Institute of Technology in Zurich (ETH-Zurich), and a Research Affiliate with the Center for the Governance of AI at the University of Oxford.

Lawrence Freedman was Professor of War Studies at King's College London from 1982 to 2014, and Vice-Principal from 2003 to 2013.

Frank Gadinger is Senior Researcher at the University of Duisburg-Essen.

Andrea Gilli is a Senior Researcher in Military Affairs at the NATO Defense College in Rome, Italy, and an affiliate at Center for International Security and Cooperation, Stanford University.

Mauro Gilli is a Senior Researcher in Military Technology and International Security at the Center for Security Studies of the Swiss Federal Institute of Technology in Zurich (ETH-Zurich).

Charles L. Glaser is Professor of Political Science and International Affairs at George Washington University, where he was the Founding Director of the Elliott School's Institute for Security and Conflict Studies from 2009-2019.

Stacie E. Goddard is Mildred Lane Kemper Professor of Political Science at Wellesley College.

Mark L. Haas is the Raymond J. Kelley Endowed Chair in International Relations and Professor of Political Science at Duquesne University.

Beatrice Heuser is Professor of International Relations in the School of Social and Political Sciences at the University of Glasgow.

William D. James is the Transatlantic Defence Research Fellow at the University of Oxford's Changing Character of War Centre and a nonresidential Hans J. Morgenthau Fellow at Notre Dame's International Security Center.

Robert Jervis is Adlai E. Stevenson Professor of International Politics at Columbia University.

Markus Kornprobst holds the Political Science and International Relations Chair at the Vienna School of International Studies.

Igor Kovac is a Pre-Doctoral Fellow at the Institute for Security and Conflict Studies at George Washington University, and a PhD Candidate at the University of Cincinnati.

Ronald R. Krebs is Beverly and Richard Fink Professor in the Liberal Arts and Professor of Political Science at the University of Minnesota, and Editor-in-Chief of the journal *Security Studies*.

Sarah E. Kreps is Professor of Government & Adjunct Professor of Law at Cornell University.

Rebecca Lissner is Assistant Professor in the Strategic and Operational Research Department at the US Naval War College.

Paul K. MacDonald is Associate Professor of Political Science at Wellesley College.

David M. McCourt is Associate Professor in the Department of Sociology at the University of California-Davis.

Lukas Milevski is an Assistant Professor in Strategic Studies at Leiden University.

Gregory Mitrovich is Research Scholar at the Arnold A. Saltzman Institute of War and Peace Studies at Columbia University.

Neville Morley is Professor of Classics & Ancient History at the University of Exeter.

Kevin Narizny is Associate Professor of International Relations at Lehigh University.

Andrew W. Neal is Senior Lecturer in Politics and International Relations and Co-Director of the Centre for Security Research (CeSeR) at the University of Edinburgh.

Daniel H. Nexon is Professor of Government and Foreign Service at Georgetown University.

Joseph M. Parent is Associate Professor of Political Science at the University of Notre Dame.

Keith Preble is a PhD Candidate in the Political Science Department at the University at Albany.

Brian C. Rathbun is Professor of Political Science and International Relations at the University of Southern California.

Norrin M. Ripsman is the Monroe J. Rathbone Professor of International Relations at Lehigh University.

Joshua Rovner is Associate Professor in the School of International Service at American University. In 2018–2019, he served as scholar-in-residence at the National Security Agency and US Cyber Command. The views here are the author's alone.

Maeve Ryan is Lecturer in History and Grand Strategy in the Department of War Studies at King's College London, where she also serves as Co-Director of the Centre for Grand Strategy.

Randall L. Schweller is Professor of Political Science at Ohio State University and was previously Editor-In-Chief of the journal *Security Studies*.

Ole Jacob Sending is Director of Research at the Norwegian Institute of International Affairs (NUPI).

Joshua Shifrinson is Assistant Professor of International Relations at Boston University.

Corina-Ioana Traistaru is a PhD Candidate in the International Legal Studies Programme of the University of Vienna and the Vienna School of International Studies.

Pascal Vennesson is Professor of Political Science and Senior Fellow at the S. Rajaratnam School of International Studies, Nanyang Technological University Singapore.

Anders Wivel is Professor of Political Science at the University of Copenhagen.

William C. Wohlforth is the Daniel Webster Professor in the Department of Government at Dartmouth College.

Rosella Cappella Zielinski is an Assistant Professor of Political Science at Boston University.

CHAPTER 1

THE ENDURING APPEAL OF GRAND STRATEGY

THIERRY BALZACQ AND RONALD R. KREBS

GRAND strategy is arguably the highest form of statecraft. In one usual definition, it is a state's "theory of victory," explaining how the state will utilize its diverse means to advance and achieve national ends. A clearly articulated, well-defined, and relatively stable grand strategy is supposed to allow the ship of state to steer a steady course through the roiling seas of global politics. When foreign policy is in line with grand strategy, the state's scarce resources are expended more efficiently, the state communicates its interests and priorities more clearly to both allies and adversaries, and the state's various arms can more smoothly harmonize their activities.

However, the obstacles to formulating and implementing grand strategy are, by all accounts, imposing. Practitioners often admit to pursuing policies without having in mind any clear strategy, let alone understanding how those particular policies advance larger national goals. They are commonly buffeted by the winds of short-term exigencies, and they often fail to do the hard work of aligning discordant interests. Grand strategy demands consistency and discipline, and both are in short supply. At times, the hortatory insistence that states really must pursue grand strategy seems like ritualized genuflection. States' efforts to pursue grand strategy are so often flawed, and so rarely do states even try to pursue anything like a grand strategy, that some have thrown up their hands and pronounced the entire venture pointless and even counterproductive.

This Handbook emerges from this paradox: that grand strategy should, according to well-established conventional wisdoms, be the center of gravity of states' relations with the outside world, yet, in practice, grand strategy often seems an unattainable ideal. It emerges also from our observation that, even though—or precisely because—the world has become seemingly more complex and unpredictable, grand strategy has had growing resonance in the world of policy and ideas and in the field of higher education. The time is right for a field-defining, interdisciplinary, and comparative text that addresses the conceptual and historical foundations, production, evolution, and future of grand strategy from an unusually diverse range of standpoints—that is, for this Handbook.

This introductory essay has four aims, corresponding to the four sections that follow. First, it introduces readers to the history of the concept of grand strategy and to the central themes of that literature. Second, it explores the abiding tensions in the literature on grand strategy—especially as manifest in the contributions to this Handbook. Third, it sets out and explains the logic of the Handbook, situating the volume's essays within that structure. Finally, it concludes with some speculative reflections on the reasons for grand strategy's recent renaissance.

What is Grand Strategy?

We cannot get very far with the study of grand strategy if we avoid discussions about its meanings and limits. Our essay therefore begins by examining the conceptual evolution of grand strategy. It studies how grand strategy's meaning has evolved in relationship to other concepts. One notable question has been whether grand strategy is most needed in times of war or peace, to win the war or construct a lasting peace. The more grand strategy is associated with war, the more it blurs into military strategy. Yet, the more grand strategy is detached from military strategy, the more it expands to encompass seemingly the entire realm of politics. Given the fundamental uncertainty about what constitutes a proper instance of grand strategy, it is little wonder that so much intellectual energy has been devoted to its definition.

Grand Strategy between Peace and War

Definitions of grand strategy have been contested and elusive since the term first emerged, probably in France, in the nineteenth century. According to Williamson Murray, we do not have, and cannot realistically aspire to, a "clear definition of grand strategy" (Murray 2011, 5). Murray's pessimistic assessment derives in part from the recognition that contending definitions of grand strategy rest on differences in underlying assumptions. Therefore, we have not imposed a definition on this Handbook's authors, which would conceal from view significant conceptual distinctions and which they would anyhow surely resist. We rather encourage readers to pay attention to explicit and tacit differences in how the contributors define grand strategy and to ascertain whether, and to what extent, their divergent definitions produce the conclusions they draw. In this section, we review extant conceptualizations of grand strategy, highlighting their tensions and contradictions, but also identifying zones of commensurability.

The relationship between grand strategy and war has long been a source of disagreement among theorists and historians. For example, Julian Stafford Corbett, who is credited with developing the modern concept of grand strategy, employed an analogous term—"major strategy"—to refer to a war-planning exercise (Corbett 1916). In contrast,

John Frederick Charles Fuller (1923, 7) considered grand strategy predominantly a peacetime activity. "Paradoxically as it may seem," he argued, "the resting time for the grand strategist is during war.... During peace time he not only calculates resources in men, supplies and moral forces of all possible enemies, but, having weighted them, he, unsuspected by the enemy, undermines them by a plan" (Fuller 1923, 20). This dispute runs rife throughout the literature. Edward Mead Earle saw grand strategy as relevant in times of both peace and war. For Earle, grand strategy "is that which so integrates the policies and armaments of the nation that the resort to war is either rendered unnecessary or is undertaken with the maximum chance of victory" (Earle 1966, viii). Basil Liddell Hart, by contrast, limits grand strategy to war situations, though he recognizes that its efficacy transcends war's moment. Thus, "grand strategy should not only conceive the various instruments but so regulate their use as to avoid damage to the future state of peace—for its security and prosperity" (Liddell Hart 1929, 151). For both Earle and Liddell Hart, however, scarred by the experience of world war, the central purpose of grand strategy is to induce peace. It is peace, or its greater likelihood, that justifies the pursuit of a given strategy.

The early literature's very focus on peace and war, together with its insistence that a well-designed grand strategy should yield peace, meant that it was deeply functionalist. The result was a conceptualization of grand strategy that was ironically, despite its functionalism, highly normative. Thus, Liddell Hart extols what he calls "true grand strategy," the object of which is "better peace, a peace of security and prosperity" (Liddell Hart [1954] 1991, 322). This normative orientation shaped attitudes toward grand strategy during the Cold War, with some prominent figures either condoning it (e.g. Kennan) or loathing it (e.g., Gerberding and Brodie 1968). Some feared that grand strategy would stretch the use of force beyond its conceptual core, within a wartime context, and others thought grand strategy both redundant to "diplomacy" (Sending 2021) and also potentially dangerous, imparting to diplomacy military overtones. For the most part, however, until the mid-1960s, many writers preferred the term "national strategy," which seemed more limited in scope and ambition. But the notion was nevertheless quite close to Liddell Hart's vision. There is indeed little daylight between Liddell Hart's view of grand strategy and the US military's 1962 definition of national strategy as "the art and science of developing and using the political, economic, and psychological powers of a nation, together with its armed forces, during peace and during war, to secure national objectives" (*Dictionary of United States Military Terms for Joint Usage* 1962, 205).

Grand strategy came back into the civilian strategist's lexicon slowly in the late 1960s, with momentum growing through the 1970s along with the renaissance of security studies (Walt 1991). Three books signaled the restoration of grand strategy (Milevski 2016, 111): Samuel Williamson's *The Politics of Grand Strategy* (1969), John Collins's *Grand Strategy* (1973), and Edward Luttwak's *The Grand Strategy of the Roman Empire* (1976). However, despite the title's explicit invocation of grand strategy, Luttwak was more concerned with the operational level of war which he thought responsible for Rome's military success. When he discussed grand strategy, Luttwak collapsed it into imperial statecraft. Collins, on the other hand, proposed a genuine and consistent engagement with grand strategy, with a promising post-Clausewitzian twist (Collins 1973, 15). Like Liddell Hart, Collins dressed grand strategy in normative garb: its purpose was to achieve a "lasting peace" (Collins 1973, 15). But Collins was clearer than his predecessors on the relationship between grand strategy and other forms of strategy, including military strategy. He thus distinguished grand strategy from both higher-level national strategy, which encompasses all strategies a nation can conceivably develop and deploy, and lower-level military strategy (Collins 1973, 15). Grand strategy, for Collins, is "the art and science of employing national power under all circumstances to exert desired degrees and types of control over the opposition through threats, force, indirect pressure, diplomacy, subterfuge, and other imaginative means, thereby satisfying national security interests and objectives" (Collins 1973, 14).

Collins' influential formulation places national security interests at the center of grand strategy, constituting its scope and specifying its frontiers (Biddle 2015, 5). This theme has featured in the literature on grand strategy ever since. Hal Brands, for example, posits that grand strategy is the "theory or logic that guides leaders seeking security in a complex and insecure world" (Brands 2014, 3). This view draws on Barry Posen's definition of grand strategy: a "state's theory about how it can best 'cause' security for itself" (Posen 1984, 13). For these writers, grand strategy's chief function is not to promote peace, but to advance state security. The specter of war, though, still looms: it is the possibility of armed conflict—"a costly and bloody business" (Posen 2014, 1)—that requires states to devote careful thought to how to marshal their resources to provide security (Dueck 2006, 10). Paraphrasing H. R. McMaster (2007, 71), "war is the final audit" of grand strategy.

Grand strategy is thus a theory, whose chief virtue, according to its proponents, is bringing coherence to and rationalizing state policy. A clearly articulated and pursued grand strategy facilitates deliberate and intentional policy planning, which is in turn most likely to produce security. Thus, Paul Kennedy puts it succinctly: "[t]he crux of grand strategy lies ... in *policy*" (Kennedy 1991, 5; emphasis in the original). In contrast to those who problematically reduce grand strategy to a bundle of policies alone (cf. Nordlinger 1995, 9–10; Christensen 1996, 7; Krasner 2010, 1), grand strategy is a theory from which an accompanying set of policies deductively flow. This view—today, arguably the dominant one—thus rests on a rationalist wager (Balzacq, Dombrowski, and Reich 2019a). Peter Feaver's definition is illustrative: "Grand strategy refers to the collection of plans and policies that comprise the state's deliberate effort to harness political, military, diplomatic, and economic tools together to advance that state's national interest" (Feaver 2009; also Walt 1987, 6). Thus John Lewis Gaddis defines grand strategy as "the calculated relationship of means to large ends", wherein "calculated" is synonymous with "preconceived," and stands opposed to faith in the "accidental, inadvertent, or fortuitous" (Gaddis 2009; also Dueck 2006, 10). Finally, grand strategy is expressly oriented to the long term, stretching by some accounts well into the future—"over decades and perhaps centuries" (Martel 2015, 32; Lobell 2003, 3).

Typologies and their Limits

Some find grand strategy's definitional and conceptual elusiveness invigorating (Baracuhy 2011, 151), and others resign themselves to an enduring muddle (Murray 2011; Goldstein 2005, 18). The concept's slipperiness seems likely to persist. Nina Silove's recent exemplary effort to bring intellectual coherence to the field distinguishes among "grand plans," "grand principles," and "grand behaviors" (Silove 2018). Grand strategy as a "grand plan" is the familiar rationalist, deductive account. Grand strategy as an "organizing principle" steers a nation's relations with the outside world, but does not provide a clear blueprint for action. Grand strategy as "grand behavior" refers to observable foreign policies, which appear to the analyst *ex post* as logically linked but which may not have been driven by any coherent vision *ex ante*. While Silove's typology seems to organize much of the existing literature, the lines between her categories are anything but bright. She concedes, for instance, that grand principles and grand plans are differentiated only by their "level of detail" (Silove 2018, 39). It is, moreover, difficult to imagine a plan without an underlying guiding set of ideas, and it is hard to see what good can be done by grand principles that support a very wide range of possible policies. At the end of Silove's sweeping review, we remain no closer to "*a* theory of *the* concept of grand strategy," which she had promised at the start. Indeed, Silove concludes that grand strategy cannot be reduced to "*one* concept" (Silove 2018, 29, 56; emphases added). The muddle remains.

A second recent exhaustive review reaches similar conclusions. Thierry Balzacq, Peter Dombrowski, and Simon Reich offer an alternative typology, grouping definitions of grand strategy based on their *logic* and *substance*. For the classicist, the logic of grand strategy is that of the use of force in a rationalist mode "to attain a given political objective" (Howard 1979, 975). Those working within the international relations tradition, in contrast, emphasize grand strategy's utility in setting priorities (Martel 2015, 32), which is necessarily a political process grounded in legitimation (Goddard and Krebs 2015). Nevertheless, they argue that grand strategy is in the end a "polythetic concept," meaning that it "combines elements which recur in political processes—through which a state articulates its ways, means, and ends" (Balzacq, Dombrowski, and Reich 2019b, 9). Grand strategy's tasks and forms, they contend, vary from case to case.

In short, a unified concept and theory of grand strategy continue to elude us. This surely frustrates those who wish knowledge would neatly cumulate. But they can take solace in the commonalities and questions that have nevertheless emerged through this conceptual inquiry. First, there is much agreement that aligning means and ends is one of the central challenges of foreign policy in general and national security policy in particular. States often have difficulty right-sizing their ambitions, and they routinely find themselves without adequate means to advance their interests. Their short-term interests are often at odds with their long-term aims, and they are unsure how to balance these intertemporal conflicts (Edelstein 2017). The enduring popularity of grand strategy reflects the persistence of both these challenges and of policymakers' desire to navigate through them. But does grand strategy, as a national security policy plan, or grand strategizing, as a process, constitute a silver bullet? Or even offer helpful answers to these perennial questions and impulses?

Second, scholars largely acknowledge that grand strategy is first and foremost an idea—a "*theory* of victory" in the security arena. They thus affirm that intellectual reflection has a place in the making of foreign policy. National security is too important a matter to be left just to the generals or the politicians. Admittedly, such a conception of grand strategy is self-serving: scholars have created a field of study that justifies their right to weigh in on affairs of state. Yet grand strategy seems to be much more than merely an academic parlor game. Its debates, though seemingly arid and theoretical, take place regularly in general-interest outlets well beyond the ivory tower. But does grand strategy resonate widely because it yields better national security policy? Or because it satisfies the human cognitive demand for interpretive frameworks that make sense of otherwise disorderly data?

Third, while some self-proclaimed realists see grand strategy as strictly responsive to international structural imperatives, there is wide implicit agreement that grand strategy is rooted in the realm of politics. Grand strategy requires answers to a series of questions that can be answered only in the political arena. Who constitutes the "we" whose interests are to be secured? What are the interests that strategy should be designed to advance? What threats to those interests are present in the international arena? Whose resources should be mobilized in the effort? Different strategies necessarily weigh more heavily and make deeper demands on some coalitions than others. They necessarily implicate different visions and ambitions. Durable grand strategy rests on stable political foundations, on well-grounded processes of deliberation and legitimation (Goddard and Krebs 2015). Politics is not the enemy of rational strategy, but is rather its necessary underpinning.

This Handbook builds on these areas of commonality. It examines the history of the grand strategy enterprise. It affirms the importance of grand strategy, while also inviting debates about its utility and purposes. It delves into the politics of grand strategy, exploring the varied actors and interests who compete to shape grand strategy. It sustains these conversations from diverse theoretical perspectives.

Tensions in Grand Strategy Scholarship

The field of grand strategy is equally defined by its enduring—and, we believe, productive—tensions. In this section, we explore briefly three such tensions.

The Status of Strategizing

The first such tension revolves around the status of grand strategizing—that is, the often raging debates over grand strategy that so exercise foreign policy elites, inside and outside government. Are these debates consequential? Or are they a matter of academic/elite navel-gazing?

One school of thought suggests that these debates matter, but only in relation to whether they produce the "right" grand strategy, as dictated to states by their position in the international system. This is the implicit view of self-identified realist analysts of global politics. But if states generally exercise little agency when it comes to strategy[1]—either because foreign policy is largely the product of rational choice or because states that make poor choices are punished by the international system (Feaver 2000)—strategy is crucial, but strategizing is moot (Lissner 2018, 7). Yet realists surely believe that strategizing matters, or they would not participate avidly in strategic debate. Some realists rail against the "blob" that, they charge, has reinforced American inclinations to liberal primacy and has prevented the United States from pursuing prudent restraint (Porter 2018). If realists' (better) argument had won, the United States would have avoided self-defeating liberal crusades. For realists, strategizing therefore matters especially when it results in error—that is, when it induces states to adopt a grand strategy that contravenes systemic imperatives (Rathbun 2008; Schweller 2006). The chief problem is that realists have little to say, from within their own theoretical tradition, about why debates over grand strategy follow a particular course and why they produce a strategic direction in line or at odds with international dictates.

Nonrealist scholars thus have far more to contribute to our understanding of how grand strategy is actually made and about the impact of grand strategizing. Liberals and constructivists are, in theoretically distinctive ways, attentive to the formation of collective identity, to processes of interest aggregation and coalition-building, and to the dynamics of discursive contest. Who legitimately participates in debates over grand strategy, and who is treated as beyond the pale and thereby silenced? How are the boundaries of legitimate debate constituted? Who dominates the narrative and sets the agenda (Krebs 2015; Krebs 2018)? What constituents and concrete interests are impacted by grand-strategic arguments, and how do they intervene in grand strategy's formulation and implementation? How do gaps arise between formal statements of grand strategy and its execution? The many flavors of liberalism and constructivism weigh and theorize these processes very differently, but they have in common an analytical focus on strategizing (Balzacq, Dombrowski, and Reich 2019b). While this comes at the expense of analytical austerity, it also grants them a purchase on the *reality* of grand strategy that realism ironically lacks.

Realists might well acknowledge that their vision of grand strategy is more normative than empirical. Yet should grand strategy ideally respond to international systemic imperatives alone? Or should it recognize as well the unique domestic configurations that render some grand strategies durably sustainable, leave some fragile, and doom still others?

Plan or Process?

For many, grand strategy is the North Star of foreign policy. In the inevitable nautical metaphor, grand strategy is a stable plan that allows the ship of state to steer a steady course across the roiling seas of domestic and international politics. Guiding the ship requires a steady but flexible hand on the tiller. One cannot sail a perfectly straight line, or one may run straight into the teeth of a storm or run aground. But the idea is that one should steer back to that course once the storm has passed. This conception of grand strategy—as a stable, clearly articulated plan—is widespread (e.g. Flournoy and Brimley 2006; Lettow and Mahnken 2009; Krepinevich and Watts 2009; Brands 2014). Planning does not guarantee success. Many plans, after all, are poorly designed, inefficient, or suboptimal. But those without a plan cannot hope to succeed in global politics.

Others question whether, given the immense complexity of global politics, one can plot a course before setting out on the journey. The inevitable storms leave the landscape so altered that the island toward which one was steering may afterwards no longer exist. From this standpoint, designing a grand-strategic plan is pointless at best, and counter-productive at worst. The obvious retort is that any grand strategy must allow for adaptation. No plan can be followed blindly, and the wise statesperson knows how to adjust in the face of altered circumstances. Indeed, claim grand strategy's defenders, there is a stronger relationship between grand strategy and pragmatism than critics allow. As Bernard Brodie once wrote, "[s]trategic thinking… is nothing if not pragmatic" (Brodie 1973, 452; also Gray 2010, 21). But how much change can grand strategy endure before it is no longer worthy of the name? How far can the ship be blown off the originally charted course before even planners must ruefully acknowledge that it is following an entirely new route? And if grand strategy routinely requires substantial emendation, what value was there in the plan in the first place? Maybe it would be better not to have one. Simon Reich and Peter Dombrowski (2017, 2) thus argue that a "one-size-fits-all grand strategy has little utility in the twenty-first century" and, as a corrective, propose a greater reliance on "calibrated strategies." Similarly skeptical of a durable grand strategy's sustainability in modern America, Daniel Drezner, Ronald R. Krebs, and Randall Schweller (2020) counsel organizational decentralization and policy incrementalism (see also Edelstein and Krebs 2015; Edelstein 2021).

These critics thus gesture toward an "emergent process" model of strategy and policymaking (Mintzberg and Waters 1985; Popescu 2018). Whereas grand strategy emphasizes intentional control, the emergent process model stresses case-by-case responsiveness. Grand strategy promotes a "designer" mindset among foreign-policymakers, but the emergent model insists that they are primarily "learners" and "pattern recognizers." Grand strategy imagines states acting off a pre-set strategic script, while the emergent approach recognizes a significant role for improvisation. Grand strategy emphasizes the reality and virtues of stability, while the emergent alternative stresses the need for nimbleness and much greater levels of adaptability.

For grand strategy advocates, emergent policymaking is too modest. How can it inform policymaking in the face of competing values? How can it prevent the ship of state from merely lurching from crisis to crisis? Cannot major states exercise some modicum of control over global affairs? And do they not then need at least a rough sense of where they are trying to push and shove a resistant world? Perhaps the *process* of grand strategy retains relevance, even if it does not produce a fixed plan. The grand strategy exercise necessitates regular meditation in the halls of power on what the nation values, whether its behavior in the world has advanced those interests, and whether it has expended its resources wisely. It provides the basis for productive self-critique. Pragmatic action informed by periodic reflection on the "big picture"—through an institutionalized grand strategy process—is presumably better than unthoughtful pragmatism.

Is grand strategy, then, best conceptualized as a plan, leavened by engagement with reality from the ground up, or as a process, informing pragmatic foreign policy? Either formulation suggests that, as Ionut Popescu maintains, "all real-world strategies have both deliberate and emergent *elements*" (Popescu 2018, 447; also Mintzberg and Waters 1985, 258). The debate, then, should not oppose two starkly different models of policymaking, but should rather revolve around where to locate policymaking between these two poles. This conceptualization gives rise to several promising lines of research: when does policymaking embraces either element more pronouncedly? How is the relationship between pragmatic action and strategic planning negotiated across time and space? And how does the resulting balance affect the performance of the state in world politics?

Who Needs Grand Strategy?

A final enduring tension lies in the question of who needs grand strategy. The dominant approach focuses on the implications of the modifying adjective "grand." By some accounts, the grandness of strategy refers to the scope of its ambitions: grand strategy entails a plan for world order, for bringing the world into line with one's values and interests (e.g. Krasner 2010). Grand strategy is then necessarily the purview of the grand in another sense—of the great powers. Only they potentially have sufficient resources to order the world. Grand strategy is a luxury of the wealthy. Smaller, weaker states, in contrast, are playthings of the powerful. They do not need a grand strategy because they have little choice but to follow structural imperatives. They are order-takers, not order-makers. Grand strategy is a mark of agency, and only the world's greatest powers enjoy such agency.

An alternative view puts more emphasis on "strategy" than on the adjective preceding it. Grand strategy is something that *all* states should do—*especially* when resources are scarce. Smaller powers, because they have limited resources, need to think carefully about where to spend their marginal dollar. The United States after the Cold War, in contrast, was so powerful relative to its rivals that it could afford to "waste" its money on peripheral projects. Much like wealthy individuals, who do not have to construct a monthly budget, great powers can allow themselves to engage the world without strategy. Small states do not have that luxury. Grand strategy is then especially valuable to the world's minor powers, because it helps them efficiently and productively allocate their scarce resources.

This tension within and between "grand" and "strategy" gives rise to at least two avenues of potentially productive research. First, do states that more consistently pursue grand strategies (as plans) and/or that conduct regular strategic reviews (grand strategy as process) do better in global politics? The presumption that they do underlies many defenses of grand strategy, but we are not aware of research substantiating the claim. There are reasons for skepticism. We can think of many examples in which states faithfully pursued grand strategies very much to their detriment—Nazi Germany, for one. We can think of many remarkable successes in foreign policy that hinged on improvisation in the face of uncertainty—such as the GHW Bush administration's management of the end of the Cold War. Perhaps rigorous research would find that smaller states need grand strategy more, and profit more from carefully formulating and executing grand strategy, than do great powers. Second, do shifts in material power affect the content and ambitions of nations' grand strategies? It seems intuitive that states' ambitions typically rise along with their power and that, conversely, their ambitions shrink along with their declining fortunes. The literature on declining powers has addressed the grand-strategic alternatives confronting these states (MacDonald and Parent 2021), but not the grandness of their grand strategies. Do states in decline abandon the "grand" and become tinkerers? Do great powers tend to mismanage their decline because their long years of plenty and wastefulness deprived them of the intellectual and bureaucratic musculature needed for careful strategic planning?

This Handbook does not seek to elide these tensions, just as it has not imposed on its contributors a single conception of grand strategy. In fact, we have tried to highlight the tensions across the chapters, by inviting our contributors to engage selectively with their interlocutors, especially those who disagree with them. The field, we believe, will not advance if we pretend that this Handbook's authors are singing in perfect harmony, out of the same hymnal, nor conversely if we throw up our hands and resign ourselves to a displeasing cacophony. Rather, we choose to place our faith in pluralistic engagement—recognizing difference, drawing attention to both commonalities and contradictions, and plumbing the depths of the tensions across this Handbook's chapters.

The Logic of the Volume

This Handbook is divided into seven sections. The first two sections are more explicitly conceptual and theoretical and are thus especially foundational. The meanings of "grand strategy" are multiple, and they are historically grounded: the purposes, the practices, and crucially the conceptual framework of grand strategy have evolved over time. Whether fully aware of this history or not, contemporary writing on grand strategy necessarily bears its fingerprints. Debates over how to conceptualize grand strategy, on the wisdom of particular grand strategies, and on the concept's very utility reflect this inheritance. The five chapters in Part I therefore address themselves to the question of "what is grand strategy?," but—in contrast to much existing literature—they employ less a theoretical or normative lens than a historical one (Chapter 2). They examine progenitors who did not explicitly reference grand strategy but to whom all later grand strategists are indebted—notably, Thucydides (Chapter 3) and Clausewitz (Chapter 4). They explore the contributions of key prominent figures in the modern grand strategy tradition, such as Liddell Hart and Earle (Chapter 5). To rectify the transatlantic bias of contemporary scholarship on grand strategy, this section also includes a chapter on grand-strategic thinking beyond the West (Chapter 6). By recovering the concept's history, the essays in this section provide crucial context for the rest of the volume. But, by revealing grand strategy's unquestioned presuppositions and giving voice to alternative traditions, these essays are potentially even more important: they can facilitate critique of and alternatives to the contemporary grand strategy exercise.

With grand strategy's historical meaning and evolution established, Part II takes an ahistorical and explicitly theoretical turn. In its chapters, distinguished theoreticians, representing an unusually diverse range of perspectives, set out the essential elements of their preferred theoretical approaches and explain what questions those approaches pose of grand strategy and what answers they offer. Much of the traditional literature on grand strategy works in a realist and rationalist theoretical vein, and Part II appropriately begins there as well (Chapter 7). But, in line with this Handbook's spirit of theoretical pluralism and its desire to promote dialogue across theoretical divides, the other essays in this section explore strategy from social constructivist and critical standpoints. While realist accounts typically conceive of grand strategy as the product of a unitary state, responding to international systematic imperatives, it can also be seen as the product of social networks—domestic, international, and even transnational—whose interests are advanced or threatened by particular strategic options and whose corresponding worldviews sustain or undermine those strategies. A social network perspective is dynamic, as grand strategy has the capacity to activate and transform social networks (Chapter 8). Strategizing is, moreover, a practice, which strategists learn and in which they then reflexively engage (Chapter 9). Whether grand strategy is consciously executed or driven by habitual practices, its form and content rely on a set of actionable ideas that forge a nation's engagement with the world—that is, ideologies (Chapter 10). In addition to practices, language is the main vehicle for promoting the systems of ideas that underlie grand strategy (Chapter 11). Finally, grand strategy hinges upon leaders' ability to develop a compelling narrative about a state's priorities and the threats it confronts. Grand strategy thus starts with securitization, advancing a "regime of truth" that empowers and silences participants in policy debate (Chapter 12). Part II introduces the reader to a broad range of theoretical perspectives on grand strategy, which are then put to work in subsequent sections.

Traditional accounts of grand strategy are often normative: they speak to what a rational, unitary, systemically inclined state *should* do, in the analyst's view, more than what real states actually do. The essays in Part III focus on the varied forces from which real grand strategies spring. No account of grand strategy can ignore the international system and geography, as well as the state of technology, and thus Part III begins with these factors (Chapters 13 and 14). But those international forces are generally not smoothly translated into strategy and policy, as they are filtered through domestic political institutions (Chapter 15) and implicate both economic interests (Chapter 16) and civil-military relations (Chapter 17). While some see such domestic forces as "impediments" to the formulation of coherent and rational grand strategy, that stance follows only if the international system speaks clearly and if it therefore provides attentive grand strategists with clear directives. Yet both dizzyingly rapid-paced events and slow-moving tectonic shifts require interpretation. The attribution of meaning to global events may be shaped by material and institutional interests, but also by individual psychology (Chapter 18) and by culture and national identity (Chapter 19). Meaning-making is not merely a matter of apolitical puzzling, but rather is deeply political and often highly contested, and the range of viable strategies of legitimation thus affects the grand strategy states can pursue (Chapter 20).

Grand strategy, we explained earlier, is typically conceived of as a theory of victory that tells a causal story about how a given set of means is to be leveraged and combined to advance a particular end. Although scholarly and popular writing on strategy often privileges military tools, stressing the use of armed force alone is in fact contrary to the spirit of the grand-strategic enterprise, which emphasizes how the full range of national means can be effectively employed. Grand strategists are most certainly not militarists: in the grand strategist's worldview, the armed forces are not an omnipurpose hammer with which to bang in the nation's many nails. The essays in Part IV therefore explore a range of instruments that any decision-maker must consider as she devises the nation's grand strategy: the use of force of course (Chapter 21), but also diplomacy (Chapter 22), economic statecraft (Chapter 23), and covert action (Chapter 24). These instruments have been updated over the decades—weapons have become more precise, the internet and social media have invigorated public diplomacy, economic and financial sanctions have become more sophisticated and impactful in a world of globalization—but the categories would have appeared on any such list half a century ago. Doing any of this naturally requires carefully collected and vetted intelligence: grand strategy can be only as good as the information underpinning it (Chapter 25). It also requires mobilizing and organizing the nation's financial base: resources are not fixed, nor are they unlimited (Chapter 26).

With previous sections having unpacked grand strategy's history, theory, sources, and instruments, the seven essays in Part V put all this together to explore, synoptically and synthetically, how international actors in practice pursue grand strategy. The section's opening essay carefully analyzes recently reinvigorated debates over US grand strategy, revealing the slate of linked semi-hidden assumptions that divide advocates of restraint from those of deep engagement (Chapter 27). It is a critical case study in the construction of grand-strategic argument—that is, the process by which strategic menus are assembled and by which persuasive rationales for particular dishes are put forward. The section's other essays examine the grand-strategic menus and choices of both familiar categories of international actors—rising great powers (Chapter 28) and declining great powers (Chapter 29)—and less familiar ones—small states (Chapter 30) and violent nonstate actors (Chapter 31). As previously discussed, the sometime claim that only great powers can have grand strategies rests on the presumption that grand strategy deserves the name only if it is grand in its ambitions. Yet all international actors can, and by some accounts should, have a rationale as to how their means and ends are aligned. Arguably, this exercise is even more important for weaker players in global politics, who enjoy less room for error.

The two final essays of Part V explore how and when international actors change grand-strategic direction (Chapters 32 and 33). The organizational and psychological obstacles to policy change are always substantial, but change is still more difficult when the policies in question touch wide-ranging elements of government action and are more deeply embedded in national discourse and identity. Grand-strategic change is therefore especially challenging. If grand strategy adapts too rapidly—if it tilts and lurches with domestic or international waves—it cannot be a steady guide for the ship of state. Yet if it does not adapt swiftly enough, that ship can crash upon the shoals. Changing grand-strategic direction at just the right time, in the right degree, and in the right way is among the central challenges of statesmanship.

With the conceptual, historical, theoretical, and empirical building blocks in place, the Handbook turns in Part VI in a more evaluative direction. Is the game of grand strategy worth the candle? The essays in this volume, echoing the conventional scholarly wisdom, generally answer that question in the affirmative. This section thus opens with a forthright and spirited defense of grand strategy's merit (Chapter 34). Of course many grand strategies fail. Yet distinguishing a poor grand strategy from a reasonable gamble that did not pay off is no easy task. Criteria for evaluating grand strategies are often implicit. In a searching essay, they become explicit (Chapter 35). However, Part VI also gives critics of grand strategy their due. Given the complexity of global politics, the inherent impossible tradeoffs, and the usual barriers to rational decision-making, grand strategy is arguably an illusion, even a self-deception, and it is perhaps even dangerous (Chapter 36). Were there no alternative to grand strategy, such critiques would carry less weight, but the authors here advance alternatives: strategic pragmatism (Chapter 37) and calibrated strategy (Chapter 38). Readers will decide for themselves whether these alternatives are superior to an always flawed grand strategy. Perhaps grand strategy is less a formal process than a "habit of mind," which changes the way scholars might appreciate its analytical relevance (Chapter 39).

Finally, Part VII explores the future of grand strategy. Global politics is rife with unknowns and is always full of surprises, and prognostication about its future course is always risky. Yet, in the editors' judgment, the five ongoing developments profiled in Part VII are fairly good bets to continue into the future. First, in contemporary liberal democracies, the marketplace of ideas has, by many accounts, become less and less functional—as trust in experts has eroded, politics has become more polarized, and the very notion of truth has come under assault (Chapter 40). Second, while polities around the globe have become increasingly pluralistic, so too have their politics become increasingly populist and nationalist (Chapter 41). Third, international politics is becoming increasingly messy. Gone are the allegedly good old days of bipolarity and multipolarity. They have been replaced by something more fluid and less predictable—a world that arguably verges on "entropy" (Chapter 42). Many contend that grand strategy is more necessary than ever if states—buffeted by domestic turmoil and international instability—are to plot a steady course. But all three essays, despite their deeply divergent theoretical roots, question whether a durable grand strategy is sustainable in a world in which the marketplace of ideas is failing, in which dominant national narratives are crumbling, and in which global politics is increasingly volatile. The three essays divide over whether grand strategy's demise is to be mourned or welcomed.

The remaining two essays in Part VII do not question the viability of the grand-strategic enterprise, but rather explore how nations will adapt to and cope with two important developments. The first is technological change. Technological innovation—from the longbow to the battle tank to the atomic bomb—bequeaths improved and sometimes radically new means, which can potentially alter the strategic equation (Chapter 43). Will the big technological changes of today and just over the horizon—the growth of computer processing speeds, the increasing automation and even autonomy of weapons systems, and artificial intelligence's gradual move from theory to lab to reality—lead to small strategic adjustments, or rather generate new strategic demands and create new strategic possibilities? The second is the graying of the world, especially in industrialized nations. As women in advanced, industrialized nations have fewer children, falling in many places well below the "replacement rate," and as these societies are reluctant to open their borders to young strivers from around the world, these polities have a diminishing resource base alongside growing welfare-state demands. As the world's wealthy nations age, and defense scrambles for a share of the shrinking budgetary pie, their grand strategies will need retooling (Chapter 44). How will they bring interests and resources into alignment in the face of these demographic pressures?

Why Now? Grand Strategy's Return

Grand strategy has always straddled the line between the worlds of the academy and policy. Its formulation requires trafficking in abstractions and distinguishing categories and types—the stock and trade of the scholar. Its payoff rests on drawing out the implications for what many arms of government do on a daily basis—the shared expertise of both scholars and policymakers. And, ultimately, the value of grand strategy lies in its consistent, yet adaptive, implementation—the exclusive purview of the policymaker.

In recent years, both scholars and policymakers across the world have embraced anew the value of thinking in grand-strategic terms and debating alternative grand strategies. Leading universities and military and diplomatic academies have established related institutes and centers (such as at King's College London, the University of Exeter, and Yale University), degree programs (including at the University of Sussex and the University of St. Andrew's), courses (such as at Sciences Po in Paris), and designated fellowships (notably, a joint Harvard-MIT program). One leading press, Oxford University Press, has established a new related book series ("Oxford Studies in Grand Strategy"). Private foundations (most notably the Charles Koch Foundation in the United States) have funneled funds into research and teaching on the subject. Government agencies—such as the Institute for Defense Higher Studies in Italy, among others—have hosted conferences on grand strategy, inviting scholars to share their views of the emerging shape of world politics and their nation's role, and they have launched large-scale bureaucratic efforts to impart greater strategic coherence to their nation's military and foreign policies. In short, there is something about this historical moment that seems to be inviting reflection and debate on grand strategy.

Why has this moment in time seen revitalized interest in grand strategy? We offer here some speculative thoughts. During the 1990s, after the Berlin Wall came down and the Soviet Union subsequently collapsed, a profound debate raged in intellectual circles about the future driving forces of global politics. Some predicted that global rivalry would soon revive but along civilizational axes (Huntington 1996), others maintained that ideological conflict and thus indeed history had reached its end with the triumph of liberalism (Fukuyama 1992), and others suggested that the developed and developing worlds were headed in opposed directions, with the latter poised for a chaotic "coming anarchy" (Kaplan 1994). Some thought that great power politics would return with a vengeance (Mearsheimer 1990), and others argued that US primacy was so overwhelming as to dissuade potential challengers (Wohlforth 1999). In other words, the shape of global politics was so uncertain in the 1990s that any talk of grand strategy seemed premature. One did not know toward what end one would be strategizing. Of course that hardly stopped policymakers from floating successors to "containment." In the Clinton White House, finding containment's heir became something of an obsession (Chollet and Goldgeier 2008). But that was as much a quest for an alluring slogan, with which to parry the administration's political critics, as a search for a substantive grand strategy to guide the nation through an uncertain world.

Nor in the 1990s, on either side of the Atlantic, did the need for grand strategy seem quite so pressing. With Russia on its heels, and eager to gain entrance to Europe's markets and Western institutions, with China still quite poor, and seemingly happy to play within the rules of the Western international economic game, with the Japanese economy swooning and stalling and then entering the doldrums for the next two decades, no major threats loomed. Instability—communal strife, civil war, dire poverty—remained mostly contained, as far as the West was concerned. Occasionally the barbarians climbed over the gate—bombing the World Trade Center in New York in 1993 and the Paris Métro in 1996—but these episodes could be treated as exceptional, and illegal migration was, with Western economies humming, merely a nuisance, albeit one with growing political resonance. Americans congratulated themselves on being "the last remaining superpower," and Europeans grumbled petulantly at American "hyperpuissance" (hyperpower), while nevertheless continuing to defer to and depend on US leadership and to ride free on US defense efforts. Strategy is needed when resources are scarce and needs are great. Both sides of the Atlantic were flush with resources in the 1990s, and the international demands on those resources did not seem urgent. The decade after the Cold War was not a time when grand-strategic debate would find fertile soil.

Nor did grand strategy become a focus of discussion among Western policymakers and pundits in the next decade. The events of September 2001, and subsequent attacks in the United Kingdom and Spain, served as a wake-up call to the West. Suddenly the homeland and international security needs seemed imposing, and the "peace dividend" of the 1990s became a distant memory of a naïve, overly sanguine time. One might have thought that, under these conditions, grand strategy would flourish in the 2000s, usefully establishing priorities and allocating resources. But it did not. For much of the decade after 9/11, the United States was the prisoner of a self-imposed "War on Terror" and its underlying narrative. There was sometimes robust debate, but only over the narrow question of how and where to wage that war. Critics who insisted that the United States faced more important threats than Islamist attacks were silenced or ignored (Lemann 2002; Krebs 2015, 145–172, 269–275). While Europeans broke with the American extension of the War on Terror to Iraq, for them too the struggle against Islamist extremism became the unquestioned, and unquestionable, priority. After 9/11, in the West, priorities abroad were not debated but presumed. It was not grand strategy that was at issue, but its particular applications and tactics. Moreover, after mass-casualty attacks in New York, London, and Madrid, resources to combat "Islamist terrorism" and "extremism" and "jihadi radicalization" were abundant on both sides of the Atlantic: what this war claimed to need, it largely got. In 2005, EU member states agreed to establish the position of EU counterterrorism coordinator, and in 2016 another new position, EU commissioner on security, was created (Bures 2020). In addition to member states' individual budgets, EU funds for fighting terrorism were spread across the EU budget, even in the ERASMUS+ program, which was primarily a cultural and scientific exchange scheme. Who needed a strategy to parcel out resources when security budgets were burgeoning? Grand strategy thus found the environment no more welcoming in the 2000s than it had in the 1990s—albeit for very different, even opposite, reasons.

Grand strategy has made a comeback in the last decade, as the War on Terror waned (Krebs 2013). The erosion of the War on Terror's stranglehold on foreign policy thought opened space. At the end of the decade, the Obama administration averred that "our global efforts to successfully counter violent extremism ... are only one element of our strategic environment and cannot define America's engagement with the world" (*National Security Strategy* 2010, 8). That breach in the Terror narrative nurtured strategic debate. It naturally prompted a series of questions: what are the other elements of that strategic environment? how do they relate to each other? and how should the country engage with the world in all its richness and with all its problems? As the narrow aperture of the War on Terror gave way to a wider lens, what followed was not a sense of relief. Partly as a result of the War on Terror's subsiding grip on the imagination, great power politics, which had of course never really gone away, seemed to make a significant return. Europeans and North Americans noticed how Russia began to reassert itself, first in its immediate region and then in the Middle East. They devoted attention to how China strengthened its hold over disputed territory in the South China Sea, launched its ambitious Belt and Road Initiative, became the lender of first resort across large portions of the world, and established a series of alternative global economic institutions. The War on Terror's fall from its dominant perch not only helped make grand strategy seem again essential, but crucially allowed for the revival of meaningful debate over grand strategy.

Grand strategy became more relevant for a second, partly related reason: across the West, claims on national resources grew in the second decade of the century. In the United States, the cumulative weight of the War on Terror, and the various wars and military missions and bases attached to it, became overwhelming. Rampant defense spending, in combination with a series of tax cuts between 2003 and 2017, had boosted the national debt to unprecedented peacetime levels. More generally, one economic challenge after another confronted the world and especially Europe—the Great Recession of 2007–2009, followed quickly by the Greek debt crisis, crises elsewhere in the Eurozone, and then Brexit. The perception of confined resources contributed to an impulse to retreat from the world, manifest fairly consistently in US public opinion after 2008, and inconsistently in US foreign policy under both President Barack Obama and his successor Donald Trump. When resources are meager, grand strategy comes to the fore. There is a good reason that, for the first time in decades, the postwar US strategy of "deep engagement" or arguably "liberal hegemony" has come under assault, and serious thinkers are putting forward arguments for "restraint." The ultimate effects of the COVID-19 pandemic are still unclear, but it is certain that, around the world, national budgets will be constrained for years to come.

In Europe, grand strategy has become *au courant* for an additional reason. From the end of the Second World War, the United States had been the undisputed linchpin of European security. Lord Ismay, NATO's first secretary general, famously said that the purpose of NATO was "to keep the Soviet Union out, the Americans in, and the Germans down." Keeping the Americans in was the real key though, since it was essential to the other two goals, and it remained the essential pivot of Europe's grand strategy even after the fall of the USSR. Europeans had thus not much exercised their strategic muscles in many a decade, because they had little choice but to place their faith in the United States—no matter their doubts as to whether Washington would sacrifice New York for Bonn. Obama's announced "pivot to Asia" in 2011–2012 served notice to Europeans that America's engagement in the continent could no longer be assured. It was time to start planning for a future without the United States, and that meant that Europeans needed to start thinking strategically again. Trump's public questioning since

2018 of NATO's mutual defense provisions suggested that the future is now and poured fuel on Europe's grand strategy fire. In addition, the European Union saw articulating a European Grand Strategy as a means of both producing a deeper European community and legitimating Europe's preeminent voice on security matters, in a world of increasing insecurity. While the fiscal effects of the COVID-19 pandemic will surely test European defense budgets and rekindle interest in American security guarantees, the United States, under the very same pressures, will presumably be even less inclined to extend them and invest in its European relationships.

That intellectual work and institutional innovation around grand strategy have flowered in recent years is a bit ironic. On the one hand, grand strategy has at the same time become subject to more criticism than ever—as reflected in several essays in Part VI. On the other hand, forward-looking thinkers, peering into the future, seem increasingly skeptical of grand strategy's ongoing relevance, sustainability, and even wisdom, given the emerging state of both domestic and international politics—as reflected in the first three essays of Part VII.

Alternative grand strategies are being debated publicly on both sides of the Atlantic and elsewhere, with a vigor not seen since the late 1940s, and serious questions are being raised about the grand strategy enterprise. The time is ripe for an Oxford Handbook that places these debates in historical, comparative, and theoretical perspective, with an eye to the past and also to the future.

Note

1. Except under conditions of unipolarity: see Monteiro 2014.

References

Balzacq, Thierry, Peter Dombrowski, and Simon Reich. 2019a. "Is Grand Strategy a Research Program? A Review Essay." *Security Studies* 28 (1): 58–86.

Balzacq, Thierry, Peter Dombrowski, and Simon Reich. 2019b. "Comparing Grand Strategies in the Modern World." In *Comparative Grand Strategy: A Framework and Cases*, edited by Thierry Balzacq, Peter Dombrowski, and Simon Reich, 1–22. Oxford: Oxford University Press.

Baracuhy, Braz. 2011. "The Art of Grand Strategy." *Survival* 53 (1): 147–152.

Biddle, Tami Davis. 2015. *Strategy and Strategy: What Students and Practitioners Need to Know*. Carlisle Barracks: United States Army War College Press.

Brands, Hal. 2014. *What Good Is Grand Strategy? Power and Purpose in American Statecraft from Harry S. Truman to George W. Bush*. Ithaca: Cornell University Press.

Brodie, Bernard. 1973. *War and Politics*. New York: Macmillan.

Bures, Oldrich. 2020. "The Counterterrorism Coordinator and the Commissioner for the Security Union: Does the European Union Need Two Top-level Counterterrorism Officials?" *Terrorism and Political Violence*. Online version. https://www.tandfonline.com/doi/full/10.1080/09546553.2020.1730329

Christensen, Thomas J. 1996. *Useful Adversaries: Grand Strategy, Domestic Mobilization, and Sino-American Conflict, 1947–1958*. Princeton: Princeton University Press.

Chollet, Derek, and James Goldgeier. 2008. *America Between the Wars: From 11/9 to 9/11*. New York: PublicAffairs.

Collins, John. 1973. *Grand Strategy: Principles and Practices*. Annapolis: Naval Institute Press.

Corbett, Julian S. 1916. *The Successors of Drake*. London: Longmans, Green & Co.

Drezner, Daniel, Ronald R. Krebs, and Randall Schweller. 2020. "The End of Grand Strategy: America Must Think Small." *Foreign Affairs* 95 (3): 107–117.

Dueck, Colin. 2006. *Reluctant Crusaders: Power, Culture, and Change in American Grand Strategy*. Princeton: Princeton University Press.

Earle, Edward Mead. 1966. "Introduction." In *Makers of Modern Strategy: Military Thought from Machiavelli to Hitler*, edited by Edward Mead Earle, vii–xi. New York: Atheneum.

Edelstein, David M. 2017. *Over the Horizon: Time, Uncertainty, and the Rise of Great Powers*. Ithaca: Cornell University Press.

Edelstein, David M. 2021. "The Limits of Grand Strategy." In *The Oxford Handbook of Grand Strategy*, edited by Thierry Balzacq and Ronald R. Krebs. Oxford: Oxford University Press.

Edelstein, David, and Ronald R. Krebs. 2015. "Delusions of Grand Strategy: The Problem with Washington's Planning Obsession." *Foreign Affairs* 94 (6): 109–116.

Feaver, Peter D et al. 2000. "Correspondence: Brother, Can You Spare a Paradigm? (Or Was Anybody Ever a Realist?)" *International Security* 25 (1): 165–169.

Feaver, Peter D. 2009. "What Is Grand Strategy and Why Do We Need It?" *Foreign Policy*. https://foreignpolicy.com/2009/04/08/what-is-grand-strategy-and-why-do-we-need-it/

Flournoy, Michele, and Shawn Brimley. 2006. "Strategic Planning for National Security." *Joint Force Quarterly* 41 (2): 80–86.

Fukuyama, Francis. 1992. *The End of History and the Last Man*. New York: Free Press.

Fuller, J. F. C. 1923. *The Reformation of War*. London: Hutchinson & Co.

Gaddis, John Lewis 2009. "What Is Grand Strategy?" Keynote address to the conference on *American Grand Strategy after War*. Duke University, February 26.

Gerberding, William P., and Bernard Brodie. 1968. *The Political Dimension in National Strategy: Five Papers*. Los Angeles: UCLA Security Studies Project.

Goddard, Stacie E., and Ronald R. Krebs. 2015. "Rhetoric, Legitimation, and Grand Strategy." *Security Studies* 24 (1): 5–36.

Goldstein, Avery. 2005. *Rising to the Challenge: China's Grand Strategy and International Security*. Stanford: Stanford University Press.

Gray, Colin. 2010. *The Strategy Bridge: Theory for Practice*. Oxford: Oxford University Press.

Howard, Michael. 1979. "The Forgotten Dimensions of Strategy." *Foreign Affairs* 57 (5): 975–986.

Huntington, Samuel P. 1996. *The Clash of Civilizations and the Remaking of World Order*. New York: Simon & Schuster.

Kaplan, Robert D. 1994. "The Coming Anarchy." *The Atlantic* 273 (2): 44–77.

Kennedy, Paul. 1991. "Grand Strategy in War and Peace: Toward a Broader Definition." In *Grand Strategy in War and Peace*, edited by Paul Kennedy, 1–10. New Haven: Yale University Press.

Krasner. Stephen D. 2010. "An Orienting Principle for Foreign Policy." *Policy Review*. https://www.hoover.org/research/orienting-principle-foreign-policy

Krebs, Ronald R. 2013. "The Rise, Persistence, and Fall of the War on Terror." In *How 9/11 Changed Our Ways of War*, edited by James Burk, 56–85. Stanford: Stanford University Press.

Krebs, Ronald R. 2015. *Narrative and the Making of U.S. National Security*. Cambridge: Cambridge University Press.

Krebs, Ronald R. 2018. "The Politics of National Security." In *The Oxford Handbook of International Security*, edited by Alexandra Gheciu and William C. Wohlforth, 259–273. Oxford: Oxford University Press.

Krepinevich, Andrew, and Barry Watts 2009. *Regaining Strategic Competence: Strategy for the Long Haul*. Washington, D.C.: Center for Strategic and Budgetary Assessments.

Lemann, Nicholas. 2002. "The War on What?" *New Yorker* 78 (27).

Lettow, Paul, and Thomas Mahnken. 2009. "Toolbox: Getting Serious About Strategic Planning." *American Interest* 5 (1): 73.

Liddell Hart, Basil. 1929. *The Decisive War of History: A Study of Strategy*. London: G. Bell & Sons.

Liddell Hart, Basil. 1991 [1954]. *Strategy*. New York: Meridian.

Lissner, Rebecca F. 2018. "What Is Grand Strategy? Sweeping a Conceptual Minefield." *Texas National Security Review* 2 (1).

Lobell, Steven E. 2003. *The Challenge of Hegemony: Grand Strategy, Trade, and Domestic Politics*. Ann Arbor: University of Michigan Press.

Luttwak, Edward N. 1976. *The Grand Strategy of the Roman Empire from the First Century A.D. to the Third*. Baltimore, MD: The Johns Hopkins University Press.

MacDonald, Paul K., and Joseph M. Parent. 2021. "Grand Strategies of Declining Powers." In *The Oxford Handbook of Grand Strategy*, edited by Thierry Balzacq and Ronald R. Krebs. Oxford: Oxford University Press.

Martel, William C. 2015. *Grand Strategy in Theory and Practice: The Need for An Effective American Foreign Policy*. Cambridge: Cambridge University Press.

McMaster, H. R. 2007. "Learning from Contemporary Conflicts to Prepare for Future War." In *Defense Strategy Air Forces: Setting Future Directions*, edited by Richmond M. Lloyd, 71–94. Newport, RI: Naval War College.

Mearsheimer, John J. 1990. "Back to the Future: Instability in Europe after the Cold War." *International Security* 15 (1): 5–56.

Mintzberg, Henry, and James A. Waters. 1985. "Of Strategies, Deliberate and Emergent." Strategic *Management Journal* 6 (3): 257–272.

Monteiro, Nuno. 2014. *Theory of Unipolar Politics*. Cambridge: Cambridge University Press.

Murray, Williamson. 2011. "Thoughts on Grand Strategy." In *The Shaping of Grand Strategy: Policy, Diplomacy, and War*, edited by Williamson Murray, Richard Hart Sinnreich, and James Lacey, 1–33. Cambridge: Cambridge University Press.

Nordlinger, Eric. 1995. *Isolationism Reconfigured: American Foreign Policy for a New Century*. Princeton: Princeton University Press.

Popescu, Ionut C. 2018. "Grand Strategy vs. Emergent Strategy in the Conduct of Foreign Policy." *Journal of Strategic Studies* 41 (3): 438–460.

Porter, Patrick. 2018. "Why America's Grand Strategy Has Not Changed: Power, Habit, and the U.S. Foreign Policy Establishment." *International Security* 42 (4): 9–46.

Posen, Barry R. 1984. *The Sources of Military Doctrine: France, Britain, and Germany between the World Wars*. Ithaca: Cornell University Press.

Posen, Barry R. 2014. *Restraint: A New Foundation for U.S. Grand Strategy*. Ithaca: Cornell University Press.

Rathbun, Brian. 2008. "A Rose by Any Other Name: Neoclassical Realism as the Logical and Necessary Extension of Structural Realism." *Security Studies* 17 (2): 294–321.

Reich, Simon, and Peter Dombrowski. 2017. *The End of Grand Strategy: US Maritime Operations in the Twenty-First Century*. Ithaca: Cornell University Press.

Schweller, Randall. 2006. *Unanswered Threats: Political Constraints on the Balance of Power*. Princeton: Princeton University Press.

Sending, Ole Jacob. 2021. "Diplomacy." In *The Oxford Handbook of Grand Strategy*, edited by Thierry Balzacq and Ronald R. Krebs. Oxford: Oxford University Press.

Silove, Nina. 2018. "Beyond the Buzzword: The Three Meanings of 'Grand Strategy.'" *Security Studies* 27 (1): 27–57.

The Joint Chiefs of Staff. 1962. *Dictionary of the United States Military Terms for Joint Usage*. Washington, D.C.

Walt, Stephen M. 1987. *The Origins of Alliances*. Ithaca: Cornell University Press.

Walt, Stephen M. 1991. "The Renaissance of Security Studies." *International Studies Quarterly* 35 (2): 211–231.

Williamson, Samuel. 1969. *The Politics of Grand Strategy: Britain and France Prepare for War, 1904–1914*. Cambridge: Cambridge University Press.

Wohlforth, William C. 1999. "The Stability of a Unipolar World." *International Security* 24 (2): 5–41.

PART I
HISTORY

CHAPTER 2

GRAND STRATEGY

The History of a Concept

LAWRENCE FREEDMAN

INTRODUCTION

THE literature on grand strategy is now vast and new contributions come rapidly, often in the form of proposals for the sort of grand strategy a country, usually the United States, should adopt. At the same time, the concept appears to lack firm theoretical foundations. There is a definite consensus to the effect that a grand strategy is a good thing to have. Being without one implies drift and a lack of direction. But there is no consensus on how it should be defined. Indeed, there is now a substantial literature devoted to help sort out the definitional confusion.

This chapter considers how the concept emerged in the early decades of the last century and the meanings that came to be attached to it. Although the word 'strategy' entered the vernacular during the late eighteenth century and became a recognised concept in the early nineteenth, focusing on the demands of battle, it took until the early twentieth century for a clear concept of grand strategy to take shape. Here the focus was on how a state must draw upon all its resources, political and economic as well as military, in order to win a war. It then came to be used in discussions of how states relate to the international system at times of peace as well as war. Here it could have a prescriptive purpose, pointing to what national leaders should do to prepare for and win wars, but also a descriptive role, providing a framework by which the strategies of past states and empires could be evaluated. As prescription, it encouraged the clear formulation of plans of action, to ensure that all national resources were fully employed in the pursuit of the most vital national interests. As description, however, the absence of any records of such plans was irrelevant, for a grand strategy might still be detected in patterns of statements and actions over a period of time, as the needs of security were identified and articulated and methods developed to meet them. The broadening of the concept has led to concerns about a loss of focus. Once everything can be included under the heading of grand strategy then perhaps nothing is.

STRATEGY: EARLY DEFINITIONS

Elsewhere I have discussed the origins of the term "strategy" (Freedman 2017; Freedman 2018). The word entered military discourse in Europe in 1771 when the French officer Paul Gédéon Joly de Maizeroy published his translation of the Byzantine emperor Leo VI's *Taktiká*. This included references to *strategía as* well as *taktiké*. *Strategía*, previously discussed as the science of the general, was now transliterated simply as *stratégie* (See Heuser 2012; Gat 1989 and 1992; Strachan 2014). It was closely related to stratagem, a word that was already often used to denote ruses and maneuvers in war. In the first instance, stratagems were seen to be at the heart of strategy, as they were about avoiding the heavy costs and risks of pitched battle. It was only at the highest level of command that these battle-winning moves could be identified and implemented. This level required an appreciation of possibilities opening up on the field of battle and often bold decisions. One issue, which is still present in debates on strategy, was whether this higher level required a special talent, founded on extraordinary insight and creativity, or whether it required learning some core principles that could be applied in an almost mechanistic manner. There is at least one example of "grand" being applied to strategy (as "the knowledge of commanding armies") at this time, but this was largely for purposes of emphasis when describing what was needed to be known by a commander in chief and his subordinate generals (Schorn 1783, 198–9). In general, references to "grand strategy" before the twentieth century can be considered etymological "false positives," with no relevance for later use (Milevski 2016).

There was, however, a term—Grand Tactics—that conveyed the same idea as strategy and was still on occasion used for the rest of the nineteenth century. It was popularized by Jacques Antoine Hippolyte Comte de Guibert at the start of the 1770s (Guibert 1772, translated in Heuser 2012) and was adopted by Napoleon, but over time "strategy" won this competition (Black 2017). Clausewitz assumed familiarity with the term in the opening of Book 2 of *On War*, to the point that he wondered whether any attempt at careful distinctions between strategy and tactics would be considered "superfluous," as the distinction between the two was "now almost universal" (Clausewitz 1989, 128). By this time, the concept had taken a slight turn. The original discussion was largely Francophone and bound up with the issue of a commander's genius. In the German-speaking world, an otherwise undistinguished figure, Heinrich von Bülow, provided an analytical framework and gave the word currency (Palmer 1986, 115). He distinguished his concept of "Strategics" from the French concept of "la stratégique," which he defined as "the science of the stratagems of war." His aim was to narrow the role of military genius by allowing command to be based on the disciplined application of set mathematical formulae. His distinction between tactics and strategy was not based on levels of command but on what happened prior to battle and in the battle. Strategics was "the science of the movements in war of two armies, out of the visual circle of each other, or, if better liked, out of cannon reach." By contrast, tactics were "the science of the movements made within sight of the enemy, and within reach of his artillery" (Bülow 2013, 88).

THE NINETEENTH CENTURY: STILL NO GRAND STRATEGY

While Bülow's mathematical models were soon forgotten, this basic distinction took root. It was when reviewing Bülow that Clausewitz developed his own formulation: tactics was the theory of using armed forces in battle, while strategy was using battle for the purposes of the war (Paret 1992, 100; Clausewitz 1989, 128–132). Baron Antoine-Henri de Jomini, a less demanding and more influential thinker, also saw strategy as being about getting forces to the point of battle, describing it as war "upon the map." "Strategy," he wrote, "decides where to act; logistics brings the troops to this point; grand tactics decides the manner of execution and the employment of the troops" (Jomini 2005, 79–100). He also proposed that tactics rather than strategy was the area of the greatest innovation. New inventions threatened a "great revolution in army organization, armament and tactics," while strategy would "remain unaltered, with its principles the same as under the Scipios and the Caesars, Frederick and Napoleon, since they are independent of the nature of the arms and the organization of the troops" (Jomini 1865, 48). This proposition was left unchallenged for the rest of the century. It is also important to keep in mind that while both Clausewitz and Jomini understood that not all conflicts were decided by large set-piece battles, that was the ideal type to which strategy should be geared. The aim was always to destroy the enemy's army to force it seek a political settlement on the victor's terms. This sharp focus on battle clarified the tasks for both tactics and strategy, and the forms of their potential interaction.

After the surge of innovative practice and theory during the first decades of the nineteenth century, the combination of this focus on battle and conviction that strategy involved timeless principles left its study in something of a rut. The circumstances encouraged orthodoxy. There were national variations on the core themes, but there was still uniformity in the approach. The contributors were normally senior military figures, still serving or recently retired, concerned with officer education. They read each other's books, if necessary in translation, and studied the same great battles of history from which they drew similar lessons (Heuser 2010, 120–1). The focus on military history encouraged conservatism. Strategy looked back even while tactics looked forward. Tactics dominated the military literature, covering a range of battlefield contingencies.

This conservatism was evident in Britain. The British were largely consumers of European military theory and made few notable contributions of their own. As late as

1894, the influential Colonel G. F. R. Henderson used the term "Grand Tactics" in one lecture to refer to the "higher art of generalship," which included "those stratagems, manoeuvres, and devices by which victories are won, and concern only those officers who may find themselves in independent command" (Henderson 1894, in Henderson 1906, 168), only then to write a few years later describing this same higher level as "strategy." The tactician, he noted, was the "more popular personage than the strategist, poring over his map, and leaving to others the perils and the glories of the fight." The strategist only really came into his own when looking beyond the principles of warfare—"which to a certain extent are mechanical, dealing with the manipulation of armed bodies"—to what he called the "spirit of warfare." This involved the moral element that could inspire troops, elements of "surprise, mystery, stratagem" (Henderson 1898). Strategy was "the art of bringing the enemy to battle, while tactics are the methods by which a commander seeks to overwhelm him when battle is joined."

Although in the United States, military thought was strongly influenced by Jomini, there was one example of a professor at West Point opening new definitional possibilities. At the close of the century, James Mercur set as strategy's first object taking "advantage of all means for securing success." This involved "questions of statesmanship and diplomacy" and included issues that would feature in later considerations of grand strategy: managing the military resources of the nation; "conducting international intercourse that when wars becomes necessary or desirable, favorable alliances may be made with strong power, and hostile combinations of nations may be avoided"; giving due weight to "financial and commercial considerations," including when choosing campaign objectives; and how military forces are organized and trained. He observed that when it came to choosing when to accept or avoid conflict "statesmanship becomes strictly strategical." Yet after that promising opening, the analysis became entirely orthodox, with the "hostile army" selected as the strategic objective. He also described "Grand Tactics" in terms close to other definitions of strategy: "planning battles, perfecting the preliminary arrangements, conducting them during their process and securing the results of victory, or avoiding the consequences of defeat" (Mercur 1898, 16, 140).

Mercur's book was only used as a text for a short period and is now largely forgotten. General Sherman did write on "The Grand Strategy of the Wars of the Rebellion," but this did not reflect any conceptual originality. Despite his own innovations late in the Civil War, he still wrote that the principles of war were fixed and unchanging. They were "as true as the multiplication table, the law of gravitation, or of virtual velocities, or any other invariable rule of natural philosophy" (Sherman 1888).

The impact of the American Civil War on the way that strategy was viewed took time to appear. They were the result of reflections on the extent to which political leaders could not step back and leave all the key decisions to their generals. President Lincoln had been actively engaged on all questions of strategy, and had hired and fired generals accordingly (Cohen 2002). A biography of Lincoln published in 1890 observed that "talk of military operations without the direction and interference of an Administration is as absurd as to plan a campaign without recruits, pay, or rations" (Nicolay and Hay 1890,

359–360). In Britain, Henderson, a close student of the war, saw the tension though his conclusion was orthodox: "Politics must always exercise a supreme influence on strategy; yet it cannot be gainsaid that interference with the commander in the field is fraught with the gravest danger" (Henderson 1903, ch. 7).

The difficulty, as Henderson was well aware, was that contextual factors were increasingly likely to determine whether an army or navy would be in a decent position for battle. In 1898, he acknowledged that strategy should be as "concerned as much with preparation for war as with war itself." He spoke of these preparations as the "Peace Strategy" (that is strategy pursued at a time of peace as opposed to one geared to achieving peace) (Henderson 1898, 761). Gradually this aspect of preparations for war gained more attention, especially given the importance of who would be allied with whom. Moreover, even accepting a clear division of labor, the "statesman and the commander" should at least understand each other. A debate developed at the Staff College in 1911 about whether it really made sense in officer education for students to write "strategical papers, referring to military operations in which they might one day be engaged," but keeping clear of political matters as they did so. One officer, Colonel Launcelot E. Kiggell, observed that when studying and teaching war he had concluded that "politics were at the back of all strategical problems" (Bond 2015, 266).

Grand Strategy Makes an Appearance

This period also saw a growing influence of naval thinking on wider strategy. The reappraisal of how strategy should be defined began with the British maritime theorist Sir Julian Corbett, an influential civilian who knew his Clausewitz (Widen 2016). His approach was shaped by the need to think about naval and military strategy in relation to each other, and his conviction that both needed to be released from the fallacy "that war consists entirely of battles between armies and fleets." The main objective was territory and not the enemy armed forces. Strategy was "the art of directing forces to the ends in view." In 1906, in his "Strategical Terms and Definitions Used in Lectures on Naval History," Corbett divided strategy into "major" (or "grand") dealing with ulterior objects and "minor" dealing with "primary objects," which were essentially concerned with war plans and operational plans respectively. The vital feature of major/grand strategy was that it involved the "whole resources of the nation for war" and not just armed force. In 1911, when he revised these notes, he left it as a distinction between major and minor (Corbett 1911, 20–22, 97, 308, 326–327).

This moved the possibilities for a discussion of "grand strategy" away from it being a higher or exemplary form of military strategy (Milevski 2016, 45–46). The shift was unavoidable after the First World War. The starting point was to recognize that the requirements of victory in war must look beyond the defeat of enemy forces to a consideration of the objectives for which the war was being fought. Here the breakthrough was made by John "Boney" Fuller and Basil Liddell Hart, two men who had fought on the Western Front and then made their names developing ideas for army mechanization. In 1923 Fuller, the senior and more original of the two, picked up on Corbett's reference to grand strategy. Accepting that the effectiveness of the military instrument had to be discussed in the context of the other instruments of state policy it was clear that a military victory was no longer adequate. The focus of war, insisted Fuller, should be "to enforce the policy of the nation at the least cost to itself and to the enemy and, consequently, to the world." The grand strategist had to understand commerce and finance, as well as politics, culture and history, in order to "form the pillars of the military arch which it is his duty to construct." (Fuller 1923, 214, 75; Gat 1998, 157)

Liddell Hart produced sharper and more lasting language. (Swain 1886; Bond 1977) As with Corbett and Fuller he saw the first step as describing the objectives of war in terms of the subsequent peace and not the elimination of the enemy army which was at most a means to an end. He sought more indirect routes to victory, avoiding the carnage of massed offensives. In this respect, it was "the function of grand strategy to discover and exploit the Achilles' heel of the enemy nation; to strike not against its strongest bulwark but against its most vulnerable spot" (Liddell Hart 1925; on its composition see Liddell Hart 1965, 75). His most lasting book, first published in 1929, was *The Decisive Wars of History*, which went through many editions, becoming *Strategy: The Indirect Approach* in 1954. At first, he offered his definition of strategy as "the distribution and transmission of military means to fulfil the ends of policy." In 1954, "transmission" was replaced with "employment." Tactics he limited to matters concerned with "the fighting." Grand strategy was about the coordination and direction of all the resources of the nation to the attainment of the political object of the war" (Liddell Hart 1929).

The influence of his view spread as he was the author of the *1929 Encyclopaedia Britannica* entry for Strategy, which described grand strategy as "practically synonymous with the policy that governs the conduct of the war, as distinct from the permanent policy which formulates its object." It served to bring out the sense of "policy in execution." At this point, therefore, he had in mind a quite tight definition of grand strategy. It was not about those aspects of policy which determined a country's place in the world and helped define allies and adversaries and so set the objectives of war. It was about those aspects of policy necessary to win wars while they were being fought.

The Concept Broadens

This tight distinction was difficult to sustain. The wider resources and efforts of the state did not suddenly make a difference once a war began but were vital to its prior preparation. If the preparations were good enough then wars might be avoided altogether. In this respect—to use Liddell Hart's distinction—was developing an alliance with another state to gain access to bases a matter of policy as "objectives" or "in execution"?

It was difficult to separate the two. It is also important to keep in mind that for Liddell Hart, setting of the "permanent policy" was at a level above grand strategy and was likely to represent deeply ingrained considerations of national interest and culture. Grand strategy was still a subordinate concept.

In the first book dedicated to the topic of grand strategy, published in Britain two years into the Second World War, H. A. Sargeaunt and Geoffrey West gave it a higher importance. They spoke of grand strategy as dealing "with the connections between war and the rest of society or civilization in which war occurs." This interaction meant that it was a matter for social science as much as military science, and their interest was more in the former. Grand strategy answered such questions as "what does this war stem from, and what is it leading to?" This was the "higher type of strategy" and must come from "the war cabinets and their advisers, above all the Prime Minister or President." They understood the tension between what a government might want from war and what war could ever achieve. When "people speak of war aims," they noted, they were often "asking for results which the human instrument and activity cannot give, just as farming cannot produce oil" (Sargeaunt and West 1941, vii, 7, 10–11; Milevski 2016, 57–59). They therefore did not take much notice of any distinction between permanent policy and policy in execution. Questions of why a war was being fought and how it was being done represented a higher level of strategy because neither could be answered in solely military terms.

The American debate followed a similar path. The term was used occasionally and somewhat randomly, often by civilians. At times, it incorporated the nonmilitary aspects of conflict and so anticipated modern usage. During the interwar years, the references grew. There was often no precise definition. Grand strategy appeared as a natural way to refer to the highest level of strategy. With war now understood to depend on all national resources, and not just the armed forces, no great conceptual leap was required to include these nonmilitary factors as a matter for grand strategy. In the landmark collection of essays *Makers of Modern Strategy*, published in the United States in 1943, the editor Edward Mead Earle remarked in his introduction that, narrowly defined, strategy was "the art of military command, of projecting and directing a campaign," where tactics was "the art of handling forces in battle." But war and society had "become more complicated," and so "strategy has of necessity required increasing consideration of nonmilitary factors, economic, psychological, moral, political, and technological." Strategy, therefore, was "an inherent element of statecraft at all times."

> In the present-day world, then, strategy is the art of controlling and utilizing the resources of a nation—or a coalition of nations—including its armed forces, to the end that its vital interests shall be effectively promoted and secured against enemies, actual, potential, or merely presumed. The highest type of strategy)sometimes called grand strategy)is that which integrates the policies and armaments of the nation that the resort to war is either rendered unnecessary or is undertaken with the maximum chance of victory. (Earle 1943, viii)

This was broader than Liddell Hart's definition, not least because the focus was on peacetime preparations for war, and on the possibility that if these were organized effectively then war could be deterred.

The heading "Grand Strategy" was given to those seven volumes of the official British history which, according to the series editor J. R. M. Butler, dealt with the "central direction of the war." The first of these was published in 1956. In a later volume in this series, published in 1972, Michael Howard opened with a definition close to Liddell Hart's.

> Grand strategy in the first half of the twentieth century consisted basically in the mobilisation and deployment of the national resources of wealth, manpower and industrial capacity, together with the enlistment of those allied and, where feasible, of neutral power, for the purpose of achieving the goals of national policy in wartime. (Howard 1972, 1)

He later described this as a "prescriptive" rather than "descriptive" definition. "All strategy," he noted, "is in principle teleological; military operations should be planned to achieve the political object." But this was also a principle "honoured more in the breach than the observance," for plans in the end were shaped by "immediate political and military necessities." Howard, quoted Lord Kitchener from 1915: "We must make war as we must; not as we would like" (Howard 1991, 31).

Any detached analysis of grand strategy, therefore, would note the extent to which actors struggled to achieve their objectives. Any actor devising a grand strategy would do well to keep this in mind when setting goals and considering how they might be achieved. Grand strategy might be a purposive activity, but what was achieved might be far removed from what was intended and not as directed by a single, controlling intelligence.

Grand Strategy as History

All of this was easier to appreciate in retrospect than prospect. Historians could expect to evaluate grand strategy in practice, looking at how states related to their environments over time. Edward Luttwak demonstrated how this might be done in 1976 when discussing how the Romans managed their empire (Luttwak 1979). Because he described this as an example of grand strategy he was accused of imposing modern concepts on classical times. Critics argued that this was a wholly modern concept, irrelevant to ancient times. How could Rome have had any grand strategy when it lacked the information-gathering and decision-making apparatus of modern states and armed forces (Whittaker 2014; Kagan 2006)? It was a criticism that he had little trouble dismissing. However leaders made their ends–means calculations, and whatever the available instruments that helped them realize their intentions, they were clearly thinking in ways that could properly be described as strategic. Luttwak wrote further books on the same theme (Luttwak 2009), as did others. Writing about the grand strategies of past powers became an accepted genre (Rahe 2015; Mitchell 2018). It could also be noted that as early as 1898, the historian Charles Oman had used the term "grand strategy" in a similar way but without definition (Oman 1898).

Luttwak dismissed the idea that grand strategy meant a grand plan. His view, as he explained in the introduction to a later edition of his book, was that "national strategies, grand or not so grand, must always be inferred from what is done or not done, and are never described in documents—or not, at any rate, in documents that might see the light of day." He challenged the idea that strategy was "systematic group thinking, based on detailed information and guided by rational choices." Strategy, he noted, was made by who "happens to be in charge," there for reasons often unrelated to the decisions they have to make, rather than trained specialists. Elsewhere he argued that

> All states have a grand strategy, whether they know it or not. That is inevitable because grand strategy is simply the level at which knowledge and persuasion, or in modern terms intelligence and diplomacy, interact with military strength to determine outcomes in a world of other states with their own "grand strategies." (Luttwak 2009, 409; see also Luttwak 1987)

This view helped justify how historians could look at the strategies of the past, but it also had implications for a more prescriptive approach to those of the future (Popescu 2017a). If strategies emerged for the complex of deliberate decision-making by a range of relevant actors over time, including their impromptu responses to events and intuitive understanding of the needs of the moment, then it would be something of a leap of faith to assume that current decision-makers could set down and then follow some master plan.

Grand Strategy as Policy

In 1987, Paul Kennedy organized a series of lectures at Yale looking a back at the grand strategies of the major powers. Kennedy had his own direct link to Liddell Hart, as did Michael Howard, who was then also at Yale. Kennedy's introduction to the book based on the series picked up on Liddell Hart's and Earle's definitions, noting how the term was concerned with peace as much as war. It was about the "balancing of ends and means," requiring consideration of costs as well as potential gains. Most importantly, it required "husbanding and managing national resources," emphasized the "vital role of diplomacy," and drew attention to the "issue of national morale and political culture." From this he concluded that:

> The crux of grand strategy lies therefore in *policy*, that is, in the capacity of the nation's leaders to bring together all of the elements, both military and nonmilitary,

for the preservation and enhancement of the nation's long-term (that is, wartime *and* peacetime) best interests. (Kennedy 1991, 1–5)

The timing of the publication of this book was perhaps serendipitous, as the international situation had been transformed since the original lectures. The end of the Cold War meant that the question of US grand strategy, which Kennedy pronounced in the book to have been remarkably successful over the previous four decades (Kennedy 1991, 172), was suddenly opened up. Yale seized the concept and almost made its own. It became the center for the study of grand strategy, with prominent contributions by Charles Hill and John Gaddis, and a teaching programme, founded in 2000, that explicitly used the study of grand strategy to prepare students for future leadership positions (Hill 2010). Its success encouraged imitators. But the programme also encouraged an ever-broadening approach to the topic. As one critique observed, its "radical contribution" was "to make a grand strategy out of everything—from national security to economics, the environment, even culture and ideology" (Meaney and Wetheim 2012).

Just as the post–First World War embrace of grand strategy reflected dissatisfaction with an overly narrow view of what strategy was about, so did the post–Cold War embrace reflect a more ambitious agenda for international security, in which all sorts of nonmilitary factors had to be addressed in order to marginalize war as an instrument of statecraft. Not long after Kennedy's edited book, in this case prompted by a 1989 conference, a group of political scientists took on grand strategy, seeing it as a chance to evaluate established realist concepts of international relations. In their introduction, the editors also used the Liddell Hart definition. Their argument was that if the economic and political dimensions were so important when it came to strategic success then it was not good enough, as realists were prone to do, to focus solely on the military dimensions and to ignore domestic factors (Rosecrance and Stein, 1993).

The stage was now set for a surge of writing on the topic of grand strategy (Martel 2015; Posen and Ross 1996). During the Cold War, few worried about the need for grand strategy. When the focus was on nuclear deterrence, grand strategy was barely mentioned. Writers such as Wohlstetter, Schelling, and Kahn did not use the term. Their focus was largely on how the decision-making of adversaries interacted. They often explicitly excluded the wider political context from their analysis, concentrating on speculative scenarios of conflict. Now that this intense period of bipolar confrontation was over the big issues of national policy, interest and purpose were suddenly opened up for the United States and its allies. The nature of the choices and how they were to be made were seen as properly matters for grand strategy. There were, however, no obvious boundaries to the discussion. The only continuities were in believing a grand strategy was a good thing to have, because without it, government would lack direction, and seeing it as something to be decided at the highest level of government. But the focus had shifted from how to use all national resources to win a war; to using these resources to prepare for war and if possible deter war; to deciding on what, when, and with whom it might be worth going to war; to explaining how national objectives might be achieved by nonmilitary means; to weighing different objectives against each other and trying to coordinate a policymaking process so that the best outcomes could be achieved. At this point, grand strategy became indistinguishable from foreign policy.

Without evident boundaries, the literature moved from discussions of what a grand strategy might look like in both form and content to efforts to determine the main competing approaches (Silove 2018; Lissner 2018; Avery, Markowitz, and Reardon, 2018). This effort was conducted less with any expectation of finding a consensus than in identifying different strands of activity connected with the study of grand strategy—from developing policy prescriptions for government, to identifying the difference that particular grand strategies might make, to the success or failure of states in conflict with each other.

Williamson Murray, in an argument similar to Luttwak's, suggested that historians had the best chance of understanding grand strategy because it was best appreciated after the fact. It was about the "ability to adjust to the reality that resources, will, and interests inevitably find themselves out of balance in some areas." Attempts to cast a grand strategy in a clear way will struggle in an "environment of constant change, where chance and the unexpected are inherent." He likened it to the making of French peasant soup, since a mixture of items is thrown into a pot, according to what was available. "In thinking about the soup of grand strategy, recipes and theoretical principles are equally useless" (Williamson 2011). For those who demanded a grand strategy as a blueprint for future action, this analogy was unfortunate. It reinforced the view that the combination of multiple and occasionally contradictory goals and the inherent uncertainties of international affairs threatened to mock anything resembling a plan (Betts 2000). Edelstein and Krebs went so far as to suggest that the very attempt to impose a strategy distorted prudent and pragmatic foreign-policymaking (Edelstein and Krebs 2015).

This undermined a search for an agreed definition, although some of those most quoted did point to important similarities. Barry Posen, writing mainly about military doctrine, and before the study of grand strategy had become so popular, described grand strategy as "a political-military, means-end chain, a state's theory about how it can best 'cause' security for itself." This raised the stakes because of the requirement for a theory of causation. Yet Posen also used a much simpler definition, as simply "a chain of political ends and military means." This fitted in with most definitions of strategy, as the aims set by politicians must be realistic and the means available sufficient. It was potentially also too narrow, for the original insight about grand strategy pointed to the need to consider both military and nonmilitary means in pursuit of security interests (Posen 1984, 13, 24). In 2018, John Gaddis, in a definition that reflected the spirit of the Yale programme by excluding very little and emphasizing the need for hard choices, described grand strategy as "the alignment of potentially unlimited aspirations with necessarily limited capabilities" (Gaddis 2018, 21). Peter Feaver set out a "purposive definition," as "the collection of plans and policies that comprise the state's deliberate effort to harness political, military, diplomatic, and economic tools together to advance that state's national interest." Yet he added that this was "the art of reconciling ends and means" (Feaver 2009). Similarly, Hal Brands offered as his definition "the purposeful and coherent set of ideas about what a nation seeks to accomplish in the world, and how it should go about doing so" (Brands 2014, 3, 5). Elsewhere, with Patrick Porter, he argued that grand strategy was best understood "not as a formal planning process, but as a guiding intellectual framework ... It is an ecological worldview, formed from a mix of different influences—experience, study, values, ideology—that helps officials make sense of complexity and bring resources and commitments into alignment" (Brands and Porter, 2015).

Conclusion

Ionut Popescu queried the long-term forward look implied by a grand strategy and argued instead for an emergent strategy, based on learning and adaption (Popescu 2017b). At the end of the book he co-edited with Williamson Murray, Richard Sinnreich noted that its case studies would lead to doubts about "whether grand strategy, in the sense of the consistent execution over time of a preconceived strategic design, is even possible, let alone likely" (Sinnreich 2011, 254). As we have seen, this has been a regular observation by historians. In contrast to those who saw grand strategy as a policy aspiration, a yearning for a more coherent and coordinated approach to policy and its implementation, historians have taken a more skeptical, rueful approach, noting that the instances of government sticking to a plan for any length of time, in the face of chance events and the resistance of other actors, has been the exception rather than the rule.

Even the more optimistic, prescriptive approaches to grand strategy have pointed to the need to bring ends and means into balance, and accepted that this is unlikely to be captured in an early blueprint. Whatever the advantages of proclaiming a grand strategy as a statement of intent and as a guide to policy endeavors, in practice the strategy followed will be "emergent" as unexpected developments require reappraisals and changes of course. This is an issue with any form of strategy, and it is not at all unique to the higher levels. This is why strategy is always best discussed as a process rather than a plan, starting with the immediate problem at hand rather than the ultimate objective. It may be better to think of acting strategically than having a strategy (Freedman 2013).

Here, grand strategy does not pose different problems to any other form of strategy. The real problem is the lack of boundaries. In his original definition, Liddell Hart focused on how a war should be prosecuted. This was too narrow. Grand strategy begins at times of peace and continues once a war is over. It also must be conducted at the highest level of government. It refers to an executive responsibility because it involves the coordination of the national effort. But it does not need to address, all at once, all of the big issues confronting a government. Grand strategy comes into its own at a time of war or when war threatens because a focus imposes itself on a government. All other issues become secondary. That is quite different from a government wondering about what it should be worrying about and trying to set priorities among multiple possible objectives. If there is little natural focus, then there should be no surprise if the strategy is incoherent.

Crisis and conflict, therefore, are the natural domain of grand strategy. Without the special imperatives they provide, then too much discussion of grand strategy becomes just another way of talking about foreign policy and speculating about future threats or lapsing into vague generalizations about a nation's standing and interests. It may be that governments can manage perfectly well without grand strategies. They need not be under any obligation to produce one to impose some sort of order on what is an unavoidably disorderly and uncertain situations, when they must cope with contradictory pressures and shifting priorities. As governments like to suggest that they are in control of events, they may still wish to promulgate a forward-looking grand strategy, even if their actual grand strategy may only be discerned with hindsight. For those with a responsibility for acting strategically, the most helpful advice may be to worry less about having a plan and more to think hard about what is important in the current situation, the opportunities and dangers opening up, the interests and potential actions of others, the challenges of implementing any move that needs to be made, and so on. The way to think about grand strategy might therefore involve putting a bit more emphasis on the "strategy" and a bit less on the "grand."

References

Avery, Paul C., Jonathan N. Markowitz, and Robert J. Reardon. 2018. "Disentangling Grand Strategy: International Relations Theory and U.S. Grand Strategy." *Texas National Security Review* 2 (1): 29–51.
Betts, Richard. 2000. "Is Strategy an Illusion?" *International Security* 25 (2): 5–50.
Black, Jeremy. 2017. *Plotting Power; Strategy in the Eighteenth Century*. Bloomington: Indiana University Press.
Bond, Brian. 1977. *Liddell Hart: A Study of his Military Thought*. London: Cassell.
Bond, Brian. 2015. *The Victorian Army and the Staff College 1854–1914*. London: Routledge.
Brands, Hal. 2014. *What Good Is Grand Strategy? Power and Purpose in American Statecraft from Harry S. Truman to George W. Bush*. Ithaca, NY: Cornell University Press.
Brands, Hal, and Patrick Porter. 2015. "Why Grand Strategy Still Matters in a World of Chaos." *The National Interest*. https://nationalinterest.org/feature/why-grand-strategy-still-matters-world-chaos-14568
Bülow, Dietrich Heinrich von. 2013. *The Spirit of the Modern System of War*, trans. Malorti de Martemont. Cambridge, UK: Cambridge University Press.
Clausewitz, Carl von. 1989. *On War*. Translated by Michael Howard and Peter Paret. Princeton: Princeton University Press.
Cohen, Eliot. 2002. *Supreme Command: Soldiers, Statesmen, and Leadership in Wartime*. New York: Simon & Schuster.
Corbett, Julian S. 1911. *Some Principles of Maritime Strategy*. London: Longmans, Green and Co.
Drezner, Daniel W. 2011. "Does Obama Have a Grand Strategy? Why We Need Doctrines in Uncertain Times." *Foreign Affairs* 90: 4.

Earle, Edward Meade, ed. 1943. *Makers of Modern Strategy*. Princeton: Princeton University Press.
Edelstein, David M., and Ronald Krebs. 2015. "Delusions of Grand Strategy." *Foreign Affairs* 94: 6.
Feaver, Peter. 2009. "What Is Grand Strategy and Why Do We Need It?" *Foreign Policy*. https://foreignpolicy.com/2009/04/08/what-is-grand-strategy-and-why-do-we-need-it/
Freedman, Lawrence. 2013. *Strategy: A History*. New York: Oxford University Press.
Freedman, Lawrence. 2017. "The Meaning of Strategy, Part I: The Origins." *Texas National Security Review* 1 (1): 90–105.
Freedman, Lawrence. 2018. "The Meaning of Strategy, Part 2: The Objectives." *Texas National Security Review* 1 (2): 34–57.
Fuller, J. F. C. 1923. *The Reformation of War*. 2nd edition. London: Hutchinson and Co.
Gaddis, John. 2018. *On Grand Strategy*. New York: Penguin Press.
Gat, Azar. 1989. *The Origins of Military Thought: From the Enlightenment to Clausewitz*. Oxford: The Clarendon Press.
Gat, Azar. 1992. *The Development of Military Thought: The Nineteenth Century*. Oxford: The Clarendon Press.
Gat, Azar. 1998. *Fascists and Liberal Visions of War*. Oxford: The Clarendon Press.
Gray, Colin S. 2010. *The Strategy Bridge: Theory for Practice*. Oxford: Oxford University Press.
Guibert, Jacques de. Antoine Hippolyte Comte. 1772. *Essai général de Tactique*. London: chez les libraires associés.
Henderson, F. R. 1894. "Lessons from the Past for the Present, *Lecture at the United Services Institution*." In F. R. Henderson, 1906 *The Science of War: A Collection of Lectures and Essays*, edited by Neil Malcolm. London: Longmans.
Henderson, F. R, 1898. "Strategy and its Teaching." *Journal of the Royal United Services Institution* 42 (245): 761–786.
Henderson, F.R. 1903. *Stonewall Jackson*. Vol. 1. London: Longmans.
Heuser, Beatrice. 2010. *The Evolution of Strategy*. Cambridge: Cambridge University Press.
Heuser, Beatrice. 2012. *The Strategy Makers: Thoughts on War and Society from Machiavelli to Clausewitz*. Santa Barbara, CA: Praeger Security International.
Hill, Charles. 2010. *Grand Strategies: Literature, Statescraft, and World Order*. New Haven, CT: Yale University Press.
Howard, Michael. 1972, *Grand Strategy,* Vol. 4, *U.K. Official History of the Second World War*. London: HMSO.
Howard, Michael. 1991. "British Grand Strategy in World War 1." In *Grand Strategies in War and Peace*, edited by Paul Kennedy. New Haven: Yale University Press.
Jomini, Antoine-Henri. 1865. Translated by Col. S.B. Holabird. *Treatise on Grand Military Operations: or A Critical and Military History of the Wars of Frederick the Great as Contrasted with the Modern System*, 2 vols. New York: D. van Nostrand.
Jomini, Antoine Henri de. 2005. *The Art of War*. Translated by G.H. Mendell and W.P. Craighill [1838]. Texas: El Paso Norte Press.
Kagan, Kimberly. 2006. "Redefining Roman Grand Strategy." *The Journal of Military History* 70 (2): 333–362.
Whittaker, C. R. 2004. *Rome and its Frontiers: The Dynamics of Empire*. London: Routledge.
Kennedy, Paul, ed. 1991. *Grand Strategies in War and Peace*. New Haven: Yale University Press.
Kennedy, Paul. 1991. "Grand Strategy in War and Peace: Toward a Broader Definition." In *Grand Strategies in War and Peace*, edited by Paul Kennedy. New Haven: Yale University Press.

Liddell Hart, B. H. 1925. "The Napoleonic Fallacy; The Moral Objective in War." *Empire Review* 1: 510–520.

Liddell Hart, B. H. 1929. *The Decisive Wars of History*. London: G. Bell and Sons.

Liddell Hart. B. H. 1965. *Memoirs*. Vol. 1. London: Cassell.

Lissner, Rebecca Friedman. 2018. "What is Grand Strategy? Sweeping a Conceptual Minefield." *Texas National Security Review* 2 (1): 53–73.

Luttwak, Edward. 1979. *The Grand Strategy of the Roman Empire: From the First Century A.D. to the Third*. Baltimore: Johns Hopkins University Press.

Luttwak, Edward. 1987. *Strategy: The Logic of War and Peace*. Cambridge, MA: Harvard University Press.

Luttwak, Edward. 2009. *The Grand Strategy of the Byzantine Empire*. Cambridge MA: Harvard University Press.

Martel, William. 2015. *Grand Strategy in Theory and Practice: The Need for an Effective American Foreign Policy*. Cambridge, MA: Cambridge University Press.

Meaney, Thomas, and Stephen Wertheim. 2012. "Grand Flattery: The Yale Grand Strategy Seminar." *The Nation*. https://www.thenation.com/article/archive/grand-flattery-yale-grand-strategy-seminar/.

Mercur, James. 1898. *The Art of War: Prepared for the Cadets of the United States Military Academy*. New York: John Wiley.

Milevski, Lukas. 2016. The *Evolution of Modern Grand Strategic Thought*. Oxford: Oxford University Press.

Palmer, R. R. 1986. "Frederick the Great, Guibert, Bülow: From Dynastic to National War." In *Makers of Modern Strategy: From Machiavelli to the Nuclear Age*, edited by Peter Paret. Princeton, NJ: Princeton University Press.

Mitchell, A. Wess. 2018. *The Grand Strategy of the Habsburg Empire*, Princeton: Princeton University Press.

Murray, Williamson. 2011. "Thoughts on Grand Strategy." In *The Shaping of Grand Strategy*, edited by Williamson Murray, Richard Hart Sinnreich, and James Lacey. New York, NY: Cambridge University Press.

Murray, Williamson, Richard Hart Sinnreich, and James Lacey, ed. 2011. *The Shaping of Grand Strategy*. New York, NY: Cambridge University Press.

Nicolay, John G., and John Hay. 1890. *Abraham Lincoln: A History*. Vol. IV. New York: The Century Co.

Oman, Charles. 1898. *A History of the Art of War: The Middle Ages from the Fourth to the Fourteenth Century*. London: Methuen.

Paret, Peter ed. 1986. *Makers of Modern Strategy: From Machiavelli to the Nuclear Age*. Princeton, NJ: Princeton University Press.

Paret, Peter. 1992. *Essays on Clausewitz and the History of Military Power*. Princeton: Princeton University Press.

Popescu, Ionut C. 2017a. "Grand Strategy vs. Emergent Strategy in the Conduct of Foreign Policy." *Journal of Strategic Studies* 41 (3): 438–460.

Popescu, Ionut. 2017b. *Emergent Strategy and Grand Strategy: How American Presidents Succeed in Foreign Policy*. Baltimore: Johns Hopkins University Press.

Posen, Barry R. 1984. *The Sources of Military Doctrine: France, Britain, and Germany between the World Wars*. Ithaca: Cornell University Press.

Posen, Barry R., and Andrew L. Ross, 1996. "Competing Visions for U.S. Grand Strategy." *International Security* 21 (3): 5–53.

Rahe, P. 2015. *The Grand Strategy of Classical Sparta: The Persian Challenge*. New Haven: Yale University Press.
Rosecrance, Richard, and Arthur Stein, ed. 1993. *The Domestic Bases of Grand Strategy*. Ithaca: Cornell University Press.
Sargeaunt, H. A., and Geoffrey West. 1941. *Grand Strategy*. New York: Thomas Y Cromwell.
Schorn, De Nockhern. 1783. *Idees Raisonnees Sur Un Systeme General Suivi Et De Toutes Les Connoissances Militaires Et Sur Une Methode Etudier Lumineuse Pour La Science De La Guerre Avec Ordre Et Discernement En Trois Parties Avec Sept Tables Methodiques*. Nuremberg et Altdorf: chez George Pierre Monath.
Sherman, General W. T. 1888. "The "Grand Strategy of the Wars of the Rebellion." *The Century Magazine* 13: 582–598.
Silove, Nina. 2018. "Beyond the Buzzword: The Three Meanings of 'Grand Strategy.'" *Security Studies* 27 (1): 27–57.
Sinnreich, Richard. 2011. "Patterns of Grand Strategy." In *The Shaping of Grand Strategy*, edited by Williamson Murray, Richard Hart Sinnreich, and James Lacey. New York, NY: Cambridge University Press.
Strachan, Hew. 2005. "The Lost Meaning of Strategy." *Survival* 47 (3): 33–54.
Strachan, Hew. 2014. *The Direction of War: Contemporary Strategy in Historical perspective*. Cambridge, UK: Cambridge University Press.
Swain, Richard M. 1986. *B. H. Liddell Hart; Theorist for the 21st Century*. Fort Leavenworth, KA: Advanced Operational Studies School for Advanced Military Studies, US Command and General Staff College.
Widen, J. J. 2016. *Theorist of Maritime Strategy: Sir Julian Corbett and His Contribution to Military and Naval thought*. Abingdon: Routledge.

CHAPTER 3

THUCYDIDES' LEGACY IN GRAND STRATEGY

NEVILLE MORLEY

IN the mid-1970s, students arriving at the US Naval War College were sometimes disconcerted to discover that their first seminar in the new curriculum developed by Admiral Stansfield Turner would focus on the ancient Greek author Thucydides, "an unknown book about an apparently irrelevant war by an author with an unpronounceable name" (Gaddis 2018, 60–61; cf. Stradis 2015). Such a response is much less likely today; Thucydides and the Peloponnesian War are now familiar names in the field of politics and military strategy, cited as authoritative by generals, international relations theorists, politicians, and journalists. Quotations from his work—above all the doctrine of "might makes right" from the so-called Melian Dialogue, and the summary of the "truest cause" of the war popularized recently as the "Thucydides Trap"—are regularly deployed to explain the dynamics of contemporary geopolitics (e.g. Welch 2003; Allison 2017). Recent studies of grand strategy likewise present him as a brilliant and pioneering analyst of the subject (e.g. Gray 2010, 264; Murray 2011, 6; Martel 2015, 24) or take for granted principles derived from his work such as the primacy of the motives of "fear, honor and interest" (e.g. Gray 1999, 196, 348; Gray 2015; Baylis, Wirtz, and Gray 2016, 7).

However, the place of Thucydides in Grand Strategy is paradoxical, or at least confused, in three respects, which echo his reception within International Relations theory (cf. Lebow 2012; Keene 2015). Firstly, Thucydides is presented as both ancient and modern. Like Sun Tzu, he is invoked to establish the antiquity of the discipline and the timelessness of certain key principles of statecraft, as a figure who transcended the limited perspective of his time to understand events in an essentially modern manner. At the same time, however, he is offered as evidence for the limited development of strategic thought before the second half of the twentieth century, not least because of the undeveloped condition of his society (e.g. Martel 2015, 24–25; Gaddis 2018, 33–36). Secondly, he is praised as a pioneering theorist of strategy and interstate relations, but discussions of his work then focus not on any exposition of theory but on the historical events that he described—that is, drawing on the alternative tradition of interpreting

Thucydides since the Renaissance, as a "scientific" and uniquely reliable historian and source of information about the past, and taking his account at face value (e.g., Tsakiris 2006; Platias and Koliopoulos 2010). Thirdly, while Thucydides is mentioned as an important figure by most (though not all) writers on grand strategy, he is rarely discussed in any detail; the majority of references are rhetorical rather than substantive, establishing him as a mythical founding figure of the discipline and drawing on his accumulated cultural authority (cf. Ruback 2015 on the comparable practice in IR) while side-stepping awkward questions about the actual nature and content of his work and how this might affect its relevance to modern strategic analysis.

The majority of references to Thucydides in grand strategy literature, therefore, are either superficial or problematic. However, this does not make him irrelevant. The argument of this chapter is that Thucydides' exploration of the events of a specific period of distant history offers an important complement to more explicit theoretical approaches to the subject. While he does not offer anything resembling a theory or precepts of grand strategy, despite the claims of a few of his admirers, we can read his work as a kind of case study, a thought-provoking source of analogies and examples that is "good to think with", and even as a metacommentary on the possibilities and problems of grand strategy in the contemporary world.

The Nature of Thucydides' Project

Theorists of grand strategy are certainly not alone in assimilating Thucydides' text to the norms and assumptions of their own modern discipline, at the expense of ignoring or obscuring its more awkward and anachronistic aspects. What is striking in this case is the attempt at combining, or at least juxtaposing, the two divergent traditions of modern reception. Since his work was rediscovered, translated, and disseminated in Western Europe in the fourteenth century, having been known for the previous millennium or so only through passing remarks of authors like Cicero, Thucydides has been taken as an intellectual model and inspiration (Harloe and Morley 2012; Lee and Morley 2015). Most such readings have involved a combination of familiarization and defamiliarization: Thucydides is presented as an example or template for imitation, because of the perfection of his work and/or its innovative qualities, but generally within the present conception of a given genre or discipline—but with no agreement as to which discipline has the strongest claim to his legacy. In concrete terms, historians have tended to see him as a model historian, and political theorists as a kind of political theorist (cf. Ober 2001; Lebow 2012).

The historians' claim is, on the face of it, the more obvious and convincing, given that the bulk of Thucydides' text is an apparently straightforward narrative of the events of what we know as the Peloponnesian War, the 30-year war between the Lacedaimonians (Spartans) and the Athenians in the second half of the fifth century BCE. Not only was his subject matter historical; so too, it is frequently argued, was his methodology. The widespread conviction that Thucydides was an especially reliable, objective, and trustworthy reporter of information about the past is based partly on considering his text in the context of his biography. Although he identified himself as an Athenian, he did not spare his fellow citizens from criticism (and was criticized for a lack of patriotism by at least one ancient commentator); conversely—with the possible exception of his depiction of one or two Athenian politicians—he does not appear vindictive either, despite being exiled by Athens for his own failure as a general (Morley 2015, 71–96). Still more important are his stated methodological precepts at the beginning of his first book, which underpinned the case that his work anticipated modern critical historiography: his rationalizing interpretations of mythical traditions and events like plagues and eclipses, his insistence on the need to enquire carefully into the past and emphasis on the difficulty of doing so, and his contempt for those who accept the first story they hear and those who write history for entertainment rather than truth (Greenwood 2006; Forsdyke 2017).

> It is difficult to be sure of every detail in the evidence since people accept quite uncritically any reports of the past they get from others, even those relating to their own country. (1.20.1)

> I investigated ever detail with the utmost concern for accuracy. This was a laborious process of research, because eyewitnesses at the various events reported the same things differently, depending on which side they favored and on their power of memory. (1.22.2–3)

This version of Thucydides exemplifies the historian's duty to the truth of the past as an end in itself, and the critical methods required to achieve this, and his work is then taken as a wholly reliable source of historical information—including about the strategic thinking of his protagonists. However, there are multiple grounds on which this image might be questioned. For most of the events described, we have no contemporary sources other than Thucydides' account, and he rarely discusses or describes his evidence; we are required to take a great deal of his narrative on trust. Even more problematic are the speeches that he put into the mouths of important individuals, while admitting the impossibility of recording them verbatim and instead offering a formulation that has troubled historians ever since: "What I have set down is how I think each of them would have expressed what was most appropriate in the particular circumstances, while staying as close as possible to the overall intention of what was actually said" (1.22.1). This blurs the distinction, which historians are keen to maintain, between Thucydides' supposedly critical and objective account and other, more literary and rhetorical—and hence less reliable and scientific—forms of historiography, associated with premodern approaches.

However, Thucydides' own description of the purpose of his work casts doubt on the idea that he aimed to chronicle events as an end in itself:

> [My work] will have served its purpose well enough if it is judged useful by those who want to have a clear idea of what happened in the past and what—the human condition being what it is—can be expected to happen again some time in the future in similar or much the same ways. It is composed to be a possession for all time, and not just a performance-piece for the moment. (1.22.4)

Historians have been happy to accept this as a boilerplate statement about the value of knowing about the past. Since the nineteenth century, however, and especially in political theory and international relations since the Second World War, the passage has been understood in a much stronger sense, as the foundational statement of a normative social science. If there are constants in human affairs—the phrase "the human condition being what it is" is often translated as "according to human nature"—then Thucydides appears to be asserting the possibility of identifying consistent laws or principles that will continue to hold true in future, on the basis of his study of past data.

The most familiar example of such an interpretation is the Realist school of international relations theory, which gives Thucydides credit for identifying some basic principles of interstate relations: for example, the primacy of rational motives of fear, interest, and honor; the irrelevance of issues of justice and ethics in conflicts between states; and the ability of the stronger power to dictate terms while weaker powers are forced to comply (e.g. Gilpin 1986; Gustafson 2000; Forde 2012). The actual course of the war in Thucydides' account, especially its outbreak, is understood as exemplary, blurring the distinction between events and their interpretation and providing a template for understanding future occurrences:

> In summary, according to Thucydides, a great or hegemonic war, like a disease, follows a discernible and recurrent course. The initial phase is a relatively stable international system characterized by a hierarchical ordering of states with a dominant or hegemonic power. Over time, the power of one subordinate state begins to grow disproportionately; as this development occurs, it comes into conflict with the hegemonic state. The struggle between these contenders for pre-eminence and their accumulating alliances leads to a bipolarization of the system. In the parlance of game theory, the system becomes a zero-sum situation in which one side's gain is by necessity the other side's loss. As this bipolarization occurs the system becomes increasingly unstable, and a small event can trigger a crisis and precipitate a major conflict; the resolution of that conflict will determine the new hegemon and the hierarchy of power in the system. (Gilpin 1988, 596–597)

The confident assertions of these scholars about Thucydides' supposed thesis are rendered somewhat questionable by the absence from the work of any such statements of transhistorical principles or general laws in the historian's own voice, let alone detailed elaboration or analysis of them. As Thomas Hobbes, one of the first and most perceptive of Thucydides' English translators, noted, "Digressions for instruction's cause, and other such open conveyances of precepts (which is the philosopher's part), he never useth" (1629, xxii).

Instead, it is necessary to extract statements of general principle from the words that Thucydides puts into the mouths of characters in his account: for example, the Athenian representatives, in a debate at Sparta, who claim to have been motived by fear, honor, and interest like any other state (1.75), or the Athenians at Melos who refused to consider anything other than pragmatic arguments from the Melians, on the grounds that issues of justice were relevant only between those of equal power (5.89). The problem, as critics of Realism have long observed, is that this rests on a series of problematic assumptions: that Thucydides intends us to read these claims as transhistorical principles rather than as contingent, historically specific arguments; that they are supposed to be axiomatically true; and that we should identify them without question as Thucydides' own views (e.g. Johnson 1993 and 2015; Crane 1998; Ahrensdorf 1997; Welch 2003). These statements are more plausibly understood as Thucydides' characterization of the thinking and assumptions of the speakers—the different attitudes that led to the outbreak of war; the arrogance of the Athenians at Melos, just before they launched their disastrous expedition to Sicily—and indeed we should see him as offering them to us for analysis and criticism, especially as they most often appear in dialogue or debate with opposing arguments.

It is not simply that Thucydides was not, in any doctrinaire sense, a Realist, although he was undoubtedly interested in similar issues about state motivation and decision-making and the relationship between power and justice (cf. Morley 2018). He was not in fact concerned to advance any specific theory about human behavior, even if we can identify recurring concerns in his work with the problems of rhetoric, emotion, and democratic deliberation, or with the role of chance in events and the limits of human foresight (Lebow 2001; Hawthorn 2014). But it is equally obvious that he did not intend simply to impart information about past events as an end in itself. Rather, as Hobbes observed, Thucydides deployed various literary techniques to present events in a manner which immersed his readers in the action as spectators or even—hearing speeches in major debates and having to weigh the opposing arguments—as vicarious participants. Readers primed by his introduction to identify possible analogies and lessons, and to recognize their own times in the events he described, would thus come to reflect on wider questions about the course of the war, the causes of events, the role of chance and contingency, the influence of individual leaders versus the force of larger developments and structures, the nature of political deliberation, and much else. The best explanation of the long tradition of contradictory interpretations of what Thucydides *really* meant is that he was entirely successful in creating something which anyone could find useful in trying to understand their world; it is always possible to identify some analogies with later events, and to hear echoes of present concerns, while passing over the many sections which fail to speak to *this* present.

The implications of this for the study of grand strategy are obvious. We should not expect to find Thucydides advancing any explicit theory of strategy, and should not assume that the strategic precepts and arguments expounded by characters in his account can be straightforwardly ascribed to him (*pace* Platias and Koliopoulos 2010). Further, we should be cautious about taking his description of Athenian and Spartan strategy at face value; certainly, he intended to offer a true account, but his version of events is an interpretation, not a simple chronicle (cf. Kagan 2010). We are engaged with "Thucydides' Peloponnesian War", a complex artifact intended above all to open up questions and provoke further thought.

Grand Strategy in the Peloponnesian War

Thucydides did not talk in terms of "strategy", let alone "grand strategy"; *stratēgia* for him refers simply to the holding of the position of *stratēgos*, one of the Athenians' ten annually elected generals, including his own unsuccessful term of office in 422 (e.g. 1.95.6, 5.26.5; Martel 2015, 61–62). This neglect of the concept is a general feature of classical antiquity, rather than a personal blind spot. There is no discussion anywhere in Greek or Roman literature of the idea that the relationship between generalship and other forms of the exercise of power should be considered explicitly, and even the concepts of "policy" or "planning" are alien to the classical worldview, despite the fact that some translations make it appear that ancient leaders pursued such things (on ancient strategy, cf. Wheeler and Strauss 2007, 186–187, 213–223). It is nevertheless entirely reasonable to say that Thucydides did study these themes, regardless of whether he had a name for them or treated them as a unity.

This is true not just in the trivial sense that Thucydides described not only battles and military maneuvers but the whole course of the war, including the political debates and decisions that shaped military activity (Freedman 2013, 29–30). In terms of William Martel's definition of grand strategy, Thucydides' subject matter is long term (the war lasted for three decades, on and off), concerned with the highest ends of the state, and employing all means—primarily military, but also diplomacy and elements of "soft power" (compare for example the arguments, in the Mytilenean Debate and Melian Dialogue, about how the actions of Athens will affect its reputation and hence influence the future behavior of other states; 3.39.7, 3.45–47, 5.95–99). More importantly, he clearly aspired to an understanding of the war as a complete phenomenon, offering a perspective that goes well beyond that of any of the participants in both chronological scope and analytical depth. His account of "why the Peloponnesians and Athenians fought with one another" begins not with an account of escalating tensions between the two sides over previous years or decades, but with a schematic overview of early Greek history that establishes the dynamic relationship between resources and conflict, framed by doubts about human capacity to evaluate strengths and advantages, offering a broader sociological context for the war (1.1–20; Foster 2010).

The multilayered nature of his interpretation is seen most clearly in his account of the actual outbreak of the war. On the one hand, he concludes his introductory remarks with the claim (recently popularized as "The Thucydides Trap" and applied to current US–China relations: Allison 2015, 2017) that "the truest cause but the one least discussed" was the rise of Athens and the fear this provoked in Sparta, so that the latter were compelled to war; this remark, complex and ambiguous in the original Greek, emphasizes the underlying structural factors compelling actors without their knowledge, a precursor of the "sleepwalkers" interpretation of the origins of the First World War (Jaffe 2017). However, Thucydides' narrative immediately moves on to the specific events that led to Sparta's declaration of war, highlighting the different motives of multiple actors, not only the two protagonists, and the many ways in which the debates about war on each side could have turned out differently (even if only to delay the inevitable) (Robinson 2017). He is concerned with the ability of decision-makers and deliberative bodies to evaluate situations successfully, and their susceptibility to having their judgment swayed by wishful thinking or other emotions; with the conditions under which strategic decisions are made, and the capacity of different political organizations—the difference between Athenian and Spartan politics is an important theme—to develop and maintain a grand strategy.

The bulk of Thucydides' narrative of the war can be divided between two categories of action: deliberations and decision-making, and maneuvers, sieges, and battles. He shifts backwards and forwards between the development of strategy, however inchoate, and its attempted implementation. None of this is shown to be straightforward; people and deliberative bodies make decisions, but as readers with the benefit of hindsight and a broader perspective, we are conscious of the weaknesses in their reasoning—and these decisions can rarely if ever be put fully into practice with the intended consequences. One example of Thucydides' technique is the speech of the Corinthian representatives at a meeting of the Peloponnesian allies, denouncing the Spartans for their failure to act against Athens (cf. Badian 1993):

> Spartans, your faith in your own constitution and society makes you mistrustful of outsiders like ourselves when we have something to tell you. This does give you your quality of self-discipline, but it also leaves you in greater ignorance when it comes to dealing with anything outside Sparta. Many are the times, for example, that we warned you of the threat the Athenians posed to us, but you refused to learn the lessons we were giving you and preferred instead to suspect the speakers of being motivated by our domestic feuds with Athens. (1.68.1–2)

> We ought not to be still considering whether we have been wronged but how we should be responding in our defense. Men of action make their plans and then strike decisively and at once against those who dither… Of all the Greeks you Spartans are the only ones to be so passive: you defend ourselves against attack not by the use of power but by being *about* to use it; and you alone put an end to an enemy's expansion not in its early stages but when they are twice their original size. (1.69.2–4)

This speech serves multiple purposes. It presents to the reader reasons why war could have been seen as desirable, necessary, or unavoidable from the Peloponnesian side (without implying that these claims were necessarily true); it implies possible interpretations of events (Spartan failure to act in a timely fashion—"You are the ones to blame for all this" (1.69.1)—versus Corinthian aggression in forcing the issue because of their own long-standing enmity towards Athens); and above all it offers a characterization of the Spartans and their approach to strategic thinking (cf. Gaddis 2018, 36, on the link made between culture/character and strategy). It is made clear that the Spartans do indeed lack overall strategy, beyond a wish to be left alone if possible, which has led them to delay taking any action, and now prompts a precipitate reaction. Following this debate, one of the Spartan kings, Archidamus, argued for a policy of building up resources and preparing for war, not being afraid of their reputation for slowness— "On no account must we let ourselves be carried away by the hope that the war can be brought to a speedy end if we devastate their land" (1.81.6)—but the people had now been roused to anger and were easily manipulated by another prominent Spartan into voting for immediate war, although "it was still impossible for them to give effect to it immediately given their state of unreadiness" (1.125.2).

Thucydides' characterization of the absence of Spartan grand strategy, ventriloquized through the Corinthians, is borne out by subsequent events. With the partial exception of explicitly un-Spartan individuals like the energetic general Brasidas, their approach to fighting Athens is thoroughly traditional, based on the invasion of Athenian territory in the hope of bringing them to battle, largely reactive, and regularly ineffective, as on multiple occasions—even after the Sicilian disaster—they fail to take advantage of opportunities or Athenian errors (Hunt 2006). This account is historically plausible, as the fundamental imperative of Spartan policy was to avoid any risk of their subject population of helots revolting and hence to avoid committing too many of their own forces to any action outside their own territory (Kelly 1982). However, Thucydides clearly presents their caution as both culturally embedded and problematic; the Spartans lack any wider vision or imagination, and hence are incapable of pursuing victory effectively against a more imaginative and/or less predictable enemy.

For much of the war, this absence of strategic thinking was equally true of the Athenians; as presented by the Corinthians in the same speech, they appear as a force of relentless but poorly directed energy, constantly trying something new and daring. They themselves, perhaps disingenuously, echoed the claim that their power had been allowed to develop through Spartan inaction, and that their empire was acquired almost by accident:

> It was only when you were unwilling to stay on to deal with what was left of the barbarian forces that the allies approached us and of their own accord asked us to assume the leadership. These were the circumstances that first forced us to develop the empire to its present point. Fear was the strongest motive, followed later by honor and then by self-interest as well. (1.75.1–3)

The idea of Athens lacking any longer-term strategy is echoed on several subsequent occasions, when Athenian leaders chide their citizens for their unwillingness to do what is necessary to maintain an empire—which "is like a tyranny, which it seems wrong to take but perilous to let go" (2.63.2). This emphasizes the crucial point that, while Spartan strategy was driven by caution and conservatism rather than any coherent plan, Athenian strategy was volatile and short term, shaped by the emotional reactions of the *demos* to immediate events and the ways in which these could be manipulated or channeled by competing speakers in the assembly (Wohl 2017).

This theme is highlighted—as is Thucydides' concern with the subject—by the sole exception to the absence of conscious and coherent grand strategy in the Peloponnesian War: the policy of Pericles, Athens' leader at the outbreak of the war (Foster 2010; Taylor 2010; Azoulay 2010). Pericles' strategy was simple: to refuse to engage with the militarily superior Spartan soldiers when they invaded Athenian territory, but instead to withdraw within the city's walls, using Athenian naval dominance to maintain food supplies and attack Spartan interests elsewhere. What is important is that this approach is clearly presented by Thucydides, through a series of speeches he puts in the mouth of Pericles, as an explicit and coherent strategy, grounded in understanding and foresight (Kagan 2010; Platias and Koliopoulos 2010, 35–60). Pericles reassures the Athenians that his plan is based not only on evaluating both sides' resources but on analyzing these in relation to wider principles—"Capital is what sustains a war rather than forced contributions" (1.141.2–4)—and anticipating likely developments. He insists on the need for long-term consistency rather than short-term reaction, even in the face of difficulty and uncertainty: "I know that the mood in which people in general are persuaded to go to war does not remain the same when they actually undertake it, but that they change their minds with their circumstances. So I see that I must now give you very much the same advice as before ..." (1.140.1). Further, the famous and much-quoted Funeral Oration offers a coherent statement of the state's highest political ends to be pursued globally over the long term (to echo Martel 2015, 31), with Pericles emphasizing Athenian exceptionalism in democracy, freedom, and openness as the foundation of the approach and, as he claims, the source of their destined victory. As with any other speech in Thucydides, none of this is to be taken at face value—in a number of ways, Pericles' exposition of Athenian values is idiosyncratic and manipulative (cf. Roberts 2012)—but it reinforces the sense that he possessed a clear vision of grand strategy and sought to implement it—and often, though never consistently, to articulate it to his fellow citizens (as Walling 2013 notes, he just as frequently sought simply to reassure them that he had such a plan).

Whether Pericles' strategy, deeply unpopular with many Athenians, would have prevailed in time is unknown, due to his death in the plague that struck Athens in the second year of the war; this is one of the most important counterfactual possibilities in the whole work. Thucydides praises Pericles' foresight in avoiding direct engagement or other risks and suggests that the wisdom of this was confirmed by subsequent events (2.65.5–11)—but the nicely ambiguous language could mean that his successors took risks and so brought disaster, without necessarily implying that Pericles' avoidance of risk would certainly have brought success. Certainly, Thucydides emphasizes the dependence of this strategy on the personality of Pericles, able to overrule the short-term thinking and emotions of the people through personal authority; "what was nominally a democracy was really the rule of the first man" (2.65.9), implying that Athens was capable of pursuing a grand strategy only if it became less democratic and less Athenian. The nature of political leadership is shown to be central to the successful development of any sort of strategy (*contra* Platias and Koliopoulos 2010, 4).

The Mytilene Debate (3.36–49), in which the Athenians first voted to massacre the entire population of a revolted ally and then changed their minds the next day, offers one case study of their lack of consistent strategy and susceptibility to manipulation (Macleod 1978). An even more crucial example is the Sicilian Debate, in which Thucydides depicted the defeat of a cautious, quasi-Periclean strategy of the avoidance of ambitious overseas adventures, albeit badly articulated, by a combination of ignorance of the enemy and the situation, overconfidence in the predictability of events, arrogant belief in Athenian power, and the lack of any long-term perspective (6.1–26; Kallet 2001). And in the aftermath of the subsequent disaster, Thucydides caustically remarked, the Athenians denounced the orators who had proposed the expedition, as if they themselves had not voted for it (8.1.2).

Principles and Problems of Ancient Grand Strategy

Thucydides' account is always overtly focused on the specifics of historical events: he shows how the combination of Pericles' coherent strategy and the Spartan lack of strategy led to the outbreak of war at that time and in that manner, while the death of Pericles and the lack of grand strategy on either side thereafter was one of the crucial factors determining how events subsequently played out and prolonged the war (Platias 2002; Tsakiris 2006). But it is easy to see how one might draw wider conclusions from this account, potentially relevant to the present. In his depiction of Pericles, Thucydides showed that grand strategy in the full meaning of the term was possible in classical Greece, albeit rare, dependent on specific conditions and individuals, and fragile. There is no guarantee of the success of such an approach—if the planner's grasp of conditions or available resources is faulty, or their anticipation of developments is overly optimistic or pessimistic, as Thucydides arguably implied of Pericles (Foster 2010), let alone if the plan is impacted by chance events—but the lack of such a grand strategy clearly leaves a state more vulnerable, or at any rate more subject to the vagaries of events or the changeable emotions of people. Pericles' early death invites counterfactual reflection: would his strategy have succeeded, if he had lived, and if not why not? Could Athens ever have prevailed without such a plan, unless by sheer chance? Did the Spartans win simply because Athens made too many serious errors, given their own lack of grand strategy?

This offers a basis for considering other episodes in the narrative. The Melian Dialogue, for example, can be read in multiple ways. The Athenian expedition can be evaluated against the original Periclean strategy of avoiding overseas conquests, and against Thucydides' claims about the strategies of Pericles' successors. Further, and perhaps more illuminating, we can explore the claims made by the Athenians in the Dialogue about the dominance of power and self-interest and the superiority of being feared to being liked in dealings with other states, and the responses offered by the Melians—not in search of timeless principles that can be elevated into a theory of grand strategy, but rather as deliberately contentious claims and would-be principles that need to be interrogated. Thucydides staged a debate between competing conceptions of the world and how to engage with it, raising questions about the relationship between means and ends and the extent to which any strategy depends on assumptions about the predictability of events (cf. Ober and Perry 2014). As readers, we are not supposed to adopt the Athenians' strategy or the assumptions that underpinned it; they are presented in this unusual dramatic form to compel us to question them, so as both to understand the ways that other states and powerful groups may think and to reflect on our own assumptions.

For an equally illuminating and less familiar example, we can consider the speech made by the representatives of Corcyra before the war, seeking to persuade the Athenians to enter into alliance with them against Corinth (1.32–36). A crucial element in Thucydides' presentation is that the Corcyreans put forward their arguments as answers to the questions the Athenians ought, they claim, to be considering, in terms of their own behavior—"What we used to think of as prudent behavior on our part—avoiding any external alliance that could expose us to sharing the risks in a neighbor's policy—is now revealed as a misjudgment and a source of weakness" (1.32.4)—and in relation to long-term strategy, motives, and the anticipation of future developments.

> If you accept into an alliance people whose most vital interests are at stake, you can expect to see abiding proofs of their gratitude; and furthermore, we have built up a navy which is greater than any but yours. Just think—what could be a greater stroke of luck for you, or more irksome to your enemies, if an additional force you would have paid so much to have and would have been so grateful for comes to you of its own accord, unsolicited, and offers itself up at no risk or expense on your part, bringing you honor in the world at large, the gratitude of those you are directly helping, and more power to your own cause? (1.33.1–2)

Thucydides then prompts his readers to question every statement and assumption by offering counterarguments. The Corinthians seek to dissuade Athens from the proposed alliance largely by raising issues of justice, duty, and past behavior, rather than advantage or expediency—which becomes part of the explanation for Athens eventually deciding to ignore them—but they include a broader statement of principle about choosing strategy: "One's advantage is in fact best served by making the fewest mistakes; and the future prospect of war, with which the Corcyreans are trying to scare you and lead you astray, remains an uncertain possibility" (1.42.2). And of course the untrustworthiness of this claim—or at least the impossibility of being certain how to decide on the relative likelihood of different events occurring—is emphasized by the fact that the Athenians, having ignored Corinthian advice, later offer some very similar advice to the Spartans in *their* deliberations about war:

> Think in advance about how unpredictable war can be before you find yourself involved in one. The longer a war lasts the more likely it is to turn on matters of chance, which we are all equally unable to control and whose outcome is a matter of risk and uncertainty. Men go to war and launch into action as their first rather than what should be their last resort, and only when they come to grief do they turn to discussion. (1.78.1–2)

This is, we may surmise, less about establishing a useful principle for the development of strategy—it is clearly already a truism in fifth-century BCE Greece—than about identifying difficulties with the enterprise. Successful development and implementation of strategy and grand strategy depend on being able to anticipate events, or having a plan that is invulnerable to chance; but Thucydides' narrative offers a series of examples which highlight the inability of human beings to predict or anticipate successfully, and which emphasize instead their tendency towards excesses of optimism or pessimism, confirmation biases, and groupthink—the Sicilian Debate being simply the most prominent example (Turner 2018).

Conclusion

In important respects, Thucydides' account echoes Martel's view (2015, 24) on the absence of grand strategy in the premodern era. Even in the case of Pericles—whose example serves above all to prove the general rule—it is too dependent on individual inspiration, rather than being sustained by any form of institution, and too vulnerable to the vagaries of politics, whether the whims of the *demos* or the infighting of oligarchs or the suspicions of a monarch. The pressure to respond to immediate events, in the absence of a strong commitment to consistency, is usually overwhelming. It is typical of Thucydides' provocative approach that the most eloquent denunciation of the tendency of democratic systems to be swayed easily by emotions and manipulative rhetoric is put into the mouth of the arch demagogue Cleon, a figure we are primed to mistrust:

> The most dire prospect of all is if none of our decisions remain firm and if we fail to recognize the following facts: that a city is in a stronger position if it has bad laws which are always enforced than it if has good laws which lack authority; that a lack of learning combined with a sense of responsibility is of more general benefit than undisciplined smartness; and that unsophisticated people are for the most part better at managing cities than their intellectual superiors. The latter always want to appear wiser than the laws and to outdo any proposals made in the public interest. (3.37.3–4)

The question is whether these are problems solely with grand strategy in the premodern era, lacking the full recognition of its power and necessity which the moderns have now developed, and without the institutional framework to ensure its adoption and consistent implementation. From this perspective, the utility of Thucydides' work is that it demonstrates the adverse consequences of an absence of grand strategy for the successful defense of a state's interests.

But that is to ignore the issues which Thucydides' account raises for any attempt at developing and implementing grand strategy. If future events are not predictable, especially given humans' tendency to exhibit a range of cognitive biases in trying to predict them, what kind of grand strategy can actually be effective? Is an effective grand strategy possible only if it is insulated from democratic control, overriding short-term popular sentiments and concerns? And—given that the Athenian attack on Syracuse was wholly consonant with Athens' self-image, and certainly justified on the basis of claims about Athenian values and character—is the common insistence on a link between the highest values of the state and its grand strategy more problematic, more open to mythical thinking and manipulation, than is entirely reassuring?

Of course, we do not need Thucydides in order to raise such questions (cf. Edelstein and Krebs 2015; Brands and Porter 2015; Betts 2019). However, he offers a powerful means for exploring them. The original idea of introducing Thucydides into the curriculum of the Naval War College was not as a source of maxims and principles or as an insight into the supposed timeless and universal laws of international relations, but as a complex, ambiguous, and unfamiliar text, describing complex and unfamiliar situations, which could be considered from multiple perspectives. His work prompts consideration of comparisons and analogies, while remaining in its essence an account of a safely distant past; it offered military officers in the 1970s a means of discussing Vietnam without mentioning Vietnam, just as for later generations it could offer a means of discussing Iraq or Afghanistan without becoming bogged down in contemporary political debates about those wars. Thucydides' name is no longer unfamiliar, but the most important and thought-provoking parts of his work for grand strategy remain underexplored.

References

Ahrensdorf, Peter J. 1997. "Thucydides' realistic critique of realism." *Polity* 30: 231–265. https://doi.org/10.2307/3235218.
Allison, Graham. 2015. "The Thucydides Trap: Are the U.S. and China headed for war?" *The Atlantic*. September 24, 2015.
Allison, Graham. 2017. *Destined for War: Can America and China Escape Thucydides's Trap?* New York: Houghton Mifflin Harcourt.
Azoulay, Vincent. 2010. *Pericles of Athens*. Princeton: Princeton University Press.
Badian, Ernst. 1993. "Thucydides and the outbreak of the Peloponnesian War." In *From Plataea to Potidaea*, 125–162. Baltimore: Johns Hopkins University Press.
Balot, Ryan K., Sara Forsdyke, and Edith Foster, eds. 2017. *The Oxford Handbook of Thucydides*. Oxford: Oxford University Press.

Baylis, John, James J. Wirtz, and Colin S. Gray, eds. 2016. *Strategy in the Contemporary World*. 5th edition. Oxford: Oxford University Press.
Betts, Richard K. 2019. "The Grandiosity of Grand Strategy." *The Washington Post Quarterly* 42 (4): 7–22. https://doi.org/10.1080/0163660K.2019.1663061.
Brands, Hal, and Patrick Porter. 2015. "Why Grand Strategy Still Matters in a World of Chaos." *The National Interest* 10/12/15.
Crane, Gregory. 1998. *Thucydides and the Ancient Simplicity: The Limits of Political Realism*. Berkeley, CA: University of California Press.
Edelstein, David M., and Ronald R. Krebs. 2015. "Delusions of Grand Strategy: The Problem with Washington's Planning Obsession." *Foreign Affairs* Nov/Dec.: 109–116.
Forde, Steven. 2012. "Thucydides and 'Realism' Among the Classics of International Relations." In Harloe and Morley, eds., 178–196.
Forsdyke, Sara. 2017. "Thucydides' Historical Method." In Balot, Forsdyke, and Foster, eds., 17–38.
Foster, Edith. 2010. *Thucydides, Pericles and Periclean Imperialism*. Cambridge and New York: Cambridge University Press.
Freedman, Lawrence. 2013. *Strategy: A History*. Oxford: Oxford University Press.
Gaddis, John Lewis. 2018. *On Grand Strategy*. London: Allan Lane.
Gilpin, Robert C. 1986. "The Richness of the Tradition of Political Realism." In *Neorealism and its Critics*, edited by Robert O. Keohane, 301–321. New York: Columbia University Press. Originally published in *International Organization* 38 (1984): 287–304. https://doi.org/10.1017/S0020818300026710.
Gilpin, Robert C. 1988. "The Theory of Hegemonic War." In *The Journal of Interdisciplinary History* 18 (4): 591–613.
Gray, Colin S. 1999. *Modern Strategy*. Oxford: Oxford University Press.
Gray, Colin S. 2010. *The Strategy Bridge: Theory for Practice*. Oxford: Oxford University Press.
Gray, Colin S. 2015. *Thucydides Was Right: Defining the Future Threat*. Carlisle Barracks, PA: United States Army War College Press.
Greenwood, Emily. 2006. *Thucydides and the Shaping of History*. London: Duckworth.
Gustafson, Lowell S., ed. 2000. *Thucydides' Theory of International Relations: A Lasting Possession?* Baton Rouge: Louisiana State University Press.
Harloe, Katherine, and Neville Morley, eds. 2012. *Thucydides and the Modern World: Reception, Reinterpretation and Influence from the Renaissance to the Present*. Cambridge: Cambridge University Press.
Hawthorn, Geoffrey. 2014. *Thucydides on Politics: Back to the Present*. Cambridge: Cambridge University Press.
Hobbes, Thomas. 1629. *Eight Books of the Peloponnesian Warre Written by Thucydides the Sonne of Olorus*. London: Henry Seile.
Hunt, Peter. 2006. "Warfare." In *Brill's Companion to Thucydides*, edited by Antonios Rengakos and Antonis Tsakmakis, 385–413. Leiden: Brill.
Jaffe, Seth N. 2017. *Thucydides on the Outbreak of War: Character and Context*. Oxford: Oxford University Press.
Johnson, Laurie M. 1993. *Thucydides, Hobbes, and the Interpretation of Realism*. DeKalb, IL: Northern Illinois University Press.
Johnson, Laurie M. 2015. "Thucydides the Realist?" In Lee and Morley, eds., 391–405.
Kagan, Donald. 2010. "Pericles, Thucydides, and the Defense of Empire." In *Makers of Ancient Strategy: From the Persian Wars to the Fall of Rome*, edited by Victor Davis Hanson, 31–57. Princeton: Princeton University Press.

Kallet, Lisa. 2001. *Money and the Corrosion of Power in Thucydides: the Sicilian Expedition and its Aftermath*. Berkeley, CA: University of California Press.

Keene, Edward. 2015. "The Reception of Thucydides in the History of International Relations." In Lee and Morley, eds., 355–372.

Kelly, Thomas. 1982. "Thucydides and Spartan Strategy in the Archidamian War." *American Historical Review* 87 (1): 25–54.

Lebow, Richard Ned. 2001. "Thucydides the Constructivist." *American Political Science Review* 95: 547–560. https://doi.org/10.1017/S0003055401003112.

Lebow, Richard Ned. 2012. "International Relations and Thucydides." In Harloe and Morley, eds., 197–211.

Lee, Christine, and Neville Morley, eds. 2015. *A Handbook to the Reception of Thucydides*. Malden MA: Wiley-Blackwell.

Macleod, Colin. 1978. "Reason and necessity." *Journal of Hellenic Studies* 98: 64–78.

Martel, William C. 2015. *Grand Strategy in Theory and Practice*. Cambridge: Cambridge University Press.

Morley, Neville. 2014. *Thucydides and the Idea of History*. London: I.B. Tauris.

Morley, Neville. 2018. "Thucydides: The Origins of Political Realism?" In *The Edinburgh Companion to Political Realism*, edited by Miles Hollingsworth and Robert Schuett, 111–123. Edinburgh: Edinburgh University Press.

Murray, Williamson. 2011. "Thoughts on Grand Strategy." In *The Shaping of Grand Strategy: Policy, Diplomacy, and War*, edited by Williamson Murray, Richard Hart Sinnreich, and James Lacey, 1–33. Cambridge: Cambridge University Press.

Ober, Josiah. 2001. "Thucydides *Theoretikos*/Thucydides *Histor*: Realist Theory and the Challenge of History." In *War and Democracy: A Comparative Study of the Korean War and the Peloponnesian War*, edited by David R. McCann and Barry S. Strauss, 273-306. Armonk and London: M.E. Sharpe.

Ober, Josiah and Tomer J. Perry. 2014. "Thucydides as a Prospect Theorist." *Polis* 31: 206–232.

Platias, Athanasios. 2002. "Grand Strategies Clashing: Athenian and Spartan Strategies in Thucydides' 'History of the Peloponnesian War.'" *Comparative Strategy* 21 (5): 377–399. https://doi.org/10.1080/01495930290043137.

Platias, Athanasios G., and Constantinos Koliopoulos. 2010. *Thucydides on Strategy: Grand Strategies in the Peloponnesian War and their Relevance Today*. New York: Columbia University Press.

Roberts, Jennifer T. 2012. "Mourning and Democracy." In Harloe and Morley, eds., 140–156.

Robinson, Eric W. 2017. "Thucydides on the Causes and Outbreak of the Peloponnesian War." In Balot, Forsdyke, and Foster, eds., 115–124.

Ruback, Timothy J. 2015. "Ever Since the Days of Thucydides: On the Textual Origins of IR Theory." In *The Ashgate Research Companion to Modern Theory, Modern Power, World Politics: Critical Investigations*, edited by Scott G. Nelson and Nevzat Soguk, 17–34. Farnham: Ashgate.

Stradis, Andreas. 2015. "Thucydides in the Staff College." In *A Handbook to the Reception of Thucydides*, edited by Christine Lee and Neville Morley, 425–445. Malden MA: Wiley-Blackwell.

Taylor, Martha C. 2010. *Thucydides, Pericles and the Idea of Athens*. Cambridge: Cambridge University Press.

Tsakiris, Theodore. 2006. "Thucydides and Strategy: Formations of Grand Strategy in the History of the Second Peloponnesian War (431–404 BC)." *Comparative Strategy* 25 (3): 173–208. https://doi.org/10.1080/01495930600956195.

Turner, Aaron. 2018. "Thucydides, Groupthink, and the Sicilian Expedition Fiasco." In *Psychology and the Classics: a Dialogue of Disciplines*, edited by Jeroen Lauwers,

Hedwig Schwall, and Jan Opsomer, 255–270. Berlin: De Gruyter. https://doi.org/10.1515/9783110482201-017.

Walling, Karl. 2013. "Thucydides on Policy, Strategy, and War Termination." *Naval War College Review* 66 (4): 47–85.

Welch, David A. 2003. "Why International Relations Theorists Should Stop Reading Thucydides." *Review of International Studies* 29: 301–319. https://doi.org/10.1017/S0260210503003012.

Wheeler, Everett, and Barry Strass. 2007. "Battle." In *The Cambridge History of Greek and Roman Warfare, Volume I: Greece, the Hellenistic World and the Rise of Rome*, edited by Philip Sabin, Hans van Wees, and Michael Whitby, 186–247. Cambridge: Cambridge University Press.

Wohl, Virginia. 2017. "Thucydides on the Political Passions." In Balot, Forsdyke, and Foster, eds., 443–458.

CHAPTER 4

CLAUSEWITZ, *DIE POLITIK*, AND THE POLITICAL PURPOSE OF STRATEGY

BEATRICE HEUSER

CLAUSEWITZ AND TWO TRADITIONS OF THINKING ABOUT STRATEGY

IT is an act of bravery to accommodate a chapter on Carl von Clausewitz in a handbook dealing with Grand Strategy. As the subsequent chapter (Milevski) shows, there is no agreement on the meaning of the term "grand strategy." As I have shown elsewhere, even the terms "*stratégie/Strategie*/strategy" were invented in Western Europe only in Clausewitz's own times (Heuser 2010a, I). To this day, authors are struggling to make sense both of the narrower term "strategy" and the term "grand strategy" in contexts of ever-evolving war, against the background of changing technology, scale, resources but also ideologies, worldviews, beliefs, and values. What they all have in common, however, is that they relate the use (or threat of use) of armed force, and thus warfare, to a higher political purpose. In propagating this political dimension of warfare and of strategy, Clausewitz played an important role.

This chapter will sketch two traditions of writing about strategy making (in our modern sense) to which he contributed. The first, which we should name after Paul-Gédéon Joly de Maizeroy (1719–1780), introduced the Byzantine term "strategy" to the West and defined it narrowly in a purely military way that Clausewitz espoused and passed on to later generations. (We must insert a note of caution here: Clausewitz rarely acknowledged his debts to other authors, so we must rely on echoes of their writings in his (Heuser 2018, 185–207).) The second I shall call the Political Strategy Tradition, and it is one that sees strategy as subordinate to a higher political purpose. Clausewitz is usually credited with having been the first to formulate this, but as we shall see, the idea precedes him, and here, too, he stands in a longer tradition of thinking about a political–military nexus. His contribution to promoting this second tradition is crucial, however, and this link between higher politics and the use of military force as an instrument underlies all current definitions of grand strategy.

The Maizeroyan Tradition

So, focusing on the first tradition, we must start with the narrow sense in which Clausewitz himself understood the word "strategy," to explain why this cannot provide the link with more recent notions of "grand strategy." In the Age of Enlightenment, several authors had been groping for some term to describe something bigger than considerations of how to deploy forces on a battlefield and how to lead them into combat. Shortly before the French Revolution, both Joly de Maizeroy (1771) and the Austrian Wilhelm von Bourscheid (1781), stumbled across a Byzantine text dating from around 900 AD attributed to the Emperor Leo VI the Wise that employed the Greek term "*strategía*." In translating this, both created neologisms in their own languages. Joly de Maizeroy (1785 [1765], xxii) defined his own term, "*la stratégie*," as follows:

> La Stratégie comprises plans of operations, the movements of armies, the art of establishing camps, marches, distributions of troops in relation to particular projects, and generally the sciences of reasoning such as the *coup d'oeuil* [the intuitive interpretation of a situation]: that is why one calls [strategy] more habitually "military dialectic," which is the higher part of war and the particular science of the general.

Joly de Maizeroy got himself into a pickle as he wrote this in an updated version of his own earlier work called *Course of Tactics*; originally published in 1765 when he had not yet come across Leo's text. In the original version he had used "tactics" in a sense that in the revised version he would call "strategy." He had by no means been the only one to use "tactics" in such a larger sense—a widely read manuscript by a young officer, Count Guibert (1772) did so, too.

In the century after Joly de Maizeroy (1771) published his translation of Leo's text, definitions of "strategy" abounded, but were usually very technical and limited to military dimensions. One of the most influential German language authors of the period, Heinrich von Bülow (1835 [1799], 84f; Kuhle 2018), defined the relationship between strategy and tactics thus:

> The science of the military [*kriegerische*] movements outside the view of the adversary in the context of two armies at war with one another, or ... outside the range of the largest artillery piece etc, is strategy. The science of the military movements in the

presence of the enemy, as they can be observed by the same, or ... within the firing range of the largest artillery piece, is tactics.

Elsewhere Bülow (1805; quoted in von Courtlary 1819) summed it up flippantly, "where there is a punch-up, it's tactics, where there isn't, it's strategy."

It is against this background that we find Clausewitz (1832, II.1; 1976, 6) giving us the neither original nor very useful definition of strategy as "the use of engagements for the object of the war", as though strategy consisted only of "engagements" or battles. Further on, he opined, "the art of war" must "be broken down into tactics and strategy. The first is concerned with the form of the individual engagement, the second its use" (Clausewitz 1976 [1832], II.1, 132). And

> Strategy decides the time when, the place where, and the forces with which the engagement is to be fought, and through this threefold activity exerts considerable influence on the battle's [*Gefecht*] outcome. Once tactics has produced the battle, once the outcome is clear, whether that be victory or defeat, then strategy may make whatever use of it which can be made in view of the purpose of the war.
>
> And he noted that "the ultimate purpose of the whole war is specific to almost every war." (Clausewitz 1976 [1832], III. 8, 194. My slightly amended translation)

Strikingly, in the entire section of Book III chapter 8 from which this quotation hails, Clausewitz not once uses the term *die Politik* or *politisch*.[1] So we are left wondering whether Clausewitz thought of "the purpose" or "object of war" as a mere campaign aim—a victory in battle or the seizure of territory—or as something we would today consider a strategic aim such as knocking one adversary out of the war so as to be able to concentrate all forces on another front. In these writings, we cannot yet find in Clausewitz's definition firm evidence that he saw the need to couple strategy to politics.

In short, the Clausewitzian definitions of "strategy," which are really a rephrasing of what had been said in many ways since Joly de Maizeroy, do not much advance our understanding of war. It was indirectly that Clausewitz contributed to a second (pre-existing!) tradition of thinking about war, which put the political purpose at the center of strategy.

The Political Strategy Tradition and the Meaning of *Die Politik*

What the second tradition of defining of "strategy" and the later term "grand strategy" have in common is that they see the use (or the threat of the use) of armed forces in war and peace as in some way subordinate to a greater political purpose. Moreover, "grand strategy" tends to assume that there are tools and resources other than the purely military—albeit perhaps largely in support of the military—being employed in the pursuit of this higher purpose (Balzacq, Dombrowski, and Reich 2019).

It was again Heinrich von Bülow (not Clausewitz!) who first introduced a new level of analysis by distinguishing a "political strategy" from a "military strategy." In one of his latest works, dedicated to the campaign of 1805, he wrote

> political strategy relates to military [strategy] as the latter does to tactics, and political strategy is the highest. For just as the military [strategy] commands operations of a campaign or at best of a single war, political [strategy] concerns itself with the brilliance and durability of kingdoms over centuries or millennia. (Bülow 1806, 150f)

This proves that Clausewitz was far from being the first to have understood that there is (or should be) a higher political purpose to war, even though his would be the punchiest formulation of that relationship. It was only in *On War*, written in the 15 years after the Napoleonic Wars, that Clausewitz (1832, I.1, para. 24) that he came up with the famous section title which everybody knows, that "war is the mere continuation of *die Politik* with other means." But what did Clausewitz himself mean by *die Politik*? Translated into today's English, would it mean "politics" or "policy," or "political decision-makers," indeed "the government," "the state," or perhaps only "the minister/ministry responsible"?

Translating Clausewitz into English was complicated by the negative connotations that developed around the word "politics." Machiavelli (whom Clausewitz admired) had explained how power struggles influenced political decision-making. Machiavelli's unjudgmental analysis led his moralistic critics to see "politics" as immoral, akin to "politicking," and it did not sound right to subordinate the conduct of war to the whims of politicking leaders. This negative connotation of the term "politics" persuaded Michael Howard (2007, v–x) and Peter Paret in their translation of Clausewitz's *On War* (1976) frequently to use the term "policy" rather than "politics" for Clausewitz's *die Politik*. This has in turn been criticized by scholars, because "policy" has a narrower meaning, concerned with carefully crafted governmental approaches to and positions on certain issues (Honig 2007; Bassford 2007; see also Echevarria 2007). George Dimitriu (2018) has made a good case for seeing strategy-making as a function, not of rationally derived government policy, but also of politicking, political power games, both in Clausewitz's times and now; this certainly helps us better to understand strategy-making today.

We need to establish how Clausewitz himself understood the word *Politik* before we can then take the next step and see what larger insights Clausewitz has for us on the nature of the interface between a military strategy and a higher political purpose. To do so let us look, first, at what the term *Politik* meant in Clausewitz's own times, and how the authors he read (or presumably read) used the word before him. Secondly, let us home in on particularities of Clausewitz's views of the relationship between *die Politik* and the use of armed force, compared and contrasted with the views of the others.

In *Grimm's Dictionary*, which the Grimm brothers compiled during Clausewitz's lifetime, *die Politik* is defined as "*die Kunst des Staatslebens*," literally, the art of "State life" or public affairs, a curious word elsewhere defined in the *Dictionary* as "life of a State, or life as it is conducted within the State" (Grimm and Grimm 1854). Clausewitz also read works in French. In French, the term *la politique* had been used since the thirteenth century with a variety of meanings. Probably the earliest, thirteenth-century use referred to "the science and practice of government." Since Corneille had used the term in the seventeenth century, it could be taken to mean "the particular way of governing" ("Politique" 2012). Montesquieu in his *Spirit of Laws* of 1748 which Clausewitz greatly admired, only used the term "*la politique*" 13 times, without ever defining it, but apparently in the sense of "the particular way" or "process of governing." (For example, he wrote, "In monarchies, *la politique* achieves great things with the least effort [*vertu*] possible; just as in the most beautiful machines, as few movements, forces and wheels as possible are used by craftsmanship" (Montesquieu 1979 [1748], I.iii.5, 147).)

From the seventeenth century onwards, "*la politique*" could also mean "principles guiding action" (as in the English: "policy"), "public affairs, activities relating to the exercise of power in a State," and "behaviour in the public domain," but also "in the private domain." At the same time, it could mean "agility, subtleness in one's conduct." Last not least for our purposes, we should note that Germaine de Staël—in whose intellectually highly charged household in Switzerland Clausewitz stayed for several weeks in 1807—in her reflections on the French Revolution published in 1817 used "*la politique*" to mean "*parler politique*," which might be loosely translated as "political discourse" or "political talk" ("Politique" 2012).

A work to which Clausewitz may have been introduced by Germaine de Staël who in her youth had known the author well, and which Clausewitz (1812; see Heuser 2018, 204–207) definitely read before 1812, was the *Essai général de Tactique* by Guibert (1772), the long introduction to which begins with the words:

> If by *la politique* we mean the art of negotiating, or rather intriguing, that of blindly fomenting some revolution, or in the obscurity of cabinets to conclude or break some treaties…, we are in this regard without doubt superior to the Ancients.… But if *la politique* is the vast and sublime science of ruling a State, internally and externally; to direct individual interests towards a general interest; to render the peoples happy and to attach them to [make them supportive of] their governments, let us agree that [*la politique*] is entirely unknown to modern administrations … (translation in Heuser 2010b, 154)

Guibert thus criticized the French government of his own times, and what followed was a series of suggestions for the improvements of things. Clausewitz was so impressed with this book that he translated whole passages of it into German and also paraphrased them in his own *On War* (Heuser 2018, 204–207).

Turning to Clausewitz's use of *die Politik* in his earlier writings, in his ruminations on the Peace of Tilsit (1807), he clearly used the term in the meaning of "policy" or in the modern sense of overall strategy. Having accused Tsar Alexander of Russia of having, first, supported Prussia, and then, helped himself to a small portion of Prussian territory (the area of Byalystok), he argued that (even) Machiavelli would have turned away with disgust from such a *Politik*. He went on to extol the greatness of Machiavelli's thoughts, and spoke of the "*Politik* towards other States, which Machiavelli counselled to such States that are too weak to take the direct approach" (quoted in Rothfels 1922, 62–64).

In notes he penned sometime between 1819 and 1823, Clausewitz blamed Napoleon's conquests in Europe not only on French military acumen, but also on the "*liederliche Politik des Augenblicks*" of Europe's other princes, perhaps best translated as the shameful short-sighted politics of ad-hockery that focused on one day at a time rather than on the greater task of defeating Napoleon. Elsewhere he wrote that some German polities asked for constitutional changes, inspired by "ancient Rome with its enormous *Politik*." Here the word could either mean "policy/strategy of expansion," or its great political system. (Interestingly, he went on, like Montesquieu before him, to emphasize the link between the constitution of the polity and its foreign policies, and the indirect influences of parliaments—he meant representatives of the social classes and guilds—on foreign policy (Rothfels 1922, 173f).)

And now for a crucial passage of *On War*, concerning Prussia's defeat of 1806, translated here by Alan Cromartie who deliberately refrained from replacing the word *Politik* itself. "Did the disaster arise from the influence of *die Politik* on war or from the mistaken *Politik* itself?" Clausewitz asked, and continued: although the mistakes only revealed themselves in wartime,

> This did not happen because *die Politik* omitted to take counsel from the art of war. The very art of war in which an exponent of *die Politik* might have believed—i.e. the one from the real world, which belonged to the *Politik* of the day as its familiar tool—*this* art of war, I say, was naturally caught up in *die Politik*'s mistake and couldn't inform it of a better way.

War itself had changed, but not because

> the French government had freed itself from the leading strings of *die Politik*, but arose from the altered *Politik* which was produced by the French Revolution for the whole of Europe as much as for France. This *Politik* introduced other means, other forces, and in so doing made possible an energy in the conduct of war that would not otherwise have been thinkable. (Clausewitz 1832, VIII.6B; this translation by Cromartie 2015)

Let us attempt to paraphrase this by replacing "*die Politik*" with a more precise expression each time, assuming this is what Clausewitz meant. We would thus read: "Did the disaster arise from the influence of *policy-makers (the king and the diplomats)* on war or from the mistaken *policy* itself?" And:

> This did not happen because *the king* omitted to take counsel from *his generals*. The very art of war in which *the political leadership* might have believed—i.e. the one from the real world, which belonged to the *political context* of the day as its familiar tool—*this* art of war, I say, was naturally conditioned by *the mistaken overall policies (grand strategy?)* and couldn't inform *policy makers* of a better way.... [This was not

because] the French government had freed itself from the leading strings of *cabinet politics*, but arose from the altered *political dynamics* which was produced by the French Revolution for the whole of Europe as much as for France. This *revolutionary political dynamic* introduced other means, other forces....

It seems impossible to settle for a one-to-one consistent translation using only one English word.

Why did Clausewitz choose the word *Politik* for all of these?[2] There are several plausible answers. One is that in *On War*, Clausewitz was not concerned with criticizing King Frederick William III on whose favor his livelihood depended. If elsewhere he was less discreet in his implicit criticism of this monarch, Frederick William is not as much as mentioned in *On War*.

Secondly, we should recall that Clausewitz had set out to write something akin to Montesquieu's *Esprit des Lois*. Montesquieu himself had been on the lookout for (a limited number of) higher principles that, he claimed, governed all the laws about which he was writing. Montesquieu (1979 [1748], I:119) explained, "once I had discovered my principles, all that I was looking for came to me ..." Montesquieu's principles included the subordination of private law to public law, and of the state (and its governments) to the rule of law. If it is—as we may assume from his own statement—this sort of principle that Clausewitz was in search of, then writing about the subordination of warfare to *die Politik* as a higher principle, a big generic term that could encompass many different aspects, made perfect sense. Clausewitz took little interest in the mechanism of politics, in decision-making processes or "process tracing." To the contrary, one can assume that he wanted to boil down the manifold manifestations of political activity to one bigger principle—*die Politik*—just as elsewhere he introduced the principle of chance, or the principle of passion. Considering also his interest in Newton (mentioned in Clausewitz 1976 [1832], 112, 146), who with his concept of "force" had found a common descriptor for the horse's muscle power pulling a chariot and the mutual attraction of planets by gravitation, one could see the attractiveness of one such comprehensive term.

But there is a third, much simpler explanation: the meanings of words change over time. As we have seen from the etymological survey of the use of the term *la politique* in French and *die Politik* in German, these were terms used widely to encompass a variety of meanings and nuances. Where today one might, for the sake of precision and after a century of the existence of Political Science as a discipline at universities, choose a number of different expressions, all these terms seem to have come together in the heads of Clausewitz's contemporaries writing both in French and in German.

Die Politik and War

Having thus explored how Clausewitz might have understood *die Politik*, let us now see what light other works on the interface between *die Politik/la politique* and the use of force might shed on Clausewitz's ideas about it. The first to turn to is again the *Essai général*, where Guibert identified two strands of the policymaking of a government, and the need for them to interact for the State to have a robust defense posture:

> By Politics [*la politique*] I mean the art of governing a State in such a manner that the subjects may be happy, the State powerful, and respected by her neighbours; ... from thence Politics is naturally divided into two parts, *domestic* and *foreign* Politics [*Politique intérieure et Politique extérieure*].
>
> The first is the foundation of the second. All that belongs to the happiness and strength of a people falls under the first [category]: laws, manners, customs, preconceived opinions, national spirit, justice, police, population, agriculture, trade, revenues of the nation, expenses of government, duties, application of their produce...

Guibert went on to explain the complementary contributions that the two branches of government should make to the wellbeing of the State and its people, clearly thinking in terms of the duties of two complementary but distinct branches of government.

> While domestic Politics thus prepares and perfects every tool [of governing the State] internally, foreign Politics examines what weight and consideration the application of those tools can give to a State externally ... [Foreign Politics] must be acquainted with every kind of relation of its own country and the interests of others.

It must distinguish illusionary from real interests, ephemeral alliances from lasting ones. Foreign Politics

> must afterwards calculate what military force a State requires to impose respect on its neighbours, to give weight to its negotiations. [Foreign Politics] should tailor its military force in relation to the spirit and strength of the country, so it is not too great for its means, or else it would exhaust the State...

Foreign politics could guide the education of the armed forces so that great skill, valor, and discipline allowed the state to keep the size of the army small and thus "less burdensome to the subjects" (translation in Heuser 2010b, 150–70). So for Guibert, a healthy state was needed for a strong defense posture. Meanwhile, he did not differentiate between the exercise of diplomacy and the tasks of dealing with the military. (This predominance of foreign policy over defense policy continues to resonate in France.) Guibert's *Essai général* must have encouraged Clausewitz to reflect further on the nexus between foreign policy making and warfare.

Guibert was not the only one to be writing about the relationship between politics and warfare. In 1774, two years after the first publication of Guibert's *Essai général*, an anonymous work was published by the Royal Saxon Court's printer with the title *Attempt to establish rules according to which a concept for a war in its entirety, as well as operational plans for each individual campaign, are to be drawn up* (Anon. 1774). As passages in a work by Friedrich Wilhelm von Zanthier published in the following year summarize its key points, Zanthier is likely to have been its author or co-author (Zanthier

1775, 66f.). (A copy of this book existed in the library of the General War School the director of which Clausewitz was from 1818.[3]) In simple terms, this work on how to draw up a strategy for war or for an operation explained that if a prince's Cabinet [*Cabinett*] or council of ministers wanted to decide whether and how to wage a war, they should produce two plans: one concerning the war as a whole (today one might say the overall strategy in all its planning dimensions) and one an operational or campaign plan[4] [*Operationsplan*]. The work suggested that the two plans might effectively coincide, for example in the case of a small power fighting defensively only on one frontier. In a more complex scenario in which choices would have to be made, however, one would need the expertise or skill [*Kunst*] to make the best choices, i.e., how to prioritize or prefer some choices of action over others, to find "the shortest and easiest way to a secure an advantageous peace" (Anon. 1774, 3ff).

On what we would now call a strategic or grand-strategic level, a war plan would have to take into account the specific attributes of enemies and allies. Some powers would be enemies from the start, others might become enemies. One might have to seek new allies as the war evolved (ibid., 15f). Meanwhile, one should consider ways to undermine the enemy alliance, and how to behave towards neutrals (ibid., 146–156).

The author (Zanthier?) underscored that in order to draw up a good campaign plan, one needed "the skill [*Kunst*] to choose, among the different possible steps one could take against an individual enemy, the most decisive ones, and to identify the means that would in the fastest and most reliable way execute this plan." The author explained that each campaign plan and the plan for the war as a whole had to be thought out jointly, so that implications of each for the other could be taken into account: one could not allocate the same manpower and resources to several campaign plans simultaneously, and one would have to prioritize at the level of the plan for the war as a whole (we would say: the strategic level), with implications for resources at the level of the operational plans (ibid., 5). Consequently, resource constraints might lead one to the decision to avoid the war altogether, or else "to conduct the war, not as one would like to, but as one can" (ibid., 19).

Who should be charged with drawing up the war plan and the operational plans?

> A general of a certain standing will always have the talent to draw up [the concept for] the war as a whole from the operational plans of the individual campaigns. The minister by contrast, if he is not also a soldier, is never capable of designing the operational plan of an individual campaign, or even to judge its quality. Nor should one ever leave it to the minister alone to draw up [the concept for] the war as a whole. Instead, one must listen to the [respective] generals who are to be put in charge of the different frontiers, so that one can base the design for the war as a whole on their knowledge of war [*Kriegswissenschaft*] and simultaneously on the art of [governing] the State [*Staatskunst*] (ibid., 13).[5]

To be balanced, the wisdom and expertise of the minister would be needed for the conduct and termination of the war as a whole. A soldier might always be tempted to push further into enemy territory and to make further conquests. The minister, however, would take a larger (as we would say strategic) view and realize that there are limits to territorial conquest which statecraft [*Staatskunst*] must impose, as this would lengthen the frontiers one would henceforth have to defend and create new enemies. The wise prince, counselled by the minister, would return conquered territory little by little, in return for concessions elsewhere which would help bring about "a secure and lasting peace." The minister would contribute his knowledge of the enemy country, of the obstacles to a successful campaigns and war, and would see what parts of the military plans had to be adapted to these external realities. To conclude, we read, in order to determine all this properly,

> one has to comprehend the war in its entirety, and think it through from the beginning to the end [*bis zu seinem Ende durchdenken*], otherwise one runs the risk of already making a mistake with the first step, of embarking on it wrongly from the beginning, of getting confused about the game, and losing. (ibid., 159)

(It is perhaps this passage that inspired Clausewitz's (1976 [1832], VIII.3A, 584) admonition that one must not take the first step in war without thinking about the last.) The anonymous author (Zanthier?) concluded, "Thus the art of war and *die Politik* go hand in hand, jointly to determine the design of the war as a whole. He who follows only the sign posts of one or the other will go astray" (Anon. 1774, 157–159).

Clausewitz's (1976 [1832], VIII.6B, 606–610) own musings about the need for the Cabinet to consult the commander-in-chief also reads as though it might have been inspired by this text. In any case, while this anonymous author did not produce a punchy line about how warfare must be subordinated to higher purposes of *die Politik*, this is clearly its message.

A couple of decades later, we find this implication again in the writing of Immanuel Kant. Dwelling on war as the recourse of the State to pursue its legal claims in the absence of a court, he wrote, "*Die Anwendung, die der Staat von seiner Gewalt macht, um sein Recht zu verfolgen, ist also der Krieg*" (quoted in Mellin 1801, 715)—loosely translated, "war is the state's application of its power, in pursuit of its rights"; war is thus an instrument of state power. This formulation in turn resonates in an essay by Clausewitz's colleague Otto August Rühle von Lilienstern (1818), originally written in 1813, which had the same title "*Vom Kriege*" ("On war") that Clausewitz later gave to his own work. Here Rühle wrote that "war is the way and method to decide quarrels of the peoples through luck and the use of force." Summarizing a lengthy argument, Rühle homed in once again on the need to keep in mind "relationship between war and the state," and how the state had to "dominate the raw violence [of war] in such a way that [war] allows itself to become a useful instrument of an enlightened statecraft [*Staatskunst*]" (Rühle 1818, 159). In short, through the exercise of statecraft, war fare is a tool of politics.

We do not have explicit proof that Rühle had read Guibert, but there seem to be echoes of Guibert in Rühle's writing. While instead of *la politique* or *die Politik*, Rühle used the term *die Staatskunst*, this fits perfectly Guibert's definition of *la politique* as "the vast and sublime science of ruling a State" (see above). In any case, Rühle took

Guibert's differentiation between domestic and foreign-policymaking a conceptual step further. Rühle saw both as part of statecraft but postulated the division of the latter into two sub-areas. In a section originally written in 1811 he noted, "One tends to label the art of the conduct of relations among States in the state of peace as *Diplomatic Art*, while in times of war it is called *Art of the Conduct of War* [Rühle's emphasis]" (ibid., 180). He also used his own neologism *Diplomatik* as shorthand for "diplomatic art," which should ensure that the state was at all times prepared for defense, but also to prepare a particular war, and should determine when to initiate a state of war. He called for the recruitment of practitioners of a "*diplomatische Kriegskunst*," a diplomatic art of war, which should straddle the civilian aspect of the art of governing a country and the art of war. Such practitioners, he thought, could be educated by sending civil servants - i.e. aspiring diplomats - to attend courses in military academies (ibid., 185).

To underscore that the conduct of state policy in both peace and war must not be conducted in separate silos, Rühle explained, in a passage which again seems to echo the Saxon anonymous' (Zanthier's?) *Attempt to establish rules...*:

> Throughout history we only see great political results where *die Diplomatik* (or *die Politik*, as it is also called) goes hand in hand with the art of war, where either both are directly united in the person of the prince himself, or where the joint supreme command is left to the supreme military commander, or where the foreign minister is sufficiently well initiated into the secrets of the art of war to be capable of designing military operations, and to assess the military situation of the State and its neighbours in their entirety (ibid., 180f).

Regrettably, Rühle thought, the latter two were rarely the case: neither was the supreme military commander usually given the necessary political instructions, nor had the foreign minister usually made the effort to learn about the simplest rules of the art of war. The prevailing processes of government decision-making kept both compartments of the state well apart, especially in times of peace. "Thus when war breaks out, there is ... a lack of the necessary harmony [between them]. [They] cannot come to an agreement about the purpose [of the war] nor about the means" to pursue it. Foreign minister and military commander-in-chief poison each other's lives, "and it is by sheer luck if the survival or the actual interests of the State are not buried under the hostile sparring of *die Diplomatik* and art of war" (ibid., 181).

Against the background of this earlier literature Clausewitz (1832, I.1, 23–24. My translation), writing between the late 1810s and 1830, formulated his own ideas about peace and war, including of course the passage for which he is most famous:

> War is thus a political act.... If we keep in mind that war springs from some political purpose, it is natural that the prime motive of its existence will remain the supreme consideration conducting it.... *Die Politik* will thus permeate the entire war-act and will have a continuous influence on it, as far as the nature of the exploding forces allow.

> 24. War is a mere continuation of *die Politik* with other means.
> Thus we see that war is not just a political act, but a true political instrument, a continuation of political intercourse, a completion of the same with other means. What remains distinctive about war relates only to the particular nature of its means.... the political intention is the purpose, war is the means, and the means can never be thought of without the purpose.

These passages both comprise the idea of war as an instrument of state policy and allow for the influence of the complexity of politics at home and in interstate relations. It would be on this foundation that our own political–military understanding of strategy would ultimately be built from the twentieth century onwards.

THE MAIZEROYAN TRADITION AFTER CLAUSEWITZ

Initially, however, it was the narrow Maizeroyan definition of strategy, reinforced by Clausewitz's own use of the term, that would prevail in the Western literature well into the twentieth century. Most famously, Napoleon's Swiss general Baron Henri de Jomini (1992 [1838], 69–71), whose works would dominate the teaching in military academies from America to Russia while Clausewitz was still all but unknown, produced the following definitions independently of (and probably originally earlier than[6]) Clausewitz, but clearly, once more, inspired by the Maizeroyan tradition:

> Strategy is the art of making war upon the map, and comprehends the whole theatre of operations. Grand Tactics is the art of posting troops upon the battlefield according to the accidents of the ground, or bringing them into action, and the art of fighting upon the ground in contradistinction to planning upon a map.... Strategy decides where to act ... grand tactics decides the manner of execution and the employment of the troops.

And further on in his famous and frequently re-published *Art of War*, he wrote "Strategy ... is the art of bringing the greatest part of the forces of an army upon the important point of the theatre of war or the zone of operations" (ibid., 322).

In 1840, one of Clausewitz's successors as instructors of the Prussian Army, Wilhelm von Willisen (1868 [1840], I:26), told his disciples that "the task of the art of war is [to bring about] victory ... Victory merely means the achievement of the military aim as it arises directly from the fighting." And, "strategy is the doctrine of joint [operations]," "the doctrine of battle [*Schlagen*] is tactics (ibid., vol. I, 30–32)." Five years later, the French Maréchal Marmont (1845, 17, 25), once Napoleon's Aide de Camp, continued the Jominian tradition, writing "the general movements that take place beyond the vision of the enemy and before battle are called strategy" and "tactics is the science of the application of manoeuvres."

Twenty years later, again echoing Jomini, the Briton Sir Edward Bruce Hamley (1872 [1866], 60) lectured his students that "The theatre of war is the province of strategy," while "The field of battle is the province of tactics." Writing for the British Army, Colonel J.F. Maurice (1891, 7) requoted Hamley's words. At much the same time, the Jominian definitions were still repeated verbatim by French General Derrécagaix (1890 [1885], 1:4). Even at the turn of the nineteenth to the twentieth century, G.F.R. Henderson (1905, 39), Instructor in Tactics at the Royal Military Academy at Sandhurst, could lecture the British army that

> Strategy ... is the art of bringing the enemy to battle, while tactics are the methods by which a commander seeks to overwhelm him when battle is joined.... strategy leads up to the actual fighting—that is, to the tactical decision: but that while the two armies are seeking to destroy each other it remains in abeyance, to spring once more into operation as soon as the issue is decided.... the end of strategy is the pitched battle; ... the encounter at which strategy aims is one in which every possible advantage of numbers, ground, supplies, and *moral[e]* shall be secured ..., and which shall end in his enemy's annihilation.

It was the Soviets who most tenaciously clung to the Maizeroyan tradition because it had found its confirmation of Clausewitz's writings, and Clausewitz in turn had been approved of by Lenin. Even after the Second World War, Soviet military literature defined strategy "as the preparation and execution of the war as a whole and tactics as the organization and conduct of battle. The content of strategy and of tactics is the same—armed struggle" (Rasin 1958). The Cold War was already in full swing when Soviet definitions thus still continued in the Maizeroyan tradition derived from Emperor Leo, as echoed also by Clausewitz.

THE POLITICAL STRATEGY TRADITION WITH CLAUSEWITZ'S CONTRIBUTION

It was the alternative Political Strategy Tradition with inputs from Guibert, Rousseau, Kant, Bülow (with his "political strategy") and Rühle that turns on the role of political aims in the formulation of a strategy that in the end would outlast the Maizeroyan Tradition. Thus, for example, today's official Russian definition of "strategy" (there is no Russian definition of "grand strategy") reads as follows: "Politics determines the goals of the war and the methods of waging it, mobilizes human and material resources to achieve victory in the war, creates favorable internal and foreign policy conditions for S[trategy]. In turn, S[trategy] has an opposite effect on politics." (Russia 2020).

As we have seen, Clausewitz was merely a link in the chain of the Political Strategy Tradition. It is in this tradition that Captain Basil Liddell Hart (1944, 229) would later define "strategy" as "the art of distributing and applying military means to fulfil the ends of policy." In turn, on this definition of strategy, he and others would later build their definitions of grand strategy, to which policy or the overarching political purposes are central.[7]

Notes

1. Presumably this is something he would have changed, had he had time to complete the revision of his work.
2. I am grateful to Hew Strachan for having raised this question.
3. After the dissolution of the *Kriegsakademie* (as the General War School had been renamed in 1859) at the end of the Second World War, its library was originally loaned to the State Library of Lower Saxony, but the books formally became property of the Bundeswehr when this was set up, and are now mainly located in the library of the Centre for Military History and Social Sciences of the Bundeswehr (ZMSBw) in Potsdam.
4. Operational plan and campaign plan will be used synonymously here.
5. In this context, and more generally in German and French, as in English at the time, the word "art" referred to the skill and ability to do something practical, while "science" was used to refer to impractical, theoretical reflection (See Heuser 2016).
6. Earlier publications of Jomini with similar formulations go back to 1806.
7. The author wishes to thank Dr George Dimitiu, Professors Alan Cromartie, Andreas Herberg-Rothe and Alexander Querengässer for their precious comments and advice. All remaining errors are but her own.

References

Anon. *Versuch über die Regeln, nach welchen der Entwurf zu einem Kriege im Ganzen, sowohl als der Operational Plan eines Einzelnen Feldzugs einzurichten ist*. 1774. Dresden: Churfürstliche Hof- und Buchdruckerei.

Balzacq, Thierry, Peter Dombrowski, and Simon Reich. 2019. "Is Grand Strategy a Research Program? A Review Essay." *Security Studies* 28 (1): 58–86. https://doi.org/10.1080/09636412.2018.1508631.

Bassford, Christopher. 2007. "The Primacy of Policy and the 'Trinity' in Clausewitz's Mature Thought." In *Clausewitz in the Twenty-First Century*, edited by Hew Strachan and Andreas Herberg-Rothe, 74–90. Oxford: Oxford University Press.

Bourscheid, Johann W. von, trans. 1781. *Kaisers Leo des Philosophen Strategie und Taktik*. Vienna: Joseph Edler von Kurzboeck.

Bülow, Heinrich von. 1805. *Neue Taktik der Neuern sie sie seyn sollte*. Berlin: Himburg.

Bülow, Heinrich von. 1806. *Der Feldzug von 1805 Militärisch-Politisch Betrachtet*. Published by the author.

Bülow, Heinrich von. 1835. *Geist des Neuern Kriegssystems hergeleitet aus dem Grandsatze einer Basis der Operationen*. 3rd edition. Hamburg: August Campe.

Clausewitz, Carl von. 1812. *Confession Memorandum*.

Clausewitz, Carl von. 1832. *Vom Kriege*. Berlin: Dümmler.

Clausewitz, Carl von. 1976. *On War*. Translated by Michael Howard and Peter Paret. Princeton, NJ: Princeton University Press.

Colonel Maurice, J.F. 1891. *War*. London: Macmillan.
Courtlary, V.E. Thellung von. 1819. *Versuch über Taktik und Strategie*. Leipzig: Friedrich Christian Wilhelm Vogl.
Cromartie, Alan. 2015. "Introduction." In *Liberal Wars: Anglo-American Strategy, Ideology, and Practice*, edited by Alan Cromartie. Contemporary Security Studies. London: Routledge.
Derrécagaix, Victor Bernard. 1890. *La Guerre moderne*. 2nd edition. Vol. 1. Paris: L. Baudoin.
Dimitriu, George. 2018. "Clausewitz and the Politics of War: A Contemporary Theory." *Journal of Strategic Studies* (October): 1–41. https://doi.org/10.1080/01402390.2018.1529567.
Echevarria, Antulio J. 2007. "On the Clausewitz of the Cold War: Reconsidering the Primacy of Policy in On War." *Armed Forces & Society* 34 (1): 90–108. https://doi.org/10.1177/0002764206294175.
Grimm, Jacob, and Wilhelm Grimm. 1854. "Staatsleben." In *Deutsches Wörterbuch*. Leipzig: Verlag von S. Birzel. http://woerterbuchnetz.de/cgi-bin/WBNetz/wbgui_py?sigle=DWB&sigle=DWB&mode=Vernetzung&lemid=GS38261#XGS38261
Guibert, Jacques-Antoine-Hippolyte de. 1772. *Essai général de Tactique*. London: Associated Librarians.
Hamley, Edward Bruce. 1872. *The Operations of War Explained and Illustrated*. 3rd edition. Edinburgh: William Blackwood & Sons.
Henderson, George Francis Robert. 1905. *The Science of War: A Collection of Essays and Lectures, 1892–1903*. London: Longmans, Green & Co.
Heuser, Beatrice. 2010a. *The Evolution of Strategy*. Cambridge: Cambridge University Press.
Heuser, Beatrice, ed. 2010b. *The Strategy Makers: Thoughts on War and Society from Machiavelli to Clausewitz*. Praeger Security International. Santa Barbara, CA: Praeger.
Heuser, Beatrice. 2016. "Theory and Practice, Art of Science of Warfare: An Etymological Note." In *War, History and Strategy; Essays in Honour of Professor Robert O'Neill*, edited by Daniel Marston and Tamara Leahy, 179–196. Canberra: ANU Press. https://press-files.anu.edu.au/downloads/press/n1879/pdf/book.pdf
Heuser, Beatrice. 2018. "What Clausewitz Read." In *Strategy Before Clausewitz: Linking Warfare and Statecraft, 1400-1830*, edited by Beatrice Heuser, 185–207. Cass Military Studies. Abingdon: Routledge.
Honig, Jan Willem. 2007. "Clausewitz's On War: Problems of Text and Translation." In *Clausewitz in the Twenty-First Century*, edited by Hew Strachan and Andreas Herberg-Rothe, 56–73. Oxford: Oxford University Press.
Howard, Michael. 2007. "Foreword." In *Clausewitz in the Twenty-First Century*, edited by Hew Strachan and Andreas Herberg-Rothe, v–x. Oxford: Oxford University Press.
Joly de Maizeroy, Paul-Gédéon. 1771. *Institutions militaires de l'empereur Léon le Philosophe*. Paris: Claude-Antoine Jombert.
Joly de Maizeroy, Paul Gédéon. 1785. *Cours de Tactique théorique, pratique et historique*. Paris: Claude-Antoine Jombert. (First edition published in 1765.)
Jomini, Antoine Henri Baron de. 1838. *Précis de l'Art de la Guerre: Des principales Combinaisons de la Stratégie, de la Grande Tactique et de la Politique militaire*. Brussels: Meline, Cans et Copagnie.
Jomini, Antoine Henri Baron de. 1992. *The Art of War*. Translated by G.H. Mendell and W.P. Craighill. London: Greenhill Books.
Kennedy, Paul M. 1991. "Grand Strategy in War and Peace: Toward a Broader Definition." In *Grand Strategies in War and Peace*, edited by Paul M. Kennedy, 1–8. New Haven: Yale University Press.

Kuhle, Arthur. 2018. *Die Preußische Kriegstheorie um 1800 und ihre Suche nach dynamischen Gleichgewichten*. Berlin: Duncker & Humblot.

Liddell Hart, Basil. 1944. *Thoughts on War*. London: Faber and Faber, n.d.

Marmont, Maréchal Auguste de, Duc de Raguse. 1845. *De l'Esprit des Institutions militaires*. Paris: J Dumaine.

Mellin, G.S.A. 1801. *Encyclopädisches Wörterbuch der kritischen Philosophie*. Jena & Leipzig: Friedrich Frommann.

Montesquieu, Charles Louis de Secondat, baron de La Brède et de. 1979. *De l'Esprit Des Lois*. Originally 1748. Vol. I. Paris: Flammarion.

"Politique." 2012. In *Trésor de la Langue française*. https://www.cnrtl.fr/etymologie/politique

Rasin, J.A. 1958. "Die Bedeutung von Clausewitz Für Die Entwicklung Der Militärwissenschaft." *Militärwesen* 2 (3): 377–392.

Rothfels, Hans, ed. 1922. *Carl von Clausewitz: Politische Schriften und Briefe*. Munich: Drei Masken Verlag.

Rühle von Lilienstern, Otto August. 1818. *Aufsätze über Gegenstände und Ereignisse aus dem Gebiete des Kriegswesens*. Berlin: Ernst Siegfried Mittler.

Russia, Ministry of Defence. 2020. *Encyclopedia-Dictionary*, http://xn--d1abichgllj9dyd8a.xn--90anlfbebar6i.xn--p1ai/encyclopedia/dictionary/details.htm?id=10395@morfDictionary, accessed February 6, 2021.

Willisen, Wilhelm von. 1868. *Theorie des Großen Krieges*. Vol. I. Leipzig: Verlag Duncker & Humblot.

Zanthier, Friedrich Wilhelm von. 1774. *Freyer Auszug aus des Herrn Marquis de Santa Cruz de Marzenado, Gedanken von Kriegs- und Staatsgeschäften, nebst einem Versuch über die Kunst den Krieg zu studieren*. Göttingen und Gotha: Johann Christian Dieterich.

CHAPTER 5

LIDDELL HART'S IMPACT ON THE STUDY OF GRAND STRATEGY

LUKAS MILEVSKI

It is widely believed that Basil Liddell Hart made a vital contribution to grand strategy as a topic of study, although the exact character of this contribution has not been entirely settled. Many believe that it was Liddell Hart who first introduced the concept of grand strategy to strategic studies (Dueck 2006, 9; Lahn 1997, 185; Rosencrance and Stein 1993, 3). Although this would have been a truly significant contribution if it were true, it is not historically accurate. Liddell Hart did not even introduce the first modern interpretation of grand strategy, regardless of how one determines the modernity of individual iterations of the concept.

Nonetheless, Liddell Hart had lasting impact on the study of grand strategy. His definition has been nearly universally cited by subsequent scholars writing about grand strategy. Moreover, he remained a major figure in the nascent British academic strategic studies community and was also well connected to American strategic studies until his death in 1970. As Michael Howard noted, "[s]cores if not hundreds of students and disciples were bound to this implacable and loving master," and further that "the depth and intensity which he brought to it over fifty years have transformed the nature of military thought itself" (Howard 1984, 198, 199). What was his real impact on the study of grand strategy?

Liddell Hart himself only ever dedicated a single eight-page chapter to the discussion of grand strategy, much of which is less conceptual than application of his basic ideas to historical discussion—for all his presumed importance to the field of grand strategy, he did not leave much about the concept to posterity through the written word. Most understanding of his grand-strategic thought is derived from only a small handful of constantly cited paragraphs, which barely changed at all between their first writing in 1929 in *The Decisive Wars of History* and their final republication three decades later in *Strategy*. Liddell Hart lamented that grand strategy was barely developed as a concept, but throughout his career hardly contributed to that endeavor himself. This leads to the perhaps outsized importance of Liddell Hart's later interpreters. How does one distinguish between the effect of Liddell Hart's own grand-strategic thought and that of his later interpreters, especially Paul Kennedy, the most influential? In a single introductory chapter to *Grand Strategies in War and Peace*, Kennedy provided a quick interpretation of Liddell Hart's grand-strategic thought which has ever since colored mainstream understanding of Liddell Hart's ideas. Arguably, it has been Kennedy not Liddell Hart who has been the more influential in the subsequent study of grand strategy.

This chapter examines Liddell Hart's impact upon the study of grand strategy and differentiates between his grand-strategic thought and that of his later interpreters. It begins by briefly introducing Liddell Hart's best known paragraphs on grand strategy within his intellectual context, including not just the impact of the First World War upon his thought but also the ideas of grand strategy posited by his predecessor Julian Corbett and his contemporary JFC Fuller. Thereafter, the work of his most influential interpreter, Paul Kennedy, is introduced. The two competing interpretations, Kennedy's of Liddell Hart versus Liddell Hart's own, are examined to determine the extent to which Liddell Hart's particular understanding actually survives in modern work on grand strategy. Finally, a caveat is made concerning Liddell Hart's influence through Kennedy's interpretation, as Kennedy was also influenced by American grand-strategic theorists such as Edward Mead Earle, to whose concept Kennedy's is much closer than to Liddell Hart.

Liddell Hart's Intellectual Context

American authors and those writing for an American audience dominate the history of grand-strategic thought. They first invoked grand strategy during the nineteenth century and have also substantially dictated the evolution of the concept from the 1970s to the present. In this highly American context, the anomaly of three British theorists writing for a British audience emerged in the first half of the twentieth century: Sir Julian Stafford Corbett, John Frederick Charles Fuller, and Basil Henry Liddell Hart. These three authors transformed grand strategy into a recognizably modern concept through roughly similar but largely mutually independent interpretations of the term, and set the basis for its American readoption in the latter half of the Cold War. These British authors have been so crucial in shaping subsequent grand-strategic thought that one author suggests that "surely Britain can lay claim to the important idea of grand strategy" (Layton 2012, 56). To understand the changes these British theorists brought to the concept of grand strategy, one must not only recognize what the changes are but also the context in which those changes occurred.

During the nineteenth century, the term grand strategy was never strictly defined, but its usage indicates that it was analogous to generalship or to certain aspects of generalship. Charles James, British rather than American, first used the term in the English language in *A New and Enlarged Military Dictionary* in 1805. He suggested that grand strategy was a subset of strategy, one which focused on commanding the main army on the main campaign in the main theater of war (James 1805, 862–863). The meaning of grand strategy throughout this century was never consistent but varied with the author, yet all were related to generalship. They included military maneuver on campaign, the commander's vital *coup d'oeil*, the more abstract notion of using military power for political consequence, and coordinating strategy across multiple theaters (Milevski 2016, ch. 1).

Corbett redefined grand strategy in the first decade of the twentieth century into something which today may begin to be recognized as grand strategy. "First there is Grand Strategy, dealing with whole theatre of war, with planning the war. It looks on war as a continuation of foreign policy. It regards the object of the war & the means of attaining it. It handles all the national resources together, Navy, Army, Diplomacy & Finance" (Corbett CBT/31, 117). Corbett expanded grand strategy beyond the military realm to encompass not just maritime power but also a nonmilitary instrument in the form of finance. This first time a nonmilitary element was included in an interpretation of grand strategy may arguably be considered the first modern definition.

The nonmilitary addition to the concept reflected the context in which Corbett was writing. As a British maritime strategic thinker, he was interested particularly in the maritime context in which Britain could employ power in war. This context permitted nonmilitary instruments more readily than the European Continent, as Alfred Thayer Mahan, another naval theorist, also noted: "The diplomatist, as a rule, only affixes the seal of treaty to the work done by the successful soldier. It is not so with a large proportion of strategic points upon the sea." Indeed, "[s]uch possessions are obtained so often without actual war, because the first owners on account of weakness are not able to make the resistance which constitutes war; or, for the same reason of weakness, feel the need of political connection with a powerful naval state" (Mahan 1911, 123, 124). This more expansive and more permissible maritime perspective led Corbett to develop an idea of what he considered a particular way of warfare: "the British or maritime form is in fact the application of the limited method to the unlimited form, as an ancillary to the larger operations of our allies—a method which has usually been open to us because the control of the sea has enabled us to select a theatre in effect truly limited" (Corbett 1988, 66). Prefiguring Liddell Hart's own British way in warfare, it was an interpretation of British strategic history which emphasized the confluence of military and nonmilitary power to win wars (Lambert 2010).

After Corbett came JFC Fuller's core definition of grand strategy which never wavered but whose details were constantly shifting. His fundamental definition of grand strategy was "[t]he transmission of power in all its forms, in order to maintain policy" (Fuller 1923, 219). Here again the definition of grand strategy is broadened from military-centric interpretations popular during the nineteenth century to one which encompassed *all* forms of power, continuing a trend which Corbett began (although it remains unknown to what extent Fuller was or was not aware of Corbett's writings and particularly his concept of grand/major strategy).

Yet the context in which Fuller broadened grand strategy differed from that of Corbett. Fuller was not a maritime strategist, but rather one whose focus was always on land warfare on the European Continent, largely impermissible to nonmilitary instruments. The defining context for his writing on grand strategy was the experience of the First World War. Fuller believed that the character of war reflected the character of peace and international affairs in general, that "[t]he immoralities of war are normally but a continuation of the immoralities of peace" (Fuller 1923, 69). He identified the age in which he lived as the age of economics: "War is not an altruistic but an economic question; it is a continuation of peace policy, and the foundations of peace policy, in the present material age, are economic." Even more explicitly, he suggested that "[w]ar is a continuation of economic policy in another form" (Fuller 1932a, 83). The First World War reflected this, being an industrial war whose economic strain became ultimately one of the decisive factors in the Entente success. Thus anything which could affect the enemy economy was a valid method, even though it was easily possible to push those instruments too far. "The economic attack is without question the most brutal of all forms of attack, because it does not only kill but cripple, and cripples more than one generation. Turning men, women and children into starving animals, it is a direct blow against what is called civilization" (Fuller 1932b, 230).

Due to the Continental European context's impermissibility and his personal diagnosis of the ultimate inutility of nonmilitary instruments in war to attack the civilian population and the bases of the adversary's national power, Fuller for a brief period developed a wholly unique interpretation of grand strategy. As he wrote,

> Paradoxical as it may seem, the resting time of the grand strategist is during war, for it is during peace that he works and labours. During peace time he not only calculates the resources in men, supplies and moral forces of all possible enemies, but, having weighed them, he, unsuspected by the enemy, undermines them by a plan. (Fuller 1923, 220)

Early in his interwar writings, Fuller conceived of grand strategy as a purely peacetime concept, one whose task was to prepare for the next war. Presumably, this was the only context in which he believed nonmilitary power could be usefully employed in the practice of grand strategy.

Last of the three major British theorists of grand strategy was Basil Liddell Hart (1895–1970). The decisive influence on his thinking was the same as on Fuller, only more so: the First World War. Younger than Fuller, Liddell Hart had been affected more traumatically by the war. His reaction to it was primarily emotional, largely as a result of his experience. "One must conclude that Liddell Hart was so emotionally involved in attacking the inept conduct of the First World War and its legacy that he was unable to approach its more general causes with detachment. Instead, he found a plausible scapegoat in what he mistakenly believed to be Clausewitz's notion of strategy" (Bond 1977, 51). Although he and Fuller shared the same goal, to limit the overall damage done by warfare, they differed both in their interpretation of this task and the means by which it could be accomplished. Whereas Fuller thought in terms of an international economic system, Liddell Hart thought as much in terms of lives as of national economy. This is unsurprising, given that "[o]f Liddell Hart's matriculation year in Corpus Christi, Cambridge, (1913) 27 per cent were killed in the war" (Gat 2001, 654). Indeed, Hew Strachan has noted that he "belonged to those groups, both in society as a whole and in the army, which suffered disproportionately in the Great War. The middle class, the professions, the public schools, the universities, contributed more men to the forces relative to their aggregate size than did working-class occupations" (Strachan 1991, 41–42).

Consequently, unlike Fuller, Liddell Hart believed much more strongly in the utility and especially the desirability of nonmilitary, especially economic, forms of coercion. This led him to develop his own interpretation of the British way in warfare, possibly influenced by Corbett's earlier version, in which economic power was vital in financing both the war and Britain's allies in the war, while economic pressure in the form of naval blockade was crucial in coercing Britain's enemies to submit. Britain's own army would operate in subsidiary theaters of war, where it could achieve substantial gains at little cost (Liddell Hart 1931; Liddell Hart 1932).

Unlike Fuller, Liddell Hart did not consider the longer term economic damage dealt to the enemy by economic means. His orchestra of multiple means was to be concluded through peace negotiations, which in turn were to ensure that the ensuing peace would be durable. Although Liddell Hart's concept of the British way in warfare became quite influential and remains much referenced, especially in British academic, professional military, and policymaking circles, it has rarely been connected with his more basic definition of grand strategy, nor will this be the task here. Instead, subsequent interpretations of Liddell Hart's grand-strategic thought tend to be based on his two best known paragraphs on grand strategy:

> If practically synonymous with the policy which governs the conduct of war, as distinct from the permanent policy which formulates its object, the term "grand strategy" serves to bring out the sense of "policy in execution." For the role of grand strategy is to co-ordinate and direct all the resources of a nation towards the attainment of the political object of the war—the goal defined by national policy. (Liddell Hart 1929, 150–151)

> Furthermore, while the horizon of strategy is bounded by the war, grand strategy looks beyond the war to the subsequent peace. It should not only combine the various instruments, but so regulate their use as to avoid damage to the future state of peacefulness, secure and prosperous. Little wonder that, unlike strategy, the realm of grand strategy is for the most part *terra incognita!* (Liddell Hart 1929, 151)

These are familiar paragraphs, but perhaps their original meaning has been altered by later interpretations.

Liddell Hart never ascribed grand strategy an actual peacetime role. He was quite clear in this regard, noting that "[w]hile practically synonymous with the policy which guides the conduct of war, as distinct from the more fundamental policy which should govern its object, the term 'grand strategy' serves to bring out the sense of 'policy in execution'" (Liddell Hart 1991, 321–322). Perhaps somewhat confusingly, he distinguishes between two types of policy: the fundamental policy which seeks benefit from war versus wartime policy whose aim is to guide the conduct of war. Liddell Hart's grand strategy was the latter. It was the conduct of war.

Liddell Hart introduced peace into the definition of grand strategy to counterbalance strategy, which he interpreted as an exaggerated fixation on the conduct of military operations. He noted how

> [h]istory shows that gaining military victory is not in itself equivalent to gaining the object of policy. But as most of the thinking about war has been done by men of the military profession there has been a very natural tendency to lose sight of the basic national object, and identify it with the military aim. (Liddell Hart 1991, 338)

He associated this tendency with Clausewitz, but even more with his followers, especially Moltke the Elder. Moltke indeed espoused this type of thinking, arguing that "strategy must always direct its endeavors toward the highest aim attainable with available means. Strategy thus works best for the goals of policy, but in its actions is fully independent of policy" (Hughes 1993, 44). Liddell Hart believed that it was this line of thought which had led to the apparently futile bloodletting of the First World War:

> [i]t became evident there was something wrong with the theory, or at least with its application—alike on the planes of tactics, strategy, and policy. The appalling losses suffered in vain pursuit of the 'ideal' objective, and the post-war exhaustion of the nominal victory, showed that a thorough re-examination of the whole problem of the object and aim was needed. (Liddell Hart 1991, 345)

Liddell Hart's concept of grand strategy was meant to counter this type of thinking and impetus to military action by introducing peace into the very definition of grand strategy. This resulted in an apparent direct incompatibility between grand strategy and standard ideas of strategy: "while grand strategy should control strategy, its principles often run counter to those which prevail in the field of strategy." Moreover, he tied his notion of grand strategy to Clausewitz.

> The object in war is a better state of peace—even if only from your point of view. Hence it is essential to conduct war with constant regard to the peace you desire. This is the truth underlying Clausewitz's definition of war as a "continuation of policy by other means"—the prolongation of that policy through war into the subsequent peace must always be borne in mind. (Liddell Hart 1991, 353)

Liddell Hart's argument is clear: despite Clausewitz's efforts, as a concept, strategy was ultimately incapable of maintaining the continuity of political intention suggested by war being a continuation of policy by other means. Instead, strategy devolved into mere operations. Liddell Hart sought to rescue the conduct of war by introducing the concept of grand strategy to revitalize that necessary political continuity by keeping military operations in their place. Liddell Hart's theoretical structure of policy, grand strategy, strategy, and tactics was functionally identical to Clausewitz's theoretical structure of policy, strategy, and tactics—except that in Liddell Hart's view Clausewitz's theory had failed during the First World War since strategy suffered grave difficulties simultaneously facing in opposite directions and interacting with both tactics and policy.

In line with moderating military operations, part of Liddell Hart's focus was broadening strategy beyond the military alone. Just as with the introduction of peace into his definition, this conceptual expansion implied an apparent belief that the introduction of nonmilitary instruments might moderate the conduct of, and subsequent damage caused by, war. Liddell Hart's *first* definition of grand strategy was quite nineteenth century in its outlook: "It is the function of grand strategy to discover and exploit the Achilles' heel of the enemy nation; to strike not against its strongest bulwark but against its most vulnerable spot" (Liddell Hart 1925, 27). This is grand strategy as the *coup d'oeil*, the identification of the enemy's vital spot in strategy. This formulation nearly survived into his 1941 revision of *The Decisive Wars of History*, which was published as *Strategy of the Indirect Approach*. Here Liddell Hart wrote in a galley insertion that "[i]t should be the aim of grand strategy to discover and pierce the Achilles' heel of the opposing government's power to make war. And strategy, in turn, should seek to penetrate the joint in the harness of the opposing forces" (Liddell Hart 9/6, 1). This insertion did not endure to publication, but if it had it would have coexisted alongside the enunciation of Liddell Hart's better known definition of grand strategy.

A connection between use of nonmilitary instruments and the *coup d'oeil*, which clearly existed in Liddell Hart's mind although not in his published writing, implies that the enemy's Achilles heel might not be military, or that the most effective—and cheapest—way of attacking it might not be military. Elsewhere I have suggested that "[t]he structure of Liddell Hart's entire strategic theory was to serve as a straightjacket on military strategy to prevent a repetition of the First World War" (Milevski 2016, 55). This observation is based on the vertical structure of Liddell Hart's theory, wherein grand strategy as wartime policy sought to control the direction and intensity of military strategy.

Yet it is crucial to recognize that the horizontal dimension of Liddell Hart's grand-strategic thought, the inclusion of nonmilitary instruments to act beside the military, also reinforces that straitjacket. Unfortunately, Liddell Hart never wrote a book specifically on grand strategy, which he believed to be necessary as his single chapter could not do the topic justice: "To deal adequately with this wider subject [of grand strategy] would require not only a much larger volume, but a separate volume" (Liddell Hart 1991, 353). Among the topics Liddell Hart does not discuss is the actual relationship among the myriad instruments of power, military and nonmilitary, in war. One can only speculate on the exact logic of how including nonmilitary power might restrain the thirst for military victory which Liddell Hart believed afflicted the practitioners of strategy. Indeed, on the one occasion in which he did discuss the relationship between nonmilitary and military power in war, while writing on the British way in warfare,

Liddell Hart simply assumed that sea power and naval pressure worked and that economic coercion was possible and effective. He did not explain his logic on the integration of military and nonmilitary power, but to moderate military strategy was surely the purpose for including nonmilitary instruments in his definition of grand strategy; moderating military strategy was the ultimate purpose of virtually all of his major writing.

The Kennedy Interpretation

A handful of men took the lead in revitalizing grand strategy as a concept in the latter half of the Cold War: John Collins, Edward Luttwak, Barry Posen, and Paul Kennedy. Of these, Kennedy most influenced subsequent writing about grand strategy as his broad interpretation became the basis for the further conceptual evolution of grand strategy. He explicitly cited Liddell Hart's (as well as Edward Mead Earle's) interpretations of grand strategy as the basis for his further development:

> his [Liddell Hart's] contribution to the study and understanding of grand strategy as a whole was very important. What he and, slightly later, Earle were arguing for was a substantial broadening of the definition of the term, to show what a complex and multilayered thing proper grand strategy had to be—and thus to distinguish it very firmly from the strictly operational strategy of winning a particular battle or campaign. (Kennedy 1991, 4)

Kennedy explicitly premised his interpretation of grand strategy on that of Liddell Hart, but not only on him. What part of Kennedy's interpretation was likely derived from Liddell Hart as opposed to Earle is discussed below.

Kennedy was clearly embarking on the endeavor of expanding the concept of grand strategy beyond what previously existed and along these lines he identified two fundamental aspects to grand strategy:

> To begin with, a true grand strategy was now concerned with peace as much as (perhaps even more than) with war. It was about the evolution and integration of policies that should operate for decades, or even centuries. It did not cease at a war's end, nor commence at its beginning. (Kennedy 1991, 4)

> Second, grand strategy was about the balancing of ends and means, both in peacetime and in wartime. It was not enough for statesmen to consider how to win a war, but what the *costs* (in the largest sense of the word) would be; not enough to order the dispatch of fleets and armies in this or that direction, but to ensure that they were adequately provided for, and sustained by a flourishing economic base; and not enough, in peacetime, to order a range of weapons systems without careful examination of the impacts of defense spending. (Kennedy 1991, 4)

The natural result of Kennedy's conceptual expansion of grand strategy was a changed relationship with policy. "The crux of grand strategy lies therefore in *policy*, that is, in the capacity of the nation's leaders to bring together all the elements, both military and nonmilitary, for the preservation and enhancement of the nation's long-term (that is, in wartime *and* in peacetime) best interests" (Kennedy 1991, 5). Rather than strategy serving policy, Kennedy flipped the relationship so that policy was meant to serve grand strategy. In no other way could grand strategy possibly safeguard the economic health of the great power over decades or centuries.

Although Kennedy's grand strategy is hegemonic, his own personal interest limits how he approaches the concept in practice. From the beginning of his career he focused on the interaction between economic and military bases and forms of power over the long term. Moreover, although he recognized that military and economic power could strengthen one another, he believed that it was much easier for them to be mutually antagonistic instead (Kennedy 1981). Thus, although the purpose of grand strategy was to integrate coherently such diverse policy issues as the military, diplomacy, economics, technology, science, education, etc., his overriding concern about the relationship between economics and military power led Kennedy to state that "the greatest problem of all is, predictably, the one that dogged grand strategists from Louis XIV to Winston Churchill: the lack of money to build up and organize the nation's forces for their many roles" (Kennedy 1988).

Kennedy characterizes this admittedly fundamental relationship between military power and economic and financial strength as a question of making and meeting commitments on one hand and maintaining and improving one's own economic base on the other:

> whether, in the military/strategic realm, it [this relationship] can preserve a reasonable balance between the nation's perceived defense requirements and the means it possesses to maintain those commitments; and whether, as an intimately related point, it can preserve the technological and economic bases of its power from relative erosion in the face of the ever-shifting patterns of global production. (Kennedy 1989, 514–515)

He also emphasized the time lag often at play with regard to the defense and military commitment decisions being made, as once made they still had to be met later even as economic strength might be faltering. "[T]he fundamental grand-strategical dilemma remains: the United States today has roughly the same massive array of military obligations across the globe as it had a quarter-century ago, when its shares of world GNP, manufacturing production, military spending, and armed forces personnel were so much larger than they are now" (Kennedy 1989, 521). As a result of Kennedy's embrace of including peacetime alongside wartime over the long term, his concept of grand strategy is no longer strategic, but rather altogether political.

Kennedy's reinterpretation of grand strategy combined with his emphasis on the sustainability of great power status prefaced the subsequent and ongoing grand strategy debate in the United States between those seeking more versus less restraint in America's global conduct. From his writings on both great powers and grand strategy, Kennedy clearly falls on the restraint side of the debate. However, his reasoning is distinct from the extant debate, as he deplored action and especially commitments made in times of strength, which, if waning, makes commitments more difficult to honor and may lead the United States to overexert itself economically and financially. While all strategy and policy is future-oriented, Kennedy's notion of grand strategy is truly fixated on the future, with the purpose of moderating activity and commitments made today to ease their economic burden not just years but decades into the future.

Kennedy Versus Liddell Hart

In terms of inheriting the essence of Liddell Hart's concept, the key element which Kennedy got right is the explicit, indeed definitional, awareness of the costs of grand strategy. In Liddell Hart's understanding, the costs of grand strategy were the costs of war and were felt primarily during the subsequent peace. Kennedy interprets the costs of grand strategy more broadly as the resources which a great power must spend to maintain its place in the world, especially by force. This is unsurprising given Kennedy's earlier work on the rise and fall of the great powers: "the historical record suggests that there is a very clear connection *in the long run* between an individual Great Power's economic rise and fall and its growth and decline as an important military power (or world empire)" (Kennedy 1989, xxii). Indeed, grand strategy is for Kennedy naturally a great power concern, one irrelevant to small and medium powers.

Yet this broader interpretation of the costs of grand strategy is also related to Kennedy's first conceptual point about grand strategy, that it focuses as much if not more on peace than on war and may endure for decades or even centuries. With regard to the role of peace in grand strategy, Kennedy diverges from Liddell Hart. Given its subsequent influence and popularity, Kennedy's interpretation of grand strategy sends the further study of grand strategy awry from the direction which Liddell Hart intended. This, however, is not to deny that Liddell Hart participated in the early twentieth-century British broadening of the concept—he very clearly did.

The focus of Kennedy's interpretation of grand strategy contrasted significantly with that of Liddell Hart, although ostensibly derived from the latter's earlier efforts. Liddell Hart's grand strategy was still fundamentally strategic in that it sought some end, whereas Kennedy's interpretation instead emphasized husbanding one's strength over the long term with otherwise no particular goal in mind. As he noted, "the student of grand strategy needs to take into consideration a whole number of factors that are not usually covered in traditional military histories, including ... [t]he critical importance of husbanding and managing national resources, in order to achieve that balance between ends and means touched upon above." However, from Kennedy's long-term perspective, any ends mentioned are ultimately only individual destinations within a much longer journey (Kennedy 1991, 4).

This long-term, indeed virtually endless, perspective shifts the crux of grand strategy from moderating military strategy in war as Liddell Hart suggested to managing policy and politics over decades or centuries. Maintaining the moderating hierarchy was Liddell Hart's original intention in introducing his interpretation of grand strategy. Kennedy, in partly relying on Liddell Hart's wording to expand grand strategy into war *and* peace, either misinterprets or misrepresents Liddell Hart's concept. Kennedy transformed grand strategy into a hegemonic concept effectively responsible for the entire health of the great power:

> there is still a long way to go before we get a full comprehension of what a number one power's peacetime grand strategy is all about. Only when the military dimension is properly "integrated" with this country's diplomacy, economic structure, technology, science, education, and all of the other components of national strength will we be able to have a real long-term strategy. (Kennedy 1988)

For grand strategy, this is a far cry from what appears in retrospect to be a modest early life as a concept dedicated to moderating military strategy, let alone an even older period of nascence when it was synonymous in part or in whole with generalship.

Influencing Kennedy: Liddell Hart or Earle?

The combination of both wartime and peacetime responsibilities under a single conceptual umbrella, a key factor in Kennedy's definition of grand strategy, is a characteristic more likely to have been drawn from World Wars–era American strategic thought than from Basil Liddell Hart, even though Kennedy cites both. Kennedy explicitly referred to the best known of the American theorists, Edward Mead Earle, as the other major source for his own broadening of grand strategy, although Earle was neither the first nor the only to expand the concept in the United States. These key differences between the interpretations of grand strategy proffered by Liddell Hart and Kennedy change the very point of the two concepts.

Earle's famous definition of strategy reflected a wider American attitude. Earle's work was preceded by that of George Meyers, a US Navy captain and lecturer on strategy at the US Army War College. Meyers defined strategy—not grand strategy—in a similar way as did Earle define grand strategy, as "the provision, preparation, and use of diplomacy and of the nation's armed forces in peace and war to gain the purpose of national policy. Strategy in war is the provision, preparation, and use of diplomacy and of the armed forces to gain the purpose of the war" (Meyers 1928, xiv). Meyers considered any concept of strategy which did not incorporate both war and peace to be incomplete and prone to contradiction, although he unfortunately never explained the potential contradictions. Although Meyers' perspective was undoubtedly shaped by his naval background, it was also reflective of American experience during the First World War. One of the United States' formative experiences of the time were the attempts, sometimes even conspiracies, of European powers to widen the war and drag the United States in, one way or another. Thus, Meyers could feel justified in stating that strategy had to extend into peacetime to prevent war from touching the United States altogether.

Edward Mead Earle noticed and accepted the expanding definition of strategy in the late 1930s. In an address to the Academy of Political Science in 1940 he argued that any military-centric definitions of strategy left out "[w]hat has become universal usage of the word" (Earle Box 35). He argued in a similar vein after the Second World War that

> of course it is possible to make a discussion of grand strategy merely a play on words. That is to say, you may deal with the term "grand strategy" in such a way as to make it synonymous with "over-all national policy." And, in a sense, that's what it is: the grand strategy is the over-all national policy. But to some extent the question is one of emphasis and proportion rather than clearly defined boundaries. (Earle Box 37)

Earle thus famously defined grand strategy, in his classic *Makers of Modern Strategy*, as: "The highest type of strategy—sometimes called grand strategy—is that which so integrates the policies and armaments of the nation that the resort to war is either rendered unnecessary or is undertaken with the maximum chance of victory" (Earle 1966, viii).

These American interpretations of strategy and grand strategy truly encompassed both peace and war in a way that Liddell Hart's definition and discussion never had. However, in contrast to Liddell Hart, the conceptual order of peace and war differed. Liddell Hart considered peace to be the result of war, and thus it was vital to wage war in a way that contributed to the character of the peace. Peace followed war. In the American interpretations, peace *preceded* war. As Michael Howard noted,

> [g]rand Strategy involves not only war *fighting*, but war *avoidance*, including what later became known as "deterrence". Again, this was a definition that came naturally to an observer of the international scene in the 1940s. A better peacetime "grand strategy" on the part of the democracies, Earle implied, might have made it unnecessary to fight the Second World War at all, or at least to do so with a better prospect of winning it. (Howard 2001, 2)

Although Howard describes this as a natural perspective born of the 1940s, Liddell Hart never shared it. It might be more accurate to say that it was naturally an American perspective, stemming not just from the American experience of the diplomacy surrounding two World Wars, but also from American geographical isolation from

Europe. Notably, Earle's concept of grand strategy still ended with that quite un-Liddell Hartian word: "victory."

The question of whether, without Liddell Hart's writing on grand strategy, Kennedy's evolution in grand strategy would not have happened, is counterfactual; we simply do not know. Kennedy's influential reinterpretation of grand strategy, and the peculiar understanding of Liddell Hart which was its byproduct, draw fairly equally from British and American traditions. Kennedy draws moderation from the British line of grand-strategic thought and conceptual expansiveness from American grand-strategic thought. He then adds his particular interest in extended historical timescales to top off his own concept of grand strategy.

Conclusion

Over time, Basil Liddell Hart gradually mellowed in relation to Clausewitz's theory of war. Liddell Hart originally depicted Clausewitz as the "mahdi of mass and mutual massacre," as someone who "looked only to the end of a war, not beyond war to the subsequent peace" (Liddell Hart 1933, 120, 121). By his second and last revision of *Strategy*, he blamed Clausewitz's successors more than Clausewitz himself for the bloodshed of the First World War, in that the successors misinterpreted Clausewitz—although he still emphasized that the way Clausewitz structured and wrote his theory contributed to misunderstandings: "As so often happens, Clausewitz's disciples carried his teaching to an extreme which their master had not intended" (Liddell Hart 1991, 339). Nonetheless, by his second revision, Liddell Hart was sufficiently comfortable with Clausewitz to associate his own notion of grand strategy overtly with Clausewitzian thinking about war as the continuation of politics by forceful means, by explicitly extending that notion to the end of war, which he felt was the logical conclusion never reached by Clausewitz.

It is thus somewhat ironic that a similar fate befell Liddell Hart himself, with reference to his definition of grand strategy. Much as Clausewitz's meaning was in fact apparent, at least to careful readers, so too was Liddell Hart's actual meaning of grand strategy as clearly printed—but nonetheless misinterpreted by later readers who have transformed the idea into something which Liddell Hart would probably not recognize. Paul Kennedy derived an impossibly expansive interpretation of grand strategy ostensibly from Liddell Hart's definition of strategy, although he was probably also substantially influenced by World Wars–era American grand-strategic thinking.

Liddell Hart's purpose in considering grand strategy was undoubtedly to moderate the practice of military strategy. Given the importance he attached to this goal of grand strategy, he may well have hoped that his short discussion of grand strategy in *Strategy*—a chapter hardly seven or eight full pages long, besides various mentions elsewhere—would both spark and shape a larger research agenda on the topic. This did not occur for reasons unrelated to Liddell Hart, specifically the birth of the nuclear age and the eclipse of grand strategy between the end of the Second World War and the late 1970s. At this point came a new generation of writers, analysts, and scholars, working in a substantially different context from that in which Liddell Hart wrote, and reshaping the concept of grand strategy to suit their own needs or interests.

Although this wave of evolution of the concept of grand strategy often positioned itself as the heir to Liddell Hart (and sometimes Earle), Liddell Hart would probably not recognize such interpretations of grand strategy. Liddell Hart's idea of grand strategy emphasized the conduct of war, the combination of military and nonmilitary instruments for a single purpose in war, and imposition of a policy-generated straitjacket on military strategy as practiced by generals. Modern interpretations of grand strategy fulfill none of these emphases. Instead, altogether unintended, Liddell Hart's effect on the study of grand strategy was to create a definitional baseline from which grand strategy was spun off in various unforeseen directions by his successors and interpreters.

The results have been unfortunate. We now have few concepts with which we can understand war at all, let alone strategically, and those which remain, such as operational art, present the same weaknesses which Liddell Hart originally identified in military strategy. Moreover, the actual issue of combining military and nonmilitary power into a single strategic effort, which was a core focus of Liddell Hart's idea of grand strategy, has become a piously invoked but not actually well studied or understood facet not just of grand strategy, but even of the many definitions of strategy. To this day, this issue of combining different types of power is poorly understood in both logic and practice. Instead, the West has simply kept rediscovering it in different forms from the comprehensive approach to hybrid warfare—without ever understanding the logic of combination. Liddell Hart's original idea of grand strategy represents a road not traveled by the literature, which is all the poorer for not following that path. To adapt his words about grand strategy from his 1929 *The Decisive Wars of History*, repeated in 1954, and reprinted in 1967 in his second revision of *Strategy*: little wonder that, unlike employing military power, combining nonmilitary and military power together is for the most part *terra incognita!*

Bibliography

Bond, Brian. 1977. *Liddell Hart: A Study of His Military Thought*. London: Cassell.
Corbett, Julian S. *Lectures on Naval Strategy*. CBT/31, Julian Stafford Corbett Papers, National Maritime Museum.
Corbett, Julian S. 1988. *Some Principles of Maritime Strategy*. Annapolis: Naval Institute Press.
Dueck, Colin. 2006. *Reluctant Crusaders: Power, Culture, and Change in American Grand Strategy*. Princeton: Princeton University Press.
Earle, Edward Mead. 1966. "Introduction." In *Makers of Modern Strategy: Military Thought from Machiavelli to Hitler*, edited by Edward Mead Earle, vii–xi. New York: Atheneum.

Earle, Edward Mead. "Lecture on Grand Strategy to Army War College," March 26, 1951, Earle Papers, Box 37, Folder "Drafts/Transcripts-Lectures-Army War Coll. [2 of 4]."

Earle, Edward Mead. "Political and military strategy for the United States," November 13, 1940, Edward Mead Earle Papers, Seeley G. Mudd Manuscript Library, Princeton University, Box 35, Folder "Post-WW2: Strategy."

Fuller, J.F.C. 1932a. *The Dragon's Teeth: A Study of War and Peace*. London: Constable & Co.

Fuller, J.F.C. 1923. *The Reformation of War*. London: Hutchinson & Co.

Fuller, J.F.C. 1932b. *War and Western Civilization 1832–1932: A Study of War as a Political Instrument and the Expression of Mass Democracy*. London: Duckworth.

Gat, Azar. 2001. *A History of Military Thought*. Oxford: Oxford University Press.

Howard, Michael. 1984. *The Causes of War and Other Essays*. Cambridge, MA: Harvard University Press.

Howard. Michael. 2001. "Grand Strategy in the Twentieth Century." *Defence Studies* 1 (1) (Spring): 1–10.

Hughes, Daniel, ed. 1993. *Moltke on the Art of War: Selected Writings*. Novata: Presidio Press.

James, Charles. 1805. *A New and Enlarged Military Dictionary, or, Alphabetical Explanation of Technical Terms*. London: The Military Library.

Kennedy, Paul. 1991. "Grand Strategy in War and Peace: Toward a Broader Definition." In *Grand Strategies in War and Peace*, edited by Paul Kennedy, 1–7. New Haven: Yale University Press.

Kennedy, Paul. 1988. "Not So Grand Strategy." *The New York Review of Books* 35 (8) (May 12) https://www.nybooks.com/articles/1988/05/12/not-so-grand-strategy/, accessed December 28, 2018.

Kennedy, Paul. 1981. "Strategy versus Finance in Twentieth-Century Great Britain," *The International History Review* 3 (1) (January): 44–61.

Kennedy, Paul. 1989. *The Rise and Fall of the Great Powers: Economic Change and Military Conflict from 1500 to 2000*. New York: Vintage Books.

Lahn, Peter. 1997. "Grand Strategy." In *US Foreign Policy After the Cold War*, edited by Randall B. Ripley and James M. Lindsay, 185–214. Pittsburg: University of Pittsburg Press.

Lambert, Andrew. 2010. "The Naval War Course, *Some Principles of Maritime Strategy* and the Origins of the 'British Way in Warfare.'" In *The British Way in Warfare: Power and the International System, 1856–1956: Essays in Honour of David French*, edited by Keith Neilson and Greg Kennedy, 219–256. Farnham: Ashgate.

Layton, Peter. 2012. "The Idea of Grand Strategy," *RUSI Journal* 157 (4) (August/September): 56–61.

Liddell Hart, Basil. 1931. "Economic Pressure or Continental Victories." *RUSI Journal* 76 (503) (August), 486–510.

Liddell Hart, Basil. "Insertion on Galley 77," Basil Liddell Hart Papers, Liddell Hart Centre for Military Archives, King's College London, 9/6/14.

Liddell Hart, Basil. 1925. *Paris, or the Future of War*. London: Kegan Paul, Trench, Trubner & Co.

Liddell Hart, Basil. 1991. *Strategy*. New York: Meridian.

Liddell Hart, Basil. 1932. *The British Way in Warfare*. London: Faber & Faber.

Liddell Hart, Basil. 1929. *The Decisive Wars of History: A Study in Strategy*. London: G. Bell & sons.

Basil Liddell Hart. 1933. *The Ghost of Napoleon*. London: Faber & Faber.

Mahan, Alfred Thayer. 1911. *Naval Strategy Compared and Contrasted with the Principles and Practice of Military Operations on Land*. London: Sampson Low, Marston & Company.

Meyers, George J. 1928. *Strategy*. Washington, D.C.: Byron S. Adams.

Milevski, Lukas. 2016. *The Evolution of Modern Grand Strategic Thought*. Oxford: Oxford University Press.

Rosencrance, Richard, and Arthur A. Stein. 1993. "Beyond Realism: The Study of Grand Strategy." In *The Domestic Bases of Grand Strategy*, edited by Richard N. Rosencrance and Arthur A. Stein, 3–21. Ithaca: Cornell University Press.

Strachan, Hew. 1991. "'The Real War': Liddell Hart, Cruttwell, and Falls." In *The First World War and British Military History*, edited by Brian Bond, 41–68. Oxford: Clarendon Press.

CHAPTER 6

GRAND STRATEGY BEYOND THE WEST

K.M. FIERKE

"Beyond the West" suggests a very broad church, spanning the greater part of the globe, making it difficult to generalize in such a short space. This chapter seeks to examine two of the most famous strategies with origins in Asia, identified with Sun Tzu and Gandhi. On the surface they would appear to be unfit for comparison. Sun Tzu belongs to a tradition of military strategy, and is now part of the classical canon (Morrow 2015). Gandhi is identified with the nonviolent strategy of nonstate actors. My intention in examining the two together is to explore a family resemblance in their respective conceptions of grand strategy, even while recognizing that they are very distinct.

This brief look at two strategies is not representative of all strategy that has originated outside the West, and indeed, for a number of reasons, a binary West/non-West distinction is problematic. There is now and arguably has always been far more global cross-fertilization than is suggested by the dichotomy (Hobson 2004). For instance, we can see the influence of the American, Henry David Thoreau, on Gandhi (Hendrick 1956), and the latter's influence on nonviolent campaigns across the world since, or we can see the impact of Sun Tzu's thought on Western military strategy, whether through, for instance, its influence on the strategic thought of Liddell Hart and John Boyd (Yuen 2014, 2) or in interpreting the counterinsurgency strategies of contemporary enemies, such as al-Qaeda or the Taliban (Coker 2003; Bartley 2005; Love 2010).

As ideas travel, they are uprooted from the culture of origin and replanted in foreign soil. For example, the translation of Gandhi's thought by Martin Luther King, in the context of the US Civil Rights movement, resituated his strategy within Christianity. The process of translation may expose tensions. A History Channel documentary (2009) on Sun Tzu's *Art of War* examined a series of major military blunders on the part of Western powers asking what difference it would have made if Sun Tzu had been taken seriously. In so doing, it drew on a contrast between the logic of attrition that underpins the game of Chess, which is the dominant metaphor for Western strategy, in contrast to the logic of the Chinese or Japanese game of Go, which, like Sun Tzu, emphasizes capturing the maximum territory with the most efficient use of resources. The contrast between two distinct logics suggests translation may be less than straightforward. Rather than a "West"/"non-West" distinction, this chapter rests on a contrast between two understandings of "reality." For both Sun Tzu and Gandhi, strategy begins with the context of a relationship, consciousness of the other, and, to varying degrees, a desire sustain relationship, rather than destroying the other through instrumental or gratuitous violence. While few "Western" strategists would embrace the latter, the heavy focus on aerial carpet bombing and a strategy of attrition in conflicts from World War II to Vietnam or Iraq might suggest otherwise (see, e.g., McNamara 2004). For Sun Tzu and Gandhi, relationality suggests not an absence of difference or boundaries but begins with the whole, which is more than the sum of its parts.

Strategy as a plan of action designed to achieve an overall or grand aim is put to work in the world. Success requires working with the world, rather than against it. But what constitutes "reality" cannot be taken for granted. The two non-Western conceptions of grand strategy rest on assumptions about the nature, components, and operating principles of reality that contrast with the Western. The "realism" of the latter, building on Newtonian principles, includes an emphasis on the primacy of "brute" matter (Bilgrami 2008), the intrinsic separateness of objects or individuals, assumptions of changeless form, and of instrumental rationality, to which both modernity and the social sciences are indebted (Wendt 2015). By contrast, Sun Tzu and Gandhi highlight the role of consciousness, impermanence, and change, of the relationality of all life, and thus the importance of socio-ethical issues (Li and Perkins 2015, 1–14), which is compatible with a quantum metaphysics of indeterminism, consciousness, entanglement, and complementarity. The nuclear physicist, Niels Bohr ([2010] 1961, 20) drew a parallel between quantum physics and Eastern traditions such as Daoism and Buddhism (see also Fierke 2017, 2019). While grand strategy is always about a relationship between multiple parties, this broad metaphysical distinction has implications for how relationships are understood and acted upon.

The proliferating literature on grand strategy can be difficult to navigate due to a large degree of conceptual inconsistency (Lissner 2018: 2). The literature has tended to focus not only on states, but great powers, and the United States, in particular (Balzacq et al. 2019). Sun Tzu and Gandhi call this emphasis into question. As already suggested, Sun Tzu's thought is of relevance to state and nonstate actors alike, and for economic strategy as well as military. Gandhi's "grand" strategy of seeking India's independence, against the backdrop of British imperial rule, challenges any notion that the state, as a repository of community that seeks security, is ontologically prior. The potential for the state to be an object of contestation comes clearly into view, when placed in the context of a fight that ran counter to the grand strategy of Great Britain, the global imperial power of the time. India's independence campaign was precisely one about the means and ends to improve India's security vis a vis what was implicitly, and came to be defined explicitly, as an external power.

While a strand of the grand strategy literature highlights the pursuit of security through the effective mobilization of a range of resources (Balzacq et al. 2019), there has been a tendency to equate grand strategy with military strategy, the objective of establishing control over others, and the use of sheer force and technology in doing so (Yuen 2014). By contrast, for both Sun Tzu and Gandhi, achieving objectives without recourse to force is a priority. The emphasis is less on controlling a system than causing the least disturbance to it and thus some notion of harmony. Both are "grand," if primarily in the sense highlighted by Silove (2018, 27) of "grand plans, grand principle and grand behaviours." Removing the specific reference to states, they both establish priorities for the mobilization of sources of power to insure their perceived interests (van Hooft 2019). Both raise high order questions of avoiding recourse to force, while detailing specific means to achieve this objective, with a vision that emerges from a particular understanding of "reality."

One might compare a Western and non-Western tradition, looking at, for instance, Sun Tzu and Carl von Clausewitz (e.g. Yuen 2008; Lord 2000, 303–304) or violent and nonviolent resistance to imperial power, such as Gandhi and Franz Fanon (see, e.g., Srivastava 2010). I instead explore the reliance of Sun Tzu and Gandhi's "grand" strategies on holism and relationality. The central point is not to deny that all strategy is relational, or to suggest that relationality is entirely absent from Western strategy, but rather to reinforce the claim made by Brands (2014, as cited in Balzacq et al. 2019, 4) that grand strategy is not only "as contingent on domestic politics as on the structural forces of IR," but is also as much constitutive of these distinctions as a reflection of them. In this regard, there is a difference between strategic interactions that begin with an assumption that the "other" is ontologically prior, and entirely separate from the self—and thus the potential to treat them as "brute matter" or for purposes of control—as contrasted with one in which relationality goes "all the way down," such that self and other are mutually implicated within an organic whole, where harmony or disharmony arise from a particular type of relationship. A relationship of mutual implication, as distinct from mutual exclusion, is more effectively depicted as *intra-action* (Barad 2007) by which self and other are shaped and transformed through their engagement, where the distinction between subject and objects becomes evident only at the moment of encounter. Wendt (2015) argues that intra-action, or what constructivists have referred to as mutual constitution, is only physically tenable within a quantum framework.

After setting out some broad contrasts regarding cosmology, ontology, and epistemology below, I zoom in on Sun Tzu and Gandhi. I conclude with some reflections on why the contrasts are important in a globalizing world. Both cases highlight the importance, if possible, of achieving objectives without recourse to military force, which, I argue arises from a relational cosmology, where harmony and diversity coexist, and in which truth is not uniform but multi-perspectival. Gandhian nonviolence has more often been adopted by those who lack the capacity to overwhelm with military force. Sun Tzu highlights the potential to succeed in battle even against overwhelming odds. In both cases, the psychological dimensions of strategy, and the primacy of outwitting or transforming an enemy, rather than wielding superior force, take center stage.

Cosmology, Ontology, Epistemology

The strategies of Sun Tzu and Gandhi rely on cosmologies that share more in common with quantum physics than classical. This difference, which is often lost in translation, is important for understanding how the strategies work. Contrary to Newtonian assumptions that the world is composed of mindless matter, Daoism and Buddhism (as well as Hinduism), like quantum physics, see a universe of continuous movement, of flux and change, with a dynamic relationship between matter and consciousness. The source of this dynamism is the mutual implication of particles and waves, or what is referred to in quantum physics as complementarity. If in classical physics a particle is a particle and a wave is a wave, in quantum physics, a particle can, in certain circumstances, become a wave and a wave can become a particle. The mutual implication of matter and wave turns the Newtonian conception of "brute matter" on its head. The very thing that realists point to as "reality," which our language is said to merely describe, correctly or incorrectly, is formed through language and is thus dependent on context and the manifestation of potentials. In Daoism, Buddhism, or Hinduism, this suggests two "realities" or "truths," although they are mutually implicated. The one truth is universal, relating to a consciousness and intelligence that is entangled and infuses all material life. The other is conventional, resting on an illusion of separateness, and, at the level of humans, constituted in language.

Consciousness, as Wendt (2015) argues, can't be accounted for if one begins with mindless matter. While the Western concept of lifeforce or *elan vital* has been largely discredited within Newtonian science, it has many counterparts "beyond the West," and not least *ch'i* in Daoism and *prana* in Hinduism. In these traditions, consciousness pervades all life, from the universe to the body to political engagements, and is at the heart of strategy. If *ch'i* or *prana* relate to a universal life force and a relational ontology of entanglement, the illusory nature of conventional reality relies on an epistemology in which truth can never be fully grasped but is multispectral. While "Truth is one," according to a famous verse of the Hindu *Rig Veda*, truth can have various names (Easwaren 2007, 22, 85), much like snapshots of the same object from different angles. In this view, form is imposed on a world that is otherwise without form. Forms are themselves conventional constructs. Wang Chen, in the classic *Dao of Peace* (Sawyer 1999, 18–19), identifies the cause of suffering in the human tendency to conceptualize. He states that "as soon as things have names and people emotions, love and hate arise and attack each other, warfare flourishes." The contrast between two realities or truths reinforces a claim, also applicable to grand strategy more broadly, that the manipulation of perception is the essence of strategy (Hammond 2001, 181). For Sun Tzu, this manipulation involves a violent or nonviolent blow to the enemy's psychological center of gravity (O'Dowd and Waldron 1991, 28). Gandhi's purely nonviolent strategy is directed at the enemy's moral center of gravity which is knocked off balance by exposure of the distinction between an appearance of moral legitimacy and the reality of widespread suffering. In both cases, harmony, balance, and avoiding the use of force form the heart of strategy. Each of the two sections that follow explore a cosmology, the mutual implication of oppositions, the role of the "lifeforce," and the significance of this vision for ethics, planning, and tactics, as well as the objective of avoiding or minimizing recourse to the use of force.

Sun Tzu

Bohr's (2010) parallel between Daoism and quantum physics provides a physical basis for Sun Tzu's grand strategy, placing it in a world characterized by indeterminism, a life force (*ch'i*), entanglement, and relationality, where oppositions are complementary and mutually inclusive, rather than mutually exclusive. While the language of quantum science may be no more familiar than the Chinese concepts, it provides a framework for understanding the Daoist cosmology as more than myth or specific to a culture. The *Dao de Jing* (2000, ch. 42) presents the universe as a Grand Unity that began as a vast field of undifferentiated primal *qi*, which separated into polarities of yin and yang, which further interacted to create the diverse and complex world we live in. Within this cosmology, all things in the universe are constantly engaged in a cycle of dynamic transformation, breakdown, and return to a state of primordial *ch'i* (Meyer 2012). The dynamic relationship between opposites, yin and yang, formed from *ch'i*, is fundamental to Sun Tzu's *Art of War*, which, Yuen (2014, 68) highlights, preceded the *Dao de Jing*. There is a strong resemblance between the dialectics contained within the two texts.

The mutual implication of opposites is evident in one of the *Art of War*'s most famous passages, that "Warfare is the Dao of Deception" (Sawyer 1993, 158). Sun Tzu states that "although capable, display incapability. When committed to employing your forces, feign inactivity. When your objective is nearby, make it appear as if distant; when far away, create the illusion of being nearby" (Sawyer 1993, 158). The "Dao of Deception" provides a framework for understanding the string of oppositions contained within Daoist military strategy, all of which relate to fundamental Chinese philosophical concepts. The Dao of Deception rests in particular on the manipulation of *ch'i* and *cheng*. *Ch'i* translates as "crafty" or "unorthodox," but ancient strategy documents also use this spelling to refer to *qi*, as it relates to the spirit or morale of troops, which I will discuss shortly. The "unorthodox" or "crafty" (*ch'i*) refers to the unusual, unexpected, marvelous, or strange, in contrast with the more orthodox or straightforward (*cheng*) or, more simply, a contrast between indirect and direct strategy. As mutually inclusive oppositions, *cheng* can become a *ch'i* force and *ch'i* can become a *cheng* force. Concepts in the *Dao de Jing* from the natural world, that things, while remaining in a complementary dynamic tension, revert to their opposite after reaching their extreme, resonate with Sun-Tzu's dynamic characterization of the unorthodox turning into the orthodox (Sawyer 2007, 55). *Ch'i* and *cheng* relate, among others, to the ability of the strategist to concentrate his own forces while dividing those of the enemy. It is here that the manipulation of appearance and reality is key, as the general, for instance, creates the illusion of attacking in one or multiple places, thereby dividing enemy forces, while concentrating his own at another location. For Sun Tzu, at the start of battle one should "be as coy as a virgin; when your enemy lowers his guard and offers an opening, rush in like a hare out of its cage and the enemy will be unable to defend in time" (Khoo 1992, 45). The ability to manipulate the orthodox and unorthodox is key to success in a context where one is severely outnumbered. Sawyer (2007, 5) recounts Tien Tan's multistate, unorthodox strategy, where only 7000 exhausted soldiers and another 10,000 inhabitants trapped in Chi-mo defied a siege of some 100,000.

The indeterminism at the heart of strategy is evident in a further opposition between form (*hsing*) and power (*shih*). Yuen (2008, 194–195) notes that the primary job on the battlefield is to identity the enemy's form while concealing one's own. He draws on Sun Tzu's use of a water metaphor to elaborate the significance of a strong army's ability to change form. "[T]he army's disposition of force [*hsing*] is like water ... Water configures [*hsing*] it flows in accord with the terrain; the army controls its victory in accord with the enemy. Thus the army does not maintain any constant strategic configuration of power [*shih*], water has no constant shape [*hsing*]." He further states that if the pinnacle of military deployment [*hsing*] approaches the formless, then "even the deepest spy cannot discern it or the wise make plans against it." *Shih* and *hsing* relate to other oppositions such as emptiness (hsu) and solidness (shih), which involve creating the illusion that no position or force is permanently empty or solid, thereby presenting the opponent with an ongoing dilemma of what to defend or what to attack.

Another meaning of *ch'i* References to phonetic translations of the Chinese are based on Wade and Giles is expressed in a single passage of the *Art of War* and is the earliest reference to be found in military manuals: "The *ch'i* of the Three Armies can be snatched away; the commander's mind can be seized" (Sawyer 2007, 170). During the classic Warring States period, military writings developed a martial motivational science centered on the concept of *ch'i* that articulated numerous measures and methods for moderating the army's energy and controlling the soldier's commitment (Sawyer 2007, 50). *Ch'i* was at the heart of a psychology of fear and courage, which involved going to battle at the point that the *ch'i* of one's own forces was strong and that of the enemy was weak (Sawyer 2007, 49). The strategist is engaged in a dynamic process, where he must first and foremost be concerned with conserving his own *ch'i*, while also trying to identify the psychological, moral, and political qualities that make up the adversary's *ch'i*, in order to dissipate it or attack at the more propitious moment (O'Dowd and Waldron 1991, 29), when the energy of the enemy has abated. The wise general seeks to attack doubt and weakness in the enemy, while exercising control of the spirit of one's own army. Wei Liao, a strategist in the fourth century BC, believed that the army's *ch'i* essentially determined a battle's outcome (Sawyer 1993, 229, 236).

Ch'i and the mind, though intangible, constitute the "information" or "intelligence" that Sun Tzu considers most important (Yuen 2008, 190). Consciousness relates in part to what today is referred to in security circles as intelligence, but given Sun Tzu's reliance on a roughly translated "divine skein" (Warner 2006, 486), it is arguably more than just information *about* the other. The concept relates to spying, and in particular

Sun Tzu's elaboration of five types of spy, who work simultaneously, with none of them knowing the overall method of operation. A skein is a length of yarn or silken thread coiled loosely or in some sort of reel. The image resonates with quantum notions of entanglement, which in the German *Vershrankung*, originally posed by the physicist Erwin Schrodinger, suggests an unfolding or crossing over in an orderly manner, akin to a finely woven tapestry (Clegg 2006, 3). Sun Tzu's reference to divine spirit suggests the value of the web of intelligence as a "treasure of the ruler" and a system by which s/he coordinates, secures, and exploits the findings of the agents (Warner 2006, 486). The web as greater than the sum of its parts, is a whole and, against a Daoist backdrop, connects to a concept of the universe. *Ch'i*, as the "life force," relates to a form of intelligence that pervades all "life." Sun Tzu's emphasis on knowing not only the enemy but the environmental conditions, e.g., the "terrain," points to the importance of this broader context of intelligence. Knowing the enemy while remaining "formless" and adaptable oneself, makes it possible to attack when the former are at their weakest point, throw them off balance, and thus achieve victory with minimal effort.

After the victory, when one's own forces are exhausted, Sun Tzu emphasizes that it is far better to rebuild or restore what has been gained than to destroy it (Khoo 1992, 48). One can see several reasons for this emphasis. The first regards the dangers of protracted war. Coker (2003, 18) argues that Sun Tzu first and foremost feared the consequences of escalation in war, as this would potentially end in total defeat rather than total victory. An exhausted army can subsequently be attacked by a third party or may be unable to police the peace. Sun Tzu was very clear that no country has benefitted from protracted warfare.

The second is a moral position, consistent with a maxim, repeated in texts of the Warring States period and early Han, of "sustaining the perishing, reviving the extinct," which became a litmus test for the legitimate use of coercive force and found expression in the idea that victorious rulers shouldn't profit from the resources of a vanquished state but should return the assets to a people in exchange for submission or, among others, a claim that the annihilation of a state and its sacred institutions through terror and violence defies deep structural patterns of the cosmos (Meyer 2012).

A third relates to the focus of grand strategy on the system and concern about the unintended or undesired consequences of prolonged action beyond what is needed, and not least the consequences of the hatred generated by war. Chapter 79 of the *Dao de Ching* raises a question of how reconciliation can be successful if, in the face of peace, enmity remains. Yuen (2014, 95) highlights the amount of time it takes to reverse the consequences of hate, which suggests that excessive measures or the prolongation of conflict will be counterproductive and disruptive to the overall harmony of the system. Hate is an emotion that arises in the context of a relationship, which, in the argument of Sun Tzu, is best avoided to the end of preserving the system within which the relationship is entangled.

As a military strategist, Sun Tzu was perhaps less concerned with morals per se than with the efficient use of resources or effectiveness in battle. Nonetheless, moral law is one of five fundamental factors of Sun Tzu's strategy. By moral law, he means that which brings people into alignment with their ruler so that they will follow him without fear, although this law also suggests its opposite, i.e., an ability to undermine the coherence of popular will can debilitate an enemy, as was, for instance, evident in Soviet efforts to destabilize and demoralize Western societies during the Cold War (Corneli 1987, 441). The further factors include "heaven" (the working of natural forces on the conduct of military operations), the earth (working with the terrain rather than against it), command (the virtues of the general), and doctrine (the organization of the army), all of which highlight the importance of planning (Khoo 1992, 2–3). In laying out the five fundamentals, Sun Tzu claims that success or defeat of either side will depend on whether they accept or reject his advice. This holistic approach to planning places emphasis on creating the conditions by which an outcome can come about on its own, rather than creating a blueprint that may be unable to adapt to a continuously changing environment.

Unlike Confucius or Gandhi, Sun Tzu does not reject violence altogether. Indeed, he sees war as a necessary evil but argues that the most effective strategy will avoid war altogether. It is better to subjugate other states without actually engaging in armed combat, through deception or diplomatic coercion, thwarting the enemy's plans and alliances and frustrating their strategy (Sawyer 2007, 57). The objective to avoid the use of force if possible is evident in how Sun Tzu devises the strategy of attack, beginning with the enemy's plans, then their alliances, followed by their army. Attacking fortified cities is at the very bottom of the list. As Sun Tzu states, "Fighting to win one hundred victories in one hundred battles is not the supreme skill. However, to break the enemy's resistance without fighting is the supreme skill" (Khoo 1992, 9). Placing these claims in the larger context of Daoism reveals that a central objective of grand strategy not only regards the efficient use of resources, given that war is costly. It further points to the primacy of complementarity, by which oppositions (*yin* and *yang*), including self and enemy other, are always mutually implicated and thus in a relationship, where fates cannot be entirely separated, as expressed in Sun Tzu's maxim, "If you know yourself and know your enemy, in a hundred battles you will never fear the results ..." (Khoo 1992, 11). Minimizing recourse to the use of force is bound up in the further objective of restoring balance and harmony to the system.

Gandhi

Gandhi's Art of Politics would seem to be an entirely different kettle of fish than Sun Tzu's *Art of War*. The emphasis of Sun Tzu on deception, secrecy, or striking the enemy when they are weak, would seem contrary to a strategy that is associated with a willingness to suffer. Yet, Gandhi's strategy resonates with aspects of Daoist military strategy, even while derived from a different tradition of thought and situated in the modern context of imperialism. At the level of cosmology, the Dao finds a counterpart in the Hindu "supreme science" of consciousness (*brahmavidya*) going back to the first millennium

BC. The universe was understood to be a manifestation of *prana* or pure consciousness that transcends all creation, and a force of creation itself. *Prana* has many levels of meaning, from the physical breath to consciousness itself, and is at work at every level of life. In contrast to the focus of Western science on the external material world, this conception of science looked inward, to knowledge of reality that might be discovered through the mind (see Davidson and Harrington 2002). The rishis or "see'ers" of ancient India believed that the single most important purpose of life was to discover this reality experientially in order to realize compassion on earth. They found, in going beyond the senses, a continuous process of change, with matter coming together, dissolving, and coming together again in different forms (Easwaren 2007 [1985], 10). In Hindu meditation, consciousness, when acutely focused, is withdrawn from the body and mind, entering into a singularity in which the sense of the individual as separate dissolves. It was in this state that the "seers" discovered a core of consciousness that is beyond time and change.

Atman, the spiritual life principle of the universe, is nonlocal and larger than the individual, yet understood to infuse the individual. The mutual implication of opposites in Gandhi's thought begins with the tension between two notions of self, i.e., a "true self" and the more illusory self of the ego. The true desires—and with them the true self—are said to be hidden by other, false desires (Ganieri 2013, 25). Gandhi's reforms began with the egoistic self. The external battle could not be separated from the internal battle against the ego. Self-reform was the point of departure for beginning to make conscious choices that would transcend and transform divisions within society.

The central objective of Gandhi's campaign was *Swaraj*, which means self-rule. This sacred Vedic word, which is far more than political independence in the Western sense, connotes both self-rule and self-restraint. Indeed, it rests on a fundamental critique of modernity, including the reification of violence, widespread among realists, as a "natural" and thus "inevitable" feature of human nature (Steger 2006, 332), an atomic notion of the self as independent and prior to any social relations or the notion of matter as brute and inert, and the desire to control nature, thereby disengaging us from life within a habitat. As Bilgami (2008, 63–4) argues, these Newtonian orthodoxies remove any normative constraints on action and abdicate any notion of a first person, as distinct from third person view of agency.

Gandhi viewed Western modernization as alienating, materialist, exploitative of both nature and human beings, and lacking in moral purpose. He understood the self to be intrinsically relational and interdependent with both context and its social relations, such that living in harmony with oneself could not be detached from membership in a community of all-encompassing Spirit. The unity and oneness of life provides the foundation of truth, nonviolence, and tolerance, which then underpin concepts of political self-government for the many. Individual self-government meant that India's freedom began with each individual taking personal responsibility for changing attitudes of intolerance and exclusivity. Individual reform was the basis for social reform, including Hindu–Muslim religious conflict, the evils of the caste system, and economic inequality.

If *Swaraj* was the objective, *Satyagraha* was the core of the strategy. As William (Shirer 1979, 84), who reported on Gandhi's revolution in the 1930s, said in his memoirs, "satyagraha was Gandhi's 'supreme achievement, which taught us all that there was a greater power in life than force which seemed to have ruled the planet since men first sprouted on it. That power lay in the spirit, in truth and love, in nonviolent action." Gandhi described *Satyagraha* in terms of a metaphor that likened it to a banyan tree with innumerable branches (Iyer 1973, 265). The trunk consisted not only of nonviolence (*ahimsa*) but also of truth (*satya*). The branches consisted of the many forms of nonviolent action, from civil disobedience and noncooperation to fasting and social reform.

As regards truth, he warns of the need to continually remind ourselves of our fallibility and limitations. Human understanding is always imperfect and thus incapable of possessing absolute truth (Steger 2006, 345). We have to believe in truth, but we cannot possess complete knowledge, and any claim to infallibility would be dangerous. Truth is vindicated not by inflicting suffering on others but through self-suffering. Precisely because none of us can see reality "from everywhere at once," we are not in a position to know the full truth and thus to punish others. Gandhi's philosophy rests on a deeply relational understanding of our entanglement with others. As stated in the *upanisad*—the "hidden connection" or "secret teaching"—the self that gazes out from within my body is the same self that gazes out from within yours (Ganieri 2013, 31). Gandhi (2009, 97), who like Sun Tzu relies on a water metaphor, claims that "as ice becomes what it is from water, so we have all come from the same water and it shall turn again into that water."

The ideal of nonviolence has its origins in the realization that when life is full of suffering we should cause suffering to none (Gandhi 2009, 115). It is thus better to transform the enemy than to destroy them. The transformation was not to be realized through passivity or doing nothing, but through action that strikes at the enemy's moral sense of gravity by destabilizing the conventional truth and turning the relationship between appearance and reality on its head. In suggesting that, given a choice, the use of violence is preferable to passive acquiescence born of cowardice (Ostergaard 1974), Gandhi, far from condoning violence, stresses the importance of agency in effectively realizing one's objectives. Ganieri's (2013, 5) claim that the "self *is* an activity" (italics added), is consistent with Gandhi's stance. The *Satyagrahi* general sought not retribution but to transform a conflict situation so that warring parties could find a mutual interest in resolution. *Satyagraha* rests on a combination of withdrawing cooperation from a state that has become corrupt, which assumes its dependence on the support of oppressed populations, and civil disobedience, which involves disobeying unjust laws in order to register protest.

Like *ch'i* in Daoist military strategy, the life force or *prana* has an important place. While violence is the law of the brute, who knows only physical might, Gandhi (151, 133–134) refers to nonviolence as the law of our species. He claims that dignity requires obedience to this higher law and the strength of the spirit. Power comes from complete control over the senses, and the preservation and sublimation of, he states, "the vitality that is responsible for the creation of life. If this vitality is mobilized rather than dissipated by evil, it can be transformed into a powerful creative energy. Power involves control over not only action but thought" (151, 97). The *Satyagrahi* general examines himself continuously, listening to the dictates of the inner self and obeying his inner voice. *Brahmacharya*, which relates to the conservation of vital energy, is the source of the inner strength "to stand unarmed against the whole world" (151, 95). With *Satyagraha*, no less than military warfare, the discipline of the soldier, and obeying the general's command is crucial, even when hostilities have been suspended. But in this war, there is no space for violence, in any shape or form, including thought, speech, or deed. There is only space for soul-force, which is universal and makes no distinction between kin and strangers, young and old, male and female, nor friend and foe (151, 78). While some are believed to follow the law of the brute, the *Satyagrahi* begins with the assumption that no one is so fallen that they cannot be converted by love (151, 25).

Remaking the individual self, and finding the higher Self within, is inextricable from transforming the world. The struggle between good and evil, both internal and external, rests on a recognition that evil can only flourish in the world if allied with something good (Gandhi 2009, 4). Based on Gandhi's principle of noncooperation, the evil system, represented by the British colonial regime, would only be able to endure so long as it received the support of good people. Once this support was withdrawn, the government could not survive (Gandhi 2009, 4). Likewise, the selfless action that underpins noncooperation requires shedding attachment to the body, or to forms of cooperation that bolster the system.

Gandhi's nonviolence struck at the moral center of gravity of British rule in India. It challenged the appearance of British goodness and their right to rule India, turning it on its head and revealing the structural violence that underpinned the presence. Here I highlight just two forms of this noncooperation in the context of the Indian campaign. One was the renunciation of foreign clothing (*Swadeshi*), replacing it with the spinning of one's own cloth and living more simply according to Indian traditions. The symbolism is important in so far as India's economy, which was based on textiles, was destroyed by colonialism. However, Gandhi (1951, 146) specified that the boycott was aimed not merely at the British but extended to all foreign cloth. Dumping had reduced millions to pauperism. To focus on British goods was indefensible from the perspective of nonviolence as it would be retaliatory and punitive.

A second form of noncooperation required letting go of attachment to bodily comfort. During the Salt Marches, rows of nonviolent "soldiers" were bludgeoned by the forces of her Majesty's army, as they approached the sea to collect salt, a basic necessity of human life. Action motivated by the desires of the ego, and not least comfort, had to be replaced by voluntary suffering, if need be, and compassion. As Gandhi (2009, 90) states, "nonviolence will have become direct experience for us ... when our whole life comes to be permeated with the spirit of compassion, when nonviolence manifests itself in its true essence." This relies on a spirit of sacrifice or *yayna*, which requires letting go of the impermanent ego, and seeing the other and oneself as inseparable. At the heart of *satyagraha* was an assumption that suffering will move the heart of an oppressor or opponent. The strategy was conceived as a practical experiment with employing nonviolence within the political realm.

The unwillingness to cooperate with acts that legitimate and manifest the power of an oppressor evokes a reaction from the latter, who then attempts to enforce cooperation, often with violence. The willingness to absorb punishment and to suffer is key to the moral destabilization. Either submitting to the punishment or reacting with violence reinforces the position of the oppressor. In the latter case, the use of violence by the agent makes it possible for the powers that be to delegitimize them as a criminal or terrorist, and thus divert attention away from the underlying cause of the action. In accepting the blows of violence in response to a refusal to cooperate, a question is raised in the minds of the audience about the moral legitimacy and authority of those who claim to rule (Fierke 2012).

Conclusions

The agent of grand strategy, as articulated by Sun Tzu and Gandhi, is not the entirely separate individual who instrumentally maximizes their self-interest, or whose primary constraint is the materiality of the world, as is so prominent in modern thinking. For both strategists, the self who acts is instead entangled in a web that extends outward to the universe, which includes the enemy, but is also infused with its life-force. The self is embedded and informed by a consciousness of the impact of thought and action on the dynamics that flow through this web. While suggesting a degree of constraint, strategy is not without reason or agency, but both begin from the perspective of the whole, with attention to context, as well as to the dynamic polarity of opposites and their mutual implication, including self and other or appearance and reality.

As Bilgami (2008, 72) notes, "to view nature and the world not as brute matter but as containing value that makes normative demands on agency is not by any means to be unscientific." Datta-Ray (2015, 135), who argues that modernity is coded in violence, examines the influence of the ancient *Mahabharata*, not only on Gandhi, but Indian diplomacy following independence, and states that it provides a means of "navigating a crowded cosmos without damaging it," of negotiating it without causing harm. Gandhi's nonviolence is often interpreted as a "weapon of the weak; he claims, however, that it is in fact superior to the force of arms (Gandhi 1951, 51). *Art of War* is a military strategy, with a potential to cause harm, but its core message regards the importance of avoiding unnecessary violence. Sun Tzu highlights the importance of planning, and emphasizes the psychological relationship between self and other, in order to achieve one's objectives with the minimal use of force, and with attention to restoring balance and restoring the enemy in its aftermath.

Sun Tzu's *Art of* War is most often drawn on by Western actors in a context of asymmetry, such as guerrilla warfare, going back to Mao, or contemporary terrorism in the case of al-Qaeda or ISIS. In the Chinese context, the strategy has relevance at the interstate level and might, for instance, provide a different take on Xi Jinping's Belt and Road Initiative (BRI) than the China threat thesis that dominates in the United States (see, e.g., Yung 2018). Drawing on symbolism of the ancient Silk Roads and a language of respect and relationality, the strategy, much like a game of Go, might be seen as the efficient use of resources to spread Chinese influence while avoiding, to the extent possible, the use of force. This preserves a role for threat and force, while recognizing the tension between older relational strategies and the logic of a state system based on sovereign states. Gandhi's strategy preserved a friendship with Britain after independence, but was followed by the violent separation of India and Pakistan into separate states. This tragic irony can be situated within a larger international context where the meaning of independence is inseparable from status as a separate sovereign state. This logic of separation is in tension with the relationality that underpinned Gandhi's thought. Both Sun Tzu and Gandhi present "grand" strategies of importance to a globalizing world and in the face of climate change, a battle that ultimately depends on our ability to reimagine the world as a relational whole, to rethink self and other, and the implications for the use of violence and the conduct of war within it.

References

Balzacq, Thierry, Peter Dombrowski, and Simon Reich. 2019. "Is Grand Strategy a Research Program? A Review Essay." *Security Studies* 28 (1).
Barad, Karen. 2007. *Meeting the Universe Halfway*. Durham, NC: Duke University Press.
Bartley, Caleb M. 2006. "The Art of Terrorism: What Sun Tzu Can Teach us about International Terrorism." *Comparative Strategy* 24 (3): 237–251.
Bilgrami, Akeel. 2008. "Gandhi, Newton and the Enlightenment." *Philosophical Exchange* 38 (1): Art, 4: 2–18, accessed April 5 2019, at http://digitalcommons.brockport.edu/phil_ex/vol38/iss1/4
Bohr, Niels. 2010 [1961]. *Atomic Physics and Human Knowledge*. New York: Dover Publications.
Brands, Hal. 2014. *What Good is Grand Strategy?: Power and Purpose in American Statecraft from Harry S. Truman to George W. Bush*. Ithaca, NY: Cornell University Press.
Carnes, Lord. 2000. "A Note on Sun Tzu." *Comparative Strategy* 19 (4): 301–307.
Clegg, Brian. 2006. *The God Effect: Quantum Entanglement, Science's Strangest Phenomenon*. New York: St. Martin's Griffin.
Coker, Christopher. 2003. "What would Sun Tzu say about the War on Terrorism?" *The RUSI Journal*, 148 (1): 16–20.
Corneli, Alessandro. 1987. "Sun Tzu and the Indirect Strategy." *Revista di Studi Politici Internazionali*, 54 (3): 419–445.
Datta-Ray. 2015. *The Making of Indian Diplomacy: A Critique of Eurocentrism*. London: Hurst & Co.
Davidson, Richard J., and Anne Harrington, eds. 2002. *Visions of Compassion: Tibetan Buddhists and Western Scientists Examine Human Nature*. OUP USA.
Easwaren, Eknath. 2007 [1985]. *The Bhagavad Gita*, translation. Tomales, CA: Nilgiri Press.
Fierke, K.M. 2019. "*Contrary sunt Complementa*: Global Entanglement and the Constitution of Difference." *International Studies Review* 21 (1): 146–169.

Fierke, K.M. 2017. "Consciousness at the Interface: Wendt, Eastern Wisdom, and the Ethics of Intra-action." *Critical Review* 29 (2): 141–169.

Fierke, K.M. 2012. *Political Self Sacrifice: Agency, Body and Emotion in International Relations.* Cambridge: Cambridge University Press.

Gandhi, Mohandus. 1951. *Nonviolent Resistance (Satyagraha).* New York: Schocken Books.

Gandhi, Mohandus. 2009. *The Bhagavad Gita According to Gandhi.* Berkeley, CA: North Atlantic Books.

Ganieri, Jonardon. 2013. *The Concealed Art of the Soul: Theories of the Self and Practices of Truth in Indian Ethics and Epistemology.* Oxford: Oxford University Press.

Hammond, Grant T. 2001. *The Mind of War: John Boyd and American Security.* Washington, DC: Smithsonian Institution Press.

Hendrick, George. 1956. "The Influence of Thoreau's "Civil Disobedience" on Gandhi's Satyagraha." *The New England Quarterly* 29 (4): 462–471.

Hobson, John. 2004. *The Eastern Origins of Western Civilization.* Cambridge: Cambridge University Press.

Iyer, Raghavan. 1973. *The Moral and Political Thought of Mahatma Gandhi.* New York: Oxford University Press.

Khoo Kheng-Hor, ed. 1992. *Sun Tzu's Art of War.* Translated by Hwang Chung-Mei. Darul Eshan, Malaysia: Pelanduk Publications.

Li Chenyang, and Franklin Perkins, eds. 2015. *Chinese Metaphysics and its Problems.* Cambridge: Cambridge University Press.

Lissner, Rebecca Friedman. 2018. "What is Grand Strategy? Sweeping a Conceptual Minefield." *Texas National Security Review* 2 (1): 1–22.

Love, Kevin M. 2010. "A Sun Tzu Approach to Counter Al-Qaeda's Global Insurgency." *Strategy Research Project*, U.S. Army War College. https://www.hsdl.org/?abstract&did=724478, accessed November 25, 2019.

McNamara, Robert. 2004. *The Fog of War.* Sony Pictures.

Meyer, Andrew Seth. 2012. *The Dao of the Military: Liu An's Art of War.* New York: Columbia University Press.

Morrow, Nicholas. 2015. "Sun Tzu, The Art of War (c. 500–300 B.C.)." *Classics of Strategy and Diplomacy*, 24 November. https://www.classicsofstrategy.com/2015/11/sun-tzu-the-art-of-war-c-500-300-bc.html, accessed April 28, 2019.

O'Dowd, Edward, and Arthur Waldron. 1991. "Sun Tzu for Strategists." *Comparative Strategy* 10 (1): 25–36.

Ostergaard, Geoffrey. 1974. "Gandhian Nonviolence and Passive Resistance." *Civil Resistance. info.* https://civilresistance.info/ostergaard, accessed November 25, 2019.

Sawyer, Ralph. 2007. *The Dao of Deception.* New York: Basic Books.

Sawyer, Ralph. 1999. *The Dao of War.* New York: Basic Books.

Sawyer, Ralph. 1993. *The Seven Military Classics of Ancient China.* New York: Basic Books.

Shirer, William. 1979. *Gandhi: A Memoir.* New York: Simon and Schuster.

Silove, Nina. 2018. "Beyond the Buzz Word: Three Meanings of "Grand Strategy,"" *Security Studies* 27 (1): 27–57.

Srivastava, Neelam. 2010. "Towards a Critique of Colonial Violence: Fanon, Gandhi and the Restoration of Agency." *Journal of Postcolonial Writing* 46 (3–4): 303–319.

Steger, Manfred B. 2006. "Searching for *Satya* through *Ahimsa*: Gandhi's Challenge to Western Discourses of Power." *Constellations* 13 (3): 332–353.

Van Hooft, Paul 2019. "Grand Strategy." *Oxford Bibliographies*. oxfordbibliographies.com, accessed December 23, 2019.
Warner, Michael. 2006. "The Divine Skein: Sun Tzu on Intelligence." *Intelligence and National Security* 21 (4): 483–492.
Wendt, Alexander. 2015. *Quantum Mind and Social Science*. Cambridge, UK: Cambridge University Press.
Yuen, Derek M.C. 2014. *Deciphering Sun Tzu: How to Read the Art of War*. London: Hurst & Co.
Yuen, Derek M.C. 2008. "Deciphering Sun Tzu." *Comparative Strategy* 27 (2): 183–2000.
Yung Sun Lai. 2018. "Sun Tzu's 'Art of War' is China's Strategy to the 'One Belt One Road.'" *Daily FT*, 26 January. www.ft.lk/columns/Sun-Tzu-s--Art-of-War--is-China-s-strategy-to--One-Belt-One-Rad-/4-648092, accessed November 5, 2019.

PART II

THEORETICAL APPROACHES

CHAPTER 7

RATIONAL ANALYSIS OF GRAND STRATEGY

CHARLES GLASER

THIS chapter describes the basic structure of a rational analysis of grand strategy. Rational analysis is an approach, not a school or a theory. It is the approach that is required by and supports sound policy analysis; it is not controversial. Nevertheless, appreciating the structure and requirements of a rational analysis can provide guidance for performing high-quality analysis and for critiquing ongoing debates over grand strategy. The terminology "rational grand strategy" does not have currency in current grand strategy debates, but all of the major schools of grand strategy in the US debate are built on a rational analysis.

The chapter begins with a brief discussion of how I use the terms "grand strategy" and "rational." It then describes the basic components of a rational grand-strategic analysis: state's interests, the international environment, theories of state interaction, the options available to a state, the comparison of these options, and a conclusion about which grand strategy will best serve a state's interests. The final section briefly highlights the analytic value of understanding the structure and requirements of rational analyses of grand strategy.

WHAT IS A RATIONAL GRAND STRATEGY?

What is "grand strategy"? The term "grand strategy" is used in a variety of different, albeit related, ways (Silove 2018; Milevski 2016, 1–9; Lissner 2018). Although the different definitions each have virtues, this chapter uses the term to refer to a state's broad policies for achieving its vital interests (following Goldstein 2005, 17–20). Some analyses of grand strategy focus exclusively on a state's national security interests (e.g., Posen 2014); others include a range of additional interests, including economic and ideological interests (e.g., Brooks and Wohlforth 2016). A state's grand strategy can be comprised of military, economic, and diplomatic policies, although some analyses of grand strategy focus solely on military policy.

This definition is different from another that is commonly used—"grand strategy is a political-military means-end chain, a state's theory about how best it can 'cause' security for itself" (Posen 1984, 13). As discussed below, the analysis of grand strategy employs a variety of types of theory, but grand strategy itself is a policy, not a theory or the analysis that employs the theory.

What qualifies as a "broad" policy is necessarily a judgment call. For a major power, which regions of the world it commits to protect, which countries it includes in its security alliances, and whether it favors an open international economic system are clearly among its broad choices. More specific choices about whether to deploy forces on allies' territory are also among its broad choices, as are its choice of the type of military doctrine.[1] The size and type of its military forces are on the boundary between grand strategy and military policy, and are often not included in characterizations of a state's grand strategy.

What is a "rational" analysis? By rational grand strategy I mean simply a grand strategy that is based on a rational analysis of a state's grand strategy options. A rational analysis explores a state's options for achieving its interests, given the opportunities and constraints imposed by its international environment/situation. This analysis must identify the variables that influence the grand strategies that are available to the state, assess the range of strategies that are feasible, and compare the costs, benefits, and risks of key alternative grand strategies across this range.

The analysis must also be strategic—that is, it must take into account the anticipated reactions of opposing states, both adversaries and allies.[2] Clearly, whether an action will produce the desired result will often depend at least partly on whether and how an adversary reacts to offset it.

A state will usually face uncertainties about its international environment. These uncertainties could be about its potential adversaries' motives and objectives, about states' power, about the effectiveness of various military technologies and strategies for employing them, and about how an adversary will interpret the state's actions. A rational analysis should include these uncertainties in its evaluation.

Due to the sheer complexity of the analytic task, and possibly limits on the time available for analysis, a rational analysis may not be fully complete. For example, it may not address the full spectrum of possible alternative policies and it may not include all imaginable uncertainties. In addition, a rational analysis of grand strategy will typically not quantify the costs, benefits, and probabilities that various options are projected to generate. It will, however, compare the size of these outputs, as this is necessary to compare the overall desirability of the analyzed options. This analysis may not meet certain standards of rational analysis. It would be a "bounded rational" analysis.[3] Given the scope and complexity of the issue, this is what we can reasonable expect, or strive for, in the analysis of a state's grand strategy.

Rational analyses of a state's grand strategy produced by different analysts will not necessarily produce an agreed-upon result. Different analysts performing a rational analysis of the same quality and comprehensiveness can reach different conclusions because they disagree about inputs to the analysis. The most basic disagreement would be over the state's interests. These disagreements are fundamental, reflecting inherent values, and cannot be adjudicated by further analysis. Other disagreements can reflect disagreements about the state's international environment, including other states' motives and military capabilities. For example, experts disagreed throughout the Cold War about both Soviet motives and intentions and about the probability that a Soviet invasion of Western Europe would succeed. Yet another source of disagreement can be beliefs/theories about the nature of international politics, including the probability that deterrence—nuclear and conventional—will succeed in a specific situation, the probability that an adversary will interpret actions/signals as the sending state intends, and whether a state's credibility for defending one interest is closely connected to its willingness to defend another interest.[4]

A complete rational analysis of a state's grand strategy addresses a number of essential components:

- The state's interests.
- The state's international situation/environment—as I explain below, how this is characterized depends on the theoretical perspective the analysis employs.
- Theories of state interaction—that is, theories about how an opposing state will understand and react to the state's policies.
- Options—a state's interests, its international environment, and theories of interaction provide the foundation for identifying the state's grand-strategic options and evaluating their feasibility, costs, and benefits.
- Tradeoffs and Conclusions.

Although a state's grand strategy can have security, economic, and diplomatic dimensions, the following discussion is cast primarily in terms of security. This simplification helps to clarify the key features of a rational grand-strategic analysis. Expanding the framework developed below to include these other dimensions is straightforward.

Interests

Fundamental Interests

A state can hold a spectrum of fundamental interests that should be factored into its grand strategy. By "fundamental," I mean an interest that has inherent value for the state; it is pursued for its own sake, not to contribute to achieving another interest. In contrast, I term interests that are pursued to achieve a fundamental interest as "derivative interests," which I discuss below. This distinction is important in the grand strategy debate, because derivative interests are often conflated with fundamental interests, which can significantly weaken the analysis.

States can have four types of fundamental interests. Virtually all states value the first two—security and prosperity. In addition, states can have political-ideological interests and/or humanitarian interests.

Security is commonly considered a state's most important interest. A state is secure when it does not face threats to its territorial integrity and sovereignty. Security can reflect a state's ability to protect its territory from invasion and destruction and its ability to prevent opposing states from posing effective coercive threats. Security can also reflect the absence of opposing states that have an interest in posing these types of threats. Even if an opposing state is capable of invading or coercing, the state can be highly secure if the opposing state has no intention of employing these capabilities.

Some analyses identify security as a derivative interest, not a fundamental interest. In this framing, prosperity and consumption are fundamental, and security is valued because it is necessary to protect consumption (e.g. Powell 1999, ch. 2). Although the logic of this framing is strong, for grand-strategic analysis there is substantial efficiency in envisioning security as a fundamental interest. Many of a state's key choices affect its security directly; translating this security into protected future prosperity abstracts too far from the concrete terms of the analysis. A full grand-strategic analysis should, however, consider the economic investments required by various grand strategy options and identify them as costs, which result in reduced consumption.

The second interest that states have is prosperity. A state's GDP is a basic, but far from adequate, measure of its prosperity. GDP per capita can be a much better indicator of the prosperity of individuals living in the state. Even this measure fails to capture distributional issues, which raises questions about how leaders and outside analysts should even evaluate a state's prosperity and overall well-being. Evaluation is further complicated by non-economic factors that affect people's well-being, including the quality of the environment. While all of these considerations are important, and could influence how a state pursues its interest in prosperity, the central point is that prosperity, however understood, is a key interest for virtually all states.

Beyond security and prosperity, a state could have a variety of political-ideological-ideational interests. A state could be interested in spreading its regime type. For example, the United States has been committed to spreading democracy, including in some cases via the use of force. To the extent that these efforts have reflected the United States' preference simply for a world with more democratic states, in contrast to a belief that more democracies would benefit US security and economic interests, they have reflected a fundamental interest. A state could have an interest in status—its standing or rank in the relevant international community (Renshon 2017). A state could be interested in spreading its type of economic system, simply because it reflects its view of a desirable world. Part of the US–Soviet competition to spread market capitalism vs. communism reflected this type of interest. And a state could have an interest in spreading its defining/dominant religion. All of these political and ideological interests could be sufficiently important to influence a state's grand strategy.

Finally, a state could have humanitarian interests—interests in the prosperity and well-being of the people of other states. This interest could be reflected in a state's willingness to provide economic support for economic development, to use military force to save lives in a civil war, or to provide logistical support in disaster relief operations. Whether these humanitarian interests rise to the level of importance that they should be included as a component of grand strategy will vary across states and is open to debate; I include them here for the sake of completeness.

Prosperity, ideology, and even humanitarian interests can, but do not always, create incentives for a state to take territory. Distinguishing between these motives for expansion and security-driven motives for expansion is analytically valuable; as sketched in the section on theories, a state will sometimes want to pursue different grand-strategic policies when it faces a purely security-seeking state that wants to expand and a state that wants to expand for these other nonsecurity reasons.

From the perspective of grand-strategic analysis, there is no right or wrong to fundamental interests. In a sense, that is what it means to be fundamental—they reflect a state's values and in their purest form are not subject to debate. Of course, analysts may not agree about a state's fundamental interests. Analysts who hold different fundamental interests or disagree about their relative importance may reach different conclusions about grand strategy, and these disagreements cannot be resolved by further analysis. In contrast, as discussed below, disagreements about the cost of pursuing a fundamental interest and of the state's prospects for success are more amenable to research and analysis.

The proportion of its resources that a state should expend to achieve each of its fundamental interests can change even when their relative importance is unchanged. This can occur when the state's international environment changes, specifically when changes occur in the threats and opportunities facing the state. For example, in the decade following the Cold War, the United States significantly reduced defense spending and increased its involvement in humanitarian intervention. The shift did not reflect a decrease in the importance that the United States placed on security, but instead the disappearance of the Soviet threat, which increased US security, thereby freeing up resources for and reducing the risks of humanitarian intervention.

Derivative Interests

By "derivative interest," I mean an interest that, once achieved, will increase a state's prospects for achieving a fundamental interest. The derivative interest is not valued for its own sake, but instead because its achievement contributes to achieving a fundamental interest.[5]

Derivative interests are usually linked to fundamental interests by a theory—a causal logic that holds that achieving the derivative interest will contribute to achieving the fundamental interest. For example, many analysts hold that spreading democracy will increase US security and therefore call for the United States to make large investments toward this end. This argument is based on democratic peace theory, which holds that democracies do not fight other democracies. Concluding that spreading democracy is a derivative security interest requires more, however, than accepting democratic peace theory. In addition, the wars that would be avoided by specific countries becoming democratic would have had to have posed a threat to US security. Would the nondemocratic state have attacked the United States? Would the United States have been drawn into a war involving that nondemocratic state? Consequently, one could argue that spreading democracy is not a derivative security interest for two sets of reasons. First, an analyst could reject democratic peace theory; she could nevertheless believe that spreading democracy achieves a fundamental US political-ideological interest. Second, an analyst who accepts democratic peace theory could judge that US security would not have been at risk if the states in question remained nondemocratic. This analyst could nevertheless believe that the United States has fundamental humanitarian interests in preventing these wars and, therefore, favor US efforts to spread democracy.

In contrast, some derivative interests, instead of reflecting theories of how states interact, are based on other forms of analysis. For example, during the Cold War, a central presumed derivative interest of US grand strategy was to ensure that Eurasia remained divided—that is, not dominated by a single major power. This was not a fundamental interest because US security is distinct from Eurasian security. The most direct logic supporting this derivative interest was that a Eurasian hegemon would have sufficient resources to invade or at least economically strangle the United States. Whether a hegemon would in fact have possessed this capability depends on a military assessment of the feasibility of attacking or strangling the United States. The most thorough such assessments raised serious doubts about this danger, which in turn raised questions about the security importance of keeping Eurasia divided (Art 1991, 14–23).

Analyses of grand strategy often present derivative interests as though they were fundamental interests. This conflation can greatly weaken the analysis by submerging important theoretical debates and disagreements and by giving the derivative interest the mistaken appearance of being uncontroversial (Avey, Markowitz, and Reardon 2018). Treating a derivative interest as a fundamental interest skips a critical step in grand-strategic analysis: identifying the relevant theory (or other form of analysis) and then applying it to the situation the state faces. When this occurs, not only is the analysis less clear and transparent than it should be, but its conclusions are not fully supported.

In US grand strategy debate, some of the key disagreements between schools of thought hinge on whether achieving an assumed derivative interest would actually increase US security. There are numerous examples of divergent analysis that are essentially decided by treating an unexplored, or at least underexplored, derivative interest as though it were a fundamental interest. Other important examples include: preventing war between other major powers, which depends on whether the United States would get drawn into such a war; preventing nuclear proliferation, which depends on whether proliferation increases the probability of war and on whether these wars would involve the United States; maintaining access to Persian Gulf oil, which depends on whether a disruption of this oil's flow would actually pose a security or significant economic threat to the United States; and preserving peace through strength, which depends on whether the called-for military dominance is required to perform necessary missions (Department of Defense 2019, 15). Each of these derivative interests is potentially contentious, based on disagreements about international relations theories and/or military-technical assessments.

The quality of grand-strategic analysis would be improved if analysts began their analysis only with fundamental interests, then worked their way to derivative interests. This would increase the transparency of the analysis and clarify the theories that were being employed, thereby exposing key potential sources of disagreement between analyses.

International Environment

A state's ability to achieve its interests depends on its international environment.

How a state's international environment is characterized depends upon the theoretical perspective employed. This is unavoidable because the theory identifies the variables that should (that is, that are believed to) influence a state's policy; the two are inherently intertwined. In this section I describe a defensive realist/rationalist characterization of the international environment. Other theories provide different characterizations that would also be compatible with a rational analysis of grand strategy. I present the defensive realist framing both because it has a variety of analytic strengths and because it captures much of the US grand strategy debate, which I have been using throughout this chapter to illustrate various features of rational grand-strategic analysis.

A defensive realist approach characterizes the international environment in terms of both material and information variables (Glaser 2010). Material variables determine the state's potential military capabilities. Information variables reflect the state's understanding of its adversary's motives and interests.[6] These information variables inform the state's assessment of which other states are adversaries/threats and which are potential allies, and, in turn, influence the risks of cooperative and competitive policies. Other theories include or exclude different variables. For example, an offensive realist framing would not include information variables, focusing instead simply on opposing states' power because it holds that states should assume the worst about opposing states (Mearsheimer 2001). A liberal framing could include variables that capture states' regime types, key international institutions, and the degree of economic interdependence.

Material variables are comprised of power and offense–defense variables. Power is the ratio of the state's resources that can be converted into military assets to the adversary's resources. The relevant resources can include the state's wealth, population, human capital, and level of technological development. Power indicates the potential relative size and quality of states' military forces, not the actual size of their forces. A different conception of power would focus on states' deployed forces, not their potential forces.

Which of the two understandings of power to employ depends on the time frame of the analysis. Grand strategy tends to provide long-term guidance, which makes the more basic understanding of power—power as potential—the more appropriate variable/measure. For example, the US grand strategy of containment, as formulated by George Kennan, was designed for a sustained competition with the Soviet Union. However, under certain conditions a shorter time frame can be appropriate. For example, a shorter time frame can be necessary if an opposing state is changing relatively rapidly—experiencing unanticipated economic growth or deploying military forces more quickly than anticipated. A shorter time frame can also be necessary if the state concludes that an opposing state's interests/goals have changed, which can happen more quickly than material changes.

Power, however, is insufficient for assessing a state's ability to defend itself against attack and to successfully attack others. This is because power does not translate directly into potential military capability—that is, the ability to perform specific military missions. The relative ease of attacking versus defending also matters. Thus, the offense–defense balance—defined as the ratio of the cost of the offensive forces an attacker requires to take territory to the cost of the forces the defender has deployed—is an essential variable (Glaser and Kaufmann 1998; Jervis 1978).[7] The offense–defense balance depends on a variety of factors, including the nature of military technology and geography. When defense has the advantage, equally powerful states will have excellent prospects for successfully defending themselves. When defense has a large advantage, a less powerful state will have good prospects for defending itself against a more powerful state. Defense advantage, however, does not make successful offense infeasible under all conditions; a sufficiently powerful state will be able to invest sufficient resources in military forces to successfully attack a much weaker state even when defense has the advantage.

A couple of examples illustrate the importance of the offense–defense balance and the role it plays in the US debate over grand strategy. Nuclear weapons create a large advantage for deterrence, which is functionally equivalent to defense. Neo-isolationists, who argued following the Cold War that the United States should end its major power alliances in Europe and Asia, built their argument partly on the defense advantage provide by nuclear weapons. According to this analysis, a European hegemon, even if far more powerful than the United States, could not successfully invade or coerce the United States because in an arms race the United States would be able to retain its nuclear retaliatory capabilities. Thus, the United States need worry little about the power—military potential—of such a hegemon (Gholz, Press, and Sapolsky 1997).

Distance and challenging terrain also favor defense. The Atlantic and Pacific Oceans provide the United States with defensive buffers. Thus, in addition to nuclear weapons, neo-isolationists argued that geography further reduces the potential military capability of a Eurasian hegemon. In contrast, states that share borders tend to have greater potential to attack each other. Long borders can also make attack relatively easy because defending the entire border can be beyond the resources of the defending state, which means some positions will be underdefended and thus more vulnerable to attack.

Information about an adversary's motives and interests can play a central role in influencing a state's grand strategy. A state that believes an opposing state—whether driven by security or other motives—is interested in attacking or coercing it or its allies should view the opposing state as a threat to its security and should plan to protect against that state. In contrast, a state that believes an opposing state is not motivated to attack it or its allies should not view the state as a threat and should not invest much to defend against it.[8]

A state's assessment of the threats it faces will be determined by the combination of material variables and this information variable: The extent of the threat posed by an opposing state will depend on its power, the offense–defense balance, and the state's assessment of the opposing state's intentions/motives. An opposing state poses a larger threat when it is more powerful, the offense–defense balance favors offense, and the state believes the opposing state is interested in attacking it (Walt 1984).

A second information variable should influence the state's policy choices: the state's beliefs about the adversary's understanding of the state's own motives. This variable matters because the state is more secure when the opposing state believes that the state is uninterested in attacking it. This is because an insecure adversary might be able to increase its security by attacking the state. Consequently, the state needs to judge whether it should pursue policies that will signal its benign motives, which depends partly on the opposing state's beliefs.

Although many analyzes of grand strategy do not describe the state's international environment is such general terms, they do reflect analysts' understandings of how to characterize the international environment. For example, an assessment that takes as its starting point the threats a state faces is implicitly taking into account the opposing states' capabilities (material variables) and, depending on the theory, may also include the state's beliefs about whether the opposing states have an interest (or derivative interest) in attacking it (which is captured in information variables).

The Cold War grand strategy debate provides an important example of disagreements about these information variables. While so-called hawks and doves agreed on the broad policy of containment, they disagreed about the Soviet Union. Hawks believed that the Soviet Union was a secure state that was driven by ideology and culture to dominate Western Europe. In addition, they believed that Soviet leaders did not see NATO as a threat, possibly because it was comprised of democracies. In contrast, doves believed that Soviet military and foreign policy was driven at least partly by insecurity generated by the combination of NATO's military capabilities and Soviet beliefs about NATO's malign intentions, and were far less convinced that the Soviet Union was determined to conquer Western Europe. These disagreements generated a deep divide—hawks favored competitive policies and were skeptical of arms control, while doves favored more cooperative policies designed to avoid fueling negative political spirals, while providing NATO with adequate deterrent capabilities.

Theories

Theories shape and inform grand-strategic analysis in a variety of ways. As the preceding section highlights, theories play a central role in determining how an analysis characterizes a state's international environment. In addition, theories necessarily play a central role in grand-strategic analysis (and the analysis of international policy more generally) because they provide the *causal links* between a state's policy options, which are intended to achieve its interests and derivative interests, and the outcomes those options are expected to produce. Different theories can, therefore, support different grand strategies. We have already seen this role for theory when discussing derivative interests, with theories establishing the connection between a fundamental interest and derivative interests. Theories arguably play a more visible role, albeit not necessarily a more important one, in grand-strategic analysis of policy options and outcomes.[9]

Deterrence theory, which is among the most intuitive of IR theories, plays an important role in grand-strategic analysis. It holds that a state that faces a threat can increase its security by improving its military capabilities, thereby enhancing its ability to deter by convincing the adversary that the prospects for winning are too low and/or that the costs of war will be too high. Investing more in military forces (internal balancing) and/or forming alliances (external balancing) can accomplish this.

Disagreements about the effectiveness of US military forces and about the requirements of deterrence have significantly influenced the grand strategy debate. For example, disagreements about the effectiveness of NATO conventional forces in Europe, which reflected different beliefs about the requirements of deterrence and about how to model the outcomes of conventional battles, contributed to disagreements about NATO nuclear doctrine. Some analysts argued that NATO conventional forces provided a sufficiently effective deterrent that NATO did not need to also rely on the threat of first use of nuclear weapons; others disagreed, either because they doubted the effectiveness of the conventional forces or because they believed that nuclear threats provided a necessary supplement to conventional deterrence. A second prominent example involves the prospects for deterring nuclear proliferators from using nuclear weapons. Doubts about the effectiveness of deterrence underpinned the Bush administration's policy of preventive war and specifically the US invasion of Iraq. Analysts who were more confident in the United States' ability to deter a nuclear Iraq from using nuclear weapons tended to oppose preventive war.

Defensive realism warns us that the seemingly straightforward policies identified by deterrence theory may under certain conditions not increase the state's security, and could even decrease it. If the adversary believes the state poses a threat (or more precisely, if the state believes its adversary holds this view), then the state needs to consider whether acquiring additional military capabilities will reduce its adversary's security. The adversary's reduced security could pose a danger in two ways—increasing the value the adversary places on expansion that would increase its security and leading the adversary to build forces that offset or more than offset the state's increase.

When in this type of situation, the state faces a security dilemma (Jervis 1978; Glaser 1997; Kydd 2005). In this situation, the state should consider policies that are less threatening, which might include foregoing certain types of weapons systems or building smaller forces. These policies could, however, increase the state's own military vulnerability and in turn its insecurity. How to balance these cooperative and competitive policies depends on the state's understanding of the opposing state's beliefs. When the state believes that the opposing state sees it as a threat, the case for cooperative/restrained policies is stronger; in contrast, if the state believes the opposing state is confident that it is not a threat, then more competitive policies are relatively more attractive. China's grand strategy of peaceful rise was based in large part on this logic: increasing multilateral cooperation was expected to reduce hostile views of China, which would in turn convince states not to balance against its growing military capabilities (Goldstein 2005, 119–128).

Theories of costly signaling explain how a state can use its policy choices to communicate benign motives and demonstrate resolve to protect its interests, and how it can interpret an adversary's policies to update its assessments of opposing states' motives and intentions. A cooperative policy that would be more likely to be chosen by a security seeker than by a state with other reasons for expansion can lead a rational adversary to increase its assessment that the state is in fact a security seeker. If, however, this policy would reduce the state's own military capability, then signaling its benign motives may be too risky. This is another perspective on the security dilemma. Of course, theories that hold that states should assume the worst or consider only states' power, and not their intentions, reject these signaling arguments and also much of the security dilemma's warning against overly competitive policies.

Studies of the US grand strategy debate—both immediately following the Cold War and recently—find that the some of the most basic theoretical questions in IR theory play a defining role in the debate and can be used to provide an insightful mapping of the spectrum of schools of thought (Avey, Markowitz, and Reardon 2018; Posen and Ross 1996/97). All the established schools of thought in the current US grand strategy debate employ some form of realism, with its emphasis on the importance of power and capabilities for deterring attack and producing peace. Different schools, however, favor different strands of realism, which generates significant disagreements about the proper scope of US geopolitical commitments and the broad policies it should pursue to protect them.

Even more fundamental disagreements also play out in the current grand strategy debate in which a triad of liberal arguments support more extensive US global engagement. Some grand strategies complement the realist dimension of their analysis with arguments about the importance of international institutions, which among other virtues are said to provide a hegemonic power with legitimacy that is vital to sustaining the international order (Ikenberry 2012). Other grand-strategy schools place weight on the multiple benefits of democracy, and therefore call for promoting and protecting democracy to achieve US interests, which further expands the recommended reach of US grand strategy. A third liberal argument holds that economic interdependence increases the prospects for peace among major powers. This argument, when wedded to the argument that US global security commitments contribute to preserving the open international economic, also supports calls for global engagement. In contrast, analysts who believe that the open system will persist if the

United States terminates its security commitments tend to support more limited, neo-isolationist policies.

Options—Feasibility, Costs, and Benefits

The state's interests, its international environment, and theories of interaction provide the foundation for identifying and evaluating the state's grand strategy options. Options do not come prepackaged: identifying and fleshing out options is one of the central tasks of a grand-strategic analysis or, for that matter, any policy analysis. That said, in mature debates, the key options have often been identified and much of the debate focuses on their feasibility and desirability—costs and benefits.[10]

Assessments of the feasibility of the state's options will largely reflect its material environment. For example, whether a state can achieve a specific military capability—the ability to perform a military mission—will depend on the state's power and the offense–defense balance. However, even this assessment includes some basic theoretical considerations. For example, how much will the adversary build up in reaction to the state's arming? Will the adversary be willing and able to devote more of its resources to denying this capability than the state is willing to invest, thereby neutralizing the initial investment's impact?

The feasibility of other options may depend even more heavily on theories of interaction. Some theories hold that states balance against power, while others hold that states balance against threats. The feasibility of the United States building its Cold War alliances depended partly on which theory was correct, with the latter turning out to be the stronger. Other theories of alliance formation disagree over whether states are inclined to balance against, or instead bandwagon with, threats. If the latter is correct, the United States will have increasing difficulty holding together its alliances in East Asia as China's power increases, which could require a major revision to US grand strategy. But the balancing arguments tend to be stronger, which means China's rise is unlikely to require such a revision.

The overall desirability of the feasible options—the combination of their costs and benefits—also depends heavily on theories of interaction. All else being equal, a state will prefer to have more military capability than less. But all else is almost never equal. Most obviously, greater military capability usually costs more than less capability. Because a state values prosperity and consumption, there is a tradeoff between greater military capability and greater consumption. This in turn requires the state to assess how much additional security would be provided by the additional military capability. If the state has already achieved a high level of security, then additional military capability may not be worth the additional economic/consumption costs. In addition, greater military capability may not increase a state's security. As described above, the state could face a security dilemma, in which case the pursuit of more ambitious military capabilities could decrease its adversary's security and, in turn, its own security.

Tradeoffs and Conclusions

The final step in a grand-strategic analysis is to assess the overall benefits of the identified options and reach a conclusion. In some ways, this stage of the process is the most subjective: while theories can identify costs and benefits, their size is much harder to estimate. And states will often be comparing apples and oranges. Relevant examples include an incremental increase in security compared to an estimated economic cost; an improvement in deterrence compared to an increased risk of escalation if deterrence fails; benefits that accrue if the adversary is primarily a security-seeking state compared to the costs if the adversary is instead a more malign type of state; and investments required to protect allies compared to the economic benefits of the open international economy (if such benefits actually exist).

Brief examples illustrate the complicated tradeoffs that underpin key grand strategy choices the United States has faced. First, certain policies that a state pursues to increase its military capabilities and increase the credibility of its deterrent threats may not increase its security, even when the policies increase its capability and/or credibility, and do not decrease the adversary's security. During the Cold War, the United States deployed large conventional forces on European soil to enhance both the credibility of its commitment and to improve its conventional deterrent. However, while effective in achieving these purposes, these deployments also virtually guaranteed that the United States would be involved in a large war against the Soviet Union if deterrence failed. During the 1990s, neo-isolationists judged that the best way to stay out of a war in Europe, and thereby increase US security, was to stay out of Europe altogether—that is, not to forward deploy US forces and to leave NATO entirely. This tradeoff continues to apply to current US grand strategy.

A similar example concerns US deployment of nuclear weapons in the European theater: while these weapons likely enhanced deterrence of a Soviet conventional attack, they also increased the probability that, if deterrence failed, the conventional war would go nuclear. There is no clear-cut way to weigh this tradeoff, but a decision had to be made. Finally, adopting an offensive conventional doctrine or a damage-limitation nuclear posture, which could be required by a grand strategy of primacy, could enhance deterrence by increasing the likelihood that a conventional war would escalate to nuclear war, but, if deterrence fails, the probability of nuclear war would be higher. Current debates over US policy toward China reflect analysts' divergent assessments of how to balance these risks (Glaser and Fetter 2016; Talmadge 2017; Green et al. 2017).

In the end, transparency in how an analyst reached a conclusion may be as valuable, probably more valuable, than the specific conclusion she reaches. Identifying tradeoffs and explaining why one side of the ledger is greater enable other analysts to consider those tradeoffs, reevaluate them, and reach their own conclusions. In contrast, masking somewhat intangible comparisons can provide a crisper conclusion, possibly even a more persuasive one. But the quality of the analysis and its contribution to understanding a state's grand strategy options will be smaller.

Appreciating the Rational Approach

Although the rational approach to grand strategy applies to a central set of questions—what grand strategy should a state adopt?—it does not address all the issues that have concerned analysts of grand strategy. For example, it does not attempt to explain why a state adopted one grand strategy over another. Nor does the rational approach attempt to explain why a state adopted a flawed grand strategy—that is, one that lies outside the range of grand strategies that can reasonably be identified with a rational analysis (e.g. Snyder 1991). It does, however, provide the necessary baseline for this analysis. Relatedly, the approach does not engage the question of whether states are capable of effectively formulating and implementing a grand strategy.[11]

A potentially more challenging question concerns the value of the rational approach itself. Given that it is generic and flexible—able to accommodate a full spectrum of state interests and any combination of theories—what does the rational approach help us understand? The rational approach provides a guide to the structure and necessary components of grand-strategic analysis. Employing the approach imposes discipline on analysis. Carefully applied, it produces rigorous and transparent analysis. These result from fully identifying a state's interests and the features of its international environment, and applying theories to establish all of the causal links in the analysis. Derivative interests should be unmasked, shown to be based on fundamental interests and various theoretical and/or empirical judgments. Clear descriptions of the state's international environment facilitate the careful application of theories because most theories are conditional and depend on the specifics of the international environment.

The rational approach can also facilitate the comparison and evaluation of alternative grand strategies. When all of the necessary components of a grand-strategic analysis are clearly laid out, the sources of disagreement have been made explicit. Finally, the discipline imposed by the rational approach can advance research by exposing or clarifying questions—theoretical and empirical—that influence the grand strategy debate but have not been fully explored.

Notes

1. On broad types of military doctrine, see Posen 1984, 16–24, who identifies offensive, defensive, and deterrent types.
2. On strategic choice theories more generally, see Lake and Powell 1999.
3. Bounded rationality is usually applied to the decision-making of individuals and organizations, not to policy analysis. However, even high-quality policy analysis will share some of the limits exhibited by individuals, although maybe not the biases and use of heuristics. For an overview of bounded rationality, see Jones 1999.
4. There is an important question of why analysts looking at the same evidence and body of knowledge disagree about facts and theories; in an ideal rational analysis, they would reach

the same conclusions, which would incorporate agreed upon uncertainties about facts and theories. This standard is not met in real-world debates that I include as rational.
5. In making essentially the same distinction, Avey, Markowitz, and Reardon (2018), use the term "objectives" instead.
6. A complete characterization would also include the state's beliefs about its adversary's understanding of its motives.
7. There is, however, debate over the analytic value of offense–defense variables (see, for example, Lieber 2005), which influences whether they should be included in analyses of grand strategy.
8. This statement includes a simplification: the state would also need to consider whether the opposing state might want to attack it in the future and thus whether to hedge against this possibility.
9. Theories also play a role in explaining how states initially acquire and then update their information about each other. A strategic choice theory takes a state's initial information about opposing states as given—that is, not explained by the theory. However, in the context of grand-strategy debate, loosening this assumption and welcoming a somewhat broader type of rational theory is reasonable, among other reasons because it matches well with the analysis that underpins the actual US debate. And the rationality assumption itself includes theoretical claims, including that states will correctly interpret other state's actions.
10. Desirability and feasibility cannot be entirely separated because a state should be willing to spend more to achieve highly desirable options; nevertheless, this simplification helps shed light on the basic structure of the analysis.
11. For skeptical views, see Betts 2021; Edelstein and Krebs 2015; Edelstein 2021.

References

Art, Robert J. 1991. "A Defensible Defense: America's Grand Strategy After the Cold War." *International Security* 15 (4): 5–53.

Avey, Paul C., Jonathan N. Markowitz, and Robert J. Reardon. 2018. "Disentangling Grand Strategy: International Relations Theory and US Grand Strategy." *Texas National Security Review* 2 (1): 29–51.

Betts, Richard K. 2021. "Is Grand Strategy an Illusion? Or, the Grandiosity of Grand Strategy." In *The Oxford Handbook of Grand Strategy*, edited by Thierry Balzacq and Ronald R. Krebs. Oxford: Oxford University Press.

Brooks, Stephen G., and William C. Wohlforth. 2016. *America Abroad: The United States' Global Role in the 21st Century*. Oxford: Oxford University Press.

Department of Defense. 2019. *Indo-Pacific Strategy Report: Preparedness, Partnership, and Promoting a Networked Region* (June).

Edelstein, David. 2021. "The Limits of Grand Strategy." In *The Oxford Handbook of Grand Strategy*, edited by Thierry Balzacq and Ronald R. Krebs. Oxford: Oxford University Press.

Edelstein, David M., and Ronald R. Krebs. 2015. "Delusions of Grand Strategy: The Problem with Washington's Planning Obsession." *Foreign Affairs* 94 (6): 109–116.

Glaser, Charles L. 1997. "The Security Dilemma Revisited." *World Politics* 50 (1): 171–201.

Glaser, Charles L. 2010. *Rational Theory of International Politics: The Logic of Competition and Cooperation*. Princeton: Princeton University Press.

Glaser, Charles L., and Chaim Kaufmann. 1998. "What is the Offense-Defense Balance and Can We Measure It?" *International Security* 22 (4): 44–82.

Glaser, Charles L., and Steve Fetter. 2016. "Should the United States Reject MAD?: Damage Limitation and US Nuclear Strategy toward China." *International Security* 41 (1): 49–98.

Gholz, Eugene, Daryl G. Press, and Harvey M. Sapolsky. 1997. "Come Home, America: The Strategy of Restraint in the Face of Temptation." *International Security* 21 (4): 5–48.

Goldstein, Avery. 2005. *Rising to the Challenge: China's Grand Strategy and International Security*. Stanford: Stanford University Press.

Green, Brendan Rittenhouse, Austin Long, Matthew Kroenig, Charles L. Glaser, and Steve Fetter. 2017. "Correspondence: The Limits of Damage Limitation." *International Security* 42 (1): 193–207.

Ikenberry, G. John. 2012. *Liberal Leviathan: The Origins, Crisis, and Transformation of the American World Order*. Princeton: Princeton University Press.

Robert Jervis. 1978. "Cooperation Under the Security Dilemma." *World Politics* 30 (2): 167–214.

Jones, Bruce D. "Bounded Rationality." 1999. *Annual Review of Political Science* 2: 297–321.

Kydd, Andrew H. 2005. *Trust and Mistrust in International Relations*. Princeton: Princeton University Press.

Lake, David A., and Robert Powell, eds. 1999. *Strategic Choice and International Relations*. Princeton: Princeton University Press.

Lieber, Keir A. 2005. *War and the Engineers: The Primacy of Politics over Technology*. Ithaca: Cornell University Press.

Lissner, Rebecca Friedman. 2018. "What is Grand Strategy? Sweeping a Conceptual Minefield." *Texas National Security Review* 2 (1): 52–73.

Mearsheimer, John J. 2001. *The Tragedy of Great Power Politics*. New York: W.W. Norton.

Milevski, Lucas. 2016. *The Evolution of Modern Grand Strategic Thought*. Oxford: Oxford University Press.

Posen, Barry R. 1984. *The Sources of Military Doctrine: France, Britain, and Germany Between the World Wars*. Ithaca: Cornell University Press.

Posen, Barry R., and Andrew L. Ross. 1996–97. "Competing Visions for US Grand Strategy." *International Security* 21 (3): 5–53.

Posen, Barry R. 2014. *Restraint: A New Foundation for US Grand Strategy*. Ithaca: Cornell University Press.

Powell, Robert. 1999. *In the Shadow of Power: States and Strategies in International Politics*. Princeton: Princeton University Press.

Renshon, Jonathan. 2017. *Fighting for Status: Hierarchy and Conflict in World Politics*. Princeton: Princeton University Press.

Snyder, Jack. 1991. *Myths of Empire: Domestic Politics and International Ambition*. Ithaca: Cornell University Press.

Silove, Nina. 2018. "Beyond the Buzzword: The Three Meanings of 'Grand Strategy.'" *Security Studies* 21 (1): 27–57.

Talmadge, Caitlin. 2017. "Would China Go Nuclear? Assessing the Risk of Chinese Nuclear Escalation in a Conventional War with the United States." *International Security* 41 (4): 50–92.

Walt, Stephen M. 1987. *The Origins of Alliances*. Ithaca: Cornell University Press.

CHAPTER 8

NETWORK THEORY AND GRAND STRATEGY

DANIEL H. NEXON

IN standard parlance, a "network" is a "group or system of interconnected people of things" ("Network" n.d.). We do not have to look that hard to find mentions of networks in work on grand strategy; writing on the subject often refer to "alliance networks," "economic networks," "terrorist networks," and the like. However, these phrases are often simply descriptive; explicit efforts to *theorize* the relationship between networks and grand strategy remain relatively rare.

The literature that does exist comes in two major, although sometimes overlapping, categories. The most common treats networks as *a specific form of organization*, one distinct from markets and hierarchies. These approaches usually focus on how states should adapt their grand strategies in light of transnational terrorism and other network phenomena. The less common understands networks as part of a more general theoretical approach—associated with social-network analysis and some other relational frameworks. It *describes and compares the structure of all organizations, political orders, and other systems of relationships*, as well as the ways in which networks position actors or entities in relation to one another (see Hafner-Burton, Kahler, and Montgomery 2009).

This essay considers how each approach relates to the study and practice of grand strategy. I argue that both provide plausible ways of theorizing grand strategy in terms of networks, but that the latter holds significantly more promise for scholars and is likely to produce more important insights for practitioners. I conclude with some avenues for further research.

Networks as Specific Organizational Forms

Powell (1990, 300–304) argues that in networks participants are "interdependent" and bound by "norms of reciprocity." In contrast, actors in markets are "independent" from one another; self-interest drives their interactions, such as when firms try to maximize their own profits. Actors in hierarchies exist in relations of dependency. They interact on the basis of "formal" and "bureaucratic" logics, such as in a military chain of command marked by increasing levels of formal authority (see Figure 8.1). Others view networks as less a distinct type of organization and more an intermediate position along the continuum from ideal-typical markets to ideal-typical hierarchies.

As Borgatti and Foster (2003, 995) note, "During the 1980s and 1990s, 'network organization' (and related terms) became a fashionable description for organizational forms characterized by repetitive exchanges among semi-autonomous organizations that rely on trust and embedded social relationships to protect transactions and reduce their costs." This literature often claims that processes of globalization—from greater economic interdependence to new communications technologies—explains the rise of such networks. It also often sees network organizational forms as better suited to a globalized world, as they balance "the flexibility of markets with the predictability of traditional hierarchies."

A number of such networks receive attention in discussions of grand strategy. Examples include *transnational advocacy networks* that link together activists, activist organizations, governments and government officials, and other like-minded actors across national borders (Keck and Sikkink 1998; Betsill and Bulkeley 2004;

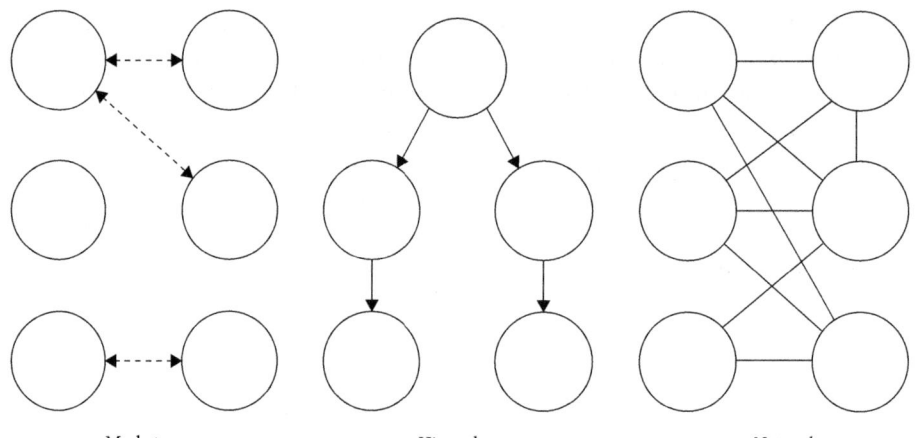

Market:
Temporary Contract-Based Exchange

Hierarchy:
Formal, Institutionalized Lines of Authority

Network:
Interpendent, Reciprocal Connections

FIGURE 8.1 Markets, hierarchies, and networks

Carpenter 2007); *global governance networks*, "defined as networks of interdependent actors that contribute to the production of public governance" in the international arena (Torfing 2012) and that link together non-state actors, international organizations, national-states, private regulatory bodies, and other actors (see Betsill and Bulkeley 2004); and *economic networks*, generally seen in terms of transnational supply and production chains, global financial flows, multinational corporations, and other forms of transnational economic ties that make the world more economically interdependent (Blanchard 2011; Norrlof and Wohlforth 2019; Zhao and Liu 2010).

'Networked Politics Changes Everything'

One subgenre of work on grand strategy claims that states need to adapt to a world increasingly dominated by networks, whether conceptualized as actors (such as "terrorist networks") or mediums for political action (such as "telecommunications networks"). Within this work, we find a continuum between *strong* and *weak* versions. The strongest variant holds that the new networked politics requires a fundamental rethinking of significant aspects of grand strategy. In the late 1990s, Arquilla, Ronfeldt, and Zanini (1999, 75) argued that "the rise of network forms of organization is a key consequence of the ongoing information revolution. Business organizations are being newly energized by networking, and many professional militaries are experimenting with flatter forms of organization." They predicted that "the recent bombings of U.S. embassies in East Africa, along with the retaliatory American missile strikes, may prove to be the opening shots of a war between a leading state and a terror network." It should come as no surprise, then, that after the September 11, 2001, attacks on the United States a number of analysts framed the "War on Terror" as pitting relatively flat-footed state hierarchies against flexible networks. Such observers often argued that nation-states needed to adopt more network-oriented organizational forms in order to successfully compete (Arquilla and Ronfeldt 2001; Sangiovanni 2005).

Slaughter (2009) argues that virtually every important dimension of international affairs—war, diplomacy, business, media, and society—is now networked. "The emerging networked world of the twenty-first century ... exists above the state, below the state, and through the state." Thus "the state with the most connections will be the central player, able to set the global agenda and unlock innovation and sustainable growth." Some suggest that a networked world is dangerous. They recommend that the United States respond by reasserting national sovereignty against multilateral institutions, free trade, and the movement of people across borders. This is one way to interpret the grand strategy of the Trump administration and its criticisms of the "liberal international order": as an argument that efforts to pursue a more "networked world" of transnational trade, governance, and security relationships reduce American security, undermine national identity, and benefit foreign interests (Dombrowski and Reich 2017; Ikenberry 2017; Norrlof 2018; Stokes 2018).

However, many of these recommendations largely track with traditional approaches to grand strategy. For example, Slaughter's recipe for success in a networked world is basically traditional liberal internationalism abroad—multilateral approaches to collective problems, a reduced emphasis on the exercise of hegemony—and liberal politics at home (see also Slaughter 2016). Similarly, the pursuit of greater economic and political autarky is hardly a new principle in the study of grand strategy (see Lobell 2003, 92–94).

Networked Politics Involves New Actors and New Instruments

More subdued approaches argue that states need to adjust, but not completely rethink, their grand strategies in light of the rise of networked politics. This can involve, first, recognizing the ways in which networks—such as nuclear-proliferation networks—can threaten the goals of states, and, second, adopting policies designed specifically to interdict them (Byman 2006; Montgomery 2005). After September 11, the United States used its position within international financial networks to disrupt terrorist funding, and otherwise targeted the financial flows that sustained transnational violence-wielding networks (Acharya 2009).

In this sense, networked politics less undermine the state than provide it with a variety of new power-political instruments (Goddard, MacDonald, and Nexon 2019). Insofar as grand strategy is the "art of reconciling means and ends" (Feaver 2009), this has grand-strategic implications. Growing complexity in global governance networks allows states to "forum shop" and choose friendly international organizations to adjudicate their disputes, implement sanctions, or mobilize military alliances (Alter and Meunier 2009; Busch 2007). Similarly, states should, when formulating grand strategy, take seriously the influence of transnational advocacy networks on state behavior and find ways to exploit or undermine them (Petrova 2016).

Farrell and Newman (2019c) make a compelling version of this claim about "weaponized interdependence." As they (2019b) explain, "new flows of money, information and manufacturing components required the construction of a correspondingly vast infrastructure. Global finance relied on a complex system of institutions to clear transactions and facilitate messaging and communications between different financial institutions." For example, the "Internet was built on routing systems, physical 'pipelines' and redundant information storage facilities to move and house data. Complex supply chains needed equally complex networks that drew together a myriad of assemblers, suppliers and sub-suppliers." These apparently "apolitical" developments "tended to channel global flows through a small number of central data cables and switch points." This "did not just transform economies; it transformed international security. A global economy meant that states' economies were interdependent with each other." The ability of the United States to use the SWIFT system—designed to facilitate international financial flows—to target terrorist financing, and also to enforce sanctions on countries like Iran and Russia, stemmed from its central position in global financial networks (Farrell and Newman 2019b; see also Carter and Farha 2012; Veebel and Markus 2016).

Consider also arguments about "sharp power"—the exploitation by authoritarian powers of the relative openness of liberal democracies for political ends (Walker 2018). Moscow, often through Kremlin-affiliated oligarchs, has backed convivial parties and political movements in other countries. As of 2017, "some 40 pro-Russian NGOs in the Baltic States have received at least €1.5 million," and "Russia has also developed relations with a wide range of anti-EU political parties as well as made loans to the French National Front" (Seely 2017, 54). Russian meddling in foreign elections, such as its pro-Trump and pro-Brexit activities in 2016, exploit networked media and economic environments to undermine political cohesion in NATO and the EU. Moscow has also attempted—with some success—to insert itself as a broker among transnational reactionary and conservative networks in the West. This appears to be part of a broader grand strategy that aims to undermine liberal political and security institutions that Moscow views as a threat, but cannot compete with in direct economic and military terms (Cooley and Nexon 2020, ch. 7; Michael 2019; Walker and Ludwig 2017).

Those who view networked politics as important but not revolutionary see contemporary developments as affecting the specific instruments, but not the general logics, of grand strategy. Cyberspace provides a new medium for espionage and sabotage; social media offers a new environment for propaganda, active measures, and information warfare. While networked politics need to be incorporated into grand-strategic thought, the argument goes, they don't force a rethink of basic principles (see Lindsay 2013; Maness and Valeriano 2015).

Everything Old is New Again

The critics of "networked politics" approaches to grand strategy fall into two camps. Some—usually realists—dismiss the significance of most networks for grand strategy. As they are quick to point out, variations on the "networked politics" theme go back a long way. Similar claims appeared in the 1960s and 1970s under such rubrics as the growth of "interdependence," "complex interdependence," and "transnationalism" (see Keohane and Nye 1971; Keohane and Nye 1973; Morse 1969). Some skeptics consider "networked politics" merely the latest flavor of liberal (or "idealist") arguments that trade interdependence and international institutions can ameliorate power-political competition and reduce the likelihood of the use of force (see Mearsheimer 1993; Sterling-Folker 2000). When it comes to the "dark side" of networked politics—transnational terrorist and criminal networks—skeptics point out that it is relatively easy to make much of such threats in the absence of great-power competition. At the end of the day, they believe states and their policies drive international politics (for a discussion, see Nexon 2009, 33).

Other critics argue that networked politics are not a new development in international politics. They point to the importance of networks—from transnational terrorists to ideological movements, from economic networks to communication flows—in past periods of human history, especially in the context of the rise and decline of great powers and the security of political communities. For them, good grand-strategic thought should *always* pay attention to networks, and networks' absence is less a function of their importance to international politics than an indictment of mainstream work on grand strategy (Cooley and Nexon 2020, chs. 1–3, 6; Goddard and Nexon 2016; Goddard 2018).

Much of the research that emphasizes the enduring role of transnational forces in world politics works with understandings of networks derived from social-network analysis rather than those used in the "networked politics" approach. Doing so helps make sense of historical variation in the salience of nonstate actors, mobilization dynamics, and the broader texture of power politics. Scholars in this camp argue that we should avoid thinking of "networks versus markets versus hierarchies," but think instead in terms of the network structures of organizations, financial flows, alliances, and the like. This is particularly true for theorizing grand strategy, where network and relational analytics likely help us understand the significance of variation not just in the structure of international order, but also in the kinds of political communities that populate world politics.

Network Analytics and Grand Strategy

The other major approach to the intersection of networks and grand strategy treats networks as a *general analytic device* for picturing, measuring, and conceptualizing *any* structural context. In this approach, every organizational form—let alone every social context—is comprehensible in terms of its network characteristics. The opportunities and constraints faced by states and other actors derive, to one degree or another, from these actors' position within political, economic, social, or other networks of interaction (Avant and Westerwinter 2016; Hafner-Burton, Kahler, and Montgomery 2009; see also Wasserman and Faust 1994).

Within this approach we find a variety of related traditions. These include international-relations scholars who adopt the tools and techniques of formal, quantitative network analysis (see Cranmer and Desmarais 2016; Duque 2018; Hafner-Burton and Montgomery 2006; Kinne 2014; Maoz et al. 2006), as well as scholars who draw upon Charles Tilly's "relational realism" (Tilly 1998; Tilly 2005; see also Diani 2007) and more qualitative, informal approaches that use network concepts (see Jackson and Nexon 2019).

All of these scholars generally share a social ontology, called *relationalism*, that treats interactions and relationships as its basic building blocks. It views agents and structures as constituted by ongoing patterns of interaction and relations. This contrasts with the more common international-relations frameworks, individualism and holism (Wendt 1999, 26).

Individualism treats entities—such as states, firms, and individuals—as the locus of analysis and explains outcomes primarily with reference to their attributes. For example, standard interpretations of the democratic peace hold that *being* a democracy *affects* state behavior such that it will be much less likely to initiate military conflict against another democracy (see Chernoff 2004). Holism treats ordered systems as the starting point of its analysis and "implies a top-down conception of social life ... [that] works downward from irreducible social structures" (Wendt 1999, 26). The logics of systems, often understood in terms of their functional requirements, explain behavior. For example, standard interpretations of structural realism—an approach ubiquitous in scholarly discussions of grand strategy—hold that the anarchical character of the international system creates strong pressures on great powers to pursue balance-of-power politics. If it did not, then it would see itself transformed from anarchy to hierarchy, with a *de jure* or de facto world government (Waltz 1979; see Goddard and Nexon 2005; Nedal and Nexon 2019, 169–74).

Network approaches are not the only variants of relational theory, which also includes many field theories, a number of practice theories, and actor-network theory (see McCourt 2016). Moreover, we find some differences in vocabulary among network approaches, but for our purposes the following will suffice as key concepts and their definitions:[1]

- *Social sites*—any individual, organization, political community, or other entity that forms a "node" in a network. Most social sites are themselves composed of networks, bounded in some way with respect to other social sites in the larger network.
- *Ties*—every interaction or relationship (social, economic, political, or cultural) between two or more social sites forms a tie. Ties may be fleeting or durable, conflictual or cooperative, hierarchical or equitable. Some approaches treat joint affiliation in a common social site, such as an international organization, as generating a tie. Others require evidence of an actual interaction.[2]
- *Networks* are composed of ties, especially relatively durable ones. Analysts might focus on the networks generated by a specific kind of interaction (such as financial flows, alliances, diplomatic relations, or formal governance relationships) or by more general interactions (all economic exchanges, all instances of international cooperation, or any interaction in a specific setting). Networks have measurable properties, such as *density*—the number of actual ties compared to the total number of possible ties (see Figure 8.2). Networks also can take specific structural forms, such as core–periphery arrangements (see Figure 8.3).
- *Positionality* is one way of describing the various structural locations that social sites might occupy in networks and can be compared across networks—that is, make two or more social sites *structurally equivalent*. Positionality might involve

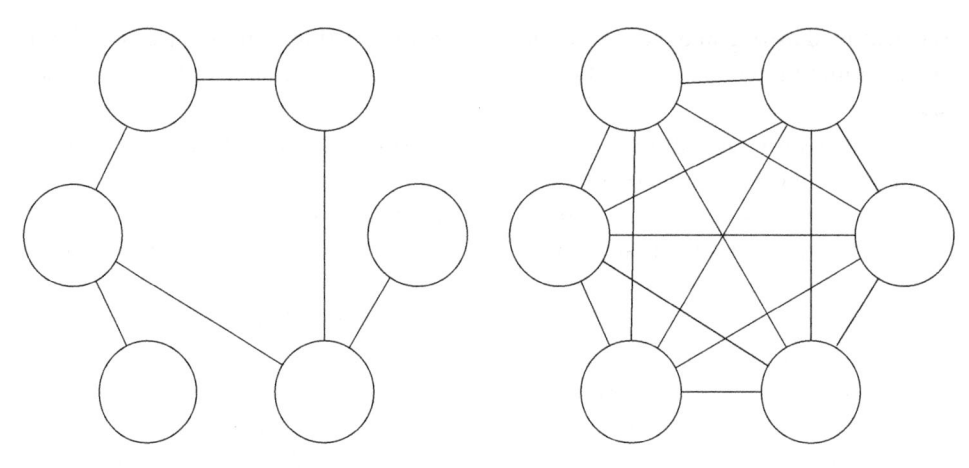

Relatively Sparse Network with
Six Social Sites/Nodes

Maximally Dense Network with
Six Social Sites/Nodes

FIGURE 8.2 Network density

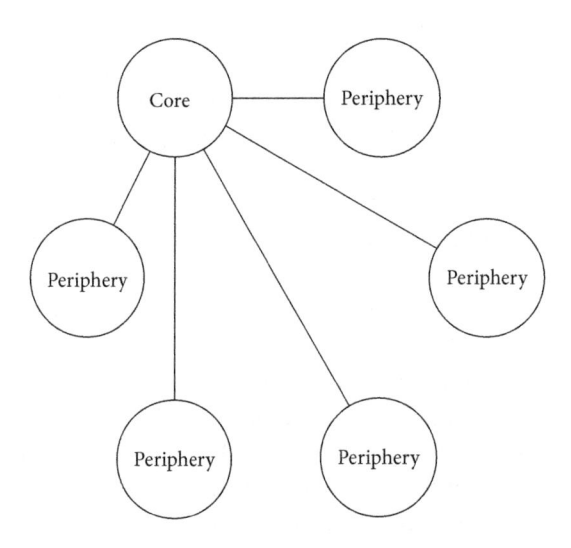

Core–Periphery Network Structure with
Six Social Sites/Nodes

FIGURE 8.3 Core–periphery structure

measurements of various kinds of centrality, such as *degree centrality*, which is measured by "the sum of the value of the ties between that node and every other node in the network" and "tells us how much access a particular node has to the other nodes," or *betweenness centrality* which "corresponds to the number of shortest paths in the network that pass through a particular node, and therefore ... measures the dependence of a network on a particular node for maintaining connectedness." (Hafner-Burton et al. 2009, 563–564)

The qualitative network literature on grand strategy, for its part, often focuses on concepts such as *brokerage*. A social site enjoys a brokerage position when it is tied to two or more other sites that themselves lack ties—that is, a broker bridges structural holes. The core in Figure 8.3 occupies a brokerage position between its five peripheries. Brokerage can also refer to the activation of that bridging position, such that a broker links two or more previously disconnected movements or organizations (per the earlier discussion of the Kremlin attempting to position itself as a broker among right-wing and culturally conservative political movements).

To get a sense of how this approach differs in a concrete setting from the "networks versus hierarchies" framework, consider Farrell and Newman's argument about weaponized interdependence. On its face, it looks like a claim about networked politics—indeed, we examined it in that context. But it actually focuses on *specific* network properties that obtain in *some* domains of interdependence. These properties are inconsistent with the "networked politics" model; weaponized interdependence is not made possible by flat networks with multiple redundancies that depend on trust, but rather by ones characterized by "asymmetric network structures, in which some nodes are 'hubs,' and are far more connected by others"—that is, in which some social sites occupy brokerage positions or have high degree centrality (Farrell and Newman 2019c, 5). States that control those nodes can exercise power by virtue of their ability to choke off access by other states or because they enjoy regulatory authority over the flows that pass through those nodes. States that do not control those nodes find themselves vulnerable, and either need to live with that vulnerability or construct new ties that flatten the overall network (Farrell and Newman 2019b; Farrell and Newman 2019c).

Thus, Farrell and Newman (2019a) note that after pulling out of the Joint Comprehensive Plan of Action (JCPOA)—the multilateral agreement on Iranian nuclear proliferation—and reimposing sanctions on Iran, the United States began to use SWIFT to force compliance from the other signatories of the JCPOA. This has led Washington's European allies to look for ways of routing around SWIFT, including via the Special Purpose Vehicle (SPV). If this shift continues, it would erode Washington's network-positional power in the global financial system and, with it, an important source of American structural (or infrastructural) power.

This kind of network power is not a unique feature of the contemporary period. Before the First World War, the British considered using their control over the hubs of global commerce to collapse the world economy (Lambert 2012). In 1941, Washington famously froze Japanese assets in the United States, effectively cutting off Japan from the overwhelming majority of its imported petroleum and thereby contributing to Tokyo's decision to launch a preemptive war against the United States (Anderson 1975, 201–2).

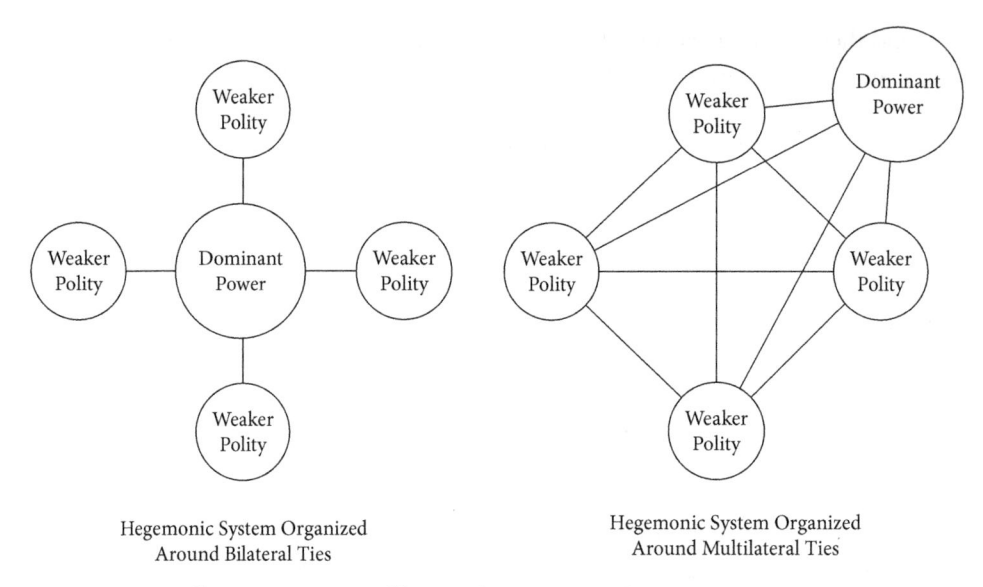

FIGURE 8.4 Different organizational logics of hegemonic orders

Network analytics often provide a way of describing (or recoding) important concepts in debates about grand strategy. This can make it possible to approach old questions in new ways, such as whether relative inclusion or exclusion from the institutions of international order makes conflict more likely (Hafner-Burton and Montgomery 2006), or the nature of the relationship between hegemony and economic processes (Norrlof and Wohlforth 2019; Oatley 2015). Similarly, we can represent the difference between hegemonic orders characterized by multilateralism and bilateralism in network terms (see Figure 8.4), which opens up the possibility of understanding their dynamics using mechanisms and dynamics derived from network theory.

These approaches share a broad analytic sensibility rather than a set of arguments about the direction of world politics and how that matters for grand strategy. Thus, the best way to get a sense of them is to work through some existing lines of scholarship.

Networks as Drivers of Grand Strategy

Network analysis can identify how position in international networks affects grand strategy. For example, Washington's overseas basing network likely not only contributes to its global dominance, but also shapes its grand strategy. It gives the United States a stake in the fate of specific regimes and regions that provide bases and military access to American forces; it makes it possible—and therefore plausible—to project military power. As Heath (2018, 2) argues, the U.S. military developed its expeditionary capability on the foundations of a post–World War II global network of alliances that China conspicuously lacks. The alliances both enabled and drove demand for a powerful U.S. military presence abroad. The United States fought major wars in Korea and Vietnam ... in part to defend key allies and uphold the credibility of its security commitments.

However, as "China has no such network, it faces little demand for such a robust capability."

In general, the location of states in economic, security, and other networks—as well as the structure of those networks—should affect their opportunities and constraints, and hence their grand strategies. For example, MacDonald (2014) finds that the structure of local networks—as well as that of ties between the British and local collaborators—helps account for patterns of British imperial expansion. Goddard (2018) shows how the network-position of rising powers within international orders pushes them toward different kinds of revisionist aims and means. She argues that rising powers vary in terms of how they are plugged into existing networks along two dimensions: their opportunities for access—how "integrated into the dominant [institutional] network"—and brokerage—the extent to which they "bridge structural holes." Access gives rising powers "institutional power," in that they can leverage the existing infrastructure of the international order to pursue their goals. Brokerage provides "entrepreneurial power," in that they can mobilize resources outside of, or on the periphery of, the existing order.

In Goddard's account, these two different positional characteristics generate four ideal-typical kinds of revisionists: isolated revisionists, who enjoy high brokerage and low access, and pursue change in international order via exit; bridging revisionists, who enjoy high access and high brokerage and engage in "rule-based revolution" as they can also bring external leverage to bear on other great powers; rogue revisionists, who face low brokerage and low access and can only proceed by directly challenging the order; and integrated revisionists, who have low brokerage and high access—the fact that they wield influence in the existing order and lack outside options means that they generally limit their effort to transform international order or simply accept the status quo (Goddard 2018, 765–775). For instance, during the interwar period, Imperial Japan found itself marginalized in existing institutions—largely due to the racism of the European powers—and lacked any outside options, as East Asia was already a fairly dense ecosystem of sovereign states and imperial possessions. Thus, Tokyo ultimately embarked on an effort to carve out its own order—which from 1930 onward it called the "Co-Prosperity Sphere"—through the aggressive use of force. In contrast, until the end of the nineteenth century, the United States had low access to European institutions—by design and geography—but extensive opportunities to build relationships in Central and South America. It therefore operated as an isolated revisionist (Goddard 2018, 789–792, 777).

The Creation and Manipulation of Networks as Grand Strategy

The examples above focus on how networks may help explain grand strategies. But states may also create and manipulate network ties as part of their grand strategies. Arguments such as MacDonald's and Goddard's suggest why: international actors—whether states, diplomats, or transnational movements—generate power and influence from their position within various economic, political, and social networks. This gives them incentives to create and alter network ties; it also means that they can deliberately use those ties as power-political instruments.

Network accounts therefore provide an important corrective to traditional work on grand strategy, which tends to see power primarily as a function of military capabilities and economic wealth. For example, Henke (2017) shows that the number of independent ties that the United States has with other countries—common membership in international organizations, bilateral relationships, and so forth—affects Washington's ability to recruit those countries into its multilateral military coalitions. The more ties, the greater likelihood of recruitment. Her explanation focuses on information: the greater the number of ties, the more opportunities for American diplomats and officials to learn information about another country, such as what kind of bargain will entice the government to contribute troops to the coalition.

The United States has generally enhanced its power by building an extensive network of alliances and partnerships and by rooting that network in interpersonal and inter-organizational ties—such as between the US Department of Defense and overseas counterparts. But such networks can prove a double-edged sword. Some case studies suggest that such connections can prove a source of influence for client states and other weaker partners. In the period before and immediately after the 2008 Russia–Georgia war, Georgian officials cultivated close ties with their American counterparts; they used the social capital that they built up through those relationships to convince Washington to forge closer military and economic ties with Georgia (Cooley and Nexon 2016; Kreiger, Souma, and Nexon 2015). The specific structure of those networks almost certainly affects the balance of influence and the flow of information; "fractured social networks," for example, "can foster information bias and distrust" and therefore increase "the likelihood of bargaining failure" (Henke 2018, 120).

Such scholarship suggests that the nature, extent, and structure of networks should factor into grand strategy. There is evidence that it does, such as China's Belt and Road Initiative (BRI) which seeks to leverage the construction of a global infrastructure network as a source of political influence and a mechanism for altering international order in Beijing's favor (Nordin and Weissmann 2018). Moscow, for its part, has attempted to position itself as an important broker for (and supporter of) far-right ideological networks. These include linkages among political parties, such as the post-fascist Freedom Party (FPÖ) in Austria and Lega in Italy, and cultural conservative groups, such as the World Congress of Families (WCF)—which is part of a global anti-LGBTQ network. The aim here seems to be to wedge apart NATO and the EU, or at least undermine their political cohesion (Cooley 2015; Cooley and Nexon 2020, chs. 2 and 6; Klapsis 2015; Michael 2019; Shekhovtsov 2018; on wedge strategies in general, see Crawford 2011).

Along these lines, a number of analysts have noted that hegemonic orders based on bilateral ties (see Figure 8.4) produce a network structure reminiscent of imperial systems. Empires manifest as rimless hub-and-spoke political orders, in which the imperial center relies on divide-and-rule logics and its brokerage position to maintain control of its peripheral territories (see Galtung 1971; Ikenberry 2004; Nexon and Wright 2007; Nye 2002). Indeed, Cha (2010) has found evidence that Washington opted for a bilateral security system in East Asia in order to prevent collusion among clients such as Taiwan and South Korea—collusion, Washington feared, that might entrap the United States into war with North Korea or China. On the other hand, the network structure of multilateral arrangements (see Figure 8.4) may resemble those of confederative and federative political systems. Treating NATO as a security confederation might not only help explain its longevity—its persistence after the end of the Cold War—but also help to illuminate the underlying logic of so-called "liberal order" (see McConaughey, Musgrave, and Nexon 2018).

Conclusion

Casual references to networks are quite common in discussions of grand strategy. Some proponents of specific grand strategies make much of the supposed growth of "networked politics." But only in recent years have scholars and analysts begun to look at grand strategy through the lens of network analysis. Doing so offers promising avenues for understanding the causes of grand strategy, better grappling with the mechanisms and logics that undergird grand-strategic considerations, and identifying new instruments relevant to grand strategy. Moreover, once we move away from the notion that "networked politics" changes everything, a number of the historical cases that inform grand strategy—such as the rise and decline of the Spanish monarchy—may turn out to look rather different than analysts tend to assume (Nexon 2009, ch. 6).

My hope is that this chapter will help orient readers toward a number of different research trajectories involving networks and grand strategy. But let me close by elaborating on a few possibilities. First, a lot of work remains to be done on how governments manipulate transnational network ties in the pursuit of power and influence (see MacDonald 2014). Farrell and Newman (2019c), along with a number of scholars working in international political economy (see also Winecoff 2015), are producing some of the most interesting work here—especially for the study of grand strategy, which is weaker on economic statecraft than on the use of military instruments.

Second, current debates about the fate of the "liberal order" call attention to the close relationship between grand strategy and international order. Grand strategies often focus on altering or maintaining aspects of international order; for states, including hegemonic powers, international orders are "means, mediums, and objects of cooperation and contestation" (Ikenberry and Nexon 2019, 395; see also Goh 2019). But to understand how international orders create opportunities and constraints for grand strategy, we need to move beyond describing them as a catalog of rules and norms. Network approaches likely provide a useful way of understanding the topography of orders and how states are positioned within them. Order has an infrastructure made up of alliance, financial, trade, and other ties among states and other actors. There's a lot more work to do on how the structure of those infrastructures—and how states are positioned within them—shapes their interests, as well as creates opportunities and constraints for influence. At the same time, we might learn a great deal about grand strategy by treating it as a collection of instruments and strategies oriented towards maintaining or altering those networks.

Third, and related, network and relational approaches give us new tools for comparing different kinds of political systems and identifying them in informal manifestations. While no shortage of scholarship exists on how regime type influences state behavior, that scholarship overwhelmingly focuses on matters of democracy and authoritarianism. Thus, we know comparatively little about how, say, confederative, federative, and imperial arrangements shape grand strategy. For example, how much does it matter for their grand strategies that some states have strong imperial characteristics, or that others are federal systems? Some aspects of Chinese foreign policy—such as settling territorial disputes involving cross-national ethnic groups—might reflect imperial management strategies. Both within the Russian Federation—such as viz. Chechnya—and in its "near abroad"—such as Ukraine and Georgia—Moscow relies heavily on an imperial repertoire including divide-and-rule tactics and manipulating territorial conflicts to exercise political control over clients. We haven't even scratched the surface of how federations might behave differently than more national-state systems. Network approaches not only provide a way to identify and compare these kinds of systems, but also to tease out their structural dynamics (MacKay 2019; McConaughey, Musgrave, and Nexon 2018; Mulich 2018).

Finally, as noted earlier, a number of research programs are seeing interesting efforts to marry insights from different relational approaches, most notably network analysis and field theory (McCourt 2016; Mische 2012; Nexon and Neumann 2018). The study of grand strategy would likely benefit by looking at the theoretical insights being generated at the intersection of different relational approaches. At the very least, the embrace of a rather distinctive understanding of relational international-relations theory by a number of Chinese scholars deserves attention, as it may directly inform Chinese grand strategy (see Qin and Nordin 2019).

Notes

1. These terms and their definitions are adapted from Hafner-Burton, Kahler, and Montgomery 2009; and Nexon 2009.

2. Some quantitative network analysts treat simply the possession of a common attribute (such as religion or regime type) as generating a tie, but this, in my view, is inconsistent with relational analysis.

References

Acharya, Arabinda. 2009. *Targeting Terrorist Financing: International Cooperation and New Regimes.* London: Routledge.
Alter, Karen J., and Sophie Meunier. 2009. "The Politics of International Regime Complexity." *Perspectives on Politics* 7 (1): 13–24.
Anderson, Irvine H. 1975. "The 1941 De Facto Embargo on Oil to Japan: A Bureaucratic Reflex." *Pacific Historical Review* 44 (2): 201–231.
Arquilla, John, and David Ronfeldt. 2001. *Networks and Netwars: The Future of Terror, Crime, and Militancy.* Washington, DC: RAND Corporation.
Arquilla, John, Paul Ronfeldt, and Michele Zanini. 1999. "Countering the New Terrorism." In *Conquering the New Terrorism*, edited by Ian O. Lesser, Bruce Hoffman, John Arquilla, David F. Ronfeldt, Michele Zanini, and Brian Michael. Jenkins, 39–84. Washington, DC: RAND Corporation.
Avant, Deborah, and Oliver Westerwinter, eds. 2016. *The New Power Politics: Networks and Transnational Security Governance.* New York: Oxford University Press.
Betsill, Michele M., and Harriet Bulkeley. 2004. "Transnational Networks and Global Environmental Governance: The Cities for Climate Protection Program." *International Studies Quarterly* 48 (2): 471–493.
Blanchard, Jean-Marc F. 2011. "China's Grand Strategy and Money Muscle: The Potentialities and Pratfalls of China's Sovereign Wealth Fund and Renminbi Policies." *The Chinese Journal of International Politics* 4 (1): 31–53.
Borgatti, Stephen P., and Pacey C. Foster. 2003. "The Network Paradigm in Organizational Research: A Review and Typology." *Journal of Management* 29 (6): 991–1013.
Busch, Marc L. 2007. "Overlapping Institutions, Forum Shopping, and Dispute Settlement in International Trade." *International Organization* 61 (4): 735–761.
Byman, Daniel L. 2006. "Remaking Alliances for the War on Terrorism." *Journal of Strategic Studies* 29 (5): 767–811.
Carpenter, R. Charli. 2007. "Setting the Advocacy Agenda: Theorizing Issue Emergence and Nonemergence in Transnational Advocacy Networks." *International Organization* 51 (1): 99–120.
Carter, Barry E., and Ryan M. Farha. 2012. "Overview and Operation of U.S. Financial Sanctions, Including the Example of Iran." *Georgetown Journal of International Law* 44: 903–914.
Cha, Victor D. 2010. "Powerplay: Origins of the U.S. Alliance System in Asia." *International Security* 34 (3): 158–196.
Chernoff, Fred. 2004. "The Study of Democratic Peace and Progress in International Relations." *International Studies Review* 6 (1): 49–78.
Cooley, Alexander. 2015. "Countering Democratic Norms." *Journal of Democracy* 26 (3): 49–63.
Cooley, Alexander, and Daniel Nexon. 2016. "Interpersonal Networks and International Security." In *The New Power Politics: Networks and Transnational Security Governance*, edited by Deborah D. Avant and Oliver Westerwinter, 74–102. New York: Oxford University Press.

Cooley, Alexander, and Daniel Nexon. 2020. *Exit from Hegemony: The Unraveling of the American Global Order*. Oxford: Oxford University Press.

Cranmer, Skyler J., and Bruce A. Desmarais. 2016. "A Critique of Dyadic Design." *International Studies Quarterly* 60 (2): 355–362.

Crawford, Timothy W. 2011. "Preventing Enemy Coalitions: How Wedge Strategies Shape Power Politics." *International Security* 35 (4): 155–189.

Diani, Mario. 2007. "Review Essay: The Relational Element in Charles Tilly's Recent (and Not so Recent) Work." *Social Networks* 29 (2): 316–323.

Dombrowski, Peter, and Simon Reich. 2017. "Does Donald Trump Have a Grand Strategy?" *International Affairs* 93 (5): 1013–1037.

Duque, Marina G. 2018. "Recognizing International Status: A Relational Approach." *International Studies Quarterly* 62 (3): 577–592.

Farrell, Henry, and Abraham Newman. 2019a. "Iran Unilateralism May Undermine America's Financial Hegemony." *Washington Post*, January 31. https://www.washingtonpost.com/news/monkey-cage/wp/2019/01/31/americas-financial-power-over-the-world-faces-a-big-big-challenge/

Farrell, Henry, and Abraham Newman. 2019b. "America's Misuse of Its Financial Infrastructure." *The National Interest*, April 15. https://nationalinterest.org/print/feature/america%E2%80%99s-misuse-its-financial-infrastructure-52707

Farrell, Henry, and Abraham L. Newman. 2019c. "Weaponized Interdependence: How Global Economic Networks Shape State Coercion." *International Security* 44 (1): 42–79.

Feaver, Peter. 2009. "What Is Grand Strategy and Why Do We Need It?" *Foreign Policy* (blog), April 8, 2009. https://foreignpolicy.com/2009/04/08/what-is-grand-strategy-and-why-do-we-need-it/

Galtung, Johan. 1971. "A Structural Theory of Imperialism." *Journal of Peace Research* 8 (2): 81–117.

Goddard, Stacie E. 2018. "Embedded Revisionism: Networks, Institutions, and Challenges to World Order." *International Organization* 72 (4): 763–797.

Goddard, Stacie E., Paul K. MacDonald, and Daniel H. Nexon. 2019. "Repertoires of Statecraft: Instruments and Logics of Power Politics." *International Relations* 33 (2): 304–321.

Goddard, Stacie E., and Daniel Nexon. 2005. "Paradigm Lost? Reassessing Theory of International Politics." *European Journal of International Relations* 11 (1): 9–61.

Goddard, Stacie E., and Daniel H. Nexon. 2016. "The Dynamics of Global Power Politics: A Framework for Analysis." *Journal of Global Security Studies* 1 (1): 4–18.

Goh, Evelyn. 2019. "Contesting Hegemonic Order: China in East Asia." *Security Studies* 28 (3): 614–644.

Hafner-Burton, Emilie M., Miles Kahler, and Alexander H. Montgomery. 2009. "Network Analysis for International Relations." *International Organization* 63 (3): 559–592.

Hafner-Burton, Emilie M., and Alexander H. Montgomery. 2006. "Power Positions: International Organizations, Social Networks, and Conflict." *Journal of Conflict Resolution* 50 (1): 3–27.

Heath, Timothy. 2018. *China's Pursuit of Overseas Security*. Santa Monica, CA: RAND Corporation.

Henke, Marina E. 2017. "The Politics of Diplomacy: How the United States Builds Multilateral Military Coalitions." *International Studies Quarterly* 61 (2): 410–424.

Henke, Marina E. 2018. "The Rotten Carrot: US-Turkish Bargaining Failure over Iraq in 2003 and the Pitfalls of Social Embeddedness." *Security Studies* 27 (1): 120–147.

Ikenberry, G John. 2004. "Liberalism and Empire: Logics of Order in the American Unipolar Age." *Review of International Studies* 30 (4): 609–630.

Ikenberry, G. John. 2017. "The Plot against American Foreign Policy: Can the Liberal Order Survive?" *Foreign Affairs* 96 (1): 2–9.

Ikenberry, G. John, and Daniel H. Nexon. 2019. "Hegemony Studies 3.0: The Dynamics of Hegemonic Orders." *Security Studies* 3 (28): 395–421.

Jackson, Patrick Thaddeus, and Daniel H. Nexon. 2019. "Reclaiming the Social: Relationalism in Anglophone International Studies." *Cambridge Review of International Affairs* 32 (5): 1–19.

Keck, Margaret E., and Katheryn Sikkink. 1998. *Activists Beyond Borders: Advocacy Networks in International Politics*. Ithaca, NY: Cornell University Press.

Keohane, Robert O., and Joseph S. Nye. 1973. "Power and Interdependence." *Survival* 15 (4): 158–165.

Keohane, Robert O., and Joseph S. Jr. Nye. 1971. "Introduction." In *Transnational Relations and World Politics*, edited by Robert O. Keohane and Joseph S. Jr. Nye, xii–xvi. Cambridge, MA: Harvard University Press.

Kinne, Brandon J. 2014. "Dependent Diplomacy: Signaling, Strategy, and Prestige in the Diplomatic Network." *International Studies Quarterly* 58 (2): 247–259.

Klapsis, Antonis. 2015. *An Unholy Alliance: The European Far Right and Putin's Russia*. Brussels: Wilfried Martens Centre for European Studies.

Kreiger, Miriam, Shannon L.C. Souma, and Daniel Nexon. 2015. "US Military Diplomacy in Practice." In *Diplomacy and the Making of World Politics*, edited by Ole Jacob Sending, Vincent Pouliot, and Iver B. Neumann, 220–255. Cambridge: Cambridge University Press.

Lambert, Nicholas A. 2012. *Planning Armageddon: British Economic Warfare and the First World War*. Cambridge, MA: Harvard University Press.

Lindsay, Jon R. 2013. "Stuxnet and the Limits of Cyber Warfare." *Security Studies* 22 (3): 365–404.

Lobell, Steven E. 2003. *The Challenge of Hegemony: Grand Strategy, Trade, and Domestic Politics*. Ann Arbor: University of Michigan Press.

MacDonald, Paul K. 2014. *Networks of Domination: The Social Foundations of Peripheral Conquest in International Politics*. Oxford: Oxford University Press.

MacKay, Joseph. 2019. "Legitimation Strategies in International Hierarchies." *International Studies Quarterly* 63 (3): 717–725.

Maness, Ryan C., and Brandon Valeriano. 2015. *Russia's Coercive Diplomacy: Energy, Cyber, and Maritime Policy as New Sources of Power*. New York: Palgrave Macmillan.

Maoz, Zeev, Ranan D. Kuperman, Lesley Terris, and Ilan Talmud. 2006. "Structural Equivalence and International Conflict: A Social Networks Analysis." *Journal of Conflict Resolution* 50 (5): 664–689.

McConaughey, Meghan, Paul Musgrave, and Daniel H. Nexon. 2018. "Beyond Anarchy: Logics of Political Organization, Hierarchy, and International Structure." *International Theory* 10 (2): 181–218.

McCourt, David M. 2016. "Practice Theory and Relationalism as the New Constructivism." *International Studies Quarterly* 60 (3): 475–485.

Mearsheimer, John. 1993. "False Promise of International Institutions." *International Security* 19 (3): 5–49.

Michael, Casey. 2019. "Hacked Emails List Right-Wing Fundraiser Partying with Russian Fascists and Oligarchs." *Think Progress*, January 30. https://thinkprogress.org/hacked-emails-list-right-wing-fundraiser-partying-with-russian-fascists-and-oligarchs-c964038dcbad/

Mische, Ann. 2012. "Bourdieu in Contention and Deliberation: Response to Lamont and Lizardo: Response to Lamont and Lizardo." *Sociological Forum* 27 (1): 245–250.

Montgomery, Alexander H. 2005. "Proliferation Determinism or Pragmatism? How to Dismantle an Atomic Bomb Network." *International Security* 30 (2): 153–187.

Morse, Edward L. 1969. "The Politics of Interdependence." *International Organization* 23 (2): 311–326.

Mulich, Jeppe. 2018. "Transformation at the Margins: Imperial Expansion and Systemic Change in World Politics." *Review of International Studies* 44 (4): 694–716.

Nedal, Dani K, and Daniel H Nexon. 2019. "Anarchy and Authority: International Structure, the Balance of Power, and Hierarchy." *Journal of Global Security Studies* 4 (2): 169–189.

"Network." n.d. Oxford Dictionaries | English. https://en.oxforddictionaries.com/definition/network, accessed June 4, 2019.

Nexon, Daniel H. 2009. *The Struggle for Power in Early Modern Europe: Religious Conflict, Dynastic Empires, and International Change*. Princeton, N.J.: Princeton University Press.

Nexon, Daniel H., and Iver B. Neumann. 2018. "Hegemonic-Order Theory: A Field-Theoretic Account." *European Journal of International Relations* 24 (3): 662–686.

Nexon, Daniel H., and Thomas Wright. 2007. "What's at Stake in the American Empire Debate." *American Political Science Review* 101 (2): 253–271.

Nordin, Astrid H. M., and Mikael Weissmann. 2018. "Will Trump Make China Great Again? The Belt and Road Initiative and International Order." *International Affairs* 94 (2): 231–249.

Norrlof, Carla. 2018. "Hegemony and Inequality: Trump and the Liberal Playbook." *International Affairs* 94 (1): 63–88.

Norrlof, Carla, and William C. Wohlforth. 2019. "Raison de l'Hégémonie (The Hegemon's Interest): Theory of the Costs and Benefits of Hegemony." *Security Studies* 28 (3): 422–450.

Nye, Joseph. 2002. *The Paradox of American Power: Why the World's Only Superpower Can't Go It Alone*. Oxford: Oxford University Press.

Oatley, Thomas. 2015. *A Political Economy of American Hegemony*. Cambridge: Cambridge University Press.

Petrova, Margarita H. 2016. "Rhetorical Entrapment and Normative Enticement: How the United Kingdom Turned From Spoiler Into Champion of the Cluster Munition Ban." *International Studies Quarterly* 60 (3): 387–399.

Powell, Walter W. 1990. "Neither Market nor Hierarchy: Network Forms of Organization." *Research in Organizational Behavior* 12: 295–336.

Qin, Yaqing, and Astrid H. M. Nordin. 2019. "Relationality and Rationality in Confucian and Western Traditions of Thought." *Cambridge Review of International Affairs* 32 (5): 601–614.

Sangiovanni, Mette Eilstrup. 2005. "Transnational Networks and New Security Threats." *Cambridge Review of International Affairs* 18 (1): 7–13.

Seely, Robert. 2017. "Defining Contemporary Russian Warfare." *The RUSI Journal* 162 (1): 50–59.

Shekhovtsov, Anton. 2018. *Russia and the Western Far Right: Tango Noir*. London, UK: Routledge.

Slaughter, Anne-Marie. 2009. "America's Edge." *Foreign Affairs* 88 (1): 94–113.

Slaughter, Anne-Marie. 2016. "How to Succeed in the Networked World," *Foreign Affairs* 95 (6): 76–89.

Sterling-Folker, Jennifer. 2000. "Competing Paradigms or Birds of a Feather? Constructivism and Neoliberal Institutionalism Compared." *International Studies Quarterly* 44 (1): 97–119.

Stokes, Doug. 2018. "Trump, American Hegemony and the Future of the Liberal International Order." *International Affairs* 94 (1): 133–150.

Tilly, Charles. 1998. "International Communities, Secure or Otherwise." In *Security Communities*, edited by Emmanuel Adler and Michael Barnett, 397–412. Cambridge: Cambridge University Press.

Tilly, Charles. 2005. *Identities, Boundaries, and Social Ties*. Boulder, CO: Paradigm Publishers.

Torfing, Jacob. 2012. "Governance Networks." In *The Oxford Handbook of Governance*, edited by David Levi-Faur. Oxford: Oxford University Press.

Veebel, Viljar, and Raul Markus. 2016. "At the Dawn of a New Era of Sanctions: Russian-Ukrainian Crisis and Sanctions." *Orbis* 60 (1): 128–139.

Walker, Christopher. 2018. "What Is 'Sharp Power'?" *Journal of Democracy* 29 (3): 9–23.

Walker, Christopher, and Jessica Ludwig. 2017. "The Meaning of Sharp Power." *Foreign Affairs*, November 16. https://www.foreignaffairs.com/articles/china/2017-11-16/meaning-sharp-power.

Waltz, Kenneth N. 1979. *Theory of International Politics*. New York: Addison-Wesley.

Wasserman, Stanley, and Katherine Faust. 1994. *Social Network Analysis: Methods and Applications*. Cambridge: Cambridge University Press.

Wendt, Alexander. 1999. *Social Theory of International Politics*. Cambridge: Cambridge University Press.

Winecoff, William Kindred. 2015. "Structural Power and the Global Financial Crisis: A Network Analytical Approach." *Business and Politics* 17 (3): 495–525.

Zhao, Quansheng, and Guoli Liu. 2010. "Managing the Challenges of Complex Interdependence: China and the United States in the Era of Globalization." *Asian Politics & Policy* 2 (1): 1–23.

CHAPTER 9

MAKING GRAND STRATEGY IN PRACTICE

CHRISTIAN BUEGER AND FRANK GADINGER

Concepts derived from social theory, such as culture, discourse, or narrative are increasingly providing new resources for the understanding of strategy, how it is made, the sources that inform it, and the effects that it has (see Nexon, Balzacq, Kornprobst, and Neal in this volume). Indeed, the renaissance of strategy studies and works on grand strategy provides ample opportunities for theoretical and methodological innovation. In this chapter we introduce and discuss scholarship on strategy that is inspired by "practice theory." Across the social sciences, practice theory has become known as a family of theorizing that argues for the importance of basing our thinking in practical activities. Practices, understood as a nexus of doing and sayings, become the main unit of analysis. What are the consequence of practice theory for understanding strategy and grand strategy? What does the perspective allow one to do and see? What kind of productive research perspectives can be developed on practice-theoretical grounds? These are the questions we aim at addressing in this chapter.

In its widest sense, practices are sets or patterns of actions—doings and sayings—organized by shared forms of knowledge. Understanding strategy as practice is to argue that strategy is the outcome of patterns of actions, might be embedded in such patterns, and as such also has impact on them. The study of strategy becomes a study of activities, relations, and the larger patterns these may form. Practice thinking shifts emphasis to the myriad of activities involved in strategy-making. Many of these activities are deliberate and conscious, others might be less grand, and more mundane. They might include analytical activities, such as the study of the state of the international system, or the quantitative analysis of a distinct threat that a strategy should consider. But what equally may influence the content of strategy are how meetings among strategists are organized, who participates in such meetings, or what technology is used to agree on common phrases. Also, the way a strategy is turned into a document that can be circulated, how it is designed, what pictures, graphs, and tables are included, and how it is circulated may well influence the effects that a strategy may achieve. Strategy-making implies arranging the world in a particular manner, and understanding these practical arrangements and their effects on actions is one of the core goals of understanding strategy as practice.

The practice approach is an emergent and increasingly prominent way across the social sciences and international relations. It is gaining a strong foothold in the study of strategy as well. In organization studies in particular, a research direction has evolved that centers on practice to understand business strategy. This direction has become known as "strategy as practice" research and constitutes one of the predominant ways that organizational strategizing is investigated. It is a rather heterogeneous movement, documented in the leading handbook (Golsorkhi et al. 2010), and to some degree it has become an open intellectual space for the introduction of various practice-oriented theories. In the discipline of international relations, practice theory has become since the late 2000s one of the most innovative research programs, with an increasingly strong voice in subfields including security studies, peacebuilding, diplomacy, and international organization research (Bueger and Gadinger 2016; Bueger 2016). In strategy studies, Iver Neumann and Henrikki Heikka (2005) are likely the first to have explored how practice theory can contribute to the understanding of strategy and strategic culture in particular. This has since been followed by a range of studies that draw on the innovation potential of practice theory to develop new ways of understanding the making of strategy in particular. For instance, Frederic Merand and Amelie Forget (2013) draw on the concepts of Pierre Bourdieu to conceptualize a field of strategy-making.

Practice theory provides an innovative and diverse conceptual and methodological tool box, but not a unified approach that relies on shared generic principles. In consequence, practice thinking has variedly been understood as a "turn"—that is an overall shift in perspective—or as a "family" of approaches which have resemblance to each other but do not necessarily fully agree on each and every aspect (Reckwitz 2002). Several different but related and overlapping lines of theorizing practice have been developed in international relations and security studies, which share a number of commitments, but tend to disagree over some fundamental questions such as how to conceive of order and change or the materiality of practice (Bueger and Gadinger 2018). While the objective of this chapter is not to discuss the foundations or the key commitments of practice theorizing, our goal in the following is to explore a range of avenues through which practice-theoretical ideas can be employed to enrich our understanding of strategy. This reflects the fact that at the time of writing and in contrast to the wider international relations discipline, the practice turn has not fully reached strategic studies yet. The range of studies is still limited. Rather than taking a backward-leaning perspective and conducting a stock-taking exercise, this chapter provides an outlook and exploration of how practice theorizing has the potential to inform strategic studies.

This chapter draws on practice-theoretical scholarship to investigate what difference it might make to understand strategy as a practice. To do so, we start from a brief review of some of the basic directions of practice thinking, largely drawing on research from organization studies but also the more general international relations discussion. We then set out different directions for studying practices, drawing on existing studies but broadening the outlook by indicating and speculating how the concepts of practice theorizing might illuminate strategy research. We start out from an exploration of how practice theorists have started to rethink two core concepts: security communities and strategic culture. We proceed in discussing how the controversial nature of strategy provides an interesting starting point for understanding strategy-making as a social struggle. We then discuss how ideas from practice-theoretical approaches known as actor-network theory (ANT), narrative theory, and new materialism provide new avenues for research. We conclude with a summary and an outlook of the potential of strategy as practice to enrich our understanding of foreign and security policymaking.

Practice Theorizing and Strategy

The introduction of practice thought in international relations and strategic studies is closely linked to the rise of culturalist and constructivist ideas (in strategic studies e.g. Neumann and Heikka 2005; van Apeldoorn and de Graaff 2014; Goddard and Krebs 2015). Practice theories offer partially complementary, and partially innovative answers to how strategy is produced and why it matters. They join culturalist and constructivist arguments that strategy as well as "grand strategy" is the outcome and effect of the practices of strategizing actors. Such strategy makers include security policymakers, security experts, bureaucrats, or civil society actors (e.g., Pirani 2016; van Apeldoorn and de Graaff 2014). Practice theory, however, foregrounds much stronger practical activities (such as the everyday production of strategy documents, or public legitimation) as well as the role of material artifacts (e.g., strategy documents) or technologies (e.g., communication tools). It also argues that strategy should be seen from a processual perspective (and hence challenges any distinctions between "grand" and "emergent strategy," see Popescu 2018).

Such a perspective may fill some of the gaps that Balzacq, Dombrowski, and Reich (2019, 22) identified in current debates on grand strategy. They argue that many important questions remain unresolved in existing literature, for example: "What drives strategic change or adjustment? How do we know when (and under what conditions) a grand strategy changes? Who is responsible for their formulation? Do heroic individual strategists (like George Kennan) develop grand strategies, or does it fall to what Williamson Murray refers to as 'corporate bodies'?" (Balzacq et al. 2018, 22). Practice theorists do not have a definite answer to these questions, but they aim at foregrounding these inner workings of strategy-making that often do not receive full attention in the traditions of grand strategy.

The potential for starting out from practice has so far been best indicated in organization studies and their focus on organizational strategy. As Spee and Jarzabkowski (2009, 69) have phrased it in an agenda-setting contribution, the practice perspective is concerned with "the doing of strategy; who does it, what they do, how they do it, what they use, and what implications this has for shaping strategy." Strategy as practice is an umbrella term that describes the myriad of activities that lead to the creation of organizational strategies. This includes strategizing in the sense of more or less deliberate strategy formulation, the organizing work involved in the implementation of strategies, and all the other activities that lead to the emergence of organizational strategies, conscious or not (Vaara and Whittington 2012, 3). As Jarzabkowski (2005, 4) summarizes it, the aim is

> to understand the messy realities of doing strategy as lived experience; to go inside the world of strategy practitioners as they struggle with competing priorities, multiple stakeholders and excessive but incomplete information in an attempt to shape some coherent "thing" that may be perceived as a strategy by markets, financial institutions and consumers. Strategy as practice is thus concerned with the detailed aspects of strategizing; how strategists think, talk, reflect, act, interact, emote, embellish and politicize, what tools and technologies they use, and the implications of different forms of strategizing for strategy as an organizational activity.

Several core tenets come through in this programmatic statement. For researchers, the most important unit are practices within organizations (businesses and corporations), yet these practices include the relations to their environments (markets, financial institutions, consumers). Researchers in particular are concerned with a micro-level, in scrutinizing the activities of strategists, their cognitive and emotional states, bodily movements, and the tools and technologies they use. This often includes detailed ethnographies, such as on the organization of meetings (Jarzabkowski and Seidl 2008), the use of PowerPoint (Kaplan 2011), or the movement of hands (Bürgi, Jacobs, and Roos 2005). In such studies, new methodological avenues are pursued that go beyond conventional interview strategies and engage in various forms of ethnography, ethnomethodology, or action research (Bürgi, Jacobs, and Roos 2005; Eikeland and Nicolini 2011). In employing such methods, researchers attempt to seek proximity to collaborate with, and contribute to the work of strategists.

Practice approaches make a number of dedicated claims. Firstly, they join other cognitive, culturalist, and constructivist approaches in arguing that strategy cannot be explained by instrumental rationality, but instead needs to be approached as a collective process of meaning-making and ordering the world. In consequence, there is no optimal, most efficient strategy or a way to evaluate a strategy as such. Nor are there predefined sources of strategy. Secondly, rather than a technical exercise driven by instrumental rationality, strategy-making is a political process in which different strategists struggle over ideas and meanings. Instead of rationality, the process is driven by taken-for-granted knowledge, routines, or the positioning of actors. Thirdly, although there is a set of actors that are more likely to participate in strategy-making, which actor strategizes and is relevant is largely an empirical question. It is not a predefined set of actors, such as military strategists that matter the most, given that strategy-making is understood as a political process. Fourthly, the perspective attends to the myriad of practices through which strategy is made. As is explored in the following, some scholars summarize practices as larger patterns, such as the formulation of doctrines, civil–military relations, and procurement, partnership programs, military planning, or threat construction. Others aim at going micro, in investigating linguistic and bodily movements, or mundane activities such as the organization of meetings, handling of PowerPoints, or the processing and analysis of data. The next sections explore these themes in more detail.

Reinterpreting Classical Concepts through Practice Lenses

One source for the introduction of practice-theoretical ideas to the strategy debate was the debate on strategic culture. The strategic culture approach was introduced as a way to study how elites and decision-makers interpret and assess the international system, and to understand how perceptions, ideas, beliefs, or norms shape understandings of foreign and security policy as well as the use of the military instrument (Bloomfield 2012). The strategic culture debate hence draws on and is grounded in concepts known in the wider discipline as cognitivist, constructivist, or sociological approaches.

As part of a special issue on the strategic cultures of the Nordic countries, Neumann and Heikka (2005) proposed a renewed conceptual framework taking practice-theoretical ideas into account. The basis for this framework was Iver Neumann's argument (2002) that conceptualized culture as a dynamic interplay between discourse and practice, drawing on the insights of Ann Swindler's sociological theory of practice (1986). Neumann and Heikka (2005) argue for the need to go beyond a reified concept of culture in order to gather a dynamic and specific framework for empirical analysis. They suggest refashioning the concept of strategic culture as dynamic interplay between the discourse of grand strategy and specific practices. For them, grand strategy is a particular discourse, a broad agreement concerning the character of the international environment and which problems need to be addressed, that comes to assume a taken-for-granted quality and as such provides the preconditions for actions. Grand strategy is reconceptualized "from being a coverall term on a par with strategic culture, to being a coverall term for all *preconditions* for action" (Neumann and Heikka 2005, 13; emphasis in original). Grand strategy, then, "is seen as a set of preconditions for action, at a specific time and in a specific place, that may exist on more or less systematized form, and that is actualized in practices" (Neumann and Heikka 2005, 14). Stressing that discourse is dependent on actualization, they outline three particular practices through which grand strategy is actualized: doctrines, civil–military relations, and procurement. Doctrines are formulations which set priorities among types of forces and how they might be used. Civil–military relations include those activities regulating the interplay between political and military leaderships, including, for instance, budgetary practices, or the military's handling of information (Neumann and Heikka 2005, 16). Procurement refers to relations to the industry and the management of resources.

Such a reformulation opens up the prospect of a different research agenda. First, it entails that we think about grand strategy not as a series of explicated statements but rather as located in the realm of preconditions for formulating such in the first instance. Second, grand strategy may or may not be consciously held, inasmuch as a grand strategy is a phenomenon that any polity has, at least potentially (Neumann and Heikka 2005, 13). Indeed, it is one of the intentions of this practice-oriented notion of grand strategy to move away from a great power focus and to argue that every state's foreign and security policy can be analyzed through such lenses.

Neumann and Heikka's innovative proposal has, at least partially, inspired a set of studies on European and African states (in particular Rasmussen 2005; Williams and Haacke 2008; Pirani 2010; Giegerich and Jonas 2012), research on European grand strategy (e.g., Edwards 2006; Rogers 2009), as well as further research exploring Swidler's theory of practice to understand the change and continuity of a country's strategic culture (Pirani 2016). Yet, their framework has been read more as a contribution to the strategic culture debate than as the outline of a genuine practice-theoretical take on strategy. As such, despite its analytical potential and its strong argument for studying activities, it has suffered the same fate as the concept of strategic culture and has fallen out of fashion.

Practice-theoretical discussions of security communities offer another means to revisit core concepts of strategic studies. Security communities, such as NATO or the EU, provide a context and form of aggregate agency for grand strategy, an instrument in strategy, as well as a potential end. The security community literature is not only important in terms of the use of military force (or restraint thereof), but also concerning whether and how political units other than the state, such as NATO, the EU, or ASEAN, develop agency and a shared grand strategy. A wave of literature offers practice-theoretical readings of security communities, arguing that it is not norms and values which provide for peaceful relations and coherence within communities, but shared patterns of practical interaction.

These reformulations of security communities have been significantly influenced by the "community of practice" framework as advanced in organization studies in particular by Etienne Wenger (1998). For Wenger (1998), a community of practice is bound together through relations in three dimensions: mutual engagement among the members of a community; joint enterprises through which they negotiate what matters to the community and what to do; as well as shared resources that the community has developed over time, including routines, concepts, and tools. For Adler and Pouliot (2011, 18) such an understanding implies that communities of practices, are "social spaces where structure and agency overlap and where knowledge, power and community intersect." They are, hence, "intersubjective social structures that constitute the normative and epistemic ground for action, but they are also agents, made up of real people, who—working via networks channels, across national borders, across organization divides, and in the halls of government—affect political, economic, and social events" (Adler and Pouliot 2011, 19).

The concept of community practice is open in scale and might hence refer to subnational, national, or transnational entities. This understanding of community has been advanced in security studies by a range of scholars, including Emmanuel Adler and Vincent Pouliot (Adler 2008; Adler and Greve 2009; Pouliot 2008).

Revising the concept of regional security communities through such lenses, Adler (2008; Adler and Greve 2009) suggests that, understood as communities of practice, these are composed of a set of intersecting repertoires of practices. Such practices including self-restraint, diplomacy, cooperative security practices, developing common enterprises and projects, as well as practices of military planning, confidence-building, or policy coordination. Adler (2008) in particular analyzes NATO through such lenses, and shows how the organization's enlargement process can be interpreted as an attempt to spread and diffuse these practices. The repertoire is learned and performed by NATO agents through practical activities, such as joint training and planning, common initiatives such as the Partnership for Peace, and mutual exchange on an everyday basis (Adler 2008, 210). This practice-based view investigates how the emergence of shared practices influences the identity and ends of states and explains how transnational communities of strategy-making evolve, as in the case of NATO.

While not explicitly addressing grand strategy, it emerges from Adler's outline that the making of strategy can be interpreted as a joint enterprise and as a form of mutual engagement that forms security communities of practice. Communities of practice are both the context and the agent of making strategy. Security community-building can be, moreover, an explicit strategic goal, as is the case for ASEAN (Adler and Greve 2009, 76), where developing the repertoire of practices through joint enterprises and mutual engagement provides the means to achieve them. In this line of research, the security communities of practice framework provide a rich tool to understand strategy-making, in particular on a regional level. The security community of practice framework and Wenger's original framework has inspired a rich literature, not least given its openness in scale. So far, it has primarily been adopted to understand security diplomacy in the European context (Bicchi and Bremberg 2017; Hofius 2016).

These practice-theoretical revisions of the constructivist conceptions of strategy culture and security communities have breathed new air into established research programs. The focus on practices here provides a different take on how culture and community is produced through everyday activities. We turn next to perspectives that take contestations around strategy as a starting point and offer a reading of the making of strategy as a field of practices or as a controversy.

Strategy as Social Struggle

What constitutes "grand strategy," what kind of object the concept refers to, and whether a dedicated government "has" grand strategy is often heavily contested. Nina Silove (2018, 28) rightly argues that despite the increasing popularity of the term, it is a slippery, fuzzy, and jumbled concept. Many foundational questions arise around the subject, as Silove (2018, 28) suggests: "Does grand strategy 'exist'? Is grand strategy intentional? Do all states have grand strategies, or only great powers? And to what extent is grand strategy constant or flexible?" Balzacq, Dombrowski, and Reich (2019, 67) similarly diagnose that definitions "refer to completely different activities and, hence, whose analytical merits are difficult to evaluate." Some authors focus exclusively on traditional military threats; others also include economic dimensions; and policymakers and official strategy documents often extend the analysis to nontraditional threats such as climate change, pandemics, and economic security. For Balzacq, Dombrowski, and Reich (2019, 67) this lack of conceptual rigor "trammels rather than facilitates communication and understanding among scholars (and indeed policymakers)." Their solution is to classify definitions into two traditions, a narrow classicist understanding and a wider International Relations one.

The de-essentialist understanding of strategy as practice challenges such proposals. It posits that the disagreement over the meaning of strategy and whether a country or government "has" strategy is not a problem to be defined away; it presents an opportunity to learn about strategy-making. The controversy over the meaning, content, and use of strategy becomes an object of research. Practice theory provides at least two promising directions to study the struggles of strategy-making.

The Bourdieusian concept of a "field" provides one of such avenues. A field is a social space of interaction. The concept aims at overcoming the division in which actors are seen as either driven by instrumental rationality, or by culture; that is, the view that actors are the victims of context, beliefs, norms, or rules and lack a strategic sense (Williams 2007, 3; Mérand and Forget 2013, 96). Through the concept of "field," spaces such as the state, or international institutions such as the EU, have been reinterpreted beyond formal institutions and rules, and deconstructed as coherent actors (Mérand and Forget 2013; Berling 2012). In the most explicit attempt to understand strategy through such lenses, Mérand and Forget (2013) propose to study strategy as a field, starting out from the question: how do certain sets of ideas become strategic policy? Addressing the question requires that we reconstruct the strategic field; that is, "the social space in which different actors who are interested in strategic policy vie to maintain and improve their position" (Mérand and Forget 2013, 102). This in turn allows us to reconstruct the particular moves of those actors, how they position themselves within the field, and aim to turn particular ideas into strategy. Such "moves" include linguistic practices, through which threats are framed; bodily moves, such as assertive gestures; and social skills, such as putting people in touch with each other, or playing with timing, such as making proposals at the right time (Mérand and Forget 2013). Paying attention to such moves offers insights into how particular individuals and groups influence the formulation of strategy. Studying the struggle between strategists and their positioning also provides important clues as to why and how certain ideas become normalized and integrated into a strategy, while others are not.

Through its focus on the struggle for power, the Bourdieusian field approach provides substantial analytical value to our understanding of the making and content of strategy.

Since it leaves open the question of who are the actors engaged in strategizing, it places significant empirical burden on the detailed reconstruction of fields of strategy. The approach risks to overemphasize the positioning of actors, and lead to a lack of attention for the substantive and normative issues that arise in the light of strategy-making.

In a second take on strategy-making as a social struggle, these substantive and normative elements come more prominently to the foreground. Here the concept of "controversy" is central. This perspective derives from the pragmatist insight that controversies are social situations in which tacit knowledge and normative foundations become articulated (Bueger 2014). Controversies are hence dedicated windows into how problems and worlds are constructed, revealing tacit practical knowledge. As Andrew Barry (2012, 330) notes, "the question of what problems or issues lie at the heart of controversies are rarely settled." Instead, "participants in a controversy may not only disagree about what is known about a problem, and why it matters, but also about the existence of the very problem about which they disagree" (Barry 2012, 330). In controversies on grand strategy, actors—including academics and experts, who are after all also strategy-makers—disagree over foundational principles of how the international system works, what the role of the state is, or what it can achieve by employing distinct instruments, such as military force. Such disputes are also struggles over which experts, non-experts, and publics should have a legitimate voice. While any controversy around strategy might be an interesting starting point, controversies over what is grand strategy, on whether a dedicated administration has a grand strategy, on what the content of a new strategy should be, or whether a new strategy is appropriate are particularly promising in this regard. Barry warns us, however, that we should not isolate controversies as single events, but study them in relation to a moving field of other controversies, conflicts, and events, including those that have occurred in the past and that might occur in the future (Barry 2012, 330).

Several practice-theoretical frameworks provide interesting angles to understand strategy as controversy: *problematization analysis*, for instance, draws on the work of John Dewey and Michel Foucault, and starts out from the claim that what requires social and political action and resources (and strategy), and as such constitutes a problem of the common, is not given or evolves naturally, but is the outcome of a collective construction process (Webb 2014). This is what is described as problematization. Taking the statements in controversies as an empirical starting point, the goal is then to reconstruct what is required to articulate an issue as problematic in the first instance (Bacchi 2012). Such an analytical angle lends itself to reconstruct the broader issues that strategy is concerned with, such as the meaning of war and protection or the appropriateness of force. Another stance is *controversy analysis*. This is an attempt inspired by ANT to map different positions and arguments within a controversy. Studying controversies allows to learn about the shared knowledge of fields and the different relations between science, technology, and politics these entail (Venturini 2012). Another variant is provided by a focus on the justifications in controversies, inspired by the sociology of Luc Boltanksi. This approach is particularly adept at revealing the normative underpinnings of practices. Gadinger (2016, 199–200), for instance, analyzes the controversy around the abuse of detainees in the Abu Ghraib prison to shed light on the normative contestation and moral ambiguity of George W. Bush's approach to a grand strategy of preemption. Public hearings in the US Congress reveal how actors disagree over the limits of the War on Terror. The controversy revolves around whether the War on Terror undermines core democratic principles and contradicts national security in the long term, or, as the administration and military argued, technocratic normative principles drawing on short-term objectives apply. The controversy hence demonstrates how actors disagree over what constitutes the most significant common good for the American people, and whether civil liberty or effectiveness should prevail and be defended.

Arranging Strategy, Fabricating Documents

Another take on the making of strategy is developed by practice theories that emphasize process and relations. Here, an understanding of strategy as an arrangement of heterogenous elements is developed. Making strategy is understood as a process of arranging and assembling. Strategy is not only interpreted as representation of the state of the world and the objectives of actors involved, but as a broader attempt at world-making. ANT provides an open framework to study such processes, while narrative theories in particular emphasize linguistic practices and understand arrangements as narratives.

Students of strategies have argued that the process of making strategy might be more important than the product: the strategy itself. Giegerich and Jonas (2012, 129), for instance, argue that the process generates the basis for the implementation but also acceptance of a strategy. Such a view is shared by strategy-makers such as the EU's High-Level Representative for Foreign Affairs and Security Policy (Tocci 2016, 463).

Practice theories such as ANT provide interesting frameworks to understand why and how process matters. They suggest that strategy-making can be interpreted as a process of assembling and arranging heterogenous elements. ANT is an approach that was initially formulated in Science and Technology Studies through empirical studies of laboratories and technological innovation processes. It has widely influenced practice research, and is increasingly promulgated in international relations and security studies research (Bueger and Stockbruegger 2017; Bueger and Gadinger 2018, 79–87). The core principle of ANT is to study practices as relations and how these are enacted, stabilized, or contested. Through such relations, actor-networks become formed between not only humans, but also nonhuman entities (e.g., technology, documents). The emphasis of the research is the process of relating.

Such an assembling process starts with convincing actors that a strategy is required and needs to be produced in the first place. ANT scholars have coined the term "interressement" to describe how actors become interested in the strategy and first relations are formed (Bueger and Stockbruegger 2017), which in other terminologies might be well conceived as initial communities or fields. Tocci (2016), one of the lead authors of the EU's 2015 grand strategy, for instance, describes the intricate process of ensuring that member states as well as the EU bodies are committed to the production process, and the myriad meetings required to do so. Through mutual engagement, the interested actors are increasingly given a role in the process of strategy-making, but also in the strategy itself, as well as the world and activities it describes. With the concept of "translation," ANT accounts for how actors and their identities transform through the process, assuming their new roles, and forming stable relations (Bueger and Stockbruegger 2017). Tocci (2016, 467), for instance, emphasizes the importance that "those who contributed would read themselves somewhere in the Strategy." Strategies might significantly redefine roles for agencies and their relations, as well as the distribution of resources between them. This is particularly the case if strategy-making is not a routine process (as in the United States), but a strategy is written for the first time, or a sub-strategy addresses a newly emerging issue. Scherrer (2012, 142), for instance, argues that in countries with weak security governance, strategy-writing is best understood "as a key element of institution-building, in that such documents inform strategic decision-making on the development of effective and accountable security institutions while ensuring that competing needs and priorities are considered. […]." Strategy-making is a crucial component of a process "that seeks to form a common identity, ethos and culture." This is also the case in emerging issue areas. For instance, the first National Maritime Security Strategy of the UK (UK Government 2014) not only redefines the role of the different agencies and ministries as they pertain to maritime space, but also creates a new governance body to ensure oversight. Through the process of translation, hence, a coherent whole such as an institution or a national or regional security sector is stabilized, and security actors are made. Actors are inscribed into the network through the strategy. Mälksoo (2016, 376) describes the EU's strategy in such terms, arguing that it "powerfully […] serves as a re-affirmation of the EU's will to survive in the first place, to maintain its position as a relevant actor on the world stage while living through a major legitimacy crisis in its history." For ANT advocates, building such relations is an act of world-making that goes beyond defining roles for the actors entangled in the network, it also performs the world in which the network is situated and with which it interacts. There is a strong claim for performativity, that a strategy might not only describe the world, but also create it. Strategy-making as such is an exercise "in ordering the world by establishing knowledge claims about 'how the world works'" (Mälksoo 2016, 376).

As Klein (1994, 27) remarks, strategy is "dependent upon the articulation of a world view in which regions and people are parceled out, divided up, and presumed to be subsumed under a master narrative." Narrative, an analytical concept originating in literary and cultural studies, is increasingly employed in both discourse and practice-oriented research on strategy. It is used, for instance, to analyze how collective sense-making unfolds in moments of crisis, such as major terrorist attacks (Devetak 2009). Practice theory offers a dedicated reinterpretation of narratives and strategy. From the viewpoint of the practice-oriented version, making strategies is a process of storytelling and narrative arrangement to make sense of and act in the world. Narrative gives purpose to practices. Strategy, then, is the temporary fixation of a narrative, for instance, in a document. To have effect, however, it needs to be read, cited, or summarized in stories.

Such a perspective develops from the understanding of narratives as a configuration device that actors use to make sense of the world and order it in a specific way to allow for action. Narratives are

> means for political actors to construct a shared meaning of the past, present and future of international politics to shape the behavior of domestic and international actors. Strategic narratives are a tool for political actors to extend their influence, manage expectations, and change the discursive environment in which they operate. They are narratives about both states and the system itself, both about who we are and what kind of order we want. (Miskimmon et al. 2013: 2)

Narrative constructions involve various practical judgments based on selective interpretation, personal experiences, or sequencing of events. Narrative is the "main device for making sense of social action" (Czarniawska 2004, 11), but also a political device for generating legitimacy. Indeed, the successful legitimation of any kind of a political project, such as a grand strategy, relies on a narrative. Narrative is a way of giving meaning to practice by constituting an overall sense of direction or purpose, refocusing identity, and enabling and constraining the ongoing activities of actors (Fenton and Langley 2011, 1171).

The search for a common understanding through the construction of narratives is, however, an often complex and flimsy affair. Stories, such as national security narratives, need to be told and retold, are influenced by the cultural repertoires of distinct communities, and are hence instable and subject to change. Narratives have effect, as Schmitt (2018) and Krebs (2015) remind us, in relation to a particular context and prior myths and stories. Russia's strategic narrative, as Schmitt (2018: 497–498) argues, works through the relation between a system narrative, that US unipolarity is detrimental to a multipolar order, and an identity narrative, which pushes the story that Russia has been "humiliated" by the West after the end of the Cold War. Krebs (2015) makes a similar argument, when he sees US national security narratives as embedded in more enduring identity narratives such as American exceptionalism.

The concept of narrative is analytically promising to explore the cultural embeddedness of strategy-making and explores why and how some interpretations of the world are included in a strategy and others not. Strategy-making becomes narrative construction and hence processes of collective sense-making, identity-building, and giving purpose to (security and diplomatic) practices.

Both ANT and narrative theory stress the importance of inscription. The arrangement, whether as actor-network or as narrative, becomes inscribed in a material artifact. One of the core features of practice theories is the claim that practices are not only linguistic, but also material. They contain bodily movements, but also the handling of artifacts, objects, and things. Earlier, we discussed examples of bodily movements, but artifacts as they pertain to strategy-making also require attention. Strategies are above all documents, and they are related to other documents. The ANT perspective may focus on the process of drafting the strategy and making the document as the more important, yet this does not imply that the strategy as document is not a powerful inscription device that has an important afterlife. Indeed, the document becomes part of other practices, nested in other documents, and might offer the beginnings of new strategy-making, when a new routine cycle of strategy-writing begins. Documents might also be used as reference in new documents, for instance, in order to indicate coherence or to legitimate certain claims. Strategies become part of a hierarchy of documents.

The focus of much of the attention on documents has been on either their production or on their content. Documents are, however, one of the core artifacts of contemporary governance. While they are temporary fixations, one of the core features is that they enable governance at distance through their circulation. As Freeman and Maybin (2011, 160) remark,

> the physical properties of policy documents extend the scope and reach of governments in space and time. Their material inscription means that a standard message can be communicated to numerous public servants in numerous and often distant locations, coordinating their actions. And the same message can serve as a reference point for successive actors and actions over time. It is the very physicality of the document that gives its temporal power.

Documents can be circulated to even the farthest distance. A strategy document can reach the diplomat in an embassy far away, just as it can reach the officer in the field. Through their materiality, they can travel and allow for the coordination of action. The power of a strategy hence lies in its physical properties. As actor-network theorists have proposed, documents can be also conceptualized as actors in their own right. As actors, they become part of a network of action and establish certain relations to other actors. This is then an invitation to "examine how documents as vital objects can drive and shape political, economic [...] and scientific activities just as much as humans do" (Prior 2008, 833). Such a perspective is hence an invitation to not only study how the propositions within a strategy are implemented, but how a strategy becomes part of a repertoire of practices, allowing us to do things differently.

Conclusion

Strategy-making can be considered as one of the foundational international practices. Strategy has the potential to anchor other practices, such as war and diplomacy. To understand strategy-making and the effect of it, recent practice-theoretical ideas provide revealing analytical frameworks and concepts. In this chapter, we set out the core premises of the practice-theoretical view and their contribution to the study of strategy. We have explored several avenues for how practice theories can inspire the study of strategy. Practice theory allows us to revisit concepts such as strategic culture or security communities as phenomena based on patterns of activities. Concepts such as "field" and "controversy" allow us to study strategy as a social struggle of power and contestation of meaning and norms. Studying strategy as arrangement gives us insights into how actors become involved in strategy, how they are transformed in the course, and how strategy has the power to reconfigure the world. Analytical tools, such as ANT, practice-oriented narrative analysis, problematization and controversy analysis, as well as materialist-oriented document analysis, hold strong promise for further research on strategy-making and rethinking existing debates and empirical material.

They offer a non-essentialist understanding of grand strategy that allows us to turn the struggle over a definition of strategy into productive empirical questions. Through their non-essentialist stances and rejection of instrumental rationality, they offer concepts and theorizing that aims to encompass process, interactions, and uncertainty. They also return politics to strategy-making in emphasizing that strategy is, above all, a political struggle between actors, but also an act of world-making. Understanding strategy as a collective achievement of various types of actors, they allow us to deconstruct the state, and to consider the diversity of strategy-makers. In placing greater emphasis on empirical analysis and rich contextual descriptions of strategy-making practices such as meetings, they invite new methods, such as ethnography or action research, to be tried out and tested. This may increase the practical relevance of strategy research and its contribution to the making of strategy. Together, these frameworks also open up new possibilities for dialogue within security studies, providing in particular new remedies for the divisions and misunderstandings between strategic studies and critical security studies, which often agree on empirical results and share many more concerns than is often appreciated. Understanding strategy-making as a basic practice of international relations, moreover, brings strategy back to the larger disciplines of international relations. It might, as well, open a further dialogue to other disciplines which are equally concerned about the production of strategy.[1]

Note

1. For comments and suggestions that have significantly improved this chapter, we are grateful to Timothy Edmunds, Henrik Breitenbauch, Andrew Neal, Anders Wivel, and the two editors. Christian Bueger acknowledges the support from the Economic and Social Research Council of the UK under the grant [ES/S008810/1] and a grant of the Danish Ministry of Foreign Affairs administered by DANIDA.

References

Adler, Emanuel. 2008. "The Spread of Security Communities: Communities of Practice, Self-Restraint, and NATO's Post-Cold War Transformation." *European Journal of International Relations* 14 (2): 195–230.

Adler, Emanuel, and Patricia Greve. 2009. "When Security Community Meets Balance of Power: Overlapping Regional Mechanisms of Security Governance." *Review of International Studies* 35 (S1): 59–84.

Adler, Emanuel, and Vincent Pouliot. 2011. "International Practices." *International Theory* 3 (1): 1–36.

Bacchi, Carol. 2012. "Why Study Problematizations? Making Politics Visible." *Open Journal of Political Science* 2 (1): 1–8.

Balzacq, Thierry, Peter Dombrowski, and Simon Reich. 2019. "Is Grand Strategy a Research Program? A Review Essay." *Security Studies* 58 (1): 58–86.

Barry, Andrew. 2012. "Political Situations: Knowledge Controversies in Transnational Governance." *Critical Policy Studies* 6 (3): 37–41.

Berling, Trine Villumsen. 2012. "Bourdieu, International Relations, and European Security." *Theory and Society* 41 (5): 451–478.

Bicchi, Federica, and Niklas Bremberg, eds. 2017. *European Diplomacy in Practice: Interrogating Power, Agency and Change*. London and New York: Routledge.

Bloomfield, Alan. 2012. "Time to Move On: Reconceptualizing the Strategic Culture Debate." *Contemporary Security Policy* 33 (3): 437–461.

Bueger, Christian, and Frank Gadinger. 2016. "International Practice Theories." In *Praxeological Political Analysis*, edited by Michael Jonas, Lorenz Lassnigg, Beate Littig, and Angela Wroblewski, 87–106. Basingstoke: Palgrave Macmillan.

Bueger, Christian, and Jan Stockbruegger. 2017. "Actor-Network Theory: Objects and Actants, Networks and Narratives." In *Technology and World Politics: An Introduction*, edited by Daniel R. McCarthy, 42–59. Abingdon: Routledge.

Bueger, Christian, and Frank Gadinger. 2018 *International Practice Theory*. 2nd edition. London: Palgrave Macmillan.

Bueger, Christian. 2014. Pathways to Practice. Praxiography and International Politics, *European Political Science Review* 6 (3): 383–406.

Bueger, Christian. 2016. "Security as Practice." In *Handbook of Security Studies*, 2nd edition, edited by Thierry Balzacq and Myriam Dunn Cavelty, 126–135. London: Routledge.

Bürgi, Peter T., Claus D. Jacobs, and Johan Roos. 2005. "From Metaphor to Practice in the Crafting of Strategy" *Journal of Management Inquiry* 14 (1): 78–94.

Czarniawska, Barbara. 2004. *Narratives in Social Science Research*. Los Angeles: Sage.

Devetak, Richard. 2009. "After the Event: Don de Lillo's White Noise and September 11 Narratives" *Review of International Studies* 35 (4): 795–815.

Edwards, Geoffrey. 2006. "Is There a Security Culture in the Enlarged European Union?" *International Spectator* 41 (3): 7–23.

Eikeland, Olav, and Davide Nicolini. 2011. "Turning Practically: Broadening the Horizon." *Journal of Organizational Change Management* 24 (2): 164–174.

Fenton, Christopher, and Ann Langley. 2011. "Strategy as Practice and the Narrative Turn." *Organization Studies* 32 (9): 1171–1196.

Freeman, Richard, and Jo Maybin. 2011. "Documents, Practices and Policy." *Evidence & Policy: A Journal of Research, Debate and Practice* 7 (2): 155–170.

Gadinger, Frank. 2016. "On Justification and Critique: Luc Boltanski's Pragmatic Sociology and International Relations." *International Political Sociology* 10 (3): 187–205.

Giegerich, Bastian, and Alexandra Jonas. 2012. "Auf Der Suche Nach Best Practice? Die Entstehung Nationaler Sicherheitsstrategien Im Internationalen Vergleich." *Sicherheit & Frieden* 30 (3): 129–134.

Goddard, Stacie E., and Ronald R. Krebs. 2015. "Rhetoric, Legitimation, and Grand Strategy." *Security Studies* 24 (1): 5–36.
Golsorkhi, Damon, Linda Rouleau, David Seidl, and Eero Vaara, eds. 2010. *Cambridge Handbook of Strategy as Practice*. Cambridge: Cambridge University Press.
Hofius, Maren. 2016. "Community at the Border or the Boundaries of a Community? The Case of EU Field Diplomats." *Review of International Studies* 42 (5): 939–967.
Jarzabkowski, Paula. 2005. *Strategy as Practice. An Activity Based Approach*. London: SAGE.
Jarzabkowski, Paula, and David Seidl. 2008. "The Role of Meetings in the Social Practice of Strategy." *Organization Studies* 29 (11): 1391–1426.
Kaplan, Sarah. 2011. "Strategy and PowerPoint: An Inquiry into the Epistemic Culture and Machinery of Strategy Making." *Organization Science* 22 (2): 320–346.
Klein, Bradley S. 1994. *Strategic Studies and World Order: The Global Politics of Deterrence*. Cambridge: Cambridge University Press.
Krebs, Ronald. 2015. *Narrative and the Making of US National Security*. Cambridge: Cambridge University Press.
Mälksoo, Maria. 2016. "From the ESS to the EU Global Strategy: External Policy, Internal Purpose." *Contemporary Security Policy* 37 (3): 374–388.
Merand, Frederic, and Amelie Forget. 2013. "Strategy. Strategizing about Strategy." In *Bourdieu in International Relations. Rethinking Key Concepts in IR*, edited by Rebecca Adler-Nissen, 93–113. London and New York: Routledge Press.
Miskimmon, Alister, Ben O'Loughlin, and Laura Roselle. 2013. *Strategic Narratives. Communication Power and the New World Order*. Abingdon: Routledge.
Neumann, Iver B. 2002. "Returning Practice to the Linguistic Turn: the Case of Diplomacy." *Millennium: Journal of International Studies* 31(3): 627–651.
Neumann, Iver B., and Henrikki Heikka. 2005. "Grand Strategy, Strategic Culture, Practice: The Social Roots of Nordic Defence." *Cooperation and Conflict* 40 (1): 5–23.
Pirani, Pietro. 2010. "'The Way We Were': The Social Construction of Italian Security Policy." *Modern Italy* 15 (2): 217–230.
Pirani, Pietro. 2016. "Elites in Action: Change and Continuity in Strategic Culture." *Political Studies Review* 14 (4): 512–520.
Popescu, Ionut C. 2018. "Grand Strategy vs. Emergent Strategy in the Conduct of Foreign Policy." *Journal of Strategic Studies* 41 (3): 438–460.
Pouliot, Vincent. 2008. "The Logic of Practicality: A Theory of Practice of Security Communities." *International Organization* 62 (2): 257–288.
Prior, Lindsay. 2004. "Documents." In *Qualitative Research Practice*, edited by Clive Seale, Giampietro Gobo, Jaber F. Gubrium, and David Silverman, 375–390. Thousand Oaks, CA: Sage Publications.
Prior, Lindsay. 2008. "Repositioning Documents in Social Research." *Sociology* 42 (5): 821–836.
Rasmussen, Mikkel Vedby. 2005. "What's the Use of It? Danish Strategic Culture and the Utility of Armed Force." *Cooperation and Conflict* 40 (1): 67–89.
Reckwitz, Andreas. 2002. "Toward a Theory of Social Practices: A Development in Culturalist Theorizing." *European Journal of Social Theory* 5 (2): 243–263.
Rogers, James. 2009. "From 'Civilian Power' to 'Global Power': Explicating the European Union's 'Grand Strategy' through the Articulation of Discourse Theory." *Journal of Common Market Studies* 47 (4): 831–862.
Scherrer, Vincenza. 2012. "UN Support to National Security Policy-Making from an Institution-Building Perspective." *Sicherheit & Frieden* 30 (3): 141–147.

Schmitt, Olivier. 2018. "When Are Strategic Narratives Effective? the Shaping of Political Discourse through the Interaction between Political Myths and Strategic Narratives." *Contemporary Security Policy* 39 (4): 487–511.

Silove, Nina. 2018. "Beyond the Buzzword: The Three Meanings of 'Grand Strategy.'" *Security Studies* 27 (1): 27–57.

Spee, Andreas Paul, and Paula Jarzabkowski. 2009. "Strategy Tools as Boundary Objects." *Strategic Organization* 7 (2): 223–232.

Swidler, Ann. 1986. "Culture in Action: Symbols and Strategies." *American Sociological Review* 51 (2): 273–286.

Tocci, Nathalie. 2016. "The Making of the EU Global Strategy." *Contemporary Security Policy* 37 (3): 461–472.

UK Government. 2014. *The UK National Strategy for Maritime Security*. London: UK Government.

Vaara, Eero, and Richard Whittington. 2012. "Strategy-as-Practice: Taking Social Practices Seriously." *The Academy of Management Annals* 6 (1): 285–336.

van Apeldoorn, Bastiaan, and Naná de Graaff. 2014. "Corporate Elite Networks and US Post-Cold War Grand Strategy from Clinton to Obama." *European Journal of International Relations* 20 (1): 29–55.

Venturini, Tommaso. 2012. "Building on Faults: How to Represent Controversies with Digital Methods." *Public Understanding of Science* 21 (7): 796–812.

Webb, P. Taylor. 2014. "Policy Problematization." *International Journal of Qualitative Studies in Education* 27 (3): 364–376.

Wenger, Etienne. 1998. *Communities of Practice: Learning, Meaning, and Identity*. Cambridge: Cambridge University Press.

Williams, Michael C. 2007. *Culture and Security. Symbolic power and the politics of international security*. London and New York: Routledge.

Williams, Paul D., and Jürgen Haacke. 2008. "Security Culture, Transnational Challenges and the Economic Community of West African States." *Journal of Contemporary African Studies* 26 (2): 119–136.

CHAPTER 10

IDEAS AND IDEOLOGY IN GRAND STRATEGY

THIERRY BALZACQ AND
PABLO BARNIER-KHAWAM

Introduction

In essence, politics is the source of grand strategy, which it serves. Although political processes and imperatives vary according to the political regime, domestic influences, including institutions, national memories, budgetary factors, and social ideas are important determinants of grand strategy's selection (Rosecrance and Stein 1993, 5). A bulk of research on Soviet Union's strategic change in the mid-80s recognizes, for example, that international pressures are neither the main nor the sole factor that explicate the Soviet Union conciliatory policy that led to the end of the Cold War. Rather, domestic considerations such as the ascent of a different group to leadership positions played a crucial role in the Soviet Union strategic adjustment (Mueller 1993). The complexity of the exact weight of each factor notwithstanding, domestic circumstances are not as permissive as realists assume. More often than not, systemic variations express outcomes of disagreements between different domestic blocs. This gives the lie to the rationalist assumption that grand strategy is generated by a unitary actor.

If politics is central to the domain of grand strategy, then, we need to pay attention to the lifeblood of politics, namely ideas and ideology (Destutt de Tracy 1804). This is what we attempt in this essay. Ideas and ideologies are the glue that hold together different components of a grand strategy together, but the two terms need to be specified, if briefly. An idea can be defined as an abstract representation of a given element of reality. There are simple or complex ideas, scientific, moral, economic, and religious ideas. In this perspective, ideas are the most basic units of thought and meaning. Ideas do not necessarily bear a political component but can be at the origin of a political movement as, for example, in the French revolution when the Third State called for the respect of the idea of "equality," which was then turned into a right. However, the politicization of ideas usually depends upon their being part of a system (better perhaps, network) of ideas (i.e., ideology).

In grand strategy, ideology refers to an interrelated set of actionable ideas, about the state's identity and place in the world, its goals, values, and interests, and the foundations of its relations to the others. Ideology forges an image of the world; shapes how actors perceive and relate to it. In pluralist societies, ideologies compete for prominence. Subnational groups that participate in the development of grand strategy are mostly divided along ideological lines (Snyder, Bruck, and Sapin 1954). Once an ideology achieves dominance, it exerts influence on grand-strategic choices by providing meaning and direction to a state's overall foreign policy action.

In this essay, we do not intend to examine how ideologies take form or why people adopt one particular ideology instead of another, and act accordingly. Our aim is more circumscribed. We argue that ideas and ideologies are both shared beliefs system and instruments of politics that aim to shape and steer a nation's grand strategy. In section I of this essay, we discuss ideology's general understanding in political science, departing from the pejorative view that has engulfed it, and revisit epistemological issues that underlie the study of ideology's repercussions on grand strategy. The essay then looks at the functions of ideology in grand strategy thought-practice. This involves threat identification, mobilization and extraction of resources, and ideological balancing.

General Characteristics of Ideology

This section discusses main approaches to ideology, following three steps. The first draws a wedge between normatively charged and neutral understandings of ideology. The second section argues that ideology's influence rests upon the intersubjective articulation of meaning structures. The final section argues that while some studies in political theory and political psychology can be content with investigating the internal structure of ideology, grand strategy is primarily interested in explicating how underlying ideological representations affect policies, that is, what kind of world does it make possible.

Positive and Negative Views

The meaning of ideology remains precarious (Mullins 1972). In political science, for example, one study identified over 27 ways of using ideology (Hamilton 1987). Another review conducted by Kathleen Night (2006) shows that the occurrence of the concept "ideology" in the *American Political Science Review* rose dramatically in the 1950s, that is, during the first wave of the Cold War, although some scholars warn that our understanding of the Cold War must not be captive of ideological lenses (Kramer 1999).

Dominant references were made to Marxism, Fascism, and Liberalism. In this context, ideology tends to conjure up two main features. First, ideology is regarded as the nemesis of (true) knowledge. That is, ideology is not testable. This may account for why ideology was generally depicted negatively. To label something "ideology" is to cast it in negative terms, and dismiss it (Morgenthau 1948, 61; Mannheim 1954, 238). Such a negative understanding of ideology has a long pedigree and still enjoys currency in certain corners of political science. This is a sentiment not so far removed from that of Giovani Sartori (1969), who construes ideology as a dogmatic, emotive politics, one that stands in opposition to, and undermines pragmatic politics.

What is known as the Marxist tradition exerted an enduring influence on the negative approach to ideology, wherein ideology is analogous to a "system of misconceived ideas" that drive action (Van Dijk 2013; Gramsci 1985; Althusser 2014; Marx and Engels 1974). For the Marxist tradition, indeed, ideology is "a system of thought that legitimated the existing economic and social order and its dominant class interests" (Maynard 2018, 481). In other words, ideology yields domination of one group over another. It is a one-way process. As Purvis and Hunt (1993, 478) put it, ideology entails "a directionality in the sense that [it] always works to favour some and to disadvantage others."

A negative view of ideology was toned down by the behaviorist school, which reduced ideology to a "benign organizing device" amenable to rigorous measurement (Knight 2006, 622). The mantra that drives behaviorists is that "what can be counted and measured is more amenable to precise formulation and presentation than other forms of human action" (Barker 2000, 223–24). The behaviorist study of ideology aimed at lifting it above the opprobrium that crippled ideology since Marx's and Engel's work. A central line of investigation, it turned out, was to quantitatively weight ideological cleavages in order to establish a causal relationship between voters' issue preference and ideological standing (Macrae 1952; Schubert 1958; Campbell et al. 1980; Converse 2006). The operationalization of ideology took center stage, but neither the arrangement nor the internal organization of ideology retained scholars' attention. This means that, at times, what appeared as ideological attitudes could not be properly connected to an ideological mindset. To do so, one first needs to ascertain what is the basic social cognition that is shared by members of the relevant group, before one can codify the relationship between the cognitive structure and a specific action. In contrast, when scholars spend a great deal of time trying to measure evidence of ideology, they often work backward, thus attempting to infer the existence of an ideology from observations of sets of behaviors. This approach faces two problems. First, meanings attached to ideology are not unequivocal. Ideologies are often ambiguous and host different semantic layers which, according to Freeden (2003, 11), "are hidden from their consumers and, frequently, from their producers as well." And while ideology can reconcile contradictory meanings, it does not suppress them altogether. Second, this approach is beset by the challenge of equifinality, as any such behavior can be provoked by a countless combination of factors. This problem echoes the epistemological debate that separates interpretivist approaches and empiricist contributions to the study of ideology.

Intersubjective Articulation

Asked to clarify whether and how ideology influences decision-making and action, IR theories take different pathways. Structural Realism, for example, reduces the ideological factor to an epiphenomenon (Waltz 1979). In the balance of power context, ideas and ideologies are not relevant as they do not belong to actors' rational behavior (Mearsheimer 2001). While liberalism has been instrumental in studying the role of ideas and ideology in world politics, it has mostly replicated the realist view that ideology is a reflection of interests (Doyle 1986). This is not the place to replay the idealism-materialism debate, if only for the fact theories of IR understand the word "material" in different ways. Moreover, material artefacts of grand strategy usually bear the mark of its ideational attributes (Wendt 1999, 92–137). Thus, we want to suggest that to explain grand strategy by reference to ideology is to focus on how it instantiates consequential meaning structures. The background of such a view is provided by those approaches that have emphasized the causal weight of ideas. One early attempt was provided by Judith Goldstein and Robert Keohane (1993).

Specifically, Goldstein and Keohane argue that ideas affect the decision-making process in three ways. First, ideas are road maps, that is, "when actors believe in the causal link they identify or the normative principles that they reflect" (Goldstein and Keohane 1993, 12). Second, ideas are focal points which "affect strategic interactions, helping or hindering joint efforts to attain 'more efficient' outcomes—outcomes that are at least as good as the status quo for all participants" (Ibid.). Finally, an absence of innovation produces an embedment of ideas in institutions and specific policies, which in turn produces a causal impact on decision-making. However, the causal link between ideas and the actors' actions remain unclear (Yee 1996). If anything, the link sounds indirect.

This indirect causation paves the way for an interpretative view. According to Brian Fay (1975, 79), "an interpretative social science is one which attempts to uncover the sense of a given action, practice or constitutive meaning ..." Although it is unable to determine direct causal relations, the interpretative approach is still concerned with establishing indirect causation, which draws on the analysis of intersubjective meaning. This intersubjective meaning is constitutive of the conditions enabling the actors to act. In other words, "these conditions must be understood not as causes but as warranting conditions which make a particular action or belief more 'reasonable,' 'justified,' or 'appropriate,' given the desires, beliefs, and expectations of the actors." They are "*quasi-causal accounts* of the ways in which certain configurations of conditions give rise to certain forms of action, rules and common meanings" (Fay 1975, 84). Intersubjectivity establishes the conditions for causation, in the sense that ideas and ideology should be considered as constitutive of social practice (Neufeld 1993, 45).

Several scholars adopt this understanding of ideology in order to study distinct processes of international relations. For example, Jeffrey Checkel (1993) mobilizes ideology as a key factor in explaining changes undergone by the Soviet regime under Gorbachev. He hypothesizes that, "[t]he appearance of a new ideology of international affairs in Soviet policy under Gorbachev was in no way preordained by a changing international system or domestic modernization processes. Rather, a changing external environment and the advent of a reformist general secretary created a series of policy windows through which aspiring policy entrepreneurs jumped" (Checkel 1993, 273). Thus, to establish the extent to which ideology matters, Checkel brings the national and international contexts together. He takes great care to show that ideology has to be embodied by individuals to influence practices, but also that these individuals need to act in a propitious institutional and political context to succeed. In this view, two environmental elements facilitate ideological influence: "(1) whether there are problems in that external setting that could be solved in whole or in part by the implementation of the entrepreneur's ideas; and (2) whether there are leaders in power who recognize that such problems do indeed exist" (Checkel 1993, 279). However, how can we identify the ideological influence he claims to study? Checkel argues that the measurement he elaborates in his analysis is indirect and relies on "a correlation between concepts, intellectual frameworks, and policies" (Checkel 1993, 296) of both the influencers and the object of influence. In other words, when actors engage relationally with one another, they are able to shape a meaning structure that, in turn, shape their practices. These intersubjectively articulated meaning structures incorporate ideologies.

In a similar vein, Mark Haas (2012) aims to measure the influence of ideology on leaders' preferences. According to Haas, ideologies affect international choices in two ways. The first is the degree of ideological differences or "ideological distance," that is, "the extent of the similarities and differences of political leaders' ideological beliefs" (Haas 2012, 5). This variable thus correlates international choices and incentives to alliances according to national leaders' ideologies. The second variable is the number of prominent ideological groups within the system or "ideological polarity," which enables him to predict the collective logic of cooperation within the international system. For example, he argues that "although the overall barriers to alliances are higher in ideological multi-polarity than in bipolarity, the likelihood of alliances among ideological enemies, somewhat paradoxically, is greater in ideologically multipolar than bipolar eras" (Haas 2012, 22). In our view, the ideological meaning structure becomes truly meaningful when it unveils choices available to actors, although it tends to be biased toward one of them. Ideology is as much present in the intersubjective meaning structure as in the alternative choices where ideological beliefs tilt the decision in the direction that serves it best. This does not forsake the causal attribute of ideology, but suggests that causal agency ascribed to ideology cannot be separated from the meaning structure that underlies interactions between actors.

Internal Structure and External Functions

We start with a simple assumption: ideologies are mainly belief systems that are common to a cluster of people. Two semantic dimensions underlie this assumption. First, ideologies are a kind of mental representation. Second, such mental representations are not individuals' properties, but are shared across a given community. It is in this very specific sense that ideologies are said to be a form of social cognition, that is, a "socially shared beliefs system" (Van Dijk 2013, 177). These two semantic dimensions are interdependent. Taken together, however, they risk validating the view that ideologies are only a set of mental propositions. We therefore direct attention to external manifestations of ideology, that is to say, enter into the ways in and through which ideologies contribute to policy functions. According to Wendt, an externalist approach means three things. "The first is that thoughts are constituted at least in part by external context rather than solely in the heads of individuals, since how thoughts get carved up or 'individuated' depends on what 'conceptual grid' is used. […] Thinking depends *logically* on social relations, not just causally," asserts Wendt (1999, 175). Second, "truth conditions are 'owned' by the community, not by individuals" (ibid.). Third, "meanings depend on the practices, skills, and tests that connect the community to the objects represented in discourse" (Wendt 1999, 176).

In grand strategy, to narrow our focus, ideology achieves its external impact in two fundamental ways: "naming" and argumentation. According to Ernesto Laclau (2005), naming gives meaning and coherence to a phenomenon. In addition, it is through naming that people come to identify themselves with an account or a policy. Thus, naming is a process through which people "come to see themselves or their interests as expressed by [ideologies]—that is, how they develop sometimes passionate emotional identification with ideological propositions or promises" (Finlayson 2013, 199). Such naming takes the form of concepts that aim to supply the grand strategy of the day with an intellectual "framework," an "organizing principle," and "orienting principle," or a "decisive point" (Martel 2015; Krasner 2010; Milevski 2016). In US grand strategy, for example, such names include "deep engagement," "restraint," "selective engagement," or "primacy" (Art 2003; Brooks and Wohlforth 2016; Posen 2014; Posen and Ross 1996).

Interestingly, these names usually work one against another, in ways that mirror ideological functions. Political ideology, argues Michael Freeden (2003, 32), refers to: "a set of ideas, beliefs, opinions, and values that (1) exhibit a recurring pattern (2) are held by significant groups (3), compete over providing and controlling plans for public policy [and] (4) do so with the aim of justifying, contesting or changing the social and political arrangements and processes of a political community." In conceiving of grand strategy as a means of identifying a decisive point, scholars tend to employ "grand strategy as an engine for their analysis and prescriptions" (Milevski 2016, 123). A prescriptive approach portrays grand strategy as a decisive point which anchors policy options and enables strategic success. If policymakers are to succeed, then, it is suggested that they remain within the coordinates set by the decisive point embodied by a name. But, because these prescriptions tend to hold normative views about the decisive point they have fashioned, they are less receptive to compromise. They become ideologies. Lukas Milveski puts it in the following words: the drive to identify and stick to a decisive point means that "grand strategic prescriptions changed the nature of grand strategy away from pragmatic instrumentality of strategy into policy, if not *ideology*" (Milevski 2016, 127; emphasis added). Milevski hints here of a process, also described by Haas, whereby unique foreign policy prescriptions tend to take ideological contours. As he notes, "if specific, usually unique, foreign policy prescriptions are central to groups' raison d'être and preferences for ordering the political world, these position are *ideological in nature*" (Haas 2012, 4; emphasis added). In other words, for Haas these prescriptions are not ideologies per se, but are susceptible to ideological leanings.

The second way through which the external manifestation of ideology can be traced is by means of rhetoric, narrative, and discourse. It is not the place to discuss the content and form of each of these concepts. Nor do we have time and space to adjudicate their relative appropriateness. Instead, what we would like to indicate is that ideologies are both conveyed by and embodied in talk and text (Krebs 2021; Kornprobst and Traistaru 2021). Ideology has a bearing upon grand strategy by virtue of its cognitive function and its argumentative leverage. But this leaves the exact magnitude of ideology's impact unspecified. We recognize that such effect is at best indeterminate, but we do not want to support the view that it is inexistent, as rationalists would encourage us to think. Rather, the most interesting question is: how does ideology produce its effect? We suggest that ideological arrangements provide actors with convenient answers to a variety of circumstances and challenges as much as a way of understanding the world and their place within it. In this sense, ideology, like culture, has a filtering effect upon decision-making processes (see McCourt 2021).

The notion of ideology as a "filter" means several things that boil down to two important ideas. On the one hand, ideology is not only a shared mental representation, but also an "argumentional resource; it is a playbook as it were, providing ready-made 'cognitive shortcuts' to assist in grasping a situation but also ways of making political claims about it" (Finlayson 2013, 199). On the other hand, ideology establishes a normative order, that is, an order of justification which throttles certain options as much as it legitimizes others (Friedberg 2000, 22). Such a palliative purpose allows ideology, among other things, to suppress ambiguity and impose whichever political alternative prevails. An essential manner in which this justification works is through argumentation and narratives (Goddard and Krebs 2015; Goddard 2021). However, what constitutes an appropriate justifying approach to grand strategy belongs to research that situates ideology within its context, which then allows it to "acquire its significance and at the same time the emotional power to inspire identification" (Forst 2017; Gries 2014).

Ideology in Grand Strategy

Grand strategy is a thought-practice. Unless one examines how the ideas embodied in a grand strategy play out in the world, it is difficult to ascertain whether such ideas exist. A.I. Richards (1936, 5) puts it in the following way, "an idea or a notion, like the physicists' ultimate particles and rays, is only known by what it does. Apart from its dress or other signs it is not identifiable." In this section, then, we identify three crucial functions of ideology. However, we do not just explore their inner workings, but rely on these functions to indicate how ideology connects thinking and practical aspects of grand strategy. Several examples illustrate our argument along the way.

Threat Perception

Grand strategy concerns the attainment of collective goals of national security. But the definition of such objectives opposes different domestic groups which hold competing ideas about what constitutes a threatening development. The ability to set threat priorities yields political benefits, both in terms of material power position and symbolic authority. Hence, the struggle between domestic blocs both over threat identification and the most appropriate remedies. In Robert Jervis' (1968, 472) words, "the way people perceive data is influenced not only by their cognitive structure and theories about other actors but also by what they are concerned with at the time they perceive the perceive the information." That is, ideology participates in threat assessment, along with material concerns. According to Mark Haas (2012, 49): "power and ideologies ... frequently work in tandem to generate threat perceptions. Power variables determine the universe of groups that possess the capacity to harm others." True, but core ideological beliefs influence what a group considers threatening and domestic politics involve groups whose singularity is in large part ideologically based. These blocs usually promote policy prescriptions that align with ideological beliefs which are not shared with competing groups. In certain contexts, ideological cleavages lead to the emergence of political factions.

Iran provides a vivid illustration of the grand-strategic effects of domestic ideological polarization. Specifically, Iran's grand strategy expresses the outcome of ideological struggles between two domestic factions, namely the progressive and the conservative. The external contrast of these ideologies is stark, while their internal coherence is mixed (Gerring 1997). Externally, then, the progressive line emphasizes economic development while the conservative line insists on the loyalty to an orthodox state ideology as the guiding principle of Iran's foreign affairs. The Islamic Revolutionary Guard Corps (IRGC), the Supreme Leader Khamenei up until 2013, and the neoconservative factions belong to the conservative line. They are up against the notion of development, which they perceive as a Western "Trojan Horse." In other words, Iran's grand strategy manifests a struggle between those who "want to preserve the revolutionary character of the state against those who believe Iran would be stronger by being perceived and dealt with as an ordinary, normal state that is nonrevisionist, with its own preferences and strategic priorities" (Balzacq and Ramadan-Alban 2019, 201).

The internal coherence of the conservative line is tighter than that of the progressive. In fact, the progressive line harbors two factions that vie for prominence. The first refers to "the post-Islamist generation, that is, religious intellectualism [...] . Reformists support political liberalism, democracy ... , and religious pluralism. Finally, they regard Western civilization as a model of freedom of thought" (Balzacq and Ramadan-Alban 2019, 199). The second pursues the following objectives: recovering Iran's international prestige, bolstering "popular sovereignty" as the cornerstone of Iran's national security, and developing regional networks of security (Kazemzadeh 2020).

These two ideological lines mirror Mark Haas's distinction between ideological hard-liners and soft-liners. The former, conservatives/hard-liners, "view diplomacy as either ineffectual, because they possess no common interests with ideological enemies that would create the basis of negotiation, or counterproductive, because talks would legitimate the regime they are trying to overthrow." While "ideological soft-liners tend to rely on more cooperative policies to provoke an ideological change in target states" (Haas 2012, 32).

Mobilization and Extraction of Resources

Grand strategizing is conducted at three levels: designing, mobilization, and implementation. While it is possible to demarcate the implementation stage from the other two, at least in theory, designing and mobilization rarely occur in separate sequences. Be that as it may, ideology does not change meaning and form to fit each level's processes and objectives. Rather, features associated with ideology are expressed in distinct ways by each level of grand strategizing. For example, at the design level, ideology manifests a community's political thinking. In this sense, ideology illuminates political principles and goals around which a nation organizes its relation with the rest of the world. According to John Gerring (1997, 972) "[b]y organizing and interpreting the world an ideology helps the subject to act within that world." That is, ideology is an action-inspiring shared beliefs system. In other words, "the significance of ideology in mobilization is not that it 'causes one to do' but that it 'gives one cause for doing'" (Mullins 1972, 509). Further, ideology plays a crucial, albeit not exclusive, role in both mobilization and implementation, including in the choice of appropriate resources to use in order to address a grand strategy's priority.

In *Sailing the Water's Edge*, for example, Helen V. Milner and Dustin Tingley (2015, 57–58), use the variance in the degree of ideological differences to account for preferences among policy instruments. For them, ideology means "beliefs about the dispositions of foreign actors and the appropriate way to deploy government resources to deal with them" (Milner and Tingley 2015, 57). Henceforth, different ideological commitments, say between conservatives and liberals, support distinct policy choices and related means to achieve them. The wider the gap between ideologies over a given policy resource, the more difficult it is for presidents to fashion consensus across the dividing lines.

Ideological Balancing

If threat assessment represents the internal, outside-in aspect of ideological competition, ideological balancing provides us with the international, inside-out dimension of ideological rivalries. A consistent tract of research in social psychology shows that ideological rivalries are zero-sum games. Because actors are pessimists about one another's intentions, they tend to assume that confrontation with the opposite ideology is unavoidable (Jost, Federico, and Napier 2013). "Ideological polarization," which is a function of the "degree of ideological differences" between two states, tends to disable cooperation between actors (Owen 2010, 40). But cooperation remains possible between nations that entertain different sets of ideological commitments, "when any one of the four major sources of alliance are extremely strong, or when there are a number of these factors in existence [balancing against a shared threat, advancing offensive international goals, countering a domestic threat, advocating and protecting shared ideological principles]" (Haas 2012, 27). Be that as it may, the default policy inclination, in context of ideological polarization, is offensive strategy, particularly in a bipolar situation, wherein ideological aversion erects uphill barriers to ideological alignment.

A typical consequence of ideological polarization is the policy of ideological outreach. Exporting ideology abroad can serve two functions. First, states may want to convert other states or groups within other states to their ideology in order to sap their social cohesion or contain the influence of the rival's sets of values, beliefs, and attitudes. Second, ideological export is suitable for widening the network of allies. Taken together, as they should, these functions indicate that the primary aim of ideological outreach is to improve a nation's security, by deterring aggression against it and raising the costs of any attack against its interests. However, the success of such a strategy hinges on the state's ability to translate any deleterious action into ideological terms, which constitutes the legitimating principle of the influence it wields.

The competition that pits Iran against Saudi Arabia in the Middle East is a typical case of ideological balancing. In the Yemeni conflict, for example, both regimes have supported groups that come closer to their ideological line. Thus, Iran sides with the Houthis, while the former Yemeni government is aided by Saudi Arabia. But this ideological balancing rests on the material power that Iran and Saudi Arabia are able to wield in favor of their allies. The ideological balancing that characterizes Iran's and Saudi Arabia's strategic moves in the region helps account for some of the dynamics that influenced the Syrian war and the 2017 Lebanese political crisis. Of course, each situation exhibits specificities that ideological balancing alone cannot fully explain or encompass.

Conclusion

A focus on ideology is a good antidote to the rationalist approach which reduces the "scope and ambition" of a nation's grand strategy to "its relative material power capabilities" (Rose 1998, 146). Structural approaches to grand strategy, which embody rationalist premises, routinely underrate the indigenous sources of a state's behavior. Yet, we do not want this to be construed as if we were asserting that all realists are ignorant of intellectual and social variables. They are not, though those who factor in such variables in their analyses remain a minority and do so in a reductionist fashion. For example, realists who examine nationalism treat it as the outcome of self-help (J. L. Snyder 1993, 181). By the same token, neoclassical realism incorporates social and intellectual elements, including ideas and ideologies. However, it confines ideologies' role to that of an intervening variable, that is, a variable that "condition[s] whether and how states respond to the international pressures" (Ripsman, Taliaferro, and Lobell 2016, 58). In this perspective, domestic variables essentially mediate or translate the exigencies of external stimuli.

This essay has sought to bestow ideology with a more proactive status in grand strategizing. While we acknowledge the relative importance of material circumstances, we have insisted that why states have the ambition they pursue and why they decide to do so is not driven by material capabilities alone (Rose 1998, 146). Rather, it is conditioned by cognitive factors, chiefly among which is ideology. Thus, the essay has shown that ideology is an actionable belief system; that is, a social representation with practical import. Some of the functions served by ideology may not fit rational standards, and ideology can be used for the purpose of manipulation. These perils are known. But to appreciate when and how they morph from possibilities to realities, we first need to take ideologies seriously.

When neoclassical realism integrates ideology in its account of a state's grand strategy, it either reduces it to an intervening variable or to a mere state's objective (Taliaferro, Ripsman, and Lobell 2012, 15). For this essay, such a view is valuable, but highly incomplete. We have therefore argued that ideology can help examine mobilization and resources extraction, which are necessary for any effective grand strategy. Here, the interesting avenue for research that opens up is to investigate the interaction effects of ideology; that is, the extent to which its role and influence varies, depending upon other factors that rationalists have usually privileged. But, and this is the rub, for such a prescription to bear fruits, scholars need to cultivate the view that the working of ideas captures the pulse of a nation's grand strategy.

References

Althusser, Louis. 2014. *On the Reproduction of Capitalism: Ideology and Ideological State Apparatuses*. London: Verso.

Art, Robert J. 2003. *A Grand Strategy for America*. Ithaca: Cornell University Press.

Balzacq, Thierry, and Wendy Ramadan-Alban. 2019. "Pivotal Powers—Iran." In *Comparative Grand Strategy: A Framework and Cases*, edited by Thierry Balzacq, Peter Dombrowski, and Simon Reich, 192–216. Oxford: Oxford University Press.

Barker, Rodney. 2000. "Hooks and Hands, Interests and Enemies: Political Thinking as Political Action." *Political Studies* 48 (2): 223–238. https://doi.org/10.1111/1467-9248.00257.

Brooks, Stephen G., and William Curti Wohlforth. 2016. *America Abroad: The United States' Global Role in the 21st Century*. Oxford: Oxford University Press.

Campbell, Angus, Philip E. Converse, Warren E. Miller, and Daniel E. Stokes. 1980. *The American Voter*. Chicago: University of Chicago Press.

Checkel, Jeffrey. 1993. "Ideas, Institutions, and the Gorbachev Foreign Policy Revolution." *World Politics* 45 (2): 271–300. https://doi.org/10.2307/2950660.

Converse, Philip E. 2006. "The Nature of Belief Systems in Mass Publics." *Critical Review* 18 (1–3): 1–74. https://doi.org/10.1080/08913810608443650.

Destutt de Tracy, Antoine. 1804. *Éléments d'idéologie*. Paris: Mme Ve Courcier, imprimeur-libraire.

Doyle, Michael W. 1986. "Liberalism and World Politics." *American Political Science Review* 80 (4): 1151–1169. https://doi.org/10.1017/S0003055400185041.

Fay, Brian. 1975. *Social Theory and Political Practice*. London: Routledge.

Finlayson, Alan. 2013. "Ideology and Political Rhetoric." In *The Oxford Handbook of Political Ideologies*, edited by Michael Freeden and Marc Stears, 197–213. Oxford: Oxford University Press. https://doi.org/10.1093/oxfordhb/9780199585977.013.0014.

Forst, Rainer. 2017. *Normativity and Power: Analyzing Social Orders of Justification*. Oxford: Oxford University Press.

Freeden, Michael. 2003. *Ideology: A Very Short Introduction*. Oxford: Oxford University Press.

Friedberg, Aaron L. 2000. *In the Shadow of the Garrison State: America's Anti-Statism and Its Cold War Grand Strategy*. Princeton Studies in International History and Politics. Princeton: Princeton University Press.

Gerring, John. 1997. "Ideology: A Definitional Analysis." *Political Research Quarterly* 50 (4): 957–994. https://doi.org/10.1177/106591299705000412.

Goddard, Stacie E. 2021. "Rhetoric and Legitimation." In *The Oxford Handbook of Grand Strategy*, edited by Thierry Balzacq and Ronald R. Krebs. Oxford: Oxford University Press.

Goddard, Stacie E., and Ronald R. Krebs. 2015. "Rhetoric, Legitimation, and Grand Strategy." *Security Studies* 24 (1): 5–36. https://doi.org/10.1080/09636412.2014.1001198.

Goldstein, Judith, and Robert O. Keohane, eds. 1993. *Ideas and Foreign Policy: Beliefs, Institutions, and Political Change*. Cornell Studies in Political Economy. Ithaca: Cornell University Press.

Gramsci, Antonio. 1985. *Selections from the Prison Notebooks*. Edited by Quintin Hoare and Geoffrey Nowell Smith. 8th edition. New York: International Publishers.

Gries, Peter Hays. 2014. *The Politics of American Foreign Policy: How Ideology Divides Liberals and Conservatives Over Foreign Affairs*. Stanford: Stanford Security Studies.

Haas, Mark L. 2012. *The Clash of Ideologies: Middle Eastern Politics and American Security*. New York: Oxford University Press.

Hamilton, Malcolm B. 1987. "The Elements of the Concept of Ideology." *Political Studies* 35 (1): 18–38. https://doi.org/10.1111/j.1467-9248.1987.tb00186.x.

Jervis, Robert. 1968. "Hypotheses on Misperception." *World Politics* 20 (3): 454–479. https://doi.org/10.2307/2009777.

Jost, John, C. M. Federico, and Jaime L. Napier. 2013. "Political Ideologies and Their Social Psychological Functions." In *The Oxford Handbook of Political Ideologies*, edited by Michael Freeden, Lyman Tower Sargent, and Marc Stears, 232–250. Oxford: Oxford University Press.

Kazemzadeh, Masoud. 2020. *Iran's Foreign Policy: Elite Factionalism, Ideology, the Nuclear Weapons Program, and the United States*. London: Routledge.

Knight, Kathleen. 2006. "Transformations of the Concept of Ideology in the Twentieth Century." *American Political Science Review* 100 (04): 619. https://doi.org/10.1017/S0003055406062502.

Kornprobst, Markus, and Corina-Iona Traistaru. 2021. "Language and Grand Strategy." In *The Oxford Handbook of Grand Strategy*, edited by Thierry Balzacq and Ronald R. Krebs. Oxford: Oxford University Press.

Kramer, Mark. 1999. "Ideology and the Cold War." *Review of International Studies* 25 (4): 539–576.

Krasner, Stephen D. 2010. "An Orienting Principle for Foreign Policy: The Deficiencies of 'Grand Strategy.'" *Policy Review*, no. 163 (October). https://www.hoover.org/research/orienting-principle-foreign-policy

Krebs, Ronald R. 2021. "Pluralism, Populism, and the Impossibility of Grand Strategy." In *The Oxford Handbook of Grand Strategy*, edited by Thierry Balzacq and Ronald R. Krebs. Oxford: Oxford University Press.

Laclau, Ernesto. 2005. *On Populist Reason*. London: Verso.

Macrae, Duncan. 1952. "The Relation Between Roll Call Votes and Constituencies in the Massachusetts House of Representatives." *American Political Science Review* 46 (4): 1046–1055. https://doi.org/10.2307/1952111.

Mannheim, Karl. 1954. *Ideology and Utopia: An Introduction to the Sociology of Knowledge*. New York: Harcourt, Brace & Co.

Martel, William C. 2015. *Grand Strategy in Theory and Practice: The Need for an Effective American Foreign Policy*. Cambridge: Cambridge University Press.

Marx, Karl, and Friedrich Engels. 1974. *The German Ideology*. Edited by C. J. Arthur. London: Lawrence & Wishart.

Maynard, Jonathan Leader. 2018. "Ideology." In *The SAGE Handbook of Political Sociology*, edited by William Outhwaite and Stephen Turner, 479–500. London: SAGE Publications. https://doi.org/10.4135/9781526416513.n29.

McCourt, David M. 2021. "Culture and Identity in Grand Strategy." In *The Oxford Handbook on Grand Strategy*, edited by Thierry Balzacq and Ronald R. Krebs. Oxford: Oxford University Press.

Mearsheimer, John J. 2001. *The Tragedy of Great Power Politics*. New York: W. W. Norton & Company.

Milevski, Lukas. 2016. *The Evolution of Modern Grand Strategic Thought*. Oxford: Oxford University Press.

Milner, Helen V., and Dustin Tingley. 2015. *Sailing the Water's Edge: The Domestic Politics of American Foreign Policy*. Princeton: Princeton University Press.

Morgenthau, Hans J. 1948. *Politics among Nations: The Struggle for Power and Peace*. New York: Alfred A. Knopf.

Mueller, John. 1993. "The Impact of Ideas in Grand Strategy." In *The Domestic Bases of Grand Strategy*, edited by Richard N. Rosecrance and Arthur A. Stein. Cornell Studies in Security Affairs. Ithaca: Cornell University Press.

Mullins, Willard A. 1972. "On the Concept of Ideology in Political Science." *American Political Science Review* 66 (2): 498–510. https://doi.org/10.2307/1957794.

Neufeld, Mark. 1993. "Interpretation and the 'science' of International Relations." *Review of International Studies* 19 (1): 39–61. https://doi.org/10.1017/S0260210500117334.

Owen, John M. 2010. *The Clash of Ideas in World Politics: Transnational Networks, States, and Regime Change, 1510–2010*. Princeton Studies in International History and Politics. Princeton: Princeton University Press.

Posen, Barry R. 2014. *Restraint: A New Foundation for U.S. Grand Strategy*. Cornell Studies in Security Affairs. Ithaca: Cornell University Press.

Posen, Barry R., and Andrew L. Ross. 1996. "Competing Visions for U.S. Grand Strategy." *International Security* 21 (3): 5–53. https://doi.org/10.2307/2539272.

Purvis, Trevor, and Alan Hunt. 1993. "Discourse, Ideology, Discourse, Ideology, Discourse, Ideology..." *The British Journal of Sociology* 44 (3): 473–499.

Richards, I. A. 1936. *The Philosophy of Rhetoric*. The Mary Flexner Lectures on the Humanities 3. Oxford: Oxford University Press.

Ripsman, Norrin M., Jeffrey W. Taliaferro, and Steven E. Lobell. 2016. *Neoclassical Realist Theory of International Politics*. Oxford: Oxford University Press.

Rose, Gideon. 1998. "Neoclassical Realism and Theories of Foreign Policy." *World Politics* 51 (1): 144–172.

Rosecrance, Richard N., and Arthur A. Stein, eds. 1993. "Beyond Realism: The Study of Grand Strategy." In *The Domestic Bases of Grand Strategy*, 3–21. Cornell Studies in Security Affairs. Ithaca: Cornell University Press.

Sartori, Giovanni. 1969. "Politics, Ideology, and Belief Systems." *American Political Science Review* 63 (2): 398–411. https://doi.org/10.1017/S0003055400262291.

Schubert, Glendon A. 1958. "The Study of Judicial Decision-Making as an Aspect of Political Behavior." *American Political Science Review* 52 (4): 1007–1025. https://doi.org/10.2307/1951981.

Snyder, Jack L. 1993. "The New Nationalism: Realist Interpretations and Beyond." In *The Domestic Bases of Grand Strategy*, edited by Richard N. Rosecrance and Arthur A. Stein, 179–200. Cornell Studies in Security Affairs. Ithaca: Cornell University Press.

Snyder, Richard C., H. W. Bruck, and Burton Sapin. 1954. *Decision-Making as an Approach to the Study of International Politics*. Princeton, NJ: Princeton University Press.

Taliaferro, Jeffrey W., Norrin M. Ripsman, and Steven E. Lobell. 2012. "Introduction: Grand Strategy between the World Wars." In *The Challenge of Grand Strategy: The Great Powers and the Broken Balance Between the World Wars*, edited by Jeffrey W. Taliaferro, Norrin M. Ripsman, and Steven E. Lobell, 1–36. Cambridge: Cambridge University Press.

Van Dijk, Teun A. 2013. "Ideology and Discourse." In *The Oxford Handbook of Political Ideologies*, edited by Michael Freeden, Lyman Tower Sargent, and Marc Stears, 175–197. Oxford: Oxford University Press.

Waltz, Kenneth Neal. 1979. *Theory of International Politics*. Long Grove, Ill: Waveland Press.

Wendt, Alexander. 1999. *Social Theory of International Politics*. Cambridge Studies in International Relations 67. Cambridge: Cambridge University Press.

Yee, Albert S. 1996. "The Causal Effects of Ideas on Policies." *International Organization* 50 (1): 69–108.

CHAPTER 11

DISCOURSE, LANGUAGE, AND GRAND STRATEGY

MARKUS KORNPROBST AND
CORINA-IOANA TRAISTARU

GRAND strategy and communication are intricately interwoven. Take, for instance, the institutionalization of the study of grand strategy in the United States. In the midst of the Second World War, Edward Earle built a network connecting the president, state department officials, members of congress, and the public. This was the infrastructure within which communication could flow amongst elites and from elites to the masses. The latter was important to him. He sought to build a broad societal consensus on grand strategy (Earle 1943; Ekbladh 2011/2012, 109). With this infrastructure in place, containment could later become a widely shared grand strategy (Dueck 2005).

Scholars of grand strategy often practice advocating a particular kind of grand strategy. If we take the United States, where studies of grand strategy are more deeply entrenched than in (most) other states, again as example, we come across all kinds of different advocacies for a US grand strategy. These are advocated in books, scholarly articles and, at least equally important, in periodicals that reach into foreign-policymaking circles such as *Foreign Affairs* and the *National Interest*. In the last decade, numerous contributions have been made to the debate between retrenchment and engagement (Brooks, Ikenberry, Wohlforth 2013; Martel 2015; Brands, Feaver, Mearsheimer, Walt 2016; Posen 2018).

Although this intricate connection between communication and grand strategy is difficult to overlook, it comes so natural to most analysts and advocates of grand strategy that they end up neglecting the study of communication (or limit it to spin-doctoring their own ideas for a grand strategy into the limelight). This chapter counters this neglect. Focusing on the relationship between communication and grand strategy, we discuss what a linguistic perspective has to offer for studying grand strategy. We investigate to what extent this perspective helps us to describe grand strategies, identify the kinds of actors who hold grand strategies, investigate how actors put grand strategies to use in concrete foreign-policymaking situations, explain the making, remaking, and unmaking of grand strategies, and examine the normative repercussions of doing research on grand strategy. To this end, we draw from what authors have written explicitly on the nexus of language and grand strategy, do a little bit of reading in between the lines of studies in which this nexus remains more or less implicit, borrow from linguistic research that does not address grand strategy, and suggest avenues for developing a linguistic perspective—very much interacting with other perspectives—further.

Our argument may be summarized in five points: first, grand strategy is, metaphorically speaking, language that has come to assume a temporary state of solid matter. It is a taken-for-granted set of commonplaces composed of representations of the international environment, identity, overall purpose, and means. Second, a variety of collective actors—ranging from states via multinational corporations, and non-for-profit organizations to terrorist organizations—may hold grand strategies. Third, actors put grand strategies to use by judging and justifying about how to make sense of a given situation, make decisions, and make meaning. Fourth, such more fluid interplays between judging and justifying have not only repercussions for foreign-policymaking but also for grand strategies themselves. They are made, remade, and unmade in these processes. Fifth, more comparative research, crisscrossing studies drawing from linguistic and other perspectives, and normative inquiries are warranted.

The organization of this chapter follows the unfolding of this argument. First, we discuss conceptualizations of grand strategy. Second, we investigate the question of who holds grand strategies. Third, we move on to the question of how actors come to put grand strategies to use. Fourth, we address how actors make, remake, and unmake grand strategies. Fifth, the conclusion summarizes our argument and sketches an agenda for further research.

What Is a Grand Strategy?

From a linguistic point of view, a grand strategy is temporarily solidified communication. There are four components of grand strategy: international environment, identity, overall purpose, and means to work towards this overall purpose. Grand strategies are characterized by intensive agreements on how these four components are to be linked together. This section discusses to what extent this conceptualization of grand strategy converges and diverges with other perspectives.

On the one hand, there are various convergences. Three of them are especially noteworthy. First, grand strategy is *intersubjective*. This is often made explicit, for instance, when grand strategy is likened to "relatively discrete and coherent arguments" (Posen and Ross 1996, 3), "a set of ideas" (Brooks, Ikenberry, and Wohlforth 2012, 11), or "a set of core ideas" (Brands and Porter 2015). This convergence extends to scholars shying away from making this ontology explicit. Even authors putting the strongest emphasis on how material forces shape grand strategy do not deny that the concept itself is part of the ideational realm (Goldman and Arquilla 1999, 306; Miller 2010). Second, grand strategy is about identifying an overall *purpose* and the *means* to work towards this purpose. When Liddell Hart (1967) coined the concept, he thought of it as a kind of meta-strategy. Kennedy's highly influential definition broadened the understanding of purpose and means but did not do away with these basic categories. On the contrary, he (1991a) underlined them even further. Third, grand strategy is something that addresses the *long run*. It is not about short-term interests and/or short-term ways to address them (Brooks and Wohlforth 2016, 75; Kennedy 1991a, 5; Brands 2015, 24; Silove 2018, 31). With regards to time, too, grand strategy is an overarching strategy.

On the other hand, there are plenty of divergences. These pertain to the components of grand strategy, the linkages across these components, and the degree of internalization of these components and linkages. Overall, a linguistic perspective strongly points towards *broadening and deepening conceptualizations of grand strategy*. Purpose and means are components of grand strategy. Analysts, however, should not a priori narrow these down to the overall purpose of, say, "fighting" (Posen 2014, 1) and the means to punishing or cooperating with competitors over hegemony (Lobell 2003), or to balance or not to balance against an opponent (Brawley 2009). It is a matter of empirical analysis whether the overall purpose of a grand strategy is about "fighting" or accumulating wealth, building international order, peaceful change, and so on, and whether the means to be used are military, economic, and/or diplomatic. Language may constitute grand strategies in a great variety of ways. These are to be explored rather than excluded by overly narrow conceptual premises.

Grand strategies are not just about purpose and means. It is telling that authors who define grand strategy in terms of purpose and means often include representations of the international environment (Luttwak 1984; Posen and Ross 1996) and the actors' identifications (Posen and Ross 1996; Brooks and Wohlforth 2016) in their empirical research. Practitioners, of course, understand the importance of weaving understandings of the security environment and identity into grand strategies very well. George Kennan (quoted in Hastedt 2017, 61), one of the early protagonists of the US grand strategy of containment, once remarked: "There seems to be a curious American tendency to search, at all times, for a single external evil, to which all can be attributed." To put this differently, positive and negative identifications are woven into grand strategies.

Linguistic approaches refrain from smuggling environment and identity into the empirical research and staying aloof from studying them conceptually. Representations of the international environment and identity are part and parcel of grand strategies (Goddard and Krebs 2015; Kornprobst 2015). Students of politics who take language seriously have long pointed out that actors do not look at purpose (Weldes 1999) and means (Schneider and Ingram 1993) in isolation. They see them in light of a broader environment and identity (Neumann and Heikka 2005; Neumann 2008; Cienki and Yanow 2013, 167). This is where linguistic approaches to grand strategy meet existing research on security environments and identity that may not address grand strategy or do so only in passing. Take securitization, for example. This literature shows that representations of international environments have come to be more and more securitized in more and more states, state alliances, and international organizations in recent decades (Wæver 1995; McDonald 2008; Balzacq and Guzzini 2015). Understandings of international environments, in other words, are not carved into stone. They evolve and with them grand strategies. Literature on identity, too, is very important for studying grand strategy. This ranges from applications of role theory to international relations (Holsti 1970; Shih 1988; Thies and Breuning 2012) to studies on how identity-constituting norms evolve from hostile towards friendly relations and vice versa (Katzenstein 1998; Bátora 2005; Kornprobst 2008).

Grand strategies are not just components but linkages across components. Other perspectives on grand strategy at times even allude to linkages in their definitions. In definitions mentioned above, the term "set" (Brooks, Ikenberry, and Wohlforth 2012, 11; Brands and Porter 2015) was mentioned twice and the formulation "coherent arguments" (Posen and Ross 1996, 3) once. For linguistic approaches, however, it does not suffice to mention linkages and then not follow up with them in further conceptual and empirical explorations of grand strategy. Grand strategies are what linguistically minded scholars who do not study this topic refer to as assemblages (Keremidchieva 2013; Walker 2016). More precisely put, they are assemblages that link representations of environment, identity, purpose, and means together (Kornprobst 2015).

Deepening research is equally important. Writers have been cautioning for some time that grand strategies are not always fully explicit (Solingen 1998, 19; Brands 2015, 6). In some cases, grand strategies may not even be recognized as such by actors embracing them (Luttwak 2009, 409). Furthermore, and related to the previous point, a number of authors contend that taken-for-grantedness is a key feature of grand strategies. Grand strategy is not just any kind of plan. It is a meta-plan or a "paradigm" (Kagan, F. 2008, 32) that comes seemingly naturally to actors who have internalized it (Nadel 1995; Gaddis 2005). Grand strategies, to use language employed outside the study of grand strategy, reside in the background rather than the foreground (Adler and Bernstein 2004; Kornprobst and Senn 2016a). This raises thorny methodological questions about how to uncover what is so taken for granted by actors that it no longer comes natural to them to even make it explicit. Linguistic research on grand strategy has shown that it can rise to the challenge (Neumann and Heikka 2005), although it has to be said that, overall, even linguistic approaches in International Relations tend to overemphasize what is explicit in discourse.

Outside the discipline, there are many voices that caution that the study of language use should not be confined to what is explicit in discourse (Sadock 1974, 292; Grice 1978, 115; van Eemeren and Grootendorst 1984, 145). This is to be taken seriously. Actors put to use grand strategies as compasses to orient themselves in the world in general and in concrete decision-making situations in particular. When they do so, they usually do not disassemble the entire compass into its components in order to be able to see the surface components as well as those that are usually hidden from the eye. They simply put it to use, the hidden components very much included. Otherwise, the components cannot work as a compass.

WHO HOLDS A GRAND STRATEGY?

It is a hardly ever questioned orthodoxy in studies on grand strategy that only states, and among these especially great powers, hold grand strategies. Being an orthodoxy, this assumption is hardly made explicit, and, if it is, it is merely asserted rather than argued for. Kennedy, for instance, flatly states that grand strategy is something for "great rather than small or medium powers" (Kennedy 1991b, 120). In line with this assumption, there is a considerable amount of research on the Soviet Union (Luttwak 1984; Gibbs 1987) and Russia (LeDonne 2003; Monaghan 2013), more and more on China (Johnston 1998; Jisi 2011, Swaine, Daly, Greenwood 2000; Goldstein 2005) and also on assertive regional powers such as Iran (Halliday 1987; Ostovar 2019), Turkey (Walker 2007; Taşpınar 2012), and Brazil (Brands 2010, 2011). Most of all, of course, there is research on the United States. The bulk of research on grand strategy, including most works cited in the previous section, focus on this state.

Authors who take language seriously venture a bit further. While there is research on great powers in general (Goddard 2015; Johnston 1998; Mitzen 2015) and the United States in particular (Tjalve and Williams 2015; Krebs 2015a, 2015b; Snyder 2015), there are also studies on middle powers (Neumann and Heikka 2005) as well as convergences on grand strategies across states, such as members of the European Union (Rogers 2009; Kornprobst 2015). Thus, linguistic approaches have started to move beyond the great power and state biases. Taken-for-granted linkages across understandings of environment, identity, purpose, and means are not confined to great powers, of course. Neither are they limited to states. Since a linguistic perspective does not share some of Realism's core assumptions, such as the great power and state biases, authors choose the actors they want to study in much less restrictive fashion.

There is plenty of empirical evidence in policy documents and existing research to suggest that analysis of the grand strategies of different types of actors is necessary to make sense of today's global politics. The International Committee of the Red Cross (ICRC)'s 2019–2022 strategy, for example, aims at providing "a compass for action for the next four years" (ICRC Strategy 2019–2022). The same applies to multinational corporations. The Boston Consulting Group (2019), for instance, likens its corporate strategy to "the overall plan for a diversified company" (Porter 1989, 234), which encompasses three areas: (1) "a clear, shared, long-term vision;" realized through a (2) portfolio strategy and (3) the establishment of "corporate policies and processes." Terrorist organizations, too, may have grand strategies. Al-Qaeda, for example, links understandings and visions of the world to its identity, overall purpose, and means (Cozzens 2006; Cornish, Lindley-French, and Yorke 2011; Jenkins 2002, 4). The literature also suggests that the Islamic State held a grand strategy (Novenario 2016).

No matter what kinds of states or organizations are put under scrutiny, a linguistic perspective cautions against assuming a priori to what extent this grand strategy is shared. Habitual assumptions that anthropomorphized states hold grand strategies

(Posen 1984, 13) are highly simplistic. An entire subfield of International Relations—Foreign Policy Analysis—cautions against this simplification. Within a state, there is usually ample contestation among different actors about what grand strategy the state ought to embrace. Yet such a focus on decision-making elites (Wohlforth 1994, 95, 98) may have its pitfalls. Actors often seek to disseminate grand strategy and anchor it in the public domain. Earle's doings, for example, have been alluded to at the very beginning of this article.

The extent to which an aggregate actor converges upon a grand strategy is a question to be examined by empirical analysis. The extent of agreement varies: it makes a major difference, for example, whether a grand strategy is widely accepted in a state or whether it is held only by a leader and a few advisors around him or her. Similarly, it is analytically significant whether a terrorist organization fully converges around a grand strategy or whether factions within such an organization hold competing grand strategies. Extensive agreement facilitates coordinated action, and leadership turnover is less problematic. The lack of such extensive agreement, by contrast, causes problems of coordination and may lead to significant changes when new leaders come to power.

How Do Actors Put Grand Strategies to Use?

Literature on grand strategy, including research that takes language seriously, rarely inquires into how actors put grand strategies to use. The analytical focus is usually more on whether a state or nonstate actor has a grand strategy and, if so, how it came into being. It is then assumed that decision-makers and advisors employ the grand strategy that they hold to orient themselves in the world.

From a linguistic perspective, however, this amounts to an oversimplification. The grand strategy alone does not do the talking. It is actors, interpreting grand strategies and applying them to a concrete situation, who do. Grand strategies, to borrow from Wiener (2009), are meaning in use. This usage, over and over in different situations, has to be explained. Existing research on grand strategy provides hints as to what kinds of usages are to be explained: sense-making, decision-making, and meaning-making.[1] Hill (2010) reminds us that grand strategy enables actors to make sense of a situation. Gaddis (2018: 17) writes that grand strategies provide actors with a "compass heading"; they "improvise" a lot when making decisions but the kinds of decisions they make are, generally speaking, in line with this compass heading. Finally, even the most powerful leaders have to justify their doings. Justifying their applications of grand strategy, they seek to engage in meaning-making to mobilize support for their doings (Christensen 1996: 11–14).

Sense-making, decision-making and meaning-making, in our view, revolve around judgments and justifications.[2] Judgment, as Beiner (1983) puts it succinctly, is subsuming particulars under universals. The particulars of a situation are made intelligible in light of the universals. What appears to actors as universals are procedural and substantive in nature (Kornprobst 2019b). They provide orientation for actors as to how much clout they have in foreign policy debates and how they can make a difference in these debates (procedural) as well as how a grand strategy and its constitutive components are to be related to a situation at hand (substantive). It will never be possible to do research on all interlocutors in debates on grand strategy, not even to speak of those who are sidelined in communicative encounters. But it is possible, following the example set by political psychologists who take judgment seriously (Tetlock 2005; Mintz and DeRouen 2010; Aronoff 2014), to inquire into how key actors come to make their judgments in sufficient depth.

Justifications are underpinned by judgments and, vice versa, shape judgments. Actors, selectively putting to use[3] a repertoire of universals—a grand strategy included—elaborate on their first hunches while communicating with one another. This communication revolves around justifications. Actors give reasons for their stances (Abulof and Kornprobst 2017). This exchange of justifications, in turn, shapes and reshapes their judgments again and again (Kornprobst 2019b).

How Do Actors Make, Remake, and Unmake Grand Strategies?

The bulk of the literature does not address questions of how grand strategies are remade or unmade. But there are many contending arguments about how grand strategies are made. The literature identifies five sets of explanatory forces: material context, social context, choice, judgment, and communication. One of these, choice, is irreconcilable with a linguistic perspective. The others, in principle, are important ingredients for developing explanations of the making, remaking, and unmaking of grand strategies that take language seriously.

Grand strategies are linked to material forces. But linguistic approaches caution that these do not determine the origins of grand strategies. A number of authors, at times self-identifying as realists, contend that grand strategies are a function of the distribution of capabilities (Posen 1984; Lobell 2003; Schweller 2004; Layne 2008). An especially bold variant of this cluster of the literature is Miller's contention that this distribution and degrees of external threat cause grand strategies. Materialism, in his words, "works as the selector of ideas", i.e., whether US grand strategy is "defensive realist", "offensive realist," "defensive liberal," or "offensive liberal" (Miller 2010, 29). This formulation postulates that materialism has quasi-agential properties. It selects.

Paying attention to language should not come at the expense of neglecting material forces. But it requires that we avoid interpretations that overburden the causal arrow from material forces to grand strategies. Linguistic approaches outside of International

Relations have generated a number of important concepts that seek to capture contextual openings available to interlocutors to make something new stick. For the Sophists, such an opening was a *kairos* (Poulakos 1997, 17–18). This concept is not all that different from what some authors in Political Science and International Relations refer to as exogenous shock (Hall 1986; Adler 1991). A perhaps more refined concept is the exigence, i.e. a tension that requires communication to be addressed (Bitzer 1968). There are various different kinds of exigences. One of them is constituted by an intersubjective tension between elements of a material and those of a social context (Kornprobst and Senn 2016b; 2018).

Social context matters. A linguistic perspective underlines the finding of several authors that grand strategies emerge out of an intersubjective context (Dueck 2005; Brands 2015). Hill (2010), a former US career diplomat, refers to this as strategic culture. Thus, work on repertoires (Benor 2010; Goddard, MacDonald and Nexon 2019), toolkits (Swidler 1986; Gill 2017), strategic culture (Johnston 1995; Meyer 2005), and related concepts provides a wealth of insights for linguistic attempts to explain the origins of grand strategies. After all, a grand strategy is a composition that connects elements of a broader repertoire firmly to one another, thus establishing an assemblage within this repertoire. Note that social context is not monolithic and homogeneous. There are tensions within the context that actors try to resolve. In other words, we are back at the concept of exigence. There are not only exogenous exigences (tensions between material and social contexts) but also endogenous ones (tensions within a context) and semi-endogenous ones (tensions between overlapping social contexts) (Kornprobst and Senn 2016b, 2018).

If contexts form one part of an explanation, agency amounts to the other. Some arguments downplay context and overplay choice. Actors are portrayed as choosing a grand strategy. Ostovar (2019), placing much greater emphasis on agency than context, contends that leaders choose a grand strategy if the costs outweigh the benefits. Choice understood this way also features prominently in Goldman and Arquilla (1999), although these authors adopt a middle ground in the structure–agency debate. Most authors, however, no matter whether they address language or not, reject such simple choice arguments, alluding to judgment instead (Kennedy 1991b; Hill 2010). Luttwak (2009, 409–418), elaborating on the nexus of judgment and the making of grand strategy in considerable detail, borrows from George (1969) and his operational code analysis in order to conceptualize how this judging works. Making grand strategies, leaders put their prior interpretations—and linkages across these interpretations—to use.

While for a long time, communication has been neglected as *explanans* of grand strategy, in the last two decades or so, a number of authors have examined it in considerable depth (Solingen 1998; Dueck 2005; Cornish, Lindley-French, and Yorke 2011, 3). A special issue in *Security Studies* (2015), edited by Stacie Goddard and Ron Krebs (2015), focused squarely on the nexus of public justification and grand strategies. Hence, scrutinizing judgments and justifications is not only of major relevance for explaining how actors put grand strategies to use. It is equally important for explaining how grand strategies are made, remade, and unmade.

Interplays of judgments and justifications appear to give rise to somewhat different—but at times related—generative mechanisms of change. First, putting to use grand strategies in concrete situations, actors make them evolve over time. If a grand strategy is employed again and again, it may develop into a rhetorical practice (De Certeau 1984).[4] Yet even these practices do not always remain the same. Adaptations happen. Actors learn lessons from putting grand strategies to use, thus making them evolve in certain directions rather than others. In the long run, this may change grand strategies quite significantly. But even after quite some evolution, there will still be what Fierke (2002), borrowing from Wittgenstein, refers to as family resemblance. Second, grand strategies can also emerge and collapse through processes that are characterized by ruptures. Simply putting to use orthodoxies no longer works. Exigences—especially exogenous ones—provide major openings for unmaking the old and making the new. Equally important, actors need to be savvy to embed the new in what is already established. Interlocutors need to make use of at least some commonplaces (Aristotle 1975; Cicero1976) that are already in the dominant repertoire. Communicative encounters that lack any familiar elements to anchor them remain unintelligible.

Conclusion

What does language have to do with grand strategy? Much more than many authors would admit! Grand strategy is, metaphorically speaking, temporarily solidified language that is made, remade, and unmade in much more fluid communicative encounters. Actors judge and justify when putting grand strategies to use. This has important policy repercussions. But their judging and justifying also has implications for grand strategy itself.

Three items for an agenda for further research come immediately to mind. First, an "explicitly comparative agenda" (Balzacq, Dombrowski, and Reich 2018, 28) for studying grand strategy should not be limited to states, not even if they are not the United States, great powers, or regional powers. Much more research is required on grand strategies shared across states. The extent to which they share grand strategies has major repercussions for their ability to do something together (Mitzen 2015; Kornprobst 2019b). Equally important, there is a need to overcome the state bias. All kinds of nonstate actors may adopt grand strategies. Even networks of nonstate actors or networks linking state and nonstate actors together may do so. The human security network, initiated by Lloyd Axworthy when he was Canadian foreign minister, is an example that comes to mind. So is, very much related to it, the Humanitarian Initiative in the nuclear arms control regime.

Second, sharp demarcations between linguistic approaches and other crisscrossing perspectives are counterproductive. It is, for example, not of much help if linguistic research is portrayed and/or portrays itself as a research program that addresses everything that is explicit and studies on practice as everything that is located underneath the radar screen of discourse. Such demarcations may make for neat scholarly pigeon holes, but they are of little help for studying the judging and justifying that make grand strategies move in certain directions rather than others. Equally important, language-sensitive research should not neglect the salience of material forces. Engaging with Realist scholarship on grand strategy and also the New Materialism in International Relations Theory (Connolly 2013; Mac Ginty 2017) serves as an important corrective against an exclusive focus on intersubjective forces.

Finally, it is of great importance to adequately address the almost inescapable normative dimension of researching grand strategy. There is simply no denying that some ideas on grand strategy make it from the scholarly realm to political decision-makers. Bits and pieces of Posen's prescriptive research on a grand strategy of restraint (Posen 2014), for example, found their way to the Trump administration (Balzacq, Dombrowski, and Reich 2018), even though Posen (2018) tried to counter this. From a linguistic point of view, it is not surprising that scholarly ideas influence the making of grand strategies. Scholars enjoy a considerable amount of epistemic authority (some more so than others), and students of grand strategy are often quite savvy in exploiting this to intervene in justificatory processes through which grand strategies are made, remade, or unmade. It is, however, highly important not to violate basic rules about how to do and disseminate research. From a linguistic point of view, these rules concern, first and foremost, debates among scholars and between scholars and other communicators. These ought to be inclusive and driven by curiosity. Instead of denying certain authors a status of ratified participants (Goffman 1981), scholars should cherish the heterogeneity of debates. This is how they can learn the most from others and critique their own work. Communicability is to be ensured by translations (Coleman 2004, 117), wherever necessary to bridge (meta-)theoretical and methodological divides. Taken together, such encounters are diametrically opposed to the shouting of spin-doctored messages, disguised as supposed scientific certainty, from the epistemic rooftops of academia and, even more so, exploiting shortcuts to the corridors of political power hidden to the public eye and established by think tanks. Instead, they point towards "deliberation type II" (Bächtinger et al. 2010, 44) or polylogue (Kornprobst 2018). Grand strategies matter for foreign policies and world politics. We'd better check their plausibility very thoroughly.

Notes

1. On this terminology, see Boin, Stern, and Sundelius (2016).
2. For a seminal account of this relationship between judgments and justifications, see Arendt (1958).
3. We borrow this formulation from Fierke (2002) and Wiener (2009).
4. On practices and discourse, see also Neumann (2002).

References

Abulof, Uriel, and Markus Kornprobst. 2017. "Introduction: The Politics of Public Justification." *Contemporary Politics* 23 (1): 1–18.

Adler, Emanuel, and Steven Bernstein. 2004. "Knowledge in Power: The Epistemic Construction of Global Governance." In *Power in Global Governance*, edited by Michael Barnett, and Raymond Duvall, 294–318. Cambridge: Cambridge University Press.

Adler, Emanuel. 1991. "Cognitive Evolution: A Dynamic Approach for the Study of International Relations and Their Progress." In *Progress in Postwar International Relations*, edited by Emanuel Adler, and Beverly Crawford, 128–173. New York: Columbia University Press.

Adler, Emanuel. 2019. *World Ordering: A Social Theory of Cognitive Evolution*. Cambridge: Cambridge University Press.

Arendt, Hannah. 1958. *The Human Condition*. Chicago: University of Chicago Press.

Aristotle. 1975. *Art of Rhetoric*. Cambridge: Harvard University Press.

Aronoff, Yael. S. 2014. *The Political Psychology of Israeli Prime Ministers*. Cambridge: Cambridge University Press.

Bächtinger, André, Simon Niemeyer, Michael Neblo, Marco R. Steenbergen, and Jürg Steiner. 2010. "Disentangling Diversity in Deliberative Democracy: Competing Theories, Their Blind Spots and Complementarities." *Journal of Political Philosophy* 18 (1): 32–63.

Balzacq, Thierry, and Stefano Guzzini. 2015. "Introduction: "What Kind of Theory—If Any—Is Securitization?"" *International Relations* 29 (1): 97–102.

Balzacq, Thierry, Peter Dombrowski, and Simon Reich. 2018. "Is Grand Strategy a Research Program? A Review Essay." *Security Studies* 28 (1): 1–29.

Bátora, Jozef. 2005. "Does the European Union Transform the Institution of Diplomacy?" *Journal of European Public Policy* 12 (1): 44–66.

Beiner, Ronald. 1983. *Political Judgment*. Chicago: University of Chicago Press.

Benor, Sarah Bunin. 2010. "Ethnolinguistic Repertoire: Shifting the Analytic Focus in Language and Ethnicity 1." *Journal of Sociolinguistics* 14 (2): 159–183.

Betts, Richard K. 2000. "Is Strategy an Illusion?" *International Security* 25 (2): 5–50.

Bitzer, Lloyd F. 1968. "The Rhetorical Situation." *Philosophy & Rhetoric* 1 (1): 1–14.

Boin, Arjen, Eric Stern, and Bengt Sundelius. 2016. *The Politics of Crisis Management: Public Leadership under Pressure*. Cambridge: Cambridge University Press.

Boston Consulting Group. 2019. "Corporate Strategy." https://www.bcg.com/capabilities/strategy/corporate-strategy.aspx, accessed April 9, 2019.

Brands, Hal, and Patrick Porter. 2015. "Why Grand Strategy Still Matters in a World of Chaos." *National Interest*, December 10, 2015. https://nationalinterest.org/feature/why-grand-strategy-still-matters-world-chaos-14568, accessed April 9, 2019.

Brands, Hal, Peter D. Feaver, John J. Mearsheimer, and Stephen M. Walt. 2016. "Should America Retrench: The Battle over Offshore Balancing." *Foreign Affairs* 95 (6): 164–169.

Brands, Hal. 2010. *Dilemmas of Brazilian Grand Strategy*. Carlisle: Strategic Studies Institute.

Brands, Hal. 2011. "Evaluating Brazilian Grand Strategy under Lula." *Comparative Strategy* 30 (1): 28–49.

Brands, Hal. 2014. *What Good is Grand Strategy? Power and Purpose in American Statecraft from Harry S. Truman to George W. Bush*. Ithaca: Cornell University Press.

Brands, Hal. 2015. "Fools Rush Out? The Flawed Logic of Offshore Balancing." *Washington Quarterly* 38 (2): 7–28.
Brawley, Mark R. 2009. *Political Economy and Grand Strategy: A Neoclassical Realist View*. London: Routledge.
Brooks, Stephen G., and William C. Wohlforth. 2016. *America Abroad: The United States' Global Role in the 21st Century*. New York: Oxford University Press.
Brooks, Stephen G., G. John Ikenberry, and William C. Wohlforth. 2013. "Lean Forward: In Defense of American Engagement." *Foreign Affairs* 92 (1): 130–142.
Brooks, Stephen G., G. John Ikenberry, and William C. Wohlforth. 2012. "Don't Come Home, America: The Case against Retrenchment." *International Security* 37 (3): 7–51.
Christensen, Thomas J. 1996. *Useful Adversaries: Grand strategy, Domestic Mobilization, and Sino-American Conflict, 1947–1958*. Princeton: Princeton University Press.
Cicero. (1976). *De Oratore*. Edited and translated by Harald Merklin. Stuttgart: Reclam.
Cienki, Alan, and Dvora Yanow. 2013. "Why Metaphor and other Tropes? Linguistic Approaches to Analysing Policies and the Political." *Journal of International Relations and Development* 16 (2): 167–176.
Coleman, Stephen. 2004. "Whose Conversation? Engaging the Public in Authentic Polylogue." *Political Quarterly* 75 (2): 112–120.
Connolly, William E. 2013. "The "New Materialism" and the Fragility of Things." *Millennium* 41 (3): 399–412.
Cornish, Paul, Julian Lindley-French, and Claire Yorke. 2011. *Strategic Communications and National Strategy*. London: Chatham House.
Cozzens, Jeffrey B. 2006. "Approaching Al-Qaeda's Warfare: Function, Culture and Grand Strategy." In *Mapping Terrorism Research: State of the Art, Gaps, and Future Direction*, edited by Magnus Ranstorp, 141–177. London: Routledge.
De Certeau, Michel. 1984. *The Practice of Everyday Life*. Berkeley: University of California Press.
Dueck, Colin. 2005. "Realism, Culture and Grand Strategy: Explaining America's Peculiar Path to World Power." *Security Studies* 14 (2): 195–231.
Earle, Edward Mead. 1943. "Power Politics and American World Policy." *Political Science Quarterly* 58 (1): 94–106.
Ekbladh, David. 2011/2012. "Present at the Creation: Edward Mead Earle and the Depression-Era Origins of Security Studies." *International Security* 36 (3): 107–141.
Fierke, Karin M. 2002. "Links Across the Abyss: Language and Logic in International Relations." *International Studies Quarterly* 46 (3): 331–354.
Gaddis, John Lewis. 2005. "Grand Strategy in the Second Term." *Foreign Affairs* 84 (1): 2–15.
Gaddis, John Lewis. 2018. *On Grand Strategy*. New York: Penguin Books.
George, Alexander L. 1969. "The "Operational Code": A Neglected Approach to the Study of Political Leaders and Decision-making." *International Studies Quarterly* 13 (2): 190–222.
Gibbs, David. 1987. "Does the USSR Have a "Grand Strategy"? Reinterpreting the Invasion of Afghanistan." *Journal of Peace Research* 24 (4): 365–379.
Gill, Timothy M. 2017. "Unpacking the World Cultural Toolkit in Socialist Venezuela: National Sovereignty, Human Rights and Anti-NGO Legislation." *Third World Quarterly* 38 (3): 621–635.
Goddard, Stacie E. 2015. "The Rhetoric of Appeasement: Hitler's Legitimation and British Foreign Policy, 1938–39." *Security Studies* 24 (1): 95–130.
Goddard, Stacie E., and Ronald R. Krebs. 2015. "Rhetoric, Legitimation, and Grand Strategy." *Security Studies* 24 (1): 5–36.

Goddard, Stacie E., Paul K. MacDonald, and Daniel H. Nexon. 2019. "Repertoires of Statecraft: Instruments and Logics of Power Politics." *International Relations* 33 (2): 304–321.

Goffman, Erving. 1981. *Forms of Talk*. Philadelphia: University of Pennsylvania Press.

Goldman O. Emily, and John Arquilla. 1999. "Structure, Agency, and Choice: Toward a Theory and Practice of Grand Strategy." In *The Politics of Strategic Adjustment: Ideas, Institutions, and Interests*, edited by Peter Trubowitz, Emily O. Goldman, and Edward Rhodes, 305–322. New York: Columbia University Press.

Goldstein, Avery. 2005. *Rising to the Challenge: China's Grand Strategy and International Security*. Stanford: Stanford University Press.

Grice, H. Paul. 1978. "Further Notes on Logic and Conversation." In *Syntax and Semantics, Vol. 9: Pragmatics*, edited by Peter Cole, 13–128. New York: Academic Press.

Hall, Peter A. 1986. *Governing the Economy: The Politics of State Intervention in Britain and France*. Oxford: Oxford University Press.

Halliday, Fred. 1987. "Iran's New Grand Strategy." *MERIP Middle East Report* 144: 7–8.

Hart, Liddell. 1967. *Strategy: The Indirect Approach*, 2nd ed. New York: Praeger.

Hastedt, Glenn P. 2017. *American Foreign Policy: Past, Present, and Future*. Lanham: Rowman & Littlefield.

Hill, Charles. 2010. *Grand Strategies: Literature, Statecraft, and World Order*. New Haven: Yale University Press.

Holsti, Kalevi J. 1970. "National Role Conceptions in the Study of Foreign Policy." *International Studies Quarterly* 14 (3): 233–309.

International Committee of the Red Cross. 2018. "ICRC Strategy 2019–2022." September 13, 2018. https://www.icrc.org/en/publication/4354-icrc-strategy-2019-2022, accessed April 9, 2019.

Jenkins, Brian Michael. 2002. "Countering Al Qaeda: An Appreciation of the Situation and Suggestions for Strategy." *RAND Corporation*. https://www.rand.org/pubs/monograph_reports/MR1620.html, accessed April 9, 2019.

Jisi, Wang. 2011. "China's Search for a Grand Strategy: A Rising Great Power Finds Its Way." *Foreign Affairs* 90 (2): 68–79.

Johnston, Alastair Iain. 1995. "Thinking about Strategic Culture." *International Security* 19 (4): 32–64.

Johnston, Alastair Iain. 1998. *Cultural Realism: Strategic Culture and Grand Strategy in Chinese History*. Princeton: Princeton University Press.

Johnston, Alastair Iain. 1998. *Cultural Realism: Strategic Culture and Grand Strategy in Chinese History*. Princeton: Princeton University Press.

Kagan Robert. 2008. "The September 12 Paradigm: America, the World, and George W. Bush." *Foreign Affairs* 87 (5): 25–39.

Kagan, Frederick W. 2008. "Grand Strategy for the United States." In *Finding Our Way: Debating American Grand Strategy*, edited by Michèle A. Flournoy and Shawn Brimley, 61–80. Washington DC: Center for a New American Security.

Kagan, Robert. 2002. "One Year After: A Grand Strategy for the West?" *Survival* 44 (4): 135–139.

Katzenstein, Peter J. 1998. *Cultural Norms and National Security: Police and Military in Postwar Japan*. Ithaca: Cornell University Press.

Kennedy, Paul. 1991a. "Grand Strategy in War and Peace: Toward a Broader Definition." In *Grand Strategies in War and Peace*, edited by Paul Kennedy, 1–10. New Haven: Yale University Press.

Kennedy, Paul. 1991b. "American Grand Strategy, Today and Tomorrow: Learning from the European Experience." In *Grand Strategies in War and Peace*, edited by Paul Kennedy, 167–184. New Haven: Yale University Press.

Keremidchieva, Zornitsa. 2013. "The Congressional Debates on the 19th Amendment: Jurisdictional Rhetoric and the Assemblage of the US Body Politic." *Quarterly Journal of Speech* 99 (1): 51–73.

Kornprobst, Markus. 2008. *Irredentism in European Politics: Argumentation, Compromise and Norms*. Cambridge: Cambridge University Press.

Kornprobst, Markus. 2009. "International Relations as Rhetorical Discipline: Toward (Re-)Newing Horizons." *International Studies Review* 11 (1): 87–108.

Kornprobst, Markus. 2015. "Building Agreements upon Agreements: The European Union and Grand Strategy." *European Journal of International Relations* 21 (2): 267–292.

Kornprobst, Markus, and Martin Senn. 2016a. "Introduction: Background Ideas in International Relations." *British Journal of Politics and International Relations* 18 (2): 273–281.

Kornprobst, Markus, and Martin Senn. 2016b "A Rhetorical Field Theory: Background, Communication, and Change." *British Journal of Politics and International Relations* 18 (2): 300–317.

Kornprobst, Markus, and Martin Senn. 2018. "Ordnung, Kommunikation und Wandel in der Weltpolitik. Entwurf einer Theorie rhetorischer Felder." *Zeitschrift für Internationale Beziehungen* 25 (2): 96–125.

Kornprobst, Markus. 2018. "Diplomatic Communication and Resilient Governance: Problems of Governing Nuclear Weapons." *Journal of International Relations and Development*, 1–26. https://doi.org/10.1057/s41268-018-0133-5.

Kornprobst, Markus. 2019a. "Framing, Resonance and War: Foregrounds and Backgrounds of Cultural Congruence." *European Journal of International Relations* 25 (1): 61–85.

Kornprobst, Markus. 2019b. *Co-Managing International Crises: Judgments and Justifications*. Cambridge: Cambridge University Press.

Korten, David C. 1987. "Third Generation NGO Strategies: A key to People-Centered Development." *World Development* 15 (1): 145–159.

Krebs, Ronald R. 2015a. "Tell Me a Story: FDR, Narrative, and the Making of the Second World War." *Security Studies* 24 (1): 131–170.

Krebs, Ronald R. 2015b. *Narrative and the Making of US National Security*. Cambridge: Cambridge University Press.

Layne, Christopher. 2008. "Security studies and the use of history: Neville Chamberlain's grand strategy revisited." *Security Studies* 17 (3): 397–437.

LeDonne, John P. 2003. *The Grand Strategy of the Russian Empire, 1650–1831*. Oxford: Oxford University Press.

Lobell, Steven E. 2003. *The Challenge of Hegemony: Grand Strategy, Trade, and Domestic Politics*. Ann Arbor: University of Michigan Press.

Luttwak, Edward N. 1984. *The Grand Strategy of the Soviet Union*. New York: Saint Martin's Griffin.

Luttwak, Edward. 2009. *The Grand Strategy of the Byzantine Empire*. Cambridge: Harvard University Press.

Mac Ginty, Roger. 2017. "A Material Turn in International Relations: The 4x4, Intervention and Resistance." *Review of International Studies* 43 (5): 855–874.

Martel, William C. 2015. *Grand Strategy in Theory and Practice: The Need for an Effective American Foreign Policy*. Cambridge: Cambridge University Press.

Martel, William. 2017. "The Making of Future American Grand Strategy." *National Interest*, January 27, 2015. https://nationalinterest.org/feature/the-making-future-american-grand-strategy-12126, accessed December 15, 2019.

McDonald, Matt. 2008. "Securitization and the Construction of Security." *European Journal of International Relations* 14 (4): 563–587.

Meyer, Christoph O. 2005. "Convergence towards a European Strategic Culture? A Constructivist Framework for Explaining Changing Norms." *European Journal of International Relations* 11 (4): 523–549.

Midford, Paul. 2002. "The Logic of Reassurance and Japan's Grand Strategy." *Security Studies* 11 (3): 1–43.

Miller, Benjamin. 2010. "Explaining Changes in US Grand Strategy: 9/11, the Rise of Offensive Liberalism, and the War in Iraq." *Security Studies* 19 (1): 26–65.

Mintz, Alex, and Karl DeRouen Jr. 2010. *Understanding Foreign Policy Decision Making*. Cambridge: Cambridge University Press.

Mitzen, Jennifer. 2015. "Illusion or Intention? Talking Grand Strategy into Existence." *Security Studies* 24 (1): 61–94.

Monaghan, Andrew. 2013. "Putin's Russia: Shaping a "Grand Strategy"?" *International Affairs* 89 (5): 1221–1236.

Nadel, Alan. 1995. *Containment Culture: American Narratives, Postmodernism, and the Atomic Age*. Durham: Duke University Press.

Neumann, Iver B. 1999. *Uses of the Other: "The East" in European Identity Formation*. Minneapolis: University of Minnesota Press.

Neumann, Iver B. 2002. "Returning Practice to the Linguistic Turn: The Case of Diplomacy." *Millennium* 31 (3): 627–651.

Neumann, Iver B. 2008. "Discourse Analysis." In *Qualitative Methods in International Relations: A Pluralist Guide*, edited by Audie Klotz and Deepa Prakash, 61–77. London: Palgrave Macmillan.

Neumann, Iver B., and Henrikki Heikka. 2005. "Grand Strategy, Strategic Culture, Practice: The Social Roots of Nordic Defence." *Cooperation and Conflict* 40 (1): 5–23.

Novenario, Celine Marie I. 2016. "Differentiating Al Qaeda and the Islamic State through Strategies Publicized in Jihadist Magazines." *Studies in Conflict & Terrorism* 39 (11): 953–967.

Ostovar, Afshon. 2019. "The Grand Strategy of Militant Clients: Iran's Way of War." *Security Studies* 28 (1): 159–188.

Porter, Michael E. 1989. "From Competitive Advantage to Corporate Strategy." In *Readings in Strategic Management*, edited by David Asch and Cliff Bowman, 234–255. London: Palgrave.

Posen, Barry R. 1984. *The Sources of Military Doctrine: France, Britain, and Germany between the World Wars*. Ithaca: Cornell University Press.

Posen, Barry R. 2002. "The Struggle against Terrorism: Grand Strategy, Strategy, and Tactics." *International Security* 26 (3): 39–55.

Posen, Barry R. 2014. *Restraint: A New Foundation for US Grand Strategy*. Ithaca: Cornell University Press.

Posen, Barry R. 2018. "The Rise of Illiberal Hegemony: Trump's Surprising Grand Strategy." *Foreign Affairs* 97 (2): 20–27.

Posen, Barry. R., and Andrew L. Ross. 1996. "Competing Vision for US Grand Vision." *International Security* 21 (3): 3–53.

Poulakos, John. 1997. "The Logic of Greek Sophistry." In *Historical Foundations of Informal Logic*, edited by Douglas Walton and Alan Brinton, 12–24. Aldershot: Ashgate.

Rogers, James. 2009. "From "Civilian Power" to "Global Power": Explicating the European Union's "Grand Strategy" through the Articulation of Discourse Theory." *Journal of Common Market Studies* 47 (4): 831–862.

Sadock, Jerrold M. 1974. *Toward a Linguistic Theory of Speech Acts*. New York: Academic Press.

Schneider, Anne, and Helen Ingram. 1993. "Social Construction of Target Populations: Implications for Politics and Policy." *American Political Science Review* 87 (2): 334–347.

John Schuessler, Joshua R. I. Shifrinson. 2018. "Making Grand Strategy Great Again." *National Interest*, July 25, 2018. https://nationalinterest.org/feature/making-grand-strategy-grand-again-26796, accessed December 15, 2019.

Schweller, Randall L. 2004. "Unanswered Threats: A Neoclassical Realist Theory of Underbalancing." *International Security* 29 (2): 159–201.

Shih, Chih-yu. 1988. "National Role Conception as Foreign Policy Motivation: The Psychocultural Bases of Chinese Diplomacy." *Political Psychology* 9 (4): 599–631.

Silove, Nina. 2018. "Beyond the Buzzword: The Three Meanings of "Grand Strategy."" *Security Studies* 27 (1): 27–57.

Snyder, Jack. 2015. "Duelling Security Stories: Wilson and Lodge Talk Strategy." *Security Studies* 24 (1): 171–197.

Solingen, Etel. 1998. *Regional Orders at Century's Dawn: Global and Domestic Influences on Grand Strategy*. Princeton: Princeton University Press.

Swaine, Michael D., Sara A. Daly, and Peter W. Greenwood. 2000. *Interpreting China's Grand Strategy: Past, Present, and Future*. Santa Monica: Rand Corporation.

Swidler, Anne. 1986. "Culture in Action: Symbols and Strategies." *American Sociological Review* 51 (2): 273–286.

Taliaferro, Jeffrey W., Norrin M. Ripsman, and Steven E. Lobell, eds. 2012. *The Challenge of Grand Strategy: The Great Powers and the Broken Balance Between the World Wars*. Cambridge: Cambridge University Press.

Taşpınar, Ömer. 2012. "Turkey's Strategic Vision and Syria." *Washington Quarterly* 35 (3): 127–140.

Tetlock, Philip E. 2005. *Expert Political Judgment: How Good Is It? How Can We Know?* Princeton: Princeton University Press.

Thies, Cameron G., and Marijke Breuning. 2012. "Integrating Foreign Policy Analysis and International Relations Through Role Theory." *Foreign Policy Analysis* 8 (1): 1–4.

Tjalve, Vibeke Schou, and Michael C. Williams. 2015. "Reviving the Rhetoric of Realism: Politics and Responsibility in Grand Strategy." *Security Studies* 24 (1): 37–60.

van Eemeren, Frans H., Rob Grootendorst, and Tjark Kruiger. 1984. *The Study of Argumentation*. New York: Irvington.

Wæver, Ole. 1995. "Securitization and Desecuritization." In *On Security*, edited by Ronnie Lipschutz, 46–86. New York: Columbia University Press.

Walker, Joshua W. 2007. "Learning Strategic Depth: Implications of Turkey's New Foreign Policy Doctrine." *Insight Turkey* 9 (3): 32–47.

Walker, Paul. 2016. "A Rhythmic Refrain: Britain's Mass-Observation as Rhetorical Assemblage." *Rhetoric Review* 35 (3): 212–225.

Walt, Stephen M. 1991. "The Renaissance of Security Studies." *International Studies Quarterly* 35 (2): 211–239.

Weldes, Jutta. 1999. *Constructing National Interests: The United States and the Cuban Missile Crisis*. Minneapolis: University of Minnesota Press.

Wiener, Antje. 2009. "Enacting Meaning-in-Use: Qualitative Research on Norms and International Relations." *Review of International Studies* 35 (1): 175–193.

Wohlforth, William C. 1994. "Realism and the End of the Cold War." *International Security* 19 (3): 91–129.

CHAPTER 12

GOVERNMENTALITY AND GRAND STRATEGY

ANDREW W. NEAL

GOVERNMENTALITY is a concept coined by the French historian Michel Foucault to capture a broader notion of the arts of government. He wanted to draw attention to the diversity of discourses and practices of government across history and society, and how these reached beyond more narrow preoccupations with sovereign and state power. Governmentality has several things in common with the grand strategy literature, such as its focus on the rational frameworks that give coherence to governmental practices and policies. Governmentality as an approach offers a way to analyze government that focuses in empirical detail on governmental practices and the discourses and assumptions that animate and support them. This chapter argues that this offers new insights about grand strategy by drawing attention to the assumptions about government that are found in its theories and concepts. This goes beyond questions about the alignment of means and ends, for example, to unpack assumptions about what means and ends it is considered possible to govern and direct.

The chapter proceeds with a general introduction to governmentality and its similarities and differences to the grand strategy literature. It then develops in more detail the role of knowledge and rationality in the literatures, followed by a discussion of how a governmentality approach functions as a form of critical analysis of assumptions about government. The final section explores international development as a case study on the insights and utility of a governmentality approach to grand strategy.

GOVERNMENTALITY AND GRAND STRATEGY

The French historian Michel Foucault (1926–1984) coined the neologism "governmentality" to denote discourses on the "art of government." His aim was to contrast this with discourses on the legitimacy and right of sovereign rule, which he thought had hitherto dominated political thought. Foucault famously called for scholars to "cut off the King's head in political theory" (Foucault 1980a, 121; Neal 2004). By this he meant getting away from sovereignty and questions of power, right, law, and legitimacy. Government, he argued, was a practice conducted not only by sovereign rulers or states, but by many other actors, institutions, and technologies in diverse contexts and through diverse methods. With the term "governmentality," Foucault invited a more heterogeneous understanding of government.

Foucault wanted to draw a distinction between different types of political and governmental writing that he identified in history. On the one hand, there were works conceived as "advice to the prince," offered most famously by Machiavelli (Foucault 1991a, 87). Machiavelli presented his "little book" explicitly as a guide for rulers to keep hold of newly acquired states (Machiavelli 1999, 1). On the other hand, Foucault identified what he called an "anti-Machiavellian" literature that emerged in Europe from the sixteenth century onwards. These were discourses on more general practices of governing beyond the immediate problems of rule (Foucault 1991a, 87). He argued that:

> there are several forms of government among which the prince's relation to his state is only one particular mode ....[P]ractices of government are ... multifarious and concern many kinds of people: the head of a family, the superior of a convent, [or] the teacher or tutor of a child or pupil. (Foucault 1991a, 91)

Claudia Aradau and Rens van Munster characterize governmentality as a "set of social practices that attempt to shape, guide or affect the behaviour of persons" (Aradau and Van Munster 2007, 91; Gordon 1991). And according to Mitchell Dean, governmentality incorporates not just the abstract legitimation of power but "multiple forms of practical, technical and calculative rationality" (Dean 1999, 28). Governmentalities thus incorporate rationalities and the governing practices and techniques they rationalize.

Foucault argued that in the modern European era, the state had become "governmentalized." It sought to govern a broadening array of processes and phenomena, and not just to increase the "might of the sovereign" (Foucault 1991a, 98). The processes and phenomena to be governed, Foucault argued, were aspects of a new object of knowledge: the population (Foucault 1991a, 100). The art of government became focused on the "the welfare of the population, the improvement of its condition, the increase of its wealth, longevity, health, etc." (Foucault 1991a, 100). This new art of government aimed to build a knowledge of these processes and phenomena that could in turn be used to foster their conditions of flourishing.

The whole literature on governmentality—from Foucault's original thoughts and inquiries to wider commentaries and applications of the concept—is a way of broadening our understanding of what it means to govern. Explicitly and implicitly, it offers a critique of the political and international thought that revolves around states and leaders as primary units and agents. Governmentality points to a wider range of actors involved in practices of government, and to the extensive forms of knowledge and technology involved in governing. It highlights more diverse objects and objectives of government—conceived more broadly than state government—such as the population, institution, family, and individual. When applied to questions of strategy and grand strategy, governmentality shifts critical focus from state-based decision-making to the wider techniques, knowledges, and objects involved in strategic governmental policies and practices.

Foucault uses governmentality to make a distinction between sovereign rule on the one hand and practices of government on the other. This offers insights for the grand strategy debate. At its simplest, Foucault's rule/government distinction loosely corresponds to the distinction between strategy and grand strategy. If strategy is a form of decisionistic rationality focused on achieving specific goals, then it comes close to the problems of rule and sovereignty Foucault saw in the "King's head" discourse. In contrast, if grand strategy is a more reflective discourse focused on wider conditions for success, then it is more akin to governmentality. In this light, there are several interesting overlaps between the debates.

We can see the strategy/grand strategy distinction in the work Sir Basil Liddell Hart, a key thinker in the grand strategy tradition. Liddell Hart emphasized the nonmilitary aspects of grand strategy, the means of which did not necessarily consist of fighting. Fighting was only one way to achieve policy ends, which could and should be achieved in other ways where possible (Liddell Hart 1967, 322). As he argued:

> Grand strategy should both calculate and develop the economic resources and manpower of nations in order to sustain the fighting services ... Grand strategy, too, should regulate the distribution of power between the several services, and between the services and industry. Moreover, fighting power is but one of the instruments of grand strategy—which should take account of and apply the power financial pressure, of diplomatic pressure, of commercial pressure, and, not least of ethical pressure, to weaken the opponent's will. (Liddell Hart 1967, 322)

Liddell Hart called for the development of diverse policy tools and national resources that were not reducible to strategic military means and ends. He stressed the importance of a range of governmental knowledges and mechanisms in developing national prosperity and vigor. We can understand Liddell Hart's vision of grand strategy—with its multiple elements, tools, and knowledges—as a specific form of governmentality.

Knowledge, Rationalization, and Government

The governmentality and grand strategy literatures are concerned with the rational frameworks that undergird specific grand strategies and modes of governing. In this vein, a governmentality approach offers a view of Liddell Hart's grand strategy as a specific "rationality of government." "Rationalities of government" are the systems of thought behind practices of government, or what Foucault called "the reasoned way of governing best" (Foucault 2008, 2). We can see parallels in Brooks and Wohlforth's argument that "grand strategy is a set of ideas for deploying a nation's resources to achieve its interests over the long run" (Brooks and Wohlforth 2016, 75). Likewise, Brands defines grand strategy as "the intellectual architecture that gives form and structure to foreign policy" (Brands 2014, 3). More succinctly, Posen characterizes grand strategy as a "theory of strategy". His oft-cited definition states: "A grand strategy is a nation-state's theory about how to produce security for itself" (Posen 2015, 1). These quotes draw attention to the intellectual rationalizations behind grand strategies.

Where the literatures differ is that, unlike grand strategy, governmentality is not concerned primarily with "higher order" questions behind governmental practices (Lissner 2018, 1). The analytical move to governmentality emphasizes the systems of thought behind all governing practices, not only those at the level of strategic rationality or state policymaking. Governmentality is concerned not only with the reason of state, or the "why" of power, but also the practical "how" of government. One of the main points is that forms of government exist within multiple social interactions and even in individual self-government. Foucault discusses a host of different questions of government beyond those centered on the state: "How to govern oneself, how to be governed, how to govern others, by who the people will accept being governed, how to become the best possible governor" (Foucault 1991a, 87).

Moral government, for example, may take a wide variety of modes and be conducted by the self or others, perhaps through parenting, formal and informal education, and religion, as well as state institutions. For example, Foucault writes of prisons as "moral technologies" which apply a specific answer to the question of "*how* does one punish?" [italics in original] (Foucault 1991b, 74). Thus when Liddell Hart calls for a grand strategy that fosters "moral resources" and "the people's willing spirit," he advocates a certain moral governmentality (Liddell Hart 1967, 322). Much of what he calls for goes beyond the governing capacities of the state and implies a broader assemblage of governmental practices that would need to reach into and shape society and economy in diverse ways.

A governmentality approach is a methodology for inquiring historically and empirically into questions and answers about government and the many forms they may take. For example, Liddell Hart wanted to "direct all the resources of a nation ... towards the attainment of the political object" including "moral resources", which he thought could be "as important as to possess the more concrete forms of power" (Liddell Hart 1967, 322). Other grand-strategic schemes contain different governmentalities, including moral ones; for example, American neoconservatism in the early twenty-first century aimed not only to deploy morality in service of foreign policy goals, but also, arguably, to use foreign policy to reshape American political morality (Williams 2005, 319; Drolet 2011, 126). To this end, the neoconservative commentator Robert Kagan criticized what he saw as the amorality of realism by arguing: "if the United States is founded upon universal principles, how can Americans practice amoral indifference when those principles are under siege around the world?" (Kagan 2000, 10; cited in Drolet 2011, 197). Liddell Hart and Kagan thus represent different grand-strategic governmentalities based on different assumptions about what it is possible and desirable to govern, and to what extent.

Considering that the grand strategy literature is under debate for its lack of coherence, common definitions, and agreed aims (Lissner 2018, 54; Silove 2018), a governmentality approach offers a way to inquire into the assumptions about government that reside in particular conceptions of grand strategy. Consider for example the question of whether grand strategy is an "output" or a "tool," as Rebecca Lissner puts it. She points out that if, on the one hand, we follow the assumptions of structural realism, such as those of John Mearsheimer, then the grand strategy of any particular state is merely the "output" of its structural position in the international state system, such as a need to seek shelter in alliances (Lissner 2018, 58; Mearsheimer 2001; see also Bailes, Rickli, and Thorhallsson 2014). On the other hand, if we see grand strategy as a "tool" then this implies the possibility of agency on the part of states or leaders, allowing them "to change the course of history by developing and implementing grand strategies that transcend structural constraints" (Lissner 2018, 58). A governmentality approach goes further by asking about the rationalities of government assumed by such positions. In the "output" strand, is it assumed, for example, that there is a functioning governmental mechanism for adapting to strategic circumstances or shaping political morality? Or if grand strategy is a "tool," is the formulation of that grand strategy assumed to reside in individual leaders, or is it the aggregate product of a range of governmental processes?

The governmentality literature does not answer these questions directly, but it does offer critical resources. Based for a large part in discursive historical analysis, it offers historical tools to put assumptions about government into context and relief. Competing visions of grand strategy carry assumptions about what states have the capacity to do and what kind of governmental structures and levers are, or should be, in place. For example, following Liddell Hart, Paul Kennedy writes:

> The crux of grand strategy lies therefore in policy, that is, in the capacity of the nation's leaders to bring together all of the elements, both military and nonmilitary, for the preservation and enhancement of the nation's long-term (that is, in wartime and peacetime) best interests. (Kennedy 1991, 5)

Yet the grand strategy literature offers little reflection on the historical context of assumptions about state capacities. For example, when Liddell Hart writes about grand strategy "economically achieved," he may only have meant this in light of Clausewitzian debates on limited warfare and economy of force, yet this has historical resonances with liberal rationalities of government identified by Foucault and others (Liddell Hart 1967, 323–324). Foucault found liberalism a particularly interesting form of governmentality because its rationalizations were based on being economical with government, or as Foucault put it, not "governing too much" (Foucault 2008, 17; 1991a, 92). Excessive rule could be a hindrance to fostering the welfare and wealth of the population. Dean characterizes the emergence of a governmentality of liberal political economy in early modern western Europe as follows:

government must become an *economic* government. To govern properly, to ensure the happiness and prosperity of the population, it is necessary to govern through a particular register, that of the *economy*. Moreover, government itself must be economical, both fiscally and in the use of power. (Dean 1999, 29)

Foucault argued that the emergence of neoliberalism in the twentieth century went further, elevating the economy—understood in terms of the market—from an aspect of human flourishing to the yardstick by which governmental success would be judged (Foucault 2008, 32–40). In light of decades of debate about the retreat of the state under Western liberalism, grand-strategic assumptions about state capacities may sound a little strange (Burnham 2001, 2014). If governments are increasingly handing responsibility for aspects of social life to the market, or increasingly hamstrung in their freedom of action by global market forces, then this raises questions about the possibility of grand strategies that rest upon a comprehensive vision of government.

If we think about Liddell Hart's implied governmentality in these historical terms, his grand strategy may take on a different hue. In 1950s Britain when he was writing, the powers of the state were extensive. Many industries and utilities had been nationalized following increased wartime state involvement, including water, electricity, fuel, telecoms, road haulage, steelmaking, and shipbuilding, not to mention the creation of the National Health Service around the same time. This was the heyday of a managed Keynesian economy, combined with low unemployment and increasing prosperity. We might say the conditions of possibility existed for Liddell Hart to think the particular governmentality contained in his grand strategy. This is more than a question of domestic impediments to grand strategy (Rosecrance and Stein 1993, 12). The point is that the same conditions or even the same assumptions do not exist in all times and all places, least of all today. To put it differently, Liddell Hart's assumptions about grand strategy and government are historically and politically contingent. His thoughts on grand strategy are not, in this light, a form of timeless strategic wisdom.

A governmentality approach is a means of critiquing assumptions about government and also a lens through which to analyze shifts in rationalities of government. For example, when the UK published its 2010 National Security Strategy (NSS), the government presented this as intrinsically linked with economic security, stating that "Our national security depends on our economic security and vice versa" (HM Government 2010, 4). This was widely interpreted as an austerity strategy predicated on spending cuts (Cornish and Dorman Andrew 2011; Hammerstad and Boas 2014). Yet this must also be understood as a shift in grand-strategic rationality in the way that the document embraces the management of "risks" alongside the more traditional countering of "threats" (Hammerstad and Boas 2014; HM Government 2010). A shift from "threat" to "risk" represents a different conception of insecurity and a profound statement on the purposes and capabilities of government. Cornish and Dorman, reflecting on the 2015 iteration, argue that it represents a choice "to prepare for some contingencies and not for others" (Cornish and Dorman 2013, 1194). For Rasmussen, a shift to "risk" means "Policy-makers must choose which risks they most need to prevent and which they have to accept" (Rasmussen 2006, 4). Indeed, the 2010 NSS document states, "we cannot prevent every risk as they are inherently unpredictable" (HM Government 2010, 25). This represents a scaling back of the traditional Hobbesian state guarantee of security and an embrace of risk assessment techniques originally developed in the insurance, finance and engineering sectors (Hagmann and Cavelty 2012, 84–85). These techniques are attached to evolving mechanisms of resilience and contingency planning found at multiple levels of government, from central ministries to local partnerships between councils, businesses, arms-length government agencies, and communities. In turn, this traces a longer genealogy in twentieth-century civil defense (Zebrowski 2015; Brassett and Vaughan-Williams 2013; Joseph 2013; Coaffee 2013). More fundamentally, the UK NSS conceives of risks arising not only from the appearance of exogenous challenges such as overseas threats, but also from endogenous systems breakdown or institutional failure in potentially any aspect of social, political, economic, or ecological life (Crowcroft 2012; Neal 2019, 245). Again, this represents a governmentality concerned not just with state security or rule, but with the government of a much wider range of socioeconomic processes, including, as Dean puts it, "the forces and capacities of living individuals, as members of a population, as resources to be fostered, to be used and to be optimized" (Dean 1999, 29).

Governmentality as an approach brings into question the very possibility of grand strategy, if that is taken to mean an overarching effort to martial and deploy a variety of means towards a particular end. If governmental practices exist in multiple dimensions of social, political, economic, and ecological life, then it cannot be assumed that they all function in the service of grand-strategic ends or can be made to do so. This is one meaning of Foucault's call to "cut off the King's head": to do away with the idea of governmental processes being directed by, and existing in the service of, a singular form of strategic agency. Dean argues that assemblages of governmental practices can nevertheless display a "strategic logic" even if that is "irreducible to the explicit intentions of any one actor" (Dean 1999, 32). He argues that governmental practices may still "evince... an orientation toward a particular matrix of ends and purposes" (Dean 1999, 32). In other words, governmental practices may appear to be directed towards the achievement of particular ends, but this does not mean it is because they have been directed that way by a strategic agent. This speaks to debates in the grand strategy literature about whether grand strategy should be understood as emergent from patterns of behavior rather than the product of any overarching strategic plan (Silove, 33; Brands 2014, 6). Dean argues that "It is necessary to be extremely careful to distinguish between the strategy of regimes of practices and the programmes that attempt to invest them with particular purposes" (Dean 1999, 32). In other words, there is a difference between, on the one hand, actually directing means towards strategic ends, and on the other, merely applying a grand-strategic narrative to particular sets of means and circumstances. The existence of a grand-strategic narrative does not necessarily mean the existence of grand-strategic control.

Case Study: Development Aid

This section will look at development aid as an example of the conjunction of governmentality and grand strategy. State development aid programs are a notable feature of post–Cold War international politics. For example, in the UK in 1997, the incoming New Labour government of Tony Blair created a Department for International Development (DFID) with the stated aim of alleviating global poverty. This had its origins in various other offices going back decades, but noteworthy in the creation of DFID as a discrete department was its separation from the Foreign and Commonwealth Office, and more specifically the separation of its policy goals from more explicit British national interests. Previously, foreign aid had often been tied to the purchase of British goods and services, but this was increasingly seen as inefficient and corrupt. A scandal in the early 1990s revealed that British aid to Malaysia to build a hydroelectric dam had been secretly dependent on a £1 billion arms purchase from the UK by the Malaysian government. The new development aid regime was predicated on the more diffuse aim of promoting the global public good, or at least a particular notion of it.

This policy shift corresponds to the governmental shift that Foucault identified: from forms of rule that aim to increase the power or wealth of the state, to arts of government that aim to promote the flourishing of populations. We can see Foucault's heterogeneous knowledges and practices of government at work in the range of activities that DFID funds and promotes. These include primary education, basic and reproductive healthcare, agricultural development, and administrative and financial reform. DFID also represents an indirect mode of governing. It does not run its own overseas development activities directly but prefers to fund other governments and nongovernmental organizations to carry out development related activities. In keeping with the emphasis on knowledge in the governmentality literature, DFID is a large funder of research that advances its poverty reduction and development goals. For example, from 2008 to 2013, DFID allocated £1 billion for development research (Department for International Development 2008). In these ways, DFID and its aims and activities represent a governmentality of development.

The rise of a governmentality of development also represents a grand-strategic shift, or least a strategic fork. While development aid is often presented in the ostensibly selfless language of altruism rather than the means/ends language of national interest, this still contributes to a wider grand strategy. If "A grand strategy is a nation-state's theory about how to produce security for itself" (Posen 2015, 1), then development aid fits the bill. It is based on a vision of world politics that sees poverty and instability as root causes of resentment and conflict. A more prosperous, better governed world with flourishing populations expands the liberal pacific union that was hoped for in the post–Cold War era (Doyle 1986). As DFID argued in a 2005 document: "DFID, working with poor people and their governments and international partners, can help build a more secure future for us all" (Department for International Development 2005, 3).

A governmentality approach, with is focus on heterogeneous elements of government, can help us to understand how development aid works as an aspect of grand strategy. Its strategic aims are diffuse and so are the actors and techniques involved. The global governance literature of the 1990s noted the increasing importance of nonstate actors in international relations, but this was often understood in terms of a corresponding, zero sum decrease in state power (Sending and Neumann 2006, 652). Sending and Neumann argue that this literature also viewed nonstate actors and civil society in hierarchical terms as objects of government "whose behavioral patterns had to be adjusted by identifying and acting upon causal relations" (Sending and Neumann 2006, 659). In contrast, using a governmentality approach, they argue that the rise of development brought a shift not only in the techniques and aims of government, but also reconceptualized nonstate actors as subjects rather than merely objects of government. This is evidenced in capacity-building projects, the funding of development research, and the empowerment and investiture of diverse agencies as "partners" to perform functions based on their reach, expertise, and professionalism (Sending and Neumann 2006, 662).

The encouragement of new governmental subjects through development practices does not necessarily mean a retreat of power or control, but rather a different conception of governing others through their own freedom (Rose 1999, 4). Like Sending and Neumann, Jonathan Joseph argues that the global poverty reduction programs that came to prominence in the 2000s were based on fostering forms of "partnership" and "ownership" on the part of recipient countries (Joseph 2010, 40). He also argues that this was accompanied by new forms of indirect government, such as mechanisms and metrics for measuring performance, progress, compliance and outcomes (Joseph 2010, 36-37). These are predicated on the ability of recipient states to collect and report data on these metrics, and thus to learn to govern themselves in a certain way. These obligations can be extensive: Carl Death claims that "The Tanzanian public services were at one point producing around 2,400 quarterly reports for external donors" (Death 2013, 780).

Development aid is a form of grand strategy built upon a governmentality of arms-length technocratic means and the constitution of ostensibly self-governing forms of political agency. This chimes with liberal ideals of freedom and autonomy, but that does not mean it is above politics or devoid of political struggle. In fact, struggles over the uses and future of development aid in the UK have taken a notably grand-strategic turn. In the context of Brexit, commentators and politicians on the British political right called for DFID to be rolled back into the Foreign and Commonwealth Office in order to refocus British foreign policy on a more national conception of the national interest, which was met with a corresponding push back from the development sector (McVeigh 2019). A year into his premiership in 2020, Boris Johnson announced the FCO/DFID merger that the right of his party had called for. This departmental reorganization followed a 2015 policy initiative which channeled £1 billion of the aid budget into a secretive "Conflict, Security and Stability Fund" (CSSF). The UK government has used this, for example, to fund the state security forces of repressive regimes, include Bahrain and Ethiopia, and has provided little public information about how the fund is used, to the extent that the parliamentary Joint Committee on the National Security Strategy argued that the fund has no effective public accountability (McVeigh 2017). At stake here is a struggle over the proper use of governmental means (development funding) and its alignment to grand-strategic ends (fostering the global good versus a more traditional and perhaps realist conception of the national interest).

Conclusion

This chapter has introduced the concept of governmentality in terms of its parallels with and utility for the grand strategy debate. Governmentality focuses on a broader understanding of government beyond state policy- and decision-making, emphasizing the governmental practices and knowledges that operate in multiple, heterogeneous aspects of social, political, economic, and ecological life. Governmentality as an approach draws attention to the empirical details of governmental practices and the assumptions about the nature and possibilities of government that support and animate them. The governmentality literature shares this interest in the intellectual frameworks that rationalize and legitimize policies with the grand strategy literature. Certain accounts of grand strategy, such as those of Liddell Hart and Kennedy, share with the governmentality approach a concern with governing the wider social and economic life of populations. Where governmentality differs is in its historical sensibility, putting assumptions about the nature and reach of government into historical context.

References

Aradau, Claudia, and Rens Van Munster. 2007. "Governing Terrorism through Risk: Taking Precautions, (Un)Knowing the Future." *European Journal of International Relations* 13 (1): 89–115.

Bailes, Alyson JK, J-M Rickli, and Baldur Thorhallsson. 2014. "Small States, Survival, and Strategy." In *Small States and International Security: Europe and Beyond*, edited by C. Archer, A. Bailes, and A. Wivel, 26–45. Abingdon and New York: Routledge.

Brands, Hal. 2014. *What Good Is Grand Strategy?: Power and Purpose in American Statecraft from Harry S. Truman to George W. Bush*. Ithaca: Cornell University Press.

Brassett, James, and Nick Vaughan-Williams. 2013. "The Politics of Resilience from a Practitioner's Perspective: An Interview with Helen Braithwaite OBE." *Politics* 33 (4): 229–239. doi: 10.1111/1467-9256.12027.

Brooks, Stephen G., and William Curti Wohlforth. 2016. *America Abroad: The United States' Global Role in the 21st Century*. New York: Oxford University Press.

Burnham, Peter. 2001. "New Labour and the Politics of Depoliticisation." *The British Journal of Politics & International Relations* 3 (2): 127–149.

Burnham, Peter. 2014. "Depoliticisation: Economic Crisis and Political Management." *Policy & Politics* 42 (2): 189–206.

Coaffee, Jon. 2013. "Rescaling and Responsibilising the Politics of Urban Resilience: From National Security to Local Place-Making." *Politics* 33 (4): 240–252. doi: 10.1111/1467-9256.12011.

Cornish, Paul, and M. Dorman Andrew. 2011. "Dr Fox and the Philosopher's Stone: The Alchemy of National Defence in the Age of Austerity." *International Affairs* 87 (2): 335–353. doi: 10.1111/j.1468-2346.2011.00976.x.

Cornish, Paul, and Andrew M. Dorman. 2013. "Fifty Shades of Purple? a Risk-Sharing Approach to the 2015 Strategic Defence and Security Review." *International Affairs* 89 (5): 1183–1202. doi: 10.1111/1468-2346.12066.

Crowcroft, Robert. 2012. "A War on "Risk"? British Government and the National Security Strategy." *The Political Quarterly* 83 (1): 172–176. doi: 10.1111/j.1467-923X.2012.02277.x.

Dean, Mitchell. 1999. *Governmentality: Power and Rule in Modern Society*. London: Sage.

Death, Carl. 2013. "Governmentality at the Limits of the International: African Politics and Foucauldian Theory." *Review of International Studies* 39 (3): 763–787. doi: 10.1017/S0260210512000307.

Department for International Development. 2005. *Fighting Poverty To Build a Safer World: A Strategy for Security and Development*. London: DfID.

Department for International Development. 2008. *Research Strategy 2008-2013*. Department for International Development.

Doyle, Michael W. 1986. "Liberalism and World Politics." *American Political Science Review* 80 (4): 1151–1169.

Drolet, Jean-François. 2011. *American Neoconservatism: The Politics and Culture of a Reactionary Idealism*. New York: Columbia University Press.

Foucault, Michel. 1980a. "Truth and Power." In *Power/Knowledge: Selected Interviews and Other Writings 1972–1977*, edited by Colin Gordon, 109–133. New York: Harvester Wheatsheaf.

Foucault, Michel. 1991a. "Governmentality." In *The Foucault Effect: Studies in Governmentality: With Two Lectures by and an Interview with Michael Foucault*, edited by Graham Burchell, Colin Gordon, and Peter Miller, 87–104. London: Harvester Wheatsheaf.

Foucault, Michel. 1991b. "Questions of method." In *The Foucault Effect: Studies in Governmentality: With Two Lectures by and an Interview with Michael Foucault*, edited by Graham Burchell, Colin Gordon, and Peter Miller, 73–86. London: Harvester Wheatsheaf.

Foucault, Michel. 2008. *The Birth of Biopolitics: Lectures at the Collège de France, 1978-1979*. Translated by Graham Burchell. Edited by Arnold Davidson. Basingstoke: Palgrave Macmillan.

Gordon, Colin. 1991. "Governmental Rationality: An Introduction." In *The Foucault Effect: Studies in Governmentality: With Two Lectures by and an Interview with Michael Foucault*, edited by Graham Burchell, Colin Gordon, and Peter Miller, 1–52. London: Harvester Wheatsheaf.

Hagmann, Jonas, and Myriam Dunn Cavelty. 2012. "National Risk Registers: Security Scientism and the Propagation of Permanent Insecurity." *Security Dialogue* 43 (1): 79–96. doi: 10.1177/0967010611430436.

Hammerstad, Anne, and Ingrid Boas. 2014. "National Security Risks? Uncertainty, Austerity and Other Logics of Risk in the UK Government's National Security Strategy." *Cooperation and Conflict* 50 (4):475–491.

HM Government. 2010. *A Strong Britain in an Age of Uncertainty: The National Security Strategy*. London: HMSO.

Joseph, Jonathan. 2010. "Poverty Reduction and the New Global Governmentality." *Alternatives: Global, Local, Political* 35 (1): 29–51.

Joseph, Jonathan. 2013. "Resilience in UK and French Security Strategy: An Anglo-Saxon Bias?" *Politics* 33 (4): 253–264. doi: 10.1111/1467-9256.12010.

Kagan, Robert. 2000. "Inside the Limo." *The New Republic*.

Kennedy, Paul M. 1991. "Grand Strategy in War and Peace: Toward a Broader Definition." In *Grand Strategies in War and Peace*, edited by Paul M. Kennedy. Yale University Press.

Liddell Hart, Basil Henry. 1967. *Strategy*. 2nd edition. New York: Meridian.

Lissner, Rebecca Friedman. 2018. "What Is Grand Strategy? Sweeping a Conceptual Minefield." *Texas National Security Review* (November 2018).

Machiavelli, Niccolo. 1999. *The Prince*. Translated by George Anthony Bull. London: Penguin.

McVeigh, Karen. 2017. "Secrecy around Aid and Security Fund Raises 'Significant Concern', Say MPs." *The Guardian*, February 7, 2017.

McVeigh, Karen. 2019. "Aid Groups Warn Boris Johnson against Combining DfID with Foreign Office." *The Guardian*, December 19, 2019.

Mearsheimer, John J. 2001. *The Tragedy of Great Power Politics*. New York; London: W.W. Norton.

Neal, Andrew W. 2004. "Cutting Off the King's Head: Foucault's *'Society Must Be Defended'* and the Problem of Sovereignty." *Alternatives: Global, Local, Political* 4 (29): 373–398.

Neal, Andrew W. 2019. *Security as Politics: Beyond the State of Exception*. Edinburgh: Edinburgh University Press.

Posen, Barry. 2015. *Restraint: A New Foundation for U.S. Grand Strategy*. Ithaca: Cornell University Press.

Rasmussen, Mikkel Vedby. 2006. *The Risk Society at War: Terror, Technology and Strategy in the Twenty-First Century*. Cambridge: Cambridge University Press.

Rose, Nikolas. 1999. *Powers of Freedom: Reframing Political Thought*. Cambridge: Cambridge University Press.

Rosecrance, Richard N., and Arthur A. Stein. 1993. "Beyond Realism: The Study of Grand Strategy." In *The Domestic Bases of Grand Strategy*, edited by Richard N. Rosecrance and Arthur A. Stein. Ithaca: Cornell University Press.

Sending, O. J., and I. B. Neumann. 2006. "Governance to Governmentality: Analyzing NGOs, States, and Power." *International Studies Quarterly* 50 (3): 651–672. doi: 10.1111/j.1468-2478.2006.00418.x.

Silove, Nina. 2018. "Beyond the Buzzword: The Three Meanings of 'Grand Strategy.'" *Security Studies* 27 (1): 27–57. doi: 10.1080/09636412.2017.1360073.

Williams, Michael C. 2005. "What is the National Interest? The Neoconservative Challenge in IR Theory." *European Journal of International Relations* 11 (3): 307–337.

Zebrowski, Chris. 2015. *The Value of Resilience: Securing life in the twenty-first century, Interventions*. Abingdon: Taylor & Francis.

PART III
SOURCES

CHAPTER 13

MATERIAL SOURCES OF GRAND STRATEGY

NORRIN RIPSMAN AND IGOR KOVAC

The purpose of this chapter is to outline the material sources of grand strategy. While we acknowledge that material inputs are not the entire story, as they must be perceived by human beings, who must respond to these inputs within a given institutional context, we do believe that the strategic environment that states face, shaped by material forces, goes a long way toward explaining their grand-strategic choices (Ripsman, Taliaferro, and Lobell 2016; Yarger 2006, 17). This position is shared in this volume by Charles Glaser, who argues that the feasibility of grand strategy options are, by and large, reflected by the material environment and the power of particular states. We therefore leave it to others in this volume to address grand strategy's ideational and institutional sources, without ourselves subscribing to material determinism.

We proceed by identifying several categories of material sources of grand strategy and by providing concrete empirical examples of how they have shaped particular grand strategies. Being limited by space, our list of material sources is not exhaustive, but we do argue that its explanatory power is sizable. We identify the following material sources of grand strategy: the state's relative power, the polarity of the international system, the regional balance of power, geography, and technology.

We continue by looking at each factor individually. Besides their independent effect on grand strategy, these sources also interact with one another. Yet, to the extent possible, we will try to isolate the effect of each factor before considering how it may interact with others. We also acknowledge that for each country, some of these causal factors might be more relevant than for others. Moreover, their hierarchy is situational—specific for each agency–environment relation (Sprout and Sprout 1965). Therefore, we are not making an argument about a particular state or group of states, but rather aspire to be as general as possible.

Relative Power

Since the inception of the disciplines of Political Science and International Relations, power has been their key object of research (e.g., Lasswell and Kaplan 1950, 75). Several conceptualizations of power have been identified (cf. Baldwin 2016). One key distinction is between power as resources ("power to") and power as a relational concept ("power over") (Pitkin 1972, 227; Schmidt and Juneau 2012). The former denotes the state's material capabilities, as well as some intangible resources. Notably, building on Morgenthau (1985, 113–165), Carr (1946, 102–145), Wight (2002, 26), and Wright (1983, 116–117), this perspective assumes that states with greater economic, political, and military resources—e.g., a larger population, greater industrial capacity, greater wealth, and more sophisticated military technology—have greater capability to influence other actors—while the latter focuses solely on a state's ability to influence other states' behavior or international outcomes (cf. Hart 1976). In general, scholars distinguish power resources from relational power—or power from influence—however, realists prefer to focus on the former in order to separate inputs from outcomes (Ripsman, Taliaferro, and Lobell 2016, 43–44; Schmidt and Juneau, 2012; Deibel 2010, 162). We do the same in this chapter. We begin by discussing the various material inputs into power—economic and military capacity, leaving natural resources for our discussion of geography below—and how their possession affects grand strategy, before we discuss the more strategically salient issue of relative power.

Economic capacity is of great importance to grand strategy. All things being equal, states with greater wealth and industrial capacity will have greater interests to protect, including securing trade routes and access to resources, and in general protecting their wealth and the welfare of their citizens (Choucri and North 1989). Moreover, such states will have greater means available to pursue their interests. For this reason, realists such as Gilpin (1981, 93) and Waltz (1979, 177) have viewed differential economic growth rates as the driving force of international politics. Indeed, many (e.g., Schweller 1998, 15–38; Singer 1987; Beckley 2018) have included industrial capacity and Gross Domestic Product (in different forms—per capita, purchasing power parity, net-GDP) as core components of their measures of national power. This explains, for example, why sustained high rates of Chinese growth in recent decades have made China a global player and a rising challenger to the United States. An economic powerhouse will also be more likely to use economic leverage as a core component of its grand strategy, employing economic incentives to stabilize distressed allies and economic sanctions to prevent and punish challenges. In this regard, the US successfully employed Marshall Plan aid as an essential component of its European containment strategy after the Second World War, and has employed economic sanctions against a variety of adversaries—including Iraq, Iran, and North Korea—in the post–Cold War era.[1]

A state's military resources, including the size of its armed forces, its weapons and equipment, its lift capacity, and its level of professionalism/training are also important determinants of its grand strategy. They help determine the scope and reach of its grand strategy and the degree to which the state can secure itself or must rely on others. Over time, military strength should loosely track a state's aggregate wealth, with wealthier states being able to invest in larger armed forces and more research and development of advanced weapons systems. Nonetheless, the two concepts must be considered separately, as at any given time a state's capabilities may reflect past, rather than present, investments. For example, Russia, though an economically struggling state, possesses a fairly large and well-equipped armed forces as a remnant of the Soviet Union's military arsenal (see Anderson, Gutmanis, and Anderson 2000, 77–94). Alternatively, poor states may dedicate a vast share of their limited economic resources to national defense, as North Korea has done (e.g., Huisken 2004). Moreover, the type of weapons a state possesses is also relevant. Thus, for example, whether a state possesses nuclear weapons will help it decide whether to pursue a defensive or deterrent posture.

What affects grand strategy more than the aggregate power resources that states possess, however, is states' relative power vis-à-vis their neighbors, rivals, and the international system as a whole. States with relative power advantages will be more secure than their rivals and can pursue more proactive, more independent, and sometimes coercive grand strategies. They are also likely to have longer time horizons and are more apt to use their power advantages to shape the strategic and economic environment to their advantage.[2] Weaker states—middle powers (Holbraad 1984; Cooper, Higgott, and Nossal 1993; Cooper 1997) and small states (Keohane 1969; Ingebritsen 2004; Thorhallsson and Wivel 2006)—will have to tether their grand strategies to great power benefactors or multilateral coalitions or institutions if they wish to be successful, since they lack the power to compel greater powers to respect their sovereignty and territorial integrity, as well as further their own political, economic, and strategic objectives in a great power world. Weaker states may also advance concepts such as international law and morality as core elements of grand strategy in an effort to restrain predatory great power behavior, whereas great powers are unlikely to pay more than lip service to arrangements that constrain their freedom of action. Relative power trends are of special importance to states' grand strategies (see Gilpin 1981; Organski and Kugler 1980; Kim and Morrow 1992; Hebron and James 1997). After all, the same absolute amount of power capabilities can mean abundance or scarcity in different contexts. Even with nuclear weapons, absolute numbers do not matter much, except in comparison to what others possess (Green and Long 2017). Rising states—those with rapidly growing capabilities that threaten to approach or eclipse the leading global or regional power—are likely to pursue more challenging and ambitious grand strategies, designed to accelerate their rise while avoiding a confrontation with the declining hegemon until they are likely to win. A good example is China's doctrine of hiding capabilities and biding time, while acting increasingly assertively in the South China Sea and on a global scale with its ambitious Belt and Road Initiative (e.g., Shambaugh 2013; Clarke 2017). The declining leader must seek ways to preserve its dominance by restraining challengers, even with a preventive use of force, or it must give way and accommodate the rising power.[3]

Power Structure of the International Community: Polarity

Another power-based determinant of grand strategy, which is in fact a byproduct of relative power, is the international distribution of power, both globally and at the level of region or subsystem. At the global level this involves the polarity of the international system, determined by the number of great powers that populate the system. Building on our previous discussion, great powers are those states that possess by far the most economic and military power resources in the world, and have a distinct step-level advantage in power resources over all the other states in system (Waltz 1979, 131). There are three types of global distribution of power, each with distinct implications for states' grand strategies: unipolarity, bipolarity, and multipolarity.

Unipolarity denotes a global system where one state has "significantly more capabilities than any other" (Jervis 2011, 255). This power distribution has profound implications for the grand-strategic choices of the unipole—the dominant power—and all the other states in the system. Facing no peer competitors and no significant constraints, the unipole can pursue an ambitious grand strategy that aims "to reshape the world in its image, pursue strategic objectives on a global scale, and prevent potential competitors from rising" (Ripsman 2019, 287; cf. Monteiro 2014). In this regard, US efforts since 1990 to expand the zone of democracy and free trade internationally, contain the spread of global terrorism and the threats posed by rogue states, and coopt rising China have been facilitated by US global hegemony.

All other states must pursue grand strategies that take the unipole into account. Aspiring competitors must pursue policies that allow them to grow economically and geopolitically, and occasionally to frustrate the unipole's global and regional objectives, yet without pushing too hard and provoking an aggressive response by the global hegemon, since that can threaten their survival.[4] Consequently, under unipolarity, states should have issue-specific grand strategies—focusing on the issues in which they have a disproportionate interest and about which the hegemon does not feel strongly, and leaving aside the issues at the core of the hegemon's interests. This, for example, can explain China's "cautious rise" strategy (Bijian 2005) and Russia's limited challenges in regions of special interest, such as Eastern Europe and Syria (Alexandrova-Arbatova 2009; Connable and Wasser 2018). Weaker states must seek to work with the dominant state—or at least not get in its way—if they wish to achieve their objectives (e.g., Labs 1992; Walt 1987, 29).[5]

Bipolarity refers to a system comprising two opposing states that are much more powerful than the rest but cannot overtake each other (Wagner 1993). Under bipolarity, the poles must set their grand strategies against one another, as no other actors in the system have the power individually or collectively to threaten them or frustrate their geopolitical ambitions. Thus, during the Cold War, the US grand strategy of containment was designed to prevent the USSR from expanding its influence and, potentially, pursuing global hegemony (Gaddis 2005, 4). Similarly, the Soviet Union sought to export Moscow-controlled communism to increase its power vis-à-vis the United States, without provoking an all-out war (Ulam 1974, ch. 8). Other states in the system would be compelled to hinge their grand strategies to one or the other of the two great powers, since only a pole would possess sufficient power to save smaller states from encroachment by the other; therefore, smaller states typically tethered their policies to a great power either by design or by coercion. Thus, the West European states sought mechanisms such as the North Atlantic Treaty Organization as a means of compelling the United States to come to their defense if attacked. In the Eastern bloc, Moscow used its military dominance to force Poland, Hungary, the German Democratic Republic, Czechoslovakia, Albania, Bulgaria, and Romania to pursue their grand strategies within institutions such as the Council for Mutual Economic Assistance and the Warsaw Treaty Organization.

Bipolarity also restricts geo-economic alternatives for all states almost exclusively to intra-alliance trade and investment (Gowa 1989). Nonetheless, a bipolar system does afford smaller states slightly more strategic freedom than does unipolarity. Because there are two great powers, in rare and extreme cases, a state can seek to switch its primary great power allegiance, although that is a risky move. During the Cold War, for example, Cuba switched from a US alignment to the Soviet camp following Fidel Castro's revolution, at the risk of US military intervention. More consequentially, China broke away from the Soviet orbit in the early 1970s after increasing tensions with Moscow, and forged better relations with the United States. Bipolar divides necessitate rigid great power competition. Relatively secure weaker states outside this main theater of competition are then left with the option of attempting a neutral and nonaligned grand strategy, such as that pursued by India and other third world states during the Cold War (Peretz 1965; Hershberg 2007; Miskovic, Fischer-Tiné, and Boskovska 2014).

A third possible global power distribution is multipolarity, an international system comprising three or more significant powers possessing capabilities that far exceed those of the remaining states, although none of the great powers can dominate the others (Lesage 2009, 13). In a multipolar system, where there is no power preponderance, states great and small have multiple alliance options and, consequently, a range of grand-strategic options. Furthermore, since multiple great powers exist, the poles could pursue security through a menu of different alternatives, including deterrence and balancing against threats, expansion and the quest for hegemony, or hiding and buckpassing (Ripsman and Levy 2008, 152; Schweller 1998, 74–75; Schroeder 1994; Walt 1987, ch. 2; Mearsheimer 2001, ch. 5). Smaller states can also seek to maximize their interests by shopping around for great power alliances, in effect creating a bidding war for their services, as Italy did by switching alliances on the eve of the First World War. Nonetheless, because of this very fluidity of alliances, cooperation, even in the economic realm, is difficult and fleeting under multipolarity, for fear that it will strengthen a potential rival (Gowa 1995, ch. 1). In short, multipolarity gives states the greatest range of choice over their grand strategies, which allows the nonmaterial sources of grand strategy discussed elsewhere in this Handbook to play a greater role in shaping each particular state's policy choices.

REGIONAL BALANCE OF POWER

While the global distribution of power has an important influence on grand-strategic choices, the regional distribution of power and regional security complex states face is no less significant (Buzan and Waever 2003; Lemke 2002; Miller 2000; Lake and Morgan 1997; Paul 2012). Some regions, such as the Middle East or South Asia, are characterized by enduring rivalries, which force states to worry more about security than advancing any broader strategic, economic, or ideological objectives. Others, however, such as Western Europe or Latin America, enjoy greater stability and have put their rivalries aside, which allows states to cast their grand strategies in terms of broader regional objectives such as economic and political integration (i.e., the European Union or MERCOSUR) and ideological objectives to promote security, such as spreading democracy.[6]

Furthermore, the regional distribution of power affects states' security calculations. One issue is whether there is a regional hegemon or not. If one regional actor is significantly more powerful than any other actors or constellation of states, it becomes pointless for the neighboring states to pursue a strategic program to counter the dominant state, unless there are viable prospects of drawing in a powerful extra-regional actor to support them. Thus, in both Western and Eastern Europe during the Cold War, the weaker states bandwagoned with the greatest power, aligning respectively with the US and the Soviet Union, since there were few credible prospects of drawing the other superpower into their rival's sphere of influence.[7] In contrast, in the post–Cold War world, states such as Georgia, Ukraine, and Poland have all attempted to counter Russian hegemony because of the higher prospects of getting US support in what used to be Moscow's sphere of influence (Janos, 2001; Toal, 2017). In regions without a clear regional hegemon, power imbalances will be perceived as very threatening and will prompt more militarized grand strategies defined in terms of containment, deterrence, and defense, with shorter time horizons, whereas regions with several larger states of comparable power will afford states more flexibility in their grand strategies. This may help explain, for example, why Middle Eastern states such as Israel, Saudi Arabia, and Egypt all have militarized grand strategies focused on the threat posed by Iran, whereas the states of Western Europe pursue security strategies focusing on nontraditional security threats using policy instruments such as international institutions and economic exchange (Ripsman and Paul 2010).

GEOGRAPHY

Geography has a profound impact on grand strategy. It shapes relative power by determining the resources that states possess. States' access to so-called "strategic goods"—food and mineral resources that are essential for national security and a functioning economy—will have a powerful impact on its grand strategy (Blanchard and Ripsman 1996). States with access to a sufficient quantity of a broad range of essential materials will be among the greatest powers in the international system and can behave with the greatest independence. Waltz (1988, 624), for example, referred to the United States and the Soviet Union during the Cold War as "continental powers" because they possessed all the critical resources they needed within their vast boundaries. These great powers possess immense resources; therefore, when designing their grand strategies, they can rely on multiple and diverse capabilities. Those who lack critical resources will necessarily be dependent on those who supply them and more susceptible to their influence, and their grand strategies will be limited (Keohane and Nye 1977, 10).

In addition, geography determines states' likely trading partners and geopolitical rivals, as states interact most with those in their neighborhoods. It is more difficult to project power across great distances, and it is more expensive to ship goods to far points. Indeed, the most durable relationships found by international relations scholars are those between proximity and trade (Isard 1954; Bergstrand, 1985), as well as between proximity and war (Wright 1983, ch. 19; Garnham 1976; Vasquez 1995).

Geography can shape grand strategy in several ways. First, as indicated, it delimits the potential power of a state by determining what natural resources it has access to (Deibel 2010, 163-175). In this regard, geography is a key determinant of the global and regional distribution of power and a state's position within it. Resource possession can also serve as a "honeypot," which can make a state vulnerable to attack, thus necessitating a defensive or deterrent grand strategy (Soysa 2002). Moreover, the discovery of important new resources in a region can lead to geostrategic competition and war (Le Billon 2004). Thus, for example, when large oil and gas reserves were confirmed in Central Asia, all great powers, regional powers, and even smaller states in the region adjusted their grand strategies to enhance their power position in relation to each other (O'Hara 2004).

Possession of scarce, specialized resources, especially strategic goods, can also enhance the array of policy options states have to advance their national security interests. Russia, for example, has developed its ability to supply or embargo oil and gas to Europe, a key industrial and military requirement, as a central component of its grand strategy (Romanova 2016; Sharples 2016). Yet, the absence of critical resources means that securing those essential commodities through trade or conquest will be a high strategic priority. In this regard, the story of the British Empire stems from an island power with limited resources seeking adequate food, fuel, and other strategic goods from abroad (see Ferguson 2012). Dealing with Arab embargoes and no oil fields of its own, Israeli grand strategy has made access to dependable supplies of oil a high priority since the state's founding (Bialer 1999, 130).

Second, the topography or terrain of the state determines how difficult and costly it is to penetrate or navigate. Difficult terrain—e.g., jungles, marshes, or mountains—facilitates defense and discourages offense, which makes a state more secure without alliances or excessive military spending. An unfavorable topography, therefore, may have a similar conflict-dampening effect to a large army (see Gray 2013, 116–152). This was the strategy Switzerland used for much of its history. It also conditions the tactics states employ, as it enables guerrilla-style combat, which comprised a key plank of Taliban strategy in recent years, as well as North Vietnamese grand strategy in the 1960s (Kapur 2016; Collins 1978). In contrast, states without obstructive natural frontiers have more intense security dilemmas and must seek more elaborate security strategies (Jervis 1978, 195). The German nightmare of a two-front war in the early part of the twentieth century, and the development of the Schlieffen Plan illustrate this dynamic (Foley 2003). Uruguay, which similarly has few geographical obstacles to its regional power neighbors Argentina and Brazil, has recently sought a regional institutional solution to this strategic dilemma, committing itself fully to MERCOSUR in the 1990s in order to manage and resolve bilateral disputes with these regional powers (Bizzozero 2003, 339–343).

Third, the state's position or location has important implications for its grand strategy. As Mahan (1890) emphasized, states located within easy access of sea lanes will rely more heavily on maritime trade and naval power as core components of grand strategy, whereas landlocked states will pursue different foreign economic policies and have a strategic forces composition that emphasizes ground forces capable of capturing and holding territory. For this reason, Parker (1985, 178–179) extrapolates that the history of geopolitics is about conflictual relations between land and sea power. Maritime borders also enable states to take advantage of "the stopping power of water" to diffuse threats and enable the state to pursue broader regional or global strategic objectives (Mearsheimer 2001, 114–128). Indeed, the two oceans that insulate the United States from the other great powers played a critical role in its rise from a revolutionary state in the eighteenth century to today's global superpower.

Beyond access to the sea, other aspects of a state's position are relevant. If a state is surrounded by other states, particularly ones with large armed forces, it faces more serious strategic dilemmas than those that are geographically removed. King Abdallah of Jordan thus quips that the Hashemite Kingdom faces a geopolitical challenge because it is "caught between Iraq and a hard place" (Gnehm 2008). Conversely, the US has benefitted from a more favorable location, which in former French Ambassador Jean-Jules Jusserand's words, amounted to the following: "On the north, she has a weak neighbor; on the south, another weak neighbor; on the east, fish, and the west, fish" (Mearsheimer and Walt 2016, 72). Australia, with no other states on its continental island, has similar strategic advantages, which reduce the urgency of the military components of its grand strategy (Hallen 2013, 105; Wesley 2016, 28–29). If a state is located at a choke point of sea-lines of communications (e.g., Iran and the Strait of Hormuz), its ability to close down this critical space can be a defining feature of its grand strategy.[8]

Fourth, the climate in which the state operates can affect the ease of power projection, the degree to which a state is threatened, the offense–defense dynamic, and the availability of resources. In the eighteenth century, Montesquieu (1989, part 3) maintained that climate affected power politics, since cold climates fostered industry, innovation, and the accumulation of wealth, all of which are conducive to the development of great power and military strength. Cold climates, however, interfere with power projection, as rivers and seas become unnavigable when frozen in the winter and travel by rail and road become more difficult in heavy snow. States in cold regions, therefore, are likely to seek the capacity to use their strategic forces and project power throughout the year. This explains why, for example, Russian grand strategy—be it Imperial or Soviet—prioritized the pursuit of a warm water port (see Cohen 2003, ch. 7; Leikin 2016). Even after the end of the Cold War, this motivation may help explain Russian actions in Syria, where it has its only warm water military port in Tartus (Parnemo 2019, 63).

A cold climate can also help a state by making it more difficult to invade, thus tipping the offense–defense dynamic in favor of the defense. Several times in Russian history, Russian leaders took advantage of their forbidding climate in order to achieve victory over more powerful adversaries, such as Napoleonic France and Nazi Germany (see Winters 2001, ch. 4). The importance of a harsh winter to Russian strategic doctrine is aptly captured in Russian Czar Nicholas I's famous quip that the two greatest Russian generals are January and February (Miller 2012, 233).

Changes to climate conditions can also have important consequences for security calculations and great power relations, by making forbidding passages navigable or habitable regions inhospitable, and by allowing states to access previously unharvestable resources. In recent years, for example, international competition has accelerated in the Arctic, as the United States, Russia, China, and other states all seek to stake their claim over the vast resource wealth becoming accessible due to climate change (Borgerson 2008). A parallel strategic dilemma could be presented if global warming were to render some waterways unnavigable due to rising waters. Thus, climate is of great potential significance to future grand strategy.

Technology

Technology affects grand-strategic choice in two ways: it changes the implications of geography; and it affects states' power potential. While geography can influence grand strategy in the manners outlined above, technological developments can alter the way in which states interact with geographical constraints. Consider, for example, the two oceans that separate the United States from the rest of the great powers. Until the Second World War, these difficult to surmount barriers made the United States largely invulnerable to great power attack, enabling it to pursue a grand strategy of unimpeded growth. With the deployment of aircraft carriers and intercontinental ballistic missiles, however, these oceans lost much of their protective value, requiring a more engaged US grand strategy to protect its interests in a more threatening global environment (Ripsman 2019; 2002, 84). The shift from coal to oil as the main source of fuel increased the importance of the Middle East for all great powers (Alnasrawi 1985), as no doubt the development of hydrogen fuel cells and better solar energy technology will reduce the region's future importance (see Cordesman and Al-Rodhan 2006; STRATFOR 2018).

More basically, however, technological innovation allows states to maximize their power, often disproportionately with their existing resource base. The possession of nuclear weapons technology, for example, offers even weaker states the prospect of deterring a more powerful rival, which may explain the eagerness of states such as North Korea, Iran, Syria and others to make acquisition of this technology a key component of their grand strategies (e.g., Sagan 1997). Cyber-technology, with its promise of being able to prevent a greater power from using its military resources or disrupt its economy and the delivery of basic services, is another potentially equalizing technology (Buchanan 2016).[9] Furthermore, changes such as the development of cruise missiles, unmanned drones, and cyber capabilities make it possible to fight conventional wars from a distance, without significant casualties to one's own soldiers, which makes it easier to contemplate the use of force with less domestic political fallout. In these and other ways, technological change can be an important driver of grand strategy.

Conclusion

We have outlined here the key material influences on grand strategy, which have a powerful causal impact on the interests that states prioritize with their grand strategies and the manner in which they pursue these interests. As we stated earlier, though, we do not believe that grand strategy is completely determined by material forces. Instead, the material setting sets the parameters within which national leaders make decisions and prioritize goals within a given set of national institutions and in a particular cultural context. This reflects a neoclassical realist worldview that state responses to the external material environment depend in part on their unique intervening leader images, strategic culture, domestic institutions, and state–society relations (Ripsman, Taliaferro, and Lobell 2016). Consequently, it will be useful to examine the other chapters in this volume—on institutions, culture, leadership, etc.—to obtain a more comprehensive understanding of the inputs into the making of grand strategy. Nonetheless, we believe that the material setting is of greatest significance for states.

Notes

1. On economics as a strategic tool, see Blanchard and Ripsman (2013); Blackwill and Harris (2016).
2. On time horizons and their impact on the grand strategies of great and rising powers see Edelstein (2017).
3. On preventive war and its alternatives, see Van Evera (1999); Levy (1987; 2011); Copeland (2001); Ripsman and Levy (2007); Reiter (2006); Trachtenberg (2007); Silverstone (2012); Paul (2016); MacDonald and Parent (2018); Shifrinson (2018).
4. On different causal pathways to conflict and war under unipolarity see Monteiro (2012).

5. Monteiro (2014) argues that even smaller states have a wide range of choice under unipolarity, but we would maintain they may pursue policies that conflict with the unipole's goals only if they wish to accept the risks of conflict with the greatest power or if they believe the unipole has too many greater interests than to get involved. For a discussion of interests, see Glaser's chapter in this volume.
6. For a discussion of how grand strategies vary across types of states and regions, see Ripsman and Paul (2010). On the stability of Latin America, see Kacowicz (2000); Mares (2001).
7. On regional hegemons see Mearsheimer (2001, ch. 2); Elman (2004); Destradi (2010). On Soviet hegemony over Eastern Europe see Jones (1977). On US hegemony over Western Europe see Layne (2015).
8. Although in her analysis Talmadge (2008) concludes that Iran has limited capabilities to shut down the straits of Hormuz beyond three months—this is still sufficient time to disrupt the oil and gas importing markets. Furthermore, Iran seeks the capacity to do so for longer, as attested to by Iran's recent cruise missile build-up and deployment, see Pasandideh (2019). Finally, with continued harassment in the region, Iran can partially reach its goals, see Katzman, Nerurkar, O'Rourke, Mason, and Ratner 2012.
9. For critical take on so-called "cyber-warfare," see Valeriano and Maness (2015); Gartzke (2013).

References

Alexandrova-Arbatova, Nadia. 2009. "The Impact of the Caucasus Crisis on Regional and European Security." *Southeast European and Black Sea Studies* 9 (3): 287–300.

Alnasrawi, Abbas. 1985. "Middle East Oil and Economic Development: Regional and Global implications." In *The Middle East: from Transition to Development*, edited by Sami G. Hajjar, 17–29. Leiden: Brill.

Anderson, Ewan W., Ivars Gutmanis, and Liam D. Anderson. 2000. *Economic Power in a Changing International System*. London: Cassell.

Baldwin, David A. 2016. *Power and International Relations: A Conceptual Approach*. Princeton: Princeton University Press.

Beckley, Michael. 2018. "The Power of Nations: Measuring What Matters." *International Security* 43 (2): 7–44.

Bergstrand, Jeffrey H. 1985. "The Gravity Equation in International Trade: Some Microeconomic Foundations and Empirical Evidence." *The Review of Economics and Statistics* 67 (3): 474–481.

Bialer, Uri. 1999. *Oil and the Arab-Israeli Conflict, 1948-63*. New York: St. Martin's.

Bijian, Zheng. 2005. "China's 'Peaceful Rise' to Great-Power Status." *Foreign Affairs* 84 (5): 18–24.

Bizzozero, Lincoln. 2003. "Uruguay: A Small Country Faces Global Challenges." In *Latin American and Caribbean Foreign Policy*, edited by Frank O. Mora and Jeanne A. K. Hey, 328–44. Boulder: Rowman & Littlefield Publishers.

Blackwill, Robert D., and Jennifer M. Harris. 2016. *War by Other Means*. Boston: Harvard University Press.

Blanchard, Jean-Marc F., and Norrin M. Ripsman. 1996. "Measuring Vulnerability Interdependence: A Geopolitical Approach." *Geopolitics* 1 (3): 225–246.

Blanchard, Jean-Marc F., and Norrin M. Ripsman. 2013. *Economic Statecraft and Foreign Policy: Sanctions and Incentives and Target State Calculations*. London: Routledge.

Borgerson, Scott G. 2008. "Arctic Meltdown: The Economic and Security Implications of Global Warming." *Foreign Affairs* 87 (2): 63–77.

Buchanan, Ben. 2016. *The Cybersecurity Dilemma: Hacking, Trust, and Fear Between Nations*. Oxford: Oxford University Press.

Buzan, Barry, and Ole Waever. 2003. *Regions and Powers: The Structure of International Security*. Cambridge: Cambridge University Press.

Carr, Edward Hallett. 1946. *The Twenty Years' Crisis, 1919–1939: An Introduction to the Study of International Relations*. London: Macmillan.

Choucri, Nazli, and Robert Carver North. 1989. "Lateral Pressure in International Relations: Concept and Theory." In *Handbook of War Studies*, edited by Manus I. Midlarsky, 289–326. Boston: Unwin Hyman.

Cohen, Saul Bernard. 2003. *Geopolitics of the World System*. New York: Rowman & Littlefield.

Connable, Ben, and Becca Wasser. 2018. "The limits of Russian Strategy in the Middle East." https://www.rand.org/blog/2018/05/the-limits-of-russian-strategy-in-the-middle-east.html, accessed June 30, 2019.

Clarke, Michael. 2017. "The Belt and Road Initiative: China's New Grand Strategy?" *Asia Policy* 24 (1): 71–79.

Collins, John M. 1978. "Vietnam Postmortem: a Senseless Strategy." *Parameters* 8 (1): 8–14.

Copeland, Dale C. 2001. *The Origins of Major War*. Ithaca: Cornell University Press.

Cooper, Andrew Fenton, ed. 1997. *Niche Diplomacy: Middle Powers After the Cold War*. London: Macmillan.

Cooper, Andrew F., Richard A. Higgott, and Kim Richard Nossal, eds. 1993. *Relocating Middle Powers: Australia and Canada in a Changing World Order*. Vancouver: University of British Columbia Press.

Cordesman, Anthony H., and Khalid R. Al-Rodhan. 2006. *The Changing Dynamics of Energy in the Middle East*. London: Praeger.

De Montesquieu, Charles. 1989. *The Spirit of the Laws*. Cambridge: Cambridge University Press.

Deibel, Terry L. 2010. *Foreign Affairs Strategy: Logic for American Statecraft*. Cambridge: Cambridge University Press.

Destradi, Sandra. 2010. "Regional Powers and Their Strategies: Empire, Hegemony, and Leadership." *Review of International Studies* 36 (4): 903–930.

Edelstein, David M. 2017. *Over the Horizon: Time, Uncertainty, and the Rise of Great Powers*. Ithaca: Cornell University Press.

Elman, Colin. 2004. "Extending Offensive Realism: The Louisiana Purchase and America's Rise to Regional Hegemony." *American Political Science Review* 98 (4): 563–576.

Ferguson, Niall. 2012. *Empire: How Britain Made the Modern World*. London: Penguin.

Foley, Robert T. 2003. "The Origins of the Schlieffen Plan." *War in History* 10 (2): 222–232.

Gaddis, John Lewis. 2005. *Strategies of Containment: A Critical Appraisal of American National Security Policy During the Cold War*. Oxford: Oxford University Press.

Garnham, David. 1976. "Dyadic International War 1816–1965: The Role of Power Parity and Geographical Proximity." *Political Research Quarterly* 29 (2): 231–242.

Gartzke, Erik. 2013. "The Myth of Cyberwar: Bringing War in Cyberspace Back Down to Earth." *International Security* 38 (2): 41–73.

Gilpin, Robert. 1981. *War and Change in World Politics*. Cambridge: Cambridge University Press.

Gnehm, Eric. 2008. "The Hashemites." *The American Interest*. http://www.the-american-interest.com/ai2/article.cfm?Id=400&MId=18, accessed April 3, 2009.

Gowa, Joanne. 1989. "Bipolarity, Multipolarity, and Free Trade." *American Political Science Review* 83 (4): 1245–1256.

Gowa, Joanne. 1995. *Allies, Adversaries, and International Trade*. Princeton: Princeton University Press.

Gray, Colin S. 2013. *Perspectives on Strategy*. Oxford: Oxford University Press.

Green, Brendan R., and Austin Long. 2017. "The MAD Who Wasn't There: Soviet Reactions to the Late Cold War Nuclear Balance." *Security Studies* 26 (4): 606–641.

Hallen, Travis J. 2013. *Great Powers, National Interests, and Australian Grand Strategy*. Canberra: Air Power Development Center.

Hart, Jeffrey. 1976. "Three approaches to the measurement of power in international relations." *International Organization* 30 (2): 289–305.

Hebron, Lui, and Patrick James. 1997. "Great Powers, Cycles of Relative Capability and Crises in World Politics." *International Interactions* 23 (2): 145–173.

Hershberg, James G. 2007. "'High-Spirited Confusion': Brazil, the 1961 Belgrade Non-Aligned Conference, and the Limits of an 'Independent' Foreign Policy during the High Cold War." *Cold War History* 7 (3): 373–388.

Holbraad, Carsten. 1984. *Middle Powers in International Politics*. London: Macmillan Press.

Huisken, Ron. 2004. *North Korea: Power Play or Buying Butter with Guns?* Canberra: Strategic and Defence Studies Centre.

Ingebritsen, Christine. 2004. "Learning from Lilliput: Small States and EU Expansion." *Scandinavian Studies* 76 (3): 369–384.

Isard, Walter. 1954. "Location Theory and Trade Theory: Short-run Analysis." *The Quarterly Journal of Economics* 68 (2): 305–320.

Janos, Andrew C. 2001. "From Eastern Empire to Western Hegemony: East Central Europe Under Two International Regimes." *East European Politics and Societies* 15 (2): 221–249.

Jones, Christopher D. 1977. "Soviet Hegemony in Eastern Europe: The Dynamics of Political Autonomy and Military Intervention." *World Politics* 29 (2): 216–241.

Jervis, Robert. 1978. "Cooperation Under the Security Dilemma." *World Politics* 30 (2): 167–214.

Jervis, Robert. 2011. "Unipolarity: A Structural Perspective." In *International Relations Theory and the Consequences of Unipolarity*, edited by John G. Ikenberry, Michael Mastanduno, and William C. Wohlforth, 252–281. Cambridge: Cambridge University Press.

Kacowicz, Arie M. 2000. "Latin America as an International Society." *International Politics* 37 (2): 143–162.

Kapur, Paul. 2016. *Jihad as Grand Strategy: Islamist Militancy, National Security, and the Pakistani State*. Oxford: Oxford University Press.

Katzman, Kenneth, Neelesh Nerurkar, Ronald O'Rourke, Chuck Mason, and Michael Ratner. 2012. *Iran's Threat to the Strait of Hormuz*. Washington: Congressional Research Service. https://apps.dtic.mil/dtic/tr/fulltext/u2/a584459.pdf, accessed December 5, 2019.

Keohane, Robert O. 1969. "Lilliputians' Dilemmas: Small States in International Politics." *International Organization* 23 (2): 291–310.

Keohane, Robert O. and Joseph Nye. 1977. *Power and Interdependence: World Politics in Transition*. Boston: Longman.

Kim, Woosang, and James D. Morrow. 1992. "When do Power Shifts Lead to War? *American Journal of Political Science* 36 (4): 896–922.

Labs, Eric J. 1992. "Do Weak States Bandwagon? *Security Studies* 1 (3): 383–416.

Lake, David A., and Patrick M. Morgan. 1997. "The New Regionalism in Security Affairs." In *Regional Orders: Building Security in a New World*, edited by David A. Lake and Patrick M. Morgan, 3–19. University Park: Penn State University Press.

Lasswell, Harold Dwight, and Abraham Kaplan. 1950. *Power and Society A Framework for Political Inquiry*. New Haven: Yale University Press.

Layne, Christopher. 2015. "America as a European hegemon." In *Paradoxes of Power: US Foreign Policy in a Changing World*, edited by David Skidmore, 39–49. London: Routledge.

Le Billon, Philippe. 2004. "The Geopolitical Economy of 'Resource Wars'." *Geopolitics* 9 (1): 1–28.

Leikin, Julia. 2016. "Across the Seven Seas: is Russian Maritime History More Than Regional History? *Kritika: Explorations in Russian and Eurasian History* 17 (3): 631–646.

Lemke, Douglas. 2002. *Regions of War and Peace*. Cambridge: Cambridge University Press.

Lesage, Dries. 2009. "Global Governance and Multipolarity, an Exploration of the Challenge." In *Contemporary Global Governance: Multipolarity Vs. New Discourses on Global Governance*, edited by Dries Lesage and Pierre Vercauteren, 13–28. Brussels: Peter Lang.

Levy, Jack S. 1987. "Declining Power and the Preventive Motivation for War." *World Politics* 40 (1): 82–107.

Levy, Jack S. 2011. "Preventive war: Concept and Propositions." *International Interactions* 37 (1): 87–96.

MacDonald, Paul K., and Joseph M. Parent. 2018. *Twilight of the Titans: Great Power Decline and Retrenchment*. Ithaca: Cornell University Press.

Mahan, Alfred Thayer. 1890. *The Influence of Sea Power upon History, 1660-1783*. New York: Scrivener.

Mares, David R. 2001. *Violent Peace: Militarized Interstate Bargaining in Latin America*. New York: Columbia University Press.

Mearsheimer, John J. 2001. *The Tragedy of Great Power Politics*. New York: W.W. Norton.

Mearsheimer, John J., and Stephen M. Walt. 2016. "The Case for Offshore Balancing: A Superior US Grand Strategy." *Foreign Affairs* 95 (4): 70–83.

Miller, Benjamin. 2000. "Explaining Variations in Regional Peace: Three Strategies for Peacemaking." *Cooperation and Conflict* 35 (2): 155–192.

Miller, William. 2012. *The Ottoman Empire and its Successors, 1801–1927*. London: Routledge.

Miskovic, Natasa, Harald Fischer-Tiné, and Nada Boskovska, eds. 2014. *The Non-aligned Movement and the Cold War: Delhi-Bandung-Belgrade*. London: Routledge.

Monteiro, Nuno P. 2012. "Unrest Assured: Why Unipolarity is not Peaceful." *International Security* 36 (3): 9–40.

Monteiro, Nuno P. 2014. *Theory of Unipolar Politics*. Cambridge: Cambridge University Press.

Morgenthau, Hans Joachim. 1985. *Politics Among Nations: The Struggle for Power and Peace*. New York: McGraw-Hill.

O'Hara, Sarah. 2004. "Great Game or Grubby Game? The Struggle for Control of the Caspian." *Geopolitics* 9 (1): 138–160.

Organski, A. F. K., and Jacek Kugler. 1980. *The War Ledger*. Chicago: Chicago University Press.

Parker, Geoffrey. 1985. *Western Geopolitical Thought in the Twentieth Century*. London: Routledge.

Parnemo, Liv Karin. 2019. "Russia's Naval Development–Grand Ambitions and Tactical Pragmatism." *The Journal of Slavic Military Studies* 32 (1): 41–69.

Pasandideh, Shahryar. 2019. "Under the radar, Iran's cruise missile capabilities advance." *War on The Rocks*. https://warontherocks.com/2019/09/under-the-radar-irans-cruise-missile-capabilities-advance/, accessed December 5, 2019.

Paul, T.V. 2012. "Regional Transformation in International Relations." In *International Relations Theory and Regional Transformation*, edited by T.V. Paul, 3–21. Cambridge: Cambridge University Press.

Paul, T.V., ed. 2016. *Accommodating Rising Powers: Past, Present, and Future*. Cambridge: Cambridge University Press.

Peretz, Don. 1965. "Nonalignment in the Arab World." *The ANNALS of the American Academy of Political and Social Science* 362 (1): 36–43.

Pitkin, Hannah. 1972. *Wittgenstein and Justice*. Berkeley: University of California Press.

Reiter, Dan. 2006. *Preventive War and its Alternatives: The Lessons of History*. Carlisle: Strategic Studies Institute.

Ripsman, Norrin M. 2002. *Peacemaking by Democracies: The Effect of State Autonomy on the Post-World-War Settlements*. University Park: Penn State University Press.

Ripsman, Norrin M., and Jack S. Levy. 2007. "The Preventive War that Never Happened: Britain, France, and the Rise of Germany in the 1930s." *Security Studies* 16 (1): 32–67.

Ripsman, Norrin M., and Jack S. Levy. 2008. "Wishful Thinking or Buying Time? the Logic of British Appeasement in the 1930s." *International Security* 33 (2): 148–181.

Ripsman, Norrin M. and T.V. Paul. 2010. *Globalization and the National Security State*. New York: Oxford University Press.

Ripsman, Norrin M., Jeffrey W. Taliaferro, and Steven E. Lobell. 2016. *Neoclassical Realist Theory of International Politics*. Oxford: Oxford University Press.

Ripsman, Norrin M. 2019. "Conclusion: The Emerging Sub-field of Comparative Grand Strategy." In *A Comparative Grand Strategy, A Framework and Cases*, edited by Thierry Balzacq, Peter Dombrowski, and Simon Reich, 284–302. Oxford: Oxford University Press.

Romanova, Tatiana. 2016. "Is Russian Energy Policy Towards the EU Only About Geopolitics? The Case of the Third Liberalisation Package." *Geopolitics* 21 (4): 857–879.

Sagan, Scott D. 1997. "Why do States Build Nuclear Weapons? Three Models in Search of a Bomb." *International Security* 21 (3): 54–86.

Schmidt, Brian C., and Thomas Juneau. 2012. "Neoclassical Realism and Power." In *Neoclassical Realism in European Politics: Bringing Power Back In*, edited by Asle Toje and Barbara Kunz, 61–78. Manchester: Manchester University Press.

Schroeder, Paul W. 1994. "Historical Reality vs. Neo-realist Theory." *International Security* 19 (1): 108–148.

Schweller, Randall L. 1998. *Deadly Imbalances: Tripolarity and Hitler's Strategy of World Conquest*. New York: Columbia University Press.

Shambaugh, David. 2013. "Chinese Thinking about World Order." In *China and the International System: Becoming a World Power*, edited by Xiaoming Huang and Robert G. Patman, 21–31. London: Routledge.

Sharples, Jack D. 2016. "The Shifting Geopolitics of Russia's Natural Gas Exports and their Impact on EU-Russia Gas Relations." *Geopolitics* 21 (4): 880–912.

Shifrinson, Joshua R. Itzkowitz. 2018. *Rising Titans, Falling Giants: How Great Powers Exploit Power Shifts*. Ithaca: Cornell University Press.

Silverstone, Scott. 2012. *Preventive War and American Democracy*. London: Routledge.

Singer, J. David. 1987. "Reconstructing the Correlates of War Dataset on Material Capabilities of States, 1816–1985." *International Interactions* 14 (2): 115–132.

Soysa, Indra de. 2002. "Ecoviolence: Shrinking Pie, or Honey Pot? *Global Environmental Politics* 2 (4): 1–34.

Sprout, Harold, and Margaret Sprout. 1965. *The Ecological Perspective on Human Affairs: With Special Reference to International Politics*. Princeton: Princeton University Press.

STRATFOR. 2018. "How Renewable Energy Will Change Geopolitics." https://worldview.stratfor.com/article/how-renewable-energy-will-change-geopolitics, accessed June 29, 2019.

Talmadge, Caitlin. 2008. "Closing Time: Assessing the Iranian Threat to the Strait of Hormuz." *International Security* 33 (1): 82–117.

Thorhallsson, Baldur, and Anders Wivel. 2006. "Small States in the European Union: What Do We Know and What Would We Like to Know? *Cambridge Review of International Affairs* 19 (4): 651–668.

Toal, Gerard. 2017. *Near Abroad: Putin, the West, and the Contest over Ukraine and the Caucasus*. Oxford: Oxford University Press.

Trachtenberg, Marc. 2007. "Preventive War and US Foreign Policy." *Security Studies* 16 (1): 1–31.

Ulam, Adam Bruno. 1974. *Expansion and Coexistence: The History of Soviet Foreign Policy, 1917–73*. New York: Holt.

Valeriano, Brandon, and Ryan C. Maness. 2015. *Cyber War Versus Cyber Realities: Cyber Conflict in the International System*. Oxford: Oxford University Press.

Van Evera, Stephen. 1999. *Causes of War: Power and the Roots of Conflict*. Ithaca: Cornell University Press.

Vasquez, John A. 1995. "Why do Neighbors Fight? Proximity, Interaction, or Territoriality." *Journal of Peace Research* 32 (3): 277–293.

Wagner, R. Harrison. 1993. "What was Bipolarity?" *International Organization* 47 (1): 77–106.

Walt, Stephen M. 1987. *The Origins of Alliances*. Ithaca: Cornell University Press.

Waltz, Kenneth N. 1979. *Theory of International Politics*. New York: McGraw-Hill.

Waltz, Kenneth N. 1988. "The Origins of War in Neorealist Theory." *The Journal of Interdisciplinary History* 18 (4): 615–628.

Wesley, Michael. 2016. "Australia's Grand Strategy and the 2016 Defence White Paper." *Security Challenges* 12 (1): 19–30.

Wight, Martin. 2002. *Power Politics*. London: Royal Institute of International Affairs.

Winters, Harold A. 2001. *Battling the Elements: Weather and Terrain in the Conduct of War*. Baltimore: Johns Hopkins University Press.

Wright, Quincy. 1983. *A Study of War*. Chicago: University of Chicago Press.

Yarger, Harry. R. 2006. *Strategic Theory for the 21st Century: The Little Book on Big Strategy*. Carlisle: Strategic Studies Institute.

CHAPTER 14

TECHNOLOGICAL CHANGE AND GRAND STRATEGY

SOPHIE-CHARLOTTE FISCHER, ANDREA GILLI, AND MAURO GILLI

WHAT is the relationship between technological change and grand strategy? Can great powers promote technological trends that allow them to pursue specific grand-strategic goals? Or is technological change beyond the reach of great powers, and thus it acts like an independent enabler or an independent constraint? The literature in international relations theory has paid only tangential attention, at best, to the role of technology and technological change in international politics. This chapter aims to fill this gap and focuses on the relationship between technological change and grand strategy.

The chapter is divided into three main sections. The first introduces technological change. The second and third sections look at the relationship between technological change and grand strategy and identify different channels through which they influence each other.

TECHNOLOGICAL CHANGE

In this section we provide a brief introduction to the role of technological change in world politics and then we summarize some of its most relevant aspects for economic, international, social, and political relations.

Technological Change in Historical Perspective

The effects and implications of technological change for world politics are self-evident when we look at the past (Brodie and Brodie 1973; Van Creveld 1989). Innovative chariot designs shortly after 2000 BC contributed to shift the balance of power in Eurasia (Mann 1986, 162). New shipbuilding techniques enabled the expansion of Muslim dynasties to North Africa, the Middle East, Europe, and Asia (Fahmy 1948). The invention of gunpowder, its application to warfare, and the diffusion of guns and artillery played a critical role in the consolidation of China under the Ming Dynasty (Andrade 2016, 54–72), the fall of Constantinople and the expansion of the Ottoman Empire (McNeill 1982, 61), and the creation of nation-states in Western Europe (Parker 1996, 6–44). At about the same time, new types of sailing ships (together with new instruments for navigation), more powerful cannons, and advances in medicine (i.e., prevention and cure of scurvy) gave rise to the age of great explorations that brought Europeans to "discover" most of the rest of the world (Cipolla 1965; Headrick 2010). These explorations notwithstanding, for more than 300 years, large parts of the world remained impenetrable to Europeans, as was the case for most of Asia other than coastal cities and for Africa. Because of advances in science and technology in the nineteenth century, however, Western Europe's control of surface land increased from 35 percent in 1800 to 84 percent in 1914 (Headrick 1981, 3). Among others, three such advances played a particularly important role in this regard. First, improvements in firepower, such as the needle-gun and the Maxim-gun, gave Europeans a definitive military edge over local populations (Headrick 1981, 83–126; 2010, 257–301; Ellis 1975, 79–109). Second, progress in medicine permitted Europeans to devise a protection against tropical diseases such as cholera, malaria, and typhoid that had until then frustrated any attempt of settling in most of Africa (Headrick 1981, 58–79; 2010, 226–256). Third, advances in naval propulsion, with the arrival of the steamboat, allowed Europeans to cruise rivers up from their deltas or in shallow coastal waters, thus projecting firepower deep into continental territories and to bring supplies to the outposts (Headrick 1981, 17–42, 129–149; 2010, 177–225). These changes were part of a much broader techno-scientific revolution that would significantly increase human control over nature—it began in in the second part of the eighteenth century with the Industrial Revolution and strengthened further about a century later, with the so-called "Second Industrial Revolution" (Landes 1972, 4; Chandler 1990, 12; Smil 2005).[1] For world politics, the direct result of this transformation was the "great divergence" between European countries (and North America) on the one hand, and the rest of the world on the other (Pomeranz 2000; and for an assessment, Broadberry et al. 2018). In other words, power over nature became a source of power over people: Europeans came to control economically, politically, and socially large parts of the world—and those who resisted were either killed, deprived of their means of subsistence, or pitted one against the other (Headrick 2010; Icenberg 2001; Silverman 2016). While this techno-scientific revolution led to divergence between the haves and the have-nots, developments from the 1870s onwards promoted convergence among the haves (Gerschenkron 1962, 31–51; Kennedy 1987, 198; Chandler 1990, 1–46). There are multiple reasons for such convergence (see, e.g., Rosenberg and Birdzell 1987), among which, the nature of technology of that time played a key role, as evidenced in the rapid economic and military growth of Germany, Japan and, subsequently, of the Soviet Union (Mowery and Rosenberg 1989, 28–31; Mokyr 1990a, 113–148).[2]

What is Technological Change?

With technological change, scholars generally refer to a broad range of activities such as invention, innovation, and diffusion of technology or of processes that lead to an increase in output without increasing the inputs (Schumpeter 1976). Accordingly, technological change is considered the only source of long-term economic growth (Solow 1956). When we look at world politics, we can identify five key features of technological change that are particularly important.

First, technological change creates new opportunities and hence alters the strategic environment—it moves the technological frontier outward (Mokyr 1990a, 1990b). Consider two of the most dramatic changes that have occurred over the past hundred years: population growth and the modern globalized economy. The synthesis of ammonia from its elements allowed for the production of large quantities of extremely effective fertilizers, which in turn paved the way for the massive population growth that we have observed over the past century (Smil 2001). China realized the strategic importance of fertilizers, after the catastrophe of the great famine in the early 1960s. Accordingly, shortly after opening to the West in 1972, it "placed orders for thirteen of the world's largest and most modern ammonia-urea complexes, the biggest purchase of its kind ever" (Smil 2001, 170). Along the same lines, consider the importance of gas turbines and diesel engines for globalization. These two extremely reliable and affordable technologies power commercial airliners and cargo ships. Without them, the speed and intensity of the world trade and exchanges would not be possible (Smil 2013, 210).

Second, technological change has distributional effects, within and without countries (Phillips 1971; Tilton 1971). Consider the demise of big corporations such as Blockbuster (rental service of movies and videogames), Nokia (Finnish mobile phone producer) or Borders (American bookstore chain), and the emergence of Netflix (online streaming), Android (Google-based operating systems for mobile devices), and Amazon (online shopping and cloud services). After Apple introduced the iPhone, Nokia almost went bankrupt. A couple of years later, Apple introduced the iPad—which, together with other tablets, dramatically reduced paper consumption. Finland happens to be both the mother country of Nokia and a leading worldwide producer of paper. These two developments significantly hit the Finnish economy in the 2010s. In the words of the then Finnish prime minister, Alexander Stubb, "The iPhone killed Nokia and the iPad killed the Finnish paper industry" (quoted in Dave 2014). The reason why technological change has distributional effects is that it can be either competence-enhancing or competence-destroying (Tushman and Anderson 1986). Some types of technological change reward existing skills, expertise, and production capabilities, thus reinforcing the leadership of incumbents, while other types of technological change require completely different skills, expertise, and production capabilities, thus allowing for the entry of new actors. In the late nineteenth and early twentieth century, for instance, bicycles and car manufacturing relied on the same machine tools, same skills and same processes, thus allowing bicycle manufacturers not only to engage in the production of cars, but also to derive an advantage from their existing capabilities (Rosenberg 1976, 9–31; Carrol et al. 1996). Similarly, the transition to fifth-generation fighter jets rewarded those countries (and companies) that had already invested extensively in stealth technology and advanced avionics (Lorell 2003, 97–114). Conversely competence-destroying technological change cancels the advantage of dominant actors. Consider the implications of the iPod and of iTunes for producers of portable CD players and for the music majors. The iPod made CD players obsolete, and significantly shrank the margins on CDs (Parker et al. 2016). To appreciate the possible magnitude of competence-destroying technological change, the case of the iPhone and Nokia described above is particularly telling. At the press conference confirming the sale of Nokia to Microsoft, the then CEO of Nokia admitted, while crying: "we didn't do anything wrong, but somehow, we lost" (quoted in Baassir 2018). That technological change has distributional effect is of central importance for IR, because it questions one of the key premises of the Offense-Defense Balance, namely that the state of technology is a systemic variable, and hence constant across countries (for a summary, see Lynn-Jones 1995, 666–667). This means that technological change can significantly weaken some countries, while strengthening others, economically, politically, or militarily, and hence possibly also affect the system as a whole.

Third, technological change can be either exogenous or endogenous to an existing competition among great powers. Countries can promote change in some technological domains to support their goals. France's investments in iron hulls, steam engines, and explosive shells in the mid-nineteenth century were aimed at challenging British naval rule, for instance (Hamilton 1993). Similarly, the United Kingdom and the United States invested in technologies aimed at detecting enemy submarines and enemy bombers (radar and sonar), in order to undermine aerial and underwater threats (see, e.g., Buderi 1996; Merrill and Wyld 1997). Alternatively, technological change can be exogenous. A technology can be the product of its time—emerging from scientific and technological progress, as was the case for the diesel engine (Smil 2005, 99–151). In other instances, a new technology can result from a competition that is external to the one of interest, and thus yield a "competitive advantage" to a given country.[3] This was the case for the firepower revolution, for example, that originated in Europe but that gave Europeans an unexpected military advantage outside of Europe (Cipolla 1965; Hoffman 2017).

Fourth, technological change creates uncertainty (Rosenberg 1996). As technology opens up new opportunities, it is difficult to understand and to identify the timing, the type, the direction, and the magnitude of technological change and of its implication—i.e., who will benefit and who will lose, as well as when and to what degree. This is a key factor given that, since the 1990s at least, the dominant narrative has pushed private and public organizations alike to adopt new innovations. In fact, under some circumstances, it might be safer not to adopt an innovation, or to postpone its adoption until it is reliable and effective. Consider the initial support for the development of submarines by British Prime Minister William Pitt—submarines that would have been used against France during the reign of Napoleon at the beginning of the nineteenth century. John Jervis, Lord St. Vincent and First Lord of the Admiralty, colorfully expressed his disagreement with that policy by stating that "Pitt was the greatest fool that ever existed, to encourage a mode of war which they who commanded the seas did not want, and which if successful would deprive them of it" (Parker 2001, 5). Along the same lines, think of the US Air Force adoption of missiles at a time when missiles were still unreliable—the running joke among US pilots was that they are called "miss-iles" and not "hitt-iles" for a reason (Michel 1997, 150–158).

Finally, technological change does not occur in a vacuum: new technologies may in fact require additional infrastructural support and new or different skills (complements) as well as new or different parts (components) (Gilli and Gilli 2016). The nature and degree of these changes impact competition among companies as well as about countries (Adner 2012). Mass production, for instance, permitted the employment of unskilled labor, thus dramatically easing the diffusion of manufacturing (Caselli 1999). Artificial intelligence, conversely, requires more skilled personnel to complement the role of machines (Agrawal, Gans, and Goldfarb 2018, 13). The evolution of military aviation provides a useful example to understand the demand for complements or components. Over the past century, air warfare has come to require much more skilled pilots and maintenance crew as well as more complex and sophisticated component parts (Prencipe 1997; Fino 2017). The Soviet Union, however, struggled dramatically in the provision of these components and complements. As a result, it could generate much less combat power than NATO countries. The end result was that complement requirements represented a competitive disadvantage for the Soviets (Epstein 1984).

The Effects of Technological Change on Grand Strategy

Grand strategy is the employment of all instruments of statecraft—including diplomacy, economic resources, intelligence, and military power—to achieve grand-strategic goals, i.e. broad and long-lasting objectives concerning the positioning of a country in the international system. As Edward N. Luttwak notes, "all states have a grand strategy, whether they know it or not" (2009, 409). Grand strategy can be analyzed by looking at its sources, at its goals, and at its instruments (Silove 2018). This is what we do in this section: we look at the effect of technological change on the sources, goals, and instruments of grand strategy.

Technological Change and the Sources of Grand Strategy

Domestic politics influence grand strategy by determining strategic needs for the country, the domestic coalitions within a country, and finally dominant narratives and ideas. Technological change can impact all the three of them.

First, technological change can make a country more independent from others in some realms, and more dependent in other realms. Early nineteenth-century shipbuilding required special types of timber oak that, in turn, could be procured only from some parts of Nordic countries and some areas in the Mediterranean (Brodie 1941; Gardiner and Lambert 1992). The transition to iron and later steel hulls relieved countries from the need to employ timber. As a result, countries like Great Britain that had vast natural supplies of iron became more independent. Along the same lines, the growing application of natural rubber made this product a key natural resource (Drabble 2000, 76). It became so important that it played a key role in Japanese imperial ambitions towards South East Asia, the primary region where rubber was grown (Wendt 1947). Similarly, the employment of the combustion engine and its diffusion in the twentieth century made oil a strategic resource, so far as to lead the United States to declare the "Carter doctrine" (Yergin 1991, 140).

Second, technological change has distributional effects both within and without countries. For instance, the logrolling coalition between the land-owning aristocracy and the emerging heavy industry significantly contributed to Germany's Weltpolitik (Snyder 1991; Herwig 1980). It is important to note, however, that such logrolling was made possible by the domestic effects of technological change: the aristocracy, on the one hand, was becoming economically weaker, and thus had a strong incentive to join the new rich; industrialists, on the other hand, were pursuing social validation in the rigid German social system, that accorded little legitimacy to the new social class (Berghahn 2000).

Third, technology can shape grand strategy by affecting dominant ideas and narratives. For example, the diffusion of the printing press favored the spread of Protestantism, which in turn altered the reach, influence, and ultimately behavior of the Vatican as well as of the different European kingdoms in the sixteenth and seventeenth centuries (Rubin 2014). Without the printing press, those religious motivations might have not arisen or might have played a much less influential role, as the failure of the Hussite movement of the early fifteenth century confirms (ibid.). The grand strategies of sixteenth-century Spain under King Charles V and of seventeenth-century Sweden under King Gustavus Adulphus can be understood only by assessing their religious motivations (Nexon 2009). Along the same lines, Ayatollah Khomeini's sermons could reach into Iranian society because of the diffusion of their audio recordings during the Shah's reign (Sreberny-Mohammadi 1990). As a result, a status quo power, which was also a pillar of the US Middle East policy and an ally of Israel, became a revisionist power, opposed to the US, Israel, and the West—and intent on transforming the geopolitics of the Middle East.

Goals of Grand Strategy

In this section we focus on the interaction between technological change and the goals of grand strategy.

First, grand strategies are generally based on assumptions about what the state of technology allows and do not allow us to do. For this reason, technological change can render some grand-strategic goals obsolete. For instance, proponents of both US deep engagement and offshore balancing share the same assumption about American military power in East Asia: namely, that US military forces will be able to deter and quickly defeat the People Liberation's Army (Montgomery 2014). However, China's growing anti-access/area-denial capabilities have made this assumption obsolete (ibid.). Similarly, the grand strategy of Imperial China under the Qing Dynasty and Imperial Japan under the Tokugawa Shonugate aimed at limiting foreign influence: both assumed that they could retrench and keep foreign intruders at bay (Zhang 2015; Toby 1984). Until the early nineteenth century, this assumption had proven largely correct. With the First and the Second Industrial Revolutions that originated in Europe, however, the military–technological gap between the two Asian countries and Western Powers widened significantly, and over the following decades, both China and Japan were forced to open up—respectively by the UK, in 1842 and by the US in 1854 (Andrade 2016, 237–244). These two cases permit a broader discussion about the "stopping power of water" discussed by John Mearsheimer and the criticism that it has generated (Mearsheimer 2001; Snyder 2002). The view that water has a "stopping power" is in fact contingent on the relative type of technology—i.e., whether technology permits us to overcome natural barriers or not (Derry and Williams 1960, 706). Until 1800, as we discussed before, this assumption was largely correct (Headrick 1981, 3). From the 1850s to the 1940s, the stopping power of water largely vanished: Western countries could invade and conquer most non-Western countries, and where invasion turned out to be difficult (such as the landing in Normandy) this had little to do with water per se, and more with coastal defenses. From the 1940s onward, Western countries found keeping their colonial empires increasingly difficult, but again this had little to do with the stopping power of water, and more to do with the diffusion of small arms and light weapons, the increasing costs these weapons imposed on colonial powers in terms of blood and treasure, and growing domestic intolerance to such costs (Gilli, Gilli, and Pischedda 2017; Areguin-Toft 2001).

Second, some grand-strategic goals such as primacy and latency are contingent on the state of technology, commercial or military. According to neorealism, primacy is self-defeating, because unrivaled power will generate incentives for other countries to balance the unrivalled power (Waltz 1979). This was the case during the Second Industrial Revolution and in the age of mass production, when industrialized countries could enter weapons manufacturing relatively easily and quickly. However, at least since the 1970s, developing state-of-the-art weapon systems has become increasingly more difficult, which in turn has made internal balancing increasingly costly and more difficult to accomplish, especially for countries that have ambitious goals such as regional hegemony (Brooks 2006; Neuman 2010; Brooks and Wohlforth 2016; Gilli and Gilli 2019). Similarly, some countries might prefer to keep defense spending to a minimum, in order to avert the domestic costs associated with it (such as crowding out effects). Japan during the Cold War and the United Kingdom in the interwar period, to some degrees, pursued a grand strategy based on latent military power—i.e., the capacity to quickly launch the production of military equipment, when the need emerges. However, such capacity is conditional on the state of technology. Since the Second World War, weapon platforms such as jet fighters or attack submarines have become increasingly more complex: nowadays it takes more than a decade to go from conceptualization to finished product, and their production poses extremely high entry barriers, such that when countries interrupt the production of this type of weapon system, they find it extremely difficult to enter it again (Alic 2013; Gholz 2007; Gilli and Gilli 2019).

Instruments of Grand Strategy

Technological change can also impact the instruments of grand strategy, such as economic resources and military capabilities.

With respect to economic resources, technological change affects productivity and thus a polity's overall wealth. This means that a country can have resources to support its overall international standing, including economic aids and free trade agreements as well as economic containment and sanctions. However, also the opposite is true. If a country cannot adopt new technologies, it will lag behind vis-à-vis its competitors. While International Relations theory generally assume that great powers could relatively easily catch up with their adversaries' technologies, this insight seems to be historically and geographically contingent (Brooks 2006; Gilli and Gilli 2019). Until the early nineteenth century, China was the wealthiest polity in the world. Yet, it could not catch up with Western inventions after that. This led to its partial submission to Western countries' demands (Andrade 2016).

Second, technological change can generate uncertainty about the instruments of grand strategies. As a result, some countries might fail to anticipate technological change, misunderstand the direction, or underestimate/overestimate its effects. For instance, France in the mid-nineteenth century tried to offset British naval supremacy through new technologies. France's leadership, however, failed also to grasp the implications of the ecosystem upon which their proposed changes were dependent. Specifically, by moving from wood to iron, and from sail to coal, naval powers required access to iron, to coal, and to coal bases, as steam-powered, iron-hulled warships required much more extensive and frequent support and maintenance than their predecessors (Lambert 1991). All three resources were scarce in France, however, and thus its technological strategy ended up strengthening, rather than weakening, British naval rule (Brodie 1941). Similarly, before the Second World War, Germany invested only limited resources in submarine production because it (mistakenly) believed that British advances with sonar had significantly reduced the effectiveness of submarines (Herwig 1996, 227–264). In fact, British sonar was much less advanced than Germany feared, and by the time Germany restarted the production of submarines in 1935, it already had the capabilities to produce submarines that would be able to escape British sonars (Showell 2006, 71 and 104). Surprisingly enough, German engineers had not realized their capabilities, and they did not develop such boats only in 1944. According to some, if Germany had developed such revolutionary submarines earlier, the Battle of the Atlantic would have lasted much longer (Polmar and Moore 2004, 8; Breemer 2010, 78).

The Effects of Grand Strategy on Technological Change

In this section, we look at how grand strategy can affect technological change. We focus on direct and indirect effects, on both strategic competition as well as long-term economic growth.

Direct Effects

A country's grand strategy can aim to develop specific technologies with the goal of securing the upper hand over a strategic rival.

At the beginning of the Cold War, the US faced a numerical imbalance in Soviet–NATO conventional forces, especially in Central Europe. A key element of US strategy to contain the Soviet Union—the so-called First Offset Strategy—consisted in relying on nuclear weapons (Friedberg 2000), which, in turn, led to additional technological developments that proved to have quite significant consequences. At first, the US Air Force enjoyed a natural monopoly over nuclear weapons, given that it had carried out the first nuclear attack in history. Yet, because of the US institutional and political system, both the US Navy and the US Army entered this domain as well—mostly to avoid being sidelined. While the nuclear project of the Army did not succeed, one of the Navy's projects, Polaris, turned out to be a terrific success (Sapolsky 1972). With the aim of preserving its status and relevance, the Navy devised a very effective way to enforce nuclear deterrence, namely by mounting ballistic missiles on submarines (Coté 1996). By cruising underwater, ballistic missile submarines would be extremely hard to detect and destroy for enemy forces, and hence would represent a much more credible deterrent than land-based intercontinental ballistic missiles and more difficult to intercept than strategic bombers (Coté 1991). The creation of the third leg of the triad of nuclear deterrence, in turn, came to play a key role throughout the Cold War, and, as we explain later, endowed the United States with a strategic advantage in comparison to the Soviet Union (Coté 2003).

In the late 1970s, the United States realized that Soviet accomplishments in conventional and nuclear weapons had eroded the strategic advantage that the US had enjoyed until then. For this reason, Washington launched the so-called Second Offset Strategy aimed at regaining strategic superiority (Mahnken 2012). In addition to investments in electronics and computers aimed at yielding a qualitative advantage in detection, data-processing, firing accuracy and range, as well as communications, the US also focused on a new revolutionary technology, so-called "low-observable" technology (more commonly known as "stealth"). The experience in South Vietnam had taught the US Air Force that its fleet of bombers and fighters was vulnerable to Soviet anti-air defense systems (Grant 2010, 23–29). Stealth technology permitted them to reduce by several orders of magnitude the radar reflections of US aircraft, and thus to shrink significantly the range at which they could be detected and engaged, thus enabling the US Air Force to enter into highly protected areas (Bahret 1993; Grant 2010, 47–53). In addition to its operational advantages, with stealth technology, the Pentagon was also intending to force the Soviet Union to increase its investments in defensive technologies, such as more advanced and hence more expensive air-defense systems, in order to reduce the resources available to Moscow for offensive capabilities (Krepinevich and Martinage 2008, 15–16).

Indirect Effects

Technologies developed for specific goals might have indirect effects later on, which in turn provided unexpected additional benefits. The case of US ballistic missile submarines provides two additional examples in this regard.

First, US investment in underwater acoustics date back to well before the Second World War and were massively increased immediately afterward (Lasky 1974; Lasky 1976). In the 1940s and 1950s, these investments were intended to address the risk that the Soviet Union might use new, quieter submarines to disrupt strategic lines of communications (Coté 2003, 15–18). US investments in underwater acoustics led to significant improvements in passive sonar, to the discovery and understanding of the deep sound channel, and to the installment of a network of fixed underwater hydrophones at key strategic chokepoints (Stefanick 1987, 1–32, 217–365; Whitman 2005).[4] Such investments yielded a massive advantage to the US, as it enabled it to easily detect, identify, and track Soviet ballistic missiles submarines (Sontag et al., 133–134; Coté 2003, 72). As a result, from the mid-1960s until the early 1980s, the Soviets lacked credible sea-based second-strike capabilities (Coté 2003, 79; Long and Green 2015).

Second, when ballistic missile submarines were invented, their operation posed two main challenges: how to assess their precise location, which was necessary in order to calculate the precise trajectory of their missiles, and hence to ensure their accuracy; and how to ensure efficient and reliable command and control, which would allow for a prompt retaliation in case of need. To provide such geolocation capabilities and command and controls, the US Navy developed both satellite navigation and satellite communication systems (Friedman 2000, 74). With time, US satellites have come to play a fundamentally important role for the US military and its capacity to gather and share intelligence and information (Posen 2003; Gilli and Gilli 2016). In fact, the entire

US command and control system, as well as its beyond-visual-range power projection capabilities, depend on the complex constellation of US satellites. This could hardly have been predicted when ballistic missile submarines were first conceived.

Additional Indirect Effects

Grand strategy can both promote or hinder long-term technological development and hence economic growth. The Cold War offers interpretations that are consistent with both accounts.

When the Cold War started, the US could count on a bigger and more vibrant economy than the Soviet Union, but many of the key technologies that would define the confrontation between the two blocs had still to be invented and developed (Lake 2019; United States Senate, 1979). Investments in many key technologies led to a major scientific, technological, and industrial transformation. According to some, such investments yielded significant long-term benefits for the US economy (Mazzuccato 2013). In particular, the transition of military technologies to the commercial realm, generally known as "spin-offs," enabled the integration into the civilian economy of powerful technologies such as microprocessors, computers, internet, advanced materials, and propulsion systems, to name just a few (ibid.). Ultimately, this spin-off process played a crucial role also in the American victory in the Cold War. The increasing employment of computers in the US economy yielded significant productivity gains, which generated additional wealth, and hence resources to be deployed in the fight against community. This meant that for the Soviet Union, competing with the US became increasingly costly and ultimately unsustainable, given that it had not been able to close the gap in the new advanced sector (Heinrich 2002; Etzkowitz 1983; Brooks and Wohlforth, 2000).

Despite some outstanding cases of successful military spin-offs such as GPS, semiconductors, and ARPANET, some have argued that this focus on military technology came at the expense of the US civilian economy. During the Cold War, the US Department of Defense in fact became the largest direct and indirect employer of scientists and engineers in the United States, with a third of all US scientists dependent on military spending for their livelihood (Ullmann 1984, 106). It is not unconceivable that this constrained the technical capabilities of the American civilian economy, also because military requirements often set highly complex, high-performance objectives that have ultimately very limited commercial applications (DiFilippo 1990; Markusen 1986).

A proper balance of these two opposing forces is inevitably difficult, not leat because of the very political nature of the topic—investments in weapons. Such a difficulty serves as a reminder of the trade-offs that any policy choice presents, especially when technological change, as well as its primary consequences (such as uncertainty and distributional effects), are involved.

Conclusions

In 1983, the then Chief of the Soviet General Staff, Nikolai Orgakov, conceded that "modern military power is based on technology, and technology is based upon computers." He added that, for the Soviet Union to catch up technologically with the United States, it needed an economic revolution. But the question was whether it could "have an economic revolution without a political revolution" (quoted in Gelb 1992). Orgakov's remarks are not only one of the first assessments of the inherent weaknesses of the Soviet Union from a Soviet official, but also an implicit, and important, reminder to International Relations scholars: economics, politics, and technology are all tightly integrated. The field of international relations has paid more attention to the relationship between economics and politics than to their interaction with technology. This chapter has provided a brief overview of the role of technology in world politics, and of how it affects and is affected by grand strategy, with the ambition of introducing students to this topic and of promoting further research on it.

Disclaimer

The views expressed in this article do not represent those of the German Government, of NATO, of the NATO Defense College, or of any other institution the authors are or have been affiliated with.

Notes

1. Particularly insightful in this regard is David Landes' remark that "the Englishman of 1750 was closer in material things to Caesar's legionnaires than his own great-grand-children" (1972, 5).
2. For each of the countries mentioned in the text, see, e.g., Herwig (1980); Overy (1994); Evans and Peattie (2012); and Allen (2003).
3. This is consistent with Porter's (1989) logic on competitive advantages.
4. The deep sound channel is a natural phenomenon created by hydrostatic pressure, water density, and temperature that permits the sound to propagate underwater for thousands of miles (see, e.g., Stefanick 1987: 232–238).

References

Adner, Ron. 2012. *The Wide Lens: A New Strategy for Innovation*. New York: Portfolio.

Agrawal, Ajay, Joshua Gans, and Avi Goldfarb. 2018. *Prediction Machines: The Simple Economics of Artificial Intelligence*. Boston: Harvard Business Review Press.

Alic, John A. 2013. "Managing US Defense Acquisition." *Enterprise & Society* 14 (2) (March): 1–36.

Allen, Robert C. 2009. *Farm to Factory: A Reinterpretation of the Soviet Industrial Revolution*. Princeton, NJ: Princeton University Press.

Andrade, Tonio. 2016. *The Gunpowder Age: China, Military Innovation and the Rise of the West in World History*. Princeton, NJ: Princeton University Press.

Baassir, Ramez. 2018. "Complacency Will Be the Death of You." *Forbes*, October 10, 2018.

Bahret, William F. 1993. "The Beginnings of Stealth Technology." *IEEE Transactions on Aerospace and Electronic Systems* 29 (4) (Oct.): 1374–1385.

Berghahn, Volker. "Demographic growth, industrialization and social change." In *Nineteenth-Century Germany: Politics, Culture and Society, 1790–1918*, edited by John Breuly, 169–212. London: Bloomsbury Academic.

Breemer, Jan S. 2010. *Defeating the U-boat: Inventing Antisubmarine Warfare*. Newport, RI: Naval War College Press.

Broadberry, Stephen, Hanhui Guan, and David Daokui Li. 2018. "China, Europe, and the Great Divergence: A Study in Historical National Accounting, 980–1850." *The Journal of Economic History* 78 (4): 955–1000.

Brodie, Bernard. 1941. *Seapower in the First Machine Age*. Princeton, NJ: Princeton University Press.

Brodie, Bernard, and Fawn M. Brodie, 1973. *From the Crossbow to H-Bomb: The Evolution of the Weapons and Tactics of Warfare*. Bloomington: Indiana University Press.

Brooks, Stephen G. 2006. *Producing Security: Multinational Corporations, Globalization, and the Changing Calculus of Conflict*. Princeton, NJ: Princeton University Press.

Brooks, Stephen G., and William C. Wohlforth. 2000. "Power, Globalization, and the End of the Cold War: Reevaluating a Landmark Case for Ideas." *International Security* 25 (3): 5–53.

Brooks, Stephen G., and William C. Wohlforth. 2015/16. "The Rise and Fall of the Great Powers in the Twenty-First Century: China's Rise and the Fate of America's Global Position." *International Security* 40 (3) (Winter): 7–53.

Buderi, Robert. 1996. *The Invention that Changed the World: How A Small Group of Radar Pioneers Won the Second World War and Launched a Technical Revolution*. New York, NY: Touchstone.

Carroll, Glenn R. et al. 1996. "The Fates of De Novo and De Alio Producers in the American Automobile Industry, 1885–1981." *Strategic Management Journal* 17 (1) (Summer): 117–137

Caselli, Francesco. 1999. "Technological Revolutions." *American Economic Review* 89 (1) (March): 78–102.

Chandler, Alfred D. Jr. 1990. *Scale and Scope*. Cambridge, MA: The Belknap Press.

Cipolla, Carlo M. 1965. *Guns, Guns, Sails, and Empires: Technological Innovation and the Early Phases of European Expansion, 1400–1700*. Manhattan, KS: Sunflower University Press.

Coté, Owen. 1991. "The Trident and the Triad: Collecting the D-5 Dividend." *International Security* 16 (2): 117–145.

Coté, Owen. 1996. *The Politics of Innovative Military Doctrine: The US Navy and Fleet Ballistic Missiles*. PhD Dissertation. Massachusetts Institute of Technology.

Coté, Owen. 2003. *The Third Battle: Innovation in the US Navy's Silent Cold War Struggle with Soviet Submarines*. Newport, R.I.: Naval War College.

Derry, T.K., and Trevor I. Williams. 1960. *A Short History of Technology: From the Earliest Times to A.D. 1900*. New York: Dover Publications.

DiFilippo, Anthony. 1990. *From Industry to Arms: The Political Economy of High Technology*. Westport, CT: Greenwood Press.
Dave, Paresh. 2014. "Apple ruined two key export markets for Finland, prime minister says." *The Los Angeles Times*, October 13, 2014.
Drabble, John D. 2000. *An Economic History of Malaysia, c.1400–1990: The Transition to Modern Economic Growth*. London: Macmillan Press.
Ellis, John. 1975. *The Social History of the Machine Gun*. Baltimore, MD: The Johns Hopkins University Press.
Epstein, Joshua M. 1984. *Measuring Military Power: The Soviet Air Threat to Europe*. Princeton, NJ: Princeton University Press.
Etzkowitz, Henry. 1993. "Clinton Administration Unites Science, Technology, and Industrial Policies." *Technology Access Report* 6 (12): 1.
Evans, David C. and Mark R. Peattie, *Kaigun: Strategy, Tactics, and Technology in the Imperial Japanese Navy, 1887–1941*. Annapolis, MD: Naval Institute Press).
Fahmy, Aly Mohamad. 1948. *Muslim Sea-Power in the Eastern Mediterranean from the Seventh to the Tenth Century*. PhD Dissertation. School of Oriental and African Studies, University of London.
Fino, Steven A. 2017. *Tiger Check: Automating the US Air Force Fighter Pilot in Air-to-Air Combat, 1950–1980*. Baltimore, MD: Johns Hopkins University Press.
Friedberg, Aaron L. 2000. *In the Shadow of the Garrison State: America's Anti-Statism and its Cold War Grand Strategy*. Princeton, NJ: Princeton University Press.
Friedman, Norman. 2000. *Seapower and Space: From the Dawn of the Missile Age to Net-Centric Warfare*. Annapolis, MD: Naval Institute Press.
Gardiner, Robert, and Andrew D. Lambert. 1992. *Steam, Steel and Shellfire: The Steam Warship, 1815–1905*. London: Conway Maritime Press.
Gelb, Leslie H. 1992. "Foreign Affairs; Who Won the Cold War?" *The New York Times*, August 20, 1992. A27.
Gerschenkron, Alexander. 1962. *Economic Backwardness in Historical Perspective: A Book of Essays*. Cambridge, MA: Belknap Press.
Gholz, Eugene. 2007. "Globalization, Systems Integration, and the Future of Great Power War." *Security Studies* 16 (4) (October–December): 615–636.
Gilli, Andrea, and Mauro Gilli. 2016. "The Diffusion of Drone Warfare? Industrial, Infrastructural, and Organizational Constraints." *Security Studies* 25 (1) (Winter): 50–84.
Gilli, Andrea, and Mauro Gilli. 2018/19. "Why China Has Not Caught Up Yet: Military-Technological Superiority and the Limits of Imitation, Reverse Engineering, and Cyber Espionage." *International Security* 43 (3) (Winter): 141–189.
Gilli, Andrea, Mauro Gilli, and Costantino Pischedda. 2017. "The Other Side of COIN Insurgent Firepower and Counterinsurgency Outcomes." Paper Presented at the *American Political Science Association Annual Conference*. San Francisco, CA.
Gilpin, Robert. 1981. *War and Change in World Politics*. Cambridge: Cambridge University Press.
Grant, Rebecca. 2010. *The Radar Game: Understanding Stealth and Aircraft Survivability*. Arlington, VA: Mitchell Institute Press.
Hamilton, C. I. 1993. *Anglo-French Naval Rivalry 1840–1870*. Oxford, UK: Clarendon Press.
Headrick, Daniel R. 1981. *The Tools of Empire: Technology and European Imperialism in Nineteenth Century*. New York: Oxford University Press.

Headrick, Daniel R. 2010. *Power over People: Technology, Environments, and Western Imperialism, 1400 to the Present*. Princeton, NJ: Princeton University Press.

Heinrich, Thomas. 2002. "Cold War Armory: Military Contracting in Silicon Valley." *Enterprise & Society* 3 (2) (June): 247–284.

Herwig, Holger H. 1980. *"Luxury" Fleet: The Imperial German Navy, 1888–1918*. London: George Allen and Unwin.

Herwig, Holger H. 1996. "Innovation Ignored: The submarine problem—Germany, Britain, and the United States, 1919–1939." In *Military Innovation in the Interwar Period*, edited by Williamson Murray and Allan R Millet, 227–264. Cambridge: Cambridge University Press.

Hoffman, Philip T. 2017. *Why Did Europe Conquer the World?* Princeton, NJ: Princeton University Press.

Isenberg, Andrew C. 2001. *The Destruction of the Bison*. New York, NY: Cambridge University Press.

Kania, Elsa. 2018. *Battlefield Singularity: Artificial Intelligence, Military Revolution, and China's Future Military Power*. Washington DC: Center for a New American Security.

Kennedy, Paul. 1987. *The Rise and Fall of the Great Powers: Economic Change and Military Conflict from 1500 to 2000*. New York: Random House.

Krepinevich, Andrew F., and Robert C. Martinage. 2008. *Dissuasion Strategy: Thinking Smarter About Defense*. Washington, DC: Center for Strategic and Budgetary Assessments.

Lake, Daniel R. 2019. *The Pursuit of Technological Superiority and the Shrinking American Military*. London: Palgrave Macmillan.

Lambert, Andrew D. 1991. *The Last Sailing Battlefleet: Maintaining Naval Mastery, 1815–50*. London: Conway Maritime Press.

Landes, David S. 1972. *The Unbound Prometheus: Technological Change and Industrial Development in Western Europe from 1750 to the Present*. New York, NY: Cambridge University Press.

Lasky, Marvin. 1974. "A Historical Review of Underwater Acoustic Technology 1916–1939 with Emphasis on Undersea Warfare." *US Navy Journal of Underwater Acoustics* 24 (4) (October): 601–606.

Lasky, Marvin. 1976. "Historical Review of Undersea Warfare Planning and Organization 1945–1960 with Emphasis on the Role of the Office of Naval Research." *US Navy Journal of Underwater Acoustics* 26 (2) (April): 327–355.

Lynn-Jones, Sean M. 1995. "Offense-Defense Theory and Its Critics." *Security Studies* 4 (4) (Summer): 660–691.

Long, Austin, and Brendan Rittenhouse Green. 2015. "Stalking the Secure Second Strike: Intelligence, Counterforce, and Nuclear Strategy." *Journal of Strategic Studies* 38 (1–2) (Winter): 38–73.

Lorell, Mark A. 2003. *The US Combat Aircraft Industry, 1909–2000: Structure, Competition, Innovation*. Santa Monica, CA: RAND Corporation.

Luttwak, Edward N. 2009. *The Grand Strategy of the Byzantine Empire*. Cambridge, MA: Harvard University Press.

Mahnken, Thomas P. 2012. *Competitive Strategies for the 21st Century: Theory, History, and Practice*. Palo Alto, CA: Stanford University Press.

Mann, Michael. *Sources of Social Power: History of Power from the Beginning to A.D.1760 Vol 1*. New York, NY: Cambridge University Press, 1986.

Markusenm, Ann Roell. 1986. "The Militarized Economy." *World Policy Journal* 3 (3): 495–516.

Mazzuccato, Marianna. 2013. *The Entrepreneurial State: Debunking Public vs. Private Myths in Risk and Innovation*. London: Anthem Press.

McNeill, William H. 1982. *The Pursuit of Power: Technology, Armed Force, and Society since A.D. 1000*. Chicago, IL: University of Chicago Press.

Mearsheimer, John J. 2001. *The Tragedy of Great Power Politics*. New York: W.W. Norton.

Merrill, John, and Lionel D. Wyld. 1997. *Meeting the Submarine Challenge: A Short History of the Naval Underwater Systems Center*. Washington, DC: Department of the Navy.

Michel, Marshall L. III. 1997. *Clashes: Air Combat over North Vietnam 1965-1972*. Annapolis, MD: Naval Institute Press.

Mokyr, Joel. 1990a. *The Lever of Riches: Technological Creativity and Economic Progress*. New York: Oxford University Press.

Mokyr, Joel. 1990b. *Twenty-Five Centuries of Technological Change: An Historical Survey*. New York: Harwood.

Montgomery, Evan Braden. 2014. "Contested Primacy in the Western Pacific: China's Rise and the Future of US Power Projection." *International Security* 38 (4) (Spring): 115-149.

Mowery, David C., and Nathan Rosenberg. 1989. *Technology and the Pursuit of Economic Growth*. New York: Cambridge University Press.

Neuman, Stephanie. 2010. "Power, Influence and Hierarchy: Defense Industries in a Unipolar World." *Defence and Peace Economics* 21 (1): 105-134.

Nexon, Daniel H. *The Struggle for Power in Early Modern Europe: Religious Conflict, Dynastic Empires, and International Change*. Princeton, NJ: Princeton University Press.

Overy, Richard J. 1994. *War and Economy in the Third Reich*. Oxford: Clarendon.

Parker, Geoffrey. 1996. *The Military Revolution: Military Innovation and the Rise of the West, 1500-1800*. New York: Cambridge University Press.

Parker, Geoffrey G., Marshall W. Van Alstyne, and Sangeet Paul Choudary. 2016. *Platform Revolution: How Networked Markets Are Transforming the Economy—and How to Make Them Work for You Hardcover*. New York, NY: W.W. Norton & Co.

Parker, John. 2001. *The Silent Service: The Inside Story of the Royal Navy's Submarine Heroes*. London: Headline Publishing.

Phillips, Almarin. 1971. *Technology and Market Structure: A Study of the Aircraft Industry*. Lexington, MA: Lexington Books.

Polmar, Norman, and Kenneth J. Moore. 2004. *Cold War Submarines: The Design and Construction of US and Soviet Submarines*. Washington, DC: Potomac Books, Inc.

Porter, Michael E. 1989. *The Competitive Advantage of Nations*. New York: Free Press.

Pomeranz, Kenneth. 2000. *The Great Divergence: China, Europe, and the Making of the Modern World Economy*. Princeton, NJ: Princeton University Press.

Posen, Barry R. 2003. "Command of the Commons: The Military Foundation of US Hegemony." *International Security* 28 (1) (Summer): 5-46.

Prencipe, Andrea. 1997. "Technological Competencies and Product's Evolutionary Dynamics: A Case Study from the Aero-engine Industry." *Research Policy* 25 (8) (January): 1261-1276.

Rosenberg, Nathan. 1976. *Perspectives on Technology*. New York: Cambridge University Press.

Rosenberg, Nathan. 1996. "Uncertainty and Technological Change." In *The Mosaic of Economic Growth*, edited by Ralph Landau, Timothy Taylor, and Gavin Wright, 91-125. Palo Alto, CA: Stanford University Press.

Rosenberg, Nathan, and L. E. Birdzell Jr. 1987. *How the West Grew Rich: The Economic Transformation of the Industrial World*. New York, NY: Basic Books.

Rubin, Jared. 2014. "Printing and Protestants: An Empirical Test of the Role of Printing in the Reformation." *The Review of Economics and Statistics* 96 (2) (May): 270–286.

Sapolsky, Harvey M. 1972. *The Polaris System Development: Bureaucratic and Programmatic Success in Government*. Cambridge, MA: Harvard University Press.

Schumpeter, Joseph A. 1976. *Capitalism, Socialism and Democracy*. New York, NY: Harper and Row Publishers.

Showell, Jay Mallman. 2006. *The U-Boat Century: German Submarine Warfare 1906–2006*. Annapolis, MD: Naval Institute Press.

Silove, Nina. 2018. "Beyond the Buzzword: The Three Meanings of Grand Strategy." *Security Studies* 27 (1) (Winter): 27–57.

Silverman, David J. 2016. *Thundersticks: Firearms and the Violent Transformation of Native America Hardcover*. Cambridge, MA: Belknap Press.

Sayler, K. M. 2019. *Artificial Intelligence and National Security*. Washington DC: Congressional Research Service.

Smil, Vaclav. 2001. *Enriching the Earth: Fritz Haber, Carl Bosch, and the Transformation of World Food Production*. Cambridge, MA: MIT Press.

Smil, Vaclav. 2005. *Creating the Twentieth Century: Technical Innovations of 1867–1914 and Their Lasting Impact*. New York: Oxford University Press.

Smil, Vaclav. 2013. *Prime Movers of Globalization: The History and Impact of Diesel Engines and Gas Turbines*. Cambridge, MA: MIT Press.

Snyder, Glenn H. 2002. "Mearsheimer's World-Offensive Realism and the Struggle for Security: A Review Essay." *International Security* 27 (1): 149–173.

Snyder, Jack. 1991. *Myths of Empire: Domestic Politics and International Ambition*. Ithaca, NY: Cornell University Press.

Solow, Robert M. 1956. "Contribution to the Theory of Economic Growth." *The Quarterly Journal of Economics* 70 (1) (February): 65–94.

Sontag, Sherry, and Christopher Drew, with Annette Lawrence Drew. 1998. *Blind Man's Bluff: The Untold Story of American Submarine Espionage*. New York: PublicAffairs.

Sreberny-Mohammadi, Annabelle. 1990. "Small Media for a Big Revolution: Iran." *International Journal of Politics, Culture, and Society* 3 (3) (Summer): 341–371.

Stefanick, Tom. 1987. *Strategic Antisubmarine Warfare and Naval Strategy*. Lexington, MA: Lexington Books.

Tilton, John E. 1971. *International Diffusion of Technology: The Case of Semiconductors*. Washington DC: The Brookings Institution.

Toby, Ronald P. 1984. *State and Diplomacy in Early Modern Japan: Asia in the Development of the Tokugawa Bakufu*. Princeton, NJ: Princeton University Press.

Tushman, Michael L., and Philip Anderson. 1986. "Technological Discontinuities and Organizational Environments." *Administrative Science Quarterly* 31 (3) (September): 439–465.

Ullmann, John E. 1984. "The Pentagon and the Firm." In *The Militarization of High Technology*, edited by John Tirman. Ballinger Publishing Company Pensacola, FL.

United States Department of Defense. 2019. *Summary of the 2018 Department of Defense Artificial Intelligence Strategy: Harnessing AI to Advance our Security and Prosperity*.

United States Senate, Committee on Appropriations, Subcommittee on Department of Defense Spending. 1979. *DoD Defense Authorization for Appropriations for Fiscal Year 1980: Procurement*.

van Creveld, Martin. 1989. *Technology and War: From 2000 B.C. to the Present*. New York: Touchstone.
Waltz, Kenneth N. 1979. *Theory of International Politics*. New York: McGraw-Hill.
Wendt, Paul. 1947. "The Control of Rubber in World War II." *Southern Economic Journal* 13 (3) (January): 203–227.
Whitman, Edward C. 2005. "The 'Secret Weapon' of Undersea Surveillance." *Undersea Warfare* 7 (2) (Winter).
Yergin, Daniel. 1991. *The Prize: The Epic Quest for Oil, Money, and Power*. New York, NY: Simon & Schuster.
Zhang, Feng. 2015. *Chinese Hegemony: Grand Strategy and International Institutions in East Asian History*. Palo Alto, CA: Stanford University Press.

CHAPTER 15

THE DOMESTIC SOURCES OF GRAND STRATEGY

JONATHAN D. CAVERLEY

A romantic notion still exists that grand strategy is something statesmen produce by responding objectively to the pressures of the international system. So let us get the obligatory Kennan reference out of the way. Despite being held up, correctly, as one of the great realist policy statements, Kennan's "The Sources of Soviet Conduct" argued that Soviet political and cultural affinity for a certain geopolitical approach necessitated a response appropriate and sensitive to the West's own political economy and culture. Eliminating domestic politics from grand strategy would surely have puzzled Bismarck, Metternich, Kissinger, or any other person reputed to be good at it.

Academia tends to be a lagging indicator of important global events. This chapter therefore predicts resurgent interest in the domestic sources of grand strategy given the current state of international politics, specifically the intensifying competition between the United States and China. However, research to date will not be sufficient to understand the next several decades of this dyad (or even the past ones), and this chapter proposes some new avenues of inquiry.

Much research already exists on how democracy (and nondemocracy) can drive grand strategy, and important states in contemporary international politics differ with respect to regime type. On the other hand, almost all the major powers in the international system remain quite liberal in their international economic relations—the other major concern of research on domestic influences on grand strategy. This chapter delves further into the grand-strategic role of regime type and the form of capitalism practiced within the state. It then suggests two additional under-researched domestic-level factors—militarism and nationalism—that will shape grand strategy in the coming years.

I leave it to other Handbook chapters to define grand strategy (see also Lissner 2018). This chapter concentrates on the conceit that grand strategy can be stable, in the words of the Handbook's introduction, on the "roiling seas" of domestic politics. Moreover, this chapter does not care whether a grand strategy is formally stated or adopted, only consistent. As Edelstein and Krebs (2015, 111) observe, the United States' constant pursuit of liberal hegemony since the Second World War has not been the "product of a formal grand strategy." Instead, they argue that this stable orientation is the result of several "enduring structural features," which they list as "material preponderance, the powerful corporate interests that profit from global integration, [and] the dominance of core liberal tenets in American political culture."

Edelstein and Krebs are surely correct that domestic preferences do not alone drive grand strategy. But while Narizny's (2017a) claim that "grand strategy is not a response to systemic imperatives; rather, it is the product of domestic preferences" overstates the case, forces within the state remain an often overlooked factor. Grand-strategic discussion, in the United States at least, rarely considers them. For example, the most prominent American grand strategy debate, that between "deep engagement" (Brooks, Ikenberry, and Wohlforth, 2012) and "restraint" (Posen 2014), has gone back and forth for decades with little reference to domestic politics. This chapter suggests some ways to change that.

Two Teetering Legs of the Kantian Tripod: Regime Type and Variety of Capitalism

This chapter does not weigh in on the debate between the two primary theories of domestic sources of grand strategy: liberalism and neoclassical realism (Fiammenghi et al. 2018; Narizny 2017b).[1] Instead, this chapter identifies a division of labor between the two, in which liberalism concentrates on the goals of grand strategy and neoclassical realism focuses on the resources mobilized for grand strategy.

Over the past decades of American-dominated International Relations, research has largely coalesced around the liberal theoretical approach. Specifically, a rich research program exists on the two domestic legs of the "Kantian tripod": whether a state is a democracy and whether it participates in a liberal trading system (Russett and Oneal 2001).[2] It is no coincidence that these largely American-dominated research programs rhyme with the US policy, at least since the end of the Second World War, of promoting free markets and elections.

Many have ascribed to the United States a post–Cold War grand strategy, particularly vis-à-vis China, of liberalizing trade to eventually encourage democratization and a "responsible stakeholder" approach to international politics. To many American policymakers, this strategy is now judged a failure (Brands and Cooper 2019; Campbell and Ratner 2018), although it is perhaps too early to tell (Jisi et al. 2018). This would suggest that the liberal American research program on grand strategy will also adjust. This next tranche of research should take a broader approach to a state's type of regime and type of (capitalist) economy and should focus not just on the ends of grand strategy but the means devoted to it.

The Irrelevance of the Dyadic Democratic Peace

Linking regime type to grand-strategic ends is a well-established research program. That democracies do not fight each other is both commonly accepted and largely irrelevant to contemporary great power politics (for a recent review, see Hobson 2017). Indeed, given the most important dyad in contemporary international politics, the more relevant questions are: how conflictual are relations between democracies and nondemocracies, and what are the relative advantages of each regime type?

More recent work has focused on the structures *within* democracies and the even broader "authoritarian" category. Selectorate theory shows that democracies can act in authoritarian ways, and leaders of nondemocracies must often appease a broad cross-section of elites (Bueno de Mesquita, Smith, Siverson, and Morrow 2003). Weeks (2016) explodes the distinction between democracies and nondemocracies by arguing that, at least when it comes to conflict initiation, the difference between personalist and nonpersonalist states matters far more. According to Weeks, a large-selectorate authoritarian state and a democracy do not differ much in conflict behavior.

Rather than the strategic ends each regime type pursues, more recent research addresses means—that is, the resources that states can mobilize. Democracies may have more difficulty mobilizing resources for large wars (Carter 2015) and shifting away from nonmilitary spending (Carter and Palmer 2016). Schultz and Weingast (2003) argue that states with better access to credit, specifically democracies, enjoy a significant military advantage in long-standing rivalries (see also DiGiuseppe 2015). On the other hand, Shea (2014) finds that not only do borrowing costs have a substantial effect on war outcomes, but democracies are more sensitive to these costs than are nondemocracies.

Beyond Free Trade

Apart from some realists, few have advocated the economic containment of China.[3] In this sense, liberal confidence in the pacifying effects of "free trade" will be put to the test; the Biden administration seems almost as skeptical as its predecessor. But there is more to the economy than international economic exchange. While every major state in the system remains tied into a large trading network and subscribes to some form of capitalism, how markets and trade manifest in each state plausibly influences grand strategy. Perhaps a Washington Consensus once existed, if only in Washington, but it is time to move beyond the American International Political Economy preoccupation with liberalism (McNamara 2009) and take a broader view. Just as research on authoritarian foreign policy has only begun to catch up to the rather triumphalist democratic peace program, research on alternative forms of capitalism remains far behind the curve of actually existing practices in international politics.

China is certainly a trading state, but it is not internally capitalist in McDonald's (2009) sense of having a constrained government, economic freedom, and the rule of law. Indeed, the standard variables of the variety of capitalism literature (Hall and Soskice 2001; Katzenstein, 1978) do not capture important differences between large capitalist countries (including but not limited to China) and their impact on grand strategy (McNally 2012; Nölke, ten Brink, Claar, and May 2015).[4]

It is well understood that economic interests often drive grand-strategic ends (Fordham 2008; Fordham 2019; Solingen 1998; Trubowitz 1998). Narizny (2007, 16–22) lists three factors: a governing coalition's dependence on "exports, imports, foreign investment, and defense spending," the geographic location of foreign economic activity, and the state's vulnerability to foreign competition. While partisan divides and political shifts (via elections or otherwise) can change the governing coalition, these factors are often stable enough to shape grand strategy.

Many important economies continue to be driven by exports, regardless of which political coalition is in power. The United States has a strong middle class of consumers that purchase huge amounts of domestic and foreign goods. While many fear China's use of its massive reserves of US debt as an economic weapon, it is just as plausible that this reserve leads to Chinese caution (Drezner 2009). A China that successfully develops a middle class that is less reliant on export-led growth and thus less dependent on the US-led financial system might act quite differently abroad. A domestic political economy approach is simply essential for understanding the most important (or, at least, the most visible) "grand-strategic" development of the past decade: China's "One Belt One Road" initiative. The domestic political need to export surplus infrastructure-building capacity largely by state-owned-enterprises is just as feasible an explanation for this Chinese policy as any outwardly facing grand-strategic design (Jones and Zeng 2019; Ye 2019).

As with work on regime type, a body of work is growing on how types of economic systems shape the means for grand strategy rather than the goals. The state's ability to extract funds from society, particularly tax revenue and debt, underpins the projection of military power (Cappella Zielinski 2016, 5). War made the tax system (Scheve and Stasavage 2010), and the tax system made war (Caverley 2014; Kreps 2018; Kriner, Lechase, and Cappella Zielinski 2015).

A state's variety of capitalism shape not only the funding but the tools of grand strategy. A tendency to use contractors rather than uniformed personnel is informed by ideas of efficiency and freedom, as well as the domestic economy (Avant 2005). Many argue that the existence of conscription shapes a state's grand strategy, and conscription and military recruitment are shaped by the economy (Asal, Conrad, and Toronto 2017; Cohn and Toronto 2017). The ability to build weapons also rests in part on a state's variety of capitalism (Devore 2014). Indeed, the venerable topic of links between the military and civilian economies will no doubt receive renewed attention. Two centers of gravity in US grand strategy—Silicon Valley and the Pentagon—form an interdependent, if sometimes uneasy, nexus (Weiss 2014). China is pursuing its own civil–military fusion to grow both its economy and its military power (Cheung 2016; Kania and Laskai 2021).

The ability of a state's domestic political economy to generate military power, often described as an S-shaped production curve, will grow in relevance in grand-strategic thinking. At the higher end of this curve, marginal costs increase steeply (Gilpin 1981), and small differences may have large effects on the means available to great powers (Caverley and Kapstein 2016). It remains to be seen whether China's domestic political economy can enable it to produce the materiel needed to catch up with the United States (Brooks 2019; Gilli and Gilli 2019).

Beyond Economic Factors: Militarism and Nationalism

So far, this chapter has pointed out the synergy during the unipolar era between liberal International Relations (IR) theory—focusing on domestic, largely economic factors as the drivers of grand strategy—and the liberal political project—spreading political and economic freedom. This section suggests that the theory and the project will diverge, with the former concentrating on two decidedly illiberal domestic forces: militarism and nationalism.

These forces differ from the variables found in traditional liberal IR in two important ways. First, treating either as a purely sectoral or economic factor underestimates their causes and their power. Second, while existing IR research on both militarism and nationalism has tended to focus on them as mobilization strategies, they quite clearly can also shape the ends of grand strategy.

What Publics Want from Their Militaries, and What Militaries Want from Their Publics

While work on the domestic sources of grand strategy tends to focus on the role played by economic interests, this chapter suggests expanding this lens to include other important social groups within states, starting with the military's role in grand strategy, a traditional concern in security studies (Brooks 2008; Kier 1997; Posen 1984). In this section I examine two separate but related developments under the umbrella term of "militarism": when the military becomes the dominant means of grand strategy and how the military's domestic role determines grand strategy's ends (Caverley 2014, 3).[5]

The military enjoys sufficient popularity to influence grand strategy not just in the United States but around the world. Each of eight recently polled western European democracies ranked the military as its most respected institution (Simmons, Silver, Johnson, Taylor, and Wike 2018), as did each of seven Arab states (Arab Barometer

2017). In each of 17 Latin American countries polled the military was second only to the Catholic Church (Latinobarómetro 2018). A Russian poll shows respondents trusting the military even more than Putin (ANO Levada Center 2018). In India, Indonesia, and South Africa, majorities polled in 2017 thought "rule by the military" would be a good way of governing the country (Gramlich 2017). Does military popularity translate into influence on grand strategy, especially among great powers?

Work to date on the military in IR tends to focus, understandably, on the military's effectiveness as a tool of foreign policy. At the comparative level, there is a deep methodological divide on whether politically influential militaries prefer the aggressive use of war. Whereas the qualitative literature suggests that military regimes are often reluctant to use military force abroad (Avant 1996; Desch 1999; Feaver and Gelpi 2004), statistical analysis suggests otherwise (Lai and Slater 2006; Sechser 2004; Weeks 2016). Clearly, more needs to be done to reconcile these findings (White 2017).

Beyond conflict initiation, the military plays a foreign policy role not just in military dictatorships or juntas: states that fear military overthrow will be unable to produce an externally focused grand strategy and are unlikely to generate effective military power to counter one's external rivals (Talmadge 2016). Heavily capitalized militaries reduce the cost of conflict for the median voter, leading to large defense budgets and aggressive use of military force (Caverley 2014).

Military politics may shape the ends of grand strategy as well. For example, the ability to buy military loyalty and use it for repression encourages states to send soldiers abroad on peacekeeping missions (Caverley and Dillon Savage 2019; Wilén, Ambrosetti, and Birantamije 2015). The fact that the US military's popularity is remarkably impervious to decline despite the outcomes of its several recent wars (Burbach 2017) suggests that it is not being evaluated simply as a tool of the state's foreign policy. Its popularity may lead elites and publics to turn to the military, not just for expertise but for legitimacy, taking on deeply political roles that raise concern of civil–military experts (Brooks 2019; Golby, Feaver, and Dropp 2018; Golby and Karlin 2018; Krebs, Ralston, and Rapport 2021) even before the crises of the Trump administration.

In the United States what happens when the immovable object of "the troops'" popularity meets the irresistible force of partisan polarization (Caverley 2021)? The partisan difference over "confidence" in the military is comparable in magnitude to such divisive institutions as the executive branch, organized religion, and science. Democrats and Republicans agree less on the military relative to banks, the press, the Supreme Court, Congress, and organized labor (Smith, Davern, Reese, and Hour 2018). If political elites in the United States are effectively campaigning at all times, the public receives a continuous stream of partisan cues (Iyengar, Lelkes, Levendusky, Malhotra, and Westwood 2018; Lee 2016). This self-reinforcing cycle is likely to ensnare the military regardless of what it does, because affective partisanship has little to do with the military's actions or announcements.

China's civil–military relations differ greatly from its democratic rival but are no less likely to shape the ends of grand strategy. The People's Liberation Army (PLA) formally works for the Chinese Communist Party and has little direct connection to the state, much less the people. Thus, Party unification is necessary for strategic adjustment to outside forces (Fravel 2017). Under the current, apparently unitary leadership of Xi Jinping, China's military shift from an internal and continental orientation to a more maritime, regional approach rests on the ability to demobilize 300,000 personnel, encourage traditionally rival services to work together jointly, and tamp down a massive corruption problem (Blasko 2016; Kokoshin 2016). All these efforts involve intense domestic politics, and its success will shape China's grand strategy for decades. As part of a strategy to ensure the military stays on the Chinese Communist Party's side (as opposed to that of the state or the nation), Xi Jinping's regime appears to be stoking fears of foreign interference among PLA officers, as opposed to the broader public (Johnston 2017, 38).

The implications of politicized militaries for grand strategy remain to be seen. But it is clear that the role of the military cannot be understood in isolation from another global trend: growing nationalism and populism.

From Nationalism to Populism to Civilizations

Many scholars describe grand strategy as a battle between two economic blocs: nationalists and internationalists (Narizny 2001; Solingen 1998; Trubowitz 1998). Such a distinction underestimates the power of the ideas underpinning these categories, especially given budding research on the role of discourse in determining both grand strategy's means and ends (Balzacq, Léonard, and Ruzicka 2016; Goddard and Krebs 2015; Krebs 2015; Kornprobst and Traistaru 2021; Goddard 2021).

Most writing on the role of domestic ideas and grand strategy tends to focus on "strategic culture" (Kier 1997; Legro 2007; Lock 2010). To date, while much work identifies and describes a strategic culture, this research is less successful in showing its effect on grand strategy. In the US case, Dueck (2006, 4) identified classical liberal assumptions—chiefly a deep-seated and often naïve belief in spreading liberal democracy and open markets abroad as the means to United States security—that filter policy options, making "reluctant crusaders." Layne (2007), however, looks at the same culture and finds the impetus for perpetual expansionism. Similar analysis of Chinese strategic culture gives us even less of a clear outcome. After all, relative to the United States, China has a lot more history to draw on, "mixing facts with myths through selective use of the country's vast historical and cultural experiences" (Zhang 2013). No one can quite agree on what this culture is: a devotion to a tributary system, contented pacifism, or a combination of the two (Kang 2003). Whereas Zhang (2013) describes Chinese exceptionalism as "great power reformism, benevolent pacifism, and harmonious inclusionism," Johnston (1998) argues that while China does indeed have a strategic culture, it does not differ much from the *realpolitik* associated with Western societies.

Nationalism

Perhaps the biggest omission in discussion of strategic culture is nationalism, which clearly can serve as both a tool of and a force upon grand strategy (Weiss 2013). For the past few decades, American nationalism has largely been conflated with a liberal strategic culture, sometimes crusading and sometimes content being the city on the hill (Monten 2005). But it is clearly becoming less tenable to state that "the core classical liberal belief in individual liberty and equality ... binds all Americans, conservatives and liberals alike" (Nau 2013, 13–14). A large section of the public that believes it represents the "real America" is not liberal in any sense of the term.

Realists have associated nationalism with the means of grand strategy, most specifically mobilization of state resources. Nationalism has been attributed to a revolution in military power generation (Posen 1993). Schweller's (2006) work on underbalancing suggest that politics lacking nationalism will have difficulty mobilizing national resources to foreign policy ends. Mearsheimer (2019) forcefully argues that liberal internationalist policymakers have failed to contend with the enduring, resistant power of nationalism, the ultimate defensive technology (Edelstein 2008). Schweller (2018) goes so far as to credit nationalism with allowing "a soft landing as the world moves from unipolarity to bipolarity."

But an older literature considers nationalism as a force shaping grand strategy's ends, rarely for the better. Indeed, hyper-nationalism has been considered an international problem since the very founding of the discipline (Cox 2019; Van Evera 1994). It is this aspect of nationalism that is most pressing in terms of grand strategy research.

Walter Russell Mead (2017) labelled the 2016 US presidential election a rare moment of "Jacksonian revolt." Jacksonians, while relatively isolationist in outlook, support building a strong military to defend against external enemies. A similar mechanism drives "Jacksonian political engagement." Mead identifies a "perception that Jacksonians are being attacked by internal enemies, such as an elite cabal or immigrants from different backgrounds. Jacksonians worry about the US government being taken over by malevolent forces bent on transforming the United States' essential character." Significant amounts of research link support for Jacksonianism/populism to a sensed loss of status of one's ingroup relative to outgroup members (Inglehart and Norris 2017). This ingroup is tied to categories such as social class, race, gender, rural versus urban location, and education.

Given domestic politics in major states as diverse as Britain, Russia, Brazil, Japan, India, as well as the United States, the role of populist nationalism around the world is clearly an important phenomenon with which the field is only beginning to come to grips intellectually. It is a complicated product of the nation-state, the global economy, and the distribution of benefits within each. While feelings of nationalism may be caused in part by economic pressures (Solt 2011), it is clearly too simplistic to describe "nationalists" and "internationalists" as two economic blocs contending over grand strategy. Populistm is at best weakly connected to economic factors, but instead a reaction to cultural change and immigration (Inglehart and Norris 2017). While this research on populism tends to concentrate on domestic politics, clearly there are grand-strategic implications. There is a complicated, and as yet poorly understood, link between economic inequality, cultural anxiety, populism, and international politics.

Civilizations

Populist nationalist discourse often resonates with that of "civilizations." Despite Huntington's "clash" thesis being one of the most consistently debunked arguments in International Relations (Gartzke and Gleditsch 2006; Henderson and Tucker 2001), the political discourse in the United States and elsewhere does not agree. Consider the quite remarkable 2019 quotation from Kiron Skinner, the US State Department's Director of Policy Planning, the office that epitomizes grand strategy in the United States, describing "a fight with a really different civilization and a different ideology." Her remarks echoed Trump's own language in a Warsaw speech (2017):

> The fundamental question of our time is whether the West has the will to survive. Do we have the confidence in our values to defend them at any cost? Do we have enough respect for our citizens to protect our borders? Do we have the desire and the courage to preserve our civilization in the face of those who would subvert and destroy it?

In this short speech Trump invoked "civilization" ten times, "trade" and "individual freedom" once each, and "democracy" not at all. This is a remarkable reversal of America's self-conception of its relationship to the world. Moreover, it arises at a time of growing discourse about "civilization-states," specifically in reference to China (Coker 2019; Jacques 2012; Zhang 2012).

Race and Gender as Domestic Sources of Grand Strategy

The intersection of this civilizational discourse with that of populism prompts related questions: who are the people, and which civilization gets defended? Nationalism, populism, and civilization generally distinguish among ethnicity, race, gender, and other important non-economically defined subgroups within and outside a state.

In her same speech on civilization, Skinner also remarked that "it's the first time that we'll have a great power competitor that is not Caucasian." While Skinner was relieved soon afterwards, she is clearly not the first grand strategist to incorporate race explicitly or implicitly into their worldview. Skinner's most illustrious predecessor, George Kennan was no stranger to racism. The original title of *Foreign Affairs* was the *Journal of Race Development* after all (Vitalis 2015).

Perception of racism by the other great powers drove a considerable portion of aggressive Japanese grand strategy, and earlier presidents tried to tamp down such rhetoric to manage US–Japanese relations (Ward 2013). What happens when leaders maintain their political power by emphasizing these racial divisions? In the United States, Burbach (2018) notes a growing gap in confidence in the military between whites and nonwhites. One fascinating experiment designed to overcome social desirability bias showed a very large 25-point difference in support for veterans benefit spending between white people and Black people (Kleykamp, Hipes, and MacLean 2018).

This relatively newfound, mainstream concern for the role of racism in grand strategy joins the long-established Feminist IR observation that state legitimacy and coercion are founded through socially constructed power relations built on both militarism and gender exclusion (Cohn 1987; Enloe 2014; Tickner 1992). Hudson et al. (2009) show a strong and substantively large correlation between gender inequality and conflict onset. In short, when considering forces like militarism and populism, we should consider: who gets to make grand strategy and whom is grand strategy for?

Conclusion: All for Naught?

The post–Cold War era was a moment when domestic politics (or at least one state's domestic politics) drove international politics (Ikenberry, Mastanduno, and Wohlforth 2009; Jervis 2011). American political science's generational concern with democracy and trade liberalization stems from the absence of power politics in a unipolar era. With the rise of China, this chapter predicts growing attention to a number of domestic factors previously masked by American unipolarity. It concludes, however, by reviewing three important arguments claiming that these domestic factors will have little effect on grand strategy moving forward.

First, great power competition may force states increasingly to resemble each other domestically. US grand strategy looked the way it did over the past several decades in part because no powerful state or states existed to push back. It is an open question whether regimes' behaviors converge due to competition (Waltz 1979)—the venerable second image reversed argument (Gourevitch 1978). We may therefore see shrinking variation in domestic politics should great power rivalry continue to grow.

Second, one can go still further and suggest that even this realist approach may be irrelevant. Domestic variables may ensure there is no grand strategy to study. Grand strategy cannot matter, indeed does not meaningfully exist, if the political system does not allow the strategist to follow it. Many observers, especially in the West, ascribe to Russia or China a more monolithic leadership and thus an apparently more stable grand strategy. But in the words of Yuen Yuen Ang (2018), "even Chinese policymakers cannot come to a consensus on what the China model is."

Consider Narizny's (2001) useful simplification of grand strategy as the product of competition between two blocs of economic actors within a state. Perhaps in some preference aggregation systems this can produce a consistent policy aligned along the median selector's references. But if the policy gap between parties is vast, and the blocs frequently trade power, there is little prospect for consistency. For two decades since the Cold War's end, little partisan divide existed over whether Russia represents the "greatest danger" to the United States. Both parties' adherents moved in lockstep with each other, with the biggest difference in 2008 (Republicans 16 percent, Democrat 13 percent). But the divide is now a whopping 18 percent (21 percent and 39 percent respectively, Suls 2017).

Third, and more troubling still, the causal arrow may reverse, with grand strategy helping to secure advantage in tumultuous domestic politics. Taking a page from Midge

Decter's neoconservative maxim that "domestic policy was foreign policy and vice versa," Brands (2019), fretting about polarization's effect on US grand strategy, states hopefully that "one can now see, however faintly, the outlines of a new consensus"—that the greatest threat to the United States is "the form of aggressive behavior by hostile authoritarian powers." Rather than simply resulting from domestic politics, grand strategy, up to and including war, can be a means of tamping it down.

This chapter concludes by extending this logic to suggest that, in a hyper-partisan environment such as the present United States, even domestic political unity through threat-mongering may be too much to hope for. Donald Trump has after all been credibly accused of leveraging the US foreign policy apparatus, specifically military aid to Ukraine, to acquire information on his political opponent in service of his reelection. While its domestic sources remain worth studying, it may be less useful to use the actual term "grand strategy," with all its portentousness, once its potential for mischief has been so fully realized.

Notes

1. The other cleavage traditionally used in describing grand strategy research is the relative weight of material influences versus more ideas-based ones. I consider both factors without refereeing between them (see Ripsman and Kovac 2021; Goddard 2021; McCourt 2021).
2. The third leg being international institutions.
3. See this fascinating interview between John Mearsheimer and Peter Navarro, director of trade and industrial policy during the Trump Administration (Navarro 2016).
4. Varieties of Capitalism has focused almost exclusively on mature industrialized democracies and the limited institutional variation found within. However, the key variables—"corporate governance (understood as the ability for corporate control); corporate finance (the governance (understood as the ability for corporate control); corporate finance (the means by which companies raise funds for investments); labour relations; education and training; and the transfer of innovations"—are relevant beyond the states originally considered (Nölke et al., 2015).
5. For a comprehensive overview of militarism, see Mabee and Vucetic (2018).

References

Ang, Yuen Y. 2018. "The Real China Model: It's Not What You Think It Is." *Foreign Affairs* 99 (3).

ANO Levada Center. 2018. Institutional Trust. https://www.levada.ru/en/2018/10/22/institutional-trust-4/, accessed March 19, 2021.

Arab Barometer. 2017. "Arab barometer wave IV." https://www.arabbarometer.org/waves/arab-barometer-wave-iv/, accessed February 18, 2020.

Asal, Victor, Justin Conrad, and Nathan Toronto. 2017. "I Want You! The Determinants of Military Conscription." *Journal of Conflict Resolution* 61 (7): 1456–1481.

Avant, Deborah D. 1996. "Are the Reluctant Warriors Out of Control? Why the U.S. military is Averse to Responding to Post-Cold War Low-Level Threats." *Security Studies* 6 (2): 51–90.

Avant, Deborah D. 2005. *The Market for Force*. Cambridge: Cambridge University Press.

Balzacq, Thierry, Sarah Léonard, and Jan Ruzicka. 2016. "'Securitization' revisited: theory and cases." *International Relations* 30 (4): 494–531.
Blasko, Dennis J. 2016. "Integrating the Services and Harnessing the Military Area Commands." *Journal of Strategic Studies* 39 (5–6): 685–708.
Brands, Hal. "America's Foreign Policy Isn't Dead. Yet." https://www.bnnbloomberg.ca/america-s-foreign-policy-isn-t-dead-yet-1.1247478, accessed April 22, 2019.
Brands, Hal, and Jack Cooper. 2019. "After the Responsible Stakeholder, What? Debating America's China Strategy." *Texas National Security Review* 2 (2): 68–81.
Brooks, Risa. 2008. *Shaping Strategy: The Civil-Military Politics of Strategic Assessment.* Princeton, NJ: Princeton University Press.
Brooks, Risa. 2019. "Integrating the Civil–Military Relations Subfield." *Annual Review of Political Science* 22 (1): 379–398.
Brooks, Stephen G. 2019. "Power Transitions, Then and Now: Five New Structural Barriers That Will Constrain China's Rise." *China International Strategy Review* 1 (1): 65–83.
Brooks, Stephen G., G. John Ikenberry, and William C. Wohlforth. 2012. "Don't Come Home, America: The Case against Retrenchment." *International Security* 37 (3): 7–51.
Burbach, David T. 2017. "Gaining Trust While Losing Wars: Confidence in the U.S. Military after Iraq and Afghanistan." *Orbis* 61 (2): 154–171.
Burbach, David T. 2018. "Partisan Dimensions of Confidence in the U.S. Military, 1973–2016." *Armed Forces and Society* 45 (2): 211–233.
Campbell, Kurt M., and Ely Ratner, E. 2018. "The China Reckoning: How Beijing Defied American Expectations." *Foreign Affairs* 97 (2): 1–7.
Carter, Jeff. 2015. "The Political Cost of War Mobilization in Democracies and Dictatorships." *Journal of Conflict Resolution* 61 (8): 1768–1794.
Carter, Jeff, and Glenn Palmer. 2016. "Regime Type and Interstate War Finance." *Foreign Policy Analysis* 12 (4): 695–719.
Caverley, Jonathan D. 2014. *Democratic Militarism: Voting, Wealth, and War.* Cambridge: Cambridge University Press.
Caverley, Jonathan D., and Ethan B. Kapstein. 2016. "Who's Arming Asia?" *Survival* 58 (2): 167–184.
Caverley, Jonathan D., and Jesse Dillon Savage. 2019. "Peacekeeping for Rent and Repression." Unpublished manuscript, U.S. Naval War College and Trinity College Dublin.
Caverley, Jonathan D. 2021. "When an Immovable Object Meets an Irresistible Force: Military Popularity and Affective Partisanship." In *Reconsidering American Civil-Military Relations: The Military, Society, Politics, and Modern War*, edited by Lionel Beehner, Risa Brooks, and Daniel Maurer. Oxford: Oxford University Press.
Cheung, Tai Ming. 2016. "Innovation in China's Defense Technology Base: Foreign Technology and Military Capabilities." *Journal of Strategic Studies* 39 (5–6): 728–761.
Cohn, Carol. 1987. "Sex and Death in the Rational World of Defense Intellectuals." *Signs* 12 (4): 687–718.
Cohn, Lindsay P., and Nathan W. Toronto. 2017. "Markets and Manpower: The Political Economy of Compulsory Military Service." *Armed Forces and Society* 43 (3): 436–458.
Coker, Christopher. 2019. *The Rise of the Civilizational State.* Cambridge: Polity.
Cox, Michael. 2019. "Nationalism, Nations and the Crisis of World Order." *International Relations* 33 (2): 247–266.
Desch, Michael. C. 1999. *Soldiers, States, and Structure: Civilian Control of the Military in a Changing Security Environment.* Baltimore: Johns Hopkins University Press.
Devore, Marc R. 2014. "Defying Convergence: Globalisation and Varieties of Defence-Industrial Capitalism." *New Political Economy* 20 (4): 569–593.

DiGiuseppe, Matthew. 2015. "Guns, Butter, and Debt: Sovereign Creditworthiness and Military Expenditure." *Journal of Peace Research* 52 (5): 680–693.

Drezner, Daniel W. 2009. "Bad Debts: Assessing China's Financial Influence in Great Power Politics." *International Security* 34 (2): 7–45.

Dueck, Colin. 2006. *Reluctant Crusaders: Power, Culture, and Change in American Grand Strategy*. Princeton, NJ: Princeton University Press.

Edelstein, David M. 2008. *Occupational Hazards: Success and Failure in Military Occupation*. Ithaca, NY: Cornell University Press.

Edelstein, David M., and Ronald R. Krebs. 2015. "Delusions of grand strategy: The problem with Washington's planning obsession." *Foreign Affairs* 94 (6): 109–116.

Enloe, Cynthia. 2014. *Bananas, Beaches and Bases: Making Feminist Sense of International Politics*. Berkeley: University of California Press.

Feaver, Peter D., and Christopher Gelpi. 2004. *Choosing Your Battles: American Civil-Military Relations and the Use of Force*. Princeton, NJ: Princeton University Press.

Fiammenghi, Davide, Sebastian Rosato, Joseph M. Parent, Jeffrey W. Taliaferro, Steven E. Lobell, Norrin M. Ripsman, and Kevin Narizny. 2018. "Correspondence: Neoclassical Realism and Its Critics." *International Security* 43 (2): 193–213.

Fordham, Benjamin O. 2008. "Economic Interests and Public Support for American Global Activism." *International Organization* 62 (1): 163–182.

Fordham, Benjamin O. 2019. "The Domestic Politics of World Power: Explaining Debates over the United States Battleship Fleet, 1890–91." *International Organization* 73 (2): 435–468.

Fravel, M. Taylor. 2017. "Shifts in Warfare and Party Unity: Explaining China's Changes in Military Strategy." *International Security* 42 (3): 37–83.

Gartzke, Erik, and Kristian Skrede Gleditsch. 2006. "Identity and Conflict: Ties that Bind and Differences that Divide." *European Journal of International Relations* 12 (1): 53–87.

Gilli, Andrea, and Mauro Gilli. 2019. "Why China Has Not Caught Up Yet." *International Security* 43 (3): 141–189.

Gilpin, Robert. 1981. *War and Change in World Politics*. Cambridge: Cambridge University Press.

Goddard, Stacie E. 2021. "Rhetoric and Legitimation." In *The Oxford Handbook of Grand Strategy*, edited by Thierry Balzacq and Ronald R. Krebs. Oxford: Oxford University Press.

Goddard, Stacie E., and Ronald R. Krebs. 2015. "Rhetoric, Legitimation, and Grand Strategy." *Security Studies* 24 (1): 5–36.

Golby, James, Peter Feaver, and Kyle Dropp. 2018. "Elite Military Cues and Public Opinion About the Use of Military Force." *Armed Forces & Society* 44 (1): 44–71.

Golby, James, and Mara Karlin. 2018. "Why 'Best Military Advice' Is Bad for the Military—and Worse for Civilians." *Orbis* 62 (1): 137–153.

Gourevitch, Peter. 1978. "The Second Image Reversed: The International Sources of Domestic Politics." *International Organization* 32 (4): 881–912.

Gramlich, John. 2017. "How countries around the world view democracy, military rule and other political systems." https://www.pewresearch.org/fact-tank/2017/10/30/global-views-political-systems/, accessed February 18, 2021.

Hall, Peter A., and David Soskice. 2001. *Varieties of Capitalism: The Institutional Foundations of Comparative Advantage*. Oxford: Oxford University Press.

Henderson, Errol A., and Richard Tucker. 2001. "Clear and Present Strangers: The Clash of Civilizations and International Conflict." *International Studies Quarterly* 45 (2): 317–338.

Hobson, Christopher. 2017. "Democratic Peace: Progress and Crisis." *Perspectives on Politics* 15 (3): 697–710.

Hudson, Valerie M., Mary Caprioli, Bonnie Ballif-Spanvill, Rose McDermott, and Chad F. Emmett. 2009. "The Heart of the Matter: The Security of Women and the Security of States." *International Security* 33 (3): 7–45.

Ikenberry, G. John, Michael Mastanduno, and William C. Wohlforth. 2009. "Unipolarity, State Behavior, and Systemic Consequences." *World Politics* 61 (1): 1–27.

Inglehart, Ronald, and Pippa Norris. 2017. "Trump and the Populist Authoritarian Parties: The Silent Revolution in Reverse." *Perspectives on Politics* 15 (2): 443–454.

Iyengar, Shanto, Yphtach Lelkes, Matthew Levendusky, Neil Malhotra, and Sean J. Westwood. 2018. "The Origins and Consequences of Affective Polarization in the United States." *Annual Review of Political Science* 22 (1): 129–146.

Jacques, Martin. 2012. *When China Rules the World: The End of the Western World and the Birth of a New Global Order*. New York: Penguin.

Jervis, Robert. 2011. "Unipolarity: a Structural Perspective." In *International Relations Theory and the Consequences of Unipolarity*, edited by G. John Ikenberry, Michael Mastanduno, and William C. Wohlforth, 252–281. Cambridge: Cambridge University Press.

Jisi, Wang, J. Stapleton Roy, Aaron L. Friedberg, Thomas Christensen, Patricia Kim, Joseph S. Nye Jr, Eric X. Li, Kurt M. Campbell, and Ely Ratner. 2018. "Did America Get China Wrong? The Engagement Debate." *Foreign Affairs* 97 (4): 183–195.

Johnston, Alastair Iain. 1998. *Cultural Realism: Strategic Culture and Grand Strategy in Chinese History*. Princeton, NJ: Princeton University Press.

Johnston, Alastair Iain. 2017. "Is Chinese Nationalism Rising? Evidence from Beijing." *International Security* 41 (3): 7–43.

Jones, Lee, and Jinghan Zeng. 2019. "Understanding China's 'Belt and Road Initiative': Beyond 'Grand Strategy' to a State Transformation Analysis." *Third World Quarterly* 40 (8): 1415–1439.

Kang, David C. 2003. "Getting Asia Wrong: The Need for New Analytical Frameworks." *International Security* 27 (4): 57–85.

Kania, Elsa B. and Lorand Laskai. 2021. *Myths and Realities of China's Military-Civil Fusion Strategy*. https://www.cnas.org/publications/reports/myths-and-realities-of-chinas-military-civil-fusion-strategy, accessed March 19, 2021.

Katzenstein, Peter J. 1978. *Between Power and Plenty: Foreign Economic Policies in Advanced Industrial States*. Madison: University of Wisconsin Press.

Kier, Elizabeth. 1997. *Imagining War: French and British Military Doctrine between the Wars*. Princeton, NJ: Princeton University Press.

Kleykamp, Meredith, Crosby Hipes, and Alair MacLean. 2018. "Who Supports U.S. Veterans and Who Exaggerates Their Support?" *Armed Forces and Society* 44 (1): 92–115.

Kokoshin, Andrei A. 2016. *2015 Military Reform in the People's Republic of China: Defense, Foreign and Domestic Policy Issues*. Cambridge, MA: Belfer Center for Science and International Affairs, Harvard Kennedy School. https://www.belfercenter.org/sites/default/files/legacy/files/Military%20Reform%20China%20-%20web2.pdf

Kornprobst, Markus, and Corina-Ioana Traistaru. 2021. "Language and Grand Strategy." In *The Oxford Handbook of Grand Strategy*, edited by Thierry Balzacq and Ronald R. Krebs. Oxford: Oxford University Press.

Krebs, Ronald R. 2015. *Narrative and the Making of US National Security*. Cambridge: Cambridge University Press.

Kreps, Sarah E. 2018. *Taxing Wars: The American Way of War Finance and the Decline of Democracy*. New York: Oxford University Press.

Krebs, Ronald R., Robert Ralston, and Aaron Rapport. "No Right to Be Wrong: What Americans Think about Civil-Military Relations." *Perspectives on Politics*, 2021, 1–19.

Kriner, Douglas, Breanna Lechase, and Rosella Cappella Zielinski. 2015. "Self-interest, Partisanship, and the Conditional Influence of Taxation on Support for War in the USA." *Conflict Management and Peace Science* 35 (1): 43–64.

Lai, Brian, and Dan Slater. 2006. "Institutions of the Offensive: Domestic Sources of Dispute Initiation in Authoritarian Regimes, 1950–1992." *American Journal of Political Science* 50 (1): 113–126.

Latinobarómetro. 2018. *Informe 2018*. Santiago, Chile. http://www.latinobarometro.org/lat.jsp, accessed March 19, 2021.

Layne, Christopher. 2007. *The Peace of Illusions: American Grand Strategy from 1940 to the Present*. Ithaca, NY: Cornell University Press.

Lee, Frances E. 2016. *Insecure Majorities: Congress and the Perpetual Campaign*. Chicago: University of Chicago Press.

Legro, Jeffrey W. 2007. *Rethinking the World: Great Power Strategies and International Order*. Ithaca, NY: Cornell University Press.

Lissner, Rebecca F. 2018. "What is Grand Strategy? Sweeping Conceptual Minefield." *Texas National Security Review* 2 (1): 52–73.

Lock, Edward. 2010. "Refining Strategic Culture: Return of the Second Generation." *Review of International Studies* 36 (3): 685–708.

Mabee, Bryan, and Srdjan Vucetic. 2018. "Varieties of Militarism: Towards a Typology." *Security Dialogue* 49 (1–2): 96–108.

McCourt, David M. 2021. "Culture and Identity." In *The Oxford Handbook of Grand Strategy*, edited by Thierry Balzacq and Ronald R. Krebs. Oxford: Oxford University Press.

McDonald, Patrick J. 2009. *The Invisible Hand of Peace*. Cambridge: Cambridge University Press.

McNally, Christopher A. 2012. "Sino-Capitalism: China's Reemergence and the International Political Economy." *World Politics* 64 (4): 741–776.

McNamara, Kathleen R. 2009. "Of Intellectual Monocultures and the Study of IPE." *Review of International Political Economy* 16 (1): 72–84.

Mead, Walter Russell. (2017). "The Jacksonian Revolt: American Populism and the Liberal Order." *Foreign Affairs* 96 (2): 2–7.

Mearsheimer, John J. 2019. *The Great Delusion: Liberal Dreams and International Realities*. New Haven, CT: Yale University Press.

Mesquita, Bruce Bueno de, Alastair Smith, Randolph M. Siverson, and James D. Morrow. 2003. *The Logic of Political Survival*. Cambridge, MA: MIT Press.

Monten, Jonathan. 2005. "The Roots of the Bush Doctrine: Power, Nationalism, and Democracy Promotion in US Strategy." *International Security* 29 (4): 112–156.

Narizny, Kevin. 2001. *The Political Economy of Grand Strategy*. Princeton, NJ: Princeton University Press.

Narizny, Kevin. 2017a. "American Grand Strategy and Political Economy Theory." In *Oxford Research Encyclopedia of Politics*, edited by William R. Thompson. Oxford: Oxford University Press. https://doi.org/10.1093/acrefore/9780190228637.013.316

Narizny, Kevin. 2017b. "On Systemic Paradigms and Domestic Politics: A Critique of the Newest Realism." *International Security* 42 (2): 155–190.

Nau, Henry R. 2013. *Conservative Internationalism: Armed Diplomacy under Jefferson, Polk, Truman, and Reagan*. Princeton, NJ: Princeton University Press.

Navarro, Peter. 2016. "Crouching Tiger: John Mearsheimer On Strangling China And The Inevitability of War." Real Clear Defense. https://www.realcleardefense.com/articles/2016/03/10/crouching_tiger_john_mearsheimer_on_strangling_china_and_the_inevitability_of_war_109127.html

Nölke, Andreas, Tobias ten Brink, Simone Claar, and Christian May. 2015. "Domestic Structures, Foreign Economic Policies and Global Economic Order: Implications from the Rise of Large Emerging Economies." *European Journal of International Relations* 21 (3): 538–567.

Posen, Barry R. 1984. *The Sources of Military Doctrine*. Ithaca, NY: Cornell University Press.

Posen, Barry R. 1993. "Nationalism, the Mass Army, and Military Power." *International Security* 18 (2): 80–124.

Posen, Barry R. 2014. *Restraint: A New Foundation for U.S. Grand Strategy*. Ithaca, NY: Cornell University Press.

Ripsman, Norrin, and Igor Kovac. 2021. "Material Sources of Grand Strategy." In *The Oxford Handbook of Grand Strategy*, edited by Thierry Balzacq and Ronald R. Krebs. Oxford: Oxford University Press.

Russet, Bruce, and John R Oneal. 2001. *Triangulating Peace: Democracy, Interdependence, and International Organizations*. New York: W. W. Norton and Company.

Scheve, Kenneth, and David Stasavage. 2010. "The Conscription of Wealth: Mass Warfare and the Demand for Progressive Taxation." *International Organization* 64 (4): 529–561.

Schultz, Kenneth A., and Barry R. Weingast. 2003. "The Democratic Advantage: Institutional Foundations of Financial Power in International Competition." *International Organization* 57 (1): 3–42.

Schweller, Randall. 2018. "Opposite but Compatible Nationalisms: A Neoclassical Realist Approach to the Future of US–China Relations." *The Chinese Journal of International Politics* 11 (1): 23–48.

Schweller, Randall. 2006. *Unanswered Threats: Political Constraints on the Balance of Power*. Princeton, NJ: Princeton University Press. https://doi.org/10.5860/choice.44-1785

Sechser, Todd S. 2004. "Are Soldiers Less War-Prone than Statesmen?" *Journal of Conflict Resolution* 48 (5): 746–774.

Shea, Patrick E. 2014. "Financing Victory: Sovereign Credit, Democracy, and War." *The Journal of Conflict Resolution* 58 (5): 771–795.

Simmons, Katie, Silver, Laura, Johnson, Courtney, and Richard Wike. 2018. "In Western Europe, Populist Parties Tap Anti-Establishment Frustration but Have Little Appeal Across Ideological Divide." https://www.pewresearch.org/global/2018/07/12/in-western-europe-populist-parties-tap-anti-establishment-frustration-but-have-little-appeal-across-ideological-divide/

Smith, Tom W., Michael Hout, and Peter V. Marsden. 2018. *General Social Surveys, 1972–2016*. Chicago. https://gssdataexplorer.norc.org

Solingen, Etel. 1998. *Regional Orders at Century's Dawn: Global and Domestic Influences on Grand Strategy*. Princeton, NJ: Princeton University Press.

Solt, Frederick. 2011. "Diversionary Nationalism: Economic Inequality and the Formation of National Pride." *The Journal of Politics* 73 (3): 821–830.

Suls, Rob. 2017. "Share of Democrats calling Russia 'greatest danger' to U.S. is at its highest since end of Cold War." http://www.pewresearch.org/fact-tank/2017/04/20/share-of-democrats-calling-russia-greatest-danger-to-u-s-at-its-highest-since-end-of-cold-war/, accessed September 10, 2018.

Talmadge, Caitlin. 2016. "Different Threats, Different Militaries: Explaining Organizational Practices in Authoritarian Armies." *Security Studies* 25 (1): 111–141.

Tickner, J. Ann. 1992. *Gender in International Relations: Feminist Perspectives on Achieving International Security*. New York: Columbia University Press.

Trubowitz, Peter. 1998. *Defining the National Interest: Conflict and Change in American Foreign Policy*. Chicago: University of Chicago Press.

Trump, Donald J. 2017. "Remarks to the People of Poland." Warsaw, Poland. https://www.whitehouse.gov/briefings-statements/remarks-president-trump-people-poland/

Van Evera, Stephen. 1994. "Hypotheses on Nationalism and War." *International Security* 18 (4): 5–39.

Vitalis, Robert. 2015. *White World Order, Black Power Politics: The Birth of American International Relations*. Ithaca, NY: Cornell University Press.

Waltz, Kenneth N. 1979. *Theory of International Politics*. Boston, MA: Addison-Wesley Pub. Co.

Ward, Steven. 2013. "Race, Status, and Japanese Revisionism in the Early 1930s." *Security Studies* 22 (4): 607–639.

Weeks, Jessica L. 2016. *Dictators at War and Peace*. Ithaca, NY: Cornell University Press.

Weiss, Jessica C. 2013. "Authoritarian Signaling, Mass Audiences, and Nationalist Protest in China." *International Organization* 67 (1): 1–35.

Weiss, Linda. 2014. *America Inc.? Innovation and Enterprise in the National Security State*. Ithaca, NY: Cornell University Press.

White, Peter B. 2017. "Generals in the Cabinet: Military Participation in Government and International Conflict Initiation." https://cidcm.umd.edu/sites/cidcm.umd.edu/files/peter_white_cidcm_5_1_2017_1.pdf

Wilén, Nina, David Ambrosetti, and Gérard Birantamije. 2015. "Sending Peacekeepers Abroad, Sharing Power at Home: Burundi in Somalia." *Journal of Eastern African Studies* 9 (2): 307–325.

Ye, Min. 2019. "Fragmentation and Mobilization: Domestic Politics of the Belt and Road in China." *Journal of Contemporary China* 28 (119): 696–711.

Zhang, Feng. 2013. "The Rise of Chinese Exceptionalism in International Relations." *European Journal of International Relations* 19 (2): 305–328.

Zhang, Weiwei. 2012. *The China Wave: Rise of a Civilizational State*. Hackensack, NJ: World Century Publishing Corporation.

Zielinski, Rosella Cappella. 2016. *How States Pay for Wars*. Ithaca, NY: Cornell University Press.

CHAPTER 16

ECONOMIC INTERESTS AND GRAND STRATEGY

KEVIN NARIZNY

Economic activity that crosses borders can have far-reaching consequences for international politics. Whether it involves trade, investment, or plunder, it is typically undertaken by politically powerful elites, those with considerable influence over the state and the making of foreign policy. They call on the state to protect and promote their interests, and it obliges by expanding its commitments abroad. This inevitably brings it into conflict with other states, giving rise to security competition and the risk of escalation to militarized disputes. Consequently, the state invests considerable military, diplomatic, and economic resources into preparing for war. By this logic, economic interests are a fundamental cause of grand strategy and should be central to its study.

What sort of economic interests, then, might affect grand strategy? Grand strategy often entails extensive mobilization of resources from society, and it invariably provides greater benefits to and imposes greater costs on some groups than others. It has enormous potential to affect the wealth of societal actors; thus, it creates distributional conflict among them. Different schools of thought disagree on the significance of that conflict, however. In one view, the state is autonomous from society and unbiased by the concerns of domestic groups; this is conventional realism. In other perspectives, which include liberalism, Marxism, and neoclassical realism, the state is biased in favor of a particularistic set of interests. When this bias is consistent across governments, it constitutes a national preference; when it varies across governments, it is a subnational preference.

This chapter will flesh out each of these analytic frames, review the different sources of economic interest within them, and suggest how domestic preferences come to be represented at the highest levels of the making of foreign policy. Given space constraints, I exclude research on how politicians set agendas and manipulate public opinion (rather than straightforwardly represent economic interests), and I cover work only by social scientists, not historians. I proceed in four sections. First, I discuss how realism treats the relationship between economic interests and grand strategy. Realism's insights are essential; however, its assumption that grand strategy is predominantly security-seeking sharply limits its analytic utility. The next two sections review various types of economic interests and their hypothesized effects on state behavior. I begin with national characteristics, like a country's socioeconomic structure or level of economic interdependence. Then, I turn to sources of subnational variation. Finally, in the conclusion, I briefly suggest several lines of research that are likely to generate progress in the study of economic interests in grand strategy.

THE SURVIVAL MOTIVE

International relations paradigms play a vital role in structuring research into the sources of grand strategy. The most influential paradigm in security studies is realism, which assumes the state to be a rational, unitary actor that seeks above all to ensure its survival. In realism, grand strategy is a response to external pressures, not an expression of internal preferences, and private economic interests are irrelevant. The only economic interests that matter are collective, per the unitary state assumption, and these matter only to the extent that they affect security, per the survival assumption.

Within these theoretical constraints, realism makes important contributions to the literature. For a survival-motivated state, cross-border economic activity impacts national security in two broad categories. First, in the long term, it can either add to or drain from the resource base that underpins military power (Copeland 2014; Rowe 1999). Trade often generates economic growth, but it can also contribute to relative decline; foreign investment can provide a steady stream of repatriated profits, but it can also divert productive capital out of the home market; and technological exchange can keep an economy at the cutting edge of innovation, but it can also allow for the rapid advancement of less-developed competitors. How a state is affected by and responds to these considerations may be a central concern of its grand strategy. In general, realists expect states to take advantage of opportunities to increase their wealth by expanding their military power and diplomatic commitments abroad. In this view, grand strategy is a form of capital investment that generates security-improving profits.

Second, in the short term, cross-border economic activity can be a source of either advantage or vulnerability. Consider interwar Japan, which imported much of its oil and metals from the United States (Copeland 2014, chs. 4–5; Sagan 1988). Losing this source of raw materials would wreak havoc not only on Japan's economy but also on its military power. When the Roosevelt administration ramped up an embargo in 1941, Japanese policymakers were left with a stark choice: either accept their subordination to the United States or acquire another source of raw materials. For Americans, the imbalance in trade was a source of coercive leverage; for the Japanese, it was a threat to their status as a great power. Thus, it weighed more heavily on the grand strategy of Japan than that of the United States.

Another contribution of realism is its insight into the endogeneity of cross-border economic activity. In international economic theory, trade and foreign investment follow opportunities for profit based on transportation costs, factor endowments, and other considerations that are exogenous to grand strategy. In this view, the causal relationship between economic interests and grand strategy should be uncomplicated and unidirectional, pointing from the former to the latter. Realists, in contrast, ask how grand strategy shapes economic interests. Survival-motivated states will incentivize firms and manipulate markets to avoid becoming vulnerable to potential rivals (Copeland 2014), make other countries vulnerable to them (Hirschman 1945), strengthen their allies (Gowa 1994; Skålnes 2000), and weaken their adversaries (Mastanduno 1992). Thus, realists argue that "trade follows the flag." Much research contests this claim (Davis 2008; Fordham 2008c, 2010; Hamilton-Hart 2012; Kastner 2009; Layne 2006, ch. 5; Narizny 2003c; Papayoanou 1999), but the point remains that the direction of causality cannot simply be assumed.

Realism is indispensable to the study of economic interests and grand strategy. Its emphasis on the high stakes and complex dynamics of competition among states draws attention to the interactive elements of grand strategy and provides a necessary corrective to the naïve optimism of idealists. It excels in explaining how states respond to situations and behaviors that they deem to threaten their interests. However, this is not the entire, or even the most important, task for the analysis of grand strategy. Where realism falls short is in its account of how states decide what constitutes a threat and what tradeoffs are justified in response to it. Realism has much of value to say about the *means* of foreign policy, but it has an impoverished view of the *ends* of foreign policy.

Consider, again, the case of Japan in 1941. It is true that Japan's reliance on imports of raw materials from the United States made it vulnerable to coercion, and it is reasonable to believe that Japan's strategic autonomy and great power status were threatened by the US embargo. It does not follow, however, that Japan's survival was at stake. Suppose Japanese policymakers had conceded to US demands, which were for Japan to withdraw from southeast Asia, end its war with China, and refrain from hostilities against the Soviet Union. Suppose, furthermore, that the United States, encouraged by its success, continued to place new demands on Japan, and that Japan, still vulnerable to the threat of a trade embargo, continued to make concessions. Did Japanese policymakers have any reason to believe that this chain of events would lead to the occupation of Tokyo by a foreign army? No: survival was not at stake, and any plausible scenario involving Japanese concessions would have left Japan with far more autonomy and status than it has at present, after seven decades of willing subordination to the United States. Survival was only at stake if Japan refused to concede, because that could lead to total war with the United States. Facing a choice between a certain loss of some autonomy and a substantial chance of utter defeat, Japanese policymakers opted for the latter.

In view of cases like this, some realists propose an expansive definition of survival, one that incorporates values like strategic autonomy and great power status (see Kadercan 2013). Doing so only begs the question; it is akin to trying to explain the American Civil War as a dispute over states' rights. The leaders of the Confederacy often framed their actions in these terms, but it would be naïve to accept them at their word and inquire no further. One must ask, "states' rights to do what, and in whose interests?" It is no less naïve to accept "strategic autonomy" as an explanation for Japan's decision to fight. Rather, one must ask, "strategic autonomy for what, and in whose interests?" For Japan, the answer was the exploitation of China, particularly Manchuria, by and for the Japanese military and industrial monopolies (Drea 2009, chs. 9–10; Snyder 1991, 137–42). These groups' economic interests were not the "national interest," and the behavior of their government was jarringly inconsistent with any reasonable conception of survival.

Recognizing the inadequacy of the survival motive to explain grand strategy, some scholars have turned to other approaches. One perspective, neoclassical realism, seeks to reformulate realism to allow for greater analytic flexibility. It encourages attention to a wide range of domestic variables while insisting on the ultimate priority of systemic factors (Ripsman, Taliaferro, and Lobell 2016; Rose 1998). Liberalism, in contrast, asserts the analytic priority of preferences; it is designed specifically to focus attention on the domestic factors underlying foreign policy (Moravcsik 1997; see also Frieden 1999). It does not ignore systemic variables, but it treats them as constraints on the pursuit of preferences, not as the underlying motive for state behavior. Finally, a third paradigm, Marxism, specializes in the study of class conflict (Teschke 2008).

These three schools of thought have generated an abundance of theoretical insight into the connection between economic interests and grand strategy. They have sharp differences over analytic methods and theoretical framing (Narizny 2017b), and they reach different conclusions about the causal weight of economic interests in grand strategy, but they also overlap in important ways. Thus, intramural debates are not the focus of this chapter. Instead, I focus on the logics that connect economic interests to grand strategy. Rather than organize these logics according to paradigms, I divide them by level of analysis. That is, I distinguish between economic interests that can be attributed to a country as a whole and those that are contested by specific groups within it. The former have been researched extensively but have important limits in their application to grand strategy; the latter offer more detailed insight into grand strategy but are not as well established in the field.

National Preferences

Most claims about national-level economic interests originate in one of two literatures: Marxism and liberalism. Classical Marxist theories of imperialism assert that capitalist countries have an inherent tendency to undertake an aggressively expansionist grand strategy (Hobson 1938; Brewer 1990; see also Layne 2006). In a capitalist economy, the state and capitalists suppress wages, which results in an excess of profit. At first, capitalists invest those profits in increased productive capacity, but rising capacity soon outstrips demand. Workers with suppressed wages cannot afford to consume all of the goods that their economy produces; thus, a crisis of overproduction arises. Unwilling to raise wages, but desperate for new sources of income, capitalists look for new markets abroad in which to sell their surplus goods and invest their surplus profits. Foreign countries often resist such efforts, so capitalists enlist the help of their state to force open new markets. At maximum, this entails the annexation of colonies and formation of an empire; at minimum, it involves the subordination of clients and creation of spheres of influence. In an international system with multiple capitalist great powers, the search for new markets will inevitably bring those powers into conflict. As the world becomes increasingly divided into empires and spheres of influence, conflict will intensify, and a systemic war may become inevitable.

Implicit in classical Marxist theories of imperialism is the idea that noncapitalist states behave less aggressively than capitalist states. Under socialism, the means of production are owned by the state, which has no reason to extract surplus capital or create excess capacity. No crisis of overproduction occurs; thus, there is no need to expand into new markets abroad. Judging from the historical record, this may be true. The only states that have attempted full-scale socialism have been communist, and communist states do not seem to have expanded for reasons of economic interest.[1] It does not follow, however, that communist states are more peaceful than capitalist states, because they may have other, non-economic reasons to act aggressively (Kennan 1947; Walt 1996, ch. 4).

Furthermore, communism is not the only alternative to capitalism. A different strand of Marxist theory, political Marxism, seeks insight into the behavior of modern, capitalist states by contrasting them with premodern, precapitalist states (Lacher 2006; Teschke 2003; Wood 2003). Feudal states, for example, had an intense economic interest in territorial expansion. Their socioeconomic elite, the landed nobility, specialized in control over the means of coercion, which they used to extract rents from peasants. Within this socioeconomic structure, their best prospects for increasing their wealth were the plunder of towns and the conquest of land. Meanwhile, the merchant elites who ruled towns, particularly seaports, found that their fortunes rose and fell on their ability to monopolize trade routes. The most successful among them, like the leading city-states of Italy and provinces of the Dutch Republic, invested enormous resources in military power that they used to exclude competition. Capitalist states, in contrast, seek to create a free market with access for all. They are willing to coerce anticapitalist resisters and "rogue states" at the point of a gun, but their ultimate goal is to open borders, not change them, so as to make the world safe for the capitalist exploitation of labor. Thus, they create an ever-expanding "Lockean heartland" of liberal internationalism at the core of the international system (van der Pijl 1998, ch. 3), and their shared transnational interests may trump the national interests of individual states (Robinson 2004).

Another intellectual tradition, the classical liberalism of Enlightenment Europe, has spawned a vast literature on the pacifying effects of trade (see Mansfield and Pollins 2003; Schneider, Barbieri, and Gleditsch 2003). In this view, trade is profitable, and war disrupts trade; thus, trade increases the opportunity costs of war. Two historical shifts reinforce this logic. First, the increasing integration of the world economy over the past century allows states and firms to acquire any sort of goods they desire at competitive prices (Brooks 2013, 874–877). As a result, there is no longer a need for conquest. Second, economic progress has come to depend less on the exploitation of natural resources (Markowitz, Fariss, and McMahon 2019) than on a complex interplay of information, organization, and technology, all of which are vulnerable to disruption (Rosecrance 1986). The more the wealth of a society would be destroyed by its conquest, the less attractive it becomes as a target of conquest, and the incidence of war declines.

Each of these claims has been subject to criticism (e.g., Barbieri 2002; Liberman 1995), and theoretical refinement continues. The most recent contribution to the literature is the idea of a "capitalist peace," in which the likelihood of conflict between two countries is determined not just by their economic interdependence but also their internal socioeconomic structures (see Schneider and Gleditsch 2013). Whereas classical liberals and classical Marxist theorists of imperialism disagreed sharply on the significance of capitalism for grand strategy, this "neoclassical liberalism" (McDonald 2009, 46) and political Marxism have converged on the view that capitalist dyads are more peaceful than mixed or noncapitalist dyads.

A final set of perspectives on national preferences concerns the distribution of the costs of war. According to the institutional logic of democratic peace theory, elites can insulate themselves from such costs, whereas the median voter is vulnerable to conscription. Democratic leaders, who are elected by the median voter, thus seek to avoid unnecessary conflicts. Authoritarian leaders, who rely mainly on the support of elites, can act more aggressively (Bueno de Mesquita et al. 2003; Doyle 1983, 229–30). Caverley (2014; see also Rowe, Bearce, and McDonald 2002), however, reaches a different conclusion. Under the influence of the median voter, democracies' military spending should be capital-intensive, rather than labor-intensive, and military service should be voluntary, rather than conscripted. As a result, the fiscal burden of defense should fall primarily on the rich. As income inequality increases, moreover, the share of taxes paid by the median voter will decline. Ever more insulated from the costs of war, the median voter will become ever more hawkish, supporting frequent small wars. Contrary to democratic peace theorists, Caverley suggests that democracies act more aggressively than authoritarian states.

Each of the research traditions discussed in this section makes an important contribution to international relations theory. Their impact on the literature on grand strategy, however, has been limited. First, Marxist ideas rarely receive much attention from mainstream academics. I suspect this is due in part to bias, which is unfair, and in part to Marxists' disdain for "positivist" hypothesis testing, which is their own fault. Second, classical liberal research is focused overwhelmingly on quantitative methods. Most studies are designed to estimate average causal effects, not explain an individual state's behavior at a given point in time. As a result, they cannot engage fully in interpretive debates over grand strategy decision making (Copeland 2014, ch. 2). Third, regardless of method or paradigm, all of these perspectives' ability to account for change is constrained. In the short term, national attributes like socioeconomic structure, economic interdependence, and regime type tend not to vary much, and a constant cannot explain change. Yet sudden change in grand strategy does occur, often associated with turnover in the executive. On March 4, 1921, for example, American grand strategy transitioned from Woodrow Wilson's liberal internationalism to Calvin Coolidge's near-isolationism. This shift cannot be attributed to national characteristics, nor was it a response to a sudden change in the external environment. An effective theory of grand strategy must go deeper than national preferences; it must be able to explain variance across individual leaders.

Subnational Preferences

Subnational theories of economic interests do not address factors typically associated with the study of individual leaders, such as cognitive biases, ideological commitments, and causal beliefs. They can, however, suggest an answer to a more fundamental question: how do individuals with particular personal characteristics come to lead their countries? Subnational theories begin with the assumption that politicians in a position of power, including those who make grand strategy, represent a societal constituency (Fordham 1998, 6–9; Moravcsik 1997, 516–520; Narizny 2007, 25–32). That constituency is the politician's ruling coalition, which is a subset of either the electorate, as in a democracy, or the selectorate, as under authoritarianism. To rise to power, as well as to fend off challengers once in power, politicians support policies that benefit the distributional interests of their coalition. Individuals whose biases, commitments, and beliefs happen to correspond to the aggregated preferences of a ruling coalition will be most likely to reach the heights of power. Those who are flexible in their biases, commitments, and beliefs, and who are able to adjust their views to attract the support of enough constituents to assemble a ruling coalition—but who are not so flexible as to appear unreliable—will also have an advantage over their competitors. In this view, leaders' personal characteristics matter to policymaking, but they are not causally independent. Rather, they are the result of a process of interest aggregation that matches individuals' biases, commitments, and beliefs to the economic interests of societal groups. To explain grand strategy, therefore, we must begin not with psychoanalysis but rather political economy.

Economic interests at the subnational level take various forms, which I classify as either sectoral or class-based. Sectoral interests are those that are shared by owners, managers, and laborers within a set of firms. Perhaps the most important sectoral characteristic is the geographic locus of firms' exposure to the international economy (Fordham 1998, 86–88; Narizny 2007, 18–21; Trubowitz 1998, 17–18; see also Davis 2008). In general, firms that engage in trade or foreign investment have an interest in an expansive grand strategy that protects and promotes their activities abroad. The content of that strategy, however, depends on the location of their activity. Weak countries at the periphery of the international system can be made to open their markets through conquest, regime change, and other forms of coercion. Firms that derive income from them have an interest in a grand strategy that specializes in power projection and the unilateral use of force. If such a strategy involves the annexation of colonies, it is imperialism; if not, it is interventionism.[2] Strong countries at the core of the international system, in contrast, are not so easily pushed around. To threaten them with military force would only undermine the interests of firms that trade with and invest in them. A grand strategy designed to protect and promote the interests of such firms must attempt to resolve existing international disputes and prevent the escalation of future ones. It can lay the foundation for closer economic cooperation only through increasing reliance on multilateralism and international law, not coercion. Often referred to as liberal internationalism, or simply internationalism (Kleinberg and Fordham 2013; Narizny 2003b; Nolt 1997, 99–100; Trubowitz 1998, 134–137), it is designed to promote economic interdependence among great powers and is closely associated with globalization.[3] Finally, some firms have little connection to the world outside their national borders. They do not engage in trade or foreign investment, nor are they directly dependent on firms that do. Given their inward focus, they have little to gain from an expansive, ambitious grand strategy. The fewer commitments, the better; a strategy that attempts to accomplish anything more than to secure their homeland from invasion will be a waste of their taxes.

A second sectoral characteristic that impacts firms' interest in grand strategy is their international competitiveness. This category addresses only firms whose output is potentially tradeable, such that they might compete with imports or engage in export. At one end of the spectrum are firms that are at a competitive disadvantage and that receive no assistance from their state. They compete with imports and have poor prospects for economic survival in the long term. Such firms, the stereotypical losers from globalization, have a similar interest in grand strategy as the previously described firms that have no connection to the international economy. Indeed, the two groups should partially overlap. There should, however, be a subtle difference: one is largely unaffected by the international economy, whereas the other is actively harmed by it. Thus, the losers from globalization have an interest not just in a parsimonious grand strategy but also in opposing any form of internationalism (Frieden 1988, 67; Musgrave 2019; Narizny 2017a, 12–14; Trubowitz 1998, 146–147), which, as described above, is designed to promote globalization.

When internationally uncompetitive sectors have the active assistance of their state, their interest in grand strategy shifts. If their state can gain control over foreign markets, it can provide them with competitive advantages for export and investment in those markets (Blanken 2012, 43–46; McDonald 2009, 69–71; Nolt 1997, 99). In the late nineteenth and early twentieth centuries, Britain, France, Germany, Italy, and Japan had many weakly competitive manufacturing firms that lobbied for the creation or expansion of empire as a means of gaining privileged access to captive consumers and exploiting natural resources. A century later, France still has an informal empire in West Africa in which it intervenes for the benefit of politically well-connected firms, while China is forming close relationships with otherwise isolated "rogue states" for the same purpose.

At the other end of the spectrum of international competitiveness are firms that successfully export without state assistance. In contrast to the losers from globalization, they have an interest in an active, expansive grand strategy. The focus of that strategy, however, cannot be predicted without more information, particularly the geographic locus of their overseas activity, as described above.[4] In the late nineteenth and early twentieth centuries, the manufacturing sector in the northeastern United States was becoming increasingly competitive, but its ability to export to the core of the international system was sharply constrained by protectionism therein. Countries like France, Germany, and Italy raised tariffs to promote their own industrialization and had little interest in reciprocal liberalization. Locked out of markets in the core, American manufacturers focused instead on the periphery (Narizny 2007, 44–47; see also Trubowitz 1998, 43–47).[5] Thus, they favored interventionism, not internationalism. Not until the 1930s, when the Great Depression and the collapse of the international economy created a unique opportunity and strong incentive for both the United States and some European states to cooperate to reduce tariff rates, did a significant number of American manufacturers begin to embrace internationalism (Frieden 1988; Trubowitz 1998, 106–118).

A third sectoral characteristic is asset specificity. This perspective originates with Frieden (1989, 1994), who argues that the rise and fall of imperialism in the nineteenth and twentieth centuries were a response to the changing nature of North–South trade and investment. At the start of this period, the most profitable economic activity overseas was the exploitation of natural resources, which required large capital investments that were vulnerable to expropriation by native peoples and colonial rivals. Protecting them required direct control over territory, thus imperialism. Over time, however, they were eclipsed by other kinds of economic activity. Firms that invested in small-scale manufacturing, like textiles, had lower capital requirements and were more mobile; likewise, firms that exported goods and services to developing markets had little to lose from expropriation. As a result, they had less need for intervention, and empire became superfluous. This argument has much merit, but the last step is overly ambitious. Many factors contributed to the decline of imperialism, and there were countervailing reasons for firms to continue to support imperialism, such as a desire for competitive advantages, without having high asset specificity.

Fourth, some sectors' economic interest in grand strategy is industry-specific. Many classical Marxists argue that finance drives the imperialism of capitalist states. Investors seek the highest possible rate of return, which is consistently to be found in the least developed parts of the world. Often these markets are not governed by strong states, or the strong states that govern them resist external penetration, so the political risk of investment is high. To defray that risk, the financial sector demands that its own state intervene aggressively, even to the point of war. Yet Kirshner (2007) argues that Marxists have it backward: foreign conflicts rattle markets and cause steep losses in stock valuation, so bankers lobby their state for caution. In fact, these two positions are not irreconcilable. The financial sector may favor imperialism when the costs of expansion are expected to be low, yet prefer to avoid military conflict with powerful states when their overseas investments are not endangered. In this light, it should be of no surprise that Hobson (1938) finds British finance to have been hawkish over mineral-rich southern Africa in the 1890s, while Kirshner (2007, ch. 6) finds British finance to have been dovish over the desolate Falkland Islands in the 1980s.

The best-known sector with industry-specific interests in grand strategy is defense contractors. Firms that sell goods and services to the military benefit straightforwardly from foreign policies that require increased defense spending. In the short term, what is best for business is war; in the long term, it is great power rivalry. They should prefer a grand strategy that is as active and expansionist as possible, one that sees threats everywhere and that responds to them through arms races and military action. Such a strategy should make numerous commitments to the defense of other countries, both to require the expansion of the military and to provide additional markets for arms exports. Defense contractors are unlikely to make their preferences public; doing so would result in a political backlash. Instead, they exert influence indirectly, contributing to the political campaigns of hawkish politicians and parties. Wherever defense industries are a major employer, moreover, they gain significant support from public opinion. As a result, politicians with constituencies that benefit from defense spending tend to be the strongest supporters of a hawkish, expansionary grand strategy (Fordham 2008a, 2008b; Thorpe 2014; Trubowitz 1998).

Another sector with industry-specific interests is think tanks. They play a critical role in the foreign policy establishment, not so much as incubators of ideas, but as shapers of public opinion and employers of would-be policymakers whose party is out of power. Most major American think tanks are funded by multinational corporations that have a stake in an active grand strategy due to their trade, foreign investment, or military contracts. This sponsorship ensures that think tanks employ only liberal internationalists and nationalist hawks, making it difficult for isolationists or advocates of "restraint" to establish themselves in the policy community (Van Apeldoorn and de Graaff 2016; Walt 2018, ch. 3).

Not all subnational economic interests are sectoral. In subnational theories of class interests, the salient cleavage is between the rich and the poor. Unlike classical Marxism, such theories do not assume that the state represents a single, dominant class; rather, the class composition of governments can vary. In the realm of grand strategy, class comes into play in the question of a "guns versus butter" tradeoff in military spending. Research on this topic tests the hypothesis that governments that represent the upper class attempt to redirect budgetary resources from welfare to defense, whereas governments that represent the lower class do the opposite. For several decades, the literature failed to reach consensus either in favor of or against this proposition. In my own work (Narizny 2003a; see also Anievas 2014, ch. 6), I explain why: its basic premise is flawed. Although the poor have a class interest in butter, the rich do not have a class interest in guns. If an upper-class government has surplus revenue, its priority should be to cut taxes on the rich, not increase defense spending. Furthermore, a dramatic increase in defense spending often harms holders of wealth. It consumes resources, so it tends to cause inflation and increase the bargaining power of labor; it is costly, so it leads to increased taxation; and it generates economic distortions that necessitate heavy-handed regulation of markets. To avoid these effects, governments that represent the upper class look for diplomatic means to counter major threats, in the form of either alliances or appeasement, before undertaking a full-scale rearmament program. Governments that represent the lower class are less reluctant to cause labor scarcity, raise taxes, and increase the size of government, so they pursue guns and butter simultaneously.

The diverse array of economic interests in grand strategy poses a methodological dilemma for researchers. Should one make an exhaustive accounting of every relevant variable and try to evaluate its relative weight, or is parsimony preferable? Some scholars have responded to this dilemma by clustering together different types of group according to their hypothesized interest in grand strategy. For example, a number of sectors described above are expected to support an aggressively expansionist grand strategy: those with a geographical focus on the periphery of the international system, those that are weakly competitive but receive assistance from their state, those with immobile assets abroad, and defense contractors. These can be described collectively as members of the "nationalist" or "cartelized" coalition, while those with an interest in the rule of international law and multilateral diplomacy constitute the "internationalist" or "free trade" coalition (Lobell 2003, 21–26; Nolt 1997, 95–100; Snyder 1991, 31–55; Solingen 1998, 8–13). This practice can facilitate our understanding of cases in which societal groups separate into rival coalitions as expected. However, that separation does not always occur: political coalitions are often based on issues other than foreign policy and can include strange bedfellows (Fordham 1998, 9–12; Kirshner 2007, 17, 215–216; Narizny 2017a, 14). Thus, researchers should be careful not to assume a nationalist-internationalist divide. Instead, they should start case studies by investigating which societal groups are part of which coalitions and determine how much influence each has within its coalition. Only then should they formulate hypotheses about what strategy that coalition will pursue.

Conclusion

The literature on economic interests and grand strategy is large and growing. It is not, however, anywhere near to exhausting its potential. On the theoretical side, more research about subnational preferences is needed. Page and Jacobs (2005) find that certain industry-specific sectors have strong preferences and extraordinary influence over the making of foreign economic policy, yet there are few monographs about the preferences of industry-specific sectors over grand strategy. Kirshner's (2007) book on finance is a valuable contribution, but much more remains to be said. Also useful would be further research into the connection between economic interests and other domestic factors associated with grand strategy, like nationalism and ideology. Snyder (1991) offers a grand synthesis but does not sort out the details, whereas Hamilton-Hart (2012) goes deeper but does not address cases of great power grand strategy.

On the empirical side, there are huge gaps in the literature, especially on subnational preferences. Most research focuses on the United States, with Great Britain as a distant second, while all other countries have been relatively neglected, at least by scholars who publish in English. Snyder (1991) touches on economic interests in the grand strategies of Germany and Japan, but more in-depth analysis is imperative. Subnational preferences in Austria-Hungary, France, Italy, and Russia have been almost completely ignored by social scientists. More encouraging is the emerging body of work on contemporary China, a case of undeniable importance (Jones and Zeng 2019; Shirk 2014, 403–406; Ye 2019). The more that scholars address new cases, the more likely they are to contribute new theoretical insights that shed light on old cases, and the more evident it will be that economic interests deserve close attention as a fundamental cause of grand strategy.

Notes

1. The Soviet Union did extract resources from East Germany at the end of the Second World War, but the occupation of Central and Southeast Europe became a drain on the Soviet economy over the long run (Bunce 1985).
2. For different theoretical perspectives on how states choose between these two strategies, see Narizny (2007, 19–21), Blanken (2012, 43–47), and Frieden (1994).
3. Internationalism also promotes interdependence among states that are not great powers; see Solingen (1998, 22–32) and Kastner (2009, 21–28).
4. For a related logic that differs in important details, see McDonald (2009, 67–69).
5. For a different interpretation, see Fordham (2019). Fordham claims that the negotiation of an "especially important" trade reciprocity agreement with France in 1898 demonstrates that Europeans were, in fact, willing to open their markets to American manufacturing exports (443). This is incorrect: France agreed to lower its tariffs only on certain foodstuffs and construction materials, not manufactures (New York Times 1898; see also De Molinari 1890, 313–15).

References

Anievas, Alexander. 2014. *Capital, the State, and War: Class Conflict and Geopolitics in the Thirty Years' Crisis*. Ann Arbor: University of Michigan Press.

Barbieri, Katherine. 2002. *The Liberal Illusion: Does Trade Promote Peace?* Ann Arbor: University of Michigan Press.

Blanken, Leo J. 2012. *Rational Empires: Institutional Incentives and Imperial Expansion*. Chicago: University of Chicago Press.

Brewer, Anthony. 1990. *Marxist Theories of Imperialism: A Critical Survey*. 2nd edition. London: Routledge and Kegan Paul.

Brooks, Stephen G. 2013. "Economic Actors' Lobbying Influence on the Prospects for War and Peace." *International Organization* 67 (4): 863–888.

Bueno de Mesquita, Bruce, Alastair Smith, Randolph M. Siverson, and James D. Morrow. 2003. *The Logic of Political Survival*. Cambridge, MA: MIT Press.

Bunce, Valerie J. 1985. "The Empire Strikes Back: The Evolution of the Eastern Bloc from a Soviet Asset to a Soviet Liability." *International Organization* 39 (1): 1–46.

Caverley, Jonathan D. 2014. *Democratic Militarism: Voting, Wealth, and War.* Cambridge: Cambridge University Press.

Copeland, Dale C. 2014. *Economic Interdependence and War.* Princeton: Princeton University Press.

Davis, Christina L. 2008. "Linkage Diplomacy: Economic and Security Bargaining in the Anglo-Japanese Alliance, 1902–1923." *International Security* 33 (3): 143–179.

De Molinari, Gustave. 1890. "The McKinley Bill in Europe." *North American Review* 151 (406): 307–318.

Doyle, Michael. 1983. "Kant, Liberal Legacies, and Foreign Affairs, Part I." *Philosophy and Public Affairs* 12 (3): 205–235.

Drea, Edward. 2009. *Japan's Imperial Army: Its Rise and Fall.* Lawrence: University Press of Kansas.

Fordham, Benjamin O. 1998. *Building the Cold War Consensus: The Political Economy of U.S. National Security Policy, 1949–51.* Ann Arbor: University of Michigan Press.

Fordham, Benjamin O. 2008a. "Economic Interests and Congressional Voting on Security Issues." *Journal of Conflict Resolution* 52 (5): 623–640.

Fordham, Benjamin O. 2008b. "Economic Interests and Public Support for American Global Activism." *International Organization* 62 (1): 163–182.

Fordham, Benjamin O. 2008c. "Power or Plenty? Economic Interests, Security Concerns, and American Intervention." *International Studies Quarterly* 2 (4): 737–758.

Fordham, Benjamin O. 2010. "Trade and Asymmetric Alliances." *Journal of Peace Research* 47 (6): 685–696.

Fordham, Benjamin O. 2019. "The Domestic Politics of World Power: Explaining Debates over the United States Battleship Fleet, 1890–91." *International Organization* 73 (2): 435–468.

Fordham, Benjamin O. 1988. "Sectoral Conflict and Foreign Economic Policy, 1914–1940." *International Organization* 42 (1): 59–90.

Fordham, Benjamin O. 1989. "The Economics of Intervention: American Overseas Investments and Relations with Underdeveloped Areas, 1890–1950." *Comparative Studies in Society and History* 31 (1): 55–80.

Frieden, Jeffry A. 1994. "International Investment and Colonial Control: A New Interpretation." *International Organization* 48 (4): 559–593.

Frieden, Jeffry A. 1999. "Actors and Preferences in International Relations." In *Strategic Choice and International Relations*, edited by David A. Lake and Robert Powell, 39–76. Princeton: Princeton University Press.

Gowa, Joanne. 1994. *Allies, Adversaries, and International Trade.* Princeton: Princeton University Press.

Hamilton-Hart, Natasha. 2012. *Hard Interests, Soft Illusions: Southeast Asia and American Power.* Ithaca: Cornell University Press.

Hirschman, Albert O. 1945. *National Power and the Structure of Foreign Trade.* Berkeley: University of California Press.

Hobson, John A. 1938. *Imperialism: A Study.* 3rd edition. London: Allen and Unwin.

Jones, Lee, and Jinghan Zeng. 2019. "Understanding China's 'Belt and Road Initiative': Beyond 'Grand Strategy' to a State Transformation Analysis." *Third World Quarterly* 40 (8): 1415–1439.

Kadercan, Burak. 2013. "Making Sense of Survival: Refining the Treatment of State Preferences in Neorealist Theory." *Review of International Studies* 39 (4): 1015–1037.

Kastner, Scott L. 2009. *Political Conflict and Economic Interdependence Across the Taiwan Strait and Beyond.* Stanford: Stanford University Press.

Kennan, George F. 1947. "The Sources of Soviet Conduct." *Foreign Affairs* 25 (4): 566–582.
Kirshner, Jonathan. 2007. *Appeasing Bankers: Financial Caution on the Road to War*. Princeton: Princeton University Press.
Kleinberg, Katja B., and Benjamin O. Fordham. 2013. "The Domestic Politics of Trade and Conflict." *International Studies Quarterly* 57 (3): 605–619.
Lacher, Hannes. 2006. *Beyond Globalization: Capitalism, Territoriality and the International Relations of Modernity*. Abingdon: Routledge.
Layne, Christopher. 2006. *The Peace of Illusions: American Grand Strategy from 1940 to the Present*. Ithaca: Cornell University Press.
Liberman, Peter. 1995. *Does Conquest Pay? The Exploitation of Occupied Industrial Societies*. Princeton: Princeton University Press.
Lobell, Steven E. 2003. *The Challenge of Hegemony: Grand Strategy, Trade, and Domestic Politics*. Ann Arbor: University of Michigan Press.
Mansfield, Edward D., and Brian M. Pollins. 2003. *Economic Interdependence and International Conflict: New Perspectives on an Enduring Debate*. Ann Arbor: University of Michigan Press.
Markowitz, Jonathan, Christopher Fariss, and R. Blake McMahon. 2019. "Producing Goods and Projecting Power: How What You Make Influences What You Take." *Journal of Conflict Resolution* 63 (6): 1368–1402.
Mastanduno, Michael. 1992. *Economic Containment: CoCom and the Politics of East-West Trade*. Ithaca: Cornell University Press.
McDonald, Patrick J. 2009. *The Invisible Hand of Peace: Capitalism, the War Machine, and International Relations Theory*. Cambridge: Cambridge University Press.
Moravcsik, Andrew. 1997. "Taking Preferences Seriously: A Liberal Theory of International Politics." *International Organization* 51 (4): 513–553.
Musgrave, Paul. 2019. "International Hegemony Meets Domestic Politics: Why Liberals Can Be Pessimists." *Security Studies* 28 (3): 451–478.
Narizny, Kevin. 2003a. "Both Guns and Butter, or Neither: Class Interests in the Political Economy of Rearmament." *American Political Science Review* 97 (2): 203–220.
Narizny, Kevin. 2003b. "Rational Idealism: The Political Economy of Internationalism in the United States and Great Britain, 1870–1945." *Security Studies* 12 (3): 1–39.
Narizny, Kevin. 2003c. "The Political Economy of Alignment: Great Britain's Commitments to Europe, 1905–39." *International Security* 27 (4): 184–219.
Narizny, Kevin. 2007. *The Political Economy of Grand Strategy*. Ithaca: Cornell University Press.
Narizny, Kevin. 2017a. "American Grand Strategy and Political Economy Theory." In *Oxford Research Encyclopedia of Politics*, 1–24. Oxford: Oxford University Press.
Narizny, Kevin. 2017b. "On Systemic Paradigms and Domestic Politics: A Critique of the Newest Realism." *International Security* 42 (2): 155–190.
New York Times. 1898. "Reciprocity with France." *New York Times*: 7.
Nolt, James H. 1997. "Business Conflict and the Demise of Imperialism." In *Contested Social Orders and International Politics*, edited by David Skidmore, 92–127. Nashville: Vanderbilt University Press.
Page, Benjamin, and Lawrence R. Jacobs. 2005. "Who Influences US Foreign Policy?" *American Political Science Review* 99 (1): 107–123.
Papayoanou, Paul A. 1999. *Power Ties: Economic Interdependence, Balancing, and War*. Ann Arbor: University of Michigan Press.
van der Pijl, Kees. 1998. *Transnational Classes in International Relations*. London: Routledge.

Ripsman, Norrin M., Jeffrey W. Taliaferro, and Steven E. Lobell. 2016. *Neoclassical Realist Theory of International Politics*. Oxford: Oxford University Press.

Robinson, William I. 2004. *A Theory of Global Capitalism: Production, Class, and State in a Transnational World*. Baltimore: Johns Hopkins University Press.

Rose, Gideon. 1998. "Neoclassical Realism and Theories of Foreign Policy." *World Politics* 51 (1): 144–172.

Rosecrance, Richard N. 1986. *The Rise of the Trading State: Commerce and Conquest in the Modern World*. New York: Basic.

Rowe, David M. 1999. "World Economic Expansion and National Security in Pre-World War I Europe." *International Organization* 53 (2): 195–232.

Rowe, David M., David H. Bearce, and Patrick J. McDonald. 2002. "Binding Prometheus: How the 19th Century Expansion of Trade Impeded Britain's Ability to Raise an Army." *International Studies Quarterly* 46 (4): 551–578.

Sagan, Scott D. 1988. "The Origins of the Pacific War." *Journal of Interdisciplinary History* 18 (4): 893–922.

Schneider, Gerald, Katherine Barbieri, and Nils P. Gleditsch, eds. 2003. *Globalization and Armed Conflict*. Lanham: Rowman and Littlefield.

Schneider, Gerald, and Nils P. Gleditsch, eds. 2013. *Assessing the Capitalist Peace*. London: Routledge.

Shirk, Susan. 2014. "The Domestic Context of Chinese Foreign Security Policies." In *The Oxford Handbook of the International Relations of Asia*, edited by Saadia M. Pekkanen, John Ravenhill, and Rosemary Foot. Oxford: Oxford University Press, 391–410.

Skålnes, Lars S. 2000. *Politics, Markets, and Grand Strategy: Foreign Economic Policies as Strategic Instruments*. Ann Arbor: University of Michigan Press.

Snyder, Jack L. 1991. *Myths of Empire: Domestic Politics and International Ambition*. Ithaca: Cornell University Press.

Solingen, Etel. 1998. *Regional Orders at Century's Dawn: Global and Domestic Influences on Grand Strategy*. Princeton: Princeton University Press.

Teschke, Benno. 2003. *The Myth of 1648: Class, Geopolitics, and the Making of Modern International Relations*. London: Verso.

Teschke, Benno. 2008. "Marxism." In *The Oxford Handbook of International Relations Theory*, edited by Christian Reus-Smit and Duncan Snidal, 163–187. Oxford: Oxford University Press.

Thorpe, Rebecca U. 2014. *The American Warfare State: The Domestic Politics of Military Spending*. Chicago: University of Chicago Press.

Trubowitz, Peter. 1998. *Defining the National Interest: Conflict and Change in American Foreign Policy*. Chicago: University of Chicago Press.

Van Apeldoorn, Bastiaan, and Naná de Graaff. 2016. *American Grand Strategy and Corporate Elite Networks*. Abingdon: Routledge.

Walt, Stephen M. 1996. *Revolution and War*. Ithaca: Cornell University Press.

Walt, Stephen M. 2018. *The Hell of Good Intentions: America's Foreign Policy Elite and the Decline of U.S. Primacy*. New York: Farrar, Straus, and Giroux.

Wood, Ellen M. 2003. *Empire of Capital*. London: Verso.

Ye, Min. 2019. "Fragmentation and Mobilization: Domestic Politics of the Belt and Road in China." *Journal of Contemporary China* 28 (119): 696–711.

CHAPTER 17

CIVIL–MILITARY RELATIONS AND GRAND STRATEGY

RISA BROOKS

Introduction

SCHOLARS have long argued that relations between a state's civilian and military leaders are among the most important determinants of its international relations. Civil–military relations can affect everything from how a state fights, to the types of wars in which it engages. Yet, with some important exceptions, there has been minimal research that explores their impact on states' grand strategies.

This essay seeks to address that deficit, arguing that civil–military relations can have profound effects on states' grand strategies. Specifically, I elucidate alternative causal pathways, arguing that relations between the military, society and political leadership can potentially impact three major dimensions of grand strategy. First, civil–military relations can affect the core principles, or substance of a state's grand strategy. Civil–military relations may influence, for example, whether a state is inclined toward a grand strategy that entails significant global commitments and military ventures, one that is revisionist towards the regional or global order, or that is more cautious in its use of military power and foreign interventions. Second, civil–military relations can affect whether a state is able to align its grand strategy's political, diplomatic, military, and economic components, or whether the state instead is prone to pursue a poorly integrated strategy composed of irreconcilable approaches across these different domains. Last, relations between military and civilian leaders can affect the execution or implementation of a grand strategy and therefore, whatever its putative merits, whether the state can in fact achieve the promise of the principles they espouse.

Below I explore each of these dimensions of grand strategy, focusing first on its substance.

The Substance of Grand Strategy

The first way that civil–military relations shape grand strategy is by affecting its overall orientation or "substance." Grand strategies reflect different premises and causal beliefs about international relations, which translate into different organizing principles or "blueprints" (Lissner 2018; for overviews see CNAS 2019; Posen 2015). Civil–military relations can affect these grand-strategic choices through several causal pathways.

One way is via what might be called societal-military relations, or the relationship between the mass public and the military.[1] In particular, widely held societal beliefs about the efficacy of military force and the social prestige of the military institution may affect how central a role the military versus other tools play in grand strategy.[2] In the most acute cases, these societal factors could contribute to a militarist ethos, which is "a set of attitudes and social practices which regards war and the preparation for war as a normal and desirable social activity" (Mann 1987; Levy 2014, 76), or more specifically, as the "the vast array of customs, interests, prestige, actions, and thought associated with armies yet transcending true military purposes" (Vagts 1959, 13; also see Desch 2006, 576). Militarist attitudes may shape the social and domestic political context in which leaders make decisions about grand strategy (Bacevich 2005).

Recent years, for example, have seen the rise of cultural tendencies of this kind in the United States. As Richard Kohn has observed, since the 1930s, the US public has become increasingly militarized, in that "the American people's identification with and use of war images and thinking, and a belief in the primacy of standing military forces for American safety, have become normalized" (Kohn, 2009, 177). Similarly, as Andrew Bacevich (2005) describes it,

> Americans in our time have fallen prey to militarism, manifesting itself in a romanticized view of soldiers, a tendency to see military power as the truest measure of national greatness, and outsized expectations regarding the utility of military force. To a degree without precedent in US history, Americans have come to define the nation's strength and well-being in terms of military preparedness, military action, and the fostering of (or nostalgia for) military ideals.

The United States military, as indicated in commonly cited polling by the Gallup organization, is the most socially esteemed of all the country's social and political institutions (Gallup 2019). This esteem is also accompanied by a lack of knowledge or interest in the activities or nature of the military, such that the American public evinces a sort of blind reverence toward the United States military (Fallows 2015). Moreover, this reverence for the military is not limited just to the United States. There has been a surge in popularity of militaries in countries around the world, which may contribute to the growth of a global wave of militarist attitudes. The cases of Brazil and Israel are exemplary (Albertus 2018; Kershner 2019).

Societal attitudes of this kind, in turn, could have two consequences for a state's grand strategy. First, they might affect resource allocation in the state: how much is spent on the military versus other instruments of statecraft. Grand strategies reflect different conceptualizations for how military, diplomatic and economic means of statecraft are to be employed; they reflect decisions about the relative investments and roles each plays in attaining security for the state. Militarist attitudes may skew the emphasis within it toward reliance on the military, affecting the balance of tools available to political leaders as they make decisions about grand strategy.

Second, militarist attitudes might affect how often military tools are conceptualized as the appropriate means for addressing national security challenges. That is, are military solutions seen as superior or better than alternative means of influence? If, as Yagil Levy (2014, 79) puts it, "the legitimacy to use force ... is socially accepted as a normal, pervasive, and enduring strategic preference," the resort to military tools to solve a variety of problems may seem natural to members of society. All problems begin to appear as solvable with military force (Bacevich 2005; Brooks 2016).

Today, for example, some contend that the United States is using military operations to confront global challenges that cannot be addressed primarily with force, such as extremist violence (Kizer 2019 39). In 2018, the United States, for example, had active bombing campaigns in seven countries and troops involved in military operations for counterterrorism purposes in 14 countries, as well as military forces deployed for a variety of purposes in over 80 countries across the globe (Kizer 2019 39). Since 1992, the US has used military force abroad more than 200 times, relative to 46 "armed overseas deployments" during the Cold War (Lissner 2019, 50). As Richard Kohn has observed in the US case, despite historical apprehensions toward standing military forces, the sweeping and amorphous character of the United States' Global War on Terror has both reflected and promoted militarist values, "transforming the United States incrementally, over time, into a nation its founders would recognize, but abhor" (Kohn, 2009, 177). Even ideas about what constitutes war and peace may succumb to militarist pressures, as with the growing popularity of using the concept of "gray zone operations" to frame political phenomena like subversion, influence operations and sabotage as acts of war (Stoker and Whiteside 2020).

In turn, with societies willing to sustain high levels of defense spending because of their reverence or faith in the military, or belief in the efficacy of force, a more ambitious and resource intensive grand strategy becomes possible; pursuit of such a grand strategy, in turn, may reinforce a sense that the state should invest heavily in defense and regularly employ force and engage in military interventions. Lasswell (1941), for example, famously argued that the growth of a large military establishment in response to external threats would intensify a state's martial tendencies and sustain the military's influence in the state. Such public support also enables an expansive force posture, including forward deployments of troops, extensive alliance commitments and the capability for foreign military interventions and operations overseas. In the United States, for example, the public's willingness to spend on the military has been essential to sustaining what some contend is the country's prevailing grand strategy of Liberal Hegemony (Posen

2015). As a corollary, Americans' belief in the efficacy of force and faith in the military could complicate efforts by adherents of a grand strategy of Restraint (who retain doubts about what can be accomplished with military force), or pacifist approaches to create constituencies beholden to their worldview. In short, relations between society and the military—and the public's views towards the utility of force—are an important influence on, or enabling factor for reliance on particular grand strategies, and an obstacle to the pursuit of others.

A country's strategic culture may also influence its grand strategy. Strategic culture can be conceptualized in different ways: as a factor in leaders' decision-making calculus or as informing the entire context of those decisions. Scholars of strategic culture might anticipate that deeply embedded strains of beliefs about the efficacy and appropriateness of force will yield continuities within a state's grand strategy over time. States are predisposed to different grand-strategic principles, premised on different roles and dependencies on force, for reasons rooted in their strategic cultures (Gray 1999; Johnston 1995; Poore 2003).

Civil–military relations may also constrain the resources available to leaders in formulating grand strategy via the cultural beliefs or preferences over the use of force that a particular military organization, or its subunits, hold. Both Jeff Legro (1995) and Elizabeth Kier (1997), for example, detail how different military organizations acquire distinctive beliefs about the efficacy of different weapons or doctrines. Theo Farrell (2005) describes how in the nineteenth century the Irish adopted a conventional structure for their military effort against the British when guerilla methods were better suited to their resources, in part because of global norms about what constitutes a legitimate state military. These cultural biases and preferences shape what the military sees as conceptually possible in the operational and tactical domain, how it develops doctrine, as well as the capabilities it can bring to bear on the battlefield. They therefore constrain the availability and nature of military tools in grand strategy.

The military's organizational interests in self-preservation and protecting its resources may also be another factor that checks political leaders' grand-strategic choices. In a fascinating study, for example, Stefano Recchia (2015) describes how US military leaders pressured political leaders to seek allies and endorsement from international organizations for military interventions in humanitarian crises in the 1990s. Military leaders sought to alleviate burden sharing and mitigate the risks and costs of unilaterally prosecuting these operations, even threatening to "veto" the interventions if multilateral support was not obtained. This reticence makes sense in context of Deborah Avant's (1996/97) analysis of the American military in the immediate post–Cold War era. She details resistance among many in the 1990s in the United States military to engage in military operations for humanitarian purposes, or for the purposes of stabilizing failing states. The preferences of the country's "reluctant warriors," as Avant put it, were a background factor in shaping the politics of US grand strategy. In fact, combined, Recchia's and Avant's analyses help explain a seeming paradox in US grand strategy in the 1990s: while military preferences may have constrained the pursuit of humanitarian intervention entailed by Liberal Internationalism (the reluctance of the military to intervene in the 1994 genocide in Rwanda being one example), they also promoted that grand strategy by requiring buy-in from international organizations in the interventions that occurred.

Similar dynamics may help illuminate the potential grand strategies available to political leaders in the United States in the contemporary era. On the one hand, military leaders may be amenable to a grand strategy of Restraint, in part because it reserves military force for major conventional threats, and discourages reliance on counterinsurgency in military interventions (Posen 2015). Restraint aligns better with military preferences to address conventional threats from peer competitors (Zenko 2018). Notwithstanding the rise of military leaders in the mid-2000s, central among them David Petraeus, which enabled a shift among some in the army and marines in favor of counterinsurgency doctrine, this is potentially a serious constraint on US grand strategy. Indeed, the abrupt shift back to great power competition in the United States under Donald Trump's presidency might be seen in part as a resurgence of these cultural views (Kaplan 2013). Hence, some features of Restraint may resonate well with military preferences and could push the US in that direction.

Alternatively, the military's organizational interests may push against those pro-Restraint impulses. The desire to reduce uncertainty and mitigate risk may compel military leaders to maintain extensive military alliances, including sustaining the North Atlantic Treaty Organization in its present form, which is at odds with the tenets of Restraint (Posen 2015). The desire to minimize uncertainty (Posen 1984; Van Evera 1984) may create a bias toward preventive war doctrines to mitigate potential threats, which could align military commanders' preferences with the views of proponents of a bellicose grand strategy (Kizer 2019, 39). Organizational interests in reducing uncertainty could also support a preference by military leaders for forward basing and robust alliances—measures that may allow for better scripted military plans with less contingencies for which to account, and ensure resources and allies are available. In sum, a grand strategy of Restraint, or of Liberal Hegemony, becomes more viable and available politically to leaders if an influential military buys in to its respective precepts—or each becomes more challenging to adopt, if it does not.

The impact of military preferences on grand strategy are likely to be even more acute in authoritarian or illiberal democracies. In these regimes, the military may exercise a veto over security matters and strategy, if not control them outright; military preferences are therefore paramount in understanding why a state adopts a particular grand strategy. In Pakistan, for example, civilian leaders have long needed to accommodate military leaders whose views shape the country's grand strategy (Shah 2014; Siddiqa 2003; Talbot 2002; Fair 2014). In Turkey, the military's dominance in the country's National Security Council in the latter twentieth century allowed it significant influence over security matters under successive civilian governments (Ozcan 2001; Robins 2003). Historically, political influence by militaries has at times proven profoundly pathological to the formulation and execution of grand strategy. Indeed, some authoritarian states may be inherently inclined toward revisionist aims because of the military's prominence in politics. Jessica Weeks (2012), for example, argues that when military leaders dominate in autocracies, states adopt strategies that incite wars or deliberately seek them out. Military dominance in a regime is a crucial explanatory variable in assessing the substance of a state's grand strategy.

THE CHARACTER OF GRAND STRATEGY

Civil–military relations may also affect the character of a state's grand strategy, and especially how integrated is that strategy. Integration refers to the internal consistency among the constituent elements of grand strategy such that they are self-reinforcing and synergistic (Brooks & Stanley 2007; Rosencrance and Stein 1993, 4). An example of disintegration would be a grand strategy that emphasized attaining security goals through active military interventions in failing states without a concomitant and complementary diplomatic approach or resource commitment to those conflicts. Integration also encompasses connections across the means–end chain, such that integration entails that military activity supports overarching political goals. Integration in the latter sense contributes to a state's strategic (in)effectiveness, or the ability to ensure that peacetime force structures and deployments and military operations and tactical engagements in wartime serve strategic purposes and political objectives. An example of this kind might be consistently supporting ongoing military operations that do not translate into success on the strategic or political level; winning battles, while failing to achieve the essential political objectives for which the war is ostensibly being fought. Through these mechanisms, civil–military relations can lead to bottom-up flaws in the military dimensions of grand strategy.

Scholars of civil–military relations have long warned of their potentially dire effects on political-military integration. Posen's (1984) seminal book, *The Sources of Military Doctrine*, explores the disconnect between how force is conceptualized and employed (what he frames as military doctrine) and the attainment of a state's political goals. Posen contends that incentives from competition in the international arena incline the political leadership to adopt a grand strategy, or doctrine, attuned to that stimuli. The military's organizational parochialism, however, favors the pursuit of force structures and strategies that protect autonomy and insulate the institution from uncertainty—whether or not those methods are attuned to external conditions and stimuli. The presence of civilian control, or the capacity of civilian leaders to oversee and rationalize military strategy, determines whether there is course correction, or disintegration persists; civilian influence is essential to assure that the military instrument is calibrated to political objectives (Snyder 1984, 1991).

Similarly, Eliot Cohen (2002) contends that civilian intervention in military affairs in wartime is essential to ensure that military activity aligns with larger politico-strategic objectives along the means–end chain. Building on Clausewitz's famous dictum about war's inherently political character, Cohen identifies sage civilian leadership in wartime as essential to accomplishing integration. Civilians' intervention in military activity at all levels is necessary to assure that the military is being employed in a manner that serves larger politico-strategic aims of the state. Without effective and comprehensive civilian control of the military, states are prone to adopt disintegrated grand strategies.

Other scholars argue the opposite: that civilian forbearance and respect for military autonomy will enable integration. They contend that civilian "micromanagement" leads to misguided or politically motivated plans and policies that are disconnected from the functional requirements of prosecuting military operations and thereby inhibit wartime success. These "professional supremacists," as Peter Feaver (2011) terms them and whom build from arguments in Samuel Huntington's (1957) seminal *The Soldier and the State*, link disintegration to overweening intrusion by civilians into what is seen as the military's proper domain of responsibility (Brooks 2020a). In other words, it is also possible that disintegrated grand strategy is more likely if civilians exercise too much control and intrude into military autonomy to design and execute military operations. Regardless, for many scholars, the balance of civilian authority and oversight over military affairs is a key determinant of the capacity to create an efficacious and integrated military component within states' grand strategies.

Yet, another body of scholarship focuses less exclusively on the presence or absence of civilian oversight, and more on the qualitative character of the strategic assessment process in which military and political leaders engage. Strategic assessment involves several key dimensions, including coordination among military and political officials, information sharing, a clear process for making decisions, and the bureaucratic competence of those state entities that provide supporting intelligence and analysis to officials at the apex (Brooks 2008).

Some configurations of civil–military relations have particularly damaging effects on strategic assessment, which harms their capacity to attune political goals with military activity. One set of cases prone to such pathologies occurs in states where political and military leaders both wield significant domestic political power and have divergent preferences over when and how force is to be used (Brooks 2008). It is harder to share information, rationalize analysis, and make authoritative decisions in these contexts. In Egypt, for example during the crisis prior to the start of the June 1967 war with Israel, the country's political and military leadership were intensely competing for control of the military with different preferences over the use of force; these dynamics greatly impeded the quality of strategic assessment and contributed to inciting a war that the country was ill-prepared to fight (Brooks 2008). This war damaged President Nasser's bid for leadership in the Arab world, and arguably proved the *coup de grâce* of his grand strategy of pan-Arabism and nonalignment. Similarly, in Iraq, Saddam Hussein's tendency to appoint loyalists to key positions in the military and to punish dissenters fostered an echo chamber for the autocrat's own biased assessments, leading to miscalculations and distortions in decision-making in its 1991 and 2003 wars led by the United States (Woods et al. 2006).

The provision of military advice within strategic assessment—how it is provided and the substance of that advice—is another factor that scholarship suggests might impact grand strategy, and especially how military tools are employed in pursuit of political and security objectives. Dick Betts (1977/1991) has shown that during the Cold War, US military leaders often were reticent to use force in international conflicts, but supported a major resource commitment once the choice to fight was made by political leaders. States in which military leaders often succeed in pushing civilians to approve a massive and enduring commitment of force in overseas conflicts could be prone to disintegrated grand strategies if those resource constraints are at odds with political goals.

Recent years have also seen an emerging debate about whether civil–military relations in the United States are well-suited to the process of strategic assessment at the senior levels of the US military and civilian leadership in the Department of Defense and White House. Some worry that prevailing norms governing military roles in those processes are harmful to strategic assessment (Golby and Karlin 2018; Davidson 2013). These norms reflect Samuel Huntington's objective control approach to civilian control of the military, outlined in his seminal book, *The Soldier and The State* (Huntington 1957). Objective control implies a modal form of interaction between military and political leaders with clear boundaries in the content and format of their exchanges: it supports a transactional approach, whereby military leaders deliver options when provided with clearly articulated goals and objectives, or what is often referred to as "guidance" (Brooks 2020a). These conventions, however, may not be well suited to the expedients civilians face in national security decision-making. Political leaders often want to know what is possible in the military domain before deciding among goals and priorities when managing a crisis or contemplating the use of force. As Golby and Karlin (2018, 144) put it, "In many cases, even setting political objectives requires a textured understanding of expected costs, troop commitments, conflict duration, the likelihood of success, the impact on other global contingencies, and military and political risks." Similarly, Huntington's norms may also undermine strategic assessment by hindering intellectual engagement with how political factors might bear on the efficacy of strategy or conduct of military operations (Binkley 2016, 251).

Consequently, scholars and analysts contend that those activities that blend or combine political and military activity and considerations may be "orphaned" in the advisory process (Lord 2015; Owens 2015, 92). These deficits in strategic assessment, in turn, could help explain why the US has experienced a pronounced political-strategic disconnect in its recent wars in Iraq and Afghanistan (Strachan 2010; Brooks 2020a). In sum—and broadly—how political and military leaders in states conceive of and carry out their respective roles could impact the strategic assessment process, with important implications for the integration of military tools with larger strategic and political goals.

EXECUTION AND IMPLEMENTATION OF GRAND STRATEGY

Civil–military relations may also affect grand strategy via their influence on the implementation and execution of those strategies. Execution refers to the capacity to win the wars, forge the alliances, and defend the interests pursuant to the principles underlying a state's grand strategy. Implementation refers to the capacity to develop supportive policies and capabilities consistent with grand strategy. States need to translate grand-strategic principles into actual behavior (Silove 2018), and especially into policies, doctrines, deployments, and equipment.

Civil–military relations can impede the execution of grand strategy when there are diverging policy preferences and mistrust among military and political leaders, and when politicians marginalize military leaders with whom they disagree. Donald Rumsfeld's relationship with the US military in the lead-up to the 2003 Iraq War is exemplary of this dynamic. Fundamental disagreements over "Transformation" of the US military plagued the relationship from the start; this disagreement then intensified over divergent expectations about the force commitment needed to stabilize Iraq after an invasion (Brooks 2008). Consequently, Rumsfeld marginalized those within the military with whom he disagreed, truncating search and analysis, which contributed to poor planning for the post-combat stabilization phase (Phase IV) of the war. The execution of George W. Bush's grand strategy, in which a transformative war in Iraq was a cornerstone, was hindered by dysfunctional civil–military relations and poor planning for the 2003 invasion.

One way that implementation suffers is through military contestation and pressure on procurement decisions. Military organizations, as described above, often have preferences over procurement and doctrinal choices that are shaped by their cultures, or organizational interests. States' grand strategies involve decisions about how military forces are structured and deployed that may conflict with those interests or preferences. They may require reductions or shifts in the type of equipment or forces on which a state relies and how many, and where they are based. A grand strategy of Restraint for example envisions significant cuts in the US Army, a narrowing of the roles and missions in the marines, while supporting the maintenance of naval capacity (Posen 2015). One can imagine major resistance from the army and marines, in particular, to the implementation of such a grand strategy. If a country cannot allocate resources appropriately and trim or adjust force structure, the state is unable to translate its grand strategy into supporting capabilities.

Military planning processes and organizational conventions may further complicate the translation of grand strategy into supporting capabilities, as Reich and Dombrowski (2018) contend occurs with the US Navy. Some have argued, for example, that the US military's economic and bureaucratic structure is ill-suited to adaptation of artificial intelligence (AI) and other emerging technologies (Olney 2019; Zegart and Childs 2018). Indeed, one possible impact of the adoption of AI and robotics is to reduce the role of the tactical warfighter and attenuate the command structure as machines take a greater role on the battlefield (Brooks 2018; Brooks 2020b). Combat arms engaged in tactical warfighting may consequently resist the adoption of technologies that produce these effects, stymieing essential innovation and organizational adaptation. The implementation of grand strategies that rely on these tools to reduce the costs of war might suffer as a consequence (Shifrinson 2019, 56).

Military leaders have a variety of means to subvert civilian leaders' power to translate grand-strategic goals into defense policy, deployments, doctrine, or procurement decisions. Some of these are inherent in the delegation relationship, in which military officers may exploit information asymmetries to slow-roll or shirk in carrying out decisions made by civilians (Feaver 2003). Yet the tactics can be far more direct and overt than bureaucratic resistance and delay. Even in democracies, in which militaries generally do not assume overt roles in politics, military leaders have a variety of political tactics they may employ that increase the domestic political costs or mobilize societal opposition to particular outcomes sought by civilians. These include making public statements in the press to appeal to public opinion, or leaking their views about the wisdom of a civilian leader's choices; they also include forging alliances with members of a country's legislative branch or aligning with interest groups (Brooks 2009).

One such example occurred during the Obama administration's 2009 review of strategy for the war in Afghanistan. During the review, a report by then commander of NATO forces in Afghanistan, General Stanley McChrystal, was leaked to the press. At the time, the military leadership strongly supported a troop intensive counterinsurgency (COIN) approach to the Afghan war, over a lighter footprint counterterrorism-centric orientation (Woodward 2010; Brooks 2020a). The number of troops recommended by McChrystal exceeded what Obama sought to commit, given his desire to move toward a reduced military commitment in the region. While the president ultimately signed on to a troop increase (although not the number McChrystal sought) and endorsed the COIN approach, as accounts of the episode frame it, Obama was constrained in his options by the leaked report. He would conceivably have faced a domestic political backlash had he chosen the counterterrorism approach at odds with military advice (Feaver 2009). While military leaders rejected claims that they were purposely seeking to limit the president, their political maneuvering likely complicated the ability to adjust US strategy in the war and pursue Obama's goal of reducing military commitments abroad. Obama is not alone in facing significant resistance from prominent military leaders as they pursued their political goals. President Bill Clinton faced efforts by then Chairman of the Joint Chiefs of Staff Colin Powell to marshal public opinion against US intervention in the Bosnian civil war (Kohn 1994). Decades earlier, President Dwight Eisenhower faced significant mobilization by elements in the military in opposition to his preferred military doctrine, massive retaliation, which was a key pillar of his grand strategy. In particular, General Matthew Ridgway saw the approach as a threat to the military profession's exclusive domain in regulating the conduct of war (Bacevich 1997).

Some political institutions, such as the presidential system in the United States, which divides executive and legislative authority, may provide particular opportunities for such mobilization. States in these circumstances may have a hard time translating their grand strategies into viable politico-military strategies, as Avant suggests the United States did during the Vietnam War (Avant 1994). Alternatively, military services may coalesce with civilian groups to influence military strategy and doctrine. Eisenhower foresaw the dangers that the "military industrial complex," as he termed it in his final speech as president, could produce for a grand strategy that emphasized economic growth and investment in the civilian sector over defense expenditure. Finally, a cartelized political system may also enable military services to coalesce with parts of society in "logrolls" to advance their interests. Jack Snyder (1991) describes how this process undermined both Wilhelmine Germany's grand strategy and that of Imperial Japan. A contemporary variant of that dynamic involves military services coalescing with defense industry corporations and members of the legislative branch to create "iron triangles" as leverage in procurement decisions.

One final pathway through which civil–military relations may affect the execution of grand strategy is through their effect on the military's effectiveness in armed conflict with the country's external adversaries. If a grand strategy is premised on defending against particular adversaries, or requires offensive action against others, the military's effectiveness in armed conflict will affect the execution of the state's grand strategy: that is, the military's capacity to translate basic resources into actual fighting power is essential to achieve grand-strategic aims.

One set of states, in particular, is likely to have major deficits in this regard: those whose autocratic leaders fear potential *coup d'etats* from their militaries. A large body of literature has explored how states that must coup-proof their militaries suffer serious deficiencies in their effectiveness in armed conflict. Leaders in these regimes organize civil–military relations in order to insulate themselves from coups, using tactics that complicate the coordination necessary for these conspiracies, or eliminate the incentive of military officers to engage in them (Brooks 1998; Quinlivin 1999). These measures can include distortions or overcentralization in command structures; suppression of training and junior officer initiative; appointments and promotions that heavily emphasize political versus meritocratic criteria; and a range of other measures. These methods can have deleterious effects on a military's organizational structure and its preparation for war; they impede the ability to marshal force effectively in battle against an adversary (Brooks 1998; Narang and Talmadge 2018; Pilster and Bohmelt 2011).

Research on autocracies in the Middle East, for example, has explored these tensions between organizing the military to prevent coups and to promote effective performances in war. Saddam Hussein, as Talmadge (2015) recounts, was only able to salvage his performance in his 1980s war with Iran when he relaxed some of the measures he employed to protect his regime against military coups. Other scholars have highlighted the deleterious effects of coup-proofing, especially when it involves privileging ethnic or sectarian allies in the regime, on the state's capacity to fight civil wars and fend off internal threats (Roessler 2016). These measures inhibit the acquisition of intelligence about opposing communities, undermining military effectiveness. Other scholars observe that external threats can harmonize civil–military relations (Desch 1999), potentially facilitating military effectiveness. While this literature exploring tensions between regime security and military effectiveness does not speak directly to "grand strategy," it clearly has implications for it. This scholarship suggests an entire class of states that will have a hard time implementing their grand strategy in the military domain, if not in formulating those strategies in the first place—this is especially dangerous in cases where these states harbor territorial ambitions or must guard against external and internal threats.

Conclusion

Civil–military relations have major implications for grand strategy. They can affect its substance, influencing the principles that comprise a state's grand strategy at any given time. They can affect grand strategy's character, and whether it is integrated across political, military, diplomatic, and economic domains, or instead fosters irreconcilable approaches. Civil–military relations can affect the implementation and execution of grand strategy, and whether the state is able to translate principles into supporting capabilities and policies and to employ resources effectively to prevail in wars and achieve diplomatic breakthroughs. Future research should do more to theorize and validate empirically these alternative impacts on grand strategy.

Today, scholars are engaged in an important debate about the merits of alternative grand strategies, seeking to identify through argumentation and empirical analysis the principled approaches that might best protect a state's security. Yet, pressures from civil–military relations may have an important effect not only in shaping the context in which analysts and scholars consider these options, and political leaders choose among them, but in the potential that the goals required of particular strategies can be realized. Understanding these constraints is therefore essential for both positive and normative analysis of grand strategy.

Notes

1. Civil–military relations encompass a variety of relationships. Many scholars focus on relations between civilian officials, political leaders and military leaders at the apex of state decision-making. Yet, civil–military relations also encompasses relations between society and the military institution, between state institutions and the military, and for some scholars includes aspects of intra-military relationships among leaders or units. See Brooks (2019).
2. Militarism pertains to societally held political values and cultural inclinations (Levy 2014). In may be useful to disaggregate the idea of militarism into social esteem for the

military institution; views toward the efficacy of force and its appropriate uses; and views towards war itself. It is possible that these attitudes may co-vary, but they might also be distinct. Despite the seeming contradictions, it is possible that a society could evince significant esteem for the military, belief in the efficacy of force over other tools of statecraft, amidst significant antiwar sentiment, or some other combination.

REFERENCES

Albertus, Michael. 2018. "The Military is Back in Brazil." *Foreign Policy*, October 29, 2018. https://foreignpolicy.com/2018/10/29/the-military-is-back-in-brazil/

Avant, Deborah. 1994. *Political Institutions and Military Change*. Ithaca, NY: Cornell University Press.

Avant, Deborah. 1996/97 "Are the Reluctant Warriors out of Control." *Security Studies* 6 (2) (winter) 1996–97): 51–90.

Bacevich, Andrew. 1997. "The Paradox of Professionalism: Eisenhower, Ridgway, and the Challenge to Civilian Control, 1953–1955." *Journal of Military History* 61 (2) (April): 3030–3033.

Bacevich, Andrew. 2005. *The New American Militarism*. Oxford University Press.

Betts, Richard K.1991/1977. *Soldiers, Statesmen, and Cold War Crises*. Columbia University Press.

Binkley, John. 2016. "Clausewitz and Subjective Civilian Control: An Analysis of Clausewitz's Views on the Role of the Military Advisor in the Development of National Policy." *Armed Forces and Society* 42 (2): 251–275.

Brooks, Risa. 1998. "Political-Military Relations and the Stability of Arab Regimes," Adelphi Paper 324, New York: Oxford University Press, 1998

Brooks, Risa. 2008. *Shaping Strategy: The Civil-Military Politics of Strategic Assessment*. Princeton, NJ: Princeton University Press.

Brooks, Risa. 2009. "Militaries and political activity in democracies." In Nielsen and Snider, eds., 213–239.

Brooks, Rosa. 2016. *How Everything Became War and the Military Became Everything: Tales from the Pentagon*. New York: Simon & Schuster.

Brooks, Risa. 2018. "Future War will Test US Civil-Military Relations." *War on the Rocks*, November 26, 2018. https://warontherocks.com/2018/11/technology-and-future-war-will-test-u-s-civil-military-relations/

Brooks, Risa. 2020a. "Paradoxes of Professionalism: Rethinking Civil-Military Relations in the United States." *International Security* 4 (4) (Spring): 7–44.

Brooks, Risa. 2020b. "The Civil-Military Implications of Emerging Technology." In *Reconsidering American Civil-Military Relations: The Military, Society, Politics, and Modern War*, edited by Lionel Beehner, Risa Brooks, and Daniel Maurer, 221–244. New York: Oxford University Press.

Brooks, Risa, and Elizabeth Stanley, eds. 2007. *Creating Military Power: the Sources of Military Effectiveness*. Stanford: Stanford University Press.

Center for a New American Security (CNAS). 2019. "New Voices in Grand Strategy." https://www.cnas.org/publications/reports/new-voices-in-grand-strategy

Cohen, Eliot A. 2002. *Supreme Command: Soldiers, Statesmen and Leadership in Wartime*. New York: Simon and Schuster.

Davidson, Janine. 2013. "The Contemporary Presidency: Civil-Military Friction and Presidential Decision-making: Explaining the Broken Dialogue." *Presidential Studies Quarterly* 43 (1).

Desch, Michael C. 1999. *Civilian Control of the Military: The Changing Security Environment*. Baltimore, MD: Johns Hopkins University Press.

Desch, Michael. 2006. 'Civil-Militarism: The Origins of the New American Militarism." *Orbis* 50 (3).

Fallows, James. 2015. "The Tragedy of the American Military." *The Atlantic*, January/February 2015.

Fair, C. Christine. 2014. *Fighting to the End: The Pakistan Army's Way of War*. New York: Oxford University Press.

Farrell, Theo. 2005. "World Culture and Military Power." *Security Studies* 14 (3) (July–September): 448–488.

Feaver, Peter D. 2003. *Armed Servants: Agency, Oversight, and Civil-Military Relations*. Cambridge, MA: Harvard University Press.

Feaver, Peter. 2011. "The Right to Be Right: Civil-Military Relations and the Iraq Surge Decision." *International Security* 35 (4).

Peter Feaver, "Bob Woodward Strikes Again! (McChrystal Assessment Edition)." *Foreign Policy*, September 21, 2009. https://foreignpolicy.com/2009/09/21/bob-woodward-strikes-again-mcchrystal-assessment-edition/

Gallup. 2019. "Confidence in Institutions." https://news.gallup.com/poll/1597/confidence-institutions.aspx

Golby, James, and Mara Karlin. 2018. "Why 'Best Military Advice' is Bad for the Military—and Worse for Civilians." *ORBIS* 68 (1) (Winter): 137–153.

Gray, Colin S. 1999. "Strategic Culture as Context: The First Generation of Theory Strikes Back." *Review of International Studies* 25: 49–69.

Huntington, Samuel P. 1957. *The Soldier and the State: The Theory and Politics of Civil-Military Relations*. Cambridge, MA: Harvard University Press.

Johnston, Alastair Iain. 1995. *Cultural Realism: Strategic Culture and Grand Strategy in Chinese History* Princeton, NJ: Princeton University Press.

Kaplan, Fred. 2013. "The End of the Age of Petraeus." *Foreign Affairs*, January 1, 2013.

Kershner, Isabel. 2019. "Generals are Back in Israel's Political Vanguard." *New York Times*, March 22, 2019.

Kier, Elizabeth. 1997. *Imagining War: French and British Military Doctrine between the Wars*. Ithaca, NY: Cornell University Press.

Kizer, Kate. 2019. "A US Grand Strategy for a Values Driven Foreign Policy." New Voices in Grand Strategy, CNAS, April 11, 2019. https://www.cnas.org/events/new-voices-in-american-grand-strategy

Kohn, Richard. 2009. "The Danger of Militarization in an Endless 'War' on Terrorism." *The Journal of Military History* 73 (1) (January).

Kohn, Richard. 1994. "Out of Control: The Crisis in Civil-Military Relations." *The National Interest*, March 1, 1994. https://nationalinterest.org/article/out-of-control-the-crisis-in-civil-military-relations-343

Lasswell, Harold D. 1941. "The Garrison State." *The American Journal of Sociology* 46 (4): 45–68.

Legro, Jeffrey. 1995. *Cooperation under Fire: Anglo-German Restraint during World War II*. Ithaca, NY: Cornell University Press.

Levy, Yagil. 2014. "What is Controlled by Civilian Control of the Military? Control of the Military vs. Control of Militarization." *Armed Forces & Society* 42 (1): 75–98.

Lissner, Rebecca. 2018. "What is Grand Strategy? Sweeping a Conceptual Minefield." *Texas National Security Review* 2 (1) (November): 52–73.

Lissner, Rebecca Friedman. 2019. "Military Intervention and the Future of American Grand Strategy." New Voices in Grand Strategy, CNAS, April 11. https://www.cnas.org/events/new-voices-in-american-grand-strategy

Lord, Carnes. 2015. "On Military Professionalism and Civilian Control." *Joint Force Quarterly* 78 (3rd Quarter).

Mann, Michael. 1987. "The Roots and Contradictions of Modern Militarism." *New Left Review* 1 (162) (March/April).

Narang, Vipin, and Caitlin Talmadge. 2018. "Civil-Military Pathologies and Defeat in War." *Journal of Conflict Resolution* 62 (7).

Nielsen SC, Snider DM, eds. 2009. *American Civil-Military Relations: The Soldier and the State in a New Era*. Baltimore, MD: Johns Hopkins University Press.

Olney, Rachel. 2019. "The Rift Between Silicon Valley and the Pentagon is Economic, Not Political." *War on the Rocks*, January 28, 2019.

Owens, Mackubin. 2015. "Military Officers: Political Without Partisanship." *Strategic Studies Quarterly* 9, no. 13 (Fall): 88–101.

Ozcan, Gencer. 2001. "The Military and the Making of Foreign Policy." In *Turkey in World Politics*, edited by Barry Rubin and Kemal Kirisci. Boulder: Lynne Rienner Press.

Pilster, Ulrich, and Tobias Bohmelt. 2011. "Coup-Proofing and Military Effectiveness in Interstate Wars, 1967–99." *Conflict Management and Peace Science* 28 (4): 1–20.

Poore, Stuart. 2003. "What Is the Context? a Reply to the Gray-Johnston Debate on Strategic Culture." *Review of International Studies* 29 (2) (April).

Posen, Barry. 2015. *Restraint: A New Foundation for US Grand Strategy*. Ithaca, NY: Cornell University Press.

Posen, Barry. 1984. *The Sources of Military Doctrine : France, Britain, and Germany between the World Wars*. Cornell Studies in Security Affairs. Ithaca, NY: Cornell University Press.

Quinlivin, J. 1999. "Coup-Proofing: Its Practice and Consequences in the Middle East." *International Security* 24 (Fall): 131–165.

Roessler, P. 2016. *Ethnic Politics and State Power in Africa: The Logic of the Coup–Civil War Trap*. Cambridge: Cambridge University Press.

Recchia, Stefano. 2015. *Reassessing the Reluctant Warriors: US Civil-Military Relations and Multilateral Intervention*. Ithaca, NY: Cornell University Press.

Robins, Philip. 2003. *Suits and Uniforms: Turkish Foreign Policy since the Cold War*. Seattle: University of Warosenshington Press.

Rosecrance, Richard, and Arthur A. Stein, "Beyond Realism: The Study of Grand Strategy." In *Domestic Bases of Grand Strategy*, edited by Richard Rosecrance and Arthur Stein, 3–21. Ithaca, NY: Cornell University Press.

Shaw, Aqil. 2014. *The Army and Democracy: Military Politics in Pakistan*. Cambridge, MA: Harvard University Press.

Shifrinson, Joshua R. Itzkowitz. 2019. "Requiem for a Dream: American Grand Strategy, 1991–2018." New Voices in Grand Strategy, CNAS, April 11, 2019. https://www.cnas.org/events/new-voices-in-american-grand-strategy

Siddiqa, Ayesha. 2003. *Pakistan's Arms Procurement and Military Buildup, 1979-99: In Search of a Policy*. London: Palgrave.

Silove, Nina. 2018. "Beyond the Buzzword. Three Meanings of Grand Strategy." *Security Studies* 27 (1).

Simon Reich and Peter Dombrowski. 2018. *The End of Grand Strategy: US Maritime Operations in the 21st Century*. Ithaca, NY: Cornell University Press.

Snyder, Jack. 1991. *Myths of Empire: Domestic Politics and International Ambition*. Ithaca, NY: Cornell University Press.

Snyder, Jack. 1984. "Civil-Military Relations and the Cult of the Offensive, 1914–1984." *International Security* 9 (1): 108–146.

Stoker, Donald, and Whiteside, Craig. 2020. "Blurred Lines: Gray-Zone Conflict and Hybrid War—Two Failures of American Strategic Thinking." *Naval War College Review* 73 (1/ 4). https://digital-commons.usnwc.edu/nwc-review/vol73/iss1/4

Strachan, Hew. 2010. "Strategy or Alibi? Obama, McChrystal, and the Operational Level of War." *Survival* 52 (5) (October–November): 157–182. doi.org/10.1080/00396338.2010.522104.

Talmadge, Caitlin. 2015. *The Dictator's Army: Battlefield Effectiveness in Authoritarian Regimes*. Ithaca, NY: Cornell University Press.

Talbot, Ian. 2002. "Does the army shape Pakistan's foreign policy?" In *Pakistan: Nationalism without a Nation?*, edited by Christophe Jaffrelot, 311–337. New Delhi, IN: Manohar.

Vagts, Alfred. 1959. *A History of Militarism: Civilian and Military*. Greenwich, Conn.: Meridian.

Van Evera, Stephen 1984. "The Cult of the Offensive and the Origins of the First World War." *International Security* 9 (summer): 58–107.

Weeks, Jessica. 2012. Strongmen and Straw Men: Authoritarian Regimes and the Initiation of International Conflict. *American Political Science Review* 106, no. 2, 326–347.

Woods, Kevin, et al. 2006 "Iraqi Perspectives Project: A View of Operation Iraqi Freedom from Saddam's Senior Leadership - Hussein's Distorted Worldview, Desert Storm, Regime Prepares for War, Baghdad Bob, Final Days" Joint Center for Operational Analysis (JCOA),United States Joint Forces Command (JFCOM).

Woodward, Bob. 2010. *Obama's Wars* New York: Simon and Schuster.

Zegart, Amy and Kevin Childs. 2018. "The Divide Between Silicon Valley and Washington is A National Security Threat." *The Atlantic*, December 13, 2018.

Zenko, Micah. 2018. "America's Military Is Nostalgic for Great Power Competition" Chatham House. https://www.chathamhouse.org/expert/comment/america-s-military-nostalgic-great-power-competition

CHAPTER 18

INDIVIDUAL PSYCHOLOGY AND GRAND STRATEGY

Romancing the State

BRIAN C. RATHBUN

THERE are two ways in which we can speak of individual psychology and its relevance for grand strategy. The first is at the level of elites. How is it that individual leaders have an effect on the substance and success of grand strategy? The other is at the level of the masses. What can we say about the psychology of the everyday man or woman, and how it bolsters or frustrates the efforts of their leaders in their grand-strategic pursuits? While both questions are located at the "first-image" of analysis, they are very different questions.

In this chapter, I first review the epistemological challenges of showing individual agency in international politics in a way that satisfies "positivist" criteria for good social science. The study of a single individual's impact on international relations is fraught with difficulty, and all the more so if one seeks to establish generalizable patterns with clearly specified causal mechanisms. It is one thing to show that individuals "matter," quite another to show how they matter and why and in such a way that can explain the impact of multiple leaders in different structural contexts. This is particularly challenging in the study of individuals' impact on grand strategy.

I then turn to how these problems are particularly pronounced for establishing how and why individuals matter for grand strategy, which likely explains why there is so little research on the subject. I make the case for a turn away from the substance of grand strategy towards a focus on leadership style. Whereas the substance of a grand strategy is hardly every truly individualist in origin, how and whether leaders pursue grand strategy is a function of their sense of agency, which varies across individuals. Romantics believe in the power of individuals to remake politics, whereas realists believe that individuals must conform to structural barriers, making the former much more likely than the latter to define grand foreign policy projects for their states. These two leadership styles emerge out of fundamentally different patterns of cognition: romantics are marked by their emotional, intuitive, and less procedurally rational psychology and realists by their deliberative and objective thinking style. Finally, I make the case that romantics are also better positioned, and more likely, to make the kind of appeals to public opinion that provide a mass basis for a grand strategy.

INDIVIDUALS, AGENCY, AND INTERNATIONAL RELATIONS

The study of individual action in international relations poses particular problems for those who embrace a "neopositivist" epistemological stance, which aims at establishing causal patterns that hold true across a variety of cases.[1] Whether this actually *is* the benchmark for scientific success remains a matter of contestation in the international relations field and beyond (Levine and Barder 2014). But for those who endorse it, neopositivist explanation aims "at showing that the event in question was not 'a matter of chance,' but was to be expected in view of certain antecedent or simultaneous conditions," and "seek[s] to identify *systematic* (rather than nonsystematic, or random) connections between factors that hold true across cases" (Jackson 2003, 229).

Showing that individuals have an impact on international relations is methodologically difficult because our focus of study involves the largest social collectives ever known to man. Given the sheer number of people involved, not to mention the causal factors operating at other levels of analysis—domestic institutions, the balance of power, cultural norms, transnational constitutive rules—it is almost impossible to pinpoint the causal effect of a single individual. How does one herd millions of figurative cats, what more against a pack of million dogs that fiercely resist?

However, the problem runs still deeper because IR scholars generally have (and I would say, *should* have) ambitions greater than establishing that individuals "matter" in foreign affairs (Byman and Pollack 2001). Although it is methodologically difficult to establish that the course of history would have been different had a state been led by a different leader, it is still, even if successful... boring. To "matter" is simply to say that things would have been different had a different individual been in the same place and made different choices. It meets a narrow definition of causal explanation in that X can be shown to have caused Y if Y only occurs in the presence of X and never in its absence (Campbell and Stanley 1966). However, it avoids the more intellectually satisfying contribution of explaining *how* things were different, or *why* it was that they were different.

Showing that individuals "matter" is useful as a corrective to deterministic structural theories that deny the effect of individuals in favor of the domestic and institutional structures that constrain them (Waltz 1979). Parachute pants were not the worst part of the 1980s for many IR scholars. Byman and Pollack's (2001) call to pay attention to the "great men" of history is really a rallying cry against systemic realism. However, this is only a negative contribution in that it tells us what is insufficient without offering much its place. Showing that individuals matter is generally just an effort to fill in what a positivist would call the "error term."

A more satisfying theoretical agenda for the individual level of analysis would be establishing systematic patterns in international politics and foreign-policymaking based on variation in individual-level traits, likely those of state leaders, with a clear articulation of causal mechanisms between those dispositional attributes and individuals' choices and behavior. Those attributes cannot be reduced simply to structural circumstances, whether ideational or material (Rathbun 2014). It might be, for instance, that domestic revolutions lead to revolutionary foreign policy by selecting for risk-tolerant leaders and undermining the usual institutional constraints that would tie their hands (Colgan and Weeks 2015). However, that is not an individual-level account of foreign affairs in any meaningful way since the true causal action operates at a higher level of analysis.

In other words, a proper individual-level account has to demonstrate agency (Dessler 1989). Most work in international relations—grand strategy studies included—tends to deny the significance of individual choices and decisions. Indeed, the absence of agency to some degree goes part and parcel with the neopositivistic epistemological standard to which so many aspire. Mainstream IR theory seeks to generate general theories by placing particular events in broader categories (Jackson 2003, 229). However if explanation amounts to arguing that "similarly positioned actors … would have arrived at the same conclusions and undertaken the same set of actions" then this amounts to "an elimination of agency—understood as the capacity to have acted otherwise," leaving so-called "agents who lack the ability to make meaningful choices." There are "mere throughputs for environmental factors," "*sites* in which factors beyond their control combine … to produce outcomes beyond their control" (Jackson 2003, 232).

Of course, individual-level attributes are themselves conditioned by structural factors, particularly social environment. The scholar must draw the line at some point in an individual's life when he or she has taken on a particular essence or disposition, whether it be ideology or risk propensity, and then assess the influence of those inclinations, while trying to hold other potential causal factors at other levels of analysis constant.

In doing so, there are a number of potentially dangerous and interrelated pitfalls. The first is establishing the relevant set of individual-level factors of potential causal relevance to the phenomenon of study. Individuals vary on so many dimensions that it can be hard to narrow down a list. There is the danger of both idiosyncrasy and availability. With respect to the former, it might be true that Napoleon sought to conquer Europe because he was short or that Kaiser Wilhelm II had a chip on his shoulder (figuratively) because his arm was withered (literally). To the extent that there are not a lot of withered arms (although probably more variation in height), this is not a good candidate for the establishment of patterns beyond the specific case. Again, it might be true that the Kaiser's boyhood injury "mattered" by affecting his behavior later in life, but this is different than a theoretical account based on systematic individual differences.

Unsurprisingly, there is a strong correlation between the low bar of leaders mattering and idiosyncratic explanations.

In the search for less idiosyncratic data, however, we face the temptation of the drunkard's search, in which the souse looks for his keys under the lamp post, not because they are likely to be there, but because that is where the light is. Looking for patterns, we need multiple observations, so we look for things that are easily observable, even if these are not necessarily the most relevant factors. In international relations, the tendency is to measure whatever factors we can, even if they lack clear causal implications. For instance, Horowitz et al. (2015) code the professional background, educational level, and military service of hundreds of leaders—factors that, even if statistically associated with certain foreign policy behaviors, are confounded with any number of factors that are more plausibly important but harder to measure.

Yet in choosing the most interesting and promising individual-level factors, the analyst must be careful to avoid tautology. The most likely "causes" of behavior "Y"— whether it be the nation's use of force, its propensity to join international organizations, or its inclination to incite trade wars—are beliefs about the likely utility of military force, the gains of multilateralism, or the benefits of economic coercion, respectively. Yet reducing foreign economic policy to the belief that "trade wars are good and easy to win" is akin to showing that leaders have beliefs and act on the basis of those beliefs—likely true, but not much of an explanation. Moreover, we are likely to find such supporting evidence expressed in the context of the event to be explained itself, making it hard to establish a firm causal order.

Individuals, Agency, and Grand Strategy

The difficulties inherent in establishing the effect of individuals on international relations in a way that goes beyond saying that individuals matter, while steering clear of the pitfalls identified above, is particularly acute in the study of grand strategy. This likely explains why there are so few contributions to this literature that systematically account for the phenomenon by reference to variation in individual-level attributes. In fact, I cannot find any. Leaders play a role in many social scientific accounts but largely as the sites and throughputs that Jackson (2003) identifies. There are of course innumerable and valuable accounts of the exploits of great men of history, but these are, understandably, more descriptive and historiographic rather than generalizable and social scientific.

Any grand strategy seems to require an ideational component (Legro 2016). Grand strategy identifies at its minimum a set of long-term goals of the state and a sense of how to achieve them (Edelstein and Krebs 2015). Were these not ideational and instead forced upon the state by its material environment, there would be no need to strategize, which is an active, cognitive, deliberative process. Grand strategy, given its grandness, must likely be supplemented by a sense of meaning, a narrative of the country's purpose with reference to historical achievements and guiding values that hold the state together (Krebs 2015). The material environment does not just provide this, although it likely shapes the plausibility and therefore possibility of adopting different strategies. It would be hard for the leader of Bulgaria to maintain that his state had a special mission to spread freedom around the world.

An individual-level account of grand strategy could therefore demonstrate the effect of a leader's truly unique worldview on its foreign policy and potentially international relations more broadly, for better or for worse. Yet even a quick, top-of-the-head rundown of the "great men" of history does not yield many plausible candidates for such an individualist account. The ideas that have driven the grand strategies of those to whom we have erected monuments are rarely original but rather emerge out of broader ideological movements. Wilson did not invent, but rather championed, the application of progressive liberal ideas to international affairs. Where would Lenin have been without Marx? Reagan's vision owed substantially to the neoconservative movement that had done the intellectual legwork (Krebs 2015; Rathbun 2019). Bush's War on Terror seemed to be a warmed-over version of the latter, substituting al Qaeda for the Communist International (Krebs and Lobasz 2007). In other words, many of our potential individual game-changers are throughputs for the ideas they adopted in social milieus operating at a different level of analysis. These are not second-image but more of a meso-level of small groups that we could call domestic politics as opposed to domestic institutions (Rathbun 2004).

Moreover, if it were the case that some grand strategies are born in the figurative vacuum of a truly individual mind, these ideas become by definition idiosyncratic and therefore nongeneralizable. In other words, there is a constant tension between demonstrating the causal impact of individuals' ideas on grand strategy and developing generalizable theories. Even if we can establish that Mao had a fundamentally different set of ideas about international politics than anyone who had ever come before him, we just then call it Maoism, which is another way of saying that it has no broader implication for any other state's grand strategy. It is relevant only to a particular time and place since it was wholly original. The study of individuals and grand strategy becomes the documentation of the great feats of great men—which is to say, history. Individual-level accounts are too... individual.

An individual's contribution to grand strategy likely consists of packaging in a novel way ideas already present in the surrounding social milieu. Hitler, for whom we can make a pretty good case that he had a grand strategy with international effects, wedded social Darwinist "theories" with a new populism already present in the German right before the First World War (Weikart 2004; Eley 1980). Even so, this is not really a social scientific account of Nazi grand strategy at the individual level. Either these ideas would have eventually come together anyhow, under the leadership of some other entrepreneurial psychopath, or Hitler was a political genius, which is another way of saying that he was *sui generis* and cannot serve as the foundation for some broader individualist account of grand strategy.

Most ideational accounts of grand strategy (or other related constructs such as foreign policy culture) note the presence of distinct ideological subgroups offering alternative ways of thinking about a state's foreign policy purpose and how to achieve it. For instance, many note the struggles in the United States between isolationists, unilateralists, neoconservatives, liberals internationalists, and multilateralists throughout the years (Legro 2016; Krebs 2015; Rathbun 2008; Dueck 2008). In linking these alternative foreign policy grand strategies to political parties, Rathbun (2012) tries to avoid the pitfalls of idiosyncrasy while simultaneously offering a systematic account of who is most likely to favor a multilateral grand strategy. Joining NATO and the UN, and designing them in a particularly multilateral way, was not unique to President Harry Truman, for instance. As part of a progressive strategy with roots that go back to Woodrow Wilson, these policies were natural expressions of the Democratic Party's core ideological values. There is therefore agency, but individuals are still sites.

What about a more comprehensive account of grand strategy based on systematic variation in individual-level variables other than ideology? Here again the nature of grand strategy makes this methodological approach more difficult than in the study of other areas of foreign-policymaking. Many of the variables we find under the lamp post are much more likely candidates for affecting the general conflict behavior of states than for accounting for sustained efforts at grand strategy. Consider risk again. The relationship between risk tolerance and grand strategy is unclear. Grand strategy implies a deliberate strategy to achieve goals, and potentially therefore some dissatisfaction with the status quo, suggesting that risk-acceptant leaders are more likely to formulate such designs. However, grand strategy also implies a deliberate process of cost–benefit analysis, which is more likely to mark risk-neutral or risk-avoidant individuals.

Horowitz and Stam (2014) also evaluate the effect of military background. Even if leaders with military experience are more likely to include a coercive element in their grand strategy, this is hopelessly indeterminate. Coercion takes many forms. Is it the creation of buffer zones through territorial conquest or simply balancing power? Military background could lead to a preference for either of these very different strategies. This same indeterminacy could be said to mark other individual-level variables identified by Byman and Pollack (2001) as relevant for showing that individuals "matter." Does being delusional make one more likely to pursue a grand strategy? Does it encourage the grandiosity inherent in believing that one control the destiny of a state's future? Or does it make the leader incoherent and incapable of sustained action?

Other variables are potentially more useful. Resolve as an individual trait seems to be a likely necessary or sufficient condition for sustained effort at grand strategy. Kertzer (2016) shows that a concern for honor, longer time horizons, and higher risk propensity predict a willingness to persevere. Honor can change the decision-making calculus of individuals (Renshon 2017), adding an intrinsic desire for face, prestige, and status that might make the use of force more likely. Yarhi-Milo (2018) argues that some leaders are more concerned with their images than others, and it might be that these types need a prestige project like a grand strategy. Longer time horizons focus the leader's mind on the desirability of the abstract goals one is pursuing rather than the short-term constraints and problems that one has to solve in getting there (Rapport 2015).

Style over Substance: Leadership Style, Psychology, and Grand Strategy

I propose that the individual-level variables most likely to systematically affect grand strategy are those that determine the style rather than the substance of foreign-policymaking. This requires a new focus on how leaders govern rather than what they try to accomplish (Hermann et al. 2001), although the two are linked. A complete empirical account would of course necessitate specifying the latter but with an acknowledgment that substance cannot truly emerge spontaneously from the individual level. This is certainly not the only potentially fruitful avenue.

Herrmann et al. note a consistent dichotomy in the conceptualizations of leadership style between "one type of leader ... guided by a set of ideas, a cause, a problem to be solved, or an ideology" and another that "arises out of the nature of the leadership context or setting in which the leader finds him or self" (2001, 86). The distinction goes by various names: crusader vs. pragmatist, ideologue vs. opportunist, and transformational vs. transactional. In recent work (Rathbun 2019), I have made use of a distinction between *realists* and *romantics* that is heavily reliant on this bifurcation, and I use those terms in the following discussion. The framework seems ready-made for application to grand strategy in both specifying whether leaders even attempt anything like a grand strategy and also, if they do, how they will attempt to implement it. Not every leader will attempt a grand strategy. Most will probably muddle through. And even if they have such ambitions, there are different ways at going about it that will also likely vary based on leadership style.

The most important distinction between the realist and the romantic is their sense of agency, in life and in international relations. A belief in agency is inherent in any attempt to shape a grand strategy. There is no point in planning if one is powerless against the structural forces of international politics. Foreign policy will be a pure function of events, dear readers, events. Yet not all leaders are in agreement about how much room for choice there is even when they share the same structural position. Just as international relations scholars disagree about how much room there is for agency in international politics, so do actual foreign-policy practitioners. We might think of them as lay IR theorists. To the extent that structural circumstances are not the ultimate cause of these beliefs—which might be the case, for instance, if the leaders of weak and vulnerable countries always eschew grand strategies whereas those of stronger countries always formulate an overall design—these different views are themselves the product of human agency. In other words, leaders have the agency and choice about whether to believe in structure and how much weight to give it.

Variation in beliefs about agency is not new in international relations but has been largely forgotten. It is a crucial element in the operational code literature. George (1969) identifies as a core element of the "philosophical content" of an operational code, "How much 'control' or 'mastery' can one have over historical development?" This will have obvious implications for the answers of other central elements such as "What are the prospects for the eventual realization of one's fundamental political values and aspirations?", "What is the role of 'chance' in human affairs and in historical development?", "Is the political future predictable? In what sense and to what extent?" These questions can all be asked of leaders independently of any knowledge about their foreign policy goals, although answers to them will affect how leaders define goals.

Romantics have a profound sense of agency. As Hermann et al. describe, for romantics, "constraints are things to be overcome or dealt with, not accepted; they are obstacles in the way but are viewed as not insurmountable" (2001, 88). For romantics, according to Isaiah Berlin,

> The necessities of which the universe is composed are no longer "given," no longer imposed upon us as an objectively necessary reality whose laws are either recognized for what they are or else ignored to our cost. Man is not... a passive observer who can accept or reject a world which is what it is, whether he likes it or not. He is in virtue of being a "subject" wholly active. His "activity" consists not in contemplation but in imposing principles or rules of his own making upon the prima facie inert mass of nature. (2014, 236)

Romantics believe in the power of individuals, even when pitted against broad, impersonal structural forces.

Realists, in contrast, believe that policy must adjust to circumstances. According to E.H. Carr, "The realist analyses a predetermined course of development which he is powerless to change" (1964, 12). Realism "tends to emphasize the irresistible strength of existing forces and the inevitable character of existing tendencies" (1964, 10). The "utopian is necessarily voluntarist; he believes in the possibility of more or less radically rejecting reality," whereas realists "arrange their policies to suit the realities of world." As Herrmann et al. describe, "They seek to tailor their behavior to fit the demands of the situation in which they find themselves" (2001, 87).

We should not hastily conclude, however, that realists have *no* sense of agency in international relations. Classical realists at least spend just as much effort prescribing good foreign policy practice as they do explaining and describing the true nature of foreign affairs (Zarnett 2014, 3). Morgenthau admits this, "Political realism contains not only a theoretical but also a normative element" (1948, 7). This indicates that, for many prestructural realists, we should not take for granted that international structure will dictate foreign policy. Individual leaders have differing abilities and willingness to recognize the constraints that they are under. Heeding structure is itself an act of individual agency. Nevertheless, classical realists advise against the pursuit of a romantic foreign policy, a crusade with little connection to the vital interests of a country (Morgenthau

1948). Making the world safe for democracy might be desirable, but it is not feasible. Resources must be conserved for the more important and achievable battles. The fact that these classical realists bother offering their advice rather than just their analysis indicates that they think there is some room for maneuver.

Moreover, realist practitioners at least have an appreciation for the great complexity of international affairs. Agency matters a great deal, but it is entirely clear what consequences leaders' actions might have in a world that might go to war when a butterfly flaps its wings. Bismarck for instance had a profound sense of intellectual modesty. Given the inability to predict the consequences of one's actions—how others will react, how others will react to that reaction—the best thing to do is often to do nothing (Rathbun 2019).

For these reasons, realists are practitioners of pragmatic statecraft (Rathbun 2014). Therefore it is not surprising that those who advocate against the articulation of fixed grand strategy term their approach "pragmatic" (Edelstein and Krebs 2015). That approach is realist in that it identifies "specific challenges in lieu of searching for an overarching foreign policy doctrine" and advises an "experimental approach" to foreign policy. That approach exhibits agency, not in the form of a stubborn belief that the world is of our making, but rather by adapting strategy to circumstances based on whether it is working or not. Morgenthau would be proud: "A statesman ... is to be guided by circumstances; and judging contrary to the exigencies of the moment, he may ruin his country forever" (Morgenthau 1946, 221). Realists judge each problem on its own merits and eschew the formulation of universal principles or solutions (Carr 1964, 16). To the extent that realists have a grand strategy, it is a grand strategy of not being grand.

Romantics are therefore more likely to pursue a grand strategy in the first place. Based on their belief in agency, they do not trim their own sails or pull their punches. They believe that their state can achieve great things. Realists are more likely to simply manage the ship of state, careful not to set out ambitions that cannot be achieved.[2] Romantics are more likely to offer a narrative, an idealistic cause that their country symbolizes, whereas the latter will likely define state goals in narrower, material terms. It is not impossible for the realist to have a grand strategy. Bismarck had the ultimate aim of the unification of Germany under Prussian dominance. However, he did so in a particularly realistic way—with long time horizons, a carefully plotted series of steps, and a recognition that he was likely not to succeed given factors beyond his control. This recognition of structural forces is likely crucial for explaining his agentic legacy.

Where does this variation come from? Romantics and realists have very different cognitive styles. The former

> act like the classic cognitive misers from the information processing literature ... The cognitive miser ... is guided by schemas or images that define the nature of reality. They rely on simple rules or heuristics in making a choice, engaging in top-down information processing in which information is sought to maintain or strengthen the original schema. These leaders start with the conceptualization of what might be

present and then look for confirming evidence biasing the processing mechanism to give the expected result. (Hermann 2001, 92)

In Tetlock's (2017) terms, romantics are hedgehogs, more reliant on what psychologists call System I thinking (Kahnemann 2011). Their cognition is based more on gut instinct and emotion, rather than active and conscious deliberation and more likely to exhibit the heuristics and biases uncovered by generations of behavioral economists and psychologists (Rathbun 2019).

Realists, in contrast,

> engage in bottom-up information processing; rather than imposing structure on the data, they are guided by the evidence they are receiving from the environment. They are likened to naïve scientists who seek to learn if their initial reactions to a problem are supported by the facts, or to use information from the environment to develop a position. In other words, such leaders consider what among a range of alternative scenarios is possible in the current context. (Hermann et al. 2001, 92–93)

Their cognition is more procedurally rational. These foxes rely more than hedgehogs on System II processing. Realists also have an uncanny ability to suppress common emotional reactions that interfere with good judgment, such as belief assimilation, sunk-cost bias, short-term thinking, and an inability to understand objectively how others might perceive our actions.

More committed to developing an objective picture of the world around them, realists are less likely to simply see what they want to see, and more likely to be honest about the constraints that impinge on the achievement of their desires. Their objectivity makes them more structuralist. The romantic, in contrast, is resistant to an acknowledgment of the obstacles in his or her path, facilitating the belief in agency.

As a result, romantics and realists exhibit different levels of resolve and risk-acceptance. The former place great emphasis on the importance of will, highlighted as important in recent research on conflict behavior (Kertzer 2016). Although there is no guarantee of success, what heroes lack in objective power, they make up for in their intensity of commitment and their force of will. "Those with great will simply do not accept structural barriers to action." Instead, "the general or statesman or thinker ... knows how to will, that is, how to shape the less or more recalcitrant materials with which his life provides him to the pattern which is demanded by the real self whose presence he feels at his most exalted" (Berlin 2014, 225). Central to romanticism is the concept of *Streben*, or "striving." In colloquial terms, where there is a will, there is a way. Resolve is the manifestation of a belief in agency. Realists are more inclined to believe in the objective constraints of power.

Romantics are likely to be more risk-acceptant in their choices, although they are unlikely to acknowledge that fact. Rather they allow the desirability of their goals to influence their beliefs about feasibility, thus downplaying the risk–reward tradeoff generally inherent in any political action. Romantics are best described as risk-oblivious, leading them to act in such a manner that could be described by outsiders as risk-acceptant. Realists are more inclined to independently evaluate desirability and feasibility, making them more risk-averse in contrast. They will exhibit risk-acceptant tendencies only in situations in which vital interests are in question. The resolve and risk-acceptance of romantics is likely a double-edged sword when it comes to the implementation of a grand strategy. On the one hand, an inability to adjust in light of incoming information, what a rationalist calls "updating," can drain the resources of a state in a failing endeavor. On the other hand, by virtue of their strong commitments and resolve, they are more willing to pay such costs, contributing to an ability to wear out opponents.

Extreme realists and extreme romantics are likely to be rare in international relations, albeit for different reasons. Nevertheless, the extremes serve as a useful dimension for thinking about relative differences between leaders that might affect their tendency towards grand-strategic thinking. Realism is a demanding cognitive standard, as it presumes a deep commitment to rational thinking (Rathbun 2018). All human beings rely on heuristics, for instance, to save psychological energy, something likely to be particularly pronounced in situations of high workload common to state leaders. Moreover, international politics is often more complicated than other types of politics given the interdependence among states and the ambiguity of information (Rathbun 2007), making heuristics particularly attractive. Extreme romantics are rare because they are less likely to rise to the highest levels of politics. Not knowing how to lose battles and win wars, they are bad chess players. To the extent that getting to the point of implementing a grand-strategic vision requires that one reach the top levels of politics, an unwillingness to compromise, to go along to get along, are hindrances to achievement (Rathbun 2019).

Tell Me a Story: Romantics and Public Opinion

Leaders cannot pursue grand strategies alone. Even in nondemocratic societies, they require societal buy-in. Grand strategies, unless retrenching in nature, are major efforts at mobilization of a country's resources. This raises the question of mass psychology. How is it that leaders are able to rouse public opinion towards such an endeavor, particularly when it might require some degree of personal sacrifice on the part of the everyman?

This question was long ignored during the structural turn in international relations, which black-boxed the state and implicitly assumed that external threat would do the trick in sobering up even the biggest louses in the saloons towards a collective effort. But even (perhaps especially) realists are now taking this question seriously (Taliaferro 2006). Christensen treats the ability to mobilize the public as an intervening variable between external challenges and strategies to cope with them. This "neoclassical" realist approach turns back to classical forefathers. Morgenthau writes, in pages of *Politics among Nations* that are almost never read,

> National morale is the degree of determination with which a nation supports the foreign policies of its government in peace or war. It permeates all activities of a nation, its agricultural and industrial production as well as its military establishment and diplomatic service. In the form of public opinion, it provides an intangible factor without whose support no government, democratic or autocrat, is able to pursue its policies with full effectiveness. (1948, 140).

Pure material power is not enough to pursue a grand strategy, Morgenthau implies.

> A government may have a correct understanding of the requirements of foreign policy and of the domestic politics to support them, but if it fails in marshaling public opinion behind these policies, its labors will be in vain, and all the other assets of national power of which the nation can boast will not be used to best advantage. (1948, 154)

By one prominent way of thinking about public opinion, generating mass support is not particularly problematic so long as elites themselves agree. "Elite cue" theory argues that people, being uninformed about politics in general and foreign policy in particular, rely on information given to them by those who govern them (Kertzer and Zeitzoff 2017). If they see agreement, they follow along. If this is the case, mass public opinion is endogenous to the elite game of politics and therefore the first image matters little.

This school of thought implies that *how* leaders talk to their citizens makes little difference, just that they do. They could make a simple pragmatic case based on dollar and cents, and the public would dutifully follow along. Others, however, argue that precisely because the public is different than elites they respond to different types of arguments—more simple, moralistic, and emotional. Morgenthau writes,

> The kind of thinking required for the successful conduct of foreign policy must at times be diametrically opposed to the kind of considerations by which the masses and their representatives are likely to be moved. The peculiar qualities of the statesman's mind are not always likely to find a favorable response in the popular mind. The statesman must think in terms of the national interest, conceived as power among other powers. The popular mind, unaware of the fine distinctions of the statesman's thinking, reasons more often than not in the simple moralistic and legalistic terms of absolute good and absolute evil. (1948, 152)

Christensen takes this line as well, "Citizens are more likely than state elites to adopt highly stylized and ideological views of international conditions and proper policy responses to them. Therefore, leaders need to sell expensive policies by stating them in easily digestible ways, shunning complicated logic about abstract or long-term threats" (1993, 17). In Krebs' terms, popular mobilization requires not an "argument" but a "story."

The former "seeks to persuade the audience of the correctness of a course of action"; the latter is characterized instead by "setting the scene, organizing events into a causal sequence, identifying and characterizing protagonists ... [It] transports audiences into a world of meaning" (2015, 37–38).

In the terms used above, romantics are better positioned to inspire public opinion. Romantics articulate foreign policy in terms of a struggle between good vs. evil. They highlight the necessity of sacrifice, but also tell a story about how the good guys will eventually win (or at least maintain their honor by trying). After all, the term romantic comes from the Latin stem "roman," meaning story. Realists will not do as well in mobilizing the public, however. Even realists generally acknowledge this. Carr observes, "The necessity, recognized by all politicians both in domestic and international affairs, for cloaking interests in a guise of moral principles is in itself a symptom of the inadequacy of realism." Morgenthau notes, "The statesman must take the long view, proceeding slowly and by detours, paying with small losses for great advantage; he must be able to temporize, to compromise, to bide his time. The popular mind wants quick results; it will sacrifice tomorrow's real benefit for today's apparent advantage" (1948, 152). No one likes a political realist, as has been observed. He or she will likely need to sell a realist strategy by cloaking it in moralistic and emotional language.

So far, however, there has been nothing in the way of systematically testing how variation in the nature of public appeals matters for sustaining public opinion in the pursuit of a grand strategy. There is good reason for this. Grand strategies occur over long periods of time, yet most efforts to gauge public opinion are snapshots at a particular point in time given the inherent difficult in measuring mass attitudes over decades. Moreover, the effect of framing is best established experimentally through manipulation, which is only suited to cross-sectional data.

Conclusion

Any complete empirical account of grand strategy cannot rely exclusively on style. If leaders have a cause bigger than themselves that they pursue despite, indeed oblivious of, the odds, what is that cause? However, given that very few individuals have purely individual ideas (and if they did, these would by definition be nongeneralizable and therefore difficult to incorporate into a generalizable account), the substance of grand strategy is best thought of as exogenous in an individual-based account. This points the way towards a division of labor between the study of grand strategy at other levels of analysis. Whereas leadership style is more than other variables truly dispositional in nature, the substance of grand strategy likely comes from an ideational milieu operating at a higher level of analysis.

The individual level is therefore likely indispensable for the study of grand strategy but also inherently incomplete. Grand strategy implies grandiosity, a sense of agency that one can make a fundamental impact in a highly structured environment, that we should not assume is equivalent across leaders. And yet, just what individuals do with this agency is never wholly a function of their own dispositional nature.

The substance of their agenda, and how it is framed, is also likely to greatly affect public opinion, whose support is certainly necessary for the success of any strategy that is truly grand. Given that there has not been much in the way of social scientific research on individual psychology and grand strategy, this essay is more a call to arms (with specific marching orders) than anything else.

Notes

1. Under this understanding, "scientific realism" would also be considered neopositivistic. For a review of epistemology and IR, see Monteiro and Ruby (2019). For defenses of scientific realism, see Wendt (1999); Joseph and Wight (2010).
2. There is an irony in this, in that contemporary academic realists are very taken with grand strategy. I would argue that they have a grand strategy that consists merely of undoing liberal American grand strategy.

References

Berlin, Isaiah. 2014. *Political Ideas in the Romantic Age: Their Rise and Influence on Modern Thought*. Princeton: Princeton University Press.

Byman, Daniel L., and Kenneth M. Pollack. 2001. "Let Us Now Praise Great Men: Bringing the Statesman Back in." *International Security* 25 (4): 107–146.

Campbell, Donald T., and Julian C. Stanley. 1966. *Experimental and Quasi-Experimental Designs for Research*. Chicago: Rand Mcnally.

Carr, E.H. 1964. *The Twenty Years' Crisis, 1919–1939: An Introduction to the Study of International Relations*. London: Macmillan.

Colgan, Jeff D., and Jessica Weeks. 2014. "Revolution, Personalist Dictatorships, and International Conflict." *International Organization* 69 (1): 163–194.

Dessler, David. 1989. "What's At Stake in the Agent-Structure Debate?" *International Organization* 43 (3): 441–473.

Dueck, Colin. 2008. *Reluctant Crusaders: Power, Culture, and Change in American Grand Strategy*. Princeton: Princeton University Press.

Edelstein, David M., and Ronald R. Krebs. 2015. "Delusions of Grand Strategy: The Problem with Washington's Planning Obsession." *Foreign Affairs* 94 (6): 109–116.

Eley, Geoff. 1980. *Reshaping the German Right: Radical Nationalism and Political Change after Bismarck*. New Haven: Yale University Press.

George, Alexander L. 1969. "The 'Operational Code': A Neglected Approach to the Study of Political Leaders and Decision-Making." *International Studies Quarterly* 13 (2): 190–222.

Hermann, Margaret G., Thomas Preston, Baghat Korany, and Timothy M. Shaw. 2001. "Who Leads Matters: The Effects of Powerful Individuals." *International Studies Review* 3 (2): 83–131.

Horowitz, Michael C., and Allan C. Stam. 2014. "How Prior Military Experience Influences the Future Militarized Behavior of Leaders." *International Organization* 68 (3): 527–559.

Horowitz, Michael C., Allan C. Stam, and Cali M. Ellis. 2015. *Why Leaders Fight*. Cambridge: Cambridge University Press.

Jackson, Patrick Thaddeus. 2003. "Defending the West: Occidentalism and the Formation of NATO." *Journal of Political Philosophy* 11 (3): 223–252.

Joseph, Jonathan, and Colin Wight, eds. 2010. *Scientific Realism and International Relations*. Houndmills, Basingstoke: Palgrave Macmillan.

Kahneman, Daniel. 2011. *Thinking, Fast and Slow*. New York: Farrar, Straus and Giroux.

Kertzer, Joshua D. 2016. *Resolve in International Politics*. Princeton: Princeton University Press.

Kertzer, Joshua D., and Thomas Zeitzoff. 2017. "A Bottom-Up theory of Public Opinion About Foreign Policy." *American Journal of Political Science* 61 (3): 543–558.

Krebs, Ronald R. 2015. *Narrative and the Making of US National Security*. Cambridge: Cambridge University Press.

Krebs, Ronald R., and Jennifer K. Lobasz. 2007. "Fixing the Meaning of 9/11, Hegemony, Coercion, and the Road To War in Iraq." *Security Studies* 16 (3): 409–451.

Legro, Jeffrey W. 2016. *Rethinking the World: Great Power Strategies and International Order*. Ithaca: Cornell University Press.

Levine, Daniel J., and Alexander D. Barder. 2014. "The Closing of the American Mind: American School International Relations and the State of Grand theory." *European Journal of International Relations* 20 (4): 863–888.

Monteiro, Nuno P., and Keven G. Ruby. 2009. "IR and the False Promise of Philosophical Foundations." *International Theory* 1 (1): 15–48.

Morgenthau, Hans J. 1946. *Scientific Man vs. Power Politics*. Chicago: University of Chicago Press.

Morgenthau, Hans J. 1948. *Politics Among Nations: The Struggle For Power and Peace*. New York: Alfred A. Knopf.

Rapport, Aaron, 2015. *Waging War, Planning Peace: US Noncombat Operations and Major Wars*. Ithaca: Cornell University Press.

Rathbun, Brian C. 2004. *Partisan Intervention: European Party Politics and Humanitarian Intervention in the Balkans*. Ithaca: Cornell University Press.

Rathbun, Brian C. 2007. "Uncertain about Uncertainty: Understanding the Multiple Meanings of a Crucial Concept in International Relations Theory." *International Studies Quarterly* 51 (3): 533–557.

Rathbun, Brian C. 2008. "Does One Right Make A Realist? Conservatism, Neoconservatism, and Isolationism in the Foreign Policy Ideology of American Elites." *Political Science Quarterly* 123 (2): 271–300.

Rathbun, Brian C. 2012. *Trust in International Cooperation: International Security Institutions, Domestic Politics and American Multilateralism*. Cambridge: Cambridge University Press.

Rathbun, Brian C. 2014. *Diplomacy's Value: Creating Security in 1920s Europe and the Contemporary Middle East*. Ithaca: Cornell University Press.

Rathbun, Brian C. 2018. "The Rarity of Realpolitik: What Bismarck's Rationality Reveals About International Politics." *International Security* 43 (1): 7–55.

Rathbun, Brian C. 2019. *Reasoning of State: Realists, Romantics and Rationality in International Relations*. Cambridge: Cambridge University Press.

Renshon, Jonathan. 2017. *Fighting For Status, Hierarchy and Conflict in World Politics*. Princeton: Princeton University Press.

Taliaferro, Jeffrey W. 2006. "State Building For Future Wars: Neoclassical Realism and the Resource-Extractive State." *Security Studies* 15 (3): 464–495.

Tetlock, Philip E. 2017. *Expert Political Judgment, How Good Is It? How Can We Know?* Princeton: Princeton University Press.

Waltz, Kenneth N. 1979. *Theory of International Politics*. Reading: Addison-Wesley.

Weikart, Richard. 2004. *From Darwin to Hitler: Evolutionary Ethics, Eugenics and Racism in Germany*. New York: Palgrave MacMillan.

Wendt, Alexander. 1999. *Social Theory of International Politics*. Cambridge: Cambridge University Press.

Yarhi-Milo, Keren. 2018. *Who Fights For Reputation: The Psychology of Leaders in International Conflict*. Princeton: Princeton University Press.

Zarnett, David. 2017. "What Does Realist Foreign Policy Activism Tell Us About Realist theory?" *Foreign Policy Analysis* 13 (3): 618–637.

CHAPTER 19

CULTURE, IDENTITY, AND GRAND STRATEGY

DAVID M. MCCOURT

"An America that is safe, prosperous, and free at home is an America with the strength, confidence, and will to lead abroad. It is an America that can preserve peace, uphold liberty, and create enduring advantages for the American people." So begins the 2017 Security Strategy of the United States (NSS 2017). In a sharp turnaround, NSS 2017 names geopolitical competition from China and Russia—rather than terrorism—as America's most pressing threat and develops an "America first" strategy with echoes of isolationism.

What do culture and identity have to do with a seemingly objective assessment—and a long overdue one for many—of America's national interests and the principal threats facing the country, shaped by the priorities of President Donald Trump? Surely grand strategy is the preserve of politics and power, and the timeless wisdom of *realpolitik*? What role is there for culture and identity?

In this chapter, I argue that culture and identity are essential components of any realistic account of grand strategy. NSS 2017 does much more than assess America's strategic environment: it tells a story of who America *is*, and who it *should be*, in world politics. Grand strategy reflects a state's strategic culture—note the unquestioned assumption of global leadership, and the strongly liberal values. Grand strategies also reflect international political culture more broadly, as when NSS 2017 proclaims "peace, security, and prosperity depend on strong, sovereign nations that respect their citizens at home and cooperate to advance peace abroad." Security strategies are *performative*, making the world at the same time as speaking of it, and fashioning an identity for an international actor.

The centrality of culture and identity in international politics are key insights from the constructivist approach to IR theory. Here I outline the constructivist challenge to mainstream approaches that emphasize material conceptions of power and interests. I then illustrate the ubiquity of culture and identity in the formulation of UK and US grand strategy, noting that the prominence of realism in the US is itself historically contingent. I then explore recent developments in culturalist theorizing that caution against taking culture and identity as stable entities rather than often contradictory processes. This serves to connect the insights from this chapter to others in the volume on practice, discourse, legitimation, power, and expertise.

The Constructivist Challenge in IR and Security Studies

Grand strategy, Colin Dueck (2006, 1) explains, "involves the prioritization of foreign policy goals, the identification of existing and potential resources, and the selection of a plan or road map that uses those resources to meet those goals." Decisions driven by, and bearing on, matters of grand strategy, include levels of defense spending, foreign aid provision, alliance behavior, troop deployments, and diplomatic activity. American grand strategy since 1945, for example, has been liberal internationalist in content and hegemonic in form: seeking to promote liberal goals such as free markets and democratic governance structures, while preventing states with opposed ideologies from predominating in specific regions around the world (Dueck 2006). High levels of defense spending, the maintenance of a global network of bases, and the creation of ingrained foreign aid, are all hallmarks of this grand strategy, which has endured despite frequent criticism.

In IR theory, the standard account of where grand strategies come is realist. From this perspective, international politics is the never-ending struggle for power between states in an anarchical world—power used to secure national interests (Morgenthau 1948). Grand strategies in that context fundamentally reflect the objective distribution of power in the international system. Larger and more powerful states have greater latitude to define their national interests as they desire, and sufficient power to achieve their aims. Realists are thus fond of Greek historian Thucydides' famous exhortation: "the strong do what they can, the weak suffer what they must."

Constructivism emerged in IR theory to nuance this realist picture (Adler 1997; Bertucci, Hayes, and James 2018; Ruggie 1998). As Jeffrey Checkel (1998, 324) noted in an early review, constructivists took aim at the narrow debate at the time between neorealists and neoliberal institutionalists over whether states seek absolute or relative gains in world politics (Baldwin 1993). For constructivists, both approaches ignored "the content and sources of state interests and the social fabric of world politics" (Checkel 1998, 324) By looking to the broader social sciences for guidance on how to theorize that social fabric, constructivists sought to expand the conceptual horizons of the field's mainstream (Finnemore 1996b; McCourt 2016). Constructivist views of grand strategy center on the concepts of *culture* and *identity*.

The Culture of National Security

For Peter Katzenstein (1996a, 6), culture is "a broad label that denotes collective models of nation-state authority or identity, carried by custom or law." Hard to pin down—of which more later—some early proponents deliberately avoided firm definitions of culture (Lapid and Kratochwil 1996, 6–9). Most agree, however, that culture inheres in some combination of collective beliefs, practices, identities, rules, and shared meanings: "Humans live in a web of intersubjective meanings, expressed through, and embedded within, language, images, bodies, practices, and artefacts," Christian Reus-Smit (2018, 1) argues. Culture forms the background knowledge of a community—how one typically thinks and acts. In anthropologist Clifford Geertz's (1973, 5) well-known formulation, culture is the "webs of meaning" within which humans live, which they "themselves have spun." Culture therefore has both descriptive and prescriptive content. Culture is both a matter of "is" and "ought" (Kratochwil and Ruggie 1986), referring to "both a set of evaluative standards (such as norms and values) and a set of cognitive standards (such as rules and models) that define what social actors exist in a system, how they operate, and how they relate to one another" (Katzenstein 1996a, 6).

The actors in the international system and how they relate to one another is the locus of Alexander Wendt's oft-cited analysis of the culture of international relations (Wendt 1992, 1999). Wendt took head-on the structural realist theorizing of Kenneth Waltz (1979), showing that it is far from lacking in culture. The structural realist approach describes a "Hobbesian" world of entrenched enmity. Noting how for many states this does not characterize their relations, Wendt described two alternative "cultures of anarchy" states can inhabit and construct in their international relations: a "Lockean" world of cautious rivalry and a "Kantian" world of peaceful coexistence. Wendt's approach helps explain differences in, for example, US grand strategy toward the West and Latin America—where Washington has forged long lasting "security communities" (Adler and Barnett 1998)—and with parts of the world where more conflictual relations continue.

While influential, Wendt's account maintains the parsimony of structural realism, and as such offers a thin vision of the effects of culture on grand strategy. A more generative constructivist literature offered a deeper understanding of culture, stressing how the sort "social facts"—societal constraints on individual behavior—sociologist Emile Durkheim described in domestic society holds for international society too (see Ruggie 1998). For norms researchers, international politics is far from the anomic world described by realists. It is filled with expectations about legitimate behavior, expectations that put often-strict bounds on what states can do and want to do (Acharya 2004; Klotz 1995; Keck and Sikkink 1998a. For a good overview see Hoffman 2017). Nina Tannenwald (2008), for example, has demonstrated the powerful effects of a taboo against first use of nuclear weapons. Taboos, Tannenwald (2008, 45) explains, are a certain type of cultural norm that have both *regulative* effects—the injunction in international law against first use—and *constitutive* effects—placing nuclear weapons in the "do not use" category and creating a "non-first user" category states can aspire to join and uphold (Tannenwald 2008, 48). Culture is thus normative in a dual sense, with the nuclear first-use taboo constitutive of what it means to be a civilized country.

Accounts of culture that rest at the level of the structure of international politics inform our understanding of grand strategy formulation in the much same way as do structural realist and liberal theories. International culture is an important shaping factor that resolves in diverse political units differently. A distinction between rationalist and non-rationalist understandings of culture is important to make here, however (see Keohane 1988; Zürn and Checkel 2005). Rationalists view social expectations deriving from culture as inputs to be weighed like other costs in the cost–benefit analyses they see as the basic feature of social life. Nonrationalists, by contrast, argue that culture is "thicker" than rationalists allow, *constituting* the way social situations are made up—what moves are even thinkable for certain in bargaining scenarios. While these differences in perspective come with implications for data and methodological approach, especially concerning the potential for formalization, from both perspectives, at the nation-state level "strategic cultures" are seen as a central driver of grand strategy (compare Johnston 1995, Katzenstein 1996b; Meyer 2007).

For Dueck (2006), consequently, structural realist and structural-cultural accounts of American grand strategy both give insufficient weight to its uniquely *American* nature. The centrality of US culture is evident in a commitment to a specific form of antiauthoritarian and market-oriented liberalism, and internationalism vacillating between moral crusading and reluctant leadership. Similarly, Katzenstein (1996b) and Andrew Oros (2008) demonstrate the culturally unique understanding of security in Japan, which is far more expansive than the American focus on the police and military, underpinning Japan's hesitation toward the use of force.

If culture shapes political action at the international and state levels, it also operates at the substate level, in domestic governing organizations. Lynn Eden (2004), to illustrate, demonstrates the profound effects of organizational culture in American planning for the use of nuclear weapons. Addressing the puzzle of why American military organizations in the postwar period developed very accurate predictions about the blast radius from nuclear weapons, but consistently underestimated the radius for fire damage—which had such impact at Hiroshima. The answer, Eden emphasizes, influenced weapon procurement decisions, leading both the United States and the Soviet Union to build tens of thousands of, effectively unusable, bombs. Eden explains the puzzle with reference to the social construction of knowledge in US war planning organizations, specifically the "Knowledge-laden organizational routines" and "organizational frames" that shaped the way American war planners understood nuclear weapons. In brief, they came to fold nuclear weapons into a "blast damage frame" that had emerged during the 1930s in military studies of bombing and was reaffirmed during conventional bombing in Second World War studies—a frame that utterly failed to fit the world of nuclear weapons. Eden's analysis is a powerful example of organizational culture and the frames through which culture influences action (also Foley 2013; Kier 1997).

A related literature of special significance to scholars of grand strategy addresses the routines and "habits" underpinning the construction of grand-strategic knowledge (Hopf 2010). Patrick Porter (2018), for example, locates the sources of continuity in US grand strategy since the end of the Cold War in the habits and routines of the American foreign policy "Establishment"—the many think tanks, research centers, and academic departments, mainly in Washington DC, that provide knowledge to the US government when it comes to foreign policy. Porter describes how the Establishment narrows strategic debate to some version of US primacy along more or less liberal internationalist lines, limiting voices for other grand strategies such as restraint, pullback, or offshore balancing. Crucially, members of the Establishment are often unaware of how US foreign policy reproduces itself as an unintended consequence of their common modes of thinking and talking about global problems and American options.

Grand Strategy as Identity Affirmation

The second master concept from the constructivist approach to grand strategy is *identity*. Identity-based accounts posit that grand-strategic formulation is as much about affirming a state's sense of self—of who it *is*—in world politics, as it is about material interests. Identity and culture are deeply entwined. The identities states perform in international affairs are manifestations of cultures at each of the levels noted above— the international, national, and subnational. For example, whereas securing the US national interest in Northeast Asia might suggest a preemptive strike on North Korea, such action would violate America's collective sense of self. In the American collective imagination, the United States is not the *type* of actor that violates norms of national sovereignty and the peaceful resolution of international disputes unless it must.

Like culture, identity too is a contested concept. Competing definitions abound (see Berenskoetter 2018; Vucetic 2017). Invoking identity opens up tricky philosophical questions about what identities are and where they come from. How *exactly* do considerations of "American-ness" influence grand strategy? In addition, the implication that identities are unique raises concerns about generalizability. Scholars take different stances on these questions and develop quite different approaches to identity in international relations therefore (on the disciplinary politics of identity, see Price and Reus-Smit 1998; Rousseau 2006; and Zehfuss 2006). While any classificatory scheme might do some violence to the diversity of this body of work, four broad and interrelated approaches to identity can be identified: (1) identity as a story of a community's place in international relations; (2) identity as state's "Self"; (3) critical approaches on the exclusionary practices of foreign policy; and (4) the constitutive role of sovereignty as expressing the moral purpose of the state in world politics.

National Identity Stories

Perhaps the most straightforward approach to identity and state action is to assess the national identity stories that form the basis of foreign policy (e.g. Hall 1999). In an influential early illustration, Eric Ringmar (1996) addressed the question of why Sweden became involved in the Thirty Years' War (1618–1948). Sweden's embroilment in the Europe-wide conflict, Ringmar showed, was made possible by the construction during the late sixteenth and early seventeenth century of a Swedish national identity as a unified country—separate from Norway and Denmark with whom its history had been intertwined for 300 years. As a proud and separate country, founded by the ancient Goths, and a member of the Protestant countries of Europe, King Gustav Adolf (1594–1632) believed his purpose to be to take Sweden into the Thirty Years' War.

Again, foregrounding the identity-based motives for foreign policy has been a crucial move for constructivists because it responds to a puzzle left over from realist accounts of grand strategy, namely where national interests come from. Realists downplay the question of how supposedly material conditions like national interests are interpreted as interests in the first place. Similarly, rationalists downplay the origins of the preferences that structure bargaining games between states, as between individuals in domestic society. But as Alexander Wendt (1992, 398) has argued, "identities are the basis of interests," like Sweden's identity as a unified protestant country (see also Mark Lynch 1999). In Martha Finnemore's (1996, 1) formulation, before someone or some state can know what they *want*, have to know who or what they *are*. National identity stories provide this crucial aspect of state action missing from realist and rationalist accounts (see Ruggie 1997).

The *story* part of the national identity stories should not be neglected. For Ringmar (1996: 95), "Our definitions of interest and identities are intimately related to the way in which we make sense of our world ... it is on the basis of the meanings we construct that interests and identities are defined." Meanings are constructed as and through narratives. Narratives, Friedrich Kratochwil (2006) shows, construct meaning by plotting events in the structure of a story, providing logical and chronological coherence by showing why something is the way it is by retelling its story of becoming (Polkinghorne 1988). Grand strategies do the same thing. As Ron Krebs (2015, 14) has shown, national security narratives set out "the broad contours for policy. Whether explicitly articulated or left implicit, it is the reason some beliefs seem naïve and that others seem realistic."

While highly generative, national identity stories make relatively little *conceptual* use of the concept of identity. Again, identities are stories about a national sense of community, betrayed in public rhetoric. In certain renderings, identity-based explanations of foreign policy are largely indistinguishable from those based on "ideas" or "belief systems" (Goldstein and Keohane 1993; Little and Smith 1998). Other approaches, consequently, foreground the concept of identity, in diverse ways.

Identity and the National "Self"

For Brent Steele (2008) and Jennifer Mitzen (2006), identity is not simply a national story but a natural drive of the state to counter threats to its "ontological security." This view expands the concept of security from the physical world—territory, borders, and population—to the core beliefs about who or what a state is and the motivations that derive from threats to them. Jarrod Hayes (2013), for example, shows how America's identity as a democratic country had crucial implications when it came to whether Cold War disputes with China and India would become security issues. Democratic India was viewed by elites and the public in America as less threatening to the American Self than nondemocratic China—an insight which usefully socializes the long-standing thesis in IR that democracies are more cooperative with fellow democracies than alternative regime types (Russett 1993).

The move to social psychology has also brought with it an increased sensitivity to emotions and affect in threat perception (Ross 2014). Jacques Hymans (2006), for example, explains nuclear proliferation on the basis of the identity-based meanings and emotions that nuclear status carries for different states. National identity conceptions, he shows (2006, 22–23), have two dimensions: a *solidarity* dimension that corresponds to ideas about what a community stands for; and a *status* dimension made up of beliefs about where a state ranks in world politics. The decision to cancel South Africa's nuclear program after the end of Apartheid, then, can be explained by the feeling of its leaders that South Africa's status and national purpose were not enhanced by nuclear capability. India and Pakistan, by contrast, had strong status concerns and solidarity reasons for wanting nuclear weapons, beyond threat posed by the other. Hymans' work exemplifies a rich literature focused on recognition and status-seeking, one that moves beyond constructivism's confines (see, among others, Larson and Shevchenko 2019; Lindemann and Ringmar 2011; Murray 2018; Renshon 2017).

Identity, Difference, and Foreign Policy

The move to social psychology brings with it theoretical specificity absent from some national identity stories. Yet it also relies on cognitive and psychological processes in ways that can downplay the social and cultural factors initially attractive to constructivists. Both ontological security and national identity approaches can fail to grapple with the question of where state identities come from (for an important exception that situates identities in societal understandings, see Hopf 2001). The problem of the origins of identities has been common to philosophical discourse since Hegel's discussion of the master–slave dialectic. There Hegel affirmed that identity—what something is—and difference—what something is not—are mutually constitutive. A master could not *be* a master without the slave, and *vice versa*. A third identity-based literature has thereby stressed the inherently *relational* nature of identities and the mutual constitution of Self and "Other" (Jackson and Nexon 1999).

"Broadly conceived as the mutual, cognitive, sociological, or emotional ties through which states understand themselves, especially in relation to others," Janice Bially Mattern (2005, 42) notes, "identity is an *embodiment* of shared categories of Self-Other understanding." Identities are formed through an "on-going process of interaction and social learning" (Mattern 2005, 52). Iver Neumann (1998) and Ayse Zarakol (2011), for example, each foreground the social origins of foreign policies in the case of the "problematic" identities of Russia and Turkey (see Adler-Nissen 2014 on the stigma that goes along with such "transgressive" state identities). Both countries have struggled to situate themselves against the West—neither fully within nor fully outside. What goes for marginal and stigmatized identities goes for seemingly unproblematic identities too. All identities are constructed against Others. These Others may be concrete other states, diffuse notions of what is different in international political culture, and even past understandings of the state in question.

Identity affirmation, therefore, both at the individual and state level, is achieved through the playing of distinct *social roles*. Roles exist at the intersection of the unique and the general, mediating between identity and social structure. Contra Waltz and Wendt's thin visions of international culture as populated by the roles of enemy, friend, and rival, international society is filled with richer sets of roles for states to enact, from great power, hegemon, to regional powers (which, it should be noted, English School theorists in particular have long acknowledged, see Bull 1977; Clark 2011). As Neumann and Ole Jacob Sending (2010) explore, Russian foreign policy since before the reign of Peter the Great (1672–1725) has been shaped by repeated—frequently frustrated—attempts to play role of *great power* in international affairs, a role defined by the Western Powers (Hopf 2012). Russian foreign policy has vacillated between an intense desire for acceptance into the Western club and fierce rejection of all it stands for, as evidenced today in Vladimir Putin's attempts to play a distinctly non-Western great power role. Russia's identity and the urge to affirm its preferred self in international politics is foregrounded from a role-based approach, but so too are the social and cultural constraints within which the process has taken place, mediated through the shifting expectations constitutive of the great power role.

A connected literature adopts a more critical tack, foregrounding the *political* as opposed to merely social constitution of identity. For David Campbell (2001), foreign policy is the activity constitutive of identity. Rather than the foreign—the other—foreign policy "makes foreign" certain events and actors (Campbell 1991, 61). US foreign policy, Campbell argues, has been based on a series of shifting foreign threats constitutive of American identity: Britain, communism/the Soviet Union, drugs, and more recently terrorism. As Richard K. Ashley (1987, 51) argues, foreign policy is "a specific form sort of *boundary producing political performance*."

Sovereignty, Identity, and the State's Moral Purpose

A final literature connects the socially constructed nature of state identity with its fundamentally moral character, returning us to the beginning of our discussion of how culture constitutes identities in international relations. For Christian Reus-Smit (1999), national stories represent identities at the surface level of international society. At a deeper level, fundamental institutions of international society—from multilateralism (see Ruggie 1993) and great power management (Raymond 2019), to the many regimes that structure functional spheres of international cooperation—"comprise the basic rules of practice that structure regime cooperation" (Reus-Smit 1999, 13). Underpinning them all are "the deep constitutive metavalues that comprise the normative foundations of international society" (Reus-Smit 1999, 6). Again, as Peter Katzenstein (1996b, 22) notes, "Cultural-institutional contexts do not merely constrain actors by changing the incentives that shape behavior. They do not simply regulate behavior. They also constitute the very actors whose conduct they seek to emulate." Centrally, the notion of sovereign statehood is the foundational metapractice of modern world politics, constituting the moral purpose of the state, constituting actors as knowledgeable social agents, at the same time as regulating their behavior (Reus-Smit 1999, 12–13; see Biersterker and Weber 2011; Bartelson 1995; Havercroft 2011; Philpott 2001).

The constructivist challenge in security studies is, in sum, rich in variety and richer still in its controversy. So long as theoretical dispute is empirically generative, there is no reason to consider diversity as a negative condition. In the next section, I continue to argue the payoff of identity-based and cultural explanations of grand strategy in the cases of the United States and Britain.

THE CULTURE OF NATIONAL SECURITY IN BRITAIN AND THE UNITED STATES

The value-added of identity-based and cultural accounts of grand-strategy formulation is to demonstrate how supposedly objective national interests and security threats rest on understandings of who a state is in world politics and what it wants to achieve in its relations with others. The previous section followed the custom of presenting culture- and identity-based accounts of grand strategy as opposed to realist-inflected approaches stressing power and material interests. But the perspectives are more complementary than conflictual. As scholars like Jeffrey Legro (2005) and Fareed Zakaria (1998) have demonstrated, no understanding of America's grand strategy over the twentieth century can ignore its economic rise. Yet neither was the liberal internationalist form of its predominance inevitable. Some scholars have coined the termed "realist-constructivism" to blend concerns with power and cultural and identity (Barkin 2010).

America's recent move from a terrorism-focused security strategy towards a strategy rooted in great power competition, which opened this chapter, is a good illustration. As late as 2015, terrorism was the main overarching concept in US thinking about security, with China a potential ally in the Global War on Terror (US NSS 2015). Fast-forward to 2017 and China and Russia are described as strategic competitors (NSS 2017). While commentators might debate whether such a shift constitutes a clear change in grand strategy away from liberal internationalism, or a change in midrange strategy only, certainly the frame—a cultural concept concerning America's identity in world politics—impacts grand strategy in Dueck's formulation (2006, 6).

From a realist perspective, the change to a great-power competition strategy has a clear material foundation in the shift in global power from West to East. America's "unipolar moment" is coming to an end, with China—unlike Russia—emerging as a peer challenger. For the moment, arguably, China's military challenge is confined to East Asia, and the force component of the security strategy reflects a desire to maintain naval superiority in the theater. But Beijing's economic and diplomatic clout carries with it a more serious challenge to America's role or social identity as hegemon. The Belt and Road Initiative sparks worries among many grand strategists in Washington of an alternative Chinese-led international order. In ways that could be rendered drawing on any or all of the approaches to identity and culture described above, many voices in Washington now speak of the need for a "whole of government" approach to the China challenge.

The British case also suggests that constructivist and materialist accounts of grand strategy can be complementary. As I have explored elsewhere (McCourt 2014), British foreign policymakers and grand strategists have since 1945 endeavored to maintain a *residual great power* role in world politics, and have been facilitated in doing so by the American hegemon and the equally powerful desire to continue playing the great power role of their French counterparts. Britain, like France, no longer has the economic power to support the kind of worldwide military and diplomatic posture adopted by the United States. But equally, elites and masses in each country expect their leaders to continue to play prominent roles in international affairs—to be something significant in the world, and not become "another Belgium."

Note, for example, the recent "Brexit" vote in the United Kingdom. As many commentators noted before the referendum, a leave victory has profound implications for UK foreign policy (see Glencross and McCourt 2018). "Europe" has been one of the central pillars of British foreign policy for centuries, well before former Prime Minister Winston Churchill placed it alongside the US alliance and the Commonwealth as one of the "three circles" of Britain's postwar role. Brexit risks a serious loss in standing: no longer America's access point to the EU and likely economically weakened as a result. None of that, however, has prevented British leaders like Theresa May from developing a new label for an essentially unchanged British role in the world post-Brexit: "Global Britain."

Culture and identity are thus every bit as important to grand strategy as material interests. Beyond the Anglosphere, cases such as Japan, Germany, China, and India all suggest that what states *can* do relates at best indirectly to what they *want to do*, their national interests. Each of these states has the material capacity to develop the sort of grand strategy one might expect from a great power. Yet each shies away from a great power identity in different ways, for reasons relating to their history and culture, and what being a great power would mean in each specific case.

Where critics of culture and identity approaches in world politics argue that international relations "at base" has a material underpinning, they are engaging in clever philosophical sleight of hand: as if we could with enough effort "dig" our way down to something solid, and hence real. Here realism as an international theory—with all its useful advice about the lure of power and the need for prudence—becomes realism as a philosophical position about the nature of the world and its contents—about what is *really* real. Scholars who stress the role of culture and identity in world politics, by contrast—whatever their differences in approach and emphasis—share the conviction that culture and its constitutive relationship to identity *is really real*.

As scholars such as Michael C. Williams (2007) have shown, the notion that security and culture form a dichotomy is false. "The very idea that culture is somehow separable from security—that there is a 'material' domain of *strategic* relations largely separable from a (usually derivative or epiphenomenal) realm of culture—can itself be understood as an historical construction and cultural legacy with deep roots in Western political thought and culture," Williams (2007, 3) explains. Noting how culture burst onto the scene after the end of the Cold War in the form of human rights, democracy, and the civilizational component of EU and NATO expansion, Williams asserts that the struggle over the nature of world politics did not disappear, but became a struggle for a form of *symbolic* power (see also Neumann and Sending 2010; Pouliot 2010). Once again, the relationship between conception of security and interests is culturally specific (McSweeney 1999; Buzan, Waever, and de Wilde 1997).

The clinching argument for the primacy of the cultural is historical. Realist IR theory, IR scholars have recently begun to accept, is a cultural artifact (Guilhot 2011). It emerged in the early 1950s in the United States in the crucible of America's rise to hegemony and the formation of IR as a distinct academic specialty with theory at its core. The realist worldview reflected the concerns of émigré scholars like Hans Morgenthau as well as American grand strategists like George Kennan. Indeed, the label "national security" itself was born of the same constellation (see Hogan 1998). Realism, in theory and in practice, is thus a distinctly *American* way of seeing the world. This does not make it wrong so much as culturally unique, reaffirming the centrality of culture and identity to grand strategy.

Recent Developments in Culturalist Theorizing

Scholarship foregrounding culture and identity continues to enrich the field (Lebow 2016; Lebow 2009; Solomon 2015). As realism gives way to rationalism as the baseline of explanations of world politics in US political science—a constructivist sensibility accounts for the background assumptions underpinning rational agents and institutions (Checkel 1997; Zürn and Checkel 2005; see also McCourt 2016). At the same time, however, as Christian Reus-Smit (2018) has recently explored in detail, much culturalist work in IR has imported a set of blinders when it comes to its view of culture, blinders that have tended to overemphasize cultural homogeneity at the expense of a more variegated view of culture. The constructivist challenge in security studies is therefore in the process of augmentation.

For Reus-Smit (2018: 7), "IR's understanding [of culture] is marooned in debates that last thrived in the 1930–1950s." Cultural anthropologists and sociologists working in that era saw culture as a relatively uniform stratum of human interaction. Geertz's "webs of significance" held every member of a cultural group in their catchment.

This "default conception" of culture has characterized much work from the English School and the early generations of constructivism that imported culture into IR. In the case of constructivism, both work on individual norms—like no first use of nuclear weapons—and the deep cultural structures of international society—like the constitutive role of sovereign statehood—implies a coherence and unity to culture that is, in reality, absent. Culture is not a discrete object—a web or glue holding society together. Culture and identities are multiple and contested: state identities do not go unchallenged; international norms are rarely uniformly apprehended and accepted.

A homogeneous view of culture was initially useful as a means of demarcating the "social" disciplines like sociology and cultural anthropology from Economics and Psychology (Reus-Smit 2018, 16–49). Still today within the scientific culture of American political science, conceptualizing culture a discrete "thing" that can be measured and operationalized is attractive to many scholars. Yet, the default conception badly errs by essentializing culture.

The dominant view of culture beyond IR today, by contrast, is as something "highly variegated, often contradictory, only loosely integrated, and fluidly and porously bounded" (Reus-Smit 1998, 7). In sociologist Ann Swidler's (1986) influential reimagining, culture is less a coterminous web than a toolkit. Culture's toolkit provides skilled social agents resources in their practical day-to-do activities, while denying access to other tools. What holds for culture is true of identity also. As Friedrich Kratochwil, for one, has urged, the notion of "identity" is best understood as the story an individual—or state—tells themselves to provide coherence to an entity undergoing constant changes in terms of participants and roles played. Identity, in other words, must not be conceptualized as a coherent entity, but as part of the conceptual toolkit of culture as agent's struggle to maintain their ontological consistency despite the ubiquity of change.

Rejecting the default conception of culture, with Reus-Smit, has important implications for how we should think about the cultural and identity-based origins of grand strategy, building bridges between the present chapter and others in this volume along the way.

First, and most clearly, new approaches in IR theory focused on practices (by Christian Bueger and Gadinger, Chapter 9) and social networks (Daniel Nexon, chapter 8) are part of the de-essentialization of the culture and identity perspective. Scholars whose work underpins the practice turn—like Pierre Bourdieu, Anthony Giddens, Charles Taylor, and Foucault—explore the practical, everyday, or background conceptions that orient social action, without assuming the sort of homogeneous cultural blanket typical of structural functionalism and structuralist approaches. Similarly for social networks: if culture is a toolkit of practically oriented resources, one's social position within a network, field, or whatever similar concept one chooses, determines to a great extent how one perceives the world and acts upon it.

Second, and relatedly, adopting an explicitly nonessentialist view of culture connects culture and identity to approaches that foreground language, discourse, and legitimation in grand strategy (Epstein 2010; Epstein 2008; Goddard 2018, see Chapter 11 in this volume by Marcus Kornprobst and Corina-Ioana Traistaru). Language is not a neutral medium that unproblematically confers cultural expectations to individuals. Language is part of culture's toolkit, representing the world to political agents at the same time as providing rhetorical resources. As Stacie Goddard and Ron Krebs (2015) have recently argued, "Legitimation is integral to how states define the national interest and identify threats, to how the menu of policy options is constituted, and to how audiences are mobilized." Elsewhere, Patrick Jackson (2007) employs a topological metaphor to explain how the language of political debate provides certain powerful resources to actors in political contestation. The key points here are that discourse has effects on political outcomes that are independent of material and symbolic power, and actor beliefs and motivations.

Third, a variegated perspective on culture maintains that cultural processes are political and hence shot through with power. None other than Max Weber—perhaps the foremost cultural social theorist—showed how politics is its own sphere of social life, defined by the struggle over political power. The grubby world of power and politics often gets overlooked in work on the cultural and identity-based motivations underpinnings state action in world affairs (Williams 2007, 1; Checkel 1999). Yet much early constructivist work acknowledged power in ways that later representations of the approach have downplayed (see especially Onuf 1989). Recall Jutta Weldes' (1999, 13) account of the social construction of national interests:

> drawing on and constrained by the array of cultural and linguistic resources already available within the security imaginary, state officials create representations that serve, first, to populate the world with a variety of objects, including both the self (that is, the state in question, and its authorized officials) and others ... Each of the objects is simultaneously given an identity; it is endowed with characteristics that are sometimes precise and certain, at other times vague and unsettled.

The strategic actions of state officials in the political arena are here paramount.

Fourth, and again related, if cultural processes are political, then a concern with the activities of cultural producers in the form of experts should be central to culture and identity-based accounts of grand strategy (e.g. Allen 2018; Guilhot 2005. See Chapter 40 of this volume by Daniel Drezner). Experts and elites are entrepreneurs of norms, as early constructivist works emphasized (Cecilia Lynch 1999; Keck and Sikkink 1998b; Price 1997, but later characterizations have generally ignored. Lisa Stampnitzky (2013), for example, shows how the taken-for-granted notion of "terrorism" was a cultural product formulated in the 1970s as the basis for an emerging social science field of terrorism studies. Terrorism's meaning, Stampnitzky shows, has shifted as the academic experts have brought their Western cultural biases—including the entrenched dichotomy between the rational and the irrational—to a wide-ranging set of activities grouped as terrorism.

Fifth, and finally, as something politically contested and variegated, culture and identity must not be considered the domain of the normatively "good"—with realism and *realpolitik* the domain of the "bad." Constructivists have, it is true, tended to focus on progressive norms. Ann Towns (2010), for one, showing how norms towards gender equality in national legislatures have diffused internationally. Yet, if culture and identity are central to community constitution, part of their very nature is to exclude and create hierarchies within—rankings-based class, status, race and ethnicity, sex and gender. For every story of a national or civilizational identity underpinning state action, in other words, there is a story of othering within and without. Consider, for example, the gendered organizational culture in American planning for nuclear war (Cohn 1987), and the racialized Anglo-Saxon identity (Vucetic 2011), and even the race-based origins of International Relations itself (Vitalis 2015; see Price 2008 on the question of constructivist ethics).

Conclusion

This chapter has urged the student of grand strategy to take culture and identity seriously as baseline drivers of how states do and should think about their international relations. The task is complicated by a cultural tendency in many countries to view grand strategy–making as absent culture—an arena in which cold material calculations match national power to national interests. Nothing could be further from the truth. From the rules and practices defining who gets to participate in international relations, to the ways individuals in domestic organizations view their own positions as producers of expertise and knowledge useful to governments, culture and identity are central to the making of grand strategy.

More programmatically, two implications follow from this chapter. First, scholars of grand strategy who focus on its culture and identity should not be content to play second fiddle to their realist and rationalist counterparts. Culture and identity do not merely explain what is left over from materialist factors; they account for the basic ways strategies are designed and implemented. Examinations of culture and identity in grand strategy should therefore be the first word on the subject, not an afterthought. Second, and relatedly, making such a shift requires placing culture and identity alongside other culturally sensitive approaches and methodologies, many of which are on display in this volume. A culturalist perspectives has natural affinities with approaches based on narratives, practice, experts, and habit, which together should be considered a powerful toolkit for the explication of grand strategy–making in world politics.

References

Acharya, Amitav. 2004. "How Ideas Spread, Whose Norms Matter? Norm Localization and Institutional Change in Asian Regionalism." *International Organization* 58 (2): 239–275.
Adler, Emanuel. 1997. "Seizing the Middle Ground: Constructivism in World Politics." *European Journal of International Relations* 3 (3): 319–363.

Adler, Emanuel, and Michael Barnett. 1998. *Security Communities*. Cambridge: Cambridge University Press.

Adler-Nissen, Rebecca. 2014. "Stigma Management in International Relations: Transgressive Identities, Norms, and Order in International Society." *International Organization* 68 (1): 143–176.

Allen, Bentley B. 2018. *Scientific Cosmology and International Orders*. Cambridge: Cambridge University Press.

Ashley, Richard K. 1987. "Foreign Policy as Political Performance." *International Studies Notes* 13: 51.

Baldwin, David. 1993. *Neorealism and Neoliberalism: The Contemporary Debate*. New York: Columbia University Press.

Barkin, J. Samuel. 2010. *Realist Constructivism: Rethinking International Relations Theory*. Cambridge: Cambridge University Press.

Bartelson, Jens. 1995. *A Genealogy of Sovereignty*. Cambridge: Cambridge University Press.

Berenskoetter, Felix. 2018. "Identity in International Relations." In *The International Studies Encyclopedia, Vol. 6*, edited by Robert A. Denemark. Oxford: Wiley-Blackwell.

Bertucci, Mariano E., Jarrod Hayes, and Patrick James, eds. 2018. *Constructivism Reconsidered: Past, Present, and Future*. Ann Arbor: University of Michigan Press.

Biersteker, Thomas J., and Cynthia Weber, eds. 2011. *State Sovereignty as Social Construct*. Cambridge: Cambridge University Press.

Bull, Hedley. 1977. *The Anarchical Society: A Study of Order in World Politics*. London: Macmillan.

Campbell, David. 1991. *Writing Security: United States Foreign Policy and the Politics of Identity*. Minneapolis: University of Minnesota Press.

Checkel, Jeffrey T. 1997. "International Norms and Domestic Politics: Bridging the Rationalist-Constructivist Divide." *European Journal of International Relations* 3 (4): 473–495.

Checkel, Jeffrey T. 1998. "The Constructivist Turn in International Relations Theory." *International Security* 50 (2): 324–348.

Checkel, Jeffrey T. 1999. "Norms, Institutions, and National Identity in Contemporary Europe." *International Studies Quarterly* 43 (1): 83–114.

Clark, Ian. 2011. *Hegemony in International Society*. Oxford: Oxford University Press.

Cohn, Carol. 1987. "Sex and Death in the Rational World of Defense Intellectuals." *Signs: Journal of Women in Culture and Society* 12 (4): 687–718.

Dueck, Colin. 2006. *Reluctant Crusaders: Power, Culture, and Change in American Grand Strategy*. Princeton: Princeton University Press.

Eden, Lynn. 2004. *Whole World on Fire: Organizations, Knowledge, and Nuclear Weapons Devastation*. Ithaca: Cornell University Press.

Epstein, Charlotte. 2008. *The Power of Words in International Relations: The Birth of an Anti-Whaling Discourse*. Cambridge: The MIT Press.

Epstein, Charlotte. 2010. "Who Speaks? Discourse, the Subject, and the Study of Identity in International Relations." *European Journal of International Relations* 17 (2): 327–350.

Finnemore, Martha. 1996a. *National Interests in International Society*. Ithaca: Cornell University Press.

Finnemore, Martha. 1996b. "Norms, Culture, and World Politics: Insights from Sociology's Institutionalism." *International Organization* 50 (2): 325–347.

Foley, Frank. 2013. *Countering Terrorism: Institutions, Norms, and the Shadow of the Past*. Cambridge: Cambridge University Press.

Glencross, Andrew, and David M. McCourt. 2018. "Living Up to a New Role in the World: The Challenges of "Global Britain." *Orbis* 62 (4): 582–597.

Goddard, Stacie E. 2018. *When Might Makes Rights: Rising Powers and World Order*. Ithaca: Cornell University Press.

Goddard, Stacie E., and Ronald R. Krebs. 2015. "Rhetoric, Legitimation, and Grand Strategy." *Security Studies* 24 (1): 5–36.

Goldstein, Judith, and Robert O. Keohane, eds. 1993. *Ideas and Foreign Policy: Beliefs, Institutions, and Political Change*. Ithaca: Cornell University Press.

Guilhot, Nicolas. 2005. *The Democracy Makers: Human Rights and the Politics of Global Order*. New York: Columbia University Press.

Guilhot, Nicolas, ed. 2011. *The Invention of International Relations Theory: Realism, the Rockefeller Foundation, and the 1954 Conference on Theory*. New York: Columbia University Press.

Hall, Rodney Bruce. 1999. *National Collective Identity: Social Constructs and International Systems*. New York: Columbia University Press.

Hayes, Jarrod. 2013. *Constructing National Security: U.S. Relations with China and India*. Cambridge: Cambridge University Press.

Havercroft, Jonathan. 2011. *Captives of Sovereignty*. Cambridge: Cambridge University Press.

Hoffman, Matthew. 2017. "Norms and Social Constructivism in International Relations." *The International Studies Association Encyclopedia*. https://oxfordre.com/internationalstudies/view/10.1093/acrefore/9780190846626.001.0001/acrefore-9780190846626-e-60?print=pdf, accessed May 2019.

Hogan, Michael J. 1998. *A Cross of Iron: Harry S. Truman and the Origins of the National Security State, 1945–54*. Cambridge: Cambridge University Press.

Hopf, Ted. 2002. *Social Construction of International Politics: Identities and Foreign Policies, Moscow, 1955 and 1999*. Ithaca: Cornell University Press.

Hopf, Ted. 2010. "The Logic of Habit in International Relations." *European Journal of International Relations* 16 (4): 539–361.

Hopf, Ted. 2012. *Reconstructing the Cold War: The Early Years, 1945–1958*. Oxford: Oxford University Press.

Hymans, Jacques E.C. 2006. *The Psychology of Nuclear Proliferation: Identity, Emotions, and Foreign Policy*. Cambridge: Cambridge University Press, 2006.

Jackson, Patrick Thaddeus. 2007. *Civilizing the Enemy: German Reconstruction and the Invention of the West*. Ann Arbor: University of Michigan Press.

Jackson, Patrick Thaddeus, and Daniel H. Nexon. 1999. "Relations Before States: Substance, Process, and the Study of World Politics." *European Journal of International Relations* 5 (3): 291–332.

Johnston, Alastair Iain. 1995. "Thinking about Strategic Culture." *International Security* 19 (4): 32–64.

Katzenstein, Peter, ed. 1996a. *The Culture of National Security: Norms and Identity in World Politics*. New York: Columbia University Press.

Katzenstein, Peter, ed. 1996b. *Cultural Norms in National Security: Police and Military in Postwar Japan*. Ithaca: Cornell University Press.

Keck, Margaret, and Kathryn Sikkink, 1998a. "International Norm Dynamics and Political Change." *International Organization* 52 (4): 887–917.

Keck, Margaret, and Kathryn Sikkink, 1998b. *Activists Beyond Borders: Transnational Advocacy Networks in International Relations*. Ithaca: Cornell University Press.

Keohane, Robert O. 1988. "International Institutions: Two Approaches." *International Studies Quarterly* 32 (4): 379–396.

Kier, Elizabeth. 1997. *Imagining War: French and British Military Doctrine between the Wars*. Princeton: Princeton University Press.

Klotz, Audie. 1995. *Norms in International Relations: The Struggle against Apartheid*. Ithaca: Cornell University Press.

Kratochwil, Friedrich V. 2006. "History, Action, and Identity: Revisiting the 'Second' Great Debate and Assessing its Importance for Social Theory." *European Journal of International Relations* 12 (1): 5–29.

Kratochwil, Friedrich V., and John Gerard Ruggie. 1986. "The State of the Art on an Art of the State." *International Organization* 40 (4): 753–775.

Krebs, Ronald R. 2015. *Narrative and the Making of US National Security*. Cambridge: Cambridge University Press.

Lapid, Yosef, and Friedrich Kratocwhil. 1996. *The Return of Culture and Identity in IR Theory*. Boulder: Lynne Reinner.

Larson, Deborah Welch, and Andrei Shevchenko. 2019. *Quest for Status: Chinese and Russian Foreign Policy*. New Haven: Yale University Press.

Lebow, Richard Ned. 2009. *A Cultural Theory of International Relations*. Cambridge: Cambridge University Press.

Lebow, Richard Ned. 2016. *National Identities and International Relations*. Cambridge: Cambridge University Press.

Legro, Jeffrey. 2005. *Rethinking the World: Great Power Strategies and International Order*. Ithaca: Cornell University Press.

Lindemann, Thomas, and Eric Ringmar. 2011. *The International Politics of Recognition*. New York: Routledge.

Little, Richard, and Steve Smith, eds. 1988. *Belief Systems in International Relations*. Oxford: Blackwell.

Lynch, Cecilia. 1999. *Beyond Appeasement: Interpreting Interwar Peace Movements in World Politics*. Ithaca: Cornell University Press.

Lynch, Marc. 1999. *State Interests and Public Interests: The International Politics of Jordan's Identity*. New York: Columbia University Press.

Mattern, Janice Bially. 2005. *Ordering International Politics: Identity, Crisis, and Representational Force*. New York: Routledge.

McCourt, David M. 2014. *Britain and World Power since 1945: Constructing a Nation's Role in International Politics*. Ann Arbor: University of Michigan Press.

McCourt, David M. 2016. "Practice Theory and Relationalism as the New Constructivism." *International Studies Quarterly* 60 (3): 475–485.

McSweeney, Bill. 1999. *Security, Identity and Interests: A Sociology of International Relations*. Cambridge: Cambridge University Press.

Meyer, Christoph O. 2007. *The Quest for a European Strategic Culture: Changing Norms on Security and Defense in the European Union*. Basingstoke: Palgrave.

Mitzen, Jennifer. 2006. "Ontological Security in World Politics: State Identity and the Security Dilemma." *European Journal of International Relations* 12 (3): 341–370.

Morgenthau, Hans. 1948. *Politics among Nations: The Struggle for Power and Peace*. New York: McGraw-Hill.

Murray, Michelle. 2018. *The Struggle for Recognition in International Relations: Status, Revisionism, and Rising Powers*. New York: Oxford University Press.

Neumann, Iver B. 1998. *Uses of the Other: "the East" in European Identity Formation*. Minneapolis: University of Minnesota Press.

Neumann, Iver B., and Ole Jacob Sending. 2010. *Governing the Global Polity: Practice, Mentality, and Rationality*. Ann Arbor: University of Michigan Press.

Onuf, Nicholas. 1989. *World of Our Making: Rules and Rule in Social Theory and International Relations*. Columbia, SC: University of South Carolina Press.

Oros, Andrew. 2008. *Normalizing Japan: Politics, Identity, and the Evolution of Security Practice*. Stanford: Stanford University Press.

Philpott, Daniel. 2001. *Revolutions in Sovereignty: How Ideas Shaped Modern International Relations*. Princeton: Princeton University Press.

Polkinghorne, Donald E. 1988. *Narrative Knowledge and the Human Sciences*. Albany: SUNY Press.

Porter, Patrick. 2018. "Why America's Grand Strategy Has Not Changed: Power, Habit, and the U.S. Foreign Policy Establishment." *International Security* 42 (4): 9–46.

Pouliot, Vincent. 2010. *International Security in Practice: The Politics of NATO-Russia Diplomacy*. Cambridge: Cambridge University Press.

Price, Richard M. 1997. *The Chemical Weapons Taboo*. Ithaca: Cornell University Press.

Price, Richard, ed. 2008. *Moral Limit and Possibility in World Politics*. Cambridge: Cambridge University Press.

Price, Richard M. and Christian Reus-Smit. 1998. "Dangerous Liaisons? Critical International Theory and Constructivism." *European Journal of International Relations* 4 (3): 259–254.

Raymond, Mark. 2019. *Social Practices of Rule-Making in World Politics*. New York: Oxford University Press.

Renshon, Jonathan. 2017. *Fighting for Status: Hierarchy and Conflict in World Politics*. Princeton: Princeton University Press.

Reus-Smit, Christian. 1999. *The Moral Purpose of the State: Culture, Social Identity, and Institutional Rationality in International Relations*. Princeton: Princeton University Press.

Reus-Smit, Christian. 2018. *On Cultural Diversity: International Theory in a World of Difference*. Cambridge: Cambridge University Press.

Ringmar, Eric. 1996. *Identity, Interest and Action: A Cultural Explanation of Sweden's Intervention in the Thirty Years' War*. Cambridge: Cambridge University Press.

Ross, Andrew A.G. 2014. *Mixed Emotions: Beyond Fear and Hatred in International Conflict*. Chicago: Chicago University Press.

Rousseau, David L. 2006. *Identifying Threats and Threatening Identities: The Social Construction of Realism and Liberalism*. Stanford: Stanford University Press.

Ruggie, John Gerard. 1993. *Multilateralism: The Anatomy of an Institution*. New York: Columbia University Press.

Ruggie, John Gerard. 1997. "The Past as Prologue? Interests, Identity, and American Foreign Policy." *International Security* 21 (4): 89–125.

Ruggie, John Gerard. 1998. "What Makes the World Hang Together? Neo-utilitarianism and the Social Constructivist Challenge." *International Organization* 52 (4): 855–885.

Russett, Bruce. 1993. *Grasping the Democratic Peace*. Princeton: Princeton University Press.

Solomon, Ty. 2015. *The Politics of Subjectivity in American Foreign Policy Discourses*. Ann Arbor: University of Michigan Press.

Stampnitzky, Lisa. 2013. *Disciplining Terror: How Experts Invented "Terrorism"*. Cambridge: Cambridge University Press.

Steele, Brent J. 2008. *Ontological Security in International Relations: Self-Identity and the IR State*. New York: Routledge.
Swidler, Ann. 1986. "Culture in Action: Symbols and Strategies." *American Sociological Review* 51 (2): 273–286.
Tannenwald, Nina. 2008. *The Nuclear Taboo: The United States and the Non-Use of Nuclear Weapons since 1945*. Cambridge: Cambridge University Press.
Towns, Ann E. 2010. *Women and States: Norms and Hierarchies in International Society*. Cambridge: Cambridge University Press.
US NSS 2015. "Security Strategy of the United States of America." https://obamawhitehouse.archives.gov/sites/default/files/docs/2015_national_security_strategy_2.pdf, accessed May 2019.
US NSS 2017. "Security Strategy of the United States of America." https://www.whitehouse.gov/wp-content/uploads/2017/12/NSS-Final-12-18-2017-0905.pdf, accessed May 2019.
Vitalis, Robert. 2015. *White World Order, Black Power Politics: The Birth of American International Relations*. Ithaca: Cornell University Press.
Vucetic, Srdjan. 2011. *The Anglosphere: A Geneaology of a Racialized Identity in International Relations*. Stanford: Stanford University Press.
Vucetic, Srdjan. 2017. "Identity and Foreign Policy." *The Oxford Research Encyclopedia of Politics*. https://oxfordre.com/politics/view/10.1093/acrefore/9780190228637.001.0001/acrefore-9780190228637-e-435, accessed May 2019.
Waltz, Kenneth. 1979. *Theory of International Politics*. Reading: Addison-Wesley.
Weldes, Jutta. 1999. *Constructing National Interests: The United States and the Cuban Missile Crisis*. Minneapolis: University of Minnesota Press.
Wendt, Alexander. 1999. *Social Theory of International Politics*. Cambridge: Cambridge University Press.
Wendt, Alexander. 1992. "Anarchy is What States Make of It: The Social Construction on Power Politics." *International Organization* 46 (2): 391–425.
Williams, Michael C. 2007. *Culture and Security: Symbolic Power and the Politics of International Security*. New York: Routledge.
Zakaria, Fareed. 1998. *From Wealth to Power: the Unusual Origins of America's World Role*. Princeton: Princeton University Press.
Zarakol, Ayse. 2011. *After Defeat: How the East Learned to Live with the West*. Cambridge: Cambridge University Press.
Zehfuss, Maja. 2006. Constructivism and Identity: A Dangerous Liaison, in Stefano Guzzini and Anna Leander, eds. *Constructivism in International Relations*. New York: Routledge, 93–117.
Zürn, Michael, and Jeffrey T. Checkel. 2005. "Getting Socialized to Build Bridges: Constructivism and Rationalism, Europe and the Nation-State." *International Organization* 59 (4): 1045–1079.

CHAPTER 20

RHETORIC, LEGITIMATION, AND GRAND STRATEGY

STACIE E. GODDARD

Scholars associated with diverse research traditions have increasingly agreed that legitimacy is significant in the formulation and operation of grand strategy. Despite the field's embrace of legitimacy, scholars of international relations have shown less interest in the role of *legitimation*—the public justification of policy—in creating and sustaining grand strategies. This oversight is puzzling. Grand strategy only becomes legitimate when leaders articulate the reasons why policies are justifiable, and only if audiences accept those claims. Empirically, moreover, leaders devote substantial time, energy, and resources to justifying their strategy to audiences at home and abroad. To overlook legitimation is to overlook much of global politics. This chapter makes the case for treating legitimation as central to the study of grand strategy. It explains what legitimation is, why it matters, and how it drives grand strategy at every stage, from the articulation of national interest, to the interpretation of threat, to the selection of instruments. The essay concludes with challenges to the legitimation of grand strategy in contemporary international politics.

Legitimation and Grand Strategy

By legitimation, I mean how political actors publicly justify their policy stances before concrete audiences (Jackson 2006; Stein 2000; Goddard and Krebs 2015; Goddard 2018). All humans engage in legitimation. Living in communities and craving approval, human beings are governed by what Jon Elster has termed "the civilizing force of hypocrisy": when we speak in public, we must offer socially acceptable reasons or face the censure of our peers (Elster 1995). In a similar way, all states engage in legitimation, justifying their aims and actions to various audiences: to get their own publics to support their foreign policies and to convince other nations to accept their aims.

The fact that states legitimate their actions points to some significant features of international politics. It implies that the international system contains rules and norms that identify what counts as appropriate behavior, ascribe meaning to action, and set the boundaries of appropriate action in world politics (see, e.g., Finnemore 2003). The principles used to justify grand strategies vary across time and space. Grand strategies justified as "keeping the balance" were central to the grand strategies of European states in the Concert period (Elrod 1976); in contrast, "peaceful hegemony" guided China's grand strategy up through the late nineteenth century (Kang 2010). In the early twentieth century into the present day, the United States' grand strategy has embraced the principles of the liberal institutional order. The maintenance of free markets, and the pursuit of self-determination and human rights, have all appeared in justifications of contemporary US grand strategy.

Legitimation is both a social and strategic process. While actors are social, they do not mindlessly obey the norms and rules of the international system. Norms and rules, instead, provide what Ann Swidler calls a "cultural tool-kit," which includes the rhetorical resources that can be used to justify grand strategy (Swidler 1986). When leaders seek to formulate a grand strategy, they do so understanding that they should deploy rules and norms in ways that are more likely to galvanize their domestic populations than others. Likewise, they understand that some appeals, while able to mobilize an audience at home, might also appear illegitimate and threatening to others abroad. Leaders therefore pay careful attention to how they legitimate their grand strategies, understanding that how they justify their actions influences their power at home and abroad.

To paraphrase Richard Betts, without legitimation, there is no rationale for how the nation will achieve purposes worth blood and treasure (Betts 2000). But this does not mean that legitimation is integral to grand strategy at all times and all places; indeed, there are moments when legitimation is unlikely or even unnecessary. The importance of legitimation is driven by two demands: first, audiences' demand for reasons for a strategy and, second, leaders' need for publics, at home and abroad, to mobilize in support of grand strategy (Goddard and Krebs 2015). On the one hand, the importance of legitimation depends on the extent to which audiences demand justification for a foreign policy. At home, there are times that the public is not paying attention to foreign affairs—when domestic issues dominate political debate, for example. Likewise, a grand strategy that is rote or institutionalized need not be justified, either at home or abroad. Until recently, there was little need for the United States to justify its continued support of NATO in Western European countries. In contrast, departures from traditional foreign policies provoke more scrutiny, especially if they seem to break the "rules of the game" (Stein 2000).

On the other hand, the need for legitimation also depends on leaders' demand for collective mobilization: leaders need to justify their foreign policies only when they require support from publics at home and abroad or when, conversely, they hope to undercut mobilization against their grand strategies. Obviously, the more a nation must sacrifice in pursuit of a grand strategy, the more justification becomes necessary. To persuade the American public to commit the resources for containment, Truman needed to explain why the United States must rescue European economies and create permanent alliances to contain the Soviet threat. Abroad, the need for mobilization varies as well. A grand strategy that can be pursued unilaterally may not require legitimation. Even then, failing to legitimate a unilateral grand strategy may result in resistance over time, as the United States found in the wake of the war in Iraq. Multilateral efforts, in contrast, may require mobilizing allies.

In sum, legitimation matters either when audiences demand a justification or when the need for collective mobilization is substantial. Using this framework, we can now turn to how and when legitimation operates in the key processes of grand strategy formation: the construction of the national interest; the interpretation of threats; and the selection of the instruments of foreign policy.

Legitimating the National Interest

Formulating a grand strategy requires a well-defined national interest, one that specifies what ends a collective actor, usually the state, should pursue in world politics. In its absence, leadership cannot identify threats or select appropriate means. The national interest transcends the trivialities of everyday politics; it rests on the articulation of a shared vision of the political community's goals, not the mere amalgamation of or compromise among private interests or the domination of a powerful individual's whims. Despite its centrality to theories of international relations and foreign policy, the national interest remains one of the most contested concepts in international relations theory. Neorealists assume that an enduring national interest flows from the competitive pressures of international politics, shaping not only the polity's pursuit of security or power, but its very cohesion: when security is scarce, lesser ends fall by the wayside, parochial interests are overcome, and the nation and its purpose emerge.

The problem is that there is no such thing as a "national interest" or, more precisely, at any given time most political communities fail to demonstrate consensus on any issue of foreign policy. And most of the time, this is not a problem. Much of politics not only operates, but actually thrives, in contestation. Indeed, there are some that see the "national interest" as little more than antidemocratic propaganda, an instrument for shutting down debate over the ends of foreign policy, denouncing it as "a weapon that saps democratic processes" (David Wood, in Clinton 1994, 495). But if there is no national interest, then scholars should abandon the concept of "grand strategy" altogether (e.g., Mitzen 2015, 64). The national interest may not be enduring and objective, but for grand strategy to exist, it must be a social fact: because grand strategy aligns *collective* means and ends, it therefore requires some definition of the national interest.

The key then becomes understanding how the national interest is constructed. A rhetorical politics approach suggests that legitimation is central to understanding the creation of a national interest, a commitment by the whole of a political community to act in concert in the name of a collective purpose. At the heart of grand strategy are the reasons a political community must act together. As Jutte Weldes puts it, the national interest "functions as a rhetorical device that generates the legitimacy of and political support for state action. The national interest thus wields considerable power in that it helps to constitute and legitimize the state's actions as important" (Weldes 1996, 4).

That leaders use rhetoric to construct the national interest is not solely a constructivist insight. As Schou Tjalve and Williams argue, during the Cold War, realist scholars, including Morgenthau, Niebuhr, and Schlesinger, understood the necessity of legitimation in creating and maintaining a collective entity at home. They worried that "the absence of a mobilized public sphere within which to negotiate a collective sense of purpose" would undercut grand strategy and create a "weak and inconsistent foreign policy" (Schou Tjalve and Williams 2015, 46). Not just strong but responsible rhetorical leadership—appeals that would not rely on threat inflation or outright lies to build "we-ness"—was necessary for a robust grand strategy.

As discussed above, legitimation is not necessary in all times and all places; using rhetoric to construct a national interest becomes necessary under two conditions. First, the greater the threat, the greater the need to articulate a national interest. This may seem surprising, since realists suggest that it is under cases of extreme objective threat that a national interest will emerge (Wolfers 1962, 67–80). Yet even in the face of significant threats, societies can fail to overcome the forces of fragmentation and generate collective purpose—a source of grand-strategic failure, as Schweller has shown (Schweller 2006). The greater the threat, the more leaders must rely on the rhetoric of national interest to bind the nation together. Second, there are moments when domestic audiences are more likely to demand leaders justify a strategy as in the "national interest." An attack on the homeland may need little in the way of legitimation; in contrast, why Hitler's expansion into France or communist influence in Greece threatened the "American way of life" required more explanation.

Under these conditions, leaders must rely on legitimation to construct a national interest. When leaders justify their grand strategies, they are doing more than buying off key constituencies or fooling the masses with myths. Rather, when successful, the act of publicly justifying grand strategy mobilizes the collective identity that the strategy promises to make secure. Public debates over grand strategy mobilize a political community, which is always rife with cleavages, into a coherent and unified entity whose security must be assured. Through legitimation, leaders articulate a collective interest that resonates and binds together political communities, mobilizing support behind collective purpose. It is through this process of public definition that actors come to see themselves as a cohesive political community.

More often than not, this rhetorical process is aimed towards constituting the nation, so the audience for legitimation lies within state boundaries. But legitimation can also construct political communities beyond states that lay claim to a collective interest. Patrick Jackson, for example, argues that appeals to "Western Civilization" constructed the United States, Western Europe and—at the time, oddly—Germany as a singular collective entity with a shared political purpose that must be protected from the Soviet threat (Jackson 2006). Mitzen argues that leaders of the Concert of Europe shaped the idea that "the great powers" were a cohesive group with a shared collective intention and thus could formulate a grand strategy (Mitzen 2015). But whatever the actor in question, it is the act of legitimation that constructs the shared sense of purpose.

Legitimation and the Construction of Threat

Second, grand strategy demands that leaders define the threat to the national interest. Poor threat assessment leads to poor grand strategy. Without an understanding of threat, leaders cannot choose appropriate remedies, or which resources are necessary to protect the national interest. Threat inflation leads to a waste of resources at best; at worst, it sparks a security dilemma and even ultimately war (Jervis 1978). Underestimating a threat leads to no better results. Moreover, states often face numerous threats to their national interest, and thus need to prioritize among them. Given the uncertainty inherent to international politics, threat assessment is no easy task. While neorealists continue to argue that states should understand threats to their national interest in terms of power—evaluating whether their opponents have the capabilities to challenge their vital interests (Mearsheimer 2002)—in practice, this is not how leaders operate. Capabilities, as Stephen Walt argued over three decades ago, drive only part of states' threat assessment (Walt 1986). Even when a potential opponent has significant capabilities, if it has benign aims, there is no reason to treat it as a threat to the national interest.

Thus, most scholars agree that, when creating their grand strategies, leaders look not only to their opponents' might but also their intentions: they strive to determine what challengers will do with their wealth and power, and whether those aims will threaten their vital interests. What this means, in both theory and practice, is that threat assessment rests on how states divine the intentions of other states. How is this accomplished? Most rationalist models argue that states will look to a challenger's behavior for some form of costly signal to tell whether an opponent is a threat to its national interest (Glaser 2010; Kydd 1997). For example, if a potential challenger is investing heavily in offensive technology, seemingly building the capacity for force projection and conquest, then other states are right to be worried. In this view, the United States correctly viewed the Soviet decision to maintain its forces after the Second World War, deployed outside of the country's borders, as a costly signal that the Soviets were a significant threat, one that suggested that a grand strategy of containment was necessary. In contrast, Britain correctly surmised that the initial American restraint during the South American revolutions in the early nineteenth century was a signal that the rising power harbored limited aims.

This seems straightforward on the face of it. The problem is that behavior—even costly actions—rarely provides actors with clear information. To give an example, when Japan invaded Manchuria in 1931, this could be seen as a limited conquest of a territory in which Japan had long claimed to have special interests, or as the beginning of a larger campaign to dominate China (Goddard 2018). There was nothing inherent within the invasion—as costly as it was—that could serve as an indicator of Japan's future strategy. Likewise, as the United States decides how to formulate its grand strategy in the twenty-first century, it must determine whether China is a threat to its national interest. How to understand, then, China's expansionist efforts in the South China Sea, or its efforts to build up infrastructure through its Belt and Road initiative? Certainly, both are "costly" signals. But should these actions in the South China Sea be construed as an attempt to challenge American dominance in the Asia Pacific? Or do they constitute a return to the nineteenth-century territorial status quo, as China claims?

It is not simply that the United States lacks information about China's behavior; it is that China's behavior can be reasonably read in a number of different ways. And this is hardly unusual: most signals are indeterminate, subject to multiple understandings. Scholars have long recognized this, and focused then on threat perception, asking why it is state leaders are likely to see particular actions as threatening and other actions as benign (Yahri-Milo 2014). A rhetorical politics approach suggests that responding to threats is not only a matter of perception but also of *interpretation*. When faced with a threat, leaders must tell a story to their audiences about the nature of that threat, imparting meaning to the challenger's behavior and making sense of those actions to the audience.

As with the national interest, the importance of legitimation in threat construction varies. The need for legitimation is greatest when states face a particularly powerful challenger that is engaged in rule-breaking—that is to say, when a challenger appears to be violating the rules and norms of the international system. Acts of rule-breaking make visible the question of whether or not a challenger is a threat and create demands for legitimation. For example, it is one thing to ask in the abstract if a rising power is a threat. Scholars and policymakers can debate abstract questions without much scrutiny. When rising powers decide to invade neighboring powers, their actions become visible, and the public demands interpretation.

Moreover, some rule-breaking demands more active mobilization than others. There are brute facts in international politics, and threat is not entirely what an actor makes of it. Signals, as Jervis argues, "are not natural; they are conventional. That is, they consist of statements and actions that the sender and receiver have endowed with meaning in order to accomplish certain goals" (Jervis 1989, 139). For some behavior, with relatively settled interpretations attached, there is less need for leaders to explain the nature of the threat. When Japan attacked Pearl Harbor, this did not require much interpretation—although even here, Roosevelt had to explain why Japan's actions were part of the overarching threat of fascism (Krebs 2015). Other rule-breaking needs more explanation. Some rule-breaking may be argued to be legitimate: invading another state preemptively in the name of self-defense is an example. At other times, leaders must explain to their publics why an action that looks relatively benign demands a response.

This is when legitimation becomes critical in the social construction of threat: when the threat becomes visible, and there is a demand for interpretation, leaders must actively define the nature of their adversary to their audience. At times, a lack of rhetorical leadership leads to an inability to form a coherent grand strategy. Whatever Chamberlain *really* thought about Hitler—and the field remains rife with arguments about this (Yarhi-Milo 2014; Ripsman and Levy 2008)—the narratives surrounding Hitler's intentions remained unsettled through the 1930s. Despite a pattern of clear revisionist behavior, it was not until late 1938 that British leaders developed a cohesive story of Germany as a threat to Britain's national interest. At other moments, rhetorical leadership successfully interprets actions as threatening. It was not clear, for example, that the Truman administration would successfully convince the American public that the Soviet Union was a threat to the US national interest; its efforts to do so were necessary to mobilizing the public behind a strategy of containment. In each of these cases, legitimation was critical to the emergence of a coherent grand strategy.

Legitimation and Instruments

Finally, grand strategy requires the careful selection of instruments, decisions about how a state will deploy military, economic, or social power to secure the nation's interest against a threat. While George Kennan saw the Soviet Union as a significant threat to the United States, his vision of containment relied primarily on economic and diplomatic instruments to contain the Soviet Union; only after NSC-68 did containment shift to a military strategy. China's grand strategy uses some military resources in its South China Sea expansion but relies primarily on economic and institutional resources to expand its influence.

In a purely rationalist model, we would expect that leaders would select those instruments that would most effectively and efficiently produce the ends of grand strategy. As straightforward as this sounds, it assumes a world where leaders can conceive of infinite instruments available to them, and that the only "costs" that shape their choices are material ones. Empirically, we know that this is not the case. Leaders instead operate within a limited "toolkit" of statecraft: at any given time, there are a set of instruments of grand strategy that are seen as more or less legitimate (Goddard, MacDonald, and Nexon 2019). During the nineteenth century, it was legitimate for great powers to call a congress and settle disputes through the horse-trading of territory. By the end of that century, both the practice of calling congresses and the instrument of territorial exchange had lost legitimacy. In the contemporary international system, the legitimate use of force often rests on institutional channels and procedures, most notably gaining the support of the UN Security Council (Hurd 2007).

This is not to say that states select only instruments that are seen as legitimate; the argument here is not that states act within a "logic of appropriateness" at all times (March and Olsen 1998). It is to say, rather, that leaders understand that there are constraints on what instruments can be deployed and that there are costs to behaving illegitimately. Nor does this mean that legitimation is always necessary or significant. Indeed, during the normal course of foreign policy, the conventions surrounding what counts as "legitimate" instruments might be so well understood that no public justification is necessary. Much of diplomacy is conducted in a world where audiences are paying little attention and the need for mobilization is low.

But when the demand for legitimation is high, rhetoric will have significant effects on the instruments of grand strategy. To begin with, how leaders legitimate their nation's grand strategies makes particular instruments more salient than others. For example, as Rosa Brooks, Neta Crawford, and others argue, legitimating counterterrorism as a "war on terror" was more than mere rhetoric; it had significant effects on the instruments that could be used to fight terrorism at home and abroad. At the broadest level, the "war on terror" frame securitized terrorism, making it a threat that necessitated an offensive, preemptive, military response. A different legitimation would have opened up a different toolkit of grand strategy. Both Brooks and Crawford argue that, after 9/11, the Bush administration could have talked about terrorism as a crime, violence deployed by illegitimate actors against law-abiding citizens across the globe. Conceived in this way, a different toolkit becomes salient (Brooks 2017; Crawford 2003. See also Krebs and Lobasz 2007).

Moreover, a legitimation approach suggests that leaders understand that deviating from a recognized toolkit will come with costs, both at home and abroad. At home, populations might be less willing to support a grand strategy that operates with suspect instruments. Abroad, illegitimate strategies are more likely to provoke resistance. What this means is that, even when states select illegitimate instruments, they are still likely to claim that they are operating within the rules and norms of the international system. When the United States turned to military force in Iraq, despite the UN Security Council's decision to reject the use of force, the Bush administration claimed that it was still acting in the spirit of international norms and rules, protecting both democracy and principles of nonproliferation. Likewise, Russia's invasion and eventual annexation of Crimea was justified with appeals to liberal practices, claims that the Russian minority was being persecuted, and Russian protection necessary. These claims largely fell on deaf ears, however, and failed to stave off a punishing sanctions regime.

Indeed, so cognizant are leaders of the costs of illegitimate instruments that they will make attempts, where possible, to render their choices invisible to the public. Before attempting to legitimate the invasion and annexation of Crimea, Russia attempted to hide its efforts, using so-called "little green men" instead of uniformed soldiers in its operations. In doing so, Russia perhaps intended to create an "open secret" (Carson 2018), where all sides could ignore Russian involvement, and no justification would be necessary. For years, the Bush administration hid and then denied the existence of its targeted killing program; only after considerable pressure from human rights groups, especially Human Rights Watch, did the Bush administration began to articulate a normative rationale for targeted killings (Jose 2017). At times, so eager are officials to avoid the costs of legitimation that they adopt inefficient and even ineffective strategies. Covert regime change, as Lindsey O'Rourke demonstrates, rarely worked during the Cold War, but it did keep an illegitimate instrument of containment out of the public eye (O'Rourke 2018).

Winning the War of Words

Legitimation, in sum, shapes every aspect of grand strategy, from how nations define their collective interests, to how they perceive threats, to how they select instruments.[1] Yet explaining the demand and significance of legitimation does not account for the outcome. While leaders will always justify their grand strategy, they are not always successful. Before the Gulf War, President George H.W. Bush's attempts to legitimate US involvement were clumsy; the president "kept shifting his emphasis among various justifications for the U. S. military deployment in the Gulf, as if he were market-testing ads for a new deodorant" (quoted in Stein 2000, 240). Putin's appeals to liberal norms to justify his invasion and annexation of Crimea were largely dismissed by American and European audiences.

All of this raises the question: under what conditions will leaders successfully legitimate a grand strategy? Scholars of rhetorical politics have offered a range of answers to why legitimations work in some instances and not others. At the core of most of these theories is the concept of "resonance." Resonance is defined as whether the rhetoric is seen as having "pertinence, relevance, or significance" with a targeted audience (Kniss 1996. See also Checkel 2001; Keck and Sikkink 1998; Finnemore and Sikkink 1998; Payne 2001; Price 1998). For legitimation to matter, the appeals have to be heard.

Despite the concept's centrality, resonance remains an elusive concept. We know resonant rhetoric when we hear it. Indeed, that's the point. At times, a state's leaders attempt to legitimate its actions, but their language falls on deaf ears: other powers dismiss their justifications as ineffective, unimportant, or insincere. For example, the United States never found an effective justification for its 2003 intervention in Iraq, one that appeared as more than window-dressing on its interests. At other times, states struggle to cobble together an effective justification, even though everyone understands the rules of the game. It is tempting to establish the resonance of rhetoric after the fact: we know that a leader's legitimation strategies "resonated" when they convinced audiences that a grand strategy was justified. Doing so obviously risks tautology.

While there is no one generalizable theory of resonance, studies of legitimation have emphasized five factors as contributing to resonance:

(1) *Speaker*. As the literature on "securitization" has emphasized, not everyone "can 'do' or 'speak' security successfully," and some are "more or less privileged in articulating security" (Buzan, Wæver, and Wilde 1998, 27, 32). And, as Bourdieu observed, linguistic power is underpinned by the "belief in the legitimacy of words and of those who utter them" (Bourdieu 1991, 170). Some have authority to legitimate policy, while others shout from the sidelines. Some enjoy credibility as spokespersons for the public interest, while others are dismissed as self-serving. Some are more able than others to transcend rhetorical constraints and creatively design novel legitimation strategies. Some rhetorical approaches to politics emphasize the importance of agents, often seeming to embrace "great man theories" or charismatic approaches to rhetorical authority. We expect

skilled speakers like Franklin Delano Roosevelt or Winston Churchill to successfully legitimate their grand strategies.

Yet the recent literature of legitimation questions this focus on rhetorical skill, noting variation in even the best orators' ability to construct a national interest. However formidable Roosevelt's skill, during the 1930s, he failed to convince the United States that confronting Nazi Germany was a national interest (Krebs 2015). However much we remember Churchill's call for collective resistance, it is worth remembering that, during the interwar period, his attempts to name Hitler's Germany as a threat fell upon mostly deaf ears (Goddard 2015). Recent scholarship thus looks less at an individual's skill, and more at how certain individuals are positioned in ways to access rhetorical resources and legitimate grand strategy. In the United States, the authority to articulate the national interest often lies with the president, whose authority to speak for "the nation" may instead lie in his position partly outside partisan networks and everyday political squabbling, as the holder of the only nationally elected office. As Krebs and Lobasz argue, for example, George W. Bush's shaping of the national narrative in the wake of the 9/11 attacks was not the product of his unusual rhetorical skills, but rather of the authority he wielded in that moment to speak on the nation's behalf and make sense of what had transpired (Krebs and Lobasz 2007).

(2) *Context*. National security debate is also shaped by the institutional and discursive context: where and when they speak. Institutions affect not only whether legitimation is required and is politically significant, but also how legitimation contests play out. Institutional rules may grant some authority to speak security and impart agenda-setting power to others, making them more likely to win the legitimation battle. Those rules may also make subsequent challenge easier or harder, by subjecting officials to regular oversight or shielding them from it. The more institutional rules provide openings to opposition politicians or civil society to express alternative perspectives, the less enduring legitimation victories are. For example, as argued earlier, Mitzen's work on legitimation and the creation of a "European" collective identity focuses on the use of public forums (Mitzen 2013). It was both within and because of these institutional spaces that European leaders could persuade each other of their collective intention. It was in public forums, Mitzen demonstrates, that Metternich and Castlereagh managed to persuade Alexander that any action against the Ottomans during the Greek revolt would be a European issue, and convinced him to act in their collective interest.

Legitimating grand strategy depends upon the discursive context as well. Like other structures, discursive structures vary in their degree of slack: they can be very tight, reducing choice so dramatically that individuals feel suffocated, or they can be very loose, allowing individuals to perceive a world of possibility (Swidler 1986). As Krebs argues, for example, during "settled" times, a dominant discourse constitutes an unspoken common sense, and elites on both sides of debates must legitimate their preferred policies in its terms (Krebs 2015a). Challenges to grand strategy during such periods of routine politics are necessarily narrow. Those who ignore these discursive constraints when engaging in legitimation meet with a rude reception: leading elites and mainstream media either ignore them or treat them as beyond the bounds of respectability. In contrast, during "unsettled" times, debates over national security are comparatively unstructured. "Policy entrepreneurs" then enjoy the freedom to redefine the national interest and to advance new stories about threats.

(3) *Audience*. Audiences are central to legitimation, for it is they who determine the victor. As described above, when justifying their grand strategies, leaders are working not solely, nor even primarily, to persuade each other, but to mobilize the support of key constituencies behind their preferred strategy. This is challenging in large-scale, diverse polities with multiple constituencies. A policy justification that resonates with one constituency may strike another as illegitimate. When legitimation reinforces societal cleavages or appeals too narrowly, it cannot mobilize the support necessary for grand strategy.

For this reason, much of the work on legitimation examines how leaders attempt to legitimate across multiple audiences. For example, this may be one reasons that leaders are always tempted to "securitize" issues to mobilize support for grand strategy. By framing a challenge as an existential threat, leaders attempt to convince a fragmented audience to put aside their differences in order to ensure their own survival (Buzan, Waever, and Wilde 1998; Balzacq 2011). Other scholars have emphasized how leaders might effectively use "multivocal" strategies, legitimations that are heard differently by different audiences (Padgett and Ansell 1993; Goddard 2018; Nexon 2009).

4) *Content*. To recognize that what political actors say—the content of their legitimating appeals—matters is not to say that some arguments are naturally more persuasive or compelling than others. Whether framing is effective depends on whether the deployed frames draw on and are consistent with common rhetorical formulations or sit in tension with them. Weldes argues, for example, that leaders use collective meanings, or "security imaginaries" to define, "Who are we as a collectivity? What are we for one another? Where and in what are we? What do we want; what do we desire; what are we lacking?" (Weldes 1999, 10).

This explains why the collective interest so often remains the "national" one. As well-established repositories of collective identity, nation-states contain a trove of shared commonplaces that can be deployed to construct a shared purpose. In contrast, beyond the nation-state, whether shared commonplaces are available is more variable. Kornprobst argues, for example, that there was a dearth of shared commonplaces available to Europeans who wanted to construct a grand strategy. Without those commonplaces, Europe remained fragmented across state lines (Kornsprobst 2015). In constructing narratives of threat, leaders too rely on resonant language, telling stories of threat designed to mobilize publics. Milosevic's use of the Field of Blackbirds to mobilize Serbians in the 1990s was designed to link the threat of Kosovo secessionism to battles against the Ottoman Empire.

(5) *Technique*. The fate of legitimation rests not just on what is said, but how it is said, or rhetorical technique. Speakers strike audiences as skilled based in part on what metaphors, analogies, figures of speech, and tone they choose (Lakoff and Johnson 1980; Hart, Childers, and Lind 2013) as well as how they conform to the rhetorical conventions

associated with particular forms of public address, or genres (Fairclough 2003, chs. 4–6; see also Campbell and Jamieson 1990, 2008). Some argue, for example, that leaders are more successful when they rely on a transcendental language that goes beyond the often instrumental rhetoric of ordinary politics. Schou Tjalve and Williams, for instance, urged leaders to adopt religious language forms, specifically a jeremiad, to bind together their fractured polities (Schou Tjalve and Williams 2015). Krebs' work on narrative argues that presidents must adopt a "story-telling mode" if they are to effectively mobilize publics (Krebs 2015). Jack Snyder, likewise, suggests that public intellectuals who embed their policy recommendations in rich narratives, and purposefully conflate the empirical with the normative, are more likely to appeal to public audiences than do those that rely on a presentation of fact (Snyder 2015).

Conclusion: The Future of Legitimation

Human beings always give reasons for their actions. This essay makes the case that doing so matters, even in the high politics of grand strategy. It is the reasons that leaders give that constitute what collective interests are, what threats exist, and what instruments are available to preserve the nation, all of which are essential elements of grand strategy. All of that being said, many of the examples in this essay are drawn from a time when international institutional orders seemed more robust, when leaders held more power over their populations, when the masses relied on the same media for their message about foreign policy.

While some might suggest that increasing fragmentation abroad and polarization at home have made legitimation futile, there is reason to believe it has also made legitimation all the more necessary. There was a time where it was not necessary for the United States to explain why Western Europe was vital to American national interests and why continued investment in NATO was necessary. The decline of international institutions might also intensify legitimation contests among states. As rules and norms fragment, leaders can appeal to different norms and rules to justify their grand strategies at home and abroad. China can counter American appeals to human rights with a demand that the United States respect norms of sovereignty. Likewise, increasing domestic polarization in the United States may seem to undercut the possibility of legitimating a grand strategy and, in particular, of creating a coherent national interest (Schultz 2018). Scholars and policymakers are right to be worried about polarization, but it has never been the case that the national interest emerges neatly from domestic consensus. The more polarized domestic politics, the more demand there is for leaders to articulate the national interest, and why and how they intend to protect it. In other words, increasing uncertainty and contestation at home and abroad may have made legitimation difficult, but it has also rendered it even more essential to a successful grand strategy.

Note

1. The discussion below draws extensively on Goddard and Krebs 2015.

References

Balzacq, Thierry, ed. 2011. *Securitization Theory: How Security Problems Emerge and Dissolve.* Abingdon, UK: Routledge.
Betts, Richard K. 2000. "Is Strategy an Illusion?" *International Security* 11 (2): 5–50.
Bourdieu, Pierre. 1991. *Language and Symbolic Power.* Cambridge, MA: Harvard University Press.
Brooks, Rosa. 2017. *How Everything Became War and War Became Everything.* New York: Simon and Schuster.
Bukovansky, Mlada. 2002. *Legitimacy and Power Politics.* Princeton: Princeton University Press.
Bukovansky, Mlada. 2007. "Liberal States, International Order, and Legitimacy: An Appeal for Persuasion over Prescription." *International Politics* 44 (2): 175–193.
Buzan, Barry, Ole Wæver, and Jaap de Wilde. 1998. *Security: A New Framework for Analysis.* Boulder, CO: Lynne Rienner.
Campbell, Karlyn Kohrs, and Kathleen Hall Jamieson. 1990. *Deeds Done in Words: Presidential Rhetoric and the Genres of Governance.* Chicago: University of Chicago Press.
Carson, Austin. 2018. *Secret War: Covert Conflict in International Politics.* Princeton University Press.
Checkel, Jeffrey. 2001. "Why Comply: Social Learning and European Identity Change." *International Organization* 55 (1): 553–588.
Clark, Ian. 2007. *Legitimacy in International Society.* New York: Oxford University Press.
Clinton, W.C. 1994. *The Two Faces of National Interest.* Baton Rouge: Louisiana State University Press.
Crawford Neta. 2003. "The Slippery Slope to Preventive War." *Ethics & International Affairs* 17 (1): 30–36.
Elrod, Richard B. 1976. "The Concert of Europe: A Fresh Look at an International System." *World Politics* 28 (2): 159–174.
Elster, J. 1995. "Strategic Uses of Arguments." In *Barriers to Conflict Resolution*, edited by K. Arrow, 237–255. New York: Norton.
Finnemore, Martha. 2003. *The Purpose of Intervention: Changing Beliefs About the Use of Force.* Ithaca: Cornell University Press.
Finnemore, Martha. 2009. "Legitimacy, Hypocrisy, and the Social Structure of Unipolarity: Why Being a Unipole Isn't All It's Cracked Up to Be." *World Politics* 61 (1): 58–85.
Finnemore, Martha, and Kathryn Sikkink. 1998. "International Norm Dynamics and Political Change." *International Organization* 52 (4): 887–917.
Glaser, Charles. 2010. *Rational Theory of International Politics.* Princeton: Princeton University Press.
Goddard, Stacie E. 2015. "The Rhetoric of Power Politics: Hitler's Legitimation Strategies and the Creation of Uncertainty, 1935–1939." *Security Studies* 24 (1): 95–130.
Goddard, Stacie E. 2018. *When Right Makes Might: Rising Powers and World Order.* Ithaca: Cornell University Press.
Goddard, Stacie E., Paul K. MacDonald, and Daniel H. Nexon. 2019. "Statecraft: Instruments, Logics, and International Order." *International Relations* 33 (2): 304–321.

Goddard, Stacie E., and Ronald R. Krebs. 2015. "Rhetoric, Legitimation, and Grand Strategy." *Security Studies* 24 (1): 5–37.

Hall, Rodney Bruce. 1999. *National Collective Identity: Social Constructs and International Systems*. New York: Columbia University Press.

Hart, Roderick P., Jay P. Childers, and Colene J. Lind. 2013. *Political Tone: How Leaders Talk and Why*. Chicago: University of Chicago Press.

Helleiner, Eric. 2010. "A Bretton Woods moment? The 2007–2008 Crisis and the Future of Global Finance." *International Affairs* 86 (3): 619–636.

Hurd, Ian. 1999. "Legitimacy and Authority in International Politics," *International Organization* 53 (2): 379–408.

Hurd, Ian. 2007. "Breaking and Making Norms: American Revisionism and Crises of Legitimacy." *International Politics* 44 (2): 194–213.

Hurrelmann, Achim et al., eds. 2007. *Legitimacy in an Age of Global Politics*. Basingstoke: Palgrave Macmillan.

Ikenberry, G. John. 2001. *After Victory: Institutions, Strategic Restraint, and the Rebuilding of Order after Major Wars*. Princeton: Princeton University Press.

Ikenberry, G. John. 2011. *Liberal Leviathan*. Princeton: Princeton University Press.

Jackson, Patrick Thaddeus. 2006. *Civilizing the Enemy: German Reconstruction and the Invention of the West*. Ann Arbor, MI: University of Michigan Press, 2006.

Jervis, Robert J. 1978. "Cooperation under the Security Dilemma." *World Politics* 30 (2): 167–214.

Jervis, Robert J. 1989. *The Logic of Images in International Relations*. New York: Columbia University Press.

Jose, Betcy. 2017. "Not Completely the New Normal: How Human Rights Watch Tried to Suppress the Targeted Killing Norm." *Contemporary Security Policy* 38 (2): 237–259.

Kang, David C. 2020. *East Asia before the West: Five Centuries of Trade and Tribute*. New York: Columbia University Press.

Keck, Margaret, and Kathryn Sikkink. 1998. *Activists Beyond Borders, Advocacy Networks in International Politics*. Ithaca: Cornell University Press.

Kennedy, Paul, ed. 1992. *Grand Strategies in War and Peace*. New Haven, CT: Yale University Press.

Kornsprobst, Markus. 2015. "The European Union and Grand Strategy." *European Journal of International Relations* 21 (2): 267–292.

Kniss, Fred. 1996. "Ideas and Symbols as Resources in Intrareligious Conflict: the Case of American Mennonites." *Sociology of Religion* 57 (1): 7–23.

Krebs, Ronald K. 2015a. *Narrative and the Making of US National Security*. Cambridge: Cambridge University Press.

Krebs, Ronald K. 2015b. "Tell Me a Story: FDR, Narrative, and the Making of the Second World War." *Security Studies* 24 (1): 131–170.

Krebs, Ronald R. and Jennifer K. Lobasz. 2007. "Fixing the Meaning of 9/11: Hegemony, Coercion, and the Road to War in Iraq." *Security Studies* 16 (3): 409–451.

Kreps, Sarah. 2018. *Taxing Wars: The American Way of War Finance and the Decline of Democracy*. New York: Oxford University Press.

Kydd, Andrew. 1997. "Sheep in Sheep's Clothing: Why Security Seekers do not Fight Each Other." *Security Studies* 7 (1): 114–155.

Lakoff, George, and Mark Johnson. 1980. *Metaphors We Live By*. Chicago: University of Chicago Press.

March, James G., and Johan P. Olsen. 1998. "The Institutional Dynamics of International Political Orders." *International Organization* 52 (4): 943–969.

Mearsheimer, John J. 2002. *Tragedy of Great Power Politics*. New York: W. W. Norton.
Mitzen, Jennifer. 2013. *Power in Concert: The Nineteenth Century Origins of Global Governance*. Chicago: University of Chicago Press.
Mitzen, Jennifer. 2015. "Illusion or Intention: Talking Grand Strategy into Existence." *Security Studies* 24 (1): 61–94.
Mitzen, Jennifer, and Randall Schweller. 2011. "Knowing the Unknown Unknowns: Misplaced Certainty and the Onset of War." *Security Studies* 20 (1): 2–35.
Nexon, Daniel H. 2009. *The Struggle for Power in Early Modern Europe: Religious Conflict, Dynastic Empires, and International Change*. Princeton: Princeton University Press.
O'Rourke, Lindsey A. 2018. *Covert Regime Change: America's Secret Cold War*. Ithaca: Cornell University Press.
Padgett, John, and Christopher Ansell. 1993. "Robust Action and the Rise of the Medici, 1400-1434." *American Journal of Sociology* 98 (6): 1263.
Payne, Roger. 2001. "Persuasion, Frames and Norm Construction." *European Journal of International Relations* 7 (1): 38–39.
Price, Richard. 1998. "Reversing the Gun Sights: Transnational Civil Society Targets Land Mines." *International Organization* 52 (3): 613–644.
Ripsman, Norrin and Jack Levy. 2008. "Wishful Thinking or Buying Time? The Logic of British Appeasement in the 1930s." *International Security* 33 (2): 148–181.
Reus-Smit, Christian. 2004. *American Power and World Order*. Cambridge: Polity Press.
Schou Tjalve, Vibeke, and Michael C. Williams. 2015. "Reviving the Rhetoric of Realism: Politics and Responsibility in Grand Strategy." *Security Studies*, 24 (1): 37–60.
Schultz, Kenneth. 2018. "The Perils of Polarization," *Washington Quarterly* 40 (4): 7–28.
Schweller, Randall. 2006. *Unanswered Threats: Political Constraints on the Balance of Power*. Ithaca: Cornell University Press.
Snyder, Jack. 2015. "Dueling Security Stories: Wilson and Lodge Talk Strategy." *Security Studies* 24 (1): 171–197.
Steffek, Jens. 2003. "The Legitimation of International Governance: A Discourse Approach." *European Journal of International Relations* 9 (2): 249–275.
Stein, Arthur. 2000. "The Justifying State." In *Peace, Prosperity, and Politics*, edited by John Mueller, 235–255. New York: Westview Press.
Swidler, Ann. 1986. "Culture in Action," *American Sociological Review* 51 (2): 273–286.
Walt, Stephen. 1986. *The Origins of Alliances*. Ithaca: Cornell University Press.
Walt, Stephen. 2005. *Taming American Power: The Global Response to U.S. Primacy*. New York: W.W. Norton.
Weldes, Jutta. 1999. *Constructing National Interests: The United States and the Cuban Missile Crisis*. Minneapolis: University of Minnesota Press.
Wolfers, Arnold. 1962. *Discord and Collaboration*. Baltimore: The Johns Hopkins University Press.
Yarhi-Milo, Keren. 2014. *Knowing the Adversary: Leaders, Intelligence, and Assessment of Intentions in International Relations*. Princeton: Princeton University Press.
Zaum, Dominik, ed. 2013. *Legitimating International Organizations*. Oxford: Oxford University Press.

PART IV
INSTRUMENTS

CHAPTER 21

GRAND STRATEGY AND MILITARY POWER

PASCAL VENNESSON

MILITARY power is the crucible of grand-strategic thinking and action. Yet, the role and relative importance of military power in grand strategy has been ambivalent from the start and even contradictory. On the one hand, by bringing together all the state's industrial, societal, psychological, diplomatic, and other resources, grand strategy can magnify military power and unleash its destructive capacity in a total war. On the other, grand strategy can have the opposite effect and, if well executed, render the resort to force limited and the shift to full-blown war unnecessary. Moreover, the ongoing contest between narrow and broad accounts of grand strategy is fundamentally about military power. In this chapter, I examine military power through the lens of grand strategy succinctly understood as the vision, plans, and policies that comprise organized political actors' deliberate effort to harness all their resources to advance their long-term interests (these political actors do not have to be states: Luttwak 2001, 210; Vennesson 2010). By military power I mean the set of instruments and capabilities which confer to a given collective actor the capacity to bring about intended political objectives through the display, threat, and use of force. These instruments and capabilities include all organized forces, their doctrines and concepts of operations, as well as their personnel and armaments, either already existing or in the making and projected to exist in the future.

This chapter is organized as follows. I begin by identifying the First World War as the main origin of the distinctive idea of grand strategy resulting in its core meaning and ambivalence. I then show that grand strategy acts as a force multiplier, before exploring the ways in which military successes and failures affect grand-strategic effectiveness. Finally, I discuss how military power as a component of peacetime grand strategy can produce its psychological effects on the will of the adversary through the display and threat of force or competitive defense procurement rather than actual fighting. I conclude by arguing that the specific characteristics of military power help identify some of the limits of grand strategy, notably its underestimation of contingency arising from the dynamic interaction with a thinking adversary.

World War I, Military Power, and the Meaning of Grand Strategy

As a distinctive conception of strategy and set of practices, grand strategy was born from the profound crisis of military power during the First World War. Prior to the 1920s, the term "grand strategy" appeared rarely, was not anchored to a particular meaning, and remained virtually indistinguishable from (military) strategy (Milevski 2016, 15–27). To be sure, naval strategy and colonial expansion during the nineteenth and early twentieth century were important antecedents of grand-strategic thinking by bringing together military power and a wide range of other instruments and resources. Still, it was mostly between 1914 and 1918 that the commonly accepted understanding of plain "strategy"— the use of battle in a particular theater for the purpose of the war (what is generally seen today as the operational level of war)—proved insufficient to shape and to help understand the war and its conclusion (Strachan 2013, 14–15). This classical meaning of strategy left out too much of what had been crucially important for the conduct and outcome of the war and, many feared, was bound to characterize future wars: the mobilization of mass armies; the need to coordinate land, sea, and increasingly air power; the home front; the involvement of industries, coalition warfare; the worldwide geographical extension of theaters of operation; the systematic military exploitation of technical and scientific inventions; economic blockade; finance; domestic unrest; social revolution; propaganda and tight control of opinions; concentration of political power; diplomacy vis-à-vis allies and adversaries, etc. Of course, some of these aspects of warfare and statecraft preexisted, but crucially they were understood as lying in separate domains *outside* the scope of strategy (Poirier 1997, 33; Strachan 2013). Arising from the total experience of the war, grand strategy was originally designed to supplement and help military power achieve the political objectives that for four years seemed out of reach.

The emergence of integrated plans to mobilize the industry or use propaganda systematically, for example, and their explicit connection with military power in a broader or "grand" strategy may sound self-evident today, but it was revolutionary in the interwar period. It triggered a flurry of ideas and debates worldwide, in democracies and authoritarian regimes alike (Coutau-Bégarie 1999, 66–68). "Major strategy" and "grand strategy" became first J. F. C. Fuller's and then B. H. Liddell Hart's favored phrase to designate the range of ideas, plans, and policies designed to address this challenge in the United Kingdom. In the 1920s, Soviet strategists Mikhaïl Frunze and Alexander Svechin called for an "integral strategy" to bring together coherently military strategy on the one hand and political and economic strategy on the other. At the same time, the strategist of the Imperial Japanese Army, General Ishiwara Kanji, and other "total war" officers argued that Japan should prepare for a protracted war by skillfully meshing military and foreign policy tools, mobilizing the entire resources of the nation and promoting autarky (Barnhart 1987, 22–49). The ideas and abilities of both military and civilian leaders should be integrated in a broad "war leadership" which would require centralization of control over all aspects of Japanese government and society on an unprecedented scale (Peattie 1975, 71–74, 82). General Erich Ludendorff also emphasized the need for such a coordination of resources in the service of war understood as the supreme end of the state, and in the 1930s, Nazi leaders referred to "broadened strategy," while in Fascist Italy "integral war" was the phrase of choice. In the United States, political leaders and war planners used "global" and later "national" strategy, while "total," "global" or "integral" strategy became prominent in France, particularly after 1945 (Beaufre 1965, 30–31; Coutau-Bégarie 1999, 66–68). In sum, the First World War significantly broadened the scope of strategy, and the Second World War consolidated that trend, exacerbated by the advent of nuclear weapons (Vennesson 2017, 2020). Adding the term "grand" may appear needlessly grandiose, but it simply refers to a higher level of strategy, above tactics and operations. Irrespective of the preferred vocabulary, the central idea was similar: to recognize explicitly and to affirm the existence of a new, wider level and type of strategic thinking and practices, more complex and multifaceted than pure (military) strategy. This mode of strategic action had not been previously identified by prominent strategic thinkers such as Carl von Clausewitz or Antoine de Jomini.

Two main implications emerge from this history of the concept of grand strategy. First, we can now recast the alleged contest between narrow and broad understandings of grand strategy. In fact, I argue, there is no such contest (for a different perspective: Balzacq et al. 2019, 68–76). Instead, scholars focus either on strategy or on grand strategy depending on what they seek to explain and what they see as significant. Some, such as Barry Posen (2014), pay particular attention to plain (military) strategy. They examine preparations for war and ways of war; study military capabilities and how they are employed during wars. This is a rich and complex (certainly not "narrow") domain and a worthwhile endeavor devoted to strategy—but *not* to grand strategy. The reason is straightforward: grand strategy is not merely about subjecting military power to the discipline of policy, nor is it focused ultimately on fighting. Both political-military integration and combat long predated the notion of grand strategy and are already key components of what (military) strategy itself does. By contrast, others such as Stephen Brooks and William Wohlforth (2016), examine the interplay of military power, economics, technology, and institutions in the quest for core, long-term political objectives. Their endeavor, equally worth pursuing, is indeed about grand strategy, *not* (military) strategy. Calling such focus on grand strategy an "international relations" perspective is confusing (Balzacq et al. 2019, 71–76). The broadening scope of strategy beyond the use of battles to win wars did not originate in international relations in a generic sense but specifically within strategic thinking and practices, indeed within war itself as it became total (Vennesson 2017, 2020). Moreover, many dimensions of grand strategy are actually domestic, not international. Hence, there is no need to distinguish a military-focused "classicist" conception of grand strategy from a more holistic "international relations" one (Balzacq et al. 2019). There is only one tradition, although certainly diverse, of grand-strategic thinking which extends beyond the purely strategic conception of military power. The notion of grand strategy ultimately captures the historical and conceptual evolution of strategic theory after total war and the nuclear revolution.

Second, the experience of grand-strategic thinking and action is by no means limited to the West (see, for example, Weldemichael 2013). In the anticolonial struggles to achieve independence in Africa, Asia, Latin America, and the Middle East, liberation movements found ways to combine their initially limited military capabilities with a range of other resources, such as powerful mobilizing ideologies, popular support, and a range of diplomatic initiatives. For example, they took advantage of the United Nations General Assembly to put forward their demands and reduce the freedom of action of colonial powers. They forged the Non-Aligned Movement to shift the international political and economic agenda, and gain the support of fellow revolutionary regimes to create safe havens and benefit from logistical and other support.

Grand Strategy as Force Multiplier

Grand strategy is not synonymous with military statecraft, but military statecraft is one of its central components. Overall, grand strategy seeks to generate in a sustained way, including in peacetime, disproportionate power from a given level of military capability, by combining it with other instruments and resources (Luttwak 2009, 6). It is connected to, yet distinct from, and subordinated, to policy. Its central role is to distribute missions, coordinate and direct action, and balance resources among different domains, such as political, economic, diplomatic, cultural, psychological, and military, in order to achieve political objectives. These different domains act both autonomously and in connection to the others. The list of these policy instruments varies but generally includes diplomatic exchanges, "the public communication of propaganda, secret operations, the perceptions of others formed by intelligence, and all economic transactions of more than purely private significance" (Luttwak 2001, 209). Such a shrewd grand strategy can dramatically augment the impact of military power. For example, in his famous June 18, 1940 BBC Radio broadcast, General Charles de Gaulle, then aspiring leader of the Free French, offered a grand-strategic counternarrative projected into the future to react to an immediate setback (De Gaulle 1998, 83–84). Facing the prospect of the government of occupied France signing an armistice with the Nazi invaders, he admitted a severe defeat. However, he pointedly noted that what had actually been lost was only the battle of France, not the war itself, which could not be decided by a single battle. That war, he argued, was a world war, and military power had to be put in the context of a wide range of resources: France's colonial empire, its fleet and financial assets, as well as its allies, those engaged in the war such as the United Kingdom and those who may soon join, like the United States, who retained extensive capabilities and the command of the sea. He publicly used a grand-strategic frame to give meaning to what had just happened and offered a coherent response which integrated the short-term shock in a long-term view leading to ultimate victory. Revolutionary war, notably theorized and put to the task by Mao Zedong and Vo Nguyen Giap, is at its core a multidimensional struggle conceived and fought at the grand-strategic level in which military power is inserted within a set of other resources equally, if not more, significant at least in the initial phases.

Strategy is expected to say how military power can contribute to victory. Grand strategy is supposed to say how military power, together with a wide range of other (nonmilitary) resources, can weigh on the will of the adversary without military victory (Poirier 1985, 16). The key problem here is not the efficient application of force as in military strategy and tactics but the exploitation of potential force, including in peacetime (Schelling 1960, 5). Naval forces have been frequently used in their political role due to their mobility, flexibility, and wide geographic reach (Luttwak 1974). The workings of these missions are not based on the direct, destructive, or constraining, effect of military power. It depends instead on the reactions that the naval deployments may evoke for others. For example, between 1815 and 1918, the Royal Navy implemented the UK's grand strategy but did not fight a major action (Strachan 2013, 156). Alfred Mahan, Julian Corbett, and Raoul Castex emphasized the maritime sources of grand-strategic thinking and action (Strachan 2013, 155, 32; Milevski 2016, 27–44). During the Cold War, nuclear weapons became progressively consonant with the exploitation of potential force in their deterrent role but also by affecting the distribution of power in the international system. Over time, nuclear planning came to be seen as predictive, stabilizing, and long term (Strachan, 2013, 248).

The force multiplier effects of grand strategy on military power can be both fast and slow. Attrition or exhaustion is the gradual wearing down of an enemy, materially and psychologically, through the accumulation of damage. It is commonly contrasted with strategies of annihilation based on a swift, overwhelming victory leading to the political surrender of the defeated force. In some cases, the grand-strategic effects of military power operate slowly through attrition, like during the Cold War, notably characterized by the protracted arms race between the US and the Soviet Union (Milevski 2019). However, the grand-strategic uses of military power, through a mixture of deterrence, persuasion, and propaganda, can also be effective quickly, as shown by the annexation of the Crimean Peninsula by Russia in February–March 2014. Hitler's "extended (or broadened) strategy" brought about a string of successes from 1936 until 1938 through the skillful display of military power combined with other resources, such as propaganda and economic pressures, and without actual fighting. The forced domestic unity of the totalitarian regime, the militarization of its economy, and its presentation of an allegedly inevitable "new order" also contributed to intimidate the outside world. The intense, multiform propaganda effort, including ideas, slogans, movies, and rallies, formed an ideological offensive designed to undermine the unity of potential adversaries. The domestic use of secrecy, deception, and intimidation in peacetime was projected internationally. As Edward Mead Earle pointed out: "war to the Nazis no longer consisted solely, or even primarily, of military operations, the policy of the state in time of so-called peace was only a 'broadened strategy' involving economic, psychological, and other non-military weapons" (Mead Earle 1948, 513). In short, grand-strategic thinking and action is not intrinsically attritional.

While grand-strategic action aspires to be a force multiplier, this is not to say that in practice the coordinated action of diplomacy, economy, soft power, and military capabilities is easy or frequently achieved. Grand strategists strive to think and act in such a way as to provide military strategists with the best possible conditions in peacetime and wartime. Yet, the consequences of their action can be contradictory. They can create a situation in which military power devours resources and controls multiple policy areas, from industrial production to school curriculum, in the logic of total war. By helping organize mass mobilization and direct all the resources of a political community toward the war effort, it considerably expands military power and gives it the dominant role in peacetime and wartime. Grand strategy can also be designed in such a way to minimize as much as possible the relative importance of military power and ensure that a strictly limited, but well prepared from a diplomatic and propaganda perspective, display or threat of force is sufficient to reach the expected political goal. Grand strategy, by tightly integrating the policies and armaments of a nation, could render the resort to war unnecessary (Mead Earle 1948, 513). Similarly, for John Collins, grand strategy "if successful, alleviates any need for violence" (Collins 1973, 15). In fact, some grand-strategic thinking and practices are rooted in the acknowledgment of the distinct limits of the use of military force. As Edward Luttwak puts it: "In the imperial period [of Roman history] at least, military force was clearly recognized for what it is, an essentially limited instrument of power, costly and brittle. Much better to conserve force and use military power indirectly, as the instrument of political warfare" (Luttwak 1976, 2).

Moreover, from the perspective of military power, it is unclear whether grand strategy can actually be practiced over time, outside of the specific context of total war (Poirier 1997, 49). The leaders of the Soviet Union tried to put into place a military power–focused grand strategy, but it contributed to their demise. In times of war or major crisis, grand strategy tends to become more focused. In peacetime, it tends to be neglected, and the diversified bureaucracies of modern states, combined with the dispersion of power in democracies, often prove to be an impediment to the integration of plans and operations (Strachan 2013, 216).

Grand-Strategic Effectiveness of Military Power

Grand strategy introduces a distinctive way to assess the effectiveness of military power. A general can be skillful in the conduct of battles and campaigns, yet the government he serves may prove unable to integrate his ways and means with a wide range of other, nonmilitary, resources and to align them with larger political goals. The general may also misunderstand, or even disagree with, the grand strategy, leading to uses of force that may be irrelevant or counterproductive. Conversely, a grand strategy can prove successful despite military failures or stalemates at the tactical or operational level.

Military Successes, Grand-Strategic Failures

I take two examples, the Trafalgar Campaign (1805) and the generalship of Robert E. Lee during the American Civil War, to show that grand-strategic thinking casts military operations in a different light. In his *Campaign of Trafalgar* (1910), British naval strategist Julian Corbett provides a masterly assessment of the complex articulation between military effectiveness in a specific battle and its grand-strategic impact. He critically analyzes Prime Minister William Pitt's intricate offensive grand strategy designed to forge the Third coalition between England, Prussia, Russia, Austria, and Sweden, to encircle and destroy Napoleon's France. What matters to Corbett is not merely the naval battle of Trafalgar itself, but the interlocking and mutually supporting land, maritime, economic, and diplomatic instruments that brought it about. Pitt's audacious grand strategy attempted to reform domestic taxation, combine land and naval operations, and connect distant theaters of operation from the West Indies to the Mediterranean, from the English Channel to Southern Germany and Italy. These actions were articulated to a series of intricate diplomatic moves targeted at Russia and Prussia in order to encourage Austria to join and ultimately shift from alliance to war coalition. Instead of being centered on Admiral Nelson's decisions as Commander-in-Chief of the Mediterranean Fleet, British grand strategy involved a wider cast of decision-makers in the higher direction of the war who played a decisive role, notably Prime Minister Pitt, Lords Melville and Barham, successive First Lords of the Admiralty, as well as Lord Castlereagh, Secretary of War and the Colonies.

The battle of Trafalgar (October 21, 1805), fought by the Royal Navy against the combined fleets of the French and Spanish Navies off the southwest coast of Spain, was a stunning tactical success for the British. The perception that this naval victory saved Britain from invasion and the dramatic death of Admiral Nelson during the engagement ensured its symbolic significance. However, from a grand-strategic standpoint, the *campaign* of Trafalgar was a failure. While Nelson's fleet was able to keep command of the Mediterranean, sea power by itself was an insufficient instrument with which to defeat the French Empire. British land forces were too small to be committed without allies. Diplomatic negotiations proved lengthy and cumbersome, and Napoleon's quick and daring offensive against Austrian and Russian forces culminated in his victory at Austerlitz (December 2, 1805). As Corbett pointed out with the battle of Austerlitz: "the fatal blow was delivered, and Pitt's grand fabric was in ruins. Though at first the truth was not realised, the Third Coalition had ceased to exist" (Corbett 1910, 415).

Alan Nolan's critical appraisal of Robert E. Lee's generalship during the American Civil War provides another assessment of military effectiveness grounded in grand-strategic thinking (Nolan 1991). While often successful tactically and operationally, he maintains, General Lee was deficient at the grand-strategic level. In fact, President of the Confederacy Jefferson Davis and his administration never really defined the South's grand strategy in the first place (Nolan 1991, 72). While general Lee fully accepted civilian control, he autonomously developed his own sense of the grand strategy of the Confederacy and how his Army of Northern Virginia would implement it. He believed that the South's grand strategy was, and should be, offensive and his view translated in the specific troop movements that he advocated and planned for. However, Lee's grand strategy of the offensive and his single-minded attempt to defeat the Federal Army outright was counterproductive and hurt the Confederacy's prospects for victory over the Union. The South notably suffered from a manpower disadvantage and, in addition to battle losses, the demanding offensive also extracted a price in illness and desertions. To be sure, siege warfare would not have been sustainable, and it had to keep its armies in the field. Yet, General Lee's offensives "produced high casualty rates, and these casualties exacerbated the manpower differential, made a siege more likely, and reduced the Confederacy's ability to maintain an effective fighting force" (Nolan 1991, 88–89). In short, according to Alan Nolan, insisting on the offensive regardless of defensive opportunities may have been tactically and operationally bold, but it was not grand-strategically sound. General Lee's direction of military forces undermined the capacity of resistance of the Confederacy.

The cases of the Trafalgar Campaign and the generalship of Robert E. Lee, examined through the lens of grand strategy, help bring to light three patterns. First, military power is dependent on, and connected to, a wider range of capabilities and instruments such as maritime, economic, and diplomatic initiatives or, in the case of the Confederacy, a demographic disadvantage. The central challenge is not only the use of force itself but the complexity of mutual dependence and joint action under constraint, even if there is an agreement on the political goal being pursued. In any given campaign or battle, the military commanders' decisions at the tactical and operational level are important but incomplete. Their performance cannot be considered outside of their grand-strategic contexts. Second, and related, in addition to the military commanders, here Admiral Nelson and General Lee, a wider cast of decision-makers in the higher direction of the war are influential and need to be taken into account because they contribute to shape military power. However, as the case of the Confederacy shows, the civilian leadership does not always define the grand strategy and generals may then develop their own grand-strategic sense of the war, which may or may not help reach the expected political ends. Third, there is no straightforward or necessary transmission belt from success at the tactical or operational level to desirable grand-strategic consequences. In fact, tactical or operational successes may remain inconsequential, or even counterproductive, for grand strategy. These two cases are obviously far from unique. For example, Napoleon proved ultimately unable to translate his almost continuous tactical and operational successes until the invasion of Russia in 1812 into durable grand-strategic achievements. Lieutenant General Erwin Rommel's operational successes in North Africa in 1941 could not translate into a decisive victory at the grand-strategic level. Imperial Japan's tactical and operational success at Pearl Harbor was counterproductive at the level of grand strategy (Luttwak 2001, 239, 248).

Military Failures, Grand-Strategic Successes

During the Vietnam War, North Vietnamese forces never defeated any large body of American troops in battle and did not exhaust US military superiority. Yet, the stalemate and their occasional limited military successes helped prolong the war, allowing diplomacy and propaganda to weaken US relations with its allies and, most importantly, erode the political consensus that sustained the war effort (Luttwak 2001, 250). In 1973, the crossing of the Suez Canal by Egyptian forces was not expected to bring about a military victory over Israel and impose a settlement. After some early successes in the Sinai, combined with Syrian force progression on the Golan Heights, the Arab forces found themselves in a precarious position. The Israel Defense Forces counteroffensive pushed back the Syrian army, crossed the Suez Canal into Egypt, and encircled their adversary. However, President Sadat's limited offensive activated Egypt's diplomatic strength, notably its ability to rely on the Soviet Union's influence in world affairs and on the support of the Arab world, as well as Western anxiety regarding access to oil (Luttwak 2001, 250–256). Despite the partial and short-lived tactical and operational achievements, these mixed diplomatic and economic pressures on Israel, combined with force, helped Egypt achieve a grand-strategic success with the 1974 disengagement agreement that left it in control of both banks of the Suez Canal (Luttwak 2001, 250–256).

Beyond the Use of Force: Grand-Strategic Effects of Military Power

Grand strategy does not approach military power as a fixed set of instruments that should be employed in only one way. Instead, particularly in peacetime, grand-strategic thinking pushes some of its dimensions in the background and brings others to the fore. Success does not necessarily depend on actual fighting but in exploiting in multiple ways different facets of military power. From the perspective of grand strategy, the linkage between strategy and tactics is not central. What matters instead is the link between military capabilities (land, naval, air, cyber) and economic and geopolitical effects, not necessarily or not primarily, mediated by the actual the use of force. The wager of peacetime grand strategy is that military power can produce its required psychological effects on the will of the adversary *directly*, bypassing the clash of arms. This runs directly counter to the notion that tactical results are the only things that matter in war and that where there is no battle, nothing is accomplished. Such a change of emphasis does not dilute the fact that states exist in a world where war is possible, on the contrary. War remains the horizon of all grand-strategic choices and forces policymakers to operate in a climate of uncertainty and under constraints (Poirier 1985, 15–16). The preparation for war does not cease to be a core military task, but in a grand-strategic perspective, some dimensions of military power become more salient than others. Specifically, grand strategy gains in relative emphasis over war, the display and threat of force over its employment and defense procurement over operations.

Grand Strategy, Not Just War

The striking scope and destruction during the First and particularly the Second World War magnified by the implications of the nuclear age put into question the preeminent role of war as a strategic instrument (this section is based on Vennesson 2017). An exclusive reliance on war fighting could not be decisive and, in the case of a war among nuclear armed belligerents, could even prove catastrophic. Compared to the prenuclear era, the warcentric aspects of military power lost their preeminence. While for Clausewitz, strategy was incorporated into war, Cold War grand strategies released strategy from the confines of war. As Bernard Brodie famously pointed out: "Thus far the chief purpose of our military establishment has been to win wars. From now on its chief purpose must be to avert them. It can have almost no other useful purpose" (Brodie 1946, 76).

In the 1950s and 1960s, with the end of the US monopoly on nuclear weapons and the spread of ballistic missiles, the Cold War strategic thinkers, such as Thomas Schelling, Herman Kahn, Bernard Brodie, Albert Wohlstetter, and André Beaufre, reconceptualized strategy as incorporating the vast range of virtual modes of employment of coercive capacities designed to influence the will of political and military actors as well as societies in peacetime as well as in times of crisis (Vennesson 2017; Mahnken 2012). This grand-strategic thinking indicated that military power could not be limited to war anymore, since it came to include nuclear deterrence that sought to make war impossible. These practitioners, thinkers, and analysts who were not for the most part soldiers but predominantly engineers, economists, sociologists, and mathematicians, were not bounded by traditional "military" perspectives and developed different views of military power. Deterrence, compellence, and arms control were the emblematic components of Cold War grand-strategic thinking. In addition to war as a specific mode of force employment, an entire body of knowledge about coercive means and action, such as economic coercion, covert action, or information operations, became components of grand strategy. In such an altered strategic context, military organizations took on nonwar fighting roles such as surveillance and monitoring, peace support, humanitarian relief, and security operations. Political objectives could still be achieved by combining a limited military action with a range of psychological, economic, and diplomatic instruments. Consequently, the grand-strategic effects of military power became more widespread and pervasive. They are felt not primarily in war but equally, and even more prominently, in peacetime as well as in all the crises situations, which lay at the fuzzy boundary between war and peace (Zenko 2010).

Display and Threat, Not Just Use of Force

In peacetime grand strategy, military power plays a significant role through the display and the intended or unintended threat of force. This mix of armed diplomacy and propaganda is the everyday, latent, and continuous grand-strategic effects of military power on world order (Luttwak 2001, 224). As Edward Luttwak points out: "Any instrument of military power that can be used to inflict damage upon an adversary, physically limit his freedom of action, or reveal his intentions may also affect his conduct, and that of any interested third parties, even if force is never actually used" (Luttwak 1974, 6). He labeled "armed suasion" "all reactions, political or tactical, elicited by all parties—allies, adversaries, or neutrals—to the existence, display, manipulation, or symbolic use of any instrument of military power, whether or not such reaction reflects any deliberate intent of the deploying party" (Luttwak 1974, 10–11). Crucially, the perception of the party to be influenced, be they friends or adversaries—not the military power of the sender as such—is what produces the persuasion or the deterrence effects (Luttwak 1974, 6). Their perceptions, emotions, calculations lead these friends and adversaries to decide (or not) to be convinced or deterred. The goal of military power–focused diplomacy and propaganda, such as a naval deployment for example, is to manipulate these subjective evaluations. These uses of military power to influence and convince can include "symbolic" uses of force, as long as they are perceived as symbolic, i.e. that the damage has been deliberately minimized by the target.

The display of the instruments of military power is also designed to intimidate. The notoriously secretive North Korean regime publicly displays its weapons, including nuclear missiles, during its Day of the Foundation of the Republic military parade. The belief that during the Ukrainian crisis, Russian decision-makers put into practice a preexisting strategy of "hybrid warfare" is another illustration of these manipulations of beliefs about military power. During the 1930s, Nazi Germany and Fascist Italy went at great length to project a facade of awesome military power, especially air power, which generated exaggerated assessments and erroneous beliefs in a rapid shift in the balance of power. As Edward Luttwak notes, the spectacular long-range flights of the Italian Air Force to the North Pole and South America as well as the massive military parades contributed to deter Britain and France to interfere with Italy's conquest of Ethiopia, its intervention in the Spanish Civil War, and its annexation of Albania (Luttwak 2001, 221). Similarly, in the 1950s Soviet leaders used impressive imagery of space exploration to magnify their nuclear capabilities and give credence to their claim that they had achieved superiority over the United States. Of course, there are trade-offs between a military policy of stage management exclusively focused on grand-strategic effects and the specific needs of war preparation. As in the case of Mussolini, some political actors can be tempted to sacrifice combat strength for the sake of a manipulative image of military power, designed for propaganda and grand-strategic effects (Luttwak 2001, 220–221). Finally, military doctrines are another component of this display of intentions. In addition to their tactical or operational significance, they can have direct international political effects (Strachan 2013, 247–248). A doctrinal preference for the offensive, for example, could have destabilizing consequences at the grand-strategic level, such as affecting the likelihood that wars will break out or the outcome of wars that have already begun. The doctrines shaping the potential (non) uses of nuclear weapons had such a political impact that they were seen in grand-strategic terms (Strachan 2013, 247). To be sure, such everyday grand-strategic effects of military instruments are significantly less constraining than the wartime uses of force. Yet, they have other advantages, as Edward Luttwak pointed out: "power born of *potential* force is not expended when used, nor is it a finite quantity. Force, on the other hand, is just that: if directed to one purpose, it cannot simultaneously be directed at another, and if used, it is *ipso facto* consumed" (Luttwak 1976, 33).

Defense Procurement, Not Just Military Operations

In *On War*, Carl von Clausewitz excluded the preparation of forces from his conception of strategy. By contrast, grand strategy is anchored in the profound consequences of mid-nineteenth-century industrial and technological development for military power. In the twentieth century, the research and development effort to improve existing weapons or create new ones became permanent and had far-reaching implications in peacetime and in wartime. The cost of weapon systems as well as the duration of their conception and fabrication gave them a greater relative importance in strategic practices, particularly with nuclear weapons. This is not just to say that the planning, programming, and budget execution cycle, with its long-term temporal dimension and complex assessment of risk, is an important component of grand strategy. It is a stronger statement: beyond acquiring weapon systems, arms procurement increasingly became an important way to put military power to the task to help achieve directly grand-strategic objectives. The theory and process of arms control illustrates this connection between the instruments of military power and grand-strategic outcomes. In the context of the Cold War, nuclear competition, arms control negotiations, and agreements served to divert the great power conflict and channel it away from its aspects deemed undesirable by the belligerents. As Thomas Schelling indicated, arms control sought to "reshape military incentives and capabilities with a view to stabilizing mutual deterrence" (Schelling 1966, 248). Irrespective of whether or not these negotiations and partial agreements would bring the conflict to an end, arms control restrained specific features of some weapons while releasing resources to build new weapons or weapons with novel configurations (Luttwak 2001, 214–217).

Most importantly, armament programs became in themselves a component of grand-strategic influence. Even future programs for weapon systems only projected or partially built are used politically in the context of a larger power competition. In the early 1980s, director of the US Department of Defense's Office of Net Assessment Andrew Marshall contributed to the adoption of cost-imposing or "competitive" armament strategy, exploiting US technological advantages and imposing disproportionately large costs on the USSR's military efforts (Mahnken 2012; Krepinevich and Watts 2015; Mahnken 2020). Armament procurement policy helped the United States to compete more effectively in the continuing peacetime rivalry with the Soviet Union. Andrew Marshall urged to move the rivalry into areas where the USSR would have to expend far more resources than the United States to remain competitive and to create conditions that would lead Soviet leaders to invest in less threatening capabilities (Krepinevich and Watts 2015, 167). The United States capitalized on its advantages such as stealth air technology (B2 bomber) and submarine detection and quieting. Ronald Reagan's Strategic Defense Initiative (SDI) was a prominent competitive strategy. Even minimally effective missile defenses would force Soviet planners to significantly increase the allocation of warheads to ensure a sufficiently high success rate and also reinforce the deterrent effect (Krepinevich and Watts 2015, 169). The instruments of military power exerted a direct grand-strategic influence, not through their actual use in war, but through their contribution to exhaust the Soviet Union economically. Similarly, being ahead in concepts of operation and organizational innovation at the core of the revolution in military affairs would produce desirable grand-strategic effects, such as preserving US preeminence (Krepinevich and Watts 2015, 220). In this grand strategy of attrition, the ways and means are scientific research and technological innovation applied to military power. In sum, armament programs and their constantly renewed rationale are important facets of military power at the grand-strategic level. They are used not just to acquire weapon systems but also to send signals to, and to shape the preferences and behaviors of enemies and allies, while coopting public opinion and pressure groups domestically. For example, China and the United States competitively develop technologies and doctrines of "anti-access/area denial" (A2/AD) and "AirSea Battle" (ASB) in the South China Sea (Mahnken 2012). This long-term trajectory of technical and acquisition trends, as well as strategies and operational concepts, between two states which at present cannot outspend each other, has an important grand-strategic, diplomatic, dimension in addition to its military technological aspect.

Military Power and the Limits of Grand Strategy

British strategic thinker Basil Liddell Hart noted that "while grand strategy should control strategy, its principles often run counter to those which prevail in the field of strategy" (Liddell Hart 1991, 353). In what ways do the principles of grand strategy run counter those which prevail for military strategy? Grand strategy is, at least in part, a declaration of intent oriented towards future, high-level goals and an indication of the possible resources and means required to achieve these goals (Strachan 2013, 235; Silove 2018). It promises to increase effectiveness and improve action by being systematic, efficient, coordinated, and consistent. Since the late 1990s, among

Western countries, grand strategy is understood as managing and controlling future risks reactively, wedded to the status quo and assuming predictability (Strachan 2013, 235–252). In short, grand strategy seeks to project linear-logical, long-term goals and solutions into the realm of conflict. However, military power is a persistent reminder that contingency and the dynamic interaction among adversaries are likely to frustrate grand-strategic projects.

To be sure, grand strategy is designed to help political and military leaders subjugate force to the reign of political reason. Indeed, military leaders often lament the absence of grand strategy (Strachan 2013, 216). Moreover, translating political goals into operational plans and resolutely executing them are certainly important aspects of military power. However, the top-down, planning-oriented understanding of grand strategy contradicts a number of central dimensions of military power, which also belongs to the realm of contingency, uncertainty, and interaction (Strachan 2013, 235–252). The distinctive characteristics of force, its embeddedness into politics, as well as the interactive characteristics of conflict point to serious limits of common, peacetime grand-strategic thinking (this section is based on Vennesson 2020). For example, at the core of Carl von Clausewitz theory lies the "remarkable (wondrous) trinity" which establishes that wars are not only made of "pure reason": emotions interact with the play of chance and probabilities of military art, as well as the rational finality that shape action. Instead of claiming that the use of force unfolds in a necessary dynamic, he stressed contingencies, distortion, and errors which are an integral part of the phenomena. Morale, emotions, and perceptions come into play, and uncertainty is not merely a lack of information but a problem of how to process and understand information.

Military leaders are acutely aware of the tendency of the use of force to elude, at least partially, rational control. Friction, another key component of Clausewitz's conceptual system, designates the imponderable elements, both natural and social, like the imperfection of knowledge, the uncertainty vis-à-vis one's own army and the army of the enemy, spatial and temporal inaccuracies, or the resistances due to the characteristics of organizations, that insert themselves between the reasonable calculations of the political and military actors and their, often problematic, implementation (Clausewitz 1832, 69). The display, threat, or use of force alters circumstances, contexts, and objectives. In short, core dimensions of military power remind grand strategists that the results that they envision are not as predictable as they think, that an element of surprise is likely to interfere, and that the outcomes are likely to be different from those sought by any single participant to the complex making of the grand strategy.

Grand strategy cannot be solely approached as a means of technical control over an objectified set of future risks but should be able to respond to immediate preoccupations. In a conflicting environment, the display, threat, or use of force face an active adversary consciously pursuing his own coercive goals. It is inherently characterized by the reciprocity of voluntary actions. Military leaders recognize the significance of longer-term aspiration, but they must work with contingency (Strachan 2013, 103). Having in place the right coordinating institutions, such as a National Security Council or its equivalent for example, and controlling a range of preexisting, economic, diplomatic, and societal resources, is only a start. These preconditions cannot be a substitute for facing the logics of conflictual situations and their interlocking features. These interactions have logics of their own, and tend to take off and become independent from the conditions of their genesis. Military leaders discover empirically, in the course of the conflictual interaction, what the actual constraints under which grand-strategic ideas may expect to operate and how they perform under uncertainty. Many of these constraints remain hidden in the planning stage at the grand-strategic level. They only become clearer in the implementation process, notably when friction becomes intertwined with action. Military power is about exploiting the opportunities which arise in the course of action. Far from rigidly executing orders, military leaders exercise their capacity for judgment to process the complexity of a specific situation and act reasonably, meaning thoughtfully and appropriately (Sumida 2008, 135–153; Vennesson 2020). Instead of the Cold War, the exercise of grand strategy during the Second World War was more attuned to the logic of military power. As historian Hew Strachan emphasized, grand strategy was then reactive and prudential, and often proved to be an exercise in flexibility and adaptability in the short term sustained by a narrative projected into the future (Strachan 2013, 243).

In the end, success is not based on abstract knowledge of decision rules or on obedience to directives; it cannot be derived by purely analytical means from a priori considerations (Schelling 1960, 162–163). Military power and military strategy are a reminder that ways and means cannot always be bypassed but need to be included in the conceptual stage of grand strategy. A desired future is likely to amount to nothing if the actual interactive process and its unintended consequences is ignored or neglected. The danger of grand strategy understood exclusively as a peacetime plan is that it may rob military strategy from some of the flexibility needed when confronting a specific crisis. Grand strategy is not something that could be learned and analyzed uniquely in terms of coordinated action and rational precepts. Strategic thinking which accompanies military power, but is sometimes lost at the grand-strategic level, is indispensable to approach what Lucia Seybert and Peter Katzenstein call "protean power," i.e. "the effect of improvisational and innovative responses to uncertainty that arise from actors' creativity and agility in response to uncertainty" (Seybert and Katzenstein 2018, 4).[1]

Note

1. An earlier version of this chapter was delivered as the Pierre Hassner Lecture at the 12th Conference of the Italian Standing Group on International Relations, Trento, Italy, June 2019. I thank Filippo Andreatta and Vittorio Emanuele Parsi for their kind invitation and friendship over the years, the participants for their questions, as well as Thierry Balzacq, Kenneth Kuniyuki, Anit Mukherjee, Ong Weichong, and Evan Resnick for their thoughtful suggestions.

References

Balzacq, Thierry, Peter Dombrowski, Simon Reich. 2019. "Is Grand Strategy a Research Program? A Review Essay." *Security Studies* 28 (1) 2019: 58–86.

Barnhart, Michael A. 1987. *Japan Prepares for Total War. The Search for Economic Security, 1919-1941*. Ithaca, NY: Cornell University Press.

Beaufre, André. 1965 [1st ed. 1963]. *Introduction to Strategy*. London: Faber and Faber.

Brodie, Bernard, ed. 1946. *The Absolute Weapon: Atomic Power and World Order*. New York: Harcourt, Brace.

Brooks, Stephen, and William Wohlforth. 2016. *America Abroad: The United States' Global Role in the 21st Century*. Oxford: Oxford University Press.

Clausewitz, Carl von. 1832/1976. *On War*. Princeton, NJ: Princeton University Press.

Collins, John M. 1973. *Grand Strategy: Principles and Practices*. Annapolis, MD: Naval Institute Press.

Corbett, Julian S. 1910. *The Campaign of Trafalgar*. London: Longman, Green and Co.

Coutau-Bégarie, Hervé. 1999. *Traité de stratégie*. Paris: Economica-Bibliothèque stratégique.

De Gaulle, Charles. 1998 [1st ed. 1954]. *The Complete War Memoirs of Charles de Gaulle*. New York: Carroll & Graf Publishers.

Krepinevich, Andrew, and Barry Watts. 2015. *The Last Warrior. Andrew Marshall and the Shaping of Modern American Defense Strategy*. New York: Basic Books.

Liddell Hart, Basil. H. 1991 [1st ed. 1929]. *Strategy*. New York: Meridian.

Luttwak, Edward N. 1974. *The Political Uses of Sea Power*. Baltimore: The Johns Hopkins University Press.

Luttwak, Edward N. 1976. *The Grand Strategy of the Roman Empire. From the First Century A.D. to the Third*. Baltimore: The Johns Hopkins University Press.

Luttwak, Edward N. 2001 [1st ed. 1987]. *Strategy. The Logic of War and Peace*. Cambridge, MA: The Belknap Press of Harvard University Press.

Luttwak, Edward N. 2009. *The Grand Strategy of the Byzantine Empire*. Cambridge, MA: The Belknap Press of Harvard University Press.

Mahnken, Thomas G., ed. 2012. *Competitive Strategies for the 21st Century. Theory, History, and Practice*. Stanford: Stanford University Press.

Mahnken, Thomas G., ed. 2020. *Net Assessment and Military Strategy. Retrospective and Prospective Essays*. New York: Cambria Press.

Mead Earle. Edward. 1948 [1st ed. 1943]. "Hitler: the Nazi Concept of War." In *Makers of Modern Strategy. Military Thought from Machiavelli to Hitler*, edited by Edward Mead Earle, 504–516. Princeton: Princeton University Press.

Milevski, Lukas. 2016. *The Evolution of Modern Grand Strategic Thought*. Oxford: Oxford University Press.

Milevski, Lukas. 2019. *Grand Strategy Is Attrition: The Logic of Integrating Various Forms of Power in Conflict*. Carlisle Barracks, PA: United States Army War College Press.

Nolan, Alan T. 1991. *Lee Considered. General Robert E. Lee and Civil War History*. Chapel Hill: The University of North Carolina Press.

Peattie, Mark R. 1975. *Ishiwara Kanji and Japan's Confrontation with the West*. Princeton, NJ: Princeton University Press.

Poirier, Lucien. 1985. *Les voix de la stratégie*. Paris: Fayard.

Poirier, Lucien. 1997. *Le chantier stratégique*. Paris: Hachette-Pluriel.

Posen, Barry. 2014. *Restraint: A New Foundation for U.S. Grand Strategy.* Ithaca, NY: Cornell University Press.

Schelling, Thomas C. 1960. *The Strategy of Conflict.* Cambridge: Harvard University Press.

Schelling, Thomas C. 1966. *Arms and Influence.* New Haven: Yale University Press.

Seybert, Lucia A., and Peter J. Katzenstein. 2018. "Protean Power and Control Power: Conceptual Analysis." In *Protean Power. Exploring the Uncertain and Unexpected in World Politics*, edited by Lucia A. Seybert and Peter J. Katzenstein, 3–26. Cambridge: Cambridge University Press.

Silove, Nina. 2018. "Beyond the Buzzword: The Three Meanings of 'Grand Strategy.'" *Security Studies* 27 (1): 27–57.

Strachan, Hew. 2013. *The Direction of War. Contemporary Strategy in Historical Perspective.* Cambridge: Cambridge University Press.

Sumida, Jon Tetsuro. 2008. *Decoding Clausewitz. A New Approach to On War.* Lawrence, KS: University Press of Kansas.

Vennesson, Pascal. 2010. "Competing Visions for the European Union Grand Strategy." *European Foreign Affairs Review* 15: 57–75.

Vennesson, Pascal. 2017. "Is Strategic Studies Narrow? Critical Security and the Misunderstood Scope of Strategy." *The Journal of Strategic Studies* 40 (3): 358–391.

Vennesson, Pascal. 2020. "Is Strategic Studies Rationalist, Materialist and a-Critical?" *Journal of Global Security Studies* 5 (3): 494–510.

Weldemichael, Awet Tewelde. 2013. *Third World Colonialism and Strategies of Liberation. Eritrea and East Timor Compared.* Cambridge: Cambridge University Press.

Zenco, Micah. 2010. *Between Threats and War. U.S. Discrete Military Operations in the Post-Cold War World.* Stanford: Stanford University Press.

CHAPTER 22

DIPLOMACY AND GRAND STRATEGY

OLE JACOB SENDING

IN his book, *On Grand Strategy*, John Lewis Gaddis notes that strategy has to "proportion aspirations to capabilities" stressing that "These are opposites—the first being free from limits and the second bound by them." (2018,175). Schematically, we may say that grand strategy here takes the form of a plan for how to reach these aspirations, whereas capabilities is the tool box available to implement it.[1] As such, Gaddis can be said to include diplomacy under grand strategy, in that the former features as part of the toolbox, or capabilities, for the latter. Gaddis goes further, suggesting that succeeding in grand strategy requires that aspiration and capabilities "must connect," which only happens when "you hold both in mind simultaneously." (2018, 117). Presented in this way, we get a sense of the intellectual trajectory of grand strategy that is discussed elsewhere in this volume (XX, this volume), where the *locus* of balancing between aspiration and capabilities, and of succeeding or failing in conducting grand strategy, is very much the statesmen who, operating through diplomacy to engage other states, succeed or fail in formulating and implementing a good strategy.

This image of statesmen who operate to shape world events—Bismarck, Roosevelt, de Gaulle, Bush, Xi, Trump—is very much on display in Kissinger's *Diplomacy* (1994). The book is said to "illuminate just what diplomacy *is*" but is perhaps more accurately described as an international political history of the West, and where diplomacy is the sum total of decisions of political leaders and their effects. It describes the emergence of the state system, based on sovereignty and the balance of power from the seventeenth century onwards, and proceeds to take on the Concert of Europe, revolutionary projects (Napoleon III, Bismarck), the causes and consequences of the First and Second World Wars, international crises during the Cold War (Suez 1956–1957, Hungary 1956, Berlin 1958–1963), and the end of the Cold War. Kissinger's implicit rendering of diplomacy is of interest in this context, because it comes close to equating grand strategy with diplomacy: it features discussions of how different statesmen understood, and misunderstood, the context in which they were operating, and assessments of the strategies they used to achieve their aims. In this sense, Kissinger's *Diplomacy* is as much a book about grand strategy as Gaddis's (2018) *On Grand Strategy* is about diplomacy.

Both place statesmen at the heart of their analyses. Kissinger zooms in on the decisions of such leaders at decisive moments, stressing their ability (or lack thereof) to see and navigate in the political terrain of their time. Gaddis (2018) approaches it from a similar perspective, stressing the importance of leaders being able to hold both aspiration and capabilities in mind when making decisions. To understand the relationship between grand strategy and diplomacy, however, it is useful to broaden the perspective and consider diplomacy as more than the decisions of statesmen *qua* diplomats. In this chapter, I do so by exploring in some detail the *institution* of diplomacy. There are two versions of such an institutional perspective, one which foregrounds diplomacy as a set of meaning-defining and action-facilitating rules and practices, in keeping with a new institutionalist perspective (Powell and Dimaggio 1991; cf. Sending, Pouliot, and Neumann 2015). The other version draw insights from work on performance and performativity (Butler 1997) to explore how these same institutionalized rules and practices is what makes possible the acting out or performance of particular forms of states, or state identity, in the first place (Neumann and Sending 2020). In the first version, institutions enable and constrain preconstituted actors. In the second version, institutions are constitutive of them, as there is "no doer before the deed" (Duvall and Chowdhury 2011).

I discuss central insights from both views of diplomacy, but spend more time on the latter, as it has received less attention and may offer some avenues for future research. In particular, I reflect on the editors' point that grand strategy can be seen as an "unattainable yet regulative ideal" for states (Balzacq and Krebs, this volume). The institutional perspective helps us see why this is so, as it captures the institutionalized requirements for the performance of certain types of statehood: regardless of the effectiveness of any given grand strategy, it is something that particular types of state are expected to have.

Diplomacy and Strategy

The etymology of strategy is linked to warfare. From ancient Greek, it is composed of "stratós" (army) and "àgo" (I lead, I conduct). It signals control and agency. It is something that an actor or a polity does to others, or the environment in which it operates. The etymology of diplomacy, by contrast, is much less straightforward. From latin "diploma" which means folded paper/license or more specifically letter of recommendation or authority. It is far removed from the institution of diplomacy as we know it, but already here we can detect an uneasy relationship between the two. Strategy describes a universe of deliberate action and their effects. Diplomacy by contrast, is about exchange of information, representation, and negotiation between recognized polities.

While it is not surprising that strategy has historically been closely linked to military practice, it is noteworthy that it carries many of the same connotations also today. References to Machiavelli and Clausewitz are legion, where war-making is the primary means to achieve political ends. Posen refers to strategy as the state's "theory about how it can best 'cause' security for itself" (1984, 13). In his review of the literature on strategy, Richard Betts notes along similar lines that it is the "essential ingredient for making war either politically effective or morally tenable" (2000, 5). The key reason why strategy is closely linked to military issues is of course the primacy of state security and survival: in an international environment of ever-present threats to a state, strategy necessarily focuses first and foremost on state survival. The establishment of US dominance during the 1990s led some scholars and commentators to note that strategy was no longer needed, as there were no threats that were specific enough to develop a proper strategy to combat. Robert Jervis argued in the late 1990s, for example, that when both the seriousness of the threat and the probability of its occurrence is low, strategy becomes "mission impossible" (1998, 1). As Jervis explains, the absence of dominant threat on which everyone agrees undermines the viability of strategy, leaving it open to shifting coalitions of domestic groups to advance different foreign policy objectives (1998, 33).

The issue of agreement on threats is an important one. Kissinger stress that a shared conceptual framework is necessary to withstand the pressure from different actors seeking to insert themselves to advance parochial interests (1979, 130). This is where the particularity of grand strategy relative to foreign policy comes to the forefront: it is more prescriptive, more ambitious. Valerie Hudson and Christopher Vore argue, for example, that foreign policy analysis (FPA) treats "national interests" as the "interests of various players—not all of which may coincide, and not all of which are coherently related to anything resembling an objective national interest" (1995, 210). Explicitly criticizing the tendency to associate the state with the statesman, Hudson and other FPA scholars seek to "break apart the monolithic view of nation states as unitary actors." While the meaning of foreign policy has changed over time (Leira 2019), it represents a much broader category than that of grand strategy. It is the sum total of interests and official relations with other states. Moreover, all states can be said to have a foreign policy. The same cannot be said of grand strategy. Uganda, Norway and Chile all have an official foreign policy, but none of them have a government white paper or similar that sets out a (grand) strategy. In this sense, grand strategy is closely associated not only with the severity of a threat and the ability to calculate its probability. It is also associated with the category of great powers, and the level of perceived agency or autonomy. Foreign policy, by contrast, is much broader, and includes an inventory of all the positions that a government takes on issues with bearing on its security, welfare, status, etc. Strategy is thus much more specific than foreign policy, as it is defined by a hierarchy of goals, and where some means are deemed more effective than others (Goddard and Krebs 2015, 8).

The scholarship on grand strategy revolves in part around how to define it. Some see it primarily as revolving around security (and thus war), whereas others see it more as the overarching framework within which foreign policy is conducted. Reviewing four key works on grand strategy over the last five years—those of Brands (2015) on US grand strategy; Brooks and Wohlforth's (2016) defense of US global engagement; Posen's (2014) argument for restraint as US grand strategy; and Milevski's (2016) more conceptual and historical treatise—Balzacq, Dombrowski, and Reich (2019) differentiate between a classicist view of grand strategy, on the one hand, and a view of grand strategy emerging from within the discipline of International Relations (IR), on the other. These two views on grand strategy differs both in their scope and temporality. The classicist view zooms in on war and territorial security as the overriding concern, while the latter revolves around broader foreign policy interests.

The IR version of grand strategy provides—in my view—a better platform from which to analyse the relationship between grand strategy and diplomacy. That is: a classicist reading provide less leeway for discussing how diplomacy relates to grand strategy, given its primary focus on war and security, which downplays the role of diplomacy also in conducting war. For example, the United States exercised significant diplomatic pressure on allies in the buildup to the war in Iraq, seeking to win support from members of the UN Security Council. More broadly, the classicist view overlooks the extent to which the ends and the means of grand strategy includes economic interests (cf. Farrell and Newman 2019), and often takes place on other arenas and with other tools than warfighting (Goddard and Nexon 2016). For these reasons, grand strategy is better understood as being both broader in its aims (military and other) and its means, running the whole gamut of tools at the disposal of a state from warfighting to cultural diplomacy.

Diplomacy is for sure a tool or resource: states can mobilize its representatives in different capitols to negotiate with other states, and use diplomatic tools to signal support or criticism of other states. But diplomacy is also much more than a resource: it is a structure that make it possible to communicate with and signal to other states, where certain institutional agreements are in place, which may shape both the process and the outcomes of power political competition (Sharp 2009). There is significant historical variation, of course, in how diplomacy has conditioned grand strategy. The transition from "old" diplomacy of nineteenth-century Europe to the "new" diplomacy that would reflect the rule of law, where arbitration and some form of world "government" would replace war is a case in point. Woodrow Wilson, for example, is reported to have written to Senator Hitchcock in 1920 that "I am not willing to trust to the council of diplomats the working out of any salvation of the world from the things which it has suffered" (Morgenthau 1946, 1069). Here, the profession of diplomacy is associated with great power rivalry, war-making, and secret alliances. Commenting on the emergence of the liberal demands for a "new" diplomacy reflected in the aspirations of the League of Nations and later with the establishment of the United Nations, Morgenthau notes that:

> "It is, ... one thing to have a low opinion of the intellectual and moral qualities of a group of professional men, and it is quite another to believe that they and their work fulfil no useful function, that they have become obsolete, and that their days

are numbered. While the former opinion is as old as the profession of diplomacy itself, the latter belief has its roots in the liberal philosophy of the nineteenth century. (Morgenthau 1946, 1067)

The Hague Peace conferences (1899 and 1907) aimed precisely to effectuate such a shift away from the old diplomacy, placing international lawyers on a par with state leaders in the settling disputes through arbitration (Sacriste and Vauchez 2007; Koskenniemi 2001). The multilateralism of the Hague conferences, along with the impartiality attributed to the legal profession, later formed the model for a new type of "diplomatic" actor—the international civil servant of the League of Nations and the United Nations system (Sending 2014). These international civil servants would later become the "international twin" of western diplomats as the US and its allies implemented the strategy of embedding US power within multilateral institutions in the formative decades after the Second World War (cf. Kratochwil and Ruggie 1986). When seen in this way, the rules and practices that make up the institution of diplomacy establish opportunities and constraints on what can and cannot be done.

It was arguably the writings of the English School that most forcefully established diplomacy as an institution. Hedley Bull (1977) defined diplomacy as one of four institutions of international society. As Neumann (2003, 349) argues, Bull's concept of "diplomatic culture ... is part of a wider international political culture which Bull, following Wight, sees as a *necessary precondition* for the emergence of what he (again famously) calls an international society." In this way, the English School was an important precursor to later works which begun to historicize diplomacy as a social practice for how polities signal to and engage one another. Cornela Navari (2011) highlights, for example, that English School scholars zoomed in on many of the same issues that contemporary practice theorists (Adler and Pouliot 2011) see as constitutive of diplomacy (Neumann 2012). Indeed, as Hopf (1998, 178) has noted, Robert Jervis's (1970) application of Erving Goffman's work on self-presentation treats diplomacy as a practice based on intersubjective meaning.

While the English School saw diplomacy as an institution that enable and constrain interaction between states, it was not until the late 1980s that scholars began to theorize the institution of diplomacy in a broader sense. Crucial here was James Der Derian's *On Diplomacy* (1987), which introduced something qualitatively new by treating diplomacy as a foundational *social* activity of "mediating estrangement," whether between man and God, sovereign and suzerain, or between formally recognized polities. While Bull had seen diplomacy as reflective of more fundamental features of international society—state survival etc.—this conception of diplomacy saw diplomacy as countering alienation. What emerges here is diplomacy as the condition of possibility for engaging others, which other authors subsequently took further to explore diplomacy as a structuring force of world politics more generally. Costas Constantinou (1996) analyzed diplomacy as the broader negotiation of meaning; Paul Sharp (2009) elaborated a diplomatic theory of world politics, organized around representation, and Iver Neumann demonstrated how the logics of diplomacy intertwined with that of bureaucracy to shape the workings of a foreign ministry (Neumann 2012).

While not explicitly taking on its implications for grand strategy, these authors offered new analytical tools with which to explore the micro-level diplomatic practices through which strategy necessarily had to be implemented. Vincent Pouliot (2008) has shown how NATO members are heavily conditioned by diplomatic practices and shared knowledge which make some action alternatives unthinkable. In this perspective, the institution of diplomacy is what diplomats think *from*. In a similar vein, Rebecca Adler-Nissen (2014) has shown how the United Kingdom and Denmark's strategies for seeking influence yet retaining autonomy within the EU are made possible by diplomatic practices of negotiating "opt-outs." This literature reverses the relationship between strategy and diplomacy: it is no longer the statesmen who stand above the toolbox of diplomacy and skillfully use it to achieve a given end. Rather, diplomacy is a condition of possibility to engage in grand strategy at all: diplomatic practices condition what can be done and what can be thought. This hails from a view of diplomatic practices—and practices more generally (Schatzki and Knorr-Cetina 2001)—as defining *meaning*. An ambassador can be summoned to the Foreign Ministry to convey criticism, or the ambassador can be expelled from the country. Conversely, the sending state may dispatch their ambassador to signal criticism, or recall their ambassador. All of this depends on mutually recognized rules that are embedded in diplomatic practice. It is in this sense that diplomacy provides an infrastructure within which strategy can be formulated and implemented (Sending, Pouliot, and Neumann 2015). This infrastructure can change over time, of course: diplomacy in the era of the European Concert was different from what it was in the two decades after the Second World War. It changes again with decolonization, where all states are nominally recognized as sovereign equals within a system of substantive hierarchy (Lake 2009; Zarakol 2017; Holm and Sending 2018).

Since the end of the Cold War, diplomacy has become populated by a plethora of nonstate actors, which again modifies the toolbox through which strategies can be conducted. Under the heading of "global governance" scholars have demonstrated that nonstate actors can shape political outcomes. The most clear-cut examples are arguably from areas that are considered inconsequential from the perspective of grand strategy—such as humanitarianism (Barnett 2018; Sending 2015), human rights (Carpenter 2011), or climate change (Abbott, Greene, and Keohane 2016). Nonetheless, insights from these fields have been brought to bear on the functioning of diplomacy as well, in terms of changes in what type of expertise and skills are considered important, where market-based skills and networks are increasing in importance (Melissen 2016; Seabrooke 2015).

An emerging literature on the different modalities of power-political competition similarly reflect changes in diplomacy (Goddard, MacDonald, and Nexon 2019). Some scholars have brought out how, for example, global financial and information networks—populated by nonstate actors—are key to contemporary US strategy (Farrell and Newman 2019). Others have brought attention to how Russia and China are increasingly using international organizations and nongovernmental organizations to counter norms advanced by Western governments (Cooley 2015). This suggests that the terrain on which strategy is being waged changes over time, as new tools and arenas emerge and others fall by the wayside. It also suggests that the tools used to implement a state's strategy may include tools that are not typically seen as "power political" or pertaining to strategy, such as human rights norms, or funding of international and nongovernmental organizations (Seabrooke and Sending 2020).

Statehood and Strategies

In *Politics Among Nations* (1948), Morgenthau identifies diplomacy as a site of agency which determines a state's power in engaging with others:

> Of all the factors which make for the power of a nation, the most important, and of the more unstable, is the quality of diplomacy. All the other factors which determine national power are, as it were, the raw material out of which the power of a nation is fashioned. The quality of a nation's diplomacy combines those different factors into an integrated whole, gives them direction and weight, and awakens their slumbering potentialities by giving them the breath of actual power. (1948, 109)

This is an elegant formulation of the relationship between grand strategy and diplomacy, as it captures how military and economic power are made effective and transformed into *political* power through diplomacy. This stress on the agentic power of diplomats was for Morgenthau paired with an understanding of the potentially tragic elements of such political agency, or of just how much diplomats, and statesmen, are caught up in and unable to change the conditions in which they find themselves (Arendt (2013/1958, cf. Tjalve and Williams 2015, 49). This is also on display in Kissinger's (1957) *A World Restored*. While focus is indeed on the strategies of Metternich and Castlereagh, one of Kissinger's key argument is that the new order emerged *not* because a grand strategy prevailed, but rather because "they both succeeded as they failed" to advance their primary interests. In short, the focus on the systemic conditions within which grand strategies are acted out make us see how political outcomes are rarely the result of a grand strategy. Discussing debates about US grand strategy, Daniel Drezner makes this point forcefully:

> The United States should have taken a more active role in world affairs after World War I but instead retreated into isolationism. Successive presidents bought into the domino theory of communism and expanded U.S. involvement in the Vietnam War beyond what any other strategic logic would have dictated.... These strategic mistakes were rooted in coherent strategic narratives popular with both policymakers and the public. What is striking, however, is that none of these missteps altered the trajectory of US power. The United States eventually assumed the responsibilities of primacy after World War II. The country's over-stretch in Vietnam did not change the outcome of the Cold War. (Drezner 2011, 60)

If Drezner is correct that grand strategy does not matter, what can explain the intensity of debates about it—such as in the US—and the expectation that great powers have one?

Drezner suggests that one key reason is that "there are moments when grand strategies really do count: during times of radical uncertainty in international affairs" (ibid., 61). This sounds reasonable: in unsettled or uncertain time, there is a high premium on mobilizing the resources of the state—and of allies—within a master plan on which most key actors agree. But there must be more to the story, for there is just as much debate about grand strategy also in times that are *not* uncertain.

This is where an institutional perspective that highlights how actorhood—statehood—is premised on the enactment of certain institutional rules and practices may offer additional insights (cf. Neumann and Sending 2020). While not writing about diplomacy per se, Richard Ashley foregrounds how state actors are embedded in and must make sense of contradictory structural forces, so that the core task of state actors is to try to rise above them:

> Working amidst ever-shifting factors and forces, including all of those traditionally called "elements of national power," statesmen never literally possess power and never truly hold the reins of control. Rather, competent statesmen are engaged in an unceasing struggle, at once artful and strategic, to be "empowered." They succeed to the extent that they can strike balances among all aspects of power—e.g., industrial capacity, population demands, military capability, nationalist labor, internationalist bankers, and the consent and recognition of other statesmen—to establish an at least momentary equilibrium that, in turn, defines the state and its interests. (1984, 269)

This suggests an entirely different relationship between strategy and diplomacy, where grand strategy is *the result of* how state actors seek to balance competing forces and reproduce the state in and through diplomacy. On this view, "strategy" is not first and foremost about security and state survival, but of state representation—of enacting a set of scripts for the performance of proper statehood (Butler 1997; Duvall and Chowdhury 2011; Epstein, Lindemann, and Sending 2018). Grand strategy may thus approach what Meyer and Rowan call an "institutional rule" that serve as a myth that states enact in order to be seen as legitimate within the state system (1977). Thus conceived, the fact of *having* a grand strategy and appearing to competently perform it is an integral element of what it means to be a sovereign state, independently of whether the strategy is effective or underwrites decisions and priorities. This may help account for the paradox that the editors point to in their introduction to this volume, where they note that grand strategy often appears as an "unattainable yet regulative ideal" (Balzacq and Krebs, this volume).

It is noteworthy, however, that there is significant variation in how different types of states publicly announce and present their strategy. For example, Uganda does not seem to have a grand strategy. It does have a foreign policy which is organized around three core goals: state survival, national prosperity, and well-being of the people. This is to be achieved *inter alia* through engagement primarily at the regional level, and stressing the importance of Uganda and other African states taking the lead in peace processes in the region. This is presented in bullet points at the Foreign Ministry's website, and reiterated in speeches by the president and by the foreign minister. Similarly, Peru's foreign policy is said to "Promote, protect and defend in the international system the interests of the Peruvian State and those of its citizens in order to consolidate their sustainable and inclusive development."[2] Beyond this overarching objective, the foreign policy priorities is focused on regional developments and the character of relations that Peru has with states in the Americas, in Africa, Asia, and in Europe. Austria's description of its foreign policy objectives similarly lists a range of objectives, and a set of prioritized areas, such as EU and NATO membership, respect for international law, and economic cooperation.[3] In neither case can we detect a proper "strategy." Norway's most recent foreign policy strategy document explicitly discusses changes in the strategic environment—notably a more aggressive Russia and uncertainty about US commitment to European security. But the "strategy" to deal with this new strategic environment is to do more of the same, and it illustrates the structural conditions under which Norwegian foreign policy is made: the emphasis on the alliance with the US, as a guarantor of Norwegian security, overshadows all other considerations. Contrast this with the US, whose foreign policy strategy documents are much more elaborate: President G. W. Bush's had warfighting in Afghanistan and Iraq. President Obama's had a "reset" strategy, seeking to disengage from the Middle East and solidify American preeminence in Asia, whereas President Trump's "America First" appears to entail transactional deals with both allies and rivals.

The degree to which different states have or think in terms of strategy, let alone "grand strategy," thus appears to correspond to the distribution of power in the international system: More powerful states "must" be seen to have a strategy, whereas smaller states can function well with much more limited formulations of how ends and means are linked together. The editors note that debates about the virtues of having a strategy appears like "ritualized genuflection." This seems to me to be a fundamental point. Having a strategy is important not because it helps decisions and resource allocation, but because of what it signals to others about the type of actor that a state is supposed to be. This is what is at stake in Ashley's formulation that "competent statesmen are engaged in an unceasing struggle, at once artful and strategic, to be 'empowered'" (Ashley 1984, 269). Performing "strategy" via speeches and policy documents make manifest the state as an actor that stands above events, being in control and shaping its environment rather than vice versa. There is variation, of course. For some states, it is a matter of conforming to the nominal criteria of having a foreign policy, it being recognized that the structural limitations are such that the room for maneuver is highly limited. But the more powerful the state, the more domestic and international audiences expect there to be a grand strategy.

If strategy is a script, diplomacy is the scene on which it is played out. While one should be careful not to overstate the metaphor, the meaning attached to "strategy" as something that is communicated to other states relies on the arenas defined by diplomatic practice. It may be a speech given by the head of state in the General Assembly at the UN in New York, or at a think tank or university at home or abroad. Attending diplomats, together with journalists and commentators, proceed to interpret and discuss the contents and implications of said speech, and communicating their assessment to their respective capitals. The diplomatic ecosystem around foreign policy statements and speeches are such that they serve to communicate the intentions and strategies of a state to other states. When Donald Trump gave a speech in Warsaw in June of 2017, and when Secretary of State Pompeo gave a speech in Brussels of February of 2019, they were both an integral part of communicating—on a diplomatic arena—US strategy, and US statehood, vis-à-vis Europe.

But diplomacy is also *more* than the infrastructure or arena for the communication or conduct of strategy. It is also, as Morgenthau alluded to, the practice through which the resources of a state are assembled and may be brought to bear on other states. This is typically done by diplomats, who are tasked with helping both to formulate and to translate a strategy a state has into practice. The formulation of strategy may very well be identified with a head of state or foreign minister, as it typically is when world politics is understood in terms of a "great men" theory of history. This critique has—understandably—been made of Kissinger's *Diplomacy*. Der Derian notes, for example, that "Not only does it favour the personality and testimony of a few great men . . ., but it does so at the neglect of forces and trends which cannot be reduced to the actions of individuals" (1995, 175). Students of diplomacy and foreign policy typically highlight the messy process through which foreign policy strategies are produced. One example is Neumann's ethnographically based account of the making of the Norwegian foreign minister's annual address to parliament, where it emerges that such speeches are not at all about identifying or setting out certain priorities, let alone a proper strategy. Rather, it is an exercise in bringing the foreign ministry and its diplomats together to produce, as the title of the paper tells us: "A speech that the entire ministry may stand for" (Neumann 2007). For Neumann, the story also helps explain why diplomats are not prone to innovation, since the challenge is not to produce new ideas, but to help forge a consensus of sorts between the different parts of the ministry. Others see in such quotidian practices a key virtue of diplomacy: these practices define the point from which diplomats think, which renders some courses of action unthinkable and others habitual (Pouliot 2008). Such findings suggest that the relationship between diplomacy and strategy—and between the political leader who may formulate a strategy and the diplomatic corps which are to implement it—is a complicated one. First, diplomacy makes it possible to have a strategy in the first place, since such a strategy necessarily is developed and implemented within a state system, where established diplomatic practices and institutions offers arenas and also instruments with which to implement strategy. Second, diplomacy constrains strategy, in the sense that the work processes of diplomats, organized within bureaucratic structures, define what is and what is not possible to do.

Conclusion: Strategy as Necessary Illusion?

Given that defense is an integral element of statehood, it is not surprising that we expect states to have a strategy to secure its territorial integrity and advance its interests vis-à-vis others. Waging war is qualitatively different from engaging in diplomacy, however. The former, while also shaped by rules and norms of war, concerns taking action, and breaking rules, whatever the costs (Barkawi 2015). It is what strategy scholars call a "theory of victory" (Gray 1979; Cohen 2012). As such, it is intimately linked to sovereignty understood as agency (Duvall and Chowdhury 2011). Diplomacy, by contrast, only function insofar as it does not violate or transcend the rules: War, and strategy, is not defined by rules, whereas diplomacy is (Kratochwil 1991). In this sense, strategy reflects a view of politics that zooms in on the agency of the state and its leaders to act on the world and shape it, whereas diplomacy reflects a view of politics as necessarily structured, characterized not so much by anarchy but by hierarchy, or even heteronomy (Lake 2009; Zarakol 2017; Onuf and Klink 1989). Seeing world politics through the lens of strategy thus highlights the agentic properties of states, whereas seeing it through the lens of diplomacy highlights structural constraints.

Given that strategy is associated with a theory of victory, or influence, or a level of control, it is not surprising that developing and publicly stating a strategy is something that state actors typically do, even if it is acknowledged that such strategies are never followed, and are only rarely successful. The ritualized "performance" of strategy thus reflects the structure of the state system, where the ideal of sovereignty as control or agency informs how statehood is to be performed, while at the same time such sovereignty is illusory for most states because of the structural constraints they operate under (Holm and Sending 2018). Indeed, generalized ideas about how goals are to be achieved, or how to "win" do not reflect the temporal constraints of dealing with other actors, and the uncertainty under which decisions must be taken. Rather, whatever the virtues of so-called great statesmen, their success in winning war for balancing other states may owe as much to structural factors, and luck, as the more or less smart or "strategic" decisions made in the heat of the moment. In this context, we are well advised to reflect on the metaphor provided by another state leader, US President Obama, who was asked by comedian Jerry Seinfeld: "What sport is politics? Is it chess, liar's poker?" thus reflecting the image of politics as a game of. But Obama responds by saying that it is much closer to football, being much more messy and the actors being pushed around, until you get a chance to act: "You get a yard, you get sacked .... But every once in a while, you'll see a hole and then there's open field."[4] The answer suggests that the temporal character of politics—events overtaking plans—and messiness of political life is such that only at rare moments do the tools align with the situation so that a strategy can be followed.

Acknowledgments

I am grateful to the editors for particularly instructive comments on an earlier draft, and to Maria Gilen Røysamb for copyediting and assistance with references. Funding for this work was provided by the Research Council of Norway through the project "Evaluating Power Political Repertoires," project number 250419.

Notes

1. I occasionally refer to strategy rather than grand strategy, but my focus is on grand strategy as it is used in the scholarly literature. See Balzacq et al. 2018.
2. http://www.rree.gob.pe/SitePages/ministerio_en.aspx#mision
3. https://www.bmeia.gv.at/en/european-foreign-policy/foreign-policy/
4. https://www.washingtonpost.com/news/early-lead/wp/2015/12/31/president-obama-gives-jerry-seinfeld-a-pretty-good-football-analogy/

References

Abbott, Kenneth W., Jessica Green, and Robert O. Keohane. 2016. "Organizational Ecology and Institutional Change in Global Governance." *International Organization* 70 (2): 247–277.

Adler-Nissen, Rebecca 2014. *Opting Out of the European Union: Diplomacy, Sovereignty and European Integration*. Cambridge: Cambridge University Press.

Adler, Emanuel, and Vincent Pouliot. 2011. "International Practices." *International Theory* 3 (1): 1–36.

Arendt, Hannah. 2013/1958. *The Human Condition*. Chicago: University of Chicago Press.

Ashley, Richard K. 1984. "The Poverty of Neorealism." *International Organization* 38 (2): 225–286.

Barnett, Michael. 2018. "Human Rights, Humanitarianism, and the Practices of Humanity." *International Theory* 10 (3): 314–349.

Balzacq and Krebs (this volume).

Balzacq, Thierry, and Ronald R. Krebs. 2021. "The Enduring Appeal of Grand Strategy." In *The Oxford Handbook of Grand Strategy*, edited by Thierry Balzacq and Ronald R. Krebs. Oxford: Oxford University Press.

Balzacq, Thierry, Peter Dombrowski, and Simon Reich. 2019. "Is Grand Strategy a Research Program? A Review Essay." *Security Studies* 28 (1): 58–86.

Barkawi, Tarak. 2015. "Diplomacy, War, and World Politics." In *Diplomacy and the Making of World Politics*, edited by Ole Jacob Sending, Vincent Pouliot, and Iver B. Neumann, 55–79. Cambridge: Cambridge University Press.

Betts, Richard K. 2000. "Is Strategy an Illusion?" *International Security* 25 (2): 5–50.

Brands, Hal. 2015. *What Good is Grand Strategy? Power and Purpose in American Statecraft from Harry S. Truman to George W. Bush*. Ithaca: Cornell University Press.

Butler, Judith. 1997. *The Psychic Life of Power: Theories in Subjection*. Palo Alto: Stanford University Press, Stanford California.

Bull, Hedley. 1977. *The Anarchical Society: A Study of Order in World Politics*. London: Macmillan International Higher Education.

Carpenter, R. Charli. 2011. "Vetting the Advocacy Agenda: Network Centrality and the Paradox of Weapons Norms." *International Organization* 65 (1): 69–102.

Cohen, Elliot. A. 2012. *Supreme Command: Soldiers, Statesmen and Leadership in Wartime*. New York: Simon and Schuster.

Constantinou, Costas. M. 1996. *On the Way to Diplomacy*. Minneapolis: University of Minnesota Press.

Cooley, Alexander. 2015. "Authoritarianism Goes Global: Countering Democratic Norms." *Journal of Democracy* 26 (3): 49–63.

Der Derian, James. 1987. *On Diplomacy: A Genealogy of Western Estrangement*. Oxford: Basil Blackwell.

Duvall, Raymond D., and Arjun Chowdhury. 2011. "Practices of Theory." In *International Practices*, edited by Emanuel Adler and Vincent Pouliot, 335–354. Cambridge: Cambridge University Press.

Drezner, Daniel W. 2011. "Does Obama Have a Grand Strategy? Why We Need Doctrines in Uncertain Times." *Foreign Affairs* 90 (4): 57–68.

Epstein, Charlotte, Thomas Lindemann, and Ole Jacob Sending. 2018. "Frustrated Sovereigns: The Agency That Makes the World Go around." *Review of International Studies* 44 (5): 787–804.

Farrell, Henry, and Abraham Newman. 2019. "Weaponized Interdependence: How Global Economic Networks Shape State Coercion." *International Security* 44 (1): 42–79.

Gaddis, John Lewis. 2018. *On Grand Strategy*. London: Penguin Books Ltd.

Goddard, Stacie, and Ron Krebs. 2015. "Rhetoric, Legitimation, and Grand Strategy." *Security Studies* 2 (1): 5–36.

Goddard, Stacie, and Daniel H. Nexon. 2016. "The Dynamics of Global Power Politics: A Framework for Analysis." *Journal of Global Security Studies* 1 (1): 4–18.

Goddard, Stacie E., Paul K. MacDonald, and Daniel H. Nexon. 2019. "Repertoires of Statecraft: Instruments and Logics of Power Politics." *International Relations* 33 (2): 304–321.

Gray, Colin. S. 1979. "Nuclear Strategy: The Case for a Theory of Victory." *International Security* 4 (1): 54–87.

Holm, Minda, and Ole Jacob Sending. 2018. "States before Relations: On Misrecognition and the Bifurcated Regime of Sovereignty." *Review of International Studies* 44 (5): 829–847.

Hopf, Theodore. 1998. "The Promise of Constructivism in International Relations Theory." *International security* 23 (1): 171–200.

Hudson, Valerie M., and Christopher Vore. 1995. "Foreign Policy Analysis Yesterday, Today, and Tomorrow." *Mershon International Studies Review* 39 (Supplement 2): 209–238.

Jervis, Robert. 1998. "U.S. Grand Strategy: Mission Impossible." *Naval War College Review* 51 (3): 22–36.

Kissinger, Henry. 1994. *Diplomacy*. New York: Simon & Schuster.

Kissinger, Henry. 1957. *A World Restored: Metternich, Castlereagh and the Problems of Peace, 1812–1822*. Boston: Houghton Mifflin.

Koskenniemi, Martti. 2001. *The Gentle Civilizer of Nations: The Rise and Fall of International Law 1870–1960* (Vol. 14). Cambridge: Cambridge University Press.

Kratochwil, Friedrich V. 1991. *Rules, Norms, and Decisions: On the Conditions of Practical and Legal Reasoning in International Relations and Domestic Affairs* (Vol. 2). Cambridge: Cambridge University Press.

Kratochwil, Friedrich, and John G. Ruggie. 1986. "International Organizations: A State of the Art on an Art of the State." *International Organization* 40 (4): 753–775.

Lake, David A. 2009. *Hierarchy in International Relations*. Ithaca: Cornell University Press.

Leira, Halvard. 2019. "The Emergence of Foreign Policy." *International Studies Quarterly* 63 (1): 187–198.

Meyer, John W., and Brian Rowan. 1997. "Institutional Organizations: Formal Structure as Myth and Ceremony." *American Journal of Sociology* 83 (2): 340–363.

Melissen, Jan, ed. 2016. *Innovation in Diplomatic Practice*. New York: Springer.

Milevski, L. 2016. *The Evolution of Modern Grand Strategic Thought*. Oxford: Oxford University Press.

Morgenthau, Hans J. 1946. "Diplomacy." *Yale Law Journal* 55 (5): 1067–1080.

Morgenthau, Hans J. 1948. *Politics among Nations: The Struggle for Power and Peace*. New York: Alfred Knopf

Navari, Cornelia. 2011. "The Concept of Practice in the English School." *European Journal of International Relations* 17 (4): 611–630.

Neumann, Iver B. 2003. "The English School on Diplomacy: Scholarly Promise Unfulfilled." *International Relations* 17 (3): 341–369.

Neumann, Iver B. 2007. "'A Speech That the Entire Ministry May Stand for,' or: 'Why Diplomats Never Produce Anything New.'" *International Political Sociology* 1 (2): 183–200.

Neumann, Iver. B. 2012. *At Home with the Diplomats*. Ithaca: Cornell University Press.

Neumann, Iver B., and Ole Jacob Sending. 2020. "Performing Statehood through Crises: Citizens, Strangers, Territory." *Journal of Global Security Studies*. Online version. doi: 10.1093/jogss/ogz073.

Onuf, Nicholas, and Frank Klink. 1989. "Anarchy, Authority, Rule." *International Studies Quarterly* 33 (2): 149–173.

Posen, Barry R. 1984. *The Source of Military Doctrine: France, Britain, and Germany between the World Wars*. Ithaca: Cornell University Press.

Posen, Barry R. 2014. *Restraint: A New Foundation for U.S. Grand Strategy*. Ithaca: Cornell University Press.

Powell, Walter W., and Paul Dimaggio, eds. 1991. *The New Institutionalism Organizational Analysis*. Chicago: University of Chicago Press.

Pouliot, Vincent. 2008. "The Logic of Practicality: A Theory of Practice of Security Communities." *International Organization* 62 (2): 257–288.

Sacriste, Guillaume, and Antoine Vauchez. 2007. "The Force of International Law: Lawyers' Diplomacy on the International Scene in the 1920s." *Law & Social Inquiry* 32 (1): 83–107.

Seabrooke, Leonard, and Ole Jacob Sending. 2020. "Contracting Development: Managerialism and Consultants in Intergovernmental Organizations." *Review of International Political Economy*. https://doi.org/10.1080/09692290.2019.1616601.

Seabrooke, Leonard. 2015. "Diplomacy as Economic Consultancy." In *Diplomacy and the Making of World Politics*, edited by Sending Ole Jacob, Vincent Pouliot, and Iver B. Neumann, 195–219. Cambridge: Cambridge University Press.

Schatzki, Theodore, and Karin Knorr-Cetina, eds. 2001. *The Practice Turn in Contemporary Theory*. Abingdon: Routledge.

Sending, Ole Jacob. 2015. "Diplomats and humanitarians in crisis governance." In In *Diplomacy and the Making of World Politics*, edited by Sending Ole Jacob, Vincent Pouliot and Iver B. Neumann, 256–283. Cambridge: Cambridge University Press.

Sending, O. J., Pouliot, V., and Neumann, I. B. (Eds.). 2015. *Diplomacy and the Making of World Politics* (Vol. 136). Cambridge University Press.

Sending, Ole Jacob. 2014. "The International Civil Servant." *International Political Sociology* 8 (3): 338–340.

Sharp, Paul. 2009. *Diplomatic Theory of International Relations* (Vol. 111). Cambridge: Cambridge University Press.

Tjalve, Vibeke S., and Michael C. Williams. 2015. "Reviving the Rhetoric of Realism: Politics and Responsibility in Grand Strategy." *Security Studies* 24 (1): 37–60.

Zarakol, Ayse, ed. 2017. *Hierarchies in World Politics* (Vol. 144). Cambridge: Cambridge University Press.

CHAPTER 23

GRAND STRATEGY AND THE TOOLS OF ECONOMIC STATECRAFT

BRYAN R. EARLY AND KEITH PREBLE

Introduction

Economic statecraft offers a unique set of tools for pursuing successful grand strategies, yet the role of economic statecraft is often overshadowed by military statecraft. Grand strategy is defined as "the theory of how a state produces security for itself" (Posen 2015). This production of security involves more than just building armies or establishing military alliances; it also involves the tools of economic statecraft as part of the "economic component" of grand strategy. While the economic components of grand strategy have been studied, it has been done "in a cursory way, if at all" (Posen and Ross 1996, n. 2). This chapter develops a conceptual framework for understanding how and why policymakers employ the tools of economic statecraft in pursuing grand strategy.

All states employ economic statecraft as part of their foreign policies, but major powers have more options to employ because of their larger economies, greater access to resources and technologies, and greater centrality in the global economy (Farrell and Newman 2019). While important contributions have expanded our understanding of economic statecraft (Baldwin 1985; Blanchard and Ripsman 2013; Hirschman 1945), scholars lack a concise framework that summarizes why policymakers use specific types of economic statecraft in different circumstances and why policymakers rely on some tools more than others. Economic statecraft does not operate in isolation, but rather is used in concert with diplomacy and military power to weaken adversaries or communicate threats and intentions via diplomatic channels (Drury 2001; Wiseman 2015).

We argue that policymakers employ economic statecraft in varying contexts to accomplish five major tactical objectives in pursuing their grand strategies: bargaining, balancing, generating power and prosperity, signaling and norms, and influencing nonstate actors. While realists tend to "reject the notion that policymakers can wield economic statecraft to achieve anything other than minor policy aims" (Blanchard and Ripsman 2013, 2), these tactical objectives potentially advance states' grand strategies. We identify four principal tools of economic statecraft policymakers leverage in realizing these tactical objectives: economic sanctions, foreign aid, strategic commercial policy, and institutionalized economic cooperation. We then analyze how policymakers use these tools to pursue grand strategies across five tactical objectives. Our analysis maps out areas where tools of economic statecraft can be effectively employed. Our analysis illustrates how great powers leverage sanctions and foreign aid to pursue grand strategies in varied contexts and how economic statecraft plays an underappreciated role in great power balancing behavior.

Economic Statecraft and the Tools of the Trade

Economic considerations play a role in power politics, even though some theories discount the importance of exploiting economic advantages in exercising power (Gilpin 2001; Mearsheimer 2001). Writing at the end of the Second World War, Albert O. Hirschman (1945, 13–17) argued that being engaged in foreign trade offered states the ability to both acquire national power ("supply effects") while also exercising coercive power over other states. He recognized that asymmetric economic dependencies could be exploited for foreign policy purposes, emphasizing how policymakers gain and exercise political leverage based on their foreign economic relationships. David Baldwin defines economic statecraft "as governmental influence attempts relying primarily on resources that have a reasonable semblance of a market price in terms of money" (Baldwin 1985, 30) by situating these influence attempts within a relational power structure. The use of various economic instruments allows states to exercise the power of economic statecraft through both *positive* and *negative* means. Blanchard and Ripsman (2013) have developed a theory of economic statecraft that explains how states' strategic interests shape their use of "carrots and sticks" and how the political effects these tools have on targets affect their likely outcomes.

Other scholars view economic statecraft as a set of tools meant to help countries resolve "security externalities" and situate their analysis at the macro-level of international politics (Gowa and Mansfield 1993; Norris 2016). These scholars explore the relationship between the power of the state and the effects of free trade where states provide greater resources to their military through economic gains made elsewhere. Within this framework, units of analysis, such as multinational corporations, become "soldiers" states marshal (and control) to improve their economic position vis-à-vis other states.

Scholars have also sought to encapsulate economic statecraft within the concept of "geo-economics," a term meant to capture how states employ economic means to achieve their national ends rather than engaging in war (Luttwak 1990; Blackwill and Harris 2017; Wigell, Scholvin, and Aaltola 2019). Defining geo-economics as "the application of economic means of power by states so as to realize geostrategic objectives" links the tools of economic statecraft to a specific vision of grand strategy. Geostrategic objectives involve promoting and defending a state's national interests, reaping the benefits from defending those interests, and influencing the economic actions of other states' economic goals (Blackwill and Harris 2017, 20). Geo-economics stresses the necessity of economic power not only in navigating a unipolar world (Blackwill and Harris 2017) but also in dealing with economic competition from other powers in the system (Baracuhy 2019, 22). Economic statecraft arguably plays a broader role in helping policymakers realize their grand strategies than envisioned by the geo-economics perspective.

While the tools of economic statecraft are varied, all involve the use of economic policy instruments to realize national security or foreign policy interests. The tools of economic statecraft vary in scope, from blunt instruments like comprehensive embargoes to targeted sanctions on specific individuals. Grouping the tools of economic statecraft into four broad categories necessarily entails the loss of some specificity. By categorizing the tools of statecraft along the lines of their broad functional form, we preserve their distinctiveness in terms of their utility, costs and benefits, and ease of use.

Economic Sanctions

Economic sanctions are coercive policy instruments that seek to compel changes in or impose constraints upon their targets' behavior by stigmatizing them and/or adversely affecting their economic welfare (Barber 1979; Giumelli 2011; Early and Cilizoglu 2020). Economic sanctions are versatile in scope and how they are employed; they have the potential to affect entire countries or be more narrowly crafted to target specific economic sectors, government agencies, nonstate actors, or individuals. Since the early 2000s, the global trend has moved towards more targeted forms of sanctions with a limited number of high-profile exceptions like Iran and North Korea (Biersteker, Eckert, and Tourinho 2016). Policymakers design economic sanctions to disrupt trade, investment, financial flows, membership in regimes, transportation of goods, individual travel, technology, and transfers of knowledge. Economic sanctions are unilaterally employed but may be utilized cooperatively in multilateral coalitions or under the aegis of international institutions like the European Union (EU) and United Nations (UN).

Economic sanctions imposed for compellent purposes operate via the logic that sanctions impose sufficient costs on targets so that resisting becomes too painful, forcing the target to make concessions. The "naïve" view of sanctions success (Galtung 1967; Nephew 2017) contends the senders' best approach is to impose or threaten to impose substantial, disruptive sanctions capable of inflicting significant economic costs on their targets (Bapat et al. 2013; Hufbauer et al. 2009). Contrasting views argue that leaders of sanctioned states respond to sanctions in ways that inoculate themselves from the political fallout of sanctions (Galtung 1967). Specifically, authoritarian leaders are better at resisting sanctions because they employ governmental authorities and resources in self-serving ways to maintain their grip on power (Allen 2005; Lektzian and Souva 2007).

Economic sanctions have been criticized as being ineffective for only achieving their coercive objectives a quarter to a third of the time (Hufbauer et al. 2009; Morgan, Bapat, and Kobayashi 2014). Biersteker et al. (2016) find that targeted sanctions by the UN Security Council (UNSC) achieved their compellent objectives only ten percent of the time. These figures undersell the effectiveness of economic coercion. "First off," the threat of sanctions leads to concessions from less-resolved targets (Bapat et al. 2013; Drezner 2003)". Beyond the fact that sanctions tend to be imposed against more-resolved targets, their main purpose may be to weaken or stigmatize targets or to support an international norm "instead of coercion." As Baldwin (1999) explains, the effectiveness of sanctions is also a matter of perspective. If alternatives to using sanctions are doing nothing or diplomacy alone, employing sanctions may substantially increase policymakers' chances of achieving their objectives even if the likelihood of that occurring is still low. Finally, economic sanctions can be counterproductive in some circumstances because they inflict broad-based harms on their targets' populations and are associated with significant unintended consequences (Peksen 2019).

Foreign Aid

Foreign aid refers to the transfer of economic resources to a target at a market discount or without monetary compensation, such as providing money directly, offering loans at concessional rates, loan forgiveness, providing food and medicine, humanitarian or development-related services, building infrastructure, or funding the cause-driven efforts of nongovernmental organizations (NGOs). Foreign aid is costly, as it involves the transfer of government resources to another party. It can be given to target governments, tasked to specific aid programs or NGOs, or provided directly to individuals. Foreign aid is not always "free" for recipients, as it often comes with political "strings" attached or is used as a "carrot" in negotiations. While some foreign aid may be given altruistically in response to humanitarian disasters, donors often seek to further their national interests through their aid (Alesina and Dollar 2000; Drury, Olson, and Belle 2005). Donors employ foreign aid for a variety of foreign policy purposes (Apodaca 2017) and use it to obtain *quid pro quo* concessions (de Mesquita and Smith 2007), improve political relations with the target, or gain coercive leverage over an aid recipient (Early and Jadoon 2019). For recipients, the efficacy of foreign aid is predicated on their circumstances, the conditions donors place on the aid, and the type of aid offered (Bearce and Tirone 2010).

Strategic Commercial Policy

Strategic commercial policy has historically focused on influencing international trade by emphasizing trade of strategic goods and technologies[1] that have the greatest security implications (Cupitt 2000). Beyond trade, governments use foreign direct investment policies (inflows and outflows) to gain political influence, limit access to foreign technology, or avoid foreign dependencies. Through strategic commercial policies, governments either direct or intervene in their marketplaces to shape commercial flows. Governments employ economic policies, such as subsidies and tariff reductions/eliminations, to encourage trade and investment to partners and generate positive security. Raising tariffs or imposing import/export quotas discourages trade with commercial partners, leading to greater security risks. The goal of strategic commercial policies "is to employ" economic incentives or disincentives to influence commercial flows to enhance national security (Fuhrmann 2008; Gowa and Mansfield 1993). Strategic trade controls have emerged as an important policy tool to manage trade risks associated with strategic commodities (Koch 2019). Strategic trade controls allow governments to manage the trade of strategic goods and technologies by forcing the private sector to seek governmental permission for commercial transactions involving designated strategic items (Dill and Stewart 2015). These policies work to prevent the proliferation of weapons of mass destruction (WMDs) or other strategic capabilities to state and nonstate actors (Early, Nance, and Cottrell 2017). Strategic commercial policies can affect foreign direct investment, as governments may adopt policies to limit foreign investors from taking over critical national infrastructure, sectors, or businesses. Alternatively, governments may adopt policies designed to encourage FDI in strategic and high-technology sectors. Lastly, governments promote strategic investments abroad capable of yielding technology transfers or other positive security externalities.

Strategic commercial policies have a track record of making positive contributions to states' national security. However, strategic commercial policies tend to be most successful when they align the profitability of commerce with the desired outcome of promoting or discouraging commerce. Governments have difficulty preventing constituents from trading with potential adversaries when such trade remains profitable (Barbieri and Levy 1999; Kastner 2007). Direct trade may continue to occur despite government interventions, be redirected through third parties, or shift to the black market (Barbieri and Levy 1999; Early 2015). Determined proliferators often acquire what they need on the international marketplace despite strategic trade controls (Kemp 2014). Strategic trade controls, though, have the potential to delay and discourage proliferation efforts by creating time and space for a political intervention (Koch 2019). The global movement towards the adoption of strategic trade controls has made it harder for potential terrorists and proliferators to acquire WMDs. Nascent research agendas have begun to explore the utility of sovereign wealth funds in pursuing strategic goals (Cohen 2009; Drezner 2008) and preventing critical national security resources from threats posed by foreign investment (Moran 2009).

Institutionalized Economic Cooperation

Institutionalized economic cooperation provides the greatest benefit to great powers. Since 1945, the US has heavily relied upon multilateral institutions to organize postwar relations (Ikenberry 2001, 163). While international institutions can promote cooperation between states, concerns about relative gains and cheating can hinder cooperation (Grieco 1988). When great powers *do* rely on international institutions, they prioritize their use for increasing or preserving their power and position in the international system (Evans and Wilson 1992). International institutions can also be employed strategically to reduce incentives to engage in military aggression (Lobell and Ripsman 2016).

International institutions help great powers realize the benefits of cooperation (Keohane 1984) and make their exercise of power more efficient. International institutions help states work together for "mutual gain and protection within a loosely rules-based global space" (Ikenberry 2018, 12). Great powers harness that for their own ends using international institutions to coordinate multilateral efforts consistent with their interests by mobilizing and organizing multilateral sanctioning efforts (Martin 1992). Forging economic deals also becomes much more efficient for great powers when they utilize a common regime to negotiate with other countries.

Great powers mask their use of power through international institutions (Abbott and Snidal 1998). Sbragia (2010) argues that both the United States and the EU manipulate the World Trade Organization (WTO) to gain competitive advantages over one another. Peksen and Woo (2018) show how international institutions like the International Monetary Fund (IMF) can indirectly enhance the economic isolation of sanctioned countries. Because the US wields about 17 percent of the voting power within the IMF—far greater than any other single country, the US shapes the institution's behavior according to its interests (Peksen and Woo 2018, 687; Stone 2011). Institutionalized economic cooperation can be leveraged on its own or in concert other tools of economic statecraft in pursuit of states' grand strategies.

USING ECONOMIC STATECRAFT AS PART OF GRAND STRATEGIES

Having a grand strategy provides a structured set of goals around which policymakers orient their foreign and national security policies. Grand strategies allow policymakers to identify which tactical objectives contribute to achieving their interests, but many different tools—diplomatic, military, and economic—can be used to achieve those objectives. Building on previous work (Baldwin 1985), we develop a framework that identifies five major tactical policy objectives: bargaining, balancing, generating prosperity and power, signaling and norms, and influencing nonstate actors.

We describe each objective and link them to the tools of economic statecraft best suited for achieving specific objectives. Given space limitations, our analysis focuses on describing the tools of statecraft that the literature suggests have the most salient, consistent impacts on achieving key tactical objectives. We briefly explain our rationale for why some tools are not as effective for achieving specific objectives. Our framework provides a way of matching the "foreign policy menu" of economic statecraft options available to policymakers (Most and Starr 1989) to tactical objectives having the greatest utility in pursuing grand strategies. Some tactical objectives may require the use of multiple tools of economic statecraft or hybrid forms of statecraft that combine one or more tools of economic statecraft.

Bargaining

States negotiate over policy issues in the economic, security, and domestic policy realms with conflict sometimes being a part of the negotiation process (Schelling 1966). To change a target's behavior or obtain policy concessions, leaders employ economic statecraft to provide the target with positive incentives for changing their behavior or disincentives when "bad" behaviors persist. The use of "carrots and sticks" is a common bargaining approach. Baldwin (1985) identifies bargaining as one of the chief areas in which economic statecraft can be leveraged to achieve governments' foreign policy objectives.

Economic Sanctions

Economic sanctions are frequently employed in bargaining situations over divisive issues, such as territorial or trade disputes, nuclear proliferation, terrorism, and regime change. Policymakers rely on economic sanctions to coerce targets into making concessions by threatening to impose or imposing economic costs to obtain bargaining leverage. Publicly compelling targets into making concessions is inherently difficult (Schelling 1966), but employing coercive tactics allows great powers to exploit economic dependencies of weaker states (Hirschman 1945). Since the Second World War, the United States has relied on the use of economic sanctions to achieve its foreign policy goals more than other states (Hufbauer et al. 2009; Morgan, Bapat, and Kobayashi 2014) by leveraging its dominant economic and financial positions in the global economy. Following the end of the Cold War, the EU and UN employed targeted forms of economic statecraft to address international security and political problems with greater frequency (Biersteker, Eckert, and Tourinho 2016; Morgan, Bapat, and Kobayashi 2014). Notably, sanctions tend to be most effective when goals are modest (Bapat et al. 2013).

Foreign Aid

Foreign aid can be employed productively in many bargaining situations. The difficulty of compelling targets to change their behavior means that positive forms of engagement may be more effective in some contexts (Nincic 2011). Foreign aid can be effective at striking quid pro quo deals where donors obtain policy outcomes they desire in return for providing aid (de Mesquita and Smith 2007). Illustrating this transactional approach, the US's ambassador to the UN Niki Haley (2018) stated that "President Trump and I are pushing to draw a closer connection between US foreign aid and how countries vote at the UN." China has also successfully linked its provision of foreign aid to the diplomatic status of Taiwan—convincing numerous countries to withdraw their formal diplomatic recognition of Taiwan (Jennings 2018). Relative power concerns, normative issues, and domestic politics constrain the circumstances in which foreign aid–based bargaining approaches can be utilized in bargaining situations.

Institutionalized Economic Cooperation

Great powers leverage institutionalized economic cooperation to help strike bargains or enhance the effectiveness of economic sanctions and foreign aid. International institutions allow great powers to exercise power via structures designed to favorably represent their interests, allowing them to obtain more efficiently favorable outcomes and in ways less likely to alienate partners (Abbott and Snidal 1998). The United States employed the General Agreement on Tariffs and Trade (GATT) and later the WTO to advance its international free-trade agenda. The US has relied on the UNSC to support its sanctioning efforts against Iraq, Iran, and North Korea. Researchers have found that multilateral sanctions are substantially more effective when they have the support of international institutions (Bapat and Morgan 2009; Drezner 2000).

Less Effective Tools of Economic Statecraft

Strategic commercial policy is less about helping states strike deals than about benefitting from the externalities associated with commercial policy. Imposing strategic trade controls, for example, helps countries broadly manage the security externalities of their trade rather than facilitating leverage with a particular trade partner.

Balancing

Balancing seeks to prevent states, alone or as part of a coalition, from being able to dominate their relationships with other states. Realist theory argues that, if great powers cannot become dominant themselves, they will seek to maintain a relative parity in the distribution of power between themselves and other great powers (Mearsheimer 2001; Waltz 1979). Internal balancing can involve policymakers' efforts to increase their own states' relative power, which we discuss in the next category. External balancing involves efforts to increase relative power by forming military alliances with other states. Policymakers also engage in balancing policies that seek to weaken or destabilize the power and alliance coalitions of rival great powers. Economic statecraft can play a multitude of roles in contributing to balancing efforts.

Economic Sanctions

Policymakers use economic sanctions as part of balancing efforts aimed at weakening rivals. Economic sanctions can potentially disrupt and harm their targets' economies, sapping the resources available to devote to their military forces. Before the US entered the Second World War, it had imposed an oil embargo on Japan as part of efforts to thwart its expansionist military aggression in Asia. Sanctions can also be used to bleed great powers of their strength in other ways. During the Cold War, the Soviet Union devoted tens of billions of dollars to supporting its sanctioned ally Cuba—an outflow of resources that ultimately became unsustainable in the late 1980s and contributed to the USSR's financial insolvency (Early 2015). Economic sanctions allow great powers to weaken their rivals' economic and military power, constraining the threats they pose and reducing their capacity to fight future conflicts.

Foreign Aid

Policymakers employ foreign aid to forge and maintain alliance relationships. Great powers use foreign assistance programs to lay the groundwork for stronger security relationships with other states. The US-sponsored Marshall Plan provided crucial financial assistance to European countries as they rebuilt their economies and societies after the Second World War. The program created substantial economic dependencies between Western European countries and the US and fostered a common set of shared values and interests. The North Atlantic Treaty Organization (NATO) built upon this foundation in 1949 by tying the US and Western Europe together through closer economic and security ties. Great powers also use foreign aid to help allies facing economic or humanitarian crises to prevent their alliance bloc's military strength from weakening or help prevent a friendly regime being replaced by a less friendly one. For example, the US aided many friendly authoritarian regimes during the Cold War to prevent Communist factions from taking over.

Institutionalized Economic Cooperation

Great powers augment their political and military alliances with institutionalized economic cooperation to broaden the benefit of an alliance partnership or in a more predatory way by dominant states. During the Cold War, the Soviet Union used COMECON to coordinate the joint economic policies of its junior allies in Central and Eastern Europe to its own benefit. The Trans-Pacific Partnership Trade (TPP), a (now defunct) trade deal negotiated by the US with countries in East Asia, Australia, South America, and North America, would have substantially lowered trade barriers amongst the agreement's members broadly to their benefit. One of the key US motives for the TPP is that it would have contributed to US efforts at balancing against China's growing economic and political domination of the Pacific region, adding a strong security justification for the deal.

Strategic Commercial Policy

Great powers employ strategic trade policy to strengthen allies and constrain the rivals from growing more powerful. Governments can strengthen allies by preferentially sharing strategic technologies with them (Fuhrmann 2008). Conversely, strategic trade controls help prevent the proliferation of strategically valuable commodities and technologies to rivals. During the Cold War, the US employed multilateral strategic control arrangements with its allies to prevent the export of weapons-related goods and technologies to both the Soviet Union and China via "the" COCOM and CHINCOM regimes (Cupitt 2000). While neither effort prevented the leakage of strategic commodities to the Soviet Union and China (Brooks 2005), they did impede substantial flows of capabilities to both states.

Generating Prosperity and Power

The enhanced economic efficiency from international trade frees up resources, encourages innovation, and makes supply chains more affordable, which can enhance military programs (Brooks 2005; Gowa and Mansfield 1993, 408). The tools of economic statecraft provide states with the means to ensure that these efficiencies are realized not only by generating security but also in maintaining positive externalities generated through commerce. China has leveraged its growing export-led economic expansion and access to foreign direct investment as a key means of modernizing its military over the past decade (Christensen 2015, 27–28). Governments also adopt commercial strategies to obtain access to enhanced technological capabilities, contributing to economic and military strength.

Institutionalized Economic Cooperation

Policymakers use institutionalized cooperation to promote commercial prosperity and encourage peaceful relations with other countries. Commercial ties and institutional membership constitute two "legs" of the Kantian tripod of democratic peace (Russet and Oneal 2001). Jean Monnet's motivation for the creation of the European Coal and Steel Community (the European Community and EU's precursor) sought to tie the economies of France, Germany, Italy, Belgium, Netherlands, and Luxemburg so closely together that it would become impractical for them to fight another war with one another. That effort succeeded in binding the economic relationships of those countries and those of the members that have subsequently joined the institution so closely together that none of the members have fought one another since. Membership in the EU has provided its members both peace and prosperity.

Strategic Commercial Policy

Governments adopt concerted trade, investment, and espionage strategies to enhance the strategic sectors of their economies. Arms industries are not only a source of power but also generate wealth (Krause 1992). Governments also utilize strategic commercial policy to create supply chains and export markets for their military goods that help make sustaining advanced arms industries more affordable (Brooks 2005; Krause 1992). After the Soviet Union's collapse, arms exports played a critical role in supporting Russia's economy. Following the end of the Cold War, the economic motivations for exporting arms became more salient. Arms exporters often compete with one another in seeking to capture the economic benefits of arms trade relationships. The US presently dominates arms exports with Russia a distant second (Wezeman et al. 2019).

Governments also support the acquisition of foreign companies involved in research, development, and/or production of desired strategic technologies and may adopt policies that force foreign firms to transfer technologies as part of investment packages. China adopted a requirement that foreign firms must have local partners for investments in their country and imposes technology transfer provisions. Chinese companies and the Chinese government have also engaged in rampant corporate espionage of Western companies that has substantially accelerated the growth of China's technological sophistication in the economic and military realms. As Brooks (2005, 119–120) notes, stealing technology is inferior to obtaining it via investment. Another standard practice for many developing countries making foreign arms purchases is to negotiate direct offsets, which require arms exporters to reinvest in importers' defense sectors. This practice allows countries to both purchase foreign weapons while also contributing to the buildup of their own defense sectors (Brauer and Dunne 2011).

Less Effective Tools of Economic Statecraft

Since economic sanctions harm their senders' economic welfare and foreign aid costs sender governments budgetary resources, we do not view either instrument as very effective tools for generating prosperity and power.

Signaling and Norms

Governments may want to communicate deliberate messages or to promote specific norms or ideas that align with their national interests. Signaling intentions or resolve can be difficult for a number of reasons, since "talk is cheap" and misperception are rife in international settings (Jervis 1979; Schelling 1966). Governments can also use economic statecraft for symbolic reasons or for political purposes rather than for the instrumental effects the actions will achieve.

Economic Sanctions

Policymakers often employ sanctions as "costly signals" to demonstrate their resolve in disputes (Lektzian and Sprecher 2007), but such signals may not always be perceived as a strong signal of resolve by targets (Whang and Kim 2015). Economic sanctions can be used to support international norms or stigmatize targets that engage in behavior contrary to norms or for domestic political purposes (Whang 2011). The targeting of leaders who abuse human rights stigmatizes those individuals and repudiates offending behaviors (Biersteker, Eckert, and Tourinho 2016). The international sanctions imposed against Syrian President Bashar al-Assad's regime after it used chemical weapons against its population in 2012 sought to ostracize Assad and uphold the international norms against the use of chemical weapons.

Foreign Aid

States employ foreign aid to promote international norms consistent with their foreign policies. According to Resknic (2018, 421), "democracy aid's main lever of influence is via the diffusion of norms and knowledge." The US government has promoted democratic governance, civil society, and free markets via its foreign aid programs for decades. The USAID program created by President John F. Kenney in 1961 provided a specific vehicle for US policymakers to promote their normative agenda via foreign aid. This program supported the US's grand-strategic vision that a world populated with fellow democracies would be more peaceful and more prosperous. China has recently funded a global effort to promote its values and perspectives via the creation of Confucius Institutes at universities around the world (Lo and Pan 2016). Foreign aid is a versatile instrument in promoting ideas and norms alongside the transfer of material assistance and functions as a form of "soft power" (Nye 2004).

Less Effective Tools of Economic Statecraft

Institutionalized forms of economic cooperation are less effective at promoting norms in the short term but could be used to promote norms in the longer term (Greenhill 2010). Such an approach, though, would entail significant uncertainty and longer time horizons. Additionally, strategic commercial policy tends to have longer time horizons and be more instrumentally focused.

Influencing Nonstate Actors

To achieve foreign policy goals, great powers increasingly interact with nonstate actors, such as terrorists, militant groups, civil society, and firms. We use this tactical objective serves as a catch-all for government efforts to influence foreign nonstate actors' behaviors, constrain their power, or empower them. Economic sanctions and foreign aid are better suited to address policy issues at the microlevel.

Economic Sanctions

Targeted economic sanctions are easy and cost-efficient to employ and are a better-suited tool for influencing nonstate actors. During the 1990s, US policymakers attempted to address how companies in third-party states played an active role in undermining US sanctioning efforts. The US began adopting secondary sanctions provisions to empower enforcement agencies to impose penalties against foreign firms violating US sanctions against Cuba and Iran (Early 2015). Following the 9/11 terrorist attacks, the United States deployed a new set of targeted financial sanctions to isolate terrorist groups and disrupt their financial networks (Zarate 2013). The US government used these new financial sanctions and existing anti–money laundering authorities to isolate individual terrorists and violent nonstate actors from the global financial system, imposing penalties on any parties that conducted business with them. Leveraging the

US's dominant position in the global financial system, these coercive policies proved surprisingly effective (Drezner 2015; Rosenberg et al. 2016). In the early 2000s, the UN and EU began preferentially employing targeted sanctions policies to impose specific sanctions on individuals, nongovernmental organizations, and government actors (Biersteker, Eckert, and Tourinho 2016).

Foreign Aid

Governments target foreign aid at nonstate actors to strike quid pro quo bargains, shape their policies, or empower them. As part of conflict resolution efforts, governments offer nonstate actors' financial resources in return for committing to peace. Targeted US foreign aid was employed as part of the Oslo Peace Process between the Palestinian Liberation Organization (PLO) and Israel to obtain buy-in from the PLO (Lasensky 2004). Conversely, governments often employ economic assistance to support and shape the behavior of violent nonstate actors such as militant organizations and terrorist groups (Byman 2005). Governments also provide resources to civil society organizations to support pro-democracy efforts, education and public health initiatives, or advancing issues such as women's rights (Henderson 2002). Governments also use aid to shape recipients' policies and behaviors, such as the "global gag rule" applied by the Trump administration to recipients of US public health aid that prohibits activities supportive of abortion.

Less Effective Tools of Economic Statecraft

Strategic commercial policy and institutionalized economic cooperation are less applicable for directly influencing nonstate actors.

Summarizing the Uses of Economic Statecraft for Pursuing Grand Strategies

Our conceptual framework offers several general insights into the utility of economic statecraft for pursuing grand strategies. Table 23.1 summarizes our analysis, showing which tools of statecraft are broadly useful for accomplishing specific tactical objectives in support of grand strategies. Economic sanctions and foreign aid can be used to accomplish four out of the five tactical objectives, making them very flexible tools. Governments use economic sanctions and foreign aid to advance their foreign policy interests vis-à-vis other states, influence nonstate actors, and convey information to the broader international community. Strategic commercial policy and institutionalized economic cooperation have a narrower range of applications and are less useful in situations that involve directly influencing or engaging with state or nonstate actors.

All of the tools of economic statecraft play a useful role in advancing balancing objectives, suggesting realism's focus on military balancing overlooks a key facet of how

Table 23.1 Grand strategy and the tools of economic statecraft

Tools of economic statecraft	Bargaining	Balancing	Power and prosperity generation	Signaling and norms	Influencing Nonstate actors
Economic sanctions	✓	✓		✓	✓
Foreign aid	✓	✓		✓	✓
Institutionalized economic cooperation	✓	✓	✓		
Strategic commercial policy		✓	✓		

states balance in practice (e.g., Blanchard and Ripsman 2013). Economic statecraft plays an important role in bargaining situations and can be used in concert with both diplomacy and military force. With respect to signaling and influencing nonstate actors, foreign aid and economic sanctions represent the best options within the economic statecraft toolkit.

Conclusion

Future research should continue to explore when, how, and why various instruments of economic statecraft are used as part of great powers' grand strategies. While military power undoubtedly plays a central role in realizing great powers' grand strategies, the tools of economic statecraft offer a great deal of versatility in numerous contexts. Since economic statecraft provides essential tools to policymakers for pursuing grand strategies and national interests, existing scholarship's preoccupation with the role of military power in advancing grand strategies does not capture the reality of policymaking for many countries. Could the United States have achieved its military dominance and hegemonic status without employing tools of economic statecraft after the Second World War? Would China have risen as dramatically as it has in the twenty-first century without employing tools of economic statecraft to build and modernize its military (Norris 2016)? Future research should explore fertile avenues of research, such as linkages between economic, diplomatic, and military statecraft, how the application of policies in both realms contributes to "a" state's grand strategy, and when such policies are bound to yield the greatest return.

As this chapter has highlighted, economic statecraft offers policymakers a "Swiss army knife" array of tools for achieving tactical objectives as part of their grand strategies. Future research should also comparatively explore whether our framework effectively explains the contexts in which different types of economic statecraft are employed. More broadly, few empirical studies look at how different types of economic statecraft are employed in conjunction with one another or with diplomacy and military coercion. In seeking to understand great powers' grand strategies, scholars can gain critical insights into what the use of economic statecraft is meant to accomplish and how its use may complement other policy instruments.

NOTE

1. We use the term strategic commodities to refer both to weapons and dual-use technologies that have legitimate commercial applications but can also be weaponized or used to create conventional weapons and WMDs.

REFERENCES

Abbott, Kenneth W., and Duncan Snidal. 1998. "Why States Act through Formal International Organizations." *Journal of Conflict Resolution* 42 (1): 3–32. doi:10.1177/0022002798042001001.

Alesina, Alberto, and David Dollar. 2000. "Who Gives Foreign Aid to Whom and Why?" *Journal of Economic Growth* 5 (1): 33–63. doi:10.1023/A:1009874203400.

Allen, Susan. 2005. "The Determinants of Economic Sanctions Success and Failure." *International Interactions* 31 (2): 117–138. doi:10.1080/03050620590950097.

Apodaca, Clair. 2017. "Foreign Aid as Foreign Policy Tool." In *Oxford Research Encyclopedia of Foreign Policy Analysis*. Oxford: Oxford University Press. doi:10.1093/acrefore/9780190228637.013.332.

Baldwin, David A. 1985. *Economic Statecraft*. Princeton, N.J: Princeton University Press.

Baldwin, David A. 1999. "The Sanctions Debate and the Logic of Choice." *International Security* 24 (3): 80–107.

Bapat, Navin A., Tobias Heinrich, Yoshiharu Kobayashi, and T. Clifton Morgan. 2013. "Determinants of Sanctions Effectiveness: Sensitivity Analysis Using New Data." *International Interactions* 39 (1): 79–98. doi:10.1080/03050629.2013.751298.

Bapat, Navin A., and T. Clifton Morgan. 2009. "Multilateral Versus Unilateral Sanctions Reconsidered: A Test Using New Data." *International Studies Quarterly* 53 (4): 1075–1094. doi:10.1111/j.1468-2478.2009.00569.x.

Baracuhy, Braz. 2019. "Geo-Economics as a Dimension of Grand Strategy: Notes on the Concept and Its Evolution." In *Geo-Economics and Power Politics in the 21st Century: The Revival of Economic Statecraft*, edited by Mikael Wigell, Sören Scholvin, and Mika Aaltola, 14–27. London: Routledge.

Barber, James. 1979. "Economic Sanctions as a Policy Instrument." *International Affairs* 55 (3): 367–384. doi:10.2307/2615145.

Barbieri, Katherine, and Jack S. Levy. 1999. "Sleeping with the Enemy: The Impact of War on Trade." *Journal of Peace Research* 36 (4): 463–479.

Bearce, David H., and Daniel C. Tirone. 2010. "Foreign Aid Effectiveness and the Strategic Goals of Donor Governments." *The Journal of Politics* 72 (3): 837–851. doi:10.1017/s0022381610000204.

Biersteker, Thomas J., Sue E. Eckert, and Marcos Tourinho, eds. 2016. *Targeted Sanctions: The Impacts and Effectiveness of United Nations Action*. Cambridge: Cambridge University Press.

Blackwill, Robert D, and Jennifer M Harris. 2017. *War by Other Means: Geoeconomics and Statecraft*. Cambridge, MA: Belknap Press.

Blanchard, Jean-Marc F, and Norrin M Ripsman. 2013. *Economic Statecraft and Foreign Policy: Sanctions, Incentives and Target State Calculations*. London: Routledge.

Brauer, Jurgen, and J. Paul Dunne. 2011. "Macroeconomics and Violence." In *Handbook of the Economics of Conflict*, edited by Derek L. Braddon and Keith Hartley, 311–340. Cheltenham: Edward Elgar. 10.4337/9780857930347.

Brooks, Stephen G. 2005. *Producing Security: Multinational Corporations, Globalization, and the Changing Calculus of Conflict*. Princeton: Princeton University Press.

Byman, Daniel. 2005. *Deadly Connections: States That Sponsor Terrorism*. Cambridge; New York: Cambridge University Press.

Christensen, Thomas J. 2015. *The China Challenge: Shaping the Choices of a Rising Power*. New York: W.W. Norton & Company.

Cohen, Benjamin J. 2009. "Sovereign Wealth Funds and National Security: The Great Tradeoff." *International Affairs* 85 (4): 713–731. doi:10.1111/j.1468-2346.2009.00824.x.

Cupitt, Richard T. 2000. *Reluctant Champions: U.S. Presidential Policy and Strategic Export Controls, Truman, Eisenhower, Bush, and Clinton*. New York: Routledge.

Dill, Catherine, and Ian Stewart. 2015. "Defining Effective Strategic Trade Controls at the National Level." *Strategic Trade Review* 1 (1): 2–17.

Drezner, Daniel W. 2000. "Bargaining, Enforcement, and Multilateral Sanctions: When Is Cooperation Counterproductive?" *International Organization* 54 (1): 73–102.

Drezner, Daniel W. 2003. "The Hidden Hand of Economic Coercion." *International Organization* 57 (3): 643–659.

Drezner, Daniel W. 2008. *All Politics Is Global: Explaining International Regulatory Regimes*. Princeton: Princeton University Press.

Drezner, Daniel W. 2015. "Targeted Sanctions in a World of Global Finance." *International Interactions* 41 (4): 755–764. doi:10.1080/03050629.2015.1041297.

Drury, A. Cooper. 2001. "Sanctions as Coercive Diplomacy: The U. S. President's Decision to Initiate Economic Sanctions." *Political Research Quarterly* 54 (3): 485–508. doi:10.2307/449267.

Drury, A. Cooper, Richard Stuart Olson, and Douglas A. Van Belle. 2005. "The Politics of Humanitarian Aid: U.S. Foreign Disaster Assistance, 1964–1995." *Journal of Politics* 67 (2): 454–473. doi:10.1111/j.1468-2508.2005.00324.x.

Early, Bryan R. 2015. *Busted Sanctions: Explaining Why Economic Sanctions Fail*. Stanford: Stanford University Press.

Early, Bryan R., and Amira Jadoon. 2019. "Using the Carrot as the Stick: US Foreign Aid and the Effectiveness of Sanctions Threats." *Foreign Policy Analysis* 15 (3): 350–369. doi:10.1093/fpa/orz007.

Early, Bryan R., and Menevis Cilizoglu. 2020. "Economic Sanctions in Flux: Enduring Challenges, New Policies, and Defining the Future Research Agenda." *International Studies Perspectives* 21 (4): 438–477.

Early, Bryan R., Mark T. Nance, and M. Patrick Cottrell. 2017. "Global Governance at the Energy-Security Nexus: Lessons from UNSCR 1540." *Energy Research & Social Science*, Conflict, Cooperation, and Change in the Politics of Energy Interdependence, 24 (February): 94–101. doi:10.1016/j.erss.2016.12.007.

Evans, Tony, and Peter Wilson. 1992. "Regime Theory and the English School of International Relations: A Comparison." *Millennium: Journal of International Studies* 21 (3): 329–351.

Farrell, Henry, and Abraham L. Newman. 2019. "Weaponized Interdependence: How Global Economic Networks Shape State Coercion." *International Security* 44 (1): 42–79. doi:10.1162/isec_a_00351.

Fuhrmann, Matthew. 2008. "Exporting Mass Destruction? The Determinants of Dual-Use Trade." *Journal of Peace Research* 45 (5): 633–652.

Galtung, Johan. 1967. "On the Effects of International Economic Sanctions, With Examples from the Case of Rhodesia." *World Politics* 19 (3): 378–416. doi:10.2307/2009785.

Gilpin, Robert. 2001. *Global Political Economy Understanding the International Economic Order*. Princeton: Princeton University Press. http://public.eblib.com/choice/PublicFullRecord.aspx?p=5710045

Giumelli, Francesco. 2011. *Coercing, Constraining and Signalling: Explaining UN and EU Sanctions after the Cold War*. Colchester: ECPR Press.

Gowa, Joanne, and Edward D. Mansfield. 1993. "Power Politics and International Trade." *The American Political Science Review* 87 (2): 408–420. doi:10.2307/2939050.

Greenhill, Brian. 2010. "The Company You Keep: International Socialization and the Diffusion of Human Rights Norms." *International Studies Quarterly* 51 (1): 127–145. doi: 10.1111/j.1468-2478.2009.00580.x

Grieco, Joseph. 1988. "Anarchy and the Limits of Cooperation: A Realist Critique of the Newest Liberal Institutionalism." *International Organization* 42 (3): 485–507.

Haley, Nikki. 2018. "Speech. AIPAC Annual Conference, Washington, DC (5 March)." https://www.youtube.com/watch?v=6fHSoOIGHRI, accessed February 4, 2021.

Henderson, Sarah L. 2002. "Selling Civil Society: Western Aid and the Nongovernmental Organization Sector in Russia." *Comparative Political Studies* 35 (2): 139–167. doi: 10.1177/0010414002035002001

Hirschman, Albert O. 1945. *National Power and the Structure of Foreign Trade*. Berkeley: University of California Press.

Hufbauer, Gary Clyde, Schott, Jeffrey J., Kimberly Ann Elliott, and Barbara Oegg. 2009. *Economic Sanctions Reconsidered*. Washington, DC: Peterson Institute for International Economics.

Ikenberry, G. John. 2001. *After Victory: Institutions, Strategic Restraint, and the Rebuilding of Order after Major Wars*. Princeton Studies in International History and Politics. Princeton: Princeton University Press.

Ikenberry, G. John. 2018. "The End of Liberal International Order?" *International Affairs* 94 (1): 7–23. doi:10.1093/ia/iix241.

Jennings, Ralph. 2018. "Taiwan Cannot Compete with China on Aid to Keep Foreign Allies." *Voice of America*, May 30, 2018. https://www.voanews.com/a/taiwan-s-cannot-compete-with-china-on-aid-to-keep-its-foreign-allies/4415902.html.

Jervis, Robert. 1979. "Deterrence Theory Revisited." *World Politics* 31 (2): 289–324. doi:10.2307/2009945.

Kastner, Scott L. 2007. "When Do Conflicting Political Relations Affect International Trade?" *The Journal of Conflict Resolution* 51 (4): 664–688.

Kemp, R. Scott. 2014. "The Nonproliferation Emperor Has No Clothes: The Gas Centrifuge, Supply-Side Controls, and the Future of Nuclear Proliferation." *International Security* 38 (4): 39–78. doi:10.1162/ISEC_a_00159.

Keohane, Robert O. 1984. *After Hegemony: Cooperation and Discord in the World Political Economy*. Princeton, N.J.: Princeton University Press.

Koch, Lisa Langdon. 2019. "Frustration and Delay: The Secondary Effects of Supply-Side Proliferation Controls." *Security Studies* 28 (4): 773–806. doi:10.1080/09636412.2019.1631383.

Krause, Keith. 1992. *Arms and the State: Patterns of Military Production and Trade.* Cambridge: Cambridge University Press.

Lasensky, Scott. 2004. "Paying for Peace: The Oslo Process and the Limits of American Foreign Aid." *Middle East Journal* 58 (2): 210–234.

Lektzian, David J., and Mark Souva. 2007. "An Institutional Theory of Sanctions Onset and Success." *Journal of Conflict Resolution* 51 (6): 848–871. doi:10.1177/0022002707306811.

Lektzian, David J., and Christopher M. Sprecher. 2007. "Sanctions, Signals, and Militarized Conflict." *American Journal of Political Science* 51 (2): 415–431. doi:10.1111/j.1540-5907.2007.00259.x.

Lo, Joe Tin-yau, and Suyan Pan. 2016. "Confucius Institutes and China's Soft Power: Practices and Paradoxes." *Compare: A Journal of Comparative and International Education* 46 (4): 512–532. doi:10.1080/03057925.2014.916185.

Lobell, Steven E., and Norrin M. Ripsman, eds. 2016. *The Political Economy of Regional Peacemaking.* Ann Arbor: University of Michigan Press.

Luttwak, Edward N. 1990. "From Geopolitics to Geo-Economics: Logic of Conflict, Grammar of Commerce." *The National Interest* 20: 17–23.

Martin, Lisa L. 1992. "Institutions and Cooperation: Sanctions during the Falkland Islands Conflict." *International Security* 16 (4): 143–178.

Mearsheimer, John J. 1994. "The False Promise of International Institutions." *International Security* 19 (3): 5–49.

Mearsheimer, John J. 2001. *The Tragedy of Great Power Politics.* New York: W.W. Norton & Company.

Mesquita, Bruce Bueno de, and Alastair Smith. 2007. "Foreign Aid and Policy Concessions." *Journal of Conflict Resolution* 51 (2): 251–284. doi:10.1177/0022002706297696.

Moran, Theodore H. 2009. *Three Threats: An Analytical Framework for the CFIUS Process.* Washington, DC: Peterson Institute for International Economics.

Morgan, T. Clifton, Navin Bapat, and Yoshiharu Kobayashi. 2014. "Threat and Imposition of Economic Sanctions 1945–2005: Updating the TIES Dataset." *Conflict Management and Peace Science* 31 (5): 541–558. doi:10.1177/0738894213520379.

Most, Benjamin, and Harvey Starr. 1989. *Inquiry, Logic, and International Politics.* Colombia: University of South Carolina Press.

Nephew, Richard. 2017. *The Art of Sanctions: A View from the Field.* Columbia University Press.

Nincic, Miroslav. 2011. *The Logic of Positive Engagement.* Cornell Studies in Security Affairs. Ithaca: Cornell University Press.

Norris, William J. 2016. *Chinese Economic Statecraft: Commercial Actors, Grand Strategy, and State Control.* Ithaca: Cornell University Press.

Nye, Joseph S. 2004. *Soft Power: The Means to Success in World Politics.* New York: Public Affairs.

Peksen, Dursun. 2019. "When Do Imposed Economic Sanctions Work? A Critical Review of the Sanctions Effectiveness Literature." *Defence and Peace Economics* 30 (6): 635–647. doi:10.1080/10242694.2019.1625250.

Peksen, Dursun, and Byungwon Woo. 2018. "Economic Sanctions and the Politics of IMF Lending." *International Interactions* 44 (4): 681–708. doi:10.1080/03050629.2018.1429427.

Posen, Barry R. 2015. *Restraint: A New Foundation for U.S. Grand Strategy.* Ithaca: Cornell University Press.

Posen, Barry R., and Andrew L. Ross. 1996. "Competing Visions for U.S. Grand Strategy." *International Security* 21 (3): 5–53. doi:10.2307/2539272.

Rosenberg, Elizabeth, Daniel Drezner, Julia Solomon-Strauss, and Zachary K. Goldman. 2016. *The New Tools of Economic Warfare: Effects and Effectiveness of Contemporary U.S. Financial Sanctions*. Washington, DC: Center for a New American Security.

Sbragia, Alberta. 2010. "The EU, the US, and Trade Policy: Competitive Interdependence in the Management of Globalization." *Journal of European Public Policy* 17 (3): 368–382. doi:10.1080/13501761003662016.

Schelling, Thomas C. 1966. *Arms and Influence*. New Haven: Yale University Press.

Stone, Randall W. 2011. *Controlling Institutions: International Organizations and the Global Economy*. Cambridge: Cambridge University Press.

Waltz, Kenneth N. 1979. *Theory of International Politics*. Reading, Mass.: Addison-Wesley.

Wezeman, Pieter, Aude Fleurant, Alexandra Kuimova, Nan Tian, and Siemon Wezeman. 2019. "Trends in International Arms Transfers." Stockholm International Peace Research Institute. https://www.sipri.org/publications/2019/sipri-fact-sheets/trends-international-arms-transfers-2018

Whang, Taehee. 2011. "Playing to the Home Crowd? Symbolic Use of Economic Sanctions in the United States." *International Studies Quarterly* 55 (3): 787–801. doi:10.1111/j.1468-2478.2011.00668.x.

Whang, Taehee, and Hannah June Kim. 2015. "International Signaling and Economic Sanctions." *International Interactions* 41 (3): 427–452. doi:10.1080/03050629.2015.1024242.

Wigell, Mikael, Sören Scholvin, and Mika Aaltola, eds. 2019. *Geo-Economics and Power Politics in the 21st Century: The Revival of Economic Statecraft*. London: Routledge.

Wiseman, Geoffrey, ed. 2015. *Isolate or Engage: Adversarial States, US Foreign Policy, and Public Diplomacy*. Stanford, California: Stanford University Press.

Zarate, Juan Carlos. 2013. *Treasury's War: The Unleashing of a New Era of Financial Warfare*. New York: Public Affairs.

CHAPTER 24

COVERT ACTION AND GRAND STRATEGY

GREGORY MITROVICH

Introduction

In March 1967, the journal *Ramparts* published a feature story written by journalist Sol Stern that soon became one of the most sensationalist exposés of the Cold War. His article, "The CIA and the NSA" (i.e., National Students Association), documented the spy agency's extensive use of covert operations within the United States in violation of the National Security Act of 1947 which prohibited CIA espionage within US borders (Stern 1967). Stern's reporting sparked a heated debate regarding the appropriate uses of covert action, its value to US national security, and the potential threat it poses to American democracy.

Stern's revelations that during the Cold War the CIA had developed illicit, covert ties with domestic institutions, newspapers, journals, and international student and cultural organizations (Saunders, 2013)—mundane disclosures by today's standards—shocked the country and sparked a national debate over their potential danger to American democracy and prompted a series of Congressional inquiries. The most famous investigation, the 1976 Senate Select Committee on Intelligence, also known as the Church Committee, issued a scathing report documenting countless violations of domestic laws but also revealing decades of CIA operations to destabilize foreign governments. Following these bombshell disclosures, the term "covert action" became synonymous with America's Cold War excesses, in response the US Congress passed a series of laws to prevent further covert activities inside the United States while restricting its operations abroad.

Yet just five years later, the moral repugnance that had once surrounded covert action had been replaced with calls for a new campaign to blunt the Soviet Union's intensifying overt and covert efforts to destabilize the West and win the Cold War. In 1980, Ronald Reagan ran for the presidency on a platform calling for an end to the decade-old policy of détente, a significant increase in defense spending, and a new Cold War offensive to regain the strategic initiative against the Soviet Union. With the appointment of William Casey as director of the CIA, covert action quickly became a cornerstone of Reagan's foreign policy, from arming anticommunist insurgencies in Latin America to working with the Catholic Church in support of the Solidarity movement in Poland (Bernstein 1996).

The breakup of the Soviet Union in 1991 only increased enthusiasm for covert action particularly after the 1991 Gulf War when the US sought to foment a military coup to exploit Saddam Hussein's defeat (Berkowitz and Goodman 1998). After the terrorist attacks on 9/11 and the 2003 invasion of Iraq, covert action became a critical tool in the battle against Islamic terrorism, and now its importance is again increasing given the great power challenges the United States is facing from both China and Russia.

Though its use has been a source of significant friction within the United States, covert action has long been an important and frequently used policy instrument, providing countries an opportunity to achieve their national security objectives with reduced risk of war. Most histories have focused on the activities of the United States since the end of the Second World War, which is not surprising given the outsized role covert operations played during the Cold War, reaching levels comparable to multi-theater conventional military campaigns (Miller 1973).

Though often thought of primarily as a Cold War instrument, covert action has an extensive history dating back to ancient times. Indeed, the Trojan Horse, one of the most famous stories from antiquity was itself a covert operation; 3000 years later, the story would inspire *Project Troy*, a major government study ordered by the Truman administration in 1950 to improve the administration's covert political warfare efforts to destabilize the Soviet Union (Mitrovich 2001, 75).

While the United States has certainly been one of the most prolific users of covert action, it was not the only great power to employ them. Nor was it spared covert attacks throughout its history; indeed, the US was frequently targeted by great powers who hoped to prevent its rise. Prior to the American Civil War, when America was a young nation facing enormous domestic and international challenges, the great powers of Europe launched a series of operations to discredit its republican system of government and exploit the growing divisions within the country to foster its breakup (O'Toole 2018).

By the early twentieth century, the United States, now a great power, found itself increasingly embroiled in the deepening Anglo-German rivalry, with both nations using covert means to influence American perceptions of the conflict. London hoped to turn the United States into an ally, while Berlin aimed to secure American neutrality as the power struggle escalated to war (Boghardt 2012). When that failed, the Germans launched covert operations to sabotage America's ability to support the British (Farago 1971). Today, both Russia and China are using covert cyber operations to destabilize the US electoral system. Consequently, while scholars are accustomed to focusing on America's use of covert action, we often overlook the fact that the US has frequently found itself in the crosshairs of covert campaigns launched by the world's great powers.

This chapter will examine how great powers have used covert action to achieve their strategic objectives. Part one will explore what we mean by covert action and summarize

America's experience with it. Part two will examine how the world's great powers employed covert action against the United States to contain America's rise to power, concluding with early twentieth-century British and German covert efforts to influence American attitudes regarding the Anglo-German rivalry.

Part One: What Is Covert Action and Why Do States Employ It?

Covert action is simply any policy undertaken by a state whose involvement is kept secret; from activities as mundane as secretly funneling money to philanthropic organizations to supporting paramilitary, guerrilla warfare operations against enemy governments. However, in practice the term has become a stand-in for a wide range of foreign policy instruments, including psychological and political warfare, subversion, special operations, espionage, and economic warfare. The key point is that covert actions enable nations to achieve strategic objectives by methods "short of war." Of course, belligerents have undertaken covert operations during wartime, however, they are covert to protect the mission; in peacetime, governments hope to keep aggressive operations covert to prevent sparking a war itself. While military and economic power are the two most important *overt* instruments used to attain national objectives, covert action is the hidden weapon nations use to achieve the key objectives of a nation's grand strategy.

In 1947, the National Security Council announced the first formal guidance regarding covert operations, declaring them

> activities … which are conducted or sponsored by this Government [sic] against hostile foreign states or groups or in support of friendly foreign states or groups but which are so planned and executed that any US Government responsibility for them is not evident to unauthorized persons and that if uncovered the US Government can plausibly disclaim any responsibility for them. (NSC Directive 1947)

During the Cold War, American leaders feared that if US sponsorship of covert paramilitary operations came to light, especially those aimed at the Iron Curtain, it would deepen Cold War tensions and increase the possibility of war (Mitrovich 2001, 10–12). Policymakers believed that covert action provided the United States with a weapon it could use to exploit Soviet vulnerabilities while being able to "plausibly deny" any involvement. Plausible deniability quickly became a well-known part of the Cold War lexicon, though the concept had been standard US operational behavior since the American Revolution.

Covert actions could be defensive in nature (Brands 2020), as when following the Second World War the United States engaged in a series of top secret psychological warfare operations to prevent France and Italy from falling into the Soviet Union's orbit; or offensive, as when the CIA launched Radio Free Europe and Radio Liberty (Johnson and Parta 2010), which broadcast news and information to the Soviet bloc to counter communist propaganda, or when the CIA organized a series of coups to topple foreign leaders, such the 1953 operation that led to the overthrow of Mohammed Mossadegh of Iran (O'Rourke 2018). They also provide a unique opportunity for smaller states to attack great powers, such as when North Korean and Iranian hackers infiltrated European and American computer systems, both public and private, downloading critical information and running psychological operations against business and government targets (Rosett 2015).

Covert action gives states the opportunity to pursue foreign policy objectives that normally could only be achieved by war. The most obvious example is regime change, which enables the instigator to radically change the policies of a government without having to launch conventional operations. One of the first US covert regime changes took place during the First Barbary War of 1801–1804 when a force of US Marines overthrew the Pasha of Tripoli and replaced him with his more amenable brother. In the modern era, the CIA has promoted coups in Iran in 1953, Guatemala in 1954, Cuba in 1961, South Vietnam in 1963, Chile in 1973, and in Iraq throughout the 1990s.

States have engaged in covert political warfare to destabilize, weaken, and distract rivals. The United States and the Soviet Union engaged in political warfare extensively throughout the Cold War, with the US attacking the Soviet Union and its East European satellites as well as China, while the Soviet Union launched numerous campaigns to drive wedges between the United States and Western Europe. US operatives planted disinformation to incite conflict between the Soviet Party and State apparatuses, to undermine trust between the satellite regimes and Moscow, and encourage more nationalist communists that were independent of Moscow. Radio Free Europe and Radio Liberty broadcast news and information behind the Iron Curtain to keep "the pot simmering" and the hope of freedom alive. European powers similarly tried these methods to undermine the stability of the US government, exploiting the growing divisions within the nation to hasten its fragmentation (O'Toole 2014; Wriston 1967). The Soviet Union operated extensive disinformation campaigns aimed at weakening US-West European ties during the Cold War (Bittman 1985) while today Russia has succeeded in undermining the American and British electoral systems (Mueller 2019), while China has launched a significant attack against the West as it vies for global influence.

Covert action is used to increase operational success when disclosure of nation's involvement would threaten operations. The United States has hidden its involvement with Radio Free Europe and Radio Liberty out of fear that Soviet and East European listeners would reject their programming; instead, the CIA created a cover story that the stations were founded and operated by East European émigrés. The US also provided substantial, clandestine support to independent organizations like the Congress for Cultural Freedom, magazines, and even individual artists to promote of American culture and rebut Soviet claims that American lacked a cultural heritage (Saunders 2013). The Soviet Union also employed many front organizations to promote Soviet foreign policy interests in Western Europe. Prior to the First World War, both Great Britain and

Germany similarly established front organizations to hide their influence operations within the United States (Boghardt 2012).

Coordinating Covert Action and Grand Strategy

Integrating covert operations into a foreign policy strategy has long proved tricky. In the eighteenth and nineteenth centuries, British and American diplomatic corps frequently sponsored operations to either collect intelligence or run "special operations." These operations were frequently so primitive and haphazard that they were seldom truly "covert" and often led to significant embarrassment over their use (O'Toole 2018). By the turn of the twentieth century, covert action had evolved in complexity to include sabotage, propaganda, and subterfuge; diplomats feared they would be tainted if their associations were disclosed. The British government would not even acknowledge the existence of MI6, its foreign intelligence branch, until 1994. As the First World War drew closer, the British government consolidated its foreign operations into the Secret Service Bureau, which was tasked with gathering intelligence on Imperial Germany's war making capability while also secretly launching influence operations against the US. It reported directly to the British military (Andrew 2018).

Following the war, the SSB, now renamed the Special Intelligence Service, was placed firmly within the ranks of the British Foreign Office, meaning it answered directly to the Secretary of State for Foreign Affairs. The extent of coordination between the diplomats and the foreign operations specialists still depended on the international context. During peacetime, the diplomatic core kept its distance from these operations, wishing to avoid the tarnish of association with these "less reputable" services. However, when military conflict appeared imminent, as during the 1930s, demands for intelligence and clandestine operations exploded, requiring ever greater coordination (Lomas 2019).

In July of 1936, the British government created the Joint Intelligence Committee (JIC) whose purpose was to provide a link between the Cabinet of the Prime Minister and the nation's intelligence and foreign operations services to ensure greater coordination with the nation's foreign policy (Goodman 2018). As the crisis with Nazi Germany deepened, British Foreign Minister Sir Anthony Eden became a key conduit between policy and intelligence/foreign operations and quickly became expert in British intelligence, maintaining close ties to the various intelligence branches (Lomas 2019). These ties would last throughout the Cold War and into the post–Cold War era, coming under increasing public scrutiny particularly following the Iraq War as accusations were leveled at the government of Prime Minister Tony Blair for unduly influencing JIC intelligence assessments from Iraq to justify the invasion.

Americans have always had a love–hate relationship with both intelligence gathering and covert operations, recognizing their importance in wartime while fearing that their continued use in peacetime would threaten their republican system of government. Once a conflict ended, special operations were immediately disbanded while intelligence capabilities were severely reduced. It was only during the Cold War that the United States would maintain its first sustained covert action and intelligence efforts lasting decades.

While Great Britain placed covert operations under the control of the Foreign Office, in 1947 the United States created the Central Intelligence Agency, an independent organization answering directly to the President. Relations between the State Department and the CIA were often determined by the stature of their leaders. The CIA's first director, Admiral Roscoe Hillenkoetter, frequently deferred to Secretary of State George Marshall whose advisor, George Kennan, played an outsized role in formulating the nation's first covert action programs (Corke 2007). When General Walter Bedell Smith assumed the CIA's directorship in 1950, he insisted on the agency taking the leading position on the US covert operation programs, ending the State Department's dominance (Mitrovich 2000, 64). Under President Eisenhower, the State Department and CIA enjoyed excellent relations because they were directed by two brothers, John Foster Dulles and Alan Dulles. Furthermore, President Eisenhower reformed the National Security Council to play an increasingly important role in coordinating covert action, establishing the Operations Coordinating Board as a subcommittee within the NSC to ensure that direction. This gave the Eisenhower White House significant oversight of these operations, enabling their coordination with the administration's strategic policies.

Under President John F. Kennedy, the NSC maintained its central position, and the CIA's covert programs were approved by the president and his trusted advisors, including NSC Director MacGeorge Bundy and Attorney General Robert Kennedy. President Richard Nixon also insisted that foreign policy be run from the White House, and often cut the State Department out of important decisions, especially covert action such as the CIA's role in the overthrow of Salvador Allende in Chile. Under President Jimmy Carter, disclosures of CIA activities led to reforms that significantly reduced its covert operations. President Ronald Reagan enjoyed a unique relationship with CIA Director William J. Casey, and once again, covert action took center stage. Disclosure of the Iran–Contra scandal, a covert operation where the administration illegally sold weapons to Iran to fund the Contras war against the Nicaraguan government did not diminish support for covert action in either the George H.W. Bush administration or Clinton administrations.

Part Two: The American Experience with Covert Operations

The United States has been at the epicenter of covert action since the outbreak of the Revolutionary War, through its spread across the North American continent, its emergence as a great power in the early twentieth century, and as a global superpower since

1945. Part two will examine how the United States and its rivals used covert action to influence America's rise to power.

Covert Action and the Rise of the United States

The Revolutionary war taught the Founding Fathers the importance of using the clandestine arts to secure the young nation, and the American revolutionaries quickly learned the intelligence and espionage trade; General George Washington could fairly be described as a true "spymaster" (O'Toole 2018, 827–1108; Knott 1996, 13–27). By war's end, Washington was personally operating extensive "stay-behind" networks in British-occupied Philadelphia and New York, routinely dispatching agents behind enemy lines who gathered priceless information that frequently saved the badly outgunned Continental Army from destruction. The Revolutionary War experience honed US skills in covert action, which became more important as the young United States turned its focus to its most important strategic objective—continental expansion—and faced growing European resistance.

Following its loss in the Revolutionary War, Britain's strategy was to destabilize the United States and prevent its expansion on the North American continent. The British moved quickly to isolate the United States politically and economically by refusing recognition and denying the United States trade rights with Canada and its Caribbean colonies, which the US had benefitted from throughout its colonial history. Using Quebec as their operations center, British intelligence officers—former Tory refugees who fled the US after the war—set up networks throughout the United States in especially sensitive regions such as Vermont, Florida, and the American West (Howe 1912, 332–354). Spain refused the western territories the right to ship goods down the Mississippi river, threatening to cripple their economic growth. In the meantime, the Spanish, wary of American western expansion into their own extensive territories in North America, sent agents into Kentucky and other American territories to encourage their own independence and possible annexation to Spanish territory, and conspired with Native American tribes to resist US encroachment (Bemis 1926, 113–124).

In 1787, Britain began a series of covert operations against the United States. Under the direction of Lord Dorchester, the Governor General of Canada, British agents joined their Spanish rivals in Louisville, Kentucky to investigate reports of dissension in the western territories. Lord Dorchester was himself quite familiar with the United States; during the revolution he was known as General Sir Guy Carleton Britain's commander in chief during the final 18 months of the war. Lord Dorchester recruited John Connolly, a Tory sympathizer born in Pennsylvania, supplied him with funds, and authorized him to tell Kentucky settlers that Britain was prepared to intervene on their behalf to convince Spain to allow these settlers use of the Mississippi river. In exchange, Kentucky would agree to abandon the other former colonies and pledge its loyalty to the crown.

The effort failed largely because the operation didn't remain covert—in fact it was a well-known "secret" in US government circles (O'Toole 2018, 1669).

Shortly after the creation of the new Federal government, Britain redoubled its efforts to recruit potentially pro-British American political leaders to open a confidential channel with the US government. In 1789, Lieutenant Colonel George Beckwith traveled to the United States to seek out American politicians with whom the British might engage in discussions to improve the diplomatic relations between the two countries. Among those Beckwith found most receptive was none other than Alexander Hamilton, with whom he addressed Spain's refusal to allow the US access to the Mississippi river and the port of New Orleans, permitting American trade with the British West Indies, and a broader commercial treaty between Great Britain and the US. While Beckwith never hid his identity, nor could he since he served as General Carleton's chief liaison with George Washington during the British evacuation of New York, Hamilton's discussions with him remained under cover. This has led some historians, most notably Julian P. Boyd, to conclude that Hamilton had betrayed his country (Boyd 2015).

Hamilton informed Beckwith that he could only speak with him as a private citizen and had no authorization to negotiate any deals, however, neither Washington nor any of his cabinet knew of Hamilton's discussions with Beckwith, indeed Washington had already decided to send his own representative, Gouverneur Morris, to London to begin negotiations. Historians have rejected Boyd's argument; nevertheless, as the 1790s progressed, accusations continued to be leveled at Hamilton by the Jeffersonian Republicans that he was far too sympathetic to Britain's positions.

Not to be outdone by their British and Spanish rivals, France also launched "influence operations" against the United States. In 1789, French revolutionaries stormed the Bastille, marking the eventual end of the French monarchy and the birth of a new republic inspired by the US example. American's rejoiced that republicanism had crossed the Atlantic and gained a foothold in Europe. However, the French revolution quickly disintegrated into the terror, a bloodbath of mass executions, as consistently more radicalized regimes seized power in Paris, first under Maximilien Robespierre then under the Directorate which ruled France until Napoleon seized power in 1799.

In the meantime, the French revolutionary army attacked Europe's great powers in a bid to spread the republican revolution throughout aristocratic Europe. Britain led a series of European coalitions to suppress the French Republic. In 1793, France declared war on Great Britain. This thrust the United States right into the middle of this European maelstrom as the United States was still legally bound by its 1778 Treaty of Alliance with France obligating it to defend France's Caribbean colonies from British attack. However, in 1793 the United States had no navy with which to defend these possessions.

Washington recognized that the US was unable to meet its alliance commitments, and, fearing the European conflict could ruin the young country, declared the United States neutral. The move outraged the French government and sparked a bitter debate between proponents of neutrality, led by Washington and Hamilton, and Thomas Jefferson and James Madison, who argued that a president is required to seek the consent of the US Senate before withdrawing from a treaty given legislative approval (Frisch

2007). The debate ended up reaffirming the president's right to withdraw from a treaty approved by the US Senate. However, what mattered was America's lack of naval capability, which left no other choice than neutrality.

Hoping to undermine the American stance, Edmond Genet, France's new ambassador to the US, secretly commissioned privateers in American ports to attack British Canada and Spanish possessions in Louisiana and the Florida, with the aim of drawing the United States into the French Revolutionary wars (Ammon 1973, 65–94). His goal was to create an international incident between the United States, Great Britain, and Spain, which was then allied with Great Britain against France, that he hoped would embroil the US in the conflict. Genet's gambit failed and Washington demanded the diplomats recall; however, by then the new Directorate had replaced Robespierre's Jacobin government and Genet, facing the possibility of execution upon his return, was granted asylum in the United States, later becoming an American citizen (Ammon 1973, 147–171).

Tensions between the United States and the warring parties continued to deteriorate as both the British and French launched campaigns against American shipping, capturing thousands of US merchant vessels and impressing into naval service many thousands of American sailors. Britain as well refused to withdraw its fortifications from US soil as promised in 1783, citing the need to guard Canada from US attack, and suspended American access to its colonies in West Indies. In an address to Native American chiefs, Lord Dorchester, Governor General of Canada, warned that war with the United States was imminent and encouraged the chiefs to take Britain's side. The signing of Jay's Treaty in 1794 would delay a future conflict for change to 18 years. However, the attacks on the US merchant shipping continued apace and led ultimately to the American declaration of war in 1812, which in turn gave the British another opportunity to undermine the United States.

Recognizing the increasing likelihood of war, the British government dispatched spies throughout the US to provide the military with hard intelligence regarding economic and the military preparedness of the United States (Howe 1912, 332–354). What they found was that the US was completely unprepared for conflict and that deep divisions had fractured the country which Britain could exploit, especially in New England, which remained strongly pro-British (Howe 1912, 332–354).

When war broke out, covert British intelligence services were well acquainted with the poor condition of American war planning, especially regarding the amateurish United States plans to invade Canada, which the outnumbered British forces defeated without incident. The attack would be undercut by New England states, which refused Madison's demand that their militias participate in the invasion. Pro-British sympathy was so great in the North East that that "blue-light Federalists" supposedly warned the Royal Navy's blockade fleets of American ships trying to escape by signaling the British ships with blue lights (De Roulhac Hamilton 1955). Fortunately for the United States, Great Britain failed to capitalize on these divisions and foment insurrection in New England. The British did intend to invade New York from Canada, but the invasion force turned back after the defeat of the British fleet at the Battle of Lake Champlain in 1814.

America Covert Action and the Barbary Pirates

The uncertainties regarding the country's existence, coupled with Europe's continuous covert and overt efforts to undermine the emerging American nation, taught US leaders of the wartime importance of a strong covert capability. Indeed, given the nation's military weakness, it was one of the few offensive instruments available to American policymakers.

The First Barbary War of 1801–1805 offered the best opportunity for the US to flex its new clandestine muscles. While British and French warships and privateers attacked American merchant vessels, so too did the Barbary Pirates who operated out of ports in Morocco, Algeria, and Tunis. Major European powers paid tribute to prevent these pirates from harassing their shipping, however, once it gained independence, the United States lost such protections. After paying tribute for several years, the United States decided to launch a military attack to destroy the naval power of the Barbary States and end their threat to American shipping in the Mediterranean (Leiner 2006).

The United States also launched the nation's first paramilitary operation to overthrow a foreign leader, the Pasha of Tripoli, to free the American prisoners taken in 1805 when the US frigate *Philadelphia* ran aground on a reef and was captured (Leiner 2006, 22). The paramilitary operation launched from Egypt with the goal of replacing Yusuf, the current Pasha of Tripoli, with his older brother Hamet, who the American's believed would be a more pliable leader. The small army of 400 men seized the port city of Derna as the first step in eventually capturing Tripoli. However, alarmed by the operation's success, Yusuf made a deal with US representatives to dramatically reduce the ransom for the American prisoners if they abandoned the operation. A treaty was signed, the Americans were released, but as many as 400 insurgents fell captive to Yusuf, where they met brutal fates. The treaty, however, did not end the attacks on American shipping, which would escalate during the War of 1812 as the US Navy lay trapped in American ports by the British blockade. However, shortly after the war's end in 1815, a squadron of US warships set sail for the Mediterranean, inflicting a heavy defeat on the Barbary Pirates and forcing them to abandon raids on US merchant vessels (Leiner 2006, 87–123).

US Covert Action and America's Expansion

In 1808, Napoleon Bonaparte invaded Spain, overthrowing the recently crowned King Ferdinand VII and placing his brother Joseph on the Spanish throne. The Spanish people rose in revolt, and the ensuing conflict, known as the Peninsular Wars, would play a critical role in Napoleon's eventual defeat, while also setting the stage for South America's eventual independence. Following the overthrow of Ferdinand VII, leaders throughout Spain's American empire refused to acknowledge the legitimacy of King Joseph and began pursuing policies independent of Madrid. Soon, liberation movements appeared throughout South America, and by the 1820s, Spain was forced to recognize the independence of these new nations, many with republican governments inspired by the United States (Robertson 1939, 253–296).

However, following Napoleon's defeat at Waterloo, Russia, Prussia, and Austria formed the Holy Alliance with the purpose of intervening throughout Europe to crush the last remnants of French republicanism. They believed the collapse of Spanish power and the emergence of republican governments throughout South America a dangerous threat to European stability and in 1823 announced their intention to assist Spain in reconquering its lost territories. What the alliance needed was a fleet to transport military forces across the Atlantic and approached the recently restored King Louis XVIII of France to gain his support. Alarmed by the possibility that France might lead a European effort to recover the America's for Spain, President Monroe dispatched a close friend on a secretive mission to discover Europe's plans—which he found had been scuttled at Britain's insistence in 1823 (Temperely 1906, 770–796). However, this threat refocused American attention towards discovering what was occurring within its own hemisphere. Therefore, Monroe sent secret agents throughout Mexico and Latin America to remain informed on the political situation among the Spanish colonies; their country reports convinced the administration to finally recognize their independence (O'Toole 2014, 2362) These networks would remain quite useful as the United States expanded to the Pacific Ocean.

In 1835, American colonists in the Mexican state of Texas revolted against the government of President Antonio Lopez de Santa Ana and in 1836 won independence from Mexico after Sam Houston defeated Santa Ana at the Battle of San Jacinto. Mexico refused to acknowledge Texan independence; America's annexation of Texas in 1846 would spark the Mexican American War which would eventually lead to the US annexation of the American Southwest including California.

The Mexican American war has long faded from the memory; however, it was one of the seminal moments in US history as it completed America's expansion to the Pacific Ocean. It also put the United States square in the path of British, French, and Russian interests. The Russians (Grinev 2010) and French (Willys 1929) both aspired to colonize the San Francisco Bay given its ideal location as a port along the Pacific Ocean. Great Britain hoped to contain American expansion in North America, and, under British Foreign Minister George Canning, had established close political and economic relations with Mexico with the hope of turning it into a bulwark against American expansion (Temperely 1906). Texan independence provided the British with another opportunity to contain the United States (Adams 1910). Viscount Palmerston, then British foreign minister and later prime minister, proposed to the Mexican government that they recognize Texan independence, after which Britain and France would follow with recognition, loans, and commercial agreements to support an independent Texas and use it as a buffer to further American expansion (Pletcher 1973, 425). Mexico rejected the offer and Palmerston was forced to abandon his strategy. Britain would wait until 1842 before recognizing Texan independence.

The United States government was particularly worried about British intervention; indeed, it had only recently settled a series of disputes with Britain regarding the border between the United States and Canada (Schake 2017, 39–59). To discover what the British were doing, President John Tyler dispatched a series of secret missions to uncover British policies in Texas and California and determine whether the British were committed to prevent the annexation of Texas and would support Mexico should war with the US break out (Merry 2009, 70–72). The situation in Texas was resolved when the US government formally annexed the territory in 1846, however, that move was one too many for the reeling Mexican nation, which launched a series of raids into Texas that in 1846 escalated into conflict between Mexico and the United States. The main US objective in the war was the acquisition of California, which would finalize America's march to the Pacific. President James Polk, who succeeded Tyler in 1845, feared that Britain and France might intervene and seize California before the United States, indeed, rumors were spreading that the Mexican government had offered California to wipe out their outstanding debt to the British. Polk, not aware that the British had rejected the offer, sent a secret agent to contact local leaders and inform them that the US would support Californian independence and ultimate incorporation into the United States. This he hoped would counter possible British propaganda to encourage California to join the British Empire instead. No such propaganda occurred, indeed, Britain remained surprisingly quiescent during the ensuing war, which saw the United States defeat Mexico and seize control of California, which then received statehood in 1850 (Adams 2010, 744–763).

America as a Great Power

America's victory in the 1898 Spanish-American War cemented the nation's new status as a world power and rival to the great powers of Europe. Its emergence coincided with the escalating great power conflict between Great Britain and Germany, a rivalry that led to the First World War only 15 years hence. Germany's new strategy of *Weltpolitik* coupled with massive naval buildup alerted Great Britain of Berlin's determination to replace it at the apex of world power. Meanwhile, the United States considered German inroads into Latin America a direct challenge to the Monroe Doctrine. The United States moved to defend the Western hemisphere from the Germans and to coerce the British into accepting America's leading position in the region. A three-way contest emerged: Britain sought to protect its leading position while Germany and the United States vied to replace it.

As the Anglo-German crisis escalated, the position of the United States increasingly concerned the two adversaries. The British responded by deferring to American interests in the Latin America and by stressing an Anglo-American rapprochement, while the Germans initially planned to go to war with the United States and seek a dominant position in South America. After the German General Staff dissuaded Kaiser Wilhelm II from launching an attack, Germany's strategy shifted to a contradictory combination of efforts to either ensure American neutrality in a future Anglo-German conflict or sabotage its ability to aid the British should war erupt. Following the outbreak of war in 1914, both nations launched influence operations against the United States (Boghardt 2012, 108–128).

The British effort was led by Captain William Reginald Hall, who initiated numerous intelligence and propaganda operations throughout the war, ultimately including the Zimmerman Telegram, a memo from German Foreign Minister Arthur Zimmerman to German Ambassador to Mexico Heinrich von Eckardt outlining a potential agreement offering Mexico the return of Texas, New Mexico, and Arizona in return for its alliance in war. The telegram's discovery, the fruit of two simultaneous covet operations against both the United States and Germany, inspired President Woodrow Wilson's decision to go to war.

Hall's operation benefitted greatly from the strongly pro-British sentiments of US State Department, including Secretary of State Robert Lansing. Hall and his deputy Guy Gaunt cultivated relationships with the leading Americans of the time, including former President Theodore Roosevelt, Assistant Secretary of the Navy Franklin Roosevelt, Colonel Edward House, and numerous other Anglophiles throughout American government, media, and private industry.

Great Britain's control over international telecommunications made it uniquely capable of controlling information flows to the United States. Shortly after the First World War began, the Royal Navy cut all German underwater telegraph communication cables and forced the United States to use British cable lines, yet without the ability to encode communications, British intelligence was able to eavesdrop on all information flows to and from the United States. The Germans were only able to communicate with their consulates in the United States courtesy of the US State Department cable lines, which were also monitored by the British (Winkler 2008, 100–136).

Therefore, British intelligence was uniquely placed to supply information to its allies in the United States regarding German atrocities in Belgium and German intentions in the Western hemisphere. British intelligence moved quickly to expose German covert operations within the United States; one of the most successful, not to mention innovative, operations was the Bridgeport Projectile Company, ostensibly an American munitions company prepared to sell munitions to the Allies, but in fact a German front organization which blocked sales to the allies by making enormous preemptive orders with American manufactures of machine tools, hydraulic presses, and other equipment essential to produce munitions, frustrating real buyers. In one operation, the BPC "purchased" £5 million of gunpowder from Aetna Powder Company, equivalent to one year's production (O'Toole 2014, 4839).

German operations sparked labor disputes by appealing to sympathetic, highly skilled German American workers to leave their jobs in the munitions industry. Economic sabotage operations also included purchasing strategic materials, including chlorine gas used on the German battlefields, and an attempt to buy the Wright Aeroplane Company and its patents. German operatives also planted explosive devices to sink munitions transports. Pro-German newspapers were also formed, hoping to galvanize opposition to the war among the millions of German-Americans who lived in the United States and those with anti-British sentiments, especially the Irish (O'Toole 2014, 4849). The Germans also launched a series of operations to win Mexico's sympathy during the war and to encourage attacks along the American Southwest to distract US attention from Europe (O'Toole 2014, 4607–4798).

British operatives possessed insurmountable advantages over their German rivals, since the British could feed the United States whatever information it wanted to turn them against the Germans. As there was little chance that the United States might enter the war on Germany's side, the best that German operatives could hope for was to delay America's entry until victory in Europe was achieved. However, Berlin's efforts to sabotage American assistance, along with its increasing submarine attacks against American shipping, led to a severing of US–German relations on February 3, 1917. The interception of the Zimmerman Telegram sealed America's fate as it declared war on Germany on April 6. Only 20 years later, this scenario would repeat itself once more as the Germans and British angled to define America's role in the Second World War.

Conclusion: The Future of Covert Action

For many years, cyberwarfare specialists have warned of a potential cyber 9/11, an attack that could cripple the United States infrastructure much as the al Qaeda attack on September 11 devastated New York and brought the country to a standstill. When that attack came; however, it did so in the form of the Russian cyberwarfare attack on the 2016 United States presidential election.

In launching that attack, the Russians demonstrated how complex, yet simple, covert action has become. Consider that the Russians were able to penetrate servers across the country, exposing Democratic and potentially Republican secrets, hacked into numerous state election sites, funneled disinformation to tens of millions of unsuspecting Americans, and generated countless conspiracy theories that dominated the American political discourse for two years. Not just that, but the Russians were also able to do the exact same to Great Britain in the runup to its Brexit referendum.

To accomplish such a Herculean feat during the early years of the Cold War would have entailed at the very least creating a worldwide network of operatives capable of physically penetrating state and federal government agencies across the country and accessing millions of pages of files, as well as printing and disseminating tens of millions of disinformation materials across the country. The manpower and costs required would have been immense. Today, the Russians could do it from the headquarters of the GRU Main Directorate in Moscow.

The speed and intensity of today's covert operations vastly exceed anything contemplated in years past, and with the advent of quantum computing, even the best encryption could be penetrated until quantum encryption is realized. This means that covert action will become an ever more important, and potent, weapon used by nations to achieve their grand strategies. Just as much of the literature on nuclear proliferation focused on how to deter nuclear use, so too will academic analysis of covert action need to uncover ways of deterring potentially crippling cyberattacks from ever happening. Currently, nations do not consider cyberattacks with the same dread as they did conventional or nuclear attacks; so far, Russia has paid only a marginal penalty for an attack that undermined an entire US election. Without increasing these costs, we can expect far more dangerous covert cyberattacks in the future.

References

Adams, Ephraim Douglass. 2008. *British Interests and Activities in Texas, 1838–1846*. Amazon Digital Services, Kindle Edition, originally published 1910.
Aldrich, Richard, and Rory Cormac. 2016. *The Black Door: Spies, Secret Intelligence and British Prime Ministers*. London: William Collins.
Ammon, Henry. 1973. *James Monroe: The Quest for National Identity*. Charlottesville, University Press of Virginia.
Andrew, Christopher. 2018. "Intelligence and the Coming of the First World War." In *The Secret World: A History of Intelligence*. New Haven: Yale University Press.
Bemis, Samuel Flagg. 1926. *Pickney's Treaty: A Study of America's Advantage from Europe's Distress, 1783–1800*. Baltimore: Johns Hopkins University Press.
Berkowitz, Bruce D., and Allen Goodman. 1988. "The Logic of Covert Action." *The National Interest* 51 (Spring): 38–46.
Bernstein, Carl. 1996. *His Holiness*. New York: Doubleday.
Bittman, Ladislas. 1985. *The Deception Game*. New York, Mass Market Press.
Boghardt, Thomas. 2012. *The Zimmerman Telegram: Intelligence, Diplomacy, and America's Entry into World War I*. Annapolis: Naval Institute Press.
Boyd, Julian P. 2015. *Number 7: Alexander Hamilton's Secret Attempts to Control American Foreign Policy*. Princeton Legacy Library.
Brands, Hal. 2020. *The Dark Art of Political Warfare: A Primer*. Washington DC: American Enterprise Institute.
Congressional Research Service. 2018. "Electrical Grid Cybersecurity." September. https://fas.org/sgp/crs/homesec/R45312.pdf
Corke, Sarah-Jane. 2007. *U.S. Covert Operation and Cold War Strategy: Truman, Secret Warfare, and the CIA, 1945–1953*. New York: Routledge.
De Roulhac Hamilton, J.G. 1955. "The Pacifism of Thomas Jefferson." *The Virginia Quarterly Review* 31 (4): 620.
Farago, Ladislas. 1971. *The Game of Foxes: The Untold Story of German Espionage in the United States and Great Britain During World War II*. New York: Bantam Books.

"Final Report of the Select Committee to Study Governmental Operations with Respect to Intelligence Activities." https://archive.org/stream/finalreportofselo1unit/finalreportofselo1unit_djvu.txt

Frisch, Morton, ed. 2007. *Hamilton, Alexander, and James Madison; The Pacificus-Helvidius Debates of 1793–1794: Toward the Completion of the American Founding*. Indianapolis: Liberty Fund.

Goodman, Michael. 2018. "Writing the Official History of the Joint Intelligence Committee. *Secrecy and Society* 2 (1): 1–13.

Graham, Phil. 2017. *Strategic Communication, Corporatism, and Eternal Crisis: The Creel Century*. New York: Routledge.

Grinev, Andrei V. 2010. "The Plans for Russian Expansion in the New World and the North Pacific in the Eighteenth and Nineteenth Centuries." *European Journal of American Studies* 5–2. https://journals.openedition.org/ejas/7805

Howe, John. 1912. "Secret Reports of John Howe, 1808." *The American Historical Review* 17 (2) (January): 332–354.

Jinghua, Lyu. 2019. "What are China's Cyber Capabilities and Intentions?" *Carnegie Endowment for International Peace*, April 1, 2019. https://carnegieendowment.org/2019/04/01/what-are-china-s-cyber-capabilities-and-intentions-pub-78734

Johnson, A. Ross, and Parta, Eugene. 2010. *Cold War Broadcasting: Impact on the Soviet Union and Eastern Europe*. New York: Central European University Press.

Knott, Stephen. 1996. *Secret and Sanctioned: Covert Operations and the American Presidency*. New York: Oxford University Press.

Krebs, Ronald. 2001. *Dueling Visions: U.S. Strategy Toward Eastern Europe under Eisenhower*. College Station: Texas A&M University Press.

Leiner, Frederick C. 2006. *The End of Barbary Terror: America's 1815 War Against the Pirates of North Africa*. New York: Oxford University Press.

Lomas, Daniel W. B. 2019. "Facing the Dictators: Anthony Eden, the Foreign Office and British Intelligence, 1935–1945." *The International History Review*. doi:10.1080/07075332.2019.1650092.

Lulushi, Albert. 2014. *Operation Valuable Fiend: The CIA's First Paramilitary Strike against the Iron Curtain*. New York: Arcade Press.

Meriwether, Stuart. 1973. "Operation Sanders: Wherein Old Friends and Ardent Pro-Southerners Prove to be Union Secret Agents." *The Virginia Magazine of History and Biography* 81 (2) (April): 157–199.

Merry, Robert W. 2009. *A Country of Vast Designs: James K. Polk, the Mexican War and the Conquest of the American Continent*. New York: Simon and Schuster.

Miller, Gerald. 1973. "Office of Policy Coordination, 1948–1952." https://www.cia.gov/library/readingroom/docs/1973-06-01.pdf

Mitrovich, Gregory. 2000. *Undermining the Kremlin: America's Strategy against the Soviet Bloc, 1947–1956*. Ithaca: Cornell University Press.

Mueller III, Robert S. 2019. "Report on the Investigation of Russian Interference in the 2016 Presidential Election." https://www.documentcloud.org/documents/5955118-The-Mueller-Report.html

Office of the Historian. 1948. "National Security Council Directive on Office of Special Projects." *Foreign Relations of the United States (FRUS) The Emergence of the Intelligence Establishment, 1945–1950*. https://history.state.gov/historicaldocuments/frus1945-50Intel/d292

O'Toole, G.J.A. 2014. *Honorable Treachery: A History of American Intelligence, Espionage, and Covert Action from the American Revolution to the CIA*. New York: Grove Press.

Pletcher, David. 1973. *The Diplomacy of Annexation: Texas, Oregon, and the Mexican War.* University of Missouri Press.

Robertson, William Spence. 1939. *France and Latin American Independence.* London: Oxford University Press, 253–296.

Rosett, Claudia. 2015. "How Iran and North Korea became Cyber-Terror Buddies." *FDD*, January 6, 2015. https://www.fdd.org/analysis/2015/01/06/how-iran-and-north-korea-became-cyber-terror-buddies/

Saunders, Frances Stoner. 2013. *The Cultural Cold War: The CIA in the World of Arts and Letters.* 2nd edition. New York: The Free Press.

Schake, Kori. 2017. *Safe Passage: The Transition from British to American Hegemony.* Cambridge, MA: Harvard University Press.

Stern, Sol. 1967. "The CIA and the NSA." *Ramparts Magazine* (March): 29–39. http://www.unz.com/print/Ramparts-1967mar-00029/

Temperely, Howard. 1906. "The Later American Policy of George Canning." *The American Historical Review* II (4) (July): 779–797.

Willys, Rufus Kay. 1929. "French Imperialists in California." *California Historical Society Quarterly* 8 (2) (June): 116–129.

Winkler, Jonathon Reed. 2008. *Nexus: Strategic Communications and American Security in World War I.* Cambridge, MA: Harvard University Press.

Wriston, Henry Merritt. 1967. *Executive Agents in American Foreign Relations.* Gloucester, MA: Peter Smith Publishers.

CHAPTER 25

INTELLIGENCE AND GRAND STRATEGY

JOSHUA ROVNER

GRAND strategy is a theory of security. It tells a logical story about how states keep themselves safe. The story starts with questions about the causes of stability in international politics: Does military strength deter challengers? Or should states keep a low profile to avoid provoking a hostile response? Does trade give states a powerful economic incentive to avoid conflict? Is a lasting peace founded on international institutions that can take some of the uncertainty out of anarchy? Or does it depend on a process of learning among states so they can shed mutual fears and start looking after their mutual interests?

Having arrived at answers to these weighty questions, states turn to the business of implementation. If states believe anarchy leads to insecurity, they may err on the side of restraint, reducing the size of their armed forces and avoiding foreign interventions. If they believe that security rests on conspicuous displays of power, however, they will build large militaries and project them forward. If states believe that security relies on spreading liberal values, they will provide diplomatic, military, and economic support for their ideological brethren abroad. And if they believe that enduring peace can only obtain after states overcome their mutual fear, they will focus on nonviolent diplomacy and confidence-building measures.

Intelligence agencies perform a range of functions in the service of whatever grand strategy the state pursues. In addition to traditional espionage, modern intelligence services employ a variety of technical collection platforms, which they train against a much wider set of targets. They also maintain large organizations dedicated to handling the data they collect from human assets, electronic communications, aerial and satellite imagery, and other sources. How well they utilize these resources, and how we judge their contribution to national security, depends on how closely their work is integrated into grand strategy.

This chapter explores that relationship. The first section discusses how intelligence informs grand strategy and describes several factors that limit its influence.

The second section focuses on the United States, which is particularly useful for exploring the relationship between intelligence and grand strategy. Because of its extraordinary wealth, US policymakers have the luxury of debating a range of grand strategies, along with the different intelligence postures that might support each one. I describe these postures and discuss some implications. The conclusion suggests avenues for further research.

Does Intelligence Matter?

Grand strategy rests on policymakers' beliefs about cause and effect in international politics. Intelligence agencies speak to these beliefs when they comment on trends in world affairs (National Intelligence Council 2017). Policymakers who face difficult decisions about the use of force, and who do not have strong preexisting beliefs about grand strategy, may ask intelligence advisors to assess its underlying logic. Grand strategy also relies on assessments of security threats and opportunities. Such assessments help answer basic questions about force posture and national security: Where should we send military forces, and when should we use them?

Policymakers have many sources of information and insight, of course, but intelligence agencies offer something unique, providing a "library function" for policymakers by combining classified and open source information in their estimates (Betts 2007, 5). Their ability to merge both kinds of information makes them particularly valuable for policymakers struggling with grand strategy. Access to private information also gives states a possible advantage over their rivals. International politics is a competition among states seeking security and prosperity. Intelligence helps them compete (Sims 2010. See also Fingar 2012).[1]

Having set a basic course, intelligence agencies help policymakers implement grand strategy and make adjustments over time. They monitor changes to international security and other factors that shape policy views. Such changes are important for leaders who make practical decisions about diplomacy, economic statecraft, force posture, and military intervention. Intelligence assessments attempt to describe and measure shifting security conditions, using access to secret information to give policymakers a deeper understanding than would otherwise be possible. In the ideal, they will enjoy a competitive advantage in foreknowledge that allows them to support allies and outmaneuver adversaries. We might expect intelligence agencies to have a great deal of influence over grand strategy.

Observers, however, argue that intelligence has surprisingly little impact. Intelligence officers have frequently complained about being neglected. "Let this, then, be the first axiom," one commented ruefully, "*fighting commanders, technical experts, and politicians are liable to ignore, despise, or undernote intelligence*" (Handel 1987, 15, emphasis in original). Scholars tend to agree, though as discussed below there has not been a systematic test of this proposition.[2] There is a long history of policymakers ignoring intelligence warnings. More recently scholars have taken this logic further, arguing that intelligence has little impact not just on tactical warning but also on fundamental questions of grand strategy (Marrin 2017; Immerman 2008; Jackson 2005; Betts 1978; Chan 1979; Handel 1987; and Shuker 2013).

There are many possible sources of irrelevance. Policymakers may have strong expectations and beliefs about world politics that are resistant to challenges from intelligence. Similarly, the variety of assessments may give policymakers the freedom to cherry-pick among those that support their preexisting preferences. Intelligence officials compete with others in government for influence. Military and diplomatic officials, along with informal advisors, may enjoy more sway, especially if policymakers view intelligence assessments as low quality or redundant. Intelligence officials may also struggle to navigate the complex interagency process in modern defense establishments (Thompson 2015). The result is less influence over key decisions. As one historian recently concluded, "Instances of the formulation of national security policy, or grand strategy, hinging on intelligence collection and analysis are few and far between—if they exist at all" (Immerman 2008, 7).

But perhaps this is too high a bar. The notion that grand strategy hinges on any single factor is probably unrealistic, given the complexity of decision-making. As President Lyndon Johnson's intelligence chief once told a frustrated subordinate, "How do I know how he made up his mind? How does any president make decisions? Maybe (his daughter) was in favor of it. Maybe one of his old friends urged him. Maybe it was something he read. Don't ask me to explain the workings of a president's mind" (Smith 1989, 219).

Although estimating the influence of intelligence estimates is tricky, new research has tried to be more rigorous in answering this question. One study asks three basic questions (Gallagher 2015). First, are intelligence professionals represented in key strategic planning sessions? Second, are intelligence products reflected in formal policy documents? Third, does the process of grand strategy formation and implementation clearly include a role for intelligence advice? Answering these questions would go far towards evaluating the influence of intelligence in any given case, but it would require historical scrutiny and careful judgment. Cumulative case study research might produce broader conclusions about intelligence and grand strategy.

We can imagine other approaches. Consider an alternative hypothesis: Intelligence agencies are more influential than other government organizations because they control secret information, which is particularly persuasive (Rovner 2011; Hastedt 2005; Travers, Van Boven, and Judd 2014). If this is true, we should expect policymakers to react to their first exposure to intelligence briefings in classified settings. Before taking office, these individuals likely declare their grand strategic inclinations. If intelligence matters, it should shift their views, and qualitative analysis can assess the degree and direction of the shift.

Intelligence Posture and Grand Strategy

We can also use concepts from other domains to draw intelligence into the grand strategy debate. Recent work on nuclear strategy explains why states choose different nuclear postures to support different deterrence logics (Narang 2014). Borrowing from that literature, the following discussion introduces the concept of an *intelligence posture*. It then shows how different postures map onto different grand strategies.

An intelligence posture describes how states design their intelligence agencies, what kinds of collection they emphasize, where they collect, and when and how they engage in covert action. While many questions occupy intelligence officials, four fundamental choices define a state's intelligence posture. The first has to do with the relative importance it places on secret information. States may believe that gathering secrets through clandestine means is vital for national security. It is impossible to anticipate threats and recognize diplomatic opportunities without investing deeply in espionage. Foreign states have powerful incentives to keep their intentions hidden, along with the technical details of their military capabilities. Only spies can ferret out this information, which is fundamental to assessing threats and forming grand strategy.

On the other hand, a vast amount of information is available in open sources. States can measure one another through overt diplomatic channels and by paying attention to international media. If policymakers need analysis, they can turn to think tanks or universities—or just do it themselves. Overemphasizing secrecy may mean overinvesting in data of marginal value, given the wealth of information free to all. Focusing on secrecy also risks indulging the human tendency to exaggerate the quality of information simply because it was acquired clandestinely.

The second choice has to do with how states collect intelligence. They may emphasize traditional espionage and human sources. Or they may invest more in technological collection, including aerial and space-based imagery and capabilities for intercepting and deciphering communications. There are a variety of collection disciplines, but for our purposes the main distinction is human versus technical means. Human intelligence is risky and ethically fraught. It requires convincing foreign individuals to commit treason against their countries, or to betray the trust of their associates in nonstate or transnational groups. But in some cases, there is no substitute. There is nothing like a well-placed source to reveal an adversary's real intentions, or to provide color and context for its visible routines.

Technological collection can provide extraordinary details about the capabilities of rivals. Imagery and signatures (e.g., electromagnetic emissions) allow modern intelligence agencies to develop a granular understanding of foreign capabilities. Signals intelligence (e.g., communications intercepts) can help reveal foreign intentions. Advocates of technical intelligence may argue that it produces essentially the same information without inviting the same risks. Yet there are problems here as well. Information from signals intelligence, for example, may be partial, misleading, or taken out of context. In other cases, the volume of data may overwhelm analysts' efforts to distinguish meaningful conclusions from meaningless chatter.

The third choice is between unilateral collection and foreign intelligence partnerships. Unilateral collection has important potential benefits. Relying on one's own assets, rather than reports from liaison services, reduces the risk of inadvertent misunderstanding or even deliberate misrepresentation. Much like the children's telephone game, miscommunication increases the farther raw information has to travel before reaching its destination. Developing its own intelligence gives the state more control in selecting and vetting sources. It also gives the state the opportunity to use assets as reliable agents of influence.

There are substantial opportunity costs for going it alone, however. Foreign intelligence services have important advantages. They are fluent in local languages and dialects. They know the terrain. They are a part of the social and political fabric, and possess an understanding of local mores that is impossible to replicate. Importantly, they can more easily blend in with local populations, which both increases the chances of gaining valuable information and reduces the risk of exposure. Finally, intelligence liaison arrangements provide a unique channel for diplomatic communications. This can be useful when open diplomacy breaks down.

The last choice concerns covert action as a tool of grand strategy. Such efforts often appeal to policymakers who see value in deniable activities and who seek alternatives to overt political or military intervention abroad. Covert action is not the same as clandestine work, though the categories often overlap. Clandestine operations like intelligence collection are intended to remain secret; the act itself is never supposed to come to light. Covert operations are different. In these cases, the action itself may not be secret to anyone, but the responsible party remains obscure.

Covert action includes everything from light propaganda to violent sabotage. In between are a number of activities intended to influence foreign affairs without having to claim responsibility. In some cases, the goal is to bolster the status quo, e.g., by supporting friendly but fledgling regimes without having them appear to be puppets. In other cases, the goal is to force change, e.g., by undermining unfriendly foreign powers. The same is true for covert assistance to foreign organizations and nonstate groups. The one unifying characteristic is that the external sponsor remains anonymous.

In theory, covert action provides a number of benefits to grand strategy. It provides a low-cost alternative to economic sanctions or military force. It is less risky, because plausible deniability allows leaders to claim ignorance and defuse the fallout of operations gone wrong. Wartime covert action is particularly important because it can act as a release valve and lower the risk of escalation. In this way, states can pursue limited war as a part of their grand strategies without accepting too much risk (Carson 2018. See also McManus and Yarhi-Milo 2017; Carnegie and Carson 2018).

Covert action also offers opportunities for deniable diplomacy. Because intelligence agencies operate quietly, they can pursue subterranean negotiations with adversaries in peace and war. Peacetime talks may defuse crises in advance and gradually improve relations. In other cases, they allow adversaries the chance to make common cause against shared rivals (Shulsky and Schmitt 2002, 81–82). Secret diplomacy in wartime is also important, both to establish tacit rules of engagement and to facilitate war termination. For a variety of reasons, leaders find it difficult to negotiate overtly with their enemies, not least of which is the problem of domestic blowback. Leaders frequently claim that they do not negotiate with terrorists, for example, but intelligence officials sometimes pursue "secret and deniable discussions" with nonstate armed groups in order to keep the lines of communication open (Scott 2004). Intelligence officials are less constrained. In addition, intelligence officials can pursue their own talks with their counterparts in allied states. This is especially important in periods when overt relations are frayed (Goodman 2007; Byman 2013).

ALIGNING INTELLIGENCE WITH AMERICAN GRAND STRATEGY

The choices that define a state's intelligence posture are not binary. Leaders may invest in secret intelligence and open source collection, pursue human and technical intelligence collection, and cultivate sources independently, while simultaneously making deals with foreign services. They may also engage in covert action more or less frequently, and with varying levels of enthusiasm. The question in each case is about the relative emphasis of their efforts. I simplify policy choices in order to clarify the relationship between a state's grand strategy and its intelligence posture.

The following exercise focuses on the United States, where scholars have long debated the force structure and force posture requirements for different grand strategies (Posen and Ross 1996–1997). Here I ask the same question of intelligence. The United States is a good test bed for this exercise because it is wealthy and insulated. It can afford to maintain a large and diverse intelligence community, and its favorable location makes it possible to redirect intelligence to meet different threats over time. Other states have important decisions to make about their intelligence services, but they are more constrained by resources and geography. That said, the approach used here may add a new dimension to the historical analysis of grand strategies, and it may help forecast the intelligence choices of rising great powers.

I consider three grand strategies: *restraint, liberal internationalism*, and *primacy*. Many other grand strategies occupy the spectrum from isolationism to imperialism, of course, and scholars have described these in detail (recent examples include Avey, Markowitz, and Reardon 2018; Silove 2017). I focus on these three because they reveal the basic differences underlying the current debate: whether or not a forward military posture is necessary for security, and whether ideology and institutions are important for stability.[3]

Restraint is the least assertive grand strategy. It follows the realist assumptions that anarchy forces states to be somewhat wary of one another and that international activism will cause states to push back. The best way to avoid this trap is to adopt a low-profile approach, being careful not to pick fights when national security is not at risk and avoiding the temptation to act to spread ideals and norms. In addition, states should exploit favorable geographic barriers that provide natural defenses. In so doing, states can spend less on defense while reducing the chance of having to use military force. Finally, restraint is skeptical about institutions and alliances. While restraint advocates are aware of the operational value of wartime partnerships, such agreements invite free riding. They also raise the risk of moral hazard, because allies who are confident in foreign protection have less incentive to act responsibly.

What intelligence posture is appropriate for restraint? Prominent restrainers argue that secret intelligence serves useful purposes, especially with regard to counterterrorism. Secret intelligence can help reduce the need for a large forward military presence, which is counterproductive because it aggravates anti-Americanism. The ability to penetrate terrorist groups' communications, for instance, helps provide advance warning of their plans. The ability to track their movement and financial resources adds an extra layer of protection, all without having to station US military forces in dangerous places. And by preventing attacks, intelligence helps stave off demands for revenge that would follow. Intense public pressure for military action would make restraint politically difficult, even for restraint-minded leaders. For all these reasons, military restraint requires intelligence engagement (Posen 2014, 81–85).[4]

Beyond counterterrorism, however, the logic of restraint suggests more reliance on open sources than clandestine collection. Terrorism threatens lives, but it does not change the balance of power or put sovereignty at risk. And fine-grained secret intelligence is hardly required to spot the rise of revisionist great powers. Such states make a show of their growing strength, which would be hard to hide at any rate. Secret intelligence is less important than the careful analysis of information freely available to everyone. Indeed, advocates of restraint resist the idea that accurate understandings of the balance of power require access to secret information (see Posen's comments in Mearsheimer, Posen, and Cohen 1989, 157–159).

A grand strategy of restraint would emphasize technical collection over human sources. The United States enjoys comparative technological advantages making this possible. It boasts a robust scientific and technical infrastructure and can spend lavishly on research and development. It benefits from many decades of experience with mundane and exotic collection platforms. Geography also helps. A large amount the world's internet traffic reportedly flows through the United States. This makes it easier for US intelligence agencies to intercept international communications, though some analysts suspect this is a waning advantage (Buchanan 2017a). In any case, focusing on technological collection reduce the diplomatic risks associated with recruiting foreign agents and removes the need to send forces abroad to protect them.[5] Intelligence collection would be less provocative as it would remain largely invisible to the target.[6] Advocates of restraint favor steps that reduce the likelihood of creating security dilemmas. Moving away from human intelligence, and relying on offshore collection platforms, is consistent with that logic.[7]

The logic of restraint suggests the risks of intelligence partnerships. While restraint is not opposed to all forms of partnering, it does highlight the danger of entangling alliances. Intelligence sharing is no different. A commitment to enduring intelligence arrangements creates temptations to use them in joint military activities. Conversely, providing US technical resources to smaller states might create a kind of moral hazard, if partners believe they can act with the benefit of US intelligence for their own purposes. While some kinds of cooperation fit easily in a grand strategy of restraint (e.g., sharing intelligence about the movement of individual terrorists), institutionalized arrangements can prove to be dangerous liaisons.

Finally, the logic of restraint warns against covert action because there is no guarantee that covert operations will remain hidden. The key limitation of covert action is that the number of parties involved must remain small. But because small size limits its effectiveness, policymakers have often been tempted to invest more resources in order to achieve a better return. From the perspective of restraint, covert action is a gateway drug to mission creep and overt military intervention. This can be a problem even before covert action is authorized; maintaining surreptitious links to fighters behind hostile lines can encourage leaders to use them (Gasiorowski 2019). Blown operations also reinforce foreign perceptions of malign intent, making open conflict more likely.

But in other cases, covert action may serve the interests of restraint. If covert counterterrorism successfully forestalls attacks, for instance, it will depress what would otherwise be public pressure for a military response. Similarly, covert action for the purposes of counterproliferation may slow or halt emerging nuclear threats that might one day tempt leaders into preventive or preemptive wars. A little covert action might serve the interests of restraint, despite the risks. The key issue is the balance of temptation: does covert action grease the wheels for overt intervention, or does it prevent the kind of disasters that force a military response?

Liberal internationalism is more ambitious. Its roots are in liberal international relations theory, which holds that the spread of democracy and trade help mitigate the consequences of anarchy. International institutions help states mediate disputes without resort to violence. They also facilitate multinational efforts to address transnational problems, and over time they encourage a kind of routine interaction that makes war unthinkable. Less war in the international system means fewer security risks for individual states (Ikenberry 1999).

Unlike advocates of restraint, internationalists are less confident in geography. Peripheral conflicts tend to spread, eventually drawing in the great powers. In terms of grand strategy, this means the United States should be proactive in supporting democracy and free-trade movements even in areas of little obvious value to US national security. It should also invest heavily in liberal allies and in international institutions and be ready to use force to defend them.

An intelligence posture in support of liberal internationalism would emphasize the importance of open sources. This is the same as restraint, but the reasons are different.

For internationalists, transparency is a guiding principle, and the retreat to secrecy works against international peace and prosperity (Deudney and Ikenberry 2012). Rather than maintaining large agencies capable of secret intrigues, the United States should set an example by encouraging open information exchange in international institutions. This is not to say that Washington should abandon the game entirely; clandestine work will be needed against a range of ne'er-do-wells that threaten the rules-based order. Similarly, intelligence services can increase stability by exposing malicious actors and contributing to global transparency (Herman 1996). But the need for secret intelligence should decrease as illiberal threats recede and liberal institutions become self-sustaining (Keohane 1984).

The logic of liberal internationalism tends toward technical intelligence over human spies, though it is reluctant about both. Technical intelligence from offshore and space-based platforms may feel less intrusive, and thus less a violation of liberal principles. The rise of commercial imagery has normalized this kind of collection. Signals intelligence remains controversial, however, because it involves intercepting private communications. Recruiting human spies is especially problematic for liberal internationalism, as it actively encourages foreign individuals to break the law. The combination of illegality and subterfuge is contrary to fundamental liberal principles. That said, as long as the United States is committed to a large forward military posture in the service of expanding its ideological principles, it will need a substantial foreign HUMINT capability to assess their progress.

What is truly unique about a liberal internationalist posture is its commitment to liaison agreements. These benefit the quality of intelligence by reducing the transaction costs of transactional sharing; the United States can expect to receive timely and relevant information only if the institutional groundwork is already in place. Institutionalized sharing will also encourage partners to collaborate on collection such that they can focus on their comparative advantages. And fostering liaison relationships may produce happy diplomatic byproducts. Intelligence services provide an important communication channel. Intelligence chiefs conduct their own brand of quiet diplomacy, which occasionally comes in handy. It is no accident that the United States cultivated intelligence liaison arrangements during the period of postwar liberal institution building, when alliance diplomacy was fraught (Goodman 2007).

Liberal internationalism is opposed to covert action. Its emphases on transparency and institutional agreements cut against both covert action and secret diplomacy. The first of Woodrow Wilson's "Fourteen Points" makes this clear: "Open covenants of peace, openly arrived at, after which there shall be no private international understandings of any kind but diplomacy shall proceed always frankly and in the public view" (Wilson 1918). Covert chicanery is an impediment to peace and security, according to this view, because it increases misperception and mistrust. A liberal internationalist grand strategy seeks a durable rules-based international order to ensure collective security. Covert action is anathema to this vision.

Liberal internationalists have often betrayed these principles. In the Cold War, the United States frequently pursued covert action while simultaneously building international institutions and exporting liberal ideology. Sometimes it made common cause with illiberal regimes, acting quietly against democratically elected governments it feared were entering the Soviet orbit. Covert action enabled a kind of useful hypocrisy, allowing US leaders to sustain high-sounding liberal rhetoric without having to acknowledge their illiberal activities. A more charitable interpretation is that they faced a difficult ideological tradeoff because near-term ideological purity would have put the long-term liberal project at risk. If this is the case, then covert action fit within a liberal internationalist grand strategy—but only for a while. The disappearance of threats to the liberal order meant a phasing out of covert action as a tool of grand strategy (Poznansky 2020).[8]

Primacy is the most ambitious grand strategy. It holds that security obtains when a hegemon creates a de facto hierarchy among states. In the absence of world government, a clearly dominant state can deter challengers to the international order, create space for peace and trade, and resolve collective action dilemmas. All this requires a large military presence and a demonstrated will to fight. As with restraint, primacy recognizes the perils of anarchy and doubts the value of multilateral trade and institutions as mitigating forces. And it does not put much stock in norms and ideals as substitutes for raw power. It breaks with restraint in two critical respects, however. First, it does not believe the security dilemma is the main source of violence in international affairs. The real danger is aggressive states that seek to dominate others. Second, primacists worry greatly about a state's reputation. They believe that security rests on its ability to convey credible threats and that credibility requires frequent demonstrations of force.

An intelligence posture supporting primacy would invest heavily in secret collection and treat open source intelligence warily. Weaker challengers have incentives to conceal and deceive, so revealing their capabilities and intentions is essential for a hegemon to guard its position. Primacy also views the notion of a liberal rules-based order as a façade for the true sources of international stability. For this reason, it is foolish to sacrifice aggressive collection for the sake of transparency.

Primacy asks a lot of intelligence, especially if leaders are casualty averse. The hegemon must deal with all threats to deployed forces. Primacy puts extra emphasis on human intelligence to protect them. Granular knowledge of local armed groups requires human sources to provide details about their organizational structure, funding sources, and intentions.[9] Primacists argue that gaining reliable intelligence on shadowy nonstate groups is impossible through technical means alone. Among other benefits, HUMINT helps analysts interpret information they gather from other sources. Snippets of intercepted communications or suggestive satellite imagery may not make sense otherwise. Networks of human informants are irreplaceable, and this requires a substantial HUMINT infrastructure. Boots on the ground demand intelligence, and intelligence needs boots on the ground (O'Hanlon and Reidel 2009).

Primacy calls for a flexible approach towards intelligence liaison. Local intelligence services are important for a number of missions, given their local knowledge, and technical intelligence collection is enabled by partner services. That said, primacy is wary of institutions in general, so intelligence liaison is best when it is conducted bilaterally and on a transactional basis.

Covert action is largely irrelevant for a grand strategy of primacy. There is little need for small-scale covert operations when security is premised on large forward-deployed military forces. Nor is there the same value in hypocrisy, which makes sense for a liberal internationalist approach. The foundation of primacy is the unapologetic belief in the stabilizing effects of hegemony. At most, covert action may help to secure power for local officials who are more receptive to foreign military deployments. This will make it possible to station forces without having to invade. Even in these cases, however, covert action is at best a cost-saving mechanism to facilitate overt military presence.

Table 25.1 summarizes these arguments and reveals two interesting puzzles. One is that restraint and liberal internationalism share a similar view of intelligence, despite their differences in almost all other respects. Both favor open sources and technical collection, and both are skeptical about covert action. To be sure, the rationale is different in each case. Restraint favors open sources against the most important targets, for instance, but sees clandestine collection as necessary against transnational threats. Liberal internationalism favors open sources as a matter of principle, but acknowledges the need for clandestine collection as long as the United States sustains a large forward presence. But the differences in motivation, while interesting, are less important than the areas of agreement. Debates over the military and political dimensions of grand strategy fall along neat and predictable lines. This is not so for intelligence.

A second puzzle: covert action does not fit comfortably into *any* of the major schools of American grand strategy, yet American leaders have turned to it repeatedly since the end of the Second World War. According to a recent study, the United States sought covert regime change on more than 60 occasions during the Cold War, and that total does not include covert actions that served other purposes (O'Rourke 2018). What explains this odd pattern?

It might be that policymakers simply crave freedom of action, no matter their grand strategic orientation (Gavin 2019). Flexibility means stockpiling options. The covert option may seem particularly useful in crises, as it promises a speedy and low-cost solution. Policymakers do not want to be hamstrung by the need to mobilize public opinion or large military forces to achieve their goals abroad, especially if time is short. (For restraint

Table 25.1 Intelligence postures and grand strategy

	Restraint	Liberal internationalism	Primacy
Open sources or secret collection?	Open sources	Open sources	Secret
Human or technical?	Technical	Technical	Human
Unilateral or liaison?	Unilateral	Liaison	Unilateral
Attitude toward covert action	Mostly opposed	Mostly opposed	Largely irrelevant

the allure is different: covert action may forestall the need to mobilize in the first place.) But all grand strategies find reasons to carve out exceptions to their usual skepticism about covert action, and for reasons beyond crisis management. Restrainers are willing to entertain the idea in order to pursue terrorists without having to risk the domestic outrage that would follow an attack. Liberal internationalists are sometimes willing to sacrifice a short-term liberal value in pursuit of a long-term liberal objective. And primacists may view covert action as something that helps to facilitate overt military power projection.

The turn to covert action may also reflect the peculiarities of the Cold War, when policymakers were eager to compete with the Soviet Union but desperate to avoid war. Covert action was particularly appealing in this regard. On multiple occasions Moscow and Washington proved willing to tacitly accept one another's skullduggery, because it provided a release valve for conflict. At the same time, covert operations allowed Washington to wage an intense battle against communist ideologues outside the Soviet Union, while using deniability to claim the moral and ideological high ground. It remains to be seen whether they will follow the same logic in future great power contests.

INTERNATIONAL RELATIONS, GRAND STRATEGY, AND INTELLIGENCE STUDIES

For many years, intelligence was somewhat removed from international relations theory. Intelligence was a niche field, with its own journals and professional networks. This divide was strange, given the close connection between intelligence work and the issues that animate IR scholarship. But it was understandable, given the difficulties for researchers pursuing scholarship on agencies that jealously guard their secrets. The result was that intelligence studies played little role in the debate over grand strategy.

The IR–intelligence gap has narrowed considerably over the last decade. Mainstream IR scholars have increasingly turned their attention to intelligence, partly because of the controversies surrounding the wars in Iraq and Afghanistan. The increasing availability of relevant archives has surely helped. The result is an opportunity for intelligence scholarship to inform the debate over grand strategy, which up to now has been closely tied to arguments over international relations theory.

This chapter described how intelligence informs grand strategy and why its influence is limited. It offered some propositions about the role of intelligence in different grand strategies: restraint, liberal internationalism, and primacy. It also considered the appeal of covert action to leaders with different grand strategy preferences. These propositions are certainly not the last word; they are starting points for developing and testing hypotheses. Some of them may be misleading, incomplete, or wrong.

What will it take to get better results? First, it will take a clearer definition of intelligence posture along with a more robust and generalizable typology. Not all scholars will agree with the distinguishing features I have chosen, and they may think of better ones. Second, scholars can dig more deeply into the question of influence. On this matter, we depend heavily on the insights of former intelligence officers. While their experience is important, it can provide only one perspective, and more systematic work by IR and intelligence scholars can put their experiences in theoretical and historical context.

Third, scholars can examine the mechanics of changing intelligence postures within a broader theoretical framework. Debates about posture follow surprise attacks: critics demand answers about why intelligence agencies failed to deal with specific threats and call for reorganization to meet them. Scholars can open the aperture by looking at how intelligence adapts to deeper changes in grand strategy and by exploring cases in which intelligence postures and grand strategies are misaligned.

Finally, comparative studies may shed light on how states with different resource constraints think about intelligence and grand strategy. This chapter focused on the United States because its wealth gives it a wide range of choices, which is useful for fleshing out the concept of an intelligence posture. At the same time, states with fewer resources may view intelligence as especially important, given that they cannot rely on overwhelming military power or geography to keep them safe.

Notes

1. Espionage may also help change the balance of power if states use intelligence to reverse engineer military technologies, thereby catching up with stronger rivals. Recent scholarship, however, argues that this is easier said than done (Lindsay and Cheung 2015).
2. Nor do all observers agree. New research on the last decade of the Cold War, for example, suggests that intelligence influenced grand strategy in two ways. First, the intelligence community began providing much more granular information on Soviet naval doctrine. Second, the United States devised ways of signaling its clandestine capabilities without giving away technical details to the Soviet Union. Both factors encouraged a much more assertive US force posture (See Ford and Rosenberg 2005; Long and Green 2014; and Long and Green 2017).
3. This is not to downplay alternatives. Advocates of the status quo, for example, make powerful arguments in favor of a grand strategy lying somewhere between restraint and liberal internationalism. They call for continued investments in existing alliances and institutions, but they warn against creating new ones, and above all engaging in further democracy-building measures. The intelligence requirements for such a grand strategy are not terribly different from those necessary for liberal internationalism, given the already expansive US commitments. For the purpose of this exercise, it makes sense to highlight those grand strategies with the clearest differences in order to flesh out ideal-type intelligence postures. (See Lind and Wohlforth 2019; and Brooks, Wolforth, and Ikenberry 2013.)
4. Robert Art (2012) prefers the term "selective engagement," which is related to restraint but somewhat more assertive. But his views about intelligence and terrorism are the same.
5. British officials during the period of retrenchment explicitly considered substituting intelligence for power, but also debated the risks (Aldrich 2013).

6. This is not to say that targets of SIGINT collection are blasé. Awareness of intrusion may cause considerable anxiety, especially if the target is unsure it removed the intruder from its networks and systems.
7. According to Ben Buchanan, cyberspace is an exception. Here the security dilemma is particularly intense because the same methods that enable information collection also enable offensive cyber operations. That said, there is little evidence to date that clandestine cyber intelligence collection has provoked escalation. Compare Buchanan 2017b, and Rovner and Moore 2017.
8. O'Rourke (2018), however, finds that US actions were not a product of ideological preferences.
9. In some cases, primacy may be possible without intelligence. The ancient Greek and Roman empires, for example, put little stock in espionage. Their general approach was to use military forces, rather than dedicated intelligence services, to learn about newly acquired territories (Andrew 2018, 27–53).

References

Aldrich, Richard J. 2013. "British Intelligence During the Cold War." In *Secret Intelligence in the European States System*, edited by Jonathan Haslam and Katrina Urbach. Stanford, CA: Stanford University Press.

Andrew, Christopher. 2018. *The Secret World: A History of Intelligence*. New Haven, CT: Yale University Press.

Art, Robert J. 2012. "Selective Engagement in the Era of Austerity." In *America's Path: Grand Strategy for the Next Administration*, edited by Richard Fontaine and Kristin M. Lord. Washington, DC: Center for a New American Security.

Avey, Paul C., Jonathan N. Markowitz, and Robert J. Reardon. 2018. "Disentangling Grand Strategy: International Relations Theory and U.S. Grand Strategy." *Texas National Security Review* 2 (1): 28–51.

Betts, Richard K. 1978. "Analysis, War, and Decision: Why Intelligence Failures are Inevitable." *World Politics* 31 (1): 61–89.

Betts. Richard K. 2007. *Enemies of Intelligence: Knowledge and Power in American National Security*. New York: Columbia University Press.

Brooks, Stephen G., William C. Wolforth, and G. John Ikenberry. 2013. "Lean Forward." *Foreign Affairs* 92 (1): 130–142.

Buchanan, Ben. 2017a. "Nobody but Us: The Rise and Fall of the Golden Age of Signals Intelligence." Aegis Paper No. 1708. Stanford, CA: Hoover Institute.

Buchanan, Ben. 2017b. *The Cybersecurity Dilemma: Hacking, Trust, and Fear Between Nations*. Oxford, UK: Oxford University Press.

Byman, Daniel S. 2013. "The Intelligence War on Terrorism." *Intelligence and National Security* 29 (6): 837–863.

Carnegie, Allison, and Austin Carson. 2018. "The Spotlight's Harsh Glare: Rethinking Publicity and International Order." *International Organization* 72 (3): 627–657.

Carson, Austin. 2018. *Secret Wars: Covert Conflict in International Politics*. Princeton, NJ: Princeton University Press.

Chan, Steve. 1979. "The Intelligence of Stupidity: Understanding Failures in Strategic Warning." *American Political Science Review* 73 (1): 138–146.

Deudney, Daniel, and G. John Ikenberry. 2012. "Democratic Internationalism: An American Grand Strategy for a post-Exceptionalist Era." Council on Foreign Relations *Working Paper*. https://www.ciaonet.org/record/26843?search=1, accessed March 17, 2021.

Fingar, Thomas. 2012. "Intelligence and Grand Strategy." *Orbis* 56 (1): 118–134.

Ford, Christopher A., and David A. Rosenberg. 2005. "The Naval Intelligence Underpinnings of Reagan's Maritime Strategy." *Journal of Strategic Studies* 28 (2): 379–409.

Gallagher, Michael. 2015. "Intelligence and National Security Strategy: Reexamining Project Solarium." *Intelligence and National Security* 30 (4): 461–485.

Gasiorowski, Mark. 2019. "The US Stay-behind Operation in Iran, 1948–1953." *Intelligence and National Security* 34 (2): 170–188.

Gavin, Francis J. 2019. "Rethinking the Bomb: Nuclear Weapons and American Grand Strategy." *Texas National Security Review* 2 (1): 74–102.

Goodman, Michael S. 2007. *Spying on the Nuclear Bear: Anglo-American Intelligence and the Soviet Bomb*. Stanford, CA: Stanford University Press.

Handel, Michael I. 1987. "The Politics of Intelligence." *Intelligence and National Security* 2 (4): 5–46.

Hastedt, Glenn. 2005. "Public Intelligence: Leaks as Policy Instruments—The Case of the Iraq War." *Intelligence and National Security* 20 (3): 419–439.

Herman, Michael. 1996. *Intelligence Power in Peace and War*. Cambridge, UK: Cambridge University Press.

Ikenberry, G. John. 1999. "Why Export Democracy?: The 'Hidden Grand Strategy' of American Foreign Policy." *The Wilson Quarterly* 23 (2): 56–65.

Immerman, Richard H. 2008. "Intelligence and Strategy: Historicizing Psychology, Policy, and Politics." *Diplomatic History* 32 (1): 1–23.

Jackson, Peter. 2005. "Introduction." In *Intelligence and Statecraft: The Use and Limits of Intelligence in International Society*, edited by Peter Jackson and Jennifer Siegel. Westport, CT: Praeger.

Keohane, Robert O. 1984. *After Hegemony: Cooperation and Discord in the World Political Economy*. Princeton, NJ: Princeton University Press.

Lind, Jennifer, and William Wohlforth. 2019. "The Future of the Liberal International Order is Conservative." *Foreign Affairs* 98 (2): 70–80.

Lindsay, Jon R., and Tai Ming Cheung. 2015. "From Exploitation to Innovation: Acquisition, Absorption, and Application." In *China and Cybersecurity: Espionage, Strategy, and Politics in the Digital Domain*, edited by in Jon R. Lindsay, Tai Ming Cheung, and Derek S. Reveron. Oxford, UK: Oxford University Press.

Long, Austin, and Brendan Rittenhouse Green. 2014. "Stalking the Secure Second Strike: Intelligence, Counterforce, and Nuclear Strategy." *Journal of Strategic Studies* 38 (1–2): 38–73.

Long, Austin, and Brendan Rittenhouse Green. 2017. "The Role of Clandestine Capabilities in Deterrence: Theory and Practice." U.S. Naval Postgraduate School, Project on Advanced Systems and Concepts for Countering WMD, Grant N00244-16-1-0032 Final Report.

Marrin, Stephen. 2017. "Why Strategic Intelligence Analysis has Limited Influence on American Foreign Policy." *Intelligence and National Security* 32 (6): 725–742.

McManus, Roseanne W., and Keren Yarhi-Milo. 2017. "The Logic of 'Offstage' Signaling: Domestic Politics, Regime Type, and Major Power-Protégé Relations." *International Organization* 71 (4): 701–733.

Mearsheimer, John J., Barry R. Posen, and Eliot A. Cohen. 1989. "Correspondence: Reassessing Net Assessment." *International Security* 13 (4): 128–179.

Narang, Vipin. 2014. *Nuclear Strategy in the Modern Era: Regional Powers and International Conflict*. Princeton, NJ: Princeton University Press.

National Intelligence Council. 2016. *Global Trends*, https://www.dni.gov/index.php/global-trends-home

O'Rourke, Lindsey. 2018. *Covert Regime Change: America's Secret Cold War*. Ithaca, NY: Cornell University Press.

O'Hanlon, Michael E., and Bruce Reidel. 2009. "Why We Can't Go Small in Afghanistan." *USA Today*, September 24, 2009.

Posen, Barry R. 2014. *Restraint: A New Foundation for U.S. Grand Strategy*. Ithaca, NY: Cornell University Press.

Posen, Barry R., and Andrew L. Ross. 1996–1997. "Competing Visions for U.S. Grand Strategy." *International Security* 21 (3): 5–53.

Poznansky, Michael. 2020. *In the Shadow of International Law: Covert Action in the Postwar World*. Oxford, UK: Oxford University Press.

Rovner, Joshua. 2011. *Fixing the Facts: National Security and the Politics of Intelligence*. Ithaca, NY: Cornell University Press.

Rovner, Joshua, and Tyler S. Moore. 2017. "Does the Internet Need a Hegemon?" *Journal of Global Security Studies* 2 (3): 184–203.

Scott, Len. 2004. "Secret Intelligence, Covert Action, and Clandestine Diplomacy." *Intelligence and National Security* 19 (2): 322–341.

Shuker, Stephen A. 2013. "Seeking a Scapegoat: Intelligence and Grand Strategy in France, 1919–1940." *Secret Intelligence in the European States System*, edited by Jonathan Haslam and Karina Urbach. Stanford, CA: Stanford University Press.

Shulsky, Abram N., and Gary J. Schmitt. 2002. *Silent Warfare: Understanding the World of Intelligence*. 3rd edition. Washington, DC: Potomac Press.

Silove, Nina. 2017. "Beyond the Buzzword: The Three Meanings of 'Grand Strategy.'" *Security Studies* 27 (1): 27–57.

Sims, Jennifer E. 2010. "Decision Advantage and the Nature of Intelligence Analysis." In *The Oxford Handbook of National Security Intelligence*, edited by Loch K. Johnson. Oxford, UK: Oxford University Press.

Smith, Russell Jack. 1989. *The Unknown CIA: My Three Decades with the Agency*. Washington, DC: Potomac Books.

Thompson, James. 2015. "Governance Costs and Defence Intelligence Provision in the UK: A Case-Study in Microeconomic Theory." *Intelligence and National Security* 1 (6): 844–857.

Travers, Mark, Leaf Van Boven, and Charles Judd. 2014. "The Secrecy Heuristic: Inferring Quality from Secrecy in Foreign Policy Contexts." *Political Psychology* 35 (1): 97–111.

Wilson, Woodrow. 1918. "Address to Congress." January 8, 1918. https://www.ourdocuments.gov/document_data/pdf/doc_062.pdf

CHAPTER 26

FINANCING THE GRAND STRATEGY OF GREAT AND RISING POWERS

ROSELLA CAPPELLA ZIELINSKI

How can great and rising powers finance their grand strategy? What enables and constrains a state's ability to finance its grand strategic needs? Under what conditions are leaders able to implement their desired financial strategy? While most scholars treat grand strategy holistically—its purpose being to achieve coherence between means and ends—there has been no systemic study to understand the full spectrum of financing options available, the ability of the state to implement them, and how leaders weigh the political and economic tradeoffs of each. In other words, despite the acknowledgment of a state's financial constraints in the formulation of grand strategy, less attention has been paid to the conditions under which a specific financing strategy is chosen.[1]

Understanding the full panoply of financing options available, and immediate and long-term political and economic costs and benefits, is critical for the study and practice of grand strategy. For example, the contemporary study and practice of American grand strategy places an overwhelming emphasis on debt (Kennedy 1987; Rasler and Thompson 1983; Schultz and Weingast 2003). Treating debt as the default means of financing grand strategy, however, ignores other financing options and, more importantly, results in inadequate prescription. Many grand strategy scholars argue that to correct such financial "over extension" the country must shift towards a strategy of restraint (Gholz, Press, and Sapolsky 1997; Preble 2011) while others claim that borrowing is either not financially ruinous or worth the cost (Norrlof 2008; Norrlof and Wohlforth 2019; Drezner 2013). Borrowing, however, is a political choice and not a foregone conclusion. Moreover, given the various forms of debt, not all borrowing is equal in terms of its economic costs to the state. Indeed, other forms of grand strategic finance, such as direct taxation, provide a sustainable, less economically costly form of revenue that simultaneously reduces reliance on foreign creditors and curbs inequality (Cappella Zielinski 2018).

Additionally, treating the financing of grand strategy as exogenous to strategy itself means scholars are in danger of misunderstanding the grand strategy chosen. For example, constrained financing, due to administrative and constitutional constraints, shaped Hapsburg grand strategy. The monarchy's financial constraints effectively ruled out the most obvious and efficacious means that a land empire in Austria's position might respond to threats to its territorial integrity—with robust military force. Instead, Hapsburg grand strategy was limited to securing buffers around its frontiers, constructing a defensive army to underwrite the monarchy, and investing in allied coalitions (Mitchell 2018).

In addressing this lacuna in the grand strategy literature, this chapter heeds the call put forth by Blazacq, Dombrowski, and Reich (2019) to push the study of grand strategy towards a mature research program, providing a testable framework applicable to various great and rising powers across time. Thus, this chapter provides the first analytical framework for explaining how states finance their grand strategies. First, I address the scope of the framework: how rising and great powers finance the military component of a state's grand strategy. Second, I argue that financing grand strategy presents state leaders with an intertemporal dilemma: fiscal sacrifice today for benefits accrued in the future.[2] When considering how to finance grand strategy, leaders are concerned not only with implementing grand strategy but staying in power. Thus, I address not only the means of finance—direct and indirect taxation, domestic debt, and foreign debt—but revenue sustainability and the short- and long-term political and economic costs of each approach. Third, I offer hypotheses to explain under what conditions leaders will choose a particular finance strategy. I suggest that three variables condition leaders' willingness to incur the political costs of financing grand strategy via direct resource extraction: regime type, whether or not a state is a rising or great power, and the degree of clarity in the threat environment.

Financing Grand Strategy

This chapter concerns itself with how rising and great powers mobilize economic resources over the long term to advance the military component of their grand strategies. I emphasize military costs, as they are the most expensive component of a state's grand strategy. For example, as shown in Figure 26.1, while the United States' military budget has continued to grow throughout the postwar period, the State Department's budget has remained the same.[3] Excluded from this narrow conception is financing other components of a state's grand strategy, such as trade and investment policies, diplomatic policies, and other initiatives (Hart 1957, 322).

Moreover, the scope of this chapter is limited to rising and great powers, as they are likely to spend more on the military component of their grand strategy than middle

Outlays by Agency
(in millions of dollars)

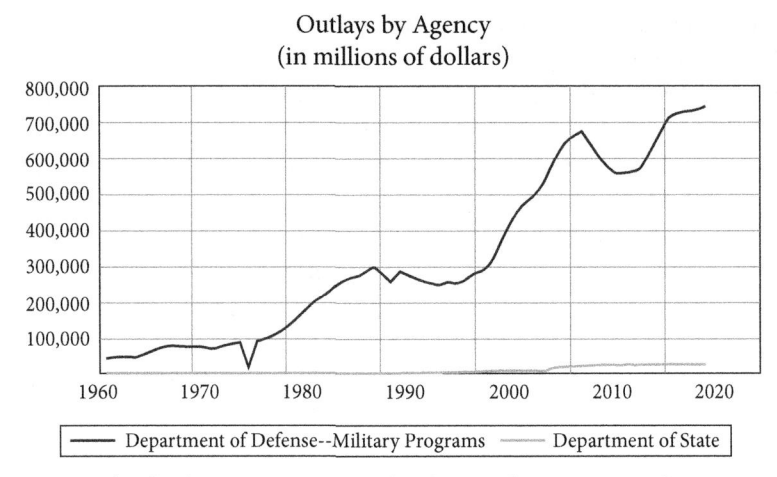

FIGURE 26.1 Outlays by the US Department of Defense and Department of State

powers.[4] Additionally, the economies of rising and great powers are relatively mature, characterized by sophisticated financial instruments and corresponding access to credit, market depth, a stable currency, and they often have or are close to having reserve currency status. Thus, rising and great powers have more financing means at their disposal than do states with less developed economies (Knorr 1975).

Also excluded from this narrow conception of financing grand strategy are the extraordinary costs associated with war onset. To be clear, preparing for war may be a distinct component of a state's grand strategy and some states may anticipate and account for future war when considering how to finance their grand strategy. For example, shaping British grand strategy in the 1930s was tension with the Treasury, which loathed overreliance on debt and the imperative of preparing for war with Germany which required raising immense sums. In 1937, the Minister for Coordination of Defence called for a defense review. The findings were clear: financing the current rearmament scheme by borrowing would undermine the economy, specifically the stability of the pound and Britain's international credit position and, therefore, the ability to confront Germany in a great power war. The report stated:

> The maintenance of credit facilities and our general balance of trade are of vital importance not merely from the point of view of our strength in peacetime, but equally for purposes of war. This country cannot hope to win a war against a major power by a sudden knock-out blow; on the country, for success we must contemplate a long war in the course of which we should have to mobilize all our resources ... If we are to emerge victoriously from such a war, it is essential we should enter it with sufficient economic strength to enable us to make the fullest use of resources overseas, and to withstand the strain ... the maintenance of our economic stability would more accurately be described as an essential element in our defense strength: one which can properly be regarded as a fourth arm in

defense, alongside the three services without which purely military effort would be of no avail. (Quoted in Shay 1977, 167)

Even accounting for such explicit considerations, financing the extraordinary costs of war upon war onset reflects unique processes outside of peacetime grand strategy spending. Wars are discrete short-term events relative to the long time horizon associated with a state's grand strategy and, consequently, are subject to distant political and budgetary conditions (see Cappella Zielinski 2016, ch. 1). Upon war onset, the state may suspend peacetime institutional budgetary constraints, freeing leaders to raise unpreceded revenue, or changes in public opinion may lower the political costs of raising revenue so that previous politically untenable sources become viable (Oatley 2015; Cappella Zielinski 2016). For example, Austria-Hungary, prior to the First World War, found it difficult to fund its military programs as the financial and manpower resources required for military forces depended upon the political support of a disaggregated constitutional structure that required the approval of two cabinets (Williamson 1991, 15). Despite borrowing to pay for its armaments programs (Bogart 1920, 136), Austro-Hungarian forces were notoriously underfunded (Mitchell 2018). However, when the First World War broke out, emergency powers allowed the Dual Monarchy to raise funds by means not previously available. Austrian Prime Minister Karl von Stürgkh invoked Paragraph 14 of the Basic Law of Representation permitting virtual emergency rule by the prime minister and eventually disbanded parliament (Williamson 1991, 16). Such actions eased the empire's ability to finance its war effort, allowing not only for domestic debt but also increases in taxation, fees, and foreign loans (Bogart 1920).

In sum, financing grand strategy is the means by which states meet the costs of armament programs, the establishment and maintenance of bases and troops at home and abroad, and military commitments and aid to allies during peacetime. It is the peacetime process by which the state redirects or procures monetary resources to meet government outlays associated with investment in the armed services, including but not limited to personnel, research and development, procurement, and associated civilian organizations, as well as military support to allies.

Financing Grand Strategy and Intertemporal Tradeoffs

How do leaders manage the imposition of immediate costs to finance a state's grand strategy long before the benefits arrive? Financing grand strategy presents an intertemporal dilemma: fiscal sacrifice today for benefits accrued in the future.[5] When considering how to finance grand strategy, state leaders concern themselves not only with implementing the state's grand strategy but also staying in power.[6] It is politically costly for leaders to raise revenue. By wresting money from individuals and households, leaders are taking the means of livelihood from the population. Not only do citizens prefer not to surrender their income to the state, but they expect something in return: to surrender revenue to the government is to contribute to the provision of general public goods (Levi 1988; Liberman 2002; Caverley 2014, 27–28). Thus, the financing manner chosen draws attention to the state's grand strategy and potential costs and rewards associated with it (Goddard and Krebs 2015, 19). In addition to political costs, leaders must consider revenue sustainability and the economic costs. Revenue stability is critical for grand strategic planners to allow them to design their budgets accordingly and invest in projects as planned. In regards to economic costs, the financial strategy chosen is subject to distributional and inflationary effects, with possible implications for state solvency and, in turn, future credit. Thus, leaders not only have to manage short-term and long-term political costs but consider revenue sustainability and short- and long-term economic costs.

To understand under what conditions leaders are more likely to incur short-term political and economic costs and when they are more likely to privilege revenue sustainability when financing grand strategy, scholars need to theorize these intertemporal tradeoffs. This section presents such an intertemporal theoretical framework that addresses the financing options available and their respective short- and long-term economic and political implications. It directly considers what degree of government intervention is entailed in each financing strategy, how these strategies affect citizens' awareness of fiscal sacrifice, and how the international economic environment shapes the available forms of extraction.

A state can finance its grand strategy by procuring funds from within the state or securing funds from outside its borders (Mastanduno, Lake, and Ikebenrry 1989). Internally, the state can extract resources directly via direct taxation or indirectly via indirect taxation or domestic debt. Externally, the state can raise funds via sovereign-to-sovereign loans or general foreign debt.

Direct resource extraction refers to resources given to the state directly by its citizens. The most typical form of direct extraction is direct taxation, including income, corporate, property, and payroll taxes. Leaders impose this method of extraction on individuals as they cannot opt out of the extraction policy or transfer the costs of said policy to others. Given the effect on them, citizens are highly aware of this policy (Cappella Zielinski 2016, 11–12; Kreps 2018). The high visibility of direct resource extraction brings attention to this financial policy, allowing citizens to reflect on the potential costs and benefits of the strategy (Goddard and Krebs 2015). Direct resource extraction is, thus, politically costly in the short term. Citizens, intrinsically reluctant to cede their hard-earned income to the state with no immediate tangible benefits due to the long time horizons of grand strategy, are unlikely to support financing strategy this way. However, the political costs of direct resource extraction may fall over time as citizens and businesses become accustomed to the prevailing tax rates and adjust their disposable spending and prices accordingly.

While the political costs of direct resource extraction are high in the short term and lower in the long term, its revenue benefits are high and economic costs low. Direct resource extraction provides a stable source of revenue. Direct tax revenue does not fluctuate with market forces or economic shocks to the same degree as indirect taxation or debt. Additionally, it is low-cost economically in the short and long term. Unlike borrowing, there is no need for the state to pay back the funds with interest. Direct resource extraction also reduces inflation and, if the tax policy is progressive, can have positive redistributive effects. Thus, in both the short and long term, direct resource extraction is characterized by low economic costs.

Indirect resource extraction refers to resources indirectly transferred from citizens to the state. Here, the government procures resources by asking nothing from citizens initially or by providing citizens with the choice of either opting out of the policy or transferring its costs. Thus, whereas direct resource extraction is compulsory and citizens are highly aware of government policy, indirect resource extraction leaves citizens relatively less aware of government extraction (Cappella Zielinski 2016, 12–13). Forms of indirect resource extraction include indirect taxation (e.g., sales taxes, value-added taxes, and tariffs) and domestic debt.[7]

Indirect taxation is less politically and economically costly than direct taxation, yet its revenue is less stable. Its political costs are diffused, as businesses can pass the costs onto the consumer and the consumer may not even be aware of the increased costs, resulting in the poor shouldering the financial burden of policy. Regarding economic costs, in the short term, the costs of indirect taxation are low, but in the long term, its costs increase as indirect taxation can push up prices, potentially resulting in inflation. Additionally, revenue collected from indirect taxation is uncertain. The elastic demand on goods means revenue garnered varies with market demand.

British rearmament policy prior to the First World War provides an example of the various political costs and economic benefits of direct and indirect taxation. At the end of the nineteenth century, the major powers of Europe embarked on major fleet-building programs to build their respective overseas empires. The British implemented an ambitious rearmament program. On March 7, 1889, Parliament passed the Naval Defence Act of 1889, establishing the "two-power standard," which called for the Royal Navy to maintain a number of battleships at least equal to the combined strength of the next two largest navies in the world, France and Russia. The First Lord associated with the new naval program made a public declaration of fundamental strategic principle: "Our establishment," he maintained in the House of Commons, "should be on such a scale that it should at least be equal to the naval strength of any two other nations" (Sumida 1989, 14). The Act called for £21.5 million over five years to construct eight first-class battleships, two second-class battleships, 29 second-class cruisers, four third-class cruisers, and 18 torpedo gunboats (Sondhaus 2001, 161).

The Conservative government initially attempted to pay for the policy through both direct and indirect means. From the outset, the Treasury argued that there would be serious political costs to a substantial increase in regressive indirect taxes, and the public's appetite for increasing direct taxes, which were already high from the Boer War, was low (Friedberg 1988, 99; Narizny 2003, 207). To meet minimal immediate revenue needs, Britain's leaders raised marginal taxes on tea, tobacco, and income

(Narizny 2003, 208). Unable to raise substantial revenue due to the high political costs, they initiated a major strategic retrenchment to curb future military expenditures (Friedberg 1988, 116–118, 169–182).

Increasing German naval capabilities, however, continued to be a threat. Once again, Britain looked to expand its naval capacity and build new dreadnoughts. This proved a costly venture and Britain again attempted direct taxation. Prime Minister David Lloyd George proposed a "People's Budget"—of the people not only in the sense that it would raise money for old-age pensions and other social welfare schemes, but also in that it would tap the required new sources of revenue in a democratic way. Rather than resort to a "stomach-tax," he introduced a series of direct taxes such as a land tax (Murray 1973, 558, 563). Despite the high political costs of the "People's Budget," Lloyd George was successful, and the increased direct and indirect taxes provided more than enough revenue for the armament program. Indeed, in 1911–1912, it was the greatest revenue surplus on record to date, providing for welfare needs and deficit payment (Sumida 1989, 188–196; Murray 1973, 570).

Domestic debt—money voluntarily lent to the government from its citizens with the explicit understanding that it will be paid back over time—is another form of indirect extraction. Domestic debt is the least visible form of domestic finance. Moreover, it can bring in large sums of revenue immediately without overburdening constituents with taxes or cutting welfare programs (Shea 2013). Additionally, contingent on the state's credit, it can also be a sustainable source of revenue for the duration of the state's grand strategy (Schultz and Weingast 2003). Thus, domestic debt is a relatively stable form of finance in the short to medium term as long as creditors are confident in repayment and willing to lend (Tomz 2007). Domestic debt, however, is economically costly, as the state has to pay back the funds with interest. Such economic costs accrue over time and are particularly notable when a state's credit is poor and or debt is sold at market rates.

A state can also finance its grand strategy via external means. External resource extraction refers to resources procured from abroad, typically securities floated on foreign markets but also sovereign-to-sovereign loans. Similar to indirect resource extraction, when a state engages in external resource extraction, it does not initially ask anything from society, further removing citizens from interacting with the state's finance policy (Cappella Zielinski 2016, 15). Borrowing from abroad, particularly at market rates, is economically costly as, akin to domestic borrowing, the state must pay funds back with interest. While external resource extraction may allow the state to secure large sums of revenue quickly, its stability as a form of long-term revenue is dubious: the debtor state is at the whim of external creditors, individuals, or states, and has little recourse if creditors decide to stop lending or demand payment.

Since the end of the Cold War, for example, the United States has financed its grand strategy via a combination of domestic and foreign debt (Oatley 2015). Ever increasing political costs to raising taxes has resulted in at least a dozen major tax cuts, starting with the Tax Relief Act of 1997, despite increases in military spending. Indeed, since 2001, military spending for the wars in Iraq and Afghanistan has been referred to as the Credit Card Wars (Bilmes 2017).

The ability of the state to raise funds domestically is contingent on state capacity, as some forms of revenue extraction require large and complex bureaucratic institutions (Cappella Zielinski 2016, 25). Direct resource extraction requires that the state be able to assess the revenue potential of many, if not all, citizens, and leaders need a statewide institutional structure to collect and process the revenue. In contrast, leaders levy indirect taxes and voluntary borrowing on a smaller segment of the population, requiring a lower volume of information and smaller supporting institutions to collect and process the resulting revenue.[8] In sum, as the number of citizens subject to the state's revenue extraction policy increases, so does the breadth and depth of the state's needed extractive capacity. Direct extraction is characterized by more state–citizen interaction than indirect extraction, while external extraction bypasses the citizenry altogether. Thus, a low extraction capacity limits states to indirect or external revenue extraction.

Japan's financing of its grand strategy at the beginning of the twentieth century illustrates the importance of state capacity. During this period, in addition to containing Russia, Japan's primary objective was to overturn the East Asian balance of power and replace China as the dominant regional power (Paine 2017). To meet these goals Japan invested in extensive land and naval forces (Paine 2017, 23; Yamamura 1977), including the purchase of warships from Britain (Jentschura, Jung, and Mickel 1977; Miller 2005). Japan's fiscal and financial capacity, however, was relatively weak. Before the Meiji Restoration, there was no central currency or central administrative tax bureaucracy. Japan introduced the yen in 1871, in 1882 the government established a central bank, and throughout the period it imposed a myriad of taxes, including a land tax and various sales taxes (Goldsmith 1983; Bird 1977, 164). Due to the newness of these institutions, Japan lacked a robust capacity to finance a large armaments program domestically. Moreover, the state had no previous experience floating debt in international markets. When Japan opened itself to world trade in 1859, it had no credit standing or national currency and little experience in floating loans (Miller 2005, 465; Patrick 1965, 207).

In light of its low state capacity, prior to the First Sino-Japanese War (1894–1895) Japan relied on debt to raise money. After a sustained effort to increase tax capacity to support its grand strategy, the government instituted for the first time a national business tax and a registration tax. In addition, Japan increased the land tax, as well as taxes on alcoholic beverages and sugar. As a result of these measures, the total tax revenue in the ten years following the Sino-Japanese War was roughly double the ten years preceding the war (Takao 1965, 433). Increased taxes to finance the Russo-Japanese War further expanded Japan's tax capacity (Cappella Zielinski 2016, 91).

While increased tax revenues financed a majority of its armaments program, Japan needed gold for purchases of ships abroad. In 1897, Japan built its credit through a $185 million gold indemnity received from China, eventually pegging the yen to gold at 0.75 grams, a value maintained for the next thirty-five years (Miller 2005, 468; Takao 1965, 447). In the words of Edward Miller, "What ensued was an international financial coup. Meiji Japan, a minor league borrower, raising only $60 million abroad since its origins thirty years earlier, tapped into global lending markets by issuing bonds with a face of $408 million, and after discounts and changes, $343 million" (Miller 2005, 472).

Structural economic variables also condition the ability of the state to resort to external borrowing. A state's ability to access resources abroad is contingent not only on its own financial market development and macroeconomic stability, but also on open capital flows and a broad and diversified investor base producing a stable demand to support revenue needs via liquidity, depth, and stability. Periods of closed and/or underdeveloped markets limit access to external debt and/or costly debt via high interest rates, liquidity premiums, and bid-ask yields. Additionally, a state's credit rating and currency status can either increase or decrease the economic cost of its external extraction strategy (Andrews 2006; Sinclair 2005). States with good credit ratings, and/or whose currency is a reserve currency, are able to run larger deficits at lower costs (Strange 1971; Kirshner 2008).

Throughout the twenty-first century, the United States has relied on foreign deficit financing to fund its military spending. The end of the Bretton Woods system in the 1970s and opening capital flows, combined with the dollar's position at the center of the international monetary system as a reserve currency, and in turn sustained demand for dollar-denominated assets, afforded the United States the unique privilege of unlimited creditors (Cohen 2006). As a result, to finance the military component of its grand strategy, instead of raising taxes or turning to domestic debt, the United States imported capital from abroad (Oatley 2015).

In sum, the various means of financing a state's grand strategy reflect a series of tradeoffs for leaders. Given the differing levels of visibility and sustainability of each means of financing, leaders must navigate the short- and long-term political and economic costs of their grand strategy. The state's capacity to extract revenue, as well as its access to external creditors, also condition its ability to implement the preferred financing option.

Navigating Costs

How do leaders decide what financing option to implement? What variables mitigate or exacerbate the political and economic costs of the financial strategy chosen? Here, I suggest three variables—regime type, state status, and clarity of the threat environment—may decrease the political costs of financing grand strategy via more direct means.

The first variable is regime type. Democracies face starker intertemporal tradeoffs than nondemocracies. Election cycles, or "political business cycles," are associated with shortened time horizons for leaders (Nordhaus 1975; Dubois 2016). Accordingly, to boost election chances, leaders implement macroeconomic policies to aid in reelection. Indeed, studies on Western democracies have shown that governments have pursued expansionary monetary and fiscal policies prior to elections (Alesina and Roubini 1992). Additionally, democracies are characterized by increased policy and budgetary transparency, particularly with respect to economic data (Hollyer, Rosendorff, and Vreeland

2018). Clearly demarcated election cycles combined with economic transparency increase political costs to democratic leaders for direct resource extraction. Thus, we should expect democratic leaders to push the political costs into the future and therefore finance their grand strategies via indirect or external resource extraction.

In contrast, nondemocracies are not subject to the same electoral constraints and associated time horizons. Nondemocracies are subject to constraints of a smaller electorate and attempt to pursue beneficial economic policies that synchronize with leadership succession or factional politics (Guo 2009; Lü and Landry 2014). Moreover, the relative timing of their political business cycle is more varied and/or longer. Additionally, nondemocracies are characterized by decreased policy and budgetary transparency relative to nondemocracies. The absence of electoral cycles and budgetary opacity increase nondemocratic leaders' time horizons and, in turn, lower the political costs of direct extraction. Thus, we should expect nondemocratic leaders, insulated from political costs, to finance their grand strategies via direct resource extraction.

The second variable is state status.[9] Leaders of rising powers can frame sacrifice today in exchange for gains tomorrow: it would produce benefits for a large segment of the population, ranging from growing national prestige and, in turn, increasing collective and individual esteem to eventual economic gains that would reward a broad coalition of citizens (Renshon 2017; Wood 2014). The potential for large gains, combined with long time horizons, lures leaders and citizens to emphasize future benefits rather than immediate costs. As Krebs and Rapport (2012) find, individuals confronting long-term challenges and opportunities systematically underweight the costs of action in favor of its desirability and, thus, are prone to wishful thinking. Furthermore, due to long time horizons, individuals often think of distant gains as greater than they are. Moreover, when actors contemplate the long term, they construe events abstractly, focusing on the desirability of their ends rather than the challenges undertaken in reaching them (Krebs and Rapport 2012, 532; Streich and Levy 2007, 204–205). Thus, leaders of rising states can effectively frame financial sacrifice as producing plentiful long-term gains that will be reaped by a broad coalition if not by all citizens. Given that leaders of rising states face lower political costs to financing grand strategy, we should expect them to finance their grand strategy in the least economically costly and most sustainable means such as direct taxation.

Unlike rising states, current great powers are more concerned with maintaining what they have (i.e., avoiding loss), rather than reaping the benefits of future gains. Leaders of great powers, therefore, are unable to frame their grand strategy around grandiose future gains. Furthermore, given the shortened time horizons associated with near-term preservation, individuals in existing great powers are less inclined to be optimistic about future payoffs and are more inclined to pay attention to the feasibility of their plans (Krebs and Rapport 2012, 532). In other words, primed to focus on feasibility, citizens of great power states focus more on the costs entailed in financing grand strategy than on the potential payoffs. In addition to great powers' inability to sell the citizenry on ambitious future benefits, potential losses are often concentrated in specific sectors. While groups facing losses are in principle willing to accept short-term financing costs to avoid even larger long-run losses, they prefer to address their long-term problems through redistributive, rather than intertemporal, means: to shift the problem's impact onto other segments of society rather than to invest in a solution (Jacobs 2008, 194). Taken together, the difficulty of selling citizens on an ambitious agenda and potential losers unwilling to confront the costs of change mean that leaders in great power states are reluctant to pay the political costs of financing their grand strategy directly and, therefore, prefer indirect or external means that work to obfuscate financial investment in grand strategy (Pierson 2012, 19–20; Cappella Zielinski 2016, 20–21; Kreps 2018, 15–20).

The third variable conditioning leader willingness to incur the various political and economic costs of financing grand strategy is threat clarity. Threat clarity is the ability to discern and rank various signals emanating from the international environment (Goldman 2010, 13). Clarity improves confidence in understanding the external threat environment, including adversary capabilities, adversary intentions and time horizons, and the nature of the threat (Knorr 1976, 90, 115; Huth, Bennett, and Gelpi 1992; Lobell 2009; Lobell 2018).[10] In turn, clarity increases leaders' confidence in the formulation and/or execution of their grand strategy. When leaders are more confident in their grand strategy, particularly vis-à-vis more immediate gains from the strategy, their inclination is to pay the economic and political costs to extract sustainable revenue (Narizny 2007, 11; Shifrinson 2018, 19–20).

When the international environment is ambiguous, leaders perceive events as indefinite or incalculable, and international circumstances no longer provide a reliable guide to strategic planning. Such ambiguity increases leaders' insecurity regarding the formulation and execution of grand strategy. Such insecurity encourages leaders to postpone public interaction with the grand strategy and, consequently, to finance it via less visible means (Edelstein 2017, 20). Moreover, the more ambiguous the external environment, the more leaders must contend with the demands and inputs of domestic actors. The clearer the cues provided by the international environment, the slighter the domestic dissension concerning their interpretation, while the more ambiguous the external threat, the more domestic social and political calculations dominate the thinking of policymakers (Ninčić, Rose, and Gorski 1999, 59). Here, leaders are less successful convincing key actors of specific strategies and less inclined to expend considerable resources on an uncertain long-term threat (Edelstein 2017, 14). Consequently, they prefer to finance their grand strategy via indirect means or external extraction.

Conclusion

Financing grand strategy, unlike other forms of government spending, is characterized by unique intertemporal tradeoffs. Leaders have to navigate how to pay for a policy today in which the benefits, themselves uncertain, accrue to citizens in the distant future. To understand how leaders manage this intertemporal tradeoff, this chapter takes the first step towards addressing this critical lacuna in the grand strategy literature. In doing so, it provides a portable and ahistorical framework of the financing options available to the state in question and the various tradeoffs leaders face when choosing among the various options. It then proposes three variables—regime type, state status, and clarity of the threat environment—that may reduce short-term political costs, enabling leaders to extract resources directly from their citizens. As this chapter is a first step in understanding the financing of grand strategy, it leaves a variety of paths open for future scholars. In addition to further understanding the financing means chosen, scholars should explore the relationship between the strategy chosen and the formulation and implementation of the strategy itself.

Notes

1. For example, see Gaddis (1982); Trubowitz (2011). For a classic study of the converse—how much is enough to fund the defense portion of a state's grand strategy—see Enthoven and Smith (1971).
2. For a discussion of temporal phenomena in the context of grand strategy see Carr (2018, 17–18).
3. Data from https://www.whitehouse.gov/omb/historical-tables/ Table 4.1.
4. For middle powers the nonmilitary components of grand strategy are much more prominent and such states are likely to need to think creatively about financing their efforts. See Worman (2018); Cha and Dumond (2017).
5. The grand strategy literature is not clear about the period of time over which it should operate—beyond vague references to the long term (Edelstein 2017). For example, Brooks and Wohlforth write, "grand strategy is a set of ideas for deploying a nation's resources to achieve its interests over the long-run" and treat grand strategy as "longest scale of time" (2016, 80). Kennedy writes that grand strategy is "about the evolution and integration of policies that should operate for decades, or even centuries" (1991, 4).
6. There is little consensus regarding the degree to which the formulation and execution of a state's grand strategy, let alone its financing, is (*ex ante*) deliberate. For a discussion of the degree to which scholars have treated grand strategy as a deliberate detailed plan see Silove (2018, 38).
7. Printing money and imposing austerity measures are other forms of indirect resource extraction yet are unsustainable in the long term. Austerity is unable to provide large sums of revenue and printing such large sums of money is so economically disastrous it is untenable. I therefore exclude these alternatives from this discussion.
8. For examples of financial market developments to float debt and the ability of a state to manage its debt portfolio, see Dickson (1967) for a historical account and Acharya and Bo (2019) for a more contemporary account.
9. For a discussion of what constitutes rising and declining powers, see Miller (2016); Shifrinson (2018, ch. 2).
10. I do not assume that observers correctly identify the threat environment, see Vertzberger (1999); Mitzen and Schweller (2011).

References

Acharya, Viral V., and Li Bo. 2019. *Establishing Viable Capital Markets*. No. 62, Basel: Bank of International Settlements (January). https://www.bis.org/publ/cgfs62.pdf

Alesina, Alberto, and Nouriel Roubini. 1992. "Political Cycles in OECD Economies." *The Review of Economic Studies* 59 (4): 663–688.

Allen, George C. 1981. *A Short Economic History of Modern Japan*. New York: Palgrave Macmillan.

Andrews, David M. 2006. *International Monetary Power*. Ithaca: Cornell University Press.

Bilmes, Linda J. 2017. "The Credit Card Wars: Post-9/11 War Funding Policy in Historical Perspective." https://watson.brown.edu/costsofwar/files/cow/imce/papers/2017/Linda%20J%20Bilmes%20_Credit%20Card%20Wars%20FINAL.pdf

Bird, Richard M. 1977. "Land Taxation and Economic Development: The Model of Meiji Japan." *Journal of Development Studies* 13 (2): 162–174.

Blazacq, Thierry, Peter Dombrowski, and Simon Reich. 2019. "Is Grand Strategy a Research Program? A Review Essay." *Security Studies* 28 (1): 58–86.

Bogart, E. L. 1920. *Direct and Indirect Costs of the Great World War*. 2nd edition. New York: Oxford University Press.

Cappella Zielinski, Rosella. 2016. *How States Pay for War*. Ithaca: Cornell University Press.

Cappella Zielinski, Rosella. 2017. "War Finance and Military Effectiveness." In *The Sword's Other Edge: Trade-Offs in the Pursuit of Military Effectiveness*, edited by Dan Reiter, 58–87. Cambridge: Cambridge University Press.

Cappella Zielinski, Rosella. 2018. "US Wars Abroad Increase Inequality at Home: Who Foots the Bill for American Hegemony?" *Foreign Affairs*, October 5, 2018. https://www.foreignaffairs.com/articles/2018-10-05/us-wars-abroad-increase-inequality-home?cid=soc-tw

Carr, Andrew. 2018. "It's About Time: Strategy and Temporal Phenomena." *Journal of Strategic Studies* 41 (6): 1–22.

Caverley, Johnathan D. 2014. *Democratic Militarism: Voting, Wealth, and War*. Cambridge: Cambridge University Press.

Cha, Victor, and Marie Dumond. 2017. *The Korean Pivot: The Study of South Korea as a Global Power*. Washington, DC: Center for Strategic and International Studies.

Cohen, Benjamin J. 2006. "The Macrofoundations of Monetary Power." In *International Monetary Power*, edited by David M. Andrews, 31–50. Ithaca: Cornell University Press.

Dickson, P. G. M. 1967. *The Financial Revolution in England. A Study in the Development of Public Credit, 1688–1756*. London: Macmillan.

Drezner, Daniel. 2013. "Military Primacy Doesn't Pay (Nearly as Much as you Think)." *International Security* 38 (1): 52–79.

Dubois, Eric. 2016. "Political Business Cycles 40 Years after Nordhaus." *Public Choice* 166 (1–2): 235–259.

Edelstein, David M. 2017. *Over the Horizon: Time, Uncertainty, and the Rise of Great Powers*. Ithaca: Cornell University Press.

Enthoven, Alain C., and K. Wayne Smith. 1971. *How Much is Enough? Shaping the Defense Program, 1961–1959*. Santa Monica: RAND Corporation.

Friedberg, Aaron. 1988. *The Weary Titan: Britain and the Experience of Relatively Decline, 1895–1905*. Princeton: Princeton University Press.

Gaddis, John Lewis. 1982. *Strategies of Containment: A Critical Appraisal of American National Security Policy During the Cold War*. Oxford: Oxford University Press.

Gholz, Eugene, Daryl G. Press, and Harvey M. Sapolsky. 1997. "Come Home, America: The Strategy of Restraint in the Face of Temptation." *International Security* 21 (4): 5–48.

Goddard, Stacie E., and Ronald R. Krebs. 2105. "Rhetoric, Legitimization, and Grand Strategy." *Security Studies* 24 (1): 5–36.

Goldman, Emily. 2010. *Power in Uncertain Times: Strategy in the Fog of Peace*. Stanford, CA: Stanford University Press.

Goldsmith, R. W. 1983. *The Financial Development of Japan, 1868-1977*. New Haven, CT: Yale University Press.

Guo, Gang. 2009. "China's Local Political Budget Cycles." *American Journal of Political Science* 53 (3): 621–631.

Hart, B. H. Liddell. 1957. *Strategy*. New York: Praeger.

Hollyer, James R., B. Peter Rosendorff, and James Raymond Vreeland. 2018. *Information, Democracy, and Autocracy Economic Transparency and Political (In)Stability*. Cambridge: Cambridge University Press.

Huth, Paul, D., Scott Bennett, and Christopher Gelpi. 1992. "System Uncertainty, Risk Propensity, and International Conflict Among the Great Powers." *Journal of Conflict Resolution* 36 (3): 478–517.

Jacobs, Alan M. 2008. "The Politics of When: Redistribution, Investment and Policy Making for the Long Term." *British Journal of Political Science* 38 (2): 193–223.

Jentschura, H., D. Jung, and P. Mickel. 1977. *Warships of the Imperial Japanese Navy, 1869–1945*. Annapolis, MD: Naval Institute Press.

Kennedy, Paul. 1987. *The Rise and Fall of the Great Powers: Economic Change and Military Conflict from 1500 to 2000*. New York: Random House.

Kirshner, Jonathan. 2008. "Dollar Primacy and American Power: What's at Stake?" *Review of International Political Economy* 15 (3): 418–438.

Knorr, Klaus. *The Power of Nations*. 1975. New York: Basic Books.

Knorr, Klaus. 1976. "Threat Perception." In *Historical Dimensions of National Security Problems*, edited by Klaus Knorr. Lawrence, KS: University of Kansas Press.

Krebs, Ronald R., and Aaron Rapport. 2012. "International Relations and the Psychology of Time Horizons." *International Studies Quarterly* 56 (3): 530–543.

Kreps, Sarah. 2018. *Taxing Wars: The American Way of War Finance and the Decline of Democracy*. Oxford: Oxford University Press.

Levi, Margaret 1988. *Of Rule and Revenue*. Berkeley: University of California Press.

Liberman, Evan S. 2002. "Taxation Data as Indicators of State–Society Relations: Possibilities and Pitfalls in Cross-National Research." *Studies in Comparative International Development* 36 (4): 89–115.

Lobell. Steven E. 2008. "A Granular Theory of Balancing." *International Studies Quarterly* 62 (3): 589–605.

Lobell, Steven E. 2009. "Threat Assessment, the State, and Foreign Policy: A Neoclassical Realist Model." In *Neoclassical Realism, the State, and Foreign Policy*, edited by Jeffrey W. Taliaferro, Norrin M. Ripsman, and Steven E. Lobell, 42–74. Cambridge: Cambridge University Press.

Lü, Xiaobo, and Pierre F. Landry. 2014. "Show me the Money: Interjurisdiction Political Competition and Fiscal Extraction in China." *American Political Science Review* 108 (3): 706–722.

Mastanduno, Michel, David A. Lake, and G. John Ikenberry. 1989. "Toward a Realist Theory of State Action." *International Studies Quarterly* 33 (4): 457–474.

Miller, E. 2005. "Japan's Other Victory: Overseas Financing of the War." In *The Russo-Japanese War in Global Perspective: World War Zero*, vol. 2, edited by J. W. Steinberg, B. W. Menning, D. Schimmelpenninck van der Oye, D. Wolff, and S. Yokote. Leiden: Konnin-klijke Brill.

Miller, Manjari Chatterjee. 2016. "The Role of Beliefs in Identifying Rising Powers." *The Chinese Journal of International* Politics 9 (2): 211–238

Mitchell, A. Wess. 2018. *The Grand Strategy of the Hapsburg Empire*. Princeton: Princeton University Press.

Mitzen, Jennifer, and Randall Schweller. 2011. "Knowing the Unknown Unknowns: Misplaced Certainty and the Onset of War." *Security Studies* 20 (1): 2–35.

Murray, Bruce K. 1973. "The Politics of the 'People's Budget.'" *The Historical Journal* 16 (3): 555–570.

Narinzy, Kevin. 2003. "Both Guns and Butter, or Neither: Class Interests. In the Political Economy of Rearmament." *The American Political Science Review* 97 (2): 203–220.

Nincic, Miroslav, Roger Rose, and Gerard Gorski. 1999. "The Social Foundations of Strategic Adjustment." In *The Politics of Strategic Adjustment: Ideas, Institutions, and Interests*, edited by Peter Trubowitz, Emily O. Goldman, and Edward Rhodes. New York, NY: Columbia University Press.

Nordhaus, William D. 1975. "The Political Business Cycle." *The Review of Economic Studies* 42 (2): 169–190.

Norrlof, Carla. 2008. "Strategic Debt." *Canadian Journal of Political Science* 41 (2): 411–435.

Norrlof, Carla, and William C. Wohlforth. 2019. "Is US Grand Strategy Self-Defeating? Deep Engagement, Military Spending, and Sovereign Debt." *Conflict Management and Peace Science* 36 (3): 227–247.

Oatley, Thomas. 2015. *A Political Economy of American Hegemony: Buildups, Booms, and Busts*. Cambridge: Cambridge University Press.

Patrick, Hugh T. 1965. "External Equilibrium and Internal Convertibility: Financial Policy in Meiji Japan." *Journal of Economic History* 25 (2): 187–213.

Pierson, Paul. 2012. *Dismantling the Welfare State? Reagan, Thatcher, and the Politics of Retrenchment*. Cambridge: Harvard University Press.

Preble, Christopher A. 2011. *The Power Problem: How American Military Dominance Makes US Less Safe, Less Prosperous, and Less Free*. Ithaca: Cornell University Press.

Rasler, Karen A., and William R. Thompson. 1983. "Global Wars, Public Debts, and the Long Cycle." *World Politics* 35 (4): 489–516.

Renshon, Jonathan. 2017. *Fighting for Status: Hierarchy and Conflict in World Politics*. Princeton: Princeton University Press.

Schultz, Kenneth A., and Barry R. Weingast. 2003. "The Democratic Advantage: Institutional Foundations of Financial Power in International Competition." *International Organization* 57 (1): 3–42.

Shay, Robert Paul. 1977. *British Rearmament in the Thirties: Politics and Profit*. Princeton: Princeton University Press.

Shea, Patrick E. 2013. "Financing Victory: Sovereign Credit, Democracy, and War." *Journal of Conflict Resolution* 58 (5): 771–795.

Shifrinson, Joshua R. Itzkowitz. 2018. *Rising Titans, Falling Giants: How Great Power Exploit Power Shifts*. Ithaca: Cornell University Press.

Silove, Nina. 2018. "Beyond the Buzzword: The Three Meanings of 'Grand Strategy.'" *Security Studies* 27 (1): 27–57.

Sinclair, Timothy J. 2005. *The New Masters of Capital: American Bond Rating Agencies and the Politics of Creditworthiness*. Ithaca: Cornell University Press.

Sondhaus, Lawrence. 2001. *Naval Warfare, 1815–1914*. New York: Routledge.

Strange, Susan. 1971. *Sterling and British Policy: A Political Study of International Currency in Decline*. Oxford: Oxford University Press.

Streich, Philip, and Jack S. Levy. 2007. "Time Horizons, Discounting, and Intertemporal Choice." *The Journal of Conflict Resolution* 51 (2): 207–208.

Sumida, Jon T. 1989. *In Defense of Naval Supremacy: Finance, Technology and British Naval Policy, 1889–1914*. Boston: Unwin Hyman.

Takao, Takeda. 1965. "The Financial Policy of the Meiji Government." *Developing Economies* 3 (4): 427–449.

Tomz, Michael. 2007. *Reputation and International Cooperation: Sovereign Debt across Three Centuries*. Princeton: Princeton University Press.

Trubowitz, Peter. 2011. *Politics and Strategy: Partisan Ambition and American Statecraft*. Princeton, Princeton University Press.

Vertzberger, Yaccov Y. I. 1999. *The World in Their Minds: Information Processing, Cognition, and Perception in Foreign Policy*. Stanford, CA: Stanford University Press.

Williamson, Samuel R., Jr. 1991. *Austria-Hungary and the Origins of the First World War*. New York: St. Martin's Press.

Wood, Steve. 2014. "Nations, National Identity, and Prestige." *National Identities* 16 (2): 99–115.

Worman, Stephen M. 2018. "The Grand Strategies of Middle Powers." Working Paper. University of Pittsburgh.

Yamamura, Kozo. 1977. "Success Ill-Gotten? The Role of Meiji Militarism in Japan's Technological Progress." *Journal of Economic History* 37 (1): 113–135.

PART V

STRATEGIC MENUS AND CHOICES

CHAPTER 27

AMERICAN GRAND STRATEGIES

Untangling the Debates

ROBERT JERVIS

DEBATES about grand strategies seem to emerge when scholars, if not decision-makers, feel that the country is in trouble. This is the case for the United States in the current era, although the diagnoses as well as the prescriptions vary. Indeed, one source of disagreement is whether the fundamental problems lie predominantly with an increasingly threatening and complex world or with America's misperception of it and misguided approach. The purpose of this chapter is to explore this and other sources of disagreement.

Note that I am looking only at the academic debate, not the proposals of political leaders and the actual policies the United States has followed in the post–Cold War years. It is not surprising that actual policies are much less consistent than the academic arguments; leaders have to react to changing environments and multiple pressures, with often conflicting incentives arising from both domestic and international politics. Academics and policy analysts value consistency; few politicians do.

TYPOLOGIES

Before analyzing debates over grand strategies, we need a typology of them. The problem here is an embarrassment of riches, with not only several candidates, but different ways of going about creating categories. Many analysts select the dimensions that they think are most crucial and then seek to populate the resulting cells of the table, with the number increasing exponentially with the number of dimensions. Henry Nau proposes a manageably simple four-fold table. "The debate about American foreign policy has always divided along two dimensions. How close in or far out should America protect its security? And for what moral or political purpose does America exist and participate in world affairs?" (Nau et al. 2017, 2; also see Green 2012). Alternatively, but with some overlap, one can make a typology out of the dimensions of how involved or assertive the United States should be and whether its engagement should be predominantly unilateral or multilateral.

In recent years, multidimensional typologies have been replaced by continua that attempt to map out different degrees of assertiveness or engagement with the international environment, with isolationism at one end and primacy or even global empire at the other (Art 2003; Art 2012; see also Jervis 1993; Huntington 1993). The two extremes have few advocates, and are designed mainly as logical exemplars and an attempt to provide an exhaustive mapping. Real debate has concentrated on the rest of the continuum and, thanks to Barry Posen's well-argued book, the term "restraint" has taken hold as the descriptor of the grand strategy that would renounce most, if not all, of America's formal alliances and that would have America withdraw from leadership positions in most international organizations. In many versions of the continuum, the next stopping-point is offshore balancing, which, as its name implies, reduces active US commitments but retains a literal and figurative presence offshore, ready to intervene if local forces are unable to maintain a balance of power in areas of vital interest. Somewhat more involved is the strategy of selective engagement, which would maintain an American presence in vital areas (most obviously, Europe) rather than wait to see if problems emerge. But, like offshore balancing and restraint, it would reduce, if not eliminate, American security presence in other areas, such as Africa and large parts, if not all, of the Middle East and Afghanistan. All three of these grand strategies call for a significant retraction of American involvement. The next strategy is more or less a reaffirmation of the broad philosophy that has characterized US foreign policy for not only most of the years since the end of the Cold War, but since the end of the Second World War as well (with the exception of episodes like Vietnam and Iraq that are seen by proponents of this view as overreaching). Stephen Brooks and William Wohlforth (2016), who are among the most careful exponents of this stance, call it "deep engagement," a term I will adopt. While shunning the excesses of the pursuit of primacy, as exemplified by the behavior of President George H. W. Bush after the terrorist attacks of September 11, 2001, this strategy involves maintaining and, where possible, strengthening America's core alliances with NATO and Japan, and providing targeted threats and security guarantees in other areas when necessary to inhibit proliferation. The United States would continue to pay a disproportionate share of the costs for major international institutions like the United Nations, and make short-run sacrifices to sustain the international economic institutions and arrangements on the grounds that they bolster international stability and American prosperity.

Why They Disagree

Maximizing the distance between alternative grand strategies brings out their differences most clearly, and so at a cost of some distortion I will focus on Restraint and

Deep Engagement, skipping over offshore balancing and selective engagement, and putting aside the calls for more assertive forms of primacy which have not received extensive academic support in the past several years. All these strategies, with the possible exception of the last, are rooted in Realism, so the differences to be explained do not lie in disputes over human nature or fundamental aspects of international politics. The fact that very serious disagreements remain reminds us that Realism is more a school of thought and an approach than a definitive theory (Avey, Markowitz, and Reardon, 2018).

For better and for worse, IR theory is strongly influenced by what is happening in the world. The greatest shock of the twenty-first century were the terrorist attacks of September 11, 2001, and for a time much focus shifted to terrorism and arguments about how to counter it. For debates about grand strategy, however, more important were the invasion of Iraq (opposed by most Realists), the rise of Chinese power and the fact that the PRC has increasingly asserted itself in ways that disturb American influence rather than become a "responsible stakeholder"—the phrase comes from a 2005 speech by Deputy Secretary of State Robert Zoelick—in the American-led world order (something that should not have surprised Realists), and, to a lesser extent, the increased conflict with Russia. These developments brought a halt to post–Cold War optimism and generated a widespread sense of decline of American power.

Whether this sense is accurate is beside the point here. My concern rather is with the common-sense claim that the dispute between Restraint and the more engaged strategies turns on the former's view that American power is no longer sufficient to reach more ambitious goals. It certainly is true that a cornerstone of prescriptive Realist thinking is that states not only have to muster the power that is necessary to procure their vital interests, but also have to adjust their interests to fit the power resources that are available (Jervis and Schweller n.d.; see also Balzacq, Dombrowski, and Reich 2019). As we will see below, however, most of the Restrainers argue not that the United States has to withdraw because it is weak, but rather that the United States is so strong that it does not have to be involved in peripheral areas and issues. While Restrainers do claim that American power is insufficient to keep China bottled up, to convert Russia and render it benign, and to bring liberal democracy to the developing world, few proponents of Deep Engagement would disagree, and Restrainers argue that their strategy would have been appropriate in the immediate post–Cold War years before the rise of terrorism, China, and Russia.

How Safe Are We?

If perceptions of American decline are not central to the debate, questions of how dangerous the world is and how large a margin of safety the US has are. Restrainers believe that the United States is extraordinarily secure (Nordlinger 1995; Cohen and Zenko 2019); Deep Engagers see the world and the American position in it as much more fragile. The latter position is close to conventional wisdom in mainstream political discourse. Two-thirds of the members of the Council of Foreign Relations reported believing that the world the United States faced in 2009 was more dangerous than it had been during the Cold War (Pew Research Center 2009), and five years later, Director of National Intelligence James Clapper similarly said, "Looking back over my more than a half century in intelligence I have not experienced a time when we've been beset by more crises and threats around the globe" (Clapper, 2014). Proponents of the need to stay deeply involved argue that, although US military spending is much greater than that of any possible opponents and although the United States remains geographically removed from possible hotspots, the world remains a dangerous place. The traditional buffers of geography and wealth, although significant, cannot guarantee national security. Not only are Russia and China hostile, but the world is more uncertain and unpredictable than was true in many past eras. Complacency simply cannot be justified. The perception of high threat requires a vigorous policy and the sacrifice of secondary values. When President Trump explained why he was supporting Saudi Arabia despite the killing of Khashoggi and other repressive acts, he replied, "The world is a dangerous place!" (White House 2018).

In part, proponents of the alternative schools of thought may differ in their fears for the future and their tolerance for risk. For example, Eliot Cohen, an advocate of Deep Engagement if not primacy, says that, "North Korea is a strategic problem ... it is by no means inconceivable that Pyongyang, at some moment of desperation or exuberance would think it in its interest to conduct a nuclear demonstration shot in the proximity of a close American ally, or even at the United States itself" (Cohen 2016). Although Brooks and Wohlforth (2016) see the United States as being in a very powerful position, they see significant dangers, especially if the United States becomes less involved. But if the impulse for an enlarged role after the Cold War arose from a belief that the United States was now dominant and had a great opportunity—and undoubtedly this was true to some extent—then one would expect the policy advocated to change as the international skies darkened. This has not happened. To the contrary, the greater dangers are now seen as providing powerful reasons not to retract. Although written during the Cold War in response to arguments for the need to be able to wage a limited nuclear war, Bernard Brodie's words encapsulate the response by many Restrainers:

> all sorts of notions and propositions are churned out, and often presented for consideration with the prefatory words: "it is conceivable that ..." such words establish their own truth, for the fact that someone has conceived of whatever proposition follows is enough to establish that it is conceivable. Whether it is worth a second thought, however, is another matter. (Brodie 1978, 83)

It would be interesting to know whether proponents of different grand strategies also differ in their perception of threat from non-human causes such as pandemics, environmental degradation, and, most obviously, climate change.

Most Restrainers ground their policy choices in the argument that the United States enjoys an unprecedented level of security and so does not need extensive alliances and military commitments (and bases) around the world (Beckley 2018; Posen 2014). Posen, pushing this argument to its limit, believes that NATO is no longer necessary. This seems to fit with one strand of standard Realist thinking; although alliances do serve multiple purposes, directly adding to national strength and national security have been their bedrock. If a country can make itself secure by its own devices, why should it take on allies?

Differing diagnoses as to the sources of the threat are as important as different perceptions of the threat's extent. Most proponents of Deep Engagement attribute developments to inherent Russian and Chinese hostility. This leads to a preference for some sort of containment policy. Most Restrainers, by contrast, believe that bad relations among the powers are largely a product of American policies that undermine the security and other vital interests of the protagonists. This is clearest in the case of Russia, where the argument is that we should not have been surprised that Russia reacted strongly to the expansion of NATO, the Western interventions in the former Yugoslavia culminating in the independence of Kosovo, US support for the "color revolutions" in the former Soviet republics, and the attempt to support anti-Putin movements within Russia (Mearsheimer 2014a, 2014b; for a rebuttal, see Sestanovich 2014). The United States will make itself safer by threatening Russia less.

How Interconnected Is the World? Credibility, Reputation, and Dominoes

Few proponents of Deep Engagement see imminent and direct threats to American security. Rather, the world is made dangerous through numerous interconnections that link different issues and events in different parts of the globe. Failing to combat terrorists in Africa or withdrawing from the Middle East, East Asia, or even Europe would not lead China, Russia, or anyone else to attack the United States, nor would it immediately collapse the international economy. These policies, however, could set in motion dynamics that would greatly harm the United States over a period of years because Deep Engagers see a variety of positive feedback mechanisms at work. American withdrawals would embolden adversaries and dishearten allies. If this sounds like the domino theory, it is because it does resemble the domino theory. But, we should not be too quick to dismiss the argument for that reason. Not only can one argue that Vietnam, which brought such ridicule on the theory, in fact did produce some domino effects, but both during the Cold War and earlier, there are cases that clearly fit.

Patrick Porter shows the extent to which the Deep Engagement perspective is underpinned by the view that modern—or postmodern—economic and political technologies and politics have produced a flattened world. Physical and political barriers that in the past reduced interconnections no longer exist. "A world linked and shrunken is a world forever on the brink of chaos, crying out for a guardian to police it. Because this world can spread insecurity anywhere anytime, the West has no choice but to act as universal guardian, taming it back into order" (Porter 2015, 33; see also Walt 2018, 18).

The mechanisms through which interconnections operate vary. Accretions of military power have been important in the past and still are relevant in some areas like the South China Sea. During the Cold War and the current era, however, credibility and reputation have been seen as more important. The literatures here are too extensive and familiar to summarize (Kertzer 2016; Harvey and Mitton 2016; Feaver et al. 2017; Crescenzi 2018; Jervis, Yarhi-Milo, and Casler forthcoming). The only point that I need to make here is that Deep Engagers see reputation as forming a greater part of credibility than do Restrainers, and the latter believe that what is crucial for credibility is the extent to which the issue engages the vital interests of the contesting states (Yarhi-Milo 2018). To take a recent example, Deep Engagers see President Trump's withdrawal from Northern Syria as not only a moral betrayal of America's Kurdish allies, but as a heavy blow to America's ability to convince others that it is a reliable partner. Restrainers reply that no one should have been surprised by Trump's move, even if it was done badly: as Realists understand, states do not continue their involvement once the cost–benefit calculations shift. As George Washington said, "It is a maxim founded on the universal experience of mankind that no nation is to be trusted farther than it is bound by its interest" (quoted in Harper 2004, 51).

For Restrainers, claims for the importance of US credibility and reputation not only are exaggerated, but are created by the very commitments that Deep Engagers see as necessary. The whole point of commitment, as Thomas Schelling (1960) famously argued, is to bolster the perceived likelihood that the state will stand firm by increasing the perceived costs it will pay if it has to back down. Formal security agreements or informal pledges then increase the incentives for the United States to live up to them. But, Restrainers argue, to the extent that powerful interconnections exist, it is because the United States has created them by making these pledges. Doing so may provide some protection—even significant protection—for countries the United States values, but this is not a choice based on security considerations given by a world shrunken by technology, globalization of various kinds, and others' perceptions of how world politics works. Instead, it is the staking of America's reputation that produces the possibility of damage that we then have to ward off. Even more than may have been true during the Cold War, commitments then create interests rather than the other way around, and they produce, rather than reduce, threats to the homeland.

Part of the reason that Restrainers believe that interconnections are muted is that many states have an interest in muting them. Negative rather than positive feedback usually characterizes international politics, and balancing dynamics are the rule; bandwagoning the exception. This is not always true, of course. Other countries have to believe that the situation is not hopeless and that their efforts will make a real difference. Leaders rarely feel helpless, however, and if anything, they are prone to exaggerate their countries' efficacy. In many areas, then, others will do more, not less, if the US does less.

Homogenization of Interests and Slippery Slopes

To see the world as tightly interconnected is to homogenize American interests because areas or issues of little intrinsic value are seen as important due to the second- or third-order consequences that are expected to flow from their fates. This is not a choice made by American leaders, but rather is a consequence of the way world politics works in a globalized era. If terrorists who gain a foothold in Africa can strike at the United States, the United States must consider Africa a vital interest even if it has no intrinsic stake in the political stability of the region; if Russia gaining greater sway over Ukraine will allow it to extend its influence throughout the rest of Europe, or if Europeans would take such Russian influence as an indication that the United States cannot stem the tide from the East, then the fact that Ukraine in and of itself does not matter to American or European interests is irrelevant. Those who favor Restraint or, even more, proponents of selective engagement, like to draw on the tradition of Realism exemplified by George Kennan when he elucidated the areas of the globe which were vital for the United States—and thereby indicated which were not. Restraint and selective engagement depend on the ability to maintain these distinctions.

Related are conflicting views about the slipperiness of slopes in international politics. Restrainers argue that once committed to the security of supposedly vital areas, the United States is very likely to be drawn into endeavors to spread democracy there and to engage in social engineering with the objective of stabilizing the region. Furthermore, if some areas are vital, then the peripheries of those areas must be defended as well. Deep Engagers reply that, although the degree of agency possessed by the United States should not be exaggerated, neither should it be dismissed. American leaders not only should but can draw lines in the future, and while decision-makers' knowledge that slopes can be slippery does not guarantee that they will be able to avoid sliding down them, it can better position them to avoid these traps or extricate themselves from them before they become too dire.

Entrapment

In parallel, Restrainers see entrapment as a major danger, and Deep Engagers believe that great powers have a number of tools at their disposal to limit it (Snyder 1984; Snyder 1997; Mandelbaum 1981). As Brooks and Wohlforth argue, the very fact that entrapment is known to be a danger leads stronger allies to carefully construct their commitments, open legal and political loopholes, and, if the situation becomes dire, confront the weaker ally with the enormous costs it will pay if the patron abandons it (Kim 2011; Press-Barnathan 2006). Consistent with this, Michael Beckley's examination of the American experience in the post–Second World War era finds that entrapment is rare (Beckley 2015; also see Lind 2016). This does make a great deal of sense; even though scholarship looks for counterintuitive patterns, Brooks and Wohlforth (2016, 134) are right to question whether we are really ready to turn Thucydides on his head, saying, in effect, that "the weak do what they can, and the strong suffer what they must." Restrainers, while not willing to renounce Thucydides, do not think that major states are always able to deal with the problem so easily. Although entrapment in the narrow sense of being drawn into an unwanted war may be rare, the broader phenomenon of entanglement in which a major power gets drawn in deeper than it had originally intended and finds its interests being shaped by those of a weaker ally is more common. The continuing existence of NATO and the US presence in Europe may be an example. If these commitments had not been made to contain Soviet power, would anyone suggest developing them now?

In democracies, domestic opinion is important, and its open political processes allow small allies to build support either with the public at large or with interested and powerful sectors. The country may then not lose agency, but the executive branch can, as Evan Resnick (2019) explains.

Temptations: Resistible or Not?

It is not only the interests and machinations of smaller allies that can entrap the United States if it adopts Deep Engagement. Perhaps more dangerous is the temptation to seek more ambitious goals, to grab what seem like cheap and worthwhile opportunities, and to fall prey to the illusion that America's key position in the international system gives it the ability and the obligation to do more than it can and should. For almost all analysts, Bush's foreign policy between September 11, 2001 and the retraction during his second term is the obvious example of the danger. For Deep Engagers, this was an unfortunate exception; for Restrainers, it was just the logical extension of the policies pursued by his predecessors, most obviously the expansion of NATO and the support for Kosovo's independence.

There seems to be little doubt that temptation is a problem, and even proponents of Deep Engagement see it as perhaps this grand strategy's greatest vulnerability (Brooks and Wohlforth 2016, 147–152, 193). They believe that it can be resisted, and indeed it can be argued that the decentralized nature of power in the American system and the larger number of veto players make it less of a danger for the United States than for other democracies, let alone for dictatorships. Furthermore, the danger exists irrespective of the grand strategy being followed and could erode even a policy of restraint. As Brooks and Wohlforth (2016, 152) argue, "in the end, the core solution to temptation lies at home, not in America's grand strategy abroad"—a point they note is also made by Beckley, who is closer to the Restraint school.

Iraq is the poster child for temptation. On this point, Restrainers and Deep Engagers agree. They diverge on the crucial question of whether it is an aberration. Deep Engagers believe that it is, and that it came about through a unique concatenation of circumstances including the unprecedented shock of 9/11, an egregious intelligence failure, and the bad luck of who held power at the time. Furthermore, the lessons of the misadventure have been learned, at least for a while. It is telling that, although the Trump administration has called for the replacement of President Nicolás Maduro of Venezuela and has repeated the mantra that all options are on the table, in fact large-scale intervention does not seem even to have been considered.

Restrainers argue that "pinning the blame on the Iraq War [in this way] overlooks how liberal hegemony makes mistakes of this sort far more likely" (Walt 2018, 259; see also Ruger 2018, 56). For many Restrainers, the temptation to overreach is a basic lesson taught by Realism, which both sees this as likely for a state that lacks a peer competitor and believes that it is unwise. Waltz (1979) argues that in bipolarity, the prime error of superpowers is to overreact, to get involved in issues and areas when not doing so would be the wiser course; Vietnam was the prime example he had in mind. In unipolarity, with the concomitant lack of any external restraint on the remaining superpower, overreaction was even more likely, and in fact as soon as the Cold War ended, Waltz predicted that at some point the United States would engage in an Iraq-like adventure (Waltz 1991). Other Restrainers locate the cause in American domestic pathologies (Mearsheimer 2018; Walt 2018).

Perceived Advantages of Entanglement

The heart of the argument for Deep Engagement is that it increases American security and prosperity. American alliances make wars less likely and suppress regional rivalries and security dilemmas, especially between countries that have current grievances like Hungary and Romania, or have fought each other in the past like Germany and France. It is no accident, to borrow the phrase from another political tradition, that the countries that have been under American security guarantees since early in the Cold War, and the states of East and Central Europe that have since been brought into NATO, form what Karl Deutsch called a "security community," which is a grouping of countries that not only are at peace, but among whom war is literally unthinkable (Jervis 2005). The community might outlast an American withdrawal because the changes that have been induced might now be permanent. But Deep Engagers see no reason to run the experiment.

American security guarantees inhibit proliferation, Deep Engagers argue, by reducing the need for these countries to gain the ultimate guarantor of their own safety and giving the United States additional leverage over them. Both halves of the claim are illustrated by the behavior of South Korea and Taiwan, which embarked on a nuclear weapons program when they thought the United States was abandoning them, and stopped when the United States issued renewed guarantees, coupled with threats to break ties if they continued.

It (almost) goes without saying that the United States has at least some interest in avoiding wars throughout the world, especially in areas of major concern to the United States, and even more when nuclear weapons might be involved. Restrainers reply that this interest is slight in most areas of the world and, where it is not, US guarantees are unnecessary—as in Europe where the local states have more than enough capability to deter or defend on their own. Of course, as it is now stands, European military capability is sharply limited, and the only way to stop free riding is for the United States to stop providing the public good. The fear that if we do less the Europeans will do even less than they are doing now contradicts basic balance of power reasoning, Restrainers note; in fact, if the United States does less, the Europeans will do more.

In East Asia, Restrainers argue, American alliances provide rigidity to a situation that needs to adjust to the fact of a rising China. Under what theory of international politics would we expect the enormous increase in the Chinese economy, with a concomitant strengthening of its military and prestige, not to lead to some sort of an adjustment of regional influence? The US stake in many of the disputes, most obviously the Senkakus/Diaoyus islands and the control of the South China Sea, come mainly from its regional alliances and alignments. For Restrainers, there is a fundamental circularity here: the United States has to stand by Japan in the dispute over the islands because it has an alliance with Japan, but it is the alliance that has created the American engagement on the issue.

Terrorism

Although America's foreign policy was upended by the terrorist attacks of 9/11, the current grand strategy debate says relatively little about the topic. This is partly because these scholars generally agree that terrorism is more frightening than it is a fundamental menace. Indeed, as the name suggests, the purpose of terrorists is to inspire terror, and short of their gaining nuclear weapons or communicable biological agents, they can do little material damage. There is a residual difference between these schools of thought, however. Restrainers point to the American military presence in Saudi Arabia as a major cause of al Qaeda, note that many more recent terrorists claim to be avenging American depredations in the Middle East and Somalia, and worry that America's chasing down of terrorists around the world (and inflicting significant civilian casualties) will create more terrorists than it will kill (Walt 2018, 175). Deep Engagers argue that it is only the overreaching and heavy-handedness of previously ill-informed policies that have fed terrorism, and that their preferred policies of supporting allies and limited but well-targeted moves against real and imminent threats will not produce blowback (Brooks and Wohlforth 2016, 141–143).

Economic Benefits and Costs

Everyone agrees that the post–Second World War prosperity of the Western world and the enormous reduction of poverty in many Asian countries owe a great deal to the relatively open economic system that the United States led—indeed, insisted on—and that this is not only intrinsically good, but allowed the West to win the Cold War and contributed to making the world more peaceful. Of course, the participants in the grand strategy debate are well aware of the backlash in recent years, including arguments about the extent to which the open system has contributed to economic inequality and migration at levels that have generated strong opposition in many countries. But these questions are not in the wheelhouse of these scholars, and as far as I can tell, there are no systematic differences between the schools of thought on possible ameliorative policies.

Where Restrainers and Deep Engagers differ is on whether the sort of American involvement in alliances and international institutions that has characterized most of American policy since 1945 is necessary to sustain the current economic system. Just as Deep Engagers see interconnections within the security area, so they believe that American alliances and guarantees underpin current international economic arrangements. The institutions involved, like the World Bank and the International Monetary Fund, act as multipliers for American power since the United States can influence the flow of resources of other countries as well as its own. In addition, American withdrawal from security commitments could lead to regional wars which would damage the American economy even if they did not directly impinge on US security.

Restrainers disagree, seeing these conflicts as less likely and less punishing to the United States (Gholz and Press 2001). Much of the international economic system could continue if the United States politically retrenched. As Walt asks, "If the United States withdrew most of its forces from the Middle East and reduced its military role in Europe ... why would Japan, China, the EU, or any other members of the G20 decide to raise new protectionist barriers, dismantle the WTO, or take other steps that would only make them poorer?" (Walt 2018, 167). The reply is that heightened fears and rivalries would eventually erode the prevailing system.

Costs and Benefits: Domestic Values

Just as Restrainers and Deep Engagers disagree about the economic costs of alternative grand strategies, so they disagree about the cost and benefits in domestic values. For Deep Engagers, the protection of democratic regimes that share many values with the United States is a significant benefit. Even though they reject imposing democracy by force, they make clear that these objections do not apply to supporting democratic regimes where they are established, especially in countries with close ties with the United States. It is not surprising that the American public rejected the Nixon and Kissinger foreign policy based on entirely Realist precepts. Despite the preaching of scholars, the public and much of the elite are willing to accept dictatorships only when extreme circumstances dictate this. Support for human rights abroad follows from parallel commitments at home. Proponents of Restraint, by contrast, see the pursuit of ambitious foreign policy goals as coming at the cost of the domestic values of liberty and a free society. The framers of the Constitution understood this tension very well, and it is exemplified by the price the public is paying in terms of privacy and civil liberties in pursuit of a frantic effort to protect against terrorism. Not only are American citizens abroad being executed without judicial process, but domestic databases are expanding at a frightening speed, and even with some recent cutbacks, American communications are no longer free from the eyes and ears of government. On this issue, the views of those on the left and right of the domestic political spectrum agree, and many would echo what President Dwight Eisenhower said to his NSC colleagues:

> We could lick the whole world ... if we were willing to adopt the system of Adolph Hitler ... After all we were engaged in defending a way of life as well as a territory, a population, or our dollar. This being the case, a recognition of this fact should comprise the first statement in the [general national security] paper. (US Department of State 1984)

Although Eisenhower would have found this flip, many Restrainers would endorse the wisdom of Pogo: "We have met the enemy, and they are us." This is true in two senses. First, by taking on excessive commitments that require extraordinary resources and the constant mobilization of public support, the United States is becoming transformed. Many would argue that the commitment to free trade generated by the supposed requirements of American leadership in the world has hollowed out not only much of the American economy, but the cohesive family structure and social fabric that is so essential to both stability and a people with strong ties to their communities and sense of a public good. Second, the cause of many of these problems is not impersonal technology, let alone foreign threats, but rather our adoption of foolish foreign policies. It is American errors that are the cause of the problem in a way that parallels what Pericles told the Athenians when he argued that Athens could defeat Sparta if it maintained self-control: "Indeed, I am more afraid of our own blunders than of the enemy's devices" (Thucydides, 1.144.1).

FEW PERCEIVED TRADEOFFS

Each of the camps offers more reasons for its views than are needed, displaying what I have earlier called belief overkill—in that all the relevant considerations point toward the same policy (Jervis 1976, 128–143; Jervis 2017). That psychology rather than logic is at work here is suggested by the fact that many of the values and considerations are not logically linked, and so there is no reason why people's beliefs on these questions should line up as neatly as they do. Restrainers believe not only that American security will not be endangered by a withdrawal of security commitments from much of the world, but that those areas are not likely to burst into flames, nor is widespread proliferation likely. They also doubt that a change in American policy will adversely affect the international economy, nor will it likely lead to a deterioration of human rights around the world. Greater restraint will then save money and preserve American values at home without requiring the sacrifice of other values that, while secondary, are still significant.

In parallel, Deep Engagers do not believe that, while their policy is best on balance, it does less well than restraint in some areas. Although Brooks and Wohlforth (2016) do acknowledge the danger of temptation as noted above, they see it as manageable. Deep Engagers also deny that their policy is much more expensive than the alternatives, or that it leads to an erosion of democratic values. It is Restraint, they believe, that would both make the United States less secure and sacrifice other American values.

Although scholars often criticize decision-makers who say that American interests and values need not conflict, their own views usually minimize such conflicts. Psychology is at work here because to perceive tradeoffs among important values is painful. For leaders to lay out the sacrifices of some values that are entailed by a policy that is best overall also is to give ammunition to their political adversaries. I do not think this is a large part of the explanation here, however. Even though scholars, like politicians, want to persuade, they are conversing with a very sophisticated audience and are accustomed to making balanced judgments. The tendency to believe that "all good things go together" comes from human nature, not the political struggle (Packenham 1973).

What Is Driving the Debate?

The search for one or two beliefs that are primarily putting people on the path to one or another grand strategy is complicated by the fact that the answer can vary from person to person. One Restrainer might be most influenced by the perception that Deep Engagement will inevitably erode domestic institutions and values, while for another this perception might trail along on the path marked out by the belief that entrapment is a major danger.

On balance, however, I think a major, if not the major, distinction between the two camps is that Restrainers believe that the United States is highly secure and that interconnections in the world are fairly loose. Domino-like dynamics are rare, and balancing is more common than bandwagoning. Despite high levels of exchange of information and economic goods, the world remains quite segmented. Of course, it is possible that events abroad could ramify through a variety of mechanisms in a way that would threaten the United States, but these are not likely to operate quickly, and the United States would have time to respond appropriately rather than putting itself on multiple front lines. Threats to American security are not direct, but at most the second- or third-order consequences, and so can be coped with if and when they appear. Gains by adversaries are more likely to dissipate than to gather momentum, and overreaction is a greater danger than is underreaction.

Deep Engagers see more numerous and important interconnections both within the security realm, and between it and the economic arena (Drezner 2013). The United States can and should make distinctions between areas and issues that are vital to it and those that are not, but what happens in the former does strongly affect the United States.

Of course, even if this analysis is correct, it does not tell us which grand strategy is. But it does clarify the arguments.[1]

Note

1. This research was supported in part by a grant from the Charles Koch Foundation.

References

Art, Robert. 2003. *A Grand Strategy for America*. Ithaca: Cornell University Press.
Art, Robert. 2012. "Selective Engagement in the Era of Austerity." In *America's Path: Grand Strategy for the Next Administration*, edited by Richard Fontaine and Kristin M. Lord, 13–28. Washington, DC: Center for a New American Security.
Avey, Paul, Jonathan Markowitz, and Robert Reardon. 2018. "Disentangling Grand Strategy: *International* Relations Theory and U.S. Grand Strategy." *Texas National Security Review* 2 (1): 28–51.
Balzacq, Thierry, Peter Dombrowski, and Simon Reich. 2019. "Is Grand Strategy a Review Program? A Review Essay." *Security Studies* 28 (1): 58–86.
Beckley, Michael. 2015. "The Myth of Entangling Alliances: Reassessing the Security Risks of U.S. Defense Pacts." *International Security* 39 (4): 7–48.
Beckley, Michael. 2018. *Unrivaled: Why America Will Remain the World's Sole Superpower*. Ithaca: Cornell University Press.
Brodie, Bernard. 1978. "The Development of Nuclear Strategy." *International Security* 2 (4): 65–83.
Brooks, Stephen G., and William C. Wohlforth. 2016. *America Abroad: The United States' Global Role in the 21st Century*. New York: Oxford University Press.
Clapper, James, 2014. "Remarks on Worldwide Threat Assessment to Senate Select Committee on Intelligence." January 29, 2014. https://www.dni.gov/files/documents/WWTA%20 Opening%20Remarks%20as%20Delivered%20to%20SSCI_29_Jan_2014.pdf
Cohen, Eliot. 2016. *The Big Stick: The Limits of Soft Power and the Necessity of Military Force*. New York: Basic Books.
Cohen, Michael, and Micah Zenko. 2019. *Clear and Present Safety: The World Has Never Been Better and Why That Matters to Americans*. New Haven: Yale University Press.
Crescenzi, Matthew. 2018. *Of Friends and Foes: Reputation and Learning in International Politics*. New York: Oxford University Press.
Drezner, Daniel. 2013. "Military Primacy Doesn't Pay (Nearly as Much as You Think)." *International Security* 38 (1): 52–79.
Feaver, Peter D., Rebecca Friedman Lissner, Danielle L. Lupton, Rupal N. Mehta, and Keren Yarhi-Milo. 2017. "Roundtable." *International Security Studies Forum* X (3). http://issforum. org/ISSF/Roundtables/10-3-credibility

Gholz, Eugene, and Daryl Press. 2001. "The Effects of Wars on Neutral Countries: Why it Doesn't Pay to Preserve the Peace." *Security Studies* 10 (4): 1–57.

Green, Brendan Rittenhouse. 2012. "Two Concepts of Liberty: U.S. Cold War Grand Strategies and the Liberal Tradition." *International Security* 37 (2): 9–43.

Harper, John Lamberton. 2004. *American Machiavelli: Alexander Hamilton and the Origins of U.S. Foreign Policy*. Cambridge: Cambridge University Press.

Harvey, Frank, and John Mitton. 2016. *Fighting for Credibility: US Reputation and International Politics*. Toronto: University of Toronto Press.

Huntington, Samuel. 1993. "Why International Primacy Matters." *International Security* 17 (4): 68–83.

Jervis, Robert, and Randall Schweller. n.d. "Realism." Unpublished manuscript. Columbia University and Ohio State University.

Jervis, Robert. 1993. "International Primacy: Is the Game Worth the Candle." *International Security* 17 (4): 52–67.

Jervis, Robert. 1976, 2nd edition. 2017. *Perception and Misperception in International Politics*. Princeton: Princeton University Press.

Jervis, Robert. 2005. *American Foreign Policy in a New Era*. New York: Routledge.

Jervis, Robert. 2017. *How Statesmen Think: The Psychology of International Politics*. Princeton: Princeton University Press.

Jervis, Robert, Keren Yarhi-Milo, and Donald Casler. Forthcoming. "Power, Interests, and Past Actions: Redefining the Debate over Credibility and Reputation." *World Politics*.

Kertzer, Joshua. 2016. *Resolve in International Politics*. Princeton: Princeton University Press.

Kim, Tongfee. 2011. "Why Alliances Entangle but Seldom Entrap States." *Security Studies* 20 (3): 350–377.

Lind, Jennifer. 2016. "Article Review 52 on 'The Myth of Entangling Alliances.' *International Security* 39:4." *H-Diplo | ISSF*. https://issforum.org/articlereviews/52-entangling-alliances

Mandelbaum, Michael. 1981. *The Nuclear Revolution: International Politics Before and After Hiroshima*. Ithaca: Cornell University Press.

Mearsheimer, John. 2014a. "Why the Ukraine Crisis is the West's Fault." *Foreign Affairs* 93 (5): 77–89.

Mearsheimer, John. 2014b. "Mearsheimer Replies." *Foreign Affairs* 93 (6): 175–178.

Mearsheimer, John. 2018. *The Great Delusion: Liberal Dreams and International Realities*. New Haven: Yale University Press.

Nau, Henry R., William Inboden, Matthew Kroenig, and Erin M. Simpson. 2017. "Roundtable 10-2 on Cohen (The Big Stick), Kaufman (Dangerous Doctrine), and Lieber (Retreat and Its Consequences)." *H-Diplo | ISSF*. https://issforum.org/roundtables/10-2-ckl

Nordlinger, Eric. 1995. *Isolationism Reconfigured: American Foreign Policy for a New Century*. Cambridge: Harvard University Press.

Packenham, Robert. 1973. *Liberal America and the Third World: Political Development Ideas in Foreign Aid and Social Science*. Princeton: Princeton University Press.

Pew Research Center for the People & the Press, in association with the Council on Foreign Relations. 2009. *America's Place in the World 2009: An Investigation of Public and Leadership Opinion About International Affairs*. Washington, DC: Pew Research Center. https://www.issuelab.org/resources/8246/8246.pdf, accessed February 2, 2021.

Porter, Patrick. 2015. *The Global Village Myth: Distance, War, and the Limits of Power*. Washington D.C.: Georgetown University Press.

Posen, Barry R. 2014. *Restraint: A New Foundation for U.S. Grand Strategy*. Ithaca: Cornell University Press.
Press-Barnathan, Galia. 2006. "Managing the Hegemon: NATO Under Unipolarity." *Security Studies* 15 (2): 271–309.
Resnick, Evan. 2019. *Allies of Convenience: A Theory of Bargaining in U.S. Foreign Policy*. New York: Columbia University Press.
Ruger, William. 2018. "Robert Kagan's Jungle Book of Forever War." *The American Conservative*, December 13, 2018. https://www.theamericanconservative.com/articles/robert-kagans-jungle-book-of-forever-war/
Schelling, Thomas. 1960. *The Strategy of Conflict*. Cambridge: Harvard University Press.
Sestanovich, Stephen. 2014. "How the West Has Won." *Foreign Affairs* 93 (6): 171–175.
Snyder, Glenn. 1984. "The Security Dilemma in Alliance Politics." *World Politics* 36 (4): 461–495.
Snyder, Glenn. 1997. *Alliance Politics*. Ithaca: Cornell University Press.
Thucydides. 1954. *The Peloponnesian War*. Translated by Rex Warner. Baltimore, MD: Penguin.
U.S. Department of State. 1984. *Foreign Relations of the United States 1952–1954*. Vol. 2, Part 1, *National Security Affairs*, edited by Lisle A. Rose and Neal H. Petersen. Washington, DC: Government Printing Office.
Walt, Stephen M. 2018. *The Hell of Good Intentions: America's Foreign Policy Elite and the Decline of U.S. Primacy*. New York: Farrar, Straus and Giroux.
Waltz, Kenneth. 1979. *Theory of International Politics*. Reading, MA: Addison-Wesley.
Waltz, Kenneth. 1991. "America as a Model for the World? A Foreign Policy Perspective." *PS: Political Science and Politics* 24 (4): 667–670.
White House. 2018. "Statement from President Donald J. Trump on Standing with Saudi Arabia." November 20, 2018. https://www.whitehouse.gov/briefings-statements/statement-president-donald-j-trump-standing-saudi-arabia/
Yarhi-Milo, Keren. 2018. *Who Fights for Reputation? The Psychology of Leaders in International Conflict*. Princeton: Princeton University Press.

CHAPTER 28

STRATEGY ON THE UPWARD SLOPE

The Grand Strategies of Rising States

JOSHUA R. ITZKOWITZ SHIFRINSON

THE initial decades of the twenty-first century have witnessed a pronounced power shift spurred by the rise of China, and concomitant relative decline of the United States and other established actors (National Intelligence Council 2012). As in prior episodes when new players disrupted the existing distribution of power, analysts focus on whether a rising China is primed to challenge the United States and its allies for power and influence (Allison 2017; Mastro 2019). Yet, despite robust research on the causes of power shifts (Organski and Kugler 1980; Gilpin 1981) and theories of particular types (e.g., satisfied, coercive, etc.) of rising state policy, little work examines rising states' grand strategies as such. The result is an asymmetry in the international relations (IR) literature: although power is widely considered a central driver of state behavior, rising state strategy remains understudied.

This chapter seeks to bring the rising state more fully into research on great power politics, grand strategy, and power shifts by asking: when great powers rise, what grand strategies do they pursue and why do they do so? It advances two interrelated arguments. First, although a wide-ranging literature touches on broad forms of rising state policy, there is little agreement on how to conceptualize rising state grand strategy; indeed, scholars even disagree over (1) what it means to be a rising state and (2) the reference point for defining risers' grand strategies. The result is an analytic muddle, yet also offers the possibility of more robustly defining rising state strategy by conceptualizing how rising state goals and means might vary and the strategic tradeoffs among these options. Second, much existing analysis of rising state behavior is undertheorized. Regardless of whether scholars ascribe rising state strategy to international or domestic factors, current research faces problems explaining shifts in strategy over time. One solution—advanced below—is thus to consider how different factors take on different salience in shaping rising state strategy as a power shift continues.

The remainder of this chapter proceeds in several sections. Following this introduction, I define core terms and clarify what it means to be a "rising state." Next, I review current approaches to typologizing rising state strategy, before advancing a potential framework to advance the theoretical discussion. Fourth, the chapter reviews and critiques different explanations for rising state strategy. Finally, the paper concludes with a brief discussion of avenues for future research.

RISING STATES: STRATEGIC CONDITIONS AND DEFINITIONS

Before defining rising state strategy, it is important to appreciate the complicated strategic backdrop against which strategy is formulated. At root, rising power presents any state with both risks and opportunities. On the one hand, a state with growing capabilities enjoys greater latitude in shaping its international environment. With comparative strength, a state's margin for strategic mistakes increases; adversary threats may no longer loom as credible (Press 2005); intra-alliance bargaining power can improve (Snyder 1997); extra resources may be available to pursue ambitious foreign agendas (Zakaria 1998); and weaker states threatened by others may turn to the riser as a source of protection (Walt 1987; Schweller 1998). On the other hand, a rising state is also prone to threaten other, relatively declining actors (Mearsheimer 2001; Morgenthau 1954). In turn, these states may seek ways—including preventive war—to slow or stop its rise (Levy 1987; Copeland 2000). Likewise, growing capabilities may yield to miscalculation and/or domestic pressure for international activism, potentially leading to crises and/or conflicts (Blainey 1988). Against this backdrop, a rising state's task is to chart a course that maximizes the advantages and minimizes the likelihood of these risks manifesting (Paul 2016, 19–20).

Defining a "Rising Great Power"

Yet, what constitutes a "rising great power"? The concept is often opaque. Many studies eschew defining the concept altogether (e.g., Kennedy 1987; Schweller 1999; Yoder 2019). Those that do, meanwhile, are often in tension with one another (Chan 2004), with major studies variously defining a rising great power as a state that is capable of challenging an existing hegemon for international dominance (Organski and Kugler 1980; Gilpin 1981); that is narrowing the relative and absolute power gap separating it from the strongest state in the international system (Chestnut and Johnston 2009); or that has growing capabilities and is "exhibiting internal recognition of its changing status" (Miller 2016).

Each of these approaches faces limitations. It makes questionable sense, for example, to limit rising powers to those states able to seek global (or even regional; see Mearsheimer 2001) hegemony: not only are hegemons rare in world politics, but, as debates surrounding the emergence of China highlight, much of the interest with rising powers involves actors that may not yet be capable of seeking hegemony. Similarly, requiring a state to recognize its changing status in international affairs risks understating how shifting power affects behavior given that perceptions of power and the actual distribution rarely track perfectly (Friedberg 1988). Combined, these conceptual divides risk inhibiting knowledge accumulation.

A cohesive definition is required. Recent work on great power decline (MacDonald and Parent 2018, 2021; Shifrinson 2018; Edelstein 2017) suggests a prospective solution. These studies define decline by examining situations where a great power begins to lose economic and military capabilities relative to one or more actors. The inverse thus offers a parsimonious definition of rise: a rising state is one experiencing *a sustained increase in its capabilities relative to one or more great powers such that it either narrows the relative gap separating it from other great powers or expands the existing gulf between it and other powers.*

This approach might seem intuitive but both breaks from and improves upon current definitions. First, the definition is inclusive as to the source of rise: states that benefit from the relative decline of another state, as well as those that sustain a higher growth rate compared to their peers, are captured by this definition. Second, it can encompass other approaches to great power rise. Thus, those interested in assessing whether a state is poised to challenge a hegemon can consider whether it is beginning to cut into a hegemon's relative lead, while those interested in assessing the role of ideas can evaluate when such factors enter into a riser's decision-making process.

Finally, because it is rooted in the idea that power in international relations is fundamentally relative in nature, the definition clarifies that rising states can include two distinct sets of actors: new states entering the leading ranks of the international system, and already powerful states that increase their dominance. The former category would encompass actors such as contemporary China. The latter category, however, is equally important: if "rising power" is to mean anything, it should capture, say, Prussia/Germany's rise from one of several roughly equal great powers in mid-nineteenth-century Europe (see Table 28.1) to perhaps first among equals before 1914, or the United States' rise from one of two superpowers in the Cold War to the world's unipole. Interestingly, both types of actors have been discussed in the relevant literature (e.g., Kennedy 1987) without explicit recognition of the distinction. The revised definition rectifies this situation, allowing for more precise discussion.

Table 28.1 Shifting power among the European great powers, 1860–1910

State	Year 1860	1870	1880	1890	1900	1910
Austria-Hungary	15	13	13	14	13	13
France	20	19	18	18	16	15
Russia	22	26	24	19	22	24
United Kingdom	24	22	24	26	25	22
Prussia/Germany	19	19	21	24	24	25

Note: Power measured as shares of Gross National Product held by Europe's leading powers. Calculated from Bairoch 1976.

RISING STATE STRATEGY: SPECIFYING THE VARIATION

Irrespective of the definition employed, the literature on rising state grand strategy is thin (Legro 2007). Of course, substantial research discusses rising state strategy either historically, or in reference to some particular issue area—usually vis-à-vis international order or other great powers. Nevertheless, these different literatures often fail to speak to one another and, in general, lack a robust framework for analyzing rising state strategy.

One approach is, in fact, not focused on rising state strategy as such, but rather examines the pathways by which particular rising states arose. Work by Kori Schake (2017) and Miranda Priebe (2015), for instance, highlights that a substantial portion of the United States' rise relied on a cautious but expansionist strategy. Similarly, Immanuel Geiss (1976) demonstrates that Germany's rise before the First World War relied on strategic circumspection in dealing with the other great powers—an effort that faltered once German politics were dominated by an aggressive mercantilist–military coalition. Studies of the postwar emergence of Japan (Samuels 2007) and China (Goldstein 2005) take a parallel tack, highlighting the centrality of adopting a limited international security profile in enabling these states to grow.

Without necessarily intending to, emerging from these studies is a general theme: rising states are often cautious. Confronting a strategic environment in which other powers are capable of challenging their growth, risers—especially early in their rise—are often reluctant to directly threaten other, relatively declining actors. This makes sense, as states that expect their power to grow have incentives to minimize confrontations until after the distribution of power has decisively shifted (Copeland 2000; Ripsman and Levy 2012). For sure, this process may be disrupted be domestic politics but, as a general proposition, "biding time" is pervasive (Edelstein 2017).

A second, more systematic approach, focuses on the tendency among rising states to challenge an extant "international order" (for definitions of order, see Tang 2016). By this logic, as their power grows, rising states have greater ability to alter international order—originally created and maintained by other powers—to better advance their particular security, ideological, or economic interests (Gilpin 1981; Tammen et al 2000; Ward 2017). Whether a riser does so hinges largely on the extent to which it is "satisfied" or "dissatisfied" with the order at hand. All things being equal, satisfied rising states are primed to adopt strategies that reinforce the existing order. What this means in practice is rarely specified (a partial exception is Johnston 2003), but seems to refer to some combination of (1) rising peacefully and avoiding issuing military changes to relatively declining states while (2) embracing the legitimacy of existing institutions, norms, and rules, even if they (3) seek greater influenlitce within existing confines (Goddard 2018a; Goddard 2018b).[1] Conversely, dissatisfied states are primed to pose problems.[2] Not only—so scholars suggest—may they challenge other states as their relative power expands, but they are predisposed to construct an alternate order so as to maximize their influence (Schweller and Pu 2011; Kupchan et al., 2001; Ward 2017).

Finally, a third approach examines rising state strategy not in terms of its attitude towards international order, but in terms of how rising states more narrowly adjudicate relations with other powers. This is an important distinction, especially as issues of order and those of relations with other great powers are often conflated (e.g., Gilpin 1981; Yoder 2019). Empirically, however, rising states may opt to challenge (or support) an order even if they support (or challenge) any particular declining state. A rising Germany, for instance, embraced a declining Austria-Hungary before 1914 even as it challenged key aspects of the pre–First World War order (Shifrinson 2018), just as a relatively rising United States preyed upon the Soviet Union in the late Cold War while trying to sustain elements of the post-1945 order it helped construct (Wohlforth 1994–1995).

In this vein, a prominent line of research suggests that the stronger rising states become, the greater their ambitions and the more likely they are to try to alter bilateral relations in their favor (Mearsheimer 2001; Mearsheimer 2010). Still, this expectation is increasingly being challenged, with recent research highlighting the possibility that states economically engaged with other actors (Lobell 2003), led by leaders aware that aggression can trigger counterbalancing (Glosny 2012; Edelstein 2017), and/or desiring partners against other threats (Shifrinson 2018; Shifrinson 2020) may selectively cooperate with other great powers. These findings more systematically echo the aforementioned case studies highlighting the tendency of rising states to behave cautiously for a large portion of their rise.

In sum, existing research on rising state strategy is problematic. Current treatments showcase that rising states often fear triggering significant opposition to their rise, yet sometimes gamble their futures anyway (for similar discussion, see Paul 2016, 19–20). Beyond this general observation, however, there is little analytic clarity. Strategies emphasizing how rising states interact with an extant order and those focused on rising states' treatment of other great powers utilize different reference points against which to conceptualize state behavior. Relatedly, many of the typologies by which analysts discuss rising state strategy present strategy using general terms or concepts and are often portrayed dichotomously, thereby missing the possibility of finer-grained variation within or across types. Reinforcing the problem is the unidimensional measurement of risers' behavior, with many typologies focused on what rising states want while excluding the means employed to seek these objectives (for an exception, see Schweller 1999). Although reasonable if one assumes state goals and means invariably overlap (i.e., if states seeking more grandiose objectives employ more expansive means), the approach elides that "grand strategy" is fundamentally about the relationship between ends and means: tools and objectives may overlap or diverge to greater or lesser degrees.

(Re)Defining Rising State Strategy

To move forward, it is worthwhile foregrounding the notion of grand strategy as a political-military-economic ends–means chain reflecting a state's "theory for how it can best 'cause' security for itself" (Posen 1984, 4). Capturing rising state grand strategy thus requires separating (1) the goals, and (2) the means or tools, by which rising states address the array of challenges and opportunities they face in international security affairs. Along the way, it is important that this framework avoid anchoring grand strategy solely on a rising state's approach towards "order" or "power" per se; these are particular aspects of one's grand strategy that may or may not overlap. Rather, a framework is needed that can more generally capture whether (as the received wisdom suggests) a rising state's overarching international ambitions expand, the degree to which they do so, and how they go about this process.

Dimensions of Rising State Strategy: Control and Assertiveness

Accordingly, and building on grand strategy's distinction between ends and means, it is useful to discuss rising state strategy in the first place as reflecting a rising state's desired *control* over its external environment. Control captures the degree to which a rising state seeks predominant influence over the policy choices of other states (Green 2010, 28). This concept is implicit in discussions of risers' behavior. In adjusting order to suit their interests, for example, dissatisfied risers seek greater control over others' strategic orientations; likewise, in opting to challenge or cooperate with individual powers, rising states aim to variously dominate or minimize their ability to shape decliners' policy options. Hence, focusing on the extent to which risers pursue control bridges existing approaches to risers' behavior without being beholden to reference points such as order or power.

Control is a continuous variable. At one end of the spectrum, rising states may seek minimal control over their international environment, affording other states the space and opportunity to pursue their interests as they see fit. Conversely, they may desire maximal control by determining others' behavior; here—in its ideal-type form—not only does a riser attempt to shape its external environment to facilitate its interests, but it may reinforce its ability to influence others by further shifting the distribution of power in its favor. Still, most rising states likely fall between these two extremes: they desire varying control over time and space as threats and opportunities wax and wane.

Besides deciding upon the desired control, states also have to select the tools to get there. Again, this may not be an easy choice. Mobilizing resources for military affairs, for instance, may hinder long-term growth and threaten other actors even though a larger military can leave a state better able to deter or defeat challengers. Similarly, enmeshing oneself in international institutions and engaging in sustained diplomacy may limit the threat posed to other states in the near term, but leave a rising state vulnerable to others' machinations. Choices in all directions are fraught.

One way to think of this decision is in terms of the *assertiveness* of a rising state's means (Narizny 2007). Assertiveness reflects the extent to which risers are (1) willing to expend economic and military resources and (2) bear significant political risks, to exert greater or lesser degrees of control (Shifrinson 2018, 19). This builds upon Schweller's discussion of a rising state's "risk propensity," that is, the "probability of success that a particular decision maker requires before embarking on a course of action" (Schweller 1999, 22). Where, however, Schweller's approach measures the foreign policy attitudes of a state's leadership, assertiveness emphasizes that a state's willingness to mobilize resources for foreign affairs is also relevant. After all, a state may be risk acceptant yet still have an understated strategy if it has not mobilized resources for foreign action.

The last point highlights an important clarification: although, *prima facie*, a state's assertiveness might seem to be causally related to a state's desired control—for instance, a state which seeks significant control might need to be highly assertive—the two are distinct. After all, and as the examples in Figure 28.1 and ideal strategic types discussed below illustrate, history is replete with states that sought differing degrees of control with distinct amounts of assertiveness. By the same measure, scholars (e.g., Posen 1984) have long known that there is nothing which automatically requires a state's ends and means to align: dis-integrated strategies in which a state's ends and means poorly align can arise due to domestic conflict, bureaucratic and organizational dynamics, and path dependency.

Like control, assertiveness can be conceptualized on a continuum. At one end are limited means, whereby a state is unwilling to pay or risk much for the sake of control. Even as American power was becoming increasingly clear to global audiences, for example, American strategists in the interwar period sought to shape European security affairs through limited diplomatic and economic engagement; they did not, however, countenance a regular US security presence on the Continent. On the other hand, rising states may opt for expansive means, whereby a state is willing to bear both costs and take risks to obtain its preferred outcome. Indeed, many analysts fear that a rising China is moving in this direction today by increasing military spending and asserting itself along its near abroad.

Strategic Logics

Combined, control and assertiveness generate important insights into the strategic logics driving rising state strategy and into the benefits and risks risers may encounter along the way (Figure 28.1). All things being equal, rising states opting for comparatively minimal control and limited means effectively eschew steps that might challenge an existing international order and/or dominate other states (minimal control) or incur significant costs and/or economic risks (limited assertiveness). The advantage from a rising state's perspective is clear: in laying low and giving no offense, it avoids incurring the wrath of existing great powers. Relatedly, in minimizing resource extraction, it sidesteps potentially fraught domestic debates over the course and purpose of one's strategic vision. The net result captures the tendency for rising states to "bide time": avoiding actions that might perturb external or internal audiences while allowing one's rise to

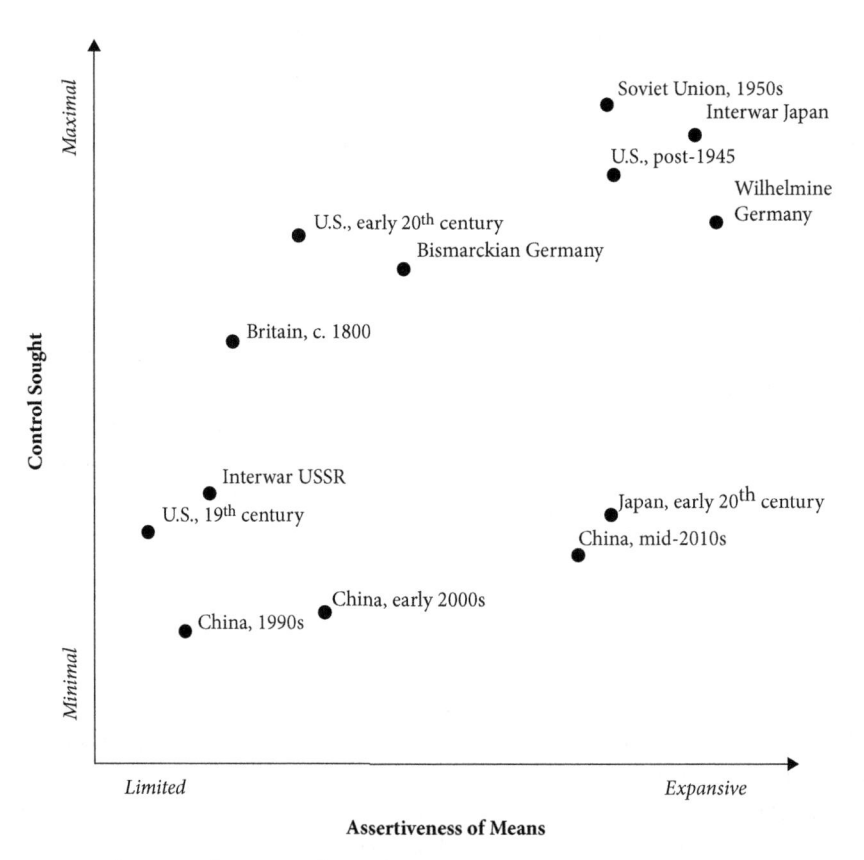

FIGURE 28.1 Conceptualizing risers' grand strategies

continue. The risk, of course, is that minimizing control and limiting assertiveness can leave states vulnerable to external actors seeking for their own reasons to limit one's rise. Given, too, that resource demands and domestic calls to find one's place in the sun can grow, the approach may prove self-limiting as rise continues.

States can also seek significant control without utilizing especially assertive means. Here, risers seek international influence on the cheap, angling to affect others' behavior without paying or risking much for the privilege. This approach has the virtue of a potentially large payoff: if control can indeed be obtained, a rising state will have not expended or risked much for the privilege. Interestingly, discussions of how to accommodate a rising China in the early-mid 2000s—granting it greater international influence in return for playing by existing international rules—implied that China should embrace such a grand strategy (e.g., Campbell and Ratner 2018). The downside, however, is simple: because states often jealously guard their sovereignty and interests, seeking greater control may generate opposition while leaving one vulnerable to any resulting blowback. A rising state may still calculate that the benefits exceed the drawbacks, but the subsequent grand strategy may be fragile—the means may not fully service the ends sought.

The mirror image is a situation where a rising state seeks comparatively minimal or limited control over its external environment but utilizes expansive means. In this scenario—captured by the lower right side of Figure 28.1—a rising state carves out a restricted domain of action for itself while still throwing meaningful resources and bearing risks for the ends sought. This might manifest, for instance, if a rising state sought a local sphere of influence and was wedded to obtaining it irrespective of domestic or international opposition; Japan's quest for local preeminence in northeast Asia in the early twentieth century—culminating in the Russo-Japanese War—suggests the strategy (Streich and Levy 2016). The virtue here is that a riser may have its way on particular interests (presumably those viewed as most vital for its security): by assertively pursuing its objectives, it may end up gaining control over the interests sought or—at minimum—making it riskier for other states to challenge the control one already has. The danger, however, is that assertively seeking even limited control can spur counterbalancing and insecurity spirals, and leave a rising state worse off than before.

Lastly, rising states may opt for both substantial control and use more assertive means. This situation roughly approximates the basic strategic expectation discussed by the likes of Gilpin and Mearsheimer: the stronger a state becomes, the greater the influence it wants and the more assertive it is in seeking it. Indeed, seeking significant control, mobilizing appropriate resources, and taking correspondingly large risks can ultimately leave a rising state in a privileged international position by overcoming threats to its security while putting its stamp on international politics. Still, it is a strategy that can also backfire: the combination of assertive means and expansive ends are likely to put a particularly large bullseye on one's back, encouraging especially strong counterbalancing. Not only may the gambit thus fail, but it can leave a rising state isolated and encircled.

APPLICATION

The control–assertiveness approach further allows comparison of rising state grand strategies across and within cases. A few—admittedly impressionistic—examples illustrate the possibilities. Rather than define both Bismarckian and Wilhelmine Germany as loosely dissatisfied but risk-acceptant states (e.g., Schweller 1999, 22), for instance, the framework acknowledges that Germany sought both greater control and utilized more expansive means as the state transitioned from the Bismarckian to Wilhelmine periods. Indeed, although Germany sought to play a leading voice in Continental circles throughout this era, there is a difference between Bismarck's efforts to limit German armaments and cooperate with other European powers, and Wilhelm II's quest for dominance and antagonistic attitude towards many peer competitors.

A similar benefit comes in discussing the rising United States. American grand strategy throughout the nineteenth century looked to assert US control in and around North America, without paying or risking much—particularly when it came to conflict with Britain—for the privilege. Shifting gears, however, US policymakers in the first half of the twentieth century sought more control over international affairs but used fairly limited means to do so. After the Second World War, meanwhile, a surging United States committed to highly assertive efforts to shape its relations with other major power in Europe, Asia, and beyond as part of the Cold War (Thompson 2015).

Above all, this approach contextualizes contemporary Chinese grand strategy. Much has been made of the ostensible turn in Chinese strategy over the last decade, with several analysts arguing that Chinese grand strategy has become increasingly revisionist (for a summary, see Johnston 2013). In reality, China's means for shaping its strategic environment have grown for decades, while the issues that China is now contesting—notably territorial disputes in the South and East China Seas and institutions shaping global governance—have long been sources of friction. Instead, the primary change seems to have been an uptick in China's desire to control the set of issues it sees as crucial to its security and its willingness to run somewhat greater risks for the privilege. This is understandably worrisome but should be considered in historical context: as the control–assertiveness framework underlines, these efforts still pale in comparison to the strategies of past rising states such as Wilhelmine Germany or interwar Japan, which sought both extensive control over other actors and were willing to gamble for the privilege.[3]

Ultimately, emerging from these sketches are important empirical implications. Consistent with existing research, rising states often bide their time—particularly the earlier they are in their rise—before becoming more ambitious. Still, the manners in which states manifest this ambition can and do vary. Some states, at some times, use their rising power to pursue more control over international affairs, whereas others hold the ends sought broadly constant while leveraging more expansive means. Meanwhile, although some rising states utilize expansive means to seek greater control over international affairs, even a cursory review of history shows (1) that this trend is far from universal, just as (2) there may not be a linear path between rising power and grandiose grand strategies. In short, treating rising state grand strategy as a reflection of control and assertiveness highlights the significant differences in rising state behavior across time and space, directing attention towards explaining these shifts.

SOURCES OF RISERS' GRAND STRATEGY

What, then, causes rising state grand strategy? Analysts are again divided. One broad set of arguments locates rising state strategy in the quest for power and security in an anarchic world. Although rising states eager to hold on to the power and security they presently enjoy and to continue growing have incentives to minimize control and assertiveness (Copeland 2000; Edelstein 2017; Shifrinson 2018), states are nevertheless expected to expand the control sought and assertiveness used at *some* point as the relative distribution of power shifts in their favor (Gilpin 1981; Mearsheimer 2001; Mearsheimer 2010). In contrast, other analysts locate rising state strategy in the nature of an extant international order: the more rising states can adapt an existing order to suit their interests (Goddard 2018a; Ikenberry 2001) while deriving material benefits (Lobell 2003; Copeland 2015; Sample 2018) and status (Murray 2018; Larson and Shevchenko 2014) from existing arrangements along the way, the more likely risers are to be satisfied. Though risers might therefore seek more control as their power grows, they should minimally do so without resorting to expansively assertive means.

Meanwhile, still a third camp locates rising state strategy in a rising state's domestic affairs. Here, major claims have been advanced that liberal democracies tend to be less prone to assertively seek influence over other actors (Lemke and Reed 1996). Others underscore the importance of motivating ideologies, suggesting that some states are driven by particular worldviews that push them to assertively seek control over other actors (Fettweis 2006; Friedberg 2018). And, in one of the more robust attempts to theorize rising state preferences to date, Ward (2013; 2017) argues that existing great powers' refusal to give rising states the status that risers feel they deserve can—under certain conditions—unleash political and social forces that may promote radical attempts at revising existing international relationships.

None of these arguments is wholly satisfying. Domestic arguments, for instance, suffer from problematic logic. Even if we allow that domestic factors drive much of state behavior, one hardly expects states to be suicidal and court conflicts with other states that can stop or slow their ascendance: international conditions ought to still matter. Similarly, arguments emphasizing the nature of international order and exchange miss that, by virtue of growing relatively stronger, a rising state has by definition managed to master existing international conditions. As Wohlforth (2009, 31) observes, it is thus unclear why a rising state would want to change the conditions that have facilitated its ascent; there ought to be a baseline incentive to cap the control sought and minimize assertiveness in order to sustain the existing relationships that have abetted one's growth. For their part, power and security arguments confront the problem of exceptional cases. Per Snyder (1991), some rising states at some times (e.g., Wilhelmine Germany, the postwar Soviet Union) embrace highly assertive and maximally controlling strategies that imperil their continued rise by triggering an overwhelming counterbalancing coalition. To belabor the obvious, this is the opposite of what one expects from a rising state driven to maximize its own power and security.

That said, it may be possible to integrate these disparate approaches into a more cohesive framework. The starting point is recognition—as power and security arguments imply—that the stronger a rising state becomes, the more choice it has in international affairs. When a state is relatively weak, it can suffer terribly if it misjudges international conditions and enacts a grand strategy that antagonizes others; hence the tendency for rising states to embrace less controlling and/or assertive strategies earlier in their rise. As their relative strength grows and states are better able to confront prospective challengers, however, such international pressures may play a less decisive role in shaping strategy as the costs of miscalculation decline. In turn, the room for strategic choice increases—or as Gilpin (1981) long ago observed, the opportunity cost for embracing more controlling and/or assertive grand strategies goes down.

This situation does not necessarily mean a rising state will alter its grand strategy. Still, as the aperture for more controlling and/or assertive strategies widens, it creates room for domestic politics to push states in particular directions; at root, with international pressures reduced, certain courses of action may no longer be seen as unappealing or strategically risky as in times past. Thus, domestic actors holding particular ideational or ideological views, with particular status grievances, representing particular economic interests, and so on, can call for new strategic approaches that might once have been viewed as beyond the pale. There is no guarantee that any particular proposal will gain traction. After all, strategies that call for gambling much of a rising state's existing power and security ought to be treated skeptically irrespective of how strong a state becomes. At minimum, however, such calls are likely to generate debate over a rising state's course. Over time, and particularly if a rising state continues growing, the net result might be a decision to pursue strategies mixing control and assertiveness to differing degrees.

In short, international conditions may play an outsized role in forming rising state strategy, but the particular degrees of control and the means selected may undergo especially pronounced changes due to domestic forces the more rise continues. This might explain why many of the rising states located towards the bottom left of Figure 28.1 (minimal control, limited means) tend to be earlier in their rise: international conditions incentivize judicious strategies that avoid antagonizing other actors. Similarly, this logic may explain why many risers seem to drift from circumspection—seeking more control and/or utilizing more expansive means—as rise continues: consistent with the above, one expects domestic actors to more readily justify departures from prior policy as relative power shifts. Above all, this approach might help explain why those states at the upper right corner (maximal control and expansive means) tended to be among the strongest states in the international system (e.g., Wilhelmine Germany, the postwar US and USSR) and/or enjoyed a large baseline level of security (e.g., Imperial Japan) before embracing highly ambitious strategies. Ultimately, rising states might become more controlling and/or assertive as their power grows, but there may be distinct domestic drivers that explain the precise rationales, pathways, and timing of strategic shifts.

Conclusion

Where does research on rising states go from here? Again, despite a large literature on the sources of great power rise and aspects of rising state policy, work on rising state strategy remains in its infancy. Research is needed to address this hole, particularly at a time when policymakers are increasingly invested in the strategies of rising great powers. Although not exhaustive, several research themes suggest themselves.

First, in what other manners can rising state strategy vary, and how do past historical episodes relate to these frameworks? As noted, scholars currently lack an accepted reference point and lexicon to even discuss rising state grand strategy. This chapter proposed the language of control and assertiveness, but this is certainly not the only approach. Indeed, other analysts might consider how strategy varies depending on the specific tools (e.g., diplomatic, military, economic) employed, whether states seek to maximize power or some other general international objective, the role of influence or prestige-seeking in defining grand strategy, and other criteria. Along the way, they would do well to survey the historical literature on risers in order to map different past behaviors onto conceptual categories (and vice versa) so as to ground social science concepts in diplomatic practice.

Second, what causes rising state grand strategy to change? The preceding discussion suggested that an array of factors located in international politics and within rising states themselves may together drive rising state behavior. Still, additional attention should be paid to (1) robustly explaining rising state strategy throughout the course of a rise, and (2) identifying the particular conditions under which strategic shifts occur. Similarly, important contributions could come in assessing how much variation in risers' strategies is explained by domestic or systemic factors alone, and in weighing what changes to current IR theories are necessary to explain this variation. Especially given the strategic dilemmas facing rising powers, a robust search for causality that leverages sustained empirical work into risers' behavior can help uncover when and why rising states are primed for caution or gamble on their futures.

Finally, scholars need to consider the implications of their findings for contemporary policy debates. At a time when policymakers in the US and beyond seek to make sense of how shifts in the distribution of power affect national and international security, scholars owe it to the world to apply their findings to policy deliberations. This effort, in turn, can suggest still additional research pathways in discussing risers' grand strategies, including consideration of whether and to what extent decliners' own behavior shapes rising state strategy, the impact of nuclear weapons on risers' policies, and whether the politics of great power rise and decline today are apt to mirror those of the past. In short, rigorously assessing rising state strategy itself is only the first step—the contemporary policy discussions surrounding rising states can inform a robust research program on grand strategies amid power shifts.

Notes

1. Interestingly, while there is a limited literature on varieties of dissatisfied strategies a state may pursue (Schweller 1999; Goddard 2018a), there does not appear to be a similar literature on varieties of satisfied strategies.
2. Several studies treat "satisfaction" and "dissatisfaction" as synonymous with a state pursuing a "status quo" or "revisionist" strategy (e.g., Chan et al. 2018; Cooley, Nexon, and Ward 2019). Although understandable, this approach confuses more than it reveals by conflating rising state strategy with international order. Again, even satisfied rising states seek adjustments to the status quo: for example, a rising United States embraced several elements (e.g., colonization, free[ish] trade) of the British-led nineteenth-century order, yet still sought leadership and dominance within this framework. Even if working within a status quo, some degree of revisionism is hard-baked into rising state strategy, raising analytic issues in describing states as "revisionist" or "status quo" actors. Referring to the scope of their "satisfaction" or "dissatisfaction" acknowledges that even satisfied states generally change the status quo.
3. Of course, the broader point holds regardless of whether one accepts the control–assertiveness typology: irrespective of how one categorizes grand strategy, any contemporary case needs to be carefully and rigorously compared to examples from the universe of cases.

References

Allison, Graham. 2017. *Destined for War: Can America and China Escape Thucydides's Trap?* Boston: Houghton Mifflin Harcourt.

Bairoch, Paul. 1976. "Europe's Gross National Product, 1800–1975." *Journal of European Economic History* 5 (2): 273–340.

Beckley, Michael. 2018. *Unrivaled: Why America Will Remain the World's Sole Superpower.* Ithaca, NY: Cornell University Press.

Blainey, Geoffrey. 1988. *The Causes of War.* Basingstoke: Macmillan.

Brooks, Stephen G., and William C. Wohlforth. 2016. "The Rise and Fall of the Great Powers in the Twenty-First Century: China's Rise and the Fate of America's Global Position." *International Security* 40 (3): 7–53.

Campbell, Kurt M., and Ely Ratner. 2018. "The China Reckoning: How Beijing Defied American Expectations." *Foreign Affairs* 97 (2): 60–70.

Chan, Steve. 2004. "Exploring Puzzles in Power-Transition Theory: Implications for Sino-American Relations." *Security Studies* 13 (3): 103–141.

Chan, Steve, Weixing Hu, and Kai He. 2018. "Discerning States' Revisionist and Status-Quo Orientations: Comparing China and the US." *European Journal of International Relations* 25 (2): 613–640.

Chestnut, Sheena, and Alastair Iain Johnston. 2009. "Is China Rising?" In *Global Giant: Is China Changing the Rules of the Game?*, edited by Eva Paus, Penelope Prime, and Jon Western, 237–260. New York: Palgrave MacMillan.

Cooley, Alexander, Daniel Nexon, and Steven Ward. 2019. "Revising Order or Challenging the Balance of Military Power? An Alternative Typology of Revisionist and Status-Quo States." *Review of International Studies* 45 (4): 689–708.

Copeland, Dale C. 2000. *The Origins of Major War*. Ithaca, NY: Cornell University Press.

Copeland, Dale C. 2015. *Economic Interdependence and War*. Princeton, NJ: Princeton University Press.

Edelstein, David M. 2017. *Over the Horizon: Time, Uncertainty, and the Rise of Great Powers*. Ithaca, NY: Cornell University Press.

Fettweis, Christopher J. 2006. "A Revolution in International Relation Theory: Or, What If Mueller Is Right?" *International Studies Review* 8 (4): 677–697.

Friedberg, Aaron. 1988. *The Weary Titan: Britain and the Experience of Relative Decline, 1895-1905*. Princeton: Princeton University Press.

Friedberg, Aaron L. 2018. "Competing with China." *Survival* 60 (3): 7–64.

Geiss, Imanuel. 1976. *German Foreign Policy, 1871–1914*. London: Routledge.

Gilpin, Robert. 1981. *War and Change in World Politics*. Cambridge: Cambridge University Press.

Glaser, Charles L. 2010. *Rational Theory of International Politics: The Logic of Competition and Cooperation*. Princeton: Princeton University Press.

Glosny, Michael A. 2012. "The Grand Strategies of Rising Powers: Reassurance, Coercion, and Balancing Responses." PhD Dissertation. Cambridge, MA: Department of Political Science, Massachusetts Institute of Technology.

Goddard, Stacie E. 2018a. "Embedded Revisionism: Networks, Institutions, and Challenges to World Order." *International Organization* 72 (4): 763–797.

Goddard, Stacie E. 2018b. *When Right Makes Might: Rising Powers and World Order*. Ithaca, NY: Cornell University Press.

Goldstein, Avery. 2005. *Rising to the Challenge: China's Grand Strategy and International Security*. Stanford: Stanford University Press.

Green, Brendan R. 2010. "The Systemic and Ideological Sources of Grand Strategic Doctrine: American Foreign Policy in the Twentieth Century." PhD Dissertation. Cambridge, MA: Department of Political Science, Massachusetts Institute of Technology.

Ikenberry, G. John. 2001. *After Victory: Institutions, Strategic Restraint, and the Rebuilding of Order After Major Wars*. Princeton: Princeton University Press.

Ikenberry, G. John. 2008. "The Rise of China and the Future of the West: Can the Liberal System Survive?" *Foreign Affairs* 87 (1): 23–37.

Johnston, Alastair Iain. 2013. "How New and Assertive Is China's New Assertiveness?" *International Security* 37 (4): 7–48.

Kennedy, Paul M. 1987. *The Rise and Fall of the Great Powers: Economic Change and Military Conflict from 1500 to 2000*. New York: Random House.

Kupchan, Charles, Emmanuel Adler, Jean-Marc Coicaud, and Yuen Foong Khong, eds. 2001. *Power in Transition: The Peaceful Change of International Order*. New York: United Nations University Press.

Legro, Jeffrey W. 2007. "What China Will Want: The Future Intentions of a Rising Power." *Perspectives on Politics* 5 (3): 515–534.

Lemke, Douglas, and William Reed. 1996. "Regime Types and Status Quo Evaluations: Power Transition Theory and the Democratic Peace." *International Interactions* 22 (2): 143-164.

Levy, Jack S. 1987. "Declining Power and the Preventive Motivation for War." *World Politics* 40 (1): 82-107.

Lobell, Steven. 2003. *The Challenge of Hegemony: Grand Strategy, Trade, and Domestic Politics*. Ann Arbor: The University of Michigan Press.

MacDonald, Paul K., and Joseph M. Parent. 2018. *Twilight of the Titans: Great Power Decline and Retrenchment*. Ithaca, NY: Cornell University Press.

MacDonald, Paul K., and Joseph M. Parent. 2021. "The Grand Strategies of Declining Powers." In *The Oxford Handbook of Grand Strategy*. Edited by Thierry Balzacq and Ronald R. Krebs. Oxford: Oxford University Press.

Mastro, Oriana Skylar. 2019. "In the Shadow of the Thucydides Trap: International Relations Theory and the Prospects for Peace in U.S.-China Relations." *Journal of Chinese Political Science* 24 (1): 25-45.

Mearsheimer, John J. 2001. *The Tragedy of Great Power Politics*. New York: Norton.

Mearsheimer, John J. 2010. "The Gathering Storm: China's Challenge to US Power in Asia." *The Chinese Journal of International Politics* 3 (4): 381-396.

Miller, Manjari Chatterjee. 2016. "The Role of Beliefs in Identifying Rising Powers." *The Chinese Journal of International Politics* 9 (2): 211-238.

Morgenthau, Hans J. 1954. *Politics Among Nations; the Struggle for Power and Peace*. 2d edition. New York: Knopf.

Murray, Michelle. 2018. *The Struggle for Recognition in International Relations: Status, Revisionism, and Rising Powers*. New York: Oxford University Press.

Narizny, Kevin. 2007. *The Political Economy of Grand Strategy*. Ithaca, NY: Cornell University Press.

National Intelligence Council. 2012. *Global Trends 2030: Alternate Worlds*. Washington, DC: National Intelligence Council.

Organski, A. F. K. 1968. *World Politics*, 2nd edition [rev.]. New York: Knopf.

Organski, A. F. K., and Jacek Kugler. 1980. *The War Ledger*. Chicago: University of Chicago Press.

Paul, T. V. 2016. "The Accommodation of Rising Powers in World Politics." In *Accommodating Rising Powers*, edited by T.V. Paul, 3-32. New York: Cambridge University Press.

Larson, Deborah, and Alexei Shevchenko. 2014. "Managing Rising Powers: The Role of Status Concerns." In *Status in World Politics*, edited by T.V. Paul, Deborah Welch Larson, and William C. Wohlforth, 33-57. New York: Cambridge University Press.

Posen, Barry R. 1984. *The Sources of Military Doctrine: France, Britain, and Germany Between the World Wars*. Ithaca, NY: Cornell University Press.

Press, Daryl G. 2005. *Calculating Credibility: How Leaders Assess Military Threats*. Ithaca, NY: Cornell University Press.

Priebe, Miranda. 2015. "Fear and Frustration: Rising State Perceptions of Threats and Opportunities." PhD Dissertation. Cambridge: Massachusetts Institute of Technology.

Ripsman, Norrin, and Jack Levy. 2012. "British Grand Strategy and the Rise of Germany." In *The Challenge of Grand Strategy: The Great Powers and the Broken Balance between the World War*, edited by Jeffrey W. Taliaferro, Ripsman, Norrin M., and Steven E. Lobell, 171-192. New York: Cambridge University Press.

Sample, Susan G. 2018. "Power, Wealth, and Satisfaction: When Do Power Transitions Lead to Conflict?" *Journal of Conflict Resolution* 62 (9): 1905-1931.

Samuels, Richard J. 2007. *Securing Japan: Tokyo's Grand Strategy and the Future of East Asia*. Ithaca, NY: Cornell University Press.

Schake, Kori. 2017. *Safe Passage: The Transition from British to American Hegemony*. Cambridge, MA: Harvard University Press.

Schweller, Randall. 2018. "Opposite but Compatible Nationalisms: A Neoclassical Realist Approach to the Future of US–China Relations." *The Chinese Journal of International Politics* 11 (1): 23–48.

Schweller, Randall L. 1998. *Deadly Imbalances: Tripolarity and Hitler's Strategy of World Conquest*. New York: Columbia University Press.

Schweller, Randall L. 1999. "Managing the Rise of Great Powers: History and Theory." In *Engaging China: The Management of an Emerging Power*, edited by Alastair Iain Johnston and Robert Ross, 1–31. New York: Routledge.

Schweller, Randall L., and Xiaoyu Pu. 2011. "After Unipolarity: China's Visions of International Order in an Era of U.S. Decline." *International Security* 36 (1): 41–72.

Shifrinson, Joshua R. Itzkowitz. 2018. *Rising Titans, Falling Giants: How Great Powers Exploit Power Shifts*. Ithaca, NY: Cornell University Press.

Shifrinson, Joshua. 2020. "The Rise of China, Balance of Power Theory and US National Security: Reasons for Optimism?" *Journal of Strategic Studies* 43 (2): 175–216.

Snyder, Glenn Herald. 1997. *Alliance Politics*. Ithaca, NY: Cornell University Press.

Snyder, Jack L. 1991. *Myths of Empire: Domestic Politics and International Ambition*. Ithaca, NY: Cornell University Press.

Streich, Philip, and Jack S. Levy. 2016. "Information, Commitment, and the Russo-Japanese War of 1904–1905." *Foreign Policy Analysis* 12 (4): 489–511.

Tammen, Ronald L., Jacek Kugler, Douglas Lemke, Alan C. Stam III, Mark Abdollahian, Carole Alsharabati, Brian Efird, and A. F. K. Organski. 2000. *Power Transitions: Strategies for the 21st Century*. New York: Chatham House.

Tang, Shiping. 2016. "Order: A Conceptual Analysis." *Chinese Political Science Review* 1 (1): 30–46.

Thompson, John A. 2015. *A Sense of Power: The Roots of America's Global Role*. Ithaca, NY: Cornell University Press.

Walt, Stephen M. 1987. *The Origins of Alliances*. Ithaca, NY: Cornell University Press.

Ward, Steven. 2013. "Race, Status, and Japanese Revisionism in the Early 1930s." *Security Studies* 22 (4): 607–639.

Ward, Steven. 2017. *Status and the Challenge of Rising Powers*. Cambridge: Cambridge University Press.

Wohlforth, William C. 1994. "Realism and the End of the Cold War." *International Security* 19 (3): 91–129.

William C. Wohlforth. 2009. "Unipolarity, Status Competition, and Great Power War." *World Politics*. 61 (1): 28–57.

Yoder, Brandon K. 2019. "Hedging for Better Bets: Power Shifts, Credible Signals, and Preventive Conflict." *Journal of Conflict Resolution* 63 (4): 923–949.

Zakaria, Fareed. 1998. *From Wealth to Power: The Unusual Origins of America's World Role*. Princeton, NJ: Princeton University Press.

CHAPTER 29

GRAND STRATEGIES OF DECLINING POWERS

PAUL K. MACDONALD AND JOSEPH M. PARENT

A lot of what we know about grand strategy comes from states in decline, and a lot of what we know about grand strategies of decline comes from a small number of states. The book that launched a thousand debates is Thucydides' *History of the Peloponnesian War*, but given that both Athens and Sparta fell from glory soon after the war, it is hard to view either city-state as a model of exemplary statecraft. Edward Gibbon's meditations in the *Decline and Fall of the Roman Empire* have influenced scholars and diplomats for centuries, but it is unclear that Rome is representative of empires in general or relevant to modern states in particular. Even on its own terms, Gibbon's explanation of Rome's grand strategy has been controversial (see Heather 2010; Luttwak 1976). Geoffrey Parker's *Grand Strategy of Philip II* highlighted how a leader's cognitive quirks could humble an empire (1998, 283–289, 292–296), but Spain's example appears rather unique, and critics have contended that its slender resource base and institutional structure stacked the deck against leaders making a large difference (Elliott 2007, 408). The canonical texts are a good place to start thinking about grand strategies of decline, but a poor place to stop.

So how do states deal with decline? There has been a great deal of work on grand strategies of decline in recent years, and that is not an accident. The great power pecking order is coming under increasing strain as an era of stable rankings comes to an end. By nearly all accounts, power is decentralizing, and even rising states such as China are struggling to impose their will on recalcitrant domestic groups, foreign allies and partners, and potential opponents abroad.

We argue that the most successful grand strategies of decline result from matching foreign policies to political conditions. The same policies that would rejuvenate one state would assassinate another, and much depends on whether leaders leverage national advantages and adapt to dynamic global conditions. The foreign policy options available to declining states are wide-ranging. They can focus on domestic adaptations, such as changes in budgetary policy, force structure, institutional configuration, and patterns of investment. They can focus on international adjustments, whether shifts in force deployment, new diplomatic demarches, attempts to redistribute burdens, or efforts to bolster strongpoint defense. Whether states succeed in using these policies depends on national attributes (such as culture, institutions, unity, and leadership) and structural constraints (such as the rank of a declining state, the rate of its decline, the availability of allies, and the conquest calculus). Yet history has not combined these policies into an infinite array of grand strategies. Instead, five grand strategies are the regular responses to decline: expansion, bluffing, binding, retrenching, and appeasing. The most common and most successful grand strategy has been retrenchment, because conditions usually favor policies that are strategically solvent and cautious, but there are no iron laws in grand strategy.

To develop these arguments, we first define central concepts and discuss the dilemmas that confront declining states. We then present the key conditions that shape how states respond to decline. We subsequently lay out the most popular policies states have used to deal with decline in the past. Pulling policies and conditions together, we then sketch the most used grand strategies of decline, broadly assessing their prospects for success. The final section highlights lingering issues and topics for future research.

DILEMMAS OF DECLINE

Grand strategy is about security scarcity and tradeoffs, and no states face both more acutely than states in decline. By grand strategy we mean the intentional bundling of a state's economic, diplomatic, and military policies to seek security from external threats. Although there are many debates in the literature, it may help to begin with the areas of agreement. There is broad consensus that states are the main actors in world politics, and great powers, the states in the heaviest weight class, tend to compete with each other for security in anarchy. Without a world state to shelter them, great powers must take steps to protect themselves, and they are very sensitive to shifts in power because power is the foundation of protection. There are many ways to think of decline–economic, financial, social, cultural, moral, military, etc.–but most of the literature tends to think of it as a political problem. It is political because fundamentally it is about power relative to peers. It is a problem because in anarchy there is no overarching authority to stop great powers from exploiting relative superiority, however temporary.

Everyone agrees that what elements compose power and the importance of these elements can change over time. But there is dissent on what the most important elements are and how they should be weighed (Lobell 2018). These disputes are usually more hypothetical than real. Most people, most of the time, agree on who the most powerful states in the world are, and on how they roughly rank relative to each other. Decline generally refers to lasting and substantial changes in the cardinal and ordinal rankings of the great powers. The assumption is that great powers are primarily concerned about relative, rather than absolute, power. Absolute gains are cold comfort if potential competitors are steadily outpacing you, while absolute declines are worrisome precisely because they allow rivals to overtake you more rapidly.

The dilemmas of decline stem from the split between what states would like to do and what states are able to do (sometimes called the "Lippmann gap," see Lippmann 1943, 7). Declining states must make tradeoffs in how they apportion defense costs and risks. On one horn of the dilemma, declining states can try to maintain their goals as costs increase. They can retain present commitments, but that entails either extracting greater resources for foreign policy, crowding out spending on other goals and possibly decreasing long-term growth rates, or keeping resources constant, providing an increasingly brittle perimeter that invites predation. On the other horn of the dilemma, states can scale back their goals at a constant or lower cost. Yet this is only the mirror image of the alternate option. Less ambitious foreign policy goals are more defensible and sustainable, but that sacrifices treasured values and longstanding commitments. On both horns, a declining great power's credibility is at risk. Either one writes checks for more commitments than one can keep, or one writes off existing commitments in potentially mortifying ways.

States confronted by decline, in short, have fundamental choices to make. They can attempt to maintain or expand their foreign policy ambitions and resources in an attempt to preserve their rank. Alternatively, they can seek to reduce their commitments and moderate their policies to manage their descent. The former risks embarrassment and defeat, the latter appears weak and invites predation. Thinking of the ship of state as an actual boat, decline is analogous to a severe storm. Some captains try to escape danger by raising sails and heading for open ocean, while others trim sails and head for shore.

Conditions Shaping Decline

In statecraft, like sailing, conditions can vary greatly, so it is only sensible that responses to decline will too. Below, we present the logic for grand strategies of decline in a linear fashion: conditions → policies → grand strategies → outcomes. Yet we must make plain that this is only a useful simplification. Which conditions matter most? We consider conditions as either domestic or international, and, to keep matters tractable, limit the list to four of each.

The most popular domestic condition in the literature is culture (Mueller 1993, 48; Dueck 2006, 4; Bacevich 2008, 5; Schake 2017, 2–3). Although all cultures have their internal debates and subcultures, dominant ideas in some national cultures may lend themselves more to expansion than others (Dafoe and Caughey 2016). For instance, Christopher Layne contends that Open Door ideology made American foreign policy counterproductively expansionist for many decades (2006, 8). Iain Johnston finds that Chinese strategic culture, though multivocal, has often favored expansion to unite "all under heaven" (1998, 31, 215; see also Yan 2013, 219–220). Great powers with more universalist cultures could be predisposed to respond to decline with aggression, while those with more particularistic cultures could be more content with the status quo. Related but distinct from culture is dominant narratives, which are culturally influenced but tend to change more quickly than national culture. Some grand strategies may be nearly impossible to attempt because dominant narratives sap public support for them or render them inconceivable (Krebs 2015, 5, 42).

A second domestic condition is internal institutions. There are several variants of this claim. For some, special interest groups block sensible responses to decline (Kennedy 1987, 523–524; Friedberg 1988, 290; Spruyt 2005, 6). For others, coalitions in the government encourage states to favor more or less aggressive policies because leaders have specific audiences to placate (Lobell 2003, 26; Weeks 2014, 35; Chiozza and Goemans 2011, 3–5). Yet regardless, the net effect is that how a great power is structured influences how it will behave. Different kinds of states will react to decline in predictably different ways.

The third domestic condition is unity. Declining great powers riven by partisan divisions may have a harder time reaching a consensus on foreign policy, sustaining a consistent foreign policy, or executing complex diplomatic or military maneuvers. Randall Schweller makes the case that consensus and cohesion at the elite and mass levels are chief factors in explaining foreign policy decisions (2006, 11–15). Others argue that consensus and cohesion are not exogenous variables but can be shaped by a state's threat environment (Bafumi and Parent 2012; Hui 2017, 284–285). On this logic, hegemons that face fewer threats are susceptible to greater domestic polarization and factionalism, but on either account, domestic unity would still shape how a state responds to decline.

The final domestic condition is leadership. There are several reasons to think that leaders could decisively influence how a state responds to decline. One is that how leaders perceive threats can vary, with some assuming that the internal workings of other countries are inherently more threatening to their own security (Saunders 2011, 3). Another reason is that leaders' rhetorical strategies shape foreign policy choices and success. How rising powers explain their intentions shapes how willing declining powers are to defend the status quo (Goddard 2018, 2), and formative experiences, especially military experience, may incline leaders to react more aggressively to decline than others (Horowitz, Stam, and Ellis 2015, 67). In a nutshell, both the character and the coherence of a state's response to decline are shaped by domestic conditions.

In terms of international conditions, the rate of decline can play a key role. States in freefall are apt to react distinctly differently than states drifting down gently or that are only declining in relative, not absolute, terms. There is some dispute about how speed affects state behavior. The traditional view is that fast falls cause fierce fights (Gilpin 1981, 191; Copeland 2000, 41). More recently, other scholars have claimed that decline makes states less dispute prone (MacDonald and Parent 2018, 63). Further, they claim, states in rapid decline are likely to adopt drastic or desperate expedients, while states in slow decline are more prone to incremental tinkering and cautious temporizing.

A second key international condition is a declining state's rank. Some scholars believe that the most dangerous and war-prone declines are hegemons. One reason for this may be because whoever is number one gets to set the rules for the international system (Gilpin 1981). Others maintain that hegemonic transitions are much like other great power transitions because, while the rules of the international order are contested, the top states have the most resources to manage their declines and ensure their interests are respected (MacDonald and Parent 2018). In fact, it could be the liminal great powers that are touchiest about power transitions because they are about to lose a seat at the great power table. Still others assert that hegemonic transitions are more contingent and depend on a variety of other factors (Copeland 2015; Shifrinson 2018). The bottom line is that the effect of rank is hotly contested.

A third factor that shapes how a state responds to decline is the availability of allies. Declining great powers may want to shed or share burdens to deal with rising challengers, but there may be no states near that challenger that are willing or able to shoulder those burdens. Conversely, declining states with access to regional allies who share their interests may have an easier time shifting costs and commitments onto others (Haynes 2015). The capacity of declining states to shift burdens may also be shaped by how alliance commitments are perceived. Sometimes states view commitments as interlinked, and renouncing a commitment in one area may be perceived as weakening commitments to defend elsewhere. At other times, pulling back in one place has no bearing on whether other commitments are perceived as credible, and retreat from a less important region can provide an important test of whether a rising power harbors revisionist intentions (Yoder 2018).

A final condition that affects grand strategies of decline is the conquest calculus. Taking and holding territory is more expensive in some eras than in others. Decision-makers must assess whether aggressive military moves are likely to raise–or drain–their capabilities in the long run. In previous periods, states were forged with iron and blood, and the acquisition of more territory was the indispensable ingredient to rising through the great power ranks. More recently, territorial expansion has gotten more expensive and less profitable, which may make it less tempting for policymakers to think they can expand their way out of decline. In brief, both the threat posed by decline and the options available to declining states are shaped by their international positions.

Policy Options during Decline

Not only do the conditions that confront declining states vary, so do the range of policy options available. To simplify matters, we group the foreign policy options described in the literature into domestic and international categories. We acknowledge that our use of these terms departs from standard usage: domestic policies refer to the implementation of foreign policies at home, while international policies indicate the implementation of foreign policies abroad. Not all domestic and international policies are employed for foreign policy purposes, of course, and we exclude those that are not. Moreover, the boundaries between these two categories may blur in practice, and states often adopt slates of policies from different categories in ways that are designed to strengthen and reinforce one another. But for the purposes of presentation, we treat them as analytically distinct.

In terms of domestic policy responses, the first avenue of dealing with decline is budgetary: foreign policy expenses can be expanded or contracted to meet new exigencies (Oatley 2015, 157–158). A state may go on a massive military spending spree to coerce and conquer its way out of an eroding position. Or, it can cut military spending to conserve resources for the long haul. In addition to the conditions described above, the willingness of a state to shift its spending in response to decline will be shaped by its particular fiscal position, revenue base, creditworthiness, and the extent to which foreign policy spending crowds out other government programs or harms macroeconomic performance. In general, studies have found that a large defense burden is associated with poorer economic performance, though this finding remains contested and is sensitive to factors such as the absolute level of defense spending, the growth cycle, the external threat environment, and defense financing (Fordham 2007; Dunne and Tian 2016).

Second, a declining power can alter its force structure to meet rising challengers. Declining states can embark on ambitious modernization efforts in an attempt to keep pace with challengers. Other options are to try to make do with fewer, more expensive weapons systems or more numerous, less expensive platforms. Declining states can also prioritize investments in different kinds of military forces. They can rely more on reserve forces than professional standing armies. They can invest in smaller, more mobile expeditionary forces rather than larger, static forward defenses. Declining states under extreme duress can reorient their investments towards homeland defense. Again, these choices are influenced by the extent to which conditions favor expansion, but also the pace of technological change, particular military operational opportunities or constraints, and whether rising threats are located closer or farther away from home.

Third, a declining power can revamp its institutions in response to decline. Sclerotic institutions are often both a potential cause of—and a potential impediment to dealing with—decline. However else they intend to manage their declines, states have incentives to reform underperforming military bureaucracies, revamp ineffective diplomatic services, resolve tangled lines of policymaking authority, and streamline inefficient policymaking processes. Professionalizing the military or civil service ranks and reducing the influence of parochial interest groups can also help increase the performance of a declining state. At the same time, efforts to revamp institutions can be expensive, disruptive, inflammatory, and generate a variety of other unintended consequences. The willingness of a state to reform its institutions, therefore, will depend not only on the severity of its decline, but also the "stickiness" of its institutions—i.e., how powerful the groups are that venerate old institutions.

Fourth, declining states may also turn to non-foreign-policy related investments, assuming they hold the key to national resurrection. Declining states can reallocate resources from foreign policy to other purposes, whether it be spending on infrastructure, innovation, or education. They can also redirect resources to pay down debt or finance tax cuts. The hope is that these kinds of investments can improve a state's standing over the long term by improving economic performance, augmenting tax receipts, and spurring technological innovation. Much as with institutions, states have traditions that may lean for or against civilian investment, and because these kinds of investments only bear fruit over the long term, they are suitable to less pressing international conditions than more urgent ones. Broadly, the ability of a declining state to use investments to slow or reverse its decline is contingent on its level of economic development, the complexity of its economy, the underlying causes of its poor performance, and the susceptibility of these problems to top-down policy interventions.

Turning to international policies, one option to deal with decline is for states to shift the deployment of military forces overseas. In some cases, declining states might seek to seize strategic territory, ports, airfields, or waterways to augment their position in advance of an impending transition. In other cases, declining states might abandon expensive, inessential, or indefensible positions. Yet policies in this category need not be as crude as simply acquiring or abandoning a base of operations. Declining powers can employ tripwire forces that credibly signal a willingness to defend exposed positions. They may make more use of rapid reaction forces that can quickly reinforce threatened possessions. Alternatively, they may make use of regional hubs, smaller concentrations of forward-deployed forces positioned in the vicinity of exposed commitments. The attractiveness of these options is shaped by the conditions described above, primarily the conquest calculus and ally availability, but prevailing communications and transportation technologies likewise influence whether these kinds of more flexible deployments will retain their effectiveness in the face of sustained decline.

Second, declining states can use diplomacy to manage relations with rising powers. This can run the range from attempts to intimidate potential rivals through bluff and bluster to efforts to negotiate spheres of influence or defuse unwinnable or marginal disputes before they escalate into war. In addition to bilateral negotiations, declining powers can use diplomacy to promote international rules, norms, and institutions designed to reinforce the status quo and limit the opportunities for future revisionism. Whether these kinds of diplomatic overtures will be effective is shaped by the severity of a declining state's fall, but also the skill of its diplomatic corps, the extent to which it has abided by diplomatic agreements in the past, its capacity to craft deals that overcome potential commitment problems, and the willingness of other states to monitor and enforce specific bargains.

Third, declining states often turn to others to help share the burden of upholding the balance of power. The types of actors that declining states can enlist run the range from major power allies, regional partners, colonial possessions, former dependencies, even nonstate clients or militias. In some cases, declining powers recruit these partners to corral a rising power. In other cases, they enlist these partners to coordinate and share defensive responsibilities in a region where the existing military balance is in flux. In extreme situations, declining powers may simply abandon prior commitments and turn responsibility for them over to someone else. Yet, as Kyle Haynes argues, declining states' decisions to devolve responsibility to "successor states" is a complicated one, which is shaped by a potential successor's capacity and willingness to defend the status quo (2015, 490–492).

Fourth, declining states can seek to bolster deterrence at select strongpoints. All states strive to signal their willingness to defend core interests, but this is a particularly challenging task for declining powers, whose capacity and will to do so is assumed to be lagging. As a result, declining states often go out of their way to signal to potential adversaries, typically rising powers, which interests they intend to preserve. Statements concerning "red lines," revamped alliance agreements, more visible deployments, more frequent or elaborate joint military exercises are among the ways declining powers can reinforce their commitment to defend potential strongpoints (Altman 2018). However declining powers choose to combine these international policies, their primary purpose is to moderate the pernicious impact of decline.

Grand Strategies of Decline

In theory, declining states could mix and match the aforementioned policies in a haphazard and uncoordinated manner. Yet, in practice, they often put them together as part of coherent grand strategies of decline. In this section, we sketch out some of the more common ways in which these policies have been boxed up, and evaluate how well these packages of policies have performed. Of course, any evaluation of the evidence is inescapably controversial because reasonable people disagree about what the standard of success should be. For example, successful grand strategy could be measured by sheer survival, endurance as a great power, staying at the top of the great power hierarchy, achieving policymakers' goals, avoiding war, or avoiding defeat in major war. To minimize controversy, in this section we stick to description and try to include as many of these standards as possible. We group the grand strategies from most to least aggressive–with the caution that these strategies are ideal types and are sometimes combined–and discuss their logic, the usual blend of policies that accompany them, and their frequency and typical outcomes.

Expansion

There are many reasons that states might try to ward off decline with war. Domestically, a great power may have a warlike culture or leader, its military institutions may be predisposed to attack, or it may have a more unified population than its adversaries. Internationally, conquest might pay, there may be no reliable allies to share burdens with, or its rank and rate of fall favor notions that war now would be more rewarding than taking one's chances later. Writings on power transition theory and hegemonic stability theory stress how changes at the top of the great power pecking order tend to exacerbate the security dilemma and to create both preventive and preemptive incentives to choose aggressive actions (Gilpin 1981; Copeland 2000; Tammen et al. 2000). The policy mix that tends to follow from a grand strategy of expansion is ramping up military spending, deferring investments in nonmilitary items, using diplomacy as cover for aggression and strongpoints as springboards for offensives, deploying forward forces, and keeping reliance on allies to a minimum. Forces in being must be large and mobile, and institutions are configured in an imperial manner to take, hold, and administer new territories.

While the bulk of the literature assumes that states should expand their way out of decline, the bulk of the cases do not follow such logic. Very few states have embraced such a grand strategy, and those that have met catastrophic ends by any measure. Germany and Japan after 1933 are exemplars of this grand strategy, and their ignominious collapses serve as a reminder of why more states do not try to conquer their way out of decline. In fact, it is hard to name any declining state that resurrected itself through conquest. The dysfunction of Nazi Germany is well known, while 1930s Japan is less known but no less spectacular. As S. C. M. Paine points out (2017, 179–187), Japanese decision-makers radically misread their environment, underestimating Chinese nationalism, overestimating how much conquest would pay, failing to coordinate with allies or employ defensible cost–benefit analysis to their grand strategy. The upshot is that if the incentives for war were as strong as many theorists say, many more great powers would have tried this route and some would have been successful (Lebow and Valentino 2009; Kirshner 2012).

Bluffing

Some states deal with decline by denying it. Either because the truth is too painful or because they have incentives to overstate their strength, a grand strategy of bluffing can be appealing. At home, leaders could be weak or flatter themselves that they have good nerves and poker faces, domestic disunity could paralyze policymaking, or national culture and institutions could embody a strong status quo bias in foreign policy. Abroad, leaders may think their decline temporary, distrust the available allies, or believe the conquest calculus buttresses weakening defenses. The policy portfolio that conveys bluffing depends on the state, but consists of leaving budget priorities, institutions, diplomacy, and military forces unchanged–in a word, inertia.

While tempting, bluffing is remarkably rare. One can make a case that some states, such as France after the Franco-Prussian War or Russia around the turn of the twentieth century, occasionally employed a strategy of bluff, but it tended to turn out badly. In the French case, a slow rate of decline and a national culture that stressed *grandeur* may have encouraged some French leaders to compensate for decline through imperial adventures on the periphery. Yet debacles in Indochina and Fashoda neither rekindled French greatness abroad nor helped French prime ministers' popularity at home. Russian bluffing was even more disastrous. For what appear to be reasons of institutional dysfunction and personal ignorance, Tsar Nicholas II bluffed his way into a war with Japan in 1904 that he neither wanted nor could win. The resulting string of defeats incited rebellion, humbled Russian power for a decade, and set the stage for revolution. As the examples attest, there appears to be no regime type especially prone to bluffing, nor an example of a state that managed to bluff its way back to greatness.

Binding

Another way to dampen the dangers of decline are international institutions. When states codify their relations more formally, it can increase predictability, legitimacy, and cooperation (Keohane 2012, 128, 133) and enhance the status of fallen powers (Zarakol 2011, 12). Instead of spending one's diminishing resource base on offense or business as usual, a binding strategy looks to normative and legal means to cope with eroding capability. This could save lives and money, avoiding arms races and security spirals that may result in tragic wars that no one wants (Ikenberry 2011, 85–86). Intuitively, this could be a compelling course when a country's national culture embraces liberal values or its leadership is steeped in legal training. Binding may be tempting at any rate of decline or rank among the great powers, but it is especially tempting with supportive allies and a prevailing belief that conquest does not pay. The policy portmanteau that follows from a binding strategy is to shift emphasis away from military statecraft to economic and diplomatic statecraft. To send a strong signal of benign intent, military spending should be slashed, forces pulled back, and mobility discouraged. Leaders should focus on economic growth, long-term investment, and shoring up domestic institutions. Overseas, only the most essential strongpoints should be buttressed, but otherwise international institutions, collective security, and multilateral diplomacy should rule the day.

The most famous example of a binding strategy is the Concert of Europe, which met regularly after the Napoleonic Wars to tamp down great power conflicts and maintain domestic tranquility in an age of smoldering nationalism. Opinions differ on when the Concert died, but for at least several years it managed to achieve its ends, and great power war did not re-erupt until the Crimean War in 1853. Less well known but also successful was the British penchant for arbitration in the nineteenth century (Langhorne 1996, 43, 47, 50). In the Americas and Asia, British arbitration efforts defused many explosive issues, and allowed policymakers in London (and elsewhere) to concentrate attention and resources on higher priorities, many of which were domestic. The Dutch used international law dexterously to justify aggressive piracy as their power waxed, as well as to legitimate their possession of weakly held territories when their power waned, but this led neither to better treatment of other people and states nor to less violence or overexpansion (Klooster 2016, 76, 254–256, 262). Moreover, Russian attempts to use arms control to blunt the consequences of decline were of little help. Though the Hague Conventions of 1899 and 1907 are impressive in historical context, they did not alleviate Russia's defense burdens or prevent war. Binding strategies do not appear very expensive, but also do not appear very effective.

Retrenchment

A straightforward solution to decline is to realign ends with means. If a state finds it has fewer capabilities than it used to relative to its peers, then it can simply adopt a less ambitious grand strategy. This has the advantage of strategic solvency, but the disadvantage of having to give up valued goals, at least temporarily. When states promptly retract their grand strategic commitments proportionate to their loss of capability, they substitute a broader, more brittle perimeter for a fiercer, more flexible defense. In addition, retrenchment frees up resources for reinvestment in more profitable undertakings, which could bend a country's growth trajectory upward. This grand strategy certainly entails risk and loss, but may be fitting under an array of conditions so long as taking and holding land is not cheap and there are capable, available allies to share burdens with. At base, retrenchment is a Fabian strategy that uses defensive strongpoints and domestic institutions to survive, reform, and recover. It demands compromise and accommodation with friends and foes. The constellation of policies that tend to go with retrenchment include a decrease in foreign policy costs alongside reforms in domestic institutions and investment in the civilian economy. More specifically, retrenching states should cut their defense spending, increasingly rely on reserves and mobile forces, direct resources to projects that promise most long-term growth, rely on defense in depth over forward-deployed forces and tough talk, defuse crises with preventive diplomacy, share burdens with allies, and reinforce crucial strongpoints.

The empirical record suggests retrenchment is the most frequent grand strategy that states use to deal with decline, but that is a mixed blessing for declining states (MacDonald and Parent 2018). The only declining states that recover their former rank are states that retrenched, but most states in serious decline do not recover their rank. Retrenching states are not more likely to be preyed upon by other great powers and are comparatively good at protecting their possessions when challenged. Retreat seldom leads to a rout. The Austrian Empire endured far longer than most by prioritizing problems, shunning war, adopting fiscal prudence, and using time as a weapon (Mitchell 2018, 317–325). Similarly, British statecraft in the nineteenth and twentieth centuries largely followed "a policy of sweet reasonableness" (Kennedy 1984, 22). For decades, Britain gave ground grudgingly and avoided quagmires until after the South African War when it reoriented foreign policy, shared burdens with aligned states, and revamped outmoded internal institutions (Rock 2000; Schake 2017). Here, too, regime type seems to make no significant difference.

Appeasement

In the sense used here, appeasement is a dramatic form of retreat, a recognition of weakness, and an attempt to sell almost anything to almost anyone at almost any price for increased security. Where retrenchment is a mild to moderate contraction of grand strategic ambition, appeasement is sustained and asymmetric concessions to allies and enemies to buy peace. The underlying logic is that if rising states have their demands satisfied, they will have little need or grounds to cause further trouble, and the declining state can refit and refuel in tranquility (Rock 2000; Ripsman and Levy 2008). The obvious downside risk is that these efforts might not only whet the appetite of adversaries but bystanders and friends too. It is a hard strategy to follow without consensus that the country is in decline, its institutions are performing poorly, and the international environment is relatively benign. A grand strategy of appeasement uses diplomatic sacrifices to shield the country while foreign policy costs are slashed and domestic institutions are massively reformed. Appeasement becomes an exercise in *sauve qui peut*, cutting military expenses to the bone, pulling back forces and stressing defense, radically restructuring uncompetitive institutions, liquidating foreign policy commitments and befriending rivals, and concentrating all assets on homeland defense. Appeasement is the grand strategy of desperate states with no options left.

It should come as little surprise that historical instances of appeasement are sad and rare. Appeasing is a grand strategy most notable among states falling quickly, and appeasing states are prone to revolutions. Steve Pincus (2009, 365) chronicles how the perceived British appeasement of France in 1687 facilitated the Glorious Revolution of 1688. China provides another example: for centuries, the Chinese Empire cycled through expansion and appeasement, typically expanding and cohering when it was in a multipolar system and contracting and fragmenting when it was in a unipolar system (Higham and Graff 2002, 14; Hui 2017, 294–295). When European empires penetrated Chinese sovereignty in the "century of humiliation," Chinese institutional reform and state-building were invigorated (Chong 2012, chs. 3–4; Halsey 2015, 5), though not quickly enough to stave off further penetration and revolution. Similarly, the Soviet Union faced mounting evidence of outmoded institutions and sclerotic growth in the 1970s and 1980s, leading to daring foreign policy agreements, painful military retreats, minimizing support for its allies, and breathtaking attempts at domestic reform, all of which failed to stave off its collapse in 1991.

Conclusion

The grand strategy literature is rich and diverse, and that can sometimes be confusing. In this chapter, we have tried to distill an essential point: that there are a finite number of policies available to decision-makers in declining great powers, those policies have been braided in a fairly limited number of ways, and their success has varied with prevailing conditions. To recap, there are two sets of influential conditions: domestic (i.e., culture, institutions, unity, and leadership) and international (i.e., rate of decline, rank, ally availability, and the conquest calculus). So, too, there are two sets of policies: domestic (i.e., budget policy, force structure, institutional configuration, and investment) and international (i.e., force deployment, diplomatic demarche, redistributive burdens, and strongpoint defense). The interaction of these conditions and policies generally leads to five grand strategies: expansion, bluffing, binding, retrenchment, and appeasement.

There remains much we do not know about grand strategy and decline. First, scholars have not done a good job identifying the root causes of decline. It stands to reason that grand strategic reactions to decline are designed to treat both the root causes and the symptoms of decline, but we know much more about the latter than the former. Second, scholars could do better distinguishing between objective measures of decline and subjective perceptions of decline. Studies typically identify decline by looking at broad macroeconomic or geopolitical indicators, yet it remains unclear how well policymakers' perceptions follow these indicators, and individual case studies suggest an imperfect match (Friedberg 1988). Third, scholars have not identified clear metrics by which to assess the performance of declining states. Because recovery is rare, it is tempting to argue that there are no good grand strategic responses to decline. Yet the counterfactual question is key here: would an alternative grand strategy have performed any better, or would it simply have accelerated decline? Finally, scholars have tended to adopt a binary description for states. They are either rising or they are declining. In practice, though, states are sometimes doing both. They are rising relative to some rivals, while declining relative to others. It is intriguing that prior to both world wars, Germany was both rising relative to Britain and declining relative to Russia. The cross pressures created by these contradictory structural trends may have generated inaccurate perceptions, spurred myths of empire, and encouraged self-defeating grand strategies.

To this point we have stuck mostly to description, but in closing we venture some modest recommendations. Over the last several centuries, the worst grand strategy of decline by any measure has been expansion. Not only is it rarely tried, it never works, and has always brought catastrophe. Only slightly less disastrous has been appeasement. This may be a somewhat avoidable fate because appeasement was not employed randomly, but only appealed to desperate leaders in weak or rapidly falling states. Bluffing appears to be much less common and effective, but at least has the merit of not being appeasement. Binding, on the other hand, seems infrequent but mildly useful. Retrenchment appears to be the dominant grand strategy in decline, and for good reason: it is the only one that has brought peaceful and reasonably prompt recovery. International conditions may vacillate, but uncertainty predominates, and solvency and flexibility appear to be the least bad approaches to coping with stormy weather. And in practice, policymakers sometimes experiment with hybrid combinations of these grand strategies: they might bluff in the short term, for example, to provide cover for a more sustained policy of retrenchment in the long term.

For US policymakers contemplating an international system where power is less concentrated in their own hands, however, this may not be comforting news. The positive headline is that decline is a golden opportunity to renew a great power: minds and efforts are focused on deteriorating fortunes, harsh conditions discipline thought and action, and there is a vast menu of options to choose from. The negative news is that adjusting to decline can be painful: leaders must overcome entrenched interests, impose painful reforms, sacrifice some national interests, empower unreliable allies, or defer to untrustworthy adversaries. Declining states are not doomed to suffer what they must, but they must accept that they cannot always do what they will.[1]

NOTE

1. For comments on an earlier draft of this chapter, the authors thank participants at a workshop held at the Modern War Institute, US Military Academy, in May 2019, as well as Stacie Goddard, Maria Parent-Quintana, Ron Krebs, and Brittany Howard.

REFERENCES

Altman, Daniel. 2018. "Advancing without Attacking: The Strategic Game around the Use of Force." *Security Studies* 27 (1): 58–88.
Bacevich, Andrew. 2008. *The Limits of Power: The End of American Exceptionalism*. New York: Metropolitan Books.
Bafumi, Joseph, and Joseph M. Parent. 2012. "International Polarity and America's Polarization." *International Politics* 49 (1): 1–35.
Brooks, Stephen, G. John Ikenberry, and William Wohlforth. 2013. "Lean Forward: In Defense of American Engagement." *Foreign Affairs* 92 (1): 130–142.
Chiozza, Giacomo, and Hein Goemens. 2011. *Leaders and International Conflict*. New York: Cambridge University Press.
Chong, Ja-Ian. 2012. *External Intervention and the Politics of State Formation*. New York: Cambridge University Press.
Christensen, Thomas. 1996. *Useful Adversaries: Grand Strategy Domestic Mobilization, and Sino-American Conflict, 1947–1958*. Princeton: Princeton University Press.
Clausewitz, Carl von. 1984. *On War*. Translated by Peter Paret and Michael Howard. Princeton: Princeton University Press.
Copeland, Dale. 2000. *The Origins of Major War*. Ithaca: Cornell University Press.
Copeland, Dale. 2015. *Economic Interdependence and War*. Princeton: Princeton University Press.
Dafoe, Allan, and Devin Caughey. 2016. "Honor and War: Southern US Presidents and the Effects of Concern for Reputation." *World Politics* 68 (2): 341–381.
Dueck, Colin. 2006. *Reluctant Crusaders: Power, Culture, and Change in American Grand Strategy*. Princeton: Princeton University Press.
Dunne, J. Paul, and Nan Tian. 2016. "Military Expenditure and Economic Growth." *The Economics of Peace and Security Journal* 11 (2): 50–56.
Elliott, J. H. 2007. *Empires of the Atlantic World: Britain and Spain in America 1492–1830*. New Haven: Yale University Press.
Fordham, Benjamin. 2007. "Paying for Global Power: Costs and Benefits of Postwar Military Spending." In *The Long War: A New History of U.S. National Security Policy Since World War II*, edited by Andrew J. Bacevich, 371–404. New York: Columbia University Press.
Friedberg, Aaron L. 1988. *The Weary Titan: Britain and the Experience of Relative Decline, 1895–1905*. Princeton: Princeton University Press.
Gibbon, Edward. 1993 [1776]. *The Decline and Fall of the Roman Empire*. New York: Everyman.

Gilpin, Robert. 1981. *War and Change in World Politics*. Princeton: Princeton University Press.

Goddard, Stacie E. 2018. *When Right Makes Might: Rising Powers and World Order*. Ithaca: Cornell University Press.

Halsey, Stephen R. 2015. *Quest for Power: European Imperialism and the Making of Chinese Statecraft*. Cambridge: Harvard University Press.

Haynes, Kyle. 2015. "Decline and Devolution: The Sources of Strategic Military Retrenchment." *International Studies Quarterly* 59 (3): 490–502.

Heather, Peter J. 2010. "Holding the Line". In *Makers of Ancient Strategy: From the Persian Wars to the Fall of Rome*, edited by Victor Davis Hanson, 227–246. Princeton: Princeton University Press.

Higham, Robin, and David Graff. 2002. "Introduction." In *A Military History of China*, edited by David A. Graff and Robin Higham, 1–18. Boulder: Westview Press.

Horowitz, Michael, Allan Stam, and Cali Ellis. 2015. *Why Leaders Fight*. New York: Cambridge University Press.

Hui, Victoria Tin-Bor. 2017. "How Tilly's State Formation Paradigm is Revolutionizing the Study of Chinese State-making." In *Does War Make States: Investigations of Charles Tilly's Historical Sociology*, edited by Lars Bo Kaspersen and Jeppe Strandsbjerg, 268–295. New York: Cambridge University Press.

Hull, Isabel. 2005. *Absolute Destruction: Military Culture and the Practices of War in Imperial Germany*. Ithaca: Cornell University Press.

Ikenberry, G. John. 2011. *Liberal Leviathan*. Princeton: Princeton University Press.

Johnston, Alastair Ian. 1998. *Cultural Realism: Strategic Culture and Grand Strategy in Chinese History*. Princeton: Princeton University Press.

Kennedy, Paul. 1984. *Strategy and Diplomacy, 1870–1945*. Aylesbury, Buckinghamshire: Fontana.

Kennedy, Paul. 1987. *The Rise and Fall of the Great Powers*. New York: Vintage.

Keohane, Robert. 2012. "Twenty Years of Institutional Liberalism." *International Relations* 26 (2): 125–138.

Kirshner, Jonathan. 2012. "The Tragedy of Offensive Realism: Classical Realism and the Rise of China." *European Journal of International Relations* 18 (1): 52–74.

Klooster, Wim. 2016. *The Dutch Moment: War, Trade, and Settlement in the Seventeenth-Century Atlantic World*. Ithaca: Cornell University Press.

Krebs, Ronald R. 2015. *Narrative and the Making of US National Security*. New York: Cambridge University Press.

Langhorne, Richard. 1996. "Arbitration: the first phase, 1870–1914." In *Diplomacy and World Power: Studies in British Foreign Policy, 1890–1950*, edited by Michael Dockrill and Brian McKercher, 43–55. New York: Cambridge University Press.

Layne, Christopher. 2006. *The Peace of Illusions: American Grand Strategy from 1940 to the Present*. Ithaca: Cornell University Press.

Lebow, Richard Ned, and Benjamin Valentino. 2009. "Lost in Transition: A Critical Analysis of Power Transition Theory." *International Relations* 23 (3): 389–410.

Lippmann, Walter. 1943. *U.S. Foreign Policy: Shield of the Republic*. New York: Little, Brown.

Lobell, Stephen. 2003. *The Challenge of Hegemony: Grand Strategy, Trade, and Domestic Politics*. Ann Arbor: University of Michigan Press.

Lobell, Stephen. 2018. "A Granular Theory of Balancing." *International Studies Quarterly* 62 (3): 593–605.

Luttwak, Edward N. 1976. *The Grand Strategy of the Roman Empire: From the First Century A.D. to the Third*. Baltimore: The John Hopkins University Press.

MacDonald, Paul K., and Joseph M. Parent. 2018. *Twilight of the Titans: Great Power Decline and Retrenchment*. Ithaca: Cornell University Press.

Mitchell, A. Wess. 2018. *The Grand Strategy of the Habsburg Empire*. Princeton: Princeton University Press.

Mueller, John. 1993. "The Impact of Ideas in Grand Strategy." In *The Domestic Bases of Grand Strategy*, edited by Richard Rosecrance and Arthur Stein. Ithaca: Cornell University Press.

Oatley, Thomas. 2015. *The Political Economy of American Hegemony: Buildups, Booms, and Busts*. New York: Cambridge University Press.

Paine, S. C. M. 2017. *The Japanese Empire: Grand Strategy from the Meiji Restoration to the Pacific War*. New York: Cambridge University Press.

Parker, Geoffrey. 2000. *The Grand Strategy of Philip II*. New Haven: Yale University Press.

Pincus, Steve. 2009. *1688: The First Modern Revolution*. New Haven, Yale University Press.

Posen, Barry R. 2013. "The Case for a Less Activist Foreign Policy." *Foreign Affairs* 92 (1): 116–128.

Ripsman, Norrin, and Jack Levy. 2008. "Wishful Thinking or Buying Time? The Logic of British Appeasement in the 1930s." *International Security* 33 (2): 148–181.

Rock, Stephen. 2000. *Appeasement in International Politics*. Lexington, Ky: University Press of Kentucky.

Saunders, Elizabeth. 2011. *Leaders at War: How Presidents Shape Military Interventions*. Ithaca: Cornell University Press.

Schake, Kori. 2017. *Safe Passage: The Transition from British to American Hegemony*. Cambridge: Harvard University Press.

Schroeder, Paul W. "Munich and the British Tradition." *Historical Journal* 19 (1): 223–243.

Schweller, Randall L. 2006. *Unanswered Threats: Political Constraints on the Balance of Power*. Princeton: Princeton University Press.

Shifrinson, Joshua R. Itzkowitz. 2018. *Rising Titans, Falling Giants: How Great Powers Exploit Power Shifts*. Ithaca: Cornell University Press.

Snyder, Jack. 1991. *Myths of Empire: Domestic Politics and International Ambition*. Ithaca: Cornell University Press.

Spruyt, Hendrik. 2005. *Ending Empire: Contested Sovereignty and Territorial Partition*. Ithaca: Cornell University Press.

Tammen, Ronald et al. 2000. *Power Transitions: Strategies for the 21st Century*. London: Chatham House.

Thucydides. 1996. *The Landmark Thucydides: A Comprehensive Guide to the Peloponnesian War*. Translated by Richard Crawley. New York: Free Press.

Weeks, Jessica. 2014. *Dictators at War and Peace*. Ithaca: Cornell University Press.

Yan Xuetong. 2013. *Ancient Chinese Thought, Modern Chinese Power*. Princeton: Princeton University Press.

Yoder, Brandon. 2018. "Retrenchment as a Screening Mechanism: Power Shifts, Strategic Withdrawal, and Credible Signals." *American Journal of Political Science* 63 (1): 130–145.

Zarakol, Ayşe. 2011. *After Defeat: How the West Learned to Live with the West*. New York: Cambridge University Press.

CHAPTER 30

THE GRAND STRATEGIES OF SMALL STATES

ANDERS WIVEL

GRAND strategies have traditionally been viewed as the prerogative of great powers (Kennedy 1991, 6). In political discourse as well as in the study of international security, debates on grand strategy seem intrinsically linked to debates on great power politics and US foreign policy (see e.g., Brown et al. 2000; Murray 2011). As the primary producers of security and order in international relations, great powers have for centuries engaged in comprehensive analyses of their strategic room for maneuver in order to device the most effective diplomatic, military, and economic means to reach their political ends. In contrast, small states have traditionally refrained from formulating explicit grand strategies. Accepting that "the strong do what they have the power to do and the weak accept what they have to accept" (Thucydides 431, B.C.E.), small states historically followed pragmatic strategies responding to the agenda set by nearby great powers and external developments rather than formulating and pursuing their own strategic goals. Consequently, there are many examples of great power grand strategies codified in national security strategies and debated publicly among politicians and experts and analysed in the academic literature, but only few and relatively recent examples of these dynamics at play in small states.

This does not mean that the concept of grand strategy is irrelevant for understanding the foreign policies of small states. Grand strategy, including the grand strategy of small states, is usually characterized by "some degree of coherence towards the outside world [...] and to be following a reasonably coherent and predictable line" (Hill 2016, 5). Coherence and predictability reflect fundamental choices of grand strategy understood as "the long-term orchestration of power and commitments to secure oneself in a world where war is possible" (Porter 2018, 9). Small state grand strategy may not be codified in official documents but nonetheless it reflects "the calculated relationship of means to large ends" (Gaddis 2009, 7). This is grand strategy in the sense that it "identifies and articulates a given political actor's security objectives at a particular point in time and describes how they will be achieved using a combination of instruments of power— including military, diplomatic, and economic instruments" (Biddle 2015, 5).

Following this introduction, the chapter proceeds in five steps followed by a conclusion. The first section identifies the general characteristics of small state grand strategy and explains how it differs from great power grand strategy. The second section discusses the domestic and international determinants of small state grand strategy. The third section unpacks two classical small state grand strategies—hiding and shelter-seeking—whereas the fourth section discusses how small state grand strategy has changed over the past decades. I argue that while the grand strategy of small states remains tied to national security concerns, they increasingly pursue "smart" strategies aimed at taking advantage of material weakness to activate nonmaterial resources and maximize international influence. The fifth section discusses the determinants of success for small state grand strategy. Finally, I sum up the analysis and conclude the chapter.

THE GRAND STRATEGIES OF SMALL STATES AND GREAT POWERS: SIMILARITIES AND DIFFERENCES

The grand strategies of small states and great powers share a number of characteristics. A grand strategy identifies the goals and prioritizes the means necessary for long-term success in the international realm. The aims and means of grand strategy are subject to debate and analysis among the foreign policy elite. For great powers in particular, the result of these debates and analyses are often codified in national security strategies, state of the union-speeches, and other documents communicating the country's position and ambitions in the world and serving as points of reference for international and domestic audiences.

Small state grand strategy tends to be less formalized than great power grand strategy. However, even for small states, grand strategy is different from both the day-to-day decisions of the foreign policy executive and the foreign policy practice. Foreign policy denotes the external behavior of the state, whereas grand strategy links the values and interests of the state to goals and means in order to identify and achieve the long-term objectives of the state (Balzacq, Dombrowski, and Reich 2019; Briffa 2019). Thus, even if small states do not codify their grand strategy in documents such as a national security strategy, small state grand strategy is discernible as a "consistent pattern of behavior over time" (Silove 2018, 34) or "key ideas" helping political decision-makers to prioritize and organize foreign policy (Brands 2014: 30).

Historically, the grand strategies of small states differed from the grand strategies of great powers. Grand strategy is the great power's "theory of victory" (Posen 1984). It "integrates the policies and armaments of the nation that the resort to war is either rendered unnecessary or is undertaken with the maximum chance of victory" (Earle 1943, viii). This understanding of grand strategy is in accordance with B.B. Lidell Hart's influential understanding of grand strategy as a combination of social, economic, and military policies in order to win not only the war but also the peace (Hart 1942). Much of the security studies literature—whether originating in assumptions about the rationality of nuclear deterrence or the need to balance the power of adversaries—also subscribes to this understanding of grand strategy without making much distinction between great powers and other states (Silove 2018, 34).

The classical literature on small states in international relations depicts the foreign policy of these countries as an antithesis to grand strategy as a theory of victory. This literature equals "small" with the absolute and relative lack of capabilities and understands this capability deficit "as a handicap to state action, and even state survival" (Browning 2006, 669). Small states are weak and vulnerable prisoners of small margins of time and error following from their capability deficit and therefore unable to defend themselves against the great powers (Jervis 1978, 172-173; Handel 1990). They have limited diplomatic power and lack the necessary diplomatic competencies to avoid war as well as the necessary military capabilities to win a war. Consequently, they have little or no voice in the peace negotiated after the war. They are the pawns of international relations. Rather than a deliberate attempt to influence their own destiny and the international realm, the behavior of small states—according to this understanding—is little more than a reflection of the balance of power with little action space for small state foreign policy decision-makers (Elman 1995).

Consequently, small states have traditionally pursued reactive and defensive foreign and security policies (Neumann and Gstöhl 2006), and "their leaders focus mostly on the protection of their territorial integrity rather than on the pursuit of more far-reaching global objectives" (Krause and Singer 2001, 16). As summed up by Robert Keohane, small states "can never acting alone or in a small group make a significant impact" (Keohane 1969, 296). Rather than a "theory of victory," small state grand strategy is historically better understood as a theory of avoiding defeat or destruction. Rather than achieving long-term success, small states have focused on avoiding short-term failure. Consequently, in the course of history, small state grand strategy has had a close fit with a defensive understanding of grand strategy as "a state's theory about how it can best 'cause' security for itself" (Posen 1984, 13).

Since 1945, changes in the international system have increasingly allowed small states to pursue offensive grand strategies aimed at maximizing influence. For this reason, the difference between great power and small state grand strategy today is a difference in degree rather than a difference in kind.

What Are the Determinants of Small State Grand Strategy?

Small state grand strategy suffers from both domestic and international constraints. In domestic politics, small states are prone to small and tightly knit political and administrative elites. The recruitment base for national leadership positions is limited, with a small group of talents courted by both the public and private sector (Sarapuu and Randma-Liiv 2020). Counterbalancing coalitions willing and able to challenge dominant elites and conventional wisdom are often weak, in particular in times of national security crisis enhancing the risk of groupthink (Janis 1982), and more generally resulting in the lack of innovation as well as corruption and personalized politics (Anckar 2020; Corbett and Veenendaal 2018). Because of their small populations, small states have a small tax base. Consequently, the opportunity for extracting resources from society for foreign and security policy is limited.

In international affairs, the most important consequence of these limitations is the inability of the small state to defend its own territory against enemies (Rothstein 1968, 29). The actions of the small state on the battlefield have only minimal influence on the outcome of war. A second consequence is the limited ability to affect diplomatic outcomes. Thus, small states have only limited ability to secure peaceful relations with other states and a stable regional and international environment, i.e., to avoid war, or more ambitiously, to facilitate peaceful change. A third consequence is the limited resources and competencies for information gathering. A limited number of diplomatic representations, often with only a few diplomats posted to each, and a small intelligence service leave small states prone to misperception and dependent upon bigger allies for intelligence as well as diplomatic support in international negotiations.

Since the end of the Second World War, both the characteristics of the international system and the interests of the great powers of this system have been modified, with important consequences for small state grand strategy (Maass 2017; Thorhallsson and Steinsson 2017). Norms of national self-determination, decolonization, and peaceful conflict resolution reduce the importance of conventional military capabilities, and, in addition, conquest rarely pays in a world of globalized, interdependent economies. At the same time, an increase in the number of international institutions helps to level the international playing field and underpin voice opportunities of small states. These developments do not put an end to the security predicament of small states, but they do transform the nature of the challenges faced by small states. Today, threats originate from many different actors above and below the state level, some of them sponsored by hostile great powers. The challenges vary in nature from military attack to terrorism and organized crime, coups, forced clientage, and internal armed conflict (Bailes, Rickli, and Thorhallsson 2014).

Small states are now less likely to be invaded but more likely to be disrupted than in the past. Today, the risks challenging small state security rarely threaten survival of the state as such, but they may risk undermining stability and changing the fabric of society. Consequently, small state grand strategy has evolved from revolving primarily around the question of military security ("war and preparations for war") to a broader understanding including also "nonmaterial sources of power" and aims beyond the battlefield, thereby reflecting a more general trend in the understanding of grand strategy (Balzacq, Dombrowski, and Reich 2019, 69).

Classical Small State Grand Strategy: Hiding and Shelter-Seeking

Unable to defend themselves from military attack on their territory, small states have historically pursued one of two grand strategies in order to cause security for themselves. The first option was to "opt out" of international relations by pursuing a so-called hiding strategy, aiming for security neutrality and political and economic autonomy. As noted in an early overview of research efforts on small states in international politics, "[t]he pursuit of a policy of neutrality is a very characteristic feature in the foreign behavior of small states" (Amstrup 1976, 170). Hiding as a grand strategy aims to protect the security interests of the small state by signaling its disinterest in great power politics and committing to impartiality. The Hague Conventions codified neutrality as legal term in 1907. Neutral states were "required not to participate in wars either directly or indirectly" (Goetchel 1999, 118). This includes maintaining impartiality in military conflicts as well as refraining from supplying weapons or credits, and making territory available for uses by one of the warring parties.

In political practice, "small states developed different variations of neutrality-centered national security strategies" (Maass 2017, 190). These practices were less ideal-typical than the legal understanding, which was "interpreted" and "adapted" by small state policymakers to fit with the external opportunities and challenges of the state (Amstrup 1976, 171; Morgenthau 1939). Neutrality as a grand strategy was originally formulated in the context of the development of the modern states system and in particular in the context of the European Concert in the nineteenth century, when the concert powers had little regard for the "Kleinstaaterei" of weaker actors potentially undermining systemic stability (Maass 2017, 123). In this context, neutrality was a means for small states to avoid conquest or annexation in the name of systemic interests and to maintain autonomy in an international system with few restrictions on great power politics (Frei 1968, 14–15). In addition, neutrality was a means to maintaining trade relations and avoiding economic dependency in times of war (Goetschel 1999, 120). This is particularly important for small states, because their domestic markets are too small for sustaining growth and wealth (Griffiths 2014). The practice of small state neutrality varies from countries such as Costa Rica and Liechtenstein with no armed forces to the armed neutrality of e.g., Sweden and Switzerland with long traditions of a relatively strong territorial defense and arms industries.

Despite its historical prominence, neutrality has been deemed a counterintuitive grand strategy in the sense that we would expect a state with a limited resource base to seek shelter from stronger allies rather than rely on its own means for protection (Karsh 1988, 4). Moreover, neutrality is only possible to the extent that the great powers respect it. Metternich respected Swiss neutrality from 1815, because it allowed Austria to deny France the Swiss territories, and the great powers recognized Belgian neutrality in 1839 and Luxembourgian neutrality in 1867 in order to maintain the stability of the European

Concert (Maass 2017, 112–113). In contrast, neutrality did not protect Belgium for German occupation in the First World War or the Baltic countries from Germany or the Soviet Union in the Second World War. Neutrality was originally a strategy for staying out of trouble by staying out of sight (Wivel and Ingebritsen 2019, 205), but this grand strategy has increasingly been used by small states as a platform for status-seeking and influence on great power politics. Prominent examples include Swedish UN activism advocating East–West détente and North–South dialogue during the Cold War and the small state–dominated nonaligned movement of developing world states in the same period calling attention to global inequality and the particular challenges of postcolonial societies.

Historically, the alternative to hiding is shelter-seeking, i.e., to seek refuge from the great power politics of international anarchy by allying with one or more strong states able and willing to shelter the small state from external threats (Bailes, Thayer, and Thorhallsson 2016; Vital 1967). Shelter-seeking involves a more or less tacit contract or a tradeoff with the great power(s) providing shelter (Morrow 1991). The great power serves as the security provider, and, in return, it gains influence over the small state's foreign policy. The small state's focus is primarily on defensive goals. The alliance provides shelter from military aggression and allows the small state to pursue core interests such as defending its territory and population. At the same time, the great power—by providing defense—is allowed to expand its influence over the small state and to deny other great powers the opportunity to do the same (Krause and Singer 2001, 18).

Small states pursuing shelter-seeking may contribute to balance of power coalitions, but they rarely pursue balancing as a grand strategy. Their main motive is to use one or more great powers as a shield against threatening great power(s), not to affect the balance of power and, by definition, their limited capabilities will have little effect on the overall balance. Small state participation in asymmetric alliances is primarily about obtaining security and defending the status quo, whereas great power participation in asymmetric alliances is about changing the status quo to widen its own autonomy and influence over international relations, in addition to preserving security (Morrow 1991). Or to put it differently, the alliance provides both the small state and the great power with a bigger margin of time and error, but as they begin from different points of departure, with the great power already being relatively safe and the small state entering the alliance to obtain basic security goals, the end result is also different for the two types of states. The great power can use its position vis-à-vis its small ally to initiate structural change, with important consequences for the future of international order (e.g., by enhancing trade and thereby further deepening dependency under the security umbrella), and in turn creating a buffer in time and space against the influence and military threat of other great powers. The consequences for the small state are mainly measured in terms of national security.

Hiding may be seen as the ultimate free-rider strategy for small states, but historically, shelter-seeking has provided small states with good opportunities for free riding as well. The most prominent example is NATO, which both during and after the Cold War has been subject to an ongoing discussion between the United States and smaller allies on their contribution to the alliance. In general, the inconsequential nature of small state contributions to the overall security of the alliance, and the unlikelihood that even a steep increase in the defense spending of small alliance members will tip the balance of power, leaves the larger allies to "bear a disproportionate share of the burden" (Olson and Zeckhauser 1966, 266). The political costs associated with bringing small states into line are most often higher than the security gains from small ally compliance. Thus, whereas alliance membership restrains the autonomy of the small state, the restraints are often the highest in the lead-up to membership, when the small state needs to demonstrate its usefulness as a future ally (Mouritzen and Wivel 2005). Once inside the club, the small state is free to enjoy security like any other member.

This strategy gives the small state a considerable action space in peacetime, but it may face important difficulties in times of war, when the small state seeks to navigate the so-called alliance–security dilemma, facing on the one hand the risk of abandonment and on the other the risk of entrapment (Snyder 1984, 466–468). The small state faces an increased risk of abandonment by stronger allies if it signals a weak commitment to alliance obligations or fails to support other alliance members in specific conflicts. However, if the small state seeks to offset this risk by pursuing a strategy of strong commitment and support to stronger allies, it runs the risk of being drawn into and ultimately entrapped in conflicts in which it has little interest and no control over when and how to end. Not all wars have the same effect on the dilemma. In military operations, such as the out of area operations that have been frequent since the end of the Cold War, the territorial integrity of the small state is not at risk. At the same time, the involvement of small states lends both legitimacy and capabilities to the operation. Consequently, the small state may use its continued involvement as an important bargaining chip. As noted by Weitsman, "during wartime, fears of abandonment may mediate the lead power's decision-making—the reverse is true for smaller states. This grants significant leverage to smaller states during wartime operations. In other words, instead of being coerced or bullied, coalition or alliance partners may be begged or bribed" (Weitsman 2014, 35).

Contemporary Small State Grand Strategy

Shelter-seeking and hiding remain important small state grand strategies, However, as a consequence of the changes in the international system since 1945, their characteristics are changing at the same time as new more offensive grand strategies become more important for small states.

Transforming Hiding and Shelter-Seeking

Hiding in its original incarnation is virtually impossible in a globalized world, and the strategy does not enjoy the prominence of the past (Wallace 1999). The rising importance of nonterritorial security problems and security interdependence makes it "questionable whether neutrality or military nonalignment has any particular strategic or security value, and, if it does, whether it currently comes in the form of their engagement in wider security initiatives" (Agius and Devine 2011, 266). However, a number of states, typically very small states with few natural resources, still aim to stay outside the entanglements of globalized international society. This allows them to increase national capabilities by serving as hubs for unregulated international financial services, tax evasion, violation of intellectual property rights, and drug trafficking (Shaw 2014; Simpson 2014), but also as (typically remote) locations of high-security prisons, refugee camps, and weapons testing and dumping sites (Baldacchino 2014). Thus, for some small developing island states, globalization combined with a virtually nonexistent threat of annexation or colonization has allowed them to build societal resilience on either serving those who want their business hidden from globalized international society or alternatively as a dumping ground for the prisoners, refugees, weapons etc. of globalized international society.

Shelter-seeking now extends far beyond military protection against great power invasion as small state security challenges now include risks such as terrorism, smuggling, piracy, and cyber threats as well as environmental and economic security. Consequently, small states seeking shelter demand a broader spectrum of services from the alliance than previously, at the same time as international and regional organizations beyond traditional alliances have come to play a key role in small state grand strategy (Bailes, Rickli, and Thorhallsson 2014, 38–39). Small states still need hard military protection, but at the same time they are dependent upon being parts of networks for the exchange of information, including intelligence, police cooperation, the effective border control of other states, etc. (Crandall 2014). Networks are not always linked to formal alliance membership but may take the form of coalitions within an alliance or between alliance members and nonmembers using the alliance as a platform for cooperation. Sometimes networks take the form of concentric circles, giving those small states that are able to forge a "special relationship" with the great power(s) at the center privileged access to information and cooperation (Haugevik 2018). These developments result in constant negotiation of security and discussions on "who does what" among alliance and coalition members, thereby multiplying the alliance–security dilemma into a series of dilemmas at many different levels of the decision-making process.

Rather than dichotomous alternatives, hiding and shelter-seeking are, increasingly, two supplementary aspects of small state grand strategy. A small state with limited capacity cannot have strong opinions, competencies, and policies on all issue areas, and it has no chance of meeting or even monitoring the threats and risks of contemporary international society effectively. Consequently, a grand strategy of shelter-seeking needs to be combined with issue-specific hiding, allowing the small state to focus its resources on issues of vital importance for national security and leaving other issues on the international security agenda for others to grapple with. In addition, small states can actively couple shelter-seeking and hiding in grand strategies, as exemplified by Malta, an EU member state preserving military neutrality as part of a grand strategy to maximize national interests by taking the role of a "Mediterranean interlocutor" between the EU and its southern neighbors (Briffa 2019).

From Defensive to Offensive Grand Strategy: The Competent Performance of Vulnerability

Small state security is no longer primarily about vulnerability to the invasion of nearby great powers, but about achieving resilience in a globalized world. In order to serve this purpose, grand strategy must be multifunctional. The multifunctionality of alliances and international institutions more broadly cuts deep into state structures and practices, thereby changing both the means and meaning of power politics (Wivel and Paul 2019). For this reason, the small state has a strong incentive to seek influence on policy and decision-making practices thus transforming the autonomy–security tradeoff into an autonomy–security–influence tradeoff (Mouritzen and Wivel 2005, 33; Rickli and Almezaini 2017, 12). Consequently, small states are likely to pursue strategies combining shelter-seeking with influence maximization. If small states are pegging their own policies to those of the strong or even adapting these policies, they have an incentive to influence these policies as well as the norms upon which they are based. Even small states living dangerously on the outside or on the margins of the rules and regulations of international society need sponsors, or at least tolerance from stronger states, and have an interest in influencing these partners in order to pursue the "creative political economy" underpinning resilience of their society (Baldacchino and Milne 2009).

In contrast to great powers competing for hegemony and dominance, the aim of small state influence-seeking is not necessarily to increase rank, but rather to engage in a "competent performance of vulnerability," taking advantage of weakness to influence international outcomes (Corbett, Xu, and Weller 2019, 1). Performing vulnerability as a grand strategy can be conceptualized under the heading "smart state strategy" (Bueger and Wivel 2018; Grøn and Wivel 2011). Rather than seeking to compensate for weakness or to move away from weakness, smart states utilize weakness by pitching their own ideas within the parameters set by the great powers. Because they are weak and viewed as nonconsequential to decision-making, they typically have more leeway to act as mediators, provide technical expertise, and champion solutions for the greater good than great powers and thereby take advantage of voice and framing opportunities if they manage to "prioritize and invest their available resources in issues of particular importance" (Panke 2012, 317).

The small state may identify a niche of particular national interest and the necessary competences to make a real and visible contribution in the name of the greater good, e.g., "peacekeeping, institution building, conflict prevention, mediation, human rights promotion or sustainable development" (Rickli and Almezaini 2017, 16). Depending on the strategic ambitions, contributions to specific wars and operations may focus on the provision of transportation or logistics, or, more ambitiously on, e.g., special operations forces (Rickli 2008). Even more ambitiously, the small state may embark on niche norm entrepreneurship by delivering policy inputs on issues that may seem marginal to the great powers but is of great relevance to the small state (Jakobsen 2009). Because of the limited coercive power of small states, they are dependent on identifying an issue that plays into the existing discourses, building a coalition in favor of the issue, and finding an organizational home for the new norm to underpin permanence and implementation (Björkdahl 2007; Grøn and Wivel 2011). If persistent, the small state may succeed in being "noticed or seen" as a state "*useful* to greater powers" and thereby enhance its bargaining position and its status as a state worthy of great power support in times of crisis (Neumann and Cavalho 2015, 2). The "virtual enlargement" strategies of, e.g., Qatar, Singapore, and the Vatican City, show how even very small states can utilize their political economy potential, models of good governance, and diplomatic mediation to achieve a status that far exceeds material capabilities (Chong 2010; Eggeling 2017).

As an alternative to, or in combination with, smart state strategies, small states may engage leash-slipping (Press-Barnathan 2012) and hedging (Tessman 2012) in an effort to maintain shelter while avoiding dependence. Leash-slipping strategies are aimed at building military capabilities in order to maximize the ability to conduct independent foreign and security policies. It is unlikely that many states will be able to achieve full independence from great power–based shelters, but they may aim to forge forerunner reputations within specific areas, allowing them to take on the role of negotiator and lead within this particular issue area (Jakobsen 2009). By hedging their choices for security shelter, small states seek to increase their security independence by increasing capabilities and strengthening diplomatic, economic, and even military ties with other states, but stop short of participating in forums or alliances balancing the shelter state. Even relatively weak small states such as Bolivia, Chile, and Ecuador have been able to use a combination of regional institutional arrangements and cooperation with South American and European states to hedge against dependency on the United States (Wehner 2020).

When Are the Grand Strategies of Small States Successful?

The grand strategies of both small states and great powers seek to reconcile political ends with limited material means (Dueck 2008, 10), but this problem is particularly acute for small states, because of their limited resource base. Small states suffer from limited influence over international affairs. This is particularly the case in security and defense policy, where material capabilities and resources remain closely tied to influence (Græger 2015). Taking their external environment as a given and viewing nonprovocation as a condition for security and survival, small state grand strategies, even when they are at their most offensive and ambitious, continue to adapt to the international environment and cater to the interests of the great powers. Still, the conditions for small state grand strategy have changed since the conclusion of the Second World War and in particular in the decades since the end of the Cold War. Today, it is not the choice between hiding and seeking shelter, which is the most important choice in small state grand strategy, but how to "mix and match" strategies to maximize security in the constantly changing contexts of a globalized security environment.

The success of small state grand strategy depends on factors both inside and outside the small state. Some small states face a more dangerous security environment than others because of their geopolitical location. Other small states suffer from limited human resources and lack of competition in the marketplace of ideas and talent. However, the success of small states in problematic locations such as the Seychelles, Singapore, and Estonia provide lessons for small state grand strategy more generally (Bueger and Wivel 2018; Chong 2010; Crandall 2014). Despite their obvious differences in terms of democratic development and geopolitical location, they share two characteristics.

First, all three countries are characterized by a pragmatic, even opportunistic, political culture. Estonia has taken advantage of its delicate geopolitical location close to Russia and its position as a victim of serious cyberattacks to build e-competencies in the private and public sector, marketing the country as *E-stonia* and open for business. It has worked closely with the United States in formulating the alliance's cybersecurity policies and contributed to US military operations, while building close political and economic ties to neighboring Baltic and Nordic countries. The Seychelles' approach to international relations begins from a Creole political culture, which combines a "genuine openness to and appreciation of difference" and a "pragmatist thinking style, which does not start from foundational principles and beliefs, but from ideas of what works and what can be achieved" (Bueger and Wivel 2018, 181–182). This allows them to work with the United States as well as China and other states at the same time. Singapore has adopted a "diplomatic style of calculated candour in addressing security issues generated by vastly larger states" (Chong 2010, 395). This approach facilitates pragmatically working towards goals for competitiveness and globalization of its domestic society; neither challenging the American world order, nor provoking China or other states in Southeast Asia.

Second, all three states have been willing and able to prioritize their goals and means and utilize their nonthreatening status as small states into "smart" or "entrepreneurial" policies, i.e., policies that are "problem-solving," "alert to opportunities," focused on transforming "an opportunity into change" in a way which is "proactive, creative and responsive" (Pedi and Sarri 2019, 12). In that sense, the lessons of these successful states come full circle. Successful small state grand strategy is pragmatic, responsive, and adaptive, although, more often now than in the past, combining defensive shelter-seeking with more offensive influence-seeking in order to hedge the security bets of the small state in a globalized security environment.

Conclusion

Grand strategy is not the prerogative of great powers. Small state grand strategy is less likely to be codified as a national security strategy, but small state grand strategy is discernible in key ideas underpinning the organization and prioritization of foreign policy by connecting values and interests with goals and means and producing consistent patterns of behavior over time. The lack of relative material capabilities has important consequences for small state grand strategy. Historically, small states have pursued defensive grand strategies. The two most prominent small state grand strategies are hiding, i.e., opting out of international affairs by pursuing military neutrality and economic and political autonomy, and shelter-seeking, i.e., seeking bi- and multilateral ties to great powers willing and able to shield the small states from the perils of international anarchy.

Developments in the international system since 1945, accelerated since the end of the Cold War, have changed the conditions for small state grand strategy, making small states less likely to be invaded or annexed by great powers but facing new disruptive security challenges. Hiding is difficult in a globalized world, but life on the margins of international society may allow some small states to take in business scorned by others, e.g., providing hubs for unregulated financial services or offering sites for prisons and refugee camps. Shelter-seeking becomes multifunctional and subject to constant negotiation, reflecting a new threat environment. New small state grand strategies are "smart" in taking advantage of material weakness to mediate, promote norms, hedge, and seek status in order to further the interests of small states. The success of these efforts depends on a pragmatic political culture and the ability and willingness to prioritize goals and means in ways which serve the interests of the small states without alienating or offending the great powers.[1]

Note

1. Research for this chapter was supported by the Erasmus+ programme of the European Union—the Jean Monnet Networks project "Navigating the Storm: The Challenges of Small States in Europe" under Grant Agreement 587498-EPP-1-2017-1-IS-EPPJMO-NETWORK. I would like to thank Thierry Balzacq, Trine Villumsen Berling, Hillary Briffa, and Revecca Pedi for comments on a draft version of the chapter.

References

Agius, Chris, and Karen Devine. 2011. "Neutrality: A Really Dead Concept? A Reprise." *Cooperation and Conflict* 46 (3): 265–284.

Amstrup, Niels. 1976. "The Perennial Problem of Small States: A Survey of Research Efforts." *Cooperation and Conflict* 11 (2): 163–182.

Anckar, Dag. 2020. "Small States: Politics and Policies." In *Handbook on the Politics of Small States*, edited by Godfrey Baldacchino, and Anders Wivel, 38–54. Cheltenham: Edward Elgar.

Baldacchino, Godfrey. 2014. "The Security Concerns of Designed Spaces: Size Matters." In *Small States and International Security: Europe and Beyond*, edited by Clive Archer, Alyson Bailes, and Anders Wivel, 241–254. London: Routledge.

Baldacchino, Godfrey, and David Milne. 2009. *The Case for Non-Sovereignty*. London: Routledge.

Bailes, Alyson, Jean-Marc Rickli, and Baldur Thorhallsson. 2014. "Small States, Survival and Strategy." In *Small States and International Security: Europe and Beyond*, edited by Clive Archer, Alyson Bailes, and Anders Wivel, 26–45. London: Routledge.

Bailes, Alyson J., Bradley A. Thayer, and Baldur Thorhallsson. 2016. "Alliance Theory and Alliance 'Shelter': The Complexities of Small State Alliance Behavior." *Third World Thematics: A TWQ Journal* 1 (1): 9–26.

Balzacq, Thierry, Peter Dombrowski and Simon Reich. 2019. "Is Grand Strategy a Research Program? A Review Essay." *Security Studies* 28 (1): 58–86.

Biddle, Stephen D. 2005. *American Grand Strategy after 9/11: An Assessment*. Carlisle, Pennsylvania: Strategic Studies Institute, US Army War College.

Björkdahl, Annika. 2007. "Swedish Norm Entrepreneurship in the UN." *International Peacekeeping* 14 (4): 538–552.

Brands, Hal. 2014. *What Good is Grand Strategy? Power and Purpose in American Statecraft from Harry S. Truman to George W. Bush*. Ithaca: Cornell University Press.

Briffa, Hillary. 2019. *Can Small States Have a Grand Strategy?* Doctoral thesis Final Draft, December 2019. London: King's College.

Brown, Michael E., Owen R. Coté Jr, Sean M. Lynn-Jones, and Steven E. Miller, eds. 2000. *America's Strategic Choices*. Cambridge, MA: The MIT Press.

Browning, Christopher. 2006. "Small, Smart and Salient? Rethinking Identity in the Small States Literature." *Cambridge Review of International Affairs* 19 (4): 669–684.

Bueger, Christian, and Anders Wivel. 2018. "How Do Small Island States Maximize Influence? Creole Diplomacy and the Smart State Foreign Policy of the Seychelles." *Journal of the Indian Ocean Region* 14 (2): 170–188.

Chong, Alan. 2010. "Small State Soft Power Strategies: Virtual Enlargement in the Cases of the Vatican City State and Singapore." *Cambridge Review of International Affairs* 23 (3): 383–405.

Corbett, Jack, and Wouter Veenendaal. 2018. *Democracy in Small States: Persisting against All Odds*. Oxford: Oxford University Press.

Corbett, Jack, Xu Yi-Chong, and Patrick Weller. 2019. "Norm Entrepreneurship and Diffusion 'from below' in International Organisations: How the Competent Performance of Vulnerability Generates Benefits for Small States." *Review of International Studies* 45 (4): 647–668.

Crandall, Matthew. 2014. "Soft Security Threats and Small States: The Case of Estonia." *Defence Studies* 14 (1): 30–55.

Dueck, Colin. 2008. *Reluctant Crusaders: Power, Culture, and Change in American Grand Strategy*. Princeton: Princeton University Press.

Earle, Edward M., ed. 1943. *Makers of Modern Strategy*. Princeton, NJ: Princeton University Press.

Eggeling, Kristin. 2017. "Cultural Diplomacy in Qatar: Between 'virtual enlargement,' National Identity Construction and Elite Legitimation." *International Journal of Cultural Policy* 23 (6): 717–731.

Elman, Miriam F. 1995. "The Foreign Policies of Small States: Challenging Neorealism in Its Own Backyard." *British Journal of Political Science* 25 (2): 171-217.

Frei, Daniel. 1968. *Neutralität-Ideal oder Kalkül? Zweihundert Jahre Aussenpolitisches Denken in der Schweiz: Mit Einem Geleitwort von alt Bundesrat Friedrich Traugott Wahlen.* Mannheim: Verlag Huber.

Gaddis, John L. 2009. *What is Grand Strategy?* New Haven: Yale University.

Goetschel, Laurent. 1999. "Neutrality, a Really Dead Concept?" *Cooperation and Conflict* 34 (2): 115-139.

Griffiths, Richard T. 2014. "Economic Security and Size." In *Small States and International Security: Europe and Beyond*, edited by Clive Archer, Alyson Bailes and Anders Wivel, 46-65. London: Routledge.

Grøn, Caroline H., and Anders Wivel. 2011. "Maximizing Influence in the European Union after the Lisbon Treaty: From Small State Policy to Smart State Strategy." *Journal of European Integration* 33 (5): 523-539.

Græger, Nina. 2015. "From 'Forces for Good' to 'Forces for Status'?" In *Small State Status Seeking: Norway's Quest for International Standing*, edited by Benjamin de Carvalho and Iver B. Neumann, 86-107. London: Routledge.

Handel, Michael I. 1990. *Weak States in the International System*. London: Frank Cass.

Haugevik, Kristin. 2018. *Special Relationships in World Politics: Inter-state Friendship and Diplomacy after the Second World War*. London: Routledge.

Hart, Basil L.1942. *The British Way in Warfare: Adaptability and Mobility*. London: Penguin.

Hill, Christopher. 2016. *Foreign Policy in the Twenty-First Century*. London: Palgrave.

Jakobsen, Peter Viggo. 2009. "Small States, Big Influence: The Overlooked Nordic Influence on the Civilian ESDP." *Journal of Common Market Studies* 47 (1): 81-102.

Janis, Irvin L. 1982. *Groupthink: Psychological Studies of Policy Decisions and Fiascoes*. Boston MA: Houghton Mifflin.

Jervis, Robert. 1978. "Cooperation under the Security Dilemma." *World Politics* 30 (2): 172-173.

Karsh, Efraim. 1988. "International Cooperation and Neutrality." *Journal of Peace Research* 25 (1): 57-67.

Keohane, Robert O. 1969. "'Lilliputians' Dilemma: Small States in International Politics." *International Organization* 23 (2): 291-310.

Kennedy, Paul M. 1991. "Grand Strategies in War and Peace: Toward a Broader Definition." In *Grand Strategies in War and Peace*, edited by Paul M. Kennedy, 1-10. New Haven, CT: Yale University Press.

Krause, Volker J., and David Singer, J. 2001. "Minor Powers, Alliances and Armed Conflict: Some Preliminary Patterns." In *Small States and Alliances*, edited by Erich Reiter and Heinz Gärtner, 15-23. Vienna: Physica-Verlag.

Maass, Matthias. 2017. *Small States in World Politics: The Story of Small State Survival, 1648-2016*. Manchester: Manchester University Press.

Morgenthau, Hans J. 1939. "The resurrection of neutrality in Europe." *American Political Science Review* 33 (3): 473-486.

Morrow, James D. 1991. "Alliances and Asymmetry: An Alternative to the Capability Aggregation Model of Alliances." *American Journal of Political Science* 35 (4): 904-933.

Mouritzen, Hans, and Anders Wivel. 2005. "Constellation Theory." In *The Geopolitics of Euro-Atlantic Integration*, edited by Hans Mouritzen and Anders Wivel, 15-42. London: Routledge.

Murray, Williamson. 2011. "Thoughts on Grand Strategy." In *The Shaping of Grand Strategy: Policy, Diplomacy, and War*, edited by Williamson Murray, Richard Hart Sinnreich, and James Lacey, 1–33. Cambridge: Cambridge University Press.

Neumann, Iver B., and Benjamin de Cavalho. 2015. "Introduction: Small States and Status." In *Small State Status Seeking: Norway's Quest for International Standing*, edited by Benjamin de Carvalho and Iver B. Neumann, 1–21. London: Routledge.

Neumann, Iver B., and Sieglinde Gstöhl. 2006. "Introduction: Lilliputians in Gulliver's World?" In *Small States in International Relations*, edited by Christine Ingebritsen, Iver B. Neumann, Sieglinde Gstöhl and Jessica Beyer, 3–36. Seattle: University of Washington Press.

Olson, Mancur, and Richard Zeckhauser. 1966. "An Economic Theory of Alliances." *The Review of Economics and Statistics* 48 (3): 266–279.

Panke, Diana. 2012. "Dwarfs in International Negotiations: How Small States Make Their Voices Heard." *Cambridge Review of International Affairs* 25 (3): 313–328.

Pedi, Revecca, and Katerina K. Sarri. 2019. "From the 'Small but Smart State' to the 'Small and Entrepreneurial State': Introducing a Framework for Effective Small State Strategies within the EU and Beyond." *Baltic Journal of European Studies* 9 (1): 3–19.

Porter, Patrick. 2018. "Why America's Grand Strategy Has Not Changed: Power, Habit, and the US Foreign Policy Establishment." *International Security* 42 (4): 9–46.

Posen, Barry R. 1984. *The Sources of Military Doctrine: France, Britain, and Germany*. Ithaca: Cornell University Press.

Press-Barnathan, Galia. 2012. "Western Europe, NATO, and the United States: Leash Slipping, Not Leash Cutting." In *Beyond Great Powers and Hegemons: Why Secondary States Support, Follow or Challenge*, edited by Kristen P. Williams, Steven E. Lobell, and Neal G. Jesse, 112–127. Stanford: Stanford University Press.

Rickli, Jean-Marc. 2008. "European Small States' Military Policies after the Cold War: From Territorial to Niche Strategies." *Cambridge Review of International Affairs* 21 (3): 307–325.

Rickli, Jean-Marc, and Khalid S. Almezaini. 2017. "Theories of Small States' Foreign and Security Policies." In *The small Gulf States: Foreign and Security Policies Before and After the Arab Spring*, edited by Khalid. S. Almezaini and Jean-Marc Rickli, 8–30. London: Routledge.

Rothstein, Robert. 1968. *Alliances and Small Powers*. New York: Columbia University Press

Sarapuu, Külli, and Tina Randma-Liiv. 2020. "Small States: Public Management and Policy-Making." In *Handbook on the Politics of Small States*, edited by Godfrey Baldacchino and Anders Wivel 55–69. Cheltenham: Edward Elgar.

Shaw, Timothy M. 2014. "What Caribbean post-2015? Developmental and/or Fragile? Old versus New Security?" In *Small States and International Security: Europe and Beyond*, edited by Clive Archer, Alyson Bailes, and Anders Wivel, 223–240. London: Routledge.

Silove, Nina. 2018. "Beyond the Buzzword: The Three Meanings of 'Grand Strategy.'" *Security Studies* 27 (1): 27–57.

Simpson, Archie W. 2014. "The Security of the European Micro-States." In *Small States and International Security: Europe and Beyond*, edited by Clive Archer, Alyson Bailes, and Anders Wivel, 167–184. London: Routledge.

Snyder, Glenn H. 1984. "The Security Dilemma in Alliance Politics." *World Politics* 36 (4): 461–495.

Tessman, Brock F. 2012. "System Structure and State Strategy: Adding Hedging to the Menu." *Security Studies* 21 (2): 192–231.

Thorhallsson, Baldur, ed. 2018. *Small States and Shelter Theory: Iceland's External Affairs*. London: Routledge.

Thorhallsson, Baldur, and Sverrir Steinsson. 2017. "Small State Foreign Policy". In *Oxford Research Encyclopaedia of Politics*. Oxford: Oxford University Press.

Thucydides, P. J. (431 B.C.E. [2009]). *The Peloponnesian War*. Oxford: Oxford University Press.

Vital, David. 1967. *The Inequality of States: A Study of the Small Power in International Relations*. Oxford: Clarendon Press.

Wallace, William. 1999. "Small European States and European Policy-Making: Strategies, Roles, Possibilities." In *Between Autonomy and Influence: Small States and the European Union*, edited by William Wallace et al., 11–26. Arena Report No. 1/99. Oslo: Arena.

Wehner, Leslie. 2020. "The Foreign Policy of South American Small Powers in Regional and International Politics." In *Handbook on the Politics of Small States*, edited by Godfrey Baldacchino and Anders Wivel, 259–277. Cheltenham: Edward Elgar.

Weitsman, Patricia A. 2014. *Waging War: Alliances, Coalitions, and Institutions of Interstate Violence*. Stanford: Stanford University Press.

Wivel, Anders, and Christine Ingebritsen. 2019. "Why Shelter Theory Matters: Ramifications for International Relations and Small State Studies." In *Small States and Shelter Theory: Iceland's External Affairs*, edited by Baldur Thorhallsson, 205–213. London: Routledge.

Wivel, Anders, and T.V. Paul, eds. 2019. *International Institutions and Power Politics: Bridging the Divide*. Washington, DC: Georgetown University Press.

CHAPTER 31

THE GRAND STRATEGIES OF VIOLENT REBEL GROUPS

DANIEL BYMAN

VIOLENT rebellion seems a losing proposition. Peaceful protest is often more successful, and the vast majority of would-be freedom fighters are quashed before their group can take up arms in large numbers (Hoffman 2017; Byman 2008, 165–200; Chenoweth and Stephan 2011). As J. Bowyer Bell argues, "The assets of the state are so apparent, so compelling, so easy to number, chart, and grasp, and the prospects of the rebel are so faint, that only the most optimistic risk an armed struggle" (Bell 1994, 115). However, a select few do form terrorist groups, insurgencies, or even mini armies that duke it out with government forces as relative equals and achieve a modicum of success. Some of these groups have at best the basic rudiments of a strategy, while still others carefully ponder how violence today might lead to victory tomorrow. Yet even those more strategic groups must wrestle with the numerous deficiencies rebel groups often face, ranging from limited and fickle international support to unskilled, rapacious, and thuggish fighters who alienate the population they claim to liberate.

This chapter examines a range of strategic options groups have used over the years with varying degrees of success. These include trying to wear down government forces, attracting significant foreign help, winning over the local population, and intimidating a range of foes in the hope of undermining the government. In many cases strategies focus on organizational survival, trying to endure and attract resources and recruits while making an area ungovernable or inhospitable for regime forces. The chapter weighs the requirements, strengths, and weaknesses of each approach and how the enemy government shapes the best strategy for the group. It illustrates its arguments with examples from history and a longer description of the Palestinian experience. The chapter concludes by discussing how states might disrupt violent rebel group strategies.

What Are Violent Rebel Groups, and What Does Strategy Mean?

The term "violent rebel groups" is a catch-all category, encompassing massive armies that fight civil wars with tens of thousands of soldiers under arms to small terrorist organizations that may have a few dozen active fighters. All, however, are rebels. That is, they are not recognized states and are usually fighting to control or create one.

Mao Zedong, the brilliant rebel leader whose small band of followers would eventually create mass armies that defeated nationalist forces and conquered China, describes stages of a revolutionary group's struggle that, as a rough guide, are applicable to other rebel movements. For Mao, the ultimate goal was to build a large conventional army. Preceding stages involved guerrilla war and political preparation. Other experts, such as French counterinsurgency specialist David Galula, describe how terrorist groups may try to bypass some of the process, using terrorism to undermine a regime and grab mass attention. Although technology and global political conditions have changed dramatically since Mao's day, the basic concepts are still relevant. A goal of some groups is simply to get to another stage in the struggle where they can they adopt a different strategy (Galula 2006, 1–42; Tse-tung 2000, 41–93).

Violent rebel groups can thus be organized along a spectrum. At one end are small terrorist groups, such as the 1970s Red Army Faction in Germany, which number several dozen members and are only capable of kidnappings, shootings, and other limited, if disruptive, terrorist attacks (Aust 2008). More capable are groups that can wage guerrilla war and mobilize at least part of the populace, enabling them to form an insurgency. The more successful insurgencies hold territory, and act as de facto, albeit unrecognized, governments in part of a territory, providing services, dispensing justice, and taxing the population. Farther along the spectrum are those that can form their own conventional military units or otherwise hope to conquer territory directly, as the Islamic State did at its peak. Strategies for victory often vary depending on where a group is along this spectrum (Central Intelligence Agency 2012, 2; Weinstein 2006).

For violent rebel groups, strategies are about not only ensuring security but "causing" victory, employing political and military means to this end. Violent rebel groups are somewhat akin to small states, where much of their security and success is beyond their control, but they still have plans, make choices, prioritize, and hold organizing principles about how their actions will lead to victory (Posen 1986, 13; Silove 2018, 51).

Impediments to Violent Rebel Group Strategies

Rebel groups have an array of weaknesses that hinder every stage of the grand strategy process, ranging from defining goals and formulating a theory of victory to implementing the strategy and adapting it as conditions change.

Some groups are simply not strategic. J. Bowyer Bell contends that for many groups their strategy of victory is simply a theory of history: the proletariat will overthrow the bourgeoisie, the foreign invaders will be ousted, God's people (whoever they are) will triumph, and so on (Bell 1994, 115–150). Other groups do not formulate a strategy and fall into one through trial and error. The Provisional Irish Republican Army, for example, at first thought that making Northern Ireland ungovernable would prompt a British withdrawal and, as that failed, switched to wearing down the British through constant attacks as a form of attrition. (Moloney 2003, 28–132) Some groups attempted multiple strategies simultaneously, heedless of possible tensions among the different options.

As rebel groups form their strategies, they may adopt unrealistic strategies of victory. From the start, rebel groups often overstate the weakness of their enemies, blithely assuming that the success of a similar group in another country or a temporary moment of weakness of a regime suggests that collapse is imminent. Yet even relatively weak states can marshal considerable power relative to the rebel group.

Groups also overstate their ability to implement strategies, in part because they frequently attract poor recruits. Although the first people to join a terrorist group are often altruists, they are usually unskilled and unprepared for a violent, underground struggle (Hoffman 2017, 37). Too often they rely on a romanticized version of a guerrilla struggle in another country when planning victory. More established groups may attract recruits who are too violent, unable to rein in their worst impulses and indeed join the rebel group because they want to commit violence. As such, rebel leaders have a hard time modulating their use of violence to achieve the results they want (Shapiro 2013, 26–81; Byman 2019; Bakke 2014, 150–187).

Most terrorist groups and many insurgencies must operate at least in part underground, which poses an additional set of challenges and makes it harder to adapt as conditions change. Underground organizations suffer from poor information flows; communication is a form of exposure that regime forces can use to identify their enemies. Thus, the constant feedback that shapes both the formulation and implementation of effective strategy is inhibited. Indeed, as Jacob Shapiro has found, groups frequently find it difficult to determine accurately how successful their own operatives are (Shapiro 2013, 26–81; Della Porta 1992). A number of groups, notably the Provisional Irish Republican Army, even found prison helpful for designing and reformulating strategy, as it allowed them a place to communicate and discuss their operational and organizational weaknesses without the demands of constant struggle (Moloney 2003, 133–162; McDonald 2003).

As groups are short on resources and many need a haven, many work with a state sponsor, which has its own objectives and strategy of victory. Although the state sponsor may provide arms, money, training, and a sanctuary, this comes at a price. In particular, the state sponsor may seek to limit the level of violence the group uses for fear of retaliation, seek to shift a group's targeting, or even sell out their proxies in exchange for a rival government's concessions in other areas. In other words, the quest to get the necessary means often interferes with the ability to pursue the desired ends (Salehyan 2007, 217–242; Salehyan, Gleditsch, and Cunningham 2011, 709–744; Byman 2005).

Many rebel groups have a de facto foreign policy, and if they fail to develop one, their strategies quickly become unrealistic and the long-term consequences can be disastrous. At times this involves seeking sponsors, but it also may involve attempts to attract international recognition or to avoid making new enemies. The Islamic State defined itself in opposition to all parts of what it deemed an infidel system. It failed to recognize its relative weakness and pursued a war against all, taking on not only the Syrian and Iraqi governments but also the United States, France, Turkey, Saudi Arabia, and other countries, thus inviting an international coalition to form against it and ultimately devastate the group's territorial control.

Finally, political causes and movements that have multiple groups frequently suffer from strategic incoherence or otherwise work at cross purposes: groups may have coherent strategies, but the movement as a whole does not. Rival groups have an incentive to amp up violence, conduct spectacular attacks, or otherwise act in ways that may not be in harmony with the most powerful groups or the best interests of the movement as a whole. Signaling confusion is a common result (Bakke, Cunningham, and Seymour 2012, 265–283).

Strategic Approaches

This section lays out an array of rebel strategies and discusses the benefits, limits, and risks of each. The initial ones presented are strategies for outright victory, but most are strategies for improvement. That is to say, they are strategies for becoming a more effective group, for weakening the government, or otherwise are transitional strategies for moving forward and being able to take on a new, more promising, strategy.

Strategies of Victory

Violent rebel groups have at least three strategies for outright victory: conquest, attrition, and outgoverning. Much of the time, however, rebel group weaknesses and the impediments listed above leave them pursuing an array of intermediate strategies designed to improve their organizational position and inch them closer to the ability to pursue true grand strategies. Several variables shape the likelihood of a strategy's success. They include: the number of groups involved in the struggle; the group's ability to recruit; the type of government the group is facing; the level of interest of the state the group is fighting; and the group's ability to attract foreign help.

Conquest

It is rare but possible for nonstate actors to win a conflict by defeating government forces on the battlefield. Vietnamese communists, the Rwandan Patriotic Front, and the Libyan rebels opposed to Qaddafi are examples of groups that fought head-to-head battles with regime forces and triumphed.

Most rebel groups, however, are militarily weak. In a conventional fight, even a weak military with tanks and other heavier systems can easily destroy lightly armed bands of rebels. Rebels, especially at the start of the fight, lack the weapons, force size, training, and other essentials to take on and win over state forces. They also need large numbers of recruits to take on conventional armies.

Because of this weakness, many of these groups win due to foreign help. Southern Vietnamese communists depended heavily on North Vietnam, which in turn depended heavily on China and the Soviet Union for support. Libyan rebels were on the brink of defeat until NATO and several Arab countries intervened, reversing the tide of battle (Michaels 2013, 37–60; Hastings 2018). Foreign help, however, is rarely sufficient to help rebel groups overcome their many weaknesses even in those rare cases when foreign sponsors are willing to provide consistent and considerable backing.

Attrition

Attrition is a time-honored strategy of warfare. As Kydd and Walter argue, attrition's goal "is to persuade the enemy that the group is strong and resolute enough to inflict serious costs, so that the enemy yields to the terrorists' demands." They further note that the state's level of interest, ability to retaliate, and cost sensitivity all shape the effectiveness of this strategy (Kydd and Walter 2006, 59). The Provisional Irish Republican Army enjoyed considerable success with an attrition strategy, using "a long war" to exhaust British and Protestant opposition (O'Brien 1999).

For attrition to succeed, the rebel group needs to be able to sustain more casualties than the government relative to the level of interest involved. Much depends on the casualty sensitivity of the combatants. Russia, for example, took over 5,000 military and interior ministry casualties in the second Chechen war without suffering unrest, while Israel and the United States are far more casualty sensitive (though the level varies considerably based on other factors) (Khalidi 2003, 101–126; Berinsky 2009; Gelpi, Reifler, and Feaver 2007, 151–174). In contrast, for the most part, rebel groups are casualty acceptant. Some rebel groups, like the Rwandan Patriotic Front, knowingly risked a genocide against their own people in order to pursue their political goals. They accepted the risk of violence and even hoped that it would generate foreign intervention against the regime they opposed (Kuperman 2005, 149–173). For the Vietnamese communists, a casualty ratio of almost ten to one against US forces was difficult but acceptable given the level of interest: existential for the Vietnamese, and marginal for the United States.

Although attrition is more realistic for most rebel groups than conquest, it too is difficult, especially for smaller groups. Rebels often take massive casualties, and they need to be able to attract large numbers of new recruits—and to keep attracting them even when the inevitable downturns in the struggle occur—to pursue an attrition strategy. If the group's overall cause is popular, as was true with the Provisional IRA, it may find more willing recruits, and some groups are able to fill their ranks via coercion. However, even a popular cause may not be enough if a group is perceived as inept. Rival groups may emerge as a result, or much of the population will simply choose to sit out the struggle altogether.

The level of government interest in a particular territory or issue also varies, and attrition is less practical when government interest is high. The Irgun, for example, was able to drive the United Kingdom out of mandatory Palestine in part because the United Kingdom was exhausted by the Second World War and did not see Palestine as a vital interest (Hoffman 2015). If a group is seeking to seize territory or change a regime, in contrast, full resistance is the norm. Thus, the level of damage inflicted by attrition, the resources a government will put into its intelligence service and military, and other factors will vary according to the relative interest of the government being attacked. If the group seeks a fundamental change in government or society, it should expect a high level of resistance and a regime willing to sustain a large number of casualties.

Outgoverning

Insurgency can be depicted as a competition in governance (Central Intelligence Agency 2012). Indeed, governance failure is often at the root of an insurgency, as it provides both grievances and operational space for rebels to organize (Jones 2008, 7–40). When a rebel group is able to control territory, it can tax, conscript, and otherwise act like a government and, in so doing, begin the process of state-building (Tilly 1985, 35–60). For groups with limited territorial ambitions, this process can lead to a de facto state and with it, possible recognition, or at least toleration. For groups with more ambitious objectives, the autonomous enclave can be a base for conquest or for intermediate strategies that advance their position relative to the state and group rivals.

For some groups, such a quasi-state enables them to better wage a war of attrition or conquest, but for others it can be an end in itself. Secessionist groups hope to turn a controlled region into a state of their own or at least to provide their people with a modicum of autonomy (Ó Beacháin, Comai, and Tsurtsumia-Zurabashvil 2016, 440–466). Megan Stewart finds that rebel groups with a secessionist agenda are more likely to provide services to all communities, in part because they seek to gain international recognition and thus want to prove the credibility of their governance (Stewart 2018, 205–226).

Outgoverning requires a high degree of military capacity relative to the state, and thus rebel groups that adopt this strategy must overcome the military weakness identified above. Simply creating a controlled territory, in fact, can be a boon for the government enemy as it puts the rebel group above ground, forcing it to defend territory in conventional military operations and enabling the state to target its personnel. The Islamic State, for example, exercised a high degree of governance over its so-called caliphate, but it fell in large part because it could not defend the territory it controlled against enemy forces (Callimachi 2018). In addition, many groups lack a strong capacity for governance. Scholars have identified preexisting cleavages and how groups raise resources as key variables explaining performance on key governance indicators (Staniland 2014; Weinstein 2006).

Intermediate Strategies

Because such true grand strategies are frequently elusive or unrealistic, at least for groups with many weaknesses that are facing a strong state, groups often focus on more immediate strategies designed to weaken the state, increase recruitment, gain foreign support, or otherwise improve their position.

For many groups, simply enduring becomes the overwhelming goal of the group—with the hope (at times implicit) that by enduring the government will collapse of its own weight or otherwise be unable to continue the struggle. In many cases groups seek to increase their recruitment, fundraising, military proficiency, or otherwise make themselves stronger and thus better able to defeat a regime via attrition or conquest or to control their own territory. The strategies below have the potential to strengthen substate groups under certain conditions, and multiple strategies may be employed by a group at the same time.

Ungovernability

Some groups try to create chaos and otherwise prevent the government from functioning. This can serve several purposes. First, it can go hand in hand with an attrition strategy, forcing a government to deploy more troops to protect government services and communities, thus increasing the cost of a struggle and making the regime more likely to concede. Second, it can decrease confidence in government, making communities more willing to seek out rebels to provide law and order and thus giving rebels a base. Third, it can enable rebels to outgovern the state by demonstrating a regime's inability to provide services and protect its people.

Jihadist groups often favor this strategy. Jihadist strategist Abu Bakr Naji, for example, has called for numerous attacks in remote parts of a country. This will stretch government forces, eventually compelling them to focus on strategic and populated areas. This in turn creates chaos in less-inhabited areas, which jihadists can then exploit by offering locals law and order and otherwise establishing their own governance and outgoverning a regime (Naji 2006, 23–61).

As with most strategies, some degree of state weakness is necessary to create an ungoverned space. A strong government facing a weak group can protect necessary areas while hunting the group, using its resource superiority to deny this strategy. At times, a group may need to contend with other strong nonstate actors. Al Qaeda, for example, tried to establish a base in the early 1990s in Somalia, but local clans robbed the group or otherwise prevented it from acting effectively (Combating Terrorism Center 2007). Many states can also function with part of their territory outside government control. If the regime dominates key cities, resources, and constituencies, it can endure indefinitely, especially if it is able to take casualties and sustain a low-level conflict. Finally, pursuing ungovernability can backfire as a strategy, leading residents to blame the group, not the government, and seeing them more as thugs while supporting a strong regime response.

Intimidation

Terrorists, insurgents, and other rebels often try to force the population to be on their side—what Kydd and Walter label a strategy of intimidation. This strategy requires the group to punish locals who work for the government such as police, village chiefs, and party leaders, or supporters of rival groups. Anyone who opposes the rebels will suffer harsh consequences. Thus, even if a population disagrees with the rebels' ideology or otherwise does not favor the group, they will still obey it out of fear (Kydd and Walter 2006, 66–67).

This achievement, however, is an intermediate goal. When groups control the population, they have more resources in terms of recruits and money, and it denies intelligence to the government (Leites and Wolf Jr. 1970). This enables them to better pursue a policy of attrition, create a parallel government, and otherwise serves their ends. Intimidation also furthers ungovernability, making the police, local officials, and others afraid to enforce order and provide services.

Intimidation is heavily dependent on government capacity, both to protect its own supporters and to threaten those of the rebels. If a government can police its own territory, an intimidation strategy is far harder, as are attempts to make a country ungovernable. Similarly, governments that can police their borders and that have a strong military make it less likely that neighboring states can intervene or provide an effective sanctuary for rebels. If an area is contested by both rebels and government forces, massacres of civilians are more likely (Kalyvas 1999, 243–285).

Provocation

Another approach taken in particular by terrorists and small rebel groups is provocation, which Kydd and Walter define as an attempt to persuade a population that the regime being opposed is evil and untrustworthy (Kydd and Walter 2006, 69–70). Provocation seeks to push the government to take politically counterproductive steps, usually an overreaction that harms civilians and otherwise makes the regime look cruel, incompetent, or both. Attacks that receive considerable media attention and/or generate massive public concern can force governments to be seen as acting. In so doing, they may demonize the entire community the rebels claim to represent, arrest indiscriminately (or worse), or otherwise drive supporters into the arms of the rebels. Provocation can thus increase the recruiting and other resource base of rebel groups. It is frequently linked to intimidation, as high-profile attacks on agents of the state can intimidate others if the state does not respond.

Provocation, however, can easily backfire. On the one hand, it can provoke a near-genocidal level of brutality or at least a high level of repression that effectively quashes the group and destroys political organization of all sorts. On the other hand, regimes with effective intelligence services are often able to arrest, kill, or otherwise disrupt the specific militants without provoking a broader backlash, thus improving their reputation for effectiveness while damaging the rebels' image among the population (Byman 2016, 62–93; Kydd and Walter 2006, 70; Byman 2014, 837–863).

Inspiration

Related to provocation, and often overlapping with it, are efforts to publicize the rebel cause and inspire others to join the fray through symbolic violence—often labeled "propaganda of the deed" (Hoffman 2017, 5–7; Bueno de Mesquita and Dickson 2007, 364–381). Violence, as such, is a form of propaganda. At times, such efforts are largely peaceful actions designed to grab attention, such as when M-19 guerrillas in Colombia stole the sword of Simon Bolivar, the liberator of South America. More ominously, M-19 also took American and other hostages, another way to grab media attention (Washington Post Foreign Service 1985).

Assassination is a common form of propaganda of the deed. Late nineteenth- and early twentieth-century anarchists, for example, sought to kill world leaders and powerful industrialists to show the vulnerability of the capitalist system, the desperate situation of ordinary workers, and the determination of those seeking change (Joll 1964, 121). By demonstrating the system's weakness and their own leadership, the silent majority of supporters would shake off their fear and lethargy and act.

For a few groups, inspiration seems an end in itself. Naïve revolutionaries of all stripes believe they are the match that will ignite a larger conflagration. How that leads to victory, however, is often less specified, and the more strategic revolutionaries link inspiration to other strategies.

Such inspiration, of course, requires that there is a silent majority and that the violence appeals to them, which it rarely does independent of a harsh and bumbling government reaction. Chenoweth and Stephan find that violence usually alienates moderates and as a result backfires (Chenoweth and Stephan 2011). Inspiration often is at odds with intimidation, which frequently requires assassinating low-level policemen, city officials, or others who have local connections and respect, and whose murder would cast the rebels more as thugs than heroes. When it is a form of provocation, it can also justify an effective state response. Russian anarchists' assassination of Czar Alexander II in 1881, for example, was meant to inspire the masses to rise up but instead led to a brutal crackdown on the plotters, their networks, and their safe houses (Hoffman 2017, 6).

Democratic governments and autocracies with some sensitivity to public opinion are better able to decrease the impact of inspiration (or the negative impact of provocation) by co-opting a group's cause and accepting measures short of absolute success—such as, say, a high degree of autonomy for an ethnic group or more privileges for a workers' movement—that may decrease a group's appeal.

Foreign Assistance

For many rebel groups, success depends on convincing neighbors, a major power, or the broader international community to assist. Some groups provide social services to rival communities or otherwise try to show their commitment to governance in order to attract international recognition and otherwise legitimate their claims to a state (Stewart 2018, 205–226). Others try to appeal to foreigners along ideological, communal, or strategic lines.

Part of the reason groups seek help is practical. Attrition, for example, is far easier if a group enjoys a nearby haven. Such a space allows them to protect their leadership, modulate the pace of operations (thus controlling their own risk of casualties), and otherwise be able to drag out a conflict. If a state is willing to arm, fund, train, and otherwise assist the rebels, they are better able to inflict casualties or even achieve military victory. Rwanda, for example, backed a minor warlord, Laurent-Désiré Kabila, with its own military forces, overthrowing in 1997 the weak government of Zaire (now Congo) led by Mobutu Sésé Seko. In a few cases foreign governments might also back groups' attempts to create parallel governments by supporting ethnic enclaves. Russia, for example, helped rebels in Ukraine, Georgia, and other parts of the former Soviet Union carve out small, often unrecognized, states protected by the umbrella of Russian military power.

Internationalization carries tremendous risks. The violence inherent in intimidation, ungovernability, and similar approaches can alienate foreign countries, convincing them to back the government. When Algerian jihadists fighting the government there in the 1990s expanded their operations to France with terrorist attacks on the Paris metro, the French government stepped up its support for the regime in Algiers. The 9/11 attacks attracted tremendous attention to al Qaeda, making it a household name, but it also brought on the wrath of the United States, with the result being the destruction of al Qaeda's global networks and the loss of its haven in Afghanistan. Al Qaeda lost more than 80 percent of its members in Afghanistan by the end of 9/11. Its training infrastructure there was destroyed, and US and allied campaigns destroyed its global networks. As one leading jihadist lamented, the 9/11 attacks "cast jihadists into a fiery furnace ... A hellfire which consumed most of their leaders, fighters, and bases" (Burke 2011, 156; Wright 2008; Byman 2015, 42–44).

The availability of foreign aid to rebels, and its scope and scale, also varies. Some ideologies are so noxious that all but the most Machiavellian or desperate regimes will shun the groups propagating them. Other groups, in contrast, may play into an enduring rivalry, being well-positioned to take advantage of a neighboring state that shares its hostility to the government. Iran and Iraq, for example, aided Kurdish rebels in each other's countries in the 1980s to undermine their enemy (McDowall 2004, 324–343). In rare but important cases, a government may take up the banner of the rebel group out of genuine conviction or ideological solidarity. As Arab nationalism spread in the Arab world in the 1950s and 1960s, an array of states aided Palestinian groups out of conviction as well as political necessity (Sayigh 1997).

Similarly, as the Palestinians and countless others have learned, foreign support is fickle. Governments may abandon rebels because they receive concessions in other areas, because of coercion, or because they see the rebels as a threat to their own regime. In addition, they may back rival factions or otherwise try to divide the movement to keep it weak. Syria in the 1970s and 1980s, for example, placed severe limits on the Palestinians within its territory and at times backed rival movements to undermine the leadership of Yasir Arafat. Iran backed Kurdish rebels against Saddam Hussein's regime in the early 1970s but, after a series of Iraqi concessions, abruptly ended its support, leading to massacres of the Kurdish rebels (Byman 2005, 117–154; McDowall 2003, 323–342).

The Palestinian Example

The Palestinian groups—among the more impressive in history in terms of their endurance, repeated uses of violence, and success in putting their issues on the world agenda—illustrate many of the impediments substate groups face in developing and implementing a coherent strategy. Their experiences also reveal the strengths and weaknesses of different strategic options. The Palestinian groups spanned the spectrum of substate groups in their diversity and strength. Some, such as the Abu Nidal Organization, were pure terrorist groups that did little else. Others, like Fatah, at times used terrorism, but also waged a guerrilla war, and held sanctuaries in neighboring countries where it acted as a state-within-a-state. Hamas, the Palestinian Islamist group, went from a small terrorist group to the de facto government of Gaza.

Palestinian groups often had naïve views of their Israeli adversary, and it took decades for them to recognize their misperceptions. After the 1967 war, Yasir Arafat, Fatah's leader and the dominant Palestinian revolutionary figure for many decades, sought to replicate the success anti-French rebels had in Algeria, driving Israeli "colonialists" back to their "homes" in Europe. This approach was a dramatic misreading of Israel's nature and level of interest in the territory it controlled, especially given the history of the Holocaust and destruction of Europe's Jewry (Yaari 1970, 133–135; Gazit 1995, 22; Sela 2014; Sayigh 1997).

Other strategies had more success. International hijackings and terrorism, for example, focused attention on the Palestinian cause and inspired Palestinians to join militant groups. Palestinian terrorists took Israeli athletes hostage in the 1972 Olympics in part because the cameras of the world were focused on Munich, the site of the games. Although the ostensible reason for the operation was the release of Palestinian prisoners, the primary goal was global attention. As George Habash, the head of the Popular Front for the Liberation of Palestine, noted before Palestinian international terrorism commenced, "World opinion has never been either with us or against us; it has just kept on ignoring us." Another Palestinian terrorist leader noted that after Munich, "world opinion was forced to take note of the Palestinian drama" (Fallaci 1970, 33; Iyad and Rouleau 1981, 112).

Over time, constant if low-level Palestinian violence did lead Israel to the negotiating table, with serious peace talks occurring throughout the 1990s—an at least partly successful strategy of attrition. These collapsed, however, in part because of continued violence by splinter groups that acted as spoilers (Pearlman 2009, 79–109). During the Second Intifada, Palestinian attacks on Israel led to harsh Israeli crackdowns and did create a sense of weariness and misery among the Israeli public conducive to the success of attrition. The response to Palestinian provocations increased support for militant violence. However, the effective Israeli response gradually suffocated Hamas and other groups. In addition, the violence strengthened a now-dominant Israeli narrative that the Palestinians were not a true partner for peace. Thus, the violence backfired in the end.

Palestinian groups also were able to control territory effectively, giving them at least some credit for governance. Fatah, for example, enjoyed significant autonomy in Lebanon for much of the 1970s and controlled Palestinian refugee camps there. Israel withdrew from Gaza in 2005 in part due to a successful attrition strategy by Hamas. In the subsequent years, Hamas became the de facto government of Gaza and developed its own military forces. It warred with Israel several times, but its strong roots and military presence enabled it to deter Israel from reoccupying Gaza (International Crisis Group 2018).

For decades, different Palestinian groups worked with different state sponsors. Some of this sponsorship was direct, as when militants conducted cross-border attacks into Israel from Egypt. In other cases it was more passive, with states like Lebanon tolerating Palestinian activity because they lacked the capacity to crush it or feared the political consequences of doing so or, in the case of Saudi Arabia, saw their own citizens' financial contributions as legitimate. As a result, the Palestinians enjoyed arms, money, and other forms of support. In addition, they enjoyed havens at different times in Egypt, Jordan, Lebanon, and Syria—all "frontline" states—as well as financial backing and organizational toleration from other Arab countries. However, some states employed different Palestinian groups such as the Abu Nidal Organization to assassinate rivals. In other cases, as in Jordan and Lebanon, Palestinian groups became involved in the politics of their haven, leading to violence there and, in the case of Jordan, a brutal crackdown that led to thousands of Palestinian casualties (Bailey 1984).

Arafat's dominant Fatah faction at times tried to limit the violence to certain targets and constrain the use of international terrorism. This caution became more pronounced after Arafat consolidated his leadership position in the mid-1970s, and his group became less convinced that Algeria or other models could easily be emulated. Rival groups, however, continued to use international terrorism in the name of the Palestinian cause (Sela 2014; Savigh 1997). Other small groups, like the Democratic Front for the Liberation of Palestine, attacked clear civilian targets, such as a school attack in Israel in 1974 that killed 27 people, tarring the overall cause, especially with international audiences. When Fatah tried to embrace peace talks in the 1990s, attacks on Israeli civilian targets by Hamas and Palestine Islamic Jihad, both sponsored by Iran, disrupted negotiations, creating a cycle of mistrust and violence that contributed to the collapse of negotiations.

Despite all these problems, the Palestinian groups enjoyed considerable public support, enabling them to recruit effectively. They suffered numerous operational defeats and political setbacks, but there was always a steady supply of recruits for militant organizations. Thus, individual groups rose and fell, but the cause in general was able to sustain itself over decades and, at times, Palestinians gained significant concessions.

The Palestinian example illustrates the need to distinguish between a group and the movement as a whole. Palestinian groups rose and fell over the years while the Palestinian national movement remained robust (Savigh 1997). In such cases, a particular group may suffer a setback or even be wiped out, but others in the movement can pick up the banner and raise it even higher. As the Palestinian experience suggests, however, the presence of multiple groups weakens a movement and hinders its ability to act strategically. Groups at times shoot at one another, weakening the movement as a whole. Group competition may lead some groups to attempt to "outbid" others, using more violence than is strategically sensible in order to siphon off popular support for a rival (Bloom 2004, 61–88; Bakke, Cunningham, and Seymour 2012, 265–283). In addition, multiple groups hinder attempts to mix violence and negotiations, as governments cannot be sure that concessions will result in a decline in violence.

Government Counterstrategies

Governments fighting insurgents, terrorists, and other nonstate violent rebels have many options that can decrease the effectiveness of rebels' grand and intermediate strategies.

Diplomacy is vital for stopping or limiting the help rebels get from outside governments. At times this can involve a public diplomacy campaign to win over a populace and decrease political support for the rebels among potentially supportive states. British efforts to tarnish the IRA and decrease support for its activities in the United States benefited tremendously when the Republic of Ireland began to cooperate with this effort. At times it may be more coercive, such as withholding aid, threatening investment, or even using military force. Sudan, for example, moved away from its policy of supporting an array of terrorist groups in the 1990s due to a mix of diplomatic, economic, and military pressure on Khartoum (Sen 2017). Diminished state support makes it harder for rebels to conquer and hold territory, have the resources necessary for attrition strategies, and otherwise achieve victory.

Government reform offers can also take the wind out of the sails of some rebel groups, satisfying some of their less committed followers and decreasing their popular support and ability to recruit, which in turns makes it hard for them to pursue attrition, conquest, or other strategies that rely on large numbers of operatives and supporters. Land reform can make left-wing causes less attractive to peasants. The Egyptian government gave nonviolent Islamist leaders greater influence over the judiciary and society in the 1990s in an attempt to isolate radical jihadist elements (Kepel 2002, 276–298). All this can make an attrition strategy less viable as a group will find it harder to sustain its losses.

Governments may also need to improve their police and militaries. Functions can include neighborhood monitoring, providing security to ordinary citizens, border protection, and defeating rebel bands of various sizes. Much of the purpose of a functioning military is to take conquest, governance, intimidation, and similar strategies off the table. In addition, security forces provide the protection necessary to ensure that governance continues.

More intelligence is always desirable. In particular, strong intelligence can avoid an overreaction to a provocation strategy, enabling a government to focus on a small subset of suspects rather than a community as a whole. This in turn enables a government response to be proportionate and avoid angering fence-sitters.

In the end, many governments are stuck with suboptimal strategies. They can build up their militaries, but often there are limits on effectiveness. The rebel havens might be diminished, but an enduring rivalry makes some form of support likely. In such cases, governments may find that some conflict is likely to endure for years and that their best bet it to try to minimize its impact rather than expect to defeat the rebels outright.

Conclusions

The best strategy for a group depends on its level of resources, popular support, and other factors that shape its size, power, and overall capabilities. Small groups, of course, cannot realistically expect to conquer or run a parallel government, and attrition would decimate their limited ranks. They must focus on inspiration and provocation to become stronger. A large group, in contrast, can attempt more ambitious strategies. A constant challenge for any group is Sun Tzu's dictum to "know the enemy and know yourself," and have a realistic awareness of the strength of the government and of its own capabilities and levels of popular support.

References

Aust, Stefan. 2008. *The Baader-Meinhof Complex*. New York: Random House.
Bailey, Clinton. 1984. *Jordan's Palestinian Challenge, 1948–1983: A Political History*. Boulder: Westview Press.
Bakke, Kristin, Kathleen Gallagher Cunningham, and Lee Seymour. 2012. "A Plague of Initials: Fragmentation, Cohesion, and Infighting in Civil Wars." *Perspectives on Politics* 10 (2): 265–283.
Bakke, Kristin M. 2014. "Help Wanted? The Mixed Record of Foreign Fighters in Domestic Insurgencies." *International Security* 38 (4): 150–187.

Bell, J. Bowyer. 1994. "The Armed Struggle and Underground Intelligence: An Overview." *Studies in Conflict and Terrorism* 17 (2): 115–150.

Berinsky, Adam J. 2009. *In Time of War: Understanding American Public Opinion from World War II to Iraq*. Chicago: University of Chicago Press.

Bloom, Mia M. 2004. "Palestinian Suicide Bombing: Public Support, Market Share, and Outbidding." *Political Science Quarterly* 119 (1): 61–88.

Burke, Jason. 2011. *The 9/11 Wars*. London: Penguin UK.

Byman, Daniel. 2005. *Deadly Connections: States that Sponsor Terrorism*. Cambridge: Cambridge University Press.

Byman, Daniel 2008. "Understanding Proto-insurgencies." *Journal of Strategic Studies* 31 (2): 165–200.

Byman, Daniel. 2014. "The Intelligence War on Terrorism." *Intelligence and National Security* 29 (6): 837–863.

Byman, Daniel. 2015. *Al Qaeda, the Islamic State, and the Global Jihadist Movement: What Everyone Needs to Know*. Oxford: Oxford University Press.

Byman, Daniel. 2016. "'Death Solves All Problems': The Authoritarian Model of Counterinsurgency." *Journal of Strategic Studies* 39 (1): 62–93.

Byman, Daniel. 2019. *Road Warriors: Foreign Fighters in the Armies of Jihad*. Oxford: Oxford University Press.

Callimachi, Rukmini. 2018. "The ISIS Files." *The New York Times*, April 4, 2018. https://www.nytimes.com/interactive/2018/04/04/world/middleeast/isis-documents-mosul-iraq.html

Central Intelligence Agency. 2012. *Guide to the Analysis of Insurgency*. https://www.hsdl.org/?view&did=713599

Chenoweth, Erica, and Maria J. Stephan. 2011. *Why Civil Resistance Works: The Strategic Logic of Nonviolent Conflict*. New York: Columbia University Press.

Della Porta, Donatella. 1992. *Social Movements and Violence: Participation in Underground Organizations*. Cambridge: Cambridge University Press.

Fallaci, Oriana. 1970. "A Leader of the Fedayeen: 'We Want a War Like the Vietnam War.'" *Life* 68 (22): 33.

Galula, David. 2006. *Counterinsurgency Warfare: Theory and Practice*. Westport, CT: Prager Security International.

Gazit, Shlomo. 1995. *The Carrot and the Stick: Israel's Policy in Judaea and Samaria, 1967–68*, Vol. 3. Washington, D.C.: Bnai Brith Books.

Gelpi, Christopher, Jason Reifler, and Peter Feaver. 2007. "Iraq the Vote: Retrospective and Prospective Foreign Policy Judgments on Candidate Choice and Casualty Tolerance." *Political Behavior* 29 (2): 151–174.

Hastings, Max. 2018. *Vietnam: An Epic Tragedy, 1945–1975*. New York: Harper.

Hoffman, Bruce. 2015. *Anonymous Soldiers: The Struggle for Israel, 1917–1947*. New York: Alfred A. Knopf

Hoffman, Bruce. 2017. *Inside Terrorism*. New York: Columbia University Press.

International Crisis Group. 2018. "Averting War in Gaza" https://www.crisisgroup.org/middle-east-north-africa/eastern-mediterranean/israelpalestine/b60-averting-war-gaza

Iyad, Abu, and Eric Rouleau. 1981. *My Home, My Land: A Narrative of the Palestinian Struggle*. New York: Times Books.

Joll, James. 1964. *The Anarchists*. London: Eyre & Spottiswoode.

Jones, Seth G. 2008. "The Rise of Afghanistan's Insurgency: State Failure and Jihad." *International Security* 32 (4): 7–40.

Kalyvas, Stathis N. 1999. "Wanton and senseless? The Logic of Massacres in Algeria." *Rationality and Society* 11 (3): 243–285.

Kepel, Gilles. 2002. *Jihad: The Trail of Political Islam*. Cambridge: Harvard University Press.

Khalidi, Noor Ahmad. 2003. "Afghanistan: Demographic Consequences of War: 1978–87." *Central Asian Survey* 10 (3): 101–126.

Kuperman, Alan J. 2005. "Suicidal Rebellions and the Moral Hazard of Humanitarian Intervention." *Ethnopolitics* 4 (2): 149–173.

Kydd, Andrew H., and Walter, Barbara F. 2006. "The Strategies of Terrorism." *International Security* 31 (1): 59–60.

Leites, Nathan and Charles Wolf Jr. 1970. "Rebellion and Authority: An Analytic Essay on Insurgent Conflicts." no. RAND-R-462-ARPA. Santa Monica: RAND Corps.

McDonald, Henry. 2003. "Bombers Jail Memoirs Reveal IRA's Long Year." *The Guardian*, March 9, 2003. https://www.theguardian.com/uk/2003/mar/09/northernireland.booksnews

McDowall, David. 2004. *The Kurds*. London: I.B. Tauris.

Michaels, Jeffrey H. 2013. "Able but Not Willing: A Critical Assessment of NATO's Libya Intervention." In *The NATO Intervention in Libya*, edited by Kjell Engelbrekt, Marcus Mohlin, and Charlotte Wagnsson, 37–60. New York: Routledge.

Moloney, Ed. 2003. *A Secret History of the IRA*. New York: W.W. Martin.

Naji, Abu Bakr. 2006. *The Management of Savagery*. Translated by William McCants. John M. Olin Institute for Strategic Studies at Harvard University. http://media.leeds.ac.uk/papers/pmt/exhibits/2800/Management_of_Savagery.pdf

Ó Beacháin, Donnacha, Giorgio Comai, and Ann Tsurtsumia-Zurabashvili. 2016. "The Secret Lives of Unrecognised States: Internal Dynamics, External Relations, and Counter-recognition Strategies." *Small Wars & Insurgencies* 27 (3): 440–466.

O'Brien, Brendan. 1999. *The Long War: the IRA and Sinn Féin*. Syracuse: Syracuse University Press.

Pearlman, Wendy. 2009. "Spoiling Inside and Out: Internal Political Contestation and the Middle East Peace Process." *International Security* 33 (3): 79–109.

Salehyan, Idean. 2007. "Transnational Rebels: Neighboring States as Sanctuary for Rebel Groups." *World Politics* 59 (2): 217–242.

Salehyan, Idean, Kristian Skrede Gleditsch, and David E. Cunningham. 2011. "Explaining External Support for Insurgent Groups." *International Organization* 65 (4): 709–744.

Sayigh, Yezid. 1997. *Armed Struggle and the Search for a State: The Palestinian National Movement, 1949–1993*. Oxford: Clarendon Press.

Sela, Avraham. 2014. "The PLO at Fifty: A Historical Perspective." *Contemporary Review of the Middle East* 1 (3) (October): 269–333.

Sen, Ashis Kumar. 2017. "Is It Time to Take Sudan Off the State Sponsors of Terrorist List?" *Atlantic Council*, July 14, 2017. http://www.atlanticcouncil.org/blogs/new-atlanticist/does-sudan-still-deserve-to-be-on-the-state-sponsors-of-terrorism-list;

Shapiro, Jacob N. 2013. *The Terrorist's Dilemma: Managing Violent Covert Organizations*. Princeton: Princeton University Press.

Silove, Nina. 2018. "Beyond the Buzzword: The Three Meanings of 'Grand Strategy.'" *Security Studies* 27 (1): 27–57.

Staniland, Paul. 2014. *Networks of Rebellion: Explaining Insurgent Cohesion and Collapse*. Ithaca: Cornell University Press.

Stewart, Megan A. 2018. "Civil War as State-Making: Strategic Governance in Civil War." *International Organization* 72 (1): 205–226.

Tilly, Charles. 1985. "War Making and State Making as Organized Crime." In *Violence: A Reader*, edited by Catherine Besteman, 35–60. New York: NYU Press.
Tse-tung, Mao. 2000. *On Guerrilla Warfare*. Translated by Samuel B. Griffith II. Champaign, Ill: University of Illinois Press.
Weinstein, Jeremy M. 2006. *Inside Rebellion: The Politics of Insurgent Violence*. Cambridge: Cambridge University Press.
Yaari, Ehud. 1970. *Strike Terror: The Story of Fatah*. New York: Hebrew Publishing Company.

CHAPTER 32

GRAND STRATEGY AND THE CHALLENGE OF CHANGE

WILLIAM D. JAMES

BRITISH statesman Lord Salisbury once observed that "the commonest error in politics is sticking to the carcasses of dead policies" (Steele 1999, 121). The same could be said for decisions of grand-strategic significance, namely those over a state's highest objectives, as well as the allocation of its finite resources. In the wake of the Second World War, several European powers came under pressure to relinquish their imperial commitments. Yet, while some chose to retrench in response to relative decline, others fruitlessly resisted the winds of change. Why do some states persist with counterproductive grand strategies? Why did Portugal and the Netherlands continue to fight for their colonies during the Cold War long after they had the means to hold them? More recently, what led successive U.S. presidents to spend vast quantities of blood and treasure on ambitious nation-building projects in the sands and valleys of the Greater Middle East, despite mounting evidence that it was a Sisyphean task?

Why have those at the helm of the state sometimes refused to change course when faced with looming political and economic storm clouds? This chapter will identify and probe the relative significance of the conditions that encourage and hinder grand-strategic adjustment (note: I treat "change" and "adjustment" as synonymous). I first offer a definition of grand strategy, as well as a framework for measuring change. I then discuss the incentives for, and impediments to, grand-strategic adjustment. The barriers to change are challenging but not insurmountable. The final section of this chapter will therefore explore the conditions under which states are able to break through the logjam and achieve change.

DEFINING GRAND STRATEGY

Scholars remain divided over the meaning and scope of grand strategy. Some think of it as "the collection of plans and policies that comprise the state's deliberate effort to harness political, military, diplomatic, and economic tools together to advance that state's national interest" (Feaver 2009). Thus, for a state to be in the business of grand strategy, it must articulate and follow a plan for navigating the complexities of international affairs. This interpretation has left the concept vulnerable to skepticism (Edelstein, this volume). Domestic and international events can quickly nullify five- or ten-year strategy documents. It would therefore be unwise to define grand strategy "as simply a prefabricated plan, carried out to the letter against all resistance" because "no world leader has ever had such a strategy, nor ever will" (Dueck 2015, 5).

The reality is that "all states have a grand strategy, whether they know it or not" because "grand strategy is simply the level at which knowledge and persuasion, or in modern terms intelligence and diplomacy, interact with military strength to determine outcomes in a world of other states with their own 'grand strategies'" (Luttwak 2009, 409). All decision-makers are inevitably faced with tradeoffs over their state's competing priorities and they make judgments—consciously or unconsciously—about which goals and threats are the most important and how resources should be deployed to meet them (Brands 2014, 6).

John Lewis Gaddis views grand strategy as "the alignment of potentially unlimited aspirations with necessarily limited capabilities" (Gaddis 2018, 21). He is, however, relaxed about the concept's scope, noting that individuals, as well as states, can have grand strategies. Gaddis believes that what constitutes *grand* is in the eye of the beholder. Thus, a sports coach can have a grand strategy for winning a competition, while an individual can even have a grand strategy for "falling in and out of love" (Gaddis, 2009). While Gaddis is right to focus on the crucial balance between means and ends, I adopt a slightly narrower definition.

Grand strategy is the art of connecting a state's highest objectives with its finite resources. It involves officials at the top level of government ranking their country's goals and evaluating how best to utilize national assets and interact with other states in order to enhance long-term security. When done well, states are likely to avoid the perils of underreach and overstretch. Whereas foreign policy describes a state's relations with the wider world, grand strategy provides an explanation for a state's behavior (James 2020, 76). It accounts for why a specific state is regarded as a threat or why a particular area is prioritized (Posen 2014, 1).

Thus, grand strategies are conceptualized by the assessment of threats and opportunities, the prioritization of the state's objectives, and the allocation of its finite resources. This is not the end of the process, however. Once conceptualized, grand strategies must be implemented and updated to reflect changing internal and external conditions (James 2020, 77). As we shall see, this is often easier said than done.

What Constitutes Grand-Strategic Change?

How can we measure grand-strategic change? Colin Dueck distinguishes between "first-order" changes, which entail "a massive shift in the extent of strategic commitments," and "second-order" changes, which are "less fundamental" and more common (Dueck 2006, 12). This is a useful distinction, although it leaves open to debate which adjustments can be considered "fundamental."

In her contribution to this handbook, Rebecca Lissner also identifies two types of change: overhauls and adjustments. For Lissner, an overhaul occurs when the state changes its "macro-theory of national security" (i.e., its "approach to the international system"). In contrast, adjustments happen when the state alters its assessment of threats and opportunities, its priorities, or its allocation of resources. This is a useful contribution, as it is relatively clear and aligns with much of the prescriptive literature on US grand strategy. Lissner's second category is, however, problematic because it is so expansive. Can we treat the allocation of means on the same level as decisions over priorities? Surely the former flow from the latter. A further issue with this framework is that it is not clear when the state reaches a tipping point between adjustments and overhauls. Are the adjustments the first pebbles of an avalanche as the grand strategy is overhauled? If so, how many adjustments are required before we think of the change as an overhaul?

Nicholas Kitchen provides the solution in linking Dueck's first-order changes to goals and those of the second-order to means (Kitchen 2010, 137–138). Thus, a first-order adjustment could involve the identification of a new threat or a reordering of existing priorities. Consider, for example, Saudi Arabia's assessment of Egypt during the Cold War. During the 1960s, Gamal Abdel Nasser's promotion of pan-Arabism was seen by Riyadh as a threat to the monarchist regimes in the region. Saudi Arabia therefore supplied arms to royalist forces fighting Egyptian soldiers in North Yemen. Yet after Nasser's death in 1970, Cairo was seen as less of a threat in Saudi eyes and the two countries underwent a thaw in relations.

A second-order change, in contrast, entails shifts in the assets employed to achieve the state's objectives. Second-order changes often follow those of the first order. With regard to hard power, we should expect shifts in force structure or military spending. In response to budget cuts and a shift towards fighting small wars, the Dutch military has sold or mothballed most of its battle tanks over the past decade. When it comes to softer forms of power, we would expect to see changes in diplomacy. An analyst could, for example, assess whether the state sought new allies in a specific region or if it increased or decreased the relative importance it placed on a particular alliance or institution. Charles de Gaulle's decision in 1959 to withdraw France's Mediterranean Fleet from NATO's integrated command could be seen in this light. Keeping NATO at a distance stemmed from the first-order shift in detaching from the Americans and British.

INCENTIVES FOR CHANGE

The ship of state will undoubtedly sail into political and economic headwinds, which means that tacking is inevitable if it is to avoid underreach or overstretch. As Lawrence Freedman observes: "with each move from one state of affairs to another, the combination of ends and means will be reappraised. Some means will be discarded and new ones found, while some ends will turn out to be beyond reach even as unexpected opportunities come into view" (Freedman 2013, 611).

Neorealists suggest that shifts in the international distribution of power provide the primary motivation for states to alter their grand strategies. Following this logic, we should therefore expect first-order changes when the state faces an emergent threat to its interests (Walt 1987, 263–265). Over one hundred years ago, the United Kingdom chose to concentrate on the danger posed by Wilhelmine Germany, at the expense of its imperial interests in the periphery. Once a threat has been identified, states balance, first by increasing defense spending and making alterations to its force structure (internal balancing) and then by forming alliances (external balancing). With its eye on revanchist Germany, the British Army was reconfigured after years of fighting imperial bush wars, while the Royal Navy constructed Dreadnought battleships. Alliances were cultivated with France and Russia to balance against the Central Powers.

Impediments to Change

Given these structural incentives, why is grand-strategic change so rare? History is replete with examples of countries that have failed to adjust to the fluctuating winds of international politics. There are factors that affect: (a) the state's willingness to change, i.e., the conceptualization stage; and (b) the state's ability to change, i.e., the implementation stage.

Psychological Explanations

Judgments over the need and extent of grand-strategic change should be objective, yet they often vary according to the demands of the problem and the abilities of particular decision-makers. We tend to think of grand strategies at the systemic level, but they are conceptualized by individuals—presidents, prime ministers, as well as ministers and officials from the foreign, defense, and finance ministries. These actors come to the table with their own beliefs, based on their own biases and life experiences. This shapes how they perceive new information concerning threats to the state's interests. The world is complex, so we use heuristics to help us cope with the plethora of confusing information we receive. These shortcuts, which range from taking an educated guess and employing rules of thumb to using one's intuition, are useful because they enable policymakers to take decisions in a timely manner. Unfortunately, they can also lead to cognitive closure as decision-makers prematurely reject new information that does not correspond with their preexisting beliefs (Jervis 2017). National leaders are likely to have particular images of certain countries or problems, which form quickly and are difficult to displace. Similarly, leaders may cherry-pick evidence to confirm prior judgments. This could impede objective threat perception.

A good example is the tendency of policymakers to reach for historical analogies to simplify their predicaments (May 1973; Khong 1992). When faced by a threat from an autocratic regime, the legacy of appeasement and the 1938 Munich Summit often springs to the minds of policymakers in London and Washington. Egypt's nationalization of the Suez Canal Company in 1956 reminded British Prime Minister Anthony Eden of Neville Chamberlain's failure to deal with Hitler and Mussolini. Across the Atlantic, the legacy of appeasement was evoked during the Vietnam War, the Cuban Missile Crisis and both Gulf wars. Decision-makers are disposed to drawing negative lessons from history to simplify complex problems, even if the context remains wildly different (Johnson and Tierney 2019).

This problem of subjective threat assessment is compounded by the fact that the system does not always provide clear signals. Leaders have to operate with imperfect information about their counterparts' intentions. Even the most rational policymakers struggle to correctly judge systemic incentives and constraints. In the buildup to the First World War, uncertainty over British intentions may have led policymakers in Berlin to believe that they could act against France and Russia without stoking British belligerence. For their part, the Germans sent London mixed messages over the sincerity of their desire to avoid conflict.

Policymakers in Washington are confronted with the same problem today but over the rise of China. Does Beijing aspire to regional or global dominance? Is President Xi's assertive foreign policy the result of domestic pressures and the need to secure raw materials? Assessments of Chinese intent will inform the US response. Should it accept Chinese hegemony of the South and East China Seas or should it push back against Beijing's territorial claims? Aaron Friedberg sagely observes that, "even if one acknowledges that structures exist and are important, there is still the question of how statesmen grasp their contours from the inside, so to speak, of whether, and if so how, they are able to determine where they stand in terms of relative national power at any given point in history" (Friedberg 1988, 8).

One of the most pertinent psychological explanations for grand-strategic change (or the lack of it) is Prospect Theory (Kahneman 2011, 318–319). People tend to be risk-averse when facing prospects of gain, and they tend to be risk-acceptant when facing prospects of loss (Welch 2011, 42). It is the latter phenomenon—loss aversion—which is particularly interesting for the study of grand-strategic change. Leaders in losing positions are often unwilling to adjust grand strategy in wartime because of this psychological reluctance to accept losses. To accept defeat after the expenditure of blood and treasure is abhorrent, while "the lure of the gamble that persevering will recoup the losses is often too great to resist" (Jervis 1992, 191). This notion of loss aversion goes some way to explaining why so many great powers have fought long and costly wars in regions of peripheral importance. In the wake of the Second World War, the French plowed resources into Indochina in a desperate bid to maintain their colonies. Their war against communist-nationalist forces in Vietnam, Laos, and Cambodia would divert finite resources away from their core interests in Europe and North Africa. The Johnson and Nixon administrations later demonstrated the same behavior during the Vietnam War. Rather than cut losses in the face of an increasingly futile and unpopular campaign, both leaders chose to escalate the conflict in the hope of securing concessions from Hanoi (Taliaferro 2004, 204).

Some leaders are more prone to motivated biases, such as revenge, status, and honor. Unlike the aforementioned cognitive biases, motivated biases are "are driven by people's emotional needs, by their need to maintain self-esteem, and by their interests—diplomatic, political, organizational, or personal" (Levy 2015). Leaders may be resistant to making substantial changes if it entails a loss in prestige. Conversely, they may undertake risky initiatives in order to satisfy their honor. Recent scholarship posits that individuals who are concerned by their personal standing relative to their peers "will be more inclined to fight in a set of crises that do not involve important material or strategic stakes but do involve reputational considerations" (Yarhi-Milo 2018, 37).

Placing status concerns above strategic interests can have dire consequences. A state may become overstretched by fighting for its reputation in a conflict that it should long since have abandoned. Such motivational biases can also cause premature grand-strategic change. If honor is at stake, the state's leaders may decide to act prematurely (i.e., before sufficient resources have been assembled and massed to counter threats). In 1914, Russian leaders had strong incentives to delay war until their military modernization was complete in 1917, yet they rushed to the defense of Serbia. The Tsar and his ministers feared their country's international standing would suffer if they backed down against Austria-Hungary and Germany. They went to war, in the words of Nicholas II, to "protect the honour, dignity and safety of Russia and its position among the Great Powers" (Renshon 2017, 223–230). Thus, status concerns can also cause premature change, as well as delays.

Cultural Explanations

The willingness to embark on first- or second-order changes can also be affected by collective ideas held by senior policymakers and wider society. The individuals responsible for conceptualizing grand strategy are socialized by prevalent ideas ingrained within their society. How leaders think about objectives, as well as the means required to attain the state's goals, is shaped by societal norms over the use of force and which areas are most deserving of attention. With regard to the latter, bodies of inherited ideas are important in explaining why countries prioritize certain regions. Winston Churchill cited Britain's "unconscious tradition" of supporting Europe's weaker states "to oppose the strongest, most aggressive" powers on the Continent (Churchill 1948, 186–187). Ideas become implanted through socialization but entrenched through institutionalization. This gives them longevity as they endure long after their creators have moved on (Kitchen 2010, 131; Goldstein and Keohane 1993).

Some scholars focus on organizational cultures, such as those of the armed forces (Kier 1999), while others examine the influence of wider societal norms on a state's behavior (Duffield 1999; Berger 1993). Charles Kupchan, for example, falls into the latter category in that he views strategic culture as "the set of images that shapes a polity's collective disposition toward the behavior of its state in the international arena." He observes that elites have the capacity to "propagate strategic images to gain support for their policies," but warns that "their actions may later come to constrain them." If, for example, they encourage the public to believe that a state's interests in the periphery are just as important as those in the core, it may be difficult to shift grand strategy away from the periphery at a later date when the core is threatened. Thus, "elites eventually find themselves unable to adjust to shifts in the international environment, entrapped in a strategic culture of their making" (Kupchan 1994, 88–101). The implication of these arguments is that policymakers may be unwilling to change grand strategy because of the domestic backlash they would face for violating accepted norms or culturally prescriptive national goals (Dueck 2006, 15).

For Patrick Porter, the United States remains wedded to a grand strategy of primacy because of "habitual ideas" held by policymakers in Washington. Decades of playing an active role in world affairs have created a "habit of primacy," which has now become so institutionalized that change is incredibly difficult. Those in charge "socialize personnel into their worldview, educating and selecting individuals who conform, excluding or penalizing those who do not." They also control public discourse, which means that they can smear alternative approaches; proposals for a more restrained grand strategy, for example, are likened to isolationism (Porter 2018, 11–17). Ronald Krebs agrees that dominant narratives "establish the common-sense givens of debate, set the boundaries of the legitimate, limit what political actors inside and outside the halls of power can publicly justify, and resist efforts to remake the landscape of legitimation" (Krebs 2015, 3). Thus, for Porter, potential alternatives to primacy are not given a fair hearing.

Organizational Explanations

The departmental loyalties of those individuals responsible for conceptualizing grand strategy can interfere with objective decision-making. Judgments over priorities and the allocation of scarce resources emerge from a tussle of ideas between a small number of players at the top level of government. They bargain with each other until one actor or a coalition can secure backing from a sufficient majority to proceed with their priorities. In his work on the Cuban Missile Crisis, Graham Allison places a great deal of importance on organizational culture (as above) and departmental loyalties. He writes that "the stance of a particular player can be predicted with high reliability from information about a person's seat" because "where you stand depends on where you sit" (Allison and Zelikow 1999, 307). Thus, decision-makers may act in their organization's interests, even if its interests conflict with the national interest. To the extent that there is grand-strategic change, it will be conditioned by the compromise reached between different bureaucratic interests, rather than as a response to systemic incentives.

The *bureaucratic politics* argument has come under sustained flak since Allison first published the theory in 1969 (Bendor and Hammond, 1992). To be sure, decisions of grand-strategic significance cannot *solely* be explained by departmental interests. Moreover, divisions between departments are fairly constant, which means that the theory struggles to account for instances of grand-strategic change. That said, Allison's argument provides another helpful explanation for delays in grand-strategic change. Departmental divisions can impede the state from responding in a timely manner. To be more specific, we should principally expect bureaucratic politics to have an impact on second-order grand-strategic changes. Decisions over force structure, for example, will be heavily influenced by the bureaucratic turf battles between different branches of the military, which are each competing for a larger slice of the defense budget.

In the wake of the First World War, British defense spending was slashed, thereby increasing competition among the armed services. With few threats to the country's interests, politicians became fairly detached from force structure debates, which meant that "each service planned for its favorite war, in a different part of the world, with little attention to the plans of its fellows" (Posen 1986, 159). The Royal Navy, unable to justify the maintenance of expensive battleships in home waters given that Germany had been disarmed, flagged the potential Japan menace in the Pacific. Meanwhile, the relatively new Royal Air Force concentrated almost exclusively on developing bombers, which it thought would "eclipse the role of navies and do away with the need for armies" (Posen 1986, 160). Even after civilian and military planners started planning for the threat posed by Germany in 1934, many RAF chiefs continued to resist the move away from strategic bombing to fighter defense (Posen 1986, 142–143). Thus, bureaucratic interests prevented a smooth second-order shift in force structure, which in turn slowed the effectiveness of the first-order change in threat perception.

Domestic Political Explanations

Even if decision-makers agree on the need to alter their state's grand strategy, it is far from certain whether they can extract the resources from society needed to implement their proposed changes. Certain groups may have the power to block or resist grand-strategic adjustment. Potential veto players (Tsebelis 2002) include political parties, interest groups, and the public. Implementing grand strategies requires immense human, material, and monetary resources. If the public, or groups that possess these resources, withhold them from the state, the government will have to divert resources in order to extract them (Ripsman, Taliaferro, and Lobell 2016, 71–72).

Weak governments may be slow to adjust to changing systemic conditions. Fareed Zakaria shows how United States was unable to translate its abundant wealth into political clout on the world stage in the late nineteenth century. The system encouraged expansion, yet the federal government lacked the executive power it enjoys today. As such, Washington was unable to harness the country's economic strength. Only when power shifted from the states to the central government, and from the legislature to the executive, were presidents able to mobilize the nation's resources for international influence (Zakaria 1998).

The degree to which power is dispersed affects a state's ability to implement grand-strategic change. Fragmented states will "underreact to dangerous threats, responding with inefficient balancing, bandwagoning, buck-passing, distancing, incoherent half measures, or ineffective policies defined by the lowest common denominator" (Schweller 2010, 12). Where power is decentralized, sectional interest groups can have a pernicious effect, particularly for those states trying to manage relative decline. Democratic systems *should* create checks on concentrated interests advocating the retention of far-flung interests in the periphery, but voters lacking good information make excellent targets for imperialist and nationalist mythmaking. Moreover, there is still the potential for cartelized blocks of interests to form within democracies. (Snyder 1991, 49–54).

In the wake of the Second World War, several European powers were unable to withdraw from their strategically burdensome colonial outposts due to the influence of business interests, settler communities, and the armed forces. Those which had decentralized states were more likely to find themselves in strategic "quagmires" due to the higher number of agents that could block changes to the status quo (Spruyt 2005, 265). In the Netherlands, for example, the multiparty system and coalition dynamics created multiple partisan veto points. Politicians who had similar interests to the settler communities and large corporations used these opportunities to block compromise solutions for Indonesia (Spruyt 2005, 147).

More recently, scholars have suggested that pro-Israeli interest groups in the United States have diverted Washington away from its own genuinely strategic goals and towards those that coincide with Tel Aviv's (Mearsheimer and Walt 2008). The system is shoving the United States towards Asia, but policymakers in Washington cannot efficiently adjust grand-strategic priorities. Riyadh and Abu Dhabi have also built formidable lobbying operations in Washington by hiring PR consultancies and funding influential think tanks.

It would be a mistake, however, to overstate the power of these interest groups. This is particularly the case in pluralistic societies, where organizations with contrasting interests often counterbalance each other. Indeed, "domestic-focused interests can be just as concentrated as their foreign-focused counterparts and often have deeper pockets" (MacDonald and Parent 2018, 18). They are also more likely to attract the attention of politicians concerned with electoral survival; healthcare and welfare are more likely to win votes than external issues relating to grand strategy.

Breaking the Logjam

States are often be unwilling or unable to adjust their grand strategies in line with changes in the international distribution of power. Grand-strategic change of the first order is possible but rare. One common assumption is that change often requires "strategic shocks" (Johnson and Madin 2008; Porter 2018, 17). The logic runs that high-impact events, which were either assigned a low probability or were unforeseen completely, are needed to break through psychological or institutional inertia.

There is fairly strong evidence to support the idea of strategic shocks triggering change. Prior to the Second World War, Australia looked to Britain as the principal underwriter of its security. The shock of Japan's entry in the war and the extent of the UK's unpreparedness forced Canberra to reconsider its grand-strategic priorities. The British were stretched thin after the fall of France in 1940 and chose to prioritize home defense and the campaign in North Africa over the deterrence of Japan. The lack of air support in Asia was evident when, on 10 December 1941, two of the Royal Navy's most powerful ships, HMS Repulse and HMS Prince of Wales, were sunk by Japanese bombers off the coast of Malaya. Australian policymakers drew a clear lesson that their principal ally was no longer able to guarantee their security. Prime Minister John Curtin told his compatriots that "Australia looks to America, free of any pangs as to our traditional links or kinship with the United Kingdom" (Curtin 1941). His arguments were strengthened two months later when the garrison in Singapore—the symbol of British power in Asia—surrendered, and the Japanese bombed Darwin. Thus, a strategic shock—the collapse of British power in Southeast Asia—led to a change in Canberra's grand strategy. For the first time in its history, the United States, not Britain, was seen as its foremost ally and protector.

It would be unwise, however, to overstate the importance of strategic shocks, as they do not *always* lead to grand-strategic change. During the Suez Crisis of 1956, the international backlash that resulted from the military operation came as a tremendous shock to policymakers in London and caused domestic political upheaval. Yet, contrary to popular belief, the Suez Crisis did not result in the swift abandonment of the UK's imperial interests. The British maintained a substantial presence in the Middle East for another 15 years. In response to the threat of Iraqi invasion, Macmillan sent troops to defend Jordan in 1958 and then Kuwait in 1961. The military base at Aden (located in modern day Yemen) quadrupled in size between 1957 and 1960 (Darby 1973, 209). Why then do strategic shocks trigger change on some occasions but not others?

There are therefore clearly degrees of strategic shock. The Japanese victories in 1941/42 came as a catastrophic shock to policymakers in Canberra, which led them to re-evaluate the emphasis they placed on their key alliances. Similarly, the defeat of the French Army in six weeks in 1940 resulted in significant changes to French grand strategy after the war. During the interwar period, Paris had sought to bind itself to allies, such as Britain, Poland, and Czechoslovakia. The events of 1939–1940 shattered France's faith in its allies. As a result, successive postwar governments pursued independence from Anglo-American security designs. France developed its own nuclear deterrent and remained aloof from NATO for much of the Cold War.

Such catastrophic strategic shocks are rare. Yet we know that states can and do change their grand-strategic priorities without such events. I posit that three conditions are necessary for first-order grand-strategic changes:

1. A hostile security environment (accentuated by strategic shocks)
2. Domestic agents of change
3. A viable alternative to the status quo

The Security Environment

The likelihood of change depends on the intensity and imminence of systemic stimuli. This harks back to neorealist arguments on the causes of adjustment. Different threat environments yield contrasting incentives. When the state is at war or faces a security crisis, domestic veto players are likely to be excluded either forcefully or voluntarily from the process. In the first instance, the need for secrecy and quick decisions will separate the key decision-makers from the rest of the bureaucracy and wider society (Ripsman, Taliaferro, and Lobell 2016, 61). The willingness of veto players to block grand-strategic change is also likely to dissipate during a crisis as the public, as well as opposition political parties and interest groups, "rally round the flag" (Mueller 1973, 61). "Opposition forces are likely to be either supportive of administration policies or stymied by broad popular support for the state" when there is an existential threat (Gibler 2010, 520). Strategic shocks can be useful in highlighting these systemic shifts both to leaders and the wider population. In summary, change is easier when the state faces a clear and existential threat.

In contrast, a more benign security environment is likely to result in implementation issues because "life is both more pleasant and more complicated when there are no threats that are both dangerous and likely" (Jervis 1998, 24). The core decision-making group is no longer the decisive stakeholder, as latent veto players *should* have greater access to information. Without a unifying existential threat, these groups no longer feel obligated to rally round the flag. As such, they can afford to push their own parochial interests. It is logical to assume that democracies face greater barriers to implementation due to a higher number of possible veto players with greater access to information. Under clearly permissive conditions, more actors are given opportunities to "shape, constrain, or defeat policies at odds with their preferences" (Ripsman, Taliaferro, and Lobell 2016, 91–94). Thus, in conditions of relative peace, leaders will have to spend more time bargaining with domestic veto players. Compromises may be necessary if they are to implement their grand-strategic priorities.

Systemic factors also help to explain shifts in strategic culture. Consider, for example, the degree of change and continuity in Japanese and German grand strategy over the past 80 years. Both harbored militarist cultures before the Second World War, but their total defeat in 1945 served as a catastrophic strategic shock, which forced them to the other end of the spectrum. This naturally resulted in seismic changes to grand-strategic assessments over priorities, as well as the use of force. These revolutionary measures have largely been upheld for the past 70 years. Only recently has Tokyo signaled a desire to amend its pacifist constitution and its defensive force structure, as a result of the growing threat posed by revisionist China. It plans to modify two of its helicopter carriers so that they can host F-35B fighter jets. These ships would therefore become Japan's first de facto aircraft carriers since the Second World War—a significant second-order shift in grand strategy. Germany, by way of contrast, faces a relatively benign security environment and still only feels comfortable projecting military force under a European Union or peacekeeping umbrella.

Domestic Agents of Change

It is not axiomatic that changes to the threat environment, whether through power shifts or strategic shocks, will result in grand-strategic adjustments. Such shifts also require determined agents of change, who have the will and political skills necessary to ensure that their priorities, as well as their judgments over alliances and force structure, are accepted (Friedberg 1988, 287–291; Porter 2018, 17). Changes to grand strategy must be politically feasible, which means that effective leaders will frame strategic choices in terms that are culturally acceptable (Dueck, 2006, 19). In the wake of 9/11, it was not clear which path the United States would take. The George W. Bush administration crafted a winning narrative which resulted in minimal resistance from domestic veto players to their interventions in Afghanistan and Iraq (Krebs 2015, 279).

It is the convergence of shifting systemic conditions (sometimes accentuated by strategic shocks) and transformational leaders that results in grand-strategic change. Without the former, leaders will struggle to implement their priorities. Consider President Franklin Roosevelt's difficulties in supplying arms to the allies in their struggle against the Axis powers in 1939–1941. Notwithstanding his disdain for the British Empire, he was keen to assist the United Kingdom in its struggle against Nazi Germany. Yet he was constrained by the US Neutrality Acts and public opinion. Geographically and economically insulated from Europe's woes, the United States faced a permissive security environment. Domestic veto players were therefore able to block and dilute Roosevelt's schemes. It took the strategic shock of Pearl Harbor to discredit the isolationist lobby, but Roosevelt's leadership was later essential in convincing the American public of his "Germany First" strategy.

A Viable Alternative to the Status Quo

The final condition of grand-strategic change is the availability of a viable alternative to the status quo. It is easier to adjust course when old ideas have been discredited by "stark failure" and when there are ready replacements, permitting for the consolidation of a new orthodoxy (Legro 2005, 34–36). There needs to be a new threat or interest for policymakers to focus upon. If there is no menace on the horizon, or if it is politically unfeasible to concentrate on a new objective or region, leaders will struggle to adjust course. The same goes for second-order grand-strategic changes. The state can only change its alliances if there are plausible substitutes available.

Consider the dilemma that many of America's allies faced in the wake of Donald Trump's election victory. President Trump embraced a zero-sum, transactional approach to international affairs with little appreciation for the efforts and interests of long-standing allies. The US withdrawal from the Trans-Pacific Trade Partnership provided an early demonstration of this for Australia. As disappointed as policymakers in Canberra were with some of the Trump administration's decisions, they had little choice other than to ride out the storm. In the twentieth century, Australia was able to make a second-order grand-strategic change in shifting its reliance on the British to the Americans. Today, however, there are no viable alternatives to the US alliance, particularly in light of the growing threat from Beijing (Beeson and Bloomfield 2019, 18–19).

Conclusion

This chapter has assessed the structural incentives for, and domestic impediments to, grand-strategic change. The international system provides signs, but these signals are not always clear; it falls to senior decision-makers to interpret and act on these warnings. Policymakers are limited by how much information they can process and are prone to cognitive, motivational, and cultural biases. Leaders may remain wedded to judgments over objectives, threats, and the allocation of resources, even as evidence mounts against their effectiveness. If policymakers do manage to agree on the degree of change that is required, domestic veto players may still prevent them from extracting the necessary resources from society to implement their planned adjustments.

These factors describe the challenge of change, but it is not instinctively clear *when* they come to the fore and prevent adjustments to a state's grand strategy. I have argued that, short of a catastrophic shock, grand-strategic change is rare but possible. It is dependent on the right systemic conditions, as well as the presence of change agents, and a viable alternative to the status quo. The ship of state takes time to adjust course, but it will likely be easier when those at the helm are faced with a clear and existential threat on the horizon.

References

Allison, Graham T., and Philip Zelikow. 1999. *Essence of Decision: Explaining the Cuban Missile Crisis*. New York: Longman.

Beeson, Mark, and Alan Bloomfield. 2019. "The Trump Effect Downunder: U.S. Allies, Australian Strategic Culture, and the Politics of Path Dependence." *Contemporary Security Policy* 40 (3): 1–27.

Bendor, Jonathan, and Thomas H. Hammond. 1992. "Rethinking Allison's Models." *American Political Science Review* 86 (2): 301–322.

Berger, Thomas U. 1999. "From Sword to Chrysanthemum: Japan's Culture of Anti Militarism." *International Security* 17 (4): 119–150.

Brands, Hal. 2014. *What Good is Grand Strategy? Power and Purpose in American Statecraft from Harry S. Truman to George W. Bush.* Ithaca: Cornell University Press.

Churchill, Winston S. 1948. *The Second World War, Vol. I: The Gathering Storm.* New York: Houghton Mifflin.

Curtin, John. 1941. "The Task Ahead." *The Herald*, December 27, 1941. http://john.curtin.edu.au/pmportal/text/00468.html, accessed 20 April, 2019.

Darby, Phillip. 1973. *British Defence Policy East of Suez, 1947–1968.* London: Oxford University Press.

Dueck, Colin. 2006. *Reluctant Crusaders: Power, Culture, and Change in American Grand Strategy.* Princeton: Princeton University Press.

Dueck, Colin. 2015. *The Obama Doctrine: American Grand Strategy Today.* Oxford: Oxford University Press.

Duffield, John S. 1999. "Political Culture and State Behavior: Why Germany Confounds Neorealism." *International Organization* 53 (4): 765–803.

Feaver, Peter. 2009. "What is Grand Strategy and Why Do We Need It?" *Foreign Policy*, April 8, 2009. https://foreignpolicy.com/2009/04/08/what-is-grand-strategy-and-why-do-we-need-it/

Freedman, Lawrence. 2013. *Strategy: A History.* Oxford: Oxford University Press.

Friedberg, Aaron L. 1988. *The Weary Titan: Britain and the Experience of Relative Decline, 1895–1905.* Princeton: Princeton University Press.

Gaddis, John Lewis. 2018. *On Grand Strategy.* New York: Penguin.

Gaddis, John Lewis. 2009. "What is grand strategy?" Karl Von Der Heyden Distinguished Lecture, Duke University, February 26, 2009, https://tiss-nc.org/wp-content/uploads/2015/01/KEYNOTE.Gaddis50thAniv2009.pdf

Gibler, Douglas M. 2010. "Outside-In: The Effects of External Threat on State Centralization." *Journal of Conflict Resolution* 54 (4): 519–542.

Goldstein, Judith, and Robert O. Keohane, eds. 1993. *Ideas and Foreign Policy: Beliefs, Institutions, and Political Change.* Ithaca: Cornell University Press.

James, William. 2020. "Grandiose Strategy? Refining the Study and Practice of Grand Strategy." *The RUSI Journal* 165 (3): 74–83.

Jervis, Robert. 1992. "The Political Implications of Loss Aversion." *Political Psychology* 13 (2): 187–204.

Jervis, Robert. 1998. "U.S. Grand Strategy: Mission Impossible." *Naval War College Review* 51 (3): 22–36.

Jervis, Robert. 2017. *Perception and Misperception in International Politics.* Princeton: Princeton University Press.

Johnson, Dominic D.P., and Dominic Tierney. 2019. "Bad World: The Negativity Bias in International Politics." *International Security* 43 (3): 96–140.

Johnson, Dominic D.P., and Elizabeth M.P. Madin. 2008. "Paradigm Shifts in Security Strategy: Why Does It Take Disasters to Trigger Change?" In *Natural Security: A Darwinian Approach to a Dangerous World*, edited by Raphael Sagarin and Jennifer Hyndman, 209–239. Berkeley: University of California Press.

Kahneman, Daniel. 2011. *Thinking, Fast and Slow*. London: Penguin.
Khong, Yuen Foong. 1992. *Analogies at War: Korea, Munich, Dien Bien Phu, and the Vietnam Decisions of 1965*. Princeton: Princeton University Press.
Kier, Elizabeth. 1999. *Imagining War: French and British Doctrine between the Wars*. Princeton: Princeton University Press.
Kitchen, Nicholas. 2010. "Systemic Pressures and Domestic Ideas: A Neoclassical Realist Model of Grand Strategy Formation." *Review of International Studies* 36 (1): 117–143.
Krebs, Ronald R. 2015. *Narrative and the Making of US National Security*. Cambridge: Cambridge University Press.
Kupchan, Charles. 1994. *The Vulnerability of Empire*. Ithaca: Cornell University Press.
Legro, Jeffrey W. 2005. *Rethinking the World: Great Power Strategies and International Order*. Ithaca: Cornell University Press.
Levy, Jack S. 2015. "Psychology and Foreign Policy Decision-Making." In *The Oxford Handbook of Political Psychology*, edited by Leonie Huddy, David O. Sears, and Jack S. Levy. Oxford: Oxford University Press.
Luttwak, Edward N. 2009. *The Grand Strategy of the Byzantine Empire*. Cambridge, MA: Harvard University Press.
MacDonald, Paul K., and Parent, Joseph M. 2018. *Twilight of the Titans: Great Power Decline and Retrenchment*. Ithaca: Cornell University Press.
May, Ernest R. 1973. *"Lessons" of the Past: The Use and Misuse of History in American Foreign Policy*. New York: Oxford University Press.
Mearsheimer, John J., and Stephen M. Walt. 2008. *The Israel Lobby and U.S. Foreign Policy*. London: Penguin.
Mueller, John E. 1973. *War, Presidents and Public Opinion*. New York: John Wiley.
Porter, Patrick. 2018. "Why America's Grand Strategy Has Not Changed: Power, Habit, and the U.S. Foreign Policy Establishment." *International Security* 42 (4): 9–46.
Posen, Barry R. 1986. *The Sources of Military Doctrine: France, Britain, and Germany Between the World Wars*. Ithaca: Cornell University Press.
Posen, Barry R. 2014. *Restraint: A New Foundation for U.S. Grand Strategy*. Ithaca, NY: Cornell University Press.
Renshon, Jonathan. 2017. *Fighting for Status: Hierarchy and Conflict in World Politics*. Princeton: Princeton University Press.
Ripsman, Norman M., Jeffrey W. Taliaferro, and Steven E. Lobell. 2016. *Neoclassical Realist Theory of International Politics*. Oxford: Oxford University Press.
Schweller, Randall L. 2006. *Unanswered Threats: Political Constraints on the Balance of Power*. Princeton: Princeton University.
Snyder, Jack. 1991. *Myths of Empire: Domestic Politics and International Ambition*. Ithaca: Cornell University Press.
Spruyt, Hendrik. 2005. *Ending Empire: Contested Sovereignty and Territorial Partition*. Ithaca: Cornell University Press.
Steele, David. 1999. *Lord Salisbury: A Political Biography*. New York: Routledge.
Taliaferro, Jeffrey W. 2004. "Power Politics and the Balance of Risk: Hypotheses on Great Power Intervention in the Periphery." *Political Psychology* 25 (2): 177–211.
Tsebelis, George. 2002. *Veto Players: How Political Institutions Work*. Princeton: Princeton University Press.
Walt, Stephen M. 1987. *The Origins of Alliances*. Ithaca: Cornell University Press.

Welch, David A. 2011. *Painful Choices: A Theory of Foreign Policy Change*. Princeton: Princeton University Press.

Yarhi-Milo, Keren. 2018. *Who Fights for Reputation: The Psychology of Leaders in International Conflict*. Princeton: Princeton University Press.

Zakaria, Fareed. 1998. *From Wealth to Power: The Unusual Origins of America's World Role*. Princeton: Princeton University Press.

CHAPTER 33

RETHINKING GRAND-STRATEGIC CHANGE

Overhauls Versus Adjustments in Grand Strategy

REBECCA LISSNER

Is the United States in the midst of a major grand-strategic reorientation? International Relations (IR) scholars vigorously debate this question, and for good reason: the course of American foreign policy, and indeed world politics, hinges on the answer. Since the Second World War and especially in the years following the collapse of the Soviet Union, the United States has served as the guarantor of the so-called liberal international order. Yet global power shifts, rapid technological innovation, the return of great power rivalry, and illiberal tendencies in Washington call into question the order's durability (Lissner and Rapp-Hooper 2018). Whether the United States intends to defend the liberal international order against emerging challenges—and, if so, how it will do so—are questions with profound implications for international politics.

Given long-standing academic interest in grand strategy, scholars should be well poised to shed light on the trajectory of American grand strategy at this critical juncture (Milevski 2016). Yet despite many valuable discrete contributions, taken as a whole, the grand strategy literature obscures more than it elucidates—a problem rooted in ongoing confusion surrounding the concept of grand strategy. Due to the lack of convergent understandings of what grand strategy is and how to measure it, IR scholars have fallen short in their attempts to theorize the origins and evolution of states' grand strategies.

Indeed, analytical shortcomings reflect basic disagreements rooted in fuzzy conceptions of grand strategy itself. For example, did Donald Trump's presidency herald a dramatic reorientation of US grand strategy? Some policy analysis emphasizes continuity: Patrick Porter, for example, identifies "more continuity than change regarding grand-strategic issues" under Trump's leadership; Matthew Kroenig argues "many of the controversial foreign policy statements that Trump has made as president have, in fact, been consistent with established U.S. policy" (Porter 2019, 39–40; Kroenig 2017). Still others associate Trump with a radical break: John Ikenberry, writing alongside Kroenig in the same issue of *Foreign Affairs*, characterizes the president as a "hostile revisionist power ... in the Oval Office," threatening the liberal international order's death by suicide; Kori Schake contends Trump's "reckless disregard for the security concerns of America's allies, hostility to mutually beneficial trade and willful isolation of the United States is unprecedented" (Ikenberry 2017; Schake 2018). Although these scholars surveyed similar bodies of evidence, they reach opposing conclusions about whether Trump's ascension to the White House produced epochal change in American grand strategy.

Beyond policy analysis, grand strategy's shaky foundations as a social-scientific concept have inhibited progress in the grand strategy research program (Lakatos 1970; Silove 2018; Balzacq, Dombrowski, and Reich 2019). Take, for example, the puzzle of why great powers change grand strategies, which is among the most important questions in IR. Although there is no shortage of excellent studies that shed light on this issue, without a clear understanding of what grand strategy entails, it is difficult to identify and evaluate competing theories of change. For Christopher Layne, the most important puzzle is explaining overwhelming continuity in American grand strategy since the 1940s, whereas Peter Trubowitz codes no fewer than six different grand strategies pursued by Washington since the beginning of Franklin Roosevelt's tenure (Layne 2007; Trubowitz 2011). Who is right?

This chapter seeks to impose order upon the IR grand strategy literature and to provide a foundation for a research program that can accumulate knowledge and, in turn, enrich debates about the craft and analysis of national strategy. Central to this endeavor is an understanding of the sources of continuity and change in states' grand strategies. In the next section, this chapter highlights the deficiencies of the existing grand strategy literature. Despite numerous individually sound studies, this literature suffers from inconsistent conceptualizations of grand strategy and, by extension, grand-strategic change as a dependent variable. The chapter then proposes a new framework for conceiving of and operationalizing grand strategy, which distinguishes between two levels of grand strategy. The first level of grand strategy is a state's orientation toward the international system, which can be considered the state's "macro-theory" of national security. The second level of grand strategy examines subordinate levels of foreign policy behavior: assumptions about current and prospective threats and opportunities, and the availability and relative utility of the tools of national power. The chapter then illustrates how this framework advances the debate about grand-strategic change by setting up a distinction between grand-strategic overhauls (changes to grand strategy's first level— or changes between grand strategies) and grand-strategic adjustments (changes to grand strategy's second level—or changes within grand strategies). Theoretically, separating overhauls from adjustments reveals that systemic shifts are a necessary but insufficient condition for the former, whereas the latter results from a more diverse array of factors. Empirically, this distinction permits a more nuanced treatment of the co-occurrence of continuity and change, as demonstrated in the ensuing case study of US grand strategy.

Finally, the chapter concludes by discussing the implications for the future course of US grand strategy.

Measuring Grand-Strategic Change

At the heart of the IR grand strategy literature are studies that treat grand strategy as a subject or, in narrower social-scientific terms, as a variable (Lissner 2018). Although there is a small yet important set of studies that addresses the determinants of grand-strategic effectiveness (Brands 2014; Brooks 2008; Popescu 2017), the preponderance of the IR grand strategy literature seeks to explain sources of continuity and change. This focus is hardly surprising. Grand-strategic reorientations—especially those of great powers—are among the most consequential events in international politics. Consider the most salient twentieth-century examples: why did Japan turn toward autarky and aggression in the late 1930s (Legro 2005, 122–142; Snyder 1991, 112–153)? Why did Germany seek to overturn the European order through expansionism in the years leading up to the Second World War (Snyder 1991, 66–112; Legro 2005, 84–122; Kennedy 1991a, 105–125; Glaser 2010, 221–227)? Why did Britain abandon its initial strategy of appeasement in favor of a more confrontational posture toward Nazi Germany (Goddard 2015; Schweller 2010, ch. 3)? Why did Russia turn toward "new thinking" in the 1980s (Rice 1991; Snyder 1991, 212–255; Legro 2005, 142–160)?

As it stands, the grand strategy literature lacks a unified and coherent approach to measuring grand-strategic change. Among studies that seek to explain variation in grand strategies, there is neither an agreed-upon threshold for identifying change nor a common taxonomy of grand-strategic types. By grouping all types of grand-strategic change, these studies have, for instance, treated the transition between status quo and revisionist approaches to international order as the same phenomenon as changes among types of revisionist strategies. Indeed, some studies of change employ a typology that recognizes a binary menu of grand-strategic options and theorizes the choice between them, whereas others see many more flavors of variation. In methodological terms, this is a problem with grand strategy as a social scientific concept: despite considerable agreement on the definition of grand strategy, scholars operationalize the concept in widely variant manners (Goertz 2012, 5). This variation, in turn, makes theories of grand-strategic change difficult to contest, falsify, and improve; moreover, it obscures the conditions that enable different forms of change.

For the study of grand strategy to advance, therefore, future research must distinguish between two types of grand-strategic change: grand-strategic overhauls, which entail changes *between* grand strategies, and grand-strategic adjustments, which entail changes *within* grand strategies. This distinction begins with a two-level framework for operationalizing grand strategy.

The core of grand strategy is a state's formulation of its national interests—that is, the abiding objectives that provide purpose for the state's exercise of power on the global stage. These interests are fundamental to grand strategy: they structure a state's concept of its role in the world, particularly its approach to the international or regional system in which it operates.[1] Interests are not *sui generis* but rather emerge in interaction with a state's international environment: the global distribution of power and other powers' grand strategies constrain a state's interests, even as interests may also seek to alter existing power configurations. Interests transform into grand strategy when they are married with the national resources available for their attainment. Together, these form what Barry Posen calls a state's "theory of security"—the causal beliefs linking national power with the attainment of national interests (Posen 2014, 1). Grand strategy is not just an intellectual construct, however; it requires enactment by policymakers. Indeed, as Paul Kennedy writes, "The crux of grand strategy lies therefore in *policy*, that is, in the capacity of the nation's leaders to bring together all of the elements, both military and nonmilitary, for the preservation and enhancement of the nation's long-term (that is, in wartime *and* peacetime) best interests" (Kennedy 1991b, 5). This broad orientation is the axiomatic, or first-order, level of grand strategy: it defines the international conditions a state seeks to create and broadly prescribes how the state will pursue them. Such conditions may include global or regional end states, like particular distributions of power, or they may describe types of interstate interaction, such as forms of institutionalization.

The first-order grand strategies that have shaped modern geopolitics are well known. Great Britain's grand strategy during the late nineteenth and early twentieth centuries sought to prevent a dominant bloc from emerging in Continental Europe by having Britain serve as an offshore balancer (Kennedy 2017). Nazi Germany's grand strategy during the Second World War was to seek power and prosperity through regional hegemony in Europe and beyond (Mazower 2009; Tooze 2008). After defeating the Axis powers, the United States sought to consolidate its position as the world's most powerful state through institutional leadership alongside efforts first to defeat the Soviet Union in the Cold War, then to deter the rise of a peer competitor from 1991 to the present (Ikenberry 2000, ch. 6; Gaddis 1982; Brands 2016).

Subordinate to first-order grand-strategic theories of security are specific assumptions about desirable ends and available means that guide discrete foreign policy choices. These second-order assumptions flow from the core of a grand strategy and are designed to support it—but secondary changes in grand strategy do not necessarily translate into primary ones. They fall into two categories. First, grand strategy's second level entails assumptions about the identity and prioritization of threats that endanger, or could endanger, national interests, as well as the opportunities presented by the international environment to advance those interests. Threats typically entail malign changes in the intentions or capabilities of extant or prospective adversaries, whether specific nations, blocs or alliances of nations, or nonstate actors. They may also include borderless challenges like pandemics or climate change. Assumptions in this category will posit some prioritization of these threats, differentiating between those that are existential and those that are grave but non-existential. The corollary of these assessments is a judgment about the permissiveness of the international environment: the opportunities

Table 33.1 Operationalizing grand strategy's first- and second-order elements

First-order elements of grand strategy
1: Macro-theory of national security: a state's approach to the international system

Second-order elements of grand strategy
2a: Identification and prioritization of current and prospective threats and opportunities
2b: Calculation of availability and relative utility of tools of national power

a state can seize to advance its national interests or forestall the emergence of threats. These can include adversary vulnerabilities ripe for exploitation, local situations of strength that can be leveraged for strategic gain, and convergent interests that facilitate the formation or fortification of alliances and partnerships.

Second, grand strategy's second level entails assumptions about the tools available to confront such threats and further such opportunities. Whereas first-order judgments set aggregate resource levels and allocations, for example by establishing the level of national means required to maintain a desired power balance, second-order calculations mediate between these broad parameters and specific foreign policy decisions, for example the allocation of troops within and across regions. These assumptions relate to the relative utility and complementarity of the elements of the foreign policy toolkit. Most consequential for international security are assumptions about the utility of military force—the political effects it can achieve when threatened or used, its utility relative to or in conjunction with other instruments of national power, and the appropriate contexts in which it can be employed. Since grand strategy goes well beyond military strategy, however, it should also entail assumptions regarding the efficacy of economic statecraft and diplomacy, as well as the interrelationship among all the components of the foreign policy toolkit (Silove 2018, 33).

Grand strategy can therefore be operationalized as a macro-theory with two categories of supporting assumptions (see Table 33.1). This model allows scholars of grand strategy to build more precise explanations of where grand strategies come from and why they change. Rather than using grand strategy as an all-encompassing term, this framework enables clear specification of which component of grand strategy is under examination.

Sources of Grand-Strategic Change

This two-dimensional model of grand strategy elucidates the distinction between two types of grand-strategic change. Changes to a state's approach to the international system ought to be considered *grand-strategic overhauls*. This genre of change—change between grand strategies—is exceedingly rare and enormously consequential.

Changes to a state's second-order strategic assumptions are best considered *grand-strategic adjustments*, or changes within grand strategies. Modifications to assumptions regarding threats and opportunities, as well as the availability and relative utility of tools of national power, are highly influential in determining foreign policy behaviors—and also more frequent. Adjustments are "not about the optimality of sustaining the core of the grand strategy but rather about how best to do so" (Brooks and Wohlforth 2016, 81; Dueck 2008, ch. 1).[2]

The rest of this chapter demonstrates the theoretical and empirical contribution of this framework. Theoretically, it clarifies the central dimensions of scholarly debate about grand strategy, isolates causal drivers of overhauls as compared with adjustments, and thereby facilitates the kind of competitive theory testing lacking in the disjointed grand strategy literature. In short, this reframing elucidates major shifts in international power distributions as the sole necessary—but nevertheless insufficient—cause of grand-strategic overhaul, whereas grand-strategic adjustments result from a more diverse array of causes.

Sources of Grand-Strategic Overhauls

Grand-strategic overhauls are distinguished from adjustments by the substance and magnitude of change they entail. Scholars employ a range of grand-strategic typologies to classify grand strategies and identify change among them. The most prevalent such typology is the distinction between status quo and revisionist orientations toward the international system: status quo grand strategies seek to preserve the system as it is, whereas revisionist grand strategies aim to transform it. This dichotomy anchors studies of grand-strategic overhaul, even as some works embellish upon it by distinguishing between subtypes. Randall Schweller, for example, assigns bestiary avatars to different degrees of revisionism: before and during the Second World War, for example, Nazi Germany was a strongly revisionist wolf, whereas the Soviet Union was a moderately revisionist fox, and so on (Schweller 1998, 19–26). Jeffrey Legro, for his part, disaggregates status quo orientations into separatist and integrationist strategies—that is, "acceptance of and cooperative participation in the prevailing international society" (illustrated by Meiji Japan and United States after the Second World War) as compared with "states that resist the norms of the extant international society and prefer to remain largely uninvolved in it" (like Tokugawa Japan and the United States before the Second World War) (Legro 2005, 8–9).

Regardless of their precise characterization, the IR literature suggests overhauls result from shifts in the structure of the international system. Realist IR theory has long emphasized relative power in accounting for these epochal grand-strategic changes. Power shifts occur, in Paul Kennedy's words, because "differentials in growth rates and technological change, leading to shifts in the global economic balances, which in turn gradually impinge upon the political and military balances" (Kennedy 2010, xx). Over time, newly powerful states modify their grand strategies in response to their elevated international positions. As Robert Gilpin argues: "As the power of a group or state increases, that group or state will be tempted to try to increase its control over the environment, it will try to expand its political, economic, and territorial control, it will try to change the international system in accordance with its particular set of interests"—which is to say, it will become revisionist (Gilpin 1981, 94–95). Established powers, by comparison, may solely seek the preservation of the status quo (Waltz 1979, 191), or they may pursue revisionist aims of their own (Mearsheimer 2001, 2), in efforts to further mold international conditions to their advantage.

As a general matter, these structural theories of grand-strategic overhaul assign little causal weight to unit-level variation (Waltz 1979, 69). Grand strategy is essentially the conveyer belt between systemic incentives and state behavior, as the material attributes of the system—most importantly the distribution of power—create pressures that "shape and shove" strategic choice (Waltz 2000, 24). As Peter Trubowitz and Edward Rhodes put it: "Big changes in a nation's strategic environment can lead to big changes in its security policies."

Yet structural explanations are manifestly insufficient in explaining states' actual grand-strategic trajectories. Even as power shifts might influence the timing and trajectory of a grand-strategic overhaul, they do not precisely determine its nature. As Trubowitz and Rhodes go on to argue: focusing exclusively on "international constraints and pressures ... is profoundly underdetermining ... rarely are external imperatives clear and unambiguous; rarely is there no range of alternative responses" (Trubowitz 1999, 5).

The IR field has therefore moved beyond purely structural theories of grand strategy; instead, analytical frameworks that reflect the necessity, as well as the insufficiency, of structural transformation for grand-strategic change are now dominant across theoretical traditions. Within the realist school, neoclassical realism embraces this insight by incorporating state-level factors into theories of change. Neoclassical realism thus accepts the importance of broad strategic parameters set by the international system while incorporating domestic-political processes as "intervening variables" that translate external pressures into particular grand-strategic choices (Rose 1998).

Similarly, scholars of ideas and domestic politics acknowledge the importance of international conditions while assigning significant causal weight to state-level factors. In the context of grand strategy, ideas constitute the menu of grand-strategic options, creating focal points for debate by characterizing alternatives (Goldstein and Keohane 1993, 12). More fundamentally, scholars of strategic culture highlight the importance of states' axiomatic national beliefs and identities in determining how they react to international events (Johnston 1998; Dueck 2008; McDougall 1997; May 1962). This strategic DNA can shape the parameters of acceptable grand-strategic choice and explain why states respond differently to similar international conditions (Goddard and Krebs 2015). Domestic political processes may reflect or interact with these ideational enablers and constraints; grand-strategic choices may also result from politicians and interest groups jockeying for political power or economic resources. Trubowitz, for example, explains the United States' late-nineteenth-century decision to become a naval power with reference to the triumph of the industrial Northeast and agrarian West over the South (Trubowitz 1999; 1998).

When attributing causality to major international events, social scientists distinguish between necessity and sufficiency. In the study of grand-strategic overhauls, changes to the international system are the sole necessary cause: in the absence of significant global power shifts (or perhaps revolutionary upheaval in domestic politics), states' first-order grand strategies should remain continuous. That relationship does not imply, however, that grand-strategic overhauls always follow from systemic change. For scholars who assign particular importance to nonmaterial variables, like ideas, this is hardly surprising. Jeffrey Legro, for instance, argues that grand-strategic overhauls occur when dramatic global events invalidate prevailing policy orthodoxy *and* when a new orthodoxy emerges to take its place. In his contribution to this Handbook, William James focuses on barriers to grand-strategic change: James affirms the necessity of "shifting systemic conditions" as a precursor to overhaul but posits "domestic agents of change, and a viable alternative to the status quo" as two additional, necessary conditions (James, this volume). For neorealists who expect grand strategies to automatically adapt to changed international conditions, however, continuity is an empirical puzzle. To address the insufficiency of structural change in producing grand-strategic overhaul, realist thinkers are increasingly drawing on ideational and domestic-political theories—a tacit admission that power may be primary, but purely materialist accounts of grand-strategic overhaul leave much variation unexplained (Porter 2019; Walt 2018).

Sources of Grand-Strategic Adjustments

Unlike grand-strategic overhauls, grand-strategic adjustments—or changes within, rather than between, grand strategies—occur with far greater frequency and reflect a wider range of causes. Even as a state's first-order theory of security remains constant, its second-order elements may vary significantly as states elevate different threats and render varying calculations of the utility of military force, diplomacy, and economic statecraft in achieving national aims. Though such changes do not entail tectonic shifts in a state's approach to the international system, they can meaningfully alter defense investments, military deployments, commitments to alliances and partnerships, participation in international institutions, foreign aid allocations, overseas investments, and diplomatic initiatives (Dueck 2008, 12).

Scholars interested in explaining the rich variation within, rather than between, grand strategies have turned toward the study of grand-strategic adjustment (e.g. Lissner forthcoming). This literature is more pluralistic and multicausal than comparable studies of grand-strategic overhauls. Most importantly, the necessity of international-systemic change is not universally accepted. Some scholars highlight modifications to the structure of the international system or major international shocks as key variables, but others focus solely on changes to actors, ideas, and domestic political processes within states.

Compared to theories of grand-strategic overhaul, theories of grand-strategic adjustment place far greater emphasis on individual agency as a driver of change. Insofar as the preferences and worldviews of political leaders shape grand strategy, leadership transitions can precipitate grand-strategic adjustments. This perspective is familiar to anyone who follows popular debates about the foreign policy doctrines of American presidents; these debates take for granted the causal role of individual agency in charting the nation's grand-strategic course (Schake 2018; Lissner and Zenko 2017; Goldberg 2016). This view is not confined to policy analysis, however; the literature on grand-strategic adjustment provides theoretical and empirical support for leaders' influence. Hal Brands locates the sources of grand-strategic adjustments in the interaction between political leaders' worldviews and international dynamics (Brands 2014). So too does John Gaddis, who associates variation in the economic assumptions underlying grand strategy with the beliefs of presidents and their most influential advisors (Gaddis 1982). Stephen Sestanovich attributes grand-strategic adjustments to the reaction of political leaders to external shocks, even as he traces recurring patterns of ambition and retrenchment over decades of American foreign policy (Sestanovich 2014). Each of these scholars presents explanations for grand-strategic adjustment that account for dynamism in the international environment as well as significant differences in the way political leaders craft national responses to geopolitical flux.

While the personal preferences of political leaders may explain changes within grand strategy, theories of adjustment also allow for the possibility that leaders are avatars for the domestic-political conditions that empowered them. Trubowitz, for example, argues that the microfoundations of American grand strategy lie in the interaction of geopolitical conditions with a president's party's preferences for guns over butter—a preference itself determined by the extent of national fiscal constraints, the electoral advantage conferred by using foreign policy as a partisan wedge issue, and distributive benefits guns and butter provide to their core constituencies (Trubowitz 2011, ch. 2). When geopolitical context changes and/or party preferences change, a leader must adjust the nation's grand-strategic path.

Another strand of the grand-strategic adjustment literature, departing even more markedly from theories of overhaul, contends that domestic-political processes may entirely explain changes within grand strategies, quite apart from shifting international conditions. Thomas Christensen highlights the mobilization of domestic publics against ideologically "useful adversaries"—an instrumentalization that can further broad strategic ends even as it inadvertently entrenches enmities that limit the range of grand-strategic possibilities available to political leaders (Christensen 1996). For Colin Dueck, grand-strategic adjustments follow from the interaction of individual leaders' preferences with their political party's preferences for guns versus butter; he explains the Obama Doctrine with reference to that president's prioritization of a transformational domestic agenda that required a grand strategy designed with Democratic party unity in mind (Dueck 2015). Finally, Ronald Krebs foregrounds wartime politics as an opportunity for strategic adjustment. Rather than construe adjustments as rational adaptation to objective battlefield conditions, he argues, wartime setbacks create surprising political incentives: failure tends to reinforce consensus around existing policy, whereas success creates political space for contestation and change (Krebs 2015).

State-level attributes and processes are thus central to theories of grand-strategic adjustment. To understand these subtler vectors of change, conceiving of states as "billiard balls" or "black boxes," as structural realists do, is simply not sufficient. Yet the particularities of national politics also make it harder for scholars to generalize the processes by which grand-strategic adjustments occur. With the exception of Christensen—whose work also examines Chinese grand strategy—each of the aforementioned works focuses exclusively on explaining US-specific mechanisms. Even so, the distinction between overhauls and adjustments is equally applicable to other states, and these general causal pathways likely obtain in non-American contexts. Indeed, the generalizability of the framework offered in this chapter distinguishes it from US-specific analytical frameworks offered by Walter MacDougall, Christopher Hemmer, Walter Russell Mead, and other scholars interested in recurring debates about American grand strategy (McDougall 1997; Hemmer 2015; Mead 2013; Sestanovich 2014).

US Post–Cold War Grand Strategy Revisited

While necessary, even tectonic structural shifts may be insufficient to produce grand-strategic overhaul—though adjustment may still result. Perhaps the most historically consequential case of continuity despite systemic change is the persistence of American first-order grand-strategic assumptions from the Cold War into the unipolar era. Scholars attribute this constancy to a range of factors including: validation of extant principles by Soviet collapse (Legro 2005; Ikenberry 2000), habits of a myopic foreign policy establishment (Porter 2019), and the essential soundness of preexisting principles, even in a changed world (S. Brooks, Ikenberry, and Wohlforth 2013; Feaver et al. 2019). While testing these competing hypotheses is beyond the scope of this chapter, the two-level framework helps parse US grand-strategic choices at this critical moment of geopolitical transition. Indeed, scholarship has suffered from the inability to distinguish dimensions of continuity and change in the early 1990s: the aforementioned works focus unduly on the absence of overhaul while giving short shrift to the important adjustments that nevertheless did occur. This case study shows how this chapter's framework adds texture and nuance to a complex historical moment.

Since the Second World War, overwhelming continuity has characterized the United States' first-order grand strategy. After a wartime overhaul, the United States' pursuit of primacy and leadership of a liberal international order has remained mostly constant since 1945. As Layne writes:

> Since the 1940s, the United States assiduously has pursued a unipolar distribution of power in the international system. And, in the three regions that matter most to it, it has maintained a permanent military presence to prevent the emergence of new

poles of power and to maintain the kind of regional peace and stability deemed essential to upholding a U.S.-dominated international order. (Layne 2007, 5)

This grand strategy has been remarkably durable and, most critically, robust to systemic change from bipolarity to unipolarity. Insofar as most theories of grand-strategic overhaul posit structural change as either a necessary or sufficient condition, the Soviet Union's collapse presents a most likely case. But even as the end of the Cold War modified the scope and intensity of the United States' liberal-hegemonic ambitions, the core principles remained basically intact.

As the Second World War was ending, American strategists set out to design a new international order that would preserve US hegemony while also ameliorating the political, economic, and security conditions that produced two major wars in 20 years. This objective animated a grand strategy with three core tenets: "Managing the external environment to reduce near—and long-term threats to US national security; promoting a liberal economic order to expand the global economy and maximize domestic prosperity; and creating, sustaining, and revising the global institutional order to secure necessary interstate cooperation on terms favorable to U.S. interests" (Brooks, Ikenberry, and Wohlforth 2013, 11). None of these tenets remained static, even during the Cold War: communism evolved from a monolithic threat to a differentiated one; Washington reimagined the economic system developed at Bretton Woods during the 1970s when it ended the gold standard; and layers of institutional cooperation, like the nuclear nonproliferation regime, developed on top of bedrock organizations like the UN. Nevertheless, the grand-strategic organizing principles remained largely unchanged.

With the Cold War's end, Washington found enduring value in each of these premises. Even as the Soviet threat waned, the George H.W. Bush administration was quick to embrace the goal of American global military primacy (Brands 2016, ch. 6; 2018). Despite vociferous calls from a Democratically controlled Congress to harvest the United States' hard-won peace dividend, the Bush administration was on guard against isolationism and sought to repurpose American power for a changed international environment. Deterrence through military strength and preservation of the United States' alliance network remained the cornerstones of such efforts.

Increasingly, domestic liberalization in the Soviet Union, combined with Moscow's remarkable cooperation on European security issues and the Gulf crisis, indicated the USSR would no longer pose a Cold War–level threat to American national security (Engel 2017). Even so, the Bush administration perceived a continued need for a forward defense posture: "In general, we must move from a defense policy designed to contain a known and powerful enemy to one that promotes and sustains our values, our interests and our allies in the face of instabilities that today are only dimly foreseen" ("Defense Planning for Theater Forces" 1990). The Gulf War validated the assumption that the United States should retain the force structure and posture necessary to deter and defend against uncertain future threats—like the one that emerged from Iraq with little warning.

As with security, the economic organizing principles of American grand strategy remained consistent despite the Soviet Union's collapse; indeed, unipolarity enabled Washington to embrace them with renewed gusto. The Bush administration sought to reap and extend the gains of Cold War victory by creating a political, economic, and security environment conducive to prosperity at home. The administration tied these outcomes to the spread of free markets, and by extension democracy (Zoellick 2011, 36), around the world through the North American Free Trade Agreement (NAFTA) (Sparrow 2015, 474), advancement of the General Agreement on Trade and Tariffs (GATT) regime, and the pursuit of market liberalization in the former Soviet Union, Latin America, South Africa, and East Asia (Brands 2016, 325). Such universalizing efforts even extended to China, an erstwhile orthodox communist state, as the administration pursued China's integration into the global economy and greater access for American businesses, Beijing's human rights record notwithstanding (Sparrow 2015, ch. 26).

Finally, the Cold War's end brought a wholesale embrace of post–Second World War institutions—the so-called "new world order" was, in fact, decidedly old. The Bush administration judged that end of the Cold War "open[ed] up the possibilities for what came to be called a new world order in which the great powers could cooperate in the way the former framers of the United Nations" had intended for the UN Security Council (Bush 1990b). Indeed, the Gulf War offered a "glimmer of the future—a new world order characterized by a growing consensus that force cannot be used to settle disputes and that when the consensus is broken, the world will respond" ("Scowcroft Citadel Commencement Speech" 1991). Similarly, the Bretton Woods Institutions could take on a new role promoting democratic capitalism "in a world where ideology no longer confronts and big power blocs no longer divide" (Bush 1990a). Thus, even as the threat orientation implied by containment died out with the Cold War's end, the United States' approach to international order—one that sought primacy through security, economic, and institutional means—remained basically constant because geopolitical events ratified, rather than impugned, its soundness.

Despite this overwhelming continuity in the United States' approach to the international system—one that persisted through the William J. Clinton administration and the subsequent post–Cold War presidencies—the Bush administration did adjust grand strategy in significant ways. In its assumptions about international threats, the administration reoriented away from the disintegrating Soviet Union. Given still-formidable military capabilities, the danger of Russian reconstitution remained in the early 1990s, but changes in the European security order—from German reunification to the Conventional Forces in Europe Treaty—rendered war increasingly unlikely (Engel 2017; Zelikow and Rice 1995). Instead, the Bush administration redirected its grand strategy toward a new type of threat: aggressive regional powers, which could upset local power balances and obstruct American interests. This concern reflected the Gulf War experience and growing worries about the proliferation of missiles and weapons of mass destruction (WMD). As President Bush warned in May 1991: "As superpower polarization and conflict melt, military thinkers must focus on more volatile regimes, regimes packed with modern weapons and seething with ancient ambitions" (Bush 1991a). This concern about regional powers' ability to erode American military primacy in vital regions with asymmetric WMD capabilities became a recurring feature of post–Cold War American grand strategy.

In its assumptions about the availability and relative utility of the tools of national power, the Bush administration came to embrace a more central role for military force in American grand strategy. Although the United States conducted several military interventions during the Cold War, its defense posture was oriented overwhelmingly toward deterrence, and the risk of US–Soviet escalation constrained the use of force (Lissner 2019). With its emergence as the world's sole superpower, however, the United States enjoyed far greater freedom of action in advancing its overseas interests by flexing its military muscle. As the 1991 National Security Strategy recognized, "the United States remains the only state with truly global strength, reach and influence in every dimension" (Bush 1991b, 2). The United States would use its military power to lock in its newfound advantages while also liberally using coercion to address emergent security challenges (Brands 2018). The propensity to use military force only increased during the 1990s with Clinton's successive military interventions and arguably culminated with the George W. Bush administration's initiation of wars in Iraq and Afghanistan, alongside an open-ended Global War on Terror.

Washington's grand-strategic response to the Cold War's end thus contained elements of both continuity and change. To focus exclusively on the first-order dimension of grand strategy, and the persistence of the United States' post–Second World War approach to international order, would be to ignore the important modifications to grand strategy's second-order dimension that set the stage for a unipolar foreign policy. Although this chapter lacks space for a thorough discussion of the United States' post–Cold War record, the case study suggests that first-order continuity was appropriate, or at least defensible, even as policymakers erred in their second-order judgments, especially overreliance on military force. Addressing first- and second-order changes enables more careful study of this crucial case by tracking both dimensions of change while clearly distinguishing between them.

Conclusion

Conceptual confusion plagues the study, analysis, and practice of grand strategy. Rather than simply critiquing the existing literature, as recent contributions by Silove and Milevski have done, this article moves scholarship forward by offering a framework for operationalizing grand strategy as a social-scientific variable (Silove 2018; Milevski 2016). This two-dimensional framework facilitates progress toward better explanations of when, why, and how states change their grand strategies. Understanding change is central to the study of IR: grand-strategic overhauls can precipitate far-reaching revisions to international order and even major war; grand-strategic adjustments can determine great powers' discrete foreign policy objectives, resource allocations, and reliance on the use of military force.

Moreover, a clearer understanding of grand strategy sheds light on the conditions under which the United States might undertake a dramatic overhaul. Framed in this article's terms, the IR grand strategy literature offers a fairly straightforward guideline: an individual leader—whether Donald Trump or another president—can produce grand-strategic adjustments. By contrast, grand-strategic overhauls are almost never driven by individual agents alone and instead generally reflect changes to the international system. As such, it is global power shifts and technological change—rather than Trump's personal proclivities—most likely to produce a fundamental reorientation of the United States' global role, though the president may shape its tenor (Lissner and Rapp-Hooper 2020, ch. 3).

Notes

1. Great powers typically operate in international as well as regional systems. Small and middle powers can have grand strategies, but these are generally oriented toward regional systems only, since such states lack the material endowments to meaningfully shape the international system.
2. Other scholars like Trubowitz and Rhodes (1999, 4) use "adjustment" to refer to changes this chapter considers grand-strategic overhauls.

References

Balzacq, Thierry, Peter Dombrowski, and Simon Reich. 2019. "Is Grand Strategy a Research Program? A Review Essay." *Security Studies* 28 (1): 58–86.
Brands, Hal. 2014. *What Good Is Grand Strategy? Power and Purpose in American Statecraft from Harry S. Truman to George W. Bush*. Ithaca: Cornell University Press.
Brands, Hal. 2016. *Making the Unipolar Moment: U.S. Foreign Policy and the Rise of the Post-Cold War Order*. Ithaca: Cornell University Press.
Brands, Hal. 2018. "Choosing Primacy: U.S. Strategy and Global Order at the Dawn of the Post-Cold War Era." *Texas National Security Review* 1 (2). https://tnsr.org/2018/02/choosing-primacy-u-s-strategy-global-order-dawn-post-cold-war-era-2/
Brooks, Risa. 2008. *Shaping Strategy: The Civil-Military Politics of Strategic Assessment*. Princeton: Princeton University Press.
Brooks, Stephen, G. John Ikenberry, and William Wohlforth. 2013. "Don't Come Home, America: The Case against Retrenchment." *International Security* 37 (3): 7–51.
Brooks, Stephen, and William Wohlforth. 2016. *America Abroad: The United States' Global Role in the 21st Century*. Oxford: Oxford University Press.
Bush, George H.W. 1990a. "Remarks at the Annual Meeting of the Boards of Governors of the International Monetary Fund and World Bank Group." http://www.presidency.ucsb.edu/ws/index.php?pid=18858
Bush, George H.W. 1990b. Interview with Brent Scowcroft, December 10, 1991, Washington Version Documentary File, Basil Liddell Hart Military Archive at King's College London.

Bush, George H.W. 1991a. "Remarks at the United States Air Force Academy Commencement Ceremony in Colorado Springs, Colorado." https://www.govinfo.gov/app/details/PPP-1991-book1/PPP-1991-book1-doc-pg575, accessed May 15, 2019.

Bush, George H.W. 1991b. "National Security Strategy of the United States (1991)." The White House.

Christensen, Thomas. 1996. *Useful Adversaries: Grand Strategy, Domestic Mobilization, and Sino-American Conflict, 1947–1958*. Princeton: Princeton University Press.

"Defense Planning for Theater Forces." 1990. CF00293, Subject Files, Heather Wilson Files, NSC Series. George H.W. Bush Library.

Dueck, Colin. 2008. *Reluctant Crusaders: Power, Culture, and Change in American Grand Strategy*. Princeton: Princeton University Press.

Dueck, Colin. 2015. *The Obama Doctrine: American Grand Strategy Today*. Oxford: Oxford University Press.

Engel, Jeffrey. 2017. *When the World Seemed New: George H. W. Bush and the End of the Cold War*. Boston: Houghton Mifflin Harcourt.

Feaver, Peter D., Hal Brands, Rebecca Friedman Lissner, and Patrick Porter. 2019. "Correspondence: The Establishment and US Grand Strategy." *International Security* 43 (4): 197–204.

Gaddis, John Lewis. 1982. *Strategies of Containment: A Critical Appraisal of Postwar American National Security Policy*. Oxford: Oxford University Press.

Gilpin, Robert. 1981. *War and Change in World Politics*. Cambridge: Cambridge University Press.

Glaser, Charles L. 2010. *Rational Theory of International Politics: The Logic of Competition and Cooperation*. Princeton: Princeton University Press.

Goddard, Stacie. 2015. "The Rhetoric of Appeasement: Hitler's Legitimation and British Foreign Policy, 1938–39." *Security Studies* 24 (1): 95–130.

Goddard, Stacie, and Ronald Krebs. 2015. "Rhetoric, Legitimation, and Grand Strategy." *Security Studies* 24 (1): 5–36.

Goertz, Gary. 2012. *Social Science Concepts: A User's Guide*. Princeton: Princeton University Press.

Goldberg, Jeffrey. 2016. "The Obama Doctrine." *The Atlantic*, April. https://www.theatlantic.com/magazine/archive/2016/04/the-obama-doctrine/471525/.

Goldstein, Judith, and Robert O. Keohane. 1993. "Ideas and Foreign Policy: An Analytical Framework." In *Ideas and Foreign Policy: Beliefs, Institutions, and Political Change*, edited by Judith Goldstein and Robert O. Keohane. Ithaca: Cornell University Press.

Hemmer, Christopher. 2015. *American Pendulum: Recurring Debates in U.S. Grand Strategy*. Cornell University Press.

Ikenberry, G. John. 2000. *After Victory: Institutions, Strategic Restraint, and the Rebuilding of Order After Major Wars*. Princeton: Princeton University Press.

Ikenberry, G. John. 2017. "The Plot Against American Foreign Policy." *Foreign Affairs*, June. https://www.foreignaffairs.com/articles/united-states/2017-04-17/plot-against-american-foreign-policy

James, William. 2021. "Grand Strategy and the Challenge of Change." In *The Oxford Handbook of Grand Strategy*, edited by Thierry Balzacq and Ronald R. Krebs. Oxford: Oxford University Press.

Johnston, Alastair Iain. 1998. *Cultural Realism: Strategic Culture and Grand Strategy in Chinese History*. Princeton: Princeton University Press.

Kennedy, Paul. 1991a. *Grand Strategies in War and Peace*. New Haven: Yale University Press.

Kennedy, Paul. 1991b. "Grand Strategy in War and Peace: Toward a Broader Definition." In *Grand Strategies in War and Peace*, edited by Paul Kennedy. New Haven: Yale University Press.

Kennedy, Paul. 2010. *The Rise and Fall of the Great Powers*. New York: Vintage.

Kennedy, Paul. 2017. *The Rise and Fall of British Naval Mastery*. New York: Penguin Books Limited.

Krebs, Ronald R. 2015. *Narrative and the Making of US National Security*. Cambridge: Cambridge University Press.

Kroenig, Matthew. 2017. "The Case for Trump's Foreign Policy." *Foreign Affairs*, June. https://www.foreignaffairs.com/articles/world/2017-04-17/case-trump-s-foreign-policy

Lakatos, Imre. 1970. "Falsificationism and Methodology of Research Programmes." In *Criticism and the Growth of Knowledge*, edited by Imre Lakatos and Alan Musgrave. Cambridge: Cambridge University Press.

Layne, Christopher. 2007. *The Peace of Illusions: American Grand Strategy from 1940 to the Present*. Ithaca: Cornell University Press.

Legro, Jeffrey. 2005. *Rethinking the World: Great Power Strategies and International Order*. Princeton: Princeton: Princeton University Press.

Lissner, Rebecca. Forthcoming. *Wars of Revelation: The Transformative Effects of Military Intervention on Grand Strategy*. New York: Oxford University Press.

Lissner, Rebecca. 2018. "What Is Grand Strategy? Sweeping a Conceptual Minefield." *Texas National Security Review* 2 (1): 52–73.

Lissner, Rebecca. 2019. "Military Intervention and the Future of American Grand Strategy." In *New Voices in Grand Strategy*. Washington, D.C.: Center for a New American Security.

Lissner, Rebecca, and Mira Rapp-Hooper. 2018. "The Day after Trump: American Strategy for a New International Order." *The Washington Quarterly* 41 (1): 7–25.

Lissner, Rebecca and Mira Rapp-Hooper. 2020. *An Open World: How America Can Win the Contest for Twenty-First-Century Order*. New Haven: Yale University Press.

Lissner, Rebecca, and Micah Zenko. 2017. "There Is No Trump Doctrine, and There Will Never Be One." *Foreign Policy*, July. http://foreignpolicy.com/2017/07/21/there-is-no-trump-doctrine-and-there-will-never-be-one-grand-strategy/

May, Ernest. 1962. "The Nature of Foreign Policy: The Calculated versus the Axiomatic." *Daedalus* 91 (4): 653–667.

Mazower, Mark. 2009. *Hitler's Empire: How the Nazis Ruled Europe*. New York: Penguin Publishing Group.

McDougall, Walter. 1997. *Promised Land, Crusader State: The American Encounter with the World Since 1776*. Boston: Houghton Mifflin.

Mead, Walter Russell. 2013. *Special Providence: American Foreign Policy and How It Changed the World*. London: Routledge.

Mearsheimer, John. 2001. *The Tragedy of Great Power Politics*. New York: Norton.

Milevski, Lucas. 2016. *The Evolution of Modern Grand Strategic Thought*. Oxford: Oxford University Press.

Popescu, Ionut C. 2017. *Emergent Strategy and Grand Strategy*. Baltimore: The Johns Hopkins University Press.

Porter, Patrick. 2019. "Why U.S. Grand Strategy Has Not Changed: Power, Habit and the Foreign Policy Establishment." *International Security* 42 (4): 9–46.

Posen, Barry. 2014. *Restraint: A New Foundation for US Grand Strategy*. Ithaca: Cornell University Press.

Rice, Condoleezza. 1991. "The Evolution of Soviet Grand Strategy." In *Grand Strategies in War and Peace*, edited by Paul Kennedy, 145–167. New Haven: Yale University Press.

Rose, Gideon. 1998. "Neoclassical Realism and Theories of Foreign Policy." *World Politics* 51 (1): 144–172.

Schake, Kori. 2018. "The Trump Doctrine Is Winning and the World Is Losing." *The New York Times*, June 15, 2018. https://www.nytimes.com/2018/06/15/opinion/sunday/trump-china-america-first.html

Schweller, Randall. 1998. *Deadly Imbalances: Tripolarity and Hitler's Strategy of World Conquest*. New York: Columbia University Press.

Schweller, Randall. 2010. *Unanswered Threats: Political Constraints on the Balance of Power*. Princeton: Princeton University Press.

"Scowcroft Citadel Commencement Speech." 1991. CF00295, Michael Hayden Chronological Files. George H.W. Bush Library.

Sestanovich, Stephen. 2014. *Maximalist: America in the World from Truman to Obama*. New York: Knopf Doubleday.

Silove, Nina. 2018. "Beyond the Buzzword: The Three Meanings of 'Grand Strategy.'" *Security Studies* 27 (1).

Snyder, Jack L. 1991. *Myths of Empire: Domestic Politics and International Ambition*. Cornell Studies in Security Affairs. Ithaca: Cornell University Press.

Sparrow, Bartholomew. 2015. *The Strategist: Brent Scowcroft and the Call of National Security*. PublicAffairs.

Tooze, Adam. 2008. *The Wages of Destruction: The Making and Breaking of the Nazi Economy*. New York: Penguin Publishing Group.

Trubowitz, Peter. 1998. *Defining the National Interest: Conflict and Change in American Foreign Policy*. American Politics and Political Economy Series. Chicago: University of Chicago Press.

Trubowitz, Peter. 1999. "Geography and Strategy: The Politics of American Naval Expansion." In *The Politics of Strategic Adjustment: Ideas, Institutions, and Interests*, edited by Peter Trubowitz, Emily Goldman, and Edward Rhodes, 105–138. New York: Columbia University Press.

Trubowitz, Peter. 2011. *Politics and Strategy: Partisan Ambition and American Statecraft*. Princeton: Princeton University Press.

Walt, Stephen. 2018. *The Hell of Good Intentions: America's Foreign Policy Elite and the Decline of U.S. Primacy*. New York: Farrar, Straus and Giroux.

Waltz, Kenneth N. 1979. *Theory of International Politics*. Reading: Addison-Wesley.

Waltz, Kenneth N. 2000. "Structural Realism after the Cold War." *International Security* 25 (1): 5–41.

Zelikow, Philip, and Condoleezza Rice. 1995. *Germany Unified and Europe Transformed: A Study in Statecraft*. Cambridge: Harvard University Press.

Zoellick, Robert. 2011. "An Architecture of U.S. Strategy After the Cold War." In *In Uncertain Times: American Foreign Policy after the Berlin Wall and 9/11*, edited by Melvyn Leffler and Jeffrey Legro. Ithaca: Cornell University Press.

PART VI
ASSESSING GRAND STRATEGY

CHAPTER 34

GETTING GRAND STRATEGY RIGHT

HAL BRANDS AND PETER FEAVER

In the last several decades, grand strategy has been a growth industry of academic study and an arena of considerable—often heated—policymaking debate. This attention justifies the writing of an Oxford University Press Handbook. But, perhaps unusually for a Handbook topic, the cottage industry of critics decrying both grand strategy as a concept and its utility in statecraft is as lively and vocal as is the cluster of scholars and practitioners who openly see value in the enterprise. We are squarely in the latter cluster, and use this chapter to explain what grand strategy is and why policymakers, even those who pooh-pooh the label, keep finding themselves engaging in it. We focus on grand strategy in the American case because this has been the focus of the most extensive study and the most sustained critique. It is also the focus of our own scholarly and policy efforts.[1]

We begin by defining the term and sketching out the basic parameters of grand strategy as it has existed in the US case. We next explain why policymakers find value in strategizing of this sort. We follow with what we call the conventional critique of grand strategy, which claims that the exercise is too demanding for harried policymakers to actually do in a meaningful way. We show how this conventional critique is grounded in a strawman misunderstanding of what policymakers actually do when they are addressing great issues of state. We next consider the revisionist critique, which makes a diametrically contrary claim about the willingness of policymakers to do grand strategy, but nevertheless concludes that in the US case such strategizing has been pernicious because of an allegedly skewed marketplace of ideas. We show how this critique fundamentally misstates how policymakers have actually wrestled with options and possible courses of action and fails to deal candidly with the advantages of the grand-strategic choices American policymakers have made over the years—and the disadvantages of the alternatives that the critics wished policymakers had chosen instead. We close with a brief discussion of how grand strategy as a field helps to bridge the divide between scholars and practitioners in American foreign policy.

American Grand Strategy: Definition and Ontology

Grand strategy is a term of art that refers to the state's effort to harness all elements of national power—political, military, diplomatic, economic, moral, and psychological—to address the threats and opportunities it confronts at any given time. Grand strategy is not limited to military tools, but it conceptually borrows from the military hierarchy of tactics in support of operations in support of a theater strategy in support of an overarching grand strategy.

The definition we find most useful is "the intellectual architecture that gives form and structure to foreign policy … a purposeful and coherent set of ideas about what a nation seeks to accomplish in the world, and how it should go about doing so" (Brands 2014, 3). Grand strategy in this sense functions something like a lawyer's "theory of the case," answering big questions such as "who are we" and "what are the threats and opportunities" (is my client better served by arguing the evidence or the law?) and from that foundation identifying a mix of military, diplomatic, and economic lines of effort that will help navigate those threats and opportunities (allocating effort between arguing the law and arguing the facts).

Properly understood, grand strategy is future-oriented and purposeful, what policymakers bring to the table as they wrestle with geopolitical challenges. It is not, therefore, merely a post-hoc rationalization of whatever pattern one can induce from the historical data of actual practice. There are times when the crush of events in a fast-moving crisis requires leaders to react and respond, improvising and adapting as fast as their government apparatus will let them. Sometimes, this ends well, and a well-meaning memoirist can try to backfill in a logic that would "retrodict" (backwards predict) what leadership was thinking and trying to do in that moment. That is not what we mean by grand strategy. To qualify as grand strategy, it must have a deeper logic beyond "getting out of this thing alive."

Even in those highly improvisational moments, however, some elements of grand strategy may be evident. For instance, the central tendencies and predictable reflexes of leaders likely stem from a deeper logic about how the world works that would qualify as a grand strategy. Hitler's tendency to double-down in a predicament was a crisis reflex, but it flowed from his deeper theory of how he thought geopolitical power worked, which fed his calamitous grand strategy. Obama's reflex to resist calls for military intervention likewise operated in the moment in a crisis, but also flowed from a larger grand strategy (Brands 2016a). In a crisis, no one says, "let's consult our grand strategy plan to see what we should do." But they do so implicitly, because the cost/benefit calculations and list of preferred options that are tried first generally do link back to grand strategies.

Grand strategy is forward-looking in the sense of recommending a course of action before it has been taken, but in the American case, grand strategy has always had a backward-looking premise: the kernel of every significant American grand strategy shift has been an attempt to avoid the last major war. George Washington's Farewell Address laid out a grand strategy aimed at ensuring the infant republic avoided another war with Britain like it had just narrowly won. The grand strategy involved eschewing permanent entangling alliances, biding time so as to build up American power for some future period when America could afford to play a more martial role on the world stage: "[t]he period is not far off when we may defy material injury from external annoyance ... when we may choose peace or war, as interest, guided by justice, shall counsel" (Washington 1796).

The grand strategy of the 1920s and 30s that informed the US decision to reject membership in the League of Nations and then to stay out of great power crises in Europe and Asia was a self-conscious effort to avoid a costly commitment to a major war, as had just happened in the Great War. Containment, the most celebrated of American grand strategies, was an effort to confront the menace of global communism without slipping back into a great power shooting war as had happened in the Second World War. The grand strategy that has animated US policy since 1990 has been an attempt to avoid another Cold War, that is, avoid confronting another hostile peer rival who has the military, diplomatic, political, and economic wherewithal to challenge US interests across multiple regions. Arguably, the shifts in American grand strategy back towards offshore balancing that Presidents Obama and Trump have both sought to impose also have the backward-looking element of an attempt to avoid another Iraq War.

Grand strategy can be articulated in text—in major speeches and white papers where the president and his principal advisors explain what they are trying to do and why, or in classified documents designed to win internal debates over different courses of action and to direct the rest of the government on key lines of action. But it is instantiated in action that is subject to continual revision and recalibration. In this way, grand strategy, at least as it has been practiced in the United States, is "emergent" (Popescu 2017). Thus, the well-worn aphorism, "no plan survives contact with the enemy."

Grand Strategy: The Benefits

If grand strategy is destined to be buffeted by crises and shocks, why bother crafting and implementing it at all? A number of modern statesmen—including President Bill Clinton—have explicitly argued that there is simply no point in doing grand strategy, and as we discuss subsequently, many scholars believe that grand strategy is simply impossible (Talbott 2002, 133). More recently, National Security Adviser John Bolton denigrated his own administration's earlier efforts to chart grand strategy, saying that the National Security Strategy produced under the guidance of his predecessor, H.R. McMaster, was "written and filed away ... consulted by no one" (Wood 2019). In reality, however, grand strategy is critical to effective statecraft, particularly for a country with as much power and as widely varying interests as the United States. There are several reasons for this.

First, the prioritizing function of grand strategy—deciding what goals, threats, and opportunities are most important—is essential to operating in a world where resources are finite. Nations rarely have enough money, military power, diplomatic capacity, or top-level attention to deal effectively with every issue they confront. Even the most dominant countries of the modern era—the United States following the Second World War, for instance—have faced agonizing tradeoffs between competing demands and priorities (Leffler 1992). If statesmen are to make these tradeoffs intelligently, if they are to avoid squandering their resources by using them on peripheral issues or dissipating those resources by spending them profligately, they must distinguish between core and secondary interests and deploy their assets accordingly.

Public documents such as the legislatively mandated National Security Strategy outlining an administration's grand-strategic approach necessarily blur these tradeoffs in carefully parsed and vague language. Yet the very act of preparing those documents can have two salutary effects. On one hand, it can force an administration to wrestle with the tensions inherent in any comprehensive set of foreign policy objectives. Thus, the awkwardness the first Clinton administration endured in drafting its initial National Security Strategy—which entailed straddling the ambition of "assertive multilateralism" with the reality of a casualty-averse president in a world of Somalias, Rwandas, and Haitis—was useful in helping the Clinton team come to terms with what they were actually willing, at the end of the day, to risk US prestige, treasure, and, above all, blood to achieve. On the other hand, when the actual results of a strategy fall so far short of what was expected, the requirement to explain the policy in public can help the administration refine its goals and bring them more in alignment with what is achievable. Thus, the challenge the second-term Bush administration faced in drafting a National Security Strategy to explain the "preemption" and the "freedom agenda" after the Iraq War and the election of Hamas in the Palestinian Authority had turned those terms into punchlines which forced the president and his advisors to reevaluate and refine the logic that undergirded and fueled their main lines of effort.

Even in periods when a state's relative power is at its apogee—for instance, the United States in the first dozen years after the collapse of the Soviet Union—the list of global problems the leaders might tackle will always be longer than the list of problems they can actually tackle successfully. Thus, at a time when many critics inside and outside government criticized the Clinton and Bush administrations for over-intervening militarily around the world, there were still many possible military entanglements the United States considered but rejected: intervening in Somalia but not Sudan, Rwanda, or the Congo; waging war to stop ethnic cleansing in Kosovo, but not Armenia, Azerbaijan, or Georgia; invading Iraq, but not Iran or North Korea; and so on. Picking and choosing amongst these potential conflicts is, of course, a classic cost–benefit exercise, but it is one in which grand strategy can play a crucial role by giving rank-ordered values to perceived costs and benefits and by forcing the administration to confront gaps between rhetoric and reality.

Second, while lesser powers can certainly have grand strategies, superpowers particularly need them to make sense of the world. Being a superpower entails pursuing dozens of foreign policy initiatives on a daily basis; it involves having a dizzying array of interests in countries and regions around the world. It is not enough simply to address these issues on an ad hoc or case-by-case basis, because doing so will inevitably result in a foreign policy that is contradictory in its parts and incoherent in its whole. "Theateritis"—the tendency to focus intensely on a specific issue at the expense of the broader global picture—will run rampant. Superpowers need an overarching idea of what they are trying to accomplish in the world, and of how individual policies fit into that broader matrix, if they are to make their policies cohesive and their power effective.

Third, grand strategy helps leaders improvise intelligently. No grand strategy can save a leader from the imperative of improvising—the world is full of surprises, even for the most intelligent strategist. All leaders will find themselves in the position of having to react, quickly and with little time for deep reflection, to unexpected and often unwelcome developments. Yet here grand strategy becomes all the more important. If leaders have done the intellectual tasks that are associated with grand strategy—setting goals, prioritizing among threats and interests, thinking hard about how to apply finite resources across an array of opportunities and challenges, and developing well-grounded theories of how the world works—they will have an intellectual framework that allows them to improvise in more effective and purposeful ways. Grand strategy, in this sense, plays the role of theory in Clausewitz's classic formulation (von Clausewitz 1984):

> Theory cannot equip the mind with formulas for solving problems, nor can it mark the narrow path on which the sole solution is supposed to lie by planting a hedge of principles on either side. But it can give the mind insight into the great mass of phenomena and of their relationships, then leave it free to rise into the higher realms of action. There the mind can use its innate talents to capacity, combining them all so as to seize on what is *right* and *true* as though this were a single idea formed by their concentrated pressure—as though it were a response to the immediate challenge rather than a product of thought.

Fourth, grand strategy is important because the world is competitive—often viciously so. Countries have enemies and rivals that seek to do them harm. Those enemies and rivals seek out a country's weaknesses and try to exploit them. A grand strategy that features a sound understanding of what one's own strengths—and an opponent's weaknesses—are can provide statesmen with an intellectual advantage in a rivalrous world. It can also help countries maintain focus on their key objectives even as they are being jostled by the actions of their competitors. Countries can have grand strategies even when they do not face a single, all-defining rivalry or competition. But when the competition becomes intense, grand strategy becomes all the more valuable.

Fifth, grand strategy matters because the consequences of messing it up are so severe. Getting foreign policy right requires mastering tactics and operations as well as grand strategy: the United States could not have won the Second World War had it not figured out, in cooperation with the British, how to safely get ships across the Atlantic or conduct opposed amphibious landings. Yet states that have an intelligent grand strategy may be better suited to surmounting initial tactical or operational difficulties, while those with a flawed grand strategy will struggle even if they achieve tactical virtuosity. During the First World War, for instance, German troops fought more effectively than their British, French, Russian, or American enemies. Yet Germany lost the war, largely because of a series of grand-strategic blunders that ensured it ultimately confronted a vastly superior allied coalition. During the Second World War, German troops were again tactically superior, and Germany again lost because a series of even more egregious grand-strategic blunders by Hitler thrust Berlin into a multi-front war that it could not win (Millett and Murray 1988). When countries get their grand-strategic choices fundamentally wrong, disaster often follows.

Finally, grand strategy is critical because grand-strategic choice is unavoidable. Even leaders who do not believe in grand strategy have to engage in grand-strategic decision-making. They must make judgments about what a country stands for, about which objectives take precedence over others, about how to make tradeoffs between competing imperatives, and about how to best use their limited resources. Given that there is simply no way of avoiding these sorts of decisions, the challenge is to make these decisions as purposefully and wisely as possible. And that requires taking grand strategy seriously.

The Conventional Critique of Grand Strategy: It Is Too Hard for Countries Like the US to Do

Many academics, however, are not inclined to do so. As a field of study, American grand strategy is unusual. A significant fraction of the scholarly and pundit commentary that uses the term "American grand strategy" uses it as a pejorative.

Eliot Cohen (2016, 203–206) offers a conventional critique of grand strategy, dismissing it as a "soothing concept," "illusory," "an idea whose time will never come, because the human condition does not permit it." Cohen claims that grand strategy is impossible because policymakers are unable to anticipate the future and thus are unable to craft overarching strategies that stand the test of time. The notion of a grand strategy that might animate leaders over several administrations or government changes ignores the crucial role of the great leaders who make the big decisions on which history hinges. Grand strategy might offer a big concept like "containment," Cohen argues, but such vague ideas are almost never dispositive in deciding tough cases. Did containment require propping up the anti-communist South Vietnamese, or did it require abandoning them to their fate? Advocates for these mutually exclusive policies—and countless intermediate hybrid approaches—argued that containment led them here and not there; if they all were right about containment, how could it be useful as a grand strategy? Thus, Cohen concludes, grand strategy "offers very little guidance" to policymakers who are wrestling with tough geopolitical choices.

David M. Edelstein and Ronald R. Krebs (2015, 110) say that grand strategy is "illusory" because a state cannot have consistent preferences, cannot evaluate the pros and cons of alternative courses of action, and cannot follow through on its choices. Geopolitics is simply too uncertain to provide the full knowledge of threats that they allege grand strategy to require. Foreign policy is "consistently unpredictable," they claim, and grand strategy does not help leaders sort through this confusion. Grand strategy must involve a "carefully charted course," which is an impossibility given the friction of bureaucratic politics and geostrategic surprises, so it simply does not exist. Enduring consistencies in strategic approaches, for instance the decades long commitment to build a liberal international order, represent merely "after the fact rationalization" of a process driven by structural realities, not purposive policies. Edelstein expands on this conventional critique in his own chapter in this volume.

The conventional critique often entails a scathing review of the major strategy documents that present aspects of American grand strategy to a public audience. The National Security Strategy, which is the top-line document purporting to lay out the president's theory of the case, is a favorite target of ridicule. Rebecca Lissner (2017, 2–3) critiques the NSS of the Bush and Obama administrations as "soaring rhetorical flourishes and extravagant goals unconstrained by material and political realities." Edelstein and Krebs (2015, 113) are unsparing, mocking it as a "laundry list of threats and challenges so long and varied that leaders can always point to some success or deflect some blame after the fact."

In sum, the conventional critique of American grand strategy dismisses the concept as grandiose, far beyond the capabilities of the policymakers toiling away on day-to-day foreign policy. Conventional critics further complain that, when required by law to produce documents purporting to be "grand strategies," the result is a disappointing mishmash of wishful thinking and laundry lists of to-do items. For a good exemplar of the conventional critique, one need look no further than Richard Betts' chapter in this very volume.

What the Conventional Critique Misses

The conventional critique sets fire to a strawman version of American grand strategy: a detailed master plan that carefully integrates all elements of national power, with branches and sequels addressing every possible contingency. Critics are right that that type of grand strategy does not exist and, if it were created, would not be very useful since it would quickly be overtaken by events.

But using a more reasonable definition of grand strategy—as a theory of the case, a way of making sense of the world—turns the figment into a fact. By this definition, most American leaders do have a grand strategy, even if they still must improvise in response to external shocks.

It is now well understood, for instance, that the Truman administration operated on the basis of a fairly coherent grand strategy during the early Cold War. That grand strategy revolved around a series of key ideas—that containment offered a preferable alternative to both appeasement and war, that checking Soviet power meant preserving an advantageous configuration of power on the Eurasian landmass, and that preserving this configuration of power required first rebuilding and protecting the core industrial regions of Western Europe and Northeast Asia.

During the late 1940s and early 1950s, the Truman administration had to IMPROVISE continually in dealing with myriad strategic shocks and unforeseen crises—the collapse of British power in the Mediterranean, the Berlin blockade, the Chinese civil war, the North Korean invasion of South Korea, and many others. How much the United States spent on defense, whether it should defend South Korea if that country were attacked, and other major questions were debated fiercely, and the Truman administration answered those questions in different ways at different times. But these basic ideas about American goals, objectives, and priorities anchored virtually all of the Truman administration's major initiatives, informing the Marshall Plan, the creation of NATO, the revival of Japan and West Germany, and the eventual buildup of Western military power amid the Korean War, and other policies that gave substance to containment.

Even the administration's improvisations were related to this core set of concepts. Although US officials had not originally envisioned creating a semi-permanent military alliance with Western Europe, for instance, that decision flowed logically from the belief that reviving that region was America's primary strategic priority, and from the realization that doing so required offering military protection as well as economic assistance. Similarly, the decision to defend South Korea in June 1950 rested largely on the belief that doing so was critical to preserving American credibility in Western Europe and Japan.

At times, the administration was diverted from its grand strategy, such as when it unwisely expanded the Korean War into North Korea and thereby triggered Chinese intervention. Yet the core logic of the grand strategy quickly reasserted itself: after December 1950, the administration recommitted to fighting a limited war in Korea so that it could focus its resources on Western Europe and, to a lesser extent, Japan (Brands 2014).

At the close of the Cold War, the Reagan administration operated on the basis of a similarly coherent grand strategy. Like Truman's grand strategy, Reagan's was based on a relatively small number of key ideas, many of which he had been articulating since the mid-1970s: that the Soviet Union was a formidable military power, but one that was geopolitically overextended and suffering from profound economic, ideological, and moral weakness; that it was therefore vulnerable to a concerted US counteroffensive using all forms of national power; and that this counteroffensive could actually set the stage for a longer-term turn to negotiation and a marked reduction of Cold War tensions on American terms.

These ideas underpinned the Reagan offensive of the early 1980s, which featured pronounced military, diplomatic, economic, ideological, and covert pressures on the Soviet Union and its allies. They also informed Reagan's shift toward coercive diplomacy from 1983 to 1984 onward, in which the administration fused continued pressure with a diplomatic engagement strategy meant to induce deep changes in Soviet behavior. There were, as always, unexpected developments along the way: Reagan himself seemed surprised by how dramatically his offensive drove up East–West tensions during the early 1980s, culminating in the war scare of 1983. But far from making it up as he went along, Reagan was acting on a grand-strategic logic that he understood—and that his administration clearly articulated in important classified documents.

National Security Decision Directive 32 (1982, 1–4), issued in 1982, outlined the "development and integration of a set of strategies, including diplomatic, informational, economic/political, and military components." America's objectives, the document stated, would be to "strengthen the influence of the US throughout the world," "to contain and reverse the expansion of Soviet control and military presence throughout the world," to "discourage Soviet adventurism, and weaken the Soviet alliance system by forcing the USSR to bear the brunt of its economic shortcomings, and to encourage long-term liberalizing and nationalist tendencies within the Soviet Union and allied countries." If the United States could hold a steady course, that document predicted, it might bring about "a fundamentally different East-West relationship by the end of this decade."

NSDD-75 (1983, 1), issued in January 1983, laid out the "escalate to de-escalate" logic of Reagan's strategy even more explicitly. US grand strategy, NSDD-75 explained, would consist of three key thrusts, or stages:

1. To contain and over time reverse Soviet expansion by competing effectively on a sustained basis with the Soviet Union in all international arenas—particularly in the overall military balance and in geographical regions of priority concern to the United States...
2. To promote within the narrow limits available to us, the process of change in the Soviet Union toward a more pluralistic political and economic system in which the power of the privileged ruling elite is gradually reduced...
3. To engage the Soviet Union in negotiations to attempt to reach agreements which protect and enhance U.S. interests and which are consistent with the principle of strict reciprocity and mutual interest.

The idea, NSDD-75 (1983, 9) noted, was to use an interlocking array of programs and policies to regain the geopolitical ascendancy over Moscow, and then to find a more "stable and constructive long-term basis for U.S.-Soviet relations."

These documents provide a veritable grand-strategic roadmap for what actually happened during the 1980s—the remarkable turning of the tide in the Cold War during the first half of the decade, and the equally remarkable Soviet retreat from that conflict that began in the second. Reagan had plenty of help from the decay of the Soviet system and the innovations introduced by Mikhail Gorbachev, of course, but the point is that his grand strategy recognized that decay and implemented policies meant to take advantage of it. Grand strategy presumes that one can trace a line from intentions to policies to results. The Reagan administration provides a good example of precisely this phenomenon.

The Revisionist Critique: The US Has a Grand Strategy, and It Is a Disaster

There is another prominent, but also flawed, strand of critique regarding American grand strategy. This, which we call the revisionist critique, rejects or assumes away most of the arguments of the conventional critique. Revisionists accept that there is such a thing as a grand strategy that helps shape policymakers' approaches to the streams of crises and opportunities that flood the inbox. Revisionists accept that leaders have theories about how the world works and seek to implement policies that are logical extrapolations of those theories. Where conventionalists dismiss grand strategy as almost a laughing matter, revisionists take it dead seriously—for they claim that in the US case, at least since the end of the Cold War and perhaps earlier, policymakers have been pursuing a disastrously wrongheaded grand strategy.

A prominent example of the revisionist critique is Patrick Porter's lament that the United States has foolishly pursued the same grand strategy of "primacy" in the post–Cold War era that it had pursued during the Cold War, spending blood and treasure in an effort to head off security threats before they metastasize into a hostile peer rival that would threaten the American-led international order rather than retreat to a more noninterventionist strategy (Porter 2018). Porter sees far more logic and consistency than do conventional critics, but he claims the logic is so faulty and the results so deleterious that the real question is: how could the United States be so stubbornly stupid? His answer is simple: benighted foreign policy elites have conspired to prevent alternative grand strategies from having a fair hearing within the policymaking process and within the broader public debate. Porter's lament follows other revisionist critics like Stephen Walt (2018) and John Mearsheimer (2018), who warn darkly about shadowy forces that wield disproportionate influence within decision-making circles. Edelstein and Krebs (2015, 112 and 114) offer a somewhat milder version of the same argument, claiming that the "playing field" of foreign policy debate is "skewed, dominated by powerful, mainstream voices." Grand strategy, they claim, is counterproductive—threat-mongering that turns imaginary problems into actual ones. Far better is a grand strategy vaguely called "restraint" that would have the United States ignore security problems in most of the world as irrelevant to its interests, and address the security problems that do matter from over the horizon with an "off-shore balancing" approach that relied primarily on local actors (Posen 2014; Walt and Mearsheimer 2016). Edelstein, in his chapter in this volume, also incorporates a revisionist critique when he claims that the mistakes the US made during the Cold War could be traced to the grand strategy of containment, and when he claims that the pivot to Asia created the self-fulfilling prophecy of a confrontational dynamic with China.

In short, revisionist critics claim that elites have duped political leaders and the public into accepting a grand strategy that is manifestly inferior to the ones advanced by the critics themselves. If the public and policymakers would give us a fair shake, the critics aver, they would see that we are right and the prevailing grand strategy is wrong.

What the Revisionist Critique Misses

The revisionists rightly recognize that conventional critics are wrong. Policymakers do tend to have a theory of how the world works and do pursue lines of action logically consistent with that theory, at least at some broad level. But revisionists grossly overstate the consensus in favor of the grand strategy that guided American leaders in the post–Cold War era, grossly understate the degree of adaptation through trial and error in the conduct of that grand strategy, and fail to provide a convincing rebuttal to the most obvious explanation for the longevity of the strategy—its effectiveness in advancing American national interest in a dangerous world (Brands and Feaver 2019).

Revisionists dismiss as secondary the very real debates over restraint options: debates over whether to reduce the US footprint in NATO in every decade of its existence—and similar debates about US commitments in Northeast Asia in the 1970s. These debates were renewed in the 1990s and, of course, were very prominent in the early Trump administration. The restraint option has been thoroughly debated in the corridors of power and exhaustively promoted in the security studies community in academic and think tank circles.

Moreover, in key respects, it has been tried and found wanting. President Obama self-consciously opted for the restraint option and began to shift the US posture in the direction of offshore balancing in the heart of the Middle East when he resisted calls to intervene more forcefully in the Syrian civil war after 2011 (as distinct from Southwest Asia, where he initially escalated the US ground commitment in Afghanistan before accelerating a drawdown), and when he brought US forces in Iraq down to zero in 2012. This experiment with a grand strategy of restraint in the Middle East core failed when Iran and Russia flowed into the vacuum created by America's departure, and when the terrorist group Islamic State (IS) used the chaos to establish a caliphate that threatened to topple the governments of Syria, Iraq, and Jordan, whilst training tens of thousands of foreigners from around the globe in terrorist techniques and shocking the world with barbarism and mass atrocities. When IS forces threatened the outskirts of the capital city Baghdad, an obviously reluctant Obama finally shifted back towards the more interventionist stance that the revisionist critics had earlier deplored. Revisionists could reasonably complain that Obama should have given their restraint grand strategy a longer test run, but they could not accurately claim that offshore balancing had not been tried.

American policymakers did give offshore balancing and the restraint grand strategy a long, two-decade run during the interwar years of 1919–1939. They came to regret it profoundly. It turns out that the short-term savings in blood and treasure that US restraint might have won in the 1920s and 1930s was paid with interest in the 1940s when the butcher's bill of the Second World War came due. For precisely this reason, American policymakers in the decades since have found the restraint grand strategy a consistently tempting option at first glance, but one that fails to pass a hardheaded cost–benefit assessment when subjected to the realistic tests of actual governance.

In this sense, revisionists fail to recognize that American grand strategy is quite pragmatic. Theories and bold notions that sound good in an academic seminar tend to wither under the rigorous cross-examination to which the policymaking process subjects any proposal. Of course, in foreign policy, the choices are often between bad and worse outcomes, and proffered panaceas that sound too good to be true usually turn out to be false hopes. Thus, policymakers are usually picking courses of action with significant unintended but anticipatable downsides. The biggest mistakes of the competing approaches—for instance, the invasion of Iraq and the abandonment of Iraq—have been subjected to due critique. Policymakers have hardly been perfect; on the contrary, there is an unfortunate tendency to overcorrect for the errors of a previous period. But the marketplace of ideas has functioned reasonably well, and the results have been superior. As Walter Russell Mead (2001, 10–12) has observed, no great power has had a better last 250 years, or 100 years, or 50 years, or even 25 years than has the United States. Over the past seventy years, American grand strategy has helped usher in an unprecedented era of global and US prosperity, helped spread democracy and human rights across continents and cultures, and managed the incredible risks of nuclear war and great power war without stumbling into either. While the revisionists have rightly drawn attention to the costs of American grand strategy, the fact remains that America is well positioned to advance its interests relative to what other great powers are confronting. Every great power would prefer to swap America's problems for their own. As grand strategies go, America's has been remarkably successful.

It is hard to imagine, moreover, that the United States would have been anywhere near as successful in foreign affairs had it simply made it up as it went along. American grand strategy was certainly facilitated by the country's superior economic power, its remarkably favorable geography, and other endowments. Yet countries can play a good hand well or poorly, and American grand strategy—a set of broadly shared ideas about how the United States should deploy its power in the service of a particular type of world order—generally allowed the United States to apply its power in a focused way (or to regain that focus after occasional periods of distraction). A country that was operating with no grand strategy at all would have found it infinitely more difficult to accomplish tasks that required persistence over many years or decades: shaping an open global economy, containing aggressive powers, pacifying formerly conflict-prone regions, and so on. It took power *and* purpose to create the world that we inhabit today: grand strategy provided the purpose that was required to make power serve great ends.

Grand Strategy Helps to Bridge the Gap

The academic critiques of grand strategy are thus unpersuasive. And yet grand strategy remains a particularly fertile field for academic study. One ironic reason, given the substance of much of the academic complaint: this is an area where scholars and other experts outside government can make meaningful contributions to policy debates precisely because here the playing field is more level. The more tactical a policy question becomes, the greater the premium on the types of information that only insiders have in abundance and high fidelity. The more grand strategic the debate is, the less decisive is classified information, and the less critical are the personality conflicts and operational processes that drive bureaucratic politics and are so hard to comprehend fully from outside of government.

It is no surprise, therefore, that most of the critics of American grand strategy cited above have all enjoyed extensive access to policymaking circles. A significant number are a staple of the think tank and study panel circuit, and, in our experience, many of their substantive critiques are read and referenced at the working level within government. They are correct when they claim that, on balance, policymakers have rarely followed their prescriptions to the letter. But they do not give themselves enough credit for the times that their arguments may have actually helped shape policy choices—for instance, the efforts by Presidents Obama and Trump to reduce the US military footprint in both the Middle East (especially Iraq and Syria) and in Southwest Asia (especially Afghanistan). Moreover, even when US policymakers have made grand-strategic choices that have run counter to those advocated by prominent academic grand strategists—for instance, the decision to reinvigorate and expand NATO after the Cold War or the decision to maintain an active internationalist agenda during the same period—the policymaking debate has duly considered, weighed, and found wanting the academic prescriptions to do something else. The contrast between how academic arguments have been able to percolate into these grand-strategic policymaking debates versus how academic considerations are all but absent in the more nitty-gritty policymaking debates of, say, how to structure partnerships with Kurdish irregular forces fighting against IS is striking. We are not claiming that academic experts do not have useful things to say on the latter; we are merely claiming that it is vastly easier to inject academic ideas into actual policy debates on the former.

At times, in fact, academic work has been quite influential in shaping US grand strategy. During the Second World War, scholars at the Brookings Institution produced a landmark study that puzzled through major questions about the postwar order.

Because the issues they considered were quite broad in scope, and because this was a time of intellectual ferment within US foreign policy, the scholars were operating on a more-or-less equal footing with American policymakers. Their report articulated ideas that would prove foundational to American grand strategy in the years that followed. They argued, for instance, that the United States must prevent any hostile power from gaining a dominant position in Eurasia, and that this meant checking efforts by the Soviet Union to extend its power through military or political means. As Melvyn Leffler recounts, the report so crystallized emerging strategic thinking about the challenges of the postwar era that the Joint Chiefs of Staff reclassified it as an official document (Leffler 1992, 11).

Similarly, the analytical practices that comprise grand strategizing as a discipline lend themselves quite readily to the kinds of intellectual work on which good policymaking depends. Strategy, as it is defined by the US military, involves developing the ends, ways, and means of policy: what are we trying to accomplish, using what techniques, and powered with what resources? Grand strategizing entails asking those questions and more—asking questions about how US actions shape the incentives and thus the possible responses of other actors in the system; directing attention to likely (or at least plausible) second- and third-order effects, especially the unintended ones; identifying the critical assumptions, especially the implicit ones, on which policy alternatives depend; carefully exploring counterfactual claims to determine which decisions are more pivotal and which are less so; and, crucially, asking the awkward tradeoff questions about how worthy ventures in one domain affect desired outcomes in other domains.

Of course, deep issue knowledge of the sort that comes from all-source intelligence analysis and lengthy experience working given policy lines all can help prepare analysts to *answer* these questions. But in our experience, we have found that a grand strategy orientation is helpful in prompting analysts and policymakers to *ask* these questions. This is partly what is meant by the aphorism, "plans are worthless, planning is everything." Grand strategy, and the work that goes into developing it, pushes policymakers to confront these questions in helpful ways. And it can just as readily be a clear-eyed academic posing these questions as a policy insider. Academic work that asks and then attempts to answer these questions in a rigorous and fair-minded way can prove particularly stimulating for those tasked with developing policies on a day-to-day basis. At a time when laments about the divide between the academy and policy world are fashionable (see Desch 2019; Walt 2018; and Maliniak et al 2020), it is worth celebrating an academic approach with a well-established record of bridging that divide.

Note

1. In this chapter, we draw extensively on our own sole and co-authored work in this area, particularly: Feaver 2009, Feaver 2012, Feaver 2013, Brands 2014, Brands 2016, Brands and Feaver 2016, Brands and Feaver 2016/17, Brands and Feaver 2017, Brands 2018, Brands and Feaver 2019, as well as numerous blog posts.

References

Brands, Hal. 2014. *What Good Is Grand Strategy: Power and Purpose in American Statecraft from Harry S. Truman to George W. Bush.* Ithaca: Cornell University Press.

Brands, Hal. 2016a. "Barack Obama and the dilemmas of American grand strategy." *The Washington Quarterly* 39 (4): 101–125. doi:https://doi.org/10.1080/0163660X.2016.1261557.

Brands, Hal. *Making the Unipolar Moment: U.S. Foreign Policy and the Rise of the Post-Cold War Order.* Ithaca: Cornell University Press.

Brands, Hal. 2018. *American Grand Strategy in the Age of Trump.* Washington: Brookings Institution Press.

Brands, Hal, and Peter Feaver. 2016. "Should America Retrench? The Risks of Retreat." *Foreign Affairs* 95 (6): 164–171.

Brands, Hal, and Peter Feaver. 2016/17. "Stress-Testing American Grand Strategy." *Survival* 58 (6): 93–120. doi: 10.1080/00396338.2016.1257199.

Brands, Hal, and Peter Feaver. 2017. "What Are America's Alliances Good For?" *Parameters* 47 (2): 15–30.

Brands, Hal, and Peter Feaver. 2019. "Correspondence: The Establishment and U.S. Grand Strategy." *International Security* 43 (4): 197–204. doi:10.1162/isec_c_00347.

Cohen, Eliot. 2016. *The Big Stick: The Limits of Soft Power and the Necessity of Military Force.* New York: Basic Books.

Desch, Michael. 2019. *Cult of the Irrelevant: The Waning Influence of Social Science on National Security.* Princeton: Princeton University Press.

Edelstein, David M., and Ronald R. Krebs. 2015. "Delusions of Grand Strategy: The Problem with Washington's Planning Obsession." *Foreign Affairs* 94 (6): 109–116.

Feaver, Peter. 2009. "Special Section: Debating American Grand Strategy After Major War," *Orbis* 53 (4): 547–552. doi:10.1016/j.orbis.2009.07.009.

Feaver, Peter. 2012. "American Grand Strategy at the Crossroads: Leading from the Front, Leading from Behind, or Not Leading at All." In *America's Path: Grand Strategy for the Next Administration*, edited by Richard Fontaine and Kristin M. Lord. Washington, D.C.: Center for New American Security.

Feaver, Peter. 2013. "Eight Myths about American Grand Strategy." In *Forging American Grand Strategy: Securing a Path Through a Complex Future*, edited by Sheila R. Ronis. Carlisle: Strategic Studies Institute, Army War College.

Leffler, Melvyn. 1992. *A Preponderance of Power: National Security, the Truman Administration, and the Cold War.* Stanford: Stanford University Press.

Lissner, Rebecca Friedman. 2017. "The National Security Strategy is Not Strategy." *Foreign Affairs*, December 19, 2017. https://www.foreignaffairs.com/articles/united-states/2017-12-19/national-security-strategy-not-strategy

Maliniak, Daniel, Susan Peterson, Ryan Powers, and Michael J. Tierney, eds. 2020. *A Seat at the Table: (When) Can International Relations Scholars Influence Foreign and International Policy?* Washington: Georgetown University Press.

Mead, Walter Russell. 2013. *Special Providence: American Foreign Policy and How It Changed the World.* New York: Routledge.

Mearsheimer, John J., and Stephen M. Walt. 2016. "The Case for Offshore Balancing." *Foreign Affairs* 95 (4): 70–83.

Mearsheimer, John. 2018. *The Great Delusion: Liberal Dreams and International Realities.* New Haven: Yale University Press.

Millett, Aaron R., and Williamson Murray, eds. 1988. *Military Effectiveness*. London: Allen & Unwin.

Murray, Williamson, MacGregor Knox, and Alvin Bernstein, eds. 1994. *The Making of Strategy: Rulers, States, and War*. New York: Cambridge University Press.

National Security Decision Directive 32: U.S. National Security Strategy. 1982. https://fas.org/irp/offdocs/nsdd/nsdd-32.pdf

National Security Decision Directive 75: U.S. Relations with the USSR. 1983. https://fas.org/irp/offdocs/nsdd/nsdd-75.pdf

Popescu, Ionut. 2017. *Emergent Strategy and Grand Strategy: How American Presidents Succeed in Foreign Policy*. Baltimore: The Johns Hopkins University Press.

Porter, Patrick. 2018. "Why America's Grand Strategy Has not Changed: Power, Habit, and the U.S. Foreign Policy Establishment." *International Security* 42 (4) (Spring): 9–46. doi:10.1162/isec_a_00311.

Posen, Barry R. 2014. *Restraint: A New Foundation for U.S. Grand Strategy*. Ithaca: Cornell University Press.

Talbott, Strobe. 2002. *The Russia Hand: A Memoir of Presidential Diplomacy*. New York: Random House.

von Clausewitz, Carl. 1984. *On War*. Edited and translated by Michael Howard and Peter Paret. Princeton: Princeton University Press.

Walt, Stephen. 2018. *The Hell of Good Intentions: America's Foreign Policy Elite and the Decline of U.S. Primacy*. New York: Farrar, Straus and Giroux.

Walt, Stephen, and John Mearsheimer. 2016. "The Case for Off-Shore Balancing: A Superior US Grand Strategy," *Foreign Affairs* (July/August). https://www.foreignaffairs.com/articles/united-states/2016-06-13/case-offshore-balancing

Washington, George. 1796. "Farewell Address." http://avalon.law.yale.edu/18th_century/washing.asp

Wood, Graeme. 2019. "Will John Bolton Bring on Armageddon—Or Stave it Off?" *Atlantic* (April). https://www.theatlantic.com/magazine/archive/2019/04/john-bolton-trump-national-security-adviser/583246/

CHAPTER 35

THE CHALLENGE OF EVALUATING GRAND STRATEGY

WILLIAM C. WOHLFORTH

A grand strategy constitutes a sustained intervention into the mind-bogglingly complex social world of international politics that is meant to advance a state's interest over the long term. To evaluate it, one must find some way to discipline a counterfactual analysis of how the state would have fared had it adopted a different grand strategy. And if the state concerned is influential enough, its grand-strategic choices might affect the international system writ large, meaning that the evaluator must now tame a counterfactual in which the international system itself might be altered in profound ways. That is an analytically fraught procedure, to put it mildly.

I address this challenge by advancing three propositions that are insufficiently appreciated in writings about grand strategy and, indeed, in scholarship on international politics more generally. First, I establish that evaluation is necessary to much, if not most, scholarship and commentary on grand strategy and to closely related efforts to test systemic theories of international politics. Evaluation can seem trivial or unnecessary only when an expert community shares a consensus about a given grand strategy, but any such consensus is fragile, and masks potential challenges that are likely to come to the fore with the passage of time or as the scholarly debate matures. Second, I show that grand strategy evaluation is much harder than is widely assumed—so hard, in fact, as to risk imposing insurmountable demands on researchers. Third, however, there are pragmatic guidelines for evaluating grand strategy that lie between the all-too-common practice of downplaying the challenge, on the one hand, and, on the other hand, delving so deeply into every possible implication of grand-strategic choice as to find oneself overwhelmed. These pragmatic suggestions for addressing the evaluation challenge make explicit what is too often hidden in international relations scholarship: that both theory and general empirical research about international politics are intimately connected to grand strategy evaluation.

The Necessity of Evaluation

The expert conversation on grand strategy has a strongly normative cast. Analysts routinely take governments past and present to task for following bad strategies or, more rarely, praise them for brilliant ones. John Lewis Gaddis's seminal book on containment in the Cold War was tellingly subtitled "a *critical appraisal*" (Gaddis 2005). The dominant tone is indeed critical, as evidenced by Williamson Murray's observation that "those who have developed successful grand strategies in the past have been much the exception" (Murray 2011). Yet scholars do periodically identify what they see as successful grand strategy, as in Luttwak's study of the Roman Empire (Luttwak 1979), or Kennedy's initially iconoclastic take on the "tradition of appeasement" in British foreign policy (Kennedy 1976). Either way, the point is that a lot of writing in this field is explicitly evaluative. The same obviously goes for another major segment of this literature, namely writings that urge a particular grand strategy on a government—a practice known in the United States as the "Kennan sweepstakes" (Silove 2019).

There is no need to belabor the point that one must evaluate a grand strategy before calling it a success or failure or before telling a government that it needs to be replaced. Less obvious but as important is the role of evaluation in studies that are not explicitly normative but rather seek to *explain* grand strategy or *test* systemic theories of international politics. Scholars usually are motivated to explain things that are puzzling. Grand strategies generally become puzzles crying out for elaborate explanations either if they seem to confound dominant theories or if they strike the observer as self-defeating or otherwise suboptimal. Because the most influential IR theories assume that states are rational, these two ways of identifying puzzles often collapse into one. Hence, a common setup for a study of this type is "State X followed a grand strategy that led to bad results, which is curious in its own right but also confounds this or that IR theory (usually realism)."

The large literature on strategic overexpansion is a case in point. In many dozens of works, scholars claim that expansion on the part of such actors as Hapsburg Spain, Hapsburg Austria, Revolutionary and Napoleonic France, nineteenth-century Russia, Wilhelmine and Nazi Germany, Imperial Japan, the Stalin- and Brezhnev-era USSR, and of course the Cold War and post–Cold War United States presents a puzzle. Having established the puzzle, scholars proceed to proffer explanations, most commonly having to do with flawed domestic institutions, ideas, or decision-making processes. The core premise of these studies is that there is a puzzle of suboptimality that needs to be explained. This presupposes an evaluation of the grand strategy pursued that demonstrates its suboptimality as well as identifies plausible alternatives that would have done better.

The same goes for the closely connected enterprise of evaluating theories of international politics. An important class of theories, notably but not exclusively realist, purports to explain patterns of state behavior over the long term. Long-term patterns of state behavior either are—or are reflections of—grand strategies (Silove 2019). In other words, grand strategies are the "dependent variable" in such theories—that is, the thing the theory seeks to explain. A common way to assess a theory is thus to check whether it is in fact consistent with the evidence about a state's grand strategy. A large swath of IR scholarship that is preoccupied with advancing and testing theories is inevitably involved deeply in the grand strategy evaluation business.

The clearest example of this analytical dependency occurs when theories assume that states seek to maximize some value, such as security, welfare, power, status, or the narrower interests of a ruler or the specific social classes the ruler represents, etc. To advance or critically evaluate any theory built on claims of this type, the analyst frequently seeks to establish whether a state's grand strategy actually appears to reflect the stipulated interest. That clearly demands evaluation: was the grand strategy followed by state X actually optimal for pursuing interest Y? If not, that is bad news for the theory that highlights interest Y, and perhaps good for some other theory that foregrounds some other interest.

Because of its popularity as a target, realism provides a good illustration. Many realist theories are built on the assumption that security, defined as protection against threats to territorial sovereignty, is the dominant interest of states. A common approach to evaluating such theories and advancing alternatives is to argue that a given state's grand strategy is inconsistent with that interest, and thus that realist theories fall short and need to be replaced or supplemented by theories that specify different interests. Evaluating grand strategy is central to this theory-testing exercise. To take an often-cited case, many scholars contend that standard realist theories cannot make sense of Germany's grand strategy in the years leading up to 1914 precisely because it poorly served that country's security interest. By provoking crisis after crisis and building a battleship fleet to challenge Britain's, Berlin seemed to put its initially robust territorial security at risk rather than protect it. Many scholars resolve the puzzle by arguing that the strategy's real purpose was to gain status on the world stage; hence the need for theories that foreground that interest (e.g., Lebow 2010; Murray 2010; Renshon 2017; Ward 2017). Key to this whole enterprise is demonstrating that there were better alternative grand strategies Berlin could plausibly have followed to advance its security.

Yet evaluations of this type are often conspicuous by their absence. This often is because the grand strategy's failure (or success) assumes a taken-for-granted quality. Such was long the case concerning Germany's pre-1914 *Weltpolitik*, which historians tended to see as self-evidently "blundering or reckless" (Renshon 2017, 40). Soviet grand strategy in the late Cold War is another case in point. Moscow's pugnacious foreign policy in the 1970s and 1980s—a seemingly contradictory mixture of cooperation and expansionism that Jack Snyder (Snyder, 1988) dubbed "offensive détente"—struck many scholars as puzzling. After all, once the USSR obtained a secure second-strike nuclear weapons capability by the mid-1960s that virtually guaranteed its security, why pursue expansionist policies whose only effect appeared to be to generate "self-encirclement" in the form of NATO, Japanese, and Chinese counterbalancing? Numerous studies found the answer in flawed Soviet institutions and strategic ideas (e.g. Griffiths 1991; Hopf 1991; Snyder 1984; Snyder 1988). From this perspective, when Mikhail Gorbachev reoriented Soviet grand strategy toward accommodation in the latter 1980s, ultimately bringing the Cold War to an end, the puzzle was not the strategy's substance but rather identifying the mechanisms through which Moscow belatedly adjusted to strategic reality (Checkel 1998; Collins 1997; Deudney and Ikenberry 1991; Mendelson 1998).

The whole question of what was puzzling and what needed to be explained hinged on assessing the grand strategy's optimality, yet at no point in this voluminous literature did anyone stop to evaluate it. The suboptimality of Brezhnev's grand strategy and optimality of Gorbachev's were matters of consensus in this research community. But those assessments are clearly debatable, and they became more suspect with the passage of time. The much-maligned Brezhnev took power in 1964, when the Western economies were in the midst of the greatest boom in capitalism's history, and the United States was engaged in a furious military buildup. In a scant seven years, he and Foreign Minister Andrei Gromyko had attained a favorable *modus vivendi* with West Germany, secured international recognition of the German Democratic Republic and most of their wartime conquests, and were engaged in a détente with the world's preeminent power, the United States, on formal terms of parity. What's not to like? For his part, the much-praised Gorbachev was sworn to advance the USSR's interests, but his concessionary grand strategy contributed to a cascade of events that led to the collapse of his country's most important alliance and ultimately his country's disappearance from the face of the earth. If that's success, many Russians shudder to think what failure might look like.

Consensus is, in short, a fragile basis for evaluating grand strategy. New perspectives afforded by the passage of time, new information as archives open, and the incentives of scholarly debate can singly or collectively upend a consensus about a grand strategy and compel scholars to address the challenge of evaluation. Scholarship on appeasement is an instructive example (Dimuccio 1998). To the early Cold War generation, it was self-evident that appeasement—attempting to engineer Nazi Germany's satisfaction with the status quo via territorial concessions—was a manifest failure, that a good alternative (containing/deterring Germany, perhaps with Soviet help) was available, and that "guilty men," flawed domestic institutions, or pernicious ideas were implicated. Many leading IR scholars built or tested theories based on this assessment of grand-strategic failure (Layne 2008). Yet historical scholarship then went through a prolonged phase of revisionism, ultimately aided by intensive archival research, that found that appeasement was the only feasible strategy under the circumstances (though perhaps poorly implemented for some of the reasons the initial postwar traditionalists had identified). By the 1990s, revisionism had itself become conventional wisdom, until post-revisionist studies appeared that once again argued for the optimality of shifting from appeasement to deterrence/containment of Hitler earlier in the game (e.g., McDonough 2002).

The Challenge of Evaluation

Research on appeasement also shows what rigorous evaluation looks like. The debate between the orthodox and revisionist camps forced scholars to grapple with vexingly complex issues: the uncertainty of intentions (given Hitler's incentive to misrepresent, when in the game should Germany's rivals have been able to determine that he was an unappeasable, unlimited-aims revisionist?); the uncertainty of assessing capabilities (did Britain and France have the capability to deter/contain Germany earlier? If not, would an arms buildup earlier in the game have done the trick or would it have just led them into more danger later?); the assessment of the strategies other players might have adopted had Britain opted for containment (given its own incentives to pass the buck, would the Soviet Union actually have stood up to Germany if London did? Could it if it wanted to? If London stood firmer, would France "entrap" it by provoking Germany?).

The more one digs into any debate featuring the evaluation of grand strategy, such as that surrounding appeasement, the more the task begins to overwhelm. Disputed questions reach deep into technical detail about weapons system capabilities (e.g., how did British aircraft stack up against German aircraft? How fast could they be produced? At what opportunity cost?), to estimates of the rationality or "reasonableness" of beliefs (e.g., what should we expect people to have known about the limits and potential of airpower in the 1930s?), and deep into domestic politics (might a harder line from London–Paris have created conditions for a coup against Hitler? Was a containment/deterrence strategy even politically sustainable in Britain without more evidence of a direct threat from Germany?). It can quickly appear as if there is no facet of 1930s European politics that one does not have to assess in minute detail before passing judgment on Chamberlain and his fellow appeasers.

Evaluating discrete strategic choices are hard enough. Strategy is a goal-oriented plan of action that matches ends and means and depends in part on the strategies of other forward-thinking actors in a competitive setting. Evaluation demands a counterfactual assessment of how an actor would have fared had it chosen some other plausible strategy, which requires the evaluator to determine what other strategies were actually plausible and estimate what strategies all other relevant actors would have chosen in that counterfactual world and how those strategies would have fared. It demands all the analytical tasks identified in the appeasement case, especially grappling with uncertainty and the incentives of strategic players—both at the time of choice and in hindsight—to misrepresent their true interests and their assessment of the strategic setting. Looming over all that is a challenge especially relevant when evaluating strategic choices by corporate actors like states: determining what the interests are that the strategy seeks to advance. Those of the leader? The elites? The people? The "state"? Do we accept a leader's definition of the national interest or, following IR theory, impute some universal overall interest to all states?

Evaluating grand strategy puts that challenge on steroids. Nina Silove adduces three meanings of the term—an identifiable plan, an overarching principle, or a definite pattern of behavior (Silove 2019). For each approach to the concept, grand strategy amounts to a set of ideas that provides a unifying logic to a state's strategies in many arenas. Following Barry Posen, these ideas can be thought of as a state's theory of how to advance its interests over the long run (Posen 2014). To evaluate grand strategy is to conduct an objective, dispassionate test of such a theory—a challenge of a much higher order than merely assessing a discrete strategic choice. Evaluating each substrategy associated with the grand strategy quickly overwhelms the researcher. Evaluating the theory itself is challenging because even though the strategy is "grand," it is not universal. Rather, it is a theory about how a specific actor can best advance its specific interest in a specific setting and time. Such a grand but specific theory is not directly amenable to testing with data according to accepted standards in modern social science.

A special challenge emerges from the fact that the actors whose grand strategies command the greatest interest are great powers. The conventionally defined great powers have over the past two centuries represented anywhere from 70–90 percent of the measurable material capabilities in the entire international system. The choices they make about the purposes to which those capabilities are put can powerfully affect the workings of the system (Braumoeller 2014). Collectively, great powers may choose grand strategies that add up to the creation of international political orders, such as the Concert of Europe. Individually, certain great powers may find themselves in a position to adopt grand strategies of regional or even global hegemony, in effect transforming all or part of the international system from anarchy to hierarchy. Evaluating grand strategies of this ilk would appear to demand a precision in modeling the workings of international systems that scholars are unlikely ever to possess.

The United States' grand strategy of deep engagement, with its manifold security commitments in multiple regions, stable, hierarchical relationships, institution-building and order-creation, is an obvious example. After US setbacks in Iraq and the global financial crisis of 2008, a consensus began to take hold among scholars of international security that post–Cold War US grand strategy has been a gargantuan failure (Brooks, Ikenberry, and Wohlforth 2012). A standard claim in this literature is that continuity in US grand strategy, despite dramatic changes in the strategic environment after 1990 that should have caused a wholesale revision, is a major puzzle (e.g., Porter 2018). Yet, as Peter Feaver and Hal Brands note (2019, 198) this ignores,

> ... the simplest explanation for why there has been substantial consistency in US strategy: because it works. As scholars have demonstrated, the past 70 years have been among the best in human history in terms of rising global and US prosperity, the spread of democracy and human rights, the avoidance of great power war, and the decline of war in general. It is also been a period when the world's leading power consistently pursued a grand strategy geared explicitly towards achieving those goals. To prove that US grand strategy persists for reasons other than utility, [critics]

would have to show that US leadership has not been necessary to those outcomes or that is no longer necessary.

What this means is that to advance this debate we need to show how a post–Second World War international system would have worked without a deeply engaged United States. And most of the theory and empirical evidence we have are products of a world with a deeply engaged United States—a tall order, given the limited explanatory power of our contested theories and models.

While this case is extreme, it is hardly unique. Any great power possessing preponderant capabilities globally or regionally faces a grand-strategic choice: conquer, dominate informally, or exercise restraint, eschewing proactive engagement. Russia took the first approach to its region, engaging in three centuries of all-azimuth expansion until it became the largest polity on earth, which it remains today (Taagepera 1997). The logic behind the strategy was that the strategic environment was one of conquer or be conquered, and so expansion was the sole grand strategy for survival (Norrlöf and Wohlforth 2019; Wohlforth 2001). In defense of that argument, one might note that non-expansionist polities in medieval and early modern Eurasia generally did fall to conquest. The problem is that most of them were conquered by Russia, making for the kind of circularity that tends to dog this kind of debate. China adopted the informal dominance approach in its region in the fourteenth to nineteenth centuries. Scholars note that East Asia was comparatively peaceful and prosperous in that epoch—yet debate whether that outcome is the result of properties of the system as a whole or chiefly the result of China's grand strategy (Kang 2010; Zhang 2015). When it attained great power capabilities after the turn of the last century, the United States opted for the third approach. That decision to reject a more deeply engaged grand strategy and pursue offshore balancing in the 1920s and 1930s remains a matter of intense controversy. How would the "twenty-years' crisis" after 1918 have unfolded with the United States in the League of Nations, and/or more willing to be involved in European security and economics? Perhaps some of the ravages of German hyperinflation might have been avoided. Perhaps, with US backing, France might have felt secure enough to make the concessions needed to stave off later German revisionism (Tooze 2014). Scholars' assessments of the overall track record of offshore balancing depend on how they model such scenarios.

Grand strategies have two further features that frustrate evaluation. Status quo strategies are often preventive, paying costs up front to prevent a worse strategic environment from emerging. To evaluate such a case, one would want to monitor the results if the government ceased pursuing the strategy. If the government in question shrinks from taking that risk, whether its strategy actually was necessary to prevent a worsening strategic environment will always remain speculative. Second, more proactive, revisionist strategies that seek to change the environment in a state's favor may face what Friedman dubs "cumulative processes," in which an actor seeks to push progressively toward an objective until some threshold is reached (Friedman 2019). Complex systems like international politics often feature feedback loops that reinforce an equilibrium up to some hard-to-estimate threshold. A revisionist grand-strategic actor that wishes to alter the system in its favor may have good reasons to think that continued pressure will yield the desired result even if initial feedback is negative.

Alternatively, a revisionist grand strategy may register highly favorable feedback until a threshold is reached that suddenly reverses the dynamic. Imagine a debate in Paris in 1811 on Napoleon's grand strategy and your task is to make the case that a grasp for lasting hegemony in Europe is a doomed ambition. After fifteen years of war, France dominated Europe, having thwarted five balancing coalitions, each collapsing as one or more members chose to bandwagon with or hide from Napoleon. You would know that British Foreign Secretary George Canning had recently offered France an *uti possedetis* ("keep-what-you-have") peace; that France ruled Spain, Italy, the Low Countries and much of Germany directly; that Austria, Prussia, Norway, and Denmark were mere satellites of the Grand Empire. Only Britain, Sweden, Portugal, and Russia would be out of Napoleon's grasp, but of these only Britain was actively balancing France. The small countries on the Continent by now had no choice but to bandwagon. And to top all that off, Russia—the one empire other than the British that could actually choose to balance—was busily collaborating with France against Britain. Take away the bias of hindsight, and try to argue for a more restrained grand strategy. Not an easy case to make!

Evaluators thus face a tough task in determining whether such strategies were flawed from the outset or perfectly reasonable bets *ex ante*. Cold War Soviet grand strategy exemplifies both issues. For most of the era, Moscow followed a classical preventive policy concerning its satellite regimes in central Europe as well as its own constituent national republics: maintain a stern reputation for resolve to convince subordinate elites and publics that the only option was continued deference. The strategy—the so-called "Brezhnev Doctrine"—entailed periodic resorts to force to nip in the bud any movement away from the Moscow-dominated equilibrium. The strategy imposed high costs, justified by the claim that it prevented a much worse environment from emerging, namely one in which restive dependencies sought exit and even alignment with the geopolitical rival. Leaders from Stalin to Chernenko were loath to test the strategy to see if it was really needed to hold things together. Ultimately, aware of the strategy's high and rising costs, Gorbachev incrementally adopted a revisionist strategy of revoking the Brezhnev Doctrine and increasing decision latitude for subordinate Communist Party leaderships that was aimed at breaking out of the Cold War equilibrium. Initial feedback was highly positive, with NATO on the defensive and the likelihood of ending the Cold War on congenial terms seemingly rising by the month. Until, that is, the nightmare that the old strategy had sought to suppress became real. In 1989, the key deterrence threshold was passed, elites and publics increasingly doubted the Kremlin's resolve and saw the chance for independence. Moscow's inner and outer empires swiftly came crashing down, along with its global position. Would-be evaluators must work hard to determine whether the fate of Gorbachev's strategy truly vindicates Brezhnev's or was the unforeseen result of a well-conceived strategic bet made in unforgiving circumstances.

The key lesson is the need to fight the temptation to let the outcome speak for itself. Given the extreme complexity of international politics, the quality of grand strategies may well be poorly related to their apparent success or failure. Some proportion of well-conceived, optimal grand strategies will appear to fail, just as some number of poor grand strategies will appear to result in success. When the strategic environment is highly favorable and permissive, many strategies may lead to normatively positive outcomes; in especially tough settings, there may well be no strategy for success, only for greater or lesser failure.

Facing the Evaluation Challenge

The upshot is that evaluating grand strategy is important but presents potentially runaway analytical challenges. An intellectually reasonable response is to eschew the entire enterprise as unrealistic, demanding more of the disciplines of political science and history than they can deliver. But to adopt that response consistently, one must also eschew all the intellectual activities for which grand strategy evaluation is necessary: criticizing states' grand strategies and testing systemic theories of international politics. If there is no responsible, rigorous, scholarly way to evaluate grand strategy, then scholars have no professional standing to comment on grand strategy. If grand strategies can't be evaluated, then neither can systemic IR theories. If you truly believe that grand strategy is a realm that is beyond the reach of responsible evaluation, then the only responsible stance to take when the discussion turns to any state's long-term approach to achieving its interests or to the veracity of competing systemic theories is to keep your mouth shut.

Those of us who believe that scholarship does have something to add to discussions of grand strategy need to face the evaluation challenge. There is no silver bullet solution, but scholars can confront it more rigorously than has been common in the past. The first step is to pay heed to four basic guidelines that emerge from the discussion so far.

First, do not rely on any evaluative consensus about a grand strategy. Here's a parlor game for grand strategy geeks: name an enduring consensus about any major power's grand strategy. In every case I can identify, even the seemingly deepest-set conventional wisdom about the efficacy of a given grand strategy has been contingent upon a research community's current preoccupations, informed by unstable (often normative) assumptions of the moment. I have already discussed the seemingly rock-solid evaluations of British, German, and Soviet grand strategies, all of which proved tenuous. Japanese grand strategy in the 1930s is another case long thought of as patently suboptimal (see, e.g., Kupchan 1994). How could anyone defend the strategic sense of a strategic course that pitted Japan against the United States, with 16 times its economic capacity? Nevertheless, that consensus ran afoul of new waves of scholarship that stressed the aggressive and racist nature of the Western powers' strategies toward Japan in the 1930s and that suggested that by 1941 Franklin Roosevelt had essentially left Imperial Japan no choice but war (Schuessler 2010; Trachtenberg 1996;

Ward 2017). These studies foregrounded the massive challenge Western nations placed on Japan's status and security, implying a far more limited array of grand-strategic options for Tokyo. Whatever one thinks of their substance, as studies of this ilk cumulated, it became impossible to take Japanese strategic blundering for granted. The lesson here is: if the evaluation of *that* grand strategy can become contentious, then any grand strategy's can. If you want your work to have a shelf life, make your evaluation explicit from the outset.

Second, be sensitive to the fact that grand strategies operate under uncertainty. Uncertainty has many meanings in social science (Rathbun 2007), but the core is that there are many crucial things that people simply cannot know when they embark upon a course of action. Grand strategies confront not only the standard problem of imperfect information concerning the capabilities and interests of other actors, but must also grapple with what Keisuke Iida (Iida 1993) calls "analytic uncertainty" about the basic workings of the social environment in which they operate. As noted, a grand strategy is a theory of how to advance interests over the long term. As such, it is a bet on how the world works, wagered by an actor with the ability to affect the world's workings. The state itself thus confronts the very same challenges of evaluation scholars do. Because the international system is so complex, the feedback generated by a state's interaction with that system may be quite ambiguous for extended periods, and updating and "learning" about the effectiveness of the strategy may take a very long time (Jervis 1997). Hence, when we observe states pursuing what strike us in hindsight as self-defeating, excessively costly, or riskily restrained grand strategies, we need to be careful before issuing judgments of failure. A grand strategy that yields poor results still might have been the best available. Needless to say, success may be down to luck.

Third, be explicit about counterfactuals. As has been stressed throughout this chapter, it is impossible to evaluate grand strategy without implying a counterfactual under which an alternative that was plausible given uncertainty performs better or worse. Taming counterfactuals is a fraught analytical enterprise, but it is better to be explicit about it and walk the reader through the reasoning behind counterfactual claims than to sweep them under the rug. Strong debates on grand strategy evaluation, such as the prolonged debate on appeasement, show how disciplined and rigorous this can get, as scholars work assiduously to establish what alternatives were truly available, what material resources existed to back them up, and what the archival evidence says about how key players would likely have responded had alternative grand strategies been in play.

Fourth, explicitly use both case-specific knowledge and more general theory and research findings to estimate counterfactuals. While observable evidence about strategic ideas, constraints, capabilities, and intentions can inform estimates about counterfactuals, general scholarly knowledge inevitably must also be deployed to model the workings of the "might-have-been" worlds that must be invoked in grand strategy evaluation. The model the evaluator constructs of the world that would unfold (or would have unfolded) under the alternative grand strategy should invoke both case-specific and general knowledge. If, say, we're assessing a grand strategy of general deterrence and containment of a rising challenger, we need to estimate whether engagement or appeasement might have worked better. Details about the challenger and its intentions surely should inform that estimate, but so should general theory and research findings about the conditions under which engagement/appeasement tends to work. Because both general theory and general empirical findings are always contested, appeals to them will never settle an evaluative debate. But any such debate will be far clearer and more productive if participants make explicit the understandings of international politics that inform their arguments.

With these guidelines in mind, most evaluative exercises are likely to entail four elements:

1. *Assess the strategic environment.* Here, the evaluator makes explicit her essential reading of the setting in which the actor's grand strategy is emerging, deploying the theory and general knowledge she judges most salient to the evaluation. For, as Charles Glaser makes clear in his essay in this volume, grand strategy and its evaluation are crucially theory dependent. Classical writings on strategy zero in on ends–means assessments for the actor concerned and those with which it interacts strategically. But for the evaluation of grand strategy, these key inputs must be folded into a more general reading of the strategic environment, which comprises material (e.g., polarity, technology) and nonmaterial factors (e.g., collectively held ideas and beliefs like nationalism, and norms of appropriate behavior like sovereignty or human rights). International relations scholarship is in large part about how to model strategic environments, how such material and nonmaterial factors interact, and how the constraints and incentives that flow from these factors influence states and other actors on the global stage. How good these models are at explaining patterns of behavior, or even how to think about the aspiration to construct such models, are both hotly disputed. My argument here is not that these models are great scientific achievements that reliably explain international politics but rather that they clarify the *evaluator's* assessment of the strategic environment. Disputes about grand strategy are often disputes about the nature of the strategic setting. Being explicit about your theory of that setting can only help the overall enterprise of evaluating grand strategy.

2. *Determine/Assess interests.* Grand strategy connects means with ends in a given strategic setting. Once the evaluator clarifies his assessment of the setting, he needs to make explicit how he understands the interests or basic preferences in play. As noted above, scholars often impute preferences, as in the popular assumption among realists that a state's territorial security is always its foremost interest. There is nothing necessarily wrong with this, as long as evaluators are clear when the debate is about interests rather than strategy. When Posen defines grand strategy as "a state's theory about how it can best 'cause' security for itself," he is implicitly criticizing any grand strategy that ever prioritizes any other interest (Posen 2014). If a state should end up following a grand strategy that accepts risks to the state's territorial security in the service of any other preference, it will come up short in Posen's evaluation even if it is

indeed the optimal strategy for the state's actual interest. The debate would then be a normative one about what interests the state *ought* to have, not about grand strategy itself. The evaluator may take an empirical approach to determining interests, carefully interrogating documents and other sources to divine how the government concerned actually defines its interest. Again, the evaluator may well find fault with the actor's interests on normative grounds, as when leaders like Hitler, Stalin, or Mao pursue odious ends. Or evaluators may take governments to task on more pragmatic grounds for failing to tailor ends to available means or to the strategic setting. The alleged error may lie in failing to prioritize interests when the evaluator thinks the strategic setting demanded the resolution of tradeoffs among them. Or the error may be said to come from a government having too expansive a definition of a specific interest. Territorial security may seem like a modest interest, but if a state's grand strategy seeks to drive the probability of even the smallest threats down to zero, at great cost to other preferences, it may come in for criticism. The key here is simply to be sure to be transparent about how interests are being determined, and to distinguish criticisms of grand strategy from criticisms of interests (Avey, Markowitz, and Reardon 2018).

3. *Identify the grand strategy.* This seems obvious and, indeed, most evaluations set forth what the analyst thinks the grand strategy in question is. But what constitutes grand strategy in general or in specific cases may itself be a matter of dispute. As noted, grand strategies may be emergent or explicit. Good evaluative practice calls for clarity rather than slavish devotion to a specific resolution of the problem. In most cases, some effort to track the existence and nature of the grand strategy empirically is likely to be needed—even if the strategy is thought to emerge from a pattern of behavior or reflect core strategic principles rather than spring forth from some explicit planning process. To clarify claims about what constitutes the grand strategy in a given case, the evaluator may want to apply some simple tests. Does it rule out certain substrategies? If I want to claim, say, that Britain followed a grand strategy of offshore balancing in some period, I ought to be able to identify plausible strategic moves it could have made that would be inconsistent with that strategy. Does it demand certain substrategies? If I want to claim that the United States pursues a grand strategy of "liberal hegemony," I ought to be able to identify what real-world commitments to liberal principles are absolutely necessary for that strategy. Is the grand strategy debated? Again, even if neither we nor the strategic actors themselves think of grand strategy in the naïve "man with grand plan" mode, the ideas, principles, and practices we are associating with the grand strategy have real-world empirical implications that ought to make appearances at critical junctures, often in the form of debates among decision-makers and elites or among the public.

4. *Assess the grand strategy with explicit comparisons to plausible alternatives.* Given the strategic environment, was/is the strategy the best way for the actor to pursue its interest? I've stressed throughout that answering that question demands

counterfactual analysis of alternatives, one held to some empirical account if possible and informed explicitly by theory and relevant bodies of empirical scholarship. The evaluator should work to establish that the alternatives are/were truly plausible. In historical cases, that means attending carefully to the problem of uncertainty and the hindsight bias; the alternative should not be one whose virtues are only apparent in light of outcome knowledge. It adds credibility if the alternatives are considered at the time. Ideally, the evaluator will seek to convince readers that the assessment of alternatives is "fair." That is, if the argument is that the grand strategy pursued is suboptimal, be sure to subject these alternatives to the same kind of stress test that the real, observable grand strategy confronts. If the argument is that the grand strategy is optimal, be sure that alternatives are not held to unrealistic standards or made to confront doomsday scenarios.

Conclusion: The Promise of Pragmatic Evaluation

Evaluating grand strategy requires ruthless discipline in defining the actor's interests, assessing its strategic environment, identifying plausible alternative strategies, and deploying theory and evidence to run grand counterfactual experiments to determine whether plausible alternative grand strategies would better have realized the actor's interests—all of this, crucially, done while remaining keenly sensitive to the challenge of uncertainty and the attendant bias of hindsight. At a minimum, the guidelines set forth in this chapter may sensitize scholars to the intellectual leaps of faith they make when they analyze a grand strategy on the assumption that the task of evaluation is easy or can be accomplished by assumption simply by observing setbacks or foreign policy failures. More ambitiously, they may prove useful for scholars seeking to transform grand strategy debates into empirical research programs.

References

Avey, Paul C., Jonathan N Markowitz, and Robert J. Reardon. 2018. "Disentangling Grand Strategy: International Relations Theory and U.S. Grand Strategy." *Texas National Security Review* 2 (1): 29–51.

Braumoeller, Bear. 2014. *The Great Powers and the International System*. Cambridge: Cambridge University Press.

Brooks, Stephen G., G. John Ikenberry, and William C. Wohlforth. 2012. "Don't Come Home, America: The Case Against Retrenchment." *International Security* 37 (3): 7–51.

Checkel, Jeffrey T. 1998. *Ideas and International Political Change: Soviet/Russian Behavior and the End of the Cold War*. New Haven: Yale University Press.

Collins, Alan. 1997. *The Security Dilemma and the End of the Cold War*. New York: St Martin's.

Deudney, Daniel, and G. John Ikenberry. 1991. "The International Sources of Soviet Change." *International Security* 16 (3): 74–118.

Dimuccio, R.A.B. 1998. "The Study of Appeasement in International Relations: Polemics, Paradigms, and Problems." *Journal of Peace Research* 35 (2): 245–259.

Feaver, Peter D., and Hal Brands. 2019. "Correspondence: The Establishment and U.S. Grand Strategy." *International Security* 43 (3): 197–204.

Friedman, Jeffrey A. 2019. *War and Chance: Assessing Uncertainty in International Politics*. Oxford: Oxford University Press.

Gaddis, John Lewis. 2005. *Strategies of Containment: A Critical Appraisal of American National Security Policy During the Cold War*. Revised edition. Oxford: Oxford University Press.

Griffiths, Franklyn. 1991. "Attempted Learning: Soviet Policy Toward the United States in the Brezhnev Era." In *Learning in U.S. and Soviet Foreign Policy*, edited by George W. Breslauer and Philip E. Tetlock. Boulder, CO: Westview.

Hopf, Ted. 1991. "Peripheral Visions: Brezhnev and Gorbachev Meet the 'Reagan Doctrine'." In *Learning in U.S. and Soviet Foreign Policy*, edited by George W. Breslauer and Philip E. Tetlock. Boulder: Westview.

Iida, Keisuke. 1993. "Analytic Uncertainty and International Cooperation: Theory and Application to International Economic Policy Coordination." *International Studies Quarterly* 37 (4): 431–457.

Jervis, Robert. 1997. *System Effects: Complexity in Political and Social Life*. Princeton, NJ: Princeton University Press.

Kang, David C. 2010. *East Asia Before the West: Five Centuries of Trade and Tribute*. New York: Columbia University Press. New York: Columbia University Press.

Kennedy, Paul M. 1976. "The Tradition of Appeasement in British Foreign Policy." *British Journal of International Studies* 2 (3): 195–215.

Kupchan, Charles. 1994. *The Vulnerability of Empire*. Ithaca, NY: Cornell University Press.

Layne, Christopher. 2008. "Security Studies and the Use of History: Neville Chamberlain's Grand Strategy Revisited." *Security Studies* 14 (3): 396–437.

Lebow, R. Ned. 2010. *Why Nations Fight: Past and Future Motives for War*. Cambridge: Cambridge University Press.

Luttwak, Edward N. 1979. *The Grand Strategy of the Roman Empire: From the First Century A.D. to the Third*. Baltimore, MD: John Hopkins University Press.

McDonough, Frank. 2002. *Hitler, Chamberlain and Appeasement*. Cambridge: Cambridge University Press.

Mendelson, Sarah E. 1998. *Changing Course: Ideas, Politics, and the Soviet Withdrawal from Afghanistan*. Princeton, NJ: Princeton University Press.

Murray, Michelle K. 2010. "Identity, Insecurity and Great Power Politics: The Tragedy of German Naval Ambition Before the First World War." *Security Studies* 19 (4): 656–688.

Murray, Williamson. 2011. "Thoughts on Grand Strategy." In *The Shaping of Grand Strategy: Policy, Diplomacy, and War*, edited by Williamson Murray, Richard Hart Sinnreich, and James Lacey. New York: Cambridge University Press.

Norrlöf, Carla, and William C. Wohlforth. 2019. "Raison de l'Hégémonie (The Hegemon's Interest): Theory of the Costs and Benefits of Hegemony." *Security Studies* 28 (3): 422–450.

Porter, Patrick. 2018. "Why America's Grand Strategy Has Not Changed: Power, Habit, and the U.S. Foreign Policy Establishment." *International Security* 42 (4): 9–46.

Posen, Barry R. 2014. *Restraint: A New Foundation for U.S. Grand Strategy*. Ithaca, NY: Cornell University Press.

Rathbun, Brian. 2007. "Uncertain about Uncertainty: Understanding the Multiple Meanings of a Crucial Concept in International Relations Theory." *International Studies Quarterly* 51 (3): 533–557.

Renshon, Jonathan. 2017. *Fighting for Status: Hierarchy and Conflict in World Politics*. Princeton, NJ: Princeton University Press.

Schuessler, John M. 2010. "The Deception Dividend: FDR's Undeclared War." *International Security* 34 (4): 133–165.

Silove, Nina. 2019. "Beyond the Buzzword: The Three Meanings of 'Grand Strategy.'" *Security Studies* 27 (1): 27–57.

Snyder, Jack L. 1984. *Myths of Empire: Domestic Politics and International Ambition*. Ithaca, NY: Cornell University Press.

Snyder, Jack L. 1988. "The Gorbachev Revolution: A Waning of Soviet Expansionism?" *International Security* 12 (3): 93–131.

Taagepera, Rein. 1997. "Expansion and Contraction Patterns of Large Polities: Context for Russia." *International Studies Quarterly* 41 (3): 475–504.

Tooze, Adam. 2014. *The Deluge: The Great War, America and the Making of the Global Order, 1916–1931*. New York: Penguin.

Trachtenberg, Marc. 1996. *The Craft of International History: A Guide to Method*. Princeton, NJ: Princeton University Press.

Ward, Steven. 2017. *Status and the Challenge of Rising Powers*. Cambridge: Cambridge University Press.

Wohlforth, William C. 2001. "The Russian-Soviet Empires, 1400–2000: A Test of Neorealism." *Review of International Studies* 27 (5): 213–235.

Zhang, Feng. 2015. *Chinese Hegemony: Grand Strategy and International Institutions in East Asian History*. Stanford: Stanford University Press.

CHAPTER 36

IS GRAND STRATEGY AN ILLUSION?

Or, the Grandiosity of Grand Strategy

RICHARD K. BETTS

EARLY in the twenty-first century, grand strategy is in vogue, but there is less in the idea than meets the eye. Distinguished from just plain strategy—a scheme for a particular campaign within a larger contest—the term implicitly conjures up unrealistic images of sweeping and far-seeing purpose, ingenuity, direction, and adroitness. Grand strategy is not always an illusion, but it is usually pretentious and grandiose as a description of what actually drives governments' actions.[1] The concept makes sense abstractly and normatively but falters in application, honored far more in principle than in practice. It is more often a description imposed by observers on the record of statesmen, or a claim made in hindsight, than a conscious and coherent plan of the statesmen in advance of events. To oversimplify only a bit, hedgehogs do grand strategy, foxes do practice. Observers devoted to the concept rescue it from evidence of practice's deviation from principle by redefining it in dubious ways.

These shortfalls do not mean that grand strategy never happens. If the occasional examples of real grand strategy are emphasized, the glass looks half full. The criticism here only means that genuine practice of grand strategy is not the norm, that when practiced it is usually very vague or little more than ad hoc application of common sense, and that the idea is more a fixation of intellectuals looking for rationality in practice than a concern of actual practitioners. If grand strategy is impractical, moreover, that may not be a bad thing, at least for strong countries.

The later part of this critique elaborates these arguments by reflecting on obstacles to grand strategy in practice and some good and bad illustrative examples. First, however, the essay asserts a proper definition of the concept and refutes challenges to it. This is not to dwell pedantically on semantics, but to counter those who affirm the concept by defining it so as to fit whatever statesmen do. Most common conceptions of grand strategy in the abstract are simple (a good thing) and rather unfocused (a necessity to distinguish it from the lower level of just plain strategy). In a book devoted entirely to the grand strategy concept, John Gaddis defines it as "the alignment of potentially unlimited aspirations with necessarily limited capabilities," usually in preparation for war, and identifies its grandness "with what's at stake" (Gaddis 2018, 21). Barry Posen defines it more directly as "a nation-state's theory about how to produce security for itself," primarily against military threats (Posen 2014, 1). To most observers, it is best distinguished from plain strategy by its concern with shaping the peace to follow war rather than the aim of military victory alone (Liddell Hart 1967, 335–336).

The definition of grand strategy that I submit is *a practical plan to use military, economic, and diplomatic means to achieve political ends over time at least feasible cost in blood and treasure*. Emphasis is on three of the points: "plan," because in some form it is the necessary condition for implementing any intention; "practical," because a strategy that cannot be implemented is irrelevant; and "over time," to distinguish concerns that are long term or at least transcend a particular incident. All this means some idea that statesmen can more or less implement about how to coordinate national resources and actions (more than reactions) to achieve objectives. (This is in line with the first conception outlined in Silove 2018, 34–38, 49, 53.) Most observers have implicitly accepted these emphases in conceptualization, but some fans of the concept reject them.

Rescue by Redefinition

To be useful analytically, a concept must be distinct from others, not synonymous. What makes grand strategy essentially distinct from the whole jumble of foreign policy is the idea of a plan for action to turn wishes into facts. When the idea of grand strategy is conceived more vaguely, in contrast, almost anything a country does can be seen as pursuing it. To evaluate a grand strategy—to judge whether the country actually won or lost because it implemented one, rather than for fortuitous reasons unconnected with it—the strategy has to be specified. For any strategy to be meaningful it should also have a modicum of coherence and consistency. When defined specifically, however, actual grand strategies—especially in democracies—often turn out to be compromises and combinations of quite different ideas. For example, after outlining four theoretical alternatives for post–Cold War US grand strategy, Posen and Ross accurately characterized the then-current administration's as a mélange of three of them: Clinton's "Selective (but Cooperative) Primacy" (Posen and Ross 1996/97, 44).

One way to make the concept sensible is the Humpty Dumpty solution, to redefine it in a way that deflects criticisms based on the gap between principle and practice. This has been done in two main ways: one expands the definition, broadening the usual vagueness to a laundry list of characteristics that cover almost any concern; the other sees it not as a plan but a process of adaptation. Neither of these redefinitions is useful.

Consider this example of salvaging the concept via all-encompassing vagueness:

> [Grand strategy is] ... the intellectual architecture that gives form and structure to foreign policy .... a purposeful and coherent set of ideas about what a nation seeks to accomplish in the world, and how it should go about doing so .... an integrated scheme of interests, threats, resources, and policies. It is the conceptual framework that helps nations determine where they want to go and how they ought to get there. (Brands 2014, 3)

This description covers too much to remain very useful analytically. It sounds as much about objectives as about ideas for how to achieve them, as much about attitudes as decisions. What notions, intentions, aspirations, or declarations are excluded? What differentiates this version of the concept from "foreign policy"? What possible behavior, however active or passive, clear or confused, would not qualify as grandly strategic? In their essay in this volume, Peter Feaver and Hal Brands retain and further expand the all-inclusive version of the concept, including the idea of deeper logic about how the world works in leaders' proclivities. Why is this evidence of grand strategy rather than motives? Moreover, as David Edelstein's essay in this volume points out, Brands attributes grand strategies without showing evidence that policymakers thought of what they were doing as grand strategy. Expansive characterizations of the concept may serve well enough (when the blanks are filled in) as a general commentary on a country's ambitions, agenda, and operating style, but they are too flabby to denote a standard by which strategic success or failure might be judged. To be worth serious causal credit a grand strategy must be more than what seems to the actors to be obvious common sense.

To paraphrase Einstein, a concept's definition should not be simplistic, but it should be as simple as possible—more than a bumper sticker but tight enough to fit in a paragraph. If specified abstractly but well enough to serve as a basis for assessment, characterizations of grand strategy become more complex and contingent. This can be useful for scholarly judgments about the variations, logic, and consistency of national behavior, as in a detailed taxonomy developed by three scholars (Avey et al. 2018, 34)—though the 5 x 13 matrix in that exercise would not be very useful to a National Security Council.

The second aspect of redefinition, compatible with the sprawling one just described, rejects the requirement that the concept be judged in terms of a plan: "Think of grand strategy as a process, not a blueprint... seeking out and interpreting feedback, dealing with surprises, and correcting course where necessary, all while keeping the ultimate objective in view" (Brands 2014, 198–199). This comports with famous aphorisms of sage practitioners, from Moltke's that no plan survives contact with the enemy, to Eisenhower's that "Plans are worthless but planning is everything." It is indeed a realistic view of how strategy is implemented—or rather changed—but it is not strategy itself. It describes what statesmen should properly do, but at the level of operations and tactics, or at most just plain strategy, not the higher level of grand strategy.

Of course, adaptation is good. Strategists should be flexible, not hidebound, and strategy should change when circumstances demand—Clausewitz saw this as fundamental to the reciprocal nature of real war. But while adaptation is good, and soundly tactical, it cannot be strategy per se. It describes how strategy should change when it does not produce the intended result. If adaptation in itself constitutes strategy, only demonstratively maladaptive behavior would discredit the rational model of strategy (Steinbruner 2002, 50n). Indeed, rats in a maze would qualify as strategists. When adaptation occurs on significant scale, strategy becomes something new, not whatever had been the grand strategy.

If *grand* strategy is conceived *ab initio*, and in broad terms of pursuing the country's security interests efficiently, deviation from it in the face of events that derail it is of course sensible. At least by some measure, however, deviation represents failure of the intended strategy, even if the result is quite acceptable for other reasons. As strategy worth the name, distinct from just sensible behavior, grand strategy should be judged by how far leaders actively apply the general plan—not exactly, but at least roughly—more than by how well they adjust reactively to events that confound it, or by how hindsight reveals faults in the original strategy and wisdom in abandoning it. An evolving accumulation of stratagems may prove a wise course, but it is not grand strategy. As Edelstein points out herein, flexibility verges on ad hoc decision, which proponents of grand strategy naturally criticize. Recognition of the process by which strategy is buffeted and adjusted is correct for understanding, but as a reflection of the *limits* of strategy. (Lawrence Freedman places a discussion of strategy as adaptation under just that subhead, "The Limits of Strategy" [Freedman 2013, 609, 611]). A better term for the idea of strategy as process is *policymaking*.

Definition of grand strategy as an adaptive process rather than a plan is closer to the concept of "emergent" strategy, which is drawn from business literature and offered as an alternative to grand strategy (Popescu 2017). Emergent strategy is seen "where a pattern realized was not expressly intended. Actions were taken, one by one, which converged over time, to some sort of consistency or pattern" (Mintzberg et al. 1998, quoted in Popescu 2017, 9). This is a dubious conception if meant in effect to salvage the record of national strategies. First, the standard of "some sort" of coherence is too vague to be very useful for evaluation: by that standard, few actions by intelligent adults could be deemed utterly lacking. Second, the conception poses strategy as more an effect than a cause of action—a notion opposite to what strategic action means to most. For action to be strategic, as distinct from successful, the strategy must precede the action, not follow it. "Emergent strategy" really denotes how alleged purpose and coherence emerge in the eye of the beholder. So, while emergent strategy is not a good normative concept, it does reflect how analysts come to detect method in the madness of practice. Policies are implemented with various confusions and dysfunctions and logic in the process is inferred, exaggerated, and imposed rhetorically after the fact rather than via a plan in advance. Grand strategy in this sense emerges as a rationalization more than an explanation.

Like Humpty Dumpty, observers are free to define grand strategy as they prefer, dragging concept into conformity with practice. But definitions that are excessively broad or evade the notion of a plan, at least a rough one, are weak because they do not differentiate the concept clearly from the more common term, foreign policy. A term that is synonymous with others rather than distinctive is less useful in itself for measuring and assessing behavior. So this critique insists on assessing the concept in terms of a plan roughly implemented in practice.

Obstacles to Grand Strategy in Practice

Grand strategy is of most interest for great powers, which have a wide range of interests and ambitions (and whose actions affect the world the most), or modern democracies (whose choices may be affected by readers of this handbook). The critique in this chapter focuses on the United States of America since it is both. The critique applies less to small or weak countries which have a narrower range of choice in security policy and fewer priorities about which to strategize beyond survival, and which therefore face fewer confusions, contradictions, and tradeoffs among goals. Nor does it apply as much to stable autocracies, which may depend on political coalitions of sorts distantly comparable to constraints of democratic politics but are likely to have more compressed decision processes and less frequent disruptive leadership turnover than in democracies. In either case, devising and executing plans is somewhat less complicated, and some measure of real and consistent grand strategy is more practical.

Israel and Switzerland illustrate the small state exception. Israel, facing enemies who want to put it out of business, has always had to rely on two main game plans: maintaining high levels of military mobilization in peacetime and cultivating support from a much larger power (France before 1967, the USA since). Switzerland, facing no local adversaries that claim ownership of its land, traditionally relies on the first solution (high military preparedness) and strict neutrality to avoid provoking other countries into enmity.

The People's Republic of China exemplifies the autocratic exception. China seems to have planned and executed an effective grand strategy when its leadership decided in the late twentieth century to rank improvement of its military capabilities as the last priority among the "four modernizations." It then shifted to increased defense spending and assertive deployments in the western Pacific a few decades later after the higher priority economic development had succeeded, thereby providing, as planned, a stronger resource base for doing so. As China has unambiguously arrived at great power status, however, it came to encounter more difficulty pursuing a clear strategy that integrates its commercial, diplomatic, and military interests in the face of the trade war launched by the Trump administration.

The first problem for great powers is the scope of objectives. The more general and varied they are, the more almost any actions can seem to reflect a strategy, but the more aims that have to be combined, the harder it becomes to do so without muddling. For the United States, two general goals are usually cited as fundamental for foreign policy since 1945: maintenance of a favorable international power position, usually conceived as either of the alternatives of military primacy or balance of power, and (at least until 2017) extension of a liberal international "order," usually conceived in terms of economic openness and promotion of democracy. Some of the resources, instruments, norms, and tactics to optimize strategy are the same for both of these general goals, but others are not. For example, covert political intervention or restrictions on trade are more likely to be compatible with the first than the second.

One solution might be to have two grand strategies, one for economic and ideological interests, the other for military or security policy. To the extent that there is more than one, however, strategies are not very grand. The norm of integration has long been well recognized in principle but limited in practice. From the original 1947 National Security Act to the legislation decades later requiring an annual presidential report on national security strategy, Congress has expected the executive to have an integrated strategy—even to include domestic matters (US Congress 1947, Section 102(d)(5)). That has scarcely ever been done, beyond boilerplate rhetoric. The criticism typically leveled at the official US national security strategy publication is that it became a Christmas tree on which all departments and interest groups hung their pet priorities and programs—and which was subsequently ignored by policymakers.

Democratic great powers face three overlapping sets of obstacles that frustrate selecting or implementing strategies (for good reasons more important than foreign policy):

- Influence of elections and public opinion, which can lead domestic political priorities to override external strategic ones;
- Frequent leadership turnover, which inhibits consistent action over a long time span;
- Constitutional dispersion of policymaking power (in presidential as opposed to parliamentary systems), which can promote either suboptimizing compromise or paralysis.

Consider some examples.

The Second World War should be a hard case for challenging the idea of grand strategy because the context was ideal for overriding the above constraints: the unconditional surrender policy made it a total war with simple criteria for success; allies and Americans both agreed on the strategic priority of "Europe First" over the Pacific theater; one political party controlled both branches of the US government before and throughout; and a single president reigned for a dozen years straight. Nevertheless, US strategists bowed to British demands to delay a cross-channel invasion of France, and they let operations in the Pacific grow and sap the pace in Europe. Franklin Roosevelt overruled his military advisors to launch the invasion of North Africa (Operation TORCH), which the military believed would divert resources and delay achievement of the main objective, because the president felt the need to deliver a military achievement to the American public in 1942. General George Marshall said the problem was that "in wartime the politicians have to do *something* important every year." As it turned out, a good case could be made that TORCH proved sensible, but for reasons evident in hindsight rather than in terms of the prior vision of strategy (Morison 1958, 45–47; Marshall quoted on 38).

The related view, anti-Clausewitzian at first glance, is that allied strategy in the Second World War was good because, with the exception of TORCH, military expediency always overrode political considerations. The paradoxical virtue seen in this was that unconditional surrender was the single goal on which all allies in the politically diverse coalition could agree, and thus, elevating military priorities over political ones held the grand alliance—the highest grand strategic priority—together (Greenfield 1963, 14–16, 23). All in all, however, did the outcome of the Second World War match the prior grand strategies of the victorious great powers? In 1942 Churchill famously said, "I have not become the King's First Minister in order to preside over the liquidation of the British Empire," but the liquidation began soon after the war. Before Pearl Harbor, Roosevelt wanted to defeat Nazi Germany, but he hardly schemed to leave other previously major powers in the dust in a new bipolar world and a hostile superpower in control of half of Europe. Great victory may validate the actions chosen despite unanticipated consequences, but it does not in itself demonstrate the impact of grand strategy.

In the Cold War, the Truman administration's planning document, NSC-68, laid out a grand strategy. It was irrelevant, however, due to lack of support for the necessary expenditures, until the completely unanticipated Korean War fortuitously reversed the resistance. The inconclusive, costly, and unpopular nature of that war, in turn, hardly fit a grand strategy. In fact, if Cold War grand strategy is characterized by reliance on deterrence, the Korean War did not follow the strategy, since there was no effort to deter the North Korean attack before it occurred.

Domestic constraints are more obvious in limited wars than in the Second World War, and together with inconstancy of leadership can easily promote compromises that undercut strategic effectiveness. In the Vietnam War, US presidents always sought to balance pressures to do more and to do less—to balance the conflicting goals of, on one hand, defeating the Vietnamese communists, and on the other, not alienating public opinion at home by mobilizing for major war over small stakes. This produced a trend of incremental escalation and then de-escalation over a period of twenty-odd years, as each president determined not to have the war lost on his watch (Gelb with Betts 1979). (A leader with indefinite tenure might have been more inclined to put a higher priority on concluding the war, either by stronger escalation or withdrawal.) Over thirty years later, Barack Obama sought a similar balance between domestic political and external strategic imperatives—not to lose in Afghanistan, but not to maximize effort to win—as he approved an increase in military forces but less than requested by military leaders (Woodward 2010, chaps. 18–19, 21–25, 28, 30).

Between Vietnam and the late phase of Afghanistan, the two George Bushes had a mixed record. In just plain strategy, Bush I had stunning success in the first war against Iraq, winning decisively at very low cost, but this ironically went with comparably huge failure in grand strategy. The whole war could almost certainly have been avoided if the United States had articulated a deterrence commitment to protect Kuwait's sovereignty. Had Saddam Hussein known that invading Kuwait would put him at war with the United States, it is hard to imagine that he would have done it. But, like Korea in 1950, the contingency that precipitated the war was not even on the radar screen of the Bush administration before the summer of 1990. Before Saddam moved, not a moment's thought had been given to how a war over Kuwait should fit in US grand strategy for the post–Cold War world, yet the unanticipated easy success, once the United States was pulled in, had a formative impact on subsequent visions and set the stage for the biggest disaster of post–Cold War foreign policy: the second war against Iraq.

Bush II's war a dozen years after his father's proceeded from a clear and more pertinent grand strategy, but its assumptions, and the military strategy employed toward it, proved a calamity. The neoconservative vision of using American primacy to keep "rogue" states from developing weapons of mass destruction, countering terrorist groups by striking their assumed support bases in such states, and promoting democracy in the Middle East—all of which animated the 2003 assault on Iraq—was clearly linked to a larger plan rooted in the logic of preventive war. The plan for the second war did fit with a grand strategy of sorts—it was just a plan that was gravely inadequate to the ambition. (The relevant thinking is in *The National Security Strategy of the United States of America* 2002, 15.) The political leadership's lack of a serious plan for occupation and stabilization beyond the conventional war (the State Department and specialists in the national security bureaucracy tried to provide such a plan but were rebuffed) reflected the error in the original plan (Bensahel et al. 2008).

Even if grand strategy is clear and sensible in principle, success depends on translating it into military strategy, operations, and tactics that will actually work toward it and produce the desired results. Grand strategy must drive plain strategy and the levels below it, not the reverse. In real war as opposed to war on paper, Clausewitz and practitioners have long known, the reverse often happens. This is why adaptation may sometimes necessarily revise policy goals. The primacy of politics "does not imply that the political aim is a tyrant. It must adapt itself to its chosen means, a process which can radically change it" (Clausewitz 1976, 87). If adaptation happens in minor ways that limit efficiency but not effectiveness, grand strategy may be seen to be applied, roughly. If the process changes outcomes substantially from what was expected by grand strategy, however, the latter is discredited even if the surprising result is good.

One huge problem confronts democratic and autocratic great powers alike: organizational complexity or technical operating requirements, which foster goal displacement in the bureaucracies that refine and implement any general strategy. National security policy may be conceived by theorists or politicians, but it must be implemented by professionals—diplomats, intelligence officers, and above all, complex and highly institutionalized military organizations. The difficulty of implementing general instructions for complicated jobs requires establishing instrumental techniques and detailed standard operating procedures and norms. These processes associated with professional expertise are usually necessary to enable organizations to function effectively, but as they are institutionalized they can make means become ends that diverge from the higher ends policymakers have in mind. For example, one might say the grand strategy of containment that the United States applied to the Vietnam War mandated "winning hearts and minds" of South Vietnamese farmers so they would support the Saigon government rather than communists of the National Liberation Front and North Vietnam. The US Army, however, had difficulty embracing the tenets of counterinsurgency theory and acted more in tune with the institution's standard orientation to conventional war, using high firepower and destructive operations more likely to alienate than endear the population in rural areas (Krepinevich 1986, chs. 6–8, 10). The institution also elected to limit personnel to one-year tours in country, and commanders to six-month rotations, in order to distribute combat experience throughout the career force for the long-term professional development of the service. This limited learning and relevant expertise of army officers on the immediate scene. As John Paul Vann put it, "The United States has not been in Vietnam for nine years, but for one year nine times" (quoted in Krepinevich 1986, 206).

Perhaps the most vivid and chilling illustration of the gap between what intellectuals see as the logic in a nation's plans and behavior, and what the underlying structures and processes actually are, can be seen in the area where the gap was never tested in war: nuclear strategy. Most observers high in the US government and throughout academia came to view American nuclear strategy as one of stable deterrence based on the danger of mutual assured destruction—that is, the idea that nuclear war would never be started because the consequences were recognized to be unthinkable, or that if started, it would be with carefully controlled limited strikes designed to force de-escalation. Late in the Cold War, however, evidence emerged that the military organizations tasked with readiness for nuclear use applied criteria for planning and deployment that envisioned fewer limitations on scale and authority for use of such weapons, and at some points frightening weakness in barriers against accidental use, barriers of which high-level strategists were unaware (Sagan 1993; Blair 1993; Ellsberg 2017, chs. 2–3, 5–6). Thus, the widespread assumption that peace endured because of a grand strategy that could assume solid stability of mutual nuclear deterrence, rather than luck, now seems wobbly.

If grand ideas are refracted when inflexible organizations translate them into action, grand strategy might be saved by giving more power to small groups of planners and by using secret diplomacy to evade bureaucratic deformation. Mechanisms designed for strategic planning have never prospered in the US government, however, with partial exceptions such as the State Department's Policy Planning Staff under George Kennan and Paul Nitze, or the National Security Council Staff under Henry Kissinger. Secret circumvention of bureaucratic constraints, in turn, may overcome inertia, but it is not always wise. Secretive Lone Ranger diplomacy can derange strategy by substituting naïve activism for plodding expertise. For example, when intervening in the Strategic Arms Limitation Talks by back channel from the White House, Kissinger came close to accepting a technical provision that would have inadvertently precluded a crucial American missile modernization program. US defense policy was saved from the gaffe only when the regular diplomat leading the official delegation found out (Smith 1980, 415–417).

At the highest level, constitutional separation of powers between Congress and president leaves room for struggle that compromises or confuses strategy. This separation has less often been an obstacle than might be expected, primarily because of the high degree of bipartisan elite consensus on the foreign policy goals of highest generality for most of the time since Pearl Harbor. Congress posed the greatest restraint when the consensus broke for a decade after the Tet Offensive, the most vivid illustrations being the Cooper-Church Amendment in 1971 limiting military operations in Indochina and the War Powers Resolution in 1973 requiring congressional approval for all lengthy US combat operations. Richard Nixon would also probably have preferred a less accommodating grand strategy toward Moscow and Beijing, but was compelled toward détente by public opinion in favor of retrenchment and lower defense spending, manifested through control of Congress by the opposition party.

The Glass Half-Full: Limitations of Good Grand Strategy

Of course, there are examples of real grand strategy, contrary to my critique, that do more or less pass the test. Otto von Bismarck's is one that most would credit. He had clear priorities among objectives—for example, German unification and neutralizing threats from other great powers—and careful plans for achieving them. The principle of always being one of three in the alliances among the five main European states was grandly strategic, and the crafty maneuvers he engineered to pursue those aims amply exceeded common sense. Bismarck's diplomacy mastered the balance of power for at least two decades. His record may look especially good in light of the mistakes of Kaiser Wilhelm, who followed him, but it is hard to think of other examples in modern times who did better in matching means to ends in ways that were more than obvious.

Few American examples match Bismarck. Feaver and Brands make a fair point in this volume that if grand strategy implies a direct line from intentions to policies to results, the Reagan administration qualifies (although its approach was rather blunt). In overall craftiness and subtlety, Richard Nixon, supported by Henry Kissinger, may come closest to the Bismarck model. It is no accident that, just months before assuming office as Nixon's assistant for national security affairs, Kissinger published an admiring essay on the Prussian statesman (Kissinger 1968). Nixon's main aims were to disentangle the United States from Vietnam and to manage what seemed at the time a trend toward US decline in the superpower balance. The twin ideas of the Nixon Doctrine (substituting military aid for American combat forces in what were then called Third

World conflicts) and détente with Moscow and Beijing were simple and compatible, went well beyond conventional wisdom, and once decided were pursued consistently. The idea of using rapprochement with China to balance Moscow was truly radical and survived counterforces in American domestic politics because of Nixon's solid status as a conservative hawk. The initiative, which would have strained the bounds of controversy if handled normally, was also accomplished in secrecy, circumventing the normal bureaucratic tendencies to obstruction and entropy.

Nevertheless, even this example has elements of "emergent" strategy. Nixon and Kissinger entered office believing that China was "the more aggressive of the Communist powers," and did not immediately plan the triangular diplomacy that marked subsequent policy. As Kissinger put it, "The new administration had a notion, but not yet a strategy, to move toward China. Policy emerges when concept encounters opportunity." In coming to reconciliation with China, "we took even ourselves by surprise" (Kissinger 1979, 172, 171, 162). Moreover, while the Nixon triangular strategy was about as grand as strategy gets in the United States, only half of it (rapprochement with Beijing) lasted long—about a quarter century. The other half, détente with Moscow, succeeded in the short term but crumbled within a decade, reversed by reinvigorated Cold War. How long a strategy must endure to qualify as grand is an unsettled question, but one of the closest American examples, Nixon's, seems at best half grand.

The Glass Half-Empty: Virtues of Ungrand Strategy

Most interesting questions in politics can be answered only subjectively, but the standards for judging the utility of the concept of grand strategy are more subjective than most. Neither success nor failure of a nation's fortunes in international politics is proof that the result was caused by its strategy, grand or otherwise. A strategy that aspires to grandness rather than grandiosity needs to be general enough to cover a wide range of contingencies but specific enough to identify priorities and sources of leverage for a particular contingency. Where that balance can be struck is hard to measure other than impressionistically. This essay is admittedly impressionistic but asks that the recently fashionable status of the concept of grand strategy be justified by value added to the term foreign policy.

The argument here is that, with some exceptions, the rough and tumble of international politics rarely leaves time for true grand strategy. Statesmen usually feel compelled to operate ad hoc, focused on the short term, animated by basic values and weakly examined premises, putting out fires most of the time, seldom cogitating deeply about long-term planning beyond their unconscious assumptions and buzzword ideas of the day. Their less than grand strategies are usually channeled by instincts, constraints, and concrete options disjunct from conscious theory. Grand strategy serves more as a rhetorical prop or motherhood statement than as a clear guide to choices that are more than obvious. Sometimes leaders in democracies come into office with genuine ambitions to pursue a markedly different course for their country, and have a serviceable grand strategy in mind, but most often they are ground down by circumstances, robustness of the status quo, and oppositional foxes in the policymaking process. They may alter their nation's course but seldom exert the amount of control and direction implied by the lofty idea of grand strategy.

This is not always bad. The dispersion of power within democratic government that is anti-strategic in tendency risks incoherent action, but effective grand strategy is not necessarily preferable. If the commander in chief happens to be radical, ignorant, confident, and impulsive all at the same time—the situation, as it happened, in the United States under President Trump—subversion of authority and frustration of grand strategy by the "deep state" (what is otherwise traditionally known as the permanent government) may be welcome. In this volume, Edelstein rightly points out other downsides of real grand strategy.

The argument here is not cynical. If authoritarian leaders are better able to set and pursue grand strategies, that is not necessarily always an advantage. In democratic theory there is a strong strand of argument against the wisdom of trying to plan and execute consistently rational strategies: the method of incrementalism, trial and error, contention in the marketplace of ideas, fashioning coalitions that agree on policies for different reasons, and other forms of suboptimization—the "science of muddling through"—accommodate interests and necessities unforeseen in singular strategies and forge less risky and more durable solutions (Lindblom 1959). Or as Fisher Ames, Federalist politician in the era of the Founders, put it, "Monarchy is a merchantman, which sails well, but will sometimes strike on a rock, and go to the bottom; whilst a republic is a raft, which would never sink, but then your feet are always in water" (quoted in Emerson 1983, 97). This less strategic approach has many deficiencies, and sometimes it produces disaster—as in the incremental American descent into Vietnam—but it often avoids the naïve disasters that can follow the combination of mistaken assumptions and bold activism.

The term grand strategy is not worthless. Sometimes it does describe reality, and it is useful within limits as a normative construct for theorists to use in prescribing how nations should try to pursue their material or moral interests. It is also perfectly serviceable as a near synonym for foreign policy when needed by drafters of good prose to avoid repetitive language. The term has simply come to be overused and the concept overvalued as a standard. Theorists should use it more sparingly, and analysts should not use the concept as the main grounds for assessing the wisdom of nations' policies and behavior.

Note

1. This chapter draws on more detailed arguments in Betts 2012a, ch. 10; Betts 2001–2; and Betts 2012b.

References

Avey, Paul C., Jonathan N. Markowitz, and Robert J. Reardon. 2018. "Disentangling Grand Strategy: International Relations Theory and U.S. Grand Strategy." *Texas National Security Review* 2 (1): 28–51.

Bensahel Nora et al. 2008. *After Saddam: Prewar Planning and the Occupation of Iraq*. Santa Monica, CA: RAND Corporation.

Blair, Bruce G. 1993. *The Logic of Accidental Nuclear War*. Washington, D.C.: Brookings Institution.

Betts, Richard K. 2001-2. "The Trouble with Strategy: Bridging Policy and Operations." *Joint Force Quarterly* 29: 23–30.

Betts, Richard K. 2012a. *American Force: Dangers, Delusions, and Dilemmas in National Security*. New York: Columbia University Press.

Betts, Richard K. 2012b. "American Strategy: Grand vs. Grandiose." In *America's Path: Grand Strategy for the Next Administration*, edited by Richard Fontaine and Kristin M. Lord, 31–42. Washington, D.C.: Center for a New American Security.

Brands, Hal. 2014. *What Good Is Grand Strategy? Power and Purpose in American Statecraft from Harry S. Truman to George W. Bush*. Ithaca, NY: Cornell University Press.

Clausewitz, Carl von. 1976. *On War*. Edited and Translated by Michael Howard and Peter Paret. Princeton: Princeton University Press.

Carroll, Lewis. 1909. *Through the Looking Glass, and What Alice Found There*. New York: Dodge.

Edelstein, David M., and Ronald R. Krebs. 2015. "Delusions of Grand Strategy." *Foreign Affairs* 94 (6): 109–116.

Ellsberg, Daniel. 2017. *The Doomsday Machine: Confessions of a Nuclear War Planner*. New York: Bloomsbury.

Emerson, Ralph Waldo. 1983. *Essays, Second Series*. New York: Library of America.

Freedman, Lawrence. 2013. *Strategy: A History*. New York: Oxford University Press.

Gaddis, John Lewis. 2018. *On Grand Strategy*. New York: Penguin.

Gelb, Leslie H., with Richard K. Betts. 1979. *The Irony of Vietnam: The System Worked*. Washington, D.C.: Brookings Institution.

Greenfield, Kent Roberts. 1963. *American Strategy in World War II*. Baltimore: Johns Hopkins Press.

Hart, B.H. Liddell. 1967. *Strategy*, 2d Edition. New York: Praeger.

Kissinger, Henry A. 1968. "The White Revolutionary: Reflections on Bismarck." *Daedalus* 97 (3): 888-924.

Kissinger, Henry A. 1979. *White House Years*. Boston: Little, Brown.

Krepinevich, Andrew F., Jr. 1986. *The Army and Vietnam*. Baltimore: Johns Hopkins University Press.

Lindblom, Charles E. 1959. "The Science of 'Muddling Through.'" *Public Administration Review* 19 (2): 79–88.

Mintzberg, Henry, Bruce Ahlstrand, and Joseph Lampel. 1998. *Strategy Safari*. New York: Free Press.

Morison, Samuel Eliot. 1958. *Strategy and Compromise*. Boston: Atlantic-Little, Brown.

The National Security Strategy of the United States of America. 2002. Washington, D.C.: The White House.

Popescu, Ionut. 2017. *Emergent Strategy and Grand Strategy: How American Presidents Succeed in Foreign Policy*. Baltimore: Johns Hopkins University Press.

Posen, Barry R. 2014. *Restraint: A New Foundation for U.S. Grand Strategy.* Ithaca: Cornell University Press.

Posen, Barry R., and Andrew L. Ross. 1996/97. "Competing Visions for U.S. Grand Strategy." *International Security* 21 (3): 5–53.

Sagan, Scott D. 1993. *The Limits of Safety: Organizations, Accidents, and Nuclear Weapons.* Princeton: Princeton University Press.

Silove, Nina. 2018. "Beyond the Buzzword: The Three Meanings of Grand Strategy." *Security Studies* 27 (1): 27–57.

Smith, Gerard. 1980. *Doubletalk: The Story of SALT I.* Garden City, NY: Doubleday.

Steinbruner, John D. 2002. *The Cybernetic Theory of Decision: New Dimensions of Political Analysis.* 2nd edition. Princeton: Princeton University Press.

U.S. Congress, National Security Act of 1947, Public Law 253, 61 Stat. 495, 80th Congress, July 26, 1947.

Woodward, Bob. 2010. *Obama's Wars.* New York: Simon & Schuster.

CHAPTER 37

THE LIMITS OF GRAND STRATEGY

DAVID M. EDELSTEIN

WHAT is grand strategy, and must states have a grand strategy to succeed in international affairs (Lissner 2018)? When asked in the midst of his presidency if the United States needed a new grand strategy, Barack Obama dismissively responded, "I don't really even need George Kennan right now" (Remnick 2014). For many scholars and observers of US foreign policy, the idea that the country could not *always* use George Kennan would border on the heretical. Kennan is viewed as the archetypical grand-strategic thinker, endowed with the rare ability and temperament to look beyond the current moment and anticipate how the United States could use all the means at its disposal to achieve its national interests over the long term (Gaddis 2011). Surely, any US president could use somebody like that, right?[1]

In fact, few topics in international relations consume as much intellectual and public energy as the grand strategies of the great powers.[2] While scholars engage in heated debates about whether the United States should act as an "offshore balancer," pursue "primacy," or take an approach of "restraint," the popular press seeks—often in vain—for a "doctrine" that defines a president's foreign policy approach in the grandest terms (Sanger 2009). Analysts wait with baited breath for the release of the latest iteration of the US National Security Strategy, and a president who appears to be guided by pragmatism rather than doctrine is sure to be criticized for lacking "vision."[3] Historian John Lewis Gaddis, perhaps the preeminent historian of the Cold War grand strategy of containment (and the authorized biographer of Kennan), seems chagrined that Bill Clinton believed that, "[Franklin Roosevelt and Harry Truman] just made it up as they went along, and he didn't see why he couldn't do the same" (Gaddis 2009, 2). But was Clinton's instinct to muddle through necessarily mistaken? Was Obama misguided when he dismissed the need for a new US grand strategy or eschewed the advice of a modern-day George Kennan? Is there a Trump Doctrine, and does it matter if there is or is not (Lissner and Zenko 2017)?

I argue, in fact, that the importance of grand strategy to successful foreign policy is often overstated and that the extent to which grand strategy can actually undermine the achievement of a state's national interests is underappreciated (Miller 2013). My argument is built on two claims. First, while the ideal-typical grand strategy might be attractive, constructing such a strategy is difficult, if not impossible. Second, grand strategies have potential downsides, including the creation of self-fulfilling prophecies and the imposition of artificial constraints. Instead, I suggest that "strategic pragmatism" will often be a more effective way for states to achieve their goals. Especially in times of uncertainty, it behooves great powers to retain the ability to be nimble and flexible in their foreign policies rather than pre-committing to a grand strategy.[4] When advocates counter that grand strategies can themselves be flexible, it raises questions about how such flexibility might undermine the supposed benefits of having a clearly articulated and credible grand strategy.

This chapter is divided into four parts. I first define grand strategy and examine the purposes of grand strategy. Next, I contend that not only are the goals of grand strategy difficult to achieve, grand strategies may also introduce certain dangers. Third, I suggest my alternative of "strategic pragmatism." Fourth, I conclude with an examination of the current debates over US grand strategy, arguing that strategic pragmatism is a more sensible approach than some of the grand strategies that others have proposed.

What Is Grand Strategy?

Grand strategy describes the ways in which states use the resources at their disposal—military, diplomatic, and economic—in conjunction to achieve their national interests.[5] A grand strategy expresses a theory for how a state can best act to achieve its national interests (Layne 1997, 88). As Hal Brands puts it, grand strategy is "the intellectual architecture that gives form and structure to foreign policy." It is the "crucial link between short-term action and medium— and long-term goals" (Brands 2014, 3–4). Conceived of as a theory, a grand strategy includes the outcomes that the state would like to achieve (i.e., its interests), the means it will use to achieve those outcomes, and a causal mechanism explaining how those means will bring about those outcomes.

Importantly, a grand strategy is not simply a statement of a state's interests or guiding principles, nor is it synonymous with a state's foreign policy. Few would dispute the need for any state to identify its national interests, but what distinguishes a grand strategy is that it must not only identify ends to be sought but also how means are to be employed to achieve those ends. Similarly, grand strategy must be more than a set of guiding principles, which may be so general as to allow a wide range of interpretations by different actors. A grand strategy also is not simply a state's foreign policy. Specific foreign policy choices ought to be derived from a country's grand strategy, but one is not the same as the other. A country's decision to pursue an arms control agreement with another country does not mean that arms control is that state's grand strategy. Instead, the arms control agreement must fit into some larger strategic agenda for the state.

The literature on grand strategy includes attempts to advocate for specific grand strategies as well as efforts to comment on the utility as well as the problems with grand strategy as a concept (Chollet and Goldgeier 2008; Jervis 1998b; Krasner 2010). In the latter category, Hal Brands' *What Good Is Grand Strategy?* discusses the general concept of grand strategy before turning to an analysis of American grand strategies since the end of the Second World War (Brands 2014). Brands concludes that leaders who consciously think about their grand strategies generally have more success than others.

Brands' analysis of grand strategy is, however, problematic. Looking back on history, he observes coordinated grand strategies without providing convincing evidence that the policymakers executing policy actually thought of what they were doing as a grand strategy. As Bruce Jentleson writes of the grand strategy literature, in general, "Rather than a genuinely guiding and overarching framework at the time, past grand strategy has been made grander by what gets read into it retrospectively" (Jentleson 2009, 70). Similarly, when the US succeeded during the period he studies, Brands has a tendency to attribute that success to a wise grand strategy without, again, presenting evidence directly connecting grand strategy to the success.

Conversely, Richard Betts offers a critical take on grand strategy, asking whether strategy is, in fact, an "illusion" (Betts 2000; Betts 2021; Dombrowski 2021). Betts focuses primarily on strategy within war and identifies ten different criticisms of the possibility of strategy. In the end, he finds some of the criticisms more justified than others, but he concludes with a defense of the continuing need for strategy, warts and all. The argument in this chapter is both more specific to grand strategy and goes further in questioning its utility. I argue that grand strategy may not only be an "illusion," but is also often counterproductive.

Why Do States Need Grand Strategies?

Barry Posen suggests that states that do not formulate clear grand strategies do so "at their peril" (Posen 2014, 4). There are three primary purposes that grand strategy might serve: coordination, signaling, and shaping (Art 2003; Drezner 2011; Posen 2014). While each of these purposes is sensible and even laudable, grand strategy is also an imperfect vehicle for their achievement. The root of the problem is the tension between flexibility and specificity that is inherent to grand strategy. On the one hand, for grand strategy to succeed, it must be specific enough to provide focal points for those purposes, especially coordination and signaling. But it is important not to build a strawman of inflexibly, overly deterministic grand strategies. No advocate of grand strategy would suggest that such strategies ought to be carved in stone and adhered to religiously. As Lawrence Freedman writes of strategy in general, "If strategy is a fixed plan that set out a reliable path to an eventual goal, then it is likely to be not only disappointing but also counterproductive, conceding the advantage to others with greater flexibility and imagination" (Freedman 2013, 610). Or as Richard Sennreich has put it, "Like a vessel under sail, grand strategy is at the mercy of uncontrollable and often unpredictable political, economic, and military winds and currents, and executing it effectively requires both alertness to those changes and constant tiller correction" (Sinnreich 2011, 256).

So, one needs to have a strategy that is flexible enough to adjust to the changing threats and opportunities that international politics provides, even as it is specific enough to allow for coordination and signaling. But how much flexibility can a strategy contain while still constituting anything legitimately labeled as a strategy? At what point does "flexibility" become the very "ad hocery" that supporters of grand strategy are so quick to dismiss? If grand strategy is to succeed, then there also must be some limits to its flexibility. I now turn to a closer look at the three main purposes of grand strategy, explaining why they are so difficult to achieve.

Coordination

Perhaps the most compelling reason given for why states need a grand strategy has to do with coordination. Modern great powers have wide-ranging interests around the globe that need to be managed by an often complicated bureaucracy. Grand strategy allows the left hand to know what the right hand is doing, preventing not only the wasteful expenditure of resources but also behavior in one country or region that might undermine a country's interests in another. Grand strategy might also allow for coordination among allies, with certain alliance partners indicating their willingness to take on particular responsibilities while leaving others to protect different interests.

To take one example of the importance of coordination through grand strategy, Wang Jisi identifies the lack of coordination as a critical impediment to the formulation of an effective Chinese grand strategy. As Wang writes, "Almost all institutions in the central leadership and local governments are involved in foreign relations to varying degrees, and it is virtually impossible for them to see China's national interests the same way or to speak with one voice. These differences confuse outsiders as well as the Chinese people" (Jisi 2011, 78–79). Coordination, therefore, is important not only for the purposes of internal management, but also for the manner in which it allows states to communicate with each other in a clear and coordinated way.

It is hard to argue that large organizations do not benefit from coordination, but one should also have modest expectations about how well grand strategy can succeed at accomplishing this purpose. As Betts notes, rather than pursuing virtuous, apolitical coordination, bureaucrats within a large government are likely to attempt to ensure that a grand strategy is coordinated around the parochial interests of their particular bureaucracy (Betts 2000, 32–37). Organizational theorists in realms far afield from grand strategy have long taught us that bureaucracies tend to promote their own health, often at the expense of larger corporate or national goals (March 1993; Simon 1947).

So, while a grand strategy might theoretically aid in coordination, it is just as likely to be a political tool used by various organizations to advance their own interests (Allison and Zelikow 1999). Finally, returning to the inherent tension in grand strategy, for grand strategy to be an effective mechanism for coordination, it must be relatively specific. An overly vague grand strategy will only beg the question of the points of coordination, but a specific grand strategy may limit the flexibility that is also necessary in the design of a reasonable grand strategy.

Signaling

Grand strategies communicate the value that great powers put on various interests, and by doing so, they reassure allies and deter adversaries. A clearly articulated grand strategy signals audiences about where their interests lie and what would be considered threats to those interests (Fearon 1997; 1994; Powell 1999). In the absence of a grand strategy, others may be tempted to behave provocatively not knowing what is and is not acceptable and allies might start to question each other's commitments. In response, those allies may begin arming themselves with potentially destabilizing consequences.

The critical and much studied question is, of course, how states can make such signals of interests credible, especially when they are embedded in a larger grand strategy. James Fearon observes that states might enhance the credibility of their grand strategies by sinking costs into those commitments by, for example, stationing troops in an ally's territory (Fearon 1997, 87). But generating such sunk cost signals for grand strategy is difficult without knowing truly how costly the signal is and, short of automated tripwires, whether or not troops would actually be used to defend an ally. Given that great powers often have the capability (and inclination) to act in inconsistent and hypocritical ways, others might reasonably question the credibility of grand-strategic commitments, especially in the challenging realm of extended deterrence.

Two additional points are worth making about the signaling role of grand strategies. First, writing about the Obama administration, Daniel Drezner contends that the simultaneous problems of coercing adversaries and reassuring allies are particularly intense in uncertain times such as the present era. Without a grand strategy in such circumstances, Drezner implies, leaders are likely to drift from crisis to crisis with no particular sense of why they should do x in one circumstance or y in another (Drezner 2011). But this only raises the question of why other states would take articulations of grand strategy under such uncertainty as a credible signal, and further, great powers might most benefit from reserving as much flexibility as possible during moments of uncertainty rather than committing themselves to a grand strategy.

Second, Posen suggests that articulated grand strategies send a signal to domestic audiences as well as international (Posen 2014, 5). In the absence of grand strategies, leaders may employ their country's military forces without having to explain the purpose of such use. Posen's argument is potentially valid, though this might simply drive leaders to craft their grand strategies in vague terms under which just about any policy could be justified to a domestic audience.

Here again, signaling raises the tension between specificity and flexibility. To be clear, credibly signaling through grand strategy is possible, but it requires specific commitments backed up by particular force deployments and sincere statements of how a state will act under certain circumstances. More specific grand strategies may make for more effective and credible signals, but as I discuss in the next section, such strategies may also lead to over- (or under-) commitment by states for the simple purpose of building credibility. More flexible grand strategies are likely to be more attractive for domestic political purposes, but such flexibility is likely to limit the effectiveness of such strategies as signals to allies, adversaries, and domestic audiences.

Shaping

According to a third logic, grand strategy is useful for shaping the future in directions amenable to what are likely to be a great power's interests. Robert Art describes his preferred "selective engagement" grand strategy for the United States as a "shaping strategy," which "emphasizes the retention of America's key alliances and forward military presence in Europe, East Asia, and the Persian Gulf, in order to help mold the political, military, and economic configurations of these regions so as to make them more congenial to America's interests" (Art 2003, 223). Left to their own devices, leaders may be inclined to focus exclusively on the short term, and grand strategy forces those leaders to be more farsighted. Such an argument is consistent with John Ikenberry's arguments about how great powers "after victory" might use their relative advantage to set the stage for long-term success (Ikenberry 2001).

That states can reliably shape the future through grand strategy is a questionable proposition. Consider the example of the contemporary United States. In the current circumstances, it is unclear how the articulation (and faithful pursuit) of a grand strategy now will secure American interests in the future. Not only is there an unavoidable element of uncertainty about how the future will evolve, but it also "takes two to tango" when shaping the future. Efforts to shape the future now may only lead others to push back in ways that make that desired future less likely to emerge. Moreover, the shaping argument about grand strategy is plagued by the same challenges as Ikenberry's. There is little reason to think that any other state once it gets relatively more powerful in the future is going to have any more respect for the interests of a powerful country, like the United States, than that powerful country has had for other states during its period of dominance.[6] Even if a unipolar power articulates a grand-strategic vision, it is not clear why any other states in the international system should trust or believe it (Suri 2009).

Despite the complexity of the international system and the difficulty of predicting the future, the premise of grand strategy is that one can devise a strategy that would be able to account for the many uncertainties of international politics. Expecting that a grand strategy would be able to incorporate complexity and its various forms of feedback seems unrealistic and, as I argue below, potentially dangerous (Jervis 1998a). As Eliot Cohen writes, "The very idea of grand strategy, then, runs on the rocks when it confronts the power of accident, contingency, and randomness that pervade human affairs" (Cohen 2016, 205). A more specific grand strategy that attempts to shape the future in certain directions may simply be premised on unreasonable assumptions about the future or fail to anticipate the many feedback effects that adopting a strategy now may have in the future. But a more flexible grand strategy may simply be too nebulous to serve the purpose of meaningfully shaping the future of international politics.

The Dangers of Grand Strategy

One might accept the problems with grand strategy that I have presented so far, but also see relatively little harm in the continued pursuit of grand strategies that might, at least, provide some of the benefits suggested by advocates. But there are at least two reasons why even clearly articulated and consistently followed grand strategies would not necessarily be good for great powers.[7]

The first danger is that a grand strategy could conceivably produce pressures for states to adopt certain policies for little reason other than to be consistent with the strategy that has been articulated. Much has been written in the international relations literature questioning the value of one's reputation and, by implication, the value of acting to uphold such a reputation (Press 2005; Tomz 2007; Mercer 1996). Even if the arguments dismissing the value of reputation are not completely convincing, most would agree that acting for the sake of reputation when direct interests are relatively low is ill-advised. The danger introduced by grand strategy is that a state's behavior anywhere in the world might be interpreted as a signal of the credibility of a country's commitment to a certain grand strategy. In turn, this potentially leads concerned great powers to feel compelled to intervene when their direct interests at stake are relatively low or to become entrapped by their allies (Snyder 1984). As Leslie Gelb and Richard Betts conclude from their examination of the US experience in Vietnam, "Doctrine and consensus are the midwives to necessity and the enemy of dissent and choice" (Gelb with Betts 1979, 365).

As an example of these dangers, during the Cold War, the United States arguably overcommitted itself to various interventions, in particular in Southeast Asia, for fear of the credibility repercussions of doing otherwise. In retrospect, it is far from clear that attempting to uphold the credibility of US grand strategy was worth the cost (Hopf 1994). Such Cold War behavior was not limited to the United States. In the context of the quagmire that the Soviet Union found itself in in Afghanistan, Soviet Premier Mikhail Gorbachev was concerned about how Soviet withdrawal would be perceived by allies. He expressed his trepidation to Alessandro Natta, the General Secretary of the Italian Communist Party, in March 1988, "In other countries ... there are forces which also do not desire the withdrawal of Soviet troops. There are even such forces in Africa. The substance of their reasoning boils down to the following: 'You're abandoning Afghanistan;

it means you're also abandoning us.'"[8] The logic of grand strategy—and its understanding of the interconnected nature of state behavior—leads a state to fear that its actions in one area of the world will be viewed as information about how that state will behave in another area of the world, no matter how unrelated the two issues may actually be. Over the course of the 1980s, such concerns contributed to a delayed withdrawal from Afghanistan even after Soviet leaders had recognized the chances of success were low (Cordovez and Harrison 1995; Kalinovsky 2011). Soviet behavior in Afghanistan was influenced by the implications of any Soviet action for Soviet credibility elsewhere, whether or not the strategy made any sense for Afghanistan specifically.

Second, in their effort to shape the future of the international system, grand strategies may create self-fulfilling prophecies.[9] As Robert Jervis observes, a "critical question is the degree to which a state's actions that are based on an initially false image have transformed the other state's intentions" (Jervis 1976, 77). If a grand strategy identifies a certain country as a threat warranting a response, then the steps taken within that grand strategy might only ensure the emergence of that other country as a threat. Forward-looking grand strategies, therefore, are not only a wager on the future, but they may also make a certain future more likely (Edelstein and Krebs 2015).

Again, a tension is evident here. Clearly, great powers would like to try to anticipate future threats and shape the international system in favorable directions, but assertive shaping may have the effect of creating—or at least accelerating—the emergence of a threat. One might argue that the US "pivot to Asia" undertaken by the Obama administration represented an important shift in US grand strategy. This pivot rested on certain beliefs about where US interests are likely to lie in the future and how best to achieve those interests. In particular, the pivot appeared, at least in part, to represent a response to the perceived rising threat posed by China to American interests in East Asia. To the extent that the pivot or "rebalancing" led to the redeployment of military assets to the Pacific, the strategy is likely viewed in Beijing as reasonably credible. The danger, though, is that such a pivot to Asia, especially if it includes related military dimensions such as the concept of "Air-Sea Battle," might create a self-fulfilling prophecy provoking conflict between the US and China (US Department of Defense Air-Sea Battle Office 2013). Whether or not the United States and China are likely to find themselves in conflict regardless of what grand strategy the US adopts now is a difficult question to answer, but all else being equal, the United States would not seem to benefit from a grand strategy that might make that conflict more likely.[10]

One final consideration affecting the utility of grand strategy is the level of uncertainty in the international system. On the one hand, one might reasonably argue that it is at times of great uncertainty when grand strategy is most needed. Without a clear strategy, states amid uncertainty are likely to wander aimlessly from one immediate threat to the next. When threats are certain, grand strategy is easier and, in a sense, less necessary. On the other hand, to the extent that grand strategies make some threats more likely to emerge, then grand strategy at times of uncertainty may be unwise. Refraining from grand strategy in favor of a more adaptive approach to international politics may serve a state better over the long term.

The Case for Strategic Pragmatism

If the only choice in the absence of grand strategy is "strategic nihilism," then it is unsurprising that grand strategy might still be viewed as preferable (Betts 2000, 16). But to question the wisdom of an articulated grand strategy is not to reject the value of acting strategically, meant simply as adopting the best policy in any given context to achieve national interests. Instead of an overarching grand strategy, I advocate here for a pragmatic approach to foreign policy that navigates between an overly specific grand strategy and its dangers and an overly flexible grand strategy and its vagueness.[11] Such an approach acknowledges that contingency and uncertainty are unavoidable in international politics and that great powers ought to seek to retain the flexibility to use their relative power to achieve their national interests without concern for consistency or reputation.[12]

In a classic article from a half-century ago, Charles Lindblom distinguishes between the "rational-comprehensive method" of policy formulation and what he calls the "method of successive limited comparisons" or what might be called "muddling through." He explains why organizations rarely act as rational actors,

> For complex problems, [the rational-comprehensive method] is of course impossible. Although such an approach can be described, it cannot be practiced except for relatively simple problems and even then only in a somewhat modified form. It assumes intellectual capacities and sources that men simply do not possess, and it is even more absurd as an approach to policy when time and money that can be allocated to a policy problem is limited, as is always the case. (Lindblom 1959, 80)

The challenge of foreign policy would seem to fit the bill of such a complex problem. While the rational-comprehensive method might represent an ideal-typical grand strategy, I argue here that strategic pragmatism is a better model for the making of foreign policy, especially as the level of uncertainty about future threats increases. Strategic pragmatism enables leaders to reconcile their need for both specificity and flexibility in the generation of strategies. More specifically, a pragmatic approach to foreign policy decision-making has five elements.

First, a pragmatic approach recognizes the inherent difficulty of predicting and shaping the future in international politics. Rather than making assumptions about the future intentions of potential allies or adversaries, a pragmatic approach would be more patient in allowing uncertainty to resolve itself before committing to a certain strategic approach to another country or region. Prematurely committing to a certain strategy introduces the dangers of creating self-fulfilling prophecies and of wasting resources. Instead, the priority of leaders should be to respond in the best, most advisable manner to acute threats as they emerge while retaining as much flexibility as possible to respond to future scenarios. As a threat becomes clearer and more predictable, a comprehensive grand-strategic response is both more advisable and more likely to be adhered to.

Clearly, leaders need to be attentive to long-term threats on the horizon, but this argument also suggests that there is virtue in avoiding overreactions to uncertain long-term threats.

Second, strategic pragmatism requires states clearly to identify their interests, but not necessarily how they will pursue and protect those interests in a particular situation. The identification and ranking of national interests is itself a significant challenge (Wolfers 1962). Despite this, much of the contemporary literature on US grand strategy seems to take interests for granted. By specifying what a state values, others can have some sense of what states would consider threatening while the state itself would retain flexibility in how to pursue and protect those interests. Interests that are well-crafted and reasonably limited will be taken more seriously than interests that are vaguely specified in an overarching grand strategy.

Third, such a strategy recognizes the limits of reputation in international politics. For a great power, reputation is less important than capabilities and the ability effectively to mobilize those capabilities. A pragmatic approach considers challenges as they occur on their own merits with less concern for how action in such situations may affect other issues or regions. While states often attempt to generate certain reputations, a pragmatic approach to strategy would resist efforts to tie specific incidents to a more general reputation (on coupling and decoupling, see Jervis 1970). Great powers would insist that each region and each commitment within a region are treated independently.

Fourth, strategic pragmatism is also opportunistic. One should not assume that a pragmatic strategy is only reactionary. Great powers may have opportunities to seize resources or expand their capabilities, and political leaders ought to retain the flexibility to pursue those interests when they present themselves without concern for how they may violate some previously devised grand strategy.[13]

Fifth and in sum, strategic pragmatism eschews efforts to devise a single coherent grand strategy to manage a country's affairs around the globe. Flexibility and hypocrisy are forms of power for states, and great powers should be reluctant to relinquish those sources of power by adopting grand strategies (Finnemore 2009). Such strategies can be unnecessary, unhelpfully vague, and generate dangerous, counterproductive behavior. Strategic pragmatism calls upon great powers to devise strategies that are tightly focused on particular challenges and threats.

The notion of strategic pragmatism is not new. To give just one example, Franklin Roosevelt admitted to lacking a consistent, coherent grand strategy during his presidency:

> You know I am a juggler, and I never let my right hand know what my left hand does... I may have one policy for Europe and one diametrically opposite for North and South America. I may be entirely inconsistent, and furthermore I am perfectly willing to mislead and tell untruths if it will help win the war. (Quoted in Kimball 1991, 7)

Elsewhere, Roosevelt denigrated the Atlantic Charter, the 1941 document laying out an allied grand strategy for the war, as essentially nice in principle, but worthless in practice

(Costigliola 2012, 228–229). George F. Kennan condemned FDR's foreign policy as that of "a very superficial man, ignorant, dilettantish, severely limited in intellectual horizon" (quoted in Kimball 1991, 18).

Through the Second World War, FDR recognized the need for pragmatic cooperation with the Soviet Union even as he anticipated the potential difficulties of managing the postwar order with the Soviets. Roosevelt, however, was not—and could not—be overly concerned with the long-term. He was less concerned about American credibility than he was with adopting what he thought was the right policy at the time, and he did not particularly concern himself with trying to come up with a single, coherent grand strategy that linked together American efforts around the world. As Robert Dallek observes, "[FDR] believed it essential to accommodate himself to changing opinion at home and altering circumstances abroad. He saw temporary compromises as inevitable in the pursuit of larger ideals" (Dallek 1979, 551). Given the complexity of the Second World War environment, such compromises, though perhaps unsavory to some and incompatible with a coherent grand strategy, made possible victory in the Second World War.

Critiques of Strategic Pragmatism

There are at least four significant critiques of strategic pragmatism (for a critique of a pragmatic approach, see Moyar 2009). First, strategic pragmatism might encourage "salami tactics" by adversaries (Schelling 1966, 66–67). Adversaries might be tempted to advance their interests piece by piece, rather than as a whole, with the hope that others, without an orienting grand strategy, might not notice what they are doing. In a similar manner, states acting in a pragmatic way may be easily distracted, unable to prioritize among the myriad issues they confront. Salami tactics are certainly a concern as is distraction, but they ought to be concerning to any state, whether or not they have a grand strategy. A state with a diffuse, global grand strategy might itself be blind to such salami tactics if it has oriented its overall grand strategy in a different direction, and expansive grand strategies are certainly not immune from the challenges of being distracted by issues that may or may not be worth the effort to confront.

Second, inasmuch as strategic pragmatism calls for decoupling, it is likely to miss truly reasonable connections between different regions and issues. If those connections are missed, then states may have to expend more resources in the future to generate credibility than they would have needed to if they had made the connection at the time. Moreover, a strategic pragmatist state might be at a disadvantage if it finds itself in an adversarial relationship with a state that has articulated its own grand strategy. These are certainly dangers, but states need to do a calculation of whether unwarranted reputation-based behavior is more or less costly than missing such connections. Is linkage or decoupling likely to be more costly? Investing in a specific reputation with a particular country may be worthwhile, but using grand strategy to develop a general reputation is less sensible. As for a state that is committed to its own grand strategy, as

I have argued, there are good reasons to think that may not be to the advantage of the other state.

Third, great powers do need to consider the allocation of resources to multiple interests in many different parts of the world, and strategic pragmatism would provide little guidance for how to do this, especially over the longer term. Is not some guidance provided by grand strategy better than the incremental guidance suggested by strategic pragmatism? Here again, though, one faces a tradeoff: grand strategy may allow the allocation of such resources, but given the inherent uncertainty and complexity in international politics, such allocation may very well turn out to be misguided. The implication of my argument is not that states ignore the need to balance resources and consider the future, but rather that they do so in a reasoned way that does not put all of one's eggs in the basket of a particular grand strategy. Strategic pragmatism encourages states to consider their resource allocations differently, focusing on flexible investments that allow states effectively to respond to the emerging threats they confront.

Fourth, grand strategy might be necessary to motivate a population to support a certain cause. Without a coherent articulation of what a country is trying to achieve, political leaders are likely to have great difficulty generating public support for foreign policy, especially if it involves the use of costly military force. While this argument makes certain intuitive sense, it is not clear that a grand strategy is necessary to garner such public support, nor does it necessarily serve a country well if grand strategy is used for this political purpose. General publics may be as myopic as their leaders and, therefore, be more inclined to respond to short-term rationales than to grand-strategic justifications.

Conclusion

In his memoirs, former US Secretary of Defense Robert Gates observes, "I don't recall ever reading the president's National Security Strategy when preparing to become secretary of defense. Nor did I read any of the previous National Defense Strategy documents when I became secretary. I never felt disadvantaged by not having read these scriptures" (Gates 2014, 144). In this chapter, I have argued that the perennial search for coherent grand strategies is, in fact, misguided. Grand strategies struggle to achieve their goals, and when they do, they might lead states to behave in ways that undermine their national interests. I have also suggested a more pragmatic alternative that would allow states to achieve their interests without the downsides of grand strategy.

Notes

1. On why great powers need grand strategies, see Feaver 2009; Gaddis 2009.
2. For a wide-ranging discussion of grand strategy, see Hill 2010.
3. For an illustrative critique of Barack Obama, see Drezner 2011.

4. For more on how states manage short- and long-term uncertainty, see (Edelstein 2017).
5. On the origins of grand strategic thinking, see Ekbladh 2011.
6. For a critique of Ikenberry, see Schweller 2001.
7. For a related critique of grand strategy, in general, see Drezner, Krebs, and Schweller 2020. For a specific critique of contemporary US grand strategy, see Porter 2018.
8. Record of Conversation of M.S. Gorbachev with the General Secretary of the Italian Communist Party Alessandro Natta, March 29, 1988, in *Cold War International History Project Bulletin*, No. 14–15 (Winter 2003–Spring 2004): 173.
9. It is at least conceivable that a grand strategy could create a positive self-fulfilling prophecy, though it is difficult to identify cases in which a grand strategy identified a particular country as a potential friend and partner that otherwise would not have been so.
10. On the potential dangers posed by the pivot to Asia, see Glaser 2012; Lieberthal 2011; Ross 2012.
11. Popescu (2017, 2018) makes the case for "emergent strategy" with an emphasis on strategy evolving through a process of learning. Popescu's analysis, however, is short on details of how this learning takes place, why certain lessons are learned and not others, and how lessons learned can be deeply politicized. See also Rose 2021.
12. One could conceive of strategic pragmatism as a grand strategy itself, but here, I attempt to distinguish an incremental, pragmatic approach from the overarching perspective of grand strategy.
13. Such an argument may be consistent with various claims about realism and the manner in which states seek to add to their power. See Mearsheimer 2001; Schweller 1994.

References

Allison, Graham T., and Philip Zelikow. 1999. *Essence of Decision: Explaining the Cuban Missile Crisis*. New York: Longman.
Art, Robert J. 2003. *A Grand Strategy for America*. Ithaca, NY: Cornell University Press.
Art, Robert J., and Patrick M. Cronin, eds. 2003. *The United States and Coercive Diplomacy*. Washington, D.C.: United States Institute of Peace Press.
Betts, Richard K. 2000. "Is Strategy an Illusion?" *International Security* 25 (2): 5–50.
Betts, Richard K. 2021. "Is Grand Strategy and Illusion? Or, the Grandiosity of Grand Strategy." In *The Oxford Handbook of Grand Strategy*, edited by Thierry Balzacq and Ronald R. Krebs. New York: Oxford University Press.
Brands, Hal. 2014. *What Good Is Grand Strategy? Power and Purpose in American Statecraft from Harry S. Truman to George W. Bush*. Ithaca, N.Y.: Cornell University Press.
Brooks, Stephen G., G. John Ikenberry, and William C. Wohlforth. 2012. "Don't Come Home, America: The Case against Retrenchment." *International Security* 37 (3): 7–51.
Chollet, Derek, and James Goldgeier. 2008. "Good Riddance to the Bush Doctrine." *The Washington Post*, July 13, 2008, sec. Opinions. http://www.washingtonpost.com/wp-dyn/content/article/2008/07/11/AR2008071102391.html
Cohen, Eliot A. 2016. *The Big Stick: The Limits of Soft Power & the Necessity of Military Force*. New York: Basic Books.
Cordovez, Diego, and Selig S. Harrison. 1995. *Out of Afghanistan: The Inside Story of the Soviet Withdrawal*. New York: Oxford University Press.

Costigliola, Frank. 2012. *Roosevelt's Lost Alliances: How Personal Politics Helped Start the Cold War*. Princeton: Princeton University Press.

Dallek, Robert. 1979. *Franklin D. Roosevelt and American Foreign Policy, 1932–1945*. New York: Oxford University Press.

Dombrowski, Peter. 2021. "Alternatives to Grand Strategy." In *The Oxford Handbook of Grand Strategy*, edited by Thierry Balzacq and Ronald R. Krebs. New York: Oxford University Press.

Drezner, Daniel W. 2011. "Does Obama Have a Grand Strategy: Why We Need Doctrines in Uncertain Times." *Foreign Affairs* 90 (4): 57–68.

Drezner, Daniel W., Krebs, Ronald R., and Schweller, Randall. 2020. "The End of Grand Strategy: America Must Think Small." *Foreign Affairs* 99 (3): 107–117.

Edelstein, David M. 2017. *Over the Horizon: Time, Uncertainty, and the Rise of Great Powers*. Ithaca, N.Y.: Cornell University Press.

Edelstein, David M., and Ronald R. Krebs. 2015. "Delusions of Grand Strategy: The Problem with Washington's Planning Obsession." *Foreign Affairs* 94 (6): 109–116.

Ekbladh, David. 2011. "Present at the Creation: Edward Mead Earle and the Depression-Era Origins of Security Studies." *International Security* 36 (3): 107–141.

Fearon, James D. 1994. "Signaling Versus the Balance of Power and Interests." *Journal of Conflict Resolution* 38 (2): 236–269.

Fearon, James D. 1997. "Signaling Foreign Policy Interests: Tying Hands versus Sinking Costs." *Journal of Conflict Resolution* 41 (1): 68–90.

Feaver, Peter. 2009. "What Is Grand Strategy and Why Do We Need It?" *Foreign Policy Blogs* (blog). April 8, 2009. http://shadow.foreignpolicy.com/posts/2009/04/08/what_is_grand_strategy_and_why_do_we_need_it

Finnemore, Martha. 2009. "Legitimacy, Hypocrisy, and the Social Structure of Unipolarity." *World Politics* 61 (1): 58–85.

Freedman, Lawrence. 2013. *Strategy: A History*. New York: Oxford University Press.

Gaddis, John Lewis. 2009. "What Is Grand Strategy?" Karl Von Der Heyden Distinguished Lecture. Duke University.

Gaddis, John Lewis. 2011. *George F. Kennan: An American Life*. New York: Penguin.

Gates, Robert Michael. 2014. *Duty: Memoirs of a Secretary at War*. New York: Alfred A. Knopf.

Gelb, Leslie H., and Richard K. Betts. 1979. *The Irony of Vietnam: The System Worked*. Washington: Brookings Institution.

Glaser, Bonnie S. 2012. "Pivot to Asia: Prepare for Unintended Consequences." *2012 Global Forecast: Risk, Opportunity, and the Next Administration*, 22–24.

Hill, Charles. 2010. *Grand Strategies: Literature, Statecraft, and World Order*. New Haven, C.T.: Yale University Press.

Hopf, Ted. 1994. *Peripheral Visions: Deterrence Theory and American Foreign Policy in the Third World, 1965–1990*. Ann Arbor: University of Michigan Press.

Ikenberry, G. John. 2001. *After Victory: Institutions, Strategic Restraint, and the Rebuilding of Order after Major Wars*. Princeton, N.J.: Princeton University Press.

Jentleson, Bruce W. 2009. "An Integrative Executive Branch Strategy for Policy Planning." In *Avoiding Trivia: The Role of Strategic Planning in American Foreign Policy*, edited by Daniel W. Drezner, 69–83. Washington, D.C.: Brookings Institution Press.

Jervis, Robert. 1970. *The Logic of Images in International Relations*. New York: Columbia University Press.

Jervis, Robert. 1976. *Perception and Misperception in International Politics*. Princeton, N.J.: Princeton University Press.

Jervis, Robert. 1998a. *System Effects: Complexity in Political and Social Life*. Princeton, N.J.: Princeton University Press.

Jervis, Robert. 1998b. "U.S. Grand Strategy: Mission Impossible." *Naval War College Review* 51 (3): 22–36.

Jisi, Wang. 2011. "China's Search for a Grand Strategy-A Rising Great Power Finds Its Way." *Foreign Affairs* 90 (2): 68–79.

Kalinovsky, Artemy M. 2011. *A Long Goodbye: The Soviet Withdrawal from Afghanistan*. Cambridge, M.A.: Harvard University Press.

Kimball, Warren. 1991. *The Juggler: Franklin Roosevelt as Wartime Statesman*. Princeton, N.J.: Princeton University Press.

Krasner, Stephen D. 2010. "An Orienting Principle for Foreign Policy." *Policy Review*, no. 163. https://www.hoover.org/research/orienting-principle-foreign-policy

Layne, Christopher. 1997. "From Preponderance to Offshore Balancing: America's Future Grand Strategy." *International Security* 22 (1): 86–124.

Lieber, Robert J. 2012. *Power and Willpower in the American Future: Why the United States Is Not Destined to Decline*. New York: Cambridge University Press.

Lieberthal, Kenneth. 2011. "The American Pivot to Asia." *Foreign Policy* 21 (December).

Lindblom, Charles E. 1959. "The Science of 'Muddling Through'." *Public Administration Review* 19 (2): 79–88.

Lissner, Rebecca, and Micah Zenko. 2017. "There Is No Trump Doctrine, and There Will Never Be One." *Foreign Policy*. July 21, 2017. https://foreignpolicy.com/2017/07/21/there-is-no-trump-doctrine-and-there-will-never-be-one-grand-strategy/

Lissner, Rebecca Friedman. 2018. "What Is Grand Strategy? Sweeping a Conceptual Minefield." *Texas National Security Review* 2 (1). https://tnsr.org/2018/11/what-is-grand-strategy-sweeping-a-conceptual-minefield/

March, James, and Herbert A. Simon. 1993. *Organizations*. Cambridge, M.A.: Blackwell.

Mearsheimer, John J. 2001. *The Tragedy of Great Power Politics*. New York: W. W. Norton.

Mercer, Jonathan. 1996. *Reputation and International Politics*. Ithaca, N.Y.: Cornell University Press.

Miller, Manjari Chatterjee. 2013. "India's Feeble Foreign Policy." *Foreign Affairs* 92 (3): 14–19.

Moyar, Mark. 2009. "Grand Strategy after the Vietnam War." *Orbis* 53 (4): 591–610.

Popescu, Ionut. 2017. *Emergent Strategy and Grand Strategy: How American Presidents Succeed in Foreign Policy*. Baltimore: Johns Hopkins University Press.

Popescu, Ionut C. 2018. "Grand Strategy vs. Emergent Strategy in the Conduct of Foreign Policy." *Journal of Strategic Studies* 41 (3): 438–460.

Porter, Patrick. 2018. "Why America's Grand Strategy Has Not Changed: Power, Habit, and the U.S. Foreign Policy Establishment." *International Security* 42 (4): 9–46.

Posen, Barry R. 2014. *Restraint: A New Foundation for U.S. Grand Strategy*. 1st edition. Ithaca, N.Y.; London: Cornell University Press.

Powell, Robert. 1999. *In the Shadow of Power: States and Strategies in International Politics*. Princeton, N.J.: Princeton University Press.

Press, Daryl G. 2005. *Calculating Credibility: How Leaders Evaluate Military Threats*. Ithaca, N.Y.: Cornell University Press.

Remnick, David. 2014. "Going the Distance." *The New Yorker*, January 27, 2014. http://www.newyorker.com/reporting/2014/01/27/140127fa_fact_remnick?currentPage=all

Rose, Gideon. 2021. "Foreign Policy for Pragmatists." *Foreign Affairs* 100 (2): 50–56.
Ross, Robert. 2012. "The Problem with the Pivot." *Foreign Affairs* 91 (6): 70–82.
Sanger, David E. 2009. "Hints of Obama's Strategy in a Telling 8 Days." *The New York Times*, April 8, 2009. http://www.nytimes.com/2009/04/08/us/politics/07web-sanger.html
Schelling, Thomas C. 1966. *Arms and Influence*. New Haven, C.T.: Yale University Press.
Schweller, Randall L. 1994. "Bandwagoning for Profit: Bringing the Revisionist State Back In." *International Security* 19 (1): 72–107.
Schweller, Randall L. 2001. "The Problem of International Order Revisited: A Review Essay." *International Security* 26 (1): 161–186.
Simon, Herbert Alexander. 1947. *Administrative Behavior: A Study of Decision-Making Processes in Administrative Organization*. New York: Macmillan.
Sinnreich, Richard Hart. 2011. "Patterns of Grand Strategy." In *The Shaping of Grand Strategy: Policy, Diplomacy, and War*, edited by Williamson Murray, Richard Hart Sinnreich, and James Lacey, 254–269. New York: Cambridge University Press.
Snyder, Glenn H. 1984. "The Security Dilemma in Alliance Politics." *World Politics* 36 (4): 461–495.
Suri, Jeremi. 2009. "American Grand Strategy from the Cold War's End to 9/11." *Orbis* 53 (4): 611–627.
Tomz, Michael. 2007. *Reputation and International Cooperation: Sovereign Debt across Three Centuries*. Princeton, N.J.: Princeton University Press.
US Department of Defense Air-Sea Battle Office. 2013. "Air-Sea Battle: Service Collaboration to Address Anti-Access and Area Denial Challenges." https://archive.defense.gov/pubs/ASB-ConceptImplementation-Summary-May-2013.pdf
Wolfers, Arnold. 1962. *Discord and Collaboration: Essays on International Politics*. Baltimore: The Johns Hopkins University Press.

CHAPTER 38

ALTERNATIVES TO GRAND STRATEGY

PETER DOMBROWSKI

THIS chapter challenges the so-called "grand strategy school" (GSS) that assumes that "the expectation is that strategic success follows from efficiently implementing an overarching grand strategic design" (Popescu 2018, 441). It describes the grand strategy school, extends it beyond its original formulation by Ionut Popescu, and critiques conventional scholarship on grand strategy by building upon my earlier work with Simon Reich and Thierry Balzacq (Balzacq, Dombrowski, and Reich 2019a). The main body of the chapter then offers three alternative perspectives to studying grand strategy that argue that: (1) grand strategy as a "normal" product of public policy processes, (2) grand strategy as an emergent strategy, and (3) grand strategy as singular approach an unattainable so nations actually pursue a series of calibrated strategies. The chapter concludes with ideas about how these three alternatives can help develop a more robust approach to studying grand strategy, regardless of whether one works within the confines of the grand strategy school or choses a more critical approach. Despite this author's professional commitment to comparative grand strategy and, more broadly, expanding the range of cases studies in terms of grand strategy, many of the examples in this chapter will focus on the American case, before, in the conclusion, returning to the ways in which grand strategy alternatives can influence cross-national and comparative research.

THE GRAND STRATEGY SCHOOL (GSS)

Scholars in the grand strategy school recommend a planning process that identifies and prioritizes threats in the international environment while prescribing the appropriate ways and means to achieve national interests, however defined, by the constitutional order, history, tradition, political culture, and outcomes of political processes.

Following Terry Deibel, Popescu summarizes this approach to strategy, grand of otherwise, as

(1) Assess the international and domestic environments,
(2) Analyze threats, opportunities, national interests, and the means of power and influence, and
(3) Plan on how to use the available instruments of power to achieve the objectives (Deibel 2004).

This is a linear, process-oriented position. It begins with identifying objectives but requires considering and evaluating the various options and instruments available for meeting those objectives. It relies on policymakers having knowledge about the both external world and the preferences of their own government; in extreme versions scholars and analysts require officials have near-perfect information. Moreover, officials must prioritize amongst competing objectives, international threats, and demands. It also assumes that officials can control bureaucracies (both in terms of gathering required inputs and in terms of ensuring that the chosen strategy is implemented) as well as provide sufficient resources to implement a grand strategy, even in the face of political disagreement and bureaucratic inefficiencies. Failures are then traced to the inability of politicians, senior civilian leaders, and/or military officials to perform all or part of the strategy-making and implementation process. Scholars in this tradition attribute strategic failures and/or successes on misidentifying national goals, not pursuing policies capable of achieving them, and/or to the inability to reconcile ends, ways, and means.

From the perspective of public policy analysis, the grand strategy school is an example of a rationale comprehensive method—decision-makers identify values or objectives, utilize a range of ways and means, within the limits of available resources. In the language of public administration and public policy scholarship, defense planning is "a service–delivery mechanism where political decision-makers act as system controllers that decide policy objectives 'upstream,' and staff/contractors implement/manage that policy 'downstream', or at least that is how it is designed to operate" (Christiansson 2018, 264). Rebecca Friedman Lissner labeled this approach as "grand strategy as blueprint" that is "a tool, rather than an automatic output, and therefore can be manipulated by agents who enact intentional designs" (Friedman Lissner 2018). Peter Layton takes this to *reductio ad absurdum* by writing a book on grand strategy that "develops an optimized strategy diagnostic process," a virtual "cook book" where he discusses the process of developing ends, ways, and means and then applying them to a diverse set of cases from a range of countries in both peacetime and war (Layton 2018, 5). A cookbook or "how to" often appeals to many practitioners, especially those who have been educated using the classic ends, ways, and means paradigm (Meiser 2016–17).[1]

Hew Strachan has stressed that the national security community, including scholars, has often "confused strategy in theory with strategy in practice" (2019, 176). The grand strategy school conflates both the institutional processes associated with strategy development and the academic scholarship theorizing about substantive strategies with strategy as practice by leaders at the highest levels of the military, political appointees to the bureaucracy, and nationally elected politicians. Moving beyond Popescu's position, underlying, and nearly overwhelming the rationalistic planning dimension of the grand strategy school is the over reliance on the classic scholarly paradigms for studying grand strategy—"strategy in theory" as opposed to strategy as practiced by government officials, military officials, and politicians.

Western scholars of grand strategy largely operate within the confines of Realist or Liberal thinking about international relations, especially with regard to the nature of nation-states and the international system. Indeed, a large body of scholarship is associated with devising typologies of grand strategies including neo-isolationism, selective engagement, cooperative security, and primacy.[2] Typologies, when used in this way, as a part of the strategy development process, rely on rational assumptions for a prescriptive purpose. Scholars currently preoccupied with strategic restraint often critique American presidential administrations for *not* pursuing restraint, as if the benefits of this grand strategy are given and the failure to pursue restraint, in one form or another, is a pathology, the function of domestic lobbying or bureaucratic paralysis.[3]

Ultimately, most, but not all, Western scholarship builds on one variant or another of Realism[4] because they prioritize security, military force, and preparations, *in extremis*, for war. Because the state is operating in an anarchic international system, because states seek power, and because the states' most important objective is survival, grand strategy must focus on how to defend the state's territorial integrity, sovereignty, and core national interests. Grand strategy in Barry Posen's formulation, for example, is "a political-military, means-ends chain, a state's theory about how it can best 'cause' security for itself" (Posen 1984, 13). The prescribed tools are preponderantly unilateral. A powerful minority view takes a Liberal view of the international system itself, and of state power, the instrument of statecraft, and the relative importance of military threats vis-à-vis other potential challenges such as the environment or other anthropogenic threats such as pandemics. Liberals rely far less on self-help and, conversely, far more on the institutional means and multilateralism to overcome the anarchic nature of the international system.[5]

The problems with the grand strategy school are manifold. To summarize, adherents to the grand strategy school, wittingly or not:

- Tend to equate grand strategy with rational planning processes;
- "[T]he strategizing ritual contributes to an overwhelming sense of insecurity;" (Krebs and Edelstein 2015, 110)
- Assume that grand strategies succeed or fail, based on the strengths and weaknesses of these rational planning and implementation processes;
- Generally, work with familiar international relations paradigms that are largely prescriptive;
- Often, believe that only great powers have grand strategies in large part because smaller states are unable to "cause security" for themselves in a world dominated by

larger, more militarily capable states *and* because they are unable to shape and influence the international order itself;
- Therefore, they spend a large portion of their scholarly energy trying to understand how great powers (and hegemons) try to shape the international system as a whole; and
- They downplay the significance of domestic politics or theorizing about the nexus between domestic politics, national security, military operations, and international affairs.

Furthermore, adherents also believe that regardless of the rational strategizing, the nature of the international environment, or how strategists interpret the environment, external factors should determine the grand strategy of the state in question. State survival is paramount: public officials, including politicians, policymakers, and public servants, use bureaucratic processes to adapt to threats and opportunities provided by the system. Realists devise strategies based on overwhelming military strength or perhaps an enduring balance of power, while Liberals seek to construct a system in which institutions and norms restrain states. In strong variants, such as held by Structural Realists, it is not even necessary to look inside the "black box" because the national state will naturally adjust (Waltz 1979, 80–100).

Given the unilateralist and personalistic tendencies of President Trump's strategic initiatives (within the wider sweep of the history of American strategies that critics such as Barry Posen characterize as "Liberal Hegemony"), scholars in the grand strategy school are left to argue about what should be done. They prescribe the ways to oppose President Trump on individual issues (e.g., withdrawing from the Iran nuclear deal or pursuing a trade war with China) or recovering from the damage he has supposedly caused American national security (writing articles how about how to recommit to NATO). They do not explain the political developments underlying the president's grand strategy[6] and/or explain his administration's divergence from their diagnoses and prescriptions (Walt 2019). To do so would require that their analyses would include a more fully formed sense of the role of domestic politics—in the United States, but also by logical extension other countries as well—not to mention political psychology and group dynamics to understand the actions of powerful leaders (Balzacq, Dombrowski, and Reich 2019b, esp. ch. 1).

THREE ALTERNATIVES TO THE GRAND STRATEGY SCHOOL

If we assume that there is such a thing as a grand strategy, but that the assumptions of the so-called grand strategy school are flawed because they fail to incorporate a

Table 38.1 Grand strategy school (GSS) versus alternatives

	GSS	Public policy	Emergent	Calibrated
Rational planning	Yes	Yes	No	Yes
Sources of failure	Strategic planning	Policy processes	Leadership	Planning and leadership
Prescriptive	Yes	Depends	No	No
International environment	Primary	Secondary	Secondary	Primary/Secondary
Domestic politics	Secondary	Primary	Primary	Primary/Secondary
Which countries?	Great powers	All states	Choice	Choice

recognition of the significance of either domestic politics or operational challenges, what are the alternatives? I highlight three major options: (1) an approach that—contra much of the work on grand strategy, foreign policy, and national security policy—treats grand strategy as a public policy output like any other produced by a political system, (2) an approach that focuses less on rationalistic planning and more on opportunistic adjustments to domestic and international conditions, and (3) a calibrated approach focusing on the role of political and military leaders, informed by bureaucrats and those working in the field, that responds to the operational challenges posed by specific threats in the international system. These are not the only alternatives; rather each represents very specific challenges to the dominant grand strategy school. Table 38.1 below summarizes the characteristics of each alternative and their relationship to GSS.

The first challenges the assumption that international affairs in general, and grand strategy more specifically, is an exception to normal politics. Instead, grand strategy, like other policy outputs, is a product of the complex processes, institutions, and democratic forces unique to each political system. The second undermines the assumption that the "ends, ways, and means" process of strategic planning is the best way to protect state interests and guard against foreign threats. It instead prescribes a more modest, adaptive and opportunistic approach, better suited to the ever-changing international environment facing the United States. Finally, the calibrated approaches focus less on comprehensive and unitary strategic planning or prescription, and more on contingent factors in explaining how specific political and military leaders interpret and respond to threats, conflicts, and the changing character of war.

The section below describes these three alternatives to the grand strategy school. Each section suggests how adopting each alternative would alter our understanding of grand strategy in general and examples of grand strategy in particular. The intent is to add greater depth to ongoing and future research into grand strategies both in the United States and, by implication, work on the grand strategies of other states, great and small.

Grand Strategy and Public Policy

A long and distinguished tradition of national security scholars has held that the United States (and many other great powers for that matter) is politically, institutionally, and culturally incapable of pursuing a grand strategy. As Samuel Huntington argued, "a national strategy is impossible because the interests, issues, institutions, and purposes involved are simply too diverse and complex to be brought together and integrated into any sort of coherent pattern" (quoted in Friedberg 1988, 65). Aaron Friedberg observes that "the power of the state is limited and the process of government is open to a wide range of influences." These remarks are, in effect, a restatement of a civics textbook version of pluralism. Many scholars of grand strategy differ, assuming that the political systems operates differently on the range of policies and programs associated with grand strategy. The questions are how and why?

The why depends on several interrelated and often unexamined assumptions. First, that the executive branch is the primary promulgator of grand strategy based on the responsibilities enumerated in the Constitution and upheld by a body of law developed over more than two centuries. Second, that the executive branch is, in the realm of foreign affairs, somewhat insulated from the other branches of government. Third, less an artifact of the constitution and centuries of tradition than the realities of America's role in the world since the 1940s, is the emergence of the "Imperial presidency" (Lindsay 2003, 530–546).[7] Specifically, the dawn of the nuclear age and the marriage of nuclear weapons to ballistic missiles has changed the logic of self-defense, greatly reducing the time available to the United State to act. The president, acting as commander in chief on the behalf of the American people, must have the freedom of action and institutional capacity to defend the United States against nuclear annihilation. Furthermore, the post–Second World War world the United States engineered included a whole set of global responsibilities, most prominently management of the West's security position vis-à-vis the Soviet Union and the Warsaw Pact. Fulfilling these grave responsibilities did not lend itself to the slow-moving, mutually reinforcing institutional design of the democratic republic. This view coincides with the belief of many foreign policy scholars that "Pluralism and interest groups are generally considered of lesser importance, the process is seen as event driven, and foreign policymaking is considered the primary domain of the president" (Wood and Peake 1998, 177).

One response to the complexities of the American political system is to argue that the United States does not pursue grand strategies so much as "muddle through" (Lindblom 1959). This entails abandoning the assumption of a reasonably frictionless process in favor of one whereby strategy lurches in the pursuit of the foreign policy interests of one domestic group or another, depending on the vagaries of elections and bureaucratic politics. Tami Biddle, following Arturo Escheverria, identifies the compelling intellectual and practical attraction of this approach: "that in the absence of 'genuine existential threats,' states may prefer to muddle through a war than to embrace a robust and coherent grand strategy that requires serious compromise over domestic preference and long-term interests" (Biddle 2015, 18; Echevarria 2014, 20–23).

In a contemporary sense, this observation provides a paradoxical explanation for why the grand strategy school has re-emerged to generate a large numbers of books and articles. An increasing number of policymakers and academics believe that potentially "genuine existential threats" do exist or will soon emerge. The rise of China as a direct challenger to US interests, including leadership of the international system, provides the main case in point, along with Russia's increased regional and global ambitions. According to the Trump administration, the potential for great power conflict has been codified in official policy documents including the *2017 National Security Strategy* and the *2018 National Defense Strategy*. The latter argues that "Long-term strategic competitions with China and Russia are the principal priorities for the Department, and require both increased and sustained investment, because of the magnitude of the threats they pose to U.S. security and prosperity today, and the potential for those threats to increase in the future" (Department of Defense 2018, 4). Under such circumstances, proponents of grand strategy argue, "muddling through" is not an option.

Yet, muddling through is more than simply a generic descriptor of grand strategy-making and implementation. The domestic public policy literature extends beyond Charles Lindblom's original formulation to a host of scholars seeking to understand policy outcomes in the domestic context. One assumption shared by IR scholars and students of domestic public policy is that "we summarize the most significant differences between the domestic and foreign policy spheres, recognizing that they are often of degree rather than kind and that different aspects of foreign policy demonstrate different values on the parameters" (Durant and Diehl 1989, 185). Yet, no less a neorealist than Stephen Krasner has acknowledged that the complexity of the Washington policy process requires the more sophisticated academic analysis of the "garbage can" and "policy stream" models (Krasner 2009, 255).

In the end, muddling through has proved to be sufficient, proponents suggest, because it has resulted in "incremental change" to arrive at "agreed-upon policies which are closely based on past experience" (Dror 1964, 153). If anything, it has allowed the United States to hold a consistent grand-strategic position across administrations and even generations of policymakers because in the Cold War, it was embedded in the national security institutions of the executive branch. Developed largely in response to the two great wars of the first half of the twentieth century, the United States possesses a formidable policymaking apparatus biased in favor of incremental change.[8]

With the election of Donald Trump, the challenge of muddling through has taken on a new urgency. Dan Drezner has argued that the Trump administration has "failed to engage in serious efforts to institutionalize its populist foreign policy ideas" while "the influence of existing foreign policy bureaucracies was weakened" (Drezner 2019a, 728). And it may be too late for the nation to recover because "the same steps that empowered the president to create foreign policy have permitted Trump to destroy what his predecessors spent decades making" (Drezner 2019b, 15). As it turns out, both the pluralistic government structures of the American democratic republic *and* the specific national security institutions developed from the time the United States emerged as a great power on the world stage in the late 1880s have proved more fragile than many suspected. An imperial president, using the special power accorded to him or her by the constitution and the evolution of American laws and institutions, could destroy the grand-strategic consensus from within and make a mockery of the role played by the permanent bureaucracy or the so-called "Deep State" in guiding American grand strategy (Cooper, Gvosdev, and Blankshain 2018).

Ultimately, scholars of grand strategy will need to heed Rosecrance and Stein's admonition by focusing on "domestic groups, social ideas, the character of constitutions, economic constraints (sometimes expressed through international interdependence), historical social tendencies, and domestic political pressures play an important, indeed, a pivotal, role in the selection of a grand strategy and, therefore, in the prospects for international conflict and cooperation" (Rosecrance and Stein 1993, 5). As Jack Snyder has reminded us, "among great powers, domestic pressures often outweigh international ones in the calculations of national leaders" (1991, 20). As an alternative to the grand strategy school, scholars should not bracket out foreign and security strategies from the study of American domestic politics and the workings of the American public policy process. Kingdon's classic research (1984), for example, centering on "problems, policies and politics," might provide an interesting starting point.[9]

While this section has, of necessity for this author, focused on the domestic politics of US grand strategy and the theoretical frames for studying American strategy as a subset of wider domestic policy processes, the point is generalizable. To understand the grand strategies of other states, great and small, may well require continuing to move beyond theories focused on the outside-in or the second-image-reversed approaches (Gourevitch 1978; Kaarbo 2015).

Emergent Strategies

Peter Layton suggests that it is possible to envision a "non-grand strategy strategy" when "grand strategy may be an inappropriate policy tool." He argues that "for these circumstances there are valid alternatives such as opportunism or risk management" (Layton 2012, 56–61). From this perspective, a state approaches grand strategy like a firm approaches opportunities and challenges in the business environment. For firms, the lodestone is profitability, and the indicators include market share, market penetration, and expansion. Historically, international relations theorists and scholars of national security have rarely employed applicable concepts developed in the literature of business management. But by the 1980s "[i]n the business world, as in the military, the loss of confidence in centralized control, quantification, and rational analysis left an opening for alternative approaches to strategy" (Freedman 2013, 504). Henry Mintzberg and James A. Waters, in drawing a potentially useful allusion, thus defined emergent strategies as "patterns or consistencies realized despite, or in the absence of, intention" (1985, 257).

As applied by Ionut Popescu to grand strategy, emergent strategizing is flexible about both the ends and the tactics of strategy—"one's later goals could change during the strategy-making process based on the lessons learned while pursuing the initial goals" (2018, 446–447). By implication, the president or chief executive should focus on learning and adapting. The process of developing a grand strategy should not rely on a static view of ends, ways, and means. Rather, senior leaders should allow their understanding of all three to evolve, given unfolding international events in the context of long-term change.

For some scholars of grand strategy, the very idea that grand strategy can be "emergent" is unsettling. Emergent strategy does not consist of a comprehensive planning process articulating ends, ways, and means and then implementing the plans using bureaucratic institutions led by like-minded individuals (Popescu 2018, 446). Of course, given the president's dominance of the executive branch, especially the national security apparatus (as discussed above), they can strategize in their own way according to their own conception of how they want to govern. Some presidents, notably Trump, have expressed frustration not only with planning and analysis but also with the entire process of governing, much less strategizing. Others appear to have stumbled upon a version of emergent strategies.

James Graham Wilson, for example, challenges journalistic and scholarly accounts that praised President Ronald Reagan's coherent grand strategy by (implicitly suggesting it was far more emergent and ambiguous in character). He argues that "Reagan's private and public rhetoric clashed," because "he remained uncertain about whether to pursue the abolition of nuclear arms or the eradication of communism" (2007, 786). Wilson labels these objectives as "peace through strength" and "a crusade for freedom" containing their "own respective set of goals and employed its own corresponding set of tactics." Reagan thus had mixed motives and adapted to the circumstances presented to him by the Soviet Union, its leaders, the international security environment, and domestic politics. Wilson's interpretation flies in the face of those offered by notable scholars such as John Lewis Gaddis, as well as a host of biographers, historians, and contemporary accounts of service in Reagan's two terms; they tend to present Reagan, despite his foibles, as a master strategist relentlessly pursing the fulfillment of Kennan's vision of containment ending in collapse from internal contradictions with the Soviet political and economic systems.

As Alexander Kirss notes, Popescu's emergent approach allows for leaders to be flexible rather than chained to a plan or even a planning process: "Policy makers are therefore free to learn from past experiences and adapt their thinking as they receive new information when embracing an emergent strategy" (2018, 121). Conceptually, however, this formulation leads to a major problem: when business leaders, for example, rely on an emergent strategy, their learning and adaptation are in service of relatively straightforward profitability goals involving transparent indicators such as market share, penetration, and perhaps firm-level growth. What is the metric for presidents or senior national security officials? Is there a consensus about the relevant metric? There may be a vague consensus about baseline security goals: protect territorial integrity, the defense of citizens at home, and national interests abroad. Yet, there is often disputes about what that means in practice, and about the ways and means of achieving grand-strategic objectives.

Pursing an emergent approach to strategy is likely to require different types of national security institutions and processes than currently exist in most countries. Systems based on rationalist planning and implementation, which imply iterative and repeatable processes staffed by subject matter experts, might give way to more streamlined, flexible groups ready to shift according the changing circumstances. More research should be done on this possibility, but it can be hypothesized that authoritarian regimes may have advantages in pursuing emergent strategies over large democracies encumbered by bureaucracies built for accountability.

Calibrated Grand Strategy

In *the End of Grand Strategy*, Simon Reich and I argue that, rhetoric aside, the United States has not pursued a universal grand strategy since the end of the Cold War (we remain agnostic on the question of whether it did beforehand). We claim that the very "notion of a grand strategy entails the vain search for order and consistency in an ever-more complex world" (Reich and Dombrowski 2018, 1). Therefore, "the very idea of a single, one size-fits-all grand strategy has little utility in the twenty-first century. Indeed, it is often counterproductive" (Reich and Dombrowski 2018, 2). Rather, there are at least six variants of grand strategy, stretching from primacy and liberal leadership to two types of sponsorship (formal and informal), restraint and isolationism in terms of their forms and degree of global engagement. The United States generally pursues all six strategies simultaneously.

In explaining this observation, we concur with Richard Rosecrance and Arthur Stein's assessment that domestic factors affect the development and implementation of grand strategy and observe that much of the recent grand strategy scholarship has largely failed to extend Rosecrance and Stein's research agenda. We thus step away from purely "systemic" explanations of grand strategy in favor of what Fearon has called "domestic-political theories" in the context of trying to understand American foreign policy. American grand strategy is therefore not simply a function of its international environment and/or the ideational interpretation of that environment by statesmen, senior policymakers, and military leaders. It is constrained, shaped, and implemented by domestic structures and bureaucratic-organizational dynamics. Grand strategies are subject to the same domestic influences as all foreign and security policies.

Yet we acknowledge that these factors coalesce with external ones. As Robert Putnam commented, in setting a high standard for explanations incorporating domestic and international variable: "[i]t is fruitless to debate whether domestic politics really determine international relations, or the reverse. The answer to that question is clearly 'Both, sometimes.' The more interesting questions are 'When?' and 'How?'" We try to address Putnam's questions. Contingency in our formulation replaces a more traditional universalistic approach to the study of grand strategy; in this it bears some commonality with the idea of emergence. Thus, we argue, inverting a traditional "top-down" formulations with a "bottom-up," empirically based one, the selection of the strategy usually begins with the reports and observations of those operating in the field. We emphasize the interaction of external and domestic factors. Military officials in theater offer strategic advice based on the nature of the threat, the nature of the conflict, and the nature of the actor/adversary. Their advice is then processed through the bureaucratic national security apparatus in the process of decision-making mediated by political considerations. How the United States actually meets these divergent threats is dependent on bureaucratic and preponderantly operational constraints, especially when the means of pursuing security policies is primarily use of the military. The consequence is a far more varied implementation of strategy than debated among scholars and those working in think tanks or the media.

In practice, national decision-makers—the military leadership and senior administration executives—then calibrate strategies—by region or issue. In some circumstances, the United States therefore pursues primacy—utilizing military forces autonomously and reserving the right to pursue American interests unilaterally. An example is the US long-term commitment to protect the flow of energy through the Persian Gulf and the Strait of Hormuz. In other cases, it pursues liberal, multilateral policies, such as the organization of large-scale military exercises, such as in the Pacific or the High North on the Russian periphery. It sponsors the initiatives of others in addressing important collective action problems where even American resources are insufficient, such as the Proliferation Security Initiative aimed at reducing the flow of illicit fissile materials or the global anti-piracy initiative. And the United States exercises restraint in its emergent Arctic strategy, while it practices a strategy of isolationism on its borders against migrants and drug smugglers as it seeks to close itself off from the world along the entire southern border of the United States.

This argument extends itself to accommodating both elements of continuity and change. The Trump administration is often associated with impetuous and even chaotic decision-making. Yet, as our operationally focused argument suggests, there were both elements of continuity in all six formulations of grand strategy in the first two years of the administration: primacist bombing in Syria, increased patrols in the Strait of Hormuz and the South China Sea, and the introduction of a welter of sanctions stretching from Venezuela to Russia and Iran; liberal multilateral exercises and increased NATO deployments in Europe along with the sustained commitment of forces in Afghanistan; a continued commitment to the Proliferation Security Initiative; and, of course, enhanced isolationism on the southern border.[10] This approach, however, also accommodates the possibility of change, contingent on the operational challenges in strategic theaters and the composition of the bureaucracy.

Our alternative is an example of what others have called a "hybrid or interface dynamics" approach to defense planning (Breitenbauch and Jakobsson 2018, 393). In effect, we respond to calls to understand

> the link between defence planning and the security environment, to the interface between administrative and budgeting systems on the one hand and policy and strategy

process on the other, and hence also to the distinction between ostensibly neutral planning processes and analyses and political level policy and strategy making, and therefore also to the difference between public administration and politics. (Ibid.)

Ours is this effort to incorporate, systematically, both domestic and international variables that distinguishes our research from those scholars who look first, and most closely, at domestic politics, institutions, and processes or focus on the external environment.

Conclusion

In most countries, the grand strategy school is the dominant approach amongst both practitioners and theorists. It will likely remain so for the foreseeable future. That work has spawned many great books and articles, helped launch numerous careers, and, of course, furthered our understanding of how great powers pursue their interests in an uncertain world. Furthermore, normalizing for different ideological traditions and institutional arrangements, many of the underlying assumptions of that work has been integrated into the thinking of leaders and policymakers in Great Britain, France, Russia, Japan, and China. It is even, or perhaps especially, true when assessing diverse Americans such as unilateralists like (former National Security Advisor) John Bolton or multilateralists such as (former Secretary of State) Hilary Clinton. Yet more can and should be done.

First and foremost, these three alternatives should be explored relative to the conventional approach. Each can and should be compared and contrasted in terms of their explanatory power against classic cases. There have been plenty of studies that examined the failures of rational approaches to formulating grand strategy; there have perhaps been even more comparing the strengths and weaknesses of grand strategy variants based on international relations paradigms. Challenging the assumptions underlying that research will serve to strengthen the scholarly discourse, extend disciplinary boundaries, and enhance its policy application.

Second, even if each alternative is found wanting, more traditional grand strategy research can be deepened by adopting some of the insights from the three. It is, for example, worth re-examining the verities that the America state has been a source of continuity in grand strategy. The election of Donald Trump raises the prospect that the state qua state is not what Patrick Porter labeled "the Blob" and is in fact unable to resist change from above (Porter 2018). The relevant questions concern if, how, and to what extent a determined leader with a political mandate can weaken the institutional underpinnings of American security and foreign policies, wrest influence away from the bureaucracy, and consequentially begin to overturn long-standing policies? Or, at the very least, whether he or she can force change by installing like-minded department and agency heads, ruthlessly routing out those within the bureaucracy that oppose change, and using the budgetary process to alter political and institutional objectives. What is to say that future American presidents will not learn this lesson? Furthermore, an application of all four formulations to other states may reveal alternative grand-strategic development processes or even other variants of grand strategy not identified by scholars working on the United States.

The emergent approach could also benefit from more attention above and beyond Popescu's initial research. There is a long-standing mantra in some circles that questions why government, and especially the military, doesn't operate more like a business.[11] Past and future leaders may have adopted aspects of emergence (as practiced in the private sector), but scholars, untrained to look for such behaviors, have missed them. The strong preference for and advocacy of rationalistic planning processes, coupled with the dominance of international relations theory (largely privileging external over internal sources of grand strategy), may have blinded scholars to contrarian evidence. But the question will remain unanswered unless future scholarship explores the possibility. It is my strong intuition that some presidents, senior military leaders, and decision-makers act in ways consistent with the emergent approach, even if they are willing participants in the strategy development and planning processes prescribed by the grand strategy school. Close readings of the historical record, if informed by the insights of emergent strategy, might reveal the gap between the precepts of the grand strategy and more flexible approaches. The conceptual challenged posed by the emergent approach can only be strengthened and extended by more empirical work.

More broadly, while this chapter has used examples from the American case to explore alternatives to the current conception of grand strategy, much more can be accomplished through comparative research. As argued elsewhere, with my colleagues Thierry Balzacq and Simon Reich, a broader conception of grand strategy allows for scholars to include many states as historical or contemporary cases that have remain unexplored. The American political system generates grand strategies in ways that differ from other states based on their own national objectives, capabilities, political dynamics, institutional settings, and strategic cultures. If we concede that our understanding of American grand strategy can be expanded by looking at internal politics and processes, we can do the same for other countries beyond a few great powers. This would allow more systematic comparisons, based not simply on an understanding of global or regional security circumstances but on how national leaders and bureaucracies interpret and act on the external environment. We may even find that the intermestic approach of Reich and Dombrowski, seeking to theorize how states pursue multiple strategies based on a dual reading of the international environment and state capabilities (military and otherwise) has value for studying other states as well.

Finally, in policy terms, more comparative work, whether building on the grand strategy school or one of the variants explored in this chapter, will surely help policymakers and military leaders develop a greater understanding of other international actors with whom the US strategically interacts. In a world of large-scale change, cartoonish images of adversary grand strategies are insufficient. More sophisticated scholarship and policy analysis, not just of how America works but how other countries do as well, is essential.[12]

NOTES

1. For the original formulation see Lykke Jr (1989).
2. The most familiar but not the first or the last typology can be found in Posen and Ross (1996/97, 5–53). Recent efforts seek to expand and deepen earlier grand strategy typologies by developing a more comprehensive "typology of five general approaches to grand strategy, typologies being the basis for establishing causative theories that can be systematically evaluated in the context of a research program." See Dombrowski and Reich (2021).
3. Posen, the leading advocate of the grand strategy of Restraint, published the most fully realized view (2015).
4. For a clear statement on grand strategy and Realism see, Rosecrance and Stein (1993, 5–11).
5. Amongst the large literature, much of it by J. John Ikenberry, see his clear statement (2009, 203–219).
6. There are exceptions. See Mead (2017, 2–7).
7. The term was first popularized by Arthur M. Schlesinger Jr (1973).
8. For a brief overview see Dombrowski and Reich (2019, esp. 31–35). For an argument describing the effects of bureaucratic continuity see Porter (2018, 9–46).
9. When all three streams come together: "when problems are coupled with policy solutions at a time when it is politically feasible to implement change. This coupling of streams can result in a policy window, generally brought on by changes in the problem or political streams. Windows can appear predictably (as a result of elections, for instance) or unpredictably (brought on, for example, by a crisis)" (Soroka 2009, 768). See also Durant and Diehl (1989).
10. For details see Dombrowski and Reich (2018, 2017).
11. See, for example, Matthews (2019).
12. I am grateful, as usual, to my long-time co-author Simon Reich for his superb editorial feedback. Frank Hoffman also offered excellent suggestions that, alas, will require a follow-on piece to address. Neither are responsible for any errors of fact, interpretation, or omission in this essay.

REFERENCES

Balzacq, Thierry, Peter Dombrowski, and Simon Reich. 2019a. "IIs Grand Strategy a Research Program? A Review Essay." *Security Studies* 28 (1): 58–86.

Balzacq, Thierry, Peter Dombrowski, and Simon Reich. 2019b. *Comparative Grand Strategy: A Framework and Cases*. New York: Oxford University Press.

Biddle, Tami Davis. 2015. *Strategy and Grand Strategy: What Students and Practitioners Need to Know*. Carlisle, PA: US Army War College Press.

Breitenbauch, Henrik, and André Ken Jakobsson. 2018. "Coda: Exploring Defence Planning in Future Research." *Defence Studies* 18 (3): 391–394.

Christiansson, Magnus. 2018. "Defense Planning beyond Rationalism: The Third Offset Strategy as a Case of Metagovernance." *Defence Studies* 18 (3): 264.

Cooper, David A., Nikolas K. Gvosdev, and Jessica D. Blankshain. 2018. "Deconstructing the 'Deep State': Subordinate Bureaucratic Politics in U.S. National Security." *Orbis* 62 (4): 518–540.

Deibel, Terry. 2004. *Foreign Affairs Strategy: Logic for American Statecraft*. New York: Cambridge University Press, 24–32.

Department of Defense. 2018. *Summary of the 2018 National Defense Strategy of the United States: Sharpening the American Military's Competitive Edge*. Washington, DC: Department of Defense.

Dombrowski, Peter, and Simon Reich. 2017. "Does Donald Trump have a Grand Strategy?" *International Affairs* 93 (5) (September): 1013–1037.

Dombrowski, Peter, and Simon Reich. 2018. "Beyond the Tweets: Continuity and Change in President Trump's Approach to Military Operations." *Strategic Studies Quarterly* 12 (2) (June): 56–81. https://www.airuniversity.af.edu/Portals/10/SSQ/documents/Volume-12_Issue-2/Dombrowski_Reich.pdf

Dombrowski, Peter, and Simon Reich. 2021. *Across Type, Time and Space: American Grand Strategy in Comparative Perspective*. London: Cambridge University Press.

Dombrowski, Peter, and Simon Reich. Forthcoming. "The Five Faces of Grand Strategy: Developing A Comparative Framework in Search of a Research Program" (under review).

Drezner, Daniel W. 2019a. "Present at the Destruction: The Trump Administration and the Foreign Policy Bureaucracy." *Journal of Politics* 81 (2): 723–730.

Drezner, Daniel W. 2019b. "This Time is Different: Why U.S. Foreign Policy Will Never Recover." *Foreign Affairs* (May/June): 10–17.

Dror, Yehezkel. 1964. "Muddling Through—'Science' or Inertia?" *Public Administration Review* 24 (3) (September): 153–157.

Durant, Robert F., and Paul F. Diehl. 1989. "Agendas, Alternatives, and Public Policy: Lessons from the U.S. Foreign Policy Arena." *Journal of Public Policy* 9 (2) (April–June): 179–205.

Echevarria, Artulio. 2014. "After Afghanistan: Lessons for NATO's Future Wars." *RUSI Journal* 159 (3) (July): 20–23.

Freedman, Lawrence. 2013. *Strategy: A History*. New York, New York: Oxford University Press.

Friedberg, Aaron L. 1988. "The Making of American National Strategy, 1948–1988." *The National Interest* 11 (Spring): 65–75.

Friedman Lissner, Rebecca. 2018. "What Is Grand Strategy? Sweeping a Conceptual Minefield." *Texas National Security Review* 2 (1) (November). https://tnsr.org/2018/11/what-is-grand-strategy-sweeping-a-conceptual-minefield/#_ftn68

Gourevitch, Peter. 1978. "The Second Image Reversed: The International Sources of Domestic Politics." *International Organization* 32 (4) (Autumn): 881–912.

Ikenberry, J. John. 2009. "Liberalism in a Realist World: International Relations as an American Scholarly Tradition." *International Studies* 46 (1&2): 203–219.

Kaarbo, Juliet. 2015. "A Foreign Policy Analysis Perspective on the Domestic Politics Turn in IR Theory." *International Studies Review* 17 (2): 189–216.

Kingdon, John W. 1984. *Agendas, Alternatives, and Public Policies*. Boston: MA Little, Brown and Company.

Kirss, Alexander. 2018. "Does Grand Strategy Matter?" *Strategic Studies Quarterly* 12 (4) (Winter): 116–132.
Krasner, Stephen D. 2009. *Power, the State, and Sovereignty*. New York, NY: Routledge.
Krebs, Ronald R., and David M. Edelstein. 2015. "Delusions of Grand Strategy: The Problem with Washington's Planning Obsession." *Foreign Affairs* 94 (6) (November): 109–111.
Layton, Peter. 2012. "The Idea of Grand Strategy." *RUSI Journal* 157 (4): 56–61.
Layton, Peter. 2018. *Grand Strategy*. Grand Strategy.
Lindblom, Charles Edward. 1959. "The Science of Muddling Through." *Public Administration Review* (Spring): 74–88.
Lindsay, James M. 2003. "Deference and Defiance: The Shifting Rhythms of Executive-Legislative Relations in Foreign Policy." *Presidential Studies Quarterly* 33 (3) (September): 530–546.
Lykke Jr., Arthur F. 1989. "Defining Military Strategy." *Military Review* 69 (5) (May): 2–8.
Matthews, Jessica T. 2019. "America's Indefensible Defense Budget." *The New York Review of Books*, July 18, 2019. https://www.nybooks.com/articles/2019/07/18/americas-indefensible-defense-budget/
Mead, Walter Russell. 2017. "The Jacksonian Revolt: American Populism and the Liberal Order." *Foreign Affairs* 96 (2) (March/April): 2–7.
Meiser, Jeffrey W. 2016-17. "Are Our Strategic Models Flawed? Ends + Ways + Means = (Bad) Strategy." *Parameters* 46 (4) (Winter): 81–91
Mintzberg, Henry, and James A. Waters. 1985. "Of Strategies, Deliberate and Emergent." *Strategic Management Journal* 6 (3) (July–September): 257–272.
Popescu, Ionut C. 2018. "Grand Strategy vs. Emergent Strategy in the Conduct of Foreign Policy." *Journal of Strategic Studies* 41 (3): 438–460.
Porter, Patrick. 2018. "Why America's Grand Strategy Has Not Changed: Power, Habit, and the U.S. Foreign Policy Establishment." *International Security* 42 (4) (Spring): 9–46.
Posen, Barry R. 1984. *The Sources of Military Doctrine: France, Britain, and Germany between the World Wars*. Ithaca, NY: Cornell University Press.
Posen, Barry R. 2015. *Restraint: A New Foundation for U.S. Grand Strategy*. Ithaca, NY: Cornell University Press.
Posen, Barry R., and Andrew L. Ross. 1996/97. "Competing Visions for U.S. Grand Strategy." *International Security* 21 (3) (Winter): 5–53.
Reich, Simon, and Peter Dombrowski. 2018. *The End of Grand Strategy: U.S. Maritime Operations in the Twenty-first Century*. Ithaca, NY: Cornell University Press.
Rosecrance, Richard, and Arthur A. Stein. 1993. "Beyond Realism: The Study of Grand Strategy." In *The Domestic Bases of Grand Strategy*, edited by Richard Rosecrance and Arthur A. Stein, 3–21. Ithaca, NY: Cornell University Press.
Schlesinger Jr., Arthur M. 1973. *The Imperial Presidency*. New York: Houghton, Mifflin, Harcourt.
Snyder, Jack. 1991. *Myths of Empire: Domestic Politics and International Ambition*. Ithaca, NY: Cornell University Press.
Soroka, Stuart. 2009. "Policy Agenda-Setting Theory Revisited: A Critique of Howlett on Downs, Baumgartner and Jones, and Kingdon." *Canadian Journal of Political Science/Revue canadienne de science politique* 32 (4) (December): 763–772.
Strachan, Hew. 2019. "Strategy in Theory; Strategy in Practice." *Journal of Strategic Studies* 42 (2): 171–190.

Walt, Stephen M. 2019. "The Tragedy of Trump's Foreign Policy." *Foreign Policy* (March 5). https://foreignpolicy.com/2019/03/05/the-tragedy-of-trumps-foreign-policy/

Waltz, Kenneth N. 1979. *Theory of International Politics*. New York: Random House.

Wilson, James Graham. 2007. "How Grand was Reagan's Strategy, 1976–1984?" *Diplomacy & Statecraft* 18 (4): 773–803.

Wood, B. Dan, and Jeffrey S. Peake. 1998. "The Dynamics of Foreign Policy Agenda Setting." *The American Political Science Review* 92 (1) (March): 173–184.

CHAPTER 39

GRAND-STRATEGIC THINKING IN HISTORY

JOHN BEW, MAEVE RYAN,
AND ANDREW EHRHARDT

THIS chapter highlights certain elements of what might be called "grand-strategic thinking" in nineteenth- and twentieth-century British foreign policy. It sets up *grand-strategic thinking* as something distinct from a clearly delineated and institutionally embedded process of grand strategizing—that is, the writing of elaborate strategic blueprints to outline the future course of a state's national security policy. Instead, this chapter suggests that in its early incarnations, grand strategy is better thought of not as a process (leading to the production of plans) but as a *habit of mind*: a conscious attempt to look beyond the confines of short-term requirements of national defense or immediate foreign policy dilemmas. In the British case, this was an approach that was antitheoretical and antidoctrinal but something more than simple pragmatism. To think grand strategically was to conceive of national interests in a more systematic and synchronized way than the day-to-day business of foreign affairs. This was not to set down certain rules of conduct that should be applied in every eventuality, but to reflect, in broader terms, about the international context in which the nation operated and the type of environment that was best suited to its pursuit of prosperity and security. It also incorporated what might be called a "historical sensibility"—that is, an understanding of the nature and pace of change in the international environment—and sought to craft a foreign policy around that. In essence, grand-strategic thinking can be understood as an intuitive appreciation of the big picture and the long term.

It is the purpose of this chapter, therefore, to establish the existence of certain grand-strategic assumptions that emerged in British foreign policy in the nineteenth century and how these ideas influenced British statecraft into the twentieth century. The chapter makes the case that a clearly identifiable British grand-strategic rationale—an understanding of the country's "place in the world"—emerged out of the Napoleonic Wars and developed across the middle decades of the nineteenth century. In the twentieth century, this grand-strategic thinking was key to the "soft landing" Britain managed to engineer in the aftermath of the Second World War as its position began to contract rapidly and radically from a world power into a continental power. The examples discussed here are Lord Castlereagh, George Canning, and Viscount Palmerston in the nineteenth century; and several Foreign Office officials in the twentieth, but most notably Gladwyn Jebb. Castlereagh, Canning, and Palmerston held office at significant and deeply consequential moments during the period from 1800 to 1865, from the Napoleonic Wars to the high-water mark of British imperial hegemony. This half-century was the crucible for developing important practices and principles of effective statecraft; a period in which each one of these leaders—Castlereagh, Canning, Palmerston—pursued the same essential goal: to sustain and expand the power base required to achieve British global commercial dominance, a key component of which was the maintenance of a favorable balance of power in Europe. Jebb and his colleagues, on the other hand, were not principal statesmen but the diplomats most responsible for developing Britain's approach to a postwar international order during the Second World War. Here the national interest remained the driving force, but this conception was dependent on the construction of a wider rules-based international order, seen most visibly in the creation of the United Nations Organization in June 1945.

This is not a story of perfect harmony or of the conscious and consistent alignment of views and approaches. After the end of the Napoleonic Wars, Britain was faced with periodic foreign policy crises and often bitter debates about its geopolitical priorities and spending commitments, and its choice of allies and enemies. What is more, the individuals discussed here differed in temperament, approach, style and disagreed on many specific issues. In some respects, in fact, Castlereagh, Canning, and Palmerston even bequeathed rival approaches to British foreign policy (Hurd). But it can nonetheless be shown that they developed a habit of grand-strategic thinking, and established some guiding assumptions, principles and practices that gave an overall sense of continuity and direction to British foreign policy. Specifically, they sought to conceive of British national interests as something shaped by the international environment; and, in turn, sought to shape that environment in a way that was conducive to British national interests. In the process, they articulated certain expectations about the historical and developmental continuum on which the other nations of the world were moving, and set a tone for their successors in the twentieth century, who set about trying to craft an advantageous new order with explicit reference to the prosperity their predecessors had carved from the ashes of the first "total war."

CASTLEREAGH

History has generally remembered Viscount Castlereagh as a quiet and calm pragmatist. His triumph was seen in his cool-headedness and temperament; his "victories" were a "series of microscopic advantages; of a judicious suggestion here, or an opportune civility there; of a wise concession at one moment, and a far-sighted persistence at another; of sleepless tact, immovable calmness, and patience," the apogee of which was the Congress of Vienna (Salisbury 1905, 12). Yet to focus on style is to neglect the substance of Castlereagh's statecraft, most notably the big-picture and long-term perspective he brought to the pursuit of British national interests. The first and most important principle of Castlereagh's statecraft was an understanding of power, rather than law, as the defining feature of the international arena. This is something that developed in Castlereagh long before his tenure as Foreign Secretary, in conversation with the Irish patriot movement with which his family was closely associated. As a young man, in his early twenties, Castlereagh had made two visits to Revolutionary France. He was initially sympathetic to the revolutionary cause, but by 1791, he saw cause for concern in the breakdown of the established order. Partially influenced by Edmund Burke's *Reflections on the Revolution in France*, he grew skeptical about the influence of natural law, and saw other forces at work in French politics that went against the prevailing winds of the Enlightenment. He was particularly doubtful about the idea that the triumph of reason was also likely to change the pattern of international relations. Small nations that aspired to act independently—relying on commerce and good will—were, he felt, likely to discover that the international arena was an unforgiving, Hobbesian sort of place where power prevailed over "abstract" rights (Castlereagh to Haliday).

While Castlereagh was influenced by Burke's writings, he was uncomfortable with the idea of Britain engaging in ideologically conditioned wars and publicly distanced himself from Burke's insistence that Jacobinism must be destroyed as an ideology. Castlereagh recognized that British national interests were best served by a period of sustained peace, as it had a head start in international commercial competition; thus, insofar as he wanted to see the monarchy restored in France it was simply because he believed this was the best means to preserve peace and stability and get back to the profitable business of peacetime trade (*The Parliamentary History of England*, December 9, 1801). As early as 1801, he was prepared to return to France the colonies which Britain had seized from her since hostilities began. Such was the strength of Bonaparte on the Continent, all Castlereagh wished for was that British manufacturers and commercial interests should not be interfered with. "Let a fair competition once be established, and I have no fear about the result" (*The Parliamentary History of England*, May 2, 1802). The same logic still applied in 1815. "It is not our business to collect trophies, but to try ... [to] bring back the world to peaceful habits," he remarked after Napoleon's final defeat at Waterloo (Phillips 1919, 1–21). This self-serving image of Britain as the impartial arbiter (an affectation which infuriated its rivals) nonetheless did convey certain realities about the position adopted by the British state throughout the two final coalitions against Napoleonic France. It was borne out by the fact that, outside the Mediterranean, Britain did not have any major territorial demands in Europe after 1815, so long as a balance of power could be maintained in which no single hegemon would emerge—particularly Russia (Davies 2012, 244–246). Self-identification as a commercial nation also led Castlereagh to be the first Foreign

Secretary to see the potential convergence of interest with the United States. As he told the House of Commons in 1816,

> there were no two countries whose interests were more naturally and closely connected: and he hoped that the course which the government of each country was pursuing, was such as would consolidate the subsisting peace, and promote harmony between the nations, so as to prevent on either side the recurrence of any acts of animosity. (Parliamentary Debates, February 14, 1816)

A further principle of Castlereagh's grand-strategic mindset was an appreciation of public opinion as the inescapable anchor of British statecraft. Again, this goes somewhat against the grain of the perception of Castlereagh put forward by both his legion of critics and by his admirers. For better or worse, the assumption is that Castlereagh sought to insulate British foreign policy from the vicissitudes of public opinion. It is certainly true that public pressure frustrated him, and he felt it weakened his hand in negotiations with other states—from European congresses to his dealings with America. But here Castlereagh displayed an appreciation of long-term policy versus short-term diplomacy that was grand strategic to its core. This came about because of his desire to keep Britain closely involved in European congress diplomacy, in the face of growing public opposition. His exasperation with other European states for failing to understand the constraints that public opinion placed upon foreign policy led to him distancing himself from those allies in 1820. There was an element of diplomacy that could be done in private, but this was not on solid or sustainable terrain. As he told the Austrians in 1820, Britain's allies could not force it to adopt a position with only the "smallest hope of rallying the national sentiment" behind it (Castlereagh to Lord Stewart). In essence, he was convinced that a strong degree of public *consent* was a prerequisite for the pursuit of a successful foreign policy that was built to last. On these grounds, he even criticized his mentor William Pitt for failing to appreciate this at the start of the war with France. It was "thereby weakened for the first ten years of the War by a divided schism of publick opinion, whether the War was of necessity or brought on by bad management." In later years, he explained, "profiting by experience, we never exposed ourselves to a question of this nature, and we were supported in the War under all its accumulated burthens by the whole energy and voice of the Nation" (Castlereagh to Lord Stewart).

The same point is central to the argument of the famous State Paper he produced in 1820, clearly evident alongside his suspicion of wars of ideology. As he put it, "if embarked in a War, which the Voice of the Country does not support, the Efforts of the strongest Administration which ever served the Crown would be unequal to the prosecution of the Conquest." Following revolutions in Spain and Portugal, it precluded the possibility of Britain taking part in a great power mission to re-establish the "legitimate" government in each. Despite its central involvement in the Treaty of Vienna, Britain had never acceded to an arrangement "intended as an Union for the Government of the World, or for the superintendence of the internal affairs of other States" (Castlereagh,

State Paper of 1820). As he further elaborated in private, a sense of "the national sentiment" must guide all long-term policy:

> This is our compass, and by this we must steer; and our Allies on the Continent may be assured that they will deceive themselves if they suppose that we could for six months act with them unless the mind of the nation was in the cause. They must not therefore press us to place ourselves upon any ground that John Bull will not maintain. (Castlereagh to Lord Stewart)

Here can see Castlereagh reiterating his earlier opposition to wars of ideology. Treaty obligations were one thing. Britain's preference for nonintervention was "not absolute" and she would obey her responsibilities "when actual danger menaces the System of Europe." But he was also emphatically clear that Britain could not "act upon the abstract and speculative principles of Precaution" (Castlereagh, State Paper of 1820).

These different strands come together in a final, underappreciated, aspect of Castlereagh's grand-strategic sensibility—an appreciation of historical change. A related aspect of this was his proto-Kissingerian conviction that the long-term stability of the domestic and international political orders depended upon their legitimacy. In the first instance, this manifested itself in a classically conservative caution about revolutionary change and political experimentation. Commenting upon the prospects for liberalism and constitutionalism in postwar Europe, he observed:

> It is impossible not to perceive a great moral change coming in Europe, and that the principles of freedom are in full operation. The danger is, that the transition may be too sudden to ripen into anything likely to make the world better or happier. We have new constitutions launched in France, Spain, Holland and Sicily. Let us see the result before we encourage further attempts. The attempts may be made, and we must abide the consequences; but I am sure it is better to retard than accelerate the operation of this most hazardous principle which is abroad. (Castlereagh to Lord W. Bentinck)

Yet Castlereagh also feared that counterrevolutionary interventions could also be a destabilizing force if they failed the test of legitimacy. The genius of the British constitution was its moderate balance of powers between monarchy and parliament; in Europe, by contrast, ultra-royalists or reactionaries tended to upset the balance the other way. This logic fed into Castlereagh's opposition to collective intervention to prop up the failing governments of the *ancien régime*. As he argued in the 1820 State Paper, many European states were

> now employed in the difficult task of casting anew their Govts. upon the Representative Principle: but the notion of revising, limiting or regulating the course of such Experiments, either by foreign Council or by foreign foe, would be as dangerous to avow as it w[ould] be impossible to execute, and the Illusion too prevalent on this Subject, should not be encouraged in our Intercourse with the Allies.

Collective intervention would lack legitimacy. It had an "air of dictation and menace," the risk of being "misunderstood," resisted and ultimately overturned as soon as the foreign armies of intervention returned home (Castlereagh, State Paper of 1820).

Canning and Palmerston

For all of the apparent differences in the personalities and foreign policy positions of Castlereagh and his successor, George Canning—to say nothing of the personal enmity that resulted in 1809 in a duel in which Castlereagh shot Canning in the leg—when it came to the fundamental guiding assumptions that gave direction to their foreign policy thinking, there existed a lot of commonality between these two old rivals. A misperception that lingered too long in the historiography of British foreign policy was that of Canning as an energetic interventionist, whose policies represented a wholesale rejection of Castlereagh's cautious, calculating pragmatism. Historians now generally recognize that Canning's accession to the Foreign Office upon Castlereagh's death in 1821 was not a radical new departure in British foreign policy (Bew 2011a, 581–584). If anything, Canning was even more staunchly anti-interventionist than Castlereagh, whose very engagement with the Congress system after 1815, in and of itself—and particularly in response to the Austrian intervention in Naples—contained the seeds of a fundamental acceptance that balance-of-power politics required at least some willingness toward interference and intervention, if only for the purposes of upholding the principle of nonintervention (Bew 2011b, 117–138). Slippage toward more frequent interventions under Canning in the mid-1820s—including in the Greek revolt at the Battle of Navarino in 1827—in this sense merely reaffirmed this principle, rather than innovating something entirely novel. Indeed, there are grounds to believe that Canning had some influence in the drafting of Castlereagh's State Paper of 1820; certainly, he took the opportunity in an April 1823 speech in the House of Commons to endorse its principles wholeheartedly (Castlereagh, *Hansard*, April 14, 1823).

While there were some important differences between the policy directions of the two men—not least in Canning's emphatic break from the Holy Alliance through his effective termination of the Congress of Verona in 1823, and his disdain for their construction of "legitimacy"—in terms of grand-strategic sensibility, Canning and Castlereagh shared many of the same core characteristics. Canning shared with Castlereagh a respect for the importance of public opinion, although again, he went further than Castlereagh on this front: his tenure at the Foreign Office and his premiership were characterized by careful cultivation of the public mood on key diplomatic issues through skillful manipulation of the press; public approval and consent, both foreign and domestic, Canning recognized, could be managed and deployed as an important tool in the toolkit of the statesman (Lady Canning 1830, 46–48).

Like Castlereagh, Canning also understood the importance of a state's capacity to project power as the most important variable that would determine the respect and maneuverability it commanded on the international stage; however, again he went further, recognizing that this same principle presented Britain with a set of dangers unique to its identity as a liberal-constitutional proto-superpower. Surveying the fleet at Plymouth in 1823, he remarked upon the tremendous latent power of the "mighty masses ... reposing on the shadows in perfect stillness," and "how soon, upon any call of patriotism or of necessity, it would ... awaken its dormant thunder." Thus "let it not be said that we cultivate peace because we fear, or because we are unprepared for war ... The resources created by peace are means of war" (Therry 1836, 423). Yet it was in this unsurpassed, historically unprecedented degree of amassed destructive power that Canning recognized—perhaps more keenly than Castlereagh—the grave danger to Britain: "The next war which should be kindled in Europe, would be a war not so much of armies as of opinions," and in that war, liberal constitutional Britain could not avoid being a magnet for the "restless and dissatisfied of any nation with which she might come in conflict." It was the "contemplation of this new *power*" which excited Canning's "most anxious apprehension," for "it is one thing to have a giant's strength, but it would be another to use it like a giant" (Corrected Report of Speeches Delivered by the Right Honourable George Canning, 1827). "The consciousness of such strength" might be a source of reassurance and security to the country, but the task of the responsible statesman was to avoid seeking "opportunities of displaying it," lest it unleash a new logic of violence in how the nation understands its place in the world, producing "a scene of desolation which no man can contemplate without horror." What Canning was essentially identifying was that the ability to project the kind of power Britain now had at its disposal was safe and sustainable only insofar as Britain sustained the studied neutrality of an "umpire" role in international affairs, involving itself in disputes and conflicts by choice more than inescapable necessity; a luxury afforded more than anything else by Britain's island status. To get drawn in on one side or another of the coming wars of ideology would be to abandon the immense benefits of this status. To be converted from "an umpire into an adversary" in wars of ideology was an outcome as unconscionable to Canning as it would have been to Castlereagh (Canning 1827, 38).

Canning's biographer, Harold Temperley, argued that the "real key" to Canning's statecraft was that "though emotional on the surface, it was intellectual in its aims and designs," "profoundly matured ... , fortified by knowledge of history and international law, and practically applied to the conditions of the time"—an evaluation that perhaps might just as easily be made of Castlereagh. In Temperley's view, Canning was more overtly guided by a code of fixed principles than his predecessor had been; a code of principles of foreign policy that boiled down, in essence, to the following list:

> no Areopagus, non-intervention; no European police system; every nation for itself, and God for us all; balance of power; respect for facts, not for abstract theories; respect for treaty rights, but caution in extending them. Provided it is sovereign and observes diplomatic obligations, a republic is as good a member of the comity of nations as a monarchy. "England not Europe"; "*Our* foreign policy cannot be conducted against the will of the nation." "Europe's domain extends to the shores of the Atlantic, England's begins there." England's function is "to hold the balance between the conflicting principles of democracy and despotism," to mediate between

two hemispheres, and the bring the New World (*pace* Monroe) into connection with the Old. (Temperley 1925, 470–471)

Certainly, as Temperley's list hints, Canning understood in ways many of his peers did not the need to rethink British global power in the era of a rising United States, and it was in the fusion of an English focus and a global outlook that Canning recognized the opportunities presented by "call[ing] the new world into existence to redress the balance of the old" (Canning, *Hansard*, December 12, 1826). Yet would Canning accept such a characterization of his own statecraft—a list of settled principles? "When people ask me ... for what is called a policy," he remarked in 1827, "the only answer is that we mean to do what may seem to be best, upon each occasion as it arises, making the Interests of Our Country one's guiding principle" (Kissinger 1994, 96).

Addressing the House of Commons 20 years later, Foreign Secretary Viscount Palmerston invoked precisely this doctrine: "If I might be allowed to express in one sentence the principle which I think ought to guide an English Minister," he remarked, "I would adopt the expression of Canning, and say that with every British Minister the interests of England ought to be the shibboleth of his policy" (Palmerston, *Hansard*, March 1, 1848). It was no idle invocation: in some ways, Palmerston was an heir of Canning—not least in his skillful fostering of public interest in the vicissitudes of foreign policy, his expert manipulation of popular opinion (merely to approve the execution of foreign policy, it is important to note—not to guide the framing of it (Brown 2002, 217)), and his understanding that appearing to give voice to the national opinion and allowing those outside politics to enjoy "a vicarious interest" could translate into a lasting power base, not only for himself but for the preservation of the dominance of the elite in an rapidly changing British political and social landscape (Brown 2002, 217).

Curiously, where Canning's five-year tenure in the Foreign Office and four-month premiership earned him a legacy as one of the most influential British statesmen of the century—and even, by some estimations, as an early pathbreaker for what became the Liberal Party—Palmerston's 30-year dominance of British foreign policy up to the zenith of its imperial power is remembered as little more than "briskly pragmatic" (Brown 2010, 481–489). Or, as Paul Smith puts it, "politics for Palmerston was largely a matter of getting from Monday to Friday without conspicuous damage" (Smith 1993, 144–145). By this account, Palmerston "held things together in his day: he neither sought a greater epitaph nor, probably, believed that there could be one" (Smith 1993, 144–145). The Duke of Argyll remembered Palmerston as "honest in his purposes, and truthful in his prosecution of them ... but he had no ideals for the future of the world, and had a profound distrust of those who professed to be guided by such ideals" (Argyll 1906, 335–344).

Palmerston's early education under Dugald Stewart at Edinburgh had indeed impressed upon him the importance of the practical, functional application of ideas; of the primacy of pragmatism over abstract principle for which his contemporaries later remembered him (Palmerston 1871). Yet like his predecessors, he developed a grand-strategic habit of mind that went beyond simple pragmatism—beyond the confines of short-term requirements of national defense or immediate foreign policy dilemmas. He shared with Castlereagh and Canning the same essential long-term, core goal for British foreign policy—to create, sustain, and expand the conditions required to achieve global commercial dominance, central to which was a favorable balance of power in Europe. However, both in substance and style, he charted quite a different course in the pursuit of this goal, most notably in the importance he placed upon the cultivation of particular liberal causes in Europe, his identification of them as connected to the British national interest, and his willingness to expend—or as some contemporaries argued, fritter—significant political and diplomatic capital on the promotion of those interests. In this sense, while a central facet of Palmerstonianism was a Canningite "English" policy, its fullest extension embodied dimensions that were Canning's worst nightmare. Like Castlereagh and Canning, though, Palmerston regarded foreign policy as an issue of unifying national importance, as operating beyond and transcending party politics and loyalties (Brown 2002, 3).

Himself notoriously difficult to categorize as realist or idealist, radical or reactionary, Palmerstonian epithets crop up to this day in support of quite divergent positions on the political spectrum. In a remark beloved of the American realist tradition, Palmerston told the House of Commons on March 1, 1848 that "We have no eternal allies, and we have no perpetual enemies. Our interests are eternal and perpetual, and those interests it is our duty to follow." This statement has been appropriated (and misquoted) widely, sometimes by those seeking an easily digestible unifying concept to summarize British grand strategy; more often as a "as part of a shorthand justification for an assertive foreign policy" and a defense of the primacy of national interest over inconvenient diplomatic obligations and ideological principles (Brands 2017, 16; Kurth 1996, 11). It is important to note that Palmerston was speaking specifically about Britain and British power, not "countries," "nations," or even great powers. Even leaving this aside, the lines were actually a qualifying remark for the wider, and more important point that while a key goal of foreign policy was "to extend the commercial relations of the country, or to place them ... upon a footing of greater security," it was at least as important that Britain was, and ought to be, a fundamentally pragmatically *moral* actor on the world stage:

> I hold that the real policy of England—apart from questions which involve her own particular interests, political or commercial—is to be the champion of justice and right; pursuing that course with moderation and prudence, not becoming the Quixote of the world, but giving the weight of her moral sanction and support wherever she thinks that justice is, and wherever she thinks that wrong has been done. (Palmerston, *Hansard*, March 1, 1848)

Alliances were an important tool in this respect, but Britain did not need to wed herself to any alliance whose strategic usefulness may fall out of alignment with the national interest, of which a moral purpose was one of several essential components. In this, Palmerston was implicitly invoking, among other things, the-then 40-year-old British foreign policy commitment to suppressing the slave trade, and the vastly complex "antislavery world system" of diplomatic, naval, military, consular, colonial, and commercial interventions over which he had long exercised personal leadership and close management (Huzzey 2012, 40–74).

> As long as England keeps herself in the right—as long as she wishes to permit no injustice—as long as she wishes to countenance no wrong—as long as she labours at legislative interests of her own—and as long as she sympathises with right and justice, she never will find herself altogether alone. (Palmerston, *Hansard*, March 1, 1848)

For Palmerston, in his framing of Britain as a moral international force, the idea of "force" was at least as important in this concept as the word "moral." Where Palmerston differed markedly from his predecessors was in how he defined the relationship between British values and the principle of sovereignty in international law, and in his willingness to deploy considerable violence to impose that "moral force." As Palmerston remarked with evident satisfaction following an unlawful unilateral antislavery intervention in Brazilian territorial waters in 1849, the gunships had "accomplished in a few weeks what diplomatic notes and negotiations have failed for years to accomplish" (Palmerston to Baring, September 3, 1850). "I have always been perfectly aware, that whenever we chose to strike the Brazilians *must* give in." In Palmerston's view

> It rarely if ever happens that a foreign gov[ernmen]t gives up its selfish interests, its passions or its prejudices to the force of argument or persuasion; and the more such a gov[ernmen]t is in the wrong, the more pig headed it generally is, because its being very much in the wrong is a proof that it is deaf and blind to reason and right. Persuasion seldom succeeds unless there is compulsion of some sort, nearer or further off behind it. (Palmerston to Baring, quoted in Ryan 2011, 231)

As Palmerston told Aberdeen 14 years later, counseling a more assertive Near Eastern policy, "Peace is an excellent thing, and war a great misfortune. But there are things more valuable than peace, and many things much worse than war" (quoted in Ashley 1879, 285).

Echoes into the Twentieth Century: The Foreign Office during the Second World War

The careers and writings of those who followed Palmerston's tenure reflect the degree to which the habit of framing British foreign policy in grand-strategic, intuitively long-term, big-picture terms had become an internalized characteristic of British policymaking, even as the basis and reach of British power contracted sharply in the twentieth century. Among others, Lord Salisbury, Lord Lansdowne, Eyre Crowe, Lord Cecil, and Austen Chamberlain offer important case studies of the way in which the post-1815 grand-strategic assumptions and instincts of Castlereagh, Canning, and Palmerston influenced—consciously and unconsciously—British diplomats and statesmen as they attempted to craft long-term British strategy in a changing international environment. Foreign Office officials during the Second World War offer a particularly clear example of how such thinking manifested within the twentieth century. It was in this period that the power of the United Kingdom, despite its empire being at its territorial zenith, was experiencing a seismic, irreversible decline relative to the United States and the Soviet Union. Senior officials wrote of the United Kingdom having passed its "dynamic phase" and that its "bluffs have been called" (Sargent, September 7, 1942; Cadogan, October 31, 1940). But far from adopting a defeatist mindset, diplomats within the Foreign Office in these years worked to balance national interests with wider designs for an international order; and importantly, they looked to the statesmen of the nineteenth century—and Castlereagh in particular—for insight.

The Foreign Office approach between 1942 and 1945 can be defined by several characteristics, a number of which had their roots in the British statecraft of the preceding century. First, diplomats and officials engaged directly with first-order questions—namely debating and planning for the reshaping of international order that would be necessary once the war was at last concluded. They recognized that they faced a challenge at least as complex as that facing Castlereagh at Vienna. However, unlike in 1815, their task was to find, if possible, an order that would allow Britain to play an outsized role given its declining military and economic strength. The reality of this coming challenge was apparent to Churchill and Attlee early in the war, as evidenced by their and the Cabinet's attempt to frame war aims (Hill 2010, 188–223). Declarations such as the Atlantic Charter were momentous and perhaps encouraging, but the question faced by British officials was to translate these rather vague ideas about a future world order into tangible results in foreign policy terms. By the spring of 1942, senior officials and several Cabinet ministers, worried that the United Kingdom was lagging behind postwar planning being undertaken in the United States and Soviet Union, began calling for a more concerted effort within the Foreign Office, in order to meet the Americans and Russians "on equal terms." Richard Law, then Parliamentary Under-Secretary, captured this sense of strategic anxiety. It was essential that the past be interrogated closely for lessons to be learned from failure, and to help develop a "grand strategy of peace": "I think whatever we had done in the tactical sphere we would have had this war, so long as our grand strategy was wrong," he argued. "And if now we do not develop a grand strategy of peace, we shall be wrong again—and we shall have another war" (Law 1942). Within the Foreign Office, several officials took on this task of developing and articulating a grand strategy for the postwar period. There was an urgency among these officials, who, like Law, felt that the United Kingdom must be guided by a coherent policy in order to both protect its interests and maintain its status as a world power. One of the great champions of this approach—and the official most responsible for developing a British postwar strategy—was Gladwyn Jebb. Early on, he was alert to the need to avoid

> creating the impression that we are a sort of ramshackle Empire, equivalent to Austria-Hungary during the last war, devoid of ideas, and overcome by the difficulties inherent in every proposal, which is unfortunately a view widely held in the United States. Only by taking up the vague ideas now floating about the world and expressing them boldly and even recklessly in our own terms can we hope to play *the role which is proper to us*. And irrespective of what we say, only by making up our minds as to what it is that we really want can we hope to be the master and not the victim of events. (Foreign Office memorandum 1942, 17)

Jebb, who later became Lord Gladwyn and the first acting Secretary-General of the United Nations, ended the document with the aphorism "*Ducunt volentum fata nolentem trahunt*" ("fate leads the willing but drags the unwilling").

Second, Foreign Office officials, like their nineteenth-century predecessors, recognized the central importance of a state's capacity to project power, and the reality that geopolitical competition would remain a key feature of the international system. The experience of the League of Nations had shown that ideas of "common humanity" and notions of states adhering to international law were feckless in the absence of power. In the words of the Permanent Under-Secretary, Alexander Cadogan, military force had now been returned to its "throne" (Cadogan, October 31, 1940). Nevertheless, an ordered international system—perhaps in the mold of the League, but with "teeth"—had major benefits to the United Kingdom. Thus, Foreign Office officials looked to create appropriate structures for a functional and robust international order in which the powers most capable of enforcing peace could assume primary responsibility for its defense.

The third characteristic of the thinking of key Foreign Office officials after 1942 was their recognition of the importance of public opinion, tempered with a wariness of allowing such views to dictate their policymaking. The United Kingdom in these years suffered no shortage of intellectuals and politicians—the historian Arnold Toynbee and Winston Churchill amongst them—who advanced their own competing visions of a future international order. Although Jebb wrote with frustration of "all the sentimentalists and idealists," nonetheless, he understood that the British public must be brought along (Jebb, November 4, 1942). The challenge he saw would be to appease the currents of opinion, seeking for the United Kingdom to "hand over the torch" of world leadership to the Americans and Russians, while yet preserving its great power identity. "Any great power which wishes to retain that title must be imbued with a sense both of its own importance and of its mission" (Foreign Office memorandum 1942, 4). Jebb and his colleagues, at times, saw their work as a kind of civilizational struggle: Britain and the democracies of Western Europe, Jebb wrote, constituted the "cradle and matrix" of Western civilization, and should Britain forego an influential role in the future, there was a risk that "our particular type of civilization must inevitably crumble" (Foreign Office memorandum 1942, 10–11). Instead, the Foreign Office sought a postwar order in which Britain was respected by all as "a realistic and temperate force capable of toning down the conflicting world ideologies possessed by other nations." But to play this role, the "nation at large" must first "be inspired with a sense of its own importance in any world order" (Jebb, October 8, 1942).

To this end, Jebb's "Four Power Plan"—first produced in the autumn of 1942—called for the United Kingdom to work with the United States, the Soviet Union, and China to create a nucleus of great powers which might be responsible for the maintenance of international peace. He originally labeled this conception a "Concert of the World" which might "keep the peace for the next hundred years in the same way as the Concert of Europe ... more or less kept the peace in Europe between the Battle of Waterloo and the beginning of World War No. 1." (Jebb, Draft Memorandum 1942, 9). Charles Webster—an historian of the Congress of Vienna, biographer of Castlereagh, commentator on the League of Nations, and advisor to the Foreign Office—recognized in Jebb's desire to create a "concert" of great powers something of "the great tradition of British policy" and grand-strategic thinking that dated back to Castlereagh, Canning, Palmerston, Salisbury, and more recently, Lord Balfour and Sir Austen Chamberlain (Webster 1944). Yet it was not a simple re-enactment of the Vienna settlement. Though Webster agreed that the great powers should reserve a distinct position in the international hierarchy, he also stressed that the legitimacy of the international order depended on whether the rights of the smaller powers were respected. The balance between the rights of the great powers and the concern for smaller nations, Webster argued, was—albeit in a different form—arguably Castlereagh's greatest contribution to the order which arose after the defeat of Napoleon (Webster 1945). It was such a conception of a postwar international order—one led by the great powers but protecting the rights of smaller nations—which guided British plans for what would become, by June 1945, the United Nations Organization.

Conclusion

What connects Castlereagh, Canning, Palmerston, and Foreign Office officials such as Jebb in the 1940s was—in the face of many different strains and pressures on foreign policy—a grand-strategic habit of mind: a conscious attempt to look beyond the confines of short-term requirements of national defense or immediate foreign policy dilemmas; an intuitive, historically anchored sense of the big picture and the long term that went beyond simple pragmatism. Yet the conclusion to be taken from this is not merely one of "great men of history," but rather that the context and trajectory of British power mattered as much as the individual officeholders in creating the conditions that necessitated and rewarded statecraft conceived of on a larger scale and timeframe than heretofore. The context of empire, with its many associated mindsets and assumptions, was evidently of central importance in helping to establish a grand-strategic culture that was, by the closing days of formal British imperialism in the twentieth century and the last gasps of its world power status, deeply internalized in the machinery of British statecraft. The statesmen discussed in this chapter were involved closely in the complex challenges of (re)constructing order in the aftermath of two immensely violent, transformative conflicts: those of 1792–1815 and 1939–1945, each of which provoked unusually urgent and acute questions of the future of British power and its place in the world. In his response, Castlereagh sought to define the national interest more clearly and expansively than had been done before 1815, and his successors—Canning and Palmerston—built consciously upon this approach, conceiving of and deploying power in ways—and for purposes—that reflected the global scope of Britain's formal and informal imperial commitments and opportunities. Alliances were in this regard deemed to be fluid and impermanent, and commercial or security interests were supposed to prevail over any abstract principles, with the sole caveat that Britain must always find ways to rationalize its interests in reassuringly moral terms, even if only for domestic audiences.

Viewed from the outside, this attempt to reconcile selfish national interests with the idea of a higher purpose could appear deeply hypocritical. And yet the story told in this chapter is more complex than that. For all his wariness about rapid political change, Castlereagh understood that Britain's liberal self-image was an inescapable influence on foreign policy. Canning eschewed interventionism and wars of ideology and yet he understood that Britain was likely to become embroiled on the liberal or democratic side, should it be forced from its preferred position as an umpire to one of a competitor. Palmerston insisted that the national interest overrode everything else and yet pushed an often counterproductive interventionist agenda that sought to portray Britain as the champion of constitutionalism and freedom, all the while constructing and maintaining a complex and expensive "antislavery world system." The point is not about whether these leaders saw Britain as *either* a moral force *or* a self-interested one, but rather that they saw the pursuit of specific moral causes as being an element of the national interest. That is, they conceived of imperial statecraft and the metropolitan national interest in a sufficiently long-term fashion to recognize the strategic value of articulating and pursuing a particular kind of global "moral order."

Seen in this way, the British strategic principles that emerged in this era cannot be reduced to simple realist tropes. They recognized the irreducible role of ideology, identity, and public opinion. They were, more than that, predicated on an assumption that humanity was set upon a developmental trajectory that would, eventually, see the world look more like Britain. They sought to conceive of British national interests as something shaped by the international environment; and, in turn, sought to shape that environment in a way that was conducive to British national interests. They did not theorize about international affairs in the abstract, but they did operate on the basis of certain expectations about the historical and developmental continuum on which the other nations of the world were set. The unexamined assumption at the core of this, of course, was a confidence—that peaked in the Victorian era—that Britain represented the highest form of constitutional, cultural, and economic development. This was the essence of British grand strategy between 1815 and 1945. It was a worldview that wove together the imperial project with the pursuit of traditional foreign policy.

The British leaders and diplomats who held responsibility for British foreign policy in the 1940s were, like their predecessors, not wantonly ideological; but at the same time, their statecraft similarly cannot be reduced to simple pragmatism. By the mid-twentieth century, it is remarkable the degree to which the grand-strategic assumptions and habits of mind born in the previous century—born, that is, in the context of an expanding power base and at the metropole of a rapidly strengthening commercial and territorial empire—had become internalized simply into "good statecraft." It was with this mindset that Jebb wrote of Britain needing to play "the role which is proper to us" and to be "the master and not the victim of events." In this approach, he sought continuity with Castlereagh, Canning, and Palmerston, who—although starting from a vastly different relative power base—understood British national interests as being both shaped by the international environment, and—with good leadership—constitutive of it. In the context of relative decline and eclipse by the newly emergent superpower blocs, the British instinct to carve out a central role in the construction and maintenance of a wider, rules-based international order reflected a preferred national self-image as architects of a better world—a new world "called ... into existence to redress the balance of the old."

References

Primary Source Material

December 9, 1801, *The Parliamentary History of England, from the Earliest Period to the Year 1803* (London, 1820), vol. XXXVI, p. 1115.

May 2, 1802, *The Parliamentary History of England, from the Earliest Period to the Year 1803* (London, 1820), vol. XXXVI, pp. 782–791.

February 14, 1816, *The Parliamentary Debates from the Year 1803 to the Present Time*, published by T.C. Hansard (London, 1816), vol. XXXII, pp. 566–568.

April 14, 1823, *Hansard* third series, vol. VIII, pp. 872–904.

Cadogan, Alexander. 1940. Minute on memorandum, October 31, 1940, UK National Archives (Kew), FO 371/25208/W11399.

Canning, *Hansard*, December 12, 1826, vol. 16 c. 397.

Castlereagh to Dr Haliday, February 27, 1792, Public Record Office of Northern Ireland (PRONI), *Castlereagh Papers*, D3030/37.

Castlereagh to Lord Stewart, February 24, 1820, PRONI *Castlereagh Papers*, D3030/5814.

Castlereagh to Lord W. Bentinck, May 7, 1814, in Vane, C.W., ed. 1853. *Correspondence of Viscount Castlereagh*, 12 vols., vol. 10, p. 18. London: John Murray.

Castlereagh 1966. "The State Paper of 5 May 1820." In *Foundations of British Foreign Policy*, edited by Temperley and Penson. London: Routledge.

Corrected Report of Speeches Delivered by the Right Honourable George Canning in the House of Commons, December 12 1826. 2nd edition. London: Ridgway, 1827.

Foreign Office memorandum. 1942. "Four Power Plan," November 8, 1942, WP (42) 516, UK National Archives (Kew), FO 371/31525/U783.

Jebb, Gladwyn. 1942. Draft memorandum on "Relief Machinery: The Political Background," August 1942, UK National Archives (Kew), FCO 73/264/Pwp/42/8.

Jebb, Gladwyn. 1942. Minute on memorandum, November 4, 1942, UK National Archives (Kew), FCO 73/264/Pwp/42/48.

Jebb, Gladwyn. 1942. Minute on memorandum, October 8, 1942, UK National Archives (Kew), FO 371/31514/U841.

Palmerston. 1848. *Hansard*, March 1, 1848 vol. 97 c. 123.

Palmerston to Baring, 3 September 1850, University of Southampton, Palmerston Papers (Broadlands MSS) [PP], GC/BA/310.

Palmerston to Howard De Walden, March 24, 1838, UK National Archives (Kew), FO 84/248.

Palmerston to Howard De Walden, March 24, 1838 and April 7, 1838, University of Southampton PP GC/HO/812-826.

Palmerston to Baring, September 3, 1850, University of Southampton PP GC/BA/310.

Sargent, Orme, minute on memorandum, September 7, 1942, UK National Archives (Kew), FO 371/31514/U636.

Webster, Charles. 1944. Draft of covering minute for Richard Law, Covering brief for "Future World Organisation: Forthcoming Conversations at Washington," April 16, 1944, UK National Archives (Kew), FO 371/40689/U3128.

Webster, Charles. 1945. Memorandum, "Castlereagh or Canning," July 1945, LSE Archives, Webster papers, 15/2.

Secondary Source Material

Argyll, George Douglas, Eighth Duke of, 1823–1900. 1906. *Autobiography and Memoirs*, ed. the Dowager Duchess of Argyll. 2 vols. New York: E. P. Dutton.

Ashley, Evelyn. 1879. *The Life and Correspondence of Henry John Temple, Viscount Palmerston*. 2 vols. London: Bentley and Son.

Bew, John. 2011a. *Castlereagh: Enlightenment, War and Tyranny*. London: Quercus.

Bew, John. 2011b. "'From an Umpire to a Competitor': Castlereagh, Canning and the Issue of International Intervention in the Wake of the Napoleonic Wars." In *Humanitarian Intervention: A History*, 117–138. Cambridge: Cambridge University Press.

Brands, Hal. 2017. "The Unexceptional Superpower: American Grand Strategy in the Age of Trump." *Survival* 59 (6).

Brown, David. 2010. *Palmerston: A Biography*. New Haven, CT: Yale University Press.

Brown, David. 2002. *Palmerston and the Politics of Foreign Policy*. Manchester: Manchester University Press.

Davies, Huw J. 2012. *Wellington's Wars*. New Haven, CT: Yale University Press.

Henderson, Gavin B. 1938. "The Foreign Policy of Lord Palmerston." *History* 22 (88): 335–344.

Hill, Christopher. 2010. *Cabinet Decisions on Foreign Policy, October 1938–June 1941*. Cambridge: Cambridge University Press.

Hurd, Douglas. 2010. *Choose Your Weapons: The British Foreign Secretary: Two Centuries of Conflict and Personalities*. London: Weidenfeld and Nicholson.

Huzzey, Richard. 2012. *Freedom Burning: Anti-Slavery and Empire in Victorian Britain*. Cornell University Press.

Kissinger, Henry. 1994. *Diplomacy*. New York: Simon & Schuster.

Kurth, James. 1996. "America's Grand Strategy: A Pattern of History." *The National Interest* 43.

Lady Canning. 1830. *An Authentic Account of Mr Canning's Policy*. London: Hatchard.

Law, Richard. 1942. "Speech to Cambridge Society for International Affairs." March 18, 1942. Reprinted in *Time and Tide*, March 21, 1942, copy in UK National Archives (Kew), FO 371/35363/U830.

Palmerston. 1871. "Autobiographical sketch." Bulwer, H.L., *The Life of Henry John Temple, Viscount Palmerston: With Selections from His Diaries and Correspondence*, 2 vols. Vol. 1, pp. 321–335. Philadelphia: Lippincott.

Phillips, W. Alison. 1919. "The Peace Settlement: 1815 and 1919." *Edinburgh Review* 230 (469) (July): 1–21.

Ryan, Maeve. 2007. "Britain, the Slave Trade and the Right of Search in Early Nineteenth Century European Diplomacy." Unpublished MPhil. dissertation, University of Cambridge.

Ryan, Maeve. 2011. "The Price of Legitimacy in Humanitarian Intervention: Britain, the Right of Search, and the Abolition of the West African Slave Trade, 1807–1867." In *Humanitarian Intervention: A History*, edited by B. Simms and D. Trim, 231–256. Cambridge: Cambridge University Press.

Smith, Paul. 1993. "Review of E.D. Steele, *Palmerston and Liberalism*." *English Historical Review* 108: 144–145.

Temperley, Harold W. 1925. *The Foreign Policy of Canning, 1822–27*. London: Bell.

The Marquess of Salisbury. 1905. *Essays by the late Marquess of Salisbury: Biographical*. New York: E.P. Dutton.

Therry, Roger. 1836. *The Speeches of The Right Honourable George Canning*. 3rd edition. London: Ridgway.

PART VII

THE FUTURE OF GRAND STRATEGY

CHAPTER 40

GRAND STRATEGY IN A FRACTURED MARKETPLACE OF IDEAS

DANIEL W. DREZNER

GRAND strategy is an attempt to marry state capabilities with social purpose. It is an intentional act of intellectual creation, guiding foreign actors, national security bureaucracies, and outside analysts about what to expect from a country's foreign policy (Drezner 2009). In theory, democracies possess an advantage in the formulation of grand strategies. Because democratic governments foster a vigorous marketplace of ideas, foreign policy elites should act as powerful critics to referee any nascent foreign policy ideas. Indeed, current debates about grand strategy have fostered a wider variety of voices than usual entering the fray (Hurlburt 2019; Goldgeier 2019). Furthermore, for grand strategies to matter, they must be clear and enduring. The ability of democracies to credibly commit should enhance the signaling power of articulated foreign policy doctrines (Cowhey 1993).

There are signs, however, that the half-life of democratic grand strategies has been shrinking. The first US grand strategy of isolationism lasted more than a century. Its most prominent grand strategy, containment, lasted less than a half-century. The post–Cold War strategy of primacy lasted only a quarter-century. Strategies need to adapt to shifts in external circumstances, but the acceleration of change cannot be denied. Nor is this limited to the United States. Democracies ranging from Great Britain to South Korea have had gyrating grand strategies over the past decade.

This chapter warns that shifts in the marketplace for foreign policy ideas render grand strategy debates in advanced industrialized democracies less significant and more superfluous. Three factors have lowered the utility of these debates. First, the erosion of trust in expertise in general and foreign policy expertise in particular has reduced the influence of foreign policy establishments. Second, the rise in political polarization has had pronounced effects on foreign policy discourse, making it harder for foreign policy intellectuals in one party to persuade elites across the political aisle. Third, decades of dysfunction and disinterest have led legislatures to cede an ever-greater share of foreign policy powers to executive branches. The reduction of legislative influence weakens a veto point in which public debate could affect choices about grand strategy.

These trends reduce the ability of foreign policy elites to fashion a sustainable grand strategy. The erosion of trust in elites weakens expert influence on strategic debates. Political polarization severely degrades the ability of parliaments to participate constructively on foreign policy. At the same time, polarization has led to the election of foreign policy leaders governing from the more extreme wings of the ideological spectrum. Grand strategies will oscillate between the parties in power, with little in the way of constancy. Credible commitments will be next to impossible to maintain. The ability to learn from past mistakes will be degraded. All of these trends reduce the ability of foreign policy elites to craft a sustainable grand strategy. Whatever grand strategy is articulated, actual foreign policy outputs will be independent of that strategy.

Grand Strategy and the Marketplace of Ideas

In theory, a country's grand strategy can and should be disciplined through the marketplace of ideas. Kaufmann (2004, 5) notes, "the marketplace of ideas helps to weed out unfounded, mendacious, or self-serving foreign policy arguments because their proponents cannot avoid wide-ranging debate in which their reasoning and evidence are subject to public scrutiny." In the absence of such a debate, policymakers and publics can fall victim to myths and misperceptions, which in turn contribute to catastrophic strategic errors (Janis 1982; Snyder 1991). An unheralded virtue of foreign policy intellectuals is to vigorously push back on bad ideas (Nichols 2017; Drezner 2017, 2019b).

Foreign policy elites are a pivotal audience for grand strategies. Government officials are the principal architects of strategy, but strategy is publicized and vetted through outside experts. These intellectuals function as a check against the implementation of bad ideas. While falling short of the definition of an "epistemic community" (Haas 1992), foreign policy elites nonetheless can act as a constraint on policymakers if they deviate from that consensus. Traditionally, politicians who proposed ideas rejected by an expert consensus—as when the Obama administration proposed quantitative restrictions on G20 trade deficits—paid a political price for that rejection.

At the onset of the Cold War, foreign policy experts played a vital role in interrogating US grand strategies. The acme of the foreign policy community was the "Georgetown Set" that debated grand strategy over Washington dinners (Herken 2014). This coterie of academics, columnists, publishers, and policymakers was small enough to exercise real leverage over the marketplace of ideas. Most of them had gone to the same schools and served together in the Second World War. This common background helped them trust each other even when they disagreed. George Kennan's direct influence over politicians and policy principals was small. The one arena where he did exercise influence, however, was over the Georgetown set (Miscamble 1992, 36; Herken 2014, 51). Those opinion writers cemented Kennan's reputation for foreign policy gravitas in the public's mind (Gaddis 2011, 270–275).

Although the range of foreign policy opinions within the Georgetown Set was narrow (Anderson 2015), there were substantive debates about methods and scope. The defining debate occurred between George Kennan and Walter Lippmann. In "The Sources of Soviet Conduct," Kennan (1947) advocated for a robust policy of containment towards the Soviet Union. Lippmann (1947) responded to Kennan's *Foreign Affairs* essay with a series of critical columns that eventually turned into *The Cold War*. Lippmann's realpolitik response was the most high-profile contemporaneous rebuttal to Kennan. Their debate demarcated the boundaries of Cold War discourse for the next four decades.

A key dynamic during this era was the push and pull between different wings of the foreign policy establishment. A rough equilibrium emerged between those who wanted the country to adopt a more interventionist posture and those who wanted to husband national power for critical junctures, between those who preferred multilateral approaches and those who preferred unilateral ones. When one camp overreached, others would seize on it to call for a course correction. Advocates of restraint invoked the excesses of Vietnam to push for retrenchment. Hawks pointed to Soviet expansionism in the 1970s to argue for a more robust posture. The partially decentralized policymaking process during this era meant that no one foreign policy camp accrued too much influence (Mead 2002, 95). When the Nixon White House pursued a strictly realpolitik approach toward the Soviet Union, for example, Congress forced human rights concerns onto the agenda. Time and time again, foreign policy reverted to the mean. Activism was eventually followed by restraint. The results of these crosscutting debates were far from perfect, but they ensured that US foreign policy did not deviate too far from containment. Past commitments remained credible in the future.

The collapse of the Soviet Union rendered containment obsolete. US officials "looked to the academy for ideas" (Byman and Kroenig 2016, 309). This sparked serious intellectual efforts to devise a grand strategy for the post–Cold War world. A number of foreign policy intellectuals stepped forward to offer new ways of thinking about world politics. Some of these worldviews were optimistic about US hegemony (Fukuyama 1989; Krauthammer 1990/91; Nye 1990); others were gloomier (Mearsheimer 1990; Huntington 1993b). Scholars debated the prospect of an expanding democratic peace (Brown, Lynn-Jones, and Miller 1996). Another debate raged over the durability and stability of American hegemony on world politics (Jervis 1993; Huntington 1993a).

America's post–Cold War grand strategy converged on the maintenance of primacy and the enlargement of a US-led liberal internationalism. Grand strategists embraced the optimistic assessments of Fukuyama and Nye and rejected the pessimistic assessments of Huntington and Mearsheimer about the future trajectory of American power. Even a policymaker as realist as Brent Scowcroft wrote in a 1989 memo to President George H.W. Bush, "When those creators of the 1940s and 1950s rested, they had done much. We now have unprecedented opportunities to do more, to pick up the task where they left off, while doing what must be done to protect a handsome inheritance" (quoted in G. Rose 2019, 16).

The power of foreign policy elites in the post–Cold War era seemed to match the influence of their predecessors during the Cold War period. Jacobs and Page (2005, 113) demonstrate that the preferences of key elite groups had a much stronger effect on policymakers than the broad public during this period. The correlation of preferences between elites and policymakers was so strong that they concluded the "foreign policy establishment" still dominated the discourse during the post–Cold War era.

The Establishment Weakens

Some observers argue that America's foreign policy community—the very definition of an unelected establishment—is *too* influential. The one thing that united presidents Obama and Trump was their disdain for foreign policy elites inside the Beltway (Drezner 2017, 4–8). Analysts argue that the post–Cold War grand strategy was too cosseting, muting debate and leading to catastrophic foreign policy decisions. Obama's deputy national security advisor Ben Rhodes referred derisively to the foreign policy community inside the Beltway as "The Blob." He vented that, "The discourse in Washington just becomes like a self-licking ice cream cone of maximalist foreign policy" (Drezner 2017, 4–5). Multiple critics of the primacy grand strategy argued that the foreign policy establishment constricted the marketplace of ideas in foreign policy (Kaufmann 2004; Friedman and Logan 2016). According to Porter (2018, 16):

> They socialize personnel into their worldview, educating and selecting individuals who conform, excluding or penalizing those who do not, and linking conformity to an axiomatic worldview with insider status; they also dominate the pool of experienced talent that makes up officialdom. They have privileged access to power via an institutional revolving door, a set of social networks, and institutions— the locations where grand strategic ideas intervene at the unit level .... The Blob dominates public discourse and sets its agenda, through privileged access to the commentariat, of which it forms a part.

Porter pointed to President Trump's first year in office as a case study of a populist candidate constrained by a foreign policy team that emanated from the Blob. The occasional disjuncture between Trump and the doctrines produced by his administration was readily observable (Woodward 2018).

The implicit critique in these analyses is that the marketplace of ideas has not functioned as advertised. There is little evidence that intellectuals are punished for past errors in judgment (Silver 2012; Drezner 2017), and this is decidedly true for foreign policy elites. The architects of the Vietnam War were subsequently praised as the "Wise Men" (Isaacson and Thomas 1986). The architects of the 2003 invasion of Iraq paid little price for that gambit. Among members of the foreign policy community, support for both the wars in Vietnam and Iraq were high. Leslie Gelb (2009, 24) admitted that his support for the 2003 Iraq War "was symptomatic of unfortunate tendencies within the foreign policy community, namely the disposition and incentives to support wars to retain political and professional credibility." Others argue that these debates have largely been disconnected from the foreign policy preferences of the American people. The gap between an interventionist foreign policy elite and a public that leans more towards restraint has been striking (Page and Bouton 2006).

While foreign policy elites may not have paid a material price for mistakes, empirical claims about the power of the Blob have not held up well either. At the rhetorical level, Trump categorically rejected the liberal internationalism of his predecessors, as did his key foreign policy subordinates. In his inaugural address, Trump (2017a) explicitly stated, "We've defended other nation's borders while refusing to defend our own, and spent trillions of dollars overseas while America's infrastructure has fallen into disrepair and decay." The Trump administration's first national security strategy (Trump 2017b) emphasized foreign economic threats to a greater extent than any previous grand strategy. Secretary of State Mike Pompeo (2018) derided the very idea of multilateral institutions, saying, "Multilateralism has too often become viewed as an end unto itself. The more treaties we sign, the safer we supposedly are. The more bureaucrats we have, the better the job gets done. Was that ever really true?" Trump's former NSC spokesperson Michael Anton (2019), in attempting to articulate a Trump Doctrine, wrote, "Let's all put our own countries first, and be candid about it, and recognize that it's nothing to be ashamed of. Putting our interests first will make us all safer and more prosperous. If there is a Trump Doctrine, that's it." None of this rhetoric was consistent with the post–Cold War grand strategy of liberal internationalism (Kupchan and Trubowitz 2007).

Trump's personnel and policy moves matched his rhetoric. By 2019 Trump had replaced all of the people Porter (2018) had identified as members of the foreign policy establishment. In his December 2018 resignation letter, Secretary of Defense James Mattis made it clear that the reason for his departure was a disagreement over US grand strategy:

> We must do everything possible to advance an international order that is most conducive to our security, prosperity and values, and we are strengthened in this effort by the solidarity of our alliances. Because you have the right to a Secretary of Defense whose views are better aligned with yours on these and other subjects, I believe it is right for me to step down from my position.

In their stead, Trump appointed policy principals who were much more unilateralist in their worldview. Over time, the Trump administration's policy actions reflected a grand strategy far closer to "America First" than liberal internationalism. On issues ranging from climate change to nonproliferation to trade policy his administration deviated significantly from the post–Cold War consensus.

The inchoate aspects of the Trump administration's grand strategy might help to explain the meager outcomes that an "America First" approach yielded (Drezner 2019c), but that does not mean the strategic shift has abated—if anything, the opposite is true. Most of Trump's foreign policy moves generated vigorous criticism from across the foreign policy community (Posen 2018; Haass 2019; G. Rose 2019). Nonetheless, that criticism had little to no effect on administration actions and strategies. Contra Porter, today's foreign policy elite have been nowhere near as influential as George Kennan and Paul Nitze. What explains this shift from the heyday of Kennan and Lippmann?

The Erosion of Trust in Elites

There are three reasons that foreign policy experts exert less influence over the marketplace of ideas. The first is the general erosion of trust in authority and expertise. The survey data showing rising levels of pessimism towards major institutions and professions is incontrovertible. Over the past half-century there has been an erosion of public trust in almost every major public institution. Vietnam and Watergate cut Americans' trust in government by half over a single decade. Pew (2019) data shows that between the immediate post-9/11 moment and March 2019, the percentage of Americas who trust the federal government fell from 54 percent to 17 percent. After examining the 2018 Edelman Trust Barometer, Ross and Kehoe (2018) concluded, "The public's confidence in the traditional structures of American leadership is now fully undermined and has been replaced with a strong sense of fear, uncertainty and disillusionment." Gallup data reveals that Americans have lost faith in most institutions: local police, unions, public schools, organized religion, business, and the healthcare system. Indeed, at no time in the past decade has the bulk of the institutions polled yielded trust levels higher than the historical average. Similarly, trust in most major sources of information—including television news and newspapers—is also at an all-time low.

Survey data on public confidence in US foreign policy elites does not exist, but it is easy to infer from other data that distrust in this kind of expertise has likely increased. The General Social Survey has polled Americans for confidence in institutions associated with learning and knowledge: the scientific community, medicine, education, and organized religion. In 1974, the average confidence level for these institutions peaked at approximately 50 percent. By 2012, confidence in all four of these institutions had dropped to an average of 31 percent (Smith and Son 2013). Americans are also more open to alternative belief systems that experts had largely discredited. On a host of scientific issues, ranging from climate change to child vaccines, public distrust and skepticism has persisted (Ricci 2015). And in politics, the public holds views that are significantly different from the consensus of political scientists (Caplan et al. 2013).

The erosion of trust in authority extends well beyond the United States. Within the advanced industrialized economies, trust in government fell by roughly 10 percentage points between 2007 and 2012 (OECD 2013). Edelman's (2015) survey revealed that "the number of countries with trusted institutions has fallen to an all—time low among the informed public." Faith in democracy as a form of government is also eroding across the advanced industrialized world (Foa and Mounk 2016).

Indeed, the erosion of trust in elites defined the Brexit debate. In the run-up to the 2016 referendum, the IMF, OECD, Bank of England, Federal Reserve, Price Waterhouse Coopers, Barclays, Moody's, and the Economist Intelligence Unit all issued reports warning that the costs of Brexit would be significant. When asked about these analyses, Michael Gove, a leader of the Leave campaign, responded confidently, "I'm glad these organizations aren't on my side." He continued: "I think people in this country have had enough of experts" (Colville 2016). A Conservative MP told the *Financial Times* that "there is a fundamental breakdown in trust not just between voters and politicians but also with the BBC, the Bank of England, the City of London, and so on" (Buck 2016). A majority of British voters favored Brexit by distrusting experts.

Healthy skepticism of experts is warranted, especially given the scandals that have plagued elite institutions over the past decade (Hayes 2012; Drezner 2017). The effect of too much skepticism on the marketplace of ideas is corrosive, however. As Teles, Hurlburt, and Schmitt note, the authority of elites and their institutions was attacked from the left in the 1960s and from the right in the 1970s. As a result, "the country lost the mediating power that these institutions had over public discourse, and in particular their ability to certify basic claims of fact" (2014, 47). Hayes (2012, 13, 25) observes that "we now operate in a world in which we can assume neither competence nor good faith from the authorities," and warned, "if the experts as a whole are discredited, we are faced with an inexhaustible supply of quackery." Nichols concludes, "The relationship between experts and citizens, like almost all relationships in a democracy, is built on trust. When that trust collapses, experts and laypeople become warring factions" (2017, 216).

The general erosion of trust in expertise has pronounced effects on the marketplace for ideas in grand strategy. Foreign policy elites possess genuine expertise, but much of their power in public discourse has traditionally come from their credentials—prestigious degrees, endowed chairs, fellowships, and sinecures in media outlets. Arguing from authority, however, only works if the authority is recognized and legitimized by others. In a world in which traditional accreditations do not carry the same prestige, foreign policy experts must work harder to make their voices heard above the din. The erosion of trust levels the playing field in the public sphere by calling into doubt the value of foreign policy expertise in the first place. Lowered barriers to entry permit individuals who lack traditional credentials to participate in public debates about grand strategy. Furthermore, new entrants can advance their arguments in part by bashing the preexisting consensus on grand strategy (Drezner 2017). They can exploit narratives about failed foreign policies of the past to argue that they can hardly be expected to do worse.

During the 2016 campaign, Donald Trump told voters at one rally, "The experts are terrible. They say, 'Donald Trump needs a foreign policy advisor.' ... But supposing I don't have one. Would it be worse than what we're doing now?" (Quoted in Nichols 2017, 210–211). His foreign policy acolytes made the same argument in articulating a populist approach to foreign policy. Indeed, the 2017 National Security Strategy explicitly criticized prior grand strategies, arguing that great power competition would "require the United States to rethink the policies of the past two decades—policies based on the assumption that engagement with rivals and their inclusion in international institutions and global commerce would turn them into benign actors and trustworthy partners. For the most part, this premise turned out to be false" (Trump 2017b, 3). Such criticism of prior grand strategies was not a feature of any prior NSS. The style befits the devalued worth assigned to establishment foreign policy experts.

The Rise of Political Polarization

The erosion of trust in expertise intersects with another trend that further devalues foreign policy expertise: the rise in political polarization. The evidence for this in the United States is incontrovertible. McCarty, Poole, and Rosenthal (2006) have shown that over the past four decades the average Democratic member of Congress has moved leftwards, and the average Republican member of Congress has moved further rightwards. Other measures of partisan conflict show that the increase in political polarization goes beyond elected officials. For both Democrats and Republicans, party elites have become more ideologically extreme than the broader party membership (Bafumi and Herron 2010). Joe Biden campaigned in 2020 as a moderate but his campaign platform was much further to the left than Barack Obama.
Indeed, political elites are now more ideologically extreme than at any time in postwar history. As one Pew survey concludes, "divisions are greatest among those who are the most engaged and active in the political process" (Dimock et al. 2014, 6). Even the data produced by polarization skeptics show that political polarization among the mass public has been on the increase since the turn of this century (Garner and Palmer 2011; Hill and Tausanovitch 2015).

There is considerable evidence showing that partisans on one side increasingly dislike and distrust partisans on the other side. Party activists now report that they dislike the other party's activists more than they did a generation ago (Shaw 2012). Between 1994 and 2014, the percentage of Republicans and Democrats who believe that the other party is "a threat to the nation's well-being" has more than doubled (Dimock et al. 2014). Compared to 30 years ago, they also believe that the other party's members are less intelligent. One recent experimental study concluded that Americans discriminated more based on political partisanship than on either race or gender (Iyengar and Westwood 2015).

As the Brexit debacle suggests, there has been an increase in political extremism across Europe as well. The Tories moved to the right to accommodate Brexit while Labor moved further to the left. Large European economies experienced a surge in nationalist populist parties: the National Front in France, Law and Justice in Poland, and AfD in Germany. Stagnating eurozone economies witnessed the rise of economically populist parties: Podemos in Spain, Syriza in Greece, and the Five-Star Movement in Italy.

The effect of polarization on the perception of foreign policy ideas in the United States has been considerable. It was often posited that foreign policy was the last preserve of bipartisanship, but Senate data show that by 2001, there was even more polarization on foreign affairs vote than domestic policy votes (Jeong and Quirk 2019). As Kupchan and Trubowitz argue: "The polarization of the United States has dealt a severe blow to the bipartisan compact between power and cooperation. Instead of adhering to the vital center, the country's elected officials, along with the public, are backing away from the liberal internationalist compact, supporting either US power or international cooperation, but rarely both" (2007, 9). Multiple analyses demonstrate that public and elite support for the liberal internationalist consensus has frayed badly (Busby and Monten 2008; Milner and Tingley 2011). Consistent with that conclusion, the bifurcation of American foreign policy is evident in public opinion polls. Across a wide array of foreign policy questions—climate change, counterterrorism, immigration, the Middle East, and the use of force—US public attitudes are polarized (Smeltz et al. 2015).

Polarization makes it difficult for foreign policy elites to affect grand strategy debates. Guisinger and Saunders (2017) ran survey experiments to see how the public responded to views from elites on an array of foreign policy questions. They found an expert consensus could alter public attitudes on issues where the public was not already polarized. When the public was already split along partisan lines, as with climate change, polarization rendered elite cues worse than useless. Expert opinions from out-of-party sources simply made respondents double down on their preexisting positions. Greater polarization imposes a tighter constraint on the ability of foreign policy experts to influence public attitudes.

Another problem with political polarization is that it makes it difficult for learning to take place (Schultz 2018). For grand strategies to improve, there has to be agreement on what failed and the lessons drawn from those failures (Brands and Edel 2019). This requires a consensus on the "stylized facts" (Hirschman 2015). The rise of political polarization means that not everyone will accept a common set of stylized facts even if there is a consensus among intellectuals. Some partisans will have a persistent incentive to craft arguments around facts not in evidence to support their foreign policy leader. As a result, in many areas of foreign policy there is no consensus about the stylized facts or common narratives that ordinarily frame a debate (Lepore 2019). For example, all available global public opinion data showed a significant deterioration in US soft power since the election of Donald Trump (A. Rose 2019). Nonetheless, when Americans were polled on this question, Republican respondents insisted that the US was more respected in the world because Trump was president.

Polarization is also weakening reservoirs of expertise within the foreign policy and national security bureaucracy. Both outside observers (Lewis 2018; Farrow 2018) and inspector general reports (Office of the Inspector General 2019a, 2019b) confirm that Trump administration officials overtly sought to purge bureaucracies of career professionals thought to be politically suspect. In the first week of the Trump administration, the White House forced several senior career ambassadors out of their positions, a move Farrow (2018, ix) labeled the "Mahogany Row massacre." Trump's first State Department policy planning director permitted conservative media attacks to prune out career diplomats believed to be sympathetic to Obama-era policies (Office of the Inspector General 2019b). One diplomat was told that a Trump appointee would oppose any Foreign Service officers for leadership positions unless they passed the "Breitbart test," in reference to the online outlet that espouses populist nationalism (Zeya 2018). Multiple career ambassadors resigned; one of them went on the record to warn about the "complete and utter disdain for our expertise" among Trump's political appointees (Cohen 2017). This was confirmed in January 2019, during which a senior Trump official penned an anonymous op-ed praising the extended government shutdown because it allowed political appointees to "weed out the saboteurs" (Drezner 2019a, 728). These attacks eroded the influence of career foreign policy experts across the bureaucracy. At the State Department, for example, departures from the Foreign Service increased, entry applications plummeted, and morale across the department fell (Stephenson 2017; Farrow 2018; Drezner 2019a).

The Enervation of Legislatures

The final trend that weakens the foreign policy establishment is the degrading of checks and balances on the executive branch's management of foreign policy. This phenomenon is evident in parliamentary democracies but is most visible in the United States. The US Constitution gives the legislative branch significant foreign policy powers, including the ability to declare war, set tariffs, and ratify treaties. Over time, however, the president has accrued unchecked operational authority over foreign policy (Schlesinger 1973; Rudalevige 2005; Drezner 2020). Azari (2019) points out that "the structure of the government puts the president in a position to both make decisions and articulate them in a way that Congress rarely can.... The government structure created by the Constitution allows the president a great deal of power and flexibility."

The other branches of government have also voluntarily ceded some of their authority. This has been most evident in foreign relations. Congress has not formally declared war since 1942, but that has not stopped the president from the use of force. Presidents have relied on the 2001 Authorization for Use of Military Force passed in the wake of the September 11th attacks to justify the use of force in Somalia, Syria, and Yemen. The vast system of alliances has further empowered the president to deploy military forces without consulting Congress (Rapp-Hopper and Waxman 2019). Congress has demonstrated little appetite to claw back those powers (Goldgeier and Saunders 2018). After passing the Smoot-Hawley Tariff Act in 1930, Congress decided it could not responsibly execute its constitutional responsibilities on trade. Over the ensuing decades, it delegated many of those powers to the president, marking the beginning of a sustained decline in congressional power.

On questions of oversight, congressional power has eroded badly. The number of hearings on questions of foreign policy has declined precipitously (Fowler 2015). Members of Congress simply lack the electoral incentive to devote time and energy into national security and foreign policy concerns (Milner and Tingley 2015). After Newt Gingrich's Contract with America, Congress handicapped itself further by reducing its own staff and resources. This has weakened its ability to rely on expertise independent of the executive branch. Again and again, Congress has eschewed responsibility and delegated authority to the president. Political polarization has further debilitated Congress, encouraging the expansion of presidential powers in response (Mann and Ornstein 2012; Schultz 2018).

The lack of congressional participation and oversight complicates the ability of foreign policy elites to influence grand strategies in multiple ways. The most obvious effect is to weaken one pathway of causal influence. When Congress holds hearings on foreign policy questions, they rely on expert witnesses from beyond the government. Committee hearings afford foreign policy experts an opportunity to weigh in publicly on an administration's foreign policy initiatives. Furthermore, if the executive branch anticipates such hearings, they have an incentive to "work the refs" and consult with experts in order to persuade them of the wisdom of their policy choices. If, however, Congress holds fewer hearings and casts fewer foreign policy votes, then the demand for expert commentary declines. Similarly, executive branch policymakers feel less of a need to preemptively seek out expert opinion.

The more significant effect is that successive presidents will be able to reverse significant portions of their predecessors' foreign policy initiatives. The absence of congressional buy-in means that presidents will execute more and more foreign policies through executive action alone. By definition, presidents can countermand or abrogate preexisting executive agreements. Polarization has eroded the notion that politicians need to govern from the center (Utych 2020). Presidents who alternate from the extremes of the American political spectrum will have an incentive to reverse their predecessors' policies. Grand strategy could represent a generalization of the "Mexico City" policy, in which Republican and Democratic presidents flip-flop rules governing global family planning depending on who controls the executive branch (Cincotta and Crane 2001). The combination of worn-down guardrails and presidents emerging from the ends of the political spectrum will whipsaw US foreign policy between ultra-conservative and ultra-liberal approaches. In such a political climate, the marketplace of ideas ceases to matter and sustainable grand strategy becomes impossible.

Conclusion

This chapter has argued that the three trends have debilitated the public sphere's ability to stress-test possible grand strategies. The erosion of trust in authority and expertise has weakened the ability of the foreign policy community to regulate the marketplace of ideas. The increase of political polarization has impaired the ability of experts to influence partisan elites and mass publics about matters of foreign policy. The growth of executive authority has removed an additional channel through which experts can influence grand strategies. Parliamentary systems of government might be partially immune from the last trend. The data, however, strongly suggests that pessimism and polarization affect democracies across the globe (Drezner 2017). These problems are hardly unique to the United States.

Can these trends reverse themselves? That possibility cannot be ruled out. There are nascent signs that legislatures are trying to recover some of their influence over foreign policy decisions. Progressive and conservative foreign policy experts are attempting to debate their worldviews, with the possibility of forging a consensus around foreign policy means and ends (Hurlburt 2019; Goldgeier 2019). Public opinion polling during the Trump era shows a surprisingly strong rejection of the foreign policy of populist nationalism (Smeltz et al. 2018). It is possible that the foreign policy missteps of the Trump administration trigger a renewed appreciation for foreign policy expertise. Mounting external threats could help forge an ideational consensus within the advanced industrialized democracies akin to containment.

There are also reasons for skepticism, however. The GOP base is far more enthusiastic about Trump's "America First" grand strategy, making it difficult for Republicans to pivot away from it. Because the parties are so closely matched in Congress, persistent foreign policy polarization in the legislative branch is likely (Jeong and Quirk 2019). Public opinion is unlikely to be a serious constraint on policymakers, because the public remains largely uninterested and unengaged on debates about grand strategy and international relations. As Halpin et al. (2019) found during their focus group research, "When asked what the phrase 'maintaining the liberal international order' indicated to them, all but one of the participants in our focus group drew a blank." Not even external threats will necessarily forge a consensus among the mass public (Myrick 2021). Without influential experts, engaged publics, and functional legislatures, grand strategy will remain the preserve of the executive. Outside expertise will matter less and less.

This is an extremely problematic political environment for the crafting of a viable grand strategy, particularly for the United States in an era of great power competition. The difference between the post–Cold War era and current moment is that in the prior era, the United States could overwhelm threats with superior power. Great power competition, however, requires a long-term strategy more akin to containment, restraint, or primacy. Brands notes, "The United States seems off-balance vis-à-vis its rivals because it has lost its familiarity with the art of long-term competition …. [it] represents the graduate level of strategy" (2019, 31). Because of the shifts discussed in this chapter, however, each president's grand strategy will only endure from four to eight years, and then be replaced by one from the opposite side of the political spectrum. In this environment, the contributions of foreign policy elites will be ephemeral. The very concept of a consistent, durable grand strategy will not be sustainable. The marketplace of foreign policy ideas will cease to matter.[1]

Note

1. Draft versions of this chapter were presented at Duke University and the US Military Academy. I am grateful to Thierry Balzacq, Barbara Bunting, Peter Feaver, Ron Krebs, and Kerney Perlik for their thoughtful feedback.

References

Anderson, Perry. 2015. *American Foreign Policy and Its Thinkers*. London: Verso.

Anton, Michael. 2019. "The Trump Doctrine." *Foreign Policy*, April 20, 2019. https://foreignpolicy.com/2019/04/20/the-trump-doctrine-big-think-america-first-nationalism/

Azari, Julia. 2019. "The Constitution Doesn't Say Enough about Limiting Executive Power." *Vox*, April 11, 2019. https://www.vox.com/mischiefs-of-faction/2019/4/11/18306412/constitution-executive-power-limits

Bafumi, Joseph, and Michael C. Herron. 2010. "Leapfrog Representation and Extremism: A Study of American Voters and their Members in Congress." *American Political Science Review* 104 (3): 519–542.

Brands, Hal. 2019. "The Lost Art of Long-Term Competition." *The Washington Quarterly* 41 (4): 31–51.

Brands, Hal, and Charles Edel. 2019. *The Lessons of Tragedy: Statecraft and World Order*. New Haven: Yale University Press.

Brown, Michael, Sean Lynn-Jones, and Steven Miller, eds. 1996. *Debating the Democratic Peace*. Cambridge: MIT Press.

Buck, Tobias. 2016. "Middle England Drives Brexit Revolution." *Financial Times*, June 15, 2016.

Busby, Joshua, and Jonathan Monten. 2008. "Without Heirs? Assessing the Decline of Establishment Internationalism in US Foreign Policy." *Perspectives on Politics* 6 (3): 451–472.

Byman, Daniel, and Matthew Kroenig. 2016. "Reaching Beyond the Ivory Tower: A How To Manual." *Security Studies* 25 (2): 289–319.

Caplan, Bryan et al. 2013. "Systemically Biased Beliefs about Political Influence." *PS: Political Science and Politics* 46 (4): 760–767.

Cincotta, Richard, and Barbara Crane. 2001. "The Mexico City Policy and U.S. Family Planning Assistance." *Science* 294 (5542): 525–526.

Cohen, Roger. 2017. "The Desperation of Our Diplomats." *New York Times*, July 28, 2017.

Colville, Robert. 2016. "Britain's Truthiness Moment." *Foreign Policy*, June 9, 2017.

Cowhey, Peter. 1993. "Domestic Institutions and the Credibility of International Commitments: Japan and the United States." *International Organization* 47 (2): 299–326.

Dimock, Michael et al. 2014. "Political Polarization in the American Public." Pew Research Center. http://www.people-press.org/2014/06/12/political-polarization-in-the-american-public

Drezner, Daniel W., ed. 2009. *Avoiding Trivia: The Role of Strategic Planning in American Foreign Policy*. Washington: Brookings Institution Press

Drezner, Daniel W. 2017. *The Ideas Industry: How Pessimists, Partisans, and Plutocrats are Transforming the Marketplace of Ideas*. New York: Oxford University Press.

Drezner, Daniel W. 2019a. "Present at the Destruction: Donald Trump and the Foreign Policy Bureaucracy." *Journal of Politics* 81 (2): 723–730.

Drezner, Daniel W. 2019b. "This Time is Different." *Foreign Affairs* 98 (3): 10–17.

Drezner, Daniel W. 2019c. "Economic Statecraft in the Age of Trump." *The Washington Quarterly* 42 (3): 7–24.

Drezner, Daniel W. 2020. "Immature Leadership: Donald Trump and the American Presidency." *International Affairs* 96 (2): 383–400.

Edelman. 2015. Trust Barometer. https://www.edelman.com/trust/2015-trust-barometer.

Farrow, Ronan. 2018. *War on Peace: The End of Diplomacy and the Decline of American Influence*. New York: W.W. Norton.

Foa, Roberto Stefan, and Yascha Mounk. 2016. "The Democratic Disconnect." *Journal of Democracy* 27 (3): 5–17.

Fowler, Linda. 2015. *Watchdogs on the Hill: The Decline of Congressional Oversight of U.S. Foreign Relations*. Princeton: Princeton University Press.

Friedman, Benjamin, and Justin Logan. 2016. "Why Washington Doesn't Debate Grand Strategy." *Strategic Studies Quarterly* 10 (4): 14–45.

Fukuyama, Francis. 1989. "The End of History?" *The National Interest* 16: 3–18.

Gaddis, John Lewis. 2011. *George F. Kennan: An American Life*. New York: Penguin.

Garner, Andrew, and Harvey Palmer. 2011. "Polarization and Issue Consistency over Time." *Political Behavior* 33 (2): 225–246.

Gelb, Leslie. 2009. "Mission Unaccomplished." *Democracy: A Journal of Ideas* (13): 10–24.

Goldgeier, James. 2019. "Is There a New Foreign Policy Consensus Forming?" *War on the Rocks*, February 1, 2019. https://warontherocks.com/2019/02/assessing-the-texas-national-security-reviews-progressive-and-conservative-foreign-policy-roundtables-is-there-a-new-consensus-forming/

Goldgeier, James, and Elizabeth Saunders. 2018. "The Unconstrained Presidency." *Foreign Affairs*, August 13, 2018. https://www.foreignaffairs.com/articles/2018-08-13/unconstrained-presidency

Guisinger, Alexandera, and Elizabeth Saunders. 2017. "Mapping the Boundaries of Elite Cues: How Elites Shape Mass Opinion across International Issues." *International Studies Quarterly* 61 (2): 425–441.

Haas, Peter. 1992. "Banning Chlorofluorocarbons: Epistemic Community Efforts to Protect Stratospheric Ozone." *International Organization* 46 (1): 187–224.

Haass, Richard. 2019. "How a World Order Ends." *Foreign Affairs* 98 (1): 22–30.

Halpin, John et al. 2019. "America Adrift." Center for American Progress, May. https://www.americanprogress.org/issues/security/reports/2019/05/05/469218/america-adrift/

Hayes, Christopher. 2012. *The Twilight of the Elites*. New York: Crown Books.

Herken, Gregg. 2014. *The Georgetown Set: Friends and Rivals in Cold War Washington*. New York: Knopf.

Hill, Seth, and Chris Tausanovitch. 2015. "A Disconnect in Representation? Comparison of Trends in Congressional and Public Polarization." *Journal of Politics* 77 (4): 1058–1075.

Hirschman, Daniel. 2015. "Stylized Facts in the Social Sciences." *Sociological Science* 3 (30): 604–626.

Huntington, Samuel. 1993a. "Why International Primacy Matters." *International Security* 17 (4): 68–83.

Huntington, Samuel. 1993b. "The Clash of Civilizations?" *Foreign Affairs* 72 (3): 22–49.

Hurlburt, Heather. 2019. "More Diplomacy, Less Intervention, but for What? Making Sense of the Grand Strategy Debate." *Lawfare*, June 7, 2019. https://www.lawfareblog.com/more-diplomacy-less-intervention-what-making-sense-grand-strategy-debate

Isaacson, Walter, and Evan Thomas. 1986. *The Wise Men*. New York: Simon and Schuster.

Iyengar, Shanto, and Sean Westwood. 2015. "Fear and Loathing across Party Lines: New Evidence on Group Polarization." *American Journal of Political Science* 59 (3): 690–707.

Jacobs, Lawrence, and Benjamin Page. 2005. "Who Influences U.S. Foreign Policy?" *American Political Science Review* 99 (1): 107–123.

Janis, Irving. 1982. *Groupthink: Psychological Studies of Policy Decisions and Fiascoes.* Boston: Houghton Mifflin.

Jeong, Gyung-Ho, and Paul Quirk. 2019. "Division at the Water's Edge: The Polarization of Foreign Policy." *American Politics Research* 47 (1): 58–87.

Jervis, Robert. 1993. "International Primacy: is the Game Worth the Candle?" *International Security* 17 (4): 52–67.

Kaufmann, Chaim. 2004. "Threat Inflation and the Failure of the Marketplace of Ideas." *International Security* 29 (1): 5–48.

Kennan, George. 1947. "The Sources of Soviet Conduct." *Foreign Affairs* 25 (4): 566–582.

Krauthammer, Charles. 1990/91. "The Unipolar Moment." *Foreign Affairs* 70 (1): 23–33.

Kupchan, Charles, and Peter Trubowitz. 2007. "Dead Center: The Demise of Liberal Internationalism in the United States." *International Security* 32 (2): 7–44.

Lepore, Jill. 2019. "A New Americanism: Why a Nation Needs a National Story." *Foreign Affairs* 98 (2): 10–19.

Lewis, Michael. 2018. *The Fifth Risk.* New York: Norton.

Lippmann, Walter. 1947. *The Cold War.* New York: Harper.

Mann, Thomas, and Norman Ornstein. 2012. *It's Even Worse than it Looks.* New York: Basic Books.

McCarty, Nolan, Keith Poole, and Howard Rosenthal. 2006. *Polarized America: The Dance of Ideology and Unequal Riches.* Cambridge, Mass: MIT Press.

Mead, Walter Russell. 2002. *Special Providence.* New York: Routledge.

Mearsheimer, John. 1990. "Back to the Future: Instability in Europe After the Cold War." *International Security* 15 (1): 5–56.

Milner, Helen, and Dustin Tingley. 2011. "Who Supports Global Economic Engagement? The Sources of Preferences in American Foreign Economic Policy." *International Organization* 65 (1): 37–68.

Milner, Helen, and Dustin Tingley. 2015. *Sailing the Water's Edge: The Domestic Politics of American Foreign Policy.* Princeton: Princeton University Press.

Miscamble, Wilson. 1992. *George F. Kennan and the Making of American Foreign Policy, 1947–1950.* Princeton: Princeton University Press.

Myrick, Rachel. 2021. "Do External Threats Unite or Divide?" Security Crises, Rivalries, and Polarization in American Foreign Policy." International Organization, 1-38. doi:10.1017/S0020818321000175.

Nichols, Tom. 2017. *The Death of Expertise.* New York: Oxford University Press.

Nye, Joseph. 1990. *Bound to Lead.* New York: Basic Books.

Office of the Inspector General, U.S. State Department. 2019a. "Review of Allegations of Politicized and Other Improper Personnel Practices in the Bureau of International Organization Affairs." ESP-19-05, August.

Office of the Inspector General, U.S. State Department. 2019b. "Review of Allegations of Politicized and Other Improper Personnel Practices Involving the Office of the Secretary." ESP-20-01, November.

Organization for Economic Cooperation and Development. 2013. *Government at a Glance.* Paris: OECD.

Page, Benjamin, with Marshall Bouton. 2006. *The Foreign Policy Disconnect.* Chicago: University of Chicago Press.

Pew Research Center. 2019. "Public Trust in Government: 1958–2019." April 11, 2019. https://www.people-press.org/2019/04/11/public-trust-in-government-1958-2019/

Pompeo, Mike. 2018. "Restoring the Role of the Nation-State in the Liberal International Order." December 4, 2018. https://www.state.gov/secretary/remarks/2018/12/287770.htm

Porter, Patrick. 2018. "Why America's Grand Strategy Has Not Changed." *International Security* 42 (04): 9–46.

Posen, Barry. 2018. "The Rise of Illiberal Hegemony." *Foreign Affairs* 97 (2): 20–27.

Rapp-Hopper, Mira, and Matthew Waxman. 2019. "Presidential Alliance Powers." *The Washington Quarterly* 42 (2): 67–83.

Ricci, Gabriel. 2015. "The Politicization of Science and the Use and Abuse of Technology." *International Journal of Technoethics* 6 (2): 60–73.

Rose, Andrew. 2019. "Agent Orange: Trump, Soft Power, and Exports." NBER Working Paper No. 25439.

Rose, Gideon. 2019. "The Fourth Founding." *Foreign Affairs* 98 (1): 10–21.

Ross, Lisa, and Stephanie Kehoe. 2018. "America in Crisis." *Edelman*, January 21, 2018. https://www.edelman.com/post/america-in-crisis

Rudalevige, Andrew. 2005. *The New Imperial Presidency*. Ann Arbor: University of Michigan Press.

Schlesinger, Arthur. 1973. *The Imperial Presidency*. Boston: Houghton Mifflin.

Schultz, Kenneth. 2018. "Perils of Polarization for U.S. Foreign Policy." *The Washington Quarterly* 40 (4): 7–28.

Shaw, Daron. 2012. "If Everyone Votes Their Party, Why Do Presidential Election Outcomes Vary So Much?" *The Forum* 10 (October).

Silver, Nate. 2012. *The Signal and the Noise*. New York: Penguin.

Smeltz, Dina. 2018. *America Engaged: American Public Opinion and U.S. Foreign Policy*. Chicago: Chicago Council on Global Affairs.

Smeltz, Dina et al. 2015. *America Divided: Political Partisanship and US Foreign Policy*. Chicago: Chicago Council on Global Affairs.

Smith, Tom, and Jaesok Son. 2013. "Trends in Public Attitudes about Confidence in Institutions." National Opinion Research Center. May. http://www.norc.org/PDFs/GSS%20Reports/Trends%20in%20Confidence%20Institutions_Final.pdf

Snyder, Jack. 1991. *Myths of Empire*. Ithaca: Cornell University Press.

Stephenson, Barbara. 2017. "Time to Ask Why." *Foreign Service Journal* (December): 7.

Teles, Steven, Heather Hurlburt, and Mark Schmitt. 2014. "Philanthropy in a Time of Polarization." *Stanford Social Innovation Review* 12 (3): 44–49.

Trump, Donald J. 2017a. Inaugural Address. January 20. https://www.whitehouse.gov/briefings-statements/the-inaugural-address/

Trump, Donald J. 2017b. *National Security Strategy of the United States of America*. Washington: Executive Office of the President.

Utych, Stephen. 2020. "Man Bites Blue Dog: Are Moderates Really More Electable than Ideologues?" *Journal of Politics* 82 (1): 392–396.

Woodward, Bob. 2018. *Fear: Trump in the White House*. New York: Simon & Schuster.

Zeya, Ursa. 2018. "Trump is Making American Diplomacy White Again." *Politico*, September 17, 2018. https://www.politico.com/magazine/story/2018/09/17/america-is-making-diplomacy-white-and-male-again-219977

CHAPTER 41

PLURALISM, POPULISM, AND THE IMPOSSIBILITY OF GRAND STRATEGY

RONALD R. KREBS

The mainstreaming of right-wing populism, across the West, is arguably the biggest political story of the twenty-first century.[1] Many Americans, both those exhilarated by Donald J. Trump's election and those deeply depressed by it, could be forgiven for believing that populism suddenly burst on the political scene in 2016. In reality, its rise over the century's first two decades was slow, gradual, and uneven, in the United States and throughout the West. But the story of populism is older still, because it is intertwined with the story of multiculturalism. The two movements are locked in a tight, uncomfortable embrace, each dancing intensely in reaction and resistance to the other. Yet their gyrations seem only to deepen the awkward embrace. Neither pluralism nor populism seems destined to fade away in the foreseeable future.[2]

Because multiculturalism and populism constitute a double helix, one cannot speak about what populism alone means for grand strategy. This essay therefore explores both in turn. It argues that, paradoxically, even though right-wing populism emerged in the West partly in reaction to multiculturalism, the two movements' effects on grand strategy have been surprisingly similar: both have made formulating and executing grand strategy much more difficult. The impediments to designing a coherent grand strategy and pursuing it consistently have always been considerable. Together, multiculturalism and populism have conspired to make those obstacles all but insurmountable. Grand strategy has become, in a word, impossible.

Since neither multiculturalism nor populism seems likely to depart the political scene anytime soon, this essay has at least two implications. First, it suggests that, while scholars may enjoy intellectual sparring over contending grand strategies, these debates are—pardon the expression—academic. Vigorously debating grand strategic alternatives may well be ingrained in the professional identities of scholars, think tankers, and pundits, and it may also serve their careerist interests. But the exercise is arguably a counterproductive distraction from less abstract, more fine-grained, and ultimately more important debates over particular policies. Second, the rationale for grand strategy presumes the virtues of a top-down policymaking process: if the hierarchy's apex issues the grand strategy, those further down the chain take their cue from it and devise their own substrategies based upon it, and their underlings in turn draw on assemblages of tactics to implement these strategic designs; the result is a coherent, consistent, and integrated set of policies across policy domains. However, if grand strategy is impossible—as this essay argues—then perhaps a more bottom-up policymaking process is more apposite.

This essay expressly takes a narrative approach, complementing the conceptual apparatuses of other essays in this section of the Handbook. After justifying and explaining this essay's narrative approach to grand strategy, it explores, through the lens of narrative and legitimation, the nature of multiculturalism and its implications for grand strategy. It then does the same for populism. The essay concludes with a normative turn: should we mourn or celebrate the demise of grand strategy? I call for burying grand strategy, not grieving its passing.

GRAND STRATEGY: A NARRATIVE APPROACH

Grand strategy is constituted by narrative.[3] As "a state's theory about how it can best 'cause' security for itself" (Posen 1984, 13), grand strategy requires strategists to define a national interest, identify threats and prioritize among them, and fashion appropriate policy responses. It therefore must rest on at least an implicit, and occasionally an explicit, narrative of national security that sets out the key *protagonists* of global politics and their attributes; the *relations* between self and other, including their respective *purposes*; the background security *scene*, including whether national and global security are divisible or seamless; and the protagonists' past and present *actions*. The resulting narrative of national security makes sense of, and orders, experience. It defines reality, weaving together past, present, and future into a cogent storyline. Some contend that security storytelling produces a policymaking environment in which emotion trumps reason. But a clear narrative of national security, by setting the foundation for debate, is in fact necessary for rational decision-making.

Debates over grand strategy are in fact often debates over narrative. Supporters of restraint, selective engagement, and deep engagement tally the costs and benefits of their preferred approaches differently because their contending stances embed different assumptions about global politics—as Robert Jervis insightfully observes in his essay for this Handbook (Jervis 2021). In other words, these grand strategies rest on different narratives of national security, especially divergent definitions of national purpose and depictions of the global scene. Advocates of restraint adopt a narrower typology of protagonists' motives. They also see global events as either fairly disconnected or as enmeshed in causal chains so complex and unpredictable that teasing them out is hopeless. With their richer conception of motives, and their greater appreciation for global interconnectedness, defenders of deep engagement charge restrainters with underestimating both the benefits of the current global order and the costs of US pullback and of the order's erosion. Rooted in different narratives, the proponents of competing strategies often talk past each other. The facts they invoke seem relevant only from within the terms of their own narrative.

Narrative matters not only to the formulation of grand strategy, but to its execution and success. Grand strategy cannot succeed unless it can endure, and it cannot endure if it remains confined to the halls of power. It requires leaders to rally broad, stable coalitions. Legitimation—the articulation before key audiences of publicly acceptable reasons for action and policy—is an essential first step toward that end. In both domestic and foreign affairs, it is necessary whenever publics of whatever scope must be mobilized and wherever there is a reasonable chance that the glare of public attention will turn (Goddard and Krebs 2015). Those who do not bother to legitimate their claims, or whose claims to legitimacy fail to pass over the bar, have few public advocates, and their few advocates are ignored or disdained. As the tendon binding concrete policies to the bones of underlying narratives, legitimation reflects the fact that narrative both enables and constrains. Narratives of national security constitute the boundaries of legitimation and therefore channel political contest, privileging particular courses of action and impeding the legitimation of others. Strategy that cannot be legitimated cannot lay claim to substantial national resources and lacks the resilience to weather setbacks. It tempts leaders to embrace covert action, which need not be legitimated, and to court controversy if their secrets come to light.

A narrative approach to grand strategy therefore highlights distinctive dynamics and processes. When strategies that are appealing to the external analyst receive little consideration in the halls of power, a narrative perspective questions the instinct to blame parochial interests for having hijacked policy and wonders rather how the menu of policy options was composed. When leaders shy away from mobilizing the public and its resources, a narrative approach does not immediately charge them with cowardice, but reflects instead on the impediments to legitimation. When strategy fails to endure, a narrative approach suggests looking to the mismatch between legitimation strategy and its narrative foundations. The sections that follow explore how, through the lenses of narrative and legitimation, two of the defining trends of our time—multiculturalism and reactionary populism—complicate the grand strategy enterprise.

The Challenge of Multiculturalism

Since the waning days of the Vietnam War, our world has been marked by growing acceptance of multiculturalism. By multiculturalism, I do not mean the reality of cultural diversity, though Western polities have certainly become more linguistically and communally diverse in recent decades.[4] Nor do I mean a designated set of policies designed to signal greater, and ideally equal, respect for the practices and identities of a nation's ethnic and religious minorities.[5] Rather, by multiculturalism I refer to these policies' underlying philosophy. As articulated by theorists like William Connolly and Charles Taylor, multiculturalism entails a profound shift away from shared societal foundations toward the recognition of diversity all the way down. This stance takes issue with the traditional claim that society should be, and is, rooted in some common identity and holds instead that the search for such fundamentals is repressive. It insists that society should be marked by contentious conversation at all levels—or, as Connolly puts it in scholarly argot, "the irreducible character of ontopolitical contestation" (Connolly 2008c, 60). This is what Taylor calls "the politics of recognition," or what Connolly terms "deep pluralism" (Taylor 1994; Connolly 1995, 2008a). The philosophy of multiculturalism is hardly uncontroversial. But it has also unquestionably gone mainstream, and it makes grand strategy—always challenging—even more so.

The Rise of Multiculturalism in the West

Societies can respond to the reality of diversity in multiple ways. The sheer fact of diversity is deeply threatening to any conception of society as homogeneous and rooted in kinship—as implied by such classic concepts as *gemeinschaft* and "organic solidarity." Diversity is compatible with civic forms of nationalism, which presume that the nation's members remain, in Benedict Anderson's famous phrase, an "imagined community" unified around a common set of political ideals and institutions (Anderson 1991). However, civic nationalists have often been quite comfortable with repressing cultural diversity in the name of national unity (Schildkraut 2011, ch. 4). Progressives like Theodore Roosevelt were good civic nationalists, but also worried that the hordes of non-Anglo-Saxons then landing on the nation's shores would not readily accept American values and join the civitas. They would need a firmer guiding hand to become "true-blue Americans." Thus, Roosevelt and others dreamed of universal military training to purge the new arrivals of their old commitments and to impart the American creed (Kennedy 1980, 30–44).

Multiculturalism represents a very different response to diversity. Unlike civic republicanism, it does not demand that prospective members of the political community earn that status by contributing to the common good. Unlike liberalism, it does not merely abide the expression of alternative viewpoints. Multiculturalism rather is rooted in the premise that all members of a society are entitled to "recognition" not only of their "unique identity ... their distinctness from everyone else," but of "the equal value of their [culture's] worth." Recognition in this sense, writes Taylor, is "not just a courtesy we owe people," but "a vital human need." Misrecognition—when people are exposed to "a confining or demeaning or contemptible picture of themselves"—constitutes "a form of oppression" because it "imprison[s] someone in a false, distorted, and reduced mode of being" (Taylor 1994, 38, 64, 26, 25). By Taylor's account, a democracy sensitive to "difference" and respectful of "recognition" must honor wildly divergent conceptions of the good life. By definition, such a democratic polity cannot rest on any unified identity, any integrated and settled "we." It must, in Connolly's formulation, be grounded in "agonistic respect ... between diverse constituencies" to facilitate the multiple, overlapping networks or "lines of connection through which governing assemblages can be constructed from a variety of intersecting constituencies" (Connolly 2008c, 44). A multicultural society, in this philosophical sense, is not, and should not be, rooted in any shared foundations. It is, therefore, at odds with any approach asserting that the polity be organized around a collective identity—even one that is a social construct and therefore changeable and contingent.

Multiculturalism emerges from an awareness that traditional liberalism's conception of pluralism is thin. The "liberalism of rights" is tolerant of diverse views, lifestyles, and practices only, according to Connolly, "within settled contexts of conflict and collective action"—that is, within certain designated bounds (Connolly 2008c, 38). It asserts that its values are universally held, but, Stuart Hall charges, "liberalism is not the 'culture that is beyond cultures' but the culture that won: that particularism which successfully universalized and hegemonized itself across the globe" (Hall 2000, 228; see similarly Taylor 1994, 43). Liberalism's pretension to universalism, critics insist, is the problem. It denies the value, and even the possibility, of alternative modes of reasoning, bases for politics, and thus "subjectivities." Despite liberalism's promise of tolerance, multiculturalists maintain, it is in fact "inhospitable to [cultural] difference"; because its universalism calls for "uniform application of the rules defining these rights," and its individualism is "suspicious of collective goals," it cannot accommodate cultural practices that run afoul of sacrosanct individual rights (Taylor 1994, 60–61). The "liberalism of rights" is laced with "strains of fundamentalism," to which its proponents are deaf (Connolly 2008b, 76). In contrast, multiculturalism abjures fundamentals and celebrates the most profound of differences.

Multiculturalism celebrates the multiplicity of identities, proclaiming their distinctiveness in the public sphere. Traditional liberalism sees identity as a private matter. It commands broad-mindedness with regard to others' expressions of opinion, but it stops short of recognizing the unique identities from which those opinions stem. Pluralism-as-tolerance is hardly to be sniffed at, for it is fragile and all too rare, across the world and across history. But, respecting only others' right to speak, it treats political views as disembodied. Multiculturalism, in contrast, asserts that politics and identity are inseparable, that ideas cannot be divorced from the personas of those advancing them, and that identity cannot be consigned to the private realm alone. Individuals and groups engaging in politics bring identities and narratives into the public sphere that need to be recognized and accorded legitimacy (Kymlicka 1995; Taylor 1994). Whereas liberalism acknowledges only a single, uniform public identity—of the rights-bearing citizen—the multicultural public sphere is awash in identities, as many as there are individuals and groups. A polity with countless identities jostling in the public sphere is not a polity that can pretend to share—or even aspire to have—a common collective identity.

Traditional liberalism was the dominant philosophy in the postwar West for two decades. But, as the 1960s came to a close, multiculturalism began to make significant headway. In the United States, the assimilative model of the "melting pot" gave way to the varied "salad," in which residents of democratic society retain their unique characters and in which ethnic identity commitments endure. Rather than sublimate prior identity commitments in favor of the nation, Americans were in the 1970s and 1980s invited to revel in their non-national identities. Weeks and months celebrating ethnic and racial heritage and history started to acquire national recognition in the United States and have since spread throughout Anglo nations. Ethnic studies programs and departments gradually took hold at colleges and universities. Multiculturalism penetrated mass opinion: most Americans, even whites, came to welcome "soft" multicultural policies accommodating cultural and linguistic diversity (Citrin and Sears 2014). Policies associated with multiculturalism became even more the norm in Europe (Koopmans 2013, 151–157). Anecdotally, one recent manifestation of multiculturalism is the now-ubiquitous expression "speak your truth." It invites speakers to share not just their opinions and considered views, but rather their "truth," as a manifestation of their selves. It valorizes speakers' expressions of their personal identity (*your* truth) in public.

Multiculturalism did not replace rights-based liberalism as the new consensus,[6] but rather it divided Western polities. Particularly in the United States, moreover, it sparked a conservative backlash that has not abated. In the late 1980s, conservative elites, fearing that the nation's foundation was eroding, sought to shore it up by defining a cultural core—"cultural literacy"—that "every American should know" (Hirsch Jr. 1988). Onetime liberals, sensing that America was coming apart at the seams, blamed new immigrants: whereas older generations had bought into the American creed, they alleged, more recent immigrants had not (Schlesinger Jr. 1992; Huntington 2005). Cultural conservatives waged war against bilingual education, rolling back federal support for native-language instruction. A nationwide campaign, which began in California in 1986, to declare English states' official language, has been successful to date in over half of US states.

The rise of multiculturalism left polities in the West without a shared national narrative. Many on the left came to view the very concept as inherently oppressive—to the point that, as Jill Lepore has observed with respect to the United States, historians stopped writing the *nation's* history decades ago (Lepore 2019). Liberal-left politicians in the United States became uncomfortable with the rhetoric of nationalism, vacillating over American exceptionalism. Meanwhile, conservatives across the West leaned into nationalism hard, while defining the nation in exclusionary ways. By the first decade of this century, there was widespread concern on both sides of the Atlantic that multicultural policies had facilitated communal self-segregation (Barrett 2013; Barry 2001; Cantle 2012; Gitlin 1995; Pickus 2005). Numerous European leaders, charging that multiculturalism had "failed," called for greater emphasis on civic integration, although they did not significantly scale back most multicultural policies (Kymlicka 2012).[7] In conclusion, growing ethnic, religious, and cultural diversity in the West did not erode national narratives. Multiculturalism—one of several possible strategies for managing this growing diversity—did.

Implications for Grand Strategy

The emergence of multiculturalism as a competing normative basis for social order presents real challenges to grand strategy.[8] To be clear, multiculturalism—even were it to become an unquestioned social norm—does not impede the *articulation* of grand strategy: pundits, scholars, and policymakers would still be free to formulate a vision of the world and its challenges, set out an account of the nation's interests, and devise a theory of victory that links national means to ends. However, multiculturalism complicates the *mobilization* of societal resources, renders the *implementation* of a consistent strategy, across policy domains, more difficult, and makes grand strategy less *sustainable* over time. Grand strategy is supposedly attractive because it imparts coherence to national policy and promises durability amidst distraction and turmoil. Multiculturalism prizes and promotes neither.

Grand strategy, I argued earlier, rests on a narrative of national security, and it is most enduring when that narrative is dominant. Under such circumstances, strategic debate is restricted to the terms of the dominant narrative. For instance, when the Terror narrative held sway in the United States, critics of the Iraq War did not challenge the underlying War on Terror, but rather launched their salvos from its terrain: the Iraq War, they contended, was a distraction from the War on Terror, which, properly conceived, would focus US energies on al Qaeda in Afghanistan and Pakistan (Krebs 2015, 269–275). Legitimating policy is a fairly straightforward, if necessarily confined, matter when narratives are dominant.

However, in societies that lack any shared foundations—that is, marked by multiculturalism—wildly divergent narratives, implying wildly divergent grand strategies, legitimately circulate. Under multiculturalism, the scope of legitimate strategic debate is unusually wide, and the potential for radical strategic shifts is therefore great. By granting all views a rightful place on the stage, by silencing none for transgressing social boundaries, by proclaiming all to lie within the pale of legitimacy, multiculturalism is radically democratic. But radical democracy—whatever its virtues—impedes the effective legitimation of broad, integrative policies like grand strategy to wide swathes of the population. Legitimation is easier to the extent that people share rhetorical commonplaces. The fewer they share, the fewer degrees of freedom political actors have to craft strategies of legitimation that are resonant. Under multiculturalism, the *legitimation* of grand strategy is more likely to fall on deaf ears.

Multiculturalism thus also hinders the state's capacity to *mobilize* national resources. Publics that view state initiatives as legitimate respond more readily to its demands for resources (Lake 1992). Because state leaders' appeals under multiculturalism resonate with narrower publics, they can expect to have fewer resources at their disposal. In addition, the radical democracy of multiculturalism implies less deference to their grand strategic vision. With a broader range of participants and perspectives involved in security debate—that is, "securitizing actors" (Buzan, Wæver, and Wilde 1998)—state leaders' preferred grand strategy less swiftly or fully commands assent. With the legitimacy of its grand strategy in question, the state needs to muster political capital and expend resources beating back challengers and offering concessions, slowing the pace and limiting the extent of mobilization.

Multiculturalism also hampers the state's capacity to *implement* grand strategy consistently and *sustain* it over time. With a narrower supportive coalition mobilized in the service of grand strategy, leaders must mobilize others selectively on behalf of particular initiatives. But they can enlist these groups' support only unevenly, because different policies implicate different interests and necessitate different legitimation strategies and concrete bargains. As a result, multiculturalism undermines the coherence of policy across domains. The passage of time introduces a further complication, as interests and coalitions necessarily shift. No political deal is ever permanent of course; all eventually outlive their usefulness. But multiculturalism renders compacts especially short-lived. The sheer complexity of the underlying social relations in a world of multiculturalism implies a less stable, or sustainable, grand strategy.

Finally, multiculturalism subverts the *performance* of grand strategy and limits its productive effects. As Thierry Balzacq and Pablo Barnier-Khawam's essay in this Handbook emphasizes (Balzacq and Barnier-Khawam 2021), grand strategy is not just a substantive guide to policy: its formal pronouncement is also a performance that both presumes and hails into being a particular image of the nation—rational and disciplined, coherent and unified. Grand strategy rests on a vision of the nation at odds with the normative underpinnings of multiculturalism. It treasures, and aims to reinforce, the very foundations that multiculturalism derides as oppressive. The more a society inclines toward multiculturalism, the greater the obstacles grand strategy faces in producing the sort of nation that would find grand strategy appealing. With multiculturalism as the backdrop, the performance of grand strategy is at best clumsy and at worst jarring.

Since the 1970s, governments across the West—especially US administrations—have often been charged with lacking a grand strategy. Critics allege that they have designed a raft of inconsistent policies to confront problems in different domains and regions; that they have merely lurched from crisis to crisis. One explanation invokes geopolitical realities: as postcolonial states across the then Third World found their footing, the Cold War could no longer be the central axis of international politics, and numerous challenges clamored for attention in a world of growing complexity. But it is perhaps not accidental that these charges accelerated alongside the rise of multiculturalism and the erosion of formerly dominant narratives.[9] As multiculturalism made legitimating and implementing grand strategy more difficult, state leaders pursued narrower foreign policy initiatives. Maybe with good reason. Elsewhere, and in line with the essays in this Handbook by David Edelstein and Peter Dombrowski (Edelstein 2021; Dombrowski 2021), I have suggested that a more pragmatic foreign policy is more consonant with multiculturalism than is grand strategy (Krebs 2017; Krebs 2018, 268–269). Varied, and at times inconsistent, legitimation strategies are less likely to prompt allegations of hypocrisy, since pragmatism makes no claim to coherence. A pragmatic foreign policy facilitates mobilization, since it requires support only for individual policies. It makes managing the politics of national security easier, as leaders can then assemble a revolving cast of otherwise strange bedfellows and shell out more limited side payments. A pragmatic approach is better suited to our fractured age.

From Pluralism to Populism

Multiculturalism thus poses a direct challenge to grand strategy. But it poses an *indirect* challenge as well, through the right-wing, nationalist, populist backlash it has helped spark. The rise of such populism cannot be reduced merely to economic dislocation. It is rooted equally, if not more, in a cultural reaction against multiculturalism. Yet, ironically, the right-wing populist reaction does not moderate the pluralist challenge to grand strategy—just the opposite.

Populism vs. Pluralism

Populism is a notoriously slippery political movement. It is, in Cas Mudde's view, a "thin-centered ideology" and thus compatible with thicker ideologies hailing from either the left or the right (Mudde 2004, 544). Nevertheless, populism is not entirely empty of content. It is, as Kurt Weyland emphasizes, a distinctive political strategy (Weyland 2001), but, because all politics requires legitimation, it also advances substantive claims about the world.

At the heart of all populisms lies a particular political imaginary, reflected in two propositions. First, populism asserts the existence of a morally pure "people," set in contrast to some smaller group—always corrupt elites, sometimes communal minorities—that pretends to be part of "the people" but actually acts contrary to the authentic people's interests and constitutes an existential threat. Second, the populist leader claims that he alone knows the people's will, that he alone has the capacity to speak on their behalf. Populism entails a "claim to *exclusive* moral representation of the real or authentic people." It is therefore both anti-elitist and anti-pluralist in its orientation. It seeks to silence its critics and competitors by denying them a place among the people—the "real people" anyway—and by accusing them of disloyalty (paradoxically, since one cannot be disloyal to a people of which one is not a part). Populism rests on the fiction that "the people" possesses a single, unified will, which only the leader knows and to which only he can give voice (Mudde 2004; Müller 2016, 19–32).

From these two propositions follow the politics of populism, in which "a personalistic leader seeks or exercises government power based on direct, unmediated, uninstitutionalized support from large numbers of mostly unorganized followers" (Weyland 2001, 14). Despite its democratic legitimation, populism tilts authoritarian. In sweeping away corrupt elites and the institutions they inhabit, the populist leader weakens all forces of opposition. By asserting his direct, unmediated line to the people, the populist leader claims that he represents their will better than can any political process. Therefore, to criticize the leader is to criticize the people and to position oneself outside its boundaries. In a populist milieu, critics are transformed into opponents; the loyal opposition is, for the populist, an oxymoron. In the populist worldview, the tyranny of the majority is a virtue, not a vice. Some praise populism's democratic potential, as a "corrective" to rule by technocrats; they credit populists with creating a more inclusive and active democracy by mobilizing the disenfranchised (Mouffe 2005; Mudde and Rovira Kaltwasser 2012). But populism actually conceives of the people as politically passive, for it is the populist leader that knows and articulates their will—better than they can themselves (Canovan 1999; Müller 2016, 41–49; Rummens 2017; Urbinati 2019).

Accounts of populism's origins, many of them complementary, abound (Rovira Kaltwasser et al. 2017; Singer 2018; de la Torre 2019). Some attribute populism to voters' alienation, particularly as a consequence of modernization and globalization. Those left materially behind feel ignored and disempowered, and they are ripe for populist politics, which offers them meaning and pledges their empowerment. Others locate populism's origins in politicians' overt and covert corruption, including their management of the political agenda, that marginalizes popular concerns and that therefore animates populism's charges of elite conspiracy. Still others ascribe populism to the hollowing out of democracy, as legislatures cede control to technocrats, both national and supranational. Populism's appeal lies in its promise to "repoliticize" governance and return power to the national political arena.

These accounts all have some merit, but they are stronger as explanations of populism's anti-elitist leanings than of its antipathy to pluralism. They overlook, and cannot easily make sense of, populism's conception of "the people" as homogeneous, unified, and possessed of a singular will. Populism cannot be comprehended without taking its nationalism and authoritarianism seriously. I propose that contemporary right-wing populism, especially in the West, reflects a backlash against the anti-foundational politics of multiculturalism.[10] For good reason, multiculturalism, and its close cousin of "political correctness," are one of contemporary populism's bogeymen. Multiculturalism imagines "the people" as heterogeneous and fragmented; any concept of "the popular will" or "the national interest" becomes meaningless and mythical. Right-wing populism is its polar opposite, insisting on firm foundations for national politics and rooted in an exclusive vision of "the nation." Populist politicians thus lean heavily on the rhetoric of morality and loyalty, casting proponents of multiculturalism as beyond the pale of both national and ethical communities. They embrace a transgressive political style, purposely crossing the boundaries of civility to emphasize that they are voicing truths that "the people" cannot express because they have been bullied into silence by "political correctness." There is no reason to show respect, the populist trumpets, to those who would water down "our" nation, "our" values, "our" traditions—that is, to defenders of multiculturalism. The rise of multiculturalism helps explain why populism today takes its distinctive form.

Populism and Grand Strategy

The populist backlash against multiculturalism presses policymaking in directions distinctly inhospitable to grand strategy.

This is not because populist leaders are necessarily unstrategic thinkers. While Donald Trump is a populist who proudly governs from his gut, not every populist leader is a Trump. Some come to office with clear worldviews and seem to have the temperament to design a well-considered grand strategy. For every Trump or Nicolás Maduro of Venezuela, there is also a Benjamin Netanyahu of Israel or a Narendra Modi of India, who, regardless of what one thinks of the substance of their strategy, certainly seem to have one. Daniel Drezner has observed that, in the bestial metaphor made famous by Isaiah Berlin, populists tend to be "hedgehogs"—that is, thinkers who know one big and important thing (Drezner 2017, 32). Rooted in a well-drawn narrative of national security, and offering a theory linking national means to national ends, grand strategy is the terrain of the hedgehog. Foxes, who know many little things and who quickly adjust their beliefs to new data, are inclined more to pragmatism and experimentation. Only a hedgehog aspires to steer the ship of state on a more-or-less straight course through turbulent seas.

However, populism, as a political strategy, militates against grand strategy and complicates its implementation. In its impulse and ambitions, grand strategy seeks to bring rationality into the making of foreign and defense policy. Populist politicians, however, traffic heavily in emotional appeals. They mobilize the people in righteous anger against their enemies, both near and far (Weyland 2017, 50, 58–59). They highlight the indignity of insults, which, because the leader claims to be the embodiment of the nation, are not just personal. With heated rhetoric always in the air, emotional responses to the crisis du jour regularly threaten to overtake rational strategy. When populist politics hold sway, grand strategy also becomes less supple, as leaders cannot smoothly shift to conciliatory tactics in a climate of affront, offense, and retribution. Appealing to raw emotion is not something of course that only populists do; all political leaders sometimes rile up the masses. But only populists make such rhetoric their daily bread and butter, and only populists conduct a continuous campaign that keeps their supporters at all times at a fever pitch (Urbinati 2019, 121–122). Consequently, even when populist leaders might like to lower the temperature, they are especially subject to "blowback" that ties their hands. Populism turns grand strategy on its head.

Populist politics also complicate grand strategy by accentuating and hardening lines of internal division. Populism narrows the sphere of the "authentic" people both vertically and horizontally, to the detriment of grant strategy. Horizontally, it defines "the people" in ways that exclude those who fall on the other side of some cleavage—whether religion, ethnicity, national origin, class, or even political affiliation. At first glance, this move might seem beneficial to grand strategy. When "the people" is limited to members of a particular ethnicity or religion, the resulting narrower community shares a larger set of rhetorical commonplaces, making it easier to craft a resonant legitimation strategy. It also more likely trusts the same circle of "securitizing actors" who are well-positioned to persuade them of the strategy's wisdom. Mobilizing its resources would be a smoother, less conflictual process, and sustaining grand strategy across domains and over time would seemingly be easier too.

However, populism's horizontal narrowing has crosscutting effects that ironically parallel those of multiculturalism—albeit like a fun-house mirror. Asserting an exclusive definition of "the people" and throwing up insurmountable barriers to entry, populism ensures that, within the nation as a territorial and legal entity, there are no broadly shared foundations. As a result, populist politics sustain deep narrative contestation, which in turn makes populism's central claim—that there is some alien population living among "us" that does not share "our" values, identity, and story—self-fulfilling. Consequently, the state will have difficulty mobilizing the resources of the excluded, for better or worse limiting the ambitions of grand strategy. Grand strategy will also be hard to sustain over time: lines of internal cleavage are fluid, and future leaders can be expected to activate different definitions of "the people." The once-excluded must always be nervous about finding themselves in the future on the outside. Whatever support they offer to grand strategy is necessarily hedged and reluctant. Populism is polarizing by design, and polarization is no friend of durable grand strategy.

Populism's vertical narrowing of "the people" has similar effects. Vertically, populism contrasts the morally pure people whose voices have for too long been silenced with the corrupt elites who have long pretended to speak in the people's name and have instead served their own parochial interests. Populism therefore undermines respect for expertise and authority. Lodging its faith in the people's common sense, it seems to call for a more inclusive, freewheeling, and democratic national conversation. Like multiculturalism, it multiplies the number of "authorized speakers" on matters of national security. This fragmentation of authority impedes any particular narrative of national security from rising to dominance, because, I have argued elsewhere, that process hinges on authoritative storytelling (Krebs 2015). When authority crumbles—by design, in the case of populism, or by accident, when deception and corruption come to light—narrative contestation becomes the norm, and *sustainable* grand strategy is a victim.

Finally, populist politics renders *durable* grand strategy impossible. It concentrates authority in the charismatic leader. It disempowers foreign policy bureaucrats, both diplomats and civilian defense experts, and it erodes governing institutions. Populist politics removes the brakes, and policy in a populist regime is thus especially a reflection of the leader—of his ideological commitments or his whims (Destradi and Plagemann 2019). If the populist leader does succeed in pursuing something akin to grand strategy, it will not outlive his rule. Whoever next takes power will confront few impediments to imposing his will. Though he does not tightly link his analysis to populism, Drezner similarly fears a future for US foreign policy "whipsaw[ed] ... between 'America First' and a new Second International" (Drezner 2019, 16). If grand strategy is desirable because it offers some measure of policy stability, populism renders grand strategy a dead letter.

Conclusion: Responding to Grand Strategy's Demise

Grand strategy is, more often than not, a pipe dream, Richard Betts suggests in his Handbook essay (Betts 2021). The forces arrayed against formulating and implementing a coherent and durable grand strategy are legion. In recent years, in a world of emergent multiculturalism and reactionary populism, those forces have become even more imposing—this essay has argued, from a narrative perspective—and there is no reason to think that these forces will weaken much in the near future. Other Handbook essays, notably those of Daniel Drezner and Randall Schweller, reach the same conclusion via very different routes: grand strategy is now, and for the foreseeable future will remain, impossible (Drezner 2021; Schweller 2021).

How should we greet the present reality and future prospect of grand strategy's demise? Genuflection toward the wisdom and even necessity of grand strategy is the norm, among both scholars and policymakers. To the extent that they accept this conclusion, they counsel mourning. If grand strategy is beyond our reach, the conventional wisdom suggests, we can expect little but frustration in the international arena.

However, I do not grieve the death of grand strategy, and I will celebrate if we get over our collective crush on Kennan. On the one hand, it is not clear that the benefits of grand strategy are great. There is no evidence that countries that pursue consistent grand strategies outperform countries that fall short of that standard. First, it obviously depends on the wisdom of the strategy itself. A self-defeating strategy—say, invading Iraq to defeat terrorism—is, by all accounts, worse for national welfare than tacking with the winds. Second, many of the most consequential and shrewd foreign policies since the Second World War—from the emergence of containment to the end of the Cold War—were the product more of seizing serendipitous opportunities and improvising than of careful strategic planning.

On the other hand, grand strategy is also associated with known pathologies that should give pause. First, grand strategists are hedgehogs, and such thinkers are known for their rigidity, their resistance to data inconsistent with their preferred theory, and their reluctance to jettison their theoretical hobbyhorse (Tetlock 2005). If it were left to US foreign policy experts, the Cold War might still be going on. Pragmatism is the foreign policy of the foxlike thinker. Second, the more we hold up grand strategy as the gold standard, the more deference is due the establishment brahmins. Not only is the track record of the "wise men" uneven at best, but it also leaves a nation vulnerable to elite-led threat inflation. A foreign policy that instead extols case-by-case judgment would allow for a wider circle of participants in security debates, who would in turn be less likely to buy into a consensus threat assessment, and it would create more openings to question the logic that leads nations to confrontation and war.

A fractured world—in which structures of authority have broken down, in which politics has become polarized and tribal, and in which populist authoritarians find fertile ground—is an unsettling one. There is something to be said for the gentility and politesse, the respect for norms and institutions, and the cross-party cooperation of yesteryear. Whether we like it or not, however, that fractured world is our world. The end of the obsession with grand strategy could be its silver lining.

Notes

1. I am grateful to Thierry Balzacq, Mark Haas, Scott Silverstone, and Daniel Wajner for comments on an earlier version of this essay, as well as to participants in "The Future of Grand Strategy" workshop, held in September 2019 at the US Military Academy at West Point.
2. When I speak of populism in this essay, I mean exclusionary/nationalist/right-wing populism—even when I do not include those modifiers. I recognize that some of my observations do not extend to the more inclusionary and progressive populism that has at times had purchase in Latin America. Thanks to Daniel Wajner for pressing me on this point.
3. The discussion that follows draws heavily and freely on Krebs (2015); Goddard and Krebs (2015).
4. Some critics of multiculturalism apply the term this way, portraying diversity itself as threatening: see, for instance, Huntington (2005); Schlesinger Jr. (1992).
5. Much empirical research on multiculturalism reduces the term to such a slate of policies: see, for instance, the literature reviewed in Koopmans (2013).
6. Philosophically as well, it has attracted many critics: for a trenchant critique, see Barry (2001).
7. Even leading advocates of multiculturalism recognize, and sometimes lament, that modern democracy depends on a degree of common identity: see Kymlicka (1995); Taylor (1998, 143).
8. See, relatedly, Huntington (1997).
9. On the absence of a dominant national security narrative in the United States from the 1960s forward, see Krebs (2015, 191–264).
10. This culturalist interpretation of populism builds on, among others, Betz (1994); Ostiguy (2017); Norris and Inglehart (2019).

References

Anderson, Benedict. 1991 [1983]. *Imagined Communities: Reflections on the Origin and Spread of Nationalism*. New York: Verso.

Balzacq, Thierry, and Pablo Barnier-Khawam. 2021. "Ideas and Ideology in Grand Strategy." In *The Oxford Handbook of Grand Strategy*, edited by Thierry Balzacq and Ronald R. Krebs. Oxford: Oxford University Press.

Barrett, Martyn, ed. 2013. *Interculturalism and Multiculturalism: Similarities and Differences*. Strasbourg: Council of Europe Publishing.

Barry, Brian. 2001. *Culture and Equality: An Egalitarian Critique of Multiculturalism*. Cambridge: Harvard University Press.

Betts, Richard K. 2021. "Is Grand Strategy an Illusion? Or, the Grandiosity of Grand Strategy." In *The Oxford Handbook of Grand Strategy*, edited by Thierry Balzacq and Ronald R. Krebs. Oxford: Oxford University Press.

Betz, Hans-Georg. 1994. *Radical Right-Wing Populism in Western Europe*. New York: St. Martin's Press.

Buzan, Barry, Ole Wæver, and Jaap de Wilde. 1998. *Security: A New Framework for Analysis*. Boulder: Lynne Rienner.

Canovan, Margaret. 1999. "'Trust the People': Populism and the Two Faces of Democracy." *Political Studies* 47 (1): 2–16.

Cantle, Ted. 2012. *Interculturalism: The New Era of Cohesion and Diversity*. Basingstoke: Palgrave Macmillan.

Citrin, Jack, and David O. Sears. 2014. *American Identity and the Politics of Multiculturalism*. New York: Cambridge University Press.

Connolly, William E. 1995. *The Ethos of Pluralization*. Minneapolis: University of Minnesota Press.

Connolly, William E. 2008a. "Deep Pluralism." In *William E. Connolly: Democracy, Pluralism, and Political Theory*, edited by Samuel A. Chambers and Terrell Carver, 85–104. London: Routledge.

Connolly, William E. 2008b. "Fundamentalism in America." In *William E. Connolly: Democracy, Pluralism, and Political Theory*, edited by Samuel A. Chambers and Terrell Carver, 61–84. London: Routledge.

Connolly, William E. 2008c. "Pluralization." In *William E. Connolly: Democracy, Pluralism, and Political Theory*, edited by Samuel A. Chambers and Terrell Carver, 37–60. London: Routledge.

de la Torre, Carlos, ed. 2019. *The Routledge Handbook of Global Populism*. London: Routledge.

Destradi, Sandra, and Johannes Plagemann. 2019. "Populism and International Relations: (Un)predictability, Personalisation, and the Reinforcement of Existing Trends in World Politics." *Review of International Studies* 45 (5): 711–730.

Dombrowski, Peter. 2021. "Alternatives to Grand Strategy." In *The Oxford Handbook of Grand Strategy*, edited by Thierry Balzacq and Ronald R. Krebs. Oxford: Oxford University Press.

Drezner, Daniel W. 2017. "The Angry Populist as Foreign Policy Leader: Real Change or Just Hot Air?" *The Fletcher Forum of World Affairs* 41 (2): 23–43.

Drezner, Daniel W. 2019. "This Time Is Different: Why U.S. Foreign Policy Will Never Recover." *Foreign Affairs* 98 (1): 10–17.

Drezner, Daniel W. 2021. "Grand Strategy in a Fractured Marketplace of Ideas." In *The Oxford Handbook of Grand Strategy*, edited by Thierry Balzacq and Ronald R. Krebs. Oxford: Oxford University Press.

Edelstein, David M. 2021. "The Limits of Grand Strategy." In *The Oxford Handbook of Grand Strategy*, edited by Thierry Balzacq and Ronald R. Krebs. Oxford: Oxford University Press.

Gitlin, Todd. 1995. *The Twilight of Common Dreams: Why America is Wracked by Culture Wars* New York: Metropolitan Books, Henry Holt.

Goddard, Stacie E., and Ronald R. Krebs. 2015. "Rhetoric, Legitimation, and Grand Strategy." *Security Studies* 24 (1): 5–36.

Hall, Stuart. 2000. "Conclusion: The Multi-cultural Question." In *Un/settled Multiculturalisms: Diasporas, Entanglements, Transruptions*, edited by Barnor Hesse, 209–241. London: Zed Books.

Hirsch Jr., E.D. 1988. *Cultural Literacy: What Every American Needs to Know*. New York: Vintage Books.

Huntington, Samuel P. 1997. "The Erosion of American National Interests." *Foreign Affairs* 76 (5): 28–49.

Huntington, Samuel P. 2005. *Who Are We? The Challenges to America's National Identity*. New York: Simon & Schuster.

Jervis, Robert. 2021. "American Grand Strategies: Untangling the Debates." In *The Oxford Handbook of Grand Strategy*, edited by Thierry Balzacq and Ronald R. Krebs. Oxford: Oxford University Press.

Kennedy, David M. 1980. *Over Here: The First World War and American Society*. Oxford: Oxford University Press.

Koopmans, Ruud. 2013. "Multiculturalism and Immigration: A Contested Field in Cross-National Comparison." *Annual Review of Political Science* 39: 147–169.

Krebs, Ronald R. 2015. *Narrative and the Making of U.S. National Security*. Cambridge: Cambridge University Press.

Krebs, Ronald R. 2017. "Pity the President." *The National Interest* (148): 34–42.

Krebs, Ronald R. 2018. "The Politics of National Security." In *The Oxford Handbook of International Security*, edited by Alexandra Gheciu and William C. Wohlforth, 259–273. Oxford: Oxford University Press.

Kymlicka, Will. 1995. *Multicultural Citizenship: A Liberal Theory of Minority Rights*. Oxford: Clarendon Press.

Kymlicka, Will. 2012. *Multiculturalism: Success, Failure, and the Future*. Washington, D.C.: Migration Policy Institute.

Lake, David A. 1992. "Powerful Pacifists: Democratic States and War." *American Political Science Review* 8 (1): 24–37.

Lepore, Jill. 2019. "A New Americanism: Why a Nation Needs a National Story." *Foreign Affairs* 98 (2): 10–19.

Mouffe, Chantal. 2005. "The 'End of Politics' and the Challenge of Right-Wing Populism." In *Populism and the Mirror of Democracy*, edited by Francisco Panizza, 50–71. London: Verso.

Mudde, Cas. 2004. "The Populist Zeitgeist." *Government and Opposition* 39 (4): 541–563.

Mudde, Cas, and Cristóbal Rovira Kaltwasser. 2012. "Populism: Corrective *and* Threat to Democracy." In *Populism in Europe and the Americas: Threat or Corrective for Democracy?*, edited by Cas Mudde and Cristóbal Rovira Kaltwasser, 205–222. New York: Cambridge University Press.

Müller, Jan-Werner. 2016. *What is Populism?* Philadelphia: University of Pennsylvania Press.

Norris, Pippa, and Ronald Inglehart. 2019. *Cultural Backlash: Trump, Brexit, and Authoritarian Populism*. Cambridge: Cambridge University Press.

Ostiguy, Pierre. 2017. "Populism: A Socio-Cultural Approach." In *The Oxford Handbook of Populism*, edited by Cristóbal Rovira Kaltwasser, Paul Taggart, Paulina Ochoa Espejo, and Pierre Ostiguy, 73–97. Oxford: Oxford University Press.

Pickus, Noah. 2005. *True Faith and Allegiance: Immigration and American Civic Nationalism*. Princeton: Princeton University Press.

Posen, Barry R. 1984. *The Sources of Military Doctrine: France, Britain, and Germany Between the World Wars*. Ithaca: Cornell University Press.

Rovira Kaltwasser, Cristóbal, Paul Taggart, Paulina Ochoa Espejo, and Pierre Ostiguy, eds. 2017. *The Oxford Handbook of Populism*. Oxford: Oxford University Press.

Rummens, Stefan. 2017. "Populism as a Threat to Liberal Democracy." In *The Oxford Handbook of Populism*, edited by Cristóbal Rovira Kaltwasser, Paul Taggart, Paulina Ochoa Espejo, and Pierre Ostiguy, 554–570. Oxford: Oxford University Press.

Schildkraut, Deborah J. 2011. *Americanism in the Twenty-First Century*. New York: Cambridge University Press.

Schlesinger Jr., Arthur M. 1992. *The Disuniting of America*. New York: W.W. Norton.

Schweller, Randall. 2021. "Grand Strategy under Nonpolarity." In *The Oxford Handbook of Grand Strategy*, edited by Thierry Balzacq and Ronald R. Krebs. Oxford: Oxford University Press.

Singer, Matthew. 2018. "The Meaning, Origin, and Consequences of Populist Politics." In *The Oxford Research Encyclopedia of Politics*, edited by William R. Thompson. New York: Oxford University Press.

Taylor, Charles. 1994. "The Politics of Recognition." In *Multiculturalism: Examining the Politics of Recognition*, edited by Amy Gutmann. Princeton: Princeton University Press.

Taylor, Charles. 1998. "The Dynamics of Democratic Exclusion." *Journal of Democracy* 9 (4): 143–156.

Tetlock, Philip E. 2005. *Expert Political Judgment: How Good Is It? How Can We Know?* Princeton: Princeton University Press.

Urbinati, Nadia. 2019. "Political Theory of Populism." *Annual Review of Political Science* 22: 111–127.

Weyland, Kurt. 2001. "Clarifying a Contested Concept: 'Populism' in the Study of Latin America." *Comparative Politics* 34 (1): 1–22.

Weyland, Kurt. 2017. "Populism: A Political-Strategic Approach." In *The Oxford Handbook of Populism*, edited by Cristóbal Rovira Kaltwasser, Paul Taggart, Paulina Ochoa Espejo, and Pierre Ostiguy, 48–72. Oxford: Oxford University Press.

CHAPTER 42

GRAND STRATEGY UNDER NONPOLARITY

RANDALL L. SCHWELLER

THERE is something about world politics today that suggests mounting chaos and randomness—what we might call a rise in international political entropy. "Any tendency towards order," in the incoherent twenty-first century, "is contradicted by big-bang disruptions, anarchic social media and Donald Trump, whose life is a masterpiece of spots and jumps" (Morrow 2018, A13). Unfolding in an extravaganza of tweets and surprises, Trump's transactional brand of *de novo* realism has set bonfires to seven decades worth of cherished concepts at the core of American grand strategy, such as support for free trade, multilateralism, and permanent friends. At the global level, populism, autocracy, and inequality are ascendant; democracy and liberalism are in retreat; and a crisis of governability has engulfed the world's most advanced democracies (Diamond 2015; Kupchan 2012; and Niblett 2017). These new arrangements, however, like flocking birds or schooling fish, promise to become incoherent again and, before long, form themselves into new patterns.

Meanwhile, artificial intelligence will soon be smarter than the human brain, making *Homo sapiens* obsolete, or so some say.[1] And the digital age's gift to humankind, the modern "infosphere"—the million-channel media universe—offers so many contradictory "facts," "truths," and "informed opinions" that people everywhere can select and interpret facts in ways that accord with their own personal, quirky, and often flat wrong versions of reality. Welcome to the post-fact world—in which knowledge no longer rests on objective truths but rather on "true enough" facts and arguments (what Stephen Colbert calls "truthiness") that make you feel good (Manjoo 2008).

International structure has played no small part in this recent surfacing of global incoherence. After 1991, the world moved from bipolarity—with its predictable fixed structures and relatively stable relationships—to unipolarity, with its capricious exercise of concentrated power. Unipolar dynamics are random because the structure does not constrain the choices of the unipole, such that most anything can happen and little can be predicted. Boundless freedom breeds randomness. Thus, the idiosyncratic beliefs of unconstrained US leaders tell us more about recent American foreign policy choices than the structure of the international system. Moreover, the structure of unipolarity exerts only weak effects on all other states in the system, as unipolar systems have less glue to hold things together than other international structures. This is because, while capabilities are concentrated under unipolarity, power and threats are diffused throughout the system. Global politics matter only for the unipolar power, the sole actor with global reach and interests. For everyone else, all politics are local.

Today, many observers see emerging bipolarity or multipolarity. I argue, instead, that the emerging world will be nonpolar, ushering in an "age of entropy" (Schweller 2014). The increasing disorder of our world will lead eventually to a sort of global ennui mixed with a disturbingly large dose of individual extremism and dogmatic posturing by states. It is the result of the unstoppable tide of entropy. A world subsumed by the inexorable forces of randomness, tipped off its axis, swirling in a cloud of information overload.

The chapter begins with a brief discussion of polarity. The next section explains why polarity means less today than it did in the past. This is followed by analysis of the current debate between realists and liberals about the likely future of world politics, and why both sides get it wrong. Next, I explore rising entropy at the global or macro level as a result of multiple power centers and globalization. Then I look at how the digital revolution has triggered increased information entropy at the individual or micro level, and how that is polarizing our politics. The chapter ends with a discussion of grand strategy under conditions of nonpolarity and rising entropy. A strategy that maximizes rapid adaptability is key in environments characterized by extreme uncertainty and risk.

Polarity

The key causal driver of neorealist theory, polarity distinguishes one international system from another in a meaningful and nontrivial way—that is, with behavioral consequences—such that changes in polarity denote changes of international systems across time. For neorealists, polarity defines the structure of the international system and, broadly speaking, explains the degree of stability expected of a given system. By system stability, neorealists mean that (1) the international system remains anarchic, (2) there is no "consequential variation" in the number of poles (e.g., changes between multi-, tri-, bi-, or unipolarity),[2] and (3) the system is not especially susceptibility to system-wide wars among all, or most, of the great powers (poles).

Like many important concepts in political science, polarity has proven somewhat elusive to define and measure. Most theorists would define a pole as a state that (1) commands an especially large share of the resources or capabilities that can be used to achieve national ends, and that (2) excels in all the component elements of state power, conventionally defined as size of population and territory, resource endowment, economic capacity, military might, political stability, and institutional competence (Ikenberry, Mastanduno, and Wohlforth 2009, 4–5). In other words, states are not placed in the top rank because they excel in one way or another. Their rank depends on how they score on all categories of capabilities. They must have a complete portfolio of power capabilities.

Determining a system's polarity boils down to counting the number of poles (that is, the number of great powers) of an era (Waltz 1979, 129–131). We ask: how many great powers are there in the international system at any given time? For Waltzian neorealists, if there are more than two great powers, then the system is said to be multipolar. Such a system existed from 1648 to 1945.[3] If there are only two great powers, then the system is called bipolar (e.g., the two superpowers, the United States and the Soviet Union, during the Cold War). If there is only one great power, then the system is unipolar. Currently, the international system is unipolar, with the US as the lone polar power; but America no longer towers over all the rest as it did in the first two decades of its reign after the Cold War.

Why Polarity Is Less Meaningful Today

Since its inception, unipolarity's *sui generis* nature has tempted observers to describe and explain its unique dynamics.[4] Its apparent lack of general properties and predictability, however, have frustrated most if not all who have sought to describe its workings. It does not behave in predictable ways like traditional multipolar or bipolar systems. Under most conditions, multipolarity breeds a classic balance of power system, in which several great powers compete and struggle with each other for power, prestige, and security. Such a system exhibits many behavioral regularities that can be reasonably explained by the interactions among the subset of great powers at the system's core.

Bipolar systems are even easier than multipolar ones to understand and predict. All the action centers on the two poles or superpowers, which do all of the important balancing on their own. The rest of the world, though viewed by the superpowers in highly competitive zero-sum terms, becomes largely superfluous to the stability of the global system. Under bipolarity, international politics boils down to a feud between the Hatfields and the McCoys. For the most part, the behavior of the two poles, the rigidity of their alliance systems, and the flexibility of their foreign policies, are structurally determined. This is not to suggest that conventional bipolar and multipolar structures explained everything that went on in international politics; rather they told us "a small number of big and important things" (Waltz 1986, 329).

Under unipolarity, by contrast, structural constraints are weak or nonexistent. With no great power rivals, the unipole makes choices unfettered by structural imperatives and constraints. It enjoys unprecedented freedom to choose, for instance, with whom to align and how tightly. Consequently, the United States should be more likely today than past great powers to form coalitions based on ideology (fellow democracies), economics, or any other idiosyncratic interests of its choosing. Alternatively, the US may prefer to put together ad hoc "coalitions of the willing" with the mission determining the coalition, as US Secretary of Defense Donald Rumsfeld declared in 2001.[5] Or it may choose to go it alone, as Donald Trump seems to favor.

On the downside, the unipole's overwhelmingly large capability advantage does not easily translate into actual power over others. Indeed, the so-called hyperpower may have less capacity to change or influence others' behavior than poles in a bi- or multipolar system. The unipole's dilemma is that the relationship between relative capabilities and relative power is not a linear one. Just as the unipolar power is largely unconstrained by the need for others, weaker powers, in turn, have less need for a polar-power patron than they would normally have under more traditional balance-of-power structures. I say "less need" rather than "no need" because many states still face local threats for which American protection and assistance is valuable, if not necessary. Moreover, there may be other ways in which the US can be extremely helpful to states and, thereby, get influence over them. Nevertheless, leadership requires followers. If the unipole is seen as unnecessary or incompetent—here, the 2007–2008 great recession caused mainly by American exports of toxic assets comes to mind—its leadership will be unneeded and unwanted. Obviously, nobody wants to follow an incompetent leader. What is unique about unipolarity is that lesser powers have fewer reasons than in the past to do so. Unipolarity exemplifies the problematic relationship between relative capabilities and usable power and influence. The extra resources that a unipole possesses over normal polar powers found in other structures are akin to what is called "useless energy" associated with entropy. In international politics, bigger is not always better.

But perhaps these weak effects of international structure in the contemporary era are due not to unipolarity per se but rather to liberal hegemony and nuclear weapons. Imagine, for instance, that the Soviet Union had won the Cold War. Its unipolar system would likely have been dominated by brute force and coercion, not legitimate authority, and it would have pressured secondary and lesser states far more heavy-handedly than the US currently does. This suggests that the social structure (or social purpose) of a given unipolar system, not its material structure, determines the kind of politics that take place within the system and the constraints exerted on the actors. Imagine further that such a nonliberal unipole existed in a world without nuclear weapons, the possession of which make states difficult to conquer and coerce. In this now offense-dominated world, the unipole's overwhelming advantage in conventional brute force would put at risk the survival of not only all other states but the states system itself.

Recognizing these alternative unipolar scenarios, the foregoing analysis of unipolar dynamics claimed both too much and too little about the predictability of such systems. It claimed too much because a predatory unipole operating in a nonnuclear world could be expected to exert significant coercive constraints on subordinate actors. It claimed too little because it is not the unipolar structure that determines whether states will be constrained but rather the unipole's specific unit-level characteristics and the military technology of the day. If the unipole's attributes and military technology so dramatically affect the properties of the given system, then unipolarity exerts even weaker effects than I have already suggested. The upshot is that polarity does not tell us much about how a unipolar system will operate.

The Current Debate

Most observers agree that the American-led international order is eroding and giving way to something new. A "return to multipolarity" is one way of describing this shift. It tells us that several great powers will emerge to challenge US supremacy. That is all. The more important question is, what sort or international order will emerge on the other side of this transition from unipolarity to multipolarity? Will it be one of peace and plenty or conflict and scarcity? On this issue, experts are divided into two camps, Pessimists and Optimists, those who think we are headed back to the future and those who believe that we are headed forward to the future.

"Back to the Future" Realists, a.k.a. Pessimists, believe that the coming multipolar world will closely resemble the one that held sway over international politics from 1648 until 1945, which was permeated by problems of insecurity, rivalry, arms races, nationalism, and fierce competition for scarce resources.[6] Embedding their arguments in examinations of historical power shifts, such as those provoked by Napoleonic France or the unification of Germany in 1871, they predict that the United States and China will soon engage in an intense security competition with considerable potential for war. This forecast is grounded in the assumption that history unfolds in repeating cycles of global war that destroy the old international order and replace it with a new one. According to this cyclical view of history, time has no direction; the world is not going anywhere it has not already been. The future, therefore, will resemble the past.

In contrast, Liberals, a.k.a. Optimists, reject the notion of a competitive, multipolar world. They see, instead, a smooth evolutionary transition from unipolarity to multipolarity, as the world's major powers (old and new) find ways to build an architecture to jointly manage and preserve the existing international system (Russett and Oneal 2001; Ikenberry 2011; Ikenberry 2001; Deudney and Ikenberry 2009). They believe in a Kantian "triangulating peace"—that democracy, economic interdependence, and a strong system of international organizations reinforce one another to promote a peaceful, just, and prosperous global community. Embracing principles and practices of restraint, accommodation, reciprocity, and cooperation, the great powers will work in concert to establish mutually acknowledged and agreed-upon roles and responsibilities to co-manage an evolving but stable international order that benefits all of them. The return of multipolarity will usher in a new age of Liberal peace, prosperity, and progress built on the rule of law. Swords will be beaten into ploughshares, and a harmony of interests will reign among the states and peoples of the world. In short, multipolarity begets cooperative multilateralism.

This is the essence of Secretary of State Hillary Clinton's vision of a "multipartner," as opposed to a multipolar, world. "It does not make sense to adapt a 19th-century concert of powers or a 20th-century balance-of-power strategy. We cannot go back to Cold War containment or to unilateralism," Clinton said in a speech at the Council on Foreign Relations in July 2009. "We will lead by inducing greater cooperation among a greater number of actors and reducing competition, tilting the balance away from a multipolar world and toward a multipartner world" (Clinton 2009). It is a view based on the assumption that history moves forward in a progressive direction—one consistent with the metaphor of time's arrow (Gould 1987).

As is often the case, reality lies somewhere between these two extremes—there is too much gloom and doom among Realists and too much dewy-eyed optimism among Liberals. Realists' fears that China's rise will provoke war with the United States are unwarranted. The destructiveness of nuclear weapons and the benefits of economic globalization have made war among the great powers unthinkable. The cycle of war among the great powers has been replaced by a perpetual peace, just as Liberals claim. Ironically, this is precisely why Liberals are too sanguine about the future. International order—particularly one that is legitimate, efficient, and dynamic—requires periodic global wars, one roughly every hundred years or so, that crown a new king, clever and powerful enough to organize the world. World order requires occasional reboots—otherwise, inertia and decay set in.

Of course, to say anything nice about war—an enterprise designed to kill people and destroy things—much less large and destructive world wars, seems ludicrous. And yet one need not be mad as a hatter to recognize something inherently indispensable about war. Great thinkers from Alexis de Tocqueville to Emile Zola, Heinrich von Treitschke to Georg Hegel, and Thomas Mann to Igor Stravinsky have sung its praises. Even those who opposed war, such as Kant, Ralph Waldo Emerson, Oliver Wendell Holmes, H.G. Wells, and William James, conceded its healthful properties (Pinker 2011, 242–243). Thus, on the eve of the Great War, Arthur Conan Doyle (1917, 308) had Sherlock Holmes conjecture: "There's an east wind coming ... such a wind as never blew on England yet. It will be cold and bitter, Watson, and a good many of us may wither before its blast. But it's God's own wind none the less, and a cleaner, better, stronger land will lie in the sunshine when the storm has cleared." The sweeping broom, the bracing wind, the cleansing storm, the purifying fire—whatever the metaphor, there remains a kernel of truth in the doctrine of romantic militarism. A world undisturbed by war cannot cleanse and renew itself; like still seas, it becomes foul.

In other words, if there is something akin to an evolving international order, as G. John Ikenberry (2001) portrays in his "constitutional order" thesis, it is not a purely linear process. It combines aspects of both time's arrow and time's cycle. Like a wheel rolling on a track up a hill, international order progresses through upwardly moving cycles, advancing as they turn, of order creation, erosion, destruction, and renewal. Before a new order can be created, the old order must be destroyed and the institutional slate wiped clean. Otherwise, new governance structures will simply be piled on top of old, moribund ones—a recipe for chaos, not order. The perpetual peace among the great powers means that there will be no future hegemonic war—the only known engine of wholesale international change and order creation.

Unless and until the world finds a new mechanism—one other than hegemonic war—for the rebirth of international order, the antiquated global architecture constructed by the United States in the aftermath of the Second World War will simply become increasingly creaky and resistant to overhaul. Entropy will increase. No one will know where international authority resides because it will not reside anywhere, and without authority, there can be no governance. The already overcrowded and chaotic landscape will continue to be filled with more and more meaningless junk; the specter of international cooperation, if it was ever anything more than an apparition, will die a slow but certain death.

Related to the absence of hegemonic war is the absence of great power wars in general (Mueller 1989; Pinker 2011). Given the new realities of the nuclear revolution and the rise of globalization and "knowledge economies," territory is no longer the coin of the realm in terms of power assets. Taking more of it no longer makes states safer or more powerful. Indeed, land grabs, naked or clothed, will certainly make the state less safe and secure in the end. The key is that great powers no longer expect to settle their differences on the battlefield. The absence of this great power expectation, as well as the devaluation of territory and the disutility of military attack as a means to power and security, have profound implications for the coming multipolar system. It means that we should not expect deep and intense security dilemmas—ones that would lead to wars—among the great powers, and consequently we should not expect new-style multipolarity to behave anything like old-style multipolarity.

Under traditional multipolar settings, the great powers armed themselves in the belief that it was not only possible, *but highly likely*, that their weapons would be used against each other. Likewise, when they formed alliances, they targeted them at one another. Balance of power—the oldest and most accepted theory of international relations—is built on the assumption that war is a legitimate instrument of statecraft: states will settle their differences by fighting and, when the odds are right, will wage wars of aggression to expand at each other's expense. Throughout history, these expectations have deeply influenced the behavior of states and the operation of the international system as a whole.

The long peace has fundamentally changed these great power behaviors and expectations. Great powers no longer build arms and form alliances in the expectation that they will settle their differences by fighting. It is no longer an acceptable practice for powerful states to waltz in and take over a country for profit. Those that ignore these global norms encounter the wrath of the entire international community, as Saddam Hussein found out when he invaded Kuwait and, more recently, Russian President Vladimir Putin found out when he annexed Crimea.

With interstate war no longer in play, balance of power theory tells us far less about what makes the clock tick in international relations than it did in the past. Contrary to the predictions of balance of power theory, today's great powers seem determined to do two things more than anything else: get rich, and avoid catastrophic military contests with each other. For these reasons, the coming world of many powerful states and nonstate actors will be very different from past multipolar systems.

That noted, three phenomena may be more important today, and in the future, than polarity. First, we see at the structural level an increase in the number and kinds of actors that can affect the system's outcomes—let us call this the emergence of multiple power centers. Second and aside from structure, process variables at the systemic and micro levels—especially those related to globalization and the digital revolution—are fundamentally reshaping the current and future dynamics of world politics and politics in general.

THE EMERGENCE OF MULTIPLE POWER CENTERS

The diffusion of power throughout the international system is causing entropy to rise. The term "power diffusion" has been used to mean several things. First, the gap in power between the US and its nearest competitor is closing. Here, power diffusion is a dynamic, long-run view of the power trajectories of the two strongest states in the system. Second, the world is becoming more multipolar. America is seeing its power decline, while others are seeing their power rise. This version of power diffusion provides a more encompassing picture than the "two-nation" view, but it is far from complete. Indeed, to say that we are witnessing a return to multipolarity—the consensus opinion among experts—is to trivialize the tectonic shift currently underway.

International relations will no longer be dominated by one or two or even several great powers. New actors—regional and global organizations, local militias, global crime and terrorist networks, nongovernmental organizations, and large corporations—are emerging to compete with states, each possessing and exerting various kinds of power. As the Cold War ended, and central and East European countries began dumping their stocks of weapons, governments across much of the developing world weakened relative to their societies.[7] Unlike the 1960s, when the state had all the guns, domestic challengers to weak governments in Africa and elsewhere were able to procure weapons on the international market. Many of these weakened governments currently find themselves at war with internal political foes or as willing or unwilling hosts to violent nonstate actors (VNSAs). Pakistan is only the most terrifying example.

Indeed, in the twenty-first century, relatively few sovereign states represented in the United Nations can truly claim a monopoly of force within their territorial borders. VNSAs are no longer minor players in a world dominated by states; they now pose a pervasive challenge to the sovereignty of nation-states. According to a study by the Federation of American Scientists, there are 385 "para-state" organizations, defined as entities that challenge the state's monopoly on the use of violence within a specified geographical territory (Federation of American Scientists, n.d.). As a global phenomenon, this fundamental change has been underappreciated largely because the VNSAs have taken different forms in different parts of the world, including tribal and ethnic groups, warlords, drug-trafficking organizations, youth gangs, terrorists, militias, insurgents, and transnational criminal organizations. These subnational challenges to the dominance of the Westphalian state will become ever more prevalent as states become increasingly deficient providers of basic governance functions (Williams 2008, 18).

Entropy dictates that systems composed of large numbers of actors tend toward greater randomness and disorder. A world populated by dozens of power centers will prove extremely difficult to navigate and control. Herding a few cats is no simple task; herding dozens of them is an impossible one. In the new global disorder, those in possession of a large advantage in traditional power capabilities (military, economic, and diplomatic) are no longer guaranteed of getting others to do what they want them to do. Indeed, it is essentially impossible for modern states, no matter how militarily and politically powerful they may be, to use diplomacy or deterrence (the threat of force to gain compliance from the target) to influence violent nonstate groups that are detached from territorial concerns and that prosper in the ungoverned spaces of failed states or within virtual communities. The problem for modern states is not only that a nonterritorial actor does not offer a clear target that can be threatened and, if necessary, destroyed (the "no-return address" problem) but that many of these violent groups are motivated by nonnegotiable religious rather than secular concerns. Worse still, violence is not a deterrent but rather a source of social cohesion for them. All of these factors weaken the ability of states to gain influence with these groups by threatening to impose clear costs on them (Grygiel 2018; Grygiel 2013, 27–29; Smith 2005, 273).

As power and influence become less and less linked, global order and cooperation will be in short supply. Instead, international relations in the twenty-first century will be defined *not* by traditional alliances held together by predictable threats, shared outlooks, and well-defined obligations but rather by selective and situational relationships—that is, by messy "multilateralism à la carte" and by networked interactions among state and nonstate actors (Haass 2017; Haass 1995; Haass 2008, 56; Slaughter 2009; Zakaria 2008, 243). One wonders what order and concerted action mean in a world that lacks fixed and predictable structures and relationships (Patrick 2009). Given the haphazard and incomplete manner by which the vacuum of lost state power is being filled, why expect order at all?

What largely defines international relations today is power's increasingly negative, limited, and conditional nature. The emergence of new and varied kinds of globally influential actors means that power, whether hard, soft, or smart, is becoming more about the ability to disrupt, block, disable, and destroy than to adopt, enable, repair, and build. It is veto power par excellence on a global scale. When power is used for constructive purposes, it will be increasingly issue-specific and, in many cases, wielded by partnerships among governments, public and private actors, and individuals.

In terms of grand strategy, the key to getting things done in a "hybrid world" of many types of actors wielding various kinds of power will be, first, for states to recognize the limitations of traditional power bases and, second, for them to identify and cooperate with private actors that possess issue-specific resources, expertise, and influence. The twenty-first century will see the emergence of a more horizontal world. Virtually all aspects of social and political activity will be linked through dense global webs of networks. Connectedness will, therefore, become a vital base of power; only the connected will thrive.

Process Variables and Rising Entropy

Globalization and Rising Entropy

Entropy is associated with the dissipation of useable energy, enervation, homogenization, and diffused or deconcentrated power. Globalization reinforces these entropic effects in four fundamental ways. First, globalization dissipates useable national power. While globalization has been going on for centuries, it is thicker, quicker, cheaper, and deeper than ever before, and this is true about the volume, velocity, and importance of contemporary cross-border flows of just about everything—capital, manufactured goods, emails, greenhouse gases, weapons, drugs, information, and viruses. These cross-border flows have become a veritable fire hose largely beyond the control of governments or any other authority, for that matter. In addition, the exponential growth of transnational channels of contact—in the number and variety of multi-continental participants in global networks—"means that more issues are up for grabs internationally, including regulations and practices (ranging from pharmaceutical testing to accounting and product standards to banking regulation) that were formally regarded as the prerogatives of national governments" (Nye 2002, 89).

Second, globalization's rapid diffusion of knowledge and technology is dramatically shifting power among nation-states, driving down America's edge in productive capacity and overall power position. And because rising powers inevitably seek enhanced prestige, status, and authority commensurate with their actual power, this leveling process will beget a crisis of international legitimacy. The stronger emerging powers become, the more determined they will be to revise: (1) their standing and voice within international institutions, (2) the current division of territory and spheres of influence, and (3) the rules of the game.

Third, the free flow of goods, information, and capital has strengthened the capacities of nonstate actors, such as energy exporters, drug cartels, terrorists, hacktivists, and Fortune 500 companies. Strong states no longer have a monopoly on power. Multifaceted networks make it easier than ever for individuals and groups to accumulate and project power, to interfere with the workings of, and penetrate the once impenetrable regions within, governments. Private information held by states, corporations, and individuals becomes more difficult to keep private; secrets cannot be kept undisclosed; confidentiality is more easily breached. Thus, for example, in September 2012, the hacking group known as AntiSec—a subset of the loose hacking collective known as Anonymous—says it obtained 12 million identification numbers for iPhone, iPad, and iPod Touch devices by hacking into the computer of an FBI agent, proving, they claim, that the FBI used device information to track people.[8] The more actors in the system, the more power centers there exist, the weaker and more diffuse power becomes within the system.

Fourth and finally, the processes that drive the global economy and information society tend to push in the direction of uniformity. We live in an increasingly homogenized global culture; "cultures have become so intermixed that there is no longer any pure or authentic culture distinct from others" (Holton 2000, 150). This is the rather benign "hybridization" or "convergence" form of the "cultural colonization" argument.[9] The less subtle, more malevolent version claims that globalization is the latest incarnation of Western imperialism. The birth of the global consumer, so the argument goes, was not merely the result of "the utilitarian convenience of global products" but was deliberately coaxed by "the sale of dreams of affluence, personal success, and erotic gratification evoked through advertising and the culture industry of Hollywood" (Holton 2000, 142). Through the force of its ubiquitous and irresistibly seductive "soft" power, the West continues to subjugate the "periphery"—a logic captured by the phrases "Coca-colonization," "McDonaldization," and "Westoxification."

The Digital Revolution and Rising Entropy

Just as the massive increase of information flows generated by the information economy has significantly increased entropy at the level of system process, the digital revolution fuels rising entropy at the micro-level—causing modern people to feel an "irremediable flatness is coming over the world."[10] Flatness here refers to a general sense of banality and loss of meaning. Rather than a heightened sense of stimulation and awareness, information overload produces boredom and alienation (Klapp 1986). As the economist Herbert A. Simon (1971, 40–41) has explained, a "wealth of information creates a poverty of attention." This is because in "an information-rich world, the wealth of information means a dearth of something else: a scarcity of whatever it is that information consumes. What information consumes is rather obvious: it consumes the attention of its recipients." A creeping sameness or, at the other extreme, variation that approaches randomness causes the brain to shut down.

Thus, information overload produces not a heightened sense of stimulation and awareness but rather boredom and alienation. This is what is known as information entropy: the degradation of information through monotonous repetition and meaningless variety. Put differently, the greater the flow and amount of information, the more likely it will degrade toward noise or sterile uniformity. People deluged by a flood of meaningless variety quickly reach a saturation point where, as a means of self-defense, they develop the capacity to tune most everything out and become extremely selective, jaded, blasé, and callous. And people bombarded by redundant information come to view life as banal, colorless, insipid, boring, and characterless.

When everything and its opposite are claimed to be true, most people stop trusting what they hear and the people from whom they hear it. They either tune it all out or heavily discount the information. This produces disinterested, cynical, and solipsistic citizens—people who scarcely fit the mold of potential warriors for various political causes. Inasmuch as increasing information entropy generates ambivalent paralysis, the main political effect of the infosphere will be a joyless peace rooted in apathy. But dangers lurk in this sea of ennui, for increasing information creates not only boredom but the possibility of extremism. Information entropy will polarize our politics and decrease our ability to reconcile our differing worldviews. Even as it bores some, it will energetically and dangerously radicalize others.

With so many competing news outlets and opinions, we can now seek out and find the kind of political views, no matter how absurd, that please us; news that tells us what we want to hear, that indulges our political preconceptions and belief systems and that is told by people who think exactly the same way we do. The result is an increase in extremist views. We see this with Donald Trump today, and on both sides of the spectrum. The mainstream media, even so-called "nonpartisan" media outlets like CNN, have been waging war on the Trump administration—a war fueled by unmistakable hatred for the man. We saw something similar (though, I would argue, with less intensity) during Barack Obama's presidency.

By producing extremist politics rooted in rigidly held competing beliefs, information entropy increases the likelihood of societal conflict and polarization that cannot be adjudicated through reasoned public debate. This is because dogmatic beliefs are little different than no beliefs. As Thomas Jefferson warned: "It is always better to have no ideas than false ones; to believe nothing, than to believe what is wrong." Worse still is to dogmatically believe that which is wrong.

Strategies for Success in a Nonpolar World

Operating within this confused and messy external environment, grand strategy—like any rigid set of guidelines for action—becomes a fool's errand. Those actors most likely to thrive, whether individuals, groups, corporations, bureaucratic organizations, or nation-states, will be the ones that can best cope with complexity and uncertainty. All actors must learn to manage discontinuous changes shaped by external forces—technological, competitive, and regulatory innovation or the decline and rise of whole industries and regional economies—that engineer radical breaks with the past. There are many strategies for reducing complexity and productively adapting to rapidly changing environments; none guarantee success.

Instead, organizations have experimented with decentralized but mutually coordinated decision-making centers. In today's world, the most valuable and complex technologies are increasingly innovated by self-organizing networks—linked organizations (e.g., firms, universities, government agencies) that create, acquire, and integrate diverse knowledge and skills required to innovate complex technologies. Self-organization here refers to the networks' capacity to constantly combine and recombine learned capabilities without centralized, detailed managerial guidance (Rycroft 2004).

Effective participation in these self-organizing innovation networks requires that long-established, inflexible operating principles be replaced with flexible learning procedures based on self-observation, networks of small production units, just-in-time production, demand flow technology, outsourcing, enterprise clusters, and so on. Because innovation is characterized by rapid, highly disruptive, and unpredictable change, managers must avoid the temptation to control every decision and, instead, learn to steer the innovation process, shaping the organizational environment within which choices emerge.

The goal is to create boundaries for effective, improvised, and self-organized solutions. As environmental uncertainty increases, therefore, smart organizations tend to become more organic—they decentralize authority and responsibility, moving it down to lower levels; they encourage employees to take care of problems through teamwork, working directly with one another; and they take an informal approach to assigning tasks and responsibilities (Courtright, Fairhurst, and Rogers 1989; Daft 2007, ch. 4). Communication becomes more horizontal, and the location of knowledge and control of tasks becomes dispersed throughout the organization, making it more fluid and able to adapt continually to changes in its external environment (Zaltman, Duncan, and Holbek 1973, 131). The safest bet in rapidly changing and uncertain environment is a strategy of incremental change. Actors prosper when they can deliver incremental improvements in performance, quality, and cost ahead of their competitors.

For nation-states, the best grand strategy in a nonpolar world of rising entropy is no grand strategy at all or, if this is politically infeasible, a very abstract one. Attempting to cope with violent and capricious changes in their external environments, rational states place a premium on flexibility and adaptability. Along these lines, leaders must resist the all-too-human tendency to impose unwarranted levels of certainty on an uncertain world.

Notes

1. As Drum (2018, 46) puts it, "smart robots will have both the muscle to do the work and the brainpower to run themselves."
2. See Waltz (1979).
3. I have argued elsewhere that we should also distinguish tripolar systems from those of four or more actors. The reason is that tripolar systems exhibit unique characteristics—especially the tendency for two of the poles to gang up on the other pole—that make it extremely unstable. For a discussion of tripolarity and triangular politics, see Schweller (1998).
4. For a fairly early and successful attempt, see Kapstein and Mastanduno (1999). See also Ikenberry, Mastanduno, and Wohlforth (2011).

5. Rumsfeld made this comment at a US Department of Defense News Briefing, 23 September 2001.
6. Pessimists are, for the most part, offensive realists. See Mearsheimer (1990, 2001).
7. Similarly, Barry Posen (2013, 557) notes: "One reason for this [a narrowing gap between the great powers' military capabilities and those of middle powers, small states, and nonstate actors] was the collapse of the Soviet Union and Warsaw Pact, which permitted a vast outflow of infantry weapons. At the same time, some of the former Soviet republics and East European Warsaw Pact states inherited arms production capabilities in search of markets." See also Herbst (2000, 255).
8. On June 22, 2018, the US Supreme Court ruled that police must get a search warrant before obtaining data showing the location of cellphone users. See Kendall and Bravin (2018). For AntiSec's antics, see Bilton (2012).
9. For hybridization, see Pieterse (2009).
10. William James, "What Makes a Life Significant" (1899), as quoted in Schweller (2010, 30).

References

Bilton, Nick. 2012. "Apple Denies Giving F.B.I. Device Information." *New York Times*, September 5, 2012. http://bits.blogs.nytimes.com/2012/09/05/apple-denies-giving-f-b-i-device-information/

Clinton, Hillary Rodham. 2009. "Foreign Policy Address at the Council on Foreign Relations." U.S. State Department, Washington, D.C., July 15, 2009. https://2009-2017.state.gov/secretary/20092013clinton/rm/2009a/july/126071.htm

Courtright, John A., Gail T. Fairhurst, and L. Edna Rogers. 1989. "Interaction Patterns in Organic and Mechanistic Systems." *Academy of Management Journal* 32 (4): 773–802.

Daft, Richard L. 2007. *Essentials of Organization Theory and Design*. 2nd edition. Mason, OH: Cengage Learning.

Deudney, Daniel, and G. John Ikenberry. 2009. "The Myth of the Autocratic Revival: Why Liberal Democracy Will Prevail." *Foreign Affairs* 88 (1): 77–93.

Diamond, Larry. 2015. "Facing Up to the Democratic Recession." *Journal of Democracy* 26 (1): 141–155.

Doyle, Arthur Conan. 1917. *His Last Bow: A Reminiscence of Sherlock Holmes*. New York: George H. Doran Company.

Drum, Kevin. 2018. "Tech World: Welcome to the Digital Revolution." *Foreign Affairs* 97 (4): 43–48.

Gilpin, Robert. 1981. *War and Change in World Politics*. New York: Cambridge University Press.

Gould, Stephen Jay. 1987. *Time's Arrow, Time's Cycle: Myth and Metaphor in the Discovery of Geological Time*. Cambridge, MA: Harvard University Press.

Grygiel, Jakub. 2013. "The Primacy of Premodern History." *Security Studies* 22 (1): 1–32.

Grygiel, Jakub. 2018. *Return of the Barbarians: Confronting Non-State Actors from Ancient Rome to the Present*. Cambridge: Cambridge University Press.

Haass, Richard N. 1995. "Paradigm Lost." *Foreign Affairs* 74 (1): 43–58.

Haass, Richard N. 2008. "The Age of Nonpolarity: What Will Follow U.S. Dominance." *Foreign Affairs* 87 (3): 44–56.

Haass, Richard N. 2017. *A World in Disarray: American Foreign Policy and the Crisis of the Old Order*. New York: Penguin Books.

Herbst, Jeffrey. 2000. *States and Power in Africa: Comparative Lessons in Authority and Control.* Princeton: Princeton University Press, 2000.

Holton, Robert. 2000. "Globalization's Cultural Consequences." *Annals of the American Academy of Political and Social Science* 570 (July): 140–152.

Ikenberry, G. John. 2001. *After Victory: Institutions, Strategic Restraint, and the Rebuilding of Order After Major Wars.* Princeton, NJ: Princeton University Press.

Ikenberry, G. John. 2011. *Liberal Leviathan: The Origins, Crisis, and Transformation of the American World Order.* Princeton, NJ: Princeton University Press.

Ikenberry, G. John, Michael Mastanduno, and William C. Wohlforth. 2009. "Introduction: Unipolarity, State Behavior, and Systemic Consequences." *World Politics* 61 (1): 1–27.

Ikenberry, G. John, Michael Mastanduno, and William C. Wohlforth, eds. 2011. *International Relations Theory and the Consequences of Unipolarity.* Cambridge: Cambridge University Press.

Kapstein, Ethan B., and Michael Mastanduno, eds. 1999. *Unipolar Politics: Realism and State Strategies After the Cold War.* New York: Columbia University Press.

Kendall, Brent, and Jess Bravin. 2018. "Court Ruling Boosts Phone Privacy." *The Wall Street Journal.* June 23–24, 2018: A1–A2.

Keohane, Robert O. 1984. *After Hegemony: Cooperation and Discord in the World Political Economy.* Princeton, NJ: Princeton University Press.

Klapp, Orrin E. 1986. *Overload and Boredom: Essays on the Quality of Life in the Information Society.* New York: Greenwood Press.

Kupchan, Charles A. 2012. "The Democratic Malaise: Globalization and the Threat to the West." *Foreign Affairs* 91 (1): 62–67.

Lasswell, Harold D., and Abraham Kaplan. 1950. *Power and Society: A Framework for Political Inquiry.* New Haven, CT: Yale University Press.

Lukes, Stephen. 2005. *Power: A Radical View.* New York: Palgrave Macmillan.

Manjoo, Farhad. 2008. *True Enough: Learning to Live in a Post-fact World.* Hoboken, New Jersey: John Wiley.

Mearsheimer, John J. 1990. "Back to the Future: Instability in Europe After the Cold War." *International Security* 15 (4): 5–56.

Mearsheimer, John J. 2001. *The Tragedy of Great Power Politics.* New York: W. W. Norton.

Morrow, Lance. 2018. "Did an Ancient Greek Anticipate Trump?" *The Wall Street Journal,* June 23–24, 2018: A13.

Mueller, John. 1989. *Retreat from Doomsday: The Obsolescence of Major War.* New York: Basic Books.

Niblett, Robin. 2017. "Liberalism in Retreat: The Demise of a Dream." *Foreign Affairs* 96 (1): 17–24.

Nye, Joseph S., Jr. 2002. *The Paradox of American Power: Why the World's Only Superpower Cannot Go It Alone.* Oxford: Oxford University Press.

Patrick, Stewart. 2009. "Prix Fixe and à la Carte: Avoiding False Multilateral Choices." *The Washington Quarterly* 32 (4): 77–95.

Patrick, Stewart. 2010. "Irresponsible Stakeholders? The Difficulty of Integrating Rising Powers." *Foreign Affairs* 89 (6): 44–53.

Pieterse, Jan Nederveen. 2009. *Globalization and Culture: Global Mélange.* Lanham, MD: Rowman and Littlefield.

Pinker, Steven. 2011. *The Better Angels of Our Nature: Why Violence Has Declined.* New York: Penguin Books.

Posen, Barry R. 2013. "Emerging Multipolarity: Why Should We Care?" In *International Politics: Enduring Concepts and Contemporary Issues*. 11th edition, edited by Robert J. Art and Robert Jervis, 552–560. Upper Saddle River, NJ: Pearson Education.

Russett, Bruce, and John R. Oneal. 2001. *Triangulating Peace: Democracy, Interdependence, and International Organizations*. New York: W. W. Norton.

Rycroft, Robert. 2004. "Self-Organizing Innovation Networks: Implications for Globalization." *Technovation* 24 (3): 187–197.

Schweller, Randall L. 1998. *Deadly Imbalances: Tripolarity and Hitler's Strategy of World Conquest*. New York: Columbia University Press.

Schweller, Randall L. 2010. "Ennui Becomes Us." *The National Interest* 105 (January/February): 27–38.

Schweller, Randall L. 2014. *Maxwell's Demon and the Golden Apple: Global Discord in the New Millennium*. Baltimore, MD: Johns Hopkins University Press.

Simon, Herbert A. 1971. "Designing Organizations for an Information-Rich World." In *Computers, Communication, and the Public Interest*, edited by Martin Greenberger, 37–52. Baltimore, MD: The Johns Hopkins University Press.

Slaughter, Ann-Marie. 2009. "America's Edge: Power in the Networked World." *Foreign Affairs* 88 (1): 94–113.

Smith, Rupert. 2005. *The Utility of Force*. New York: Knopf.

The Federation of American Scientists. n.d. "Liberation Movements, Terrorist Organizations, Substance Cartels, and Other Para-State Entities." http://www.fas.org/irp/world/para/index.html

Waltz, Kenneth. 1979. *Theory of International Politics*. Reading, MA: Addison-Wesley.

Waltz, Kenneth. 1986. "Reflections on *Theory of International Politics*: A Response to My Critics." In *Neorealism and Its Critics*, edited by Robert O Keohane, 322–345. New York: Columbia University Press.

Williams, Phil. 2008. *Violent Non-state Actors and National and International Security*. Zurich: International Relations and Security Network.

Zaltman, Gerald, Robert Duncan, and Johnny Holbek. 1973. *Innovations and Organizations*. New York: Wiley.

Zakaria, Fareed. 2008. *The Post-American World*. New York: W. W. Norton.

CHAPTER 43

GRAND STRATEGY AND TECHNOLOGICAL FUTURES

ROBERT G. CANTELMO AND SARAH E. KREPS

GRAND strategy is the integration of a state's political objectives with its capabilities to implement policies best able to advance its goals. The evolution of grand strategy, like any strategic process, is dynamic and iterative. When international or domestic factors alter the state's preferences, the state reconsiders how best to employ the instruments of national power. The resultant change in grand strategy is defined by the degree and magnitude of change from the previous. Grand-strategic change can also occur when new technology modifies the effectiveness, efficiency, or reliability of existing capabilities. New policies are adopted, or old ones abandoned, as the state recalibrates the costs, benefits, and risks of competing options in light of technical innovation. Investment in research and development may also emerge as an intermediate strategy for states optimistic about future technological breakthroughs.

Scholars have long debated the politics of technology, including the basis for strategic stability (Jervis 1978; Glaser and Kaufmann 1998; Lieber 2005), military effectiveness (Posen 1984; Rosen 1991), revolutions in military affairs (Murray and Knox 2001; Krepinevich 1994), innovation and adoption (Horowitz 2010), and the emergent consequences of social media (Kreps 2020). Fischer, Gilli, and Gilli argue in Chapter 14, however, that the specific relationship between technology and grand strategy has been under-interrogated (page XX). In their essay, they offer potential pathways through which technological change might impact grand strategy, focusing primarily on the way technology affects domestic coalitions and dominant narratives in a country, thereby creating incentives for grand-strategic stasis or change.

In this chapter, we offer a framework that is compatible with Fischer et al.'s emphasis on domestic politics while taking a different tack. We observe that technical and organizational innovation can produce significant, but indirect, shifts in the formation and implementation of grand strategy by altering the cost–benefit calculus of status quo policies and thereby expanding or moderating stated policy objectives. Alternatively, states may also prioritize future innovation through greater investment in research and development as their own intermediate goals.

The rest of this chapter proceeds as follows. First, we provide an operational definition of grand strategy as an ends–means nexus and discuss how technology can improve status quo strategies. Second, we offer a framework for how states formulate and implement new strategies in response to emergent capabilities or objectives. Finally, we evaluate these claims by applying them to three new and emerging technical innovations: precision-guided munitions, robotic autonomy, and computing.

GRAND STRATEGY AND TECHNOLOGY: CLARITY IN CONCEPT

Grand strategy is a deeply contested term in the international relations scholarship. Proponents of its usage frame their analysis in normative and positive terms. Normatively, a grand strategy is something that states and leaders should aspire to get right. In this sense, it is defined as an idealized set of policies against which the state's actions should be measured. Good grand strategy is defined by its coherence, its codification, and whether its implementation secures the state's declared objectives. Such practice has become ritualized in the United States, where each presidential administration is scrutinized over whether they possess an appropriate grand strategy (Drezner 2011; Dombrowski and Reich 2017). The US now has nearly three decades of post–Cold War deliberations over the appropriateness of competing for grand strategies of deep engagement (Brooks, Ikenberry, Wohlforth 2012/2013), offshore balancing (Mearsheimer 2001), selective engagement (Art 2003), or restraint (Posen 2014). Each of these competing policies is prescriptive and presumes that there is a correct choice for both defining and realizing American political objectives. Skeptics, by contrast, question whether debates over the significance of these policy prescriptions without clearly defined mechanisms built into grand-strategic theory (Kirss 2018).

While scholarship on grand strategy has helped us to understand the how and why of state behavior, its conceptual aspects remain muddled. One of the most cited definitions of grand strategy comes from Posen, who describes it as "a political-military, means-ends chain, a state's theory about how it can best 'cause' security for itself" (Posen 1984, 13). Though clear and concise, this fundamentally narrow definition is limited by grand strategy's theoretical heritage in security studies and neorealism. Historically, grand strategy was exclusively the domain of military theory in usage and application, "synonymous," Liddell Hart writes "with the policy which guides the conduct of war" (Liddell Hart 1991, 321–322). Assuming the primacy of security motivations in grand strategy is limiting in contemporary international politics. There is great intellectual diversity in the field that attributes interest formation to things like domestic politics

(Narizny 2007) and status-seeking (Larson and Shevchenko 2010). An alternative to the security orthodoxy is best articulated by Balzacq, Dombrowski, and Reich, as the international relations tradition which incorporates "greater attention to societal, economic, and technological dimensions" into the military factors (Balzacq, Dombrowski, and Reich 2019, 72). The more holistic approach broadens our analysis not only to other political domains, but also highlights the potential costly tradeoffs that states must weigh when setting diplomatic, economic, and military policy.

Similarly, the literature is inconsistent in terms of whether grand strategy requires clear intentionality and articulation, is just a set of overarching beliefs, or is merely the aggregation of decisions and policies a state implements (Silove 2018). Definitions are often context-dependent as well. For example, offshore balancing and selective engagement are not parsimonious or generalizable terms. Rather, they are shorthand for a bundle of policy prescriptions valid for a particular period in American foreign policy. By contrast, we retain the greatest analytical flexibility when we think about strategy as the realized actions of the state.

We define grand strategy as the set of all plans and actions that states design and implement in pursuit of their political preferences. Correspondingly, a change in grand strategy is identified as a shift in the means employed or the ends a state wishes to realize. This definition does not preclude any additional requirements. Instead, it merely provides a minimalist definition of our analytical concept. States may, for example, be explicit in how they reveal or articulate their grand strategies. The Monroe Doctrine is an example of a well-articulated grand strategy for how the fledgling United States planned to deal with European colonial powers. This process of articulation is not, however, prior to grand strategy but rather one of its products. Formalizing or declaring a grand strategy is a political act in service to a political end.

Having established a working definition of grand strategy, we now clarify how it interacts with technology. The business literature distinguishes between sustaining and disruptive technologies. The former might preserve or improve a relative advantage or otherwise provide a scaling effect to existing efficiencies; they sustain because they build on prior success (Christensen 1997, 11). By contrast, disruptive technologies can obviate existing practices in the near-term and prove damaging to the status quo (Christensen 1997, 11). In industry, the introduction of cement, glass, and the computer were technological discontinuities (Anderson and Tushman 1990). In the military domain, these disruptive technologies improve performance by increasing the efficiency, speed, or cost of a task, or by undermining the performance of an adversary's capability. Not all military technical breakthroughs are disruptive or transformative and might instead just provide sustaining incremental progress (Mukunda 2010). Distinguishing between sustaining and disruptive innovations can be challenging because it requires prior knowledge of how adoption and application of the new technology ultimately manifest themselves.

We instead define technological change as a technical or organizational innovation that increases or decreases the cost, benefit, or uncertainty associated with a particular set of actions. The introduction of technology can affect these in three ways. First, technology can increase or decrease the benefit of a given strategy. An incremental increase in the efficiency of mining technologies, for instance, may result in greater rates of resource extraction. Second, technology can increase or decrease the cost of a given strategy. The advent of nuclear submarines dramatically reduced the cost of maintaining a survivable nuclear deterrent. Third, technology can increase or decrease the uncertainty or risk associated with a set of strategies. Surface-to-ship missiles have played a large part in raising the risk of US freedom of navigation operations in the South China Sea (Biddle and Oelrich 2016). Emergent innovations might impact one or more of these different dimensions, as well as by different degrees of intensity.

Framework

In this section, we offer a framework to explain how grand strategy responds to technological change and future expectations. We argue that technology has an indirect impact on grand strategy through two main pathways. First, it may introduce new capabilities that produce changes to the cost, benefit, or risk of a certain set of strategies. We predict that when the impact of a technology is modest, the state will experience a marginal change in the effectiveness of their status quo grand strategy. The analytical expectation stands in contrast to debates around American grand strategy, where undesirable outcomes are believed to imply a suboptimal strategy. In reality, states sometimes lack good options. When the impact of technology is significant, however, we should see a shift in strategic planning and execution in the observed behavior. Second, the appeal of future innovative breakthroughs can also make investment in research and development an attractive intermediate policy objective. We predict that when states have high confidence in the yields of research investment, they will redirect existing capabilities to support this effort. Alternatively, when they have low confidence in their ability to capitalize on research, resources will be used to support status quo policy. These changes can be seen at two different levels of grand strategy: formulation and implementation.

The formulation stage of grand strategy is where states engage in the active process of marrying objectives with capabilities. States inventory and rank order their preferred political outcomes and determine the best way to achieve them. We assume that states are thinly rational: they select strategies that they believe to have the greatest chance of realizing their aims. Existing capabilities factor into the state's cost, benefit, and risk calculus as they set policy. After the emergence of a new innovation, the state re-evaluates these factors to determine how they impact the status quo. Modest improvements will produce marginal change in the net benefit of existing policy but will be unlikely to produce a new strategy altogether. Innovations that significantly impact technology are likely to produce a strategic shift. This may be because the state's political objective(s) can no longer be serviced, or because the scaling factor of technology makes more ambitious policy feasible. Nuclear weapons are perhaps the most notable example of how technological change can produce a change in strategy. As Gavin notes, the United States long practiced "strategies of inhibition" that included preventive military action, security guarantees, and treaties to help slow or halt the transfer of nuclear weapons (Gavin 2015). As Jack Levy notes, "the crossing of the nuclear threshold is the most consequential manifestation of a step-level power shift," and has commensurately large impacts on a challenger's strategic choices (Levy 2008, 7).

We also expect the future promise of innovation to have consequences for the formulation stage. When confidence in the innovation and adoption of new technologies rises, states will divert more resources from domestic consumption to invest in research and development. This strategy is maintained so long as beliefs about return on investment remain consistent. When confidence in innovation and adoption falls, states will deem the political costs of innovative research too great. Nuclear weapons again provide an illustrative example. Sagan has argued that security, domestic politics, and prestige-seeking can all serve as pathways to proliferation (Sagan 1996/97). The prestige argument, in particular, is an example of how technology investment and acquisition can become a goal unto itself.

The implementation stage of grand strategy is where plans are executed. At this level, states wrestle with the practicalities of diffusion and adoption of new innovations (Horowitz 2010), the consequences for military power and economic potential (Gilpin 1981, 65), and the interaction of the tactical, operational, and strategic dimensions of grand strategy (Luttwak 2001; Martel 2015). Modest improvement to capabilities may alter implementation by changing how soldiers, bureaucrats, and diplomats execute their daily tasks. Innovations might offer a qualitative improvement for how existing policy is implemented. The advent of modern telecommunications, for example, enabled faster and more reliable communication between diplomatic missions and their home governments. Innovations may also degrade existing practices. The introduction of the cannon in the late Middle Ages dramatically reduced the benefit of castles for defending armies and reduced the cost of siege for the attackers. It might also change the organization of force structure or force employment (Biddle 2004).

Empirical Illustrations

In this section, we examine our framework through cases of new and emerging innovations: precision-guided munitions, robotic autonomy, and computing technologies. Precision munitions are the most established and their effects have been almost fully internalized. Robotics technology is still proliferating, and states are adjusting to their implications, with several possible breakthroughs on the horizon. Lastly, computational advancements are ongoing and there is still uncertainty about what sort of strategic impact they will ultimately produce. In the section that follows, we evaluate how the technical qualities of these innovations impact the formulation and implementation of grand strategy.

To evaluate the relative impact of these technologies on the formulation and implementation of grand strategy, we discuss how they affect the cost, benefits, and risk of strategy. Technical improvements that provide increased efficiency, linear gains in the quality of use, or otherwise represent incremental improvements to the cost–benefit calculus suggest modest changes to the implementation of existing grand strategy. By contrast, technologies that produce significant changes to the state's cost–benefit considerations or alter the likelihood of success for states adopting more ambitious political objectives would be evidence of changes to the formulation of grand strategy.

Precision Munitions

During the First Gulf War, the *New York Times* reported that "for the first time in history, precision-guided bombs and missiles have played a decisive role in war paving the way for the invasion of Kuwait and Iraq" (Brown 1991). The US military brought these weapons to bear in a highly public and successful way, which fueled speculation that precision-guided munitions (PGMs) were transformative for national security and military strategy. Defense technology optimists subsequently integrated PGMs as a core component of the "third offset strategy," a Defense Department initiative intended to increase American competitiveness through military-technical improvements (Host 2015). Proponents point to the increased efficiency and reliability of PGMs and their battlefield potential. By contrast, some scholars have been more bearish on the ultimate impact of PGMs, suggesting that they "have not produced any radical change in the nature of the conventional battlefield" (Mearsheimer 1983, 200). This camp argues that PGMs do not fundamentally change the nature of military firepower or how states pursue their security goals.

The primary contribution of PGM technology has been a scaling benefit to the accuracy and lethality of airpower. With each improvement, militaries are better able to acquire and eliminate targets than they could do using previous generations' technology. Ordinance used against the Iraqi military during Desert Storm was significantly more accurate than the bombs employed during the Second World War, which "caused a great deal of collateral damage, but very often failed to destroy the intended target" (Michlovitz 2000, 557). Improved accuracy has also been accompanied by a corresponding increase in battlefield lethality (Biddle 2004, 53). Gillespie writes that though PGMs accounted for "only 8% of the total bombs expended in the Gulf War," they were responsible for "well over 75% of the serious damage inflicted on Iraqi targets" (Gillespie 2006, 138). Taken together, PGMs represent a significant improvement in the application of airpower against strategic and tactical targets.

In addition to the benefits afforded by these technical improvements, PGMs have helped to mitigate the military and political costs of employing airpower. Smart weapons reduce the number of civilian casualties, while increasing confidence in the likelihood of successful operations (Martin 2005, 6–7). Minimizing collateral damage avoids the rampant economic and human destruction resulting from traditional bombing campaigns. It may also help avoid political sanction by domestic or international audiences observing combat operations. Effective PGMs also mean that the US and other adopters require fewer weapons to produce the same effects. PGM usage has steadily increased over the last few US wars, requiring fewer sorties and total ordinance (Koplow 2009, 88). Furthermore, PGMs have also reduced the number of aircraft and pilots needed to carry out strike missions. "Instead of flying hundreds of aircraft against a single target," Martin writes "a JFC [joint force commander] will enjoy the same effects via a single strike air asset with a single bomb" (Martin 2005, 6–7). All of this points to marginal improvements and efficiencies accruing to the implementation of status quo defense policy.

Despite these qualitative technical improvements, the advent of PGMs have had negligible impact on the risk or uncertainty associated with strategic and tactical bombing. The efficiency gains do not fundamentally alter the battlefield reliance on cover and concealment that Biddle argues constitutes the foundation of the modern system (Biddle 2004, 54–55). Adversaries can utilize human shields, urban operations, and dispersion to help neutralize the advantages afforded to adversaries with PGMs. Even the aspirations of the third offset strategy are "focused on maintaining the United States' advantage in precision guided munitions," rather than reimagining warfighting (Host 2015). Lieber and Press have raised the possibility that continued improvement in precision weaponry might have the potential to transform strategic nuclear doctrine (Lieber and Press 2006; Lieber and Press 2017). This is likely an overoptimistic position, however, as counterforce remains a strategically inviable option. Even continued technical improvement in this area could be countered if other states made efforts to increase the survivability and size of their nuclear arsenals. In the nuclear dimension, deterrence is likely to remain the status quo strategic posture. Therefore, we can conclude that the modest benefits provided by PGMs do not suggest a change in the formulation of grand strategy.

Robotics

In an article from November 2018, defense technology writer Kelsey Atherton asked: "Are killer robots the future of war?" (Atherton 2018). Most definitions of robots follow "the 'sense-think-act' paradigm" and include a number of different capabilities: that the system is unmanned, remotely operated, and computer programmed to carry out a particular function; and that it is equipped with some kind of sensor, such as infrared laser beams used for object detection, sound detection equipment, and a camera connected to a data collection source (Singer 2009, 67). Examples of military robotics range from armed drones that conduct counterterrorism strikes, to robots armed with machine guns that can conduct border patrol, to underwater robots that can engage in demining operations. Robotics overlaps with computing, which provides the program that the robot implements, but this section focuses more narrowly on the hardware, and in particular, the way in which unmanned technologies may reshape war.

States relying on advances in robotic autonomy have begun to reduce the human cost of power projection. In one sense, they confer the ability to remove—or at least insulate—soldiers from the immediate effects of war itself. Unmanned aerial vehicles (UAVs) are able to conduct reconnaissance, surveillance, and strike missions that would historically have required a human pilot in the cockpit. Other innovations on the horizon suggest further ways states might remove human beings from frontline operations. A robot on patrol, for example, could be programmed to engage automatically if fired upon. The underwater sea vehicle could identify and detonate mines prior to friendly submarines going through that same territory. A drone swarm—coordinated autonomy, which might consist of a group of thousands of small drones—could obtain air superiority before sending manned aircraft for targeting (Scharre 2018, 18).

Militaries already benefit from robotics, which have become instrumental in global counterterrorism operations. The integration of robotics into existing strategy is only going to expand. The US national security strategy suggests a number of political goals where advances in robotics might prove most useful, such as counterterrorism, combating biothreats, defending against weapons of mass destruction, and strengthening border security and enforcement (NSS 2017). For example, one strategic goal outlined in the 2017 National Security Strategy is to "detect and contain biothreats at their source" (NSS 2017, 9). Automated systems embedded in robots could be programmed to identify infectious disease outbreaks in ways that facilitate the containment of those diseases. Similarly, severing the source of terrorist strength is enabled by targeted drone strikes.

The US Army has devoted considerable resources to developing units that would deploy with troops in the field. It has been using the RQ-11B Raven, a hand-thrown launch drone, for intelligence, reconnaissance, and surveillance. Soldiers assemble the system for launch and then the Raven uses its electro-optical camera to provide information back to soldiers who can then benefit from battlefield awareness about potential threats both "over the hill" and "around the corner" (Defense Industry Daily 2018). The defense industry is also generating smaller drones that are even more portable, operated from tablets, and are able to connect decision-makers with tactical developments in real time (Rempfer 2018). While current-generation combat drones have their limitations in that they flow low and slow, future-generation drones are likely to be faster and stealthier in ways that may make them more valuable in interstate conflict (Horowitz, Kreps, and Fuhrmann 2016). This could lead to greater efficiency gains in supporting air superiority missions, close air support, and even strategic bombing.

Advances in robotics could also impact the formulation of grand strategy, as these new capabilities enable states to adopt more ambitious political objectives. One prevailing view is that states have already begun to feel this transformational impact and respond accordingly. The military robotics market has grown considerably (Scharre 2018, 13), reaching about $17.34 billion in 2018 and expected to grow about 13.5% between 2019 and 2027. This evidence suggests that proficiency in robotic technology might become an intermediate policy objective for states looking to exploit existing and prospective technical breakthroughs. This logic rests on the notion that robots are not hindered by the natural limitations of humans, such as the need to sleep or fear of mortality, which means they are more enduring and resilient than their manned counterparts.

One area that has already seen some transformation as the result of robotics is the strategic innovation of light-footprint warfare. This political and legal innovation of the Obama administration has enabled the US to engage in military interventions—most famously Libya—without the political and military costs of "boots on the ground" or resorting to lengthy occupations. "Light-footprint warfare," Goldsmith and Waxman argue, "occurs largely out of public view, often from a distance, and in many cases with limited threat to U.S. personnel" (Goldsmith and Waxman 2016, 10). Robotics are essential to the implementation of this new strategy, especially because it removes some of the physical costs of war from the public debate. When debates over the War Powers Resolution arose during the Libyan intervention, the *New York Times* reported that some considered drone strikes as being outside the scope of "hostilities" (Savage 2011). This is not simply an academic distinction. One consequence of the proliferation of robotics might be to undemocratize foreign policy. Isolating the human cost of war is a double-edged sword. On the one hand, it may have a moderating effect on state resolve, since operations do not produce as many casualties. On the other, it could minimize public oversight of military interventions and further centralize foreign policy decision-making in the executive branch.

Robotics are likely to continue to have significant strategic impacts in the future. Russia and China appear to be in an arms race over autonomy (Barnes and Chin 2018). Countries that have these capabilities but have asserted that they would not use them might find themselves hard-pressed to restrain themselves if an adversary were engaged in such warfare. As former Deputy Secretary of Defense Bob Work wondered, "if our competitors go to Terminators … and it turns out the Terminators are able to make decisions faster, even if they're bad, how would we respond?" (Quoted in Scharre 2018, 8). The implication is that the United States would find it difficult to respond in kind and implement more automation in its decisions (Scharre 2018). Fully autonomous systems might thereby shift the technological balance in ways that shape strategic choices. If a fully autonomous system can go to a warzone and make decisions about targeting, whether armed ground robots or armed UAVs, then states might engage in "flash wars"—with escalation happening because algorithms respond to escalatory cues but without the human intervention to pause. Then fully autonomous robots might create the sense that offense has the advantage and therefore create an offensive-driven first-strike strategy (Scharre 2018, 298–300). If these capabilities were realized, it would represent even more significant change to the formulation of grand strategy.

Computing

In 1949, MIT math professor Norbert Wiener wrote an unpublished letter for the *New York Times* presaging "a new age of machines," one that would "replace human judgment on all levels" (Wiener 1949). As he noted, "it is already clear that this new replacement will have a profound influence upon our lives, but it is not clear to the man of the street what this influence will be" (ibid). Reacting to this letter, national security analyst Micah Zenko wrote that "if you think something is new, read anything by Norbert Wiener" (@MicahZenko 2018). Seven decades later, the warnings about computers replacing the minds of humans seem new again. Elon Musk and Stephen Hawking joined forces to campaign against artificial intelligence. According to Hawking "AI could be the worst event in the history of our civilization. It brings dangers, like powerful autonomous weapons, or new ways for the few to oppress the many. It could bring great disruption to our economy" (Kharpal 2017). AI, loosely speaking, approximates the Wiener characterization—programming computers to think like humans, in other words, performing tasks that would normally require human processing, such as speech recognition, visual perception, and decision-making—all based on large volumes of data and algorithms that teach computers to respond in certain ways to corresponding observations.

The realm of machines extends beyond AI. It includes cyber technology, such as the use of social media, encryption and decryption of information that would enable adversaries to target US personnel and military operations, and cyberattacks or operations that might include both the type of Stuxnet attack that hobbled the Iran nuclear program and election interference of the type that Russia carried out in the 2016 US presidential elections (Whittaker 2018). These technologies have been heralded as highly transformational to the costs, benefits, and risks associated with new strategic possibilities. President Reagan foreshadowed in 1989 that the "Goliath of totalitarianism will be brought down by the David of the microchip," suggesting that Silicon Valley was creating the tools through microchips that would be more effective than militaries or diplomacy in undermining authoritarian rule and implying that technology would help groups organize (Rule 1989). Whether and how these technologies have been consequential—and whom they help, whether the people on the street or their leaders—remains a matter of debate.

Advanced computing capabilities have already proven beneficial in supporting existing US strategic objectives pertaining to nuclear nonproliferation. The aforementioned case of Stuxnet provides strong evidence about the developing cost–benefit calculus. On the one hand, Slayton argues the financial cost of disrupting the Iranian nuclear program was higher than some more optimistic evidence suggests, casting doubt on the so-called dominance of cyber offense (Slayton 2016/2017). On the other hand, she acknowledges that ultimately "the costs of Stuxnet are uncertain, but they are likely to be two orders of magnitude lower than the perceived value of Iran's nuclear program" (Slayton 2016/2017, 108). If cyber operations are significantly less expensive than military intervention—often championed by hawkish leaders—then continued technical innovation provides useful new capabilities for pursuing existing strategic imperatives.

While the implications of increased computing power and machine learning point to clear changes in the implementation of grand strategy, the outstanding question about how it impacts its formulation remains. In many ways, this last case of innovation is most difficult to parse in terms of grand-strategic formulation because it is largely dual use. New breakthroughs often begin in the civilian domain, where they may be used for commercial activity or domestic consumption. Over time, states identify ways in which they can exploit civilian developments to pay political dividends. Social media is representative of this dual use, where civilian usage was widespread, and the political consequences were under-interrogated (until the 2016 election). Facebook, for example, appears to be self-consciously apolitical, but the way it advertises, the decisions it makes to censor objectionable news, and the regulatory measures it takes to enforce the guidelines it creates necessarily affects the way that billions of users consume politically relevant information (Kreps 2020). In other words, Facebook's very efforts to remain on the sidelines of politics directly implicate it in key decisions about the political process, including who is elected (Fisher 2018). Another illustrative political application is Project Maven, which is aimed at using large volumes of data collected from drone footage to generate algorithms about the identity and location of militants. Google had initially used its big data program, Tensorflow, to generate algorithms, but withdrew from the project due to public censure. The software is open source, a symbolic math library in service of deep learning—not expressly political. Yet it found an application that could dramatically shape how states target and achieve political aims.

Given the relatively underdeveloped nature of these technologies and sparse empirical record, it would be overly speculative to evaluate this question as a hard test. We can offer, instead, certain indicators that would support or undermine support for the argument that computing innovations can influence the formulation of grand strategy. More states altering their public diplomacy or information operations to target citizen mobilization and education efforts during elections, for example, could be seen as suggestive evidence. Integration of machine learning with static or dynamic weapons platforms could produce a technical shift in the offense–defense balance. Further movement toward digital currency or electronic commerce could create demand for new policies to deal with domestic political economic interests on issues of taxation and public finance. None of these developments should be taken individually to suggest a transformation of grand strategy, but as these technologies continue to develop and proliferate, their collective impact might produce significant and measurable shifts in how state service their overarching political objectives.

Discussion

In this chapter, we have offered an argument for how technical innovations indirectly impact the formulation and implementation of grand strategy. In our framework, we argue that technological progress intervenes on existing grand strategy in an iterative process. States do not start from scratch as new technologies and organizational practices emerge, rather, they look for ways to integrate new capabilities and improvements into their existing practices. One virtue of our approach is treating the gains from innovation as continuous, rather than discrete. We do not focus on "types" of innovations, but rather the aggregation and size of the effect on the state's existing capabilities. This enables us to investigate how technological progress may interact with grand strategy while holding the foundational interests of the state constant.

When new technologies produce modest efficiency gains, states will use these new capabilities to realize marginal benefits in implementing status quo strategies. By contrast, significant technical improvements may alter the choice set available to states and lead to the adoption of new strategies or the pursuit of future technology as its own end. When this occurs, states may set more ambitious political objectives enabled by new capabilities or even pursue further technological progress as an intermediate end. Our empirical illustrations explicate the logic of our framework and discuss how three different innovations interacted with the formulation and implementation of grand strategy.

The primary technical benefit of precision-guided munitions has been the increased accuracy and lethality of military firepower. This has impacted the implementation of national security and military strategies by increasing the efficiency of combat operations, easing the burden on pilots, and reducing collateral damage and civilian casualties. Precision-guided munitions have not had a noticeable impact on the formulation of grand strategy, as these marginal benefits have fallen short of fundamentally altering the modern system of battle.

Robotics present more of a middle ground, as they provide efficiency gains on the implementation of existing strategy and have also helped to formulate new policy objectives and strategic approaches to conflict. On the one hand, robotics improves the implementation of grand strategy, improving the safety and reliability of military tasks that might otherwise be hazardous for individual soldiers. On the other hand, the advent of light-footprint warfare is a new strategic formulation that capitalizes on new capabilities to wage war where the US might not be sufficiently resolved to commit boots on the ground. Global investment in robotics also suggests that pursuit of this technological edge is an end unto itself for some states.

Finally, advancements in computing are simultaneously some of the newest and potentially most impactful innovations. Cyber capabilities have enabled states to develop alternative capabilities to pursue existing strategic priorities—a fact illustrated by the case of the US employing Stuxnet to undermine the Iranian nuclear program. Computing has also established an entirely new domain of information operations, as evidenced by the Russian exploitation of social media to affect the 2016 US presidential elections. As computing technologies develop and proliferate, strategies may continue to adjust their political aims to exploit or safeguard vulnerabilities in networked defense, electronic commerce, or information systems.[1]

Note

1. The authors would like to thank Ronald Krebs, Thierry Balzacq, Max Margulies, Mark Haas, Sally White, and Alexander Kirss for their thoughtful comments and suggestions. We would also like to thank participants of the Department of Social Sciences "Grand Strategy Workshop" at West Point for their enthusiastic participation and insightful contributions.

References

Anderson, Philip, and Michael Tushman. 1990. "Technological Discontinuities and Dominant Designs: A Cyclical Model of Technological Change." *Administrative Science Quarterly* 35 (4) (December): 604–633.

Art, Robert J. 2003. *A Grand Strategy for America*. Ithaca: Cornell University Press.

Atherton, Kelsey D. 2018. "Are Killer Robots the Future of War? Parsing the Facts on Autonomous Weapons." *The New York Times*, November 15, 2018. https://www.nytimes.com/2018/11/15/magazine/autonomous-robots-weapons.html

Balzacq, Thierry, Peter Dombrowski, and Simon Reich. 2019. "Is Grand Strategy a Research Program? A Review Essay." *Security Studies* 28 (1): 58–86.

Barnes, Julian, and Josh Chin. 2018. "The New Arms Race in AI." *Wall Street Journal*, March 2, 2018. https://www.wsj.com/articles/the-new-arms-race-in-ai-1520009261

Biddle, Stephen. 2004. *Military Power: Explaining Victory and Defeat in Modern Battle*. Princeton: Princeton University Press.

Biddle, Stephen, and Ivan Oelrich. 2016. "Future Warfare in the Western Pacific: Chinese Antiaccess/Area Denial, U.S. AirSea Battle, and Command of the Commons in East Asia." *International Security* 41 (1) (Summer): 7–48.

Brooks, Stephen G., G. John Ikenberry, and William C. Wohlforth. 2012/13. "Don't Come Home America: The Case Against Retrenchment." *International Security* 37 (3) (Winter): 7–51.

Brown, Malcolm W. 1991. "Invention that Shaped the Gulf War: The Laser-Guided Bomb." *New York Times*, February 26, 1991. https://www.nytimes.com/1991/02/26/science/invention-that-shaped-the-gulf-war-the-laser-guided-bomb.html

Christensen, Clayton M. 1997. *The Innovator's Dilemma: When New Technologies Cause Great Firms to Fail*. Boston: Harvard Business School Press.

Defense Industry Daily staff. 2018. "Digital Raven: Hand-Launched UAV Goes Binary." *Defense Industry Daily*, October 4, 2018. https://www.defenseindustrydaily.com/digital-raven-up-to-666m-to-aerovironment-for-uav-upgrades-06050/

Dombrowski, Peter, and Simon Reich. 2017. "Does Donald Trump Have a Grand Strategy?" *International Affairs* 5: 1013–1037.

Drezner, Daniel W. 2011. "Does Obama Have a Grand Strategy?" *Foreign Affairs* 90 (4) (July/August): 57–68.

Fischer, Sophie-Charlotte, Andrea Gilli, and Mauro Gilli. 2021. "Technological Change and Grand Strategy." In *The Oxford Handbook of Grand Strategy*, edited by Thierry Balzacq and Ronald R. Krebs, XX–XX. Oxford: Oxford University Press.

Fisher, Max. 2018. "Inside Facebook's Secret Rulebook for Global Political Speech." *New York Times*, December 27, 2018. https://www.nytimes.com/2018/12/27/world/facebook-moderators.html

Gavin, Frank. 2015. "Strategies of Inhibition: U.S. Grand Strategy, the Nuclear Revolution, and Nonproliferation." *International Security* 40 (1) (Summer): 9–46.

Gillespie, Paul G. 2006. *Weapons of Choice: The Development of Precision Guided Munitions*. Tuscaloosa: University of Alabama Press.

Gilpin, Robert. 1981. *War and Change in World Politics*. Princeton: Princeton University Press.

Glaser, Charles L., and Chaim Kaufmann. 1998. "What is the Offense-Defense Balance and Can We Measure It?" *International Security* 22 (4) (Spring): 44–82.

Goldsmith, Jack, and Matthew Waxman. 2016. "The Legal Legacy of Light-Footprint Warfare." *The Washington Quarterly* 39 (2): 7–21.

Horowitz, Michael C. 2010. *The Diffusion of Military Power: Causes and Consequences for International Politics*. Princeton: Princeton University Press.

Horowitz, Michael, Sarah Kreps, and Matthew Fuhrmann. 2016. "Separating Fact from Fiction in the Debate over Drone Proliferation." *International Security* 41 (2) (Fall): 7–42.

Host, Pat. 2015. "DoD Developing Third 'Offset' Strategy Focused on Precision Munitions." *Defense Daily*, March 17, 2015. https://www.defensedaily.com/dod-developing-third-offset-strategy-focused-on-precision-munitions/pentagon/

Jervis, Robert. 1978. "Cooperation Under the Security Dilemma." *World Politics* 30 (2) (January): 167–214.

Kharpal, Arjun. 2017. "Stephen Hawking says A.I. Could Be 'Worst Event in the History of Our Civilization.'" *CNBC*, November 6, 2017. https://www.cnbc.com/2017/11/06/stephen-hawking-ai-could-be-worst-event-in-civilization.html

Kirss, Alexander. 2018. "Does Grand Strategy Matter?" *Strategic Studies Quarterly* 12 (4) (Winter): 116–132.

Koplow, David A. 2009. *Death by Moderation: The U.S. Military's Quest for Usable Weapons*. Cambridge: Cambridge University Press.

Krepinevich, Andrew. 1994. "Cavalry to Computer: The Pattern of Military Revolutions." *The National Interest* 37 (Fall): 30–42.

Kreps, Sarah E. 2020. *Social Media and International Politics*. Cambridge: Cambridge University Press.

Larson, Deborah Welch, and Alexei Shevchenko. 2010. "Status Seekers: Chinese and Russian Responses to U.S. Primacy." *International Security* 34 (4): 63–95.

Levy, Jack. 2008. "Preventive War and Democratic Politics." *International Studies Quarterly* 52 (1): 1–24.

Liddell Hart, B.H. 1991. *Strategy*. London: Meridian.

Lieber, Keir A. 2005. *War and the Engineers: The Primacy of Politics Over Technology*. Ithaca: Cornell University Press.

Lieber, Keir A., and Daryl G. Press. 2006. "The End of MAD? The Nuclear Dimension of U.S. Primacy." *International Security* 30 (4) (Spring): 7–44.

Lieber, Keir A., and Daryl G. Press. 2017. "The New Era of Counterforce: Technological Change and the Future of Nuclear Deterrence." *International Security* 41 (4) (Spring): 9–49.

Luttwak, Edward N. 2001. *Strategy: The Logic of War and Peace*. Cambridge: Belknap Press.

Martel, William C. 2015. *Grand Strategy in Theory and Practice: The Need for an Effective American Foreign Policy*. New York: Cambridge University Press.

Martin, John D. 2005. "Misfire: An Operational Critique of OIF Targeting Strategy." *Joint Military Operations Department*. Newport: Naval War College.

Mearsheimer, John J. 1983. *Conventional Deterrence*. Ithaca: Cornell University Press.

Mearsheimer, John J. 2001. *The Tragedy of Great Power Politics*. New York: W.W. Norton and Company.

Michlovitz, David E. 2000. "Precision-Guided Munitions." In the *Oxford Companion to American Military History*, edited by John Whiteclay Cambers, 556–557. Oxford: Oxford University Press.

Mukunda, Gautam. 2010. "We Cannot Go On: Disruptive Innovation and the First World War Royal Navy." *Security Studies* 19 (1): 124–159.

Murray, Williamson and MacGregor Knox. 2001. "Thinking about Revolutions in Warfare." In *The Dynamics of Military Revolution, 1300–2050*, edited by MacGregor Knox and Murray Williamson, 1–14. Cambridge: Cambridge University Press.

National Security Strategy of the United States of America. 2017. Washington, DC: Government Printing Office.

Narizny, Kevin. 2007. *The Political Economy of Grand Strategy*. Ithaca: Cornell University Press.

"National Security Council Report. NSC 68. 'United States Objectives and Programs for National Security.'" History and Public Policy Program Digital Archive, U.S. National Archives, April 14, 1950. http://digitalarchive.wilsoncenter.org/document/116191

Posen, Barry. 1984. *The Sources of Military Doctrine: France, Britain, and Germany between the World Wars*. Ithaca: Cornell University Press.

Posen, Barry. 2014. *Restraint: A New Foundation for U.S. Grand Strategy*. Ithaca: Cornell University Press.

Rempfer, Kyle. 2018. "Man-Portable, Multi-Tool Drones Coming to Ground Troops Near You." *Army Times*, October 8, 2018. https://www.armytimes.com/2018/10/08/man-portable-multi-tool-drones-coming-to-ground-troops-near-you/

Rosen, Stephen P. 1991. *Winning the Next War: Innovation and the Modern Military*. Ithaca: Cornell University Press.

Rule, Shelia. 1989. "Reagan Gets a Red Carpet from British." *New York Times*. June 14, 1989. https://www.nytimes.com/1989/06/14/world/reagan-gets-a-red-carpet-from-british.html

Sagan, Scott. 1996/1997. "Why Do States Build Nuclear Weapons?: Three Models in Search of a Bomb." *International Security* 21 (3): 54–88.

Savage, Charlie. 2011. "2 Top Lawyers Lost to Obama in Libya War Policy Debate." *New York Times*, June 17, 2011. https://www.nytimes.com/2011/06/18/world/africa/18powers.html

Scharre, Paul. 2018. *Army of None: Autonomous Weapons and the Future of Warfare*. New York: W.W. Norton and Company.

Silove, Nina. 2018. "Beyond the Buzzword: The Three Meanings of 'Grand Strategy.'" *Security Studies* 27 (1): 27–57.

Singer, Peter. 2009. *Wired for War: The Robotics Revolution and Conflict in the Twenty-First Century*. New York: The Penguin Press.

Slayton, Rebecca. 2016/2017. "What is the Cyber Offense-Defense Balance?: Conceptions, Causes, and Assessment." *International Security* 41 (3) (Winter): 72–109.

Whittaker, Zack. 2018. "US Intelligence Community says Quantum Computing and AI Pose an 'Emerging Threat' to National Security." *TechCrunch*, December 13, 2018. https://techcrunch.com/2018/12/13/us-intelligence-quantum-computing-artificial-intelligence-national-security-threat/

Wiener, Norbert. 1949. "The Machine Age." Unpublished Editorial: Massachusetts Institute of Technology. https://libraries.mit.edu/app/dissemination/DIPonline/MC0022/MC0022_MachineAgeV3_1949.pdf.

Zenko, Micah (@MicahZenko). 2018. "If you think something is new, read anything by Norbert Wiener. He wrote this for the NYT in 1949, but it was never published. bit.ly/2Tc5WWH." Tweet. December 27, 2018.

CHAPTER 44

POPULATION AGING AND GRAND STRATEGY

MARK L. HAAS

THE world is experiencing an era of unprecedented demographic change. Due to major reductions in fertility levels and significant increases in life expectancies over the course of the last century—and especially since the end of the Second World War—a majority of countries are growing older, many at fantastic rates and extent. In 2018, 13 countries were what the United Nations classifies as "super aged" based on at least 20 percentof their population ages 65 and older. By 2050, 82 countries are projected to reach this level of extreme aging, which is roughly 42 percentof the world's states (PRB 2018). Significantly, the world's most powerful countries are not immune from this trend. To the contrary, China, France, Germany, Japan, Russia, the United Kingdom, and the United States are among the oldest states in the world, and all will continue to age as the century progresses. By 2050, the median ages of all these states will be at least 41, and several (China, Germany, and Japan) will have median ages above 48.[1]

This chapter analyzes the impact of population aging on states' grand strategy. Following Barry Posen, I define grand strategy as "a political-military, means-ends chain, a state's theory about how it can best 'cause' security for itself ... A grand strategy must identify likely threats to the state's security and it must devise political, economic, military, and other remedies for those threats" (1984, 13). A grand strategy, in other words, consists of leaders' understandings of: (1) their state's core interests; (2) threats to these interests; (3) the appropriate policies designed to advance these interests in the face of the threats to them; and (4) the capabilities available to achieve policy success. Population aging will have important effects on all four dimensions of grand strategy. The following analysis is ordered based on the extent of aging's likely impact on these components, discussing from most to least affected. I focus primarily on aging in the great powers because their grand strategies are the most consequential for the evolution of international relations.

The Effects of Population Aging on States' Capabilities

Aging's largest impact on grand strategy will result from the major negative effects that it will have on states' capabilities, including economic and military power and societal cohesiveness (I discuss the last in a subsequent section).[2] The effects of aging on states' economies will be particularly important. A state's gross domestic product (GDP) is a product of the number of workers and overall productivity. As a country's workforce shrinks due to population aging as more people enter retirement than enter the labor market, so, too, will its GDP unless productivity levels rise sufficiently to compensate for this loss. Between 2015 and 2050, Japan's working-age population (ages 15 to 64) is expected to shrink by 29 percent, Russia's and China's by 20 percent, and Germany's by 17 percent. To prevent these workforce reductions from translating into overall GDP decline, states' productivity must increase proportionally. Although this is likely to be the case in most of the industrialized countries, workforce contraction is nevertheless likely to significantly hinder economic expansion.

Compounding this problem, significant societal aging is also likely to limit productivity growth. An International Monetary Fund (2016, 6–8) report, for example, predicted that Europe's aging workforce was likely to reduce productivity by roughly 0.2 percentage points per year through 2035. Aging may hurt productivity because people become less innovative as they age and less adept in adopting new technologies and methods in the workplace (Irmen and Litina 2017). The elderly also tend to be more risk-averse than younger individuals, which will make them less inclined to switch careers, start new businesses, or invest in high-risk, high-reward ventures.

Population aging is already having major negative effects on states' economies, and these effects are likely to become worse in coming decades as the extent of aging intensifies. A 2016 study of US states from 1980 to 2010 found that a 10 percentincrease in the percentage of 60 year-olds and over decreased the growth rate of GDP per capita by 5.5 percent(Maestas, Mullen, and Powell 2016).

The impact of slowing economic growth on the capabilities component of grand strategy is obvious. The slower states' economic expansion, the less we should expect significant increases in any of the instruments of international relations that require substantial expenditures, most notably spending on military hardware and personnel, international aid and development and other dimensions of economic statecraft, and the diplomatic corps. Reductions in these expenditures are instead more likely in periods of economic stagnation.

Population aging is likely to negatively affect states' military capabilities (which many analysts consider to be the most important instrument of grand strategy) not only indirectly due to slowing economic growth, but directly by creating crowding out dynamics and increasing military personnel costs. Regarding crowding out, the more that governments spend on elderly welfare, the less they are likely to spend on all other purchases, including on the military. All governments in the industrialized world have made commitments to pay for substantial portions of the retirement and healthcare costs of their elderly citizens. The older a society, the greater the number seniors for which its government is potentially responsible.

In his analysis of national power, Michael Beckley argues that a country's capabilities are best understood as net resources calculated by subtracting costs from assets. A major set of costs that reduces national power are "welfare" or "subsistence" costs, which "include outlays on basic items such as food, health care, social security, and education" (2018, 15). These expenses (especially social security and healthcare) will dramatically increase in aging states, thereby significantly reducing these countries' net power.

The projected increases in governmental spending for the elderly in coming decades are massive. One study forecasts that annual public benefits to the elderly (both pension and healthcare) as a percentage of GDP will rise between 2010 and 2040 by 7.4 percentage points in the United States (to an overall percentage of 18.5), by 7.3 percentage points in Germany (to an overall percentage of 24.3), by 5.8 percentage points in Japan (to an overall percentage of 20.9), by 5.7 percentage points in France (to an overall percentage of 24.3), and by 5 percentage points in the United Kingdom (to an overall percentage of 18.9) (Jackson, Howe, and Peter 2013, 14). Another study predicts that China's public spending on pensions and healthcare as a percentage of GDP based on current benefit levels will increase by roughly 13 percentage points between 2015 and 2050 (to an overall level of 19.9). If China increases benefit levels to be on par with high-income countries—which is a stated goal of China's government—this increase will be roughly 21 percentage points (to an overall level of 28 percentof GDP) (Cai, Feng, and Shen 2018, 825–827). These expenditures on the elderly will create a very tight fiscal environment that will pressure all other areas of spending.

Population aging does not necessarily mean that governments will increase spending on elderly welfare at the expense of funding the military. Russia's government, for example, is currently cutting welfare spending for seniors in order to increase military expenditures (Khodarkovsky 2016). Leaders, especially in illiberal regimes where elites are much less likely to be penalized for neglecting citizens' preferences, can try to ignore the incentives created by aging that push for increased spending on elderly welfare and instead favor other priorities.[3] These incentives are, however, very powerful and they will only intensify the older a population becomes. The reasons are clear. Population aging results in the significant growth—both absolutely and as a percentage of a state's population—of a demographic cohort that is traditionally very politically active and in high need of governmental support. Older individuals' demand for governmental support is very high for two main reasons. First, the need for healthcare grows substantially as people age. Studies have shown that seniors use three to five times more medical care than younger people, and this trend only accelerates as the elderly age (CIA 2001, 27; Jackson 2002, 22). Second, few people possess sufficient savings to finance their retirement. According to a 2017 study by the World Economic Forum, the gap between what most individuals across the world have saved and what they need to retire is massive. By 2050, this gap will be $137 trillion in the United States (in 2015 US dollars), $119 trillion in China, $33 trillion in the United Kingdom, and $26 trillion in Japan. Roughly 24 percent of this gap results from inadequate personal savings and almost all of the remainder from underfunded public pensions.[4] This gap will put tremendous pressure on governments to significantly increase welfare spending on the elderly.

When high demand for governmental services is coupled with high political activism (seniors typically vote at much higher levels than younger cohorts), leaders ignore this demand at their peril. Although seniors' demand for increased spending on their welfare will be most politically salient in democracies, leaders in illiberal regimes will also confront incentives to avoid angering this growing demographic group.[5] It is therefore not surprising that the dominant trend over the last century, even in many illiberal regimes, is the expansion of welfare payments for the elderly. China between 2009 and 2014, for example, increased public spending on pensions and healthcare as a share of GDP by two percentage points. According to Yong Cai, Wang Feng, and Ke Shen, this increase "was mainly driven by increases in benefit generosity, not population change." China's government has committed to continue to increase the generosity of its welfare payments in coming decades even as the number of seniors in the country explodes (2018, 818 (quotation), 823–824).

Aging is also likely to negatively impact states' military power by significantly increasing military personnel costs. This outcome will occur for two main reasons. The first results from increasing labor costs in an era of falling fertility. When fertility rates decline, the size of the pool of military-age recruits shrinks. Fewer babies today means fewer potential soldiers tomorrow. As the supply of military-age labor falls, its per unit price will increase (assuming constant demand). In this environment, states' militaries will have to pay more per soldier if they want to be able to attract and keep the best personnel in vital areas of operation. This analysis is most true for volunteer militaries that depend to a great extent on the attractiveness of compensation to secure recruits. Even conscripted armies, though, confront incentives not to let the disparity between civilian and military wages get too great lest dissatisfaction in the ranks become excessive.

Numerous sources highlight growing difficulties for governments in attracting military recruits as their societies age. According to Alison Smale, for example, "Germany is confronting a demographic crisis, and its all-volunteer army is just one of many enterprises seeking every-scarcer skilled labor ... 'The time when we could pick and choose from a large pool of conscripts is over,' [argued Germany's defense minister Ursula von der Leyen in 2014] ... We are facing a huge challenge" (2014). Xie Xiaobo, the chief of staff at the Guizhou Xingyi military command in southern China, similarly observed in 2015 that "working against [China's] military is the country's one-child policy ... which has led to a generation of only children in China's cities who have a variety of career choices other than a rigorous soldier's life" (Forsythe 2015). Given the shrinking pool of prime military-age cohorts in aging states, it is not surprising that per-soldier costs have tended to increase considerably in these countries (Brooks et al. 2019, 70–71, 85, 88–89).

A second factor that is likely to increase states' military personnel costs at the expense of weapons procurement is the aging of the military itself. The great powers' pension obligations to retired military personnel are considerable. Russia in the 2000s consistently spent more on military retirees than on either weapons procurement or military research and development (Haas 2007, 142). Rising pension costs (along with pay increases for active personnel), according to China's government, were the most important reason for increases in Chinese military spending in the 1990s and 2000s (PRC 2004). In fiscal year 2017, the US military spent nearly $58 billion on pensions, which was roughly 9 percent of its total budget (Office of the Comptroller, US Department of Defense 2017, 57). These costs alone would have made the United States the seventh largest military spender in the world (Tian et al. 2018, 2).

Growing military personnel expenditures due to increasing per-unit labor and pension costs will impact states' grand strategies by reducing their ability to project power. When per-unit labor costs are increasing, the same amount of money will pay for fewer soldiers. Growing pension costs for military retirees not only do not add to states' capabilities, but likely subtract from them due to crowding out dynamics.

The Effects of Population Aging on States' Policies

Population aging is also likely to have a significant impact on the policy component of grand strategy. This dimension of grand strategy refers to the types of international choices that leaders make in order to protect their interests against anticipated threats.

Two varieties of choices, broadly speaking, are particularly important in defining the policy dimension of grand strategy (Narizny 2007, 11–15). The first is leaders' willingness to use force to achieve their international objectives. The second is states' level of activity in the international arena along an internationalist–isolationist continuum. An internationalist grand strategy is one that dedicates significant resources to promoting and protecting a state's international influence, an isolationist one the reverse. There are good reasons to expect that the dominant incentives created by population aging will push for the adoption of more peaceful and less internationalist policies.

Population aging will push states to adopt less aggressive and less active international policies for four principal reasons (one of which is discussed in the next section). The first results from the findings presented earlier. All other things being equal, internationalist and aggressive grand strategies are more likely during eras of expanding capabilities, while isolationist and peaceful grand strategies are more likely during periods of shrinking or stagnating capabilities. Population aging makes it more likely that states will be operating in the latter situation than the former. In a time of fiscal austerity brought on by societal aging, more restrained grand strategies are likely to become more compelling because they mesh with the need to reduce spending. President Donald Trump, for example, clearly indicated sympathy for these prescriptions, indicating that fiscal constraints require that US leaders think hard about pulling back from the world, including withdrawing from long-standing alliance commitments. As he said while campaigning in April 2016,

> we have spent trillions of dollars over time on planes, missiles, ships, equipment, building up our military to provide a strong defense for Europe and Asia. The countries we are defending must pay for the cost of this defense, and if not, the U.S. must be prepared to let these countries defend themselves. We have no choice ... [I]n this time of mounting debt ... not one single dollar can we waste. (Trump 2016)

The second reason why aging states are likely to adopt more isolationist and less aggressive grand strategies results from the effects that shrinking fertility (which is the primary cause of population aging) are likely to have on casualty aversion. Both governments and societies are likely to become more casualty sensitive as fertility shrinks, thereby creating enhanced barriers to aggressive international policies.

The linkage between falling fertility rates and increasing casualty sensitivity at the governmental level is straightforward. As I detailed above, shrinking fertility will result in a decline in the number of people of prime military age, which will tend to force militaries to spend more on each soldier as this cohort of labor becomes scarcer. When both the pool of potential military recruits shrinks and the amount of money invested in each individual soldier increases as per unit labor costs grow, leaders' casualty aversion is likely to intensify (Brooks et al. 2019, 70). The more scarce and valuable a resource (in terms of money and time invested in it), the more careful leaders will be with it. A government in an era of falling fertility should therefore be more hesitant to initiate conflicts that risk soldiers' lives.

An early, though critical, example of how low fertility rates, population aging, and a dearth of potential military recruits can push leaders to adopt a risk-averse and highly casualty-sensitive grand strategy even in a highly threatening security environment is France in the 1930s. Due to very low fertility rates and the deaths of nearly 1.4 million soldiers during the First World War (which was roughly 3.5 percent of France's population and all from younger cohorts), France in the 1930s was the oldest country in the world, with nearly 15 percent of its population 60 or older (which meets the United Nations' definition of an "aged" state). In every year between 1935 and 1939 (and continuing through 1945), more people died in France than were born, which is another hallmark of an advanced aged society. France's prime military age cohort (ages 20–29) shrunk by roughly 10 percent between 1931 and 1936, making it less than 60 percent of Germany's (Dyer 1978, 66–67, 83–84; Ogden and Huss 1982, 285; Mitchell 2003, 20, 22).

The constraints and strategic pessimism created by these demographic variables played a major role in pushing French leaders to adopt a defensive and highly casualty-sensitive grand strategy. As Richard Tomlinson, Marie-Monique Huss, and Philip Ogden explain, in the second half of the 1930s

> the fear of depopulation assumed unprecedented political importance in France. The cause was [a soldier] recruitment crisis ... Military planners traced the roots of this

crisis back to the Great War, when the number of births had fallen by almost 50%. It was therefore a statistical certainty that twenty years later the level of recruitment would fall by the same proportion. What no one could have foreseen was that the arrival of this "hollow" period of recruitment in 1935 would coincide with a resurgence of German militarism ... The army command had no solution to this problem except to continue to fortify the Maginot Line, and hope that in the meantime the Germans would not invade. (1985, 28; also Dyer 1978, 85)

France's aging problem even pushed some French leaders to prefer an early surrender to Germany after its invasion in 1940. This preference is the ultimate example of a grand strategy of restraint and casualty aversion due to demographic decline. According to Colin Dyer:

If the French did not wish to die for Danzig, neither did they wish to die for France. In view of the disastrous demographic situation, to die for France would probably have meant the death of France. The French therefore had to lose, whether they fought or not. It was better to surrender and to live than to fight and kill France forever. On 26 May 1940 Marshal [Philippe] Pétain [then Deputy Prime Minister and Prime Minister beginning the following month] had declared it was "stupid to speak of France fighting to her last man. It is also criminal", he added, "in view of our losses in the first war and of our feeble birth rate." French blood was scarce and had to be spared at all costs. (Dyer 1978, 93; also 103)

Falling fertility rates are likely to increase casualty sensitivity not only at the governmental level but at the societal level as well. Edward Luttwak argues that low-fertility families in the modern era are more casualty sensitive and thus more opposed to war because they are less used to losing children to disease (1995). Brooks et al. utilize a different logic and evidence to reach the same conclusion (2019, 71–74). Their data, which comes from the multistate, multigenerational "Value of Children" surveys, indicates that the fewer children parents have, the more that highly valued and nonsubstitutable psychological and emotional goals (such as having someone to love and care for, enjoyment, self-esteem, gender balance, and carrying on the family name) are tied to each individual child (Arnold and Albores 1975; Nauck and Klaus 2007). The greater the "value" of any one child, the greater the loss that the child's death creates, thereby making casualty sensitivity especially high for parents with few children (Bulatao 1981, 2). Analyzing the level of parents' investments in terms of time and money (especially in terms of educational costs) in individual children leads to the same prediction. Studies have demonstrated that parents' human capital expenditures per child are substantially higher when fertility is lower (Lee and Mason 2010). As these investments in what have been labeled "high quality" children expand, we would expect casualty sensitivity in lowerfertility societies to also increase. Numerous studies indicate that societies have become more sensitive to casualties over the last fifty years (e.g., Everts and Isernia 2001). This timeframe corresponds with significant reductions in fertility levels across most of the world.

A third reason why population aging is likely to incentivize the adoption of more peaceful grand strategies is by empowering a group that tends to be more pacific that others. As olderage cohorts grow as a percentage of a state's population, their political power, especially in democracies, is likely to increase. If people tend to become more opposed to war as they age, then the increasing political power of older people would create an enhanced disposition to peace.

Quantitative analyses have found that there is indeed a strong relationship between age and preferences against aggression. Gelpi, Feaver, and Reifler find that in the United States "age is ... a significant predictor of casualty tolerance; older respondents [in surveys] are less willing to tolerate casualties than younger ones." Moreover, the older a person becomes, the less likely he or she will support the use of force for either security or humanitarian reasons, or the escalation of existing military conflicts (2009, 35–36, 84–88, quotation from 88). Surveys of older people in other countries, including France, Germany, the Netherlands, and the United Kingdom, reveal similar results (Brooks et al. 2019, 80–83).

Seniors' political interests go a long way in explaining why individuals become more opposed to aggressive international policies as they age (Brooks et al. 2019, 75). The elderly could fairly reason that the more war-prone their country's foreign policies, the less money that will be available for spending on seniors. Less militaristic policies, in contrast, would increase the likelihood of higher levels of welfare spending. These calculations, according to some reports, played an important role in pushing thousands of Japanese pensioners in 2015 to participate in mass protests against Prime Minister Shinzo Abe's efforts to weaken Japan's pacifist constitution (Funabashi 2015).[6]

THE EFFECTS OF POPULATION AGING ON STATES' INTERESTS

The "interest" component of grand strategy is typically defined in terms of protecting states' security from others' encroachment. The effects of population aging may help advance this core goal. If the analysis in the preceding two sections is correct and aging societies' capacity and preferences for aggression are likely to be significantly lower than in younger countries, then states will tend to be more secure the more their international relations are dominated by interactions with aged countries (Haas 2007;Brooks et al. 2019). This relationship will create unique opportunities for states to protect their safety. If older states are likely to be less aggressive, then leaders will have a security-based interest in other countries becoming older. These elites, as a result, have an interest in supporting international policies that decrease other states' fertility rates while increasing life expectancies, which together are the causes of population aging. The most effective policies that result in these outcomes are ones that improve economic development, women's rights, and public health.

At the same time that population aging is likely to create unique opportunities for leaders to protect their state's security, it may also temper the importance of this interest in favor of advantaging another one: improving citizens' welfare. By "welfare," I am referring to the health, comfort, and prosperity of a group's members. State security is obviously a critical component of individuals' welfare because a high threat of violence compromises the ability to enjoy all other goods. Welfare, though, is more comprehensive because it goes beyond the protection of individuals' lives to the advancement of their quality of life. In an aging world, leaders may decide to risk higher levels of international insecurity (by, for example, lowering levels of military spending or eschewing costly preventive measures against enemies) if this allows enhanced levels of domestic spending to improve seniors' quality of life.

These claims relate to the crowding out dynamics between old-age security and military spending that I discussed above. Costly efforts to promote states' international security interests are in tension with the provision of domestic welfare if the resources dedicated to one results in significantly fewer resources spent on the other. The more that governments respond to the very high demand in aging societies for major increases in spending on the elderly, the more the security interest of grand strategies may be jeopardized. Indeed, the demand for the provision of elderly welfare in aging countries may be so great that leaders come to define their state's international interests and grand strategy success to an important extent by how well they help advance this domestic objective. This last development, according to Seongho Sheen, is already occurring in China, which is aging faster than any country in history. Because "rapidly aging populations... create more demand for social security than military security," leaders are likely to give more thought to privileging the provision of elderly welfare even if this means risking higher levels of international insecurity. Thus, Sheen argues, "one organizing principle for China's grand strategy will be the improvement of living standards, welfare, and happiness." Hence Chinese leaders' claim that they are pursuing a "'peaceful rise' as the country's geopolitical goal, in an effort to continue economic development" (2013, 294, 318).[7]

A final way in which population aging could affect the interest component of states' grand strategies is by stoking nationalist sentiments and parties based on a growing interest in protecting a state's majority ethnic culture against the advance of minority ones. Nationalists are fixated on the ethnocultural differences between groups, perceive their group to be under threat from others, and aim to preserve their group's traditions. The rise of nationalist parties is bound to affect not only domestic politics, but foreign relations as well as nationalists are likely to oppose internationalist grand strategies in favor of more isolationist ones. (The rise of nationalist parties, which is often accompanied by the polarization of society along ethnic lines, is also likely to negatively affect states' international capabilities: intense domestic divisions and the decline of societal cohesiveness frequently result in policy paralysis while inclining leaders and society to be inwardly focused.)

The most obvious way in which population aging is likely to aid the rise of nationalist parties is by contributing to major demographic shifts within a state. If a country is divided into different ethnic groups (which I define broadly based not only on ethnicity, but race, language, and/or religion), and if the dominant ethic group is aging faster than minority ones due to lower fertility rates (which will cause it to shrink as a percentage of the state's overall population), ethnicity is likely to become increasingly salient to how members of the dominant group view the world. As is often the case, the more a group's political position is threatened—in this case by demographic decline—the more important the characteristics that define the group will become to perceptions and policies. In this environment, members of the dominant but declining identity group are likely to fear that the fundamental character of the regime is under threat as other groups increase in numbers.

These dynamics are likely already at work, playing a central role in the rise of populist nationalist parties and candidates across much of Europe and the United States, beginning in the 2014 elections to the European Parliament. Survey data and statistical analyses confirm that support for these parties was primarily a product of cultural and not economic fears, and the former were rooted in demographic shifts. As Eric Kaufmann summarizes:

> The populist story is primarily one of culture and identity, in particular the fear among white voters across the West that their cultures and identities are under threat ... The rise of populism stems, first and foremost, from ethnocultural anxiety. Members of the majority populations fear an erosion of the connection between their communities of shared ancestry and their perceived homelands.

This "ethnocultural anxiety" is the result of "the shrinking demographic weight of the West's ethnic majorities" due to a combination of aging by the dominant group and higher immigration levels by minority groups (2018, 224, 231; also Kaufmann 2019, 2, 5, 18, 222–223; Norris and Inglehart 2019, 16, 40–41, 44–45, 47, 49, 182, 189, 200).

Helping to create demographic shifts among different ethnic groups within a state is not the only way in which population aging is likely to contribute to the rise of nationalist parties. The same outcome will occur if older people tend to be more nationalistic and focused on cultural threats than younger individuals. Evidence indicates that this is often the case. In an analysis of individuals' values in 32 European and Middle Eastern countries, Pippa Norris and Ronald Inglehart find that age is strongly associated with authoritarianism (what I have called nationalism), with "older cohorts always endorsing authoritarian values more than the Millennials" (individuals born between 1980 and 1996) (2019, 120).[8] Consistent with this finding, there was a major generational divide both in the 2016 US presidential election and the 2016 referendum in Britain regarding whether Britain should leave the European Union ("Brexit").[9] Older people were much more likely than younger people to vote for Trump and for Britain to leave the European Union. Cultural anxieties, including fear of ethnic change, were a dominant motivating factor for older voters in both countries (Norris and Inglehart 2019, 52, 77, 345, 385, 397–398; Kaufmann 2019, 207, 433, 516). Older people are also consistently the most hostile to immigration, especially by people of different ethnicities, which makes nationalist parties' anti-immigrant programs (which is central to virtually all of these parties) particularly appealing to this demographic group (Norris and Inglehart 2019, 200).[10]

Growing ethnic nationalism in aging societies and the resulting enhanced interest in preserving a particular culture against the advance of different ones is likely to result in more isolationist and less internationalist grand strategies. The more leaders are fixated on the preservation of their ethnic-national culture, the more likely they are to prioritize domestic interests over international ones. (Trump's campaign and governing slogan "American First" nicely captures this sentiment.) Nationalists are thus likely to reject international commitments, membership in international organizations, globalization, and the mobility of peoples across borders. As Norris and Inglehart summarize, populist nationalist parties' foreign policies favor "the protection of national sovereignty, secure borders, a strong military, and trade protectionism ... rather than membership of the European Union, diplomatic alliances, human rights, international engagement, and multilateral cooperation within the G7, NATO, and United Nations" (2019, 8). Increasing power of nationalist parties in aging societies will therefore reinforce the economic and fiscal incentives for isolationist and restrained grand strategies (discussed above) that are likely to exist in these countries.[11]

The Effects of Population Aging on Leaders' Perceptions of Threat

The biggest impact that population aging is likely to have on the threat component of grand strategy is by increasing leaders' hostility to immigration. I have already discussed the reason for this escalation. Older people, whose political power is likely to grow in aging states, tend to view immigration as a much greater cultural danger than do younger individuals. Older societies, as a result, are likely to help empower nationalist parties that make anti-immigration a central component of their political platform.

The same factors that are likely to make immigration a threat in aging societies will also make ideologies that support the privileging of other cultures (most notably multiculturalism) and the (largely) free movement of peoples across borders a danger. An aging world could thus result in important geopolitical shifts as fellow nationalists band together against internationalists and cultural liberals. These dynamics help explain, for example, Eastern European nationalists' growing tensions with various Western European states as well as enhanced admiration for Vladimir Putin's Russia. Hungary's Prime Minister Viktor Orbán described the growing cultural danger from Western European countries in his February 2018 stateofthe union address:

> The great old European nations in Western Europe have become immigrant countries. Day by day their cultural foundations are being transformed, the population raised in a Christian culture is declining, and the major cities are undergoing

Islamisation ... The danger [of cultural subversion based on multiculturalism] is threatening us from the West. This danger to us comes from politicians in Brussels, Berlin and Paris. They want us to adopt their policies: the policies that made them immigrant countries and that opened the way for the decline of Christian culture and the expansion of Islam ... We shall never express solidarity with those European leaders who want to take Europe into a post-Christian and post-national era.[12]

The calculations that are pushing populist nationalist parties in Eastern Europe to view Western European governments as a threat are also likely to result in warmer views of Putin's Russia, thereby reversing dominant threat perceptions since the end of the Cold War. As Ronald Brownstein explains:

European populist parties share a common set of priorities focused on restricting immigration, unwinding global economic and political integration (by renouncing the European Union, and, for some of these parties, NATO as well), taking tougher steps to fight Islamic radicalism, and, in most cases, opposing cultural liberalism and secularization at home. On all those fronts, they view Putin not as a threat, but as an ally. (2017)

Conclusion

Demography is not destiny, but it is an extremely powerful force. Population aging's political effects will be both profound and in important ways paradoxical. Aging is likely to contribute to growing domestic tensions and polarization, with the chief axes of dispute between younger and older cohorts and between majority and minority ethnic groups. Older and younger generations are likely to clash over both resources (because a growing percentage of a country's resources is likely to be dedicated to elderly welfare and away from other objectives) and values (because older cohorts tend to be more nationalistic and culturally conservative than younger ones). These domestic tensions will intensify if a country's majority ethnic group is aging faster (and thus declining demographically) in relation to minority groups. This condition will tend to stimulate the growth of ethnonationalist sentiments and thus the likely polarization of society along ethnic lines.

The effects of population aging on international politics and grand strategies are much more salutary. Demographically aged states are likely to be less aggressive internationally than younger ones (Brooks et al. 2019). Declining military capabilities and increased incentives for more restrained foreign policies point strongly to this conclusion. And because most countries (including the great powers, which have typically been the most aggressive states in the system) are aging, the future of international relations is likely to be more peaceful than the past.[13] This is clearly an outcome to be celebrated, even though it comes with an enhanced likelihood of growing domestic tensions and fractures.[14]

Notes

1. Unless otherwise noted, all demographic data were calculated from UN (2017).
2. For related analysis, see Haas (2007, 116–120, 140–144); Brooks et al. (2019, 68–71); Haas (2018, 91–93).
3. Elites can also try to avoid the tradeoff between increased spending on the elderly and reduced expenditures in other areas, including on the military, by levying new taxes and acquiring more debt. The problem with these policies, especially for the great powers, is that taxation rates and debt levels are in many cases already extremely high, which makes significant increases in either politically and economically difficult. See Haas (2007, 120–122).
4. In accordance with OECD guidelines, the study defines the resources necessary to fund retirement as 70 percent of pre-retirement income (WEF 2017, 7–8).
5. Consistent with the claim that aging is likely to affect policies in both liberal and illiberal regimes, Brooks, Brooks, Greenhill, and Haas (2019) find that population aging significantly reduces the likelihood of international aggression even after controlling for regime type.
6. The preceding analysis focuses on how population aging is likely to result in more peaceful grand strategies. The effects of aging, could, however, create incentives for more bellicose foreign policies by creating closing windows of opportunity. The costs created by aging could incentivize states to aggress in order to achieve revisionist international objectives before the full costs of aging come due. Closing windows of opportunity, though, are rarely the key source of war. (See Lebow 1984.)
7. For similar dynamics in Germany, see Apt (2014, 22).
8. The two Middle Eastern countries analyzed were Israel and Turkey. The rest were European. I prefer the term "nationalist" rather than "authoritarian" to describe individuals who are focused on ethnocultural differences among groups because the latter term is often used synonymously with illiberal regimes. The growth of nationalist parties can occur in both liberal and illiberal states, though nationalists' high threat perceptions and responses to them can undermine liberal values and institutions.
9. For details see Raisher (2016).
10. On the relationship between increasing age and increasing hostility to immigration, see Winkler (2015); Pettigrew, Wagner, and Christ (2007). Increasing hostility to immigration in aging states is ironic. Increased immigration is a potential solution to one of the principal costs created by aging: slowing economic growth due to reductions in the number of workers. Yet this solution will often be viewed as highly threatening to the identity of a country's declining ethnic group. Aging thus simultaneously creates a need as well as opposition to a principal means of meeting it.
11. This is not to say that nationalist identities could not result in increased incentives for international aggression. Nationalists in aging countries could be inclined to use force abroad to protect or unify with ethnic kin in other countries, to try to stop a source of immigration, or to harm the international brethren of growing minority groups in their country (for a particularly important example of the last, see Toft (2014)). In the 2010s, increasing nationalism and concerns over immigration led to increased tensions—but not armed hostilities—between the Trump administration and Mexico and some European countries and Turkey. Nevertheless, because the dominant inclination of nationalists in aging states is to focus on domestic politics while rejecting international commitments,

we should expect their grand strategies to most often be ones of restraint. The rise of ethnonationalist parties is also likely to increase the level of domestic polarization at both the elite and popular levels, which is an outcome that tends to decrease the likelihood of activist foreign policies. On the last, see Schweller (2004).
12. Quoted in Orbán (2018).
13. Sub-Saharan Africa is the main exception to the trend of worldwide aging.
14. A more peaceful world internationally is also likely to facilitate the growth of domestic polarization. States that confront a benign security environment tend to be more divided than those that confront a threatening one (Desch 1996).

References

Apt, Wenke. 2014. *Germany's New Security Demographics: Military Recruitment in the Era of Population Aging.* Dordrecht, Netherlands: Springer.

Arnold, Fred, and Sonia Albores. 1975. *The Value of Children: A Cross-National Study.* Honolulu: East-West Population Institute.

Beckley, Michael. 2018. "The Power of Nations: Measuring What Matters." *International Security* 43 (2): 7–44.

Brooks, Deborah Jordan, Stephen G. Brooks, Brian Greenhill, and Mark L. Haas. 2019. "The Demographic Transition Theory of War: Why Young Societies Are Conflict Prone and Old Societies Are the Most Peaceful." *International Security* 43 (3): 53–95.

Brownstein, Ronald. 2017. "Putin and the Populists: The Roots of Russia's Political Appeal in Europe and the United States." *The Atlantic*, January 6, 2017. https://www.theatlantic.com/international/archive/2017/01/putin-trump-le-pen-hungary-france-populist-bannon/512303/

Bulatao, Rodolfo. 1981. "Values and Disvalues of Children in Successive Childbearing Decisions." *Demography* 18 (1): 1–25.

Cai, Yong, Wang Feng, and Ke Shen. 2018. "Fiscal Implications of Population Aging and Social Sector Expenditure in China." *Population Development Review* 44 (4): 811–831.

Central Intelligence Agency (CIA). 2001. "Long-Term Global Demographic Trends: Reshaping the Geopolitical Landscape." CIA. https://www.hsdl.org/?abstract&did=2810

Desch, Michael C. 1996. "War and Strong States, Peace and Weak States?" *International Organization* 50 (2): 237–268.

Dyer, Colin. 1978. *Population and Society in Twentieth Century France.* New York: Holmes & Meier.

Everts, Philip, and Pierangelo Isernia, eds. 2001. *Public Opinion and the International Use of Force.* London: Routledge.

Forsythe, Michael. 2015. "As China Prospers, the Military Recruiter's Job Gets Harder." *New York Times*, March 19, 2015. https://sinosphere.blogs.nytimes.com/2015/03/19/as-china-prospers-the-military-recruiters-job-gets-harder/

Funabashi, Yoichi. 2015. "Japan's Gray-Haired Pacifism." *New York Times*, August 12, 2015. http://www.nytimes.com/2015/08/13/opinion/japans-gray-haired-pacifism.html

Gelpi, Christopher, Peter Feaver, and Jason Reifler. 2009. *Paying the Human Cost of War: American Public Opinion and Casualties in Military Conflicts.* Princeton, N.J.: Princeton University Press.

Haas, Mark L. 2007. "A Geriatric Peace? The Future of U.S. Power in a World of Aging Populations." *International Security* 32 (1): 112–147.

Haas, Mark L. 2018. "Population Aging and International Conflict." In *The Oxford Encyclopedia of Empirical International Relations Theory*, Vol. 3, edited by William R. Thompson, 91–105. New York: Oxford University Press.

IMF (International Monetary Fund). 2016. "Euro Area Policies." IMF Country Report No. 16/220. https://www.imf.org/external/pubs/ft/scr/2016/cr16220.pdf

Irmen, Andreas, and Anastasia Litina. 2017. "What a Study of 33 Countries Found About Aging Populations and Innovation." *Harvard Business Review*, January 18, 2017. https://hbr.org/2017/01/what-a-study-of-33-countries-found-about-aging-populations-and-innovation

Jackson, Richard. 2002. *The Global Retirement Crisis*. Washington, D.C.: Center for Strategic and International Studies.

Jackson, Richard, Neil Howe, and Tobias Peter. 2013. *The Global Aging Preparedness Index*. 2nd edition. Washington, D.C.: Center for Strategic and International Studies.

Kaufmann, Eric. 2018. "Good Fences Make Good Politics: Immigration and the Future of the West." *Foreign Affairs* 97 (5): 224–231.

Kaufmann, Eric. 2019. *Whiteshift: Populism, Immigration, and the Future of White Minorities*. New York: Abrams Press.

Khodarkovsky, Michael. 2016. "Playing with Fear: Russia's War Card." *New York Times*, October 26, 2016. https://www.nytimes.com/2016/10/27/opinion/playing-with-fear-russias-war-card.html

Lebow, Richard Ned. 1984. "Windows of Opportunity: Do States Jump Through Them?" *International Security* 9 (1): 147–186.

Lee, Ronald, and Andrew Mason. 2010. "Fertility, Human Capital, and Economic Growth over the Demographic Transition." *European Journal of Population* 26 (2): 159–182.

Luttwak, Edward. 1995. "Toward Post-Heroic Warfare." *Foreign Affairs* 74 (3): 109–122.

Maestas, Nicole, Kathleen J. Mullen, and David Powell. 2016. "The Effect of Population Aging on Economic Growth, the Labor Force and Productivity." NBER Working Paper No. 22452. http://www.nber.org/papers/w22452.pdf

Mitchell, B. R. 2003. *International Historical Statistics: Europe, 1750–2000*. 5th edition, Basingstoke, England: Palgrave Macmillan.

Narizny, Kevin. 2007. *The Political Economy of Alignment*. Ithaca: Cornell University Press.

Nauck, Bernhard, and Daniela Klaus. 2007. "The Varying Value of Children: Empirical Results from Eleven Societies in Asia, Africa, and Europe." *Current Sociology* 55 (4): 487–503.

Norris, Pippa, and Ronald Inglehart. 2019. *Cultural Backlash: Trump, Brexit, and Authoritarian Populism*. Cambridge: Cambridge University Press.

Office of the Comptroller, U.S. Department of Defense. 2017. "Fiscal Year 2017: Military Retirement Fund Audited Financial Report." https://comptroller.defense.gov/Portals/45/documents/cfs/fy2017/13_Military_Retirement_Fund/FY2017_MRF_AFR_Final.pdf

Ogden, Philip E., and Mari-Monique Huss. 1982. "Demography and Pronatalism in France in the Nineteenth and Twentieth Centuries." *Journal of Historical Geography* 8 (3): 283–298.

Orbán, Viktor. 2018. "Viktor Orbán's 'State of the Nation' Address." Transcript, *Visegrád Post*, February 20, 2018. https://visegradpost.com/en/2018/02/20/the-west-will-fall-as-europe-is-occupied-without-realising-it-said-viktor-orban-christianity-is-the-last-hope-full-speech/

Pettigrew, Thomas F., Ulrich Wagner, and Oliver Christ. 2007. "Who Opposes Immigration? Comparing German and North American Findings." *Du Bois Review* 4 (1): 19–39.

Posen, Barry R. 1984. *The Sources of Military Doctrine: France, Britain, and Germany between the World Wars*. Ithaca: Cornell University Press.

PRB (Population Reference Bureau). 2018. "Featured Graphic: Many Countries' Populations Are Aging." PRB. https://www.prb.org/insight/featured-graphic-many-countries-populations-are-aging/

PRC (People's Republic of China). 2004. *China's National Defense in 2004*. Beijing: State Council Information Office. https://fas.org/nuke/guide/china/doctrine/natdef2004.html.

Raisher, Josh. 2016. "Europe by Numbers: Old Europe." *Berlin Policy Journal*, July 5, 2016. https://berlinpolicyjournal.com/europe-by-numbers-old-europe/

Schweller, Randall L. 2004. "Unanswered Threats: A Neoclassical Realist Theory of Underbalancing." *International Security* 29 (2): 159–201.

Sheen, Seongho. 2013. "Northeast Asia's Aging Population and Regional Security: 'Demographic Peace?'" *Asian Survey* 53 (2): 292–318.

Smale, Alison. 2014. "Memo from Germany: A Dwindling Army Tempts New Recruits with a Charm Offensive." *New York Times*, June 27, 2014. https://www.nytimes.com/2014/07/28/world/europe/german-army-a-dwindling-army-tempts-new-recruits-with-a-charm-offensive.html

Tian, Nan, Aude Fleurant, Alexandra Kuimova, Pieter D. Wezeman, and Siemon T. Wezeman. 2018. *Trends in World Military Expenditure, 2017*. Stockholm: SIPRI.

Toft, Monica Duffy. 2014. "Death by Demography: 1979 as a Turning Point in the Disintegration of the Soviet Union." *International Area Studies Review* 17 (2): 184–204.

Tomlinson, Richard, Marie-Monique Huss, and Philip E. Ogden. 1985. "'France in Peril': The French Fear of Dénatalité." *History Today* 35 (4): 24–31.

Trump, Donald. 2016. "Donald Trump's Foreign Policy Speech." Transcript, *New York Times*, April 27, 2016. https://www.nytimes.com/2016/04/28/us/politics/transcript-trump-foreign-policy.html

UN (United Nations). 2017. *World Population Prospects: The 2017 Revision*. United Nations Department of Economic and Social Affairs. https://esa.un.org/unpd/wpp/

WEF (World Economic Forum). 2017. "We'll Live to 100—How Can We Afford It?" WEF. http://www3.weforum.org/docs/WEF_White_Paper_We_Will_Live_to_100.pdf

Winkler, Hernan. 2015. "Why Do Elderly People Oppose Immigration When They're Most Likely to Benefit?" Brookings Institute. https://www.brookings.edu/blog/future-development/2015/07/22/why-do-elderly-people-oppose-immigration-when-theyre-most-likely-to-benefit/

INDEX

A

Abu Ghraib prison scandal, controversy analysis of, 150–51
Abu Nidal Organization, 516–18
academia. *See* scholarship and academia
actor-network theory (ANT)
  controversy analysis and, 150–51
  practice theory and, 151–54
  strategy assembly and, 151–52
actors in grand strategy, 12–13
  change made by, 526–28
  culture of national security and, 305
  diplomacy and, 363
  linguistics research and, 177–78
  multiple power centers and, 697–99
  nonpolarity and strategies for, 701–2
  practice theory and, 145–46
  remaking and unmaking of strategies and, 179–81
  technology and role of, 223–25
  use of strategies by, 178–79
adaptation, in grand strategy, 181
adjustments, changes in grand strategy as, 524–25, 539–52
Adler, Emanuel, 147–48
Adler-Nissen, Rebecca, 361
adversary insecurity, state strategy and, 114–15
Afghanistan war
  civil-military relations and, 280–81
  Soviet grand strategy during, 610–11
African states
  diplomacy in, 363–64
  practice theory in, 147
agency
  diplomacy and, 365–66
  governmentality and, 194–96
  grand strategy and, 290–93

international relations theory and, 288–90
leadership style and psychology and, 293–97
linguistics of grand strategy and, 180
realist sense of, 294–95
romantic sense of, 294, 295
Alexander (Tsar of Russia), 331–32
  Clausewitz on, 61–62
Alexander II (Tsar of Russia), 514–15
Allende, Salvador, 394
alliances
  declining states and role of, 477–78
  Palmerston on, 644–46
  small state shelter-seeking and, 495–96
Allison, Graham, 529–30
Al Qaeda, 177–78, 512–13, 515–16
alternatives to grand strategy
  change based on, 534–35
  identification of, 525
altruism, governmentality and, 197–99
America First strategy, emergence of, 660–62
American Civil War
  grand strategy thinking and, 28–29
  military success and strategic failure in, 345–46
American grand strategy theory, British influence on, 74–80
American Political Science Review, 160–61
analytic uncertainty, evaluation of grand strategy and, 584
Anderson, Benedict, 676
Anglo-German crisis, US hegemony and, 400–2
Anonymous collective, 699–700
AntiSec hacking group, 699–700
Anton, Michael, 660–62
appeasement
  change in grand strategy and, 524–27
  as declining power strategy, 484–85
  evaluation of, 578, 579

Aradau, Claudia, 191
Arafat, Yasir, 516–18
Arant, Deborah, 274–75
argumentation
   cultural theory and, 313–14
   ideology and, 164–65
armament programs, as strategic instrument, 350–51
armed conflict. *See* war
arms control, military power and, 348
arms exports, economic statecraft and, 379–80
Arquilla, John, 125–26, 180
Art, Robert, 609–10
artificial intelligence, strategic impact of, 714–15
Art of War (Jomini), 68–69
Art of War (Sun Tzu), 82–83, 93–94
Ashley, Richard, 363
Asia
   financing of grand strategy in, 429–30
   grand strategy theories in, 89–101
   US policy change toward, 571–72
Assad, Bashar al-, 380
assassination, violent rebel groups use of, 514–15
assemblages, linguistics of grand strategy and, 176
assertiveness, rising states' strategy of, 462–64, 466–67
asset specificity, subnational preferences and, 264–65
Association of Southeast Asian Nations (ASEAN), 147–48
asymmetric alliances, shelter-seeking by small states and, 495–96
Athenians, Thucydides' criticism of, 48–49
Atlantic Charter (1941), 613–14
atman (Hindu spiritual life), 97
Attempt to establish rules according to which a concept for a war in its entirety, as well as operational plans for each individual campaign, are to be drawn up (Anon.), 64–66, 67
Attlee, Clement, 647–48
attrition, logic of
   foreign aid to rebels and, 515–16
   rebel groups' strategy and, 510–11
   Western grand strategy and, 82–83

audience, legitimation and role of, 323, 332
austerity strategies, governmentality and, 195–96
Australia
   geography and security of, 212
   strategic shock and policy change in, 531–33
Austria-Hungary
   military spending in, 425
   retrenchment by, 484
authoritarianism
   civil-military relations and, 281–82
   cost navigation in grand strategy financing and, 430–32
   costs of war and, 261–62
   military preferences in, 275–76
   obstacles to grand strategy in, 594
   population aging and, 730–31
   populism and, 682
   resistance to economic sanctions in, 372–73
   selectorate theory and, 241
authority, populism and fragmentation of, 684
Authorization for Use of Military Force (US), 666
autonomy-security-influence tradeoff
   Palestinian rebel groups and, 517
   small state strategies and, 498–99
Avant, Deborah, 280–81
Axworthy, Lloyd, 181–82

B

Bacevich, Andrew, 272
balance of power theory. *See also* offshore balancing
   declining states use of, 480–81
   economic statecraft and, 377–79
   ideology and, 162–63
   multiple power centers and, 697–99
   multipolarity and, 696
   shelter-seeking by small states and, 495–96
Baldwin, David, 371, 372–73, 376
Balzacq, Thierry, 1–18
   on debt financing of grand strategy, 422–27
   on foreign policy and grand strategy, 358–59
   grand strategy school and, 620, 631–33, 708
   on ideology and grand strategy, 159–69
   on performativity of grand strategy, 680–81
   practice theory and, 144–46
   strategy as social struggle and, 148

Barbary Pirates, 398
bargaining
    change in grand strategy and, 529–30
    in economic statecraft, 376–77
Barnier-Khawam, Pablo, 159–69, 680–81
Barry, Andrew, 150
Basic Law of Representation (Austria), 425
battle, strategy in, 27
Battle of Navarino, 642–44
Beaufre, André, 348
Beckley, Michael, 447–48, 723
Beckwith, George, 396
behaviorist school, ideology and, 161
Beiner, Ronald, 178–79
belief systems
    civil-military relations and, 274–75
    ideas and ideology and, 163–65
Bell, J. Bowyer, 506, 508–9
Belt and Road Initiative (China)
    domestic grand strategy and, 241–43
    emergence of, 16–17
    networks as grand strategy in, 134–35
    transnational politics and, 207
    US foreign policy and, 311–12
Berlin, Isaiah, 294, 683–84
Betts, Richard
    on civil-military relations and strategic assessment, 277–78
    on coordination of grand strategy, 607
    on dangers of grand strategy, 610–11
    on demise of grand strategy, 685–86
    on illusion of grand strategy, 590–601, 606
    on legitimation and leadership, 323
betweenness centrality, networks, 129–31
Bew, John, 637–51
Biddle, Tami, 625–26
Biersteker, Thomas J., 372–73
bilateral agreements, networks and, 134–35
Bilgrami, Akeel, 100
binding strategy, declining powers use of, 483
bipolarity
    decline of, 690–91
    dynamics of, 692–93
    global power distribution and, 208–9
Bismarck, Otto von, 295, 356–57, 466–67, 599–600

black market, commercial policy strategies and, 373–74
Blair, Tony, 197–99, 393
Blanchard, Jean-Marc, 371
bluffing, by declining states, 482–83
bodily movements, practice theory and, 149–50, 153–54
Bohr, Nils, 90, 93
Boltanski, Luc, 150–51
Bolton, John, 561, 631–33
Borgatti, Stephen P., 124
Bosnian civil war, 280–81
Boston Consulting Group, 177–78
bottom-up policymaking
    calibrated grand strategy and, 629–31
    civil-military relations and, 276–78
    grand strategy based on, 673–74
    realist perspective on, 296
bounded rationality
    rational grand strategy, 108–9
Bourdieu, Pierre, 143–44, 149–50, 314, 330–31
Bourscheid, Wilhelm von, 58–59
Boyd, John, 89
Boyd, Julian P., 396
Brahmacharya, 98–99
Brands, Hal
    on change in grand strategy, 546–47
    on Clausewitz, 91
    evaluation of US grand strategy, 559–72, 580–94
    on foreign policy and grand strategy, 358–59, 605–6
    on governmentality, 192–93
    grand strategy scholarship of, 4, 35–36
Brazil, grand strategy research on, 177–78
Bretton Woods system, 428–29, 430, 549, 550
Brexit
    aging demographics and, 730–31
    developmental aid and, 198–99
    erosion of trust and debate on, 663
    political polarization and, 664–66
Brexit vote, foreign policy implications of, 312
Brezhnev, Leonid, 577–78
Brezhnev Doctrine, 582
British theorists of grand strategy, 74–80
Brodie, Bernard, 8–9, 348, 444
brokerage, networks and, 131–32

Brooks, Deborah Jordan, 727
Brooks, Rosa, 271–82, 329, 358–59, 379–80
Brooks, Stephen G., 192–93, 341–42, 442, 444, 447–49, 453
Brownstein, Ronald, 732
Buchanan, Ben, 419n.7
Buddhism, 90
  non-Western grand strategy theory and, 92
Bueger, Christian, 142–55
Bull, Hedly, 360
Bülow, Heinrich von
  on grand strategy, 26–27, 58–59
  on political *vs.* military strategy, 60
Bundy, MacGeorge, 394
burden-shifting, by declining states, 477–78
bureaucratic politics, change in grand strategy and, 529–30
Burke, Edmund, 638–40
Bush, George H. W., 442, 549, 597
Bush, George W.
  change in grand strategy under, 534
  diplomacy and grand strategy by, 356–57
  failed grand strategy of, 329
  grand strategy under, 562
  legitimation of strategy under, 331
  obstacles to grand strategy for, 597
Butler, J. R. M., 32
Byman, Daniel L., 288, 506–19

C

Cadogan, Alexander, 648–49
calibrated grand strategy, 629–31
Campaign of Trafalgar (Corbett), 345–46
Campbell, David, 310
Canada, US border dispute with, 400
Canning, George, 399–400, 582, 637–38, 642–44
Cantelmo, Robert G., 706–699
capabilities, grand strategies and distribution of, 179–81
capacity-building projects, state power and, 198
capitalism
  Kantian tripod and varieties of, 240–43, 249n.4
  national economic interests and, 259–62
capitalist peace concept, 260–61

Carr, Edward Hallett, 206–7, 294
carrot and stick approach
  economic bargaining and, 376
  economic statecraft and, 371
  foreign aid and, 373
Carter, Jimmy, 394
Casey, William, 389–90, 394
Castex, Raoul, 343
Castlereagh (Viscount)
  Canning and, 637–38, 642–44
  history of grand strategy and, 637–38, 649–51
  Kissinger on, 362
  legitimation and, 331–32
  statecraft under, 638–42
Castro, Fidel, 209
casualties
  population aging and sensitivity to, 726
  rebel groups and acceptance of, 510–11
causality
  individual agency and, 288
  rational grand strategy and, 115–18
Caverley, Jonathan D., 239–49
Central Intelligence Agency (CIA), 389
  covert actions and, 391–93
  creation of, 394
Chamberlain, Neville, 327–28
change in grand strategy
  adjustment-based change, 524–25, 539–52
  alternatives to status quo, 534–35
  bias as motivation in, 528
  challenge of, 523–35
  cultural explanations for, 528–29
  domestic influences on, 530–31, 534
  first- and second-order change, 524–25, 542–43
  impediments to, 526–31, 546
  incentives for, 525–26
  linguistics of grand strategy and, 181
  marketplace of ideas and, 657–58
  measurement of, 524–25, 541–43
  organizational culture and, 529–30
  overcoming barriers to, 531–35
  overhaul-based change., 524–25, 539–52
  psychological explanations for, 526–28
  security environment and, 533–34
  sources of, 543–48
  statecraft and management of, 523
  US post-Cold War strategy revisions, 548–51

Checkel, Jeffrey, 162–63, 304
cheng, Dao of Deception and, 93–94
Chenoweth, Erica, 514–15
ch'i
   Dao of Deception and, 93–94
   in Sun Tzu's *Art of War,* 94–96
China
   appeasement strategy in, 484–85
   break with Soviet Union by, 209
   cautious rise strategy in, 208–9
   changes in strategy due to rise of, 524–27
   competition with US from, 303–4
   control-assertiveness as rising state, 466–67
   coordination of grand strategy in, 607
   covert actions by, 390, 391–93
   cultural factors in foreign policy of, 476–77
   Deep Engagement policy and, 444–45
   economic capacity and relative power of, 206
   economic statecraft in, 379–80
   evaluation of grand strategy in, 581
   foreign aid programs in, 381
   foreign firm acquisition in, 379–80
   grand strategy in, 177–78, 594
   hidden capacities and relative power of, 207
   international relations theory and rise of, 443
   Japanese grand strategy concerning, 429–30, 533–34
   Japanese invasion of, 326–27
   military politics in, 243–45
   military procurement strategy in, 350–51
   multipolarity and power status of, 697–99
   Nixon's policies in, 599–600
   nonstate actors and diplomacy by, 361–62
   obstacles to grand strategy in, 594
   population aging and, 723–24
   population aging in, 722
   population growth in, 223–25
   as rising state, 460
   robotics technology in, 714
   strategic culture in, 245
   strategic logics as rising state, 465
   technology innovation and strategic goals in, 226–28
   US free trade with, 241–43
   US post-Cold War strategy towards, 240–43, 311–12, 550
   US security policy and perceptions of, 308–9, 311, 326–27
CHINCOM program, 378–79
choice, linguistics of grand strategy and, 180
Christensen, Thomas J., 297–99, 546–47
Churchill, Winston, 312, 330–31, 528, 595–96, 647–49
"The CIA and the NSA" (Stern), 389
civic republicanism, multiculturalism and, 676–78
civilization discourse
   domestic grand strategy and, 247
   multiculturalism and, 676–78
civil-military relations
   character of strategy and, 276–78
   grand strategy and, 271–82
   indirect effects of technology on, 230–31
   military economic and bureaucratic structure and, 279–81
   practice theory and, 146–48
   strategy execution and implementation and, 279–82
   substance of grand strategy and, 272–76
   use of force paradigm and, 273–74
   variety in, 282n.1
Clapper, James, 443–44
clash of civilizations thesis, 247
class-based interests
   economics and, 262–66
   subnational interests as, 265–66
classical liberalism, national economic interests and, 260–61
Clausewitz, Carl von, 10–11
   on friction, 352
   grand strategy and legacy of, 27, 57–58, 340–41, 358, 563, 593
   Liddell Hart on, 76–77, 78–79, 85–86
   Maizeroyan tradition and, 58–59
   on military strategy, 350–51, 597
   origins of *die Politik* and, 60–61
   Political Strategy tradition and *die Politik* of, 59–68
   Sun Tzu and, 91
   on tactics, 26–27
   on war and *die Politik,* 63–68
Cleon, Thucydides' rhetoric on, 52–53

climate change
  power and role of, 212–13
  US grand strategy debate and, 444
Clinton, Bill, 280–81
  grand strategy under, 561–64
Clinton, Hilary, 631–33, 694–95
COCOM program, 378–79
coercive diplomacy, Reagan's shift to, 566–68
cognitive closure, change in strategy and, 526–28
cognitive style, individual psychology and, 295
Cohen, Eliot, 276–77, 444, 564–65, 609–10
Cold War. *See also* post-Cold war era
  bipolarity of power during, 208–9
  covert actions in, 389, 391–93, 413–15, 416–17
  credibility during, 445–46
  dangers of grand strategy during, 610–11
  derivative interests during, 111–13
  effects on technology of, 229–30
  force multiplier effect in, 343
  foreign policy during, 658–60
  grand strategy during, 3, 9–10, 15
  ideology and, 160–61
  indirect effects of technology in, 230–31
  intelligence strategy during, 417–18, 418n.2
  obstacles to grand strategy in, 596
  policy changes during, 525
  regional balance of power during, 210
  Soviet destabilization efforts during, 95–96
  Soviet grand strategy during, 576–78
  US grand strategy during, 566
  US national identity in, 308–9
The Cold War (Lippmann), 658–59
collective mobilization
  legitimation and, 323–24
  national interest legitimation and, 324–26
Collins, John, 3–4, 80, 344
colonialism
  financial sector preference for, 264–65
  nonviolent resistance to, 99–100
  policy change and the end of, 523
  political resistance to ending, 531
  subnational preferences and, 262–66
  technology innovation and, 226–28
COMECON program (USSR), 378
commercial policy, economic statecraft and strategy of, 373–74, 377, 378–80

communication
  in diplomacy, 364–65
  grand strategy and, 173–82
  indirect effects of technology on, 230–31
  nonpolarity and strategies for, 701–2
  violent rebel groups and, 508–9
community of practice framework, practice theory and, 147–48
competitiveness
  grand strategy as aid to, 563
  sectoral interests and, 262–66
computer technology
  indirect effects of, 230–31
  strategic impact of, 714–16
Concert of Europe, 325–26, 360, 483, 494, 580–94
Conflict, Security and Stability Fund (UK), 198–99
Confucius Institutes, 381
Congress for Cultural Freedom, 391–93
Congress of Vienna, 638–40
Connolly, William, 675–76
conquest, violent rebel group strategy of, 510
consciousness
  Hindu concept of, 96–97
  non-Western grand strategy theory and, 92–93
  Sun Tzu on, 94–95
conscription, domestic grand strategy and, 242–43
Constantinou, Costas, 360
constitutive effects of cultural norms, 305–6
constructivism
  cultural theory and, 305–6, 313–16
  identity and, 307–11
  international relations and security studies and, 304–11
  practice theory and, 144–46
  status of strategizing in, 7–8
consumption, security and, 110–11
containment strategy
  bipolarity of power and, 208–9
  international environment and, 113–15
  legitimation of, 323–24, 328
  Soviet Union collapse and obsolescence of, 659–60
  US grand strategy and role of, 560–61
containment strategy, critique of, 564–65

control, rising states' strategy of, 462–64, 466–67
controversy
 analysis, 150–51
 practice theory and, 150
conventional weapons development, technology and, 229–30
cooperation
 ideological balancing and, 167–68
 institutionalized economic cooperation, 374–75, 377, 378
 prosperity and power generation and, 379
Cooper-Church Amendment (1971), 599
coordination, state grand strategy and, 607–8
Co-Prosperity Sphere (Japan), 133
Corbett, Julian Stafford
 grand strategy theory and, 2–3, 29, 74–80
 Liddell Hart and, 74
 on military power and grand strategy, 343, 345–46
Corcya representatives, Thucydides on speech by, 51–52
Corinthians, Thucydides on speech of, 47–49, 51–52
Cornish, Paul, 195–96
cosmology, non-Western grand strategy and, 92–93
cost-benefit analysis
 state strategy options and, 118
 US domestic values *vs.* grand strategy and, 451–52
 in US grand strategy, 450–51
costly signaling
 legitimation instruments and, 329
 rational grand strategy and, 117
costs of war
 financing of grand strategy and, 424–25
 national preferences and, 261–62
Council for Mutual Economic Assistance, 208–9
Council on Foreign Relations, 443–45
counterfactuals, evaluation of grand strategy and, 584
counterinsurgency doctrine
 civil-military relations and, 275–76, 280–81
 government counterstrategies to rebel groups, 518–19

counterterrorism
 legitimation of, 329
 policies of, 16
 robotics technology and, 712–14
Course of Tactics (Joly de Maizeroy), 58–59
covert actions. *See also* intelligence
 Anglo-German crisis and, 400–2
 Barbary Pirates and, 398
 characteristics of, 391–93
 foreign policy integration with, 393–94
 future of, 402–3
 grand strategy and, 389–400
 history of, 390
 as illegitimate instruments, 329
 intelligence gathering and, 410–11
 liberal internationalism opposition to, 413–15
 Mexican-American War and, 399–400
 primacy and irrelevance of, 415–16
 restraint in intelligence strategy and, 413
 United States history of, 395–97
 US great power strategy and, 400–2
 US intelligence strategies and, 416–17
Crawford, Neta, 329
credibility
 signaling in grand strategy and, 608–9
 US grand strategy and, 445–49
Credit Card Wars, 428–29
credit financing for grand strategy
 economic impact of, 424–25
 in Japan, 429–30
Crimea, Russian annexation of, 329, 343–44, 349–50
Crimean War, 483
critical standpoint theory, grand strategy in, 11
Cromartie, Alan, 62–63
cross-border economic activity, survival motive and, 257–59
cross-border violence, Palestinian rebel groups and, 517
Cuba
 Soviet alliance with, 209, 377–78
 US economic sanctions in, 381–82
Cuban Missile Crisis, 524–27, 529–30
cultural literacy, multiculturalism and, 678

cultural theory
    change in grand strategy and, 528–29
    civil-military relations and, 274–75
    conditions for decline in, 476–77
    diplomacy and, 360
    globalization and homogeneity and, 700
    identity and, 303–16
    national security and, 305–7
    population aging and, 728–31
    practice theory and, 144–46
    recent developments in, 313–16
    security culture, US-British comparisons of, 311–13
    societal-military relations and, 272
    strategic culture, 146–48
    toolkit metaphor of, 314, 323
Curtin, John, 531–33
cyber security
    covert actions and infiltration of, 391–93, 402–3
    security dilemma in, 419n.7
    small state grand strategy and, 500
    technology innovation and, 714–15
cyber-technology, power and, 213–14

D

dangers of grand strategy, 610–11
Dao de Jing, 93, 95
Daoism, 90
    Gandhi and, 96–97
    non-Western grand strategy theory and, 92
    quantum physics and, 93–96
Dao of Deception, 93–94
Dao of Peace, 92–93
Datta-Ray, 100
Davis, Jefferson, 345–46
Dean, Mitchell, 191, 194–96
Death, Carl, 198
debt financing
    for American grand strategy, 422–27
    declining power and paydown of, 479–80
    grand strategy funding with, 428–30
decision-making
    change in grand strategy and structure of, 529–30
    intelligence and, 408
    judgments and justifications for, 178–79

military power and grand strategy and, 346
nonpolarity and strategies for, 701–2
The Decisive Wars of History (Liddell Hart), 30, 73–74, 79
Decline and Fall of the Roman Empire (Gibbons), 474–75
declining powers
    appeasement by, 484–85
    binding strategies of, 483
    bluffing by, 482–83
    conditions for decline in, 476–78
    dilemmas of, 475–76
    domestic institutions and, 477
    future research issues, 485–87
    grand strategies, 474–87
    history of, 474–75
    international environment, 477–78
    policy options of, 478–81
    retrenchment by, 484
    rising states and, 458–59
Decter, Midge, 248–49
Deep Engagement
    advantages of entanglement and, 449–50
    cost-benefit analysis of US grand strategy and, 450–51
    entrapment and, 447–48
    evaluation of, 580–94
    global interconnectivity and, 445–49
    perceived tradeoffs in, 452–53
    Restraint theory and, 443
    risk tolerance and debate over, 444
    temptation of ambitions and, 448–49
    terrorism and, 450
    threat perception in US and, 443–45
    US disagreement over, 442–49
    US domestic values and, 451–52
    US foreign policy and, 442
de-essentialist perspective, practice theory and, 149–50
defense contractors, economic interests of, 265–66
defense spending, civil-military relations and, 273–74
defensive realism
    deterrence theory and, 116–17
    international environment and, 113–15

de Gaulle, Charles (Gen.), 342–43, 356–57, 525
degree centrality, networks, 129–31
delegation relationship, military economic and bureaucratic structure and, 279–81
deliberation and decision-making
　ideology and, 162–63
　Thucydides on war and, 47–49
Democratic Front for the Liberation of Palestine, 517
democratic peace theory, 111–13
　costs of war and, 261–62
　Kantian tripod and, 241
democratic states, cost navigation in grand strategy financing and, 430–32
demographic shifts, population aging and, 728–31
density, networks, 129–31
Department for International Development (DFID) (UK), 197–99
Der Derian, James, 360, 365
derivative state interests
　grand strategy and, 111–13
　security as, 110–11
de Staël, Germaine, 61
deterrence theory, 116–17
　military power and, 348
　US grand strategy and role of, 560–61
Deutsch, Karl, 449–50
developmental aid. *See also* foreign aid
　as governmental case study, 197–99
Dewey, John, 150–51
Diebel, Terry, 621
die Politik
　Clausewitz's definition of, 60
　in Clausewitz's *On War*, 62–63
　historical origins of, 60–61
　Political Strategy tradition and, 59–68
　war and, 63–68
diesel engine, globalization and, 223–25
difference, identity and foreign policy and, 309–10
digital revolution, rising entropy and, 700–1
diplomacy
　British Foreign Office in World War II and, 647–48

contemporary scholarship on, 360
covert actions and, 393–94
declining states use of, 480–81
grand strategy and, 356–66
as illusion, 365–66
international comparisons of, 363–64
small states' grand strategy and, 492
statehood and, 362–65
strategy and, 357–62
as tool or resource, 359–60
violent rebel groups and, 518–19
Diplomacy (Kissinger), 356–57, 365
direct resource extraction, financing of grand strategy through, 425–30
discourse
　discursive structure of rhetoric and, 331–32
　grand strategy and, 173–82
　ideology and, 165
disintegrated strategy, civil-military relations and, 276–78
diversity, societies' responses to, 676–78
doctrines, practice theory and, 146–48
documents
　benefits in grand strategy of, 562
　critique of, 565
　governance and role of, 154
Dombrowski, Peter
　on alternatives to grand strategy, 620–33
　on civil-military relations, 279–81
　on debt financing of grand strategy, 422–27
　on foreign policy and grand strategy, 358–59, 680–81
　grand strategy scholarship and, 708
　on logic and substance in grand strategy, 5
　on practice theory, 144–46
　on strategy as social struggle, 148
domestic institutions, declining powers and, 477, 478–81
domestic polarization
　change in grand strategy and, 546–47
　grand strategy and, 248–49
　marketplace of ideas and, 664–66
　military politics and, 243–45
　populism and, 683–84
　technological change and, 225–26
　threat perception and, 166–67

domestic policy, as grand strategy
    source, 239–49
    change resistance from, 530–31, 534, 546–47
    crossnational similarities in, 248–49
    dyadic democratic peace and, 241
    military capacity and, 243–45
    nationalism and, 245–46
    race and gender in, 247–48
    in rising states, 467–69
    US policies and strategies and, 451–52, 626–27, 629–31
domino theory, US grand strategy and, 445–49
Dorchester (Lord), 395–97
Dorman Andrew, M., 195–96
Drezner, Daniel
    on domestic policy and grand strategy, 626–27
    on emergent grand strategy, 8–9
    on ideas and ideology, 657–68
    on nonstate actors, 362–63
    on populism, 683–84
    on signaling in grand strategy, 608–9
drone technology, 713, 715–16
Dueck, Colin, 245, 304, 306, 311, 524–25, 546–47
Dulles, Allan, 394
Dulles, John Foster, 394
Durkheim, Emile, 305–6

E

Earle, Edward Mead, 2–3, 343–44
    Cold War and grand strategy theory of, 80, 84
    on communication, 173
    grand strategy theory of, 10–11, 31–32
    Kennedy and influence of, 83–85
Early, Bryan R., 370–84
Eckardt, Heinrich von, 401
economic interests and statecraft
    balancing strategies in, 377–79
    bargaining tools for, 376–77
    cost-benefit analysis of US grand strategy and, 450–51
    cost navigation in grand strategy financing and, 430–32
    declining powers and, 478–81
    Deep Engagement and, 445–49
    domestic grand strategy and, 241–43
    economic sanctions and, 372–73, 376, 377–78, 380
    financing of grand strategy and, 425–30
    foreign aid and, 373, 376–77, 378, 381, 382
    future research issues, 383–84
    grand strategy and, 256–67, 370–84
    incentives for grand strategy change and, 525–26
    indirect effects of technology on, 230–31
    institutionalized economic cooperation, 374–75, 377, 378, 379
    in Kennedy's grand strategy theory, 81–82
    military power and, 347–51
    military spending and, 424–25
    national preferences and, 259–62
    networks and, 124–25
    nonstate actors and, 381–82
    objectives and tools of, 375–83
    population aging and capabilities of, 725–28
    population aging impact on, 722–25
    prosperity and power goals of, 379–80
    relative power and, 206–7
    signaling and norms in, 380–81
    strategic commercial policy, 373–74, 377, 378–80
    subnational preferences and, 262–66
    summary of, 382–83
    survival motive, 257–59
    technological innovation and, 226, 228–29
    tools of, 370–71
    US grand strategy and, 450–51, 549
economic sanctions, 372–73, 376, 377–78, 380, 381–82
Edelman Trust Barometer, 662–64
Edelstein, David M.
    on domestic grand strategy preferences, 239–40
    on foreign policy and grand strategy, 565, 680–81
    on grand strategy, 35
    on limits of grand strategy, 604–15
    on policymaking and grand strategy, 593
    revisionist critique of grand strategy and, 568–69
Eden, Anthony, 524–27
Eden, Lynn, 306

Egypt, Suez Canal nationalization by, 347, 524–27
Ehrhardt, Andrew, 637–51
Eisenhower, Dwight D., 280–81, 394, 452–49
elections
 cost navigation in grand strategy financing and, 430–32
 digital technology impact on, 714–15
 financing of grand strategy impact on, 425–30
 population aging and, 723–24
 sharp power in, 127
elite cue theory, public opinion and, 297–98
elites
 change in grand strategy and role of, 528–29
 cultural production and, 315
 decline in US foreign policy of, 660–62
 erosion of trust in, 662–64
 marketplace of ideas and, 658–60
 political polarization among, 664–66
 populist typology of, 681
 small states and role of, 492–93
 US foreign policy and role of, 659–60
Elster, Jon, 322–24
emergent grand strategy
 examples of, 599–600
 guidelines for, 616n.11
 policymaking and, 8–9, 593
 scholarship on, 627–29, 631–33
Encyclopaedia Britannica, grand strategy in, 30
engagement, retrenchment and, 173
English School
 cultural theory and, 313–14
 diplomacy and, 360
Enlightenment era, Maizeroyan tradition and, 58–59
entanglement, 94–95
 small states' avoidance of, 496–98
 US grand strategy and advantages of, 449–50
entrapment
 small state shelter-seeking and, 495–96
 US grand strategy and fear of, 447–48
entropy
 digital revolution and, 700–1
 globalization and, 699–700
 multiple power centers and, 698

environmental degradation, US grand strategy debate and, 444
epistemology, non-Western grand strategy and, 92–93
ERASMUS+ program, 16
Escheverria, Arturo, 625–26
Essai général de Tactique (Guibert), 61, 63–68
ethnocultural anxiety, population aging and, 730
ethnography, organization studies and, 144–45
European security
 grand strategy and, 17–18
 population aging and, 728–31
 technological change, 228–29
 US post-Cold War strategy and, 550–51
European states
 political polarization in, 664–66
 practice theory in, 147
 shifting power among, 458–59
European Union (EU)
 counterterrorism policies and, 16
 diplomacy in, 363–64
 diplomatic practices and, 361
 economic sanctions strategy of, 376
 grand strategy research on, 177–78
 practice theory and, 147–48
 security concerns in, 17–18
 strategy assembly in, 151–52
evaluation of grand strategy
 challenges in, 579–83
 guidelines for, 583–87
 necessity of, 576–78
 US grand strategy evaluation, 559–72
exigences, linguistics of grand strategy and, 179–80, 181
exogenous shocks
 change in grand strategy and, 531–33
 linguistics of grand strategy and, 179–80
 US Cold War grand strategy and, 566
expansionist policies
 declining states and pitfalls of, 481–82
 failure of, 576
experts, cultural production and, 315
explicit comparative agenda, grand strategy studies and, 181–82
exports
 economic impact of, 241–43
 subnational preferences and, 262–66

external context, ideology and, 164–65
external financing, grand strategy funding with, 428–30

F

failed grand strategy
  legitimation failure, 329, 330–33
  military success and, 345–46
family resemblance, evolution of grand strategy and, 181
Farrell, Henry, 126–27, 131–32
Farrell, Theo, 274
Fatah organization, 516–18
Fay, Brian, 162–63
Fearon, James, 608–9, 629–31
feasibility assessments, state strategy options, 118
Feaver, Peter, 4, 35–36, 277, 580–94, 599–600, 728
Federation of American Scientists, 697–99
fertility rates
  population aging and, 724–25, 726
  social impact of decline in, 727
feudalism, national economic interests and, 260
field, strategy as, practice theory and, 149–50
Fierke, K. M., 89–101, 181
financial sector, asset-specific preferences and, 264–65
financing of grand strategy, 422–33. *See also* cost-benefit analysis; costs of war
  declining states and, 478–81
  intertemporal tradeoffs in, 425–30
  in Japan, 429–30
  military costs and, 423–25
  navigation of costs in, 430–32
Finland, technology innovation and, 223–25
Finnemore, Martha, 307–8
firepower, grand strategy and development of, 221–22
First Barbary War (1801-1804), 391–93, 398
First Offset Strategy, 229–30
First Sino-Japanese War (1894-1895), 429–30
First World War. *See* World War I
Fischer, Max, 706
Fischer, Sophie-Charlotte, 221–32

force, use of
  civil-military relations and, 273–74
  declining state structure for, 478–81
  limited strategic effectiveness of, 351–53
  non-Western grand strategy without, 90–91
  strategic assessment and, 277–78
  Sun Tzu on legitimate use of, 95, 96
  US intelligence strategies and, 411–17
force multiplier effect, 342–44
force structure
  changes in grand strategy and shifts in, 525, 533–34
  civil-military relations and, 276
  declining power alteration of, 479
  grand strategy implementation and role of, 279
  Palmerston on, 646
  US grand strategy debate over, 411–17
Fordham, Benjamin O., 246–249n.5
Foreign Affairs, 173, 539–41
foreign aid. *See also* developmental aid
  economic statecraft and, 373, 376–77, 378, 381, 382
  to violent rebel groups, 510, 515–16
foreign debt financing, grand strategy funding with, 428–29, 430
foreign direct investment, economic statecraft and, 373–74
foreign firms, economic statecraft and acquisition of, 379–80
foreign policy
  adjustment to grand strategy and, 546–47
  British grand strategy and, 647–48, 649–51
  covert actions and, 391–94
  culture and security in, 307
  in declining states, 476, 478–81
  economic statecraft and, 370–71
  enervation of legislatures and, 666–67
  grand strategy and, 358–59, 563–64
  identity and difference in, 309–10
  individual style and psychology and, 293–97
  limits of grand strategy in, 565
  marketplace of ideas and, 657–58
  military capability and, 243–45
  multiculturalism and, 680–81
  national identity stories and, 307–8
  political polarization and, 664–66

population aging and, 725–28
rising states' assertiveness in, 463–64
strategic pragmatism and, 612–13
think tanks and, 265–66
US debates over, 441–42
of violent rebel groups, 509
Foreign Policy Analysis, grand strategy research and, 177–78, 358
Forget, Amelie, 143–44, 149–50
form *(hsing)*, strategy and, 94–96
forum shopping, networked actors and instruments and, 126–27
forward defense posture, US grand strategy adherence to, 549
Foster, Pacey C., 124
Foucault, Michel, 150–51
  on anti-Machiavellian literature, 191
  on governmentality, 190–93, 195–96
  on liberalism, 194–96
  on moral technologies, 193–94
  on practice theory, 314
  on rule-governmentality shift, 197–99
fragmentation of authority, populism and, 684
France
  Algerian rebellion against, 515–16
  Castlereagh in, 638–40
  colonization attempts in America by, 399–400
  covert actions by, 399
  as declining state, 482–83
  evaluation of grand strategy in, 582
  history of covert actions by, 396
  la politique in, 60–61
  loss aversion and policy change in, 527–28
  political polarization in, 664–66
  population aging and policy reform in, 726–27
  post-war change in grand strategy of, 531–33
Franco-Prussian War, 482–83
Frederick William III, Clausewitz and, 63
Freeden, Michael, 161, 164–65
Freedman, Lawrence, 525–26, 606–7
Freeman, Lawrence, 25–37
free markets, US post-Cold War grand strategy and role of, 549
free-riding, small state shelter-seeking and, 495–96

free trade policy
  domestic grand strategy and, 241–43
  economic statecraft and, 371
friction, Clausewitz's concept of, 352
Friedberg, Aaron, 625
Friedman, Jeffrey A., 581–83
Frunze, Mikhaïl, 340–41
Fukuyama, Francis, 659–60
Fuller, John Frederick Charles
  grand strategy theory and, 2–3, 29–30, 74–80, 340–41
  Liddell Hart and, 74
fundamentalism, liberalism *vs.*, 677–78
fundamental state interests, rational grand strategy and, 109–11
Funeral Oration (Thucydides), 49–50

G

Gaddis, John Lewis
  on actors' use of grand strategy, 178–79
  on change in grand strategy, 524, 546–47
  definition of grand strategy by, 591
  on diplomacy and grand strategy, 356–57
  evaluation of grand strategy and, 576
  grand strategy scholarship of, 34, 35–36, 604–5
  on statecraft and grand strategy, 4
Gadinger, Frank, 142–55
Galula, David, 507
Gandhi, Mahatma
  cosmology, epistemology and ontology in theories of, 92–93
  grand strategy theory and nonviolence of, 89–91, 96–100
  nonviolent strategies of, 92–93
gas turbines, globalization and, 223–25
Gates, Robert, 615
Gaunt, Guy, 401
Gavin, Frank, 709–10
Geertz, Clifford, 305, 313–14
Geiss, Immanuel, 460
Gelb, Leslie, 610–11, 660–62
Gelpi, Christopher, 728
gemeinschaft, multiculturalism and, 676
gender, domestic grand strategy and, 247–48
General Agreement on Tariffs and Trade (GATT), 377, 550

General Social Survey, 662–64
Genet, Edmond, 397
geo-economics, 371–72
geography
   grand strategy and, 210–13
   indirect effects of technology on, 230–31
   technological change and innovation and, 221–22
   US intelligence strategies and, 412–13
geopolitics
   bipolarity and, 692–93
   chaos and randomness in, 690–91
   culture and identity in, 303–4
   Deep Engagement and, 445–49
   erosion of trust and, 662–64
   evaluation of grand strategy and, 576–78
   grand strategy development and, 541–43
   homogenization of interests and, 447
   limits of grand strategy and, 565
   military power and, 347–51
   multiculturalism and, 675–81
   multiple power centers and, 697–99
   small state grand strategy and, 492–93, 494–95, 499–500
George, Alexander L., 180, 294
Georgetown Set, US foreign policy and, 658–59
Germany
   Anglo-German crisis and, 400–2
   changes in postwar grand strategy of, 533–34
   control-assertiveness approach as rising state, 466–67
   covert actions by, 390, 401–2
   evaluation of grand strategy in, 576–78
   expansionist failure in, 481–82
   political polarization in, 664–66
   population aging in, 722, 724–25
   as rising state, 460
   technology innovation and politics in, 226
Gerring, John, 167
Gibbons, Edward, 474–75
Giddens, Anthony, 314
Giegerich, Bastian, 151–54
Gillespie, Paul, 711–12
Gilli, Andrea, 221–32
Gilli, Mauro, 221–32

Gilpin, Robert, 206–7, 465, 467–69, 544–45
Glaser, Charles, 107–20, 205
global events, international relations theory and impact of, 443
global governance networks, 124–25
   diplomacy in, 361–62
globalization
   populism and, 682
   rising entropy and, 699–700
   small state grand strategy and, 492–93, 496–98
   technology innovation and, 223–25
   trade policies and, 260–61
global politics
   civil-military relations and, 272–73
   culture and, 305–6, 312
   developmental aid in, 197–99
   diplomacy and, 365–66
   domestic sources of grand strategy and, 239–40
   geographic location and, 212
   grand strategy and, 3, 15
   identity and, 312
   linguistics in grand strategy and, 177–78
   polarity of relative power and, 208–9
   technology innovation and, 221–22, 226
global positioning systems (GPS), 230–31
Glorious Revolution of 1866, 484–85
Goddard, Stacie E., 133, 180, 314–15, 322–33
Goffman, Erving, 360
Goldman, O. Emily, 180
Goldsmith, Jack, 714
Goldstein, Judith, 162–63
Gorbachev, Mikhail, 577–78, 582, 610–11
Gove, Michael, 663
governmentality. See also ungovernability of rebel groups
   Clausewitz's understanding of, 60–61
   defined, 190
   developmental aid case study, 197–99
   documents and, 154
   enervation of legislatures and, 666–67
   erosion of trust in, 662–64
   Foucault's analysis of, 190–92
   grand strategy and, 190–99
   insurgency as competition for, 511–12
   knowledge and rationalization in, 192–96

multiple dimensions of, 196
practices of, 193–94
recent scholarship on, 191, 194–96
reform efforts, violent rebel groups and, 518–19
Grand Strategies in War and Peace (Kennedy), 73–74
grand strategy
  actors in, 12–13
  ancient grand strategy, principles and problems in, 50–52
  benefits of, 561–64
  civil-military relations and, 271–82
  communication and, 174–76
  contemporary relevance of, 14–18
  covert action and, 389–400
  critical evaluation of, 13, 564–65, 605–6
  culture and identity in, 303–16
  dangers of, 610–11
  declining powers, 474–87
  defined, 2–6, 523–24, 560–61
  demise of, 685–86
  developmental aid and, 198
  diplomacy and, 356–66
  domestic sources of, 239–49
  early definitions of, 26–27
  economic interests and, 256–67
  effects on technology of, 229–31
  evaluation of, 575–87
  expanded concepts of, 30–32
  financing of, 422–33
  first- and second-order elements of, 524–25, 542–43
  as force multiplier, 342–44
  functions of, 9–10
  future of, 13–14, 631–33
  good strategy examples of, 599–600
  governmentality and, 190–99
  historical evolution of, 10–11
  in history, 637–51
  identification of, 586
  identity affirmation in, 307–11
  ideology and, 159–69
  as illusion, 365–66, 590–601
  individual agency and, 290–93
  individual psychology and, 287–300
  instruments for, 12
  intelligence and, 406–18
  international forces in, 12
  legitimation and rhetoric in, 322–33
  limits of, 351–53, 604–15
  marketplace of ideas in, 658–60
  material sources of, 205–14
  military power and, 243–45, 339–53
  multiculturalism and, 679–81
  narrative approach to, 674–75
  network analytics and, 128–35
  nineteenth-century precursors to, 27–29
  nonpolarity and, 690–702
  non-western theories of, 89–101
  obstacles in practice to, 594–99
  between peace and war, 2–4
  plan *vs*. process perspectives on, 8–9
  population aging and, 721–32
  populism and, 683–84
  in practice, 142–55
  prioritization function of, 562
  public policy alternative to, 625–27
  rational analysis of, 107–20
  redefinition of, 590–80
  research issues about, 541–43
  revisionist critique of, 568–69
  rising powers, 457–70
  of small states, 490–501
  strategic pragmatism alternative to, 612–15
  technological innovation and, 221–32, 706–699
  tensions in scholarship on, 6–10, 341–42
  theories of, 11
  Thucydides' legacy in, 41–53
  twentieth century emergence of, 29–30
  typologies of, 27–29
  ungrand strategy *vs.*, 600–1
  of violent rebel groups, 506–19
  World War I and emergence of, 340–42
Grand Strategy (Collins), 3–4
Grand Strategy of Philip II (Parker), 474–75
grand strategy school (GSS)
  alternatives to, 623–24
  analysis of, 623–24
Grand Tactics, 26–27
The Grand Strategy of the Roman Empire (Luttwak), 3–4
gray zone operations, civil-military relations and, 273–74

Great Britain. *See* United Kingdom (UK)
great power status
    British residual great power role in, 312
    evaluation of grand strategies and role of, 580–94
    financing of grand strategy and, 431–32
    grand strategy financing and, 422–33
    military spending and, 423–25
    multipolarity and, 696
    obstacles to grand strategy and, 595–98
    small state comparisons with, 491–92
    US foreign policy debate and role of, 441–42
    US strategy for, 311–13, 400–2
Great Recession of 2007-2009, grand strategy and, 17
Grimm's Dictionary, 60–61
Gromyko, Andrei, 577–78
gross domestic product (GDP)
    as fundamental state interest, 110–11
    population aging impact on, 722–25
    relative power and, 206
guerrilla-style combat
    topography and terrain and, 211–12
    violent rebel groups and, 507
Guibert, Jacques Antoine Hippolyte (Comte de Guibert), 26–27, 61, 63–68
    Rühle von Lilienstern and, 66–67
Guisinger, Alexandrea, 664–66
Gulf War of 1991, 389–90, 524–27
    US grand strategy and, 549
guns *vs.* butter tradeoff
    change in grand strategy and, 546–47
    subnational interests and, 265–66
Gustav Adolf (King), 307–8

H

Haas, Mark L., 163, 164–65, 166–67, 721–32
Habash, George, 516–18
habit of mind
    British grand strategy and, 649–51
    grand strategy as, 637
Hague Conventions, 360, 483
    small state strategies and, 494–96
Haley, Nikki, 376–77
Hall, Stuart, 677–78
Hall, William Reginald, 400–2
Hamas, 516–18
Hamilton, Alexander, 396
Hamley, Edward Bruce, 69
hard power, changes in grand strategy and shifts in, 525
Hawking, Stephen, 714–15
Hayes, Christopher, 663
Hayes, Jarrod, 308–9
Haynes, Kyle, 480–81
health care costs, population aging and, 723–24
hedging, small states' strategy of, 498–99
Hegel, G. F. W., 309–10
hegemonic orders, network logics of, 131–32
Heikka, Henrikki, 143–44, 146–48
Henderson, G. F. R. (Col.), 27–29, 69
Hermann, Margaret G., 293–97
Heuser, Beatrice, 57–70
hiding strategy, for small states, 494–98
hierarchies
    networks *vs.*, 131–32
    primacy in intelligence and, 415–16
hijackings, by violent rebel groups, 516–18
Hill, Charles, 34, 178–80
Hillenkoetter, Roscoe, 394
Hinduism
    consciousness in, 96–97
    non-Western grand strategy theory and, 92
Hirschman, Albert O., 371
history
    Castlereagh's grand strategic concept of, 641–42
    change in grand strategy and reliance on, 524–27
    governmentality and, 194–96
    grand strategy in, 32–33
    of technological change and innovation, 221–22
    Thucydides' discussion of, 42–44
History of Peloponnesian War (Thucydides), 474–75
Hitler, Adolf, 291, 327–28, 343–44, 349–50
Hobbes, Thomas, 44, 45
Hobson, John A., 264–65
holism, networks and, 128–32
Holy Alliance, 399
homogeneity, globalization and, 700
Horowitz, Michael, 292

Houston, Sam, 399–400
Howard, Michael, 32
    Kennedy and, 33–34
    on Liddell Hart, 73
    on peace and grand strategy, 84–85
    on politics, 60
Hudson, Valerie, 358
Humanitarian Initiative, 181–82
humanitarian interest, as fundamental state interest, 110–11
Human Rights Watch, 329
human security network, 181–82
Hunt, Alan, 161
Huntington, Samuel, 277, 278, 625
Hurlburt, Heather, 663
Hussein, Saddam, 277–78, 281–82, 389–90, 696
hybrid warfare, Russian strategy of, 349–50
Hymans, Jacques, 309

I

ideas and ideology
    balancing of, 167–68
    Castlereagh's criticism of, 640–41
    change in grand strategy based on, 528–29, 545
    defined, 160
    as fundamental state interest, 110–11
    ideological outreach and, 167–68
    individual agency and, 290–93
    internal structure and external functions, 163–65
    intersubjective articulation, 162–63
    marketplace of ideas, grand strategy in, 657–68
    politics and, 159–60
    populism *vs.* pluralism and, 681–82
    positive and negative views, 160–61
    resource mobilization and extraction and, 167
    rising states grand strategy and, 467–69
    technological change impact on, 225–26
    threat perception and, 166–67
identity
    cultural theory and, 303–16
    difference and foreign policy and, 309–10
    grand strategy as affirmation of, 307–11
    international environment and, 175–76
    multiculturalism and, 677–78
    national identity stories, 307–8
    national self concept and, 308–9
    power and politics and, 315
    recent theorizing on, 313–16
    sovereignty and moral purpose and, 310–11
ideological distance, leadership preferences and, 163
ideological polarity, 167–68
    leadership preferences and, 163
idiosyncratic data, individual agency and, 289–90
Iida, Keisuke, 584
Ikenberry, John, 539–41, 609–10, 695
immigration, population aging and hostility to, 731–32
imperialism
    British history of grand strategy and, 637–38
    financial sector preference for, 264–65
imperial presidency paradigm
    barriers to US grand strategy and, 625, 626–27
    enervation of legislatures and, 666–67
improvisation
    grand strategy as tool for, 560–61, 563
    in US Cold War grand strategy, 566
India, US national identity and perceptions of, 308–9
indirect government, developmental aid and, 198
indirect resource extraction, financing of grand strategy through, 427
individual agency
    adjustment to grand strategy and, 546–48
    grand strategy and, 290–93
    international relations theory and, 288–90
individualism, networks and, 128–32
individual psychology. *See* psychology
Indochina
    as declining state, 482–83
    French grand strategy in, 527–28
industry-specific preferences, 264–65
influence
    intelligence and role of, 417–18
    small state strategies for, 498–99

information variables
    digital revolution and rising entropy, 700–1
    intelligence and, 407–8
    international environment and, 113–15
    state strategy and, 114–15
infrastructure investment, declining power
        strategies and role of, 479–80
Inglehart, Ronald, 730–31
inscription, narrative theory and, 153–54
inspiration, as violent rebel group strategy, 514–15
institutional rule and reform
    declining powers and, 477, 478–81
    in diplomacy, 363
instruments for grand strategy, 12
    illegitimate instruments, 329
    legitimation and, 328–29
    military power and, 346, 349–50
    networked actors and instruments
        in, 126–27
    technological change and, 228–29
insurgencies
    as governance competition, 511–12
    violent rebel groups and, 507
integrated strategy, civil-military relations
        and, 276–78
intelligence
    grand strategy and, 406–18
    international relations theory and, 417–18
    liberal internationalism in, 413–15
    primacy in, 415–16
    relevance of, 407–8
    restraint in, 412–13
    US strategic alignment and role of, 411–17
    on violent rebel groups, 518–19
interaction theories, state strategy options
        and, 118
interconnectivity
    Deep Engagement perspective and, 445–49
    homogenization of interests, 447
    Restrainer perspective, 446
interest groups, declining powers and, 477
interests
    grand strategy evaluation and assessment
        of, 585–86
    in rational grand strategy, 109–13
International Committee of the Red Cross
        (ICRC), grand strategy research and, 177–78

international environment
    assessment of grand strategy and, 585
    declining states and, 477–78
    great powers' shaping of, 611
    legitimation in, 325–26
    networks and, 125–26
    polarity in, 208–9, 692–93
    political cost of grand strategy financing
        and, 432
    population aging and, 725–28
    representations of, 175–76
    state interests and, 113–15
    US grand strategy for management of, 549
international forces, grand strategy and, 12
international institutions
    declining powers binding with, 483
    institutionalized economic cooperation
        and, 374–75, 377, 378
internationalism
    foreign aid to rebel groups and, 515–16
    subnational preferences and, 262–66
International Monetary Fund (IMF), 375
    aging workforce predictions of, 722
    US power and, 450–51
international relations theory
    distributional effect of technology
        and, 223–25
    economic capacity and, 206–7
    foreign policy and, 358–59
    geography and, 210–11
    global events impact on, 443
    ideology and, 162–63
    individual agency and, 288–90
    intelligence studies and, 417–18
    Kantian tripod and, 240–43
    linguistics of grand strategy and, 179–81
    military capability and, 243–45
    multiple power centers and, 697–99
    network analytics and, 128–35
    practice theory and, 144–46
    relative power and, 207
    rising states and, 458–59
    small states' grand strategy and, 492
    structivist challenge in, 304–11
    technological change in, 228–29
    Thucydides and, 41–42
    US grand strategy reorientation and, 539–41

interpretative social science, ideology and, 162–63
interressement principle, actors' interest in strategy and, 151–54
interstate relations
 Thucydides' account of, 44
 US grand strategy for management of, 549
intersubjectivity
 ideology and, 162–63
 linguistics of grand strategy and, 179–80
intertemporal framework, financing of grand strategy and, 425–30
interventionism
 subnational preferences and, 262–66
 US grand strategy and, 659–60
intimidation, violent rebel group strategy of, 513
investments, declining power strategies and role of, 479–80
Iran
 covert actions by, 391–93
 grand strategy research on, 177–78
 Palestine rebel groups supported by, 518
 regional balance of power and, 210, 215n.8
 threat perception and grand strategy in, 166–67
 US economic sanctions in, 381–82
Iran-Contra scandal, 394
Iraq War
 civil-military relations during, 279
 competing grand strategy approaches in, 570
 diplomatic pressure for support of, 358–59
 failure of US legitimation strategy for, 329, 330–33
 grand strategy and, 16
 international relations theory and impact of, 443
 policy failures of elites in, 660–62
 temptation of ambitions and, 398–400
Ishiwara Kanji, 340–41
Islamic Revolutionary Guard Corps (IRGC) (Iran), 166–67
Islamic State, 177–78, 507, 509
Israel
 Palestinian rebel groups and, 516–18
 small state grand strategy, 594
 US policy change toward, 531

J

Jackson, Patrick Thaddeus, 290, 325–26
Jacksonian revolt, 246
Jacobs, Lawrence, 660
James, Charles, 74–75
James, William D., 523–35, 546
Japan
 Australian perception of threat from, 531–33
 changes in postwar grand strategy of, 533–34
 Chinese threat and grand strategy of, 429–30, 533–34
 culture and national security in, 306
 expansionist failure in, 481–82
 financing of grand strategy in, 429–30
 grand strategy theory in, 340–41
 invasion of Manchuria by, 326–27
 Pearl Harbor attack by, 327–28
 population aging in, 722
 as rising state, 460
 survival motive and pre-war economic interests in, 257–59
 technology innovation and strategic goals in, 226–28
Jarzabkowski, Paula, 144–45
Jay's Treaty, 397
Jebb, Gladwyn, 637–38, 648–49
Jefferson, Thomas, 396–97
Jentleson, Bruce, 606
Jervis, Robert, 166–67, 327–28, 358, 360, 441–54, 611
jihadist groups, 512–13
Johnson, Boris, 198–99
Johnston, Alastair Iain, 245, 476–77
Joint Committee on the National Security Strategy (UK), 198–99
Joint Comprehensive Plan of Action (JCPOA), 131–32
Joint Intelligence Committee (JIC, UK), 393
Joly de Maizeroy, Paul Gédéon, 26, 57–58
 Clausewitz and, 58–59
Jomini, Antoine-Henri de, 27, 68–69, 340–41
Jonas, Alexandra, 151–54
Jordan, geopolitics and, 212
Joseph, Jonathan, 198
judgment, in grand strategy, 178–79
Jusserand, Jean-Jules, 212

justifications
  for grand strategy, 178–79
  legitimation and, 323–24

K

Kabila, Laurent-Désiré, 515–16
Kagan, Robert, 193–94
Kahn, Herman, 348
Kahn, Hermann, 34–35
Kant, Immanuel, 66–67
Kantian tripod
  institutional economic cooperation and, 379
  multipolarity and, 697–99
  regime type and capitalism, 240–43
Katzenstein, Peter, 305, 306, 310–11
Kaufmann, Chaim, 658–60
Kaufmann, Eric, 730
Kehoe, Stephanie, 662–64
Kennan, George
  CIA and, 394
  containment strategy and, 113–15, 328
  on culture and foreign policy, 313
  domestic sources of grand strategy and, 239–40, 247–48
  Georgetown Set and, 658–59
  grand strategy and legacy of, 604–5
  on homogenization of interests, 447
  practice theory and, 144–46
  Roosevelt and, 613–14
  security policy and international environment and, 175–76
  strategic planning mechanisms and, 598–99
Kennedy, John F., 394
Kennedy, Paul, 4, 33–34, 544–45
  American and British influences on, 83–85
  Cold War and grand strategy theory of, 80–82
  evaluation of grand strategy and, 576
  Liddell Hart and, 33–34, 73–74, 82–83, 85–86
  on power and grand strategy, 177–78
  on purpose and means in grand strategy, 174–75
  on state capacity, 194–96
Kennedy, Robert F., 394
Keohane, Robert, 162–63
Kertzer, Joshua D., 292–93

Kier, Elizabeth, 274
King, Martin Luther, 82–83
Kirshner, Jonathan, 264–65
Kirss, Alexander, 628–29
Kissinger, Henry, 356–57, 358, 365, 451–52, 598–600
Kitchen, Nicholas, 525
knowledge
  globalization and diffusion of, 699–700
  governmentality and, 192–96
  ideology and, 160–61
Kohn, Richard, 272, 273–74
Korean War
  obstacles to grand strategy in, 596
  US strategy during, 566
Kornprobst, Markus, 173–82, 332
Kovac, Igor, 205–14
Krasner, Stephen, 626–27
Kratochwil, Friedrich, 307–8, 314
Krebs, Ronald R., 1–18, 35, 153
  on change in grand strategy, 546–47
  on communication and grand strategy, 180
  critiques of grand strategy and, 565
  on domestic preferences in grand strategy, 239–40
  on legitimacy, 314–15
  on national security narratives, 307–8, 332–33
  on pluralism and populism, 673–86
  on popular mobilization, 298–99
  revisionist critique of US strategy and, 568–69
  on rhetorical resonance, 331
  on status factors in grand strategy financing, 431–32
  on strategic culture, 528–29
Kreps, Sarah E., 706–699
Kriegsakademie, 70n.3
Kroenig, Matthew, 539–41
Kupchan, Charles, 528–29, 665–66
Kurdish rebels, 515–16
Kydd, Andrew H., 510–11, 513

L

Laclau, Ernesto, 164–65
land warfare, grand strategy scholarship and, 76

language
  cultural theory and, 314–15
  grand strategy and, 173–82
  rhetorical technique and, 332–33
Lansing, Robert, 401
Lasswell, Harold, 273–74
latency, technology innovation impact on, 226–28
Law, Richard, 647–48
law enforcement, violent rebel groups and, 518–19
Layne, Christopher, 245, 476–77, 539–41, 548–49
Layton, Peter, 36, 621, 627
leadership
  adjustment to grand strategy and role of, 546–47
  audience for, 323, 332
  change in grand strategy by, 526–28, 534
  civil-military relations and strategic assessment, 277–78
  in declining states, 477
  diplomacy and, 356–57
  financing of grand strategy political impact and, 425–30
  grand strategy and, 292–93
  ideology and, 163
  improvisation in, grand strategy basis for, 560–61
  individual agency and, 290–93
  legitimation and, 323
  population aging impact on, 731–32
  populism and, 683–84
  rhetorical resonance and, 330–31
  in small states, 492–93
  style and psychology and, 293–97
  threat construction and, 326–28
League of Nations
  diplomacy and, 360
  US rejection of, 560–61
leash-slipping, small states' strategy of, 498–99
Lebanon, Palestinian rebel groups and, 517
Lee, Robert E., 345–46
legislatures, enervation of, foreign policy and, 666–67
legitimacy and legitimation
  audience role in, 323, 332
  context of, 331–32
  cultural theory and, 314–15
  definition of, 322–24
  discursive constraints on, 331–32
  future of, 333
  grand strategy and, 322–33
  instruments of, 328–29
  military capability and, 243–45
  multicultural narrative as threat to, 679–81
  narrative as tool of, 675
  of national interest, 324–26
  rhetorical politics of, 329, 330–33
  speakers' skills and, 331
  threat construction and, 326–28
Legro, Jeffrey, 274, 311, 546
Leo VI (Byzantine emperor, Leo the Wise), 26, 58–59
Lepore, Jill, 678
Levy, Jack, 710
Levy, Yagil, 273
liaison agreements
  liberal internationalism in intelligence and, 413–15
  primacy in intelligence and, 415–16
Liberal Hegemony strategy, civil-military relations and, 273–74
liberal internationalism
  grand strategy school and, 622–23
  political polarization about, 664–66
  primacy in intelligence and, 415–16
  US embrace of, 539–41
  US grand strategy for promotion of, 549
  US intelligence strategies and, 413–15
liberalism
  domestic sources of grand strategy and, 240–43
  free trade and, 241–43
  ideology and, 162–63
  multiculturalism and, 676–78
  multipolarity and, 697–99
  national economic interests and, 259–62
  nationalism and, 245–46
  status of strategizing in, 7–8
  strategic culture and, 245
  survival motive and, 259
  unipolarity and, 693
Libya, rebel groups in, 510

Liddell Hart, Basil
    on Clausewitz, 76–77, 78–79, 85–86
    Earle's theory contrasted with, 83–85
    First World War influence on, 76–77, 340–41
    on governmentality, 193–96
    grand strategy scholarship and, 2–3, 10–11, 29–30, 707–9
    impact on grand strategy scholarship of, 73–86
    intellectual context in work of, 74–80
    Kennedy and, 33–34, 82–83
    on limits of military power strategy, 351–53
    meta-strategy view of grand strategy and, 174–75
    on nonmilitary grand strategy, 192
    Political Strategy tradition and, 69–70
    on rationality of government, 192–93
    Sun Tzu's influence on, 89
    on war and strategy, 36–37
Lieber, Kier A., 711–12
Lincoln, Abraham, 28–29
Lindblom, Charles, 612, 626–27
linguistics
    actors' use of grand strategy and, 178–79
    definitions in grand strategy and, 176
    grand strategy and, 174–76
    remaking and unmaking of strategies and, 179–81
    rhetorical resonance and, 330–33
Lippman gap, 476
Lippmann, Walter, 658–59
Lissner, Rebecca Friedman, 194–96, 524–25, 539–52, 565, 621
Lloyd George, David, 428–30
Lobasz, Jennifer, 331
logic, grand strategy and, 5
logrolling coalitions
    civil-military relations and, 280–81
    technology innovation and, 226
long run perspective
    Castlereagh's views on, 640–41
    grand strategy and, 174–75
loss aversion, change in grand strategy and, 527–28
Ludendorff, Erich (Gen.), 340–41
Luttwak, Edward
    Cold War strategy and, 80
    evaluation of grand strategy and work of, 576
    on fertility rates and social practice, 727
    grand strategy theory and, 3–4, 32–33
    on military power as strategy, 344, 349–50

M

MacDonald, Paul K., 133, 474–87
Machiavelli, Niccolo, 60, 61–62, 191, 358
macroeconomics, cost navigation in grand strategy financing and, 430–32
Madison, James, 396–97
Maduro, Nicolás, 448, 683–84
Mahabharata, 100
Mahan, Alfred, 75, 212, 343
Maizeroyan tradition
    Clausewitz and, 58–59
    modern legacy of, 68–69
Makers of Modern Strategy (Earle), 31–32, 84
Mälksoo, Maria, 151–52
maneuvers, sieges, and battles, Thucydides on war and, 47–49
Mao Zedong, 291, 342–43, 507
maritime strategic thinking
    geography and, 212
    grand strategy theory and, 75
    technological change impact on, 226
market economy, governmentality and, 195–96
marketplace of ideas, grand strategy in, 657–68
    decline of elites in, 660–62
    enervation of legislatures and, 666–67
    erosion of trust in elites and, 662–64
    polarization and, 657–58, 664–66
Marshall, Andrew, 350–51
Marshall, George, 394
Marshall Plan, 206, 378
Martel, William, 46, 52–53
Martin, John D., 711–12
Marxism
    ideology and, 161
    national economic interests and, 259–62
    positivist hypothesis testing and, 261–62
    survival motive and, 259
mass production, technology and, 223–25

material sources of grand strategy. *See also* resource mobilization and extraction
  change sources, 543–48
  defined, 205–14
  diplomacy as, 359–60
  geography and, 210–13
  ideology and, 162–63
  international community polarity and, 208–9
  international environment and variables in, 113–15, 205
  regional balance of power and, 210
  relative power as, 206–7
  remaking and unmaking of grand strategies and, 179–81
  in rising states, 467–69
  technological change and innovation and, 225–26
  technology, 213–14
Mattern, Janice Bially, 309–10
Mattis, James, 660–62
Maurice, J. F. (Col.), 69
maximum territorial capture, logic of, 82–83
May, Theresa, 312
McCarty, Nolan, 664–66
McChrystal, Stanley, 280–81
McCourt, David M., 303–16
McDonald, Patrick J., 242
McMaster, H. R., 561
Mead, Walter Russell, 246, 570
meaning making
  judgments and justifications for, 178–79
  practice theory and, 145–46
means, in grand strategy, 174–76
means research, democratic mobilization and, 241
Mearsheimer, John, 194–96, 226–28, 246, 465, 568–69
medical innovation, grand strategy and development of, 221–22
Melian Dialogue (Thucydides), 41, 46, 50–51
Mérand, Federic, 143–44, 149–50
MERCOSUR, 211–12
Mercur, James, 28–29
Metternich, Klemens von, 331–32, 362, 494–95
Mexican-American War, 399–400
Meyer, John W., 363

Meyers, George, 83–84
MI 6 (UK), 393–94
Middle East
  British grand strategy changes in, 531–33
  civil-military relations in, 281–82
  Cold War policy changes in, 525
  energy technology and, 213–14
  population aging in, 733n.8
  regional balance of power in, 210
  restraint strategy failure ion, 569–71
  US policy change toward, 531, 571–72
middle powers
  financing of grand strategy by, 423–25, 433n.4
  grand strategy research on, 177–78
Milevski, Lukas, 73–86, 164–65, 358–59
militarism
  civil-military relations and, 282–83n.2
  grand strategy and, 292
military power
  change in grand strategy and, 529–30
  declining states use of, 476, 480–81
  display and threat using, 349–50
  domestic politics and, 243–45
  global interconnectivity and, 445–46
  grand strategy and, 339–53, 563–64
  indirect effects of technology on, 230–31
  military economic and bureaucratic structure and, 279–81
  military failure and strategic success, 347
  military success and strategic failure of, 345–46
  national economic interests and, 260
  nationalism and, 245–46
  non-force aspects of, 347–51
  nuclear weapons and strategies of, 348
  population aging and, 722–25, 726
  procurement strategies and, 350–51
  rebel group outgoverning and, 511–12
  rebel groups' lack of, 510
  relative power and, 206–7
  statecraft and, 342–44
  state strategy options and, 118
  strategic display of, 349–50
  strategic effectiveness of, 344–47
  strategic limitations of, 351–53
  sustaining and disruptive technologies and, 708–9
  technology and, 223–25, 226–28, 229–30

military power (*cont.*)
   topography and terrain and, 211–12
   US post-Cold War strategy and, 550–51
   violent rebel groups and, 518–19
   World War I and impact of, 340–42
military spending
   changes in grand strategy and shifts in, 525
   in declining states, 478–81
   financing of grand strategy with, 423–25
   Japanese grand strategy financing and, 429–30
   population aging impact on, 722–23
   robotics technology, 713
   US grand strategy financing and, 428–29, 430
military strategy. *See also* civil-military relations
   character of, 276–78
   Clausewitz's understanding of, 60–61
   obstacles to grand strategy and, 597, 599–600
   precision munitions and, 711–12
   robotics and, 712–14
   tactics and, 27
   US grand strategy and, 629–31
Miller, Benjamin, 179–81
Miller, Edward, 429–30
Milner, Helen V., 167
Mintzberg, Henry, 627
Mitrovich, Gregory, 389–400
Mitzen, Jennifer, 308–9, 325–26, 331–32
modernization, Gandhi's critique of, 97–98
Modi, Narendra, 683–84
Moltke the elder, 78
monitoring, military power and, 348
Monnet, Jean, 379
Monroe, James, 399
Monroe Doctrine, 400, 708
Montesquieu (Charles de Secondat), 60–61, 63, 212–13
moral government, theory of, 193–94
moral law, Sun Tzu on, 95–96
moral purpose
   populism and, 681
   sovereignty and identity and, 310–11
Morgenthau, Hans Joachim, 206–7, 294–95, 297–99, 313
   on diplomacy, 359–60, 362
   on legitimation, 325

Morley, Neville, 41–53
Morris, Gouverneur, 396
Mudde, Cas, 681
multiculturalism
   grand strategy and, 679–81
   policymaking and, 675–81
   populism and, 673
   in Western societies, 676–78
multilateral coalitions
   civil-military relations and, 274–75
   diplomacy and, 360
   institutionalized economic cooperation and, 374–75, 377, 378
   relative power and, 207
multinational corporations
   grand strategy research and, 177–78
   technology innovation and, 223–25
multipolarity
   current debate on, 697–99
   emergence of, 690–91
   global power distribution and, 208–9
Munich Summit of 1938, 327–28, 524–27
Murray, Williamson, 2, 35, 36, 144–46
   evaluation of grand strategy and, 576
Musk, Elon, 714–15
Mussolini, Benito, 349–50
Mytelenean Debate (Thucydides), 46, 50

N

Naji, Abu Bakr, 512–13
naming, ideology and, 164–65
Napoleon, 396
   Clausewitz on, 62
   evaluation of strategies of, 58–59
   invasion of Spain by, 398–400
   military power and grand strategy of, 345–46
   on tactics, 26–27
Napoleonic Wars, British history of grand strategy and, 637–38
Narizny, Kevin, 248–49, 256–67
narrative
   in grand strategy, 674–75
   ideology and, 165
   multiculturalism and, 679–81
   national identity stories, 307–8
   populism and use of, 684

as rhetorical technique, 332–33
strategy assembly and, 152–53
technological change impact on, 225–26
Nasser, Gamel Abdel, 277–78, 525
national identity stories
foreign policy and, 307–8
state identity and, 309–10
national interest
British grand strategy and, 649–51
legitimation of, 324–26
population aging impact on, 728–31
in rhetoric, 332
strategic pragmatism and, 613
National Interest, 173
nationalism
civilization discourse and, 247
domestic grand strategy and, 245–46
multiculturalism and, 678
population aging and, 728–31, 733–34n.11
populism and, 245–48, 682
National Maritime Security Strategy, 151–52
national preferences, economic interests
and, 259–62
national security. *See* security
National Security Act of 1947, 389, 595
National Security Council (US), 391–93, 394
National Security Decision Directive 32
(1982,1-4), 567–69
National Security Decision Directive 75
(1983), 567–69
National Security Strategy (NSS) (UK), 195–96
National Security Strategy documents (US), 561
criticism of, 565
national self, identity and, 308–9
National Students Association (NSA), 389
Natta, Alessandro, 610–11
natural resources, grand strategy and access
to, 210–11
Nau, Henry, 441–42
Naval Defence Act (1889, UK), 427–28
naval strategy
changes in, 529–30
financing of, 427
force multiplier effect in, 343
grand strategy and, 29, 75, 83–84
military success and strategic failure
in, 345–46

technology and advances in, 221–22, 228–30
Thucydides and, 41
Navari, Cornelia, 360
Neal, Andrew W., 190–99
Nelson, Horatio, 345–46
neoclassical realism
domestic sources of grand strategy
and, 240–43
romantic leadership and, 297–98
survival motive and, 259
neoliberalism, governmentality and, 195–96
neopositivism, individual agency and, 288
Neorealist theory
incentives for grand strategy change and,
525–26, 533–34
polarity and, 691–92
Netanyahu, Benjamin, 683–84
Netherlands, binding strategies of, 483
networks
actors and instruments in, 126–27
brokerage in, 131–32
creation and manipulation of, 134–35
criticism of, 127–28
economic networks, 124–25
global governance networks, 124–25
grand strategy and analytics of, 128–35
human security network, 181–82
key concepts in, 129–31
as organizational forms, 124–28
politics and, 125–26
relationalism theory and, 128–32
small state grand strategy and, 496–98
transactional advocacy networks, 124–25
Neumann, Iver
on developmental aid, 198
on diplomacy, 360
on identity and foreign policy, 309–10
on practice theory and strategy, 143–44
on strategic culture, 146–48
neutrality, small state strategies and, 494–96
A New and Enlarged Military Dictionary
(James), 74–75
Newman, Abraham L., 126–27, 131–32
New Materialism, 181–82
Newtonian science, Western grand strategy
theory and, 90, 92
Nexon, Daniel, 123–36

Nicholas II (Tsar), 482–83, 528
Nichols, Tom, 663
Night, Kathleen, 160–61
Nixon, Richard, 394, 451–52
　grand strategy under, 599–600
Nolan, Alan, 345–46
Non-Aligned Movement, 342
non-human threats, US grand strategy debate and, 444
nonmilitary instruments, in Liddell Hart's grand strategy theory, 79
nonpolarity
　current debate over, 697–99
　grand strategy and, 690–702
　multiple power centers and, 697–99
　successful strategies for dealing with, 701–2
nonrationalism, culture and, 305–6
nonstate actors. *See also* violent rebel groups
　counterinsurgency strategies of, 89
　developmental aid programs and, 197–99
　diplomacy and, 361–62
　economic statecraft and, 381–82
　foreign aid and, 382
　globalization and rise of, 699–700
　grand strategy and, 89–91, 181–82
　multiple power centers and, 697–99
nonviolence
　Gandhi's strategies for, 98–99
　grand strategy and, 89–91
　as resistance, 99–100
non-Western grand strategy
　cosmology, ontology and epistemology in, 92–93
　overview of, 89–101, 342
normativity
　change in grand strategy based on, 528–29
　culture and, 305–6, 315–16
　economic interests and statecraft and, 380–81
　evaluation of grand strategy in context of, 576–78
　legitimation and, 322–24
　strategic assessment and, 278
Norris, Pippa, 730–31
North American Free Trade Agreement (NAFTA), 550
North Atlantic Treaty Organization (NATO)
　bipolarity of power and, 208–9
　Cold War grand strategy and, 114–15
　deterrence theory and effectiveness of, 116–17
　diplomatic practices and, 361
　economic and security ties in, 378
　military support for, 275–76
　practice theory and, 147–48
　Restraint perspective on limits of, 444–45
　small state protections and, 495–96
North Korea
　covert actions by, 391–93
　military power in, 206–7, 349–50
Norway, diplomacy in, 365
nuclear weapons
　cultural taboos against, 305–6
　force multiplier effect of, 343
　grand strategy impact on, 229–30, 598
　intelligence posture on, 409–11
　military power and role of, 348
　as offence-defence variable, 114–15
　status dimension in capability of, 309
　technology's impact on, 709–10
　unipolarity and, 693
Nye, Joseph, 659–60

O

Obama, Barack
　change in grand strategy under, 546–47
　civil-military relations and, 280–81
　diplomacy under, 366
　economic crisis and grand strategy under, 17
　on Kennan, 604–5
　obstacles to grand strategy for, 596
　revisionist perspective on grand strategy and, 569–71
objective control approach, civil-military relations and, 278
obsolete strategies, technological change and innovation and, 226–28
offense-defense variables
　international environment and, 113–15
offshore balancing
　in grand strategy scholarship, 561, 708
　revisionist perspective on, 569–71
　US foreign policy and role of, 226–28, 307, 442

On Diplomacy (Der Derian), 360
On Grand Strategy (Gaddis), 356–57
ontology, non-Western grand strategy and, 92–93
On War (Clausewitz), 26–27, 60, 62–63, 350–51
Open Door ideology, American foreign policy and, 476–77
open sources
　liberal internationalism and use of, 413–15
　US intelligence strategies and, 412–13
operational code theory, agency in, 294
Operation Desert Storm, 711–12
Operations Coordinating Board, 394
Operation TORCH (World War II), 595–96
opportunity, pragmatic approach to, 613
Optimist ideology, multipolarity and, 697–99
Orbán, Victor, 731–32
organic solidarity, multiculturalism and, 676
organizational culture, change in grand strategy and role of, 529–30
organizational theory
　change in strategy and, 560–61
　nonpolarity and strategies in, 701–2
　obstacles to grand strategy and complexity in, 597–98
　practice theory and, 144–45
　violent rebel groups and, 508–9
Oros, Andrew, 306
O'Rourke, Lindsey, 329
Oslo Peace Process, 382
Other
　culture and role of, 315–16
　identity in foreign policy and, 309–10
outgoverning, by rebel groups, 511–12
overhauls, change in grand strategy
　as, 524–25, 539–52
　sources of, 544–46

P

Page, Benjamin, 660
Paine, S. C. M., 481–82
Palestine
　foreign aid to rebels in, 515–16
　Irgun in, 511
　violent rebel groups in, 516–18
Palestine Islamic Jihad, 518
Palestinian Liberation Organization (PLO), 382

Palmerston (Lord), 399–400, 637–38, 644–46
pan-Arabism, 525
pandemics, US grand strategy debate and, 444
paradigms, linguistics of grand strategy and, 176
Parent, Joseph M., 474–87
Paret, Peter, 60
Parker, Geoffrey, 212, 474–75
Partnership for Peace, 148
partnerships, US intelligence strategies and risk of, 412–13
Pasha of Tripoli, 391–93, 398
peace
　American grand strategy theory and, 84–85
　Liddell Hart's grand strategy and role of, 77–78
Peace of Tilsit, Clausewitz on, 61–62
peacetime strategies, military power and, 347–51
Pearl Harbor, Japanese attack on, 327–28, 346
Peksen, Dursun, 375
Peloponnesian War
　grand strategy in, 46–50
　political and military scholarship and, 41
　Thucydides' narrative of, 42–44
Peninsular Wars, 398–400
People's Liberation Army (PLA) (China), 244–45
performativity
　in diplomacy, 363, 364–65
　multiculturalism's impact on, 679–81
　small state vulnerability performance, 498–99
Pericles, Thucydides on strategy of, 49–50
Pessimist ideology, multipolarity and, 697–99
Petraeus, David, 275–76
Pincus, Steve, 484–85
Pitt, William, 345–46, 640–41
pluralism
　grand strategy and, 673–86
　multiculturalism and, 675–76
　populism *vs.*, 681–82
Polaris submarine technology, 229–30
polarity
　contemporary limits on, 692–93
　properties of, 691–92

polarization. *See also* nonpolarity
  legitimation and, 325
  marketplace of ideas and, 657–58, 664–66
  populism and, 683–84
policy and policymaking. *See also* economic interests and statecraft; foreign policy
  as alternative to grand strategy, 625–27
  in declining states, 478–81
  die Politik and, 62–63
  financing of grand strategy impact on, 425–30
  grand strategy impact on, 33–36, 541–43, 571–72, 593, 673–74
  intelligence and, 407–8
  multiculturalism and, 675–81
  population aging and, 725–28
  populism's impact on, 684
Political Strategy tradition, 57–58
  Clausewitz's *die Politik* and, 59–68, 69–70
politics. *See also* geopolitics
  change in strategy and impediment of, 530–31, 534
  civil-military relations and, 274–75, 276–78, 280–81
  cost navigation in grand strategy financing and, 430–32
  culture and, 315
  Deep Engagement and, 445–49
  developmental aid and, 198–99
  diplomacy and, 362
  financing of grand strategy, political costs of, 425–30
  as fundamental state interest, 110–11
  grand strategy in, 6, 159–60
  identity and, 310
  ideology and, 164–65
  incentives for grand strategy change and, 525–26
  in Kennedy's grand strategy theory, 81–82
  linguistics of grand strategy and, 179–80, 182
  Marxist politics, national economic interests and, 259–62
  multiculturalism and, 678
  negative connotations of, 60
  networked actors and instruments in, 126–27
  network theory and, 125–26
  pluralism in, 681–82
  population aging and, 723–24, 728
  populism and, 681–82, 683–84
  practice theory and, 145–46
  subnational preferences and, 262–66
  threat perception in US and, 443–45
  in wartime, change in grand strategy and, 546–47
Politics among Nations (Morgenthau), 297–98, 362
The Politics of Grand Strategy (Williamson), 3–4
la politique, French concept of, 60–61
Polk, James, 400
Pollack, Kenneth M., 288
Pompeo, Mike, 364–65, 660–62
Poole, Keith, 664–66
Popescu, Ionut, 9, 36, 616n.11, 621, 628–29, 631–33
Popular Front for the Liberation of Palestine, 516–18
population aging
  grand strategy and, 721–32
  policymaking and, 725–28
  state capability and, 722–25
  state interests and, 728–31
population growth, global impact of, 223–25
populism
  civilization discourse and, 247
  defined, 686n.2
  domestic sources of grand strategy and, 246
  grand strategy and, 683–84
  nationalism and, 245–48
  origins of, 682
  pluralism *vs.*, 681–82
  population aging and rise of, 728–31
Porter, Patrick
  on foreign policy, 307, 660–62
  grand strategy scholarship of, 35–36, 631–33
  on reorientation of grand strategy, 539–41, 631–33
  on reputation and credibility, 445–46
  revisionist critique of grand strategy and, 568–69
  on strategic culture, 528–29

Posen, Barry
   on civil-military relations, 276
   Cold War and grand strategy theory of, 80
   definition of grand strategy, 585–86
   evaluation of grand strategy and, 580
   on governmentality and strategy, 192–93
   grand strategy scholarship and, 4, 35–36, 182, 341–42, 622–23, 707–9
   Restraint theory and, 442, 444–45
   on signaling in grand strategy, 608–9
   on statecraft and grand strategy, 606–7
   on strategy and military power, 358
positionality, networks, 129–31
post-Cold war era. *See also* Cold War
   arms exports in, 379–80
   civil-military relations in, 274–75
   covert action in, 389–90
   culture and security in, 307
   developmental aid in, 197–99
   diplomacy in, 361–62
   grand strategy in, 33–36
   military spending in, 428–29
   Reagan's grand strategy during, 566–68
   regional balance of power in, 210
   US grand strategy in, 240–43, 548–51, 659–60
postcolonialism, multiculturalism and, 680–81
Pouliot, Vincent, 147–48, 361
Powell, Colin, 124, 280–81
power distribution. *See also* declining powers; great power status; middle powers; relative power; rising great powers; *shih* (power); small states
   Castlereagh's concept of, 638–40
   culture and concepts of, 313, 315
   developmental aid and, 198
   diplomacy and, 362
   economic statecraft and, 370–71, 379–80
   globalization and power diffusion, 699–700
   grand strategy assumptions based on, 177–78
   grand strategy change and role of, 531
   incentives for change and redistribution of, 525–26
   international environment and, 113–15
   multiple power centers and, 697–99
   population aging impact on, 722–23
   regional balance of, 210
   relative power, 206–7
   rising power, 458–59
   security strategy focus on, 311
   technology and, 213–14
   unequal distribution of, 208–9
practice theory
   arranging strategy and document fabrication and, 151–54
   cultural theory and, 314
   grand strategy and, 142–55
   international relations studies and strategy and, 144–46
   narrative and, 152–53
   obstacles to grand strategy and, 594–99
   origins of, 143–44
   strategic culture approach and, 146–48
   strategy as social struggle in, 148–51
pragmatism. *See also* strategic pragmatism
   grand strategy and, 8–9, 680–81
   multiculturalism and, 680–81
   small state grand strategy and, 500
   in US grand strategy, 570
prana (life force)
   consciousness and, 96–97
   nonviolence and, 98–99
   non-Western grand strategy theory and, 92–93
Preble, Keith, 370–84
precision-guided munitions (PGMs), 711–12
prescriptive strategy approach, ideology and, 161, 164–65
Press, Darryl G., 711–12
preventive war doctrines, military support for, 275–76
Priebe, Miranda, 460
primacy
   critique of US reliance on, 568–69
   decline in US foreign policy of, 660–62
   deep engagement as alternative to, 442
   risk tolerance and debate over, 444
   technology innovation impact on, 226–28
   in US post-Cold War strategy, 548–51
   US strategic culture based on, 415–16, 528–29, 629–31, 659–60
printing technology, religion and, 226

problematization analysis, practice theory
    and, 150–51
procurement doctrine
    civil-military relations and, 279
    culture and national security and, 306
    military power and, 350–51
    practice theory and, 146–48
productivity growth, population aging impact
    on, 722–25
professional supremacy, civil-military
    relations and, 277
Project Maven, 715–16
Project Troy, 390
propaganda of the deed, violent rebel groups
    use of, 514–15
Prospect Theory, change in grand strategy
    and, 527–28
prosperity
    economic statecraft and, 379–80
    as fundamental state interest, 110–11
    security and, 110
    US post-Cold War grand strategy and, 549
Provisional Irish Republican
    Army, 508–9, 510–11
provocation, by violent rebel groups, 513–14
proximity, grand strategy and, 210–11
psychology
    change in grand strategy and role of, 526–28
    grand strategy and, 287–300
    leadership style and, 293–97
    national identity and, 309
    Prospect Theory and, 527–28
    US perception of grand strategy tradeoffs
        and, 453
public opinion
    British foreign policy in World War II
        and, 648–49
    Castlereagh on, 640–41
    change in grand strategy and role of, 534
    erosion of trust in elites and, 662–64
    legitimation and, 323
    political polarization in, 664–66
    rebel groups' inspiration of, 514–15
    role of military in, 243–45, 272–73
    romantic leadership and, 297–99
    violent rebel groups and, 516–18
public policy, grand strategy and, 625–27

purpose, in grand strategy, 174–76
Purvis, Trevor, 161
Putin, Vladimir, 310, 696
Putnam, Robert, 629–31

Q

qi (life force)
    Daoism and, 93
    Dao of Deception and, 93–94
    non-Western grand strategy theory
        and, 92–93
quantum physics
    Daoism and, 93–96
    Eastern cultural traditions and, 90
    non-Western grand strategy theory and, 92
quasi-statehood, rebel group
    outgoverning, 511–12

R

race
    domestic grand strategy and, 247–48
    population aging and, 728–31
Radio Free Europe, 391–93
Radio Liberty, 391–93
Ramparts magazine, 389
Rapport, Aaron, 431–32
Rathbun, Brian C., 287–300
rational grand strategy
    basic principles of, 107–19
    defined, 108
    feasibility, costs and benefits of, 118
    fundamental interests, 109–11
    interests in, 109–13
    international environment and, 113–15
    theories, 115–18
    tradeoffs in, 119
    value of, 120
rationalist theory
    culture and, 305–6, 313–16
    governmentality and, 192–96
    grand strategy in, 11, 107–20
    international environment and, 113–15
    Western grand strategy and, 90
Reagan, Ronald, 714–15
    CIA and, 394
    criticism of grand strategy under, 628–29
    grand strategy under, 599–600

post-Cold War grand strategy
and, 566–68
Soviet Union and, 389–90
Realist international relations theory
culture and identity and, 312
evaluation of grand strategy and, 576–78
foreign policy and, 294–95
grand strategy in, 11
grand strategy school and, 622–23
homogenization of interests and, 447
individual agency, 288
linguistics in grand strategy and, 177–78, 181–82
multipolarity and, 697–99
national identity and, 307–8
nationalism and, 245–46
overhauls of grand strategy and, 544–46
power struggles in, 304
Restraint theory and, 444–45
status of strategizing in, 7–8
survival motive in, 257–59
Thucydides in, 44
US domestic values and, 451–52
US grand strategies and, 442–49
realist leadership, style and psychology of, 293–97
reality, non-Western grand strategy and, 90
rearmament policies, financing of grand strategy and, 427
rebel groups, government interest in, 511
Recchia, Stefano, 274–75
recognition, rising state strategy for obtaining, 467–69
recruiting strategies, violent rebel groups and, 508–9
Red Army Faction (Germany), 507
Reflections on the Revolution in France (Burke), 638–40
regime change
covert actions for, 329, 391–93
violent rebel groups and, 507
regime type
cost navigation in grand strategy financing and, 430–32
as fundamental state interest, 110–11
Kantian tripod and, 240–43
military politics and, 243–45

regional balance of power, 210
declining states and role of, 477–78
strategic pragmatism, 614–15
US post-Cold War grand strategy and, 549
regional security communities
balance of power and, 210
grand strategy research on, 177–78
practice theory and, 147–48
regulative effects of cultural norms, 305–6
Reich, Simon
on civil-military relations, 279–81
on debt financing of grand strategy, 422–27
on foreign policy and grand strategy, 358–59
grand strategy school and, 620, 631–33, 708
on logic and substance in grand strategy, 5
on practice theory, 144–46
on strategy as social struggle, 148
on US and grand strategy, 629–31
relational theory
identity and, 309–10
networks and, 128–32
relative power and, 206–7
rising states and, 461–62
relative power
grand strategy financing and, 422–33
polarity of international community and, 208–9
as resource, 206–7
religion, printing technology and, 226
remade strategies, actors role in, 179–81
reputation
dangers of grand strategy and, 610–11
Deep Engagement and, 445–46
pragmatic approach to, 613
US grand strategy and, 445–49
resonance, legitimation and, 330–33
resource mobilization and extraction. *See also* material sources
civil-military relations and, 272–73
declining states and, 478–81
financing of grand strategy through, 425–30, 433n.6, 433n.7, 433n.8
ideology and strategies for, 167
nationalism and, 246
relative power and, 206–7
rising states' strategies for, 463–64
in small states, 492–93

resource mobilization and extraction (*cont.*)
   strategic pragmatism, 615
   Sun Tzu on efficiency in, 93–96
responsible stakeholder ideology, 240–43
   international relations theory and, 443
Restraint strategy
   advantages of entanglement and, 449–50
   civil-military relations and, 275–76
   cost-benefit analysis of US grand strategy and, 450–51
   credibility and reputation and, 446
   debt financing of grand strategy and, 422–27
   entrapment and, 447–48
   global events impact on, 443
   global interconnectivity and, 445–49
   grand strategy school and, 622–23
   homogenization of interests and, 447
   perceived tradeoffs in, 452–53
   procurement decisions and, 279
   revisionist perspective on, 569–71
   temptation of ambitions and, 448–49
   terrorism and, 450
   threat perception in US and, 443–45
   US disagreement over, 442–49
   US domestic values and, 451–52
   US foreign policy and role of, 442, 659–60
   US intelligence strategies and, 412–13
retrenchment
   by declining powers, 484
   engagement and, 173
Reus-Smit, Christian, 305, 310–11, 313–14
revenue generation, financing of grand strategy and, 425–30
revisionist orientation
   of authoritarian states, 275–76
   change in grand strategy and, 470n.2, 544–46
   Chinese grand strategy and, 466–67
   critique of US grand strategy and, 568–69
   evaluation of, 581–83
   in Iranian grand strategy, 225–26
   limitations of, 569–71
   network theory and, 133
revolution, military power and, 342–43
Revolutionary War (US), covert action during, 395

rhetoric
   audience for, 332
   content of, 332
   context of, 331–32
   discursive structure in, 331–32
   ideology and, 165
   legitimation of grand strategy and, 322–33
   national interest legitimation and, 324–26
   of populism, 683–84
   resonance of, 330–33
   speakers' skills and, 331
   technique in, 332–33
Rhodes, Ben, 660–62
Rhodes, Edward, 545
Richards, A. I., 165–68
Ridgway, Matthew (Gen.), 280–81
Riefler, Jason, 728
right-wing populism, principles of, 682
Rig Veda, 92–93
Ringmar, Eric, 307–8
Ripsman, Norrin, 205–14, 371
rising great powers
   control and assertiveness of, 462–64
   definitions and strategic conditions in, 458–59
   evolution of, 460–62
   financing of grand strategy in, 422–33
   grand strategies of, 457–70
   military budgets of, 423–25
   satisfaction or dissatisfaction in, 461–62, 470n.2
   sources of strategy for, 467–69
   status factors in grand strategy financing and, 431–32
   strategic logics of, 464–65
risk tolerance
   change in grand strategy and, 527–28
   grand strategy and, 292
   rising states assertiveness and, 463–64
   status concerns, 528
   US grand strategy debate and, 444
Robespierre, Maximilien, 396
robotics, military strategy and, 712–14
roles in social structure, identity and, 310
romantic leadership
   public opinion and, 297–99
   style and psychology of, 293–97

Rommel, Erwin (Gen.), 346
Roosevelt, Franklin Delano
    changes to grand strategy by, 534
    diplomacy and grand strategy under, 356–57
    great powers conflict and, 401
    leadership qualities, 330–31
    Pearl Harbor attack, 327–28
    pragmatic leadership of, 613–14
    World War II grand strategy and, 595–96
Roosevelt, Theodore, 401, 676
Rosecrance, Richard, 627, 629–31
Rosenthal, Howard, 664–66
Ross, Lisa, 662–64
Rovner, Joshua, 406–18
Rowan, Brian, 363
RQ-11B Raven, 713
Rühle von Lilienstern, Otto August, 66–67
rule-breaking, threat perception and, 327–28
rule/government distinction
    Foucault's governmentality and, 190–92
    legitimation and, 323
Rumsfeld, Donald, 279
Russia. *See also* Soviet military scholarship
    binding strategies of, 483
    bluffing by, 482–83
    climate and power of, 212–13
    colonization attempts in America by, 399–400
    competition with US from, 303–4, 311
    covert actions by, 390
    cyber attacks by, 402–3
    Deep Engagement policy and, 444–45
    evaluation of grand strategy in, 581
    foreign policy and identity in, 310
    grand strategy theory in, 340–41
    Japanese grand strategy concerning, 429–30
    military capacity of, 206–7
    networks as grand strategy in, 134–35
    nonstate actors and diplomacy by, 361–62
    Political Strategy tradition in, 69–70
    population aging in, 722, 724–25
    regional balance of power and hegemony of, 210
    robotics technology in, 714
    sharp power in, 127
    status bias and strategy in, 528
Russo-Japanese War, 429–30

Rwandan Patriotic Front, 510, 515–16
Ryan, Maeve, 637–51

S

Sadat, Anwar, 347
Sagan, Scott, 710
Sailing the Water's Edge (Milner & Tingley), 167
salami tactics, strategic pragmatism, 614
Santa Ana, Antonio Lopez de, 399–400
Sargeaunt, H. A., 31
Sartori, Giovani, 161
satellite technology, indirect effects of, 230–31
Satyagraha, 98, 99–100
Saudi Arabia, Palestinian rebel groups and, 517
Saunders, Elizabeth, 664–66
savings rates, population aging and, 723–24
Schake, Kori, 460, 539–41
Schelling, Thomas, 34–35, 348, 350–51, 446
Scherrer, Vincenza, 151–52
Schlesinger, Arthur M., 325
Schlieffen Plan, 211–12
Schmitt, Mark, 663
Schmitt, Oliver, 153
scholarship and academia. *See also specific grand strategy scholars*, e.g., Posen
    on diplomacy and, 360
    on emergent grand strategy, 627–29, 631–33
    on governmentality, 191, 194–96
    grand strategy debates in, 34, 341–42, 571–72, 673–74
    on land warfare, 76
    policymaking and politics and, 673–74
    political and military scholarship, 41
    Soviet military scholarship, 69
    on technology and grand strategy, 707–9
    Thucydides' legacy in, 42–46
    World War I grand strategy and, 29–30, 76
Schou Tjalve, Vibeke, 325, 332–33
Schrodinger, Erwin, 94–95
Schultz, Kenneth A., 241
Schweller, Randall
    on declining states' strategies, 477
    on grand strategy demise, 544–46, 685–86
    on legitimation, 325
    on nonpolarity and grand strategy, 690–702
    on populism, 246

Schweller, Randall (cont.)
    on pragmatism and grand strategy, 8–9
    on rising states' grand strategy, 463–64
Scowcroft, Brent, 659–60
scripts, in diplomacy, 363, 364–65
Second Intifada, 517
Second Offset Strategy, 229–30
Second World War. *See* World War II
Secret Service Bureau (SSB) (UK), 393–94
sectoral interests, economics and, 262–66
securitization rhetoric, resonance of, 330–33
security policy
    change in grand strategy and, 533–34
    civil-military relations and role of, 272–73
    culture and foreign policy and, 305–7, 313
    in declining states, 475–76
    democratic peace theory and, 111–13
    deterrence theory and, 116–17
    economic statecraft and, 371
    as fundamental state interest, 110–11
    linguistic representations of, 175–76
    narrative as tool of, 674–75, 679–81
    national security narratives, 307–8
    political polarization and, 665–66
    population aging and, 728–31
    practice theory and, 147–48
    regional balance of power and, 210
    rhetorical resonance in debate on, 331–32
    robotics technology and, 712–14
    small state performance of vulnerability and, 498–99
    small states' grand strategy and, 492, 496–98
    state theory of security and, 541–43
    threat perception and, 166–67
    topography and terrain and, 211–12
    in US and UK, cultural comparison of, 311–13
    US foreign policy debate over, 441–42
Security Strategy of the United States (NSS, 2017), 303–4
security studies
    grand strategy in, 3–4, 6
    structivist challenge in, 304–11
Security Studies, 180
selective engagement
    ideology and, 164–65
    shaping grand strategy and, 609–10, 708
    US foreign policy and role of, 442
selectorate theory, 241
self-fulfilling prophecies, grand strategy and risk of, 611, 616n.11
self-preservation, civil-military relations and, 274–75
self-rule *(Swaraj)*, Ghandhi's concept of, 97–98
semiconductor technology, 230–31
Senate Select Committee on Intelligence, 389
Sending, Ole Jacob, 198, 310, 356–66
sense-making, judgments and justifications for, 178–79
September 11 2001 terrorist attacks
    changes in grand strategy following, 534
    international relations theory and impact of, 443
Sésé Seko, Mobutu, 515–16
Sestanovich, Stephen, 546–47
shaping of grand strategy, 609–10
Shapiro, Jacob, 508–9
Sharp, Paul, 360
sharp power, networks and, 127
shelter-seeking, by small states, 494–98
Sherman, William Tecumseh (Gen.), 28–29
Shifrinson, Joshua R. Itzkowitz, 457–70
shih (power). *See also* power distribution
    Chinese strategy and, 94–96
Sicilian Debate (Thucydides), 50
signaling theory
    economic interests and statecraft and, 380–81
    grand strategy and, 608–9
    rational grand strategy and, 117
    threat perception and, 327–28
Silove, Nina, 29, 90–91, 148–51, 580
Simon, Herbert A., 700–1
Sinnreich, Richard, 36
Skinner, Kiron, 247
Slayton, Rebecca, 714–15
Smale, Alison, 724–25
small states, grand strategy of, 490–501
    contemporary trends in, 496–99
    defensive to offensive strategy continuum, 498–99
    determinants of, 492–93
    great powers strategy comparisons, 491–92
    hiding and shelter-seeking and, 494–98

obstacles to, 594
performance of vulnerability and, 498–99
successful strategies, 499–500
Smith, Paul, 644–46
Smith, Walter Bedell, 394
Smoot-Hawley Tariff Act, 666
Snyder, Jack, 280–81, 332–33, 627
Snyder, Per, 467–69
social constructivism, grand strategy in, 11
social context, linguistics of grand strategy and, 179–80
socialism, national economic interests and, 259–62
social media, strategic importance of, 715–16
social network theory
  cultural theory and, 314
  grand strategy in, 11
  sites in, 129–31
social psychology. *See* psychology
social-science perspective
  change in grand strategy and, 539–41, 546
  ideology and, 162–63
societal-military relations, 272
sociological practice, 146–48
  declining fertility rates and, 727
  strategy as, 148–51
The Soldier and the State (Huntington), 277, 278
solidarity, national identity and, 309
Sophists, linguistics approach to grand strategy and, 179–80
The Sources of Military Doctrine (Posen), 276
"The Sources of Soviet Conduct" (Kennan), 239–40
South America
  Anglo-German crisis and, 400–2
  covert actions in, 399
  diplomacy in, 363–64
sovereign-to-sovereign loans, grand strategy funding with, 428–29
sovereignty
  diplomacy and, 365–66
  Foucault on governmentality and, 190–92
  identity and moral purpose and, 310–11
  nonstate actors' challenge to, 697–99
Soviet military scholarship. *See also* Russia
  Maizeroyan tradition in, 69

Soviet Union
  bipolarity of power with US and, 208–9
  China's break with, 209
  Cold War strategies of, 95–96, 577–78, 582, 610–11
  COMECON program, 378
  covert actions by, 389–90, 391–93
  critical resources in, 210–11
  as declining power, 484–85
  economic sanctions strategy of, 377–78
  grand strategy research on, 177–78
  military power in, 225, 344
  military technology innovation in, 229–30
  resource extraction by, 246–249n.1
  strategic adjustment in, 159–60, 162–63
  underwater acoustics technology and, 230–31
  unipolarity and, 693
  US covert action in, 390, 391–93
  US grand strategy following collapse of, 549, 567–69
Spain, Napoleon's invasion of, 398–400
Spanish-American War, 400
Spartans, Thucydides on Corinthians' denunciation of, 47–49
Special Intelligence Service (UK), 393–94
Spee, Andreas Paul, 144–45
Spirit of Laws (Montesquieu), 60–61, 63
spying. *See also* intelligence
  Sun Tzu on, 94–95
  with United States, 389
Stam, Allan C., 292
Stampnitzky, Lisa, 315
state bias
  change in grand strategy and, 528
  grand strategy studies and, 181–82
statehood and statecraft
  benefits of grand strategy for, 561–64
  British history of grand strategy and, 637–38
  Canning's view of, 642–44
  Castlereagh's concept of, 638–42
  change management and, 523
  coordination and grand strategy in, 607–8
  cost navigation in grand strategy financing and, 430–32
  counterstrategies to violent rebel groups, 518–19

statehood and statecraft (*cont.*)
    covert actions and, 391–93
    dangers of grand strategy in, 610–11
    in declining powers, 474–75
    derivative interests, 111–13
    developmental aid and, 198
    dilemmas of decline for, 475–76
    diplomacy and, 362–65
    domestic politics and policy change
        resistance and, 530–31
    economic statecraft, grand strategy
        and, 370–84
    emergent grand strategy and, 627
    enervation of legislatures and, 666–67
    erosion of trust in, 662–64
    evaluation of grand strategy and, 576–78
    feasibility, costs and benefits of, 118
    financing of grand strategy and impact
        on, 425–30
    function of grand strategy in, 606–10
    fundamental interests, 109–11
    globalization and rising entropy and, 699–700
    governmentality and, 191
    grand strategy and, 4, 5–6, 523
    grand strategy development by, 177–78
    identity and foreign policy and, 309–10
    international environment and, 113–15
    intimidation by rebel groups and, 513
    legitimation of, 322–26
    multicultural narrative as threat to, 679–81
    narrative as tool of, 674–75
    national interests as foundation of
        strategy, 541–43
    nonpolarity and strategies for, 701–2
    nonstate actors' challenge to, 697–99
    polarity and, 691–92
    population aging and, 722–31
    quasi-statehood, rebel group outgoverning
        as, 511–12
    rational grand strategy, 109–13
    Restraint theory and, 443
    rising states grand strategies and, 457–70
    robotics technology and, 712–14
    signaling in grand strategy and, 608–9
    small states' grand strategy and, 490–501
    sovereignty, identity and moral purpose
        in, 310–11
    subnational preferences and, 262–66
    survival motive and, 257–59
    technology's impact on, 709–10
    Thucydides on, 41–42
    tradeoffs and conclusions in, 119
    ungovernability of rebel groups and, 512–13
    ungrand strategy and, 600–1
state sponsors, of violent rebel groups, 509
status
    change in grand strategy and, 528
    cost navigation in grand strategy financing
        and role of, 431–32
    declining states and, 477–78
    as fundamental state interest, 110–11
    national identity and, 309
    small states strategies for, 494–95
status quo strategies
    change as alternative to, 534–35
    evaluation of, 581–83
    overhauls of grand strategy and, 470n.2, 544–46
stealth technology, 229–30
    as procurement strategy, 350–51
Steele, Brent, 308–9
Stein, Arthur, 627, 629–31
Stephan, Maria J., 514–15
Stern, Sol, 389
Stewart, Dugald, 644–46
stopping power of water paradigm,
    technology innovation and, 226–28
Strachan, Hew, 76–77, 621–22
stratagem, early references to, 26
strategia, early references to, 26
"Strategical Terms and Defnitions Used in
    Lectures on Naval History" (Corbett), 29
strategic assessment, civil-military relations
    and, 277–78
strategic culture approach
    change in grand strategy and, 528–29, 545
    civil-military relations and, 274–75
    domestic grand strategy and, 245–48
    linguistics of grand strategy and, 179–80
    nationalism and, 245–46
    practice theory and, 146–48
Strategic Defense Initiative (SDI), 350–51
strategic goods, access to
    commercial policy strategies and, 373–74
    grand strategy and, 210–13

strategic logics, of rising great powers, 464–65
strategic planning mechanisms, grand strategy failure and omission of, 598–99
strategic pragmatism, 612–15
    case for, 612–15
    coordination and, 607–8
    critiques of, 614–15
    dangers of grand strategy and, 610–11
    shaping and, 609–10
    signaling and, 608–9
Strategics, Bülow's concept of, 26–27
strategic shocks. *See* exogenous shocks
strategizing, academic status of, 7–8
strategy
    assembly process for, 151–54
    Clausewitzian definition of, 58–59
    early definitions, 26–27
    practice theory and, 144–46
    as social struggle, 148–51
strategy as practice research, 143–44
Strategy: The Indirect Approach (Liddell Hart), 30, 73–74, 79
structural realism
    culture and, 306
    governmentality and, 194–96
    grand strategy theory and, 545
    ideology and, 162–63
Stubb, Alexander, 223–25
Stuxnet attack, 714–15
style, leadership and, 293–97
subnational preferences, economic interests and, 262–66
subsidies, economic statecraft and, 373–74
substance, grand strategy and, 5
Suez Canal crisis
    grand strategy change following, 524–27, 531–33
    military failure and strategic success in, 347
Sun Tzu, 41–42
    Clausewitz and, 91
    cosmology, epistemology and ontology in theories of, 92–93
    grand strategy theory and, 89–91
    on manipulation of perception, 92–93
    on war and strategy, 93–96
superpower status
    benefits of grand strategy and, 561–64

bipolarity and, 448–49
geography and, 212
regional balance of power and, 210
unipolarity and, 692–93
US post-war grand strategy and, 550–51
surveillance, military power and, 348
survival motive, economic interests and, 257–59
Svechin, Alexander, 340–41
Swedish national identity, Thirty Years' War and, 307–8
Swidler, Anne, 146–48, 314, 323
SWIFT banking system, 126–27, 131–32
Switzerland
    small state grand strategy, 594
symbolic power, culture and, 313–14
Syria, Palestinian rebel groups and, 517
System I thinking, 296

T
taboos, cultural norms and, 305–6
tactics
    military focus on, 27
    topography and terrain and, 211–12
Taktiká (Leo VI), 26, 58–59
Talmadge, Caitlin, 215n.8, 281–82
Tannenwald, Nina, 305–6
targeted killing program (US), legitimation of, 329
tariff policies, economic statecraft and, 373–74
taxation, financing of grand strategy through, 425–30
Tax Relief Act (1997, US), 428–29
Taylor, Charles, 314, 675–76
technical intelligence collection
    liberal internationalism and, 413–15
    US intelligence strategies and, 412–13
technological change and innovation
    computing, 714–16
    definitions of, 223–25
    digital revolution and rising entropy, 700–1
    direct effects of, 229–30
    distributional effects of, 223–25
    globalization and diffusion of, 699–700
    goals of grand strategy and, 226–28, 709–10
    grand strategy and, 221–32, 706–699
    historical perspective on, 221–22

technological change and innovation (*cont.*)
  indirect effects of, 230–31
  intelligence gathering and, 409–11
  material sources of grand strategy and, 225–26
  military economic and bureaucratic structure and, 279–81
  post-fact ideology and, 690–91
  power distribution and, 213–14
  precision munitions development, 711–12
  robotics, 712–14
  sustaining and disruptive technologies, 708
Teles, Steven, 663
Temperley, Howard, 643–44
Tensorflow data program, 715–16
terrorism. *See also* violent rebel groups; War on Terror
  civil-military relations and, 273–74
  controversy analysis and policies on, 150–51
  counterterrorism policies and, 16
  as cultural product, 315
  Palestine rebel groups and, 516–18
  security strategy and, 308–9, 311
  US grand strategy debate and, 450
  violent rebel groups and, 507, 516–18
Tetlock, Philip E., 296
Texan independence, foreign covert action and, 399–400
"The Grand Strategy of the Wars of the Rebellion" (Sherman), 28–29
think tanks, economic interests of, 265–66
third offset strategy (US), 711–12
Thirty Years' War, Swedish national identity and, 307–8
Thoreau, Henry David, 89
thought-practice, grand strategy as, 165–68
threat perception
  change in grand strategy and, 524–27
  ideology and, 166–67
  interpretation and, 326–27
  legitimation and, 325, 326–28
  military power display and, 349–50
  political cost of grand strategy financing and, 432
  population aging and, 731–32
  small state grand strategy and, 492–93
  United States grand strategy and, 443–45, 626–27

Thucydides, 10–11
  on declining powers, 474–75
  entrapment perspective and, 447–48
  grand strategy and legacy of, 41–53
  on grand strategy in Peloponnesian War, 46–50
  historical scholarship on, 42–46
  legacy in grand strategy of, 52–53
  in military education curriculum, 41
  Peloponnesian War narrative by, 42–44
  perils and problems in analysis of, 50–52
  realist international relations theory and, 304
  Realist scholarship on, 44
Thucydides Trap, 41, 46–47
ties, networks, 129–31
time horizons
  control-assertiveness as rising state and, 466–67
  declining states and, 477–78
  financing of grand strategy and, 425–32, 433n.5
  strategic logics of rising great powers and, 464–65
Tingley, Dustin, 167
Tocci, Nathalie, 151–52
top-down policymaking
  calibrated grand strategy and, 629–31
  in declining states, 479–80
  grand strategy based on, 673–74
  military power and, 351–53
topography and terrain, grand strategy and role of, 211–12
Towns, Ann, 315–16
Toynbee, Arnold, 648–49
trade policies
  classical liberalism and, 260–61
  economic statecraft and, 373–74
  geography and, 210–11
  prosperity and power goals of, 379–80
  survival motive and, 257–59
Trafalgar Campaign, 345–46
Traistaru, Corina-Ioana, 173–82
transactional advocacy networks, 124–25
translation, in actor-network theory, 151–52
transnational politics
  networks and, 127–28
  relative power and, 207

Trans-Pacific Trade Partnership (TPP), 378, 534–35
transparency in intelligence, liberal internationalism and, 413–15
Trubowitz, Peter, 539–41, 545, 546–47, 665–66
Truman, Harry, 292, 323–24, 596
 foreign policy under, 660–62
 grand strategy under, 566
Trump, Donald
 alternatives to grand strategy and, 631–33
 calibrated strategy and, 630–31
 diplomacy under, 356–57, 364–65
 domestic impact on strategy of, 248–49
 economics and strategy choices of, 17
 foreign policy under, 660–62, 663–64, 725–28
 geopolitics and emergence of, 690–91
 grand strategy change under, 534–35, 539–41, 626–27
 media and, 701
 political polarization under, 665–66
 politics of grand strategy and, 182
 populism and election of, 673, 683–84
 preventive war strategies and, 275–76
 reputation and impact of, 445–46
Turkey, grand strategy research on, 177–78
Turner, Stansfield (Admiral), 41
Tyler, John, 400

U

uncertainty in grand strategy
 civil-military relations and, 276
 declining powers and, 485–87
 evaluation of, 579–83, 584
 military power and, 339–53
 risk of, 611
 technological change and, 223–25
 threat assessment and, 326–28
underwater acoustics technology, indirect effects of, 230–31
underwater missile technology, 229–30
ungovernability of rebel groups, 512–13
ungrand strategy, benefits of, 600–1
uniformity, globalization and, 700
unilateralism, intelligence gathering and, 410–11
unintended consequences of war, Sun Tzu on, 95

unipolarity
 ascendancy of, 690–91
 decline of, 311
 dynamics of, 692–93
 global power distribution and, 208–9, 215n.5
 US post-Cold War strategy revisions and, 548–51
United Kingdom (UK)
 arbitration efforts in nineteenth century by, 483
 Australian policy change toward, 531–33
 Canning's legacy in, 642–44
 Castlereagh's legacy in grand strategy of, 638–42
 colonization attempts in America by, 399–400
 cost of war calculations in, 424–25
 covert actions and, 390
 developmental aid programs in, 197–99
 Foreign Office strategies in World War II, 646–49
 foreign policy-covert action integration in, 393–94
 foreign policy in, 312
 French covert actions by, 396
 great power conflict and, 400–2
 history of grand strategy in, 542, 637–38, 649–51
 Palmerston's legacy in, 644–46
 political polarization in, 664–66
 rearmament policies and grand strategy financing in, 427
 retrenchment by, 484
 security culture in, 311–13
 Suez Crisis and grand strategy change in, 531–33
 tactics vs. strategy in, 27–29
 threat perception and strategy change in, 525–26
 US covert actions by, 395–97
United Nations
 diplomacy and, 360
 economic sanctions strategy of, 376
United States
 backward-looking premise in grand strategy of, 560–61
 Barbary Pirates and covert actions by, 398

United States (*cont.*)
    bipolarity of power with Soviet Union and, 208–9
    British covert actions in, 395–97
    calibrated strategy in, 629–31
    catalysts in grand strategy debate, 453–54
    change in grand strategy of, 543–548
    China as threat to, 326–27
    Cold War strategies of, 308–9, 566, 610–11
    computing technology and strategy in, 714–15
    control-assertiveness as rising state, 466–67
    cost-benefit analysis of grand strategy in, 450–51
    covert action operations by, 390
    critical resources in, 210–11
    critique of grand strategy in, 564–65
    debate over grand strategies in, 441–54, 629–31
    debt financing of grand strategy in, 422–27
    decline of Congressional power in, 666–67
    deep engagement strategy of, 442–49, 451–52, 580–94
    definition and ontology of grand strategy in, 560–61
    derivative interests in, 111–13
    diplomacy in, 363–64
    disagreement over grand strategy in, 442–49
    domestic values and grand strategy in, 451–52
    economic sanctions strategy of, 376, 377–78, 381–82
    elite foreign policy community, decline of, 660–62
    energy technology and, 213–14
    entanglement as grand strategy technique in, 449–50
    erosion of hegemony, 697–99
    erosion of trust in elite foreign policy in, 662–64
    European security policies and, 17–18
    financing of grand strategy in, 428–29
    foreign aid programs, 382
    foreign policy-covert action integration in, 393–94
    foreign policy debates in, 441–42
    French covert actions in, 396
    geographic security of, 212
    Georgetown Set grand strategy debate and, 658–59
    global interconnectivity and grand strategy in, 445–49
    grand strategy evolution in, 28–29, 31–32, 177–78, 707–9
    homogenization of interests in, 447
    intelligence alignment with grand strategy in, 411–17
    legitimation failure of Iraq War and, 329, 330–33
    marketplace of ideas and foreign policy in, 658–60
    military budget in, 423–25
    military politics in, 243–45
    military technology innovation in, 229–30
    multiculturalism in, 677–78
    networks as grand strategy in, 134–35
    nuclear weapons technology and policies of, 709–10
    obstacles to grand strategy, 594–99, 625–27, 629–31
    perceived tradeoffs in grand strategy of, 452–53
    political polarization in, 664–66
    political structure and grand strategy in, 625–27
    population aging in, 728–31
    post-Cold War grand strategy in, 240–43, 548–51
    pragmatism in grand strategy of, 570
    precision munitions development in, 711–12
    primacy as strategic culture of, 415–16, 528–29
    pro-Israeli interests of, changes to, 531
    reorientation of grand strategy in, 539–41
    revisionist critique of grand strategy in, 568–69
    as rising power, 460
    role of grand strategy in, 565–68
    security culture in, 311–13
    spying activity within, 389
    strategic commercial policy in, 378–79
    terrorism and grand strategy in, 450

threat perception and grand strategy in, 443–45
underwater acoustics technology and, 230–31
unipolar hegemony of, 208–9, 697–99
unity, in declining states, 477
universalism
  grand strategy judgment and, 178–79
  liberalism and, 677–78
unmaking of strategies, actors role in, 179–81
unmanned aerial vehicles (UAVs), 712–14
USAID program, 381
US Civil Rights movement, 82–83

V

Van Munster, Rens, 191
Vann, John Paul, 597–98
Vennesson, Pascal, 339–53
Vershrankung, entanglement and, 94–95
veto players, change in strategy and impediment of, 530–31, 533–34
victory, theory of
  diplomacy and, 365–66
  great powers' grand strategy and, 491–92
  violent rebel groups and, 509–12
victory strategies, of violent rebel groups, 509–12
Vietnam War
  appeasement during, 524–27
  civil-military relations and, 280–81
  loss aversion and policy change in, 527–28
  military failure and strategic success in, 347
  obstacles to grand strategy and, 596
  policy failures of elites in, 660–62
  rebel groups in, 510–11
violent rebel groups. *See also* nonstate actors
  attrition strategy of, 510–11
  characteristics of, 507
  conquest strategy of, 510
  foreign assistance to, 515–16
  government counterstrategies, 518–19
  grand strategies of, 506–19
  inspiration as strategy for, 514–15
  intermediate strategies of, 512–16
  intimidation strategy of, 513
  multiple power centers and, 697–99
  outgoverning by, 511–12

Palestine example of, 516–18
provocation by, 513–14
ungovernability of, 512–13
victory strategies of, 509–12
weaknesses of, 508–9
virtual enlargement strategies, small states' use of, 498–99
Vom Kriege (Rühle von Lilienstern), 66–67
Vo Nguyen Giap, 342–43
von Stürgkh, Karl, 425
Von Willisen, Wilhelm, 68–69
Vore, Christopher, 358

W

Walt, Stephen, 568–69, 691–92
Walter, Barbara F., 510–11, 513
Waltz, Kenneth N., 206–7, 210–11, 305, 448–49, 450–51
Wang Chen, 92–93
Wang Jisi, 607
war
  alternatives to, 348
  civil-military relations during, 281–82
  costs and financing of, 424–25
  die Politik and, 63–68
  diplomacy and, 357–62
  grand strategy and use of, 347–51
  against rising states, 458–59
  robotics technology and, 713
  strategic indispensability of, 695
  Sun Tzu on dangers of, 93–94, 95
Ward, Steven, 467–69
War of 1812, 397
War on Terror
  civil-military relations and, 273–74
  controversy analysis of, 150–51
  grand strategy and, 16, 308–9, 311
  legitimation of, 329
  narrative in, 679–81
war planning
  Clausewitz on strategy in, 58–59
  grand strategy and, 29–30, 31
War Powers Resolution (1973), 599, 714
Warsaw Treaty Organization, 208–9
Washington, George, 395, 396, 560–61
Washington Consensus, 241–43
Waters, James A., 627

Waxman, Matthew, 714
weaponized interdependence
   networked actors and instruments and, 126–27
   technology innovation impact on, 226–28
weapons of mass destruction (WMD)
   commercial policy strategies and control of, 373–74
   US post-Cold War grand strategy and, 549
Weber, Max, 315
Webster, Charles, 649
Wei Liao, 94–96
Weingast, Barry R., 241
Weitsman, Patricia A., 496
Weldes, Jutta, 325, 332
welfare spending, population aging and, 723–24, 728–31
Wendt, Alexander, 92–93, 163–65, 305, 307–8
Wenger, Etienne, 147–48
West, Geoffrey, 31
Western Civilization rhetoric
   legitimation using, 325–26
   multiculturalism and, 676–78
What Good Is Grand Strategy? (Brands), 606
whole of government approach, US foreign policy and, 311–12
Wiener, Norbert, 714–16
Wight, Martin, 206–7
Wilhelm II (Kaiser), 400–2, 466–67
Williams, Michael C., 313, 325, 332–33
Williamson, Samuel, 3–4
Wilson, James Graham, 628–29
Wilson, Woodrow, 292, 359–60, 401
Wivel, Anders, 490–501
Wohlforth, William Curti
   on entrapment, 447–48
   evaluation of grand strategy by, 575–87
   on foreign policy, 358–59, 442
   on governmentality, 192–93
   grand strategy scholarship of, 341–42
   psychology in grand strategy and, 453
   on rising great powers, 467–69
   on risk tolerance, 444
Wohlstetter, Albert, 34–35, 348
Woo, Byungwon, 375

Work, Bob, 714
A World Restored (Kissinger), 362
World Bank, US power and, 450–51
World Trade Organization (WTO), 375, 377
World War I
   changes in strategy during, 524–27
   covert actions during, 393–94
   grand strategy role in, 563–64
   grand strategy scholarship and, 29–30, 76
   Liddell Hart and influence of, 76–77
   military power crisis in, 340–42
   military spending during, 425
   sleepwalkers interpretation of, 46–47
   small states during, 494–95
World War II
   British Foreign Office strategies in, 646–49
   fascist military display prior to, 349–50
   grand strategy role in, 563–64
   grand strategy theory in, 31, 340–41
   obstacles to grand strategy in, 595–96
   policies on colonialism after, 531
   small states during, 494–95
Wright, Quincy, 206–7

X
Xi Jinshin, 356–57

Y
Yale University, grand strategy scholarship at, 34
Yarhi-Milo, Keren, 292–93
Yuen Foong Khong, 94–96

Z
Zakaria, Fareed, 311, 530–31
Zanthier, Friedrich Wilhelm von, 64–66
Zarakol, Ayse, 309–10
zero-sum game
   ideological rivalry as, 167–68
   US foreign policy as, 534–35
Zhang, Weiwei, 245
Zielinski, Rosella Cappella, 422–33
Zimmerman, Arthur, 401
Zoelick, Robert, 443